Fourth Edition

PRINCIPLES OF ECONOMICS

Economics and the Economy

Timothy Taylor
Journal of Economic Perspectives
Macalester College

TEXTBOOK\MEDIA

The Quality Instructors Expect.
At Prices Students Can Afford.

Replacing Oligarch Textbooks since 2004

For instructors:
• PowerPoint® slides
• Computerized test disk

When ordering this title, use ISBN 978-0-9969963-1-0

To order the Micro version, use ISBN 978-0-9969963-2-7

To order the Macro version, use ISBN 978-0-9969963-3-4

Principles of Economics: Economics and the Economy, 4th Edition

Copyright © 2017, 2014, 2011, 2008 Timothy Taylor. Published by Textbook Media.

ISBN-13: 978-0-9969963-1-0

All rights reserved. No part of this publication may be reproduced or transmitted in any form or by any means, electronic or mechanical, including photocopying and recording, or by any information storage or retrieval system without the prior written permission of the author and the publisher.

Printed in the United States of America by Textbook Media

Contents

Preface

When authors describe their reasons for writing an economics textbook, it seems customary to proclaim lofty goals, like teaching students "to think like economists" so that they can become more informed voters and citizens. Paul Samuelson, the author of the most famous introductory economics textbook for the second half of the twentieth century, famously said: "I don't care who writes a nation's laws—or crafts its advanced treaties—if I can write its economics textbooks." On my best days, I have sufficient time and energy to lift my eyes to the horizon, strike a statuesque pose, and proclaim exalted goals. But most of the time, I'm just a workaday teacher and my goals are more limited and concrete.

The pedagogical approach of this textbook is rooted in helping students master the tools that they need to solve problems for a course in introductory economics. Indeed, one of the great pleasures of writing the book is having the opportunity to share my teaching toolkit of step-by-step explanations, practical examples, and metaphors that stick in the mind. On quizzes and exams, I do not ask broad or open-ended questions about informed citizenship and thinking like an economist. At the most basic level, my goal for an economics class is that students should feel well-prepared for quizzes and exams.

The preparation that students need to perform well in an introductory economics class can be divided into three parts. First, an introductory economics class involves mastering a specialized vocabulary. I sometimes tell students that learning economics is akin to learning a foreign language—with the added difficulty that terms in economics like "demand" or "supply" or "money" sound like standard English, and thus learning economics often requires that students drop their preconceptions about what certain words mean.

Second, students need to acquire some basic analytical tools. There are four central analytical models in an introductory economics course: budget constraints, supply and demand, cost curves, and aggregate demand–aggregate supply. These four models are used for a very wide variety of applications; still, there are only four of them. There are also a few key formulas and equations to learn with regard to topics like growth rates over time and elasticity.

Third, students must learn to recognize when these terms and tools apply and to practice using them. I often tell students not to bother memorizing particular questions and answers from the textbook or homework, because my quiz and exam questions will ask them to apply what they have learned in contexts they have not seen before. To provide a variety of contexts, this book describes many economic issues and events, drawn from recent times and past history, and also drawn both from U.S. and international experiences. When students see a concept or analytical skill applied in a number of ways, they learn to focus on the underlying and unifying idea. I've also found that students do take away knowledge of many economic events and episodes—although different students seem to focus on an unpredictable (to me) array of examples, which is perhaps as it should be in an introductory course.

As a workaday teacher, the goal of helping students master the material so that they can perform well on my quizzes and exams is lofty enough—and tough enough—for me. There's an old joke that economics is the science of taking what is obvious about human behavior and making it incomprehensible. Actually, in my experience, the process works in the other direction. Many students spend the opening weeks of an introductory economics course feeling as if the material is difficult, even impossible, but by the middle and the end of the class, what seemed so difficult early in the term has become obvious and straightforward. As a course in introductory economics focuses on one lesson after another and one chapter after another, it's easy to get tunnel vision. But when you raise your eyes at the end of class, it can be quite astonishing to look back and see how far you have come. As students apply the terms and models they have learned to a series of real and hypothetical examples, they often find to their surprise that they have also imbibed a considerable amount about economic thinking and the real-world economy. Learning always has an aspect of the miraculous.

As always, my family makes a significant contribution to the existence of this book. In the nine years since the first edition, the U.S. and world economy has been convulsed by a Great Recession and then by an ungainly process of sluggish recovery, replete with questions about what is likely to happen next. The task of updating figures and examples for this fourth edition is inevitably large, but thinking about how to build connections from the concepts in the text to the economic events of the last few years made it larger. During the process of preparing this revised edition, my wife has dealt lovingly with a distracted husband; my children, with a father who was sleep-deprived or "at the office." In a very real sense, then, this book is from my dear ones to the students and instructors who use it. I hope that it serves you well.

Timothy Taylor
St. Paul, Minnesota
December 1, 2016

About the Author

Timothy T. Taylor

Timothy T. Taylor has been the Managing Editor of the *Journal of Economic Perspectives*, published by the American Economic Association, since the first issue of the journal in 1987. All issues of the journal are freely available online at http://e-jep.org. Taylor holds a B.A degree in economics and political science from Haverford College. He holds an M.S. degree in economics from Stanford University, where he focused on public finance, industrial organization, and economic history.

Taylor has taught economics in a variety of contexts. In 2012, his book *The Instant Economist: Everything You Need to Know About How the Economy Works,* was published by Penguin Plume. It was named an "Outstanding Academic Title" by *Choice* magazine of the American Library Association. He has recorded a variety of lecture courses for The Teaching Company, based in Chantilly, Virginia, including *Economics* (3rd edition), *Unexpected Economics*, *America and the New Global Economy*, *Legacies of Great Economists*, and *History of the U.S. Economy in the 20th Century*. In 1992, he won the Outstanding Teacher Award from the Associated Students of Stanford University. In 1996, he was named a Distinguished Instructor for his courses in introductory economics at the University of Minnesota. In 1997, he was voted Teacher of the Year by students at the Humphrey Institute of Public Affairs at the University of Minnesota.

He has published articles on various topics in economics in publications such as *Finance & Development*, the *Milken Institute Review*, and the *Journal of Economic Perspectives*. He blogs regularly at http://conversableeconomist.blogspot.com.

CHAPTER 1

The Interconnected Economy

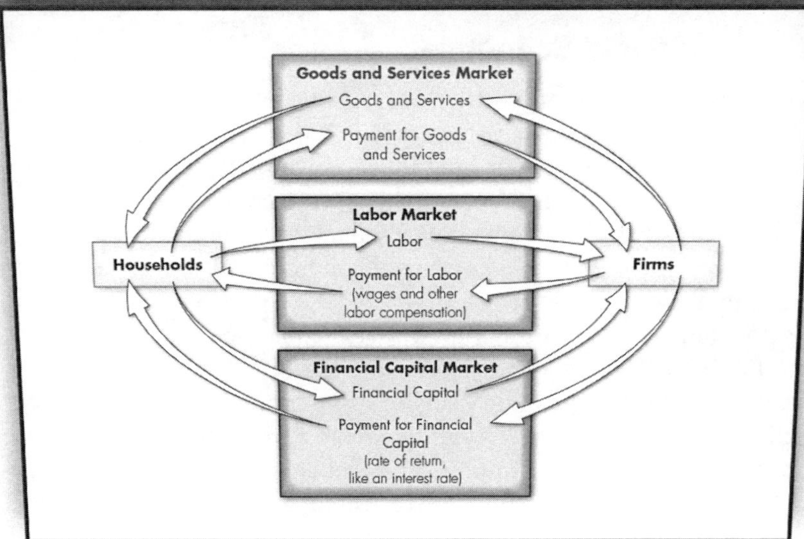

Chapter Outline

People don't produce most of what they consume. They don't grow most of their own food, make their own clothes, build their own houses, or provide their own health care and education. Instead, people mainly consume goods and services that others have produced, and in turn, what most people produce is mainly consumed by others. This pattern raises questions. What goods will be produced? What quantities of each good will be produced? How will the goods that are produced be allocated across the population? What role will be played by individuals making decisions about consuming, working, and saving? What role will be played by organizations like businesses? What role will be played by government?

Since a modern economy contains thousands upon thousands of different products that are produced, bought, and consumed, the study of economics must address an extraordinary array of topics. Are gasoline prices likely to rise? What causes a new restaurant to open or an existing restaurant to close? Will it pay off for a high school graduate to attend college? Can environmental protection go hand in hand with a rising level of consumption of goods and services? Why did the U.S. and world economies suffer such a sharp slowdown during the Great Recession from 2007–2009? What determines the number of people who want to work but cannot find jobs? When should the government cut taxes, and when should it raise them? Why do people in some countries have high incomes while those in other countries have low incomes? An introductory course in economics will help you develop the analytical tools and vocabulary for thinking and communicating about these issues.

This first chapter introduces some ways in which economies are interconnected. It discusses the range of alternatives from a market-oriented economy to a command economy. It describes how an economy divides up the tasks that are involved in production of goods and services, and how the total production of goods and services increases as a result. This chapter will also explain the difference between "microeconomics" and "macroeconomics" and preview how the chapters of this book are organized.

What Is an Economy?

economy: The social arrangements that determine what is produced, how it is produced, and for whom it is produced.

economics: The study of the production, distribution, and consumption of goods and services.

An **economy** is the set of social arrangements that answers three fundamental questions: (1) What is produced? (2) How is it produced? (3) For whom is it produced? Thus, **economics** is the study of the production, distribution, and consumption of goods and services. In an economics textbook published in 1890, the famous English economist Alfred Marshall (1842–1924) wrote more poetically that economics involved the study of people "as they live and move and think in the ordinary business of life."

Market-Oriented vs. Command Economies

market: An institution that brings together buyers and sellers of goods or services.

market-oriented economy: An economy in which most economic decisions are made by buyers and sellers, who may be individuals or firms.

command economy: An economy in which the government either makes or strongly influences most economic decisions.

Countries display a wide range of economic institutions. At one end of the spectrum is a market-oriented economy. A **market** is an institution that brings together buyers and sellers of goods or services, who may be either individuals or businesses. In a **market-oriented economy**, most economic decisions about what to produce, how to produce it, and for whom to produce it are made by these buyers and sellers. In a **command economy**, at the other extreme, the government either makes most economic decisions itself or at least strongly influences how the decisions are made.

The U.S. economy is positioned toward the market-oriented end of the spectrum. Many countries in Europe and Latin America, while primarily market-oriented, have a greater degree of government involvement in economic decisions than does the U.S. economy. Countries like China and Russia, while they are closer to having a market-oriented system now than several decades ago, remain closer to the command economy end of the spectrum. In countries such as Zimbabwe, Cuba, and North Korea, the command economy predominates.

black markets: An illegal market that breaks government rules on prices or sales.

Markets and government rules are always entangled. Even economies that are primarily market-oriented have laws and regulations to support the operation of markets. At a minimum, these laws govern matters like safeguarding private property against theft, protecting people from violence, enforcing legal contracts, preventing fraud, and collecting taxes. Conversely, even the most command-oriented economies operate with substantial **black markets**, which are markets where the buyers and sellers make transactions without the government's approval. The question of how to organize economic institutions is typically not a black-or-white choice between all market or all government, but instead involves a balancing act over the appropriate combination of market freedom and government rules.

The Interconnectedness of an Economy

In a modern economy, the economic life of every individual is interrelated, at least to a small extent, with the economic lives of thousands or even millions of other individuals. Imagine that when an economic transaction occurs, it leaves behind a line that is visible for people who wear special economist glasses.

For example, if you buy a loaf of bread at the grocery store, a blue line stretches from the store to your kitchen. When you pump gas into your car, a red line runs from the gas station to your car. A green line connects you to your employer, a purple line to the bank where you keep your checking and savings accounts, and a yellow line to the shop where you get your hair cut. This network of lines would also capture the transactions through which goods are produced. A loaf of bread would have colorful lines running to the bakery, to the company that manufactured the plastic bag for packaging, to the farm where the wheat was grown, and to the mill where the wheat was ground into flour. In turn, because the wheat farm used tractors, and trucks transported the bread to the store, lines would also extend from the loaf of bread to tractor and truck manufacturers and to trucking companies. These lines representing economic transactions also extend to those concerned with the financial side of these businesses: the bankers who provide loans and checking and savings accounts to firms, the accountants who deal with payroll and taxes, and the managers who authorize sending out the checks.

The Index of Economic Freedom

Who's in control of economic decisions? Are people free to do what they want and to work where they want? Are businesses free to produce when they want and what they choose, and to hire and fire as they wish? Are banks free to choose who will receive loans? Or does the government control these kinds of choices? Each year, researchers at the Heritage Foundation and the *Wall Street Journal* look at 10 different categories of economic freedom for countries around the world. For each component of each category, they give each nation a score based on extent of economic freedom in that category.

The 2016 Index of Economic Freedom report ranked 178 countries around the world: some examples of the most free and the least free countries are listed here. Several countries were not ranked because of extreme instability that made judgments about economic freedom impossible. These countries include Afghanistan, Iraq, Libya, Somalia, Sudan, and Syria.

The assigned rankings are inevitably based on estimates, yet even these rough measures can be useful for discerning trends. In 2016, 97 of the 178 countries ranked shifted toward greater economic freedom, although 74 of the countries shifted toward less economic freedom. In recent decades, the overall trend has been a higher level of economic freedom around the world.

Countries with the Most Economic Freedom	Countries with the Least Economic Freedom
1. Hong Kong	169. Argentina
2. Singapore	170. Equatorial Guinea
3. New Zealand	171. Iran
4. Switzerland	172. Republic of Congo
5. Australia	173. Eritrea
6. Canada	174. Turkmenistan
7. Chile	175. Zimbabwe
8. Ireland	176. Venezuela
9. Estonia	177. Cuba
10. United Kingdom	178. North Korea

If you could put on special economist glasses to see all the economic lines of connection, a single loaf of bread would appear with a network of lines that eventually reached all over town, across the state and the country, and even around the world. In a modern economy, every person, every business, and every product is at the center of a starburst of economic interconnections.

The Division of Labor

The formal study of economics began when Adam Smith (1723–1790) published his famous book *The Wealth of Nations* in 1776. Many authors had written on economic subjects in the centuries before Smith, but he was the first to address the subject in a comprehensive way. In the first chapter of *The Wealth of Nations*, Smith introduces the idea of the **division of labor**, which refers to how the work required to produce a good or service is divided into a number of simpler tasks that are performed by different workers.

division of labor: Dividing the work required to produce a good or service into tasks performed by different workers.

To illustrate the division of labor, Adam Smith used the example of how the tasks of making a pin were divided in a pin factory. He counted the multiple tasks involved with making a pin, including the steps involved in drawing out a piece of wire, cutting it to the right length, straightening it, putting a head on one end and a point on the other, and packaging pins for sale. In observing pin factories, Smith counted 18 distinct tasks that were often done by different workers. Modern businesses divide tasks as well. Even a relatively simple business like a restaurant divides up the task of serving meals into a range of jobs including top chefs, less-skilled kitchen help, servers to wait on the tables, a host at the door, janitors to clean up, and a business manager to handle paychecks and bills—not to mention the economic connections a restaurant has with suppliers of food, furniture, kitchen equipment, and the building where it is located. A complex business like a large manufacturing factory or a hospital can have hundreds of job classifications.

Adam Smith was once walking with a friend, talking enthusiastically about the division of labor, and he got so excited with the subject that he tumbled into a pit where workers were tanning hides, a foul-smelling process. Smith was the prototypical never-married, absent-minded professor. He frequently went walking, started talking to himself, and would completely lose track of time and distance. But being one of the first to put on economist glasses and perceive the division of labor must have been a highly distracting experience.

Why the Division of Labor Increases Production

When the tasks involved with producing a good or service are divided and subdivided, workers and businesses can produce a greater quantity of output. In his observations of pin factories, Smith observed that one worker alone might make 20 pins in a day, but that a small business of 10 workers (some of whom would need to do two or three of the 18 tasks involved with pin-making), could make 48,000 pins in a day. How can a group of workers, each focused on certain tasks, produce so much more than the same number of workers who try to produce the entire good or service by themselves? Smith offered three reasons.

specialization: When workers or firms focus on particular tasks in the overall production process for which they are well-suited.

First, **specialization** in a particular small job allows workers to focus on the types of production where they have an advantage. People have different skills, talents, and interests, so they will be better at some jobs than others. The particular advantages of specific workers may be based on educational choices, which are in turn shaped by interests and talents: for example, only those with medical degrees qualify to become doctors. For some goods, specialization will be affected by geography: for example, it's easier to be a wheat farmer in North Dakota than in Florida, but easier to run a tourist hotel in Florida than in North Dakota. If you live in or near a big city, it's easier to attract enough customers to operate a successful dry cleaning business or movie theater than if you live in a sparsely populated rural area.

Second, workers who specialize in certain tasks often learn to produce more quickly and with higher quality. This pattern holds true for many workers, including assembly line laborers who build cars, stylists who cut hair, and doctors who perform heart surgery. In fact, specialized workers often know their jobs well enough to suggest innovative ways to do their work faster and better. A similar pattern often operates across businesses. In many cases, a business that focuses on one or a few products (sometimes called its "core competency") is more successful than firms that attempt to make a wide range of products.

economies of scale: When the average cost of producing each individual unit declines as total output increases.

Third, specialization allows economic agents, or actors, to take advantage of **economies of scale**, which refers to the common pattern for many goods and services that as the level of production increases, the average cost of producing each individual unit declines. For example, if a factory produces only 100 cars per year, each car will be quite expensive to make on average. However, if a factory produces 10,000 or 50,000 cars each year, then it can set up an assembly line with huge machines and workers performing specialized tasks, and the average cost of production per car will be lower. The ultimate result

CLEARING IT UP

Firm, Business, Company, Corporation

What's the difference between a "business," a "firm," a "company," and a "corporation"? The short answer for practical purposes is "not much." A *business* is an organization that produces and sells, regardless of whether the customers are individuals or other businesses. A *company* is one term for the group of people who form a business. One definition of a *firm* is a "business company." A *corporation* refers to a specific legal status, where the business is treated as a separate legal entity that can sign contracts, own property, and borrow money, apart from those who manage or own the business. In this book, "business" and "firm" will typically be used to refer to all kinds of companies, whether they are officially corporations or not.

of workers who can focus on their preferences and talents, learn to do their specialized jobs better, and work in larger organizations is that society as a whole can produce and consume far more than if each person tried to produce individually all of the goods and services that the person wishes to consume.

Trade and Markets

The division of labor helps to explain why most workers do not consume most of what they produce. Instead, workers within an economy use the pay that they receive for doing their jobs to purchase the other goods and services that they desire.

As a result, you don't have to know anything about electronics or software to use a touch screen on your smartphone—you just buy the phone and start tapping away. You don't have to know anything about artificial fibers or the construction of sewing machines if you need a jacket—you just buy the jacket and wear it. You don't need to know anything about internal combustion engines to operate a car—you just climb in and drive. Instead of trying to acquire all the knowledge and skills involved in producing all of the goods and services that you wish to consume, the market allows you to learn a specialized set of skills and then use the pay you receive to buy goods and services. The economy is a social mechanism that coordinates this division of labor, specialization, and markets.

The Rise of Globalization

Recent decades have seen a trend toward **globalization**, which means that buying and selling in markets have crossed national borders to an increasing extent. As a result, firms and workers from different countries are increasingly interconnected. Globalization has occurred for a number of reasons. Improvements in shipping and air cargo have driven down transportation costs. Innovations in information and communications technology have made it easier and cheaper to manage long-distance economic connections of production and sales. Many valuable products and services in the modern economy can take the form of information—for example, computer software; financial advice; travel planning; music, books and movies; and blueprints for designing a building. These products and many others can be transported across national borders, using telephone and computer networks, at ever-lower costs. Finally, international agreements and treaties between countries have encouraged greater trade.

globalization: The trend in which buying and selling in markets have increasingly crossed national borders.

Exhibit 1-1 presents one measure of globalization. It shows the percentage of domestic economic production that was exported for a selection of countries from 1970 to 2014. **Exports** are the goods and services that are produced domestically and sold in another country; conversely, **imports** are the goods and services that are produced abroad and then sold domestically. The size of total production in an economy is measured by the gross domestic product, often abbreviated as GDP. (The details of how GDP is calculated are presented in Chapter 21.) Thus, the ratio of exports divided by GDP measures what share of a country's total economic production is sold in other countries.

exports: Goods and services that are produced domestically and sold in another country.

imports: Goods and services produced abroad and sold domestically.

In recent decades, the ratio of exports/GDP has generally risen, both worldwide and for the U.S. economy. Interestingly, the share of U.S. exports in proportion to the U.S. economy is well below the global average, in part because large economies like the United States can contain more of the division of labor inside their national borders. However, smaller economies like those of South Korea and Canada need to trade across their borders with other countries to take full advantage of division of labor, specialization, and economies of scale. In this sense, the enormous U.S. economy is less affected by globalization than most other countries. Exhibit 1-1 also shows that many medium- and low-income countries around the world, like Mexico and China, have also experienced a surge of globalization in recent decades. If an astronaut in orbit around planet Earth could put on special economist glasses that make all economic transactions visible as brightly colored lines, globalization means that the astronaut would see more connections stretching around the world.

EXHIBIT 1-1 The Extent of Globalization (Exports/GDP)

One way to measure globalization is to look at the exports/GDP ratio. For the world economy and for most individual countries, the exports/GDP ratio has risen in recent decades.

Country	1970	1980	1990	2000	2010	2014
Some High-Income Countries						
United States	6%	10%	10%	11%	13%	14%
Canada	22%	28%	26%	46%	29%	32%
France	16%	21%	21%	29%	26%	29%
Japan	11%	13%	10%	11%	15%	16%
South Korea	14%	32%	28%	39%	52%	51%
Sweden	24%	30%	30%	47%	49%	45%
Some Upper-Middle-Income Countries						
Brazil	7%	9%	8%	10%	11%	12%
China	3%	11%	16%	23%	31%	23%
Mexico	8%	11%	19%	31%	30%	32%
Some Lower-Middle-Income Countries						
India	4%	6%	7%	13%	23%	23%
Nigeria	8%	29%	43%	54%	35%	18%
Some Low-Income Countries						
Bangladesh	8%	5%	6%	14%	18%	19%
Chad	16%	17%	13%	17%	39%	34%
Nepal	5%	12%	11%	23%	10%	12%

Microeconomics and Macroeconomics

microeconomics: The branch of economics that focuses on actions of particular actors within the economy, like households, workers, and business firms.

macroeconomics: The branch of economics that focuses on the economy as a whole, including issues like growth, unemployment, inflation, and the balance of trade.

Microeconomics focuses on the actions of particular actors within the economy, like households, workers, and businesses. In contrast, **macroeconomics** looks at the economy as a whole, focusing on issues like the growth rate of production of goods and services, unemployment, price inflation, and levels of exports and imports. Microeconomics and macroeconomics are not separate subjects, but rather complementary perspectives on the overall subject of the economy.

To understand why microeconomic and macroeconomic perspectives are both useful, consider the problem of studying a biological ecosystem like a lake. One person who sets out to study the lake might focus on specific topics: certain kinds of algae or plant life, the characteristics of particular fish or snails, or the trees surrounding the lake. Another person might take an overall view and instead consider the entire ecosystem of the lake from top to bottom: what eats what, how the system stays in a rough balance, and what environmental stresses affect this balance. Both approaches are useful, and both examine the same lake, but the viewpoints are different. In a similar way, both microeconomics and macroeconomics study the same economy, but each has a different viewpoint.

Whether you are looking at lakes or economics, the micro and the macro insights should blend with each other. In studying a lake, the micro insights about particular plants and animals help to understand the overall food chain, while the macro insights about the overall food chain help to explain the environment in which individual plants and animals live. In economics, the micro decisions of individual households and businesses are influenced by whether the macroeconomy is healthy; for example, firms will be more likely to hire workers if the overall economy is growing. In turn, the performance of the macroeconomy ultimately depends on the microeconomic decisions made by households and businesses.

In this book, Chapters 1–6 introduce some basic tools of economics. This first chapter lays out the basic meaning of the economy and economics. Chapter 2 explains how economic decision-making works. Chapter 3 shows how trade can be mutually beneficial, using the example of trade between nations in the global economy. Chapters 4 and 5 discuss how forces of supply and demand determine prices—and what happens when government attempts to set prices directly. Chapter 6 discusses the debate over globalization and protectionism. With this foundation established, Chapters 7–20 focus on microeconomics and Chapters 21–34 focus on macroeconomics. Regardless of whether you are looking through the microeconomics microscope or the macroeconomics telescope, the fundamental subject material of the interconnected economy doesn't change.

circular flow diagram: A diagram that illustrates the economy as consisting of households and firms interacting in a goods and services market, a labor market, and a financial capital market.

Microeconomics: The Circular Flow Diagram

The **circular flow diagram** in Exhibit 1-2 pictures the economy as consisting of two groups—households and firms—that interact in three markets: a *goods and services market*, a *labor market*, and a *financial capital market*.

goods and services market: A market in which firms are sellers of what they produce and households are buyers.

In the **goods and services market**, firms are sellers and households are buyers, so the arrow for goods and services leads from firms to households. Payments for these goods and services flow back in the other direction, from households to firms, so the arrow for payments flows back in the opposite direction.

labor market: The market in which households sell their labor as workers to businesses or other employers.

In the **labor market**, households sell their labor to firms. Conversely, firms buy labor when they hire workers. Thus, the flow of labor runs from households to firms, but the flow of payments for labor—in the form of wages, salaries, bonuses, and benefits—flows from firms to households.

financial capital market: The market in which those who save money provide financial capital and receive a rate of return from those who wish to raise money and pay a rate of return.

In the **financial capital market**, individuals or firms who save money and make financial investments are suppliers of financial capital. Those who borrow money or receive financial investments are the recipients of financial capital. For example, someone who deposits money in a savings account at a bank is supplying financial capital, and someone who receives a loan from the bank is demanding financial capital. Individual households and firms can be either suppliers or demanders of capital, depending on whether they are

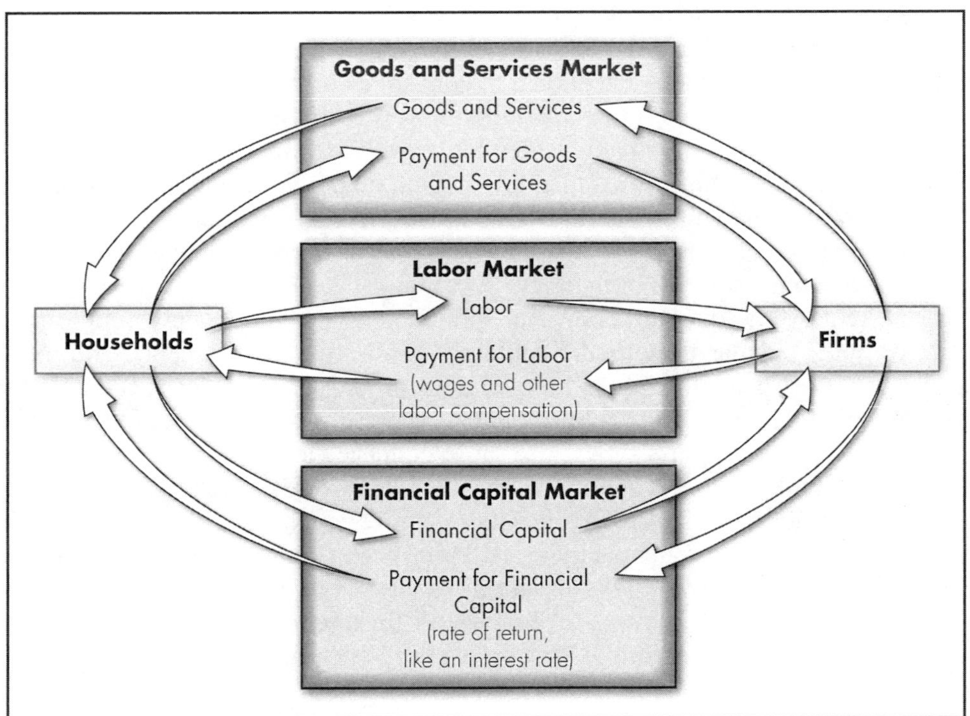

EXHIBIT 1-2 The Circular Flow Diagram

The circular flow diagram shows how households and firms interact in the goods and services market, the labor market, and the financial capital market. The direction of the arrows shows that in the goods and services market, households receive goods and services and pay firms for them. In the labor market, households work and receive payment from firms. In the financial capital market, households provide financial capital—that is, savings and financial investment—while firms pay them for that capital by providing a rate of return—for example, an interest payment.

CLEARING IT UP

Real and Financial Capital and Investment

The concept of a financial capital market can be confusing because the words "capital" and "investment" can have two different meanings. Financial capital or financial investment refers to flows of money from those people or firms who save and make a financial investment to those who borrow or receive the financial investment. Real capital or real investment usually refers to physical items like buildings or equipment, although the terms are sometimes also applied to intangible business investments, like the spending on research and development that seeks to produce new inventions. In short, you can stub your toe on real capital investment, but not on financial capital investment. Financial capital and real capital are often interrelated. Those who receive financial capital often invest those funds in real physical capital. Discussions of capital and investment throughout the book will specify whether the discussion is about real or financial capital and investment. But be warned: outside the pages of this book, and in casual conversation, the terms "capital" and "investment" can take on either meaning.

saving or borrowing. However, in the circular flow diagram, the convention is to draw the most common direction of the financial capital flow as running from households to firms—that is, households taken as a group are saving and making financial investments.

rate of return: The payment in addition to the original investment from those who have received financial capital to those who provided it.

principal: The amount of an original financial investment, before any rate of return is paid.

interest rate: A payment calculated as a percentage of the original amount saved or borrowed, and paid by the borrower to the saver.

model: A simplified representation of an object or situation that includes enough of the key features to be useful.

Payment for financial capital is called the **rate of return**. Suppliers of financial capital expect that they will eventually receive back both the amount of their original financial investment, called the **principal**, plus an additional amount called the rate of return. Conversely, demanders of financial capital expect to pay back the original principal they received, plus a rate of return, in exchange for receiving the financial investment. One common example of a rate of return is an **interest rate** charged for borrowing financial capital. If one person loans $10,000 to another person for one year at an 8% annual interest rate, then the lender—the supplier of financial capital—expects to be repaid $10,000 of principal plus $800 of interest as a rate of return. Meanwhile the borrower—the demander of financial capital—expects to pay back the $10,000 of principal plus $800 in interest. However, the rate of return is not always an interest rate. For example, a person might pay $10,000 for a half-ownership of a small business, with an agreement that the rate of return will be half of any future profits earned by the business. In this case, the actual rate of return could be high or low, depending on the profits that are eventually earned, if any.

The circular flow diagram is an example of a **model**, which is a simplified representation of an object or situation that includes enough of the key features to be useful. For example, an architect who is planning a major office building will often build a physical model that sits on a tabletop to show how the entire city block will look after the new building is constructed. Companies often build models of their new products, which are often more rough and unfinished than the final product will be, but can still demonstrate how the new product will work. Economic models like the circular flow diagram are not physical models, but instead are diagrams or graphs or even mathematical equations that represent economic patterns or theories.

The circular flow diagram shown in Exhibit 1-2 is a deliberately simple model. A more complex circular flow model could add a box for "government," and then show arrows for taxes paid flowing to the government and government spending programs going to households and firms. A box could also be added for the "rest of the world," with arrows showing the exports flowing to those countries and imports flowing back from those countries. But models should be only as complex as needed to illustrate the issue at hand—and not more so. Although issues of government and international economic connections will arise throughout the book, the structure and order of the microeconomics chapters is based on how households and firms interact in these three main markets.

Chapters 7–12 build a theoretical framework for microeconomic analysis. Chapter 7 looks at the concept of "elasticity," which is a way of measuring how quantities react to a change in prices or incomes. Chapter 8 focuses on household decision-making. Chapters 9–12 discuss how firms make decisions about production, ranging from firms that face many competitors to monopoly firms that face no competitors at all. Chapters 13–20 build on that theoretical framework to discuss some policy issues that arise in microeconomic markets. Chapters 13–15 focus on policies that involve markets for goods: assuring competition between firms, protecting the environment, and encouraging beneficial new technology. Chapters 16–17 then discuss issues that arise in labor markets: poverty, inequality, unions, discrimination, and immigration. Chapters 18–19 discuss issues that arise in financial capital markets involving insurance and financial investments like stocks and bonds. Finally, Chapter 20 discusses how economists analyze some of the political issues involved in setting microeconomic policy.

Macroeconomics: Goals, Frameworks, and Tools

When nations desire a healthy macroeconomy, they typically focus on four goals: growth in the standard of living, a low level of unemployment, low inflation, and a sustainable balance of trade between countries. After an overview of macroeconomics and how to measure the size of the economy using gross domestic product in Chapter 21, these four goals are the subject of Chapters 22–25.

Macroeconomics involves thinking about how these four goals relate to each other, and in particular how pursuing any one of these goals might necessitate trade-offs with other goals. Such analysis requires an understanding of how the macroeconomy works, both in the short-run (ranging from months to a couple of years) and in the long-run (ranging from several years to a decade and more). Chapters 26–28 present theoretical frameworks for short-run and long-run macroeconomic analysis, with names like the *aggregate supply–aggregate demand model*, the *Keynesian model*, and the *neoclassical model*.

With macroeconomic goals in mind and the frameworks for analyzing how these goals relate to each other in place, the final step is to think about how macroeconomic policy pursues these goals. The two main tools of macroeconomic policy include **monetary policy**, which involves policies that affect bank lending, interest rates and financial capital markets, and **fiscal policy**, which involves government spending and taxation. Chapters 29–34 will discuss how these policy tools can be used to pursue the four main macroeconomic goals.

monetary policy: Policy that involves altering the quantity of money and thus affecting the level of interest rates and the extent of borrowing.

fiscal policy: Economic policies that involve government spending and taxation.

Studying Economics Doesn't Mean Worshiping the Economy

Many newcomers to the study of economics either fear or hope that the subject will mainly discuss why businesses and markets are always right. Such expectations are inaccurate. Economics overlaps with the study of business decisions, but it reaches much farther to encompass all aspects of production, distribution, and consumption. Economics is concerned with the well-being of *all* people, including those with jobs and those without jobs, and those with high incomes and low incomes. Economics acknowledges that production of useful goods and services can create problems of environmental pollution. It explores the question of how investing in education helps to develop workers' skills. It probes questions like how to tell when big businesses or big labor unions are operating in a way that benefits society as a whole, and when they are operating in a way that benefits their owners or members at the expense of others. It discusses how government spending, taxes, and regulations affect decisions about production and consumption. Economics is a structured methodology for investigating these kinds of issues and many others. John Maynard Keynes (1883–1946), one of the greatest economists of the twentieth century, addressed this theme when he wrote: "[Economics] is a method rather than a doctrine, an apparatus of the mind, a technique of thinking, which helps its possessor to draw correct conclusions."

While the study of economics requires paying attention to the problems that can be generated in society's process of production, distribution, and consumption, economics is based on the belief that a higher standard of living is a goal worth pursuing. In 1900, the population of the United States had the highest average income level of any country in the world. However, from a modern perspective, people had a very low standard of living. In the United States of 1900, only one-third of all homes had running water; in rural areas, almost nobody did. Just 3 percent of homes were lit by electricity; most used coal, oil, or kerosene. About 10 percent of those aged 14–17 attended high school; about 6 percent of students graduated from high school; and about 2 percent graduated from college. Life expectancy at birth was just 47 years, and out of every 1,000 babies born, 140 died before they were a year old. (Now life expectancy is above 75 years, and out of every 1,000 babies born, fewer than 10 die in the first year.) The typical workweek for a man was 60 hours, spread over six days. While relatively few women worked in the paid labor force, the typical woman spent about 40 hours a week on meals and meal clean-up, another seven hours per week on laundry, another seven hours on cleaning the home, and an untold number of hours on child care, gardening, making and repairing clothes, fetching water, and filling the stove with wood or coal. The average woman had 10 pregnancies, so even with a high level of infant mortality, she spent about 15 years of her life either pregnant or looking after an infant. Child labor was widespread; the 1900 U.S. Census reports that one-fourth of boys aged 10–15 held a job.

Today, we look back at the people who lived 100 years ago and wonder how they managed. But remember that in 1900, the United States had the highest average income of any country in the world. It had an average standard of living slightly above that of the United Kingdom; almost double that of France or Germany; almost triple that of the richer nations of Latin America at that time, including Argentina and Chile; and quadruple the standard of living of Japan or Mexico (which had about the same standard of living at that time).

Few of us today would wish to return to the standard of living in 1900 because most of us believe that it is better to be educated than illiterate, to live longer and to have fewer babies die, to work fewer hours at less physically demanding tasks, and to have all the life-saving, labor-saving inventions that have been developed over time. This pattern of dramatic advances in the standard of living continues today. For example, consider the extraordinary advances in recent years in information and communications technology, in medicine and health, in biological sciences and genetics, and in new materials.

The economic challenge for society is to chart a course that encourages the beneficial aspects of economic growth while finding ways to curb undesirable and unwanted side effects like pollution, unemployment, and poverty. The introductory course in economics should make you more discerning about these issues. When you read newspaper or magazine articles about economic issues, you will begin to recognize terminology and arguments. When you hear classmates, co-workers, or political candidates talking about economics, you will improve your ability to distinguish common sense from nonsense. You will find new ways of thinking about current events and about personal and business decisions, as well as current events and politics. The study of economics does not dictate the answers, but it can illuminate the different choices.

Key Concepts and Summary

1. The **economy** is the way in which a society organizes the production, distribution, and consumption of goods and services. It is the set of social institutions that answers three questions: what is produced, how is it produced, and for whom is it produced.
2. In a **market-oriented economy**, individuals and businesses make most economic decisions, with government playing a background role. In a **command economy**, the government makes most economic decisions; individual and business decisions play only a background role. Most economies lie somewhere between these two extremes and have a substantial role for both the market and the government, although the emphasis varies in different countries.
3. A modern economy is amazingly interconnected. Every person and every good is linked by economic transactions—sometimes directly, often indirectly—to a vast array of other goods, people, and businesses.
4. A modern economy displays a **division of labor**, in which people earn income by specializing in what

they produce and then use that income to purchase the products they desire.

5. The division of labor allows individuals and firms to specialize and to produce more for several reasons: (a) it allows the agents to focus on areas of advantage due to natural factors and skill levels; (b) it encourages the agents to learn and invent; (c) it allows agents to take advantage of **economies of scale**.
6. The last few decades have seen **globalization** evolve as a result of growth in commercial and financial networks that cross national borders, making businesses and workers from different economies increasingly interdependent.
7. **Microeconomics** and **macroeconomics** are two different perspectives on the economy. The microeconomic perspective focuses on parts of the economy: individuals, firms, and industries. The macroeconomic perspective looks at the economy as a whole, focusing on overall issues like growth in the standard of living, unemployment, inflation, and levels of foreign trade.
8. The **circular flow diagram** shows how households and firms interact in the **goods and services market**, the **labor market**, and the **financial capital market**.
9. Macroeconomics has four main goals: growth in the standard of living, low unemployment, low inflation, and a sustainable balance of trade. It has two types of policies for pursuing these goals: **monetary policy** and **fiscal policy**.

Review Questions

1. What are the three basic questions that every economy must address?
2. What is the key difference between a market-oriented economy and a command economy?
3. What does the phrase "division of labor" mean?
4. What three reasons explain why the division of labor increases an economy's level of production?
5. What is globalization? How do you think it might have affected the economy over the past decade?
6. What is the difference between microeconomics and macroeconomics?
7. Are households primarily buyers or sellers in the goods and services market? The labor market? The financial capital market? Are firms primarily buyers or sellers in each of these three markets?
8. What are the four primary goals of macroeconomics?

Choice in a World of Scarcity

CHAPTER

2

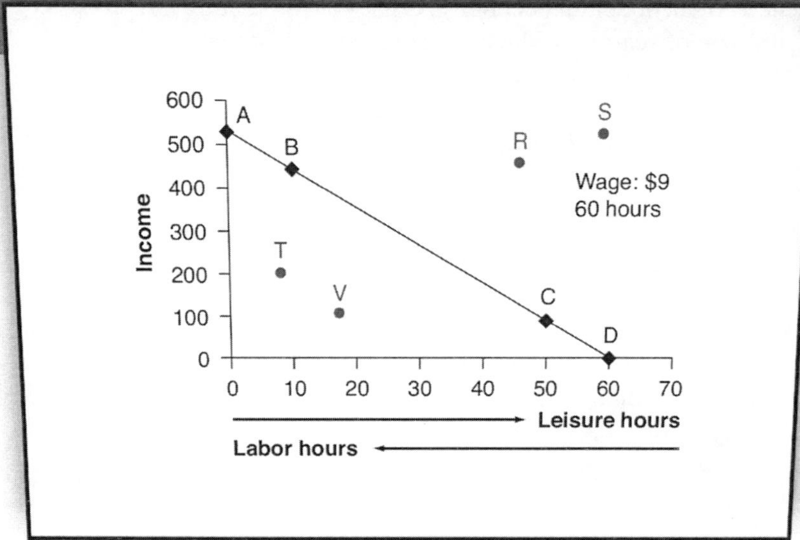

Chapter Outline

In November 1968, the Rolling Stones recorded a song called: "You Can't Always Get What You Want." But economists had already been singing a similar tune for many years. For example, an English economist named Lionel Robbins (1898–1984) wrote *An Essay on the Nature and Significance of Economic Science* in 1932, in which he described the problem of not always getting what you want in this way:

> The time at our disposal is limited. There are only twenty-four hours in the day. We have to choose between the different uses to which they may be put. The services which others put at our disposal are limited. The material means of achieving ends are limited. We have been turned out of Paradise. We have neither eternal life nor unlimited means of gratification. Everywhere we turn, if we choose one thing we must relinquish others which, in different circumstances, we would wish not to have relinquished. Scarcity of means to satisfy given ends is an almost ubiquitous condition of human nature. Here then, is the unity of subject of Economic Science, the forms assumed by human behavior in disposing of scarce means.

Economics studies how every person, every firm, and every society must make choices, because none of them can have everything that they desire.

This chapter begins with a discussion of three broad categories of choices made by individuals and households: choices about which goods to consume, how many hours to work, and how much to borrow or save. Not coincidentally, these three categories of choices match the three main markets of microeconomics discussed in the circular flow diagram in Chapter 1: the markets for goods, labor, and financial capital. The discussion then introduces a frame work for thinking about society's choices. Finally, the chapter discusses some concerns over whether the economic approach to facing scarcity and making choices describes accurately either how choices *are* actually made or how choices *should* be made.

Choosing What to Consume

People live in a world of scarcity: that is, they can't have all the time, money, possessions, and experiences they wish. Since people must choose, they inevitably face trade-offs, in which they have to give up things that they desire to get other things that they desire more. When economists analyze how individuals make these choices, they divide the decision process into two steps. The first step is to consider what choices are possible for individuals. The second step is to think about which choices individuals actually make, based on their individual preferences. The model that economists use for illustrating the process of individual choice in a situation of scarcity is the **budget constraint**, sometimes also called the **opportunity set**, a diagram that shows the possible choices.

budget constraint: A diagram that shows the possible choices.

opportunity set: Another name for the budget constraint.

A Consumption Choice Budget Constraint

To illustrate how the budget constraint model applies to choices about how much of each good to consume, consider the case of Alphonso, illustrated in Exhibit 2-1. Each graph in Exhibit 2-1 shows a different combination of Alphonso's income and the prices for two goods, burgers and bus tickets. In Exhibit 2-1*a*, Alphonso has \$10 in spending money each week that he can allocate between bus tickets for getting to work and the burgers that he eats for lunch. Burgers cost \$2 each, and bus tickets in Alphonso's town are 50 cents. Different combinations of choices that are possible for Alphonso are shown in the table and also depicted graphically in the accompanying budget constraint. Each combination of burgers and bus tickets shown in the table and the budget constraint adds up to exactly \$10. As one example, if Alphonso buys 1 burger for \$2, he has \$8 remaining and could purchase 16 bus tickets. The points along the budget constraint represent what consumption opportunities are possible for Alphonso.

How Changes in Income and Prices Affect the Budget Constraint

Changes in income will alter the budget constraint. For example, say that Alphonso's spending money increases to \$12 per week. Exhibit 2-1*b* shows both his original budget constraint and his new budget constraint. In the new budget constraint, each combination of burgers and bus tickets at the given prices now adds up to \$12. A higher income level means that the budget constraint will shift to the right of the original budget constraint; conversely, a lower income level means that the budget constraint will lie to the left of the original budget constraint.

Now suppose Alphonso's income remains the same, but the price of one of the goods increases. Changes in the price of goods will affect Alphonso's budget constraint. In other words, his income level stays at \$10 per week, but the price of bus tickets rises to \$1 each, while the price of burgers remains at \$2. Exhibit 2-1*c* shows how this change in price alters the budget constraint. A higher price for one good causes the budget constraint to move inward; more specifically, the budget constraint swings inward as if on a hinge attached to the vertical axis or the horizontal axis—depending on which good's price has

CLEARING IT UP

Sketching Budget Constraints

As an economics student, you will need to know how to sketch budget constraints quickly and accurately. When graphing a choice between two goods, it does not matter which good is on the horizontal or the vertical axis. Start by calculating, based on income and the prices of the two goods, what quantity of each good each person could buy if that person were not buying any of the other good. These calculations will determine the points on the two axes of the budget constraint. The other points then form a straight line between these endpoints.

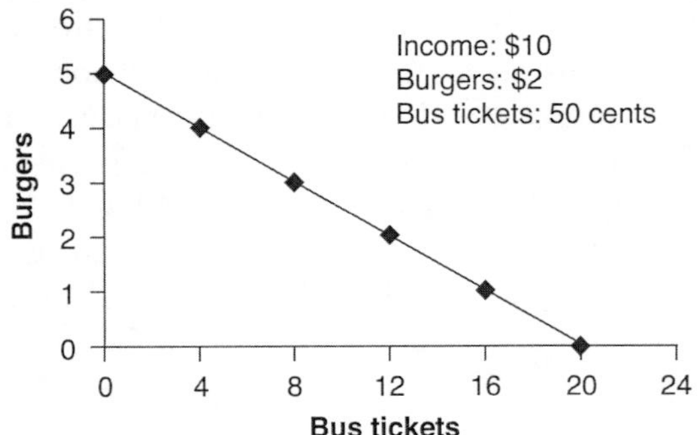

Quantity of Burgers (at $2)	Quantity of Bus Tickets (at 50 cents)
0	20
1	16
2	12
3	8
4	4
5	0

(a) First set of choices: Total income $10.

Each point on the opportunity set represents a combination of burgers and bus tickets whose total cost adds up to Alphonso's income of $10. The slope of the budget constraint line is determined by the relative price of burgers and bus tickets. All along the budget constraint, giving up a burger means gaining four bus tickets.

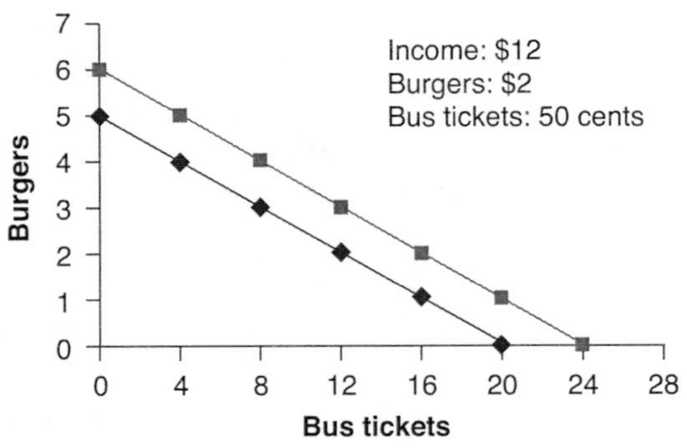

Quantity of Burgers (at $2)	Quantity of Bus Tickets (at 50 cents)
0	24
1	20
2	16
3	12
4	8
5	4
6	0

(b) Second set of choices: Total income $12.

If Alphonso's income increases from $10 to $12, his opportunity set shifts to the right of the original budget set. The lower line is the original budget constraint, and the upper line is the new budget constraint. On the new budget constraint, each combination of burgers and bus tickets now adds up to a total cost of $12. However, because the trade-off of burgers for bus tickets is unchanged—still one burger for every four bus tickets—the slope of the budget constraint line is unchanged.

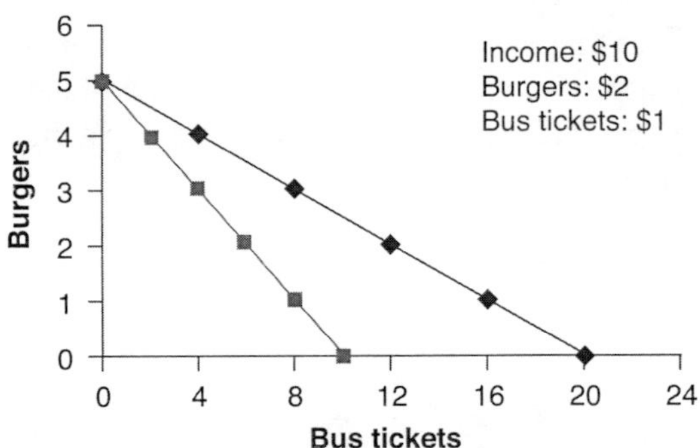

Quantity of Burgers (at $2)	Quantity of Bus Tickets (at $1)
0	10
1	8
2	6
3	4
4	2
5	0

(c) Third set of choices: Total income $10.

Alphonso's income remains at $10, as in *(a)*, but the cost of bus tickets rises from 50 cents to $1. This change causes the opportunity set to swing inward, as if on a hinge at the upper left. If Alphonso wishes to purchase only burgers, the change in price of bus tickets doesn't alter how many he can buy. However, giving up a burger now adds only two bus tickets, not four. The budget constraint line slopes more steeply as a result.

EXHIBIT 2-1 Alphonso's Consumption Choice Opportunity Set

risen. Conversely, a lower price for one good would lead to an outward movement of the budget constraint.

A change in income causes the budget constraint to shift so that the new budget constraint is parallel to the original. However, a change in prices causes the slope of the budget constraint to change so that the budget constraint is steeper or flatter. Why are the effects different? The slope of the budget constraint is determined by the relative price of the two goods, which is calculated by taking the price of one good and dividing it by the price of the other good. The *relative* price conveys the trade-off between the two goods, in this case burgers and bus tickets. In Alphonso's first budget constraint in Exhibit 2-1*a*, if he gives up 1 burger, he can take 4 additional bus trips because the price of a burger is four times the price of a bus trip (i.e., $2 versus 50 cents). The slope of this budget constraint shows that a loss of 1 burger equals a gain of 4 bus tickets. In Exhibit 2-1*b*, income changes but the relative prices of the two goods don't change, and so the slope of the budget constraint doesn't change either. In Exhibit 2-1*c*, however, giving up 1 burger means gaining only 2 bus trips (i.e., $2 versus $1), and so the slope of the budget constraint changes accordingly.

Personal Preferences Determine Specific Choices

utility: The level of satisfaction or pleasure that people receive from their choices.

What choice will Alphonso make along his budget constraint? The answer is simple: Alphonso will choose what he personally prefers. In economics, **utility** refers to the level of satisfaction or pleasure that people receive from their choices. Thus, when people make the choices that provide the highest level of satisfaction, economists say that they are "maximizing utility." In Alphonso's case, if he prefers to sit at home and eat, he buys a lot of burgers and chooses some point like *A* or *B* on the budget constraint in Exhibit 2-2. If he prefers to travel around town, he buys lots of bus tickets and chooses some point like *D* or *E* on the budget constraint. It's Alphonso's choice.

However, the logic of the budget constraint dictates that Alphonso's choice will be a point on the actual budget constraint itself—not a choice that is above the budget set or below it. Alphonso might desire a point like *H* in Exhibit 2-2 with five burgers and 16 bus tickets, offering more of both goods than choice *B*. However, choice *H* is outside the budget constraint, which means that Alphonso can't afford it. Conversely, Alphonso won't choose a point like *J* with 2 burgers and 4 bus tickets, which is inside the boundary of the budget constraint, because he could instead select a choice on the budget set itself like *B* that would have at least as much of one good and more of the other—or a choice that would offer even more of both goods. In this simple model, Alphonso doesn't have any other goods on which to spend his money, and so if he doesn't spend his money, it is wasted.

The budget constraint diagram shows what choices are possible, but it does not specify which choice is made. If two people have the same income and face the same prices, then they have identical budget constraints, but if those two people have different personal preferences, they will make different choices.

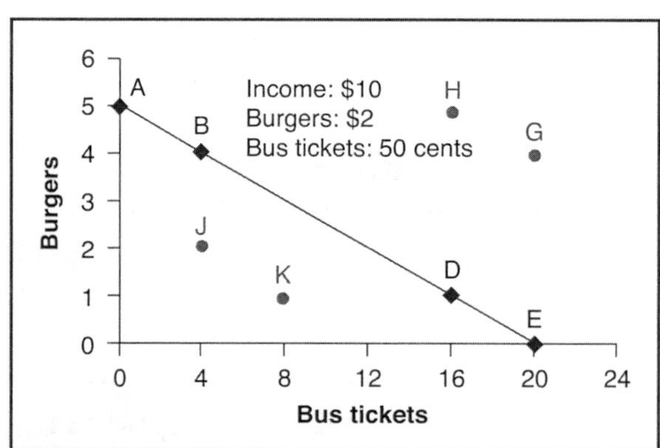

EXHIBIT 2-2 Personal Preferences Determine the Actual Choice

If Alphonso likes burgers a lot, he will probably make a choice like *A* or *B*. If he likes bus tickets a lot, he will probably make a choice like *D* or *E*. Points *H* and *G* beyond the opportunity set are unattainable for Alphonso, given his level of income, no matter how much he might like them. Points *J* and *K* would be wasteful. For example, rather than choosing point *J*, he could have both more burgers and the same number of bus tickets at point *B*. Similarly, instead of choosing point *K*, he could have the same number of burgers but many more bus tickets at point *D*.

The Origins of Economic Utility

In the late eighteenth century, a philosopher and occasional economist named Jeremy Bentham (1748–1832) constructed a philosophy called "utilitarianism," which was based on the "happiness principle" that all of society's decisions ought to be made according to the amount of pleasure and pain that they cause individuals. Bentham wrote: "The greatest happiness of the greatest number is the foundation of morals and legislation."

Utilitarianism may not sound very radical, but consider some of its implications for the world of the late eighteenth and early nineteenth century. The utilitarian philosophy did not say that the happiness of a king, queen, or member of the nobility was more important than the happiness of an average person. It did not place the happiness of men above the happiness of women. It did not say that the happiness of the unemployed, criminals, children, or the poor was any less important than the happiness of anyone else.

Bentham was the unofficial leader of a group called the Philosophical Radicals, who favored voting rights for all with a secret ballot, government programs to provide jobs for the unemployed, government-run banks to help the poor save money, better conditions in prisons, limits on child labor, and—important to economists—market competition and free trade among countries. The Philosophical Radicals weren't always right, but at least by modern standards, they were on the side of the angels more often than not.

From a Model with Two Goods to the Real World of Many Goods

The budget constraint diagram containing just two goods may seem too simple. In a modern economy, people choose from thousands of goods, not just two.

However, thinking about a model with many goods is straightforward. Instead of drawing just one budget constraint, showing the trade-off between two goods, you can draw multiple budget constraints, showing the possible trade-offs between many different pairs of goods. Or in more advanced classes in economics, you would use mathematical equations that include many possible goods and services that can be purchased, together with their quantities and prices, and show how the total spending on all of the goods adds up to the overall amount of money available. However, the graph with two goods clearly illustrates three basic concepts: (1) the budget constraint is determined by income and prices; (2) changes in income or relative prices cause a budget constraint to move; and (3) the personal preferences of an individual are represented by the point that is chosen on the budget constraint.

Choosing between Labor and Leisure

People also make choices about how to allocate their time; in particular, they choose how to divide their available hours between work and leisure. The concept of the budget constraint applies to the labor-leisure choice just as it does to the decision of what quantity of goods to consume. Again, the first step is to use the budget constraint to show what is possible, given the wage that can be earned and the number of hours in a day, while the second step is for individuals to make their personally preferred choice that maximizes utility.

An Example of a Labor-Leisure Budget Constraint

Beulah has a job as an assistant manager of a fast-food restaurant. She can work as many as 60 hours per week if she chooses. Of course, most people don't have jobs that let them choose exactly how many hours to work each week, but most people have at least some flexibility about whether to look for a part-time or a full-time job or whether to work overtime or take on a second job. Thus, it isn't unreasonable to imagine people making choices about the number of hours they work. Exhibit 2-3 shows two of Beulah's labor-leisure budget constraints.

In Exhibit 2-3*a*, Beulah's wage is $9 per hour. The table and the budget constraint show the trade-off that she faces between income and leisure. Because Beulah receives an hourly wage, the more hours she works, the more her income rises and her leisure

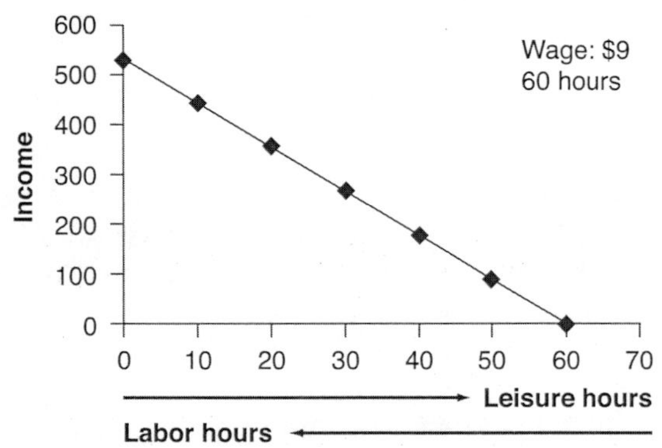

Hours Worked	Leisure Time	Income
0	60	$0
10	50	$90
20	40	$180
30	30	$270
40	20	$360
50	10	$450
60	0	$540

(a) First set of choices: Wage $9 per hour.

The points on the opportunity set show what combinations of leisure and income that Beulah can have with her 60 hours of time, given that she can earn a wage of $9 per hour. The trade-off between leisure and income, which is the wage $9 per hour, determines the slope of the line.

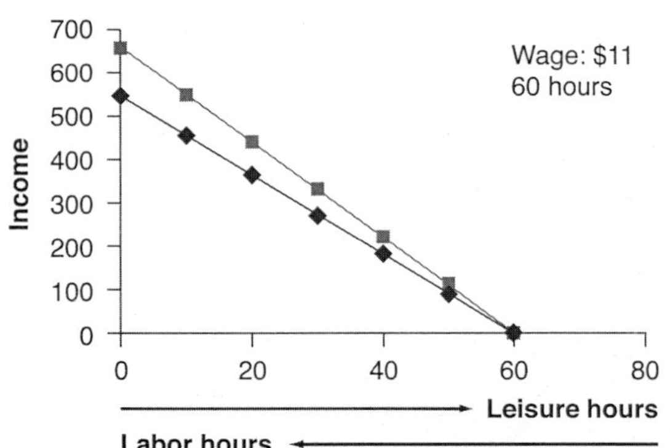

Hours Worked	Leisure Time	Income
0	60	$0
10	50	$110
20	40	$220
30	30	$330
40	20	$440
50	10	$550
60	0	$660

(b) Second set of choices: Wage $11 per hour.

If Beulah's wage increases from $9 per hour to $11 per hour, her 60 hours of time has not changed, but the trade-off that she faces between leisure and income has changed. With the higher wage, giving up a certain number of hours of leisure brings a higher income, so the budget set rotates upward.

EXHIBIT 2-3 Beulah's Labor-Leisure Opportunity Set

diminishes. The horizontal axis of the graph measures *both* labor hours and leisure hours, but in opposite directions. The quantity of hours of leisure is measured from left to right, while the quantity of hours of labor is measured from right to left. Since Beulah has a total of 60 hours available that she could work, the horizontal axis shows how she divides up this time between leisure and work.

How a Change in Wages Affects the Labor-Leisure Budget Constraint

A change in the wage will rotate Beulah's budget constraint. If her wage rises to $11 per hour, perhaps because she has gained more experience or training, then the trade-offs that she faces change as well. Both her original budget constraint and her new set of trade-offs are shown in Exhibit 2-3*b*. A new wage changes the slope of the budget constraint because a new wage means a different trade-off between hours of leisure and income.

Making a Choice along the Labor-Leisure Budget Constraint

Living in a world of scarcity—no one has more than 24 hours in a day—requires that people must make choices about how to spend their time, but the fact of scarcity doesn't dictate what choices they make. In deciding how many hours to work, Beulah will make a choice that maximizes her utility; that is, she will choose according to her preferences for leisure time and income. If she chooses to work 60 hours per week, she will have more income to spend on food, rent, clothing, cars, vacations, or other goods and services.

CLEARING IT UP

Measuring Labor and Leisure on the Same Axis

The labor-leisure budget constraint involves illustrating three factors—hours of labor, hours of leisure, and dollars of income—on only two axes. This illustration only works because the hours of both labor and leisure appear on the horizontal axis. After all, all leisure means no labor, and all labor means no leisure. On the horizontal axis, hours of leisure are measured from left to right, but hours of labor are measured from right to left. The fundamental trade-off here is between the two goods of leisure and income. In this model, labor is not a "good" in itself, but instead a mechanism for earning income.

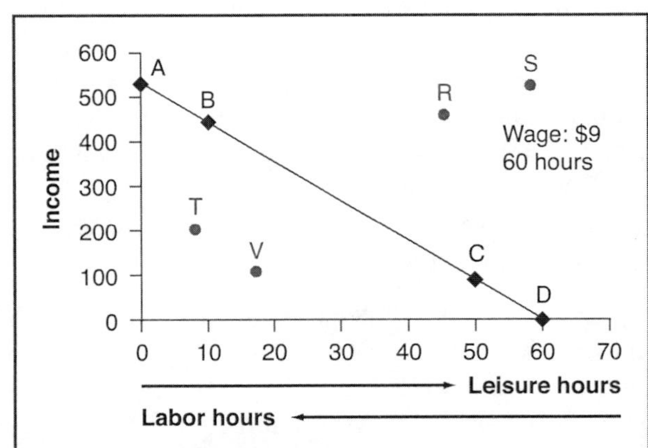

EXHIBIT 2-4 Beulah's Personal Choice on a Labor-Leisure Opportunity Set

If Beulah strongly prefers income, she will work a lot of hours and choose a point like *A* or *B*. If she strongly prefers leisure, she will work few hours and make a choice like *C* or *D*. Given that she has 60 hours of time and a wage of $9 per hour, she cannot choose points like *R* or *S* that are outside her budget set. Points like *T* or *V* inside her budget set would be wasteful; they would be like working extra hours but not being paid.

However, if she prefers leisure time, she may choose to work fewer hours so that she has more time for family, friends, and low-cost hobbies such as reading or yoga. Exhibit 2-4 illustrates both possibilities. If Beulah prefers a relatively high level of income, then she will choose a point close to *A*, with $540 of income, 60 hours of work, and no leisure. If she prefers instead a relatively high level of leisure, she might choose a point like *C* with 50 hours of leisure, 10 hours of work, and $90 in income.

Beulah might desire a combination of income and leisure that is outside her budget constraint; for example, she would probably like to have both 60 hours of leisure and $540 of income, which is the choice shown at point *S*. However, the budget constraint shows what choices are possible, given the wage and hours available, and choices beyond the budget constraint are not possible. Moreover, Beulah will not choose a point inside the budget constraint like *T*, which is 50 hours of labor, 10 hours of leisure, and $200 of income. In effect, a choice like *T* would mean that Beulah was working for only $4 per hour (i.e., $200 of income divided by 50 hours of work), when she can actually earn a wage of $9 per hour. Thus, the labor-leisure budget constraint illustrates: (1) the opportunity set of possible choices for leisure and income is determined by the wage rate and the total quantity of hours that can be worked; (2) changes in the wage rate cause the budget constraint to move; and (3) the personal preferences of an individual choosing between leisure and income are represented by the point that is selected on the budget constraint.

Choosing between Present and Future Consumption

An intertemporal choice reaches across time. Borrowing money is an intertemporal choice, because it involves borrowing money to spend in the present but promising to repay in the future. Saving money is also an intertemporal choice, because it involves less consumption in the present, but the ability to consume more in the future. The intertemporal choice budget constraint shows the trade-off between present and future consumption.

Interest Rates: The Price of Intertemporal Choice

In the consumption choice budget constraint presented earlier, the trade-off between goods is determined by the relative prices of the two goods. In the labor-leisure budget constraint, the trade-off between leisure and income is based on the wage. In the intertemporal choice budget constraint, the trade-off between present consumption and future consumption is based on the interest rate or the rate of return. The price of borrowing money is the interest that you pay on the loan. The reward for saving money is the interest that you receive. The key to understanding the economic function of interest rates is to recognize that receiving $100 in the future has less economic value than receiving $100 today. Imagine that a friend owes you $100, and when the time comes to pay, the friend says: "Hey, no problem, I'll have the money for you in five years." You protest, and your supposed friend says, "Hey, you are still getting repaid your full $100, so what are you complaining about?" You probably aren't going to persuade this loser, your former friend, to repay you sooner, but you can offer three arguments as to why $100 in the future doesn't have the same value as $100 today:

risk premium: A payment to make up for the risk of not being repaid in full.

inflation: Rise in the overall level of prices.

time value of money: The cost of having to wait for repayment.

1. *Risk of not being repaid.* The future is uncertain. Your friend could get hit by a bus. You could get hit by a bus. (The way this friendship is going, you could run over your former friend with a bus.) Having $100 in your pocket is a sure thing. Having a promise of $100 is uncertain. Anytime someone borrows money, whether the lender is a friend or a bank, the lender must be concerned about the risk of not being repaid. Part of the interest rate is a **risk premium**, that is, a payment to make up for the risk of not being repaid in full.
2. *Inflation.* In most years, there is a rise in the overall level of prices called **inflation**. In recent U.S. history, this increase has typically been 1–3% per year, but in other times and places, the rate of inflation has been much higher. If the overall level of prices rises by 3%, then on average a dollar will buy 3% less in terms of goods and services at the end of the year. As a result of the higher overall level of prices, being repaid $100 in the future will provide less buying power than receiving the money immediately. A lender demands an interest rate in part to compensate for any expected inflation, so that the money that is repaid in the future will have at least as much buying power as the money that was originally loaned. (The concept of inflation, along with its underlying causes and policy solutions, is discussed at length in the macroeconomics section of the book.)
3. *Time value of money.* Even if you knew with complete certainty that the $100 will be repaid in the future, and even if the rate of inflation is zero, it is still annoying to wait several years for repayment. If you have the money now, you can spend it on something now if you wish to do so and receive benefits from that spending. Being forced to wait is an intangible cost, but still a cost. This cost of having to wait is referred to as the **time value of money.**

Thus, when explaining to your friend why you should receive interest payments if you need to wait five years for your money, you can point out that an interest rate has three components:

Interest rate = Risk premium + Expected rate of inflation + Time value of money.

In effect, interest payments are a compensation for the risk of not being repaid, the fact that inflation tends to reduce the buying power of money over time, and the unpleasantness of having to wait to have money available.

Thinking about these three components of interest rates helps to explain why interest rates differ across times and places. At times and places when inflation is high, interest rates will also be high. Differences in interest rates at a point in time can usually be traced to the different risk premiums involved. For example, when the U.S. government borrows money, the interest rate is quite low, perhaps an annual rate of 2–4%, because the chance that the federal government will not repay what it has borrowed is quite low. A large corporation might pay an annual interest rate of 6–7% because, although the large firm is likely to pay back the loan, the risk is greater than with the federal government. A medium-size or small firm would pay an even higher interest rate because it has a greater risk of not repaying the loan. Individuals pay a relatively low interest rate when they borrow money from a bank to purchase a home because the bank (the lender) does a credit check before lending any money in the first place. The credit check is supposed to ensure that a home buyer has the financial means to cover the cost; if the buyer is unable to meet the payments, the bank can take the house and sell it. However, individuals pay a higher interest rate on credit card borrowing, in part because there is a greater risk that such loans will not be repaid.

The Power of Compound Interest

Interest rates are usually expressed in annual terms. For example, an annual interest rate of 7% means that if you borrow $100 you will need to repay $107 a year from now, or if you save $100 you will receive $7 in interest payments a year from now. But what if you are planning to save money for a period of many years, allowing the interest to accumulate over time? The formula for starting with a certain amount of money in the present, and a certain interest rate or rate of return, and figuring how much it would be worth at a date in the future is:

$$\text{Future amount} = (\text{Present amount}) \times (1 + \text{interest rate})^{\text{number of years}}$$

For example, Christopher is planning to make a financial investment of $500. He will put this money in an investment that pays an interest rate of 6% annually and leave it there for some years as the interest accumulates.

Exhibit 2-5 applies this formula for Christopher and shows what his financial investment would be worth at various dates in the future. Notice that if he leaves the financial investment alone for 20 years, the original $500 will more than triple in value to $1,603; if he leaves the financial investment alone for 40 years, it will increase more than 10-fold to $5,143. How can a seemingly moderate interest rate like 6% per year produce such large increases? The answer lies in the power of **compound interest**, when interest payments are allowed to accumulate so that in later time periods, the interest rate is paid not only on the original amount, but also on the interest that has accumulated in previous years. In the equation for how a financial investment increases in value over time, the number of years is an exponent. When quantities are raised to high exponential powers, they will eventually expand very quickly. The exponent represents the power of compound interest—as time goes by, Christopher is not just earning interest on his original $500, but also on the earlier interest he earned. If interest rates are relatively low, compound interest doesn't make much of a practical difference over a short time period of a few years. But over several decades, even a relatively low interest rate will compound in a way that yields significant returns on the initial financial investment.

compound interest: When interest payments in earlier periods are reinvested, so that in later time periods, the interest rate is paid on the total amount accumulated during previous years.

EXHIBIT 2-5 Christopher's Potential Savings

Starting with $500, Interest Rate of 6%			
After 1 year	$500 (1 + .06)^1 = $530	After 10 years	$500 (1 + .06)^{10} = $895
After 2 years	$500 (1 + .06)^2 = $562	After 20 years	$500 (1 + .06)^{20} = $1,603
After 5 years	$500 (1 + .06)^5 = $669	After 40 years	$500 (1 + .06)^{40} = $5,143

An Example of Intertemporal Choice

Consider the case of Desdemona, who is lucky enough to receive a gift of $10,000 from a wealthy aunt. She faces a choice: how much money should she consume now, and how much should she save for future consumption? Again, the first step is to use the budget constraint to show the range of possible choices, and then the second step is to illustrate the individually preferred choice that maximizes her utility.

In the intertemporal choice budget constraint, the two axes represent consumption in the present and consumption in the future. Let's assume that if Desdemona saves some of the money, she can earn an annual interest rate of 9% for the next 10 years. Exhibit 2-6 shows Desdemona's choices in both a table and a budget constraint. The levels of future consumption that are available to her 10 years from now are calculated by using the formula for compound interest. At one extreme, she can consume all of the $10,000 in the present and have nothing left in the future. At the other extreme, she can save the entire $10,000, consume none of it in the present, and have $23,673 to spend 10 years from now.

In Exhibit 2-6, both present consumption and present savings are shown on the horizontal axis. Consumption is measured from left to right; saving is measured from right to left. In effect, the horizontal axis shows how the income that is available in the present is divided into either consumption or savings. (This approach applies the same logic as the way in which hours of labor and leisure were both shown on the horizontal axis in the labor-leisure budget constraint.) If the interest rate rises, then the budget constraint has a steeper slope; a lower interest rate causes the budget constraint to rotate downward to a flatter slope.

Desdemona will seek to maximize her utility and choose the option that brings her the greatest degree of satisfaction. Inevitably, this choice will be one of the points on the budget constraint such as *A*, *B*, *C*, *D*, *E*, or *F*. Even if Desdemona wants to choose a point like *Q*, with $8,000 of consumption in the present, $2,000 of savings, and $20,000 of future consumption, she can't have it because choice *Q* is outside her budget constraint. Moreover, Desdemona will not choose a point inside the budget constraint like *R*, with $2,000 in present consumption and $10,000 in future consumption because such a choice would be like throwing away money. Instead of choosing *R*, Desdemona would certainly prefer a choice like *C* with more consumption in both the present and the future.

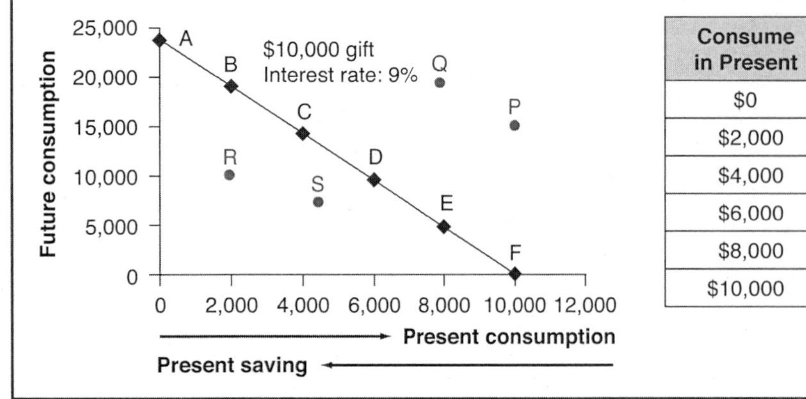

Consume in Present	Save in Present	Consume in Future
$0	$10,000	$23,673
$2,000	$8,000	$18,939
$4,000	$6,000	$14,204
$6,000	$4,000	$9,469
$8,000	$2,000	$4,734
$10,000	$0	$0

EXHIBIT 2-6 Desdemona's Intertemporal Budget Constraint

The points along the budget set represent the combinations of present and future consumption that are available to Desdemona, based on her inheritance of $10,000, an interest rate of 9% per year, and a time period of 10 years The trade-off between present consumption and future consumption—and thus the slope of the budget line—is determined by the interest rate. Choices like *Q* or *P* are unavailable to Desdemona, even if she would like them. She will not make choices like *R* or *S* because they give up present consumption without taking future consumption, which would be wasteful. Thus, she will choose among points like *A* through *F*, based on her personal preferences.

Opportunity Cost in the Airport

After the terrorist plane hijackings on September 11, 2001, many steps were proposed to improve air travel safety. For example, the federal government could provide armed "sky marshals" who would travel inconspicuously with the rest of the passengers. The cost of having a sky marshal on every flight would be roughly $3 billion per year. Retrofitting all U.S. planes with reinforced cockpit doors to make it harder for terrorists to take over the plane would have a price tag of $450 million. Buying more sophisticated security equipment for airports, like three-dimensional baggage scanners and cameras linked to face recognition software, could cost another $2 billion.

But the single biggest cost of greater airline security doesn't involve spending money. It's the opportunity cost of additional waiting time at the airport. About 750 million passengers took plane trips in the United States in 2016. Since the 9/11 hijackings, security screening has become more intensive, and consequently, the procedure takes longer than in the past. Say that, on average, each air passenger spends one extra hour in the airport per trip. Economists commonly place a value on time to convert an opportunity cost in time into a monetary figure. Let's say that the average price of time for air travelers is $25 per hour. By these estimates, the opportunity cost of delay in airports is 750 million hours × 25 dollars/hour, or $18.75 billion per year. Clearly, the opportunity costs of waiting time can be just as important as costs that involve direct spending.

In the real world, the trade-off between present and future consumption is considerably more complex than the basic intertemporal budget constraint shown here. Instead of making one decision in the present about whether to consume now or save for 10 years from now, people receive income in many different years and make decisions about how much to save over different periods of time. Moreover, financial investments often don't pay a guaranteed rate of return, so people need to take into account the risk and uncertainty of investments. Later chapters will take up the details of financial investing in greater detail. But the basic intertemporal budget constraint here illustrates three themes: (1) the budget constraint of possible choices for present and future consumption are determined by the quantity of income in the present and the interest rate; (2) changes in the interest rate will cause the intertemporal budget constraint to rotate; and (3) the personal preferences of an individual for present and future consumption are represented by the point that is chosen on the intertemporal budget constraint.

Three Implications of Budget Constraints: Opportunity Cost, Marginal Decision-Making, and Sunk Costs

The budget constraint framework has some possibly unexpected implications for how a sensible utility-maximizing individual will make decisions. Let's now draw out three of those implications, involving *opportunity cost*, *marginal decision making*, and *sunk costs*.

Opportunity Cost

When most people want to know the cost of an item or a service, they look for a price tag. When economists want to determine cost, they go one step further. They use the idea of **opportunity cost**, which is whatever must be given up to obtain something that is desired. In the examples discussed earlier, if Alphonso wants more burgers, the opportunity cost is measured in bus tickets; if he wants more bus tickets, the opportunity cost is measured in burgers. In Beulah's labor-leisure choice, if she wants more income, the opportunity cost is hours of leisure; if she wants more leisure time, the opportunity cost is dollars of income. In Desdemona's intertemporal choice, the opportunity cost of greater consumption in the present is less consumption in the future and vice versa. The idea of opportunity cost, as its name implies, is that the cost of one item is the lost opportunity to do or consume something else.

opportunity cost: Whatever must be given up to obtain something that is desired.

In many cases, it is reasonable to refer to the opportunity cost as the price. If your cousin buys a new bicycle for $300, then $300 measures the amount of "other consumption"

Can Economics Take Pride in Being the "Dismal Science"?

Economics is often called the dismal science. Yet few people would toss that phrase around so easily if they knew its origin. The "dismal science" phrase originated with British essayist Thomas Carlyle (1795–1881). In an 1849 article, Carlyle described the study of "political economy," as economics was then called, as a "dreary, desolate and indeed quite abject and distressing one; what we might call, by way of eminence, the *dismal science*."

This put-down has echoed through time. But not many people know *why* Carlyle disliked economics. The "dismal science" comment appeared in his essay "Occasional Discourse on the Negro Question." In that essay, Carlyle made the racist argument that white landowners should compel black people in the West Indies to give up their natural laziness and instead to work hard and have some purpose in their otherwise meaningless lives. Carlyle didn't just believe that black people should be ordered around by whites; he believed that all the "weak" people, black and white alike, should be compelled by the strong to do "the work they were appointed for," as he put it.

Carlyle thought economics was the "dismal science" because it rested on the assumption that people, regardless of race and social status, were best suited to make their own decisions about their own lives. Carlyle's insult is one that economists can wear with pride.

that would have been possible. For practical purposes, there may be no special need to identify the specific alternative product or products that could have been bought with that $300, but sometimes the price as measured in dollars may not accurately capture the true opportunity cost. This problem can arise when costs of time are involved. For example, consider a boss who decides that all employees will attend a two-day retreat to "build team spirit." The out-of-pocket monetary cost of the event may involve hiring an outside consulting firm to run the retreat. But an opportunity cost exists as well: during the two days of the retreat, none of the employees are doing their regular work. Attending college is another case where the opportunity cost exceeds the monetary cost. The out-of-pocket costs of attending college include tuition, books, room and board, and other expenses. But in addition, during the hours that you are attending class and studying, it is impossible to work at a paying job. Thus, college imposes both an out-of-pocket cost and an opportunity cost of lost earnings—and both costs should be taken into account.

In some cases, making the opportunity cost explicit can alter behavior. Imagine, for example, that you are an employee who goes out to lunch every day and spends $8 at a local restaurant. You may know perfectly well that bringing a lunch from home would only cost $3 a day, but somehow referring to the opportunity cost of buying lunch at the restaurant as $5 each day (i.e., the $8 it costs minus the $3 your lunch from home would cost) doesn't seem to matter much. However, if you work 250 days a year, that $5 per day adds up to $1,250 for a year—which is the cost of a decent vacation. If the opportunity cost is described as "a nice vacation" instead of "$5 a day," you might make different choices.

Marginal Decision-Making and Diminishing Marginal Utility

The budget constraint framework helps to emphasize that most choices in the real world aren't about getting all of one thing or all of another; that is, they aren't about choosing either the point at one end of the budget constraint or else the point all the way at the other end. Instead, most choices involve **marginal analysis**, which compares the benefits and costs of choosing a little more or a little less of a good.

marginal analysis: Comparing the benefits and costs of choosing a little more or a little less of a good.

The utility that a person receives from consuming the first unit of a good is typically more than the utility received from consuming the fifth or the tenth unit of that same good. When Alphonso makes his choice between burgers and bus tickets, for example, the first few bus rides that he chooses might provide him with a great deal of utility— perhaps they help him get to a job interview or a doctor's appointment. But later bus rides might provide much less utility—they may only serve to kill time on a rainy day. Similarly, the first burger that Alphonso chooses to buy may be on a day when he missed breakfast and is ravenously hungry. However, if Alphonso has a burger every single day, the last few burgers may be less appealing. Similarly, if Beulah is working 60 hours per week and thinking about whether to take a few hours of leisure, that break may provide her with a great deal of utility. But if she is working only 10 hours a week, with 50 hours of leisure already, then taking a few more hours of leisure would probably provide much less utility.

The general pattern that consumption of the first few units of any good tends to bring a higher level of utility to a person than consumption of later units is a common pattern. Economists refer to this pattern as the **law of diminishing marginal utility**, which means that as a person receives more of a good, the additional or marginal utility from each additional unit of the good declines.

law of diminishing marginal utility: As a person receives more of a good, the marginal utility from each additional unit of the good is smaller than from the previous unit.

The law of diminishing marginal utility explains why people and societies rarely make all-or-nothing choices. You wouldn't say, "My favorite food is ice cream, so I will eat nothing but ice cream from now on." Even if you get a very high level of utility from your favorite food, if you ate it exclusively, the additional or marginal utility from those last few servings would not be very high. Similarly, most workers don't say: "I enjoy leisure, so I'll never work." Instead, workers recognize that even though some leisure is very nice, a combination of all leisure and no income isn't so attractive. Thus, the budget constraint framework suggests that when people make choices in a world of scarcity, they will use marginal analysis and think about whether they would prefer a little more or a little less.

Sunk Costs

In the budget constraint framework, all decisions involve what will happen next: that is, what quantities of goods will be consumed, how many hours will be worked, or how much will be saved. These decisions do not look back to past choices. Thus, the budget constraint framework assumes that **sunk costs**, which are costs that were incurred in the past and cannot be recovered, should not affect the current decision.

sunk cost: Costs that were incurred in the past and cannot be recovered, and thus should not affect current decisions.

Consider the case of Edgar, who pays $8 to see a movie, but after watching the film for 30 minutes, he knows that it's truly terrible. Should he stay and watch the rest of the movie because he paid $8, or should he leave? The money he spent is a sunk cost and unless the theater manager is feeling kindly, Edgar won't get a refund. But staying in the movie still means paying an opportunity cost in time. Thus, Edgar's choice is whether to spend the next 90 minutes suffering through a cinematic disaster or to do something—anything—else. The lesson of sunk costs is to forget about the money that's irretrievably gone and instead to focus on the marginal costs and benefits of future options.

For people and firms alike, dealing with sunk costs can be frustrating. It often means admitting an earlier error in judgment. Many firms, for example, find it hard to give up on a new product that is selling poorly because they spent so much money in creating and launching the product. But the lesson of sunk costs is to ignore them and make decisions based on what will happen in the future.

The budget constraint or opportunity set provides a framework for thinking about how individuals make economic decisions like what to consume, how much to work, and how much to save. The purpose of this model is not to tell utility-maximizing individuals what they *should* do, but only to convey the range of available choices for what individuals *could* do, and to provide a way of showing what choices people actually make.

The Production Possibilities Frontier and Social Choices

In a world of scarcity, individuals cannot have everything they want and must instead make a choice along a budget constraint. Firms cannot have all the profits they want and must come up with new and ongoing ways of pleasing customers. Society as a whole cannot have everything it might want, either. A **production possibilities frontier** is an opportunity set for the economy as a whole. It is typically displayed as a diagram that shows the combinations of output that are possible for an economy to produce.

production possibilities frontier: A diagram that shows the combinations of output that are possible for an economy to produce.

An example of a production possibilities frontier faced by every economy is the macroeconomic choice between consumption and real investment. Consumption refers to goods

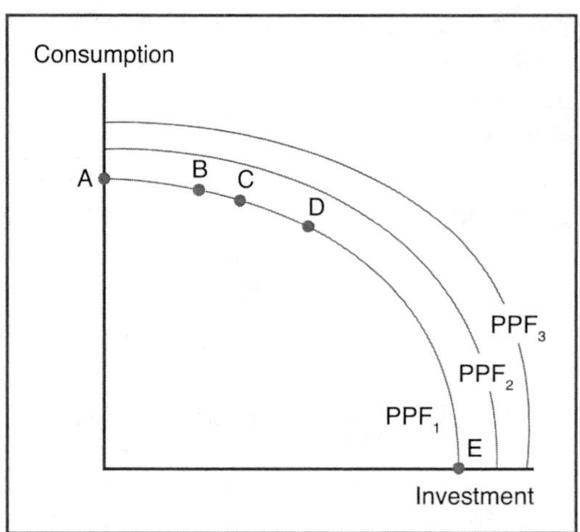

EXHIBIT 2-7 The Consumption and Investment Trade-off

A production possibilities frontier shows the possible combinations of output that a society can produce. Points *A*, *B*, *C*, and *D* illustrate some possible choices along PPF$_1$, moving from all consumption at *A* to greater investment at *B*, *C*, and *D*. PPF$_2$ and PPF$_3$ show an outward shift of the frontier, which would happen as an economy grows and can afford more of both consumption and investment.

and services that are used up this year. Real investment (as opposed to financial investment) refers to expenditures on equipment (like machinery) that can be used to produce goods or services for some years into the future. Thus, expenditures on consumption often serve a more immediate need or desire, but expenditures on investment typically help to increase the economy's level of output in the future.

A production possibilities frontier for the choice between consumption and investment is shown in Exhibit 2-7 by the line labeled PPF$_1$. At point *A*, the economy is devoting all of its resources to producing goods for current consumption and nothing to investment. At points *B*, *C*, and *D*, the economy is gradually shifting toward lower levels of consumption and higher levels of investment. At point *E*, at the other end of the production possibilities frontier, the economy is devoting all of its resources to producing goods for real investment and no resources to current consumption. In a market-oriented economy, the choice between consumption and real investment is not made by the government or by any single organization, but rather is the result of many decisions made by households and firms. However, the government can use taxes, regulations, and other policies to influence the choices of individuals as to how much they should consume or save, and also to influence the eagerness of firms to make real investments. Just as people will make choices along a budget constraint, according to their personal preferences, societies will make choices about how much to consume and to invest.

Over time, societies that invest a greater share of GDP will tend to expand their ability to produce output. Therefore, a society that chooses a high level of consumption and low level of investment, like point *B*, will find that in the future its production possibilities frontier shifts outward only a bit, perhaps from PPF$_1$ to PPF$_2$. However, a society that consumes relatively less in the present and invests more, like point *D*, will find that in the future its production possibilities frontier has shifted outward more dramatically, perhaps from PPF$_1$ to PPF$_3$. Thus, a consumption-investment production possibilities frontier shows the range of choices available to society, illustrates which choice actually happens, and even has implications for how the PPF will shift in the future.

The Shape of the Production Possibilities Frontier and Diminishing Marginal Returns

The budget constraints presented earlier in this chapter, showing individual choices about what quantities of goods to consume, how much to work, and how much to save, were all

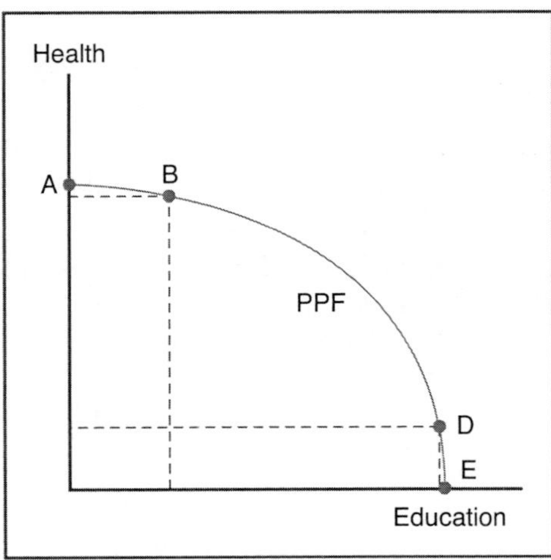

EXHIBIT 2-8 A Health vs. Education Production Possibilities Frontier

This production possibilities frontier shows a trade-off between devoting social resources to health and devoting them to education. At choices like *A* and *B*, most social resources go to health. At choices like *D* and *E*, most go to education. The curvature of the PPF shows that when a large share of resources is already devoted to health (as at point *B*), devoting still more resources to health and moving to point *A* produces only a small gain in health but a substantial loss in education. Thus, the curvature of the PPF demonstrates the law of diminishing marginal returns.

straight lines. The reason for these straight lines is that the slope of the budget constraint is determined by relative prices of the two goods in the consumption budget constraint, by the wage in the labor-leisure budget constraint, and by the interest rate in the intertemporal budget constraint. However, the production possibilities frontier for consumption and investment is often drawn as a curved line. Why does the PPF have a different shape?

Consider another example of a production possibilities frontier that arises when government decision makers must decide how much money to spend on competing government priorities, like education and health. Exhibit 2-8 shows a production possibilities frontier for this trade-off. In this diagram there are no specific numbers on the axes because there is no single way to measure levels of education and health. However, when you think of improvements in education, you can think of accomplishments like more years of school completed, fewer high-school dropouts, and higher scores on standardized tests. When you think of improvements in health, you can think of longer life expectancies, lower levels of infant mortality, and fewer outbreaks of disease. At choice *A*, the government is committing all of its resources to producing health and none to education; at choice *E*, the government is committing all resources to education and none to health. As the economy grows over time, this production possibilities frontier will shift to the right, making it possible for society to have more of both education and health. But in the immediate present, choosing more of one means choosing less of the other.

To understand why the PPF is curved, start by considering point *A* at the top left-hand side of the PPF. At point *A*, all of the available resources are being devoted to health and none to education. This situation would be extreme and even ridiculous. For example, children are seeing a doctor every day, whether they are sick or not, but not attending school. People are having cosmetic surgery on every part of their bodies, but no high school or college education exists. Now imagine that some of these resources are diverted from health to education, so that the economy is at point *B* instead of point *A*. Diverting some marginal resources away from *A* to *B* causes relatively little reduction in health because the last few marginal dollars going into health care services aren't producing much additional gain in health. However, putting those marginal dollars into education, which is completely without resources at point *A*, can produce relatively large gains. For this reason, the shape of the PPF from *A* to *B* is relatively flat, representing a relatively small drop-off in health and a relatively large gain in education.

Now consider the other end, at the lower right, of the production possibilities frontier. Imagine that society starts at choice *D*, which is devoting nearly all resources to education and very few to health, and moves to point *E*, which is devoting all spending to education and none to health. For the sake of concreteness, you can imagine in the movement from *D* to *E*, the last few doctors must become high school science teachers, the last few nurses must become school librarians, and the last few emergency rooms are turned into kindergartens. The gains to education from adding these last few resources to education are very small. However, the opportunity cost loss to health will be fairly large, and thus the slope of the PPF between *D* and *E* is steep, showing a small gain in education and a large drop in health.

The lesson here is not that society is likely to make an extreme choice like devoting no resources to education at point *A* or no resources to health at point *E*. Instead, the lesson is that the gains from committing additional marginal resources to education depend on how much is already being spent. If very few resources are currently committed to education, then an increase of a certain amount can bring relatively large gains; on the other side, if a large number of resources are already being committed to education, then an increase of a certain amount will bring relatively smaller gains. This pattern is common enough that it has been given a name: the **law of diminishing returns**, which holds that as additional increments of resources are added to a certain purpose, the marginal benefit from those additional increments will decline. This pattern arises in many contexts. When government spends a certain amount more on reducing crime, for example, the original gains in reducing crime could be relatively large. But additional increases typically cause relatively smaller reductions in crime, and paying for enough police and security to reduce crime to nothing at all would be tremendously expensive.

law of diminishing returns: As additional increments of resources are added to producing a good or service, the marginal benefit from those additional increments will decline.

The curvature of the production possibilities frontier shows that as additional resources are added to providing education, moving from left to right along the horizontal axis, the original gains are fairly large, but gradually diminish. Similarly, as additional resources are added to improving health, moving from bottom to top on the vertical axis, the original gains are fairly large, but again gradually diminish. In this way, the law of diminishing returns produces the outward-bending shape of the production possibilities frontier.

Productive Efficiency and Allocative Efficiency

The study of economics does not presume to tell a society what choice it should make along its production possibilities frontier. In a market-oriented economy with a democratic government, the choice will involve a mixture of decisions by individuals, firms, and government. However, economics can point out that some choices are unambiguously better than others. In everyday usage, the concept of efficiency refers to lack of waste. An inefficient machine operates at high cost, while an efficient machine produces without wasting energy or materials. An inefficient organization operates with long delays and high costs, while an efficient organization meets schedules, is focused, and performs within budget.

To an economist, **efficiency** refers to the situation in which it is impossible to get more of one thing without experiencing a trade-off of less of something else. The production possibilities frontier can illustrate two kinds of efficiency: *productive efficiency* and *allocative efficiency*. Exhibit 2-9 illustrates these ideas using a production possibilities frontier between consumption and investment.

efficiency: When it is impossible to get more of something without experiencing a trade-off of less of something else.

productive efficiency: When it is impossible to produce more of one good without decreasing the quantity produced of another good.

Productive efficiency means that, given the available inputs and technology, it is impossible to produce more of one good without decreasing the quantity that is produced of another good. Thus, all choices on the PPF in Exhibit 2-9, including *A*, *B*, *C*, *D*, and *E*, display productive efficiency. As a firm moves from any one of these choices to any other, either consumption increases and investment declines or vice versa. However, any choice inside the production possibilities frontier is productively inefficient and wasteful because it is possible to produce more of one good, the other good, or some combination of both goods. For example, point *R* is productively inefficient because it is possible at choice *C* to have more of both goods: investment on the horizontal axis is higher at point

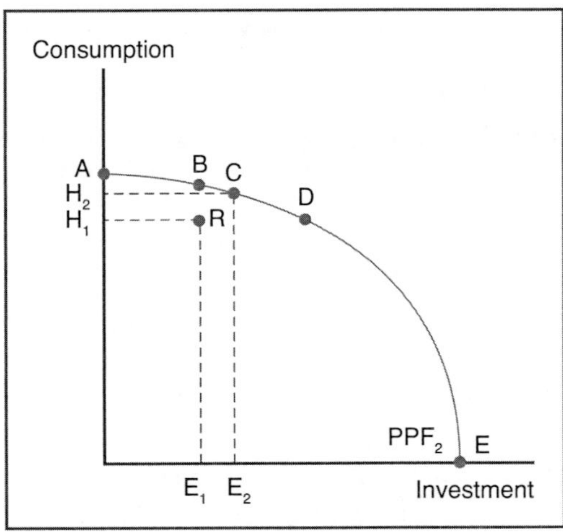

EXHIBIT 2-9 Productive and Allocative Efficiency

Productive efficiency means it is impossible to produce more of one good without decreasing the quantity that is produced of another good. Thus, all choices along a given PPF like *A*, *B*, *C*, *D*, and *E* display productive efficiency, but *R* does not. Allocative efficiency means that the particular mix of goods being produced—that is, the specific choice along the production possibilities frontier—represents the allocation that society most desires.

C than point *R* (E_2 is greater than E_1) and consumption on the vertical axis is also higher at point *C* than point *R* (H_2 is great than H_1).

Allocative efficiency means that the particular mix of goods being produced—that is, the specific choice along the production possibilities frontier—represents the allocation that society most desires. How to determine what a society desires can be a controversial question, and it will be addressed in political science, sociology, and philosophy classes as well as in economics. Only one of the productively efficient choices will be the allocatively efficient choice for society as a whole.

allocative efficiency: When the mix of goods being produced represents the allocation that society most desires.

Why Society Must Choose

Every economy should consider two situations in which it may be able to expand consumption of all goods. In the first case, a society may discover that it has been using its resources inefficiently, in which case by improving efficiency and moving to the production possibilities frontier, it can have more of some or all goods. In the second case, as an economy grows over a period of years, the production possibilities frontier for a society will tend to shift outward, and society will be able to afford more of all goods. But improvements in productive efficiency take time to discover and implement, and economic growth happens only gradually. Thus, a society must face scarcity and choose between trade-offs in the present. For government, this process often involves trying to identify where additional spending could do the most good and where reductions in spending would do the least harm. At the individual and firm level, the market economy coordinates a process in which firms seek to produce goods and services in the quantity, quality, and price that people want. But for both the government and the market economy in the short term, increases in production of one good typically mean offsetting decreases somewhere else in the economy.

Confronting Objections to the Economic Approach

It's one thing to understand the economic approach to decision-making and another thing to feel comfortable applying it. The sources of discomfort typically fall into two categories: that people don't act in the way that fits the economics model, and that even if people did act that way, they should try not to. Let's consider these arguments in turn.

A First Objection: People, Firms, and Society Don't Act Like This

The economic approach to decision-making seems to require more information than most individuals possess and more careful decision-making than most individuals actually display. After all, do you or any of your friends draw a budget constraint and mutter to yourself about maximizing utility before you head to the shopping mall? Do members of the U.S. Congress contemplate production possibilities frontiers before they vote on the federal budget? The messy ways in which people and societies actually decide doesn't much resemble neat budget constraints or smoothly curving production possibilities frontiers.

However, the economics approach can be a useful way to analyze and understand the trade-offs of economic decisions even if it doesn't describe how those decisions are actually made. To appreciate this point, imagine for a moment that you are playing basketball, dribbling to the right, and throwing a bounce-pass to the left to a teammate who is running toward the basket. A physicist or engineer could work out the correct speed and trajectory for the pass, given the different movements involved and the weight and bounciness of the ball. But when you're playing basketball, you don't perform any of these calculations. You just pass the ball, and if you're a good player, you will do so with high accuracy. Someone might argue: "The scientist's formula of the bounce-pass requires a far greater knowledge of physics and far more specific information about speeds of movement and weights than the basketball player actually has, so it must be an unrealistic description of how basketball passes are actually made." This reaction would be wrongheaded. The fact that a good player can throw the ball accurately because of practice and skill, without making a physics calculation, doesn't mean that the physics calculation is meaningless or incorrect.

Similarly, from an economic point of view, someone who goes shopping for groceries every week has a great deal of practice with how to purchase the combination of goods that will provide that person with utility, even if the shopper doesn't phrase decisions in terms of a budget constraint. Government institutions may work imperfectly and slowly, but in general, a democratic form of government feels pressure from voters and social institutions to make the choices that are widely preferred by people in that society. Thus, when thinking about the economic actions of groups of people, firms, and society, it is reasonable as a first approximation to analyze them with the tools of economic analysis.

A Second Objection: People, Firms, and Society Shouldn't Do This

The economics approach portrays people as self-interested. For some critics of this approach, even if self-interest is an accurate description of how people behave, these behaviors are not moral. Instead, the critics argue that people should be taught to care more deeply about others. Economists offer several answers to this concern.

First, economics is not a form of moral instruction. Rather, it seeks to describe economic behavior as it actually exists. Philosophers draw a distinction between **positive statements**, which describe the world as it is, and **normative statements**, which describe how the world should be. In the study of economics, positive and normative arguments often blend into each other: for example, if an economist analyzes a proposal for building a subway system in a certain city and finds that the benefits are higher than the costs, then is this study a positive analysis that merely states what *will* happen or a normative analysis that describes what *should* happen? But even if the line between positive and normative statements isn't always crystal clear, economic analysis does try to remain rooted in the study of the actual people who inhabit the actual economy. Yes, if the world were populated by saints, the economy would look different. But it isn't.

positive statements: Statements that describe the world as it is.

normative statements: Statements that describe how the world should be.

Second, self-interested behavior and profit-seeking can be labeled with other names, such as "personal choice" and "freedom." The ability to make personal choices about buying, working, and saving is an important personal freedom. Some people may choose high-pressure, high-paying jobs so that they can earn and spend a lot of money. Others may earn a lot of money and give it to charity or spend it on their friends and family. Others may devote themselves to a career that can require a great deal of time, energy,

The Budget Constraint and the Production Possibilities Frontier

When you study economics, you may feel buried under an avalanche of diagrams: diagrams in the text, diagrams in the lectures, diagrams in the problems, diagrams on exams. Your goal should be to recognize the common underlying logic and pattern of the diagrams, not to memorize each of the individual diagrams.

This chapter uses only one basic diagram, although it is presented with different sets of labels. The consumption choice budget constraint, the labor-leisure budget constraint, and the intertemporal choice budget constraint for individuals, along with the production possibilities frontier for society as a whole, are all the same basic diagram. The exhibit shows an individual budget constraint and a production possibilities frontier for two goods, Good 1 and Good 2. This kind of diagram always illustrates three basic themes: scarcity, trade-offs, and economic efficiency.

The first theme is scarcity. It is not feasible to have unlimited amounts of both goods. Budget constraints can shift, either as a result of movements of income or of prices. Production possibilities frontiers can shift, too, either as a national economy expands or as the trade-offs between the two goods shift. But even if the budget constraint or a PPF shifts, scarcity remains—just at a different level.

The second theme is trade-offs. As depicted in the budget constraint or the production possibilities frontier, it is necessary to give up some of one good to gain more of the other good. The details of this trade-off vary. In a budget constraint, the trade-off is determined by the relative prices of the goods: that is, the relative price of two goods in the consumption choice budget constraint; the relative price of labor and leisure (the wage) in the labor-leisure budget constraint; and the relative price of present and future consumption (the principal saved plus the interest rate or rate of return) in the intertemporal choice budget constraint. These trade-offs appear as a straight line. However, the trade-offs in many production possibilities frontiers are represented by a curved line because the law of diminishing returns holds that as resources are added to an area, the marginal gains tend to diminish. But regardless of the specific shape, trade-offs remain.

The third theme is economic efficiency or getting the most benefit from scarce resources. All choices on the production possibilities frontier show productive efficiency because in such cases, there is no way to increase the quantity of one good without decreasing the quantity of the other. Similarly, when an individual makes a choice along a budget constraint, there is no way to increase the quantity of one good without decreasing the quantity of the other. The choice on a production possibilities set that is socially preferred, or the choice on an individual's budget constraint that is personally preferred, will display allocative efficiency.

The basic budget constraint/production possibilities frontier diagram will recur throughout this book. Some examples include using these trade-off diagrams to analyze one source of the gains from international trade and to examine the trade-offs between environmental protection and economic output, between equality of incomes and economic output, and the macroeconomic trade-off between consumption and investment. Don't be confused by the different labels. The budget constraint/production possibilities frontier diagram is always just a tool for thinking carefully about scarcity, trade-offs, and efficiency in a particular situation.

THE TRADE-OFF DIAGRAM

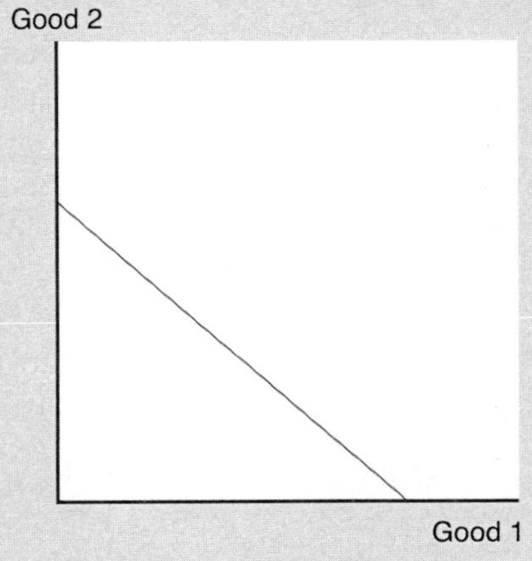

(a) An individual opportunity set.

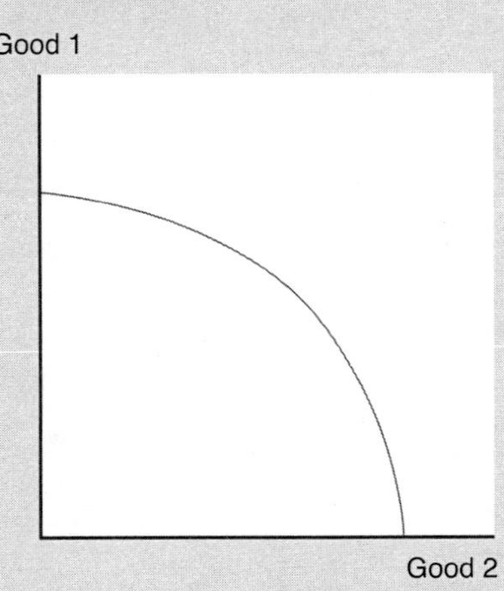

(b) A social production possibilities frontier.

and expertise but does not offer high financial rewards, like being an elementary school teacher or a social worker. Still others may choose a job that does not take lots of their time or provide a high level of income, but still leaves time for family, friends, and contemplation. Some people may prefer to work for a large company; others might want to start their own business. People's freedom to make their own economic choices has a moral value worth respecting.

Third, self-interested behavior can lead to positive social results. For example, when people work hard to make a living, they create economic output. Consumers who are looking for the best deals will encourage businesses to offer goods and services that meet their needs. Adam Smith, writing in the *Wealth of Nations*, christened this property the "invisible hand." In describing how consumers and producers interact in a market economy, Smith wrote:

> Every individual . . . generally neither intends to promote the public interest, nor knows how much he is promoting it. He intends only his own security, only his own gain. And he is in this led by an invisible hand to promote an end which was no part of his intention. By pursuing his own interest he frequently promotes that of society more effectually than when he really intends to promote it.

The metaphor of the invisible hand suggests the remarkable possibility that broader social good can emerge from selfish individual actions.

Fourth, even people who focus on their own self-interest in the economic part of their life often set aside their own narrow self-interest in other parts of life. For example, you might focus on your own self-interest when asking your employer for a raise or negotiating to buy a car. But then you might turn around and focus on other people when you volunteer to read stories at the local library, help a friend move to a new apartment, or donate money to a charity. Thus, self-interest is a reasonable starting point for analyzing many economic decisions, without needing to imply that people never do anything that is not in their own immediate self-interest.

Facing Scarcity and Making Trade-offs

The study of economics is rooted in a fundamental insight about the human condition. The world we live in is a place of scarcity, whether measured in terms of time, money, natural resources, or material goods. As a result, people must face trade-offs and make choices. The main economic trade-offs for individuals are their decisions about what to consume, how much to work, and how much to save. For society as a whole and for government decision-makers, the task is to use scarce resources as efficiently as possible to meet people's needs. Economics delves into the questions of how individuals, firms, and government will interact, and thus into the decisions that society will make about what to produce, how to produce, and for whom to produce.

Key Concepts and Summary

1. The real world is one of scarcity: that is, a world in which people's desires exceed what is possible. As a result, economic behavior involves trade-offs in which individuals, firms, government, and society must give up things that they desire to obtain other things that they desire more.
2. Individuals face three main categories of trade-offs: the consumption choice of what quantities of goods to consume, the labor-leisure choice of what quantity of hours to work, and the intertemporal choices that involve costs in the present and benefits in the future, or benefits in the present and costs in the future.
3. The **budget constraint**, sometimes called the **opportunity set**, illustrates the range of choices available. The slope of the budget constraint is determined by the relative price of the choices. Choices beyond the budget constraint are impossible. Choices inside the budget constraint are wasteful.
4. People will choose along their budget constraints in a way that maximizes their satisfaction or **utility**, which is based on their own distinctive personal preferences.
5. An interest rate has three components: the **risk premium** to cover the risk of not being repaid, the rate of expected **inflation**, and the **time value of money**, as

compensation for waiting to spend. The formula for how **compound interest** accumulates over time is:

$$\text{Future amount} = (\text{Present amount}) \times (1 + \text{Interest rate})^{\text{number of years}}$$

6. **Opportunity cost** measures cost by what is given up in exchange. Sometimes opportunity cost can be measured in money, but it is often useful to consider whether time should be included as well, or to measure it in terms of the actual resources that must be given up.
7. Most economic decisions and trade-offs are not all-or-nothing. Instead, they involve **marginal analysis**, which means they are about decisions on the margin, involving a little more or a little less.
8. The **law of diminishing marginal utility** points out that as a person receives more of something—whether it is a specific good or another resource—the additional marginal gains tend to become smaller.
9. Because **sunk costs** occurred in the past and cannot be recovered, they should be disregarded in making current decisions.
10. A **production possibilities frontier** defines a set of choices faced by society as a whole. The shape of the PPF is typically curved outward, rather than straight. Choices outside the PPF are unattainable, and choices inside the PPF are wasteful. Over time, a growing economy will tend to shift the PPF outwards.
11. The **law of diminishing returns** holds that as increments of additional resources are devoted to producing something, the marginal increase in output will become smaller and smaller.
12. All choices along a production possibilities frontier display **productive efficiency**; that is, it is impossible to use society's resources to produce more of one good without decreasing production of the other good. The specific choice along a production possibilities frontier that reflects the mix of goods that society prefers is the choice with **allocative efficiency**.
13. **Positive statements** describe the world as it is, while **normative statements** describe how the world should be. Even when economics analyzes the gains and losses from various events or policies, and thus draws normative conclusions about how the world should be, the analysis of economics is rooted in a positive analysis of how people, firms, and government actually behave, not how they should behave.

Review Questions

1. Explain why scarcity leads to trade-offs.
2. Name the three main categories of economic trade-offs that individuals face.
3. What determines the slope of the consumption choice budget constraint? The labor-leisure budget constraint? The intertemporal budget constraint?
4. Explain why individuals make choices that are directly on the budget constraint, rather than inside the budget constraint or outside it.
5. Does the economic approach specify what choices people should make? Why or why not?
6. What does it mean to "maximize utility"?
7. What are the three components of the interest rate?
8. What is the formula for how compound interest accumulates over time?
9. What is opportunity cost?
10. What is the law of diminishing marginal utility?
11. What are sunk costs?
12. What does a production possibilities frontier illustrate?
13. Why is a production possibilities frontier typically drawn as a curve, rather than a straight line?
14. Explain why societies cannot make a choice above their production possibilities frontier and should not make a choice below it.
15. What are diminishing marginal returns?
16. What is productive efficiency? Allocative efficiency?
17. What's the difference between a positive and a normative statement?
18. Is the economic model of decision-making intended as a literal description of how individuals, firms, and the government actually make decisions?

CHAPTER 3

International Trade

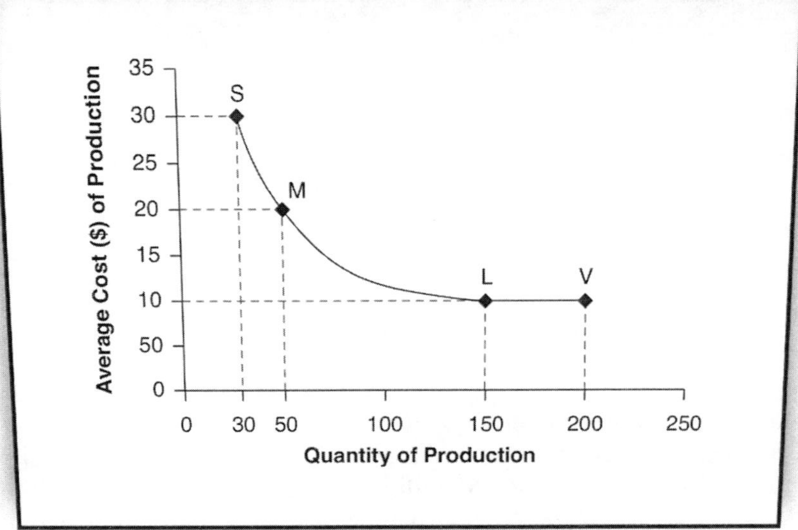

Chapter Outline

National economies are becoming more intimately interconnected in the process known as globalization. From 1970 to 2015, the size of the world economy as measured by production of goods and services almost quadrupled, and world exports—that is, goods produced in one country but sold in another country—rose by a multiple of more than 10. Similarly, the size of the U.S. economy more than tripled from 1970 to 2015, and U.S. exports rose by a multiple of more than 11. When trade as measured by exports is growing faster than the economy as a whole, international economic forces will have a greater effect on national economies. Reminders of international trade are all around. As a consumer, the food on your table might include fresh fruit from Chile, cheese from France, or bottled water from Scotland. Your phone might have been made in Sweden or Finland. The clothes you wear might be designed in Italy and manufactured in China. The toy you give to a child might have come from India. The car you drive might be from Japan, Germany, or Korea. The gasoline in the tank might be from Saudi Arabia, Mexico, or Nigeria. As a worker, if your job involves farming, machinery, airplanes, cars, scientific instruments, or many other technology-related industries, the odds are good that a hearty proportion of the sales of your employer—and hence the money that pays your salary—comes from export sales.

Exhibit 3-1 shows the volume of international merchandise trade (i.e., trade in goods) between countries in different regions of the world. The columns of the table show the region of the country where trade started; the rows show the region of the country where the exports ended up. Thus, the first entry in the top column shows that $1,251 billion in exports originated in one country in North America and went to another country in North America. The first entry in the second column shows that $214 billion in exports traveled from countries in North America to countries in South and Central America. Most of the region names should be self-explanatory, but one that may be unclear is the Commonwealth of Independent States, which includes Russia, Ukraine, and other countries that before 1991 were republics of the Soviet Union.

EXHIBIT 3-1 The Network of World Trade in Merchandise, 2014 (in billions of U.S. dollars)

The rows of the table show where trade is originating; the columns show the destination of trade. For example, the second entry in the first row shows that $214 billion in merchandise was originated in North America and was sold in South and Central America.

	Destination						
Origin	**North America**	**South and Central America**	**Europe**	**Commonwealth of Independent States**	**Africa**	**Middle East**	**Asia**
North America	$1,251	$214	$379	$17	$43	$79	$504
South and Central America	$172	$179	$114	$9	$18	$16	$170
Europe	$540	$119	$4,665	$218	$221	$229	$738
Commonwealth of Independent States	$28	$7	$385	$131	$15	$22	$134
Africa	$39	$28	$201	$2	$98	$18	$152
Middle East	$99	$11	$147	$7	$36	$113	$694
Asia	$1,064	$185	$900	$126	$207	$301	$3,093

Several patterns from this table are worth noting. First, the bulk of world trade involves high-income areas of the world, either as exporters, importers, or both. For example, the single biggest number in Exhibit 3-1 is the $4,665 billion that countries in Europe sell to each other. The level of trade between North American countries appears low compared to Europe, but this is because the European Union includes 28 nations, whereas the trade in the North American region is between the United States, Canada, and Mexico. Remember, exports from Germany to Sweden count as international trade, but sales from California to New York would not be counted in this table, since they occur within the U.S. economy.

Second, trade between high-income regions and low-income regions is fairly extensive. Perhaps the most vivid example of this point is trade of $3,093 billion between the nations of Asia, which is the second-highest number in Exhibit 3-1. The region of Asia includes the high-income economies like Japan and Korea, upper-middle-income countries like China and Thailand, lower-middle-income countries like Indonesia and Vietnam, and low-income countries like Cambodia. More generally, high-income regions of the world are important as markets for other regions. The countries of Africa, for example, export roughly twice as much to the European Union as they do to other countries of Africa. The countries of South and Central America sell as much to North America as they sell to one another.

Finally, trade between some regions is very low, for example, between Africa and South and Central America, or between the Middle East and the Commonwealth of Independent States. Indeed, some regions appear to have relatively few connections to other regions of the global economy.

The American statesman Benjamin Franklin (1706–1790) once wrote: "No nation was ever ruined by trade." Many economists would phrase their attitudes toward international trade in an even more positive manner. The circumstantial evidence that international trade confers overall benefits on the economy is strong. Trade has accompanied economic growth in the United States and around the world. Many of the national economies that have shown the most rapid growth in the last few decades—for example, Japan, South Korea, China, and India—have also dramatically expanded their international trade. There is no modern example of a country that has shut itself off from world trade and still become prosperous.

This chapter will explore the reasons that international trade provides economic gains. The discussion will draw on themes and analytic tools developed in earlier chapters. For example, Chapter 1 suggested three reasons why the division of labor and specialization, followed by trade, can increase output among individuals: specialization allows the parties to produce according to their advantages; it encourages learning and innovation; and it allows taking advantage of economies of scale. This chapter will spell out in detail how these three reasons create benefits in international trade. The production possibility frontier (PPF), introduced in Chapter 2, will be used to analyze how all countries can benefit from trade.

But although international trade provides economic gains, it is also a powerful and disruptive force. World exports of goods and services totaled over $23 trillion dollars in 2015. Domestic producers of goods often feel threatened by competition from those trillions of dollars of imports flowing into their country. Workers fear that their jobs may be at risk when foreign producers sell within their country. These fears create an awkward situation for politicians, who both want to embrace the benefits of international trade and also to block international trade from causing disruption for the firms and workers in their country. Chapter 6 will discuss public policy with regard to international trade, which often consists of a contradictory mix of international treaties to encourage trade and national actions to limit trade.

Absolute Advantage

Perhaps the most obvious case where international trade can benefit the countries that participate is the situation in which each country has a particular product that it can produce relatively cheaply compared to other countries. For example, finding oil in Saudi Arabia is pretty much just a matter of drilling a hole, but producing oil in other countries can require considerable exploration and costly technologies for drilling and extraction—if indeed other countries have any oil at all. The United States has some of the richest farmland in the world, which makes it relatively easier to grow corn and wheat here than in many other countries—like the deserts of Saudi Arabia, for example. Brazil and Colombia have climates especially suited for growing coffee. Chile and Zambia have some of the world's richest copper mines. When each country has a product that it can produce relatively cheaply, then all countries can benefit from producing that product and trading with each other.

A Numerical Example of Absolute Advantage and Trade

To illustrate the potential benefits of trade between two countries that each have a product that they produce more cheaply than the other, consider a hypothetical world with two countries, Saudi Arabia and the United States, and two products, oil and corn. Saudi Arabia can produce oil more cheaply, while the United States can produce corn more cheaply. Exhibit 3-2 illustrates the advantages of the two countries, expressed in terms of how much a worker can produce in each country. A worker in Saudi Arabia can produce six barrels of oil, while a worker in the United States can produce only two barrels of oil. However, a worker in the United States can produce eight bushels of corn, while a worker in Saudi Arabia can produce only one bushel of corn.

When one nation can produce a product at lower cost relative to another nation, it is said to have an **absolute advantage** in producing that product. In this example, Saudi Arabia has an absolute advantage in the production of oil, and the United States has an absolute advantage in the production of corn. Two nations that each have an absolute advantage in certain products can both benefit if each nation specializes (at least to some extent) in the area of its absolute advantage and then the nations trade with each other.

absolute advantage: When one nation can produce a product at lower cost relative to another nation.

EXHIBIT 3-2 Absolute Advantage: How Much Can One Worker Produce?

A worker in Saudi Arabia can produce more oil, by a margin of 6 barrels to 2 barrels. However, a worker in the United States can produce more corn, by a margin of 8 bushels to 1 bushel.

	Saudi Arabia	United States
One worker can produce	6 barrels of oil	2 barrels of oil
One worker can produce	1 bushel of corn	8 bushels of corn

EXHIBIT 3-3
Production Possibilities Frontiers and Absolute Advantage

The tables show several points along the production possibilities frontiers for each country, based on the numbers for what workers produce in Exhibit 3-2 and assuming 40 Saudi workers and 80 U.S. workers. Our assumption here is that point *A* in the two figures is the choice that each country would most prefer, given its production possibilities in the absence of trade. Each country would prefer a point like *B* in the two figures, with more of both goods, but in a world without trade, a choice like *B* is impossible. Through specialization and trade, however, a point like *B* becomes possible for both countries.

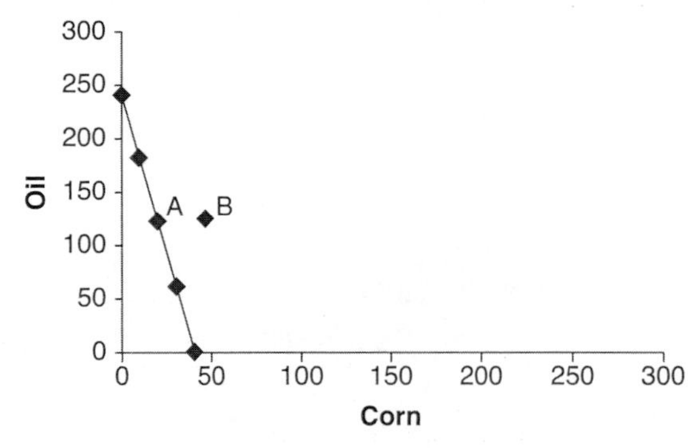

(a) Saudi Arabia *PPF* (40 workers)

Allocation of Workers	Output of Oil	Output of Corn
40 oil, 0 corn	240	0
30 oil, 10 corn	180	10
20 oil, 20 corn	120	20
10 oil, 30 corn	60	30
0 oil, 40 corn	0	40

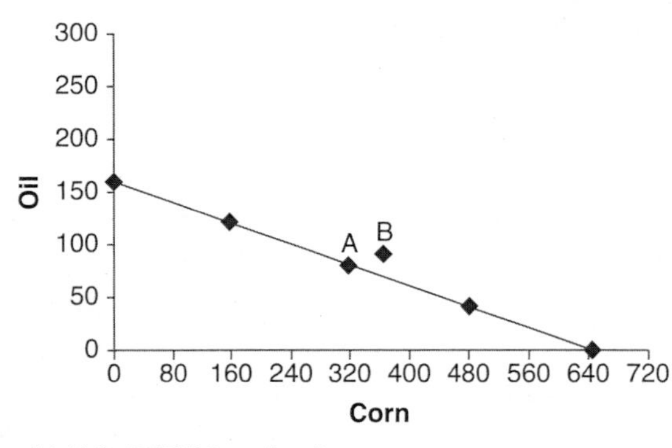

(b) U.S. *PPF* (80 workers)

Allocation of Workers	Output of Oil	Output of Corn
80 oil, 0 corn	160	0
60 oil, 20 corn	120	160
40 oil, 40 corn	80	320
20 oil, 60 corn	40	480
0 oil, 80 corn	0	640

The production possibilities frontier provides an analytical tool for illustrating this point. Exhibit 3-3 presents two production possibility frontiers for the possible levels of production in a world without trade, one for Saudi Arabia and one for the United States, based on the assumption that the economy of Saudi Arabia has 40 workers and the U.S. economy has 80 workers. If all 40 workers in the Saudi economy produced oil, that country could produce 240 barrels (i.e., $40 \times 6 = 240$); if all the Saudi workers focused on corn, that economy could produce 40 bushels ($40 \times 1 = 40$). The table next to the figure shows some of the in-between choices, and the points from the table are graphed on the production possibilities frontier. Meanwhile, if the U.S. economy devoted all 80 workers to oil, it could produce 160 barrels (i.e., $80 \times 2 = 160$), but if it devoted all 80 workers to corn, it could produce 640 bushels ($80 \times 8 = 640$).

The slope of the production possibility frontier is determined by the opportunity cost of expanding production of one good, measured by how much of the other good would be lost. The information in Exhibit 3-2 can be interpreted in terms of opportunity costs. For example, in the U.S. economy the opportunity cost of producing 2 barrels of oil, which requires one worker, is the loss of the 8 bushels of corn that the worker could have produced otherwise. Thus, in the U.S. production possibility frontier in Exhibit 3-3, every increase in oil production of 1 barrel reflects a decrease of 4 bushels of corn. In the economy of Saudi Arabia, the opportunity cost of producing 1 bushel of corn, which requires one more worker, is the loss of the 6 barrels of oil that workers could otherwise have produced. The slope of the Saudi production possibility frontier shows that every rise of 1 bushel of corn leads to a fall of 6 barrels of oil.

For the sake of the argument, let's say that before trade occurs, the most desired point for each nation—as determined by the preferences of its citizens—is the point halfway down each production possibility frontier, shown as point A on each production possibility frontier. Thus, in the world before trade, the economy of Saudi Arabia will devote 20 workers to each product, and produce 120 barrels of oil and 20 bushels of corn, while the U.S. economy devotes 40 workers to each product and produces 80 barrels of oil and 320 bushels of corn. Of course, each nation would prefer a choice like point B, which

EXHIBIT 3-4 How Specialization by Absolute Advantage Expands Output

The first two columns show the quantity of oil and corn that would be produced in each country, at its preferred point *A* as shown in Exhibit 3-3 before trade occurs. The last two columns show output after specialization has occurred, so that each country is producing only one good. The bottom "TOTAL" row shows the combined production of each good. The total quantity produced of each good is greater than in the situation before specialization, which is what allows both countries, after trade, to consume more of both goods. As a result, both countries can be better off.

	Quantity Produced before Trade		Quantity Produced after Specialization	
	Oil	*Corn*	*Oil*	*Corn*
Saudi Arabia	120	20	240	0
United States	80	320	0	640
TOTAL	200	340	240	640

offers more of both goods, but since choice B is above the production possibility frontier, that choice isn't possible for either country.

However, if each of the two nations specializes in its area of absolute advantage and then trades, it becomes possible to expand global production of both goods. Exhibit 3-4 provides the calculations. The table shows output of oil and corn in the two countries before trade, and by adding up the output in the countries, it shows global output of the two goods. Now assume that Saudi Arabia decides to specialize in its absolute advantage and produce only oil, thus producing 240 barrels of oil, and the United States specializes in its absolute advantage in farming, producing 640 bushels of corn. When each nation specializes in this way, Exhibit 3-4 shows that the total global output of both products rises. It becomes possible, with trade, to consume at higher levels than would have been possible without trade.

Consider the trading positions of the United States and Saudi Arabia after they have specialized in their areas of absolute advantage, so that the United States is producing 640 bushels of corn and zero oil, while Saudi Arabia is producing 240 barrels of oil and zero corn. If the United States can trade an amount of corn *less than* 320 bushels and receive in exchange an amount of oil *greater than* 80 barrels, it will have more of both goods than it did in the situation with no trade at all. Similarly, if Saudi Arabia can trade an amount of oil less than 120 barrels and receive in exchange an amount of corn greater than 20 bushels, it will have more of both goods than it did before specialization and trade. Exhibit 3-5 illustrates the range of trades that would benefit both sides. Any trade where the United States exports more than 20 bushels of corn but less than 320 bushels of corn, and receives in exchange imports from Saudi Arabia of at least 80 barrels of oil but no more than 120 barrels of oil, will benefit both sides. As a specific example, a trade where the United States exports 200 bushels of corn to Saudi Arabia and Saudi Arabia exports 100 barrels of oil to the United States would allow both countries to consume more of both goods than they could before specialized production and trade occurred.

EXHIBIT 3-5 The Range of Trades That Benefit Both the United States and Saudi Arabia

The U.S. Economy, after Specialization, Will Benefit If It:	The Saudi Arabian Economy, after Specialization, Will Benefit If It:
Exports no more than 320 bushels of corn in exchange for	Imports at least 20 bushels of corn in exchange for
Imports of at least 80 barrels of oil	Exports of less than 120 barrels of oil

CLEARING IT UP

Yes, a Production Possibility Frontier Can Be Straight

When the possibility frontier was introduced in Chapter 2, it was drawn with an outward-bending shape, which illustrated that as inputs were transferred from one area to another—like from producing education to producing health—there were diminishing marginal returns. In the examples in this chapter, the *PPFs* are drawn as straight lines, which means that returns are not diminishing. When a marginal unit of labor is transferred away from growing corn and toward producing oil, the decline in the quantity of corn and the increase in the quantity of oil is always the same. The linear production possibilities frontier is a less realistic model. But a straight line is easier for purposes of calculation than a curve, and it illustrates the economic themes like absolute advantage just as clearly.

Trade and Opportunity Cost

The underlying reason why trade can benefit both sides is rooted in the concept of opportunity cost. If the United States wants to expand domestic production of oil in a world without trade, its opportunity cost (based on the numbers in Exhibit 3-2) is that it must give up 4 bushels of corn for every 1 additional barrel of oil. If the United States could find a way to give up *less than* 4 bushels of corn to receive 1 barrel of oil, it would be better off. Thus, any trade where the United States gives up less than 320 bushels of corn to receive at least 80 barrels of oil—notice the 4:1 ratio—makes the United States better off. By specializing in corn production and then trading with Saudi Arabia for oil, the U.S. economy can possess more corn and oil at a cheaper opportunity cost than its own domestic production allows.

The same insight holds for Saudi Arabia. If Saudi Arabia wishes to expand domestic production of corn in a world without trade, then based on its opportunity costs (as shown in Exhibit 3-2), it must give up 6 barrels of oil for every 1 additional bushel of corn. If Saudi Arabia could find a way to give up less than 6 barrels of oil for an additional bushel of corn (or equivalently, to receive more than 1 bushel of corn for 6 units of oil), it would be better off. Thus, any trade where Saudi Arabia can export no more than 120 barrels of oil in exchange for at least 20 units of corn—notice again that the ratio of 120:20 is the country's domestic opportunity cost of 6:1—will make the country better off.

Cost is measured as opportunity cost. In this example, the opportunity cost of 1 bushel of corn is only 1/4 barrel of oil in the United States, but the opportunity cost of 1 bushel of corn is 6 barrels of oil in Saudi Arabia. Similarly, the opportunity cost of 1 barrel of oil in the United States is 4 bushels of corn, but the opportunity cost of 1 barrel of oil in Saudi Arabia is 1/6 bushel of corn. In effect, trade lets each country take advantage of the lower opportunity cost of production in the other country. This example would reach the same general conclusion showing benefits from specialization and trade if the number of workers in the two economies was altered, or if the original starting point was not assumed to be point *A* in Exhibit 3-3, but instead involved dividing up the labor in some way other than having half the workers producing each good.

Limitations of the Numerical Example

This demonstration of how both nations can benefit from specializing in their absolute advantage and trading has some limitations.

First, the example does not explain how the extra output of oil and corn will be divided up. It describes a range of trades that can benefit both sides, but it doesn't say who will receive what share of the total benefit. Perhaps the two countries will split the extra output equally. Perhaps the U.S. economy will get most of the extra output, and the Saudi economy only a little bit. Perhaps the reverse will be true. In the real economy, the price at which corn exchanges for oil will be determined by demand and supply (discussed in

CLEARING IT UP

Different Ways of Presenting Absolute Advantage

There are several different ways of presenting information that shows absolute advantage in producing at lower costs. Exhibit 3-2 showed the different quantities that a single worker could produce. Exhibit 3-6 shows the different number of workers needed to produce a fixed quantity of output. Other alternatives would be to measure work with hours, instead of workers, and to say how many hours it takes to produce a unit of a good or how many units could be produced in an hour. Don't be confused by the different labels in these kinds of tables. Focus on the underlying economic meaning: which nation can produce a certain good more cheaply, which means producing either the same amount with a lower level of inputs or producing more with the same level of inputs If in a certain nation a single worker produces more of a product, relative to the other country, or if it takes fewer workers to produce a fixed amount of a product, relative to the other country, then that nation has an absolute advantage in producing that product.

Chapter 4), which will lead to a specific price and quantity for each good. This example shows only that both countries *can* be better off with specialization and trade, not *how much* each country is better off.

Second, this example has only two hypothetical countries and two goods, while the real world has over 200 countries and tens of thousands of goods. However, the example remains useful as a model that illustrates a key underlying principle: Differences in opportunity costs can allow trade to benefit all participants.

Third, this example assumes that the opportunity costs of trading oil for corn production, or vice versa, are always constant in both countries. This premise simplifies the calculations. In the real world, countries will typically find that they have a variety of resources that are better-suited or worse-suited to producing different products. For example, Saudi Arabia has some relatively fertile land and some land where drilling for oil is more costly. Conversely, the United States has some areas of poor farmland, as well as areas where oil is more accessible. In numerical examples with constant opportunity costs, it often makes sense to specialize in the production of just one product. But in the real world, it will make sense to give up only on the more costly ways of producing certain products, and the specialization in one product won't be so extreme.

A skeptic about the gains from international trade might start asking other questions at this point. What if one nation becomes dependent on the other for oil or food, and then the exporter cuts off the supply? What if oil workers in the United States lose jobs when oil is imported from Saudi Arabia and farmers in Saudi Arabia lose jobs when corn is imported from the United States? These questions are good ones, and they will be taken up, along with many other questions, in the discussion of public policies about international trade in Chapter 6. But first, let's continue painting the picture of how international trade can provide economic benefits.

Comparative Advantage

The concept of absolute advantage is based on the assumption that each nation has a cost advantage in producing a certain product. But what happens to the possibilities for trade if one country, typically a high-income country with well-educated workers, technologically advanced equipment, and the most up-to-date production processes, can produce all products more cheaply than a low-income country? If the high-income country has a cost advantage in all products, then it may seem as if the low-income country would have nothing to trade. However, one of the most powerful insights in economic analysis, developed by the famous English economist David Ricardo (1772–1823) early in the nineteenth century, points out that even when one country has an absolute advantage in all products, trade can still benefit both sides.

The First Wave of Globalization

A second wave of globalization began in the second half of the twentieth century. But the first wave of globalization started in the nineteenth century and lasted up to the beginning of World War I. Over that time, global exports as a share of global GDP rose from less than 1% of GDP in 1820 to 9% of GDP in 1913. As the Nobel Prize-winning economist Paul Krugman of Princeton University wrote in 1995:

> It is a late-twentieth-century conceit that we invented the global economy just yesterday. In fact, world markets achieved an impressive degree of integration during the second half of the nineteenth century. Indeed, if one wants a specific date for the beginning of a truly global economy, one might well choose 1869, the year in which both the Suez Canal and the Union Pacific railroad were completed. By the eve of the First World War, steamships and railroads had created markets for standardized commodities, like wheat and wool, that were fully global in their reach. Even the global flow of information was better than modern observers, focused on electronic technology, tend to realize: the first submarine telegraph cable was laid under the Atlantic in 1858, and by 1900 all of the world's major economic regions could effectively communicate instantaneously.

This first wave of globalization crashed to a halt in the first half of the twentieth century. World War I severed many economic connections. During the Great Depression of the 1930s, many nations misguidedly tried to fix their own economies by reducing foreign trade with others. World War II further hindered international trade. Global flows of goods and financial capital rebuilt themselves only slowly after World War II. It was not until the early 1980s that global economic forces again became as important, relative to the size of the world economy, as they were before World War I.

Identifying Comparative Advantage

Consider the situation described in Exhibit 3-6 of costs of production in the United States and Mexico. In this example, it takes 4 U.S. workers to produce 1,000 pairs of shoes, but it takes 5 Mexican workers to do so. It takes 1 U.S. worker to produce 1,000 refrigerators, but it takes 4 Mexican workers to do so. In this example, the United States has an absolute advantage in productivity with regard to both shoes and refrigerators; that is, it takes fewer workers in the United States than in Mexico to produce both a given number of shoes and a given number of refrigerators. However, even in this case, Ricardo showed that both sides could benefit from trade.

Ricardo's insight was that even though the United States has an absolute advantage at producing both products with less labor, the United States does not produce both products more cheaply from an opportunity cost point of view. In Mexico, the opportunity cost of producing 1,000 extra pairs of shoes, and using the labor of 5 workers, means taking those 5 workers away from the production of refrigerators, where they would have produced 1,250 refrigerators. (Exhibit 3-6 shows that in Mexico it takes 4 workers to produce 1,000 refrigerators, so 5 workers would produce 1,250 refrigerators; that is, $5/4 \times 1{,}000$.)

EXHIBIT 3-6 Identifying Comparative Advantage

It takes fewer workers in the United States (4) to produce 1,000 pairs of shoes than it does in Mexico (5). It also takes fewer workers in the United States (1) to produce 1,000 refrigerators than it does in Mexico (4). Thus, the United States has an absolute advantage in the production of both goods. However, the comparative advantage of the United States—where its absolute advantage is relatively greatest—lies in refrigerators. The comparative advantage of Mexico—where its absolute disadvantage is relatively least—lies in shoes.

	United States	Mexico
Production	***Amount of Labor***	***Amount of Labor***
1,000 pairs of shoes	4 workers	5 workers
1,000 refrigerators	1 worker	4 workers

In the United States, the opportunity cost of producing an extra 1,000 pairs of shoes involves the labor of four workers, and moving those four workers away from refrigerator production has an opportunity cost of 4,000 refrigerators (i.e., one worker can produce 1,000 refrigerators in the United States, so 4 workers could produce 4,000). Measured in opportunity cost terms, it is cheaper to produce shoes in Mexico, where the opportunity cost is 1,250 refrigerators for every 1,000 shoes, and more expensive to produce shoes in the United States, where the opportunity cost of 1,000 pairs of shoes is 4,000 refrigerators.

Next consider the opportunity cost of producing refrigerators. Producing an extra 1,000 refrigerators in Mexico requires 4 workers. If those four workers are moved out of shoe production, the opportunity cost is 800 pairs of shoes (if it takes 5 Mexican workers to produce 1,000 pairs of shoes, than 4 workers can produce 800 shoes—4/5 × 1,000). Producing an extra 1,000 refrigerators in the United States, using one worker, would have an opportunity cost of only 250 pairs of shoes (i.e., if it takes 4 U.S. workers to make 1,000 pairs of shoes, then one worker can make 250 pairs). Measured in opportunity cost terms, producing 1,000 refrigerators is more expensive in Mexico, where it costs 800 pairs of shoes, and less expensive in the United States, where the opportunity cost is only 250 pairs of shoes.

A nation that can produce at a lower cost *when measured in terms of opportunity cost* is said to have a **comparative advantage**. Even though the United States has an absolute advantage in needing fewer workers to produce a given quantity of either shoes or refrigerators, Mexico has a comparative advantage in the production of shoes, and the United States has a comparative advantage in the production of refrigerators. Comparative advantage identifies the area where a producer's absolute advantage is greatest, or *where the producer's absolute disadvantage in productivity is least*. The United States can produce 1,000 shoes with four-fifths as many workers as Mexico (4 versus 5), but can produce 1,000 refrigerators with only one-quarter as many workers (1 versus 4). Thus, the comparative advantage of the United States, where its absolute productivity advantage is relatively greatest, lies with refrigerators, and Mexico's comparative advantage, where its absolute productivity disadvantage is least, is in the production of shoes.

comparative advantage: The goods in which a nation has its greatest productivity advantage or its smallest productivity disadvantage; also, the goods that a nation can produce at a lower cost when measured in terms of opportunity cost.

Mutually Beneficial Trade with Comparative Advantage

When nations increase production in their area of comparative advantage and trade with each other, both sides can benefit. Again, the production possibility frontier offers a useful tool. Consider a situation where the United States and Mexico each has 40 workers. The tables in Exhibit 3-7 show the level of output for different divisions of labor, using the figures for the productivity of labor given in Exhibit 3-6. For example, if the United States divides its labor so that 40 workers are making shoes, then since it takes 4 workers in the United States to make 1,000 shoes, a total of 10,000 shoes will be produced (if 4 workers can make 1,000 shoes, then 40 workers will make 10,000 shoes). If the 40 workers in the United States are making refrigerators, and each worker can produce 1,000 refrigerators, then a total of 40,000 refrigerators will be produced. The choices from the tables are graphed on the production possibility frontiers in Exhibit 3-7. As always, the slope of the production possibility frontier for each country is determined by the opportunity costs as labor is transferred from production of shoes to production of refrigerators, or vice versa.

Let's assume that in the situation before trade, each nation prefers to allocate half of its labor to production of each good, as shown at point A. Exhibit 3-8 shows the output of each good for each country and the total output for the two countries. Of course, both countries would prefer a choice like point B with more of both goods, but a choice like B that is above the production possibility frontier is impossible in a world without trade. (Choosing the halfway point is only to make a convenient example. The argument for how trade according to comparative advantage can benefit both parties works just the same if the nation's original choice is a point one-third of the way, or one-quarter of the way, or any choice between the endpoints of the production possibility frontier.)

Now, have each country transfer some amount of labor toward its area of comparative advantage. For example, the United States transfers 6 workers away from shoes

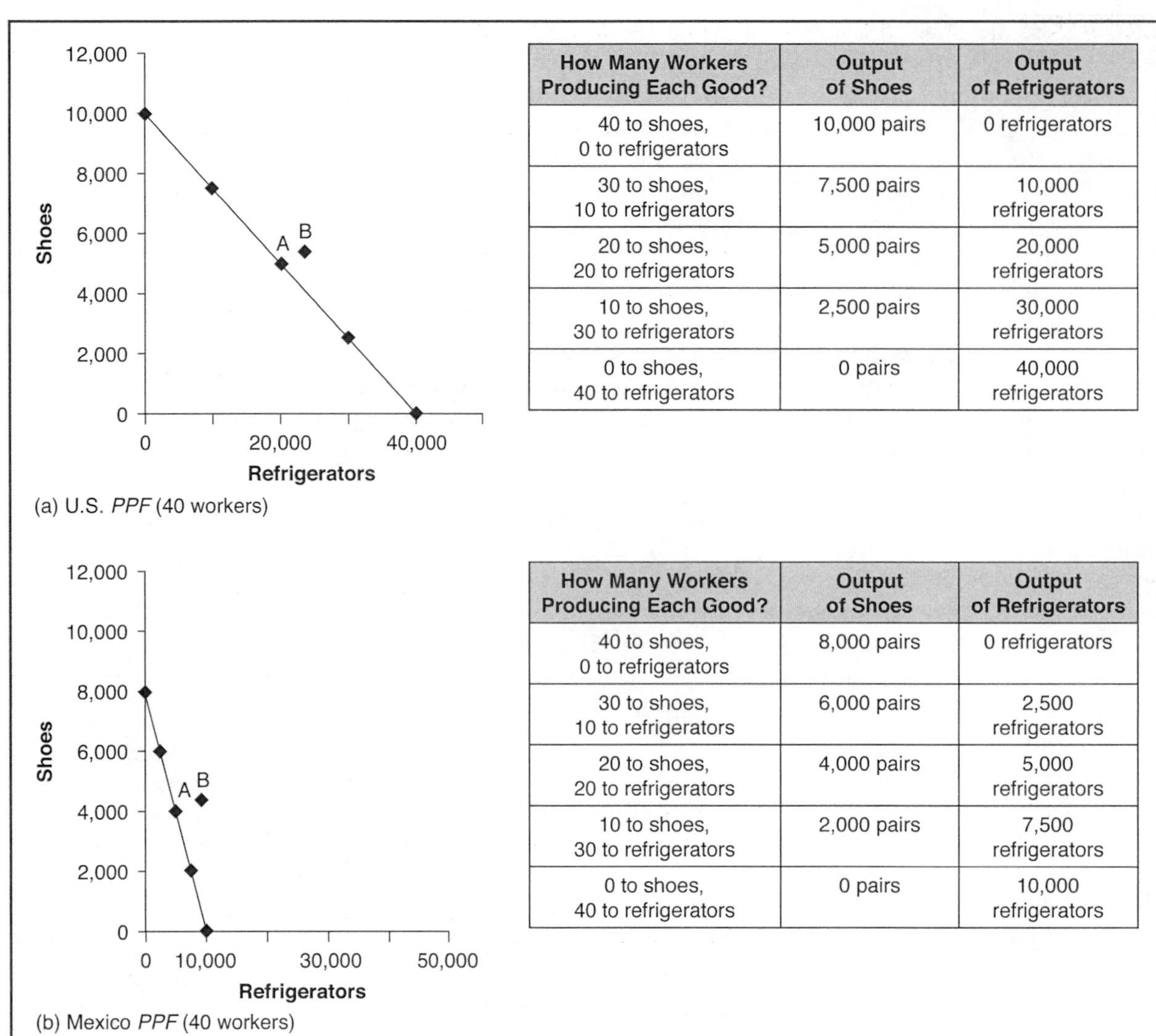

How Many Workers Producing Each Good?	Output of Shoes	Output of Refrigerators
40 to shoes, 0 to refrigerators	10,000 pairs	0 refrigerators
30 to shoes, 10 to refrigerators	7,500 pairs	10,000 refrigerators
20 to shoes, 20 to refrigerators	5,000 pairs	20,000 refrigerators
10 to shoes, 30 to refrigerators	2,500 pairs	30,000 refrigerators
0 to shoes, 40 to refrigerators	0 pairs	40,000 refrigerators

How Many Workers Producing Each Good?	Output of Shoes	Output of Refrigerators
40 to shoes, 0 to refrigerators	8,000 pairs	0 refrigerators
30 to shoes, 10 to refrigerators	6,000 pairs	2,500 refrigerators
20 to shoes, 20 to refrigerators	4,000 pairs	5,000 refrigerators
10 to shoes, 30 to refrigerators	2,000 pairs	7,500 refrigerators
0 to shoes, 40 to refrigerators	0 pairs	10,000 refrigerators

EXHIBIT 3-7 Comparative Advantage with Production Possibility Frontiers

The tables show several points along the production possibilities frontiers for each country, based on the numbers for what workers produce in Exhibit 3-6 and assuming 40 workers for each country. In the absence of trade, let's assume that each country would most prefer point A, given its production possibilities. While a point like B provides more of both goods, in a world without trade, a choice like B is impossible. Through specialization and trade, a point like B becomes possible for both countries, showing that both countries can benefit from trade.

EXHIBIT 3-8 Calculating Gains from Trade with Comparative Advantage

This table shows the total production of shoes and refrigerators before trade. It also shows total production after the United States transfers 6 workers from shoes to refrigerators and Mexico transfers 10 workers from refrigerators to shoes through specialization.

	Production before Trade		Production after Specialization	
	Shoes	*Refrigerators*	*Shoes*	*Refrigerators*
United States	5,000	20,000	5,000 – 1,500	20,000 + 6,000
Mexico	4,000	5,000	4,000 + 2,000	5,000 – 2,500
Total	9,000	25,000	9,500	28,500

CLEARING IT UP

Choosing Numbers So Comparative Advantage Examples Work

In the example in the text, why have the United States move 6 workers from shoes to refrigerators, and why have Mexico move 10 workers from refrigerators and shoes? Why 6? Why 10?

To show that specializing according to comparative advantage can benefit all parties, the shift in production must allow total combined production of both goods to increase. But here's a potential problem: If the United States shifts an equal amount of labor away from shoes that Mexico shifts toward shoes, then overall combined production of shoes will decline—because the U.S. economy has an absolute advantage in shoe production. Thus, Mexico must shift more labor toward shoes than the United States shifts away from shoes to make up for its absolute productivity advantage in shoes, so that overall combined production of shoes will increase. Having Mexico shift 10 workers toward shoes when the United States shifts 6 workers away from shoes will work for this purpose. So will any combination of numbers where the ratio of Mexican labor toward shoes to U.S. labor away from shoes is at least 5/4 to make up for the fact that it takes 5 workers in Mexico to produce the same number of shoes that takes 4 U.S. workers.

and toward producing refrigerators. As a result, U.S. production of shoes decreases by 1,500 units (6/4 × 1,000), while its production of refrigerators increases by 6,000 (i.e., 6/1 × 1,000). Mexico also moves production toward its area of comparative advantage, transferring 10 workers away from refrigerators and toward production of shoes. As a result, production of refrigerators in Mexico falls by 2,500 (10/4 × 1,000), but production of shoes increases by 2,000 pairs (10/5 × 1,000). Notice that when both countries shift toward their comparative advantage, their combined production of both goods rises, as shown in Exhibit 3-8. The reduction of shoe production by 1,500 pairs in the United States is more than offset by the gain of 2,000 pairs of shoes in Mexico, while the reduction of 2,500 refrigerators in Mexico is more than offset by the additional 6,000 refrigerators produced in the United States.

This numerical example illustrates the remarkable insight of comparative advantage: Even when one country has an absolute advantage in all goods and another country has an absolute disadvantage in all goods, both countries can still benefit from trade. Even though the United States has an absolute advantage in producing both refrigerators and shoes, it makes economic sense for the United States to specialize more in refrigerators, where it has a comparative advantage, and to import some shoes instead. Conversely, even though Mexico has an absolute disadvantage in both refrigerators and shoes, it can still play an active and productive role in world trade by focusing on its comparative advantage in shoes.

How Opportunity Cost Sets the Boundaries of Trade

This example shows that both parties can benefit from specializing in their comparative advantage and trading. By using the opportunity costs in this example, it is possible to identify the range of possible trades that would benefit each side.

Mexico started out before specialization and trade by producing 4,000 pairs of shoes and 5,000 refrigerators. Then in the numerical example given, Mexico shifted production toward its comparative advantage and produced 6,000 shoes but only 2,500 refrigerators. Thus, if Mexico can export no more than 2,000 pairs of shoes in exchange for imports of at least 2,500 refrigerators, then it will be able to consume more of both goods than before trade and it will be unambiguously better off. Conversely, the United States started off before specialization and trade producing 5,000 pairs of shoes and 20,000 refrigerators. In the numerical example given, it then shifted toward comparative advantage, producing only 3,500 shoes but 26,000 refrigerators. If the United States can export no more than 6,000 refrigerators in exchange for imports of at least 1,500 pairs of shoes, then it will be able to consume more of both goods and will be unambiguously better off. The range of trades that can benefit both nations is shown in Exhibit 3-9. For example, a trade where

EXHIBIT 3-9 The Range of Trades That Will Benefit Both the United States and Mexico

The U.S. Economy, after Specialization, Will Benefit If It:	The Mexican Economy, after Specialization, Will Benefit If It:
Exports Fewer than 6,000 refrigerators in exchange for	*Imports* at least 2,500 refrigerators in exchange for
Imports of at least 1,500 pairs of shoes	*Exports* of no more than 2,000 pairs of shoes

the U.S. exports 4,000 refrigerators to Mexico in exchange for 1,800 pairs of shoes would benefit both sides, in the sense that both countries would be able to consume more of both goods than in a world without trade.

Trade allows each country to take advantage of lower opportunity costs in the other country. If Mexico wants to produce more refrigerators without trade, it must face its domestic opportunity costs and reduce shoe production. But if Mexico instead produces more shoes and then trades for refrigerators produced in the United States, where the opportunity cost of producing refrigerators is lower, Mexico can in effect take advantage of the lower opportunity cost in the United States for producing refrigerators. Conversely, when the United States specializes in its comparative advantage of refrigerator production and trades for shoes produced in Mexico, international trade allows the United States to take advantage of the lower opportunity cost of shoe production in Mexico.

The theory of comparative advantage shows that the gains from international trade do not just result from the absolute advantage of producing at lower cost, but also from pursuing comparative advantage and producing at a lower opportunity cost.

Comparative Advantage Goes Camping

To build a greater intuitive understanding of how comparative advantage can benefit all parties, set aside examples that involve national economies for a moment and consider the situation of a group of friends who decide to go camping together. The friends have a wide range of skills and experiences, but one person in particular, Jethro, has done lots of camping before and is a great athlete, too. Jethro has an absolute advantage in all aspects of camping: carrying more weight in a backpack, gathering firewood, paddling a canoe, setting up tents, making a meal, and washing up. So here's the question: Because Jethro has an absolute productivity advantage in everything, should he do all the work?

Of course not. Even if Jethro is willing to work like a mule while everyone else sits around, he still has only 24 hours in a day. If everyone sits around and waits for Jethro to do everything, not only will Jethro be an unhappy camper, but there won't be much output for his group of six friends to consume. The theory of comparative advantage suggests that everyone will benefit if they figure out their areas of comparative advantage; that is, the area of camping where their productivity disadvantage is least, compared to Jethro. For example, perhaps Jethro is 80% faster at building fires and cooking meals than anyone else, but only 20% faster at gathering firewood and 10% faster at setting up tents. In that case, Jethro should focus on building fires and making meals, and others should attend to the other tasks, each according to where their productivity disadvantage is smallest. If the campers coordinate their efforts according to comparative advantage, they can all gain.

The Power of the Comparative Advantage Example

The two-country, two-good numerical illustration of comparative advantage, like the example of absolute advantage, has its limitations. While the example shows that both sides can benefit from specialization according to comparative advantage and trade, it doesn't explain exactly how much extra production will occur, or how the gains from trade will be divided up. It is (again) an example with two goods and two countries. It assumes production possibility frontiers that are straight lines representing constant trade-offs, rather than outward-bending curves with varying trade-offs.

These limitations can all be summarized in one basic point: this example is a model, not a literal description of the U.S. or the Mexican economy. The power of a model is to reveal the key features of how something works. The model of comparative advantage shows that even the most productive country in the world and the least productive country can both gain from trading with each other, if they each focus on the products where they possess a comparative advantage. Even the most productive country will have some product where its absolute advantage is greatest. A country can have an absolute advantage in all goods, but it is logically impossible to have a comparative advantage in all goods. Even the country with an absolute productivity disadvantage in every single product will have an area where its absolute disadvantage is smallest. Comparative advantage ranks among the most sophisticated insights in all of economics; indeed, an understanding of comparative advantage is one way of distinguishing economists from non-economists.

Intra-industry Trade between Similar Economies

Absolute and comparative advantage explain a great deal about patterns of global trade. For example, they help to explain the patterns noted at the start of this chapter, like why you may be eating fresh fruit from Chile or Mexico, or why lower productivity regions like Africa and Latin America are able to sell a substantial proportion of their exports to higher productivity regions like the European Union and North America. But absolute and comparative advantage, at least at first glance, do not seem especially well-suited to explain other common patterns of international trade.

The Prevalence of Intra-industry Trade between Similar Economies

The theory of comparative advantage suggests that trade should happen between economies with large differences in their opportunity costs of production. However, roughly half of all world trade involves shipping goods between the fairly similar high-income economies of the United States, Canada, the European Union, Japan, Australia, and New Zealand. Nearly half of U.S. trade is with the other high-income economies of the world, like Canada, Europe, and Japan, as shown in Exhibit 3-10, rather than with the much more different economies of Latin America or Africa.

Moreover, the theories of absolute and comparative advantage suggest that each economy should specialize to a degree in certain products, and then exchange those products. But a high proportion of trade is **intra-industry trade**—that is, trade of goods within the same industry. Exhibit 3-11 shows some of the largest categories of U.S. exports and imports. In all of these categories, the United States is both a substantial exporter and a substantial importer of goods from the same industry. For example, in 2015 the United States

intra-industry trade: International trade of goods within the same industry.

EXHIBIT 3-10 Where U.S. Exports Go and U.S. Imports Originate (2014)

About half of U.S. trade is with similar high-income nations of the world, like Canada, the countries of the European Union, and Japan.

	U.S. Exports Go to. . .	U.S. Imports Come from. . .
Canada	19.2%	14.9%
European Union	17.1%	17.8%
Mexico	14.7%	12.7%
China	7.6%	19.7%
Japan	4.2%	5.7%

EXHIBIT 3-11 Some Intra-Industry U.S. Exports and Imports in 2015

Many of the leading U.S. exports, as measured by these broad categories, are also leading U.S. imports. This pattern illustrates the importance of intra-industry trade for the U.S. economy.

Some Traded Products	Quantity of U.S. Exports (billions of dollars)	Quantity of U.S. Imports (billions of dollars)
Agricultural, forestry, and fishery products	$70	$56
Food	$62	$58
Manufactures	$1,112	$1,944
Paper products	$23	$20
Chemicals	$184	$217
Transportation equipment	$251	$374
Machinery (except electrical)	$123	$156
Petroleum and coal products	$80	$69
Computers and electronic products	$120	$371

exported $251 billion of transportation equipment, but imported $374 billion of transportation equipment. About 60% of U.S. trade and 60% of European trade is intra-industry trade.

Why do similar economies engage in intra-industry trade? What can be the economic benefit of having workers with fairly similar skills making cars, computers, machinery, and other products, which are then shipped in directions across the oceans to and from the United States, the European Union, and Japan? There are two reasons: how the division of labor leads to learning, innovation, and unique skills; and economies of scale.

Gains from Specialization and Learning

Consider the category of "machinery," where the U.S. economy has considerable intra-industry trade. Machinery comes in many varieties, so the U.S. may be exporting machinery for manufacturing with wood, but importing machinery for photographic processing. The underlying reason why a country like the United States, Japan, or Germany produces one kind of machinery rather than another is usually not related to U.S., German, or Japanese firms and workers having generally higher or lower skills—but just that in working on very specific and particular products, firms in certain countries have developed unique and different skills.

splitting up the value chain: When many of the different stages of producing a good happen in different geographic locations.

Specialization in the world economy can be very finely split. In fact, recent years have seen a trend in international trade called **splitting up the value chain**. The "value chain" describes how a good is produced in stages: for example, the value chain for making a toaster oven would include making metal and plastic parts, elements that provide the heat, and electrical cords; designing how the parts will fit together; assembly of the toaster ovens; packaging and shipping; and selling in a retail store. Thanks in part to improvements in technologies for communication, sharing of information, and transportation, it has become easier to split up the value chain so that instead of being done in a single large factory, these steps can be split up among different firms operating in different places and even different countries. Because of splitting up the value chain, international trade often doesn't involve whole finished products like automobiles or refrigerators being traded between nations. Instead, it can involve shipping more specialized goods like, say, automobile dashboards or the shelving that fits inside refrigerators. Intra-industry trade between similar countries produces economic gains because it allows workers and firms to learn and innovate by focusing on very particular parts of the value chain.

Economies of Scale, Competition, Variety

A second broad reason that intra-industry trade between similar nations produces economic gains involves economies of scale. The concept of economies of scale, as introduced in Chapter 1, means that as the scale of output goes up, average costs of production decline—at least up to a point. Exhibit 3-12 illustrates economies of scale for a hypothetical set of plants that produce toaster ovens. The horizontal axis of the figure shows the quantity of production by a certain firm or at a certain manufacturing plant. The vertical axis measures the average cost of production. Thus, Production Plant S, which produces a small level of output 30, has an average cost of production of $30 per toaster oven. Production Plant M, which produces at a medium level of output 50, has an average cost of production of $20 per toaster oven. Production Plant L, which produces at a large level of output 150, has an average cost of production of only $10 per toaster oven. However, Production Plant V, which produces at the very high level of output of 200, still has an average cost of production of $10 per toaster oven. In this example, a small or medium plant, like S or M, will not be able to compete in the market with a large or a very large plant like L or V, because the firm that operates L or V will be able to produce and sell at a lower cost. In this example, economies of scale operate up to point L, but beyond point L to V, additional scale of production does not continue to reduce average costs of production. (The reasons behind economies of scale, the different forms that economies of scale can take, and their implications for the size of companies will be analyzed in greater detail in Chapter 9.) Economies of scale are a common feature in many industries.

The concept of economies of scale becomes especially relevant to international trade when one or two large producers could supply the entire country. For example, a single large automobile factory could probably supply all the cars purchased in a smaller economy like the United Kingdom or Belgium in a given year. However, if a country has only one or two large factories producing cars, and no international trade, then consumers in that country would have relatively little choice between kinds of cars (other than the

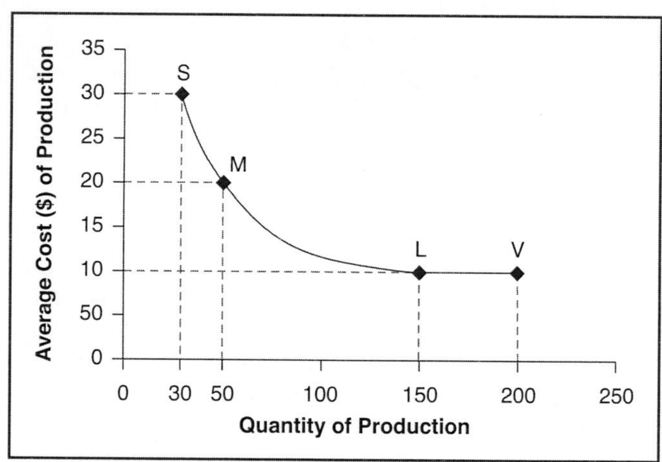

EXHIBIT 3-12 Economies of Scale

Production Plant S, which produces a small level of output 30, has an average cost of production of $30 per toaster oven. Production Plant M, which produces at a medium level of output 50, has an average cost of production of $20 per toaster oven. Production Plant L, which produces at a large level of output 150, has an average cost of production of only $10 per toaster oven. Production Plant V, which produces at the very high level of output of 200, would still have an average cost of production of $10 per toaster oven. Thus, production plant M can produce toaster ovens more cheaply than plant S because of economies of scale, and plants L or V can produce more cheaply than S or M because of economies of scale. However, the economies of scale end at an output level of 150. Plant V, despite being larger, cannot produce more cheaply on average than plant L.

color of the paint and other nonessential options), and little or no competition would exist between different car manufacturers.

International trade provides a way to combine the lower average production costs of economies of scale and still have competition and variety for consumers. Large automobile factories in different countries can make and sell their products around the world. If the U.S. automobile market was made up of only General Motors, Ford, and Chrysler, the level of competition and consumer choice would be a lot less than when the U.S. carmakers must face competition from Toyota, Honda, Suzuki, Fiat, Mazda, Mitsubishi, Nissan, Volkswagen, Kia, Hyundai, BMW, Subaru, and others. Greater competition brings with it innovation and responsiveness to what consumers want. America's car producers make far better cars now than they did several decades ago, and much of the reason is competitive pressure, especially from East Asian and European carmakers.

Dynamic Comparative Advantage

The sources of gains from intra-industry trade between similar economies—namely, the learning that comes from a high degree of specialization and splitting up the value chain and from economies of scale—do not contradict the earlier theory of comparative advantage. Instead, they help to broaden the concept of comparative advantage.

In intra-industry trade, the level of worker productivity isn't determined by climate or mineral deposits. It isn't even determined by the general level of education or skill. Instead, the level of worker productivity is determined by how firms engage in specific learning about specialized products, including taking advantage of economies of scale to the extent possible. In this vision, comparative advantage can be dynamic—that is, it can evolve and change over time as new specific skills are developed and as the value chain is split up in new ways. This line of thinking also suggests that countries are not destined to have the same comparative advantage forever, but must instead react flexibly in response to ongoing changes in comparative advantage.

Intra-industry trade between similar trading partners allows for gains from learning and innovation that arise when firms and workers specialize in the production of a certain product (and with the trend toward splitting up the value chain, this learning can become very specialized, indeed). It also allows the gains from using economies of scale for large-scale production, while avoiding the problem of having only one large supplier in a market, and instead allowing fierce competition between different producers to offer the combination of variety, price, and quantity that will satisfy their customers.

The Size of Benefits from International Trade

It's hard to measure the economic gains from international trade with precision. After all, measuring the gains from trade would require comparing the world economy with international trade to a world economy that did not have international trade—which means figuring out what the world economy would look like if international trade did not exist at all. Such calculations are bound to be controversial.

However, estimating the gains from expanding trade from existing levels is more practical. For example, the nations of the world meet together through the World Trade Organization (WTO) to negotiate ways in which they can reduce government taxes or regulations that have the effect of limiting trade. Negotiations in the WTO happen in "rounds," where all countries negotiate one agreement to encourage trade, then take a year or two off, and then start negotiating a new agreement. It often takes 7–10 years from beginning to end of a round of WTO negotiations. The current round of negotiations is called the "Doha round" because it was officially launched in Doha, the capital city in the country of Qatar, in November 2001. In a recent study, economists from the World Bank summarized recent research and found that the Doha round of negotiations would increase the size of the world economy by $160 billion per year, depending on the precise deal that ended up being negotiated. In the context of a global economy that currently produces more than $70 trillion or so of goods and services each year, this amount is not huge: it's less than 1% or less of the global economy. But before dismissing the gains from trade too quickly, it's worth remembering four points.

First, a gain of a few hundred billion dollars is enough money to deserve attention! Moreover, remember that this increase is not a one-time event; it would persist each year into the future.

Second, this estimate of $160 billion measures only the expected gains from the most recent round of trade negotiations. In other words, it measures only the economic gains from expanding international trade somewhat from the levels it had already reached a decade or so into the 21st century, before the Doha round of trade negotiations was finalized. Measuring the gains from all existing international trade would be a multiple of this number.

Third, this estimate of gains may be on the low side because some of the gains from trade are not measured especially well in economic statistics. For example, while it is possible to estimate the economic gains from taking advantage of comparative advantage or economies of scale, it is difficult to measure the potential advantages to consumers of having a variety of products available and a greater degree of competition among producers. Perhaps the most important unmeasured factor is that trade between countries, especially when firms are splitting up the value chain of production, often involves a transfer of knowledge that can involve skills in production, technology, management, finance, and law. These transfers of knowledge may be especially important in helping low-income countries improve their standard of living.

Fourth, the gains from expanding trade are probably most important for the low-income economies in the world. In some ways, the giant U.S. economy has less need for international trade, because it can already take advantage of internal trade within its economy. The United States has a variety of different climates, natural resources, and geographic areas where workers are more skilled or less skilled. It is a large enough economy that firms can become extremely specialized and focused on producing small slices of the value chain. In the huge U.S. economy, large firms can take advantage of economies of scale and still compete against each other within the U.S. economy. However, many smaller national economies around the world, in regions like Latin America, Africa, the Middle East, and Asia, have much more limited possibilities for trade inside their countries or their immediate regions. Their possibilities for gains from purely internal trade are smaller. Without international trade, they may have little ability to benefit from comparative advantage, slicing up the value chain, or economies of scale. Moreover, smaller economies often have fewer competitive firms making goods within their economy, and thus firms have less pressure from other firms to provide the goods and prices that consumers want.

The economic gains from expanding international trade are measured in hundreds of billions of dollars, and the gains from international trade as a whole probably reach well into the trillions of dollars. The potential for gains from trade may be especially high among the smaller and lower-income countries of the world.

From Interpersonal to International Trade

Most people find it easy to believe that they personally would not be better off if they tried to grow and process all of their own food, to make all of their own clothes, to build their own car and house from scratch, and so on. Instead, we all benefit from living in economies where people and firms can specialize and trade with each other.

This same argument applies at the level of the community. Most of us, whether we live in small towns or suburbs or large cities, would find it difficult if our town or city tried to be self-sufficient—for example, to produce all of its own food within the city limits, along with clothing, health care, housing, and all inputs and machinery that are used in producing these goods. There are clear economic gains when people and firms from one community trade with people and firms from other communities.

This same argument continues to apply at the level of states or provinces. The people of Vermont or New Mexico, for example, would find that their standard of living suffered considerably if they attempted to consume only what was produced inside the boundaries of their state, without trading with California, Texas, New York, and all the other states.

The benefits of trade do not stop at national boundaries, either. Chapter 1 explained that the division of labor could increase output for three reasons: workers with different characteristics can specialize in the types of production where they have an advantage (which this chapter has spelled out as comparative and absolute advantage); firms and workers who specialize in a certain product become more productive with learning and practice; and economies of scale. These three reasons apply from the individual and community level right up to the international level. If it makes sense to you that interpersonal, inter-community trade and inter-state trade offer economic gains, it should make sense that international trade offers gains, too.

International trade currently involves over tens of trillions of dollars' worth of goods and services thundering around the globe. Any economic force of that size, even if it confers overall benefits, is certain to cause disruption and controversy. This chapter has only made the case that trade brings economic benefits. Later chapters, especially Chapter 6, will discuss in detail the public policy arguments over whether to restrict international trade.

Key Concepts and Summary

1. A country has an **absolute advantage** in those products in which it has a productivity edge over other countries.
2. Two countries that each have an absolute advantage in different products can gain from specializing (at least to some extent) in the product where they have an absolute advantage and then trading.
3. A country has a **comparative advantage** where its cost of production, measured in opportunity cost terms, is lowest. Equivalently, a country has a comparative advantage in whatever product where either its absolute advantage is relatively greatest or where its absolute disadvantage is relatively least.
4. Two countries can benefit from specializing (at least to some extent) in the product where each has a comparative advantage and then trading with each other. This statement holds true even if one of the countries has an absolute advantage in both products.
5. A large share of global trade happens between high-income economies that are quite similar in having well-educated workers and advanced technology. These countries practice **intra-industry trade**, in which they import and export the same products at the same time, like cars, machinery, and computers.
6. In the case of intra-industry trade between similar economies, the gains from trade come from specialized learning in very particular tasks and from economies of scale.
7. The gains of international trade are very large, especially for smaller countries, but can be difficult to measure with precision.

Review Questions

1. What is absolute advantage?
2. In what situations does absolute advantage provide a reason for gains from trade?
3. What is comparative advantage? Explain in two ways, first using the idea of opportunity cost and second using the idea of relatively large or small absolute advantages and absolute disadvantages.
4. Is it possible to have an absolute advantage in the production of a certain good but not to have a comparative advantage in the production of that good? Explain.
5. Is it possible to have a comparative advantage in the production of a good but not to have an absolute advantage? Explain.
6. In what situations does comparative advantage provide a reason for gains from trade?
7. What is intra-industry trade?
8. What are the two main sources of economic gains from intra-industry trade?
9. What is splitting up the value chain?
10. Why might intra-industry trade seem surprising from the point of view of comparative advantage? How does intra-industry trade fit with the idea of comparative advantage?
11. Are the gains from international trade more likely to be relatively more important to larger or smaller countries?

CHAPTER

4

Demand and Supply

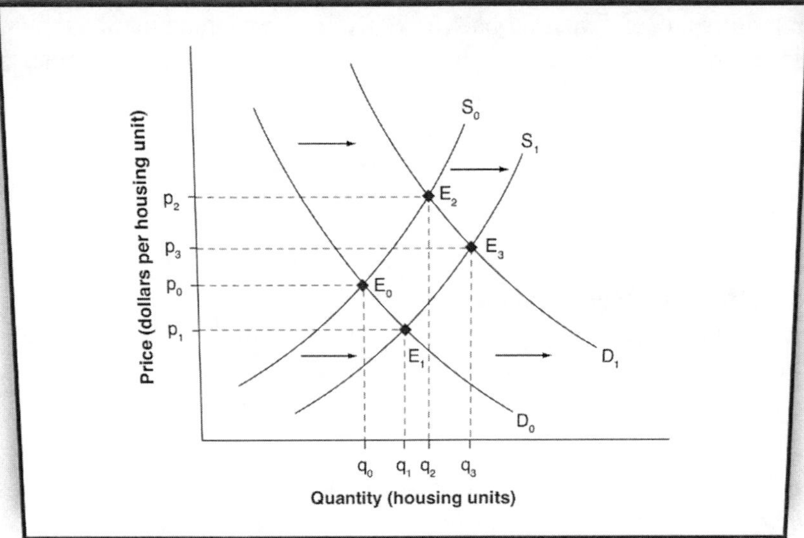

Chapter Outline

When people talk about prices, the discussion often takes a judgmental tone. A bidder in an auction pays thousands of dollars for a dress once worn by Diana, Princess of Wales. A collector spends thousands of dollars for some drawings by John Lennon of the Beatles. Mouths gape. Surely such purchases are a waste of money? But when economists talk about prices, they are less interested in making judgments than in gaining a practical understanding of what determines prices and why prices change. In 1933, the great British economist Joan Robinson (1903–1983) explained how economists perceive price:

> The point may be put like this: You see two men, one of whom is giving a banana to the other, and is taking a penny from him. You ask, How is it that a banana costs a penny rather than any other sum? The most obvious line of attack on this question is to break it up into two fresh questions: How does it happen that the one man will take a penny for a banana? and: How does it happen that the other man will give a penny for a banana? In short, the natural thing is to divide up the problem under two heads: Supply and Demand.

As a contemporary example, consider a price often listed on large signs beside well-traveled roads: the price of a gallon of gasoline. Why was the average price of gasoline in the United States $2.80 per gallon in June 2015? Why did the price for gasoline fall to $1.77 per gallon seven months later by February 2016? To explain why prices are at a certain level and why that level changes over time, economic analysis focuses on the determinants of what gasoline buyers are willing to pay and what gasoline sellers are willing to accept. For example, the price of a gallon of gasoline in June of a given year is nearly always higher than the price in January of that year; over recent decades, gasoline prices in midsummer have averaged about 10 cents per gallon more than their midwinter low. The likely reason is that people want to drive more in the summer, and thus they are willing to pay more for gas at that time. However, from June 2015 to February 2016, gasoline prices fell by much more than the average summer-to-winter fall, which suggests that other factors related to those who buy gasoline and firms that sell it changed during those six months, too.

This chapter introduces the economic model of demand and supply. The discussion begins by examining how demand and supply determine the price and the quantity sold in markets for goods and services, and how changes in demand and supply lead to changes in prices and quantities. In Chapter 5, the same demand and supply model is applied to markets for labor and financial capital. In Chapter 6, the same supply and demand model is applied to international trade. In situation after situation, in different places around the world, across different cultures, even reaching back into history, the demand and supply model offers a useful framework for thinking about what determines the prices and quantities of what is bought and sold.

Demand, Supply, and Equilibrium in Markets for Goods and Services

Markets for goods and services include everything from accounting services, air travel, and apples to zinc, zinfandel wine, and zucchini. Let's first focus on what economists mean by demand, what they mean by supply, and then how demand and supply interact in an economic model of the market.

demand: A relationship between price and the quantity demanded of a certain good or service.

quantity demanded: The total number of units of a good or service purchased at a certain price.

law of demand: The common relationship that a higher price leads to a lower quantity demanded of a certain good or service.

demand schedule: A table that shows a range of prices for a certain good or service and the quantity demanded at each price.

Demand for Goods and Services

Economists use the term **demand** to refer to a relationship between price and the quantity demanded. Price is what a buyer pays (or the seller receives) for a unit of the specific good or service. **Quantity demanded** refers to the total number of units that are purchased at a given price. A rise in price of a good or service almost always decreases the quantity demanded of that good or service; conversely, a fall in price will increase the quantity demanded. When the price of a gallon of gasoline goes up, for example, people look for ways to reduce their purchases of gasoline by combining several errands, commuting by carpool or public transportation, or taking weekend or vacation trips by car close to home. Economists refer to the relationship that a higher price leads to a lower quantity demanded as the **law of demand**.

Exhibit 4-1 gives a hypothetical example in the market for gasoline. The table that shows the quantity demanded at each price is called a **demand schedule**. Price in this

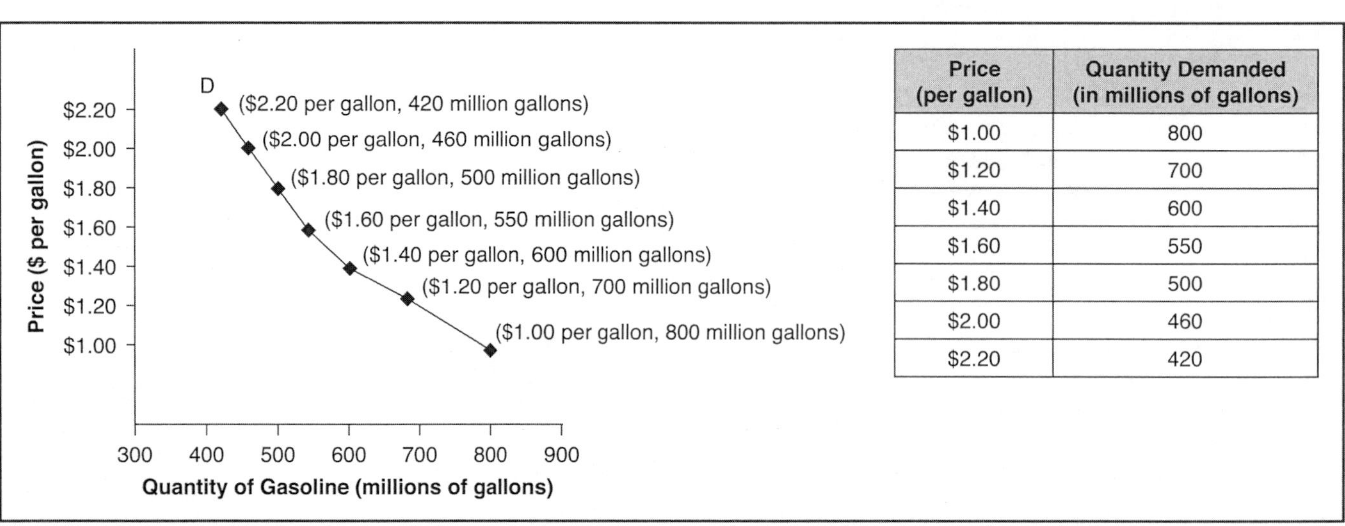

Price (per gallon)	Quantity Demanded (in millions of gallons)
$1.00	800
$1.20	700
$1.40	600
$1.60	550
$1.80	500
$2.00	460
$2.20	420

EXHIBIT 4-1 A Demand Curve for Gasoline

The table that shows quantity demanded of gasoline at each price is called a demand schedule. The demand schedule shows that as price rises, quantity demanded decreases. These points are then graphed on the figure, and the line connecting them is the demand curve D. The downward slope of the demand curve again illustrates the pattern that as price rises, quantity demanded decreases. This pattern is called the law of demand.

case is measured per gallon of gasoline. The quantity demanded is measured in millions of gallons. A **demand curve** shows the relationship between price and quantity demanded on a graph, with quantity on the horizontal axis and the price per gallon on the vertical axis. The demand schedule shown by the table and the demand curve shown on the graph are two ways of describing the same relationship between price and quantity demanded.

demand curve: A line that shows the relationship between price and quantity demanded of a certain good or service on a graph, with quantity on the horizontal axis and the price on the vertical axis.

Each individual good or service needs to be graphed on its own demand curve, because it wouldn't make sense to graph the quantity of apples and the quantity of airplanes on the same diagram. Demand curves will appear somewhat different for each product; for example, they may appear relatively steep or flat, or they may be straight or curved. But nearly all demand curves share the fundamental similarity that they slope down from left to right. In this way, demand curves embody the law of demand; as the price increases, the quantity demanded decreases, and conversely, as the price decreases, the quantity demanded increases.

Supply of Goods and Services

supply: A relationship between price and the quantity supplied of a certain good or service.

quantity supplied: The total number of units of a good or service sold at a certain price.

law of supply: The common relationship that a higher price is associated with a greater quantity supplied.

supply schedule: A table that shows a range of prices for a good or service and the quantity supplied at each price.

supply curve: A line that shows the relationship between price and quantity supplied on a graph, with quantity supplied on the horizontal axis and price on the vertical axis.

When economists talk about **supply**, they are referring to a relationship between price received for each unit sold and the **quantity supplied**, which is the total number of units sold in the market at a certain price. A rise in price of a good or service almost always leads to an increase in the quantity supplied of that good or service, while a fall in price will decrease the quantity supplied. When the price of gasoline rises, for example, profit-seeking firms are encouraged to expand exploration for oil reserves; to carry out additional drilling for oil; to make new investments in pipelines and oil tankers to bring the oil to plants where it can be refined into gasoline; to build new oil refineries; to purchase additional pipelines and trucks to ship the gasoline to gas stations; and to open more gas stations or to keep existing gas stations open longer hours. The pattern that a higher price is associated with a greater quantity supplied is so common that economists have named it the **law of supply**.

Exhibit 4-2 illustrates the law of supply, again using the market for gasoline as an example. A **supply schedule** is a table that shows the quantity supplied at a range of different prices. Again, price is measured per gallon of gasoline and quantity supplied is measured in millions of gallons. A **supply curve** is a graphical illustration of the relationship between price, shown on the vertical axis, and quantity, shown on the horizontal axis. The supply schedule and the supply curve are just two different ways of showing the same

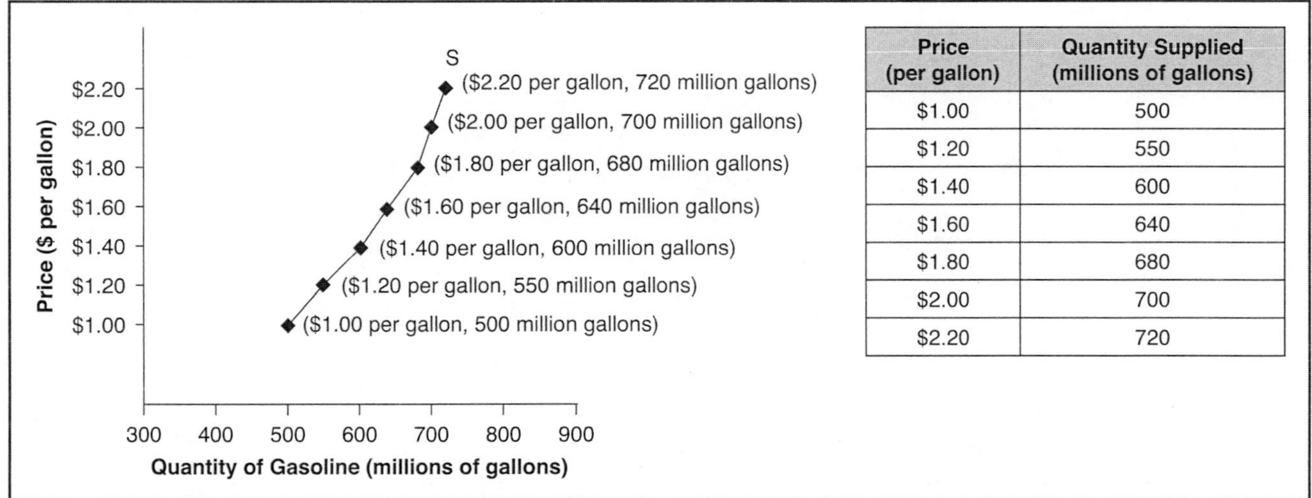

Price (per gallon)	Quantity Supplied (millions of gallons)
$1.00	500
$1.20	550
$1.40	600
$1.60	640
$1.80	680
$2.00	700
$2.20	720

EXHIBIT 4-2 A Supply Curve for Gasoline

The supply schedule is the table that shows quantity supplied of gasoline at each price. As price rises, quantity supplied also increases. The supply curve S is created by graphing the points from the supply schedule and then connecting them. The upward slope of the supply curve illustrates the pattern that a higher price leads to a higher quantity supplied—a pattern that is common enough to be called the law of supply.

CLEARING IT UP

Supply Is Not the Same as Quantity Supplied

In economic terminology, supply is not the same as quantity supplied. When economists refer to supply, they mean the relationship between a range of prices and the quantities supplied at those prices, a relationship that can be illustrated with a supply curve or a supply schedule. When economists refer to quantity supplied, they often mean only a certain point on the supply curve, or sometimes, they are referring to the horizontal axis of the supply curve or one column of the supply schedule.

information. Notice that the horizontal and vertical axes on the graph for the supply curve are the same as for the demand curve.

Just as each product has its own demand curve, each product has its own supply curve. The shape of supply curves will vary somewhat according to the product: steeper, flatter, straighter, or curved. But nearly all supply curves share a basic similarity: they slope up from left to right. In that way, the supply curve illustrates the law of supply: as the price rises, the quantity supplied increases, and conversely, as the price falls, the quantity supplied decreases.

Equilibrium—Where Demand and Supply Cross

Because the graphs for demand and supply curves both have price on the vertical axis and quantity on the horizontal axis, the demand curve and supply curve for a particular good or service can appear on the same graph. Together, demand and supply determine the price and the quantity that will be bought and sold in a market.

Exhibit 4-3 illustrates the interaction of demand and supply in the market for gasoline. The demand curve D is identical to Exhibit 4-1. The supply curve S is identical to Exhibit 4-2. When one curve slopes down, like demand, and another curve slopes up, like supply, the curves intersect at some point.

equilibrium price: The price where quantity demanded is equal to quantity supplied.

In every economics course you will ever take, when two lines on a diagram cross, this intersection means something! The point where the supply curve S and the demand curve D cross, designated by point E in Exhibit 4-3, is called the equilibrium. The **equilibrium price** is defined as the price where quantity demanded is equal to quantity supplied. The

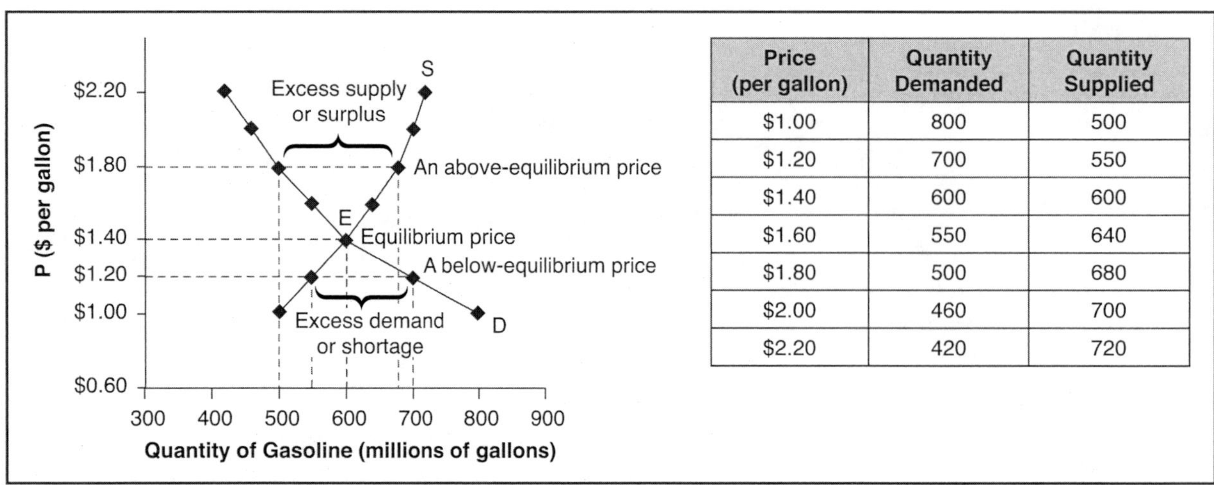

Price (per gallon)	Quantity Demanded	Quantity Supplied
$1.00	800	500
$1.20	700	550
$1.40	600	600
$1.60	550	640
$1.80	500	680
$2.00	460	700
$2.20	420	720

EXHIBIT 4-3 Demand and Supply for Gasoline

The demand curve D and the supply curve S intersect at the equilibrium point E, with a price of $1.40 and a quantity of 600. The equilibrium is the only price where quantity demanded is equal to quantity supplied. At a price above equilibrium like $1.80, quantity supplied of 680 exceeds the quantity demanded of 500, so there is excess supply or a surplus. At a price below equilibrium such as $1.20, quantity demanded of 700 exceeds quantity supplied of 550, so there is excess demand or a shortage.

equilibrium quantity is the quantity where quantity demanded and quantity supplied are equal at a certain price. In Exhibit 4-3, the equilibrium price is $1.40 per gallon of gasoline and the equilibrium quantity is 600 million gallons. If you had only the demand and supply schedules, and not the graph, it would be easy to find the equilibrium by looking for the price level on the tables where the quantity demanded and the quantity supplied are equal.

equilibrium quantity: The quantity at which quantity demanded and quantity supplied are equal at a certain price.

The word equilibrium means "balance." If a market is balanced at its **equilibrium** price and quantity, then it has no reason to move away from that point. However, if a market is not balanced at equilibrium, then economic pressures arise to move toward the equilibrium price and the equilibrium quantity.

equilibrium: The combination of price and quantity where there is no economic pressure from surpluses or shortages that would cause price or quantity to shift.

Imagine, for example, that the price of a gallon of gasoline is above the equilibrium price and is priced at $1.80 per gallon. This above-equilibrium price is illustrated by the dashed horizontal line at the price of $1.80 in Exhibit 4-3. At this higher price of $1.80, the quantity demanded drops from the equilibrium quantity of 600 to 500 million gallons. This decline in quantity reflects how people and businesses react to the higher price by seeking out ways to use less gasoline, like sharing rides to work, taking public transportation, and avoiding faraway vacation destinations. Moreover, at this higher price of $1.80, the quantity supplied of gasoline rises from the 600 to 680 million gallons, as the higher price provides incentives for gasoline producers to expand their output. At this above-equilibrium price, there is **excess supply**, or a **surplus**; that is, the quantity supplied exceeds the quantity demanded at the given price. With a surplus, gasoline accumulates at gas stations, in tanker trucks, in pipelines, and at oil refineries. This accumulation puts pressure on gasoline sellers. If a surplus of gasoline remains unsold, those firms involved in making and selling gasoline are not receiving enough cash to pay their workers and to cover their expenses. In this situation, at least some gasoline producers and sellers will be tempted to cut prices, because it's better to sell at a lower price than not to sell at all. Once some sellers start cutting gasoline prices, others will follow so that they won't lose sales to the earlier price-cutters. These price reductions in turn will stimulate a higher quantity demanded. In this way, if the price is above the equilibrium level, incentives built into the structure of demand and supply will create pressures for the price to fall toward the equilibrium.

excess supply: When at the existing price, quantity supplied exceeds the quantity demanded; also called a "surplus."

surplus: When at the existing price, quantity supplied exceeds the quantity demanded; also called "excess supply."

Now suppose that the price is below its equilibrium level at $1.20 per gallon, as shown by the dashed horizontal line at this price in Exhibit 4-3. At this lower price, the quantity demanded increases from 600 to 700 million gallons as drivers take longer trips, spend more minutes warming up their car in the driveway in wintertime, stop sharing rides to work, and purchase cars that get fewer miles to the gallon. However, the below-equilibrium price reduces gasoline producers' incentives to produce and sell gasoline, and the quantity supplied of gasoline falls from 600 to 550 million gallons. When the price is below equilibrium, there is **excess demand**, or a **shortage**; that is, at the given price the quantity demanded, which has been stimulated by the lower price, now exceeds the quantity supplied, which had been depressed by the lower price. In this situation, eager gasoline buyers mob the gas stations, only to find many stations running short of fuel. Oil companies and gas stations recognize that they have an opportunity to make higher profits by selling what gasoline they have at a higher price. As a result, the price rises toward the equilibrium level.

excess demand: At the existing price, the quantity demanded exceeds the quantity supplied, also called "shortage."

shortage: At the existing price, the quantity demanded exceeds the quantity supplied, also called "excess demand."

Shifts in Demand and Supply for Goods and Services

A demand curve shows how quantity demanded changes as the price rises or falls. A supply curve shows how quantity supplied changes as the price rises or falls. But what happens when factors other than price influence quantity demanded and quantity supplied? For example, what if demand for, say, vegetarian food becomes popular with more consumers? Or what if the supply of, say, diamonds rises not because of any change in price, but because companies discover several new diamond mines? A change in price leads to a different point on a specific demand curve or a supply curve, but a shift in some economic factor other than price can cause the entire demand curve or supply curve to shift.

The *Ceteris Paribus* Assumption

ceteris paribus: Other things being equal.

A demand curve or a supply curve is a relationship between two and only two variables: quantity on the horizontal axis and price on the vertical axis. Thus, the implicit assumption behind a demand curve or a supply curve is that no other relevant economic factors are changing. Economists refer to this assumption as ***ceteris paribus***, a Latin phrase meaning "other things being equal." Any given demand or supply curve is based on the *ceteris paribus* assumption that all else is held equal. If all else is not held equal, then the demand or supply curve itself can shift.

An Example of a Shifting Demand Curve

The original demand curve D_0 in Exhibit 4-4 shows at point Q that at a price of $20,000 per car, the quantity of cars demanded would be 18 million. The original demand curve also shows how the quantity of cars demanded would change as a result of a higher or lower price; for example, if the price of a car rose to $22,000, the quantity demanded would decrease to 17 million, as at point R.

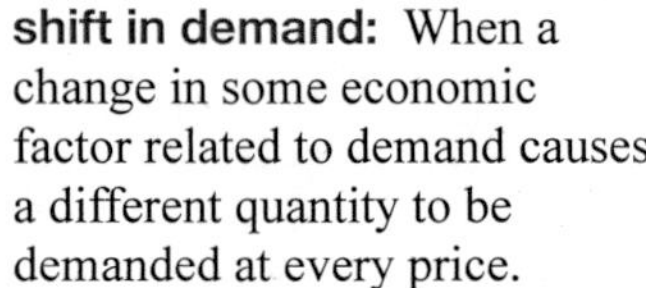

shift in demand: When a change in some economic factor related to demand causes a different quantity to be demanded at every price.

The original demand curve D_0, like every demand curve, is based on the *ceteris paribus* assumption that no other economically relevant factors change. But now imagine that the economy expands in a way that raises the incomes of many people. As a result of the higher income levels, a **shift in demand** occurs, which means that compared to the original demand curve D_0, a different quantity of cars will now be demanded at every price. On the original demand curve, a price of $20,000 means a quantity demanded of 18 million, but

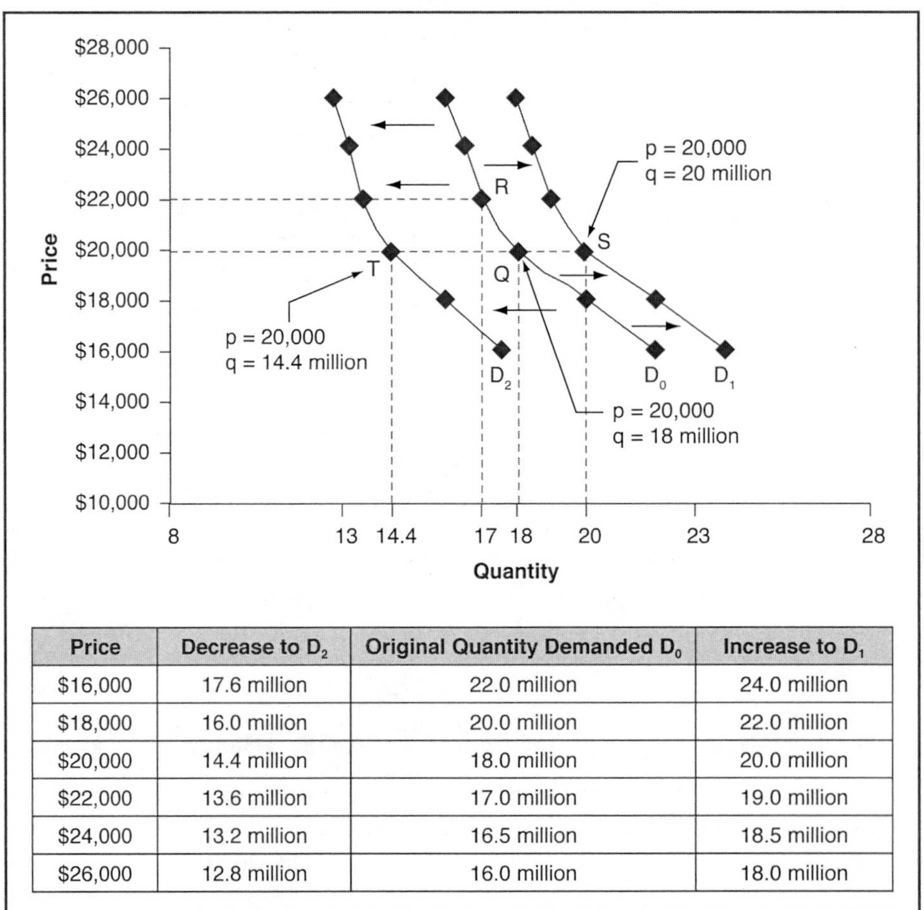

Price	Decrease to D_2	Original Quantity Demanded D_0	Increase to D_1
$16,000	17.6 million	22.0 million	24.0 million
$18,000	16.0 million	20.0 million	22.0 million
$20,000	14.4 million	18.0 million	20.0 million
$22,000	13.6 million	17.0 million	19.0 million
$24,000	13.2 million	16.5 million	18.5 million
$26,000	12.8 million	16.0 million	18.0 million

EXHIBIT 4-4 Shifts in Demand: A Car Example

Increased demand means that at every given price, the quantity demanded is higher, so that the demand curve shifts to the right from D_0 to D_1. Decreased demand means that at every given price, the quantity demand is lower, so that the demand curve shifts to the left from D_0 to D_2.

after higher incomes cause an increase in demand, a price of $20,000 leads to a quantity demanded of 20 million, at point S. Exhibit 4-4 illustrates the shift in demand as a result of higher income levels with the shift of the original demand curve D_0 to the right to the new demand curve D_1.

This logic works in reverse, too. Imagine that the economy slows down so that many people lose their jobs or work fewer hours and thus suffer reductions in income. In this case, the shift in demand would lead to a lower quantity of cars demanded at every given price, and the original demand curve D_0 would shift left to D_2. The shift from D_0 to D_2 represents a decrease in demand; that is, at any given price level, the quantity demanded is now lower. In this example, a price of $20,000 means 18 million are cars sold along the original demand curve, but only 14.4 million cars are sold after demand has decreased, at point T in Exhibit 4-4.

When a demand curve shifts, it does not mean that the quantity demanded by every individual buyer changes by the same amount. In this example, not everyone would have higher or lower income, and not everyone would buy or not buy an additional car. Instead, a shift in a demand captures an overall pattern for the market as a whole.

Factors That Shift Demand Curves

A change in any one of the underlying factors that determine what quantity people are willing to buy at a given price will cause a shift in demand. Graphically, the new demand curve lies either to the right or to the left of the original demand curve. Various factors may cause a demand curve to shift: changes in income, changes in population, changes in taste, changes in expectations, and changes in the prices of closely related goods. Let's consider these factors in turn.

A *change in income* will often shift demand curves. A household with a higher income level will tend to demand a greater quantity of goods at every price than a household with a lower income level. For some luxury goods and services, such as expensive cars, exotic spa vacations, and fine jewelry, the effect of a rise in income can be especially pronounced. However, a few exceptions to this pattern do exist. As incomes rise, many people will buy fewer bus tickets and more airplane tickets, less chicken and more steak; they will be less likely to rent an apartment and more likely to own a home; and so on. **Normal goods** are defined as those where the quantity demanded rises as income rises, which is the most common case; **inferior goods** are defined as those where the quantity demanded falls as income rises.

normal goods: Goods where the quantity demanded rises as income rises.

inferior goods: Goods where the quantity demanded falls as income rises.

Changes in the composition of the population can also shift demand curves for certain goods and services. The proportion of elderly citizens in the U.S. population is rising, from 9% in 1960, to 13% in 2010, and to a projected (by the U.S. Census Bureau) 20% of the population by 2030. A society with relatively more children, like the United States in the 1960s, will have greater demand for goods and services like tricycles and day care facilities. A society with relatively more elderly persons, as the United States is projected to have by 2030, has a higher demand for nursing homes and hearing aids.

Changing tastes can also shift demand curves. In the demand for music, for example, 50% of sound recordings sold in 1990 were in the rock or pop music categories. By 2014, rock and pop had fallen to 44% of the total, while sales of rap/hip-hop, religious, and country categories had increased. Tastes in food and drink have changed, too. From 1970 to 2014, the per person consumption of chicken by Americans rose from 40 pounds per year to 84 pounds per year, and consumption of cheese rose from 11 pounds per year to 34 pounds per year. Changes like these are largely due to movements in taste, which change the quantity of a good demanded at every price: that is, they shift the demand curve for that good.

Changes in expectations about future conditions and prices can also shift the demand curve for a good or service. For example, if people hear that a hurricane is coming, they may rush to the store to buy flashlight batteries and bottled water. If people learn that the price of a good like coffee is likely to rise in the future, they may head for the store to stock up on coffee now.

substitutes: Goods that can replace each other to some extent, so that a rise in the price of one good leads to a greater quantity consumed of another good, and vice versa.

complements: Goods that are often used together, so that a rise in the price of one good tends to decrease the quantity consumed of the other good, and vice versa.

The demand curve for one good or service can be affected by *changes in the prices of related goods*. Some goods and services are **substitutes** for others, which means that they can replace the other good to some extent. For example, if the price of cotton rises, driving up the price of clothing, sheets, and other items made from cotton, then some people will shift to comparable goods made from fabrics like wool, silk, linen, and polyester. A higher price for a substitute good shifts the demand curve to the right; for example, a higher price for tea encourages buying more coffee. Conversely, a lower price for a substitute good has the reverse effect.

Other goods are **complements** for each other, meaning that the goods are often used together, so that consumption of one good tends to increase consumption of the other. Examples include breakfast cereal and milk; golf balls and golf clubs; gasoline and sports utility vehicles; and the five-way combination of bacon, lettuce, tomato, mayonnaise, and bread. If the price of golf clubs rises, demand for a complement good like golf balls decreases. A higher price for skis would shift the demand curve for a complement good like ski resort trips to the left, while a lower price for a complement has the reverse effect.

Summing Up Factors That Change Demand

Six factors that can shift demand curves are summarized in Exhibit 4-5. The direction of the arrows indicates whether the demand curve shifts represent an increase in demand or a decrease in demand based on the six factors we just considered. Notice that a change in the price of the good or service itself is not listed among the factors that can shift a demand curve. A change in the price of a good or service causes a movement along a specific demand curve, and it typically leads to some change in the quantity demanded, but it doesn't shift the demand curve. Notice also that in these diagrams, the demand curves are drawn without numerical quantities and prices on the horizontal and vertical axes. The demand and supply model can often be a useful conceptual tool even without attaching specific numbers.

When a demand curve shifts, it will then intersect with a given supply curve at a different equilibrium price and quantity. But we are getting ahead of our story. Before discussing how changes in demand can affect equilibrium price and quantity, we first need to discuss shifts in supply curves.

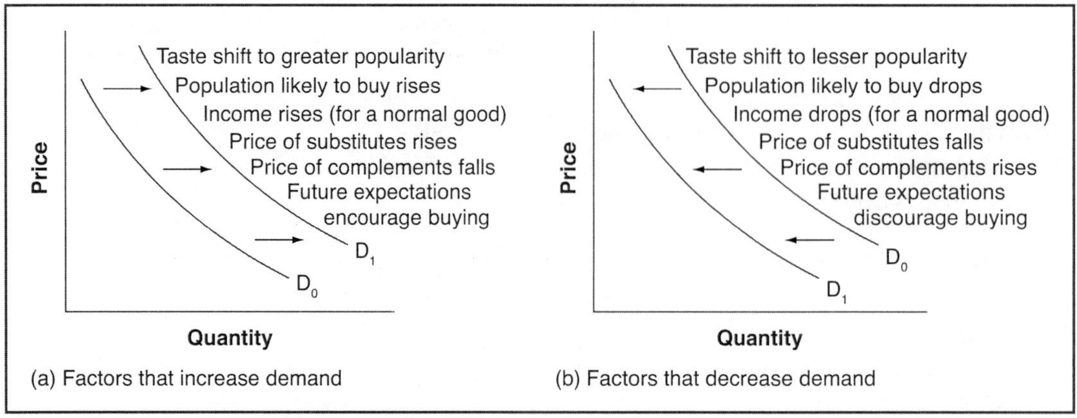

EXHIBIT 4-5 Some Factors That Shift Demand Curves

The left-hand panel *(a)* offers a list of factors that can cause an increase in demand from D_0 to D_1. The right-hand panel *(b)* shows how the same factors, if their direction is reversed, can cause a decrease in demand from D_0 to D_1. For example, greater popularity of a good or service increases demand, causing a shift in the demand curve to the right, while lesser popularity of a good or service reduces demand, causing a shift of the demand curve to the left.

An Example of a Shift in a Supply Curve

A supply curve shows how quantity supplied will change as the price rises and falls, based on the *ceteris paribus* assumption that no other economically relevant factors are changing. But if other factors relevant to supply do change, then the entire supply curve can shift. Just as a shift in demand is represented by a change in the quantity demanded at every price, a **shift in supply** means a change in the quantity supplied at every price. In thinking about the factors that affect supply, remember the basic motivation of firms: to earn profits. If a firm faces lower costs of production, while the prices for the output the firm produces remain unchanged, a firm's profits will increase. Thus, when costs of production fall, a firm will supply a higher quantity at any given price for its output, and the supply curve will shift to the right. Conversely, if a firm faces an increased cost of production, then it will earn lower profits at any given selling price for its products. As a result, a higher cost of production typically causes a firm to supply a smaller quantity at any given price. In this case, the supply curve shifts to the left.

shift in supply: When a change in some economic factor related to supply causes a different quantity to be supplied at every price.

As an example, imagine that supply in the market for cars is represented by S_0 in Exhibit 4-6. The original supply curve, S_0, includes a point with a price of $20,000 and a quantity supplied of 18 million cars, labeled as point J. If the price rises to $22,000 per car, *ceteris paribus*, the quantity supplied will rise to 20 million cars, as shown by point K on the S_0 curve.

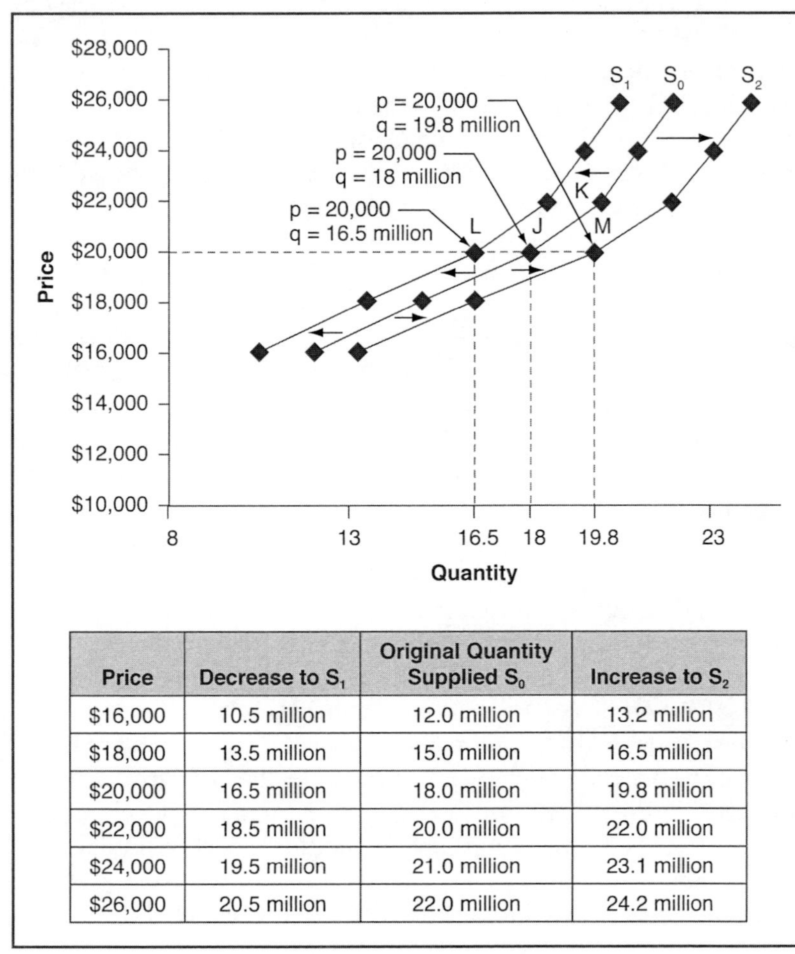

Price	Decrease to S_1	Original Quantity Supplied S_0	Increase to S_2
$16,000	10.5 million	12.0 million	13.2 million
$18,000	13.5 million	15.0 million	16.5 million
$20,000	16.5 million	18.0 million	19.8 million
$22,000	18.5 million	20.0 million	22.0 million
$24,000	19.5 million	21.0 million	23.1 million
$26,000	20.5 million	22.0 million	24.2 million

EXHIBIT 4-6 Shifts in Supply: A Car Example

Increased supply means that at every given price, the quantity supplied is higher, so that the supply curve shifts to the right from S_0 to S_2. Decreased supply means that at every given price, quantity supplied of cars is lower, so that the supply curve shifts to the left from S_0 to S_1.

Now imagine that the price of steel, an important material input in manufacturing cars, rises, so that producing a car has now become more expensive. At any given price for selling cars, car manufacturers will react by supplying a lower quantity. The shift of supply from S_0 to S_1 shows that at any given price, the quantity supplied decreases. In this example, at a price of $20,000, the quantity supplied decreases from 18 million on the original supply curve S_0 to 16.5 million on the supply curve S_1, which is labeled as point L.

Conversely, imagine that the price of steel decreases, so that producing a car becomes less expensive. At any given price for selling cars, car manufacturers can now expect to earn higher profits and so will supply a higher quantity. The shift of supply to the right from S_0 to S_2 means that at all prices, the quantity supplied has increased. In this example, at a price of $20,000, the quantity supplied increases from 18 million on the original supply curve S_0 to 19.8 million on the supply curve S_2, which is labeled M.

Factors That Shift Supply Curves

A change in any factor that determines what quantity firms are willing to sell at a given price will cause a change in supply. Some factors that can cause a supply curve to shift include: changes in natural conditions, altered prices for inputs to production, new technologies for production, and government policies that affect production costs.

The cost of production for many agricultural products will be affected by *changes in natural conditions*. For example, the area of northern China that typically grows about 60% of the country's wheat output experienced its worst drought in at least 50 years in the second half of 2009. A drought decreases the supply of agricultural products, which means that at any given price, a lower quantity will be supplied; conversely, exceptionally good weather would shift the supply curve to the right.

Goods and services are produced using combinations of labor, materials, and machinery. When *the price of a key input to production changes*, the supply curve is affected. For example, a messenger company that delivers packages around a city may find that buying gasoline is one of its main costs. If the price of gasoline falls, then in the market for messenger services, a higher quantity will be supplied at any given price per delivery. Conversely, a higher price for key inputs will cause supply to shift to the left.

When a firm discovers a *new technology*, so that it can produce at a lower cost, the supply curve will shift as well. For example, in the 1960s a major scientific effort nicknamed the Green Revolution focused on breeding improved seeds for basic crops like wheat and rice. By the early 1990s, more than two-thirds of the wheat and rice in low-income countries around the world was grown with these Green Revolution seeds—and the harvest was twice as high per acre. A technological improvement that reduces costs of production will shift supply to the right, so that a greater quantity will be produced at any given price.

Government policies can affect the cost of production and the supply curve through taxes, regulations, and subsidies. For example, the U.S. government imposes a tax on alcoholic beverages that collects about $9 billion per year from producers. There is a wide array of government regulations that require firms to spend money to provide a cleaner environment or a safer workplace. A government subsidy, on the other hand, occurs when the government sends money to a firm directly or when the government reduces the firm's taxes if the firm carries out certain actions. For example, the U.S. government pays more than $20 billion per year directly to firms to support research and development. From the perspective of a firm, taxes or regulations are an additional cost of production that shifts supply to the left, leading the firm to produce a lower quantity at every given price. However, government subsidies reduce the cost of production and increase supply.

Summing Up Factors That Change Supply

Weather patterns, changes in the cost of inputs, new technologies, and the impact of government decisions all affect the cost of production for firms. In turn, these factors affect firms' willingness to supply at a given price. Exhibit 4-7 summarizes factors that change the supply of goods and services. Notice that a change in the price of the product itself is

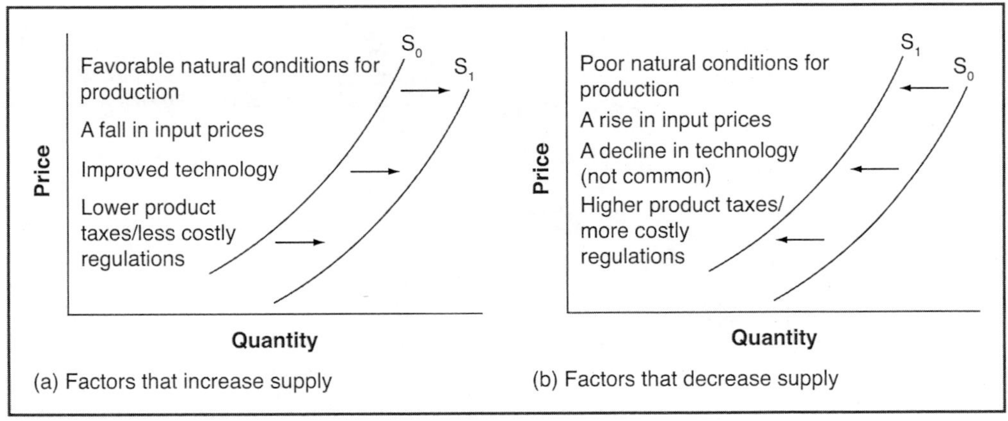

EXHIBIT 4-7 Some Factors That Shift Supply Curves

The left-hand panel *(a)* offers a list of factors that can cause an increase in supply from S_0 to S_1. The right-hand panel *(b)* shows that the same factors, if their direction is reversed, can cause a decrease in supply from S_0 to S_1.

not among the factors that shift the supply curve. Although a change in price of a good or service typically causes a change in quantity supplied along the supply curve for that specific good or service, it does not cause the supply curve itself to shift.

Shifts in Equilibrium Price and Quantity: The Four-Step Process

Because demand and supply curves appear on a two-dimensional diagram with only price and quantity on the axes, an unwary visitor to the land of economics might be fooled into believing that economics is only about four topics: demand, supply, price, and quantity. However, demand and supply are really "umbrella" concepts: demand covers all of the factors that affect demand, and supply covers all of the factors that affect supply. The factors other than price that affect demand and supply are included by using shifts in the demand or the supply curve. In this way, the two-dimensional demand and supply model becomes a powerful tool for analyzing a wide range of economic circumstances.

To understand how this works, let's begin with a single economic event. It might be an event that affects demand, like a change in income, population, tastes, prices of substitutes or complements, or expectations about future prices. It might be an event that affects supply, like a change in natural conditions, input prices, or technology, or government policies that affect production. How does this economic event affect equilibrium price and quantity? We can analyze this question using a four-step process.

Step 1: Think about what the demand and supply curves in this market looked like before the economic change occurred. Sketch the curves.

Step 2: Decide whether the economic change being analyzed affects demand or supply.

Step 3: Decide whether the effect on demand or supply causes the curve to shift to the right or to the left, and sketch the new demand or supply curve on the diagram.

Step 4: Compare the original equilibrium price and quantity to the new equilibrium price and quantity.

To make this process concrete, let's consider one example that involves a shift in supply and one that involves a shift in demand.

Good Weather for Salmon Fishing

About 90% of the shrimp consumed in the United States is imported. In 2013, Thailand, Vietnam, and China—three main global shrimp producers—experienced an outbreak of disease that affected their shrimp supplies. How did the shrimp disease affect the

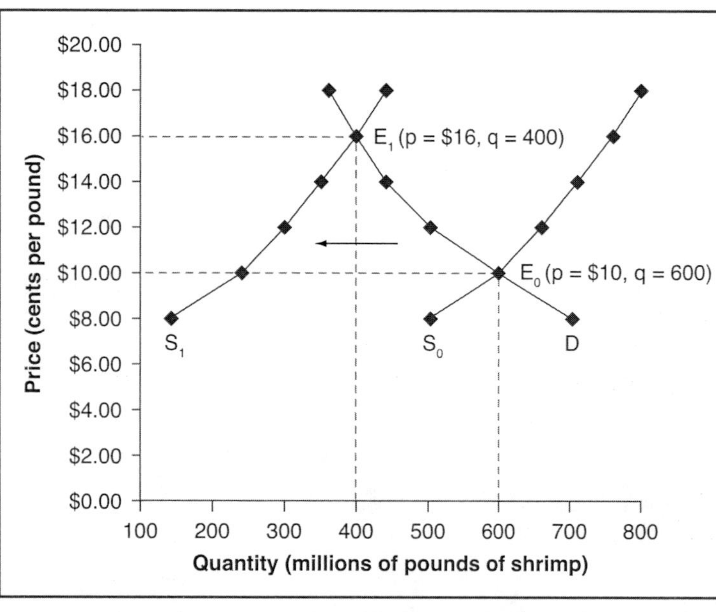

Price per Pound	Quantity Supplied in 2008	Quantity Supplied in 2013	Quantity Demanded
$8	500	140	700
$10	600	240	600
$12	660	300	500
$14	710	350	440
$16	760	400	400
$18	800	440	360

EXHIBIT 4-8 Sick Shrimp: The Four-Step Process

Step 1: Draw a demand and supply diagram to show what the market for shrimp looked like before the shrimp disease. The original equilibrium E_0 was $10 per pound, and the original equilibrium quantity was 600 million pounds of shrimp.
Step 2: Did the economic event affect supply or demand? A disease is a natural condition that affects supply.
Step 3: Was the effect on supply an increase or a decrease? Disease reduces the quantity that will be supplied at any given price. The supply curve shifts to the left from S_0 to S_1.
Step 4: Compare the new equilibrium price and quantity to the original equilibrium. At the new equilibrium, E_1, the equilibrium price rose from $10 per pound to $16 per pound, but the equilibrium quantity decreased from 600 million pounds to 400 million pounds. Notice that the equilibrium quantity demanded decreased, even though the demand curve did not move.

equilibrium quantity and price of shrimp in the United States? Exhibit 4-8 uses the four-step approach to work through this problem.

1. Draw a demand and supply diagram to show what the market for shrimp looked like before the shrimp disease. The original equilibrium E_0 was $10 per pound, and the original equilibrium quantity was 600 million pounds of shrimp.
2. Did the economic event affect supply or demand? A disease is a natural condition that affects supply.
3. Was the effect on supply an increase or a decrease? Disease reduces the quantity that will be supplied at any given price. The supply curve shifts to the left from S_0 to S_1.
4. Compare the new equilibrium price and quantity to the original equilibrium. At the new equilibrium, E_1, the equilibrium price rose from $10 per pound to $16 per pound, but the equilibrium quantity decreased from 600 million pounds to 400 million pounds. Notice that the equilibrium quantity demanded decreased, even though the demand curve did not move.

In short, the outbreak of shrimp disease decreased the supply of imported shrimp in the United States. The result was a lower equilibrium quantity of shrimp bought and sold in the market at a higher price.

Sand and Hydraulic Fracturing

The U.S. economy used about 46 million tons of sand and gravel in 2012, which is nearly twice as much as a decade earlier. In addition, the price of sand and gravel rose from $18.30/ton in 2003 to $52.80/ton in 2012. What happened? Sand is an input in products such as concrete and asphalt pavement, and it is also present in paint, paper, plastics, and glass. However, sand is also used in hydraulic fracturing, a method of extracting oil and natural gas, and use of this method expanded substantially in recent years. In some recent

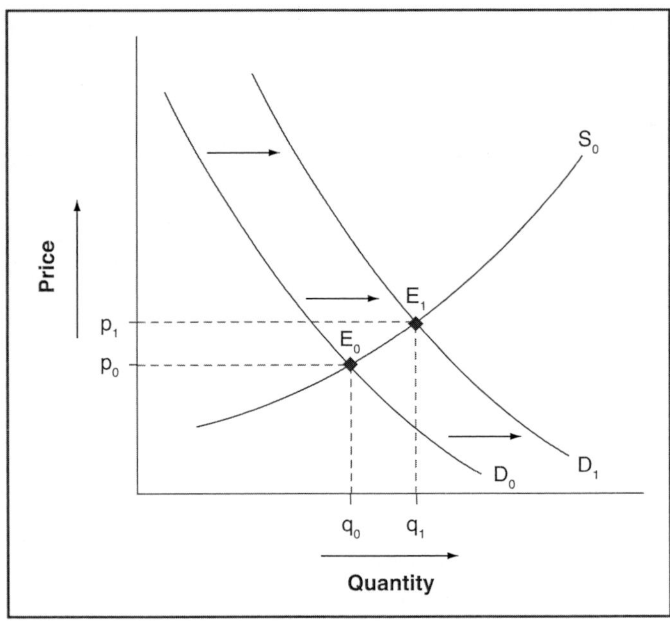

EXHIBIT 4-9 The Market for Sand: A Four-Step Analysis

Step 1: Draw a demand and supply diagram to illustrate what the market for sand looked like before the fracking boom. The demand curve D_0 and the supply curve S_0 show the original relationships.
Step 2: Will the change described affect supply or demand? The more widespread use of hydraulic fracturing technology will affect the demand for sand, which is used in that process.
Step 3: Will the effect on demand be positive or negative? The growth of fracking will tend to mean a higher quantity demanded of the product, sand, at every given price, causing the demand curve for sand to shift to the right from D_0 to D_1.
Step 4: Compare the new equilibrium price and quantity to the original equilibrium price. The new equilibrium E_1 occurs at a higher quantity and a higher price than the original equilibrium E_0.

years, when oil and gas prices were high, "fracking" accounted for more than 60% of U.S. sand consumption. How could increases in fracking affect the demand for sand? Exhibit 4-9 illustrates the four-step analysis.

1. Draw a demand and supply diagram to illustrate what the market for sand looked like in the year before the fracking boom. In Exhibit 4-9, the demand curve D_0 and the supply curve S_0 show the original relationships. In this case, the analysis is performed without specific numbers on the price and quantity axes.
2. Did the change described affect supply or demand? The widespread use of hydraulic fracturing technology, encouraged by a large rise in the price of oil and natural gas during the first decade of the 2000s, will affect demand for sand.
3. Was the effect on demand an increase or a decrease? The changes meant a higher quantity demanded of the product, sand, at every given price, causing the demand curve for sand to shift right to the new demand curve D_1.
4. Compare the new equilibrium price and quantity at E_1 to the original equilibrium price and quantity at E_0. The new equilibrium E_1 occurs at a higher quantity and a higher price than the original equilibrium E_0.

The Interconnections and Speed of Adjustment in Real Markets

In the real world, many factors that affect demand and supply can change all at once. For example, the demand for cars might increase because of rising incomes and population, and it might decrease because of rising gasoline prices (a complementary good). Likewise, the supply of cars might increase because of innovative new technologies that reduce the cost of car production, and it might decrease as a result of new government regulations requiring the installation of costly pollution-control technology. Moreover, rising incomes and population or changes in gasoline prices will affect many markets, not just cars. How can an economist sort out all of these interconnected events? The answer lies in the *ceteris paribus* assumption. Look at how each economic event affects each market, one event at a time, holding all else constant.

In the four-step analysis of how economic events affect equilibrium price and quantity, the movement from the old to the new equilibrium seems immediate. But as a practical matter, prices and quantities often do not zoom straight to equilibrium. More realistically, when an economic event causes demand or supply to shift, prices and quantities set off in the general direction of equilibrium. Indeed, even as they are moving toward one new equilibrium, prices are often then pushed by another change in demand or supply toward another equilibrium.

Price Ceilings and Price Floors in Markets for Goods and Services

Controversy often surrounds the prices and quantities that are established by demand and supply. After all, every time you buy a gallon of gasoline, pay the rent for your apartment, or pay the interest charges on your credit card, it's natural to wish that the price had been at least a little lower. Every time a restaurant sells a meal, a department store sells a sweater, or a farmer sells a bushel of wheat, it's natural for the profit-seeking seller to wish that the price had been higher. In some cases, discontent over prices turns into public pressure on politicians, who may then pass legislation to prevent a certain price

CLEARING IT UP

Shifts of Demand or Supply versus Movements along a Demand or Supply Curve

One common mistake in applying the demand and supply framework is to confuse the shift of a demand or a supply curve with the movement along a demand or supply curve. As an example, consider a problem that asks whether a drought will increase or decrease the equilibrium quantity and equilibrium price of wheat. Lee, a student in an introductory economics class, might reason:

"Well, it's clear that a drought reduces supply, so I'll shift back the supply curve, as in the shift from the original supply curve S_0 to S_1 shown on the diagram (call this Shift 1). So the equilibrium moves from E_0 to E_1, the equilibrium quantity is lower and the equilibrium price is higher. Then, a higher price makes farmers more likely to supply the good, so the supply curve shifts right, as shown by the shift from S_1 to S_2 on the diagram (shown as Shift 2), so that the equilibrium now moves from E_1 to E_2. But the higher price also reduces demand and so causes demand to shift back, like the shift from the original demand curve D_0 to D_1 on the diagram (labeled Shift 3), and the equilibrium moves from E_2 to E_3."

At about this point, Lee suspects that this answer is headed down the wrong path. Think about what might be wrong with Lee's logic, and then read the answer that follows.

Answer: Lee's first step is correct: that is, a drought shifts back the supply curve of wheat and leads to a prediction of a lower equilibrium quantity and a higher equilibrium price. The rest of Lee's argument is wrong because it mixes up shifts in supply with quantity supplied, and shifts in demand with quantity demanded. A higher or lower price never shifts the supply curve, as suggested by the shift in supply from S_1 to S_2. Instead, a price change leads to a movement along a given supply curve. Similarly, a higher or lower price never shifts a demand curve, as suggested in the shift from D_0 to D_1. Instead, a price change leads to a movement along a given demand curve. Remember, a change in the price of a good never causes the demand or supply curve for that good to shift.

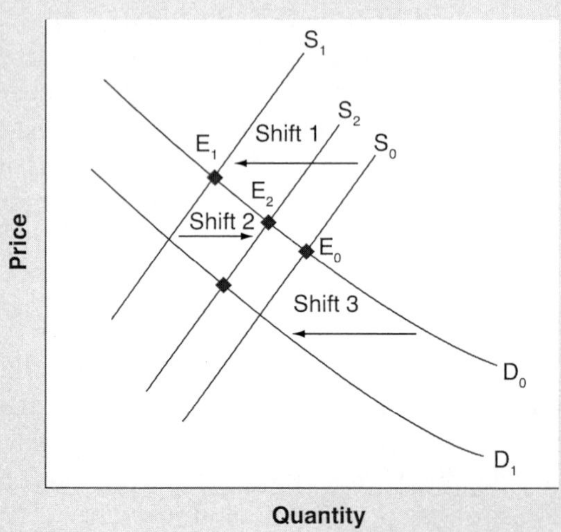

from climbing "too high" or falling "too low." The demand and supply model shows how people and firms will react to the incentives provided by these laws to control prices, in ways that will often lead to undesirable costs and consequences. Alternative policy tools can often achieve the desired goals of price control laws, while avoiding at least some of the costs and trade-offs of such laws.

Price Ceilings

Price controls are laws that the government enacts to regulate prices. Price controls come in two flavors. A **price ceiling** keeps a price from rising above a certain level, while a **price floor** keeps a price from falling below a certain level. This section uses the demand and supply framework to analyze price ceilings; the next section turns to price floors.

price controls: Government laws to regulate prices.

price ceiling: A law that prevents a price from rising above a certain level.

price floor: A law that prevents a price from falling below a certain level.

In many markets for goods and services, demanders outnumber suppliers. There are more people who buy bread than companies that make bread; more people who rent apartments than landlords; more people who purchase prescription drugs than companies that manufacture such drugs; more people who buy gasoline than companies that refine and sell gasoline. Consumers, who are also potential voters, sometimes flex enough political strength to push for a law to hold down the level of a certain price. In some cities, for example, renters have pressed political leaders to pass rent control laws, a form of price ceiling that might require that rents can only be raised by a certain maximum percentage each year.

Rent control can become a politically hot topic when rents begin to rise rapidly. Rents might rise for many reasons. Perhaps a change in tastes makes a certain suburb or town a more popular place to live. Perhaps locally based businesses expand, bringing higher incomes and more people into the area. Changes of this sort can cause a change in the demand for rental housing, as illustrated in Exhibit 4-10. The original equilibrium E_0 lies at the intersection of supply curve S_0 and demand curve D_0, corresponding to an equilibrium price of $500 and an equilibrium quantity of 15,000 units of rental housing. The effect of greater income or a change in tastes is to shift the demand curve for rental housing to the right, as shown by the data in the table and the shift from D_0 to D_1 on the graph. In this market, at the new equilibrium E_1, the price of a rental unit would rise to $600 and the equilibrium quantity would increase to 17,000 units.

Long-time apartment dwellers will dislike these price increases. They may argue, "Why should *our* rents rise because a lot of newcomers want to move in?" The current apartment-dwellers are also voters, and they may elect local politicians who pass a price ceiling law that limits how much rents can rise.

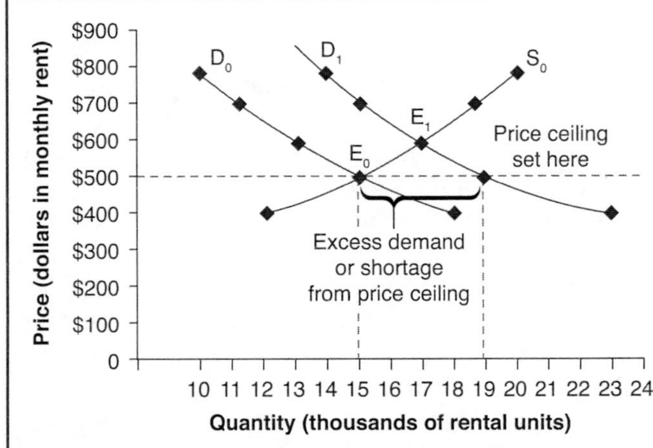

Price	Original Quantity Supplied	Original Quantity Demanded	New Quantity Demanded
$400	12,000	18,000	23,000
$500	15,000	15,000	19,000
$600	17,000	13,000	17,000
$700	19,000	11,000	15,000
$800	20,000	10,000	14,000

EXHIBIT 4-10 A Price Ceiling Example—Rent Control

The original intersection of demand and supply occurs at E_0. Demand shifts from D_0 to D_1. The new equilibrium would be at E_1—except that a price ceiling prevents the price from rising. Because the price doesn't change, the quantity supplied remains at 15,000. However, after the change in demand, the quantity demanded rises to 19,000. There is excess demand, also called a shortage.

What's a Price Bubble? A Story of Housing Prices

The average price of a U.S. single-family home rose about 1–3% per year in the first half of the 1990s; 3–5% per year in the second half of the 1990s; 7–8% per year in the early 2000s; and more than 10% per year from late 2004 to early 2006.

Although no one seriously expected price increases of 10% per year to continue for long, what happened next was still a shock. Certain metropolitan areas or states had seen declines in housing prices from time to time, but there had not been a nationwide decline in housing prices since the Great Depression of the 1930s. However, housing prices started falling in 2006, and through much of 2008 and 2009, housing prices were falling at a rate of 4–5% per year. Of course, these national averages understate the experience of certain parts of the country where both the boom and the bust were much larger.

Economists refer to this chain of events as a price "bubble." Remember that one possible reason for demand to shift is expectations about the future. If many people expect that housing prices are going to rise in the future, demand for housing will shift to the right—thus helping the prediction of higher prices come true. For a time, a cycle of expecting higher prices, increases in demand, and resulting higher prices can be self-reinforcing. But this process cannot last forever. At some unpredictable time, potential buyers recognize that the expectations of ever-higher future prices are unrealistic, at which point the expectation that future prices will stop rising or start falling causes demand to shift back in the other direction, and the price bubble deflates. Price bubbles are not just observed in housing: for example, they are also seen in markets for collectible items and in stock markets.

The bursting of the price bubble in housing—which happened in many countries around the world, not just the United States—has caused great economic difficulties. Those who owned homes watched the value of this asset decline. Some of those who borrowed money to buy a house near the peak of the bubble found a few years later, after the bubble had burst, that what they owed to the bank was much more than the house was worth. When many people began to default on their mortgage loans, banks and other financial institutions then faced huge losses. The bursting of the price bubble in housing helped to trigger the global economic slowdown that started in late 2007 and continued until 2009.

For simplicity, let's assume that a rent control law is passed to keep the price at the original equilibrium of $500 for a typical apartment. In Exhibit 4-10, the horizontal line at the price of $500 shows the legally fixed maximum price set by the rent control law. However, the underlying forces that shifted the demand curve to the right have not vanished. At that price ceiling, the quantity demanded exceeds the quantity supplied: that is, at a price of $500 the quantity supplied remains at the same 15,000 rental units, but the quantity demanded is 19,000 rental units. Thus, people who would like to rent in this area are knocking on the doors of landlords, searching for apartments. A situation of excess demand, also called a shortage, results when people are willing to pay the market price but cannot purchase (or in this case rent) what they desire.

Rent control has been especially popular in wartime and during times of high inflation. New York City, the most prominent U.S. city that has imposed rent control laws for a long period, put rent control in place as a "temporary" measure during World War II. Rent control was also especially popular during the 1970s, when all prices in the U.S. economy were rising rapidly as part of an overall process of inflation. By the mid-1980s, more than 200 American cities, with about 20% of the nation's population, had rent control laws. But in the last two decades, the political pendulum began swinging against rent control. More than 30 states adopted laws or constitutional amendments banning rent control outright. In many cities that kept some form of rent control, the focus of the law shifted from trying to hold rents below the equilibrium price to offering ways for resolving disputes between tenants and landlords, like disagreements about maintenance, pets, and noise.

Although the effect of rent control laws in the United States has faded in recent years, price ceilings are often proposed for other products. For example, price ceilings to limit what producers can charge have been proposed in recent years for prescription drugs, on doctor and hospital fees, the charges made by some automatic teller bank machines, and auto insurance rates. Many low-income countries around the world have also imposed price ceilings on basic items like bread or energy products. In the early 2000s, the gov-

CLEARING IT UP

Price Ceilings and Floors Do Not Change Demand or Supply

Neither price ceilings nor price floors cause demand or supply to change. Remember, changes in price don't cause demand or supply to change. Price ceilings and price floors can cause a different choice of quantity demanded along a demand curve, but they don't move the demand curve. Price controls can cause a different choice of quantity supplied along a supply curve, but they don't shift the supply curve.

ernment of the African country of Zimbabwe tried to help its ordinary citizens by placing ceilings on the prices of ordinary household items like bread, wheat, and cooking oil. But many producers of these items, faced with the low prices, went out of business. More recently, Venezuela tried a similar policy with similar results. The goal of the price ceiling had been to keep necessities affordable to all, but the result was that the quantity of the products declined and shortages occurred.

Price ceilings are enacted in an attempt to keep prices low for those who demand the product. But when the market price is not allowed to rise to the equilibrium level, quantity demanded exceeds quantity supplied, and thus a shortage occurs. Those who manage to purchase the product at the lower price given by the price ceiling will benefit, but sellers of the product will suffer, along with those who are not able to purchase the product at all.

Price Floors

Price floors are enacted when discontented sellers, feeling that prices are too low, appeal to legislators to keep prices from falling. A price floor is the lowest legal price that can be paid in markets for goods and services, labor, and financial capital. Price floors are sometimes called "price supports" because they prevent a price from falling below a certain level.

Around the world, many countries have passed laws to keep farm prices higher than they otherwise would be. In the annual budget of the European Union, roughly 40% of all spending late in 2014—more than $60 billion per year—was used to keep prices high for Europe's farmers. Thanks to this policy, the prices received by European farmers for such agricultural staples as wheat, barley, rice, milk, and beef have held substantially above the price prevailing in the world market for decades.

Exhibit 4-11 illustrates the effects of a government program that assures a price above the equilibrium by focusing on the market for wheat in Europe. In the absence of government

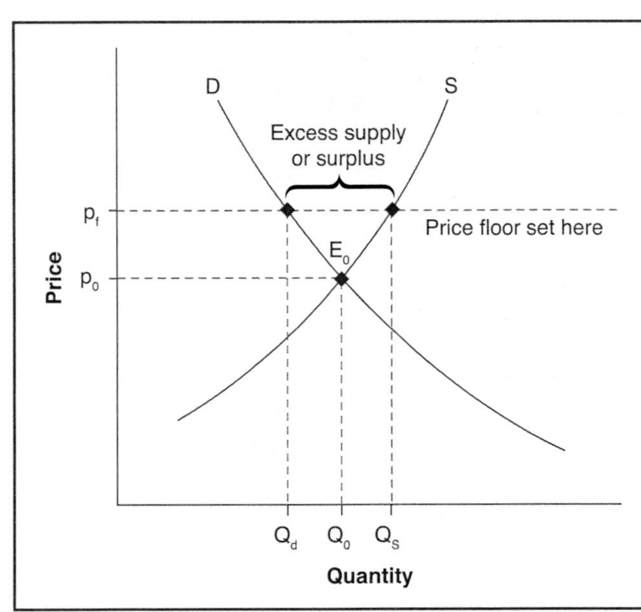

EXHIBIT 4-11 The European Wheat Prices: A Price Floor Example

The intersection of demand D and supply S would be at the equilibrium point E_0. However, a price floor set at p_f holds the price above E_0 and prevents it from falling. The result of the price floor is that the quantity supplied Q_s exceeds the quantity demanded Q_d. There is excess supply, also called a surplus.

CLEARING IT UP

When Floors Are Higher Than Ceilings

In economics, (price) ceilings often appear graphically lower than (price) floors. The reason is that binding price ceilings are below the equilibrium level, stopping the price from rising, and binding price floors are above the equilibrium level, stopping the price from falling. Thus, above-equilibrium price floors are higher than below-equilibrium price ceilings.

intervention, the price would adjust so that the quantity supplied would equal the quantity demanded at the equilibrium point E_0, with price p_0 and quantity Q_0. However, policies to keep prices high for farmers keeps the price above what would have been the market equilibrium level—the price p_f shown by the dashed horizontal line in the diagram. The result is a quantity supplied of Q_S in excess of the quantity demanded Q_d. When quantity supply exceeds quantity demanded, then a situation of excess supply exists, also called a surplus. The high-income countries of the world, including the United States, Europe, and Japan, spend roughly $1 billion per day in supporting their farmers. If the government is willing to purchase the excess supply (or to provide payments for others to purchase it), then farmers will benefit from the price floor, but taxpayers and consumers of food will pay the costs. Numerous proposals have been offered for reducing farm subsidies. But in many countries, political support for subsidies for farmers—and indirectly, for what is viewed as the traditional rural way of life—remains strong.

Responses to Price Controls: Many Margins for Action

Although a government can set price floors or price ceilings, such rules often have unintended consequences. The focus of the discussion so far has been on reactions that take the form of changes in quantity demanded or quantity supplied, and thus on understanding why price ceilings commonly lead to shortages and price floors lead to surpluses. However, buyers and sellers in real-world markets have many other ways in which they can react to price controls. The ability of households and firms to react in a variety of ways to government rules is called the problem of "many margins for action."

black market: An illegal market that breaks government rules on prices or sales.

One alternative reaction occurs when buyers and seller decide to break the government rules on prices or sales, which is referred to as a **black market**. Consider a landlord who

Price Controls of 1776

During the American Revolution, a number of states imposed price ceilings on many goods. After Rhode Island passed price control laws in 1776, the city of Providence reported on the effects to the state legislature in 1777:

> [The effect] is so intricate, variable, and complicated, that it cannot remain any time equitable. . . . It was made to cheapen the articles of life, but it has in fact raised their prices, by producing an artificial and in some respects a real scarcity. It was made to unite us in good agreement respecting prices; but hath produced animosity, and ill will between town and country, and between buyers and sellers in general. It was made to bring us up to some equitable standard of honesty . . . but hath produced a sharping set of mushroom peddlers, who adulterate their commodities, and take every advantage to evade the . . . act, by quibbles and lies.

Price control laws are often popular in the short run, because they look like an easy fix, but they become less popular over time as shortages occur, social tensions arise, and efforts to evade the laws gain force. The problems noted by the citizens of Providence, Rhode Island, in 1777 apply today as they did more than 200 years ago.

owns rent-controlled property. Suppose that although the law dictates the cap on the rent that the landlord can charge, a potential tenant is willing to pay more than the rent control law allows to live in the apartment. If this "extra rent" is paid in cash, then who will know?

A second margin for action is "side payments," which are additional payments that are made along with the actual price paid. In New York City, with its long history of rent control, landlords sometimes devise innovative charges like a "nonrefundable cleaning deposit" and a "nonrefundable key deposit," or they may require several months' rent in advance. These charges can have the effect of making the tenant pay more than the actual rent.

A third margin for action involves quality adjustment. In the case of rent control, a landlord may keep the rent low but put off needed maintenance or the installation of new appliances. The result is a lower-priced apartment—but also a lower-quality apartment.

A fourth margin for action involves shifting who is involved in the transaction. In cities with rent control, it isn't unusual for a tenant living in a rent-controlled apartment not to move out officially; instead, the tenant sublets the apartment to someone else. In this case, the original tenant pays the rent-controlled rate but charges the market rate to the new renter and pockets the difference.

Those who favor price floors and price ceilings are often quite aware of the actions that can circumvent the underlying purpose of price controls. Thus, supporters of price controls also favor rules that will include penalties for black markets, make side payments illegal, require certain quality levels, and prohibit shifts in who is involved in the transaction. However, establishing rules or laws that will limit all of the alternative margins for action is like trying to block a flowing stream with your fingers. Shutting down the many margins for action by which citizens and firms respond to price controls is much easier said than done.

Policy Alternatives to Price Ceilings and Price Floors

The economic analysis of how price ceilings can create shortages and price floors create surpluses can be disheartening. If you want to pursue a policy goal of assuring that people have a sufficient quantity of affordable housing, but rent controls are just price ceilings that cause housing shortages, what alternative policy can you advocate? If you want to pursue a policy goal of supporting farmers, but farm price supports lead to storehouses of surplus grain rotting at high cost to taxpayers and consumers, then what alternative policy can you advocate? The same demand and supply model that shows that price ceilings and price floors often have unintended, undesirable consequences of creating surpluses and shortages can also suggest alternate public policies that do not have these same trade-offs.

Let's return to the issue of rent control. If the goal is to have an expanded supply of affordable housing, then a rightward shift in a demand curve, a supply curve, or both as shown in Exhibit 4-12, can accomplish this goal. A shift to the right in the supply of affordable housing from S_0 to S_1, for example, might be achieved if a government grants subsidies to builders who construct apartment buildings that have relatively smaller rental units, which will have a more affordable price in the market. This step taken alone would cause a shift to the right from the original equilibrium E_0, to the new equilibrium, E_1, and would increase the quantity of housing from q_0 to q_1. A shift to the right in the demand curve from D_0 to D_1 might be achieved by giving a subsidy to low-income renters, perhaps in the form of cash or a voucher that the renters could use to pay some of the rent, so that low-income renters could then have more to spend on housing. This step taken alone would cause a shift to the right from the original equilibrium, E_0, to the new equilibrium, E_2, and would increase the quantity of affordable housing from q_0 to q_2. Instituting *both* sets of policies would shift supply from S_0 to S_1, demand from D_0 to D_1, the equilibrium from the original E_0 to E_3, and the quantity of affordable housing from q_0 to q_3.

Any combination of these policies is likely to be more useful in expanding affordable housing than rent control because these policies tend to increase the quantity of affordable

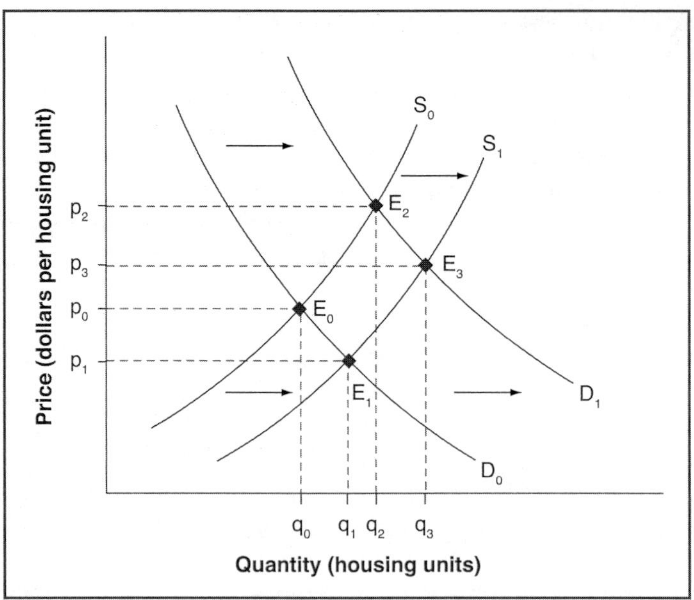

EXHIBIT 4-12 Policies for Affordable Housing: Alternatives to Rent Control

The original equilibrium is the intersection of demand D_0 and supply S_0 at the equilibrium E_0. Providing subsidies to low-income buyers of housing will shift the demand curve from D_0 to D_1, leading to a new equilibrium at E_2. Alternatively, a policy of providing subsidies to builders of affordable housing would shift the supply curve from S_0 to S_1, leading to a new equilibrium at E_1. Undertaking both demand-side and supply-side policies would move the market to equilibrium E_3, at the intersection of the new demand curve D_1 and the new supply curve S_1. As drawn here, both of these policies will increase the equilibrium quantity of affordable housing. An increase in demand will also raise the price of affordable housing, but as long as the subsidy received by buyers is larger than the higher price, buyers will not be adversely affected by the higher price that occurs from an increase in demand.

housing, whereas rent control tends to decrease it. Moreover, these alternative policies sidestep many of the problems that arise when suppliers and demanders react to price controls.

Similarly, there are a number of alternative policies to support farmers or rural areas that do not involve setting price floors for crops. For example, the government could provide income directly to farmers, especially to small-scale farmers with lower incomes. The government might also assist rural economies in many other ways: establishing new branches of state colleges and universities in agricultural areas, creating parks or nature preserves that might attract tourists, supporting research into new methods of producing and using local crops to help the local farmers stay ahead, helping to build transportation links to rural areas, and subsidizing high-speed Internet cable connections across rural areas or wireless phone service. All of these alternative policies would help rural communities while avoiding the problem of price floors, because these alternative policies don't encourage farmers to produce an excess supply of surplus food.

With alternative policies readily available, why do governments enact price floors and price ceilings? One reason is that in public policy debates over price controls, people often don't take into account the unintended but predictable trade-offs. Another reason is that government sometimes views laws about price floors and ceilings as having zero cost, while giving subsidies to demanders or suppliers requires a government to collect taxes and spend money. The point here is not to endorse every proposal for using targeted subsidies or tax breaks to change demand and supply. Each policy proposal must be evaluated according to its own costs and benefits. But before reaching for the seemingly easy policy tool of price controls, with their predictable and undesired consequences and trade-offs, it is wise to consider alternative policies to shift demand and supply so as to achieve the desired new market equilibrium.

Supply, Demand, and Efficiency

In the market equilibrium, where the quantity demanded equals quantity supplied, nothing is wasted. No excess supply sits unsold, gathering dust in warehouses. No shortages exist that cause people to stand in long lines or rely on political connections to acquire goods—alternatives that waste time and energy. All those who wish to purchase or sell goods at the equilibrium market price are able to purchase or sell the quantity that they desire, as movements of the equilibrium price bring quantity demanded and supplied into balance.

The familiar demand and supply diagram holds within it the concept of economic efficiency, which was introduced in Chapter 2. To economists, an efficient outcome is one where it is impossible to improve the situation of one party without imposing a cost on someone else. Conversely, if a situation is inefficient, it becomes possible to benefit at least one party without imposing costs on others. Thus, the definition of productive efficiency in Chapter 2 was that the economy was producing without waste and getting all it could out of its scarce resources, in the sense that it was impossible to get more of good A without a reduction in good B. Efficiency in the demand and supply model has the same basic meaning: the economy is getting as much benefit as possible from its scarce resources, and all the possible gains from trade have been achieved.

Consumer Surplus, Producer Surplus, Social Surplus

Consider the example of a market for portable music devices shown in Exhibit 4-13. The equilibrium price is $80, and the equilibrium quantity is 28 million. To see the benefits received by consumers, look at the segment of the demand curve above the equilibrium point and to the left. This portion of the demand curve shows that at least some demanders

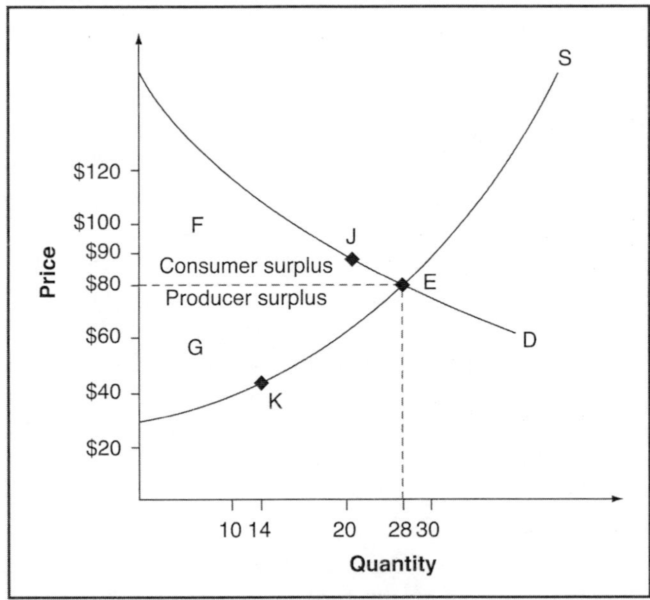

EXHIBIT 4-13 Consumer and Producer Surplus

The triangular area labeled by F shows the area of consumer surplus, which shows that the equilibrium price in the market was less than what many of the consumers were willing to pay. For example, point J on the demand curve shows that even at the price of $90, consumers would have been willing to purchase a quantity of 20 million. But those consumers only needed to pay the equilibrium price of $80. The triangular area labeled by G shows the area of producer surplus, which shows that the equilibrium price received in the market was more than what many of the producers were willing to accept for their products. For example, point K on the supply curve shows that at a price of $40, firms would have been willing to supply a quantity of 14 million. However, in this market those firms could receive a price of $80 for their production. The sum of consumer surplus and producer surplus—that is, F + G—is called social surplus.

would have been willing to pay more than $80 for a portable music player. For example, point J shows that if the price was $90, the quantity demanded of the portable music player would have been 20 million. Those consumers who would have been willing to pay $90 for a portable music player based on the utility they expect to receive from it, but who were able to pay the equilibrium price of $80, clearly received a benefit. Remember, the demand curve traces out the willingness to pay for different quantities. The amount that individuals would have been willing to pay minus the amount that they actually paid is called **consumer surplus**. Consumer surplus is the area labeled F—that is, the area between the market price and the segment of the demand curve above equilibrium.

consumer surplus: The benefit consumers receive from buying a good or service, measured by what the individuals would have been willing to pay minus the amount that they actually paid.

The equilibrium price also benefits producers. The supply curve shows the quantity that firms are willing to supply at each price. For example, point K on Exhibit 4-13 illustrates that at a price of $40, firms would still have been willing to supply a quantity of 14 million. Those producers who would have been willing to supply the portable music players at a price of $40, but who were instead able to charge the equilibrium price of $80, clearly received a benefit. **Producer surplus** is the amount that a seller is paid for a good minus the seller's actual cost. In Exhibit 4-13, producer surplus is the area labeled G—that is, the area between the market price and the segment of the supply curve below the equilibrium.

producer surplus: The benefit producers receive from selling a good or service, measured by the price the producer actually received minus the price the producer would have been willing to accept.

Social surplus is the sum of consumer surplus and producer surplus. In Exhibit 4-13, social surplus would thus be shown as the area F + G. Social surplus is larger at equilibrium quantity and price than it would be at any other quantity. At the efficient level of output, it is impossible to increase consumer surplus without reducing producer surplus, and it is impossible to increase producer surplus without reducing consumer surplus.

social surplus: The sum of consumer surplus and producer surplus.

Inefficiency of Price Floors and Price Ceilings

The imposition of a price floor or a price ceiling will prevent a market from adjusting to its equilibrium price and quantity, and thus will create an inefficient outcome. But there is an additional twist here. Along with creating inefficiency, price floors and ceilings will also transfer some consumer surplus to producers, or some producer surplus to consumers. Let's consider a price ceiling and a price floor in turn.

Imagine that several firms develop a promising but expensive new drug for treating back pain. If this therapy is left to the market, the equilibrium price will be $600 per month, and 20,000 people will use the drug, as shown in Exhibit 4-14*a*. The original level of consumer surplus is T + U, and producer surplus is V + W + X. However, the government decides to impose a price ceiling of $400 to make the drug more affordable. At this price ceiling, firms in the market now produce only a quantity of 15,000. As a result, two changes occur. First, an inefficient outcome occurs, and the total social surplus is reduced. **Deadweight loss** is the name for the loss in social surplus that occurs when the economy produces at an inefficient quantity. In Exhibit 4-14*a*, the deadweight loss is the area U + W. When deadweight loss exists, it is possible for both consumer and producer surplus to increase, in this case because the price control is blocking some suppliers and demanders from transactions that they would both be willing to make. A second change from the price ceiling is that some of the producer surplus is transferred to consumers. After the price ceiling is imposed, the new consumer surplus is T + V, while the new producer surplus is X. In other words, the price ceiling transfers the area of surplus V from producers to consumers.

deadweight loss: The loss in social surplus that occurs when a market produces an inefficient quantity.

For the case of a price floor shown in Exhibit 4-14*b*, envision a situation where a city has several movie theaters that are all losing money. The current equilibrium is a price of $8 per movie, with 1,800 people attending movies. The original consumer surplus is G + H + J, and producer surplus is I + K. The city government is worried that movie theaters will go out of business, thus reducing the entertainment options available to citizens, so it decides to impose a price floor of $12 per ticket. As a result, the quantity demanded of movie tickets falls to 1,400. The new consumer surplus is G, and the new producer surplus is H + I. In effect, the price floor causes the area H to be transferred from consumer to producer surplus, but also causes a deadweight loss of J + K.

FIGURE 4-14
Efficiency and Price Floors and Ceilings

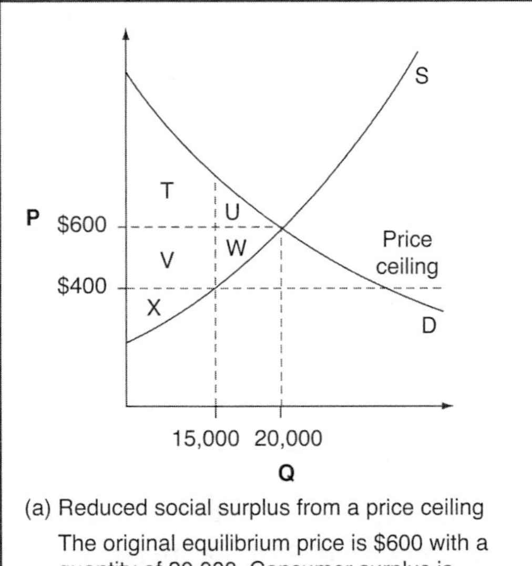

(a) Reduced social surplus from a price ceiling

The original equilibrium price is $600 with a quantity of 20,000. Consumer surplus is T + U, and producer surplus is V + W + X. A price ceiling is imposed at $400, so firms in the market now produce only a quantity of 15,000. As a result, the new consumer surplus is T + V, while the new producer surplus is X. In effect, the price ceiling transfers the surplus V from producers to consumers, but also causes deadweight loss in social surplus of U + W.

(b) Reduced social surplus from a price floor

The original equilibrium is $8 at a quantity of 1,800. Consumer surplus is G + H + J, and producer surplus is I + K. A price floor is imposed at $12, which means that quantity demanded falls to 1,400. As a result, the new consumer surplus is G, and the new producer surplus is H + I. In effect, the price floor causes the area H to be transferred from consumer to producer surplus, but also causes a deadweight loss in social surplus of J + K.

This analysis shows that a price ceiling, like a law establishing rent controls, will transfer some producer surplus to consumers—which helps to explain why consumers often favor them. Conversely, a price floor like a guarantee that farmers will receive a certain price for their crops will transfer some consumer surplus to producers, which explains why producers often favor them. However, both price floors and price ceilings block some transactions that buyers and sellers would have been willing to make and create deadweight loss. Removing such barriers so that prices and quantities can adjust to their equilibrium level will increase the economy's social surplus.

Demand and Supply as a Social Adjustment Mechanism

The demand and supply model emphasizes that prices are not set only by demand or only by supply, but by the interaction between the two. In 1890, the famous economist Alfred Marshall wrote that asking whether supply or demand determined a price was like arguing "whether it is the upper or the under blade of a pair of scissors that cuts a piece of paper." The answer is that both blades of the demand and supply scissors are always involved.

The adjustments of equilibrium price and quantity in a market-oriented economy often occur without much government direction or oversight. If the coffee crop in Brazil suffers a terrible frost, then the supply curve of coffee shifts to the left, and the price of coffee rises. Some people—call them the coffee addicts—continue to drink coffee and pay the higher price. Others switch to tea or soft drinks. No government commission is needed to figure out how to adjust coffee prices, or which companies will be allowed to process the remaining supply, or which supermarkets in which cities will receive a certain quantity of coffee to sell, or which consumers will ultimately be allowed to drink the brew. Such adjustments in response to price changes happen all the time in a market economy, often so smoothly and rapidly that we barely notice them. Think for a moment of all the seasonal foods that are available and inexpensive at certain times of the year, like fresh corn in midsummer, but more expensive at other times of the year. People alter their diets and restaurants alter their menus in response to these fluctuations in prices without fuss or fanfare. For both the U.S. economy and the world economy as a whole, demand and supply is the primary social mechanism for answering the basic questions about what is produced, how it is produced, and for whom it is produced.

Key Concepts and Summary

1. A **demand schedule** is a table that shows the **quantity demanded** at different prices in the market. A **demand curve** shows the relationship between quantity demanded and price in a given market on a graph. The **law of demand** points out that a higher price typically leads to a lower quantity demanded.
2. A **supply schedule** is a table that shows the **quantity supplied** at different prices in the market. A **supply curve** shows the relationship between quantity supplied and price on a graph. The **law of supply** points out that a higher price typically leads to a higher quantity supplied.
3. The **equilibrium price** and **equilibrium quantity** occur where the supply and demand curves cross. The **equilibrium** occurs where the quantity demanded is equal to the quantity supplied.
4. If the price is below the equilibrium level, then the quantity demanded will exceed the quantity supplied. **Excess demand** or a **shortage** will exist. If the price is above the equilibrium level, then the quantity supplied will exceed the quantity demanded. **Excess supply** or a **surplus** will exist. In either case, economic pressures will push the price toward the equilibrium level.
5. Economists often use the ***ceteris paribus*** or "other things being equal" assumption, that while examining the economic impact of one event, all other factors remain unchanged for the purpose of the analysis.
6. Factors that can shift the demand curve for goods and services, causing a different quantity to be demanded at any given price, include changes in tastes, population, income, prices of **substitute** or **complement** goods, and expectations about future conditions and prices.
7. Factors that can shift the supply curve for goods and services, causing a different quantity to be supplied at any given price, include natural conditions, input prices, changes in technology, and government taxes, regulations, or subsidies.
8. When using the supply and demand framework to think about how an event will affect the equilibrium price and quantity, proceed through four steps: (a) sketch a supply and demand diagram to think about what the market looked like before the event; (b) decide whether the event will affect supply or demand; (c) decide whether the effect on supply or demand is negative or positive, and draw the appropriate shifted supply or demand curve; (d) compare the new equilibrium price and quantity to the original ones.
9. **Price ceilings** prevent a price from rising above a certain level. When a price ceiling is set below the equilibrium price, quantity demanded will exceed quantity supplied, and excess demand or shortages will result. **Price floors** prevent a price from falling below a certain level. When a price floor is set above the equilibrium price, quantity supplied will exceed quantity demanded, and excess supply or surpluses will result.
10. Price floors and price ceilings often lead to unintended consequences because buyers and sellers have many margins for action. These margins include **black markets**, side payments, quality adjustments, and shifts in who is involved in the transaction.
11. Policies that shift supply and demand explicitly, through targeted subsidies or taxes, are often preferable to policies that attempt to set prices because they avoid the shortages, surpluses, and other unintended consequences that price ceilings and floors typically produce.
12. **Consumer surplus** is the gap between the price that consumers are willing to pay, based on their preferences, and the market equilibrium price. **Producer surplus** is the gap between the price for which producers are willing to sell a product, based on their costs, and the market equilibrium price. **Social surplus** is the sum of consumer surplus and producer surplus. Total surplus is larger at the equilibrium quantity and price than it will be at any other quantity and price. **Deadweight loss** is the loss in total surplus that occurs when the economy produces at an inefficient quantity.

Review Questions

1. In the economic view, what determines the level of prices?
2. What does a downward-sloping demand curve mean about how buyers in a market will react to a higher price?
3. Will demand curves have the same exact shape in all markets?
4. What does an upward-sloping supply curve mean about how sellers in a market will react to a higher price?

5. Will supply curves have the same shape in all markets?
6. What is the relationship between quantity demanded and quantity supplied at equilibrium?
7. How can you locate the equilibrium point on a demand and supply graph?
8. When analyzing a market, how do economists deal with the problem that many factors that affect the market are changing at the same time?
9. If the price is above the equilibrium level, would you predict excess supply or excess demand? If the price is below the equilibrium level, would you predict a shortage or a surplus?
10. Explain why a price that is above the equilibrium level will tend to fall toward equilibrium. Explain why a price that is below the equilibrium level will tend to rise toward the equilibrium.
11. Name some factors that can cause a shift in the demand curve in markets for goods and services.
12. Does a price ceiling attempt to make a price higher or lower?
13. How does a price ceiling set below the equilibrium level affect quantity demanded and quantity supplied?
14. Does a price floor attempt to make a price higher or lower?
15. How does a price floor set above the equilibrium level affect quantity demanded and quantity supplied?
16. Make a list of ways that buyers and sellers may respond to price ceilings and price floors, other than changes in quantity.
17. Why might economists commonly prefer public policies that shift demand and/or supply rather than imposing price ceilings or price floors?
18. What's the difference between demand and quantity demanded?
19. Name some factors that can cause a shift in the supply curve in markets for goods and services.
20. Is supply the same thing as quantity supplied? Explain.
21. What is consumer surplus? How is it illustrated on a demand and supply diagram?
22. What is producer surplus? How is it illustrated on a demand and supply diagram?
23. What is total surplus? How is it illustrated on a demand and supply diagram?
24. What is the relationship between total surplus and economic efficiency?
25. What is deadweight loss?

CHAPTER

5

Labor and Financial Capital Markets

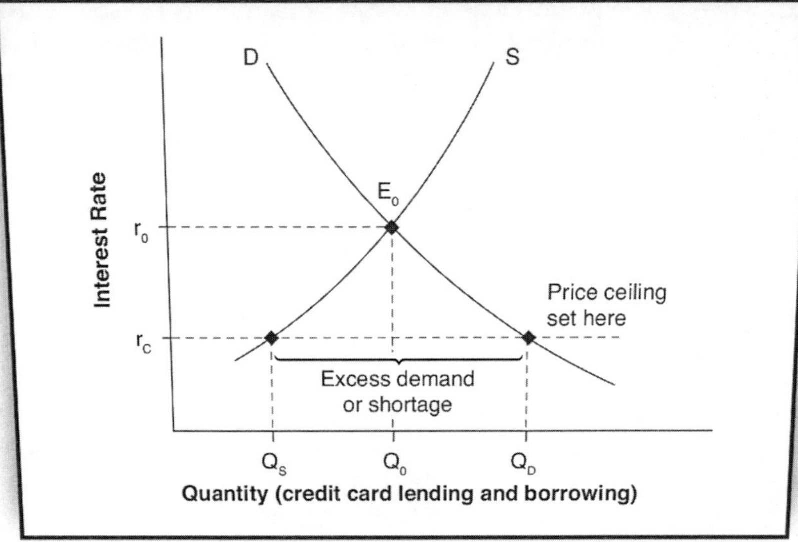

Chapter Outline

Thinking about demand and supply curves in markets for labor and markets for financial capital requires a shift in perspective about the identity of demanders and suppliers. In markets for goods and services, individuals act as consumers on the demand side of the market, while firms act as sellers on the supply side. But in labor markets, individuals are the suppliers of labor, while firms and other employers who hire labor are on the demand side. In markets for financial capital, both individuals and firms can play roles as savers who supply financial capital and also as borrowers who demand it.

Most college students play an active role in both labor and financial capital markets. Employment is a fact of life for most college students: 40% of full-time college students ages 16–24—and 76% of part-time students—were employed in 2013. Most college students are also heavily involved in financial markets, primarily as borrowers. Among full-time college students, over half take out a loan to help finance their education each year, and those loans average about $7,000 per year. Many college students also borrow using credit cards and car loans. As this chapter will illustrate, labor markets and financial capital markets can be analyzed with the same tools of demand and supply as markets for goods and services.

Demand and Supply at Work in Labor Markets

Markets for labor have demand and supply curves, just like markets for goods and services. The law of demand applies in labor markets just as it does in goods and services markets. Specifically, a higher salary or wage—that is, a higher price in the labor market—leads to a decrease in quantity of labor demanded by employers, while a lower salary or wage leads to an increase in the quantity of labor demanded. The law of supply functions in labor markets, too; that is, a higher price for labor leads to a higher quantity of labor supplied.

Equilibrium in the Labor Market

Consider the market for nurses in the Minneapolis–St. Paul, Minnesota, metropolitan area. They work for a variety of employers: hospitals, doctors' offices, schools, health clinics, and nursing homes. Exhibit 5-1 illustrates how demand and supply determine equilibrium in this labor market. Let's walk through the elements of the figure one step at a time.

The horizontal axis shows the quantity of nurses hired. In this example, labor is measured by number of workers, but another common way to measure the quantity of labor is by the number of hours worked. The vertical axis shows the price for nurses' labor—that is, how much they are paid. In this example, the price of labor is measured by salary on an annual basis, although in other cases the price of labor could be measured by monthly or weekly pay, or even the wage paid per hour. The demand and supply schedules accompanying the exhibit list the quantity supplied and quantity demanded of nurses at different salaries.

As the salary for nurses rises, the quantity demanded will fall. Some hospitals and nursing homes may cut back on the number of nurses they hire, or they may lay off some of their existing nurses. Employers who face higher nurses' salaries may also try to look after patients by investing in physical equipment, like computer monitoring and diagnostic systems, or by using lower-paid health care aides to reduce the number of nurses they need to hire.

As salaries for nurses rise, the quantity supplied will rise. If nurses' salaries in Minneapolis–St. Paul are higher than in other cities, more people will be willing to train as nurses; more nurses will move to Minneapolis–St. Paul to find jobs; and those currently trained as nurses will be more likely to pursue nursing as a full-time job, rather than trying other jobs.

At equilibrium, the quantity supplied and the quantity demanded are equal. Thus, every employer who wants to hire a nurse at this equilibrium wage can find a willing worker, and every nurse who wants to work at this equilibrium salary can find a job. In Exhibit 5-1, the supply curve S and demand curve D intersect at the equilibrium point E. The equilibrium quantity of nurses in this example is 35,000, and the average annual salary is $70,000. This example simplifies the nursing market by focusing on the "average" nurse. In reality, of course, the market for nurses is actually made up of many smaller

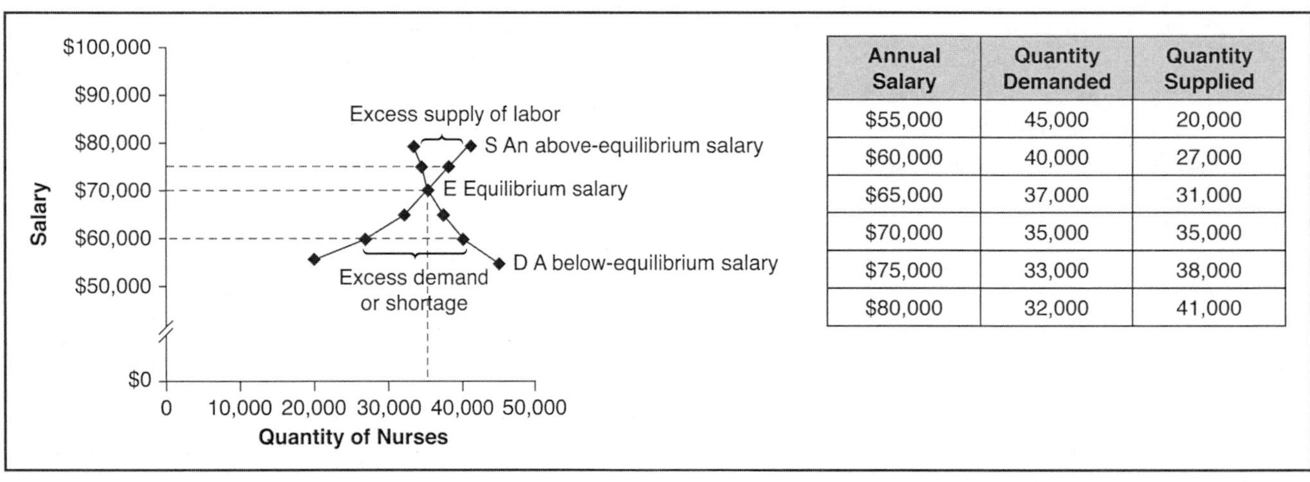

Annual Salary	Quantity Demanded	Quantity Supplied
$55,000	45,000	20,000
$60,000	40,000	27,000
$65,000	37,000	31,000
$70,000	35,000	35,000
$75,000	33,000	38,000
$80,000	32,000	41,000

EXHIBIT 5-1 A Labor Market Example: Demand and Supply for Nurses in Minneapolis–St. Paul

The demand curve D of those employers who want to hire nurses intersects with the supply curve S of those who are qualified and willing to work as nurses at the equilibrium point E. In this example, the equilibrium salary is $70,000 and the equilibrium quantity is 35,000 nurses. At an above-equilibrium salary of $75,000, quantity supplied increases to 38,000, but the quantity of nurses demanded at the higher pay declines to 33,000. At this above-equilibrium salary, an excess supply or surplus of nurses would exist. At a below-equilibrium salary of $60,000, quantity supplied declines to 27,000, while the quantity demanded at the lower wage increases to 40,000 nurses. At this below-equilibrium salary, excess demand or a shortage exists.

markets, like markets for nurses with varying degrees of experience and credentials. But many markets contain closely related products that differ in quality; for instance, even a simple product like gasoline comes in regular, premium, and super-premium, each with a different price. Even in such cases, discussing the average price of gasoline or the average salary for nurses can be useful.

When the price of labor is not at the equilibrium, economic incentives tend to move salaries toward the equilibrium. For example, if salaries for nurses in Minneapolis–St. Paul were above the equilibrium at $75,000 per year, then 38,000 people want to work as nurses, but employers want to hire only 33,000 nurses. At the above-equilibrium salary, excess supply or a surplus results. In a situation of excess supply in the labor market, with many applicants for every job opening, employers who hire nurses will have an incentive to offer lower wages than they otherwise would have. The salary will move down toward equilibrium.

In contrast, if the salary is below the equilibrium at, say, $60,000 per year, then a situation of excess demand or a shortage arises. In this case, employers encouraged by the relatively lower wage want to hire 40,000 nurses, but only 27,000 individuals want to work as nurses in Minneapolis–St. Paul. In response to such a shortage, some employers in this metropolitan area will offer higher pay in order to attract the nurses. Other employers will have to match the higher pay to keep their own employees. The higher salaries will encourage more nurses to train or work in Minneapolis–St. Paul. Again, price and quantity in the labor market will move toward equilibrium.

Shifts in Labor Demand

The demand curve for labor shows what quantity of labor employers wish to hire at any salary or wage, under the *ceteris paribus* assumption that all other relevant economic factors are held constant. At least three types of economic events can cause a shift in the demand for labor, so that a higher or lower quantity of labor is hired at every salary or wage: changes in the quantity of output produced with that kind of labor, changes in how that output is produced, and government regulations affecting firms that demand labor.

A change in the quantity of the product being produced with a certain kind of that labor will alter the demand for that kind of labor. Expenditures on health care increased from about 9% of the U.S. economy in 1980 to 17% of the economy by 2014. When people spend more dollars on health care services, the demand for nurses increases at every given wage level, too. Demand for nurses may expand even more rapidly in the future because the proportion of Americans over the age of 65 will increase in the opening decades of the twenty-first century, and the elderly tend to consume more health care. Conversely, when demand for a certain product decreases, then demand for workers who make that product decreases, too.

Demand for labor may also shift because of changes in how output is produced. Firms that want to earn high profits look for a combination of inputs—workers, materials, and equipment—to keep costs low. Hospitals have sometimes tried to hold down costs by hiring health care aides rather than better-trained and higher-paid nurses.

Government regulations can also affect the quantity of workers that firms wish to hire at any given wage. For example, government rules may require nurses, rather than less-trained health care workers, to carry out certain medical procedures, while prohibiting nurses from carrying out other procedures. Changes in government rules can increase or decrease the quantity demanded of nurses at any given price.

Shifts in Labor Supply

On the supply side of the labor market, two main factors will affect how many people want to work at a certain job at a given salary level. One issue is how the job is perceived by workers relative to other choices. For example, there seems to have been a shift in the tastes of workers such that nursing looks relatively less attractive compared to other alternative jobs. One reason for that shift is that the job options open to women in health care, law, and business have expanded in recent decades.

Government policies can also affect the supply of labor for jobs. On one side, the government may support rules that set high qualifications for certain jobs: academic training, certificates or licenses, or experience. When these qualifications are made tougher, the supply of workers in that job will decrease at any given wage. On the other hand, the government may also reduce the required level of qualifications or else subsidize training; for example, the government might offer subsidies for nursing schools or nursing students. Such provisions would shift the supply curve of nurses to the right.

A change in salary will lead to a movement along labor demand or labor supply curves, but it will not shift those curves. However, events like those sketched here will cause either the demand or the supply of labor to shift, and thus will move the labor market to a new equilibrium salary and quantity.

Technology and Wage Inequality: The Four-Step Process

Economic events can change equilibrium salary (or wage) and quantity of labor. Consider how the wave of new information technologies might affect low-skill and high-skill workers in the U.S. economy. From the perspective of employers who demand labor, these new technologies are often a substitute for low-skill laborers like file clerks who used to organize the paper records of transactions. However, these new technologies are a complement to high-skill managers, who benefit from the technological advances by being able to monitor more information, communicate more easily, and juggle a wider array of responsibilities. How would these specific effects of the new technologies affect the wages of high-skill and low-skill workers? For this question, the four-step process for analyzing how shifts in supply or demand affect a market (introduced in Chapter 4) works in this way.

1. What did the markets for low-skill labor and high-skill labor look like before the arrival of the new technologies? In Exhibits 5-2*a* and 5-2*b*, S_0 is the original supply curve for labor and D_0 is the original demand curve for labor. In each graph, the original point of equilibrium, E_0, occurs at the price w_0 and the quantity q_0. The equilibrium pay for high-skill labor in Exhibit 5-2*b* exceeds the equilibrium pay for low-skill labor.
2. Does the new technology affect the supply of labor from households or the demand for labor from firms? The technology change described here affects demand for labor by firms that hire workers.
3. Will the new technology increase or decrease demand? Based on the description earlier, as the technology substitute for low-skill labor becomes available, demand for low-skill labor will decrease and shift to the left from D_0 to D_1. As the technology complement for high-skill labor becomes cheaper, demand for high-skill labor will increase and shift to the right from D_0 to D_1.
4. The new equilibrium for low-skill labor, shown as point E_1 with price w_1 and quantity q_1, has a lower wage and quantity hired than the original equilibrium, E_0. The new equilibrium for high-skill labor, shown as point E_1 with price w_1 and quantity q_1, has a higher wage and quantity hired than the original equilibrium E_0.

Thus, the demand and supply model predicts that the new computer and communications technologies will raise the pay of high-skill workers but reduce the pay of low-skill workers. Indeed, from the 1970s through the first decade of the 2000s, the wage gap widened between high-skill and low-skill labor. In 1980, for example, a college graduate earned about 30% more than a high school graduate with comparable job experience, but by 2010, a college graduate earned about 60% more than an otherwise comparable high school graduate. Many economists believe that direct and indirect effects of the new information technologies were among the main causes behind the trend toward greater wage inequality in the United States during this period.

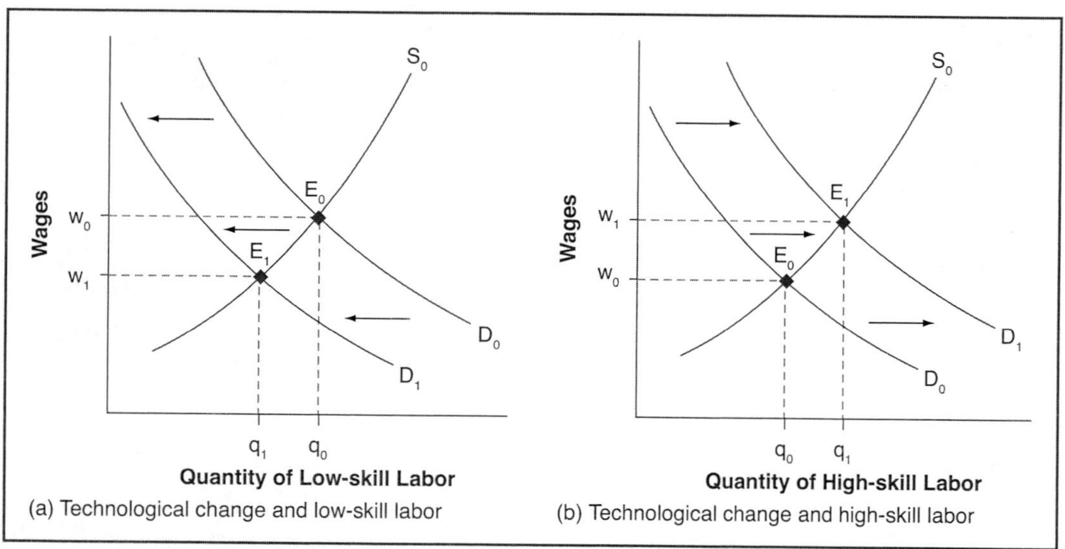

(a) Technological change and low-skill labor (b) Technological change and high-skill labor

EXHIBIT 5-2 Technology and Wages: Applying Demand and Supply

Step 1: What did the market look like before the change? In this case there are two markets: low-skill labor and high-skill labor. In each market, the original demand curve for labor is D_0, the original supply curve for labor is S_0, and the original equilibrium is E_0, where the equilibrium wage is w_0 and the equilibrium quantity is q_0.
Step 2: Does the new technology affect the supply of labor or the demand for labor? The new technology affects demand for labor.
Step 3: How will the new technology alter demand for the two types of labor? As the technology substitute for low-skill labor becomes cheaper, demand for low-skill labor will shift to the left, as shown by the shift from D_0 to D_1 in the market for low-skill labor. As the technology complement for high-skill labor becomes cheaper, demand for high-skill labor will shift to the right, as shown by the shift from D_0 to D_1 in the market for high-skill labor.
Step 4: Compare the new equilibrium to the original equilibrium. The new equilibrium for low-skill labor at E_1 has a lower wage and quantity than the original equilibrium E_0 in the market for low-skill labor. The new equilibrium for high-skill labor at E_1 has a higher wage and quantity than the original equilibrium.

Price Floors in the Labor Market: Living Wages and Minimum Wages

In contrast to goods and services markets, price ceilings are rare in labor markets because rules that prevent people from earning income are not politically popular. There is one exception: sometimes limits are proposed on the high incomes of top business executives.

The labor market, however, presents some prominent examples of price floors, which are often used as an attempt to increase the wages of low-paid workers. The U.S. government sets a **minimum wage**, a price floor that makes it illegal for an employer to pay employees less than a certain hourly rate. In mid-2009, the U.S. minimum wage was raised to $7.25 per hour. Local political movements in a number of U.S. cities have pushed for a higher minimum wage, which they call a *living wage*. Promoters of living wage laws maintain that the minimum wage is too low to ensure a reasonable standard of living. They base this conclusion on the calculation that, if you work 40 hours a week at a minimum wage of $7.25 per hour for 50 weeks a year, your annual income is $14,500, which is less than the official U.S. government definition of what it means for a family with one parent and children to be in poverty.

minimum wage: A price floor that makes it illegal for an employer to pay employees less than a certain hourly rate.

Supporters of the living wage argue that full-time workers should be assured a high enough wage so that they can afford the essentials of life: shelter, food, clothing, and health care. Since Baltimore passed the first living wage law in 1994, several dozen other cities have enacted similar laws. The living wage ordinances do not apply to all employers, but they have typically specified that all employees of the city or employees of firms that are hired by the city be paid at least a certain wage that is usually a few dollars per hour above the U.S. minimum wage.

Exhibit 5-3 illustrates the situation of a city considering a living wage law. The wage appears on the vertical axis because the wage is the price in the labor market. Before the passage of the living wage law, the equilibrium wage is $10 per hour and the city hires

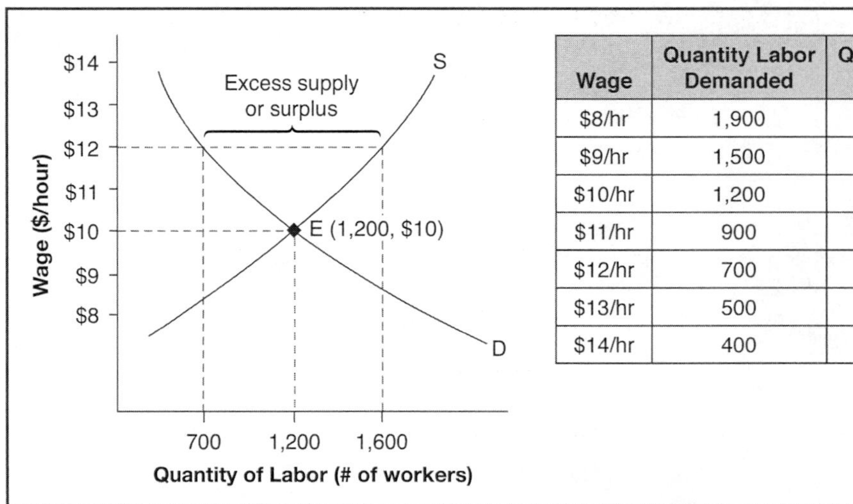

Wage	Quantity Labor Demanded	Quantity Labor Supplied
$8/hr	1,900	500
$9/hr	1,500	900
$10/hr	1,200	1,200
$11/hr	900	1,400
$12/hr	700	1,600
$13/hr	500	1,800
$14/hr	400	1,900

EXHIBIT 5-3 A Living Wage: Example of a Price Floor

The original equilibrium in this labor market is a wage of $10/hour and a quantity of 1,200 workers, shown at point E. Imposing a wage floor at $12/hour leads to an excess supply of labor. At that wage, the quantity of labor supplied is 1,600, and the quantity of labor demanded is only 700.

1,200 workers at this wage. However, a group of concerned citizens persuades the city council to enact a living wage law requiring employers to pay no less than $12 per hour. In response to the higher wage (the horizontal dashed line in the graph), 1,600 workers look for jobs with the city. At this higher wage, the city, as an employer, is willing to hire only 700 workers. At the price floor, the quantity supplied exceeds the quantity demanded, and a surplus of labor exists in this market.

The Minimum Wage as an Example of a Price Floor

The U.S. minimum wage is a price floor that is typically set very close to the equilibrium wage for low-skill labor. About 2% of American workers are actually paid the minimum wage. In other words, the vast majority of the U.S. labor force has its wages determined in the labor market, not as a result of the government price floor. In many cities, the federal minimum wage is apparently below the market price for unskilled labor because employers offer more than the minimum wage to checkout clerks and other low-skill workers without any government prodding.

Economists have attempted to estimate how much the minimum wage reduces the quantity demanded of low-skill labor. A typical result of such studies is that a 10% increase in the minimum wage would decrease the hiring of unskilled workers by 1–2%, which seems a relatively small reduction. In fact, some studies have even found no effect of a higher minimum wage on employment at certain times and places.

Let's suppose that the minimum wage set lies just slightly *below* the equilibrium wage level. Wages could fluctuate according to market forces above this price floor, but they would not be allowed to move beneath the floor. In this situation, the price floor minimum wage is said to be *nonbinding*—that is, the price floor is not determining the market outcome. Even if the minimum wage moves just a little higher, it will still have no effect on the quantity of employment in the economy, as long as it remains below the equilibrium wage. Even if the minimum wage is increased by enough so that it rises slightly above the equilibrium wage and becomes binding, only a small excess supply gap will result between the quantity demanded and quantity supplied of low-skill labor.

These insights help to explain why U.S. minimum wage laws have historically had only a small impact on employment. Because the minimum wage has typically been set close to the equilibrium wage for low-skill workers and at some times and places even below it, it hasn't had a large effect in creating an excess supply of labor. However, if the

A Peek into the Maze of Minimum-Wage Arguments

Although there is considerable controversy over just how much raising the minimum wage will affect the quantity demanded of low-skill labor, let's say for the sake of argument that a 10% rise in the minimum wage will reduce the employment of low-skill workers by 2%. Does this outcome prove that raising the minimum wage by 10% is bad public policy? Not necessarily.

If 98% of those receiving the minimum wage have a pay increase of 10%, but 2% of those receiving the minimum wage lose their jobs, are the gains for society as a whole greater than the losses? The answer is not clear, because job losses even for a small group may outweigh modest income gains for others. To complicate the issue further, if the 2% of minimum-wage workers who lose their jobs are struggling to support families, that's one thing. If those who lose their jobs are high school students picking up spending money over summer vacation, that's something else.

Another complexity arises from the fact that many minimum-wage workers don't work full-time for an entire year. Imagine a minimum-wage worker who holds different part-time jobs for a few months at a time, with some weeks in between without any work. The worker in this situation receives the 10% raise in the minimum wage when working, but also ends up working 2% fewer hours during the year. Overall, this worker's income would rise because the 10% pay raise would more than offset the 2% fewer hours worked.

Of course, the preceding arguments do not prove that raising the minimum wage is necessarily a good idea either. There may well be other, better public policy options for helping low-wage workers. (Chapter 16 discusses some possibilities.) The lesson from this maze of minimum-wage arguments is that even those who agree on the basic analysis of how a proposed economic policy affects quantity demanded and quantity supplied may still disagree on whether the policy is a good idea.

minimum wage were increased dramatically—say, if it were doubled—then its impact on reducing the quantity demanded of employment would be much larger.

Demand and Supply in Financial Capital Markets

In the U.S. economy, $3.2 trillion was saved in 2014. Some of the savings ended up in banks, which in turn loaned the money to individuals or businesses that wanted to borrow money. Some was invested in private companies or loaned to government agencies that wanted to borrow money to raise funds for purposes like building roads or public transportation. Some firms took their savings and reinvested the money in their own business.

At this point, we'll avoid becoming entangled in all the different kinds of financial investments—like bank accounts, stocks, and bonds. Chapter 19 examines these specific financial investments in more detail. The task at hand is to determine how the demand and supply model links those who wish to supply financial capital with those who demand financial investments. Those who save money and make financial investments, whether individuals or businesses, are on the supply side of the financial capital market. Those who borrow money or firms who receive financial investments are on the demand side of the financial capital market.

Who Demands and Who Supplies in Financial Capital Markets

In any market, the price is what suppliers receive and what demanders pay. In financial capital markets, those who supply financial capital through saving expect to receive a rate of return, while those who demand financial capital by receiving funds expect to pay a rate of return. This rate of return can come in a variety of forms, depending on the type of financial investment. A straightforward example of a rate of return, often used for simplicity, is the interest rate. For example, when you supply money into a savings account at a bank, you receive a certain interest rate. If you demand a loan to buy a car or a computer, you will need to pay interest on the money you borrow.

Let's consider the market for borrowing money with credit cards. The United States has about 160 million credit card holders, who hold a total of 1 billion cards (an average

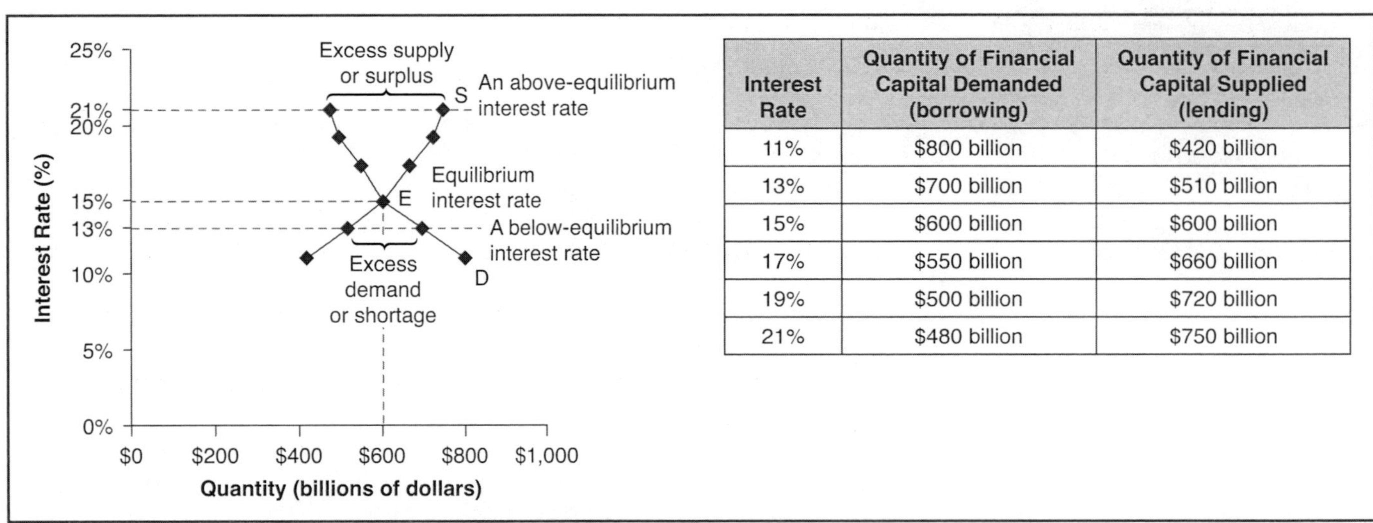

Interest Rate	Quantity of Financial Capital Demanded (borrowing)	Quantity of Financial Capital Supplied (lending)
11%	$800 billion	$420 billion
13%	$700 billion	$510 billion
15%	$600 billion	$600 billion
17%	$550 billion	$660 billion
19%	$500 billion	$720 billion
21%	$480 billion	$750 billion

EXHIBIT 5-4 Demand and Supply for Borrowing Money with Credit Cards

In this market for credit card borrowing, the demand curve D for borrowing financial capital intersects the supply curve S for lending financial capital at equilibrium E. At the equilibrium, the interest rate (the "price" in this market) is 15% and the quantity of financial capital being loaned and borrowed is $600 billion. The equilibrium is the price where the quantity demanded and the quantity supplied are equal. At an above-equilibrium interest rate like 21%, the quantity of financial capital supplied would increase to $750 billion, but the quantity demanded would decrease to $480 billion. A situation of excess supply or surplus would exist. At a below-equilibrium interest rate like 13%, the quantity of financial capital demanded would increase to $700 billion, but the quantity of financial capital supplied would decrease to $510 billion. A situation of excess demand or shortage would exist.

of about six cards per person). If you use a credit card to make a purchase, but do not pay the bill by the deadline, you have borrowed money from the credit card company and will need to pay interest. A typical credit card interest rate ranges from 12% to 18% per year. In 2015, Americans had about $900 billion outstanding in credit card debts not paid on time. About two-thirds of U.S. families with credit cards report that they almost always pay the full balance on time, but one-fifth of U.S. families with credit cards say that they "hardly ever" pay off the card in full. While credit card companies have different annual payments, different penalties for late payment, and different interest rates, let's say that on average the annual interest rate for credit card borrowing is 15% per year. Thus, Americans pay tens of billions of dollars every year in interest on their credit cards—a total that doesn't include fees, like basic fees for the credit card or fees for late payments.

Exhibit 5-4 illustrates demand and supply in the financial capital market for credit cards. The horizontal axis of the financial capital market shows the quantity that is loaned or borrowed in this market. The vertical or price axis of the financial capital market shows the rate of return, which in the case of credit card borrowing can be measured with an interest rate. The demand and supply schedule accompanying the figure shows the quantity of financial capital that consumers demand at various interest rates and the quantity that credit card firms (often banks) are willing to supply.

The laws of demand and supply continue to apply in the financial capital markets. According to the law of demand, a higher rate of return (that is, a higher price) will decrease the quantity demanded. As the interest rate rises, consumers will reduce the quantity that they borrow. According to the law of supply, a higher price increases the quantity supplied. Consequently, as the interest rate paid on credit card borrowing rises, more firms will be eager to issue credit cards and to encourage customers to use them. Conversely, if the interest rate on credit cards falls, the quantity of financial capital supplied in the credit card market will decrease.

Equilibrium in Financial Capital Markets

In the financial capital market for credit cards shown in Exhibit 5-4, the supply curve S and the demand curve D cross at the equilibrium point E. The equilibrium occurs at an interest rate of 15%, where the quantity of financial capital demanded and the quantity supplied are equal at an equilibrium quantity of $600 billion.

If the interest rate (remember, this measures the "price" in the financial capital market) is above the equilibrium level, then an excess supply, or a surplus, of financial capital will arise in this market. For example, at an interest rate of 21%, the quantity of financial capital supplied increases to $750 billion, while the quantity demanded decreases to $480 billion. At this above-equilibrium interest rate, firms are eager to supply loans to credit card borrowers, but relatively few people or businesses wish to borrow. As a result, some credit card firms will lower the interest rates (or other fees) they charge to attract more business. This strategy will push the interest rate down toward the equilibrium level.

If the interest rate is below the equilibrium, then excess demand or a shortage of financial capital occurs in this market. At an interest rate of 13%, the quantity of financial capital that credit card borrowers demand increases to $700 billion; but the quantity that credit card firms are willing to supply is only $510 billion. In this situation, credit card firms will perceive that they are overloaded with eager borrowers and conclude that they have an opportunity to raise interest rates or fees. Thus, the interest rate will face economic pressures to creep up toward the equilibrium level.

Shifts in Demand and Supply in Financial Capital Markets

The demand and supply of financial capital involves an intertemporal trade-off—that is, making a decision in the present with an eye on the future. Thus, an economic factor can shift demand or supply of financial capital if it alters the balance that people wish to strike between present and future.

Those who supply financial capital face two broad decisions: how much to save, and how to divide up their savings among different forms of financial investments. In thinking about how much to save, people must decide what they will need in the future to address expected or unexpected events. For example, the Social Security program, in which the government sends checks to workers and their families after retirement, tends to reduce the quantity of financial capital that workers save. In deciding between different forms of financial investments, suppliers of financial capital will have to consider the rates of return and the risks involved with different choices. If Investment A becomes more risky, or the return diminishes, then savers will shift some of their funds to Investment B—and the supply curve of financial capital for Investment A will shift back to the left while the supply curve of capital for Investment B shifts to the right.

Those who demand financial capital want the money now and are willing to repay in the future. For example, individuals might borrow money to purchase a long-term possession such as a condominium, a house, or a car. A business might seek financial investment so that it has the funds to build a factory or invest in a research and development project that won't pay off for five years, ten years, or more. Thus, when consumers and businesses have greater confidence that they will be able to repay in the future, the quantity demanded of financial capital at any given interest rate will shift to the right. For example, in the late 1990s many businesses became extremely confident that investments in new technology would have a high rate of return, and their demand for financial capital shifted to the right. Conversely, during the economic doldrums of 2008 and 2009, their demand for financial capital at any given interest rate shifted to the left.

Falling Global Interest Rates: The Four-Step Process

Interest rates in the global economy have declined since the late 1990s. For example, when the governments of countries with large and well-developed economies like the United States, Germany, and the United Kingdom wanted to borrow money in the late 1990s and early 2000s, they often paid an interest rate of 5–6%. By around 2015, they were typically paying an interest rate of around 2%. This pattern of falling interest rates started well before the Great Recession that rocked the global economy in 2008–2009. Economic studies have highlighted a number of factors that can affect the global interest

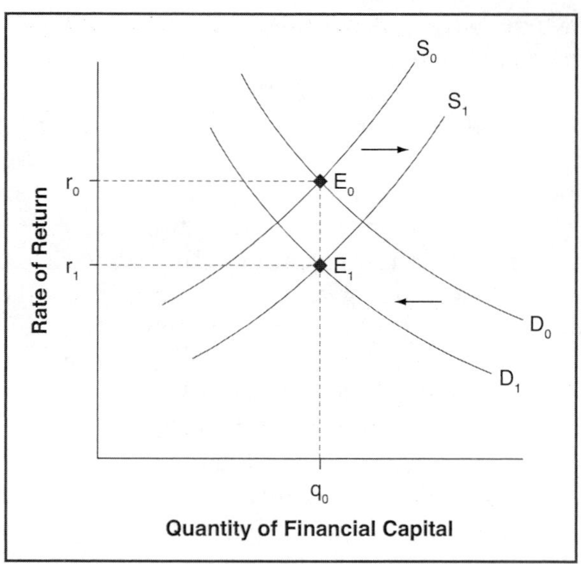

EXHIBIT 5-5 Falling Global Interest Rates: The Four-Step Process

Step 1: Draw a diagram showing demand and supply for financial capital that represents the original scenario. The demand curve D_0 intersects the supply curve S_0 of financial capital in global markets at the equilibrium E_0.
Step 2: Categorize the factors into those affecting supply and those affecting demand. An aging population, greater inequality of incomes, and the decisions of some governments around the world to hold larger financial reserves affect supply. Rapidly dropping prices of information technology and a drop in public spending on infrastructure affect demand.
Step 3: Which way will demand and supply shift? The supply-oriented factors tend to shift supply out to the right, from S_0 to S_1. The demand-oriented factors tend to shift demand back to the left, from D_0 to D_1.
Step 4: Compare the new equilibrium to the original. The new equilibrium E_1 occurs at the lower interest rate r_1, compared to r_0. In this example, the shifts in supply and demand result in the quantity of demand q_0 being the same at both equilibria.

rate: an aging population, greater inequality of incomes, the decision of some governments around the world to hold larger financial reserves against the risk of another economic and financial shock, the rapidly dropping prices of information technology, and a drop in public spending on infrastructure Using the four-step process for analyzing how changes in supply and demand affect equilibrium outcomes, how can these changing factors explain the fall in global interest rates?

Step 1: Draw a diagram showing demand and supply for financial capital that represents the original scenario in which foreign investors are pouring money into the U.S. economy. Exhibit 5-5 shows a demand curve, D_0, and a supply curve, S_0, for financial capital in global markets. The original equilibrium E_0 occurs at interest rate r_0 and quantity of financial investment q_0.

Step 2: The multiple factors affecting international capital markets can be categorized into those affecting supply and those affecting demand. In particular, three factors tend to affect the supply of capital: an aging population and rising inequality in incomes both affect people's desire to save, and when a government decides to hold larger financial reserves, it is demanding higher savings on its own behalf. Two factors tend to affect demand for capital: the rapidly dropping prices of information technology and a drop in public spending on infrastructure.

Step 3: Which way will demand and supply shift? The supply-oriented factors tend to shift supply out to the right, from S_0 to S_1. In particular, an aging population means a greater need for people to save for retirement; when incomes become more unequal, those with high incomes tend to save more; and when governments decide to hold larger financial reserves, they are desiring to save more. The demand-oriented factors tend to shift demand back to the left, from D_0 to D_1. Two factors tend to diminish demand for capital: the rapidly dropping prices of information technology, which reduce the amount firms need to spend for some of the main physical capital investments they wish to make, and a drop in public spending on infrastructure.

Step 4: Compare the new equilibrium E_1 to the original E_0. The new equilibrium E_1 occurs at the lower interest rate r_1, compared to r_0. In this specific figure, the quantity of demand q_0 is the same at both equilibria, which reflects the overall pattern that the total global saving rate doesn't seem to have moved much in the last two decades. To put it another way, the shifts in supply tended to push up the quantity supplied, but the shifts in demand tended to hold down the quantity supplied—and in this particular example, those two forces counterbalanced each other. However, you should be able to imagine a situation where the effect of shifts in supply and demand on quantity don't perfectly balance, and the quantity could end up being higher or lower at the new equilibrium.

The lower global interest rate has dramatic implications for those thinking about saving, including both households and organizations such as pension funds and life insurance companies, as well as for those thinking about borrowing, including households thinking about borrowing to buy a home and firms thinking about borrowing to purchase new plant and equipment. In a modern economy, financial capital often moves invisibly through electronic transfers between one bank account and another. Yet these flows of funds can be analyzed with the same tools of demand and supply as markets for goods or labor.

Price Ceilings in Financial Capital Markets: Usury Laws

As discussed earlier, more than 160 million Americans own credit cards, and their interest payments and fees total tens of billions of dollars each year. It's little wonder that political pressures sometimes arise for setting limits on the interest rates or fees that credit cards companies can charge. The firms that issue credit cards, including banks, oil companies, phone companies, and retail stores, respond that the higher interest rates are necessary to cover the losses created by those who borrow on their credit cards and who do not repay on time or at all. These companies also point out that credit card holders can avoid paying interest if they pay their bills on time.

Consider the credit card market as illustrated in Exhibit 5-6. In this financial capital market, the vertical axis shows the interest rate (which is the price in the financial capital market). Demanders in the credit card market are households; suppliers are the companies

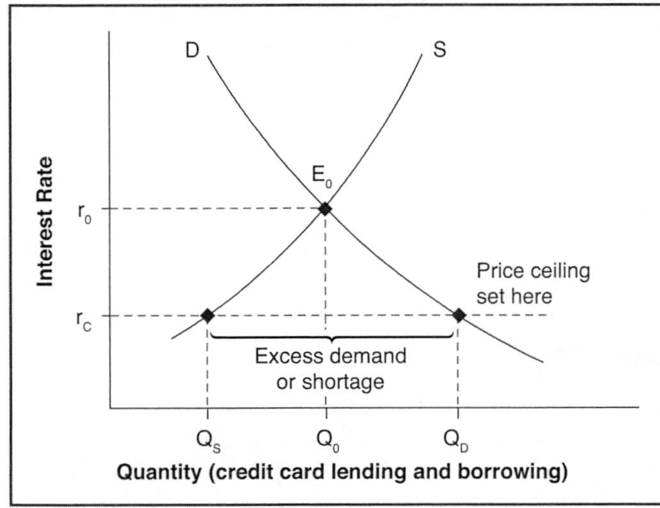

EXHIBIT 5-6 Credit Card Interest Rates: Another Price Ceiling Example

The original intersection of demand D and supply S occurs at equilibrium E_0. However, a price ceiling is set at the interest rate r_c, below the equilibrium interest rate r_0 and so the interest rate cannot adjust upward to the equilibrium. At the price ceiling, the quantity demanded, Q_D exceeds the quantity supplied, Q_S. There is excess demand, also called a shortage.

Payday Advances: Valuable Service or Predatory Lending?

A "payday advance" works this way. When you receive a payday advance, you then write a personal check to the business that is providing the advance. For example, say that the check you write is for $200. The payday advance firm gives you $180 cash on the spot. It then agrees not to cash your check for a certain period of time—usually ranging from a week to a month—until you receive your next paycheck. In this example, when the payday advance firm cashes the check, it effectively collects a charge of $20 for lending $180 for a few weeks or a month.

Consumer protection groups have asserted that this charge, which is not officially an "interest rate" but a "fee," is outrageously high, and want a price ceiling to limit what they view as excessive interest rates. After all, a 10% interest charge per month, if compounded over 12 months, works out to an interest rate of $(1 + .10)^{12} = 314\%$ per year.

Companies that offer the payday advances point out that they provide cash on the spot, without credit checks or other fees. They point out that the cash advance may offer the recipient a way to pay for unexpected expenses like an emergency car repair. They argue that many of their customers have no other options for ready cash. They admit that some customers may borrow unwisely, but observe that customers can borrow unwisely in many ways; for example, customers can end up paying fees when they don't make minimum credit card payments or when they overdraw a checking account.

About 5% of the U.S. population—call it 15 million people—have taken out a payday loan. Roughly $40 billion in payday loans are made each year. Is a price ceiling law needed in the area of payday advances, to protect consumers who may be unsophisticated, low-income, or lacking access to regular banks? Or is a payday advance just another service that people should be free to buy or not buy, as they choose, without government rules?

that issue credit cards. This exhibit does not use specific numbers, which would be hypothetical in any case, but instead focuses on the underlying economic relationships. Imagine that a law imposes a price ceiling that holds the interest rate charged on credit cards at the interest rate r_c, which lies below the interest rate r_0 that would otherwise have prevailed in the market. The price ceiling is shown by the horizontal dashed line in Exhibit 5-6. The demand and supply model predicts that at the lower price ceiling interest rate, the quantity demanded of credit card debt will increase from its original level of Q_0 to Q_D; however, the quantity supplied of credit card debt will decrease from the original Q_0 to Q_S. At the price ceiling r_c, quantity demanded will exceed quantity supplied. Consequently, a number of people who want to have credit cards and are willing to pay the prevailing interest rate will find that companies are unwilling to issue cards to them. The result will be a credit card shortage.

usury laws: Laws that impose an upper limit on the interest rate that lenders can charge.

Many states have **usury laws**, which impose an upper limit on the interest rate that lenders can charge. However, in many cases these upper limits are so high that they are well above the market interest rate. For example, if the interest rate is not allowed to rise above 30% per year, it can still fluctuate below that level according to market forces. A price ceiling that is set at a relatively high level is non-binding, and it will have no practical effect unless the equilibrium price zooms high enough to exceed the price ceiling.

Don't Kill the Price Messengers

Prices exist in markets for goods and services, for labor, and for financial capital. In all of these markets, prices serve as a social mechanism for collecting, combining, and transmitting information that is relevant to the market—namely, the relationship between demand and supply—and then serving as messengers to convey that information to buyers and sellers. In a market-oriented economy, no government agency or guiding intelligence oversees the set of responses and interconnections that result from a change in price. Instead, each consumer reacts according to that person's preferences and budget set, and each profit-seeking producer reacts to the effect on its expected profits.

Demand and Supply Curves

Just as it would be foolish to try to learn the arithmetic of long division by memorizing every possible combination of numbers that can be divided, it would be foolish to try to memorize every specific example of demand and supply in this chapter, this textbook, or this course. Demand and supply is not a list of examples; it's a model to analyze prices and quantities. Even though demand and supply diagrams have many labels, they are fundamentally the same in their logic. Your goal should be to understand the underlying model. The demand and supply analysis is the second fundamental diagram for this course. (The opportunity set model introduced in Chapter 2 was the first.)

The exhibit displays a general demand and supply curve. The horizontal axis shows the different measures of quantity: a quantity of a good or service, or a quantity of labor for a given job, or a quantity of financial capital. The vertical axis shows a measure of price: the price of a good or service, the wage in the labor market, or the rate of return (like the interest rate) in the financial capital market.

The demand and supply model can explain the existing levels of prices, wages, and rates of return. To carry out such an analysis, think about the quantity that will be demanded at each price and the quantity that will be supplied at each price—that is, think about the shape of the demand and supply curves—and how these forces will combine to produce equilibrium. Demand and supply can also be used to explain how economic events will cause changes in prices, wages, and rates of return. There are only four possibilities: the economic event may cause the demand curve to shift right or to shift left, or it may cause the supply curve to shift right or to shift left. The key to analyzing the effect of an economic event on equilibrium prices and quantities is to choose among these possibilities.

Demand and Supply Curves

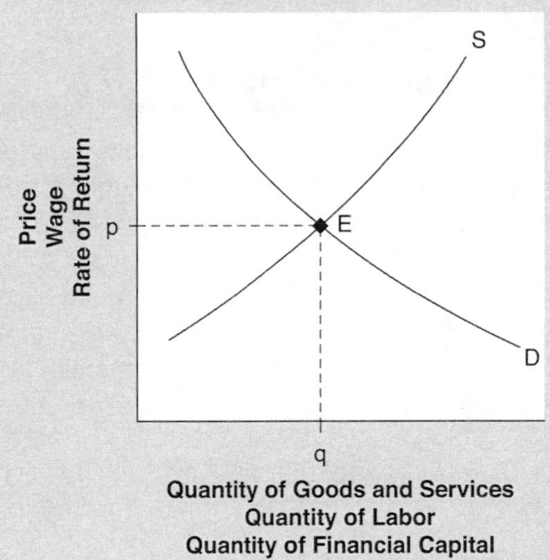

For example, if you are thinking about taking a plane trip to Hawaii, but the ticket turns out to be expensive during the week you intend to go, you merely look at the price and decide, based on the price, whether to fly. The price could be high because the cost of an input like jet fuel increased or because demand surged during that week. Or maybe the airline has raised the price temporarily to see how many people are willing to pay it. Perhaps all of these factors are present at the same time. But you don't need to analyze the market and break down the price change into its underlying factors. You just look at the price of a ticket and decide whether to fly.

Producers also commonly react to price changes without much caring why they occur. Imagine the situation of a farmer who grows oats and learns that the price of oats has risen. The higher price could be due to an increase in demand caused by a new scientific study proclaiming that eating oats is especially healthy. Or perhaps the price of a substitute grain, like corn, has risen, and people have responded by buying more oats. But the oat farmer does not need to know the details. The farmer only needs to know that the price of oats has increased and that it will be profitable to expand production as a result.

The actions of individual consumers and producers overlap and interlock as they react to prices in markets for goods, labor, and financial capital. A change in any single market is transmitted through these multiple interconnections to other markets. The role of flexible prices helping markets to reach equilibrium and linking different markets together helps to explain why price controls can be so counterproductive. There is an old proverb: "Don't kill the messenger." This saying dates back to ancient times, when messengers carried information between distant cities and kingdoms. When a messenger arrived bearing bad news, there was an emotional impulse to kill the messenger. But killing the messenger didn't eliminate the bad news. Moreover, killing the messenger had an undesirable side effect: Other messengers would refuse to bring news to that city or kingdom, depriving the citizens of future information. A custom developed that messengers should not be held personally responsible for the news that they brought.

Those who seek price controls are trying to kill the messenger—or at least to stifle an unwelcome message that prices are bringing about the equilibrium level of price and quantity. But price controls do nothing to affect the underlying forces of demand and supply. Changes in demand and supply will continue to reveal themselves through consumers' and producers' reactions with respect to quantity demanded and quantity supplied. Moreover, immobilizing the price messenger through price controls will deprive the economy of critical information. Without this information, it becomes difficult for everyone—buyers and sellers alike—to react in a flexible and appropriate manner as changes occur throughout the economy.

Key Concepts and Summary

1. In the labor market, households are on the supply side of the market, and firms are on the demand side. In the market for financial capital, households and firms can be on either side of the market: they are suppliers of financial capital when they save or make financial investments, and demanders of financial capital when they borrow or receive financial investments.
2. In the demand and supply analysis of labor markets, the price can be measured by the annual salary or hourly wage received. The quantity of labor can be measured in various ways, like number of workers or the number of hours worked.
3. Three factors can shift the demand curve for labor: a change in the quantity of the product that the labor produces, a change in the production process that uses more or less labor, and a change in government policy that affects the quantity of labor that firms wish to hire at a given wage. Two factors can shift the supply curve for labor: how desirable a job appears to workers relative to the alternatives for reasons other than pay, and how government policy either restricts or encourages the quantity of workers trained for the job.
4. In the demand and supply analysis of financial capital markets, the "price" is the rate of return or the interest rate received. The quantity is measured by the money that flows from those who supply financial capital to those who demand it.
5. Two factors can shift the supply of financial capital to a certain investment: anything that makes people want to alter their existing levels of present and future consumption; and when the riskiness or return on one investment changes relative to other investments. Factors that can shift demand for capital include business confidence and consumer confidence in the future—since financial investments received in the present are typically repaid in the future.

Review Questions

1. What is the "price" commonly called in the labor market? What is the "price" commonly called in the financial capital market?
2. Are households demanders or suppliers in the goods market? Are firms demanders or suppliers in the goods market? What about the labor market and the financial capital market?
3. Name some factors that can cause a shift in the demand curve in labor markets.
4. Name some factors that can cause a shift in the supply curve in labor markets.
5. Name some factors that can cause a shift in the demand curve in financial capital markets.
6. Name some factors that can cause a shift in the supply curve in financial capital markets.

Globalization and Protectionism

CHAPTER

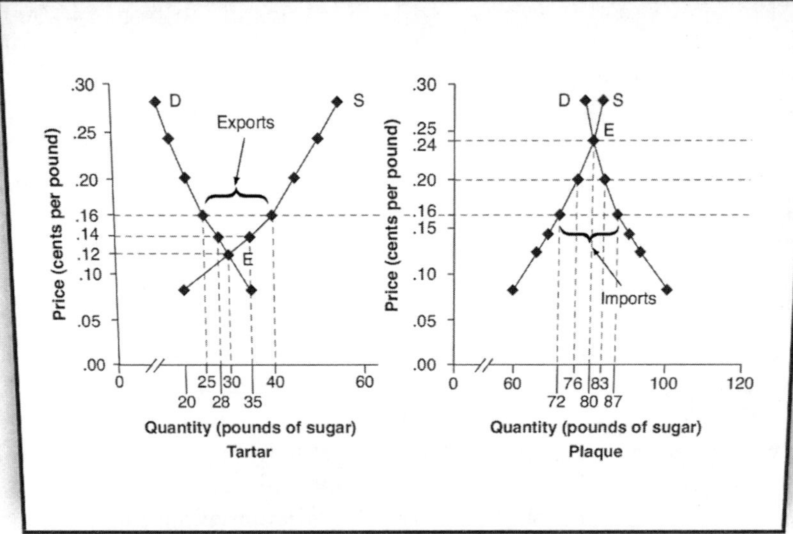

Chapter Outline

Imports of goods and services stir up worries everywhere. Some firms and workers in high-income countries like the United States, Japan, or the nations of the European Union fear that they will suffer if they must compete against firms in low-income countries of Latin America, Asia, or Africa that can pay lower wages. Conversely, some firms and workers in lower-wage countries like Mexico, India, or South Africa fear that they will suffer if they must compete against the very productive workers and advanced technology in high-income countries. Some environmentalists worry that multinational firms may evade environmental protection laws by moving their production to countries with loose or nonexistent pollution standards. Some politicians worry that their nation may become overly dependent on key imported products, like oil. All of these fears tend to reach the same basic policy recommendation: Imports of foreign products should be reduced or even cut off. Government policies to reduce or block international trade are called **protectionism** because they have the effect of protecting domestic producers from foreign competition.

protectionism: Government policies to reduce or block imports.

Protectionism takes three main forms. **Tariffs** are taxes imposed on imported products. They discourage imports by making imported products more expensive to consumers. **Import quotas** are numerical limitations on the quantity of products that can be imported. Finally, **nontariff barriers** are all the other ways that a nation can draw up rules, regulations, inspections, and paperwork to make it more costly or difficult to import products. A rule that every imported product must be opened by hand and inspected with a magnifying glass by one of just three government inspectors available at any given time can limit imports just as effectively as high tariffs or low import quotas.

tariffs: Taxes imposed on imported products.

import quotas: Numerical limitations on the quantity of products that can be imported.

nontariff barriers: All the ways a nation can draw up rules, regulations, inspections, and paperwork to make it more costly or difficult to import products.

As one example, the United States has imposed barriers to imports of textiles for decades. From the mid-1970s up to 2004, for example, the international Multi-Fibre Arrangement specified exactly the quota of textile imports that each high-income country would accept from each low-income country. By 2009, the United States had phased out its import quotas on textiles. However,

U.S. tariffs on textile and apparel imports were among the highest for any industry, averaging 10% overall, but ranging as high as 32% on man-made fiber sweaters and 28% on certain men's pants and artificial fiber coats. There are also nontariff barriers in the form of "rules-of-origin" regulations, in which certain textiles are made in the United States, shipped to other countries, combined in making apparel with textiles made in those other countries—and then re-exported back to the United States at a lower tariff rate.

Despite these interlocking import quotas, tariffs, and nontariff barriers, the share of apparel sold in the United States that is imported rose from about half in 1999 to about three-quarters today. The number of U.S. jobs in textiles and apparel fell from 541,000 in 2007 to 383,000 in 2012, and the U.S. Bureau of Labor Statistics predicts that it will decline to 245,000 by 2022. The U.S. International Trade Commission (ITC) has estimated that removing the remaining tariff and nontariff barriers would cause the number of jobs in this industry to fall by 50,000 more. However, the U.S. textile industry jobs that are saved by import quotas come at a cost. Because textile and apparel protectionism adds to the costs of imports, consumers end up paying billions of dollars more for clothing each year. The ITC also points out that when the United States eliminates trade barriers in one area, then consumers spend the money they save on that product elsewhere in the economy—so that there is no overall loss of jobs for the economy as a whole. Of course, workers in some of the poorest countries of the world who would otherwise have jobs producing textiles, but find their opportunities blocked by tariff and nontariff barriers, would gain considerably if the United States reduced its barrier to trade in textiles.

This chapter begins with an economic analysis of who benefits from protectionism and who pays the costs of protectionism, using demand and supply analysis. The chapter then considers a list of concerns raised about global trade and in particular about imports. For example, how do imports affect the number of jobs, the level of wages, and work conditions? How might imports affect promising but immature domestic industries? What about the trade and environmental issues? The primary international body through which nations negotiate over their trade rules—including rules about tariffs, quotas, and nontariff barriers—is the World Trade Organization (WTO). The membership of the WTO includes over 160 nations. The chapter closes with a discussion of the history and direction of the WTO, as well as various regional trade treaties.

Protectionism: An Indirect Subsidy from Consumers to Producers

To the noneconomist, restricting imports may appear to be nothing more than taking sales from foreign producers and allowing domestic producers to achieve greater sales. But a demand and supply analysis of protectionism shows that protectionism is not just a matter of domestic gains and foreign losses, but a policy that imposes meaningful domestic costs as well.

Demand and Supply Analysis of Protectionism

Consider international trade in sugar between two countries called Tartar and Plaque, illustrated in Exhibit 6-1. In the original supply and demand equilibrium without trade, the equilibrium price of sugar in Tartar is 12 cents per pound, with an equilibrium output of 30 tons. In Plaque, the equilibrium price of sugar in a world without trade is 24 cents per pound, with an equilibrium quantity of 80 tons. These equilibrium points are labeled with the point E.

If international trade between Tartar and Plaque now becomes possible, profit-seeking firms will spot an opportunity: buy sugar cheaply in Tartar, and sell it at a higher price in Plaque. As sugar is shipped from Tartar to Plaque, the quantity of sugar produced in Tartar will be greater than the quantity consumed in that country (with the extra production being exported) and the amount produced in Plaque will be less than the amount consumed in that country (with the extra consumption being imported). The quantity of trade

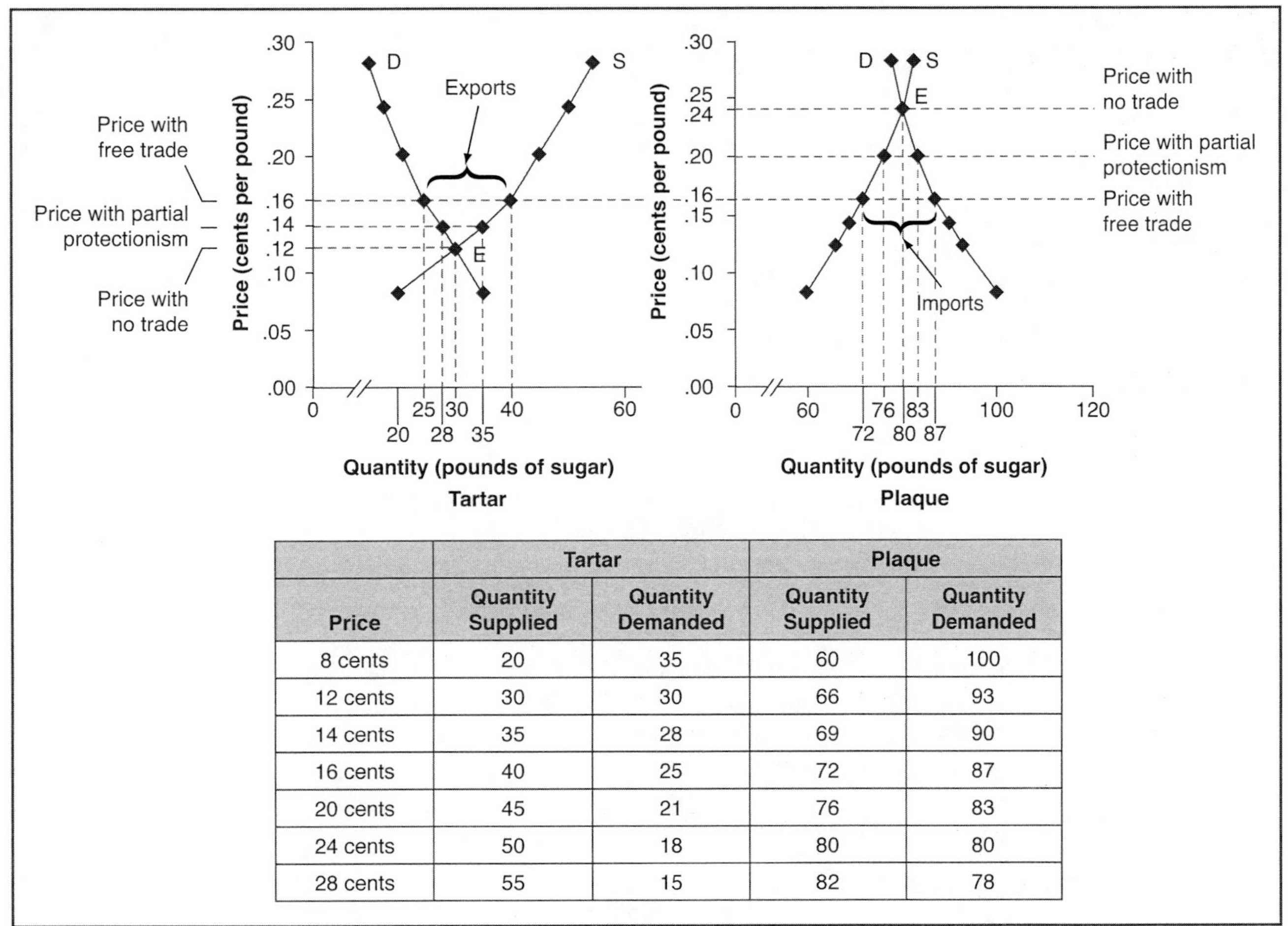

	Tartar		Plaque	
Price	Quantity Supplied	Quantity Demanded	Quantity Supplied	Quantity Demanded
8 cents	20	35	60	100
12 cents	30	30	66	93
14 cents	35	28	69	90
16 cents	40	25	72	87
20 cents	45	21	76	83
24 cents	50	18	80	80
28 cents	55	15	82	78

EXHIBIT 6-1 The Sugar Trade between Tartar and Plaque

Before trade, sugar sells in Tartar for 12 cents a pound and in Plaque for 24 cents per pound. When trade is allowed, businesses will buy sugar cheaply in Tartar and sell it in Plaque. The result with free trade will be that Tartar exports 15 pounds of sugar, Plaque imports 15 pounds of sugar, and the price is the same in the two countries at 16 cents per pound. If trade is only partly open between the countries, it will lead to an outcome between the free-trade and no-trade possibilities.

will be determined when price of sugar is the same in two countries—and thus there is no incentive to trade further. As shown in Exhibit 6-1, the equilibrium with trade occurs at a price of 16 cents per pound. At that price, the sugar farmers of Tartar supply a quantity of 40 tons, while the consumers of Tartar buy only 25 tons. The extra 15 tons of sugar production, shown by the horizontal gap between the demand curve and the supply curve in Tartar, is exported to Plaque. In Plaque, at a price of 16 cents, the farmers produce a quantity of 72 tons and consumers demand a quantity of 87 tons. The excess demand of 15 tons by the consumers of Plaque, shown by the horizontal gap between demand and domestic supply at the price of 16 cents, is supplied by imported sugar from Tartar.

The sugar farmers of Plaque are likely to argue that, if only they could be protected from sugar imported from Tartar, the country of Plaque would have higher domestic sugar production and more jobs in the sugar production industry, and Plaque's sugar farmers would receive a higher price. If the country of Plaque sets a high tariff on imported sugar, or sets an import quota at zero, then the result will be that the quantity of sugar traded between countries could be reduced to zero, and the prices in each country will return to their levels before trade was allowed.

Blocking only a portion of trade is also possible. For example, say that Plaque passed a sugar import quota of 7 tons; that is, Plaque will import no more than 7 tons of sugar, which means that Tartar can export no more than 7 tons of sugar. As can be seen in the table in Exhibit 6-1, the price of sugar in Plaque would then be 20 cents, which is the

Low-Income Countries and Agricultural Trade

Here is a stark comparison about social priorities, which has been widely publicized by the international aid organization Oxfam.

High-income countries of the world—meaning primarily the United States, Canada, countries of the European Union, and Japan—subsidize their domestic farmers by roughly $1 billion per day, including the value both of direct subsidies to farmers and indirect subsidies that come in the form of limiting imports of farm products. However, the total amount of foreign aid from these same high-income countries to the poor countries of the world is about $130 billion per year.

The support of farmers in high income countries is devastating to the chances of farmers in low-income countries. Even when their climate and land are well-suited to products like cotton, rice, sugar, or milk, the high-income countries block their exports. In some cases, the situation gets even worse when the governments of high-income countries, having bought and paid for an excess supply of farm products, gives away those products in poor countries and drives local farmers out of business altogether. In the past, shipments of excess milk from the European Union to Jamaica have caused great hardship for Jamaican dairy farmers. Shipments of excess rice from the United States to Haiti drove thousands of low-income rice farmers in Haiti out of business. The opportunity costs of protectionism aren't paid just by domestic consumers, but also by foreign producers—and for many agricultural products, those foreign producers are the world's poor.

price where the quantity demanded is 7 tons greater than the domestic quantity supplied. Conversely, if Tartar can only export 7 tons of sugar, then the price of sugar in Tartar will be 14 cents per pound, which is the price where the domestic quantity supplied in Tartar is 7 tons greater than domestic demand. In general, when a country sets a low or medium tariff or import quota, then the equilibrium price and quantity will end up in between the cases of no trade at all and completely free trade.

Who Benefits and Who Pays?

Using the demand and supply model, consider the impact of protectionism on producers and consumers in each of the two countries. For producers of the protected good, the sugar farmers of Plaque, restricting imports is clearly positive. Without a need to face imported products, these producers are able to sell more, at a higher price. For consumers in the country with the protected good, the sugar consumers of Plaque, restricting imports is clearly negative. They end up buying a lower quantity of the good and paying a higher price for what they do buy, compared to the equilibrium quantity and price with free trade.

The fact that protectionism pushes up prices for consumers in the country enacting such protectionism is not always acknowledged in public policy arguments, but it's not controversial. After all, if protectionism didn't benefit domestic producers, there wouldn't be much point in enacting such policies in the first place. Protectionism is simply a method of requiring consumers to subsidize producers. The subsidy is indirect, since it is paid by consumers through higher prices, rather than a direct subsidy paid by the government with money collected from taxpayers. But protectionism works like a subsidy nonetheless. The American humorist Ambrose Bierce defined "tariff" this way in his satirical 1911 book, *The Devil's Dictionary*: "Tariff, n. A scale of taxes on imports, designed to protect the domestic producer against the greed of his consumer."

How would Plaque's protectionism affect producers and consumers in their potential trading partner, Tartar? The sugar producers of Tartar will be unable to export to Plaque, and so they will experience lower prices. When Plaque uses import quotas to impose partial protectionism, the sugar producers of Tartar receive a lower price for the sugar they sell in Tartar—but a higher price for the sugar they are allowed to export to Plaque. Consumers of sugar in Tartar would seem to benefit from protectionism in Plaque because it reduces the price of sugar that they pay. On the other hand, remember that at least some of these consumers of sugar in Tartar also work as sugar farmers, so their incomes and jobs are reduced by protectionism. Moreover, if trade in all goods between the countries is shut down, consumers of Tartar would miss out on better prices for the goods that Tar-

Life Savers, Eh?

Life Savers, the hard candy with the hole in the middle, were invented in 1912 by Clarence Crane in Cleveland, Ohio. Starting in the late 1960s and for 35 years afterward 46 billion Life Savers a year, in 200 million rolls, were produced by a plant in Holland, Michigan. But in 2002, the Kraft Company announced that Michigan plant would be closed and Life Saver production moved across the border to Montreal, Canada.

One reason is that Canadian workers are paid slightly less, especially since the Canadian government finances health care costs. But a main reason is that the U.S. government keeps the price of sugar high for the benefits of sugar farmers, with a combination of a government price floor program and strict quotas on imported sugar. In 2012, the U.S. price for refined sugar was 70 cents a pound; the price in the rest of the world was 27 cents a pound. Life Saver production uses over 100 tons of sugar each day because the candies are 95% sugar.

A number of other candy companies have reduced U.S. production and expanded foreign production, as well. But while the candy industry is especially affected by the cost of sugar, the costs are spread more broadly. U.S. consumers pay roughly $1 billion per year in higher food prices because of elevated sugar costs. Meanwhile, sugar producers in low-income countries are driven out of business because they cannot sell their output in the U.S. market.

tar is importing—a benefit that does not appear in our single-market example of sugar protectionism.

But the central focus here is not on how protectionism affects other countries, but how it affects one's own country. Protectionism is a policy where the domestic consumers of a product (consumers may include either households or other firms) are required to pay higher prices to benefit domestic producers of that product. In addition, when a country enacts protectionism, it loses the economic gains it would have been able to achieve through the combination of comparative advantage, learning, and economies of scale that were discussed Chapter 3. With these costs and benefits in mind, let us now consider, one by one, a number of arguments that have been made for restricting imports.

International Trade and Its Effects on Jobs, Wages, and Working Conditions

In theory, at least, imports might injure workers in several different ways: fewer jobs, lower wages, or poor working conditions. Let's consider these in turn.

Fewer Jobs?

In the early 1990s, the United States was negotiating the North American Free Trade Agreement (NAFTA) with Mexico, an agreement that would reduce tariffs, import quotas, and nontariff barriers to trade between the United States, Mexico, and Canada. H. Ross Perot ran for U.S. President in 1992 as a third-party candidate, and one of his prominent campaign arguments was that if the United States expanded trade with Mexico, there would be a "giant sucking sound" as U.S. employers relocated to Mexico so that they could pay lower wages. After all, average wages in Mexico were at that time about one-eighth the U.S. level. Well, NAFTA passed Congress, President Bill Clinton signed it into law, and it took effect in 1995. For the next six years, the U.S. economy had some of the most rapid job growth and lowest unemployment in its history. Those who feared that open trade with Mexico would lead to a dramatic decrease in jobs were proven 100% wrong.

This result was no surprise to economists. After all, the trend toward globalization has been going on for decades. U.S. imports were equal to 5.4% of the U.S. economy in 1970, but to about 15% in 2015. If trade did reduce the number of available jobs, then the United States should have been seeing a steady loss of jobs for decades. While the U.S. economy does experience rises and falls in unemployment rates—like the rising unemployment rate that started in spring 2008 and reached 10% by late 2009—the number of jobs is not falling over extended periods of time. The number of U.S. jobs rose from 78 million in 1970 to 143 million in 2015.

Protectionism certainly saves jobs *in the specific industry being protected*, but for two reasons, it costs jobs in other unprotected industries. First, if consumers are paying higher prices to the protected industry, they inevitably have less money to spend on goods from other industries, and so jobs are lost in those other industries. Second, if the protected product is sold to other firms, like sugar or steel, so that other firms must now pay a higher price for a key input, then those firms will have a hard time competing against foreign producers who don't need to pay the higher price. The hidden opportunity cost of using protectionism to save jobs in one industry sacrifices the jobs that are not created in other industries. This is why the U.S. International Trade Commission, in its study of barriers to trade mentioned near the start of this chapter, predicts that reducing trade barriers would not lead to an overall loss of jobs. Protectionism reshuffles jobs from industries that are not protected from imports to industries that are protected, but it does not create more jobs.

Moreover, the costs of saving jobs through protectionism can be very high. Exhibit 6-2 shows some estimates drawn from a variety of studies of the consumer costs in higher prices of "saving jobs" through protectionism. Saving a job through protectionism typically costs much more than the actual worker's salary. For example, a study published in 2011 compiled evidence that using protectionism to save an average job in the tire industry would cost $900,000 per job saved.

Why does it cost so much to save jobs through protectionism? The basic reason is that not all of the extra money paid by consumers because of protectionism goes to save the jobs of workers. For example, if tariffs are imposed on steel imports so that buyers of steel pay a higher price, U.S. steel companies earn greater profits, buy more equipment, pay bigger bonuses to managers, give pay raises to existing employees—and also avoid firing some additional workers. Only part of the higher price of protected steel goes toward saving jobs. Also, when an industry is protected, the economy as a whole loses the benefits of playing to its comparative advantage. Thus, part of the higher price that consumers pay for protected goods is wasted by this lost economic efficiency.

There's a bumper sticker that speaks to the threat some U.S. workers feel over imported products: "Buy American—Save U.S. Jobs." A more accurate, if less catchy, bumper

EXHIBIT 6-2 Cost to U.S. Consumers of Saving a Job through Protectionism

A number of different studies have attempted to estimate the cost to consumers in higher prices per job saved through protectionism. Here is a sample of results, compiled by economists at the Federal Reserve Bank of Dallas.

Industry Protected with Import Tariffs or Quotas	Annual Cost per Job Saved
Sugar	$826,000
Polyethylene resins	$812,000
Dairy products	$685,000
Frozen concentrated orange juice	$635,000
Ball bearings	$603,000
Machine tools	$479,000
Women's handbags	$263,000
Glassware	$247,000
Apparel and textiles	$199,000
Rubber footwear	$168,000
Women's nonathletic footwear	$139,000

sticker might say: "Block Imports—Save Jobs for Some Americans, Lose a Roughly Equal Number of Jobs for Other Americans, and Also Have Consumers Pay Higher Prices."

Trade and Wages

Even if trade does not reduce the number of jobs, it could affect the wages of workers. Here, it is important to separate issues about the average level of wages from issues about whether the wages of certain workers may be helped or hurt by trade.

Because trade raises the amount that an economy can produce by letting firms and workers play to their comparative advantage, trade will also cause the average level of wages in an economy to increase. Workers who can produce more will be more desirable to employers, which will shift the demand for their labor out to the right and increase wages in the labor market.

However, even if trade increases the overall wage level, it will still benefit some workers and hurt others. Workers in industries that are confronted by competition from imported products may find that demand for their labor decreases and shifts back to the left, so that their wages decline with a rise in international trade. Conversely, workers in industries that benefit from selling in global markets may find that demand for their labor shifts out to the right, so that trade raises their wages.

One concern is that while globalization may be benefiting high-skilled, high-wage workers, it may also impose costs on low-skilled, low-wage workers. After all, high-skilled U.S. workers presumably benefit from increased sales of sophisticated products like computers, machinery, and pharmaceuticals in world markets. Meanwhile, low-skilled U.S. workers must now compete against low-wage workers worldwide for making simpler products like toys and clothing. Chapter 16 will discuss the inequality of wages in the U.S. economy in detail. But there are a number of reasons to believe that while globalization has helped some U.S. industries and hurt others, there are a number of situations in which trade does not seem likely to disproportionately injure low-skilled Americans—and indeed, it will often benefit them.

First, it seems unlikely that intra-industry trade, where the United States trades similar goods like machinery, computers, and cars with other high-wage economies like Canada, Japan, Germany, and the United Kingdom, has a heavier impact on the wages of low-skill, low-wage Americans. After all, most U.S. workers in these industries have above-average skills and wages—and many of them are doing quite well in the world of globalization. Remember, intra-industry trade makes up about half of all U.S. trade.

Second, many low-skilled U.S. workers hold service jobs that cannot be replaced by imports from low-wage countries. For example, lawn care services or moving and hauling services or hotel maids cannot be imported from countries of long distances like China or Bangladesh. Competition from imported products is not the primary determinant of their wages.

Finally, while the focus of the discussion here is on wages, it's worth pointing out that low-wage U.S. workers suffer from protectionism *in all the industries that they don't work in* because protectionism forces them to pay higher prices for basic necessities like clothing and food.

The benefits and costs of increased trade in terms of its effect on wages are not distributed evenly across the economy, and may contribute to inequality of wages. However, the growth of international trade has helped to raise the productivity of U.S. workers as a whole—and thus has helped to raise the average level of wages.

Labor Standards

Workers in many low-income countries around the world labor under conditions that would be illegal for a worker in the United States. Workers in countries like China, Thailand, Brazil, South Africa, and Poland are often paid less than the U.S. minimum wage. For example, in the United States the minimum wage is $7.25 per hour; the wage in many low-income countries might be more like $7.25 *per day*, or even less. Moreover,

The International Labor Organization

The International Labor Organization (ILO), founded in 1919, is the international body for establishing and monitoring labor standards. The ILO has passed rules, or "conventions," affecting more than 180 areas of employment, but member nations have a choice of which to ratify. For example, the first convention, passed in 1919, calls for an eight-hour workday and a 48-hour work week. An example of a more recent convention, adopted in 2010, calls for improved working conditions for those who do domestic work.

If a nation has ratified a convention, the ILO has the power to investigate complaints about violations. Complaints can come from workers, employers, or other countries. The ILO does not have power to impose financial penalties or limitations on trade. Instead, it depends on building consensus and publicity to encourage nations to sign conventions and to comply with conventions they have signed.

As of 2015, the United States has ratified just 14 of the 189 ILO conventions. This isn't necessarily unreasonable. Many countries sign off on ILO conventions, but then do little to comply. For example, 172 countries have ratified a convention against discrimination in employment and occupation that was passed in 1958. The United States has not ratified this convention. But it seems clear from a glance around the world that employment discrimination by race, gender, and religion is lower in the United States than in many of the countries that have ratified the convention. The United States is quite cautious about ratifying ILO conventions because it views workplace issues as fundamentally a domestic issue, and not the business of other countries. Of course, this makes it hard for the United States to preach to other nations about their workplace issues, too.

Country	Number of ILO Conventions Ratified, 2015
High-Income Economies	
United States	14
Canada	34
France	127
Germany	85
Japan	49
Korea, Republic of	29
United Kingdom	87
Upper-Middle-Income Countries	
Brazil	96
China	26
Mexico	79
Russian Federation	73
Lower-Middle-Income Countries	
India	45
Indonesia	19
Chana	51
Nigeria	40
Low-Income Countries	
Bangladesh	35
Cambodia	13
Chad	28

working conditions in low-income countries may be highly unpleasant, or even unsafe. In the worst cases, production may involve the labor of small children or even workers who are treated nearly like slaves. These concerns over standards of foreign labor don't affect the majority of U.S. trade, which is intra-industry and carried out with other high-income countries that have labor standards similar to the United States, but it is nonetheless morally and economically important.

In thinking about labor standards in other countries, it's important to draw some distinctions between what is truly unacceptable and what is merely painful to think about. Most people, economists included, have little difficulty with the idea that production by six-year-olds confined in factories or by slave labor is morally unacceptable, and they would support aggressive efforts to eliminate such practices—including shutting out imported products made with such labor. But many cases are less clear-cut. An article in the *New York Times* several years ago described the case of Ahmed Zia, a 14-year-old boy from Pakistan. He earned $2 per day working in a carpet factory. He dropped out of school in second grade. Should the United States and other countries refuse to purchase rugs made by Ahmed and his co-workers? If the carpet factories were to close, the likely alternative job for Ahmed is farm work, and as Ahmed says of his carpet-weaving job: "This makes much more money and is more comfortable." Other workers may have even less attractive alternative jobs, perhaps scavenging garbage or prostitution. The real problem for Ahmed and many others in low-income countries isn't that globalization has made their lives worse, but rather that they have so few better life alternatives.

Similar issues apply to adult workers in low-income counties that produce goods for export to the United States and other high-income economies like the European Union and Japan. Many of these workers receive wages that would be illegally low in the United States and other high-income countries. They are unprotected by U.S. rules that seek to assure holidays, safe workplaces, and prohibitions against discrimination and sexual harassment. Nonetheless, the jobs they have making carpets or toys or shoes often pay much better than their alternative jobs. Low wages and poor working conditions are not a clever ploy by people in low-income countries to sell more in world markets. For them, jobs with wages and working conditions that Americans wouldn't touch with a 10-foot pole can still look like a great step forward.

There is some irony when the U.S. government or U.S. citizens take issue with labor standards in low-income countries, because the United States is not a world leader in government laws to protect employees. In western European countries and Canada, all citizens are guaranteed health insurance by the government; the United States does not offer such a guarantee. Many European workers receive six weeks or more of vacation per year; in the United States, vacations are often two or three weeks per year. If European countries accused the United States of using unfair labor standards to make U.S. products cheaply, and announced that they would shut out all U.S. imports until the United States adopted government-run national health insurance, added more national holidays, and doubled vacation time, Americans would be outraged. Yet when U.S. protectionists start talking about restricting imports from poor countries because of low wage levels and poor working conditions, they are making a very similar argument.

The Infant Industry Argument

Imagine a country that wants to start its own computer industry, but at present, the country has no computer firms that can produce at a low enough price and high enough quality to compete in world markets. However, the politicians, business leaders, and workers of this country hope that if the local industry only had a chance to get established before it needed to face international competition, then a domestic company or group of companies could develop the skills, management, technology, and economies of scale that it needs to become a successful profit-earning domestic industry. The **infant industry argument** for protectionism is to block imports for a limited time, to give an infant industry time to mature, before eventually it starts competing on equal terms in the global economy.

infant industry argument: An argument to block imports for a short time, to give the infant industry time to mature, before eventually it starts competing on equal terms in the global economy.

The infant industry argument is certainly theoretically possible: give an industry a short-term indirect subsidy through protection, and then reap the long-term economic benefits of having a vibrant healthy industry. But practical implementation is tricky. In many countries, infant industries have gone from babyhood to senility and obsolescence without ever maturing. Meanwhile, infant industry protectionism that is supposed to be short-term often takes a long time to be repealed. As one example, Brazil treated its computer industry as an infant industry from the late 1970s until about 1990. Thus, in an attempt to establish its computer industry in the global economy, Brazil largely barred imports of computer products for several decades. This policy guaranteed increased sales for the Brazilian computer industry. But by the mid1980s, Brazil had a backward and out-of-date computer industry, typically lagging behind the world standards for price and performance by 3–5 years—a long time in this fast-moving industry. After more than a decade, during which Brazilian consumers and industries that would have benefited from up-to-date computers paid the costs and Brazil's computer industry never competed effectively on world markets, Brazil phased out its infant industry policy for computers.

Protectionism for infant industries imposes costs on domestic users of the product and typically has provided little benefit in the form of stronger competitive industries.

Several countries in East Asia offer an exception where infant industry protection has been used with some success. Japan, Korea, Thailand, and other countries in this region have sometimes provided a package of indirect and direct subsidies targeted at certain industries, including protection from foreign competition and government loans at interest rates below the market equilibrium. In Japan and Korea, for example, subsidies helped get their domestic steel and auto industries up and running.

Why did the infant industry policy of protectionism and other subsidies work better in East Asia than in many other regions? A study by the World Bank in the early 1990s offered some guidelines to countries thinking about infant industry protection: (1) Don't hand out protectionism and other subsidies to all industries, but focus on a few industries where your country has a realistic chance to be a world-class producer. (2) Be very hesitant about using protectionism in areas like computers, where many other industries rely on having the most advanced products available, because it's not useful to help one industry by imposing high costs on many other industries. (3) Have clear guidelines for when the infant industry policy will end. In Korea in the 1970s and 1980s, a common practice was to link protectionism and subsidies to export sales in global markets. If export sales rose, then the infant industry had succeeded and the protectionism could be phased out. If export sales didn't rise, then the infant industry policy had failed and the protectionism could be phased out. Either way, the infant industry protectionism would be temporary.

Following these rules is easier said than done. Politics often intrudes, both in choosing which industries will receive the benefits of being treated as "infants" and in choosing when to phase out import restrictions and other subsidies.

Also, if the government of a country wishes to impose costs on its citizens so that it can provide subsidies to a few key industries, it has many tools for doing so: direct government payments, loans, targeted tax reductions, government support of research and development to develop new technologies, and so on. The point here is not necessarily to advocate such subsidies, but merely to point out that when industrial subsidies are desired, it is not necessary to provide them through protectionism.

The Dumping Argument

dumping: Selling internationally traded goods below their cost of production.

anti-dumping laws: Laws that block imports sold below the cost of production and impose tariffs that would increase the price of these imports to reflect their cost of production.

Dumping means selling goods below their cost of production. **Anti-dumping laws** seek to block imports that are sold below the cost of production and to impose tariffs that would increase the price of these imports to reflect their cost of production.

The Growth of Anti-Dumping Cases

Since dumping is not allowed under the rules of the World Trade Organization, nations that believe they are on the receiving end of dumped goods can file a complaint with the WTO. Anti-dumping complaints have risen in recent years, from about 100 cases per year in the late 1980s to about 200 new cases each year in the last decade or so. Individual countries also frequently started their own anti-dumping investigations. The U.S. government has dozens of anti-dumping orders in place from past investigations. In 2016, for example, some U.S. imports that were under anti-dumping orders included wooden bedroom furniture and wax candles from China, pistachios from Iran, fresh warm-water shrimp from Brazil, wire rods from Japan and Spain, and plastic tape from Italy.

Why Might Dumping Occur?

Why would foreign firms export a product at less than its cost of production—which presumably means taking a loss? This question has two possible answers, one innocent and one more sinister.

The innocent explanation is that market prices are set by demand and supply, not by the cost of production. Perhaps demand for a product shifts back to the left or supply shifts out to the right, which drives the market price to low levels—even below the cost of production. When a local store has a going-out-of-business sale, for example, it may sell goods at below the cost of production. If international companies find that there is an excess supply of steel or computer chips or machine tools that is driving the market price down below their cost of production—well, this may be the market in action.

The sinister explanation is that dumping is part of a long-term strategy in which foreign firms would sell at below the cost of production in the short-term for a time, and when they have driven out the domestic U.S. competition, they would then raise prices. This scenario is sometimes called "predatory pricing."

Should Anti-Dumping Cases Be Limited?

Anti-dumping cases pose two questions. How much sense do they make in economic theory? How much sense do they make as practical policy?

In terms of economic theory, the case for anti-dumping laws is weak. In a market governed by demand and supply, the government doesn't guarantee that firms will be able to make a profit. After all, low prices are difficult for producers, but benefit consumers. Moreover, although there are plenty of cases in which foreign producers have taken sales from domestic U.S. firms, there are zero documented cases in which the foreign producers then jacked up prices. Instead, the foreign producers typically continue competing hard against each other and providing low prices to consumers.

But even if one could make a case that the government should sometimes enact anti-dumping rules in the short term, and then allow free trade to resume shortly thereafter, there is an additional concern that anti-dumping investigations often involve more politics than careful analysis. Calculating the appropriate "cost of production" under law can be as much an art as a science; for example, if a company built a new factory two years ago, should part of the cost of factory be counted in this year's cost of production? When a domestic industry complains loudly enough, government regulators seem very likely to find that unfair dumping has occurred. Indeed, a common pattern has arisen where a domestic industry files an anti-dumping complaint, the governments meet and negotiate a reduction in imports, and then the domestic producers drop the anti-dumping suit. In such cases, anti-dumping cases often appear to be little more than a cover story for imposing tariffs or import quotas.

In the 1980s, almost all of the anti-dumping cases were initiated by the United States, Canada, the European Union, Australia, and New Zealand. But by the 2000s, countries like Argentina, Brazil, South Korea, South Africa, Mexico, and India were filing the majority of the anti-dumping cases before the WTO. As the number of anti-dumping cases has increased, and as countries like the United States and the European Union feel targeted by anti-dumping actions of others, the World Trade Organization may well propose some additional guidelines to limit the reach of anti-dumping laws.

The Environmental Protection Argument

The potential for global trade to affect the environment has become controversial. A president of the Sierra Club, an environmental lobbying organization, once wrote: "The consequences of globalization for the environment are not good. . . . Globalization, if we are lucky, will raise average incomes enough to pay for cleaning up some of the mess that we have made. But before we get there, globalization could also destroy enough of the planet's basic biological and physical systems that prospects for life itself will be radically compromised." If free trade means the destruction of life itself, then even economists would convert to protectionism! But while globalization—and economic activity of all kinds—can pose environmental dangers, it seems quite possible that with appropriate safeguards in place, the environmental impacts of trade can be minimal. In some cases, trade may even bring environmental benefits.

In general, high-income countries like the United States, Canada, Japan, and the nations of the European Union have relatively strict environmental standards. In contrast, middle- and low-income countries of the world like Brazil, China, India, and Nigeria have lower environmental standards. The general view of the governments of such countries is that as soon as their people have enough to eat, decent health care, and longer life expectancies, then they will spend more money on sewage treatment plants, scrubbers to reduce air pollution from factory smokestacks, national parks to protect wildlife, and so on. This gap in environmental standards between high-income and low-income countries raises two worrisome possibilities in a world of increasing global trade: the "race to the bottom" scenario and the question of how quickly environmental standards will improve in low-income countries. Let us consider these two issues in turn.

The Race to the Bottom Scenario

race to the bottom: When production locates in countries with the lowest environmental (or other) standards, putting pressure on all countries to reduce their environmental standards.

The **race to the bottom** scenario of global environmental degradation runs like this. Profit-seeking multinational companies shift their production from countries with strong environmental standards to countries with weak standards, thus reducing their costs and increasing their profits. Faced with such behavior, countries reduce their environmental standards to attract multinational firms, which after all provide jobs and economic clout. As a result, global production becomes concentrated in countries where it can pollute the most, and environmental laws everywhere race to the bottom.

Although the race-to-the-bottom scenario sounds plausible, it does not appear to describe reality. In fact, the financial incentive for firms to shift production to low-income countries to take advantage of their weaker environmental rules does not seem especially powerful. When firms decide where to locate a new factory, they consider many different factors: the costs of labor and financial capital; whether the location is close to reliable suppliers of the inputs that they need; whether the location is close to customers; the quality of transportation, communications, and electrical power networks; the level of taxes; and the competence and honesty of the local government. The cost of environmental regulations is a factor, too, but typically, environmental costs are no more than 1–2% of the costs faced by a large industrial plant. The other factors that determine choice of location are much more important than trying to skimp on environmental protection costs.

When an international company does choose to build a plant in a low-income country with lax environmental laws, it typically builds a plant similar to those that it operates in high-income countries with stricter environmental standards. Part of the reason for this decision is that designing an industrial plant is a complex and costly task, and so if a plant works well in a high-income country, companies prefer to use a similar design everywhere. Also, companies realize that if they create an environmental disaster in a low-income country, it is likely to cost them a substantial amount of money in paying for damages, lost trust, and reduced sales—and by building up-to-date plants everywhere, they minimize such risks. As a result of these factors, foreign-owned plants in low-income countries often have a better record of compliance with environmental laws than do locally-owned plants.

Perhaps the hardest task for those who predict a race to the bottom scenario is explaining why it hasn't already happened. After all, globalization has been expanding for decades—and at the same time, environmental standards have been growing stronger both in high-income and in low-income countries of the world. For low-income countries, globalization has often meant importing some of the environmental values of high-income countries—and also having higher income levels to afford greater environmental protection. Apparently, the competitive pressures from mobile multinational firms that might encourage governments to reduce their environmental standards are not nearly as strong as the counterbalancing pressures to increase environmental standards.

Pressuring Low-Income Countries for Higher Environmental Standards

In some cases, the issue is not so much whether globalization will pressure low-income countries to reduce their environmental standards, but instead whether the threat of blocking international trade can be used to pressure these countries into adopting stronger environmental standards. For example, restrictions on ivory imports in high-income countries, along with stronger government efforts to catch elephant poachers, have been credited with helping to reduce the illegal poaching of elephants in certain African countries.

However, it would be highly undemocratic for the well-fed citizens of high-income countries to attempt to dictate to the ill-fed citizens of low-income countries what domestic policies and priorities they must adopt, and how they should balance environmental goals against other priorities for their citizens. Also, if high-income countries want stronger environmental standards in low-income countries, they have many other options than the threat of protectionism. For example, high-income countries could pay for anti-pollution equipment in low-income countries or could help to pay for national parks. High-income countries could help pay for and carry out the scientific and economic studies that would help environmentalists in low-income countries to make a more persuasive case for the economic benefits of protecting the environment: after all, environmental protection is very important to two industries of key importance in many low-income countries—agriculture and tourism. Environmental advocates can set up standards for labeling products, like "this tuna caught in a net that kept dolphins safe" or "this product made only with wood not taken from rain forests," so that consumer pressure can reinforce environmentalist values. The United Nations sponsors treaties to address issues such as climate change and global warming, the preservation of biodiversity, the spread of deserts, and the environmental health of the seabed, as well as other issues. Countries that share a national border or are within a region often sign environmental agreements concerning air and water rights, too. The World Trade Organization is also becoming more aware of environmental issues and more careful about assuring that increases in trade don't inflict environmental damage. Along with these other policy tools, high-income countries could refuse to import a limited number of specific products where the product is very closely linked to the environmental danger—like not importing the ivory from elephant tusks.

These concerns about the race to the bottom or pressuring low-income countries for more strict environmental standards do not apply very well to the roughly half of all U.S. trade that occurs with other high-income countries of the world. Indeed, many European countries have stricter environmental standards in certain industries than the United States.

The Unsafe Consumer Products Argument

One argument for shutting out certain imported products is that they are unsafe for consumers. This fear seems exaggerated. The World Trade Organization explains its rules in this way: "It allows countries to set their own standards. But it also says regulations must be based on science. . . . And they should not arbitrarily or unjustifiably discriminate between countries where identical or similar conditions prevail." Thus, under WTO rules, it is perfectly legitimate for the United States to pass laws requiring that all, say, food products or cars sold in the United States meet certain safety standards approved by the U.S. government, whether or not other countries choose to pass similar standards. However, such standards must have some scientific basis, and it would be unfair to impose, say, one set of health and safety standards for domestically produced goods but a different set of standards for imports, or one set of standards for imports from Europe and a different set of standards for imports from Latin America.

The National Interest Argument

It is sometimes argued that a nation should not depend too heavily on other countries for supplies of certain key products. This argument has been made for commodities that are important to the U.S. economy as a whole, like oil, and for special materials or technologies that might have weapons applications. But upon closer consideration, this argument for protectionism proves rather weak.

The issue is not whether certain products, like oil, are highly important to the U.S. economy both for personal use in transportation and heating and for a wide array of

Public Attitudes about Global Trade

How do people around the world feel about expanding trade between nations? In summer 2014, the Pew Research Center surveyed approximately 48,600 people in 44 countries. One of the questions asked about opinions on trade ties between countries. The accompanying table shows the percentages for selected countries of those who believe that growing trade ties between countries are "good."

For those who think of the United States as the world's leading supporter of expanding trade, the survey results may be perplexing. Americans actually have a less favorable view of globalization than do individuals in many other countries, whereas Vietnam, Tunisia, and Israel rank at the top. In fact, among the 44 countries surveyed, the United States was tied at fourth-lowest, higher than only Turkey, Italy, and Thailand.

Growing Trade Ties between Countries Are Good: Some Examples	
Vietnam	95%
Tunisia	95%
Spain	91%
Uganda	90%
China	89%
Brazil	80%
Mexico	71%
United States	69%
Thailand	68%
Italy	59%
Turkey	57%

industrial uses. Oil provides about 35% of all the energy in the United States, and about one-quarter of the oil used in the U.S. economy in recent years is imported. Several times in the last few decades, when the global price of oil has risen sharply, the adverse effects have been felt across the U.S. economy.

But none of this makes a very convincing argument for restricting imports of oil. If the United States needs to be protected from a possible cutoff of foreign oil, then a more reasonable strategy would be to import 100% of the United States' petroleum supply now and save the U.S. domestic oil resources for when or if the foreign supply is cut off! It might also be useful to import extra oil and put it into a stockpile for use in an emergency, as the U.S. government did by starting a Strategic Petroleum Reserve in 1977. Moreover, it may be necessary to discourage people from using oil and to start a high-powered program to seek out alternatives to oil. A straightforward way to do this would be to raise taxes on oil. (Such a tax increase on oil could be offset with cuts in other taxes, so that the total tax burden need not rise.) But it makes no sense to argue that because oil is highly important to the U.S. economy, then the United States should shut out oil imports and use up its domestic supplies of oil more quickly.

Whether to limit imports of key technologies or materials that might be important to weapons systems is a slightly different issue. If weapons builders are not confident that they can continue to obtain a key product in wartime, they might decide to avoid designing weapons that use this key product, or they can go ahead and design the weapons and stockpile enough of the key high-tech components or materials to last through an armed conflict. Indeed, a U.S. Defense National Stockpile Center has built up reserves of many materials—from aluminum oxides, antimony, and bauxite to tungsten, vegetable tannin extracts, and zinc (although many of these stockpiles have been reduced and sold in recent years). But why shut out a high technology product, like a specialized type of computer chip or screen, for all the potential civilian-sector users—including businesses that may need the technology so that their products can be competitive in world markets—just because makers of weapons are hesitant to rely on it? If the concern is to build up top-level technological capabilities for domestic producers, it is usually better to have domestic firms competing hard in world markets—perhaps with some direct government subsidies for research and development in key areas—rather than sheltering domestic producers from foreign competition.

National Security and Scissors and Shears

What follows is actual testimony before Congress in 1962 from a lobbyist arguing that the national interest demands a higher tariff on imported scissors and shears.

> [M]y name is B.C. Dueschle. I am vice president of the Acme Shear Co., located in Bridgeport, Conn. I appear before this committee as president of the Shears, Scissors & Manicure Implement Manufacturers Association, the only national trade association of domestic manufacturers of scissors and shears. The scissors and shears industry is a distinct industry and should not be confused with the larger industry and the flatware industries. . . .
>
> We have never requested or suggested that a complete embargo be placed on the import of scissors and shears. All that we have asked for and desire is a fair competitive opportunity, not an advantage. . . .
>
> We realize that the domestic scissor and shear industry with its 1,000-plus employees accounts for only a fraction of 1% of the gross national product, but we see this as no justification for letting the industry be completely destroyed by imports produced with low-cost labor.
>
> The workers in the domestic scissor and shear industry do not want to become wards of the State; they want to use their skills, which have taken many years to develop. These workers are not interested in retraining; over many years they have developed a skill they are proud of and want to continue the work they are happy doing. . . .
>
> Under the provisions of this bill, scissors and shears would be buried in a category with many other items and the duty cut 50%. This would mean a reduction of at least 20 cents per pair at the retail level for scissors and shears now being retailed at $1 to 1.29 per pair. . . .
>
> These few remaining manufacturers would be forced to close their doors and discharge their employees. The United States would then become wholly dependent on imported scissors and shears.
>
> We cannot understand how it would be in the national interest to permit such a loss. We would lose the skills of the employees and management of the industry as well as the capital investment in production equipment. In the event of a national emergency and imports cutoff, the United States would be without a source of scissors and shears, basic tools for many industries and trades essential to our defense.
>
> The scissors and shear industry is one of the oldest in the world. The skill was brought to the United States from Germany at a time when the United States needed new industry and a scissors and shear industry in particular.
>
> Scissors and shears of all sizes and types are used in every school, retail establishment, office, factory, hospital, and home in the United States. Scissors cannot be classified as a luxury, gimmick, or novelty.
>
> Scissors are used to separate us from our mothers at birth; to cut our toenails; to trim the leather in our shoes; to cut and trim the materials used in every piece of clothing that we wear.
>
> They are used to cut our fingernails, to trim our mustaches, the hair in our ears and nose, and to cut the hair on our heads—even down to the end of the road when our best suit or dress is cut down the back so that the undertaker can dress us for the last ride. Scissors are truly used from birth to death. They are essential to our health, education, and general welfare.
>
> I ask you gentlemen, is this industry one that should be permitted to become extinct in this country?

One final reason why economists often treat the national security argument skeptically is that almost any product can be touted by lobbyists and politicians as vital to national security. In 1954 the United States became worried that it was importing half of the wool required for military uniforms, so it declared wool and mohair to be "strategic materials" and began to give subsidies to wool and mohair farmers. Although wool was removed from the official list of "strategic" materials in 1960, the subsidies for mohair continued for almost 40 years until they were repealed in 1993, and then reinstated in 2002. All too often, the national interest argument has become an excuse for handing out the indirect subsidy of protectionism to certain industries or companies. After all, decisions about what constitutes a key strategic material are made by politicians, not nonpartisan analysts.

How Trade Policy Is Enacted: Global, Regional, and National

These public policy arguments about how nations should react to globalization and trade are fought out at several levels: at the global level through the World Trade Organization and through regional trade agreements between pairs or groups of countries.

The World Trade Organization

The World Trade Organization was officially born in 1995, but its history is somewhat longer. In the years after the Great Depression and World War II, there was a worldwide push to build institutions that would bind the nations of the world together. For example, the United Nations officially came into existence in 1945. The World Bank, with a focus on assisting the poorest people in the world, and the International Monetary Fund, with a focus on addressing issues raised by international financial transactions, were both created in 1946. The General Agreement on Tariffs and Trade (GATT), which provided a forum in which nations could come together to negotiate over reductions in tariffs and other barriers to trade, started in 1947. In 1995, the GATT transformed itself into the World Trade Organization.

The GATT process was to negotiate an agreement to reduce barriers to trade, sign that agreement, pause for breath, and then start negotiating the next agreement. The rounds of talks in the GATT, and now the WTO, are shown in Exhibit 6-3. Notice that the early rounds of GATT talks took a relatively short time, included a relatively small number of countries, and focused almost entirely on reducing tariffs. Since the 1970s, however, rounds of trade talks have taken years, included a large number of countries, and included an ever-broadening range of issues.

The sluggish pace of GATT negotiations led to an old joke that GATT really stood for Gentleman's Agreement to Talk and Talk. But the slow pace of international trade talks is understandable, even sensible. Having dozens of nations agree to any treaty is a lengthy process. The GATT often set up separate trading rules for certain industries, like agriculture, and separate trading rules for certain countries, like the low-income countries

EXHIBIT 6-3 Negotiating Rounds of the GATT and the World Trade Organization

Year	Place or Name of Round	Main Subjects	Number of Countries Involved
1947	Geneva	Tariff reduction	23
1949	Annecy	Tariff reduction	13
1951	Torquay	Tariff reduction	38
1956	Geneva	Tariff reduction	26
1960–61	Dillon round	Tariff reduction	26
1964–67	Kennedy round	Tariffs and anti-dumping measures	62
1973–79	Tokyo round	Tariffs, nontariff barriers	102
1986–94	Uruguay round	Tariffs, nontariff barriers, services, intellectual property, dispute settlement, textiles, agriculture, creation of WTO	123
2001–	Doha round	Agriculture, services, intellectual property, competition, investment, environment, dispute settlement	162

in the world. There were rules, exceptions to rules, opportunities to opt out of rules, and precise wording to be fought over in every case. Like the GATT before it, the WTO is not a world government, with power to impose its decisions on others. The total staff of the WTO in 2015 was about 630 people, and its annual budget was $200 million, which made it smaller in size than many medium-sized universities.

Regional Trading Agreements

Many nations belong both to the World Trade Organization and to regional trading agreements. The best-known of these regional trading agreements is the European Union. In the years after World War II, leaders of the nations of Europe reasoned that if they could tie their economies together more closely, they might be more likely to avoid another devastating war. Their efforts evolved into what is now known as the European Union. The EU, as it is often called, has a number of goals. For example, in the early 2000s it introduced a common currency for Europe—the euro—and phased out the old national forms of money like the German mark and the French franc. Another key element of the union is to eliminate barriers to the mobility of goods, labor, and capital across Europe.

For the United States, perhaps the best-known regional trading agreement is the North American Free Trade Agreement (NAFTA), which reduced barriers to trade between the United States, Mexico, and Canada. NAFTA was signed into law by President Bill Clinton in November 1993 and took effect in 1995. However, the U.S. also participates in some less-known regional trading agreements, like the Caribbean Basin Initiative, which offers reduced tariffs for imports from these countries, and a free trade agreement with Israel.

The world has seen a flood of regional trading agreements in recent years. Over 100 such agreements are now in place; a few of the more prominent ones are listed in Exhibit 6-4. Some are just agreements to talk and talk; others set specific goals for reducing tariffs, import quotas, and nontariff barriers. The current trade treaties have been described as a

EXHIBIT 6-4 Some Regional Trade Agreements

Trade Agreements	Participating Countries
Asia Pacific Economic Cooperation (APEC)	Australia, Brunei, Canada, Chile, People's Republic of China, Hong Kong, Indonesia, Japan, Republic of Korea, Malaysia, Mexico, New Zealand, Papua New Guinea, Peru, Philippines, Russia, Singapore, Chinese Taipei, Thailand, United States, Vietnam
European Union (EU)	Austria, Belgium, Bulgaria, Croatia, Cyprus, Czech Republic, Denmark, Estonia, Finland, France, Germany, Greece, Hungary, Ireland, Italy, Latvia, Lithuania, Luxembourg, Malta, Netherlands, Poland, Portugal, Romania, Slovakia, Slovenia, Spain, Sweden, United Kingdom
North America Free Trade Agreement (NAFTA)	Canada, Mexico, United States
Latin American Integration Association (LAIA)	Argentina, Bolivia, Brazil, Chile, Columbia, Cuba, Ecuador, Mexico, Panama, Paraguay, Peru, Uruguay, Venezuela
Association of Southeast Asian Nations (ASEAN)	Brunei, Cambodia, Indonesia, Laos, Malaysia, Myanmar, Philippines, Singapore, Thailand, Vietnam
Southern African Development Community (SADC)	Angola, Botswana, Democratic Republic of the Congo, Lesotho, Madagascar, Malawi, Mauritius, Mozambique, Namibia, Seychelles, South Africa, Swaziland, Tanzania, Zambia, Zimbabwe
Asia-Pacific Trade Agreement (APTA)	Bangladesh, China, India, Republic of Korea, Laos, Mongolia, Sri Lanka

"spaghetti bowl," which is what a map with lines connecting all the countries with trade treaties looks like. There is some concern among economists who favor free trade that some of these regional agreements may promise free trade, but actually act as a way for the countries within the regional agreement to try to limit trade from anywhere else. However, the more common pattern appears to be that although trade talks through the World Trade Organization have stalled, agreements to facilitate trade flows are happening through regional agreements instead.

Trade Policy at the National Level

In the arena of trade policy, there often seems to be a battle between national laws that increase protectionism and international agreements that try to reduce protectionism, like the World Trade Organization. Why would a country pass national-level laws or negotiate bilateral agreements to shut out certain foreign products, like sugar or textiles, while simultaneously negotiating at the regional and global levels to reduce trade barriers in general?

One plausible answer is that international trade agreements offer a method for countries to restrain their own special interests. A member of Congress can say to an industry lobbying for tariffs or quotas on imports: "Sure would like to help you, but that pesky WTO agreement just won't let me." In this way, international trade agreements are like hiring a personal trainer; they pressure you to follow through on the healthy behavior that you should be doing anyway.

Long-Term Trends Concerning Barriers to Trade

In the newspaper headlines, trade policy appears rife with disputes and acrimony. Countries are almost constantly threatening to challenge "unfair" trading practices of other nations. Cases are brought before the dispute settlement procedures of the WTO, the European Union, NAFTA, and other regional trading agreements. Politicians in national legislatures, goaded on by lobbyists, often threaten to pass bills that will "establish a fair playing field" or "prevent unfair trade"—although most such bills seek to accomplish these high-sounding goals by placing more restrictions on trade. Protesters in the streets may object to specific trade rules or to the entire practice of international trade.

But through all the controversy, the general trend in the last 60 years is clearly toward lower barriers to trade. The average level of tariffs on imported products charged by industrialized countries was 40% in 1946. By 1990, after decades of GATT negotiations, it was down to less than 5%. Indeed, one of the reasons that GATT negotiations shifted from focusing on tariff reduction in the early rounds to a broader agenda was that tariffs had been reduced so dramatically that there wasn't much more to do in that area. U.S. tar-

CLEARING IT UP

Trade Is Not War

People often think of international trade agreements as similar to arms control treaties. In arms control treaties, the two sides negotiate to reduce their weapons; in a trade agreement, they negotiate to reduce their trade barriers. From this point of view, nations enact trade barriers the way they build missiles, to build their strength and show their toughness, and they are willing to give up those trade barriers, like their missiles, only if other nations are also willing to disarm.

But this analogy, while it may appear reasonable on the surface, is terribly off the mark. Trade is not a form of warfare. War is fundamentally a lose-lose situation; both sides suffer losses until one side gives up. Trade is fundamentally a win-win situation, where both sides make voluntary exchanges and make mutual gains. One writer said: "As to trade as war, it is hard to think of two things more antithetical. When free to do so, buyers and sellers make deals to their mutual advantage, each walking away happy. This is some form of war? If it is, let's substitute it for all the other forms."

iffs have followed this general pattern; after rising sharply during the Great Depression, they dropped off to about 2% by the end of the century. Although measures of import quotas and nontariff barriers are less exact than those for tariffs, they generally appear to be at lower levels, too.

Thus, the last half-century has seen both a dramatic reduction in government-created barriers to trade, like tariffs, import quotas, and nontariff barriers, and also technological developments that have made international trade easier, like advances in transportation, communication, and information management. The result has been the powerful surge of international trade called globalization.

The Trade-offs of Trade Policy

Economists readily acknowledge that international trade is not all sunshine and roses and happy endings. On average and over time, the average person gains from international trade, both as a worker who has greater productivity and higher wages because of the benefits of specialization and comparative advantage, and as a consumer who can benefit from shopping all over the world for a greater variety of quality products at attractive prices. But the average person is hypothetical, not real, representing a mix of those who have done very well, those who have done all right, and those who have done poorly. It is a legitimate concern of public policy not just to focus on the average or on the success stories, but also on those who have not been so blessed. Workers in other countries, the environment, and prospects for new industries and materials that might be of key importance to the national economy are also all legitimate issues. The common belief among economists is that it is better to embrace the gains from trade, and then to deal with the costs and trade-offs with other policy tools, rather than cutting off trade to avoid the costs and trade-offs—but also losing the benefits of international trade.

To gain a better intuitive understanding for this argument, consider a hypothetical American company called Technotron. Technotron invents a new scientific technology that allows the firm to increase the output and quality of its goods with a smaller number of workers at a lower cost. As a result of this technology, other U.S. firms in this industry will lose money and will also have to lay off workers—and some of the competing firms will even go bankrupt. Should the U.S. government protect the existing firms and their employees by making it illegal for Technotron to use its new technology?

Most people who live in market-oriented economies would oppose trying to block new technology. Certainly, there is a case that society should provide temporary support and assistance for those who find themselves without work. Many would argue for government support of programs that encourage retraining and acquiring additional skills. Government might also support research and development efforts, so that other firms may find ways of outdoing Technotron. But blocking the new technology altogether seems like a mistake. After all, few people would advocate giving up electricity because it caused so much disruption to the kerosene and candle business. Few would suggest holding back on improvements in medical technology because they might cause companies selling older and less effective medical care to lose money. In short, most people view disruptions due to technological change as a necessary cost that is worth bearing.

Now, imagine that Technotron's new "technology" is as simple as this: the company imports what it sells from another country. In other words, think of foreign trade as a type of innovative technology. The objective situation is now exactly the same as before. Because of Technotron's new technology—which in this case is importing goods from another county—other firms in this industry will lose money and lay off workers. But just as it would have been inappropriate and ultimately foolish to respond to the disruptions of new scientific technology by trying to shut it down, it would be inappropriate and ultimately foolish to respond to the disruptions of international trade by trying to restrict trade.

Some workers and firms will suffer because of international trade. But in a living, breathing, market-oriented economy, some workers and firms will always be experiencing disruptions, for a wide variety of reasons. Corporate management can be better or worse. Workers for a certain firm can be more productive or less. Tough domestic competitors can create just as much disruption as tough foreign competitors. Sometimes a new product is a hit with consumers; sometimes it's a flop. Sometimes a company is blessed by a run of good luck or stricken with a run of bad luck. For some firms, international trade will offer great opportunities for expanding productivity and jobs; for other firms, trade will impose stress and pain. The disruption caused by international trade is not fundamentally different from all the other disruptions caused by the other workings of a market economy. Trying to prevent the disruptions of a market-oriented economy from happening has an opportunity cost: it means blocking the economic gains from trade.

In other words, the economic analysis of free trade doesn't rely on a belief that foreign trade is not disruptive or does not pose trade-offs; indeed, the story of Technotron begins with a particular disruptive market change—a new technology—that causes real trade-offs. But in thinking about the disruptiveness of foreign trade, or any of the other possible costs and trade-offs of foreign trade discussed in this chapter, the best public policy solutions typically don't involve protectionism, but instead involve finding ways for public policy to address the particular issues while still allowing the benefits of international trade to occur.

Key Concepts and Summary

1. There are three tools for restricting the flow of trade: **tariffs**, **import quotas**, and **nontariff barriers**. When a country places limitations on imports from abroad, regardless of whether it uses tariffs, quotas, or nontariff barriers, it is said to be practicing **protectionism**.
2. Protectionism will raise the price of the protected good in the domestic market, which causes domestic consumers to pay more but benefits producers.
3. As international trade increases, it contributes to a shift in jobs away from industries where that economy does not have a comparative advantage and toward industries where it does have a comparative advantage. Overall, however, the increase in trade does not have much effect on the number of jobs.
4. Global trade should raise the average level of wages by increasing productivity. However, this increase in average wages may include both gains to workers in certain jobs and industries and losses to others.
5. In thinking about labor practices in low-income countries, it's useful to draw a line between what is unpleasant to think about and what is morally objectionable. For example, low wages and long working hours in poor countries are unpleasant to think about, but for people in low-income parts of the world, it may well be the best option open to them. Practices like child labor and forced labor are morally objectionable, and the rules of the WTO allow any country to refuse to import products made using these practices.
6. The **infant industry argument** for protectionism is that small domestic industries need to be temporarily nurtured and protected from foreign competition for a time so that they can grow into strong competitors. In some cases, notably in East Asia, this approach has worked. But often, the infant industries never grow up.
7. **Dumping** occurs when prices are set at below the cost of production. The strategy is to set prices at a level below production costs, absorb losses until competitors are driven out of the market, and then, when competition has been eliminated or greatly reduced, to raise prices substantially and earn high profits. While there are some historical examples where this strategy has worked, it does not appear to arise very often, if at all, in global trade. More often, anti-dumping complaints seem to be a convenient excuse for imposing protectionism.
8. Low-income countries typically have lower environmental standards than high-income countries because they are more worried about immediate basics such as food, education, and health care. There are a variety of ways for high-income countries to encourage stronger environmental standards in low-income countries, including some movement to make sure that new opportunities opened up by free trade don't injure the environment. Except for a small number of extreme cases, shutting off trade seems unlikely to be an effective method of pursuing a cleaner environment.
9. Under the rules of the World Trade Organization, countries are allowed to set whatever standards for product safety they wish, but the standards must be the same for domestic products as for imported products. If there is a dispute over whether a health and safety standard is being imposed without a scientific basis, it can be appealed to the WTO.
10. The **national interest argument** for protectionism holds that it is unwise to import certain key products because if the nation becomes dependent on key imported supplies, it could be vulnerable to a cutoff. However, it is often wiser to stockpile resources and

to use foreign supplies when available, rather than preemptively restricting foreign supplies so as not to become dependent on them.

11. Trade policy is determined at many different levels: administrative agencies within government, laws passed by the legislature, regional negotiations between a small group of nations (sometimes just two), and global negotiations through the World Trade Organization.
12. During the second half of the twentieth century, trade barriers have in general declined quite substantially both in the U.S. economy and in the global economy.
13. One reason why countries sign international trade agreements to commit themselves to free trade is to give themselves protection against their own special interests. When an industry lobbies for protection from foreign producers, politicians can point out that because of the trade treaty, their hands are tied.
14. International trade certainly disrupts what would otherwise have been the pattern of an economy. This is hardly surprising, since all sorts of competitive market forces are disruptive, whether domestic or international, often causing companies and industries to rise and fall. Government has a role to play in cushioning workers against the disruptions of the market. But just as it would be unwise in the long term to clamp down on new technology and other causes of disruption in domestic markets, it would be unwise to clamp down on foreign trade. In both cases, the disruption brings with it economic benefits.

Review Questions

1. Who does protectionism protect? What does it protect them from?
2. Name and define three policy tools for enacting protectionism.
3. How does protectionism affect the price of the protected good in the domestic market?
4. Does international trade, taken as a whole, increase the total number of jobs, decrease the total number of jobs, or leave the total number of jobs about the same?
5. Is international trade likely to have roughly the same effect on the number of jobs in each individual industry?
6. How is international trade, taken as a whole, likely to affect the average level of wages?
7. Is international trade likely to have about the same effect on everyone's wages?
8. Do the jobs for workers in low-income countries that involve making products for export to high-income countries typically pay these workers more or less than their next-best alternative?
9. What's an infant industry? Why does protecting it often work better in theory than in practice?
10. What is dumping? Why does prohibiting it often work better in theory than in practice?
11. What is the race to the bottom scenario?
12. Which group of countries typically has more strict environmental standards: countries with higher incomes or lower incomes?
13. Do the rules of international trade require that all nations impose the same consumer safety standards?
14. What is the national interest argument for protectionism with regard to certain products?
15. Name several of the international treaties where countries negotiate with each other over trade policy.
16. What is the general trend of trade barriers over recent decades: higher, lower, or about the same?
17. If opening up to free trade would benefit a nation, then why don't nations just eliminate their trade barriers, and not bother with international trade negotiations?

Elasticity

CHAPTER

7

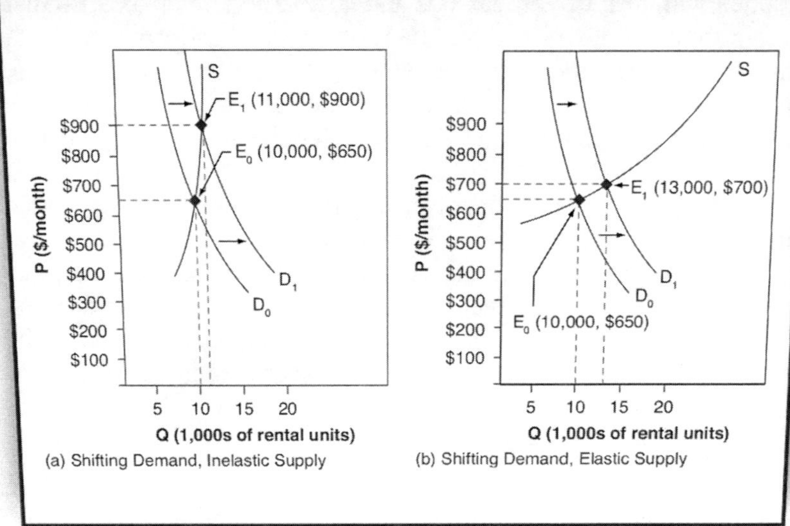

Chapter Outline

A demand curve shows that a higher price will lead to a lower quantity demanded. But how much lower? A supply curve shows that a higher price will lead to a higher quantity supplied. But how much higher? Whether a change in price will affect quantity demanded or quantity supplied by a relatively large or small amount often has real practical significance. For example, the average tax per pack on cigarettes was $2.54 in 2015, including both federal and state-level taxes. Taxes on cigarettes serve two purposes: to raise tax revenue for government and to discourage consumption of cigarettes. But if a higher cigarette tax discourages cigarette consumption by quite a lot, then because a greatly reduced quantity of cigarettes is sold, the cigarette tax on each pack won't raise much revenue for the government. Alternatively, a higher cigarette tax that doesn't discourage cigarette consumption by much will actually raise more tax revenue for the government. Thus, when a government agency tries to calculate the effects of altering its cigarette tax, it must analyze how much the tax affects the quantity of cigarettes consumed.

This issue reaches beyond governments and taxes; every firm faces a similar issue. Every time a firm considers raising the price that it charges, it must consider how much a price increase will reduce the quantity demanded of what it sells. Conversely, when a firm reduces its price, it must expect (or hope) that the lower price will lead to a higher quantity demanded of its product.

This chapter introduces the concept of **elasticity**, which measures how much a percentage change in price leads to a percentage change in quantity demanded or quantity supplied. The chapter begins with the price elasticity of demand, which looks at the responsiveness of quantity demanded to a change in price, and then examines the price elasticity of supply, which looks at the responsiveness of quantity supplied to a change in price. The concept of elasticity is then applied to a number of real-world situations, including ticket prices at concerts, cigarette taxes, airline ticket prices, changes in world oil prices, and others.

elasticity: How much a percentage change in quantity demanded or quantity supplied is affected by a percentage change in price.

Price Elasticity of Demand

When investigating how sensitive the quantity demanded is to a change in price, looking at the demand curve might seem like an obvious starting point. But the visual appearance of demand curves can be misleading. Exhibit 7-1 illustrates the problem. The data on price and quantity demanded of cheese for Exhibit 7-1*a* and 7-1*b* are identical. But in Exhibit 7-1*a*, the demand curve for cheese is graphed with a tall vertical axis and narrow horizontal axis, so that the demand curve appears to slope down steeply. In Exhibit 7-1*b*, the identical data is graphed with a short vertical axis and a wide horizontal axis, so that the demand curve appears to slope down in a relatively flat way. Remember, the data behind these two demand curves is exactly the same! In both Exhibit 7-1*a* and 7-1*b*, the demand curve slopes down, but should the shape of the demand curve for cheese be described as "steep" or "flat"? Answering this question with "it depends on how you draw it" is not very useful.

The vocabulary of elasticity offers a method of discussing how quantity demanded responds to changes in price that doesn't depend on whether the axes are drawn relatively longer or shorter. It doesn't even depend on what units are used to measure price and quantity. Instead of trying to discuss the steepness or flatness of supply and demand curves based on their visual appearance, which can be misleading, elasticity discusses the shape of demand and supply curves with numerical calculations of percentage changes.

Calculating the Elasticity of Demand

elasticity of demand: The percentage change in quantity demanded divided by the percentage change in price.

The numerical example of a demand curve D for small television sets presented in Exhibit 7-2 can help to illustrate the issues. In this case, this demand curve for small televisions is a straight line. Let's calculate the elasticity between points A and B and between points G and H. The **elasticity of demand** is defined as the percentage change in quantity demanded divided by the percentage change in price. The percentage change between two

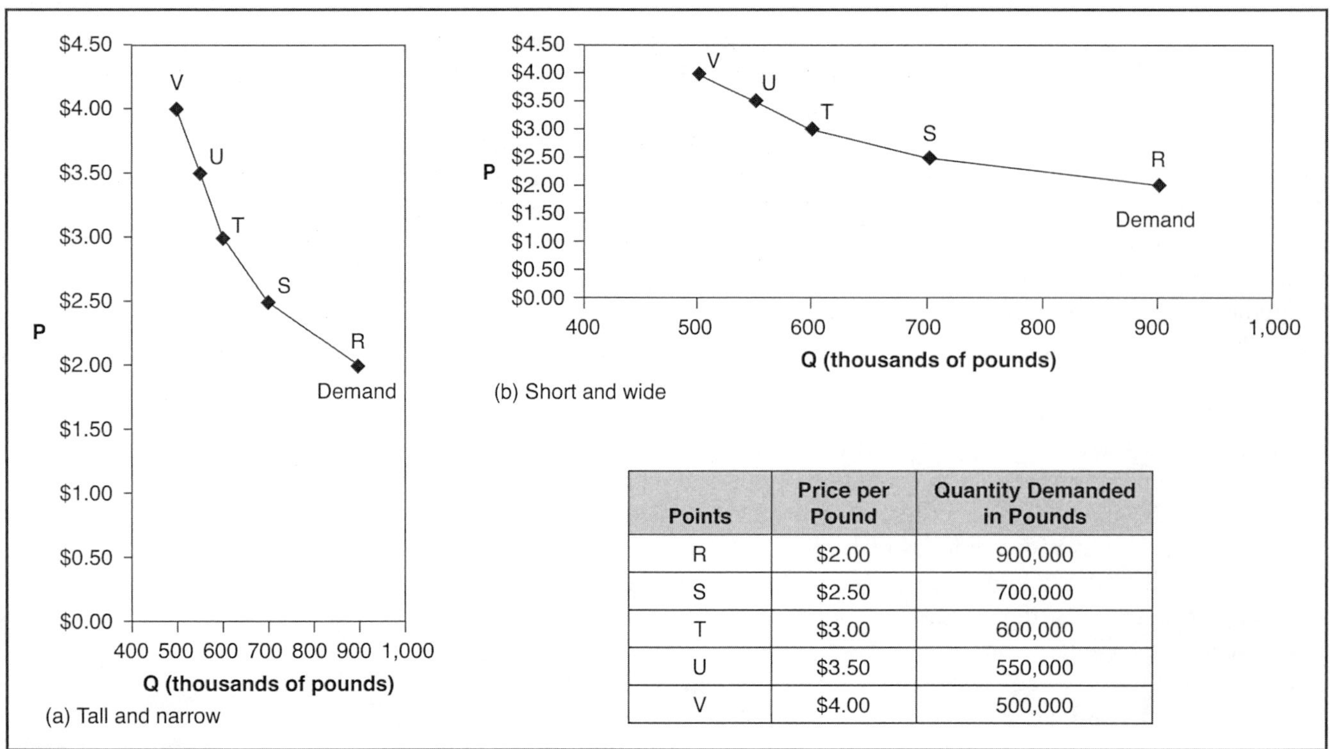

Points	Price per Pound	Quantity Demanded in Pounds
R	$2.00	900,000
S	$2.50	700,000
T	$3.00	600,000
U	$3.50	550,000
V	$4.00	500,000

EXHIBIT 7-1 Same Data for Demand Curve, Different Appearance

These two demand curves present exactly the same data on price and quantity. The only difference is that *(a)* is drawn with a longer vertical axis, while *(b)* is drawn with a longer horizontal axis. Both demand curves still slope down, but whether the slope appears steep or flat is determined by how the curve is drawn, not by the data.

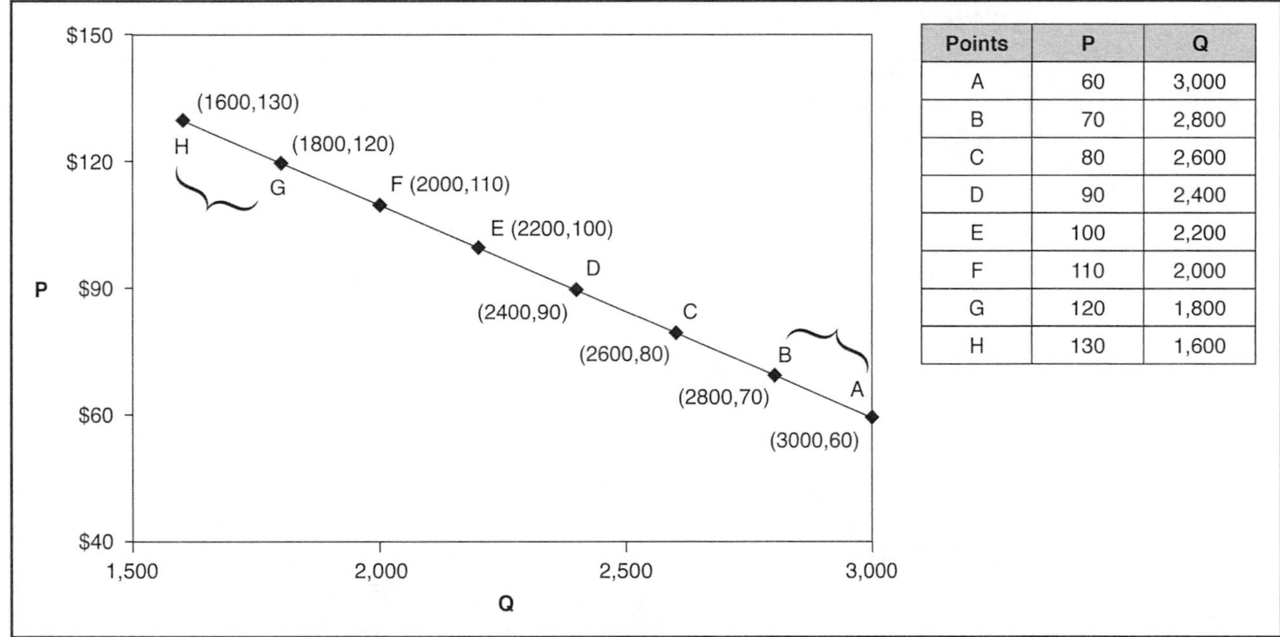

Points	P	Q
A	60	3,000
B	70	2,800
C	80	2,600
D	90	2,400
E	100	2,200
F	110	2,000
G	120	1,800
H	130	1,600

EXHIBIT 7-2 Calculating the Price Elasticity of Demand

The price elasticity of demand is calculated as the percentage change in quantity divided by the percentage change in price. Between two points like A and B, or between G and H, the formula is:

$$\text{Elasticity} = \frac{(\text{change in quantity})/[(\text{sum of the two quantities}/2)]}{(\text{change in price})/[(\text{sum of prices}/2)]}$$

quantities is calculated by taking the difference between the two quantities and dividing by the average of the two quantities—which will be the point halfway between the two quantities. Similarly, the percentage change between two prices is calculated by taking the difference between the two prices and dividing by the average of the two prices—which will be the point halfway between the two prices. Thus, the formula for elasticity of demand is:

$$\text{Elasticity of demand} = \frac{\%\text{ change in quantity demanded}}{\%\text{ change in price}}$$

$$= \frac{(\text{difference in quantity / average of original quantities})}{(\text{difference in price / average of original prices})}$$

First, apply this formula to the elasticity between A to B:

$$\frac{[3{,}000 - 2{,}800] / [(3{,}000 + 2{,}800) / 2]}{[60 - 70] / [(60 + 70) / 2]} = \frac{200/2{,}900}{-10/65} = \frac{0.069}{-0.154}$$

Therefore, the elasticity of demand between these two points is $= -0.069/0.154 = -0.448$.

As a second example, apply the same formula to calculating the elasticity of demand from G to H.

$$\frac{[1{,}600 - 1{,}800] / [(1{,}600 + 1{,}800) / 2]}{[130 - 120] / [(130 + 120) / 2]} = \frac{-200/1700}{10/125} = \frac{-0.1176}{0.08}$$

Therefore, the elasticity of demand from G to H is $= -0.1176/0.08 = -1.47$.

An elasticity number is not followed by any units. Elasticity is a ratio of one percentage change to another percentage change—nothing more.

Calculations of elasticity are all arithmetic, so what is the intuitive meaning of the number that emerges from the calculation? Hark back to the original meaning of elasticity: that is, the percentage change in quantity demanded that results from a percentage change in price. Thus, if the price started off at 65—midway between the price at points

EXHIBIT 7-3 Some Selected Elasticities of Demand

Coal	0.11	Beef	0.75
Housing	0.18	Soft drinks	0.79
Wine	0.24	New automobiles	0.87
Coffee	0.3	Air travel	1.15
Electricity	0.3	2% milk	1.22
Gasoline	0.31	Internet	1.29
Kitchen and household appliances	0.4	Restaurant meals	1.42
Poultry	0.68	Computer	2.17

A and B in the example—then a 10% increase in price of small televisions would cause a 4.48% reduction in quantity demanded, or conversely, a 10% fall in price would cause a 4.48% increase in the quantity demanded of small televisions. However, if the price started off in the range between 120 and 130—that is, midway between prices at points G and H in the example—then a 10% percent increase in price would cause a 14.7% decline in quantity demanded of small televisions, or conversely, a 10% fall in price would cause a 14.7% rise in the quantity demanded.

The word "elasticity," in its everyday use, refers to stretchiness: more elastic stretches more, while less elastic stretches less. The elasticity of demand has the same general meaning, except that in this case the stretchiness refers to how much the quantity demanded stretches or contracts in response to a change in price. Exhibit 7-3 shows a selection of demand elasticities for different goods and services drawn from a variety of different research studies by economists. A typical practice in these studies is to calculate the elasticity of demand using the current market equilibrium as the starting point.

A Possible Confusion, a Clarification, and a Warning

The most common confusion about elasticity is to think that it measures the slope of the demand curve. Elasticity is not the slope of the demand curve! The examples above have shown that whether a demand curve appears to have a steep or a flat slope depends on

Elasticity in the Vending Machine

America has 1.5 million vending machines that sell snacks and candy. Tens of millions of Americans are overweight. Could vending machines be used to nudge people toward a healthier diet? A group of researchers in the School of Public Health at the University of Minnesota have been carrying out studies to see how price and availability of snacks in vending machines affect people's purchases.

For example, one of their studies focused on vending machines at 12 worksites and 12 schools. They offered a range of price cuts for low-fat snacks. On some of the machines, they also posted signs identifying the low-fat snacks and encouraging people to buy them. The signs encouraging people to eat low-fat foods had little effect. But the study found that elasticity of demand for low-fat snacks is about 2. That is, a 10% cut in the price of low-fat snacks led to an increase of 20% in the quantity of such snacks consumed, and a 50% cut in the price of such snacks led to an increase of 100% in sales of low-fat snacks. As it turned out, the price cuts for low-fat snacks didn't even cause the average profits per vending machine to decline because an increase in the volume sold was enough to compensate for the lower prices.

Another one of their studies looked at vending machines in four metropolitan bus garages. In this study, they cut prices for healthy snack options by an average of 30% and also made sure that healthier snacks represented half of the choices in these vending machines. In this study, the elasticity of demand for health snacks was about 1: that is, the 30% fall in prices for healthy snacks led to a rise of about 30% in the quantity consumed of these snacks.

CLEARING IT UP

Elasticity Is Not Slope

Although the elasticity of a supply or demand curve is obviously related to the shape of the curve, it isn't the same as what the mathematicians call "slope." Not even close. Slope, you may remember from a high school mathematics class (or from the Appendix to Chapter 1), is "rise over run"; that is, the change on the vertical axis (the rise) divided by the change on the horizontal axis (the run). This calculation differs from elasticity in two ways. First, elasticity involves the change in what is on the horizontal axis (quantity) divided by the change in what is on the vertical axis (price). Thus, elasticity involves run/rise, not rise/run. Second, elasticity is the *percentage* change, which is a different calculation from slope. A straight line has only one slope, but as the example in the chapter shows, a straight-line demand curve has a different elasticity at every point.

how it is drawn. Even when the demand curve is a straight line, with the same mathematical slope at all points, the elasticity will differ quite substantially in different parts of that line. The calculation of elasticity is based on percentage change, which is not the same as the calculation for slope.

Many students who are confronted with the elasticity formula wonder why, in the numerator and denominator, the formula divides by the average value of either the two quantities (in the numerator) or the two prices (in the denominator). The reason is to avoid a situation where in calculating the elasticity between points A and B, one person divides the change in quantity by the quantity level at A while another divides it by the quantity level at B—thus leading to two different answers for the same question. By using the average quantity and average price between A and B, this possible confusion is eliminated. At a more advanced level of economics, using the tools of calculus, elasticity can be calculated at a specific point—in which case the need to divide by the average quantity and price at two different points doesn't arise.

Finally, here's a warning: Because demand curves slope down, the percentage change in quantity demanded in response to a percentage change in price will be a negative number—that is, either a higher price leads to a lower quantity demanded, or a lower price leads to a higher quantity demanded. However, economists have often dropped the negative sign on the elasticity of demand for decades now. After all, economists know that demand curves generally slope downward, so they don't need the reminder of the negative sign. So when you are reading or listening to something about economics and run across an elasticity of demand that has no negative sign, don't be surprised.

Price Elasticity of Supply

Just as the price elasticity of demand reveals how a percentage change in price will lead to a percentage change in quantity demanded, the price elasticity of supply measures how a percentage change in price will lead to a percentage change in quantity supplied. Again, the elasticity cannot be easily inferred from glancing at the appearance of a supply curve. Instead, elasticity requires a numerical calculation.

Calculating the Elasticity of Supply

Assume that you are renting an apartment in the Philadelphia metropolitan area, where the cost of housing for renters is about $650 per month. Say that your neighborhood has 10,000 rental units. This situation is illustrated in both Exhibit 7-4*a* and Exhibit 7-4*b*, where the original equilibrium in both graphs is at a price of $650 and a quantity of 10,000 rental apartments. Now imagine that your neighborhood suddenly becomes a more popular and fashionable place to live—that is, demand for rental housing in your neighborhood shifts to the right. Both Exhibit 7-4*a* and Exhibit 7-4*b* show an identical shift of a demand curve for rental housing out to the right from D_0 to D_1. However, the shape of the supply curve for rental housing differs in the two graphs. As a result, in

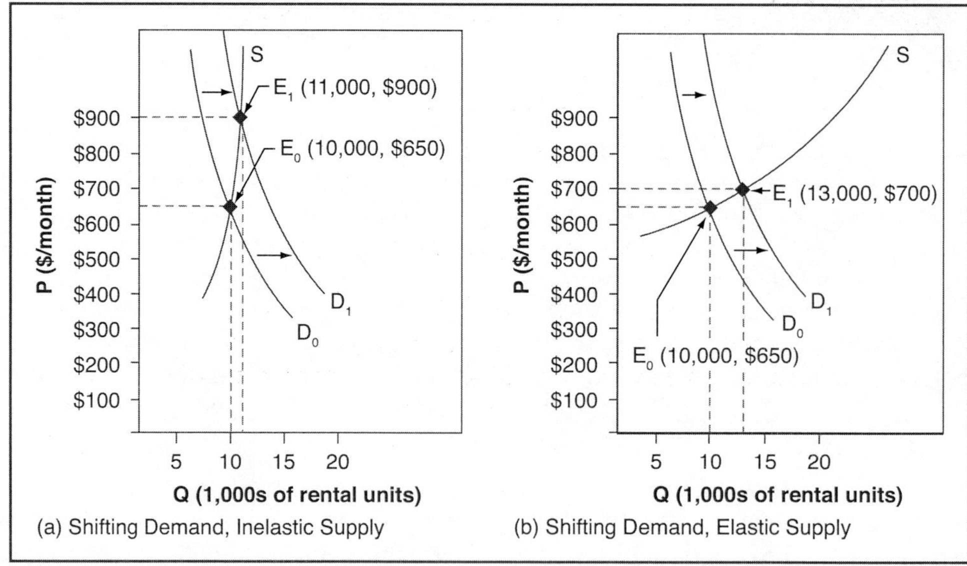

EXHIBIT 7-4 How a Shift in Demand Can Affect Price or Quantity More

The intersection E_0 between supply curve S and demand curve D_0 is the same in both *(a)* and *(b)*. The increase in demand from D_0 to D_1 is the same in both *(a)* and *(b)*. The new equilibrium E_1 has a higher price and quantity than the original equilibrium E_0 in both *(a)* and *(b)*. However, the shape of supply differs in *(a)* and *(b)*. As a result, in *(a)*, the new equilibrium E_1 happens at a much higher price but only a small increase in quantity, while in *(b)*, the new equilibrium happens at only a small increase in price but a relatively large increase in quantity.

Exhibit 7-4*a*, the new equilibrium E_1 in your neighborhood occurs at a higher rental price of $900 per month and a slightly higher equilibrium quantity of 11,000 rental units, while in Exhibit 7-4*b*, the new equilibrium E_1 results in a slightly higher rental price of $700 per month and a substantially higher equilibrium quantity of 13,000 rental units in your neighborhood. The elasticity of supply is a useful tool for explaining the different outcomes in these two situations.

elasticity of supply: The percentage change in quantity supplied divided by the percentage change in price.

Let's begin with the calculations. The **elasticity of supply** is defined as the percentage change in quantity supplied divided by the percentage change in price. Again, the percentage change between two quantities is calculated by taking the difference between the two quantities and dividing by the average of the two quantities. Similarly, the percentage change between two prices is calculated by taking the difference between the two prices and dividing by the average of the two prices. Thus, the formula for elasticity of supply is:

$$\text{Elasticity of supply} = \frac{\text{\% change in quantity supplied}}{\text{\% change in price}}$$

$$= \frac{\text{(change in quantity / average of original quantities)}}{\text{(change in price / average of original prices)}}$$

First, apply this formula to the elasticity of supply between E_0 and E_1 in Exhibit 7-4*a*.

$$\frac{[11{,}000 - 10{,}000] / [(11{,}000 + 10{,}000) / 2]}{[900 - 650] / [(900 + 650) / 2]} = \frac{1{,}000/10{,}500}{250/775} = \frac{.095}{.322}$$

The elasticity of supply in this example is .095/.322 = .295.

Now apply the same formula for elasticity of supply to the change between E_0 and E_1 in Exhibit 7-4*b*.

$$\frac{[13{,}000 - 10{,}000] / [(13{,}000 + 10{,}000) / 2]}{[700 - 650] / [(700 + 650) / 2]} = \frac{3{,}000/11{,}500}{50/675} = \frac{.261}{.074}$$

The elasticity of supply in this case is .261/.074 = 3.52.

Again, as with the elasticity of demand, the elasticity of supply is not followed by any units. Elasticity is a ratio of one percentage change to another percentage change—nothing more.

What is the intuitive meaning of these calculations? The elasticity of supply in Exhibit 7-4*a* is relatively small. A 10% rise in price causes only a 2.9% rise in the quantity supplied in Exhibit 7-4*a*. The elasticity of supply in Exhibit 7-4*b* is relatively large. In this case, a 10% rise in price would bring an increase in supply of 35%. The much greater elasticity of supply in Exhibit 7-4*b* means that quantity supplied will react much more to a certain percentage change in price.

In situations like this one, the supply curve in Exhibit 7-4*a* often reflects the situation in the short-term, when the quantity supplied of rental housing cannot increase much in a year or two. As a result, the elasticity of supply is fairly low, and the increase in demand is primarily reflected in higher prices. However, the supply curve in Exhibit 7-4*b* makes more sense from the longer run perspective of several years, when the quantity supplied of housing has time to rise more substantially because of new building activity or converting existing properties into rental units. As a result, in the long run the very same rise in demand is reflected more in a rise in the quantity of housing and less in a rise in price.

Elastic, Inelastic, and Unitary Elasticity

Numerical measures of elasticity can be usefully divided into three broad categories: elastic, inelastic, and unitary elasticity. The categories are summarized in Exhibit 7-5.

When quantity demanded or supplied is highly sensitive to changes in price, it is said to be **elastic**. Specifically, an elastic demand refers to a situation in which a certain percentage change in price leads to a larger percentage change in quantity demanded or quantity supplied. For example, a 1% rise in the price would cause a decline of more than 1%—perhaps 2%—in the quantity demanded of a good. Since elasticity refers to the percentage change in quantity divided by the percentage change in price, saying that a demand curve or supply curve is elastic means that the elasticity calculated from the formula is greater than 1.

elastic: The elasticity calculated from the appropriate formula has an absolute value greater than 1.

Demand will be elastic when consumers find it easy to shift back and forth between goods and services. For example, if the price of lamb rises, many consumers will shift to other meats and foods. Supply will be elastic when it is relatively easy to expand or contract production. For example, at a time when most of the factories in an industry are running at only about half of their full production level, it will be relatively easy to ramp up production higher.

Infinite elasticity refers to the extremely elastic situation where quantity changes by an infinite amount in response to any change in price at all. A demand curve with infinite elasticity appears in Exhibit 7-6*a*, and a supply curve with infinite elasticity appears in Exhibit 7-6*b*. Infinite elasticity creates horizontal demand and supply curves.

infinite elasticity: The extremely elastic situation where quantity changes by an infinite amount in response to even a tiny change in price.

EXHIBIT 7-5 Elastic, Unitary, and Inelastic: Three Cases of Elasticity

If . . .	Then . . .	And It's Called . . .
% change in quantity > % change in price	$\frac{\text{\% change in quantity}}{\text{\% change in price}} > 1$	Elastic
% change in quantity = % change in price	$\frac{\text{\% change in quantity}}{\text{\% change in price}} = 1$	Unitary elasticity
% change in quantity < % change in price	$\frac{\text{\% change in quantity}}{\text{\% change in price}} < 1$	Inelastic

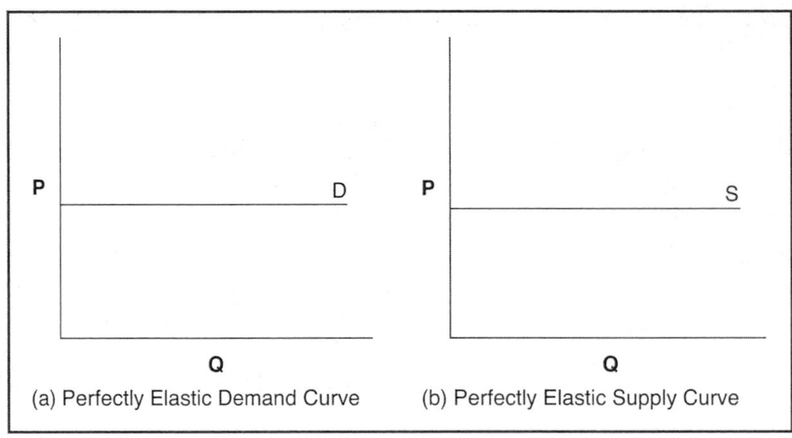

EXHIBIT 7-6 Infinite Elasticity

The horizontal lines in *(a)* and *(b)* show that an infinite quantity will be demanded *(a)* or supplied *(b)* at a specific price. This illustrates the cases of a perfectly elastic or infinitely elastic demand and supply curve.

inelastic: The elasticity calculated from the appropriate formula has an absolute value less than 1.

At the other extreme from elastic is **inelastic**—the situation where a certain percentage change in the price will cause a smaller percentage change in the quantity demanded or supplied. For example, when demand is inelastic, a 1% rise in the price would cause a decline of less than 1%—say, only 0.3%—in the quantity demanded of a good. Since elasticity is calculated as the percentage change in quantity divided by the percentage change in price, inelastic means that the level of elasticity will be less than 1.

Demand will be inelastic when consumers find it difficult to shift back and forth between goods and services. For example, if you have an illness that requires a certain drug to reduce your pain or to keep you alive, and the price of that drug rises, you may not cut back very much, if at all, on consumption of that drug, but instead you will seek ways to save money elsewhere in your budget. Supply is often inelastic in the short run because over a time period of a few months or even a year or two, businesses often have a limited ability to expand their quantity supplied in a dramatic way, given that they have only so many factories and workers on hand.

zero elasticity: The highly inelastic case in which a percentage change in price, no matter how large, results in zero change in the quantity demanded or supplied.

Zero elasticity refers to the highly inelastic case in which a percentage change in price, no matter how large, results in zero change in quantity. A demand curve with zero elasticity appears in Exhibit 7-7*a*; a supply curve with zero elasticity appears in Exhibit 7-7*b*. Zero elasticity refers to demand and supply curves that are vertical.

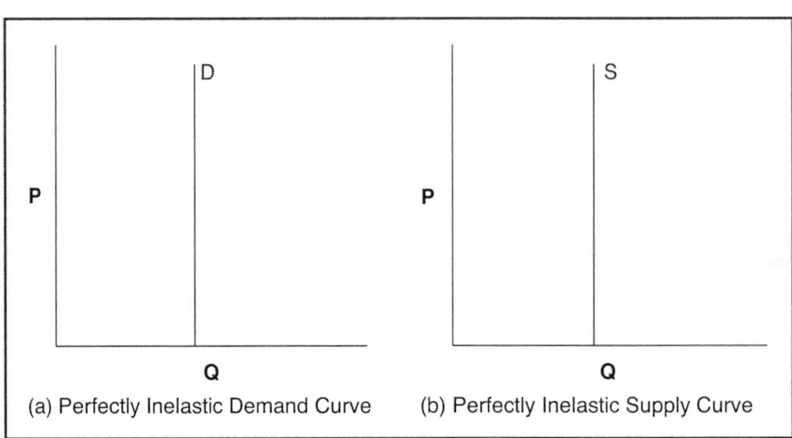

EXHIBIT 7-7 Zero Elasticity

The *(a)* vertical demand and *(b)* vertical supply curves show that there will be zero percentage change in quantity demanded or supplied, regardless of the price. This illustrates the case of zero or perfect inelasticity.

On the borderline between elastic and inelastic, the percentage change in quantity demanded is equal to the percentage change in quantity supplied, which is the case of unitary elasticity. In this case, a rise of, say, 10% in price would lead to a decline of 10% in the quantity demanded, or a fall of, say, 5% in price would lead to a fall of 5% in the quantity supplied.

When economists are sketching examples of demand and supply, it is common to sketch a demand or supply curve that is close to vertical, and then to refer to that curve as "inelastic." It is also common to sketch a demand or supply curve that is close to horizontal, and then to refer to that demand or supply curve as "elastic." Such statements must be handled with care. Remember, a close-to-horizontal or close-to-vertical demand or supply curve may appear that way because of how the axes are drawn, not because of some inherent characteristic of the underlying data. Moreover, elasticity will usually vary along a demand or supply curve, so that one zone of a demand or supply curve can be elastic while another zone is inelastic. Nonetheless, for purposes of sketching diagrams and illustrating economic intuition, it is often convenient to treat inelastic as close to vertical and elastic as close to horizontal. As long as one remembers that such statements are only approximations for the purposes of illustration, no harm is done.

Applications of Elasticity

Elasticities are useful in a wide range of circumstances. Even knowing only that a demand or supply curve is elastic or inelastic can lead to interesting insights.

Does Raising Price Bring in More Revenue?

Imagine that a band on tour is playing in an indoor arena with 15,000 seats. To keep this example simple, assume that the band keeps all the money from ticket sales. (For example, you can imagine that the owners of the arena make their money by charging for parking and concessions.) Assume further that the band pays the costs for its appearance, but that these costs like travel, setting up the stage, and so on, are the same regardless of how many people gather in the audience. Finally, assume that all the tickets have the same price. (The same insights apply if ticket prices are more expensive for some seats than for others, but the calculations become more complicated.) The band knows that it faces a downward-sloping demand curve; that is, if the band raises the price of tickets, it will sell fewer tickets. How should the band set the price for tickets to bring in the most total revenue, which in this example, because costs are fixed, will also mean the highest profits for the band? Should the band sell more tickets at a higher price or fewer tickets at a lower price?

The key concept in thinking about collecting the most revenue is the elasticity of demand. Total revenue is price times the quantity of tickets sold. Imagine that the band starts off thinking about a certain price, which will result in the sale of a certain quantity of tickets. The three possibilities are laid out in Exhibit 7-8. If demand is elastic at that price level, then the band should cut the price because the percentage drop in price will result in an even larger percentage increase in the quantity sold—thus raising total revenue.

EXHIBIT 7-8 Will the Band Earn More Revenue by Changing Ticket Prices?

If Demand Is . . .	Then . . .	Therefore . . .
Elastic	% change in Q > % change in P	A given % rise in P will be more than offset by a larger % fall in Q, so that total revenue P × Q falls
Unitary	% change in Q = % change in P	A given % rise in P will be exactly offset by an equal % fall in Q, so that total revenue P × Q is unchanged
Inelastic	% change in Q < % change in P	A given % rise in P will cause a smaller % fall in Q, so that total revenue P × Q rises

What Does a Unitary Elasticity of Demand or Supply Look Like?

A demand curve with unitary elasticity at all points is a curved line, but a supply curve with unitary price elasticity at all points is a straight line running through the origin.

To gain some intuition about why this is true, first consider the demand curve with a unitary price elasticity of demand at all points. As you move down the demand curve from A to B, the price falls by 33% and quantity demanded rises by 33%; as you move from B to C, the price falls by 25% and the quantity demanded rises by 25% (although the numbers are chosen here so that a bit of rounding off is needed); as you move from C to D, the price falls by 20% and the quantity rises by 20%. Notice that in absolute value, the declines in price as you step down the demand curve are not identical. Instead, price falls by $2.80 from A to B, by a smaller amount of $1.50 from B to C, and by a still smaller amount of $1.00 from C to D. As a result, a demand curve with constant unitary elasticity moves from a steeper slope on the left to a flatter slope on the right—and a curved shape overall.

In moving up the unitary elasticity supply curve from left to right, each increase in quantity of 20, from 50 to 70 to 90 to 110, is equal in absolute value. However, in percentage value, the steps are decreasing, from 33.3% to 25% to 20%, because the original average quantity in each percentage calculation is getting larger and larger, which expands the denominator in the elasticity calculation. Next consider the price changes moving up the supply curve. From points D to E to F and G on the supply curve, each step of $2.00 is the same in absolute value. However, if the price changes are measured in percentage change terms, they are also decreasing, from 33.3% to 25% to 20%, because the original price points in each percentage calculation are getting larger and larger in value. Along the constant unitary elasticity supply curve, the percentage quantity increases on the horizontal axis exactly match the percentage price increases on the vertical axis—so this linear supply curve has a constant unitary elasticity at all points.

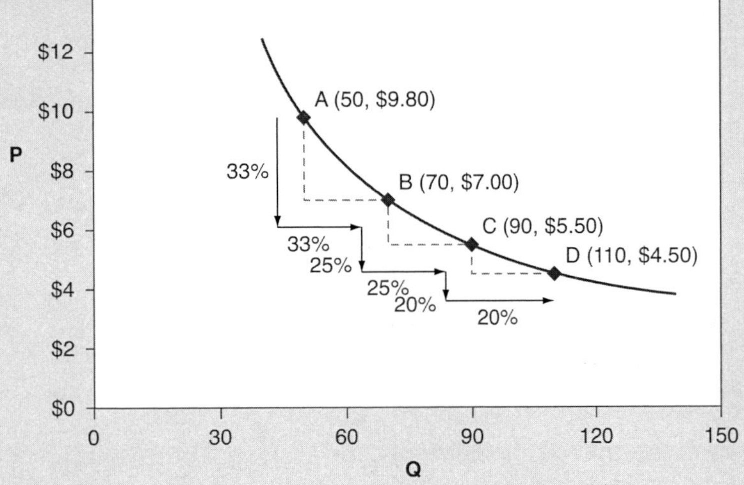

A Constant Unitary Elasticity Demand Curve

A demand curve with constant unitary elasticity will be a curved line. Notice how each step down, the demand curve has an identical percentage change in quantity demanded and in price using the elasticity formula.

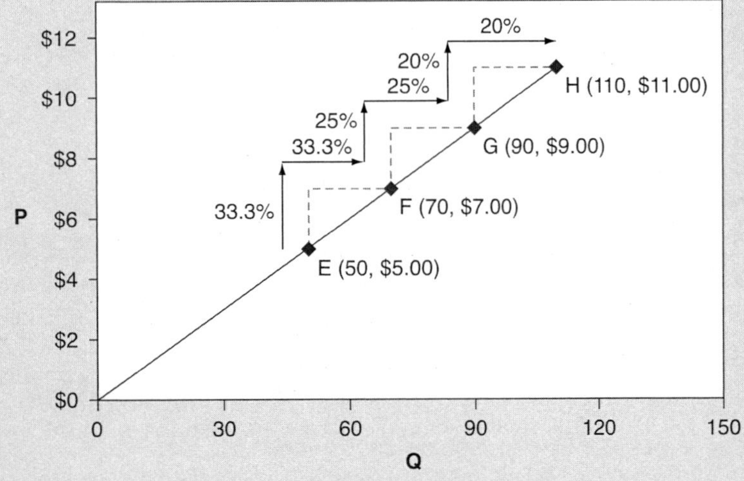

A Constant Unitary Elasticity Supply Curve

A constant unitary elasticity supply curve is a straight line reaching up from the origin. Between each point, an application of the elasticity formula shows that the percentage increase in quantity demanded is the same as the percentage increase in price.

However, if demand is inelastic at that original quantity level, then the band should raise the price of tickets because a certain percentage increase in price will result in a smaller percentage decrease in the quantity sold—and total revenue will rise. If demand has a unitary elasticity at that quantity, then a moderate percentage change in the price will be offset by an equal percentage change in quantity—so the band will earn the same revenue whether it (moderately) increases or decreases the price of tickets.

What if the band keeps cutting price, because demand is elastic, until it reaches a level where all 15,000 seats in the available arena are sold? If demand remains elastic at that quantity, the band might try to move to a bigger arena, so that it could cut ticket prices further and see a larger percentage increase in the quantity of tickets sold. Of course, if the 15,000-seat arena is all that is available or if a larger arena would add substantially to costs, then this option may not work.

Conversely, a few bands are so famous, or have such fanatical followings, that demand for tickets may be inelastic right up to the point where the arena is full. These bands can, if they wish, keep raising the price of tickets. Ironically, some bands that are extremely popular among a smaller group could make more revenue by setting prices so high that the arena is not filled—but those who buy the tickets would have to pay very high prices. However, bands sometimes choose to sell tickets for less than the absolute maximum they might be able to charge, often in the hope that fans will feel happier about attending the concert and spend more on recordings, T-shirts, and other paraphernalia.

Passing on Costs to Consumers?

Most businesses face a day-to-day struggle to figure out ways to produce at a lower cost, as one pathway to their goal of earning higher profits. However, in some cases, the price of a key input over which the firm has no control may rise. For example, many chemical companies use petroleum as a key input, but they have no control over the world market price for crude oil. Coffee shops use coffee as a key input, but they have no control over the world market price of coffee. If the cost of a key input rises, can the firm pass those higher costs along to consumers in the form of higher prices? Conversely, if new and less expensive ways of producing are invented, can the firm keep the benefits in the form of higher profits, or will the market pressure them to pass the gains along to consumers in the form of lower prices? The elasticity of demand plays a key role in answering these questions.

Imagine that as a consumer of legal pharmaceutical products, you read a newspaper story that a technological breakthrough in the production of aspirin has occurred, so that every aspirin factory can now make aspirin more cheaply than it did before. What does this discovery mean to you? Exhibit 7-9 illustrates two possibilities. In Exhibit 7-9*a*, the demand curve is drawn as highly inelastic. In this case, a technological breakthrough that shifts supply to the right from S_0 to S_1, so that the equilibrium shifts from E_0 to E_1, creates a substantially lower price for the product with relatively little impact on the quantity sold. In Exhibit 7-9*b*, the demand curve is drawn as highly elastic. In this case, the technological breakthrough leads to a much greater quantity being sold in the market at very close to the original price. If you already consume large amounts of aspirin, then you tend to benefit more from a lower price than a greater quantity sold in the market; if you are not yet an aspirin consumer, but a small decrease in price makes you willing to purchase it, you benefit more from the expanded quantity sold in the market.

Producers of aspirin may find themselves in a nasty bind here. The situation shown in Exhibit 7-9*a*, with extremely inelastic demand, means that a new invention may cause the price to drop dramatically while quantity changes little. As a result, the new production technology can lead to a drop in the revenue that firms earn from sales of aspirin! However, if strong competition exists between producers of aspirin, each producer may have little choice but to search for and implement any breakthrough that allows it to reduce production costs. After all, if one firm decides not to implement such a cost-saving technology, it can be driven out of business by other firms that do. Since demand for food is generally inelastic, farmers may often face the situation in Exhibit 7-9*a*. That is, a surge

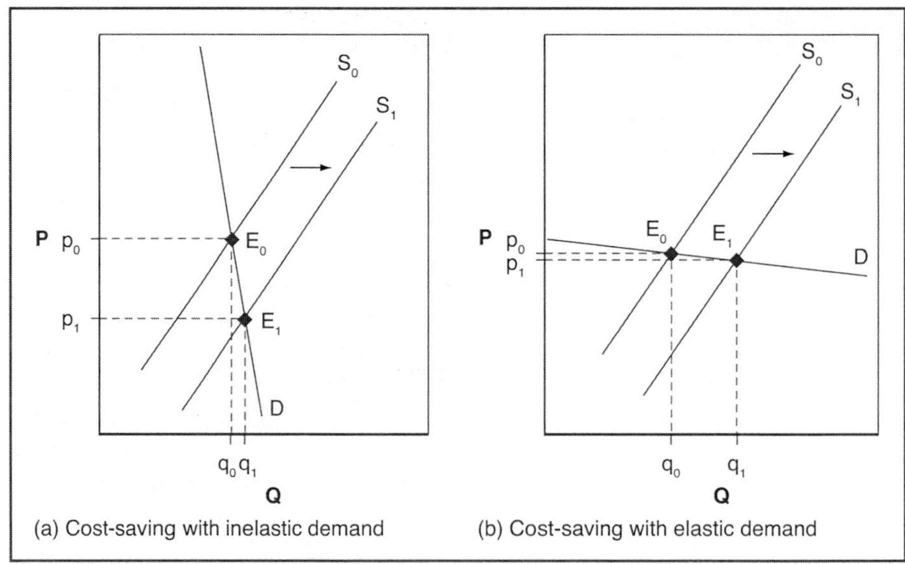

EXHIBIT 7-9 Passing along Cost Savings to Consumers

Cost-saving gains cause supply to shift out to the right from S_0 to S_1; that is, at any given price, firms will be willing to supply a greater quantity. If demand is inelastic, as in *(a)*, the result of this cost-saving technological improvement will be substantially lower prices. If demand is elastic, as in *(b)*, the result will be only slightly lower prices. Consumers benefit in either case from a greater quantity at a lower price. But the benefit takes different forms, depending on the elasticity of demand.

in production leads to a severe drop in price that can actually decrease the total revenue received by farmers. Conversely, poor weather or other conditions that cause a lousy year for farm production can sharply raise prices so that the total revenue received by farmers rises—at least for those farmers who have something to sell.

Elasticity also reveals whether firms can pass on higher costs that they incur to consumers. In this case, some of the most vivid applications involve addictive substances. For example, the demand for cigarettes is relatively inelastic among regular smokers who are somewhat addicted; economic research suggests that increasing the price of cigarettes by 10% leads to about a 4% reduction in the quantity of cigarettes smoked by adults, so

Fluctuating Coffee Prices

Coffee is an international crop. The top five coffee-exporting nations are Brazil, Vietnam, Colombia, Indonesia, and Honduras. In these nations and others, 20 million families depend on selling coffee beans as their main source of income. These families are exposed to enormous risk because the world price of coffee bounces up and down. For example, in 1993 the world price of coffee was about 50 cents per pound; in 1995 it was four times as high, at $2.00 per pound. By 1997 it had fallen by half to $1.00 per pound. In 1998 it leaped back up to $2.00 per pound. By 2002 it had fallen back to 50 cents a pound; by the end of 2005 it went back up to about $1.00 per pound. By 2009 the price had fallen back to about 65 cents per pound, before spiking up to $3.00 per pound in 2011, and then falling back to $1.60 per pound in 2015.

The reason for these price bounces lies in a combination of inelastic demand and shifts in supply. The elasticity of coffee demand is only about 0.3; that is, a 10% rise in the price of coffee leads to a decline of about 3% in the quantity of coffee consumed. When a major frost hit the Brazilian coffee crop in 1994, coffee supply shifted to the left with an inelastic demand curve, leading to much higher prices. Conversely, when Vietnam entered the world coffee market as a major producer in the late 1990s, the supply curve shifted out to the right, and coffee prices fell dramatically. When heavy rains wreaked havoc on Columbia's coffee crop in 2011, the supply curve shifted back to the left, and coffee prices spiked up.

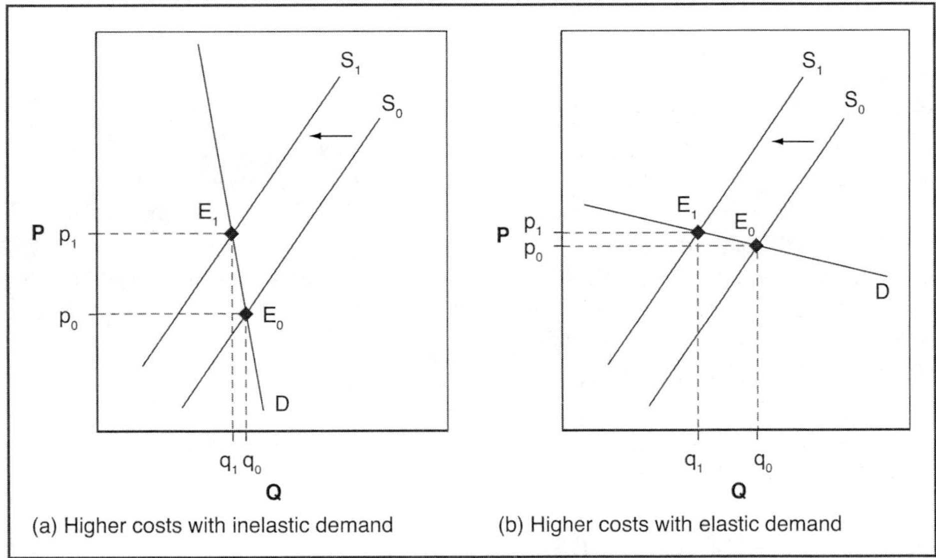

(a) Higher costs with inelastic demand (b) Higher costs with elastic demand

EXHIBIT 7-10 Passing along Higher Costs to Consumers

Higher costs, like a higher tax on cigarette companies for the example given in the text, lead supply to shift back to the left. This shift is identical in *(a)* and *(b)*. However, in *(a)*, demand is inelastic, and so the cost increase can largely be passed along to consumers in the form of higher prices, without much of a decline in equilibrium quantity. In *(b)*, demand is elastic, so the shift in supply results primarily in a lower equilibrium quantity. Consumers suffer in either case, but in *(a)*, they suffer from paying a higher price for the same quantity, while in *(b)*, they suffer from buying a lower quantity (and presumably shifting their consumption elsewhere).

the elasticity of demand for cigarettes is 0.4. If society increases taxes on companies that make cigarettes, the result, as shown in Exhibit 7-10*a*, is that the supply curve shifts from S_0 to S_1. However, as the equilibrium moves from E_0 to E_1, these taxes are mainly passed along to consumers in the form of higher prices. These higher taxes on cigarettes will raise tax revenue for the government, but they won't much affect the quantity of smoking. If the goal is to reduce the quantity of cigarettes demanded, this must be achieved by shifting this inelastic demand back to the left, perhaps with public programs to discourage the use of cigarettes or to help people to quit. For example, anti-smoking advertising campaigns have shown some ability to reduce smoking. However, if demand for cigarettes was more elastic, as in Exhibit 7-10*b*, then an increase in taxes that shifts supply from S_0 to S_1 and equilibrium from E_0 to E_1 would reduce the quantity of cigarettes smoked substantially. Youth smoking seems to be more elastic than adult smoking—that is, the quantity of youth smoking will fall by a greater percentage than the quantity of adult smoking in response to a given percentage increase in price.

The enforcement of laws against the production or sale of illegal drugs offers another application of this scenario. Laws against illegal drugs can be viewed as shifting the supply curve back to the left; that is, as a result of making certain drugs illegal, the quantity available for sale at any given price is lower than it was before. If demand for these drugs is inelastic, then producers of illegal drugs can essentially pass along the higher price from law enforcement, and these laws will not reduce the quantity consumed by much. However, if demand for these illegal drugs is quite elastic, shifting supply back to the right will reduce the quantity consumed dramatically. Many of the arguments over legalization of drugs ("Strict enforcement will cut drug use!" "No, it will only put more money in the pockets of drug dealers!") are really assertions about whether enforcement will have a greater impact on quantity or on price, and thus are really claims about the elasticities of demand and supply. But the truth is that we lack evidence on elasticities of supply and demand for illegal drugs. In 2001, the prestigious National Research Council published a report by a Committee on Data and Research for Policy on Illegal Drugs. The committee, which included several economists, concluded: "Viewing the unending public

CLEARING IT UP

For Supply Shifts, Check Elasticity of Demand, and Vice Versa

If the question is whether a shift in supply will have a greater effect on equilibrium price or quantity, the answer lies not with the elasticity of supply, but with the elasticity of demand. That's because the shifting supply curve is moving along a fixed demand curve—and the shape of that demand curve will determine the eventual outcome. Similarly, if the question is whether a shift in demand will have a greater effect on equilibrium price or quantity, the answer lies not with the elasticity of demand, but with the elasticity of supply. After all, when a shifting demand curve moves along a fixed supply curve, the shape of that supply curve will determine the eventual outcome.

debate about drug policy, the committee became painfully aware that what we don't know keeps hurting us."

Long-Run vs. Short-Run Impact

Elasticities are often lower in the short run than in the long run. On the demand side of the market, it can sometimes be difficult to change quantity demanded in the short run, but easier in the long run. Consumption of energy is a vivid example. In the short run, it's not easy for a person to make substantial changes in energy consumption. Maybe you can carpool to work sometimes or adjust your home thermostat by a few degrees if the cost of energy rises, but that's about it. However, in the long run, you can purchase a car that gets more miles to the gallon, or choose a job that is closer to where you live, or buy more energy-efficient home appliances, or install more insulation in your home. As a result, the elasticity of demand for energy is somewhat inelastic in the short run, but much more elastic in the long run.

Exhibit 7-11 is an example, based roughly on historical experience, for the responsiveness of quantity demanded to price changes. In 1973, the price of crude oil was $12 per barrel and total consumption in the U.S. economy was 17 million barrels per day. That year, the nations who were members of the Organization of Petroleum Exporting Countries cut off oil exports to the United States for six months and did not bring exports back to their earlier levels until 1975—a policy that can be interpreted as a shift of the supply curve to the left in the U.S. petroleum market. Exhibit 7-11*a* and Exhibit 7-11*b* show the same original equilibrium point and the same identical shift of a supply curve to the left from S_0 to S_1.

However, Exhibit 7-11*a* and Exhibit 7-11*b* show two different possible shapes for the demand curve for oil. Exhibit 7-11*a* shows inelastic demand for oil in the short run, while Exhibit 7-11*b* shows more elastic demand for oil in the long run. In Exhibit 7-11*a*, the new equilibrium E_1 occurs at a price of $25 per barrel and an equilibrium quantity of 16 million barrels per day. In Exhibit 7-11*b*, the new equilibrium E_1 results in a smaller price increase to $14 per barrel and a larger reduction in equilibrium quantity to 13 million barrels per day. In 1983, for example, U.S. petroleum consumption was 15.3 million barrels a day, which was lower than in 1973 or 1975. U.S. petroleum consumption was down even though the U.S. economy was about one-fourth larger in 1983 than it had been in 1973. The primary reason for the lower quantity was that higher energy prices spurred conservation efforts, and after a decade of home insulation, lower mileage cars, more efficient appliances and machinery, and other fuel-conserving choices, the demand curve for energy had become more elastic.

On the supply side of markets, producers of goods and services typically find it easier to expand production in the long term of several years, rather than in the short run of a few months. After all, in the short run it can be costly or difficult to build a new factory, hire many new workers, or open new stores. But over a few years, all of these are possible. Earlier in this chapter, the example of rental housing in Philadelphia explained how a shift in demand for rental housing is likely to increase price relatively more than quantity in the

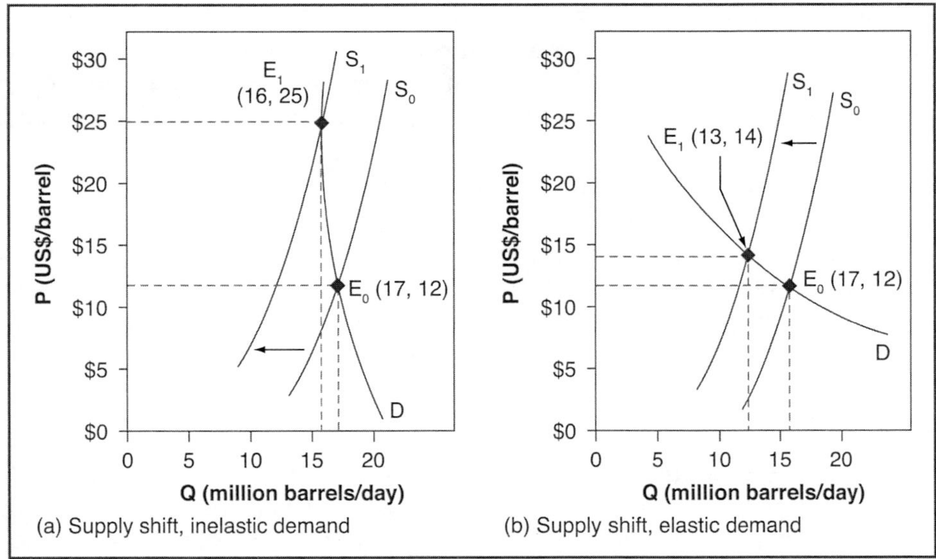

EXHIBIT 7-11 How a Shift in Supply Can Affect Price or Quantity More

The intersection E_0 between demand curve D and supply curve S_0 is the same in both *(a)* and *(b)*. The shift of supply to the left from S_0 to S_1 is identical in both *(a)* and *(b)*. The new equilibrium E_1 has a higher price and a lower quantity than the original equilibrium E_0 in both *(a)* and *(b)*. However, the shape of the demand curve D is different in *(a)* and *(b)*. As a result, the shift in supply can result either in a new equilibrium with a much higher price and an only slightly smaller quantity, as in *(a)*, or in a new equilibrium with only a small increase in price and a relatively larger reduction in quantity, as in *(b)*.

short run because it's difficult for the quantity of rental housing to adjust dramatically in the short run. However, in the long run that same shift in demand will be reflected more in a rise in equilibrium quantity than a rise in equilibrium price.

Indeed, in most markets for goods and services, prices bounce up and down more than quantities in the short run, but quantities often move more than prices in the long run. The underlying reason for this pattern is that supply and demand are often inelastic in the short run; therefore, shifts in either demand or supply can cause a relatively greater change in prices. But since supply and demand are more elastic in the long run, the long-run movements in prices are more muted, while quantity adjusts more easily in the long run.

Elasticity as a General Concept

The basic idea of elasticity—how a percentage change in one variable causes a percentage change in another variable—doesn't just apply to supply and demand curves in the markets for goods and services, but can also apply to many economic relationships. In these ways, the idea of elasticity can be used to clarify and re-explain some concepts introduced earlier in this book, like normal and inferior goods, substitute and complement goods, and others. Indeed, the concept of elasticity can also be applied to factors other than price that affect quantity.

Income Elasticity of Demand

The income elasticity of demand is the percentage change in quantity demanded divided by the percentage change in income.

$$\text{Income elasticity of demand} = \frac{\text{\% change in quantity demanded}}{\text{\% change in income}}$$

For most products, most of the time, the income elasticity of demand is positive: that is, a rise in income will cause an increase in the quantity demanded. This pattern is common enough that these goods are referred to as **normal goods**. However, for a few goods, an

normal good: A good for which the quantity demanded rises when income rises.

increase in income means that one might purchase less of the good; for example, people with a higher income might buy fewer hamburgers because they are buying more steak instead, or a person with a higher income might buy less cheap wine and more imported beer. When the income elasticity of demand is negative, the good is called an **inferior good**.

inferior good: A good for which the quantity demanded declines as income increases.

The concepts of normal and inferior goods were introduced in Chapter 4, in the discussion of supply and demand. A higher level of income causes a demand curve to shift to the right for a normal good, which means that the income elasticity of demand is positive. However, for an inferior good—that is, when the income elasticity of demand is negative—a higher level of income causes the demand curve for that good to shift to the left.

Cross-Price Elasticity of Demand

A change in the price of one good can shift the quantity demanded for another good. If the two goods are complements, like bread and peanut butter, then a drop in the price of one good will lead to an increase in the quantity demanded of the other good. However, if the two goods are substitutes, like plane tickets and train tickets, then a drop in the price of one good will cause people to substitute toward that good and to reduce consumption of the other good. Cheaper plane tickets lead to fewer train tickets, and vice versa.

cross-price elasticity of demand: The percentage change in the quantity of good A that is demanded as a result of a percentage change in the price of good B.

The **cross-price elasticity of demand** puts some meat on the bones of these ideas. The term "cross-price" refers to the idea that the price of one good is affecting the quantity demanded of a different good. Specifically, the cross-price elasticity of demand is the percentage change in the quantity of good A that is demanded as a result of a percentage change in the price of good B.

$$\text{Cross-price elasticity of demand} = \frac{\%\text{ change in quantity demanded of good A}}{\%\text{ change in price of good B}}$$

If good A is a substitute for good B, like coffee and tea, then a higher price for B will mean a greater quantity consumed of good A, and so the cross-price elasticity of demand will be positive. But if good A is a complement for good B, like coffee and sugar, then a higher price for good B will mean a lower quantity consumed of good A, and the cross-price elasticity of demand will be negative.

Elasticity in Labor and Financial Capital Markets

The concept of elasticity also applies in labor markets and financial capital markets. In the labor market, for example, the **elasticity of labor supply**—that is, the percentage change in hours worked divided by the percentage change in wages—will determine the shape of the labor supply curve. Specifically:

elasticity of labor supply: The percentage change in hours worked divided by the percentage change in wages.

$$\text{Elasticity of labor supply} = \frac{\%\text{ change in quantity of labor supplied}}{\%\text{ change in wage}}$$

The wage elasticity of labor supply for teenage workers is generally thought to be fairly elastic: that is, a certain percentage change in wages will lead to a larger percentage change in the quantity of hours worked. Conversely, the wage elasticity of labor supply for adult workers in their 30s and 40s is thought to be fairly inelastic. When wages move up or down by a certain percentage amount, the quantity of hours that adults in their prime earning years are willing to supply changes but by a lesser percentage amount.

elasticity of savings: The percentage change in the quantity of savings divided by the percentage change in interest rates.

In markets for financial capital, the **elasticity of savings**—that is, the percentage change in the quantity of savings divided by the percentage change in interest rates—will describe the shape of the supply curve for financial capital. That is:

$$\text{Elasticity of savings} = \frac{\%\text{ change in quantity of financial savings}}{\%\text{ change in interest rate}}$$

Sometimes, laws are proposed that seek to increase the quantity of savings by offering tax breaks so that the return on savings is higher. Such a policy will increase the quantity if the supply curve for financial capital is elastic because then a given percentage increase in the return to savings will cause a higher percentage increase in the quantity of savings. However, if the supply curve for financial capital is highly inelastic, then a percentage increase in the return to savings will cause only a small increase in the quantity of savings. The evidence on the supply curve of financial capital is controversial, but at least in the short run, the elasticity of savings with respect to the interest rate appears fairly inelastic.

Stretching the Concept of Elasticity

The elasticity concept doesn't even need to relate to a typical supply or demand curve at all. For example, imagine that you are studying whether the Internal Revenue Service should spend more money on auditing tax returns. The question can be framed in terms of the elasticity of tax collections with respect to spending on tax enforcement; that is, what is the percentage change in tax revenue collected resulting from a percentage change in spending on tax enforcement? Or imagine that you are interested in a policy that trims back on Social Security payments in a way that might encourage some elderly people to continue working for a few more years rather than retire. The question can be framed in terms of the elasticity of hours of work with respect to Social Security payments; that is, what is the percentage change in work hours that will result from a certain percentage change in Social Security payments?

With all of the elasticity concepts that have just been described, some of which are listed in Exhibit 7-12, the possibility of confusion arises. When you hear the phrases "elasticity of demand" or "elasticity of supply," the terms refer to the elasticity with respect to price. Sometimes, either to be extremely clear or because a wide variety of elasticities are being discussed, the elasticity of demand or the demand elasticity will be called the **price elasticity of demand** or the "elasticity of demand with respect to price." Similarly, elasticity of supply or the supply elasticity is sometimes called, to avoid any possibility of confusion, the **price elasticity of supply** or "the elasticity of supply with respect to price." But in whatever context elasticity is invoked, the idea always refers to percentage change in one variable (almost always a price or money variable) and how it causes a percentage change in another variable (typically, a quantity variable of some kind).

price elasticity of demand: Same as elasticity of demand.

price elasticity of supply: Same as elasticity of supply.

$$\text{Income elasticity of demand} = \frac{\text{\% change in quantity demanded}}{\text{\% change in income}}$$

$$\text{Cross-price elasticity of demand} = \frac{\text{\% change in quantity demanded of good A}}{\text{\% change in price of good B}}$$

$$\text{Wage elasticity of labor supply} = \frac{\text{\% change in quantity of labor supplied}}{\text{\% change in wage}}$$

$$\text{Wage elasticity of labor demand} = \frac{\text{\% change in quantity labor demanded}}{\text{\% change in wage}}$$

$$\text{Interest rate elasticity of savings} = \frac{\text{\% change in quantity of savings}}{\text{\% change in interest rate}}$$

$$\text{Interest rate elasticity of borrowing} = \frac{\text{\% change in quantity of borrowing}}{\text{\% change in interest rate}}$$

EXHIBIT 7-12 Some Applications of the Elasticity Concept

Conclusion

Framing a question in terms of elasticity is often a very useful step. When summarizing or comparing the results of a number of different studies, which are often done using different data sources, time periods, or statistical methods, it is a great help if the studies are trying to estimate a single common concept. The concept of elasticity takes the shape of demand and supply curves out of the realm of guesswork based on appearance, depending on how the curves happen to be drawn. In this way, the concept of elasticity nails down the idea of how quantity changes in response to changes in price in a way that provides a shorthand for discussion and an engine for analysis.

Key Concepts and Summary

1. **Elasticity** is a tool for measuring how much a percentage change in price causes a percentage change in quantity demanded, quantity supplied, or other economic variables.
2. The **elasticity of demand** is the percentage change in quantity demanded divided by the percentage change in price. The **elasticity of supply** is the percentage change in quantity supplied divided by the percentage change in price.
3. An **elastic** demand or supply curve is one for which a given percentage change in price leads to a larger percentage change in quantity demanded or supplied, so that the percentage change in quantity divided by the percentage change in price will be greater than 1. An **inelastic** demand or supply curve is one where a given percentage change in price will cause a smaller percentage change in quantity demanded or supplied, so that the percentage change in quantity divided by the percentage change in price will be less than one. A **unitary elasticity** means that a given percentage change in price leads to an equal percentage change in quantity demanded or supplied, so that the percentage change in quantity divided by the percentage change in price will be equal to one.
4. A demand or supply curve with **zero elasticity**, also referred to as perfectly inelastic, would be extremely inelastic, or vertical in appearance. A demand or supply curve with **infinite elasticity**, also called perfectly elastic, would be extremely elastic, or horizontal in appearance.
5. The elasticity of supply and demand determines whether a shift in supply or demand will have a larger effect on quantity or price. If demand is elastic, then shifts in supply will have a larger effect on quantity than on price. If demand is inelastic, then shifts in supply will have a larger effect on price than on quantity. If supply is elastic, then shifts in demand will have a larger effect on quantity than on price. If supply is inelastic, then shifts in demand will have a larger effect on price than on quantity.
6. In the market for goods and services, quantity supplied and quantity demanded are often relatively slow to react to changes in price in the short run but react more substantially in the long run. As a result, demand and supply often (but not always) tend to be relatively inelastic in the short run and relatively elastic in the long run.
7. *Elasticity* is a general term, referring to percentage change divided by percentage change that can be applied to many economic connections. For instance, the **income elasticity of demand** is the percentage change in quantity demanded divided by the percentage change in income. The **cross-price elasticity of demand** is the percentage change in the quantity demanded of a good divided by the percentage change in the price of another good.
8. Elasticity applies in labor markets and financial capital markets just as it applied in markets for goods and services. The wage elasticity of labor supply is the percentage change in the quantity of hours supplied divided by the percentage change in the wage. The elasticity of savings with respect to interest rates is the percentage change in the quantity of savings divided by the percentage change in interest rates.

Review Questions

1. If you wanted to make a demand or supply curve appear relatively steep, would you stretch out the horizontal or the vertical axis? What about if you wanted to make it appear relatively flat?
2. What is the formula for calculating the elasticity of demand?
3. What is the formula for calculating the elasticity of supply?
4. If demand or supply is elastic, is the response of quantity to changes in price relatively large or small?
5. If demand or supply is elastic, what is the range of the possible numerical values it can have?

6. If demand or supply is inelastic, is the response of quantity to changes in price relatively large or small?
7. If demand or supply is inelastic, what is the range of the possible numerical values it can have?
8. What is the numerical value of a unitary elasticity?
9. What units of measurement, if any, are used with elasticity?
10. Describe the general appearance of a demand or supply curve with zero elasticity.
11. Describe the general appearance of a demand or supply curve with infinite elasticity.
12. If demand is elastic, will shifts in supply have a larger effect on equilibrium quantity or on price?
13. If demand is inelastic, will shifts in supply have a larger effect on equilibrium quantity or on price?
14. If supply is elastic, will shifts in demand have a larger effect on equilibrium quantity or on price?
15. If supply is inelastic, will shifts in demand have a larger effect on equilibrium quantity or on price?
16. Would you usually expect elasticity of demand or supply to be higher in the short run or in the long run? Why?
17. What is the formula for the income elasticity of demand?
18. What is the formula for the cross-price elasticity of demand?
19. What is the formula for the wage elasticity of labor supply?
20. What is the formula for elasticity of savings with respect to interest rates?

CHAPTER

8

Household Decision Making

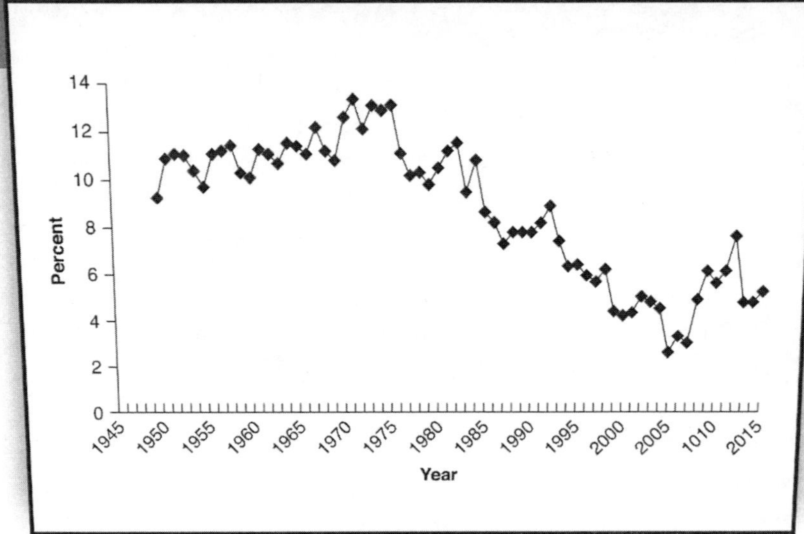

Chapter Outline

Everyone has their own personal tastes and preferences. The French say: "Chacun à son goût," or "Each to his own taste." An old Latin saying states, "De gustibus non est disputandum," or "There's no disputing about taste." But if people's decisions are based on their own tastes and personal preferences, then how can economists hope to analyze such decisions?

An economic explanation for why people make different choices begins with accepting the proverbial wisdom that tastes are a matter of personal preference. But economists also believe that the choices people make are influenced by their incomes, by the prices of goods, and by factors like climate or natural setting. This chapter will introduce the economic theory of how households make choices about what to buy, how much to work, and how much to save. The analysis in this chapter will build upon the three budget constraints introduced in Chapter 2: the consumption choice budget constraint, the labor-leisure budget constraint, and the intertemporal budget constraint. This chapter will also illustrate how economic theory offers a systematic way of thinking about the full range of possible events and responses, which can prevent jumping to possibly misguided conclusions about how households will respond to changes in prices or incomes.

Consumption Choices

Information on the consumption choices of Americans is available from the Consumer Expenditure Survey that is carried out by the U.S. Bureau of Labor Statistics. Exhibit 8-1 shows spending patterns for the average U.S. household. The first row shows income, and after taxes and personal savings are subtracted, it shows that the average U.S. household spent $53,495 on consumption. The table then breaks down consumption into various categories. The average U.S. household spent roughly one-third of its consumption on shelter and other housing expenses, another one-third of its income on food

EXHIBIT 8-1 U.S. Consumption Choices in 2014

Average income before taxes Average annual expenditure	$66,877 $53,495		
Major Categories of Spending			
Food at home	$3,971	Healthcare	$4,290
Food away from home	$2,787	Entertainment	$2.728
Housing	$17,798	Education	$1,236
Apparel and services	$1,786	Personal insurance and pensions	$5,726
Transportation	$9,073	All else: alcohol, tobacco, reading, personal care, cash contributions, miscellaneous	$3,548

and vehicle expenses, and the rest on other categories shown in the table. Of course, these patterns will vary for specific households by differing levels of family income, by the number and age of people in the household, by geography, and by preferences.

Total Utility and Diminishing Marginal Utility

To understand how a household makes its consumption choices, economists turn to the budget constraint model introduced in Chapter 2. That model uses a graph to illustrate the choice between two goods. The quantity of one good is measured on the horizontal axis and the quantity of the other good is measured on the vertical axis. The budget constraint line shows the various combinations of goods that it is possible to buy, given a certain level of income. For example, consider the situation of Jose, shown in Exhibit 8-2. Jose likes to collect T-shirts and watch movies. In the figure at the top of Exhibit 8-2, the quantity of T-shirts that Jose purchases is shown on the horizontal axis, while the quantity of movies that he attends is shown on the vertical axis. If Jose had unlimited income or goods were free, then he could consume without limit. But Jose must face a consumption choice budget constraint. Jose has a total of $56 to spend. The price of T-shirts is $14 and the price of movies is $7. Five specific choices along the budget constraint, combinations of T-shirts and movies, are shown on the graph and listed in the tables beneath the graph.

utility: The level of satisfaction or pleasure that people receive from their choices.

Jose wishes to choose the point that will provide him with the greatest **utility**, which is the term that economists use to describe a person's level of satisfaction or happiness. Let's begin with an assumption, which will be discussed in more detail later, that Jose can measure his own utility with a measurement called "utils." The first table in Exhibit 8-2 shows how Jose's utility is connected with his consumption of T-shirts or movies. The first column of the table shows the quantity of T-shirts consumed. The second column shows the total utility, or total amount of satisfaction, that Jose receives from consuming that number of T-shirts. The most common pattern of total utility, as shown here, is that consuming additional goods leads to greater total utility. The third column shows **marginal utility**, which is the additional utility provided by one additional unit of consumption. The most common pattern for marginal utility is **diminishing marginal utility**, which means that each marginal unit of a good consumed provides less of an addition to utility than the previous unit. For example, the first T-shirt Jose picks is his favorite. The fourth T-shirt is just to something to wear when all his other clothes are in the wash.

marginal utility: The additional utility provided by one additional unit of consumption.

diminishing marginal utility: The common pattern that each marginal unit of a good consumed provides less of an addition to utility than the previous unit.

The first table in Exhibit 8-2 also shows the quantity of movies that Jose could attend, his total utility from consuming each quantity of movies, and his marginal utility from attending each additional movie. Total utility follows the expected pattern: it increases as the quantity of movies rises. Marginal utility also follows the expected pattern: each additional movie brings a smaller gain in utility than the previous one. The first movie

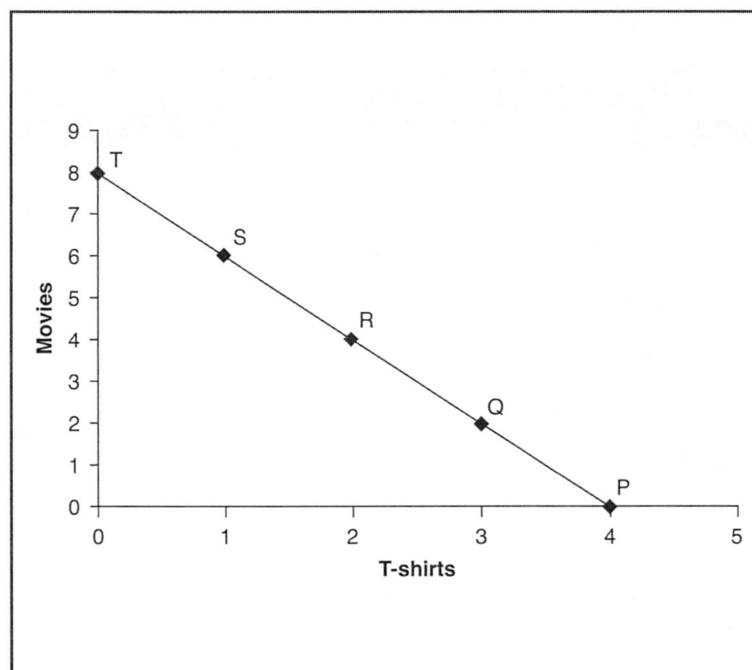

A Consumption Choice Budget Constraint

T-Shirts (Quantity)	Total Utility	Marginal Utility	Movies (Quantity)
1	24	24	1
2	46	22	2
3	66	20	3
4	84	18	4
5	100	16	5
6	114	14	6

Total and Marginal Utility

Point	T-Shirts	Movies	Total Utility
P	4	0	84 + 0 = 84
Q	3	2	66 + 31 = 97
R	2	4	46 + 58 = 104
S	1	6	24 + 81 = 105
T	0	8	0 + 100 = 100

EXHIBIT 8-2 A Choice between Consumption Goods

Jose has income of $56. Movies cost $7 and T-shirts cost $14. The points on the budget constraint show his possible choices. The first table shows total utility and marginal utility from consumption of T-shirts and movies. The typical pattern, illustrated here, is that total utility rises as the quantity consumed rises, but marginal utility falls as the quantity consumed rises. The second table shows total utility at each point along Jose's consumption choice budget set. The maximum level of utility occurs at choice S.

Jose attends is the one he wanted to see the most and thus provides him with the highest level of utility or satisfaction. The fifth movie he attends just to kill time.

Once Jose has defined in his own mind how much utility he will receive from consuming different quantities of T-shirts and movies, he is ready to make the choice that will give him the maximum amount of utility. The second table in Exhibit 8-2 looks at each point on the budget constraint , adds up Jose's total utility numbers for consuming T-shirts and movies, and calculates the total utility for each of Jose's possible choices. For Jose, the highest total utility for the possible combinations of goods occurs at point S, with a total utility of 105 from consuming 1 T-shirt and 6 movies.

Choosing with Marginal Utility

People are unlikely to carry around in their heads a mental picture of their total utility for every quantity consumed of every good. Instead, most people probably approach their utility-maximizing combination of choices in a step-by-step way. This step-by-step approach is based on looking at the trade-offs, measured in terms of marginal utility, of consuming less of one good and more of another.

For example, say that Jose starts off thinking about spending all his money on T-shirts and choosing point P in Exhibit 8-2. Jose chooses this starting point randomly; he has to start somewhere. Then Jose considers giving up the final T-shirt, the one that provides him the least marginal utility, and using the money he saves to buy two movies instead. Exhibit 8-3 tracks the step-by-step series of decisions Jose needs to make. The drop in marginal utility from giving up the fourth T-shirt is 18, but the gain in marginal utility from buying the first two movies is 31. So Jose clearly prefers point Q to point P. Now repeat this step-by-step process of decision-making with marginal utilities. Jose thinks about giving up the third T-shirt and thus surrendering marginal utility of 20, in exchange for purchasing two more movies that promise a combined marginal utility of 27. Jose

EXHIBIT 8-3 A Step-by-Step Approach to Maximizing Utility

Try	Which Has	Total Utility	Marginal Gain and Loss of Utility, Compared with Previous Choice	Conclusion
Choice 1: P	4 T-shirts and 0 movies	84 from 4 T-shirts + 0 from 0 movies = 84	—	—
Choice 2: Q	3 T-shirts and 2 movies	66 from 3 T-shirts + 31 from 2 movies = 97	Loss of 18 from 1 fewer T-shirt, but gain of 31 from 2 more movies, for a marginal utility gain of 14	Q is preferred over P
Choice 3: R	2 T-shirts and 4 movies	46 from 2 T-shirts + 58 from 4 movies = 104	Loss of 20 from 1 fewer T-shirt, but gain of 27 from two more movies for a marginal utility gain of 7	R is preferred over Q
Choice 4: S	1 T-shirt and 6 movies	24 from 1 T-shirt + 81 from 6 movies = 105	Loss of 22 from 1 fewer T-shirt, but gain of 23 from two more movies, for a marginal utility gain of 1	S is preferred over R
Choice 5: T	0 T-shirts and 8 movies	0 from 0 T-shirts + 100 from 8 movies = 100	Loss of 24 from 1 fewer T-shirt, but gain of 19 from two more movies, for a marginal utility loss of 5	S is preferred over T

prefers point R to point Q. What if Jose thinks about going beyond R to point S? Giving up the second T-shirt means a marginal utility loss of 22, and the marginal utility gain from the fifth and sixth movies would combine to make a marginal utility gain of 23, so Jose prefers point S to R.

However, if Jose seeks to go beyond point S to point T, he finds that the loss of marginal utility from giving up the first T-shirt is 24, while the marginal utility gain from the last two movies is only a total of 19. Through these stages of thinking about marginal trade-offs, Jose again concludes that S, with 1 T-shirt and 6 movies, is the choice that will provide him with the highest level of total utility. This step-by-step approach will reach the same conclusion regardless of Jose's original starting point.

A Rule for Maximizing Utility

This process of decision making suggests a rule to follow when maximizing utility. Because the price of T-shirts is twice as high in this example, the marginal T-shirt needs to provide twice the marginal utility of a marginal movie. If the marginal T-shirt provides less than twice the marginal utility of the marginal movie, then the marginal T-shirt isn't providing enough utility to justify its relative price and Jose should attend more movies. If the marginal T-shirt provides more than twice the marginal utility of the marginal movie, then Jose should buy more T-shirts. Notice that at Jose's optimal choice of point S, the marginal utility from the second T-shirt, of 22, is exactly twice the marginal utility of the sixth movie, which is 11. At this choice, the marginal utility per dollar is the same for both goods, which is the tell-tale signal that Jose has found the point with highest total utility.

This argument can be written as a general rule: the utility-maximizing choice between consumption goods occurs where the ratio of the prices of the two goods is equal to the ratio of the marginal utilities. When the price of good 1 is divided by the price of good 2, at the utility-maximizing point this will equal the marginal utility of good 1 divided by the marginal utility of good 2. This rule can be written in algebraic form:

$$\frac{P_1}{P_2} = \frac{MU_1}{MU_2}$$

Along the budget constraint, the prices of the two goods remain the same, so the ratio of the prices doesn't change. However, the marginal utility of the two goods changes with the quantities consumed. At the optimal choice of 1 T-shirt and 6 movies, point S, the price ratio of 2:1 matches the marginal utility trade-off of 22:11. A sensible economizer will only pay twice as much for something if, in the marginal comparison, the item confers twice as much utility.

Measuring Utility with Numbers

This discussion of utility started off with an assumption that it is possible to place numerical values on utility, an assumption that may smell questionable. You can buy a thermometer for measuring temperature at a hardware store, but what store sells a "utilimometer" for measuring utility? However, while measuring utility with numbers is a convenient assumption to clarify the explanation, the key assumption is not that utility can be measured by an outside party, but only that individuals can decide what they prefer.

To understand this point, think back to the step-by-step process of finding the choice with highest total utility by comparing the marginal utility that is gained and lost from different choices along the budget constraint. As Jose compares each choice along his budget constraint to the previous choice, what matters is not the specific numbers that he places on his utility—or whether he uses any numbers at all—but only that he personally can identify which choices he prefers. In this way, the step-by-step process of choosing the highest level of utility resembles rather closely how many people make consumption decisions. We think about what will make us the happiest; we think about what things cost; we think about buying a little more of one item and giving up a little of something else; we choose what provides us with the greatest level of satisfaction. The vocabulary of comparing the points along a budget constraint and total and marginal utility is just a set of tools for discussing this everyday process in a clear and specific manner. It's welcome news that specific utility numbers aren't central to the argument, because a good utilimometer is hard to find.

How Changes in Income and Prices Affect Consumption Choices

Just as utility and marginal utility can be used to discuss making consumer choices along a budget constraint, these ideas can also be used to think about how consumer choices change when the budget constraint shifts in response to changes in income or price. Indeed, because the budget constraint framework can be used to analyze how quantities demanded change because of price movements, the budget constraint model can illustrate the underlying logic behind demand curves.

How Changes in Income Affect Consumer Choices

Let's begin with a concrete example illustrating how changes in income level affect consumer choices. Exhibit 8-4 shows a budget constraint that represents Kimberly's choice between concert tickets at $50 each and getting away overnight to a bed-and breakfast for $200 per night. Kimberly has $1,000 per year to spend between these two choices. After thinking about her personal utility and marginal utility and applying the decision rule that the ratio of the prices should be equal to the ratio of marginal utilities, Kimberly chooses point M, with 8 concerts and 3 overnight getaways as her utility-maximizing choice.

Now assume that the income that Kimberly has to spend on these two items rises to $2,000 per year, causing her budget constraint to shift to the right. How does this rise in income alter Kimberly's utility-maximizing choice? Kimberly will again consider the utility and marginal utility that she receives from concert tickets and overnight getaways and seek her utility-maximizing choice on the new budget line. But how will her new choice relate to her original choice?

The possible choices along the new budget constraint can be divided into three groups, which are divided up by the dashed horizontal and vertical lines that pass through the original choice M in the figure. All choices on the upper left of the new budget constraint that are to the left of the vertical dashed line, like choice P with 2 overnight stays and 32 concerts, involve less of the good on the horizontal axis but much more of the good on

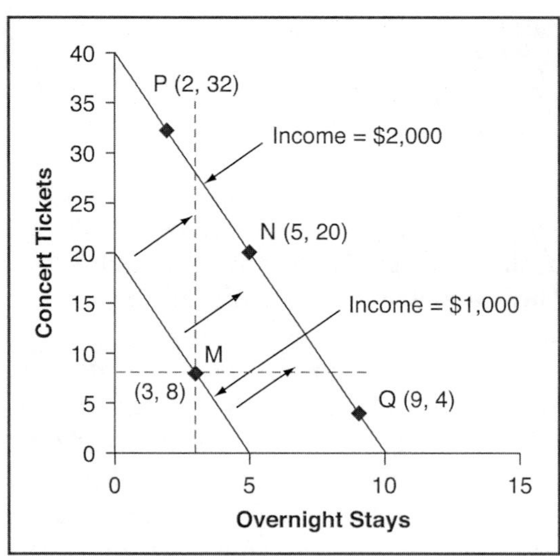

EXHIBIT 8-4 How a Change in Income Affects Consumption Choices

The utility-maximizing choice on the original budget constraint is M. The dashed horizontal and vertical lines extending through point M allow you to see at a glance whether the quantity consumed of goods on the new budget constraint is higher or lower than on the original budget constraint. On the new budget constraint, a choice like N will be made if both goods are normal goods. If overnight stays are an inferior good, a choice like P will be made. If concert tickets are an inferior good, a choice like Q will be made.

the vertical axis. All choices to the right of the vertical dashed line and above the horizontal dashed line—like choice N with 5 overnight getaways and 20 concert tickets—have more consumption of both goods. Finally, all choices that are to the right of the vertical dashed line but below the horizontal dashed line, like choice Q with 4 concert tickets and 9 overnight getaways, involve less of the good on the vertical axis but much more of the good on the horizontal axis.

All of these possibilities are theoretically possible, depending on Kimberly's personal preferences as expressed through the total and marginal utility she would receive from consuming these two goods. When income rises, the most common reaction is to purchase more of both goods like choice N, which is to the upper right relative to Kimberly's original choice M, although exactly how much more of each good will vary according to personal taste. Conversely, when income falls, the most typical reaction is to purchase less of both goods. As defined earlier in Chapter 4 and again in Chapter 7, goods and services are called "normal goods" when a rise in income leads to a rise in the quantity consumed of that good and a fall in income leads to a fall in quantity consumed.

However, depending on Kimberly's preferences, a rise in income could cause consumption of one good to increase while consumption of the other good declines. For example, a choice like P means that a rise in income caused her quantity consumed of overnight stays to decline, while a choice like Q would mean that a rise in income caused her quantity of concerts to decline. Goods where the quantity demanded declines as income rises (or conversely, where the quantity demanded rises as income falls) are called "inferior goods." An inferior good occurs when people trim back on a good as income rises because they can now afford the more expensive choices that they prefer. For example, a higher-income household might eat less hamburger or be less likely to buy a used car, and instead eat more steak and buy a new car.

How Price Changes Affect Consumer Choices

For analyzing the possible effect of a change in price on consumption, let's again use a concrete example. Exhibit 8-5 represents the consumer choice of Ichiro, who chooses between purchasing baseball bats and cameras. A price increase for baseball bats, the good on the horizontal axis, causes the budget constraint to rotate inward, as if on a hinge

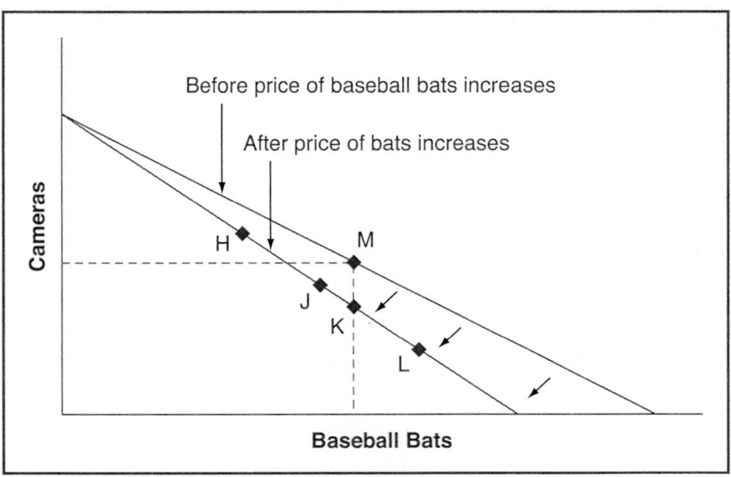

EXHIBIT 8-5 How a Change in Price Affects Consumption Choices

The original utility-maximizing choice is M. When the price rises, the budget constraint shifts to the left. The dashed lines make it possible to see at a glance whether the new consumption choice involves less of both goods, or less of one good and more of the other. The new possible choices would be fewer baseball bats and more cameras, like point H, or less of both goods, as at point J. Choice K would mean that the higher price of bats led to exactly the same quantity of bats being consumed, but fewer cameras. Choices like L are theoretically possible but often ruled out as highly unlikely in the real world because they would mean that a higher price for baseball bats means a greater quantity consumed of baseball bats.

from the vertical axis. As in the previous section, the point labeled M represents the originally preferred point on the original budget constraint, which Ichiro has chosen after contemplating his personal utility and marginal utility and the trade-offs involved along the budget constraint. In this example, the units along the horizontal and vertical axis are not numbered, so the discussion will focus on whether more or less of certain goods will be consumed, not on numerical amounts.

After the price increase, Ichiro will make a choice along the new budget constraint. Again, his choices along the new budget constraint can be divided into three segments by the dashed vertical and horizontal lines. In the upper left portion of the new budget constraint, at a choice like H, Ichiro consumes more cameras and fewer bats; in the central portion of the new budget constraint, at a choice like J, he consumes less of both goods; at the right-hand end, at a choice like L, he consumes more bats but fewer cameras.

The typical response to higher prices is that a person chooses to consume less of the product with the higher price. This effect occurs for two reasons, which occur simultaneously. The **substitution effect** is that when a price changes, consumers have an incentive to consume less of the good with a relatively higher price and more of the good with a relatively lower price. The **income effect** refers not to a change in actual income, but to a price change that affects the buying power of existing income. In this example, a higher price means that the buying power of income has been reduced (even though actual income has not changed), which lead to buying less of the good. Thus, the higher price for baseball bats would cause Ichiro to consume a lower quantity of bats because the substitution effect will encourage him to substitute consumption away from the relatively higher-priced bats and the income effect of a higher price reduces his buying power and also encourages reduced consumption of bats.

How much will a higher price for bats cause Ichiro's consumption of bats to fall? Exhibit 8-5 suggests a range of possibilities. Ichiro might react to a higher price for baseball bats by purchasing the same quantity of bats, but cutting his consumption of cameras. This choice is the point K on the new budget constraint straight below the original choice M. Alternatively, Ichiro might react by dramatically reducing his purchases of bats, and instead buying more cameras, at a choice that represents buying fewer of both goods. The key conclusion here is that it would be imprudent to assume that a change in

substitution effect: When a price changes, consumers have an incentive to consume less of the good with a relatively higher price and more of the good with a relatively lower price; always happens simultaneously with an income effect.

income effect: A change in price affects the buying power of income, with a higher price meaning that the buying power of income has been reduced, so that there is usually (with normal goods) an incentive to buy less of both goods, and a lower price meaning that the buying power of income has been increased, so that there is usually an incentive to buy more of both goods; always happens simultaneously with a substitution effect.

the price of baseball bats will only or primarily affect the good whose price is changed, while the quantity consumed of other goods remains the same. A change in the price of one good can also have a range of effects, either positive or negative, on the quantity consumed of other goods.

What about a choice like point L in the lower right of the new budget constraint? In this case, Ichiro responds to a higher price for baseball bats by purchasing more bats. A good where a higher price leads to a higher quantity demanded for a good (or a lower price leads to a lower quantity demanded for a good) is a theoretical possibility, discovered more than a century ago, called a **Giffen good**. The demand curve for a Giffen good would slope up, rather than down! However, Giffen goods should be considered a theoretical possibility that is extremely rare in actual markets, rather than a likely event. A famous economist named Francis Ysidro Edgeworth (1845–1926) summed up the situation regarding Giffen goods in this way in 1914: "Only a very clever man would discover that exceptional case; only a very foolish man would take it as the basis of a rule for general practice."

Giffen good: The theoretical but unrealistic possibility that a higher price for a good could lead to a higher quantity demanded (or a lower price leads to a lesser quantity demanded).

The Logical Foundations of Demand Curves

Changes in the price of a good lead the budget constraint to shift. A shift in the budget constraint means that when individuals are seeking their highest utility, the quantity that is demanded of that good will change. In this way, the logical foundations of demand curves—which show a connection between prices and quantity demanded—are based on the underlying idea of individuals seeking utility. Exhibit 8-6*a* shows a budget constraint with a choice between housing and "everything else." (Putting "everything else" on the vertical axis can be a useful approach in some cases, especially when the focus of the analysis is on one particular good.) The preferred choice on the original budget constraint that provides the highest possible utility is labeled M_0. The other three budget constraints represent successively higher prices for housing of P_1, P_2, and P_3. As the budget constraint shifts in, and in, and in again, the utility-maximizing choices are labeled M_1, M_2, and M_3, and the quantity demanded of housing falls from Q_0 to Q_1 to Q_2 to Q_3.

Thus, as the price of housing rises, the budget constraint shifts to the left, and the quantity consumed of housing falls. This relationship—the price of housing rising from P_0 to P_1 to P_2 to P_3, while the quantity of housing demanded falls from Q_0 to Q_1 to Q_2 to Q_3—is graphed on the demand curve in Exhibit 8-6*b*. Indeed, the vertical dashed lines stretching between the top and bottom of Exhibit 8-6 show that the quantity of housing demanded at each point is the same in both *(a)* and *(b)*. Thus, the shape of a demand curve is ultimately determined by the underlying choices about maximizing utility subject to a budget constraint.

Applications in Business and Government

The budget constraint framework for making utility-maximizing choices offers a reminder that people can react to a change in price or income in a range of different ways. For example, in the winter months of 2014, costs for heating homes skyrocketed in many parts of the country. Many people reacted by reducing the quantity demanded of energy; for example, by turning down the thermostats in their homes by a few degrees and wearing a heavier sweater inside. Even so, many home heating bills rose as much as $200 dollars per month or even more, so people adjusted their consumption in other ways, too. Each household cut back on what it valued least on the margin; for some it might have been some dinners out, or a vacation, or postponing buying a new refrigerator or a new car. Indeed, sharply higher energy prices can have effects beyond the energy market, leading to a widespread reduction in purchasing throughout the rest of the economy.

A similar issue arises when the government imposes taxes on certain products, like it does on gasoline, cigarettes, and alcohol. Say that a tax on alcohol leads to a higher price at the liquor store, the higher price of alcohol causes the budget constraint to pivot left, and consumption of alcoholic beverages is likely to decrease. However, people may also

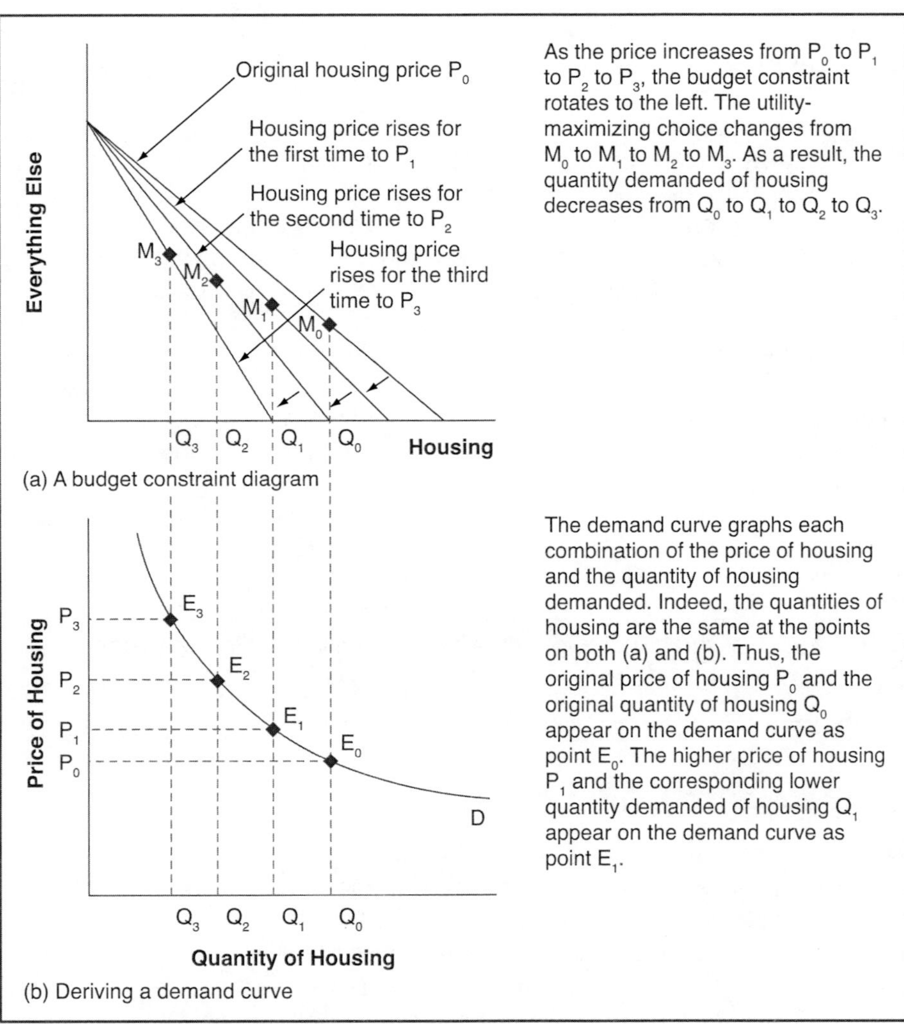

EXHIBIT 8-6 The Foundations of a Demand Curve: An Example of Housing

react to the higher price of alcoholic beverages by cutting back on other purchases; for example, they might cut back on snacks like chicken wings and nachos at restaurants. It would be unwise to assume that the alcoholic beverage industry is the only industry affected by the tax on alcoholic beverages.

As a final example of the range of possible reactions, consider a proposal that came up in the aftermath of the terrorist airplane hijackings on September 11, 2001. Congress believed that it was necessary to provide some financial assistance to airlines. One possible method of providing that assistance was in the form of coupons for airline tickets that would be distributed to all Americans, thus providing assistance to ordinary Americans as well as to the airline companies. But what if most Americans spent their coupons on airplane trips they would have taken anyway, and then use the money they saved to purchase something else? Since airline coupons free up income to spend in other ways, they are very similar to receiving additional income in the form of cash. The result could have been that air travel coupons would not provide any special assistance to the airline industry—at least no more assistance than a distribution of government checks to individuals would have provided. Of course, this argument doesn't prove that the $15 billion package of government assistance to airlines passed in October 2001 was a sensible policy. But at least handing the money directly to the airlines made sure that the airlines actually received the money, rather than opening up the possibility that the main effect of an attempt to assist the airlines would be felt in other markets.

The budget constraint framework serves as a constant reminder to think about the full range of effects that can arise from changes in income or price, not just effects on the one product that might seem most immediately affected.

Preferences Inside the Household?

In the mid-1970s, the United Kingdom made an interesting policy change in its "child allowance" policy. This program provides a fixed amount of money per child to every family, regardless of family income. Traditionally, the child allowance had been distributed to families by withholding less in taxes from the paycheck of the family wage earner—typically the father in this time period. The new policy instead provided the child allowance as a cash payment to the mother. As a result of this change, households have the same level of income and face the same prices in the market, but the money is more likely to be in the purse of the mother than in the wallet of the father.

Should this change in policy alter household consumption patterns? Basic models of consumption decisions, of the sort examined in this chapter, assume that it doesn't matter whether the mother or the father receives the money, because both parents seek to maximize the utility of the family as a whole. In effect, this model assumes that everyone in the family has the same preferences.

In reality, the share of income controlled by the father or the mother does affect what the household consumes. When the mother controls a larger share of family income, a number of studies in the United Kingdom and in a wide variety of other countries have found that the family tends to spend more on restaurant meals, child care, and women's clothing, and less on alcohol and tobacco. As the mother controls a larger share of household resources, children's health improves, too. These findings suggest that when providing assistance to poor families, in high-income countries and low-income countries alike, the monetary amount of assistance isn't all that matters: it also matters which member of the family actually receives the money.

Labor-Leisure Choices

The decision-making process of a utility-maximizing household applies to decisions about what quantity of hours to work in much the same way that it applies to purchases of goods and services. Choices made along the labor-leisure budget constraint, as wages shift, provide the logical underpinning for the labor supply curve. The discussion also offers some insights about the range of possible reactions when people receive higher wages, and specifically about the claim that if people are paid higher wages, they will work a greater quantity of hours.

U.S. workers averaged 38.5 hours per week on the job in 2012. This average includes part-timers; for full-time workers only, the average was 42.5 hours per week. Exhibit 8-7 shows that more than half of all workers are on the job 35–48 hours per week of work, but significant proportions work less or more than this amount. Exhibit 8-8 breaks down the average compensation received by private industry workers, including wages and benefits. Wages and salaries are about three-quarters of total compensation received by workers; the rest is in the form of health insurance, vacation pay, and other benefits. The compensation received by workers differs for many reasons, including experience, education, skill, talent, membership in a labor union, and the presence of discrimination against certain groups in the labor market. Issues surrounding the inequality of incomes in a market-oriented economy are explored in Chapters 16 and 17.

EXHIBIT 8-7 Persons at Work, by Average Hours Worked per Week in 2015

Hours Worked per Week	Number of Workers	Percentage of Workforce
1–14 hours	6.6 million	4.6%
15–34 hours	29.5 million	20.5%
35–40 hours	71.6 million	49.8%
41–48 hours	12.5 million	8.7%
49–59 hours	14.1 million	9.8%
60+ hours	9.4 million	6.6%

EXHIBIT 8-8 Breakdown of Average Compensation for Private Industry Workers: Wages and Benefits in 2015

Total compensation per hour	**$38.11**
Wages and salaries	25.65
Vacation and holiday pay	2.27
Sick leave and other leave	0.56
Bonuses and premium pay	1.84
Employee insurance (mainly health)	3.20
Company retirement plans	1.62
Employer payments to Social Security	1.65
Unemployment and worker's compensation insurance	0.86
Other benefits (Medicare)	0.44

The Labor-Leisure Budget Constraint

How do workers make their decisions about the quantity of hours to work? Again, let's proceed with a concrete example. The economic logic is precisely the same as in the case of a consumption choice budget constraint, but the labels are different on a labor-leisure budget constraint.

Vivian has 70 hours per week that she could devote either to working or leisure, and her wage is $10/hour. The lower budget constraint in Exhibit 8-9 shows Vivian's possible choices at this wage level. As discussed in Chapter 2, the horizontal axis of this diagram measures both leisure and labor, by showing how Vivian's time is divided between leisure and labor. Hours of leisure are measured from left to right on the horizontal axis, while hours of labor are measured from right to left. Vivian will compare choices along this budget constraint, ranging from 70 hours of leisure and no income at point S to zero hours of leisure and $700 of income at point L. She will choose the point that provides her with the

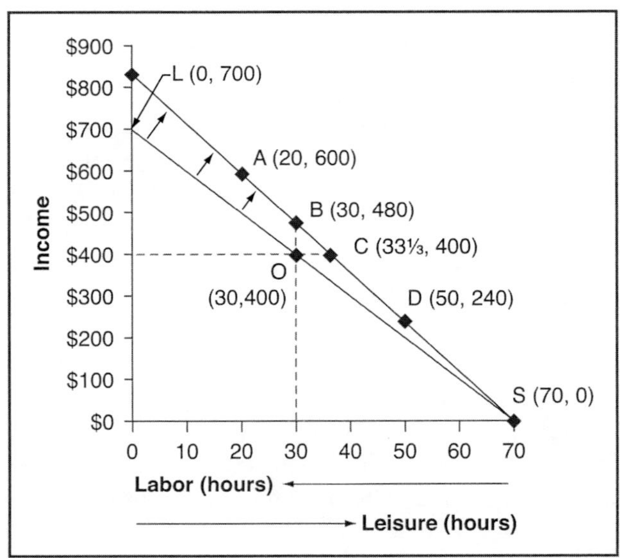

EXHIBIT 8-9 How a Rise in Wages Alters the Utility-Maximizing Choice

Vivian's original choice is point O on the lower opportunity set. A rise in her wage causes her opportunity set to swing upward. In response to the increase in wages, Vivian can make a range of different choices: a choice like D, which involves less work; and a choice like B, which involves the same amount of work but more income; or a choice like A, which involves more work and considerably more income. Vivian's personal preferences will determine which choice she makes.

highest total utility. For this example, let's assume that Vivian's utility-maximizing choice occurs at O, with 30 hours of leisure, 40 hours of work, and $400 in weekly income.

For Vivian to discover the labor-leisure choice that will maximize her utility, she doesn't have to place numerical values on the total and marginal utility that she would receive from every level of income and leisure. All that really matters is that Vivian can compare, in her own mind, whether she would prefer more leisure or more income, given the trade-offs she faces. If Vivian can say to herself: "You know, I'd really rather work a little less and have more leisure, even if it means less income," or "You know, I'd be willing to work more hours to make some extra income," then as she gradually moves in the direction of her preferences, she will seek out the utility-maximizing choice on her labor-leisure budget constraint.

Now imagine that Vivian's wage level increases to $12/hour. A higher wage will mean a new budget constraint that tilts up more steeply; conversely, a lower wage would have led to a new budget constraint that was flatter. How will a change in the wage and the corresponding shift in the budget constraint affect Vivian's decisions about how many hours to work? Vivian's choices of quantity of hours to work and income along her new budget constraint can be divided into several categories, using the dashed horizontal and vertical lines in Exhibit 8-9 that go through her original choice O. One set of choices in the upper-left portion of the new budget constraint involve more hours of work (i.e., less leisure) and more income, at a point like A with 20 hours of leisure, 50 hours of work, and $600 of income (i.e., 50 hours of work multiplied by the new wage of $12 per hour). A second choice would be to work exactly the same 40 hours and to take the benefits of the higher wage in the form of income that would now be $480, at choice B. A third choice would involve more leisure and the same income at point C (i.e., 33-1/3 hours of work multiplied by the new wage of $12 per hour equals $400 of total income). A fourth choice would involve less income and much more leisure at a point like D, with a choice like 50 hours of leisure, 20 hours of work, and $240 in income.

In effect, Vivian can choose whether to receive the benefits of her wage increase in the form of more income, or more leisure, or some mixture of these two. With this range of possibilities, it would be unwise to assume that Vivian (or anyone else) will necessarily react to a wage increase by working substantially more hours. Maybe they will; maybe they won't.

Applications of Utility Maximizing with the Labor-Leisure Budget Constraint

The theoretical insight that higher wages will sometimes cause an increase in hours worked, sometimes cause hours worked not to change by much, and sometimes cause hours worked to decline has led economists to consider labor supply curves that look like the one in Exhibit 8-10. The bottom-left portion of the labor supply curve slopes upward, which reflects the situation of a person who reacts to a higher wage by supplying a greater quantity of labor. The middle, close-to-vertical portion of the labor supply curve reflects the situation of a person who reacts to a higher wage by supplying about the same quantity of labor. The very top portion of the labor supply curve is called a **backward-bending supply curve** for labor, which is the situation of high-wage people who earn so much that they respond to a still-higher wage by working fewer hours.

backward-bending supply curve for labor: The situation when high-wage people can earn so much that they respond to a still-higher wage by working fewer hours.

These different responses to a rise in wages—more hours worked, the same hours worked, or fewer hours worked—are patterns exhibited by different groups of workers in the U.S. economy. Many full-time workers have jobs where the number of hours is held relatively fixed, partly by their own choice and partly by their employer's practices. These workers don't change their hours worked by much as wages rise or fall, so their supply curve of labor is inelastic. However, part-time workers and younger workers tend to be more flexible in their hours and more ready to increase hours worked when wages are high or cut back when wages fall.

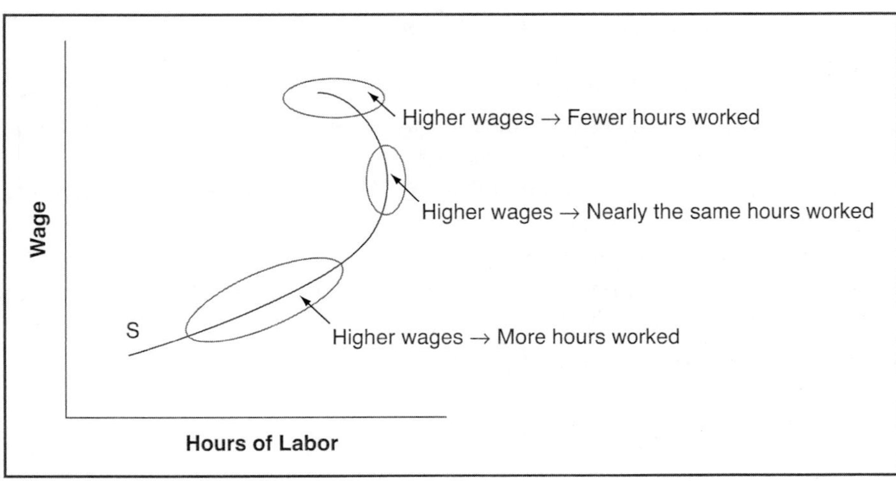

EXHIBIT 8-10 A Backward-Bending Supply Curve of Labor

The bottom upward-sloping portion of the labor supply curve shows that as wages increase over this range, the quantity of hours worked also increases. The middle, nearly vertical portion of the labor supply curve shows that as wages increase over this range, the quantity of hours worked changes very little. The backward-bending portion of the labor supply curve at the top shows that as wages increase over this range, the quantity of hours worked actually decreases. All three of these possibilities can be derived from how a change in wages causes movement in the labor-leisure budget constraint, and thus different choices by individuals.

The backward-bending supply curve for labor, when workers react to higher wages by working fewer hours and having more income, is not observed often in the short run. However, some well-paid professionals, like dentists or accountants, may react to higher wages by choosing to limit the number of hours, perhaps by taking especially long vacations or taking every other Friday off. Over a long-term perspective, the backward-bending supply curve for labor is common. Over the last century, Americans have reacted to gradually rising wages by working fewer hours; for example, the length of the average workweek has fallen from about 60 hours per week back in 1900 to the present average of less than 40 hours per week.

Is America a Nation of Workaholics?

Americans work a lot. The table shows average hours worked per year in the United States, Canada, Japan, and several European countries, with most of the data from 2014. To gain some perspective on these numbers, someone who works 40 hours per week for 50 weeks per year, with 2 weeks off, would work 2,000 hours per year. The gap in hours worked is a little astonishing; the 250- to 300-hour gap between how much Americans work and how much, say, the French work amounts to roughly 7–8 weeks less of work per year! Economists who study these international patterns debate the extent to which average Americans and Japanese have a preference for working more than, say, French or German workers, or whether French and German workers and employers face particular kinds of taxes and regulations that lead to fewer hours worked.

Average Annual Hours Worked per Employed Person	
United States	1789
Japan	1729
Canada	1704
Spain	1689
Sweden	1609
United Kingdom	1677
France	1473
Germany	1371

Recognizing that workers have a range of possible reactions to a change in wages casts some fresh insight on a perennial political debate: the claim that a reduction in income taxes—which would, in effect, allow people to earn more per hour—will encourage people to work more. The leisure-income budget set points out that this connection will not hold true for all workers. Some people, especially part-timers, probably will react to higher wages by working more. Many will work the same number of hours. Some people, especially those whose incomes are already high, may react to the tax cut by working fewer hours. Of course, cutting income taxes may be a good or a bad idea for a variety of reasons, not just because of its impact on work incentives, but the specific claim that tax cuts will lead people to work more hours is only likely to hold for specific groups of workers and will depend on how and for whom taxes are cut.

Intertemporal Choices in Financial Capital Markets

Rates of saving in America have never been especially high, but they seem to have dipped even lower in recent years, with some especially low levels during the Great Recession years from 2007–2009, as shown in Exhibit 8-11. A decision about how much to save can be represented on the intertemporal budget constraint that was introduced in Chapter 2. Household decisions about the quantity of financial savings show the same underlying pattern of logic as the consumption choice decision and the labor-leisure decision.

The discussion of financial savings here will not focus on the specific financial investment choices, like bank accounts, stocks, bonds, mutual funds, or owning a house or gold coins. The characteristics of these specific financial investments, along with the risks and trade-offs they pose, will be detailed in Chapter 19. Here, the focus is on how a household determines how much to consume in the present and how much to save in the present and spend in the future, given the expected rate of return (or interest rate), and how the quantity of savings alters when the rate of return changes.

Using Marginal Utility to Make Intertemporal Choices

Savings behavior varies considerably across households. One factor is that households with higher incomes tend to save a larger percentage of their income. This pattern makes intuitive sense; a well-to-do family has the flexibility in its budget to save 20–25% of income, while a poor family struggling to keep food on the table will find it harder to put money aside.

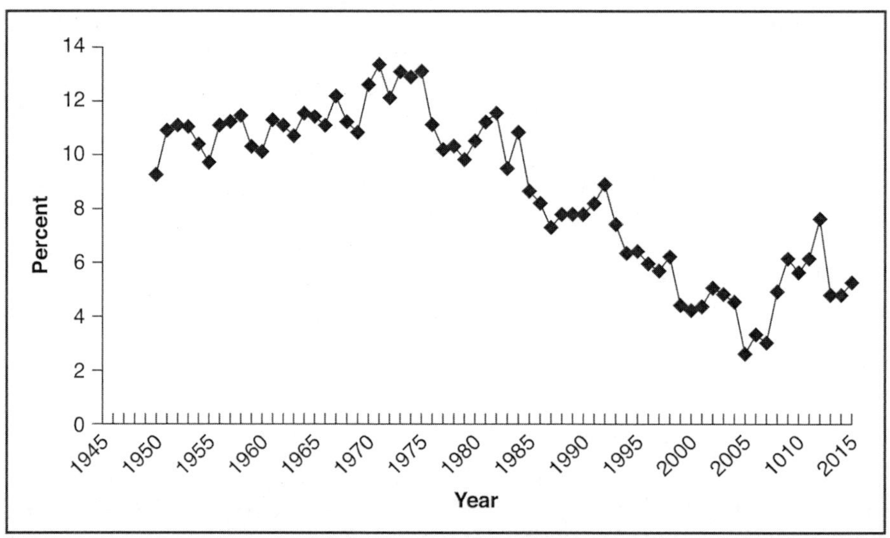

EXHIBIT 8-11 Personal Savings as a Percentage of Personal Income

Personal savings were about 7–11% of personal income for most of the years from the late 1950s up to the early 1990s. Since then, the rate of personal savings has fallen substantially.

A second key factor is linked to age. The **life-cycle theory of savings** points out a common pattern that many people save little or borrow heavily early in life, so that they can pay for a college education and buy a first home; save more in the middle of life, to pay off college and home loans and to prepare for retirement; and then draw upon their accumulated savings later in life during retirement.

life-cycle theory of savings: The common pattern that many people save little or borrow heavily early in life, save more in the middle of life, and then draw upon their accumulated savings later in life.

A third factor that causes personal savings to vary is personal preference. Some people may prefer to consume more now and let the future look after itself. Others may wish to enjoy a lavish retirement, complete with expensive vacations, or to pile up money that they can pass along to their grandchildren. There are savers and spendthrifts among the young, middle-aged, and old, and among those with high, middle, and low income levels.

Yelberton is a young man starting off at his first job. He thinks of the "present" as his working life and the "future" as after retirement. Yelberton's plan is to save money during the time period ages 30–55, retire at age 60, and then live off his retirement money during the time period from ages 60–85. On average, therefore, he will be saving for 30 years. If the rate of return that he can receive is 6% per year, then $1 saved in the present would build up to $5.74 after 30 years (using the formula for compound interest, $\$1(1{+}.06)^{30} =$ $5.74). Say that Yelberton will earn $1,000,000 over the 25 years from age 30 to age 55 (this amount is an annual salary of $40,000 multiplied by 25 years). Thus, the question for Yelberton is what share of those lifetime earnings to consume during his working life and how much to put aside until retirement. This example is obviously built on simplifying assumptions, but it does convey the basic life-cycle choice of saving during working life for future consumption after retirement.

Exhibit 8-12 shows Yelberton's intertemporal budget constraint. Yelberton's choice involves comparing the utility of present consumption during his working life and future consumption after he retires. The rate of return that determines the slope of the intertemporal budget line between present consumption and future consumption in this example is the annual interest rate compounded over 30 years, not just one year. Thus, in the lower budget constraint line on the exhibit, future consumption in this table grows by increments of $574,000 because each time $100,000 is saved in the present, it compounds to $574,000 after 30 years at a 6% interest rate. If some of the numbers on the future consumption axis look bizarrely large, remember that this occurs because of the power of compound interest over substantial periods of time and because the figure is grouping together all of Yelberton's savings for retirement over his lifetime.

Yelberton will compare the different choices along the budget constraint and choose the one that provides him with the highest utility. For example, he will compare the utility he would receive from a choice like point A, with consumption of $1 million in the present, zero savings, and zero future consumption; point B, with present consumption of $800,000, savings of $200,000, and future consumption of $1,148,000; point C, with present consumption of $600,000, savings of $400,000, and future consumption of $2,296,000; or even choice D, with present consumption of zero, savings of $1,000,000, and future consumption of $5,740,000. Yelberton will also ask himself questions like: "Would I prefer to consume a little less in the present, save more, and have more future consumption?" or "Would I prefer to consume a little more in the present, save less, and have less future consumption?" In this way, by considering marginal changes toward more or less consumption, he can seek out the choice that will provide him with the highest level of utility. Let's say that Yelberton's preferred choice is B.

Imagine that Yelberton's annual rate of return rises from 6% to 9%. In this case, each time he saves $100,000 in the present, it will be worth $1,327,000 30 years from now (using the formula for compound interest that $100,000 (1 + .09)30 = $1,327,000). A change in the rate of return alters the slope of the intertemporal budget constraint: a higher rate of return or interest rate will cause the budget line to pivot upwards, while a lower rate of return will cause it to swing downwards. If Yelberton were to consume nothing in the present and save all $1,000,000, with a 9% rate of return, his future consumption would be $13,270,000, as shown on Exhibit 8-12.

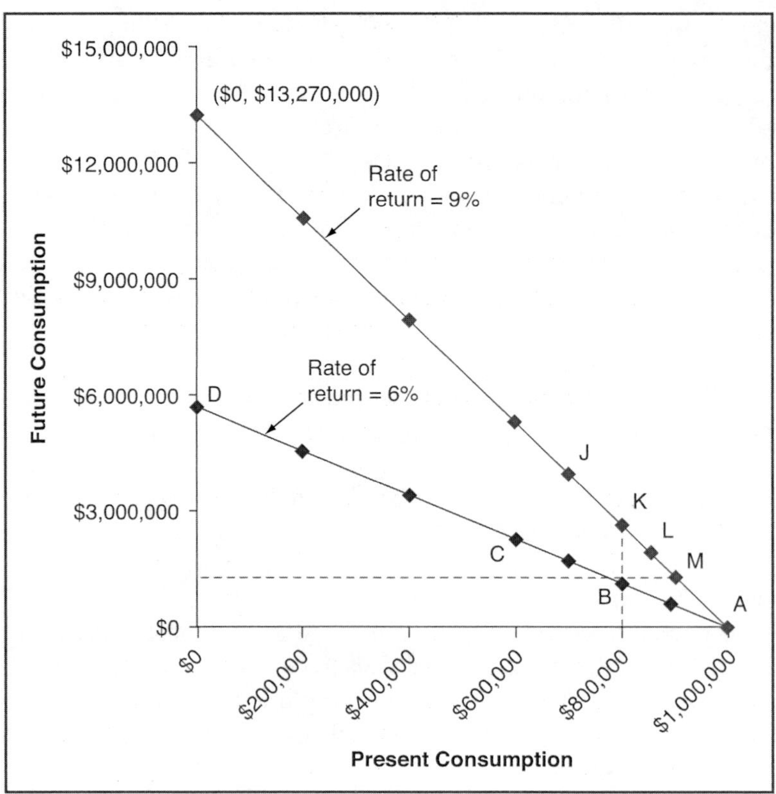

EXHIBIT 8-12 Yelberton's Choice: The Intertemporal Budget Set

Yelberton will make a choice between present and future consumption. With an annual rate of return of 6%, he decides that his utility will be highest at point B, which represents a choice of $800,000 in present consumption and $1,148,000 in future consumption. When the annual rate of return rises to 9%, the intertemporal budget constraint pivots up. Yelberton could choose to take the gains from this higher rate of return in several forms: more present saving and much higher future consumption (J), the same present saving and higher future consumption (K), more present consumption and more future consumption (L), or more present consumption and the same future consumption (M).

As the rate of return rises, Yelberton considers a range of choices on the new intertemporal budget constraint. The dashed vertical and horizontal lines running through the original choice B help to illustrate his range of options. One choice is to reduce present consumption (i.e., to save more) and to have considerably higher future consumption at a point like J above and to the left of his original choice B. A second choice would be to keep the level of present consumption and savings the same and to receive the benefits of the higher rate of return entirely in the form of higher future consumption, which would be choice K. A third choice would be that Yelberton could have both more present consumption—that is, less savings—but still have higher future consumption because of the higher interest rate, which would be a choice like L, above and to the right of his original choice B. Thus, the higher rate of return might cause Yelberton to save more, or less, or the same amount, depending on his own preferences. A fourth choice would be that Yelberton could react to the higher rate of return by increasing his current consumption and leaving his future consumption unchanged, as at point M directly to the right of his original choice B. The actual choice of what quantity to save and how saving will respond to changes in the rate of return will vary from person to person, according to the choice that will maximize each person's utility.

Applications of the Model of Intertemporal Choice

The theoretical model of the intertemporal budget constraint suggests that when the rate of return rises, the quantity of savings may rise, fall, or remain the same, depending on

America's Low Saving Rates

By international standards, Americans don't save a high proportion of their income. The rate of gross national saving includes saving by individuals, businesses, and government. By this measure, U.S. national savings amount to 16% of the size of the U.S. GDP, which measures the size of the U.S. economy. The comparable world average rate of savings is 22%.

Gross Domestic Savings as a Percentage of GDP circa 2013 and 2014			
Brazil	17%	Mexico	20%
Canada	23%	Russia	27%
China	50%	South Africa	15%
France	20%	United Kingdom	16%
Germany	26%	United States	16%
India	29%		
Japan	28%	**World average**	**22%**

the preferences of individuals. For the U.S. economy as a whole, the most common pattern seems to be that the quantity of savings doesn't adjust much to changes in the rate of return. As a practical matter, many households either save at a fairly steady pace, by putting regular contributions into a retirement account or by making regular payments as they buy a house, or they don't save much at all. Of course, some people will have preferences that cause them to react to a higher rate of return by increasing their quantity of savings; others will react to a higher rate of return by noticing that with a higher rate of return, they can save less in the present and still have higher future consumption. One prominent example in which a higher rate of return leads to a lower savings rate occurs when firms save money because they have promised to pay workers a certain fixed level of pension benefits after retirement. When rates of return rise, those companies can save less money in the present in their pension fund and still have enough to pay the promised retirement benefits in the future.

This insight suggests some skepticism about political proposals to encourage higher savings by providing savers with a higher rate of return. For example, Individual Retirement Accounts (IRAs) and 401(k) accounts are special savings accounts where the money going into the account is not taxed until it is taken out many years later, after retirement. (The main difference between these accounts is that an IRA is usually set up by an individual while a 401(k) needs to be set up through an employer.) By not taxing savings in the present, the effect of an IRA or a 401(k) is to increase the return to savings in these accounts. IRA and 401(k) accounts have attracted a large quantity of savings since they became common in the late 1980s and early 1990s. For example, the amount in IRAs rose from $239 billion in 1992 to $7,200 billion by 2015. However, overall U.S. personal savings, as discussed earlier, actually dropped from low to lower in the late 1990s and has stayed relatively low since 2000. Evidently, the larger amounts in these retirement accounts are being offset in the economy as a whole either by less savings in other kinds of accounts, or by a larger amount of borrowing (i.e., negative savings).

A rise in interest rates makes it easier for people to enjoy higher future consumption. But it also allows them to enjoy higher present consumption, if that is what individuals desire. Again, a change in prices—in this case, in interest rates—leads to a range of possible outcomes.

The Unifying Power of the Utility-Maximizing Budget Set Framework

The choices of households are determined by an interaction between prices, budget constraints, and personal preferences. The flexible and powerful terminology of utility-maximizing gives economists a vocabulary for bringing these elements together.

Not even economists believe that people walk around mumbling about their marginal utilities before they walk into a shopping mall, accept a job, or make a deposit in a savings account. However, economists do believe that individuals seek their own satisfaction or utility and that people often decide to try a little less of one thing and a little more of another. If these gentle assumptions are accepted, then the idea of utility-maximizing households facing budget constraints becomes highly plausible, too.

Key Concepts and Summary

1. Economic analysis of household behavior is based on the assumption that people seek the highest level of **utility** or satisfaction. Individuals are the only judge of their own utility.
2. In general, greater consumption of a good brings higher total utility. However, the additional utility received from each unit of greater consumption tends to decline in a pattern of **diminishing marginal utility**.
3. The utility-maximizing choice on a consumption budget constraint can be found in several ways. You can add up total utility of each choice on the budget-line and choose the highest total. You can choose a starting point at random and compare the marginal utility gains and losses of moving to neighboring points—and thus eventually seek out the preferred choice. Alternatively, you can compare the ratio of the prices of goods 1 and 2 to the ratio of the marginal utilities of goods 1 and 2 and apply the rule that at the optimal choice, the ratio of prices must equal the ratio of marginal utilities: $P1/P2 = MU1/MU2$.
4. The budget constraint framework suggests that when income or price changes, a range of responses are possible. When income rises, households will demand a higher quantity of normal goods, but a lower quantity of inferior goods. When the price of a good rises, households will typically demand less of that good—but whether they will demand a much lower quantity or only a slightly lower quantity will depend on personal preferences. Also, a higher price for one good can lead to more or less of the other good being demanded.
5. When making a choice along the labor-leisure budget constraint, a household will choose the combination of labor, leisure, and income that provides the most utility. The result of a change in wage levels can be higher work effort, the same work effort, or lower work effort.
6. When making a choice along the intertemporal budget constraint, a household will choose the combination of present consumption, savings, and future consumption that provides the most utility. The result of a higher rate of return (or higher interest rates) can be a higher quantity of savings, the same quantity of savings, or a lower quantity of savings, depending on preferences about present and future consumption.

Review Questions

1. Who makes the decision about how much utility an individual will receive from consuming a good?
2. Would you expect total utility to rise or fall with additional consumption of a good? Why?
3. Would you expect marginal utility to rise or fall with additional consumption of a good? Why?
4. Is it possible for total utility to increase while marginal utility diminishes? Explain.
5. If people do not have a complete mental picture of their total utility for every level of consumption, how can they find their utility-maximizing consumption choice?
6. What is the rule relating the ratio of prices of two goods and the ratio of marginal utilities of those goods at the optimal choice? Explain why, if this rule does not hold, the choice cannot be utility-maximizing.
7. As a general rule, is it safe to assume that a change in the price of a good will always have its most significant impact on the quantity demanded of that good, rather than on the quantity demanded of other goods? Explain.
8. How will a utility-maximizer find the choice of leisure and income that provides the greatest utility?
9. As a general rule, is it safe to assume that a higher wage will encourage significantly more hours worked for all individuals? Explain.
10. How will a utility-maximizer find the choice of present and future consumption that provides the greatest utility?
11. As a general rule, is it safe to assume that a lower interest rate will encourage significantly lower financial savings for all individuals? Explain.

CHAPTER 9

Cost and Industry Structure

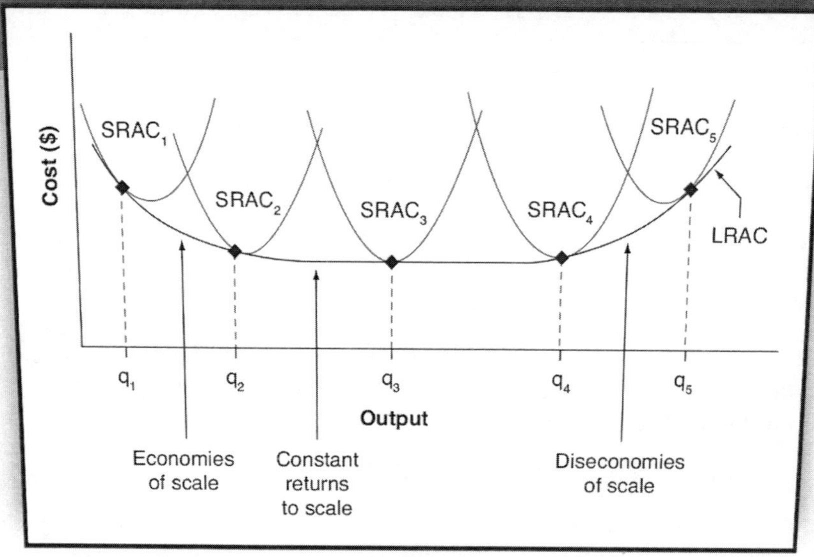

Chapter Outline

The Structure of Costs in the Short Run

The Structure of Costs in the Long Run

A business or firm is a kind of social machine. It incurs costs as it combines the labor of workers, machinery or other tools, and supplies purchased from other businesses. The firm transforms these inputs into outputs of goods and services, and collects revenue from its sales.

When people think of firms, often giants like Walmart, General Electric, or IBM—which each has over 300,000 employees—come to mind. But firms come in all sizes, as shown in Exhibit 9-1. The U.S. Census Bureau counted 6 million firms with employees in the U.S. economy. About half of all the workers in private firms are at the 17,000 large firms with more than 500 workers. But another third of workers in the U.S. economy are at firms with fewer than 100 workers. These smaller-scale businesses include everything from dentists and lawyers to businesses that mow lawns or clean houses. Indeed, Exhibit 9-1 doesn't include a separate category of millions of small

EXHIBIT 9-1 U.S. Firms by Number of Employees in 2013

U.S. firms display a wide variety of sizes. Large firms with more than 500 employees hire about one-half of the labor force. Firms with fewer than 100 employees hire about one-third of the labor force.

	Firms (% of total firms)	Number of Paid Employees (% of total employment)
Total	**5,774,000 (100%)**	**118.1 million (100%)**
0–9 employees	4,567,000 (79.1%)	12.4 million (10.5%)
10–19 employees	600,000 (10.4%)	8.0 million (6.8%)
20–99 employees	503,000 (8.7%)	19.7 million (16.7%)
100–499 employees	85,000 (1.5%)	16.6 million (14.1%)
500 or more employees	19,000 (0.3%)	61.4 million (52.0%)

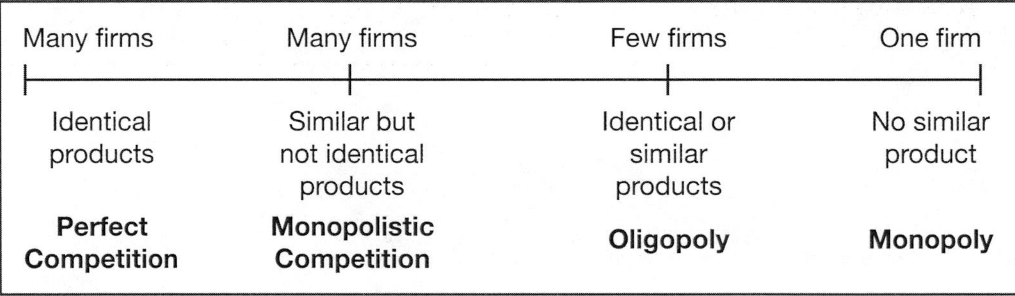

EXHIBIT 9-2 The Spectrum of Competition

Firms face different competitive situations. At one extreme—perfect competition—many firms are all trying to sell identical products. At the other extreme—monopoly—only one firm is selling a product, and this firm faces no competition. Monopolistic competition and oligopoly fall between the extremes of perfect competition and monopoly. Monopolistic competition is a situation with many firms selling similar, but not identical, products. Oligopoly is a situation with few firms that sell identical or similar products.

"nonemployer" businesses where a single owner or a few partners are not officially paid wages or a salary, but simply receive whatever they can earn. Each of these businesses, regardless of size or complexity, tries to earn a profit, where:

$$\text{Profit} = \text{Total Revenue} - \text{Total Cost}.$$

Total revenue is calculated by taking the quantity of everything that is sold and multiplying it by the sale price. Total costs include all spending on labor, machinery, tools, and supplies purchased from other firms.

The total revenue for a profit-seeking firm is determined by the price that a firm can charge and the quantity that it can sell, which in turn will be related to demand for its products and on the number of other firms that are selling similar or identical products. Exhibit 9-2 illustrates the range of different competitive conditions, which will be explored in the next three chapters. Chapter 10 examines **perfect competition**, in which each firm faces many competitors that sell identical products. Chapter 11 examines the opposite of perfect competition, which is the **monopoly** firm that faces no competitors. Chapter 12 examines two situations between perfect competition and monopoly: the case of **monopolistic competition**, where many firms sell similar but different products, and the case of **oligopoly**, where a small number of firms sell a similar product but face no other competition.

perfect competition: Each firm faces many competitors that sell identical products.

monopoly: A firm that faces no competitors.

monopolistic competition: Many firms competing to sell similar but differentiated products.

oligopoly: When a few firms have all or nearly all of the sales in an industry.

Regardless of what type of competition exists in a market, the definition of profit implies that a profit-maximizing firm will always attempt to produce its desired level of output at the lowest possible cost. After all, if any firm—from a giant like Bank of America or Boeing down to the corner gas station—can produce its desired level of production at a lower total cost, it will earn higher profits. This chapter begins by examining the costs of firms from a short-term perspective. In the short run, some costs can be adjusted quickly, like hiring or firing workers, but other costs cannot be immediately changed, like building a large factory. The discussion then takes a long-run perspective on costs, when all costs can be adjusted. Firms can use this breakdown of their cost structure into what is adjustable in the short term and what is adjustable in the long term both to understand the situation that they face in trying to earn profits and also to recognize the likely patterns of competition in their market.

The Structure of Costs in the Short Run

A list of the costs involved in producing cars will look very different from the costs involved in producing computer software or haircuts or fast-food meals. However, the cost structure of all firms can be broken down into some common underlying patterns.

When a firm looks at its total costs of production in the short run, a useful starting point is to divide total costs into two categories: fixed costs that can't be changed in the short run and variable costs that can be.

Fixed and Variable Costs

Fixed costs are expenditures that must be made before production starts and that do not change regardless of the level of production, at least not in the short run of weeks and months. Fixed costs can take many forms: for example, machinery or equipment, physical space for a retail or manufacturing business, research and development costs to develop new technology, even an expense like advertising to popularize a brand name. The level of fixed costs varies according to the specific line of business: for instance, manufacturing computer chips requires an expensive factory, but a local moving and hauling business can get by with almost no fixed costs at all if it rents trucks by the day when needed.

fixed costs: Expenditures that must be made before production starts and that do not change regardless of the level of production.

Variable costs, on the other hand, are incurred in the act of producing and will increase with the quantity produced. Labor is treated as a variable cost, since producing a greater quantity of a good or service typically requires more workers. But for many firms, variable costs also include physical inputs, like the metal and plastic involved in manufacturing a car or the cloth for making shirts and trousers.

variable costs: Costs of production that increase with the quantity produced.

As a concrete example of fixed and variable costs, consider the barber shop called The Clip Joint shown in Exhibit 9-3. Fixed costs of operating the barber shop, like the space and equipment, are $160 per day. The fixed costs are represented in the exhibit as the point where the total cost curve touches the vertical axis; that is, they are the costs incurred even if output is zero.

Variable costs are the costs of hiring barbers, which is $80 per day. The first two columns of Exhibit 9-3 show the quantity of haircuts that the barbershop can produce as it hires additional barbers. The third column shows the fixed costs, which do not change regardless of the level of production. The fourth column shows the variable costs at each level of output; these are calculated by taking the amount of labor hired and multiplying by the wage. Adding together the fixed costs in the third column and the variable costs in the fourth column produces the total costs in the fifth column.

Once production starts, total costs and variable costs rise. Variable costs often show a pattern of **diminishing marginal returns**, which occurs when the marginal gain in output diminishes as each additional unit of input is added. In the figure, diminishing marginal returns is illustrated by the ever-steeper slope of the total cost curve—that is, the cost of

diminishing marginal returns: When the marginal gain in output diminishes as each additional unit of input is added.

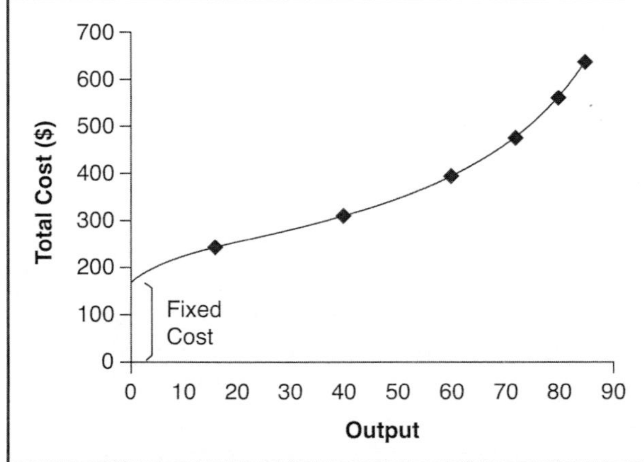

Labor	Quantity	Fixed Cost	Variable Cost	Total Cost
1	16	$160	$80	$240
2	40	$160	$160	$320
3	60	$160	$240	$400
4	72	$160	$320	$480
5	80	$160	$400	$560
6	84	$160	$480	$640

EXHIBIT 9-3 How Output Affects Total Costs

The first column shows the number of barbers hired. The second column shows the quantity of haircuts produced. The fixed costs of setting up the shop are $160, and these fixed costs do not change with the quantity of production. Fixed costs are shown by where the total cost line intersects the horizontal axis. The variable costs of hiring barbers are $80. Total costs are calculated by adding up the fixed and variable costs. Variable costs rise with production.

> **CLEARING IT UP**
>
> **What's the Difference between Business and Economics?**
>
> A certain tension exists between business and economics. Businesspeople sometimes tend to view economists as smart but theoretical and naive, with no idea of what it actually takes to run a business. One economist recalled his childhood this way: "Economists always talked a lot about business but, to my father, economists bore about the same relationship to business and the general economy as stamp collecting did to the delivery of the mail." Economists, for their part, sometimes seem to think that businesspeople are so wrapped up in day-to-day details of ordering paper clips and raking in executive bonuses that they have only a fuzzy perception of how the economic system as a whole works, or of their firm's place within that system.
>
> Although both economists and businesspeople think about business issues, they do so from different perspectives. One useful metaphor is that economists are to businesspeople as mechanics are to chauffeurs. Both jobs involve cars. But the mechanic's view of how things are working under the hood is different from the driver's view of how to get to the destination. Economists often have a better perspective on the market-oriented system as a whole and how it fits together. But businesspeople have a wealth of detailed knowledge about specific products, human relations, management, accounting, new product launches, marketing, production, strategies of specific firms, and other issues that most economists cannot match.

producing each additional unit of output is rising. As the number of barbers increases from 0 to 1, the marginal gain in output is 16; as the number rises from 1 to 2, the output gain is 24—an increasing marginal output. From that point on, the marginal gain in output diminishes as each additional barber is added. To gain some intuition for the reason behind this pattern, consider that a one-person barber shop is a very busy operation. The single barber needs to do everything: say hello to people entering, answer the phone, cut hair, sweep up, and run the cash register. A second barber reduces the level of disruption from jumping back and forth between these tasks, and allows a greater division of labor and specialization. The result can be greater increasing marginal returns. However, as other barbers are added, at some point the additional barbers will begin bumping elbows and start to produce diminishing marginal returns. As a result, the total costs of production will begin to rise more rapidly as output increases.

This pattern of diminishing marginal returns is common in many industries. As another example, consider the problem of irrigating a crop on a farmer's field. The plot of land is the fixed factor of production, while the water that can be added to the land is the key variable cost. As the farmer adds water to the land, output increases. But adding equal amounts of additional water brings smaller and smaller increases in output, until at some point the water floods the field and actually reduces output. Diminishing marginal returns arise because, given a certain level of fixed costs, marginal increases in output eventually require an ever-increasing number of inputs, and thus come at a higher cost.

Average Costs, Average Variable Costs, Marginal Costs

The breakdown of total costs into fixed and variable costs can provide a basis for other insights as well. The first five columns of Exhibit 9-4 duplicate the previous exhibit, but the last three columns offer additional calculations, where the costs are now analyzed not as a total, but on a per-unit basis. These additional calculations are also plotted on a graph.

average cost: Total cost divided by the quantity of output.

Average cost is calculated by dividing the total cost by the quantity of output. Thus, because the total cost of producing 40 haircuts is \$320, the average cost for producing each of 40 haircuts is \$320/40 = \$8. A similar calculation is performed for each entry in the average cost column.

The average cost curve is U-shaped, as shown in Exhibit 9-4. It starts off relatively high because at the far left end, average cost is calculated including all of the fixed costs and relatively little output, so the denominator in the average cost calculation is close to zero. Average costs then decline, as the fixed costs are spread over an increasing quantity

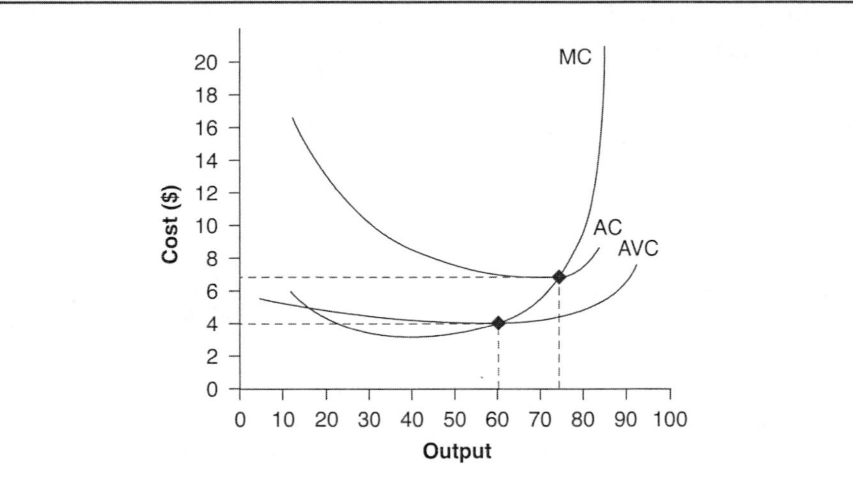

Labor	Quantity	Fixed Cost	Variable Cost	Total Cost	Marginal Cost	Average Cost	Average Variable Cost
1	16	160	80	240	5	15	5
2	40	160	160	320	03.3	8	4
3	60	160	240	400	4	6.6	4
4	72	160	320	480	6.6	6.6	4.4
5	80	160	400	560	10	7	5
6	84	160	480	640	20	7.6	5.7

EXHIBIT 9-4 Cost Curves at the Clip Joint

The information on total costs, fixed cost, and variable cost can also be presented on a per-unit basis. Average cost (*AC*) is calculated by dividing total cost by the total quantity produced. The average cost curve is typically U-shaped. Average variable cost (*AVC*) is calculated by dividing variable cost by the quantity produced. The average variable cost curve lies below the average cost curve and is typically U-shaped or upward-sloping. Marginal cost (*MC*) is calculated by taking the change in total cost between two levels of output and dividing by the change in output. The marginal cost curve is upward-sloping.

of output. In the average cost calculation, the rise in the numerator of total costs is relatively small compared to the rise in the denominator of quantity produced. But as output expands still further, the average cost begins to rise. At the right side of the average cost curve, total costs begin rising more rapidly as diminishing returns kick in.

Average variable cost is calculated by dividing the variable cost by the quantity of output. For example, the variable cost of producing 80 haircuts is $400, so the average variable cost is $400/80 = $5. The average variable cost curve will always lie below the curve for average cost, as shown in Exhibit 9-4, because average cost includes fixed costs in the numerator of the calculation and variable cost doesn't. However, as output becomes larger, fixed costs become relatively less important (because they don't rise with output), and so average variable cost sneaks closer to average cost.

average variable cost: Variable cost divided by the quantity of output.

Marginal cost is the additional cost of producing one more unit. Marginal cost can be calculated by taking the change in total cost (or the change in variable cost because that will be the same amount) and dividing it by the change in quantity. For example, as quantity produced increases from 40 to 60, total costs rise by 80. Thus, the marginal cost for each of those marginal 20 units will be 80/20 = 4. A similar calculation is performed for each entry in the marginal cost column. The marginal cost curve is generally upward-sloping because diminishing marginal returns implies that additional units are more costly to produce. A small zone of increasing marginal returns can be seen in the figure as a dip in the marginal cost curve before it starts rising.

marginal cost: The additional cost of producing one more unit.

The marginal cost line intersects the average cost line exactly at the bottom of the average cost curve—which occurs at a quantity of 72 and costs of $6.60 in Exhibit 9-4. The reason why the intersection occurs at this point is built into the economic meaning of marginal and average costs. If the marginal cost of production is below the average cost for producing previous units, as it is for the points to the left of where *MC* crosses *AC*, then producing one more additional unit will reduce average costs overall—and the *AC* curve will be downward-sloping in this zone. Conversely, if the marginal cost of production for producing an additional unit is above the average cost for producing the earlier units, as it is for points to the right of where *MC* crosses *AC*, then producing a marginal unit will increase average costs overall—and the *AC* curve must be upward-sloping in this zone. The point of transition, between where *MC* is pulling *AC* down and where it is pulling it up, must occur at the minimum point of the *AC* curve.

This idea of the marginal cost "pulling down" the average cost or "pulling up" the average cost may sound abstract, but think about it in terms of your own grades. If the score on the most recent quiz you take is lower than your average score on previous quizzes, then the marginal quiz pulls down your average. If your score on the most recent quiz is higher than the average on previous quizzes, the marginal quiz pulls up your average. In this same way, low marginal costs of production first pull down average costs, and then higher marginal costs pull them up.

The numerical calculations behind average cost, average variable cost, and marginal cost change from firm to firm. However, the general patterns of these curves, and the relationships and economic intuition behind them, do not change.

Lessons Taught by Alternative Measures of Costs

Breaking down total costs into fixed cost, marginal cost, average cost, and average variable cost is useful because each statistic offers its own insights for the firm.

Whatever the firm's quantity of production, total revenue must exceed total costs if it is to earn a profit. Fixed costs are important because at least in the short run, the firm cannot alter them. Fixed costs are sunk costs, to use a term introduced in Chapter 2. In thinking about what to do next, sunk costs should typically be ignored, since this spending has already been made and cannot be changed. However, variable costs can be changed, so they convey information about the firm's ability to cut costs in the present and the extent to which costs will increase if production rises.

Average cost tells a firm whether it can earn profits, given the price in the market. But you can rewrite the equation for profit to spell out that total revenues are the quantity produced multiplied by the price, and that total costs are the quantity produced multiplied by the average cost:

$$\begin{aligned}\text{Profit} &= \text{total revenue} - \text{total cost}\\ &= (\text{price})\,(\text{quantity produced}) - (\text{average cost})\,(\text{quantity produced}).\end{aligned}$$

This formula implies that if the market price exceeds average cost, profits will be positive; if price is below average cost, then profits will be negative.

The lesson to be learned from average variable cost is more subtle, but if a comparison between average cost and price reveals whether a firm is earning profits, then a comparison between average variable cost and price reveals whether the firm is earning profit *if fixed costs are left out of the calculation*. In certain circumstances, discussed in more detail in the next chapter, this information may prove useful.

The marginal cost of producing an additional unit can be compared with the amount of revenue gained by selling that additional unit to reveal whether the marginal unit is adding to total profit—or not. Thus, marginal cost helps in understanding how profits would be affected by increasing or reducing production.

CLEARING IT UP

Why Total Cost and Average Cost Are Not on the Same Graph

Total cost, fixed cost, and variable cost are all measured in dollars. In contrast, marginal cost, average cost, and average variable cost are all measured in dollars per unit produced. Thus, the vertical axes of the graphs are measured in fundamentally different units, and it wouldn't make practical sense to put these curves on the same graph.

A Variety of Cost Patterns

The pattern of costs varies among industries and even among firms in the same industry. Some businesses have high fixed costs, but low marginal costs. Consider, for example, an Internet company that provides medical advice to customers. Such a company might be paid by health care consumers directly, or perhaps hospitals or health care practices might subscribe on behalf of their patients. Setting up the website, collecting the information, writing the content, and buying or leasing the computer space to handle the web traffic are all fixed costs that must be undertaken before the site can work. However, when the website is up and running, it can provide a high quantity of service with relatively low variable costs, like the cost of monitoring the system and updating the information. In this case, the total cost curve might start at a high level because of the high fixed costs, but then might not rise much as the quantity of services provided rises, reflecting the low variable costs of operation. However, if the website is popular, a large rise in the number of visitors will overwhelm the website, and increasing output further would require an additional investment.

For other firms, fixed costs may be relatively low. For example, consider firms that rake leaves in the fall or shovel snow off sidewalks and driveways in the winter. For fixed costs, such firms may need little more than a car to transport workers to homes of customers and some rakes and shovels. Still other firms may find that diminishing marginal returns set in quite sharply. If a manufacturing plant tried to run 24 hours a day, seven days a week, then little time remains for routine maintenance of the equipment, and marginal costs can increase dramatically as the firm struggles to repair and replace overworked equipment.

Every firm can gain insight into its task of earning profits by dividing its total costs into fixed and variable costs, and then using these calculations as a basis for average cost, average variable cost, and marginal cost. However, making a final decision about the profit-maximizing quantity to produce and price to charge requires combining these perspectives on cost with an analysis of sales and revenue, which in turn requires looking at the competitive setting in which the firm finds itself. Before turning to the analysis of these competitive settings like perfect competition, monopolistic competition, and monopoly in the next three chapters, let's analyze the firm's cost structure from a long-run perspective.

The Structure of Costs in the Long Run

No costs are fixed in the long run. All costs are potentially variable over time. A firm can build new factories and purchase new machinery, or it can close existing facilities. In planning for the long run, the firm will compare alternative **production technologies**, where the term "technology" doesn't refer to a specific new invention like the laser beam or the assembly line, but refers to any alternative methods of combining inputs to produce output. The firm will search for the production technology that allows producing the desired level of output at lowest cost. After all, lower costs lead to higher profits—at least if total revenues remain unchanged. Moreover, each firm must fear that if it does not seek out the low-cost methods of production, then it may lose sales to competitor firms that find a way to produce and sell for less.

production technologies: Alternative methods of combining inputs to produce output.

Choice of Production Technology

Many tasks can be performed with a range of combinations of labor and physical capital. For example, a firm can have human beings answering phones and taking messages, or it can invest in an automated voicemail system. A firm can hire file clerks and secretaries to manage a system of paper folders and file cabinets, or it can invest in a computerized record-keeping system that will require fewer employees. A firm can hire workers to push supplies around a factory on rolling carts, or it can invest in motorized vehicles, or it can invest in robots that carry materials without a driver. Firms often face a choice between buying a number of small machines, which need a worker to run each one, or buying one larger and more expensive machine, which only requires one or two workers to run it. In short, physical capital and labor can often substitute for each other.

Consider the example of a private firm that is hired by local governments to clean up public parks. Three different combinations of labor and physical capital for cleaning up a single average-sized park appear in Exhibit 9-5. The first production technology is heavy on workers and light on machines, while the next two technologies substitute machines for workers. Since all three of these production methods produce the same thing—one cleaned-up park—a profit-seeking firm will choose the production technology that is least expensive, given the prices of labor and machines.

In Exhibit 9-5, example A shows the firm's cost calculation when wages are $40 and machines cost $80. In this case, technology #1 is the low-cost production technology. In example B, wages rise to $70, while the cost of machines does not change, in which case technologies #2 and #3 are tied for being the low-cost production technology. If wages keep rising up to $90, while the cost of machines remains unchanged, then technology #3 clearly becomes the low-cost form of production, as shown in example C.

This example illustrates that as an input becomes more expensive (in this case, the labor input), firms will attempt to conserve on using that input and will instead shift to other inputs that are now relatively less expensive. This pattern helps to explain why the demand curve for labor (or any input) slopes down; that is, as labor becomes relatively more expensive, profit-seeking firms will seek to substitute the use of other inputs. When

EXHIBIT 9-5 Three Ways to Clean a Park

Three Production Technologies			
Production technology 1	10 workers	2 machines	
Production technology 2	7 workers	4 machines	
Production technology 3	3 workers	7 machines	
All three technologies accomplish the same task; in this case, cleaning up one park. Production technology #1 uses the most labor and least machinery, while #3 uses the least labor and the most machinery. As the cost of labor rises from example A to B to C, the firm will choose to substitute away from labor and use more machinery.			
Example A: Workers Cost $40, Machines Cost $80			
	Labor Cost	***Machine Cost***	***Total Cost***
Cost of technology #1	10 × $40 = $400	2 × $80 = $160	$560
Cost of technology #2	7 × $40 = $280	4 × $80 = $320	$600
Cost of technology #3	3 × $40 = $120	7 × $80 = $560	$680
Example B: Workers Cost $60, Machines Cost $80			
	Labor Cost	***Machine Cost***	***Total Cost***
Cost of technology #1	10 × $60 = $600	2 × $80 = $160	$760
Cost of technology #2	7 × $60 = $420	4 × $80 = $320	$740
Cost of technology #3	3 × $60 = $180	7 × $80 = $560	$740
Example C: Workers Cost $90, Machines Cost $80			
	Labor Cost	***Machine Cost***	***Total Cost***
Cost of technology #1	10 × $90 = $900	2 × $80 = $160	$1,060
Cost of technology #2	7 × $90 = $630	4 × $80 = $320	$950
Cost of technology #3	3 × $90 = $270	7 × $80 = $560	$830

a multinational employer like Coca-Cola or McDonald's sets up a bottling plant or a restaurant in a high-wage economy like the United States, Canada, Japan, or western Europe, it is likely to use production technologies that conserve on the number of workers and focuses more on machines. However, that same employer is likely to use production technologies with more workers and less machinery when producing in a lower-wage country like Mexico, China, or South Africa.

Economies of Scale

economies of scale: When the average cost of producing each individual unit declines as total output increases.

The term **"economies of scale"** refers to the situation where as the quantity of output—the "scale" of production—goes up, average cost of production falls. When economies of scale exist, doubling of all inputs will result in more than doubling output (or equivalently, doubling all inputs will result in producing at a lower average cost). In everyday language, a larger factory can produce at a lower average cost than a smaller factory. Exhibit 9-6 illustrates the idea of economies of scale (which was originally introduced in Chapter 1), showing the average cost of producing an alarm clock falling as the quantity of output rises. For a small-sized factory like *S*, with an output level of 1,000, the average cost of production is $12 per alarm clock. For a medium-sized factory like *M*, with an output level of 2,000, the average cost of production falls to $8 per alarm clock. For a large factory like *L*, with an output of 5,000, the average cost of production declines still further to $4 per alarm clock.

The average cost curve in this economies-of-scale diagram may appear similar to the average cost curves presented earlier in this chapter, although it is downward sloping rather than U-shaped. But there is one major difference. The economies-of-scale curve is a long-run average cost curve because it allows all factors of production to change. The short-run average cost curves presented earlier in this chapter assumed the existence of fixed costs, and only variable costs were allowed to change.

One prominent example of economies of scale occurs in the chemical industry. Chemical plants have a lot of pipes. The cost of the materials for producing a pipe is related to the circumference of the pipe and its length. However, the volume of gooky chemical stuff that can flow through a pipe is determined by the cross-section area of the pipe. The calculations in Exhibit 9-7 show that a pipe that requires twice as much material to make (as shown by the circumference of the pipe doubling) can actually carry four times the volume of chemicals (because the cross-section area of the pipe rises by a factor of four). Of course, economies of scale in a chemical plant are more complex than this simple calculation suggests. But the chemical engineers who design these plants have long used what they call the "six-tenths rule," a rule of thumb that holds that increasing the quantity produced in a chemical plant by a certain percentage will increase total cost by only six-tenths as much.

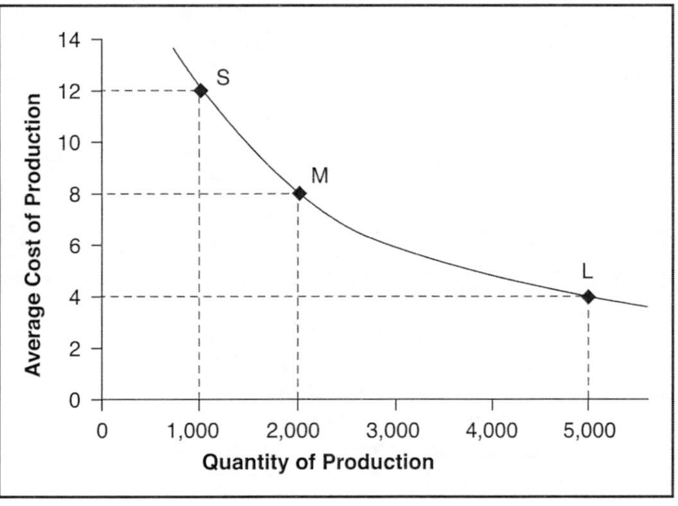

EXHIBIT 9-6
Economies of Scale

A small factory like *S* produces 1,000 alarm clocks at an average cost of $12 per clock. A medium factory like *M* produces 2,000 alarm clocks at a cost of $8 per clock. A large factory like *L* produces 5,000 alarm clocks at a cost of $4 per clock. Economies of scale exist because the larger scale of production leads to lower average costs.

EXHIBIT 9-7 Comparing Pipes: Economies of Scale in the Chemical Industry

	Circumference ($\pi 2r$)	Area (πr^2)
4-inch pipe	12.5 inches	12.5 square inches
8-inch pipe	25.1 inches	50.2 square inches
16-inch pipe	50.2 inches	201.1 square inches

A circular pipe that is 4 inches in diameter will have a circumference of 12.5 inches. A circular pipe that is 8 inches in diameter will have a circumference of 25.1 inches—so it will take twice as much material to make that pipe. However, although the pipe that is 8 inches in diameter will take twice as much material to make, and thus cost roughly twice as much, it will carry four times as much, as can be seen in the area. The area of the cross-section of an 8-inch pipe is 4 times as great as the corresponding area of a 4-inch pipe. Thus, a doubling of the cost of producing the pipe allows the chemical firm to process four times as much material. This pattern is a major reason why economies of scale occur in chemical production, which uses a large quantity of pipes.

Shapes of Long-Run Average Cost Curves

The long-run average cost curve, where all costs are allowed to vary, is actually based on a group of different short-run average cost curves, each of which represents one specific level of fixed costs. Exhibit 9-8 shows how the long-run average cost curve is built up out of a group of short-run average cost curves. Five short-run average cost or *SRAC* curves appear on the diagram. Each *SRAC* curve represents a different level of fixed costs. For example, you can imagine $SRAC_1$ as a small factory, $SRAC_2$ as a medium factory, $SRAC_3$ as a large factory, and $SRAC_4$ and $SRAC_5$ as very large and ultra-large. Although this diagram shows only five *SRAC* curves, presumably there are an infinite number of other *SRAC* curves between the ones that are shown. This family of short-run average cost curves can be thought of as representing different choices for a firm, which is planning its level of investment in fixed costs such as physical capital—knowing that different

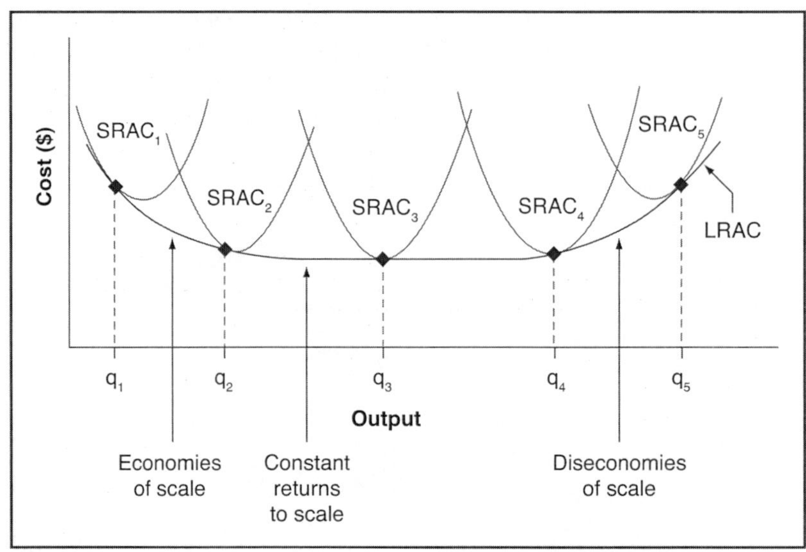

EXHIBIT 9-8 From Short-Run Average Cost Curves to Long-Run Average Cost Curves

The five different short-run average cost (*SRAC*) curves each represents a different level of fixed costs, from the low level of fixed costs at $SRAC_1$ to the high level of fixed costs at $SRAC_5$. Other *SRAC* curves, not shown in the diagram, lie between the ones that are shown here. The long-run average cost (*LRAC*) curve shows the lowest cost for producing each quantity of output when fixed costs can vary, and so it is formed by the bottom edge of the family of *SRAC* curves. If a firm wished to produce quantity q_3, it would choose the fixed costs associated with $SRAC_3$.

choices about capital investment in the present will cause it to end up with different short-run average cost curves in the future.

The long-run average cost curve shows the cost of producing each quantity in the long run, when the firm can choose its level of fixed costs and thus choose which short-run average costs it desires. Thus, if the firm plans to produce in the long run at an output of q_3, it should make the set of investments that will lead it to locate on $SRAC_3$, which allows producing q_3 at the lowest cost. A firm that intends to produce q_3 would be foolish to choose the level of fixed costs at $SRAC_2$ or $SRAC_4$. At $SRAC_2$ the level of fixed costs is too low for producing q_3 at lowest possible cost, and producing q_3 would require adding a very high level of variable costs and make the average cost very high. At $SRAC_4$, the level of fixed costs is too high for producing q_3 at lowest possible cost, and again average costs would be very high as a result.

The shape of the long-run cost curve as drawn in Exhibit 9-8 is fairly common for many industries. The left-hand portion of the long-run average cost curve, where it is downward sloping from output levels q_1 to q_2 to q_3 illustrates the case of economies of scale, which is sometimes also referred to as **increasing returns to scale**. In this portion of the long-run average cost curve, larger scale leads to lower average costs. This pattern was illustrated earlier in Exhibit 9-6.

increasing returns to scale: When a larger-scale firm can produce at a lower cost than a smaller-scale firm, also called economies of scale.

In the middle portion of the long-run average cost curve (*LRAC*), in the flat portion of the curve around q_3, economies of scale have halted. In this situation, allowing all inputs to expand does not much change the average cost of production, and this situation is called **constant returns to scale**. In this range of the *LRAC* curve, the average cost of production does not change much as scale rises or falls.

constant returns to scale: When expanding all inputs does not change the average cost of production.

Finally, the right-hand portion of the long-run average cost curve, running from output level q_4 to q_5, shows a situation where as the level of output and the scale rises, average costs rise as well. This situation is called **diseconomies of scale** or **decreasing returns to scale**. A firm or a factory can become so large that it becomes very difficult to manage, resulting in unnecessarily high costs as many layers of management try to communicate with workers and with each other, and as failures to communicate lead to disruptions in the flow of work and materials. Not many overly large factories are observed in the real world because, with their very high production costs, they are unable to compete for long against plants with lower average costs of production, and so they go out of business. However, in some planned economies, like the economy of the old Soviet Union, plants that were so large as to be grossly inefficient were able to continue operating for a long time because the government economic planners protected them from competition and assured that they would not experience losses.

diseconomies of scale: Another term for decreasing returns to scale.

decreasing returns to scale: A situation in which as the quantity of output rises, the average cost of production rises.

Although economies of scale may be easiest to visualize in terms of the size of manufacturing plants, the concept has many applications. In some cases, economies of scale may arise because doubling advertising or promotional expenses may expand sales more than proportionately, or because a larger retail space can expand sales more than proportionately, or because spreading the fixed costs of administration and record-keeping over

CLEARING IT UP

Economies of Scale vs. Diminishing Marginal Returns?

The concept of economies of scale, where average costs decline as production expands, might seem to conflict with the idea of diminishing marginal returns, where marginal costs rise as production expands. But diminishing marginal returns refers only to the short-run average cost curve, where one variable input (like labor) is increasing, but other inputs (like capital) are fixed. Economies of scale refers to the long-run average cost curve, where all inputs are being allowed to increase together. Thus, it is quite possible and common to have an industry that has both diminishing marginal returns when only one input is allowed to change, and at the same time has increasing or constant returns to scale when all inputs change together to produce a larger-scale operation.

more customers (as in the banking or insurance industries, for example) can hold down average costs. In any industry where small firms have a difficult time competing because their average costs are too high, the notion that small firms often lack economies of scale offers one plausible explanation.

The Size and Number of Firms in an Industry

The shape of the long-run average cost curve has implications for how many firms will compete in an industry and whether the firms in an industry have many different sizes or tend to be the same size. For example, say that 1 million dishwashers are sold every year at a price of $500 each and the long-run average cost curve for dishwashers is shown in Exhibit 9-9*a*. In Exhibit 9-9*a*, the lowest point of the *LRAC* curve occurs at a quantity of 10,000 produced. Thus, the market for dishwashers will consist of 100 different manufacturing plants of this same size. If some firm built a plant that produced 5,000 dishwashers per year or 20,000 dishwashers per year, the average costs of production at such plants would be well above $500, and such firms would not be able to compete.

A more common case is illustrated in Exhibit 9-9*b*, where the *LRAC* curve has a flat-bottomed area of constant returns to scale. In this situation, any firm with a level of output between 5,000 and 20,000 will be able to produce at about the same level of average cost. Given that the market will demand 1 million dishwashers per year at a price of $500, this market might have as many as 200 producers (i.e., 1 million dishwashers divided by firms making 5,000 each) or as few as 50 producers (1 million dishwashers divided by firms making 20,000 each). The producers in this market will range in size from firms that make 5,000 units to firms that make 20,000 units. But firms that produce below 5,000 units or more than 20,000 will be unable to compete because their average costs will be too high. Thus, if one observes an industry where almost all of the plants are the same size, it is likely that the long-run average cost curve has a unique bottom point like in Exhibit 9-9*a*. However, if the long-run average cost curve has a wide flat bottom like Exhibit 9-9*b*, then firms of a variety of different sizes will be able to compete with each other.

The flat section of the long-run average cost curve in Exhibit 9-9*b* can be interpreted in two different ways. One interpretation is that a single manufacturing plant producing a quantity of 5,000 has the same average costs as a single manufacturing plant with four

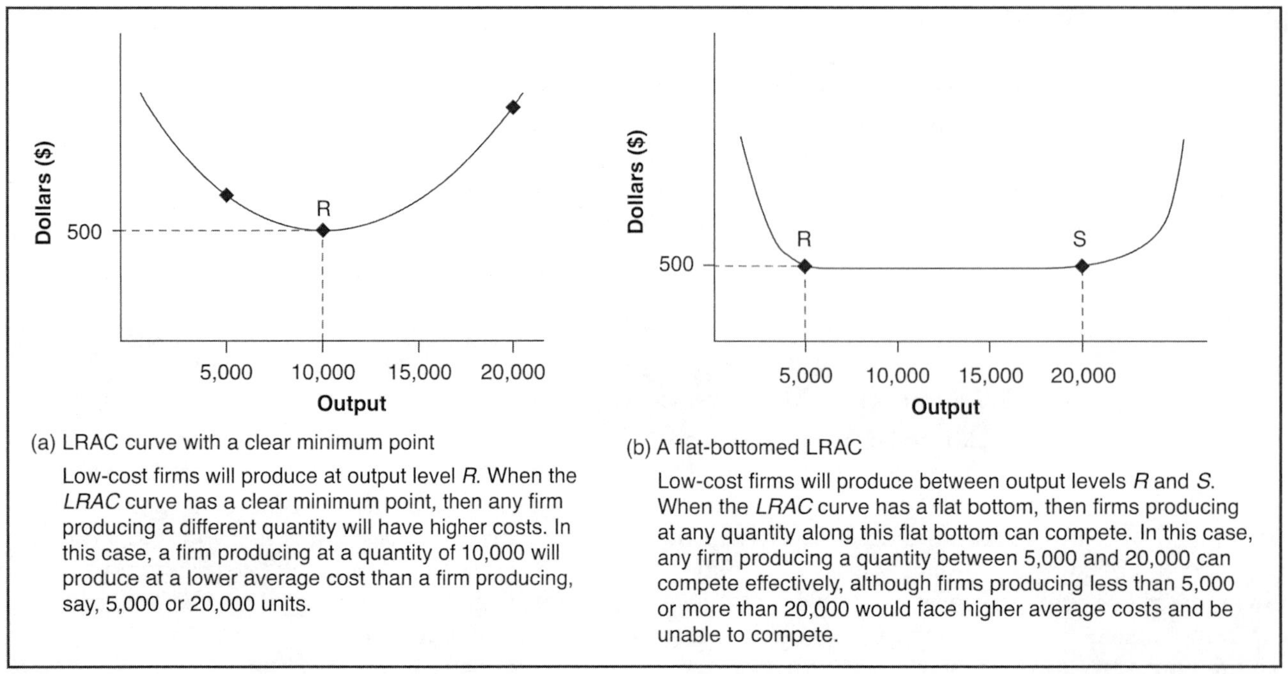

(a) LRAC curve with a clear minimum point

Low-cost firms will produce at output level *R*. When the *LRAC* curve has a clear minimum point, then any firm producing a different quantity will have higher costs. In this case, a firm producing at a quantity of 10,000 will produce at a lower average cost than a firm producing, say, 5,000 or 20,000 units.

(b) A flat-bottomed LRAC

Low-cost firms will produce between output levels *R* and *S*. When the *LRAC* curve has a flat bottom, then firms producing at any quantity along this flat bottom can compete. In this case, any firm producing a quantity between 5,000 and 20,000 can compete effectively, although firms producing less than 5,000 or more than 20,000 would face higher average costs and be unable to compete.

EXHIBIT 9-9 The *LRAC* Curve and the Size and Number of Firms

times as much capacity that produces a quantity of 20,000. The other interpretation is that one firm owns a single manufacturing plant that produces a quantity of 5,000, while another firm owns four separate manufacturing plants, which each produce a quantity of 5,000. This second explanation, based on the insight that a single firm may own a number of different manufacturing plants, is especially useful in explaining why the long-run average cost curve often has a large flat segment—and thus why a seemingly smaller firm may be able to compete quite well with a larger firm. At some point, however, the task of coordinating and managing many different plants raises the cost of production sharply, and the long-run average cost curve slopes up as a result.

In the examples to this point, the quantity demanded in the market is quite large (1 million) compared with the quantity produced at the bottom of the long-run average cost curve (5,000, 10,000, or 20,000). In such a situation, the market is set for competition between many firms. But what if the bottom of the long-run average cost curve is at a quantity of 10,000 and the total market demand at that price is only slightly higher than that quantity—or even somewhat lower?

Return to Exhibit 9-9*a*, where the bottom of the long-run average cost curve is at 10,000, but now imagine that the total quantity of dishwashers demanded in the market at that price of $500 is only 30,000. In this situation, the total number of firms in the market would only be three. A small number of firms in a market is called an "oligopoly," and Chapter 12 will discuss the range of competitive strategies that can occur when oligopolies compete.

Alternatively, consider a situation, again in the setting of Exhibit 9-9*a*, where the bottom of the long-run average cost curve occurs at a quantity of 10,000, but total demand for the product is only 5,000. (For simplicity, imagine that this demand is highly inelastic, so that it does not vary according to price.) In this situation, the market may well end up with a single firm—a monopoly—producing all 5,000 units. If any firm tried to challenge

Cities as Economies of Scale

Why are people and economic activity concentrated in cities, rather than distributed evenly across a country? The fundamental reason must be related to the idea of economies of scale—in many cases, grouping economic activity together is more productive than spreading it out. For example, cities provide a large group of nearby customers, so that businesses can produce at an efficient economy of scale. They also provide a large group of workers and suppliers, so that business can hire easily and purchase whatever specialized inputs they need. Many of the attractions of cities, like sports stadiums and museums, can only operate if they draw on a large nearby population base. Cities are big enough to offer a wide variety of products, which is what many shoppers are looking for.

These factors are not exactly economies of scale in the narrow sense of applying to the production function of a single firm, but they are related to growth in the overall size of population and market in an area. They are sometimes called "agglomeration economies."

These agglomeration factors help to explain why every economy, as it develops, has an increasing proportion of its population living in urban areas. In the United States, about 80% of the population now lives in metropolitan areas (which include the suburbs around cities), compared to just 40% in 1900. However, in poor nations of the world, including India and much of Africa, the proportion of the population in urban areas is only about 30%. One of the great challenges for these countries as their economies grow will be to manage the growth of the great cities that will arise.

If cities offer economic advantages that are a form of economies of scale, then why don't all or most people live in one giant city? At some population size, agglomeration economies turn into diseconomies. For example, traffic congestion may reach a point where the gains from being geographically nearby are counterbalanced by how long it takes to travel. High densities of people, cars, and factories can mean more garbage and air and water pollution. Facilities like parks or museums may become overcrowded. There may be economies of scale for negative activities like crime because high densities of people and businesses, combined with the greater impersonality of cities, make it easier for illegal activities as well as legal ones. The future of cities, both in the United States and in other countries around the world, will be determined by their ability to benefit from the economies of agglomeration and to minimize or counterbalance the corresponding diseconomies.

this monopoly while producing a quantity lower than 5,000 units, the prospective competitor firm would have a higher average cost, and so it wouldn't be able to compete in the longer term without losing money. A firm producing 10,000 units could produce at a lower average cost—but it could only sell 5,000 units, and so it would lose money as well. Chapter 11 discusses the situation of a monopoly firm in this situation.

Thus, the shape of the long-run average cost curve reveals whether competitors in the market will be different sizes. If the *LRAC* has a single point at the bottom, then the firms in the market will be about the same size, but if the *LRAC* has a flat-bottomed segment of constant returns to scale, then firms in the market may be a variety of different sizes.

The relationship between the quantity at the minimum of the long-run average cost curve and the quantity demanded in the market at that price will foretell how much competition is likely to exist in the market. If the quantity demanded in the market far exceeds the quantity at the minimum of the *LRAC*, then many firms will compete. If the quantity demanded in the market is only slightly higher than the quantity at the minimum of the *LRAC*, a few firms will compete. If the quantity demanded in the market is less than the quantity at the minimum of the *LRAC*, a single-producer monopoly is a likely outcome.

Shifting Patterns of Long-Run Average Cost

New developments in production technology can shift the long-run average cost curve in ways that can alter the size distribution of firms in an industry.

For much of the twentieth century, the most common change has been to see alterations in technology, like the assembly line or the large department store, where large-scale producers seemed to gain an advantage over smaller ones. In the long-run average cost curve, the downward-sloping economies of scale portion of the curve seemed to extend over a larger quantity of output.

However, new production technologies do not inevitably lead to a greater average size for firms. For example, in recent years some new technologies for generating electricity at a smaller scale have risen to prominence. The traditional coal-burning electricity plants needed to produce 300–600 megawatts of power to exploit economies of scale fully. However, high-efficiency turbines to produce electricity from burning natural gas can produce electricity at a competitive price while producing the smaller quantity of 100 megawatts of electricity or less. These new technologies create the possibility for smaller companies or plants to generate electricity as efficiently as large ones. Another example of a technology-driven shift to smaller production runs is three-dimensional printing, in which solid objects are created by putting down thin layers of material on top of each other.

Controversy has simmered in recent years over whether the new information and communications technologies will lead to a larger or smaller size for firms. On one side, the new technology may make it easier for small firms to reach out beyond their local geographic area and find customers across a state, or the nation, or even across international boundaries. This factor might seem to predict a future with a larger number of small competitors. On the other side, perhaps the new information and communications technology will create "winner-take-all" markets in which one large company will tend to command a large share of total sales, as Google has done in the market for Internet search requests or Amazon has done in online bookselling. Moreover, improved information and communication technologies might make it easier to manage many different plants and operations across the country or around the world, and thus encourage larger firms. This ongoing battle between the forces of smallness and largeness will be of great interest to economists, businesspeople, and policymakers.

Conclusion

The cost structure of a firm reveals many useful lessons. From a short-run perspective, each firm should be thinking about what costs are fixed and what costs are variable, and comparing the market price to its average costs and marginal costs. In the long run, each firm should have an idea of the extent of economies of scale in its industry, what the range of sizes is to produce at the lowest possible average cost in its industry, and how technological conditions may be shifting the long-run average cost curve over time.

While a careful examination of costs is vital, it is only half the story of the decision-making for any firm. Decisions about the profit-maximizing level of output must always include total revenues as well as total costs. Thus, the next three chapters consider the different market situations of perfect competition, monopoly, monopolistic competition, and oligopoly. In each of these setting, firms must combine their insights about total revenues and total costs, and thus reach a decision about the profit-maximizing price to charge and quantity of output to produce.

Key Concepts and Summary

1. Since profits are equal to total revenues minus total costs, every firm must consider its costs with care. Indeed, a profit-maximizing firm will always seek to produce its chosen level of output at the lowest possible cost.
2. At one end of the spectrum of competition is **perfect competition**, with many firms selling extremely similar products. At the other end is monopoly, where only one firm sells a particular product. In the middle are the cases of **monopolistic competition**, where many firms sell similar but clearly different products, and the case of **oligopoly**, where only a few firms sell a particular product.
3. In a short-run perspective, a firm's total costs can be divided into **fixed costs**, which a firm must incur before producing any output, and **variable costs**, which the firm incurs in the act of producing.
4. **Fixed costs** are sunk costs; that is, because they are in the past and cannot be altered, they should play no role in economic decisions about future production or pricing.
5. **Variable costs** typically show **diminishing marginal returns**, so that the marginal cost of producing higher levels of output rises.
6. **Marginal cost** is calculated by taking the change in total cost (or the change in variable cost, which will be the same thing) and dividing it by the change in output, for each possible change in output. Marginal costs are typically rising. A firm can compare marginal cost to the additional revenue it gains from selling another unit to find out whether its marginal unit is adding to profit.
7. **Average cost** is calculated by taking total cost and dividing by total output at each different level of output. Average costs are typically U-shaped on a graph. If a firm's average cost of production is lower than the market price, a firm will be earning profits.
8. **Average variable cost** is calculated by taking variable cost and dividing by the total output at each level of output. Average variable costs are typically U-shaped. If a firm's average variable cost of production is lower than the market price, then the firm would be earning profits if fixed costs are left out of the picture.
9. A **production technology** refers to a specific combination of labor, physical capital, and technology that makes up a particular method of production.
10. In the long run, firms can choose their production technology, and so all costs become variable costs. In making this choice, firms will try to substitute relatively inexpensive inputs for relatively expensive inputs where possible so as to produce at the lowest possible long-run average cost.
11. **Economies of scale** refers to a situation where as all inputs increase at a certain rate, the quantity of output rises at a faster rate. For example, doubling all inputs might result in more than doubling output. **Constant returns to scale** refers to a situation where as all inputs increase at a certain rate, the quantity of output rises at the same rate. **Diseconomies of scale** refers to a situation where as all inputs increase at a certain rate, the quantity of output rises at a slower rate.
12. The long-run average cost curve shows the lowest possible average cost of production, allowing all the inputs to production to vary so that the firm is choosing its production technology. A downward-sloping *LRAC* shows economies of scale; a flat *LRAC* shows constant returns to scale; an upward-sloping *LRAC* shows diseconomies of scale.
13. If the long-run average cost curve has only one quantity produced that results in the lowest possible average cost, then all of the firms competing in an industry should be the same size. However, if the *LRAC* has a flat segment at the bottom, so that a range of different quantities can produce at lowest average cost, then the firms competing in the industry will display a range of sizes.
14. If the quantity demanded in the market of a certain product is much greater than the quantity found at the bottom of the long-run average cost curve, where the cost of production is lowest, the market will have many firms competing. If the quantity demanded in the market is only slightly greater than the quantity at the bottom of the *LRAC*, the market is likely to be an oligopoly. If the quantity demanded in the market is less than the quantity at the bottom of the *LRAC*, the result is likely to be a monopoly.

Review Questions

1. How are total costs related to profits?
2. What is the difference between perfect competition, monopolistic competition, oligopoly, and monopoly?
3. What is the difference between fixed costs and variable costs?
4. Are there fixed costs in the long run? What about in the short run? Explain briefly.
5. Are fixed costs also sunk costs? Explain.
6. What are diminishing marginal returns?
7. Which costs are measured on a per-unit basis: fixed costs, average cost, average variable cost, variable costs, and marginal cost?
8. How are each of the following calculated: marginal cost, average cost, average variable cost?
9. What shape would you generally expect each of the following to have on a cost-curve diagram: fixed costs, variable costs, marginal costs, average costs, and average variable costs?
10. What is a production technology?
11. In choosing a production technology, how will firms react if one input becomes relatively more expensive?
12. What is the difference between economies of scale, constant returns to scale, and diseconomies of scale?
13. What is a long-run average cost curve?
14. What shape of a long-run average cost curve illustrates economies of scale, constant returns to scale, and diseconomies of scale?
15. Why will firms in most markets be located at or close to the bottom of the long-run average cost curve?

CHAPTER

10

Perfect Competition

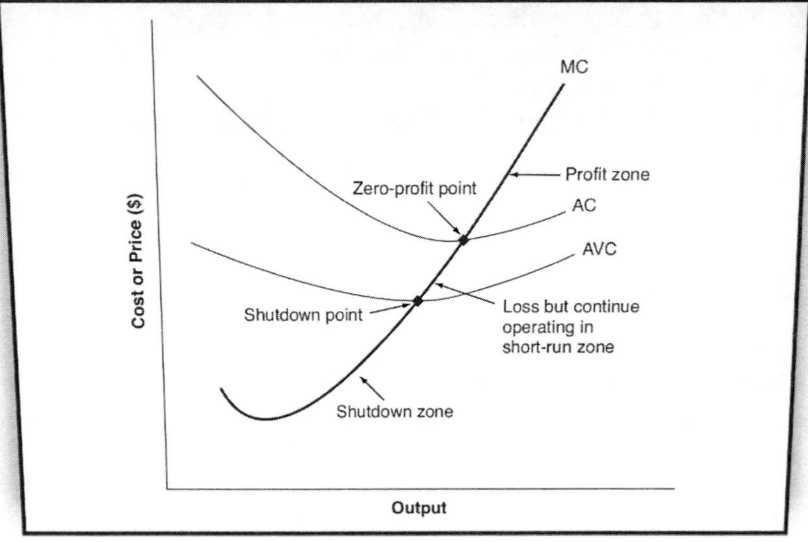

Chapter Outline

Any firm must recognize two stark realities: no consumer is required to buy the goods that it produces, and even consumers who might want its goods may choose to buy from other firms instead. Firms in a situation of **perfect competition** sell their product in a market with other firms who produce identical or extremely similar products. As a result, if a firm in a perfectly competitive market raises the price of its product by so much as a penny, it will lose all of its sales to competitors. Perfectly competitive firms are sometimes known as **price takers** because the pressure of other competing firms forces them to accept the prevailing price in the market as given. A related underlying assumption is that a perfectly competitive firm must be a relatively small player in the overall market, so that a perfectly competitive firm can increase or decrease its output without noticeably affecting the overall quantity supplied in the market.

perfect competition: Each firm faces many competitors that sell identical products.

price takers: A firm in a perfectly competitive market that must take the prevailing market price as given.

A perfectly competitive industry is a hypothetical extreme; after all, "perfect" is an extreme word. However, producers in a number of industries do face many competitor firms selling highly similar goods, in which case they must often act as price takers. For example, many farmers grow any given crop, and crops grown by different farmers are largely interchangeable. In 2015, U.S. corn farmers were receiving about $3.70 per bushel, and coffee (of the mild arabica variety) was selling for $1.60 per pound on world markets. A corn farmer who attempted to sell corn for $4.00 per bushel, or a coffee grower who attempted to sell for $2.00 a pound, would not have found any buyers. Similarly, gold was selling for $1,160 per ounce, which meant that sellers could not negotiate to receive $1,200 per ounce. Some manufactured products are similar enough that producers must sell at the price prevailing in the market. In the market for mid-sized color televisions, the quality differences are mostly not perceptible to the untrained eye, so price plays a major role in the decisions of purchasers. Gasoline is very similar between different gas stations. Blank flash drives are extremely similar, regardless of the manufacturer.

This chapter examines how profit-seeking firms make decisions about how much to produce in perfectly competitive industries. Such firms will analyze their costs as discussed in the previous chapter, using the concepts of total cost, fixed cost, variable cost, average cost, marginal cost, and average variable cost. In the short run, the perfectly competitive firm will seek out the quantity of output where profits are highest, or if profits are not possible, where losses are smallest. In the long run, the perfectly competitive firms will react to profits by increasing production further and to losses by reducing production or shutting down. Firms will tailor their decisions about the quantity of inputs like labor and physical capital to purchase according to what they need to produce the profit-maximizing quantity of output at the lowest possible average cost.

Quantity Produced by a Perfectly Competitive Firm

A perfectly competitive setting really has only one major choice to make: namely, what quantity to produce. To understand why this is so, consider a different way of writing out the basic definition of profit:

Profit = Total revenue – Total cost

= (Price) (Quantity produced) – (Average cost) (Quantity produced)

Because a perfectly competitive firm must accept the price for its output as dictated by the forces of demand and supply, it cannot choose the price that it charges. Moreover, the perfectly competitive firm must also pay the market price for inputs to production like labor and physical capital, so it cannot control what it pays for the inputs that make up its costs of production. When the perfectly competitive firm chooses what quantity to produce, then this quantity—along with the prices prevailing in the market for output and inputs—will determine the firm's total revenue, total costs, and profits.

Comparing Total Revenue and Total Cost

As an example of how a perfectly competitive firm decides what quantity to produce, consider the case of the Overdrive Production Shoppe, which makes flash drives. Exhibit 10-1 shows total revenue and total costs for the firm. The horizontal axis of the figure shows the quantity of drives produced; the vertical axis shows both total revenue and total costs, measured in dollars.

A perfectly competitive firm can sell as large a quantity as it wishes, as long as it accepts the prevailing market price. Thus, the total revenue line slopes up at an angle, with the slope of the line determined by the price. In this example, a flash drive costs \$3.50. Sales of one flash drive will bring in \$3.50, two units will be \$7, three units will be \$10.50, and so on.

The total costs for the Overdrive Production Shoppe, broken down into fixed and variable costs, are shown in the table that also appears in Exhibit 10-1. The total cost curve intersects with the vertical axis at a value that shows the level of fixed costs, and then slopes upward. (If it bothers you that these numbers don't seem more realistic, you may wish to imagine that these total cost and quantity figures represent thousands: that is, fixed costs of the plant are \$62,000, and the total cost of producing 10,000 flash drives is \$90,000. The shape of the total revenue and total cost picture does not change if both quantity and cost are expressed with extra zeros.)

Based on its total revenue and total cost curves, a perfectly competitive firm like the Overdrive Production Shoppe can calculate the quantity of output that will provide the highest level of profit. At any given quantity, total revenue minus total cost will equal profit. On the figure, the vertical gap between total revenue and total cost represents either profit (if total revenues are greater than total costs at a certain quantity) or losses (if total costs are greater than total revenues at a certain quantity). In this example, total costs will exceed total revenues at output levels from 0 to 40, and so over this range of output, the firm will be making losses. At output levels from 50 to 80, total revenues exceed total costs, so the firm is earning profits. But then at an output of 90 or 100, total costs again

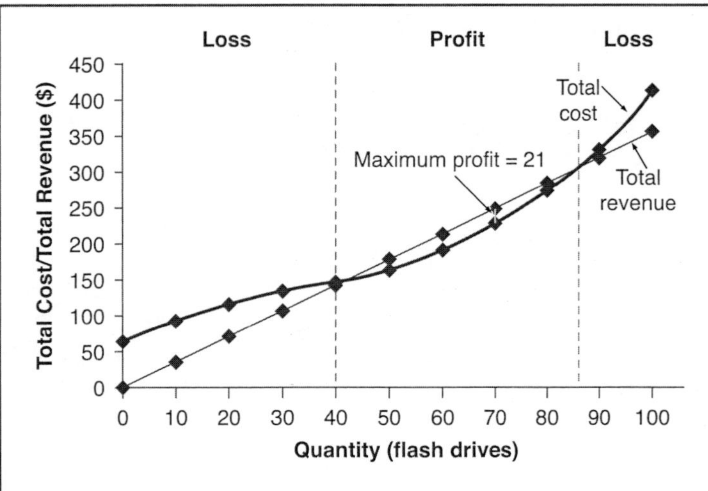

Quantity	Total Cost	Fixed Cost	Variable Cost	Total Revenue	Profit
0	$62	$62	—	0	–62
10	$90	$62	$28	$35	–55
20	$110	$62	$48	$70	–40
30	$126	$62	$64	$105	–21
40	$144	$62	$82	$140	–4
50	$166	$62	$104	$175	+9
60	$192	$62	$130	$210	+18
70	$224	$62	$162	$245	+21
80	$264	$62	$202	$280	+16
90	$324	$62	$262	$315	–9
100	$404	$62	$342	$350	–54

EXHIBIT 10-1 Total Cost and Total Revenue at the Overdrive Production Shoppe

Total revenue for a perfectly competitive firm is a straight line sloping up. The slope is determined by the price of the good. Total cost also slopes up, but with some curvature. Total cost intersects the vertical axis at the level determined by fixed costs. At higher levels of output, total cost begins to slope upward more steeply because of diminishing marginal returns. At levels of output where total cost is higher than total revenue, like 10 or 20, the firm would suffer a loss. At levels of output where total revenue is higher than total costs, like 60 or 70, the firm would earn profits. The maximum profit will occur at the quantity where the gap of total revenue over total cost is largest.

exceed total revenues and the firm is making losses. Total profits appear in the final column of the table. The highest total profits in the table occur at an output of 70, when profits will be $21.

A higher price would mean a steeper slope for the total revenue curve, so that total revenue was higher for every quantity sold; a lower price would mean a flatter slope, so that total revenue was lower for every quantity sold. What happens if the price drops low enough that the total revenue line is completely below the total cost curve—that is, at every level of output, total costs are higher than total revenues? Then the best that the firm can do is to suffer losses, but a profit-maximizing firm will still prefer the quantity of output where total revenues come closest to total costs and thus where its losses are smallest.

Comparing Marginal Revenue and Marginal Costs

Firms often do not have the necessary data they would need to draw a complete total cost curve for all different levels of production. They can't be sure of what total costs would look like if they, say, doubled production or cut production in half because they haven't tried it. Instead, firms experiment; that is, they produce a slightly greater or lower quantity and observe how profits are affected. In economic terms, this practical approach to maximizing profits means looking at how changes in production affect marginal revenue and marginal cost.

Exhibit 10-2 presents the marginal revenue and marginal cost curves based on the total revenue and total cost curves in Exhibit 10-1. The **marginal revenue** curve shows the additional revenue gained from selling one more unit. For a perfectly competitive firm, the marginal revenue curve is drawn as a flat line equal to the price level, which in this

marginal revenue: The additional revenue gained from selling one more unit.

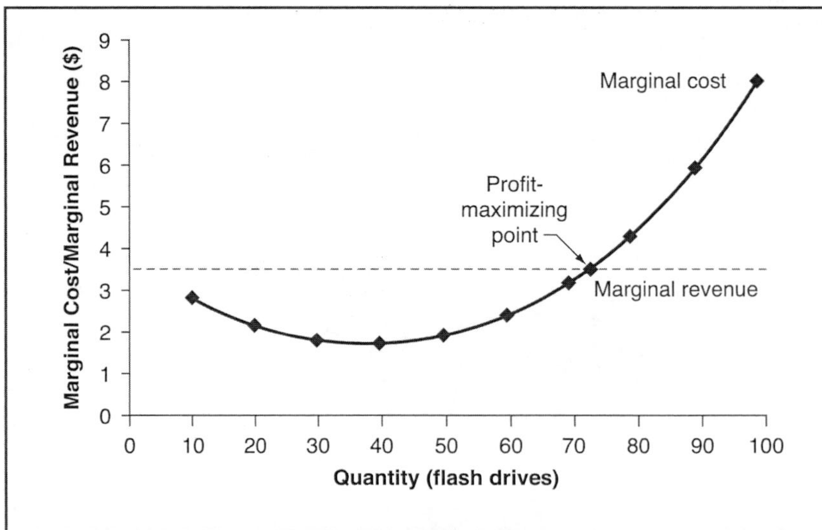

Quantity	Total Cost	Fixed Cost	Variable Cost	Marginal Cost	Total Revenue	Marginal Revenue
0	$62	$62		—	—	—
10	$90	$62	$28	$2.80	$35	$3.50
20	$110	$62	$48	$2.00	$70	$3.50
30	$126	$62	$64	$1.60	$105	$3.50
40	$144	$62	$82	$1.80	$140	$3.50
50	$166	$62	$104	$2.20	$175	$3.50
60	$192	$62	$130	$2.60	$210	$3.50
70	$224	$62	$162	$3.20	$245	$3.50
80	$264	$62	$202	$4.00	$280	$3.50
90	$324	$62	$262	$6.00	$315	$3.50
100	$404	$62	$342	$8.00	$350	$3.50

EXHIBIT 10-2 Marginal Revenues and Marginal Costs at the Overdrive Production Shoppe

For a perfectly competitive firm, the marginal revenue (MR) curve is a horizontal straight line because it is equal to the price of the good. Marginal cost (MC) is sometimes first downward-sloping, if there is a region of increasing marginal returns at low levels of output, but is eventually upward-sloping at higher levels of output as diminishing marginal returns kick in. If the firm is producing at a quantity where MR > MC, like 40 or 50, then it can increase profit by increasing output because the marginal revenue is exceeding the marginal cost. If the firm is producing at a quantity where MC > MR, like 90 or 100, then it can increase profit by reducing output because the reductions in marginal cost will exceed the reductions in marginal revenue. The firm's profit-maximizing choice of output will occur where MR = MC (or at a choice close to that point).

example is $3.50 per flash drive. The marginal revenue gained from selling one additional flash drive is just the price of that unit. Because a perfectly competitive firm is a price taker, it can sell whatever quantity it wishes at the market-determined price. Marginal cost, the cost per additional unit sold, is calculated by dividing the change in total cost by the change in quantity. In this example, marginal cost at first declines as production increases from 10 to 20, which represents the area of increasing marginal returns that is not uncommon at low levels of production. But then marginal costs start to increase, displaying the typical pattern of diminishing marginal returns.

In this example, the marginal revenue and marginal cost curves cross at a price of $3.50 and a quantity between 70 and 80 produced. If the firm started out producing at a level of 60, and then experimented with increasing production to 70, marginal revenues from the increase in production would exceed marginal costs—and so profits would rise. However, if the firm then experimented further with increasing production from 70 to 80, it would find that marginal costs from the increase in production are greater than marginal revenues, and so profits would decline.

The profit-maximizing choice for a perfectly competitive firm will occur at the point where marginal revenue is equal to marginal cost—that is, where MR = MC. A profit-seeking firm should keep expanding production as long as MR > MC because when revenue is rising faster that costs, profits increase, too. But at the level of output where MR = MC, the firm should recognize that it has achieved the highest possible level of profits and that expanding production into the zone where MR < MC will only reduce profits. Because the marginal revenue received by a perfectly competitive firm is equal to the price P, so that P = MR, the profit-maximizing rule for a perfectly competitive firm can also be written as a recommendation to produce at the quantity where P = MC. (If the firm's choices for quantity of output don't include a choice where MR is exactly equal to MC, then the highest output level where MR > MC will be the profit-maximizing choice.)

Marginal Cost and the Firm's Supply Curve

For a perfectly competitive firm, the marginal cost curve is identical to the firm's supply curve. To understand why this perhaps surprising insight holds true, first think about what the supply curve means. A firm checks the market price and then looks at its supply curve to decide what quantity to produce. Now think about what it means to say that a firm will maximize its profits by producing at the quantity where P = MC. This rule means that the firm checks the market price and then looks at its marginal cost curve to determine the quantity to produce. In other words, the marginal cost curve and the firm's supply curve contain the same information—that is, they both tell the firm what quantity to produce, given the market price.

As discussed back in Chapter 4, many of the reasons that supply curves shift relate to underlying changes in costs. For example, a lower price of key inputs or new technologies that reduce production costs cause supply to shift to the right; in contrast, lousy weather or added government regulations can add to costs of certain goods in a way that causes supply to shift to the left. These shifts in the firm's supply curve can also be interpreted as shifts of the marginal cost curve. A shift in costs of production that increases marginal costs at all levels of output—and shifts MC to the left—will cause a perfectly competitive firm to produce less at any given market price. Conversely, a shift in costs of production that decreases marginal costs at all levels of output will shift MC to the right, and as a result, a competitive firm will choose to expand its level of output at any given price.

Profits and Losses with the Average Cost Curve

If the price that a firm charges is higher than its average cost of production for that quantity produced, then the firm will earn profits. Conversely, if the price that a firm charges is lower than its average cost of production, the firm will suffer losses. Exhibit 10-3 illustrates three situations: (a) where price intersects marginal cost at a level above the average cost curve, (b) where price intersects marginal cost at a level equal to the average cost curve, and (c) where price intersects marginal cost at a level below the average cost curve.

First consider a situation where the price is equal to $4 for a flash drive. The rule for a profit-maximizing perfectly competitive firm is to produce the level of output where P = MR = MC, so the Overdrive Production Shoppe will produce a quantity of 80, which is labeled as q in Exhibit 10-3*a*. The firm's total revenue at this price will be shown by the large shaded rectangle, which represents a price of $4 per flash drive and a quantity of 80. Total costs will be the quantity of 80 times the average cost of $3.30, which is shown by the lightly shaded rectangle. Thus, profits will be the darker shaded rectangle that represents the large rectangle of total revenues minus the rectangle of total costs. It would be calculated as:

Profit = Total revenue – Total cost
$56 = (80) ($4.00) – (80) ($3.30)

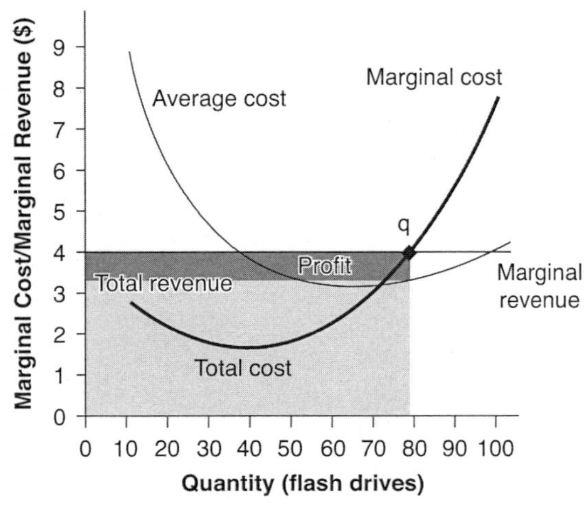

(a) Price intersects marginal cost above the average cost curve.

At a price of \$4, price is at a level where producing at the quantity where P = MC leads to a price that is above average cost. In this case, the firm is earning a profit. Total revenue is the quantity of 80 times the price of \$4, or \$320, shown by the overall shaded box. Total cost is the quantity of 80 times an average cost of \$3.30, or \$264, shown by the bottom shaded box. The leftover rectangle where total revenue exceeds total cost is the profit earned.

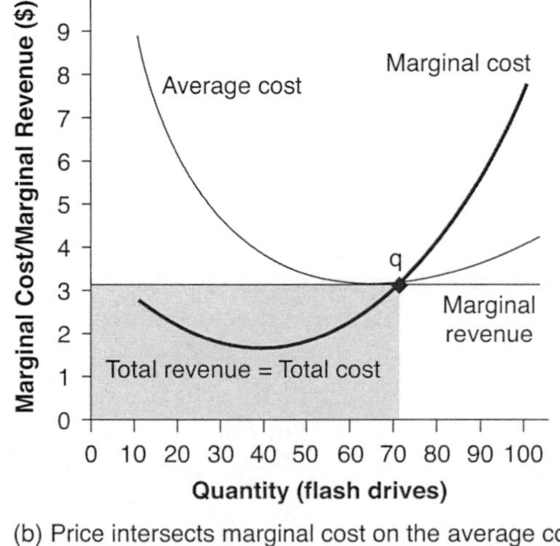

(b) Price intersects marginal cost on the average cost curve.

At a price of \$3.20, the price is now at a level where producing at the quantity where P = MC leads to a price that is equal to the average cost. Total revenue is now a quantity of 70 times a price of \$3.20. Total cost is the same: a quantity of 70 times an average cost of \$3.20. Zero profit is being earned in this situation.

(c) Price intersects marginal cost below the average cost curve.

At a price of \$2.20, when the firm produces at a quantity where P = MC, the price is below average cost. Here, the firm is suffering losses. Total costs are the large rectangle with a quantity of 50 and a price of \$3.32, for total costs of \$166. Total revenues are a quantity of 50 and a price of \$2.20, or \$110, shown by the smaller shaded box. The leftover rectangle on top thus shows the losses; that is, the amount that total cost exceeds total revenue.

Quantity	Total Cost	Fixed Cost	Variable Cost	Marginal Cost	Average Cost
0	\$62	\$62	—	—	—
10	\$90	\$62	\$28	\$2.80	\$9.00
20	\$110	\$62	\$48	\$2.00	\$5.50
30	\$126	\$62	\$64	\$1.60	\$4.20
40	\$144	\$62	\$82	\$1.80	\$3.60
50	\$166	\$62	\$104	\$2.20	\$3.32
60	\$192	\$62	\$130	\$2.60	\$3.20
70	\$224	\$62	\$162	\$3.20	\$3.20
80	\$264	\$62	\$202	\$4.00	\$3.30
90	\$324	\$62	\$262	\$6.00	\$3.60
100	\$404	\$62	\$342	\$8.00	\$4.04

EXHIBIT 10-3 Price and Average Cost at the Overdrive Production Shoppe

Now consider Exhibit 10-3*b*, where the price has fallen to \$3.20 for a flash drive. Again, the perfectly competitive firm will choose the level of output where P = MR = MC, but in this case, the quantity will be 70. At this price and output level, where the marginal cost curve is crossing the average cost curve, the price received by the firm is exactly equal to its average cost of production. Thus, the total revenue of the firm is exactly equal to the total costs of the firm, so that the firm is making zero profit.

In Exhibit 10-3*c*, the market price has fallen still further to \$2.20 for a flash drive. Again, the perfectly competitive firm will choose the level of output where P = MR = MC, and in this case the firm will choose to produce a quantity of 50. At this price and output level, the price level received by the firm is below the average cost of production. The total costs for the firm will be $166 (i.e., the average cost of $3.32 multiplied by a quantity of 50), which appear as the large rectangle. Total revenue will be $110 (price of $2.20 multiplied by a quantity of 50), which is the smaller shaded rectangle. The firm's losses of $56 are shown by the darker rectangle created by subtracting the total revenue rectangle from the total cost rectangle.

If the market price received by a perfectly competitive firm leads it to produce at a quantity where the price is greater than average cost, the firm will earn profits. If the price received by the firm causes it to produce at a quantity where price equals marginal cost, at the point where the MC curve crosses the AC curve, then the firm earns zero profits. Finally, if the price received by the firm leads it to produce at a quantity where the price is less than average cost, the firm will make losses.

The Shutdown Point

The possibility that a firm may suffer losses raises a question: Why can't the firm avoid losses by shutting down and not producing at all? The answer is that shutting down can reduce variable costs to zero, but in the short run, shutting down does not reduce fixed costs. As a result, if the firm produces a quantity of zero, it would still make losses because it would still need to pay its fixed costs. Thus, when a firm is facing the possibility of losses, it must face a question: will its losses increase or decrease if it shuts down?

As an example of this decision, consider the situation of the Yoga Center, which has signed a contract to rent space that costs $10,000 per month. If the firm continues to operate, its marginal costs for hiring yoga teachers is $15,000 for the month. If the firm shuts down, it must still pay the rent, but it would not need to hire labor. Exhibit 10-4 shows three possible scenarios. In the first scenario, the Yoga Center shuts down, in which case it faces losses of $10,000. In the second scenario, the Yoga Center remains open, earns revenues of $10,000 for the month, and experiences losses of $15,000. In the third scenario, the Yoga Center remains open and earns revenues of $20,000 for the month and experiences losses of $5,000. In all three cases, the Yoga Center loses money. In all three cases, when the rental contract expires in the long run, the store should exit this business. But in the short run, in scenario 2, the store's losses increase because it remains open, so the store should shut down immediately. In contrast, in scenario 3, the revenue that the firm can earn is high enough that the store's losses diminish when it remains open, so the store should remain open in the short run.

EXHIBIT 10-4 Should the Yoga Center Shut Down Now or Later?

Scenario 1

The firm shuts down now, so revenues are zero, but the firm must pay fixed costs of $10,000.

Total revenue – (fixed cost + variable cost) = profit

0 – 10,000 = –10,000

Scenario 2

The firm keeps operating; variable costs are $15,000 and revenues are $10,000.

Total revenue – (fixed cost + variable cost) = profit

10,000 – (10,000 + 15,000) = –15,000

Conclusion: The firm should shut down now.

Scenario 3

The firm keeps operating; variable costs are $15,000 and revenues are $20,000.

Total revenue – (fixed cost + variable cost) = profit

20,000 – (10,000 + 15,000) = –5,000

Conclusion: The firm should shut down later.

This example suggests that the key factor for a firm deciding whether to shut down is whether the firm can at least cover its variable costs by remaining open. Exhibit 10-5 illustrates this lesson for the example of the Overdrive Production Shoppe, by adding the average variable cost curve to the marginal cost and average cost curves. At a price of $2.20 per flash drive, shown in Exhibit 10-5a, the firm produces at a level of 50. It is making losses of $56 (as explained earlier), but price is above average variable cost, and so the firm continues to operate. However, if the price declined to $1.80 per flash drive, as shown in Exhibit 10-5b, and if the firm applied its rule of producing where P = MR = MC, it would produce a quantity of 40. This price is below average variable cost for this level of output. At this price and output, total revenues would be $72 (quantity of 40 times price of $1.80) and total cost would be $144, for overall losses of $72. If the firm shuts down, it must only pay its fixed costs of $62, so shutting down is preferable to selling at a price of $1.80 per flash drive.

shutdown point: When the revenue a firm receives does not cover its average variable costs, the firm should shut down immediately; the point where the marginal cost curve crosses the average variable cost curve.

The intersection of the average variable cost curve and the marginal cost curve, which shows the price where the firm lacks enough revenue to cover its variable costs, is called the **shutdown point.** If the perfectly competitive firm can charge a price above the shut-

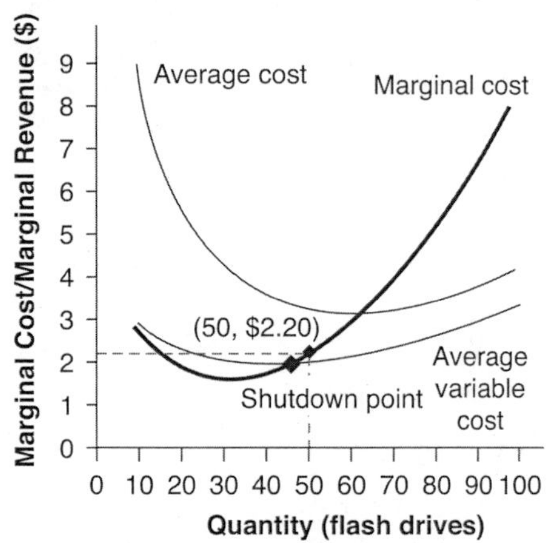

(a) Price is above the shutdown point.

Firm should not shut down because price is above shutdown point. The price is $2.20. Producing at the quantity where P = MC leads to a situation where price is below average cost but above average variable cost. Thus, the firm is suffering losses, but because it is covering its variable costs, it will continue to operate.

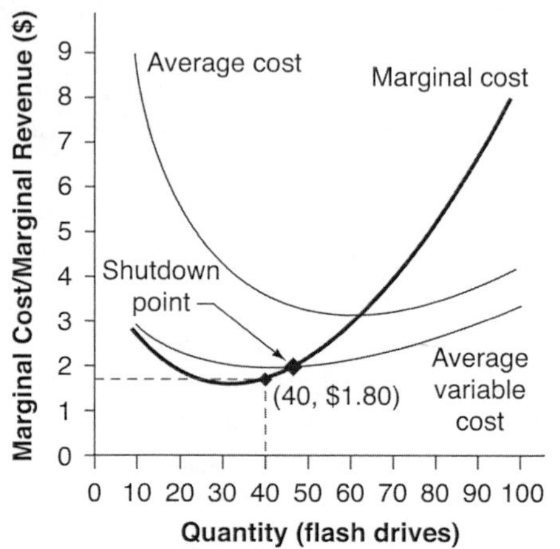

(b) Price is below the shutdown point.

Firm should shut down because price is below shutdown point. Price is $1.80, which leads to a quantity of output where price is less than average variable cost. Because the firm is now not even covering its variable costs, it should shut down immediately.

Quantity	Total Cost	Fixed Cost	Variable Cost	Marginal Cost	Average Cost	Average Variable Cost
0	$62	$62	—	—	—	—
10	$90	$62	$28	$2.80	$9.00	$2.80
20	$110	$62	$48	$2.00	$5.50	$2.40
30	$126	$62	$64	$1.60	$4.20	$2.13
40	$144	$62	$82	$1.80	$3.60	$2.05
50	$166	$62	$104	$2.20	$3.32	$2.08
60	$192	$62	$130	$2.60	$3.20	$2.16
70	$224	$62	$162	$3.20	$3.20	$2.31
80	$264	$62	$202	$4.00	$3.30	$2.52
90	$324	$62	$262	$6.00	$3.60	$2.91
100	$404	$62	$342	$8.00	$4.04	$3.42

EXHIBIT 10-5 The Shutdown Point for the Overdrive Production Shoppe

down point, then the firm is at least covering its average variable costs, and it should limp ahead even if it is making losses in the short run, since at least those losses will be smaller than if the firm shuts down immediately. However, if the firm is receiving a price below the price at the shutdown point, then the firm is not even covering its variable costs. In this case, staying open is making the firm's losses larger, and it should shut down immediately.

Short-Run Outcomes for Perfectly Competitive Firms

The average cost and average variable cost curves divide the marginal cost curve into three segments, as shown in Exhibit 10-6. At the market price, which the perfectly competitive firm accepts as given, the profit-maximizing firm chooses the output level where price or marginal revenue, which are the same thing for a perfectly competitive firm, is equal to marginal cost: P = MR = MC.

First consider the upper zone, where prices are above the level where marginal cost MC crosses AC at the zero-profit point. At any price above that level, the firm will earn profits in the short run. If the price falls exactly on the zero-profit point where the MC and AC curves cross, then the firm earns zero profits. Next consider a price that falls into the zone between the zero-profit point where MC crosses AC and the shutdown point where MC crosses AVC. In this case, the firm will be making losses in the short run—but since the firm is more than covering its variable costs, the losses are smaller than if the firm shut down immediately. Finally, consider a price below the shutdown point where MC crosses AVC. At any price like this one, the firm will shut down immediately because it cannot even cover its variable costs by operating.

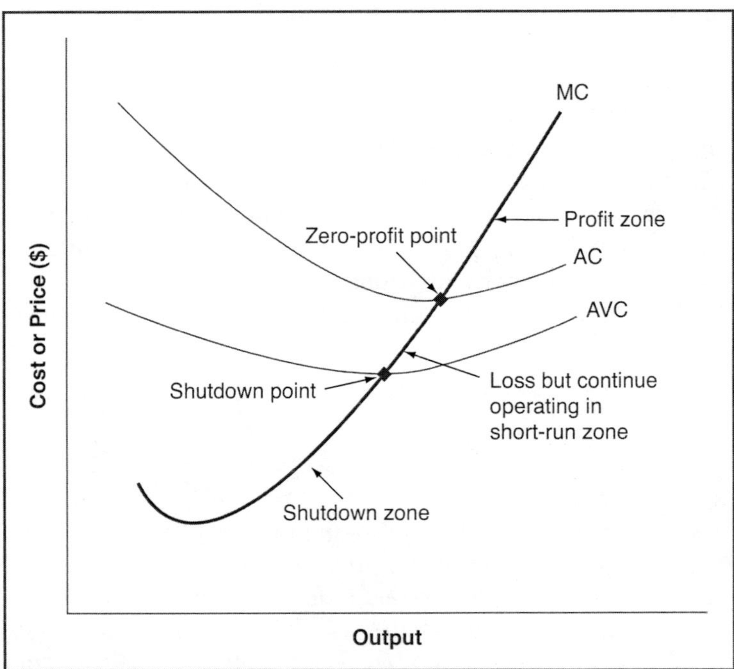

EXHIBIT 10-6 Profit, Loss, Shutdown

The marginal cost curve can be divided into three zones, based on where it is crossed by the average cost and average variable cost curves. The point where MC crosses AC is called the zero-profit point. If the market price is at a level higher than the price at the zero-profit point, then price will be above the average cost curve and the firm is earning profits. If the price is exactly at the zero-profit point, then the firm is making zero profits. If the price is below the price at the zero-profit point, then price will fall below the average cost curve and the firm will be making losses. If price falls in the zone between the shutdown point and the zero-profit point, then the firm is making losses but will continue to operate in the short run, since it is covering its variable costs. However, if price falls below the price at the shutdown point, then the firm will shut down immediately, since it is not even covering its variable costs.

Entry and Exit in the Long-Run Output

The line between the short run and the long run can't be defined precisely with a stopwatch or even with a calendar. It varies according to the specific business. But in the long run, the firm can adjust all factors of production.

In a competitive market, profits are a bugle call that incites businesses to charge. If a business is making a profit in the short run, it has an incentive to expand existing production facilities or to open new ones. New firms may start production, as well. **Entry** is the long-run process of expanding production in response to a sustained pattern of profit opportunities.

entry: The long-run process of firms beginning and expanding production when they see opportunity for profits.

Losses are the black thunderclouds that cause businesses to flee. If a business is making losses in the short run, it will either keep limping along or just shut down, depending on whether its revenues are covering its variable costs. But in the long run, firms that are facing losses will shut down at least some of their output, and some firms will cease production altogether. **Exit** is the long-run process of reducing production in response to a sustained pattern of losses.

exit: The long-run process of firms reducing production and shutting down because they expect losses.

How Entry and Exit Lead to Zero Profits

No perfectly competitive firm acting alone can affect the market price. However, the combination of many firms entering or exiting the market will affect overall supply in the market. In turn, a shift in supply for the market as a whole will affect the market price. Entry and exit are the driving forces behind a process that, in the long run, pushes the price in a perfectly competitive market to be at the zero-profit point, where the marginal cost curve crosses the average cost curve.

To understand how short-run profits for a perfectly competitive firm will evaporate in the long run, imagine that the market price starts at a level where, when the perfectly competitive firm applies the rule P = MR = MC, it produces a quantity where price is above the average cost curve and the firm is earning profits. However, these profits attract entry. Entry of many firms causes the market supply curve to shift to the right, so that a greater quantity is produced at every market price. The shift of the supply curve to the right pushes down the market price. Entry will continue to shift supply to the right until the price is driven down to the zero-profit level, where no firm is earning profits.

Short-run losses will fade away by reversing this process. Now imagine that the market price starts at a level where, when the perfectly competitive firm applies the rule

Business Failure

In the model of perfectly competitive firms, those that consistently can't make money will "exit," which is a nice bloodless word for a more painful process. When a business fails, after all, workers lose their jobs, investors lose their money, and owners and managers can lose their dreams, too. Many businesses fail. During the rough economic time period from 2009–2010, for example, 650,000 firms were born in the United States, but 720,000 firms died. About 80% of these business births and deaths involved small firms with fewer than 20 employees.

Sometimes a business fails because of poor management or workers, or because of tough domestic or foreign competition. Businesses also fail from a variety of causes that might best be summarized as bad luck. Conditions of demand and supply in the market shift in an unexpected way, so that the prices that can be charged for outputs fall or the prices that need to be paid for inputs rise. With millions of businesses in the U.S. economy, even a small fraction of them failing will affect many people—and business failures can be very hard on the workers and managers directly involved. But from the standpoint of the overall economic system, business deaths are sometimes a necessary evil if a market-oriented system is going to offer a flexible mechanism for satisfying customers, keeping costs low, and inventing new products.

P = MR = MC, it produces a quantity where price is below the average cost curve and the firm is experiencing losses. These losses lead some firms to exit. The process of exit by a number of firms causes the market supply curve to shift to the left, so that a lesser quantity is produced at every market price, and the market price rises. The process of exit will continue as long as firms are making losses, until the price rises to the zero-profit level, where firms are no longer suffering losses.

Thus, while a perfectly competitive firm can earn profits in the short run, in the long run, the process of entry will push down prices until they reach the zero-profit level. Conversely, while a perfectly competitive firm may suffer losses in the short run, firms will not continually lose money. In the long run, firms making losses are able to escape from their fixed costs, and their exit from the market will push the price back up to the zero-profit level. In the long run, this process of entry and exit will drive the price in perfectly competitive markets to the zero-profit point at the bottom of the AC curve, where marginal cost crosses average cost.

Economic Profit vs. Accounting Profit

This talk of "zero profit" in the long run must worry anyone who is thinking about starting a business—or making a financial investment in one. But the conclusion that perfectly competitive firms end up with zero profits in the long run is less dire than it may sound, because profit means something different to economists than it does to businesses. The difference arises because economists insist on considering all the opportunity costs of production, including both explicit and implicit costs.

To understand the difference between the economic view of profit and the business or accounting view of profit, think about a business where the owner plunks down $1 million to pay for fixed costs, and at the end of a year, after total revenues and total costs are tallied, the owner has a business that is still worth $1 million and in the meantime has earned a return of $50,000, or 5% of the original investment. How large a profit has the owner earned? To a business owner and the accountant, the answer is clear: the profit is the 5% or $50,000 that was earned. To put it another way, the **accounting profit** is total revenues minus the firm's expenditures on explicit costs.

accounting profit: Total revenues minus the firm's costs, without taking opportunity cost into account.

To an economist, the question is more difficult because the economist wants to take all opportunity costs, including both explicit and implicit costs, into account. Say that the business owner could have invested the money in another business, run by someone else, and it would have paid an 8% return. From the economic point of view, this implicit cost of how the financial capital could have been invested must be included as one of the firm's costs. Thus, **economic profit** is measured by total revenues minus all of the firm's opportunity costs, including both explicit expenditures and implicit costs of financial capital. From this perspective, the business owner has not experienced a gain of 5% for the year, but a loss of 3% (i.e., 5% accounting profit minus 8% in implicit costs).

economic profit: Total revenues minus all of the firm's costs, including opportunity costs.

For the economy as a whole, financial investors earn an average or "normal" level of profit. That normal level of profit determines the opportunity cost of financial investments. Thus, an economist who says that perfectly competitive firms will earn "zero profit" in the long run really means "zero profit after all opportunity costs, including implicit costs, have been taken into account," or to put it differently, that the firm will earn a normal level of profit. When an economist says that a firm will earn positive profits, the economist really means that the profits will be above the normal level. Conversely, losses to an economist include both returns that are negative in an accounting sense and also returns that are slightly positive in an accounting sense, but that do not cover the implicit cost of financial capital.

Although perfectly competitive firms will earn zero economic profits—or a normal rate of profit—in the long run, it's important to remember that not all industries are perfectly competitive, and the long run, by definition, takes some time to arrive. In the real world, businesses will often earn economic profits or losses in the short run.

The Economic Function of Profits

In popular discussions, the term "profit" is sometimes pronounced as if the speaker has been sucking on a lemon. But profits are not a dirty word, any more than "high prices" or "low prices" are dirty words. Profits have an economic rationale, which is built upon the incentives that they provide for entry and exit.

High profits are a messenger. They transmit the message that the willingness of people to pay for that good is higher than the average cost of production, and so society as a whole will benefit if more resources are allocated to production of that certain good or service. Losses are a messenger, too. They carry the message that fewer resources should be allocated to production of a certain good or service because the benefits people are receiving from that production—as measured by their willingness to pay for it—is below the cost of the resources used in the production process.

Profits also serve as a messenger to businesses to seek out the most cost-effective methods of production. As profits lead to entry or losses lead to exit, perfectly competitive firms are pressured to seek out the minimum point of the average cost curve, which is the point where economic profits are zero and also the point where output is being produced at the lowest possible average cost.

Factors of Production in Perfectly Competitive Markets

A firm in a perfectly competitive market must accept the market price for its output and must also pay the prevailing market price for its inputs like labor and physical capital. However, a perfectly competitive firm can decide what quantity of those inputs to use. The earlier discussion of how perfectly competitive firms make decisions about the quantity of output to produce was built on a distinction between short-run decisions, where certain input costs like physical capital investment were fixed, and long-run decisions, where all inputs to production could vary. In the same spirit, let's first consider how a perfectly competitive firm will determine the quantity that it uses of a variable input like labor in the short run, and then how it will determine its quantity of physical capital and its overall method of production in the long run.

The Derived Demand for Labor

When a profit-maximizing firm considers how much labor to hire in the short run, it may first calculate the profit-maximizing quantity of output, and then figure out the quantity of labor needed to produce that quantity of output. For this reason, the demand for labor (and other inputs) is sometimes called a "derived demand"; that is, the demand for labor is derived from the firm's decision about how much to produce.

For an example of how this decision process operates in the short run, consider the Cheep-Cheep Company in Exhibit 10-7, a firm in a perfectly competitive industry that

EXHIBIT 10-7 The Derived Demand for Labor: The Cheep-Cheep Birdhouse Company

Labor	Output	Fixed Cost	Variable Cost	Total Cost	Marginal Cost
0	0	$7,000	$0	$7,000	—
1	12	$7,000	$100	$7,100	$8.33
2	28	$7,000	$200	$7,200	$6.25
3	48	$7,000	$300	$7,300	$5.00
4	68	$7,000	$400	$7,400	$5.00
5	85	$7,000	$500	$7,500	$5.88
6	96	$7,000	$600	$7,600	$9.09
7	105	$7,000	$700	$7,700	$11.11

hires workers to assemble birdhouses. Assume that the cost of hiring a worker is $100 per day and that fixed costs of the birdhouse workshop are $7,000. The quantity of output for a profit-seeking perfectly competitive firm will be determined by applying the rule that production increases up to the point where P = MC. Thus, if the price for a birdhouse is $6, then the profit-maximizing level of output (from the choices in the table) is 85, and the derived demand for labor to produce that desired level of output is five workers. If a surge in demand for birdhouses drives the market price up to $10, then the optimal level of output would become 96, and the derived demand for labor rises to six workers.

Thus, one way to determine what quantity of a variable input to hire is first to determine the profit-maximizing quantity to produce, and then to work backwards and determine what quantity of the input is needed.

The Marginal Revenue Product of Labor

Instead of calculating the amount of labor to hire based on the profit-maximizing quantity, an alternative but equivalent approach is to compare the cost of hiring a worker to the value of what a worker produces.

The cost of hiring a worker is straightforward: it is the wage or compensation paid to the worker. To calculate the value of what a worker produces, find the quantity of production attributable to the marginal worker and multiply it by the price of that output. Exhibit 10-8 takes a different look at the basic cost information from Exhibit 10-7, focusing on the output of workers at the Cheep-Cheep Birdhouse Company. The first column repeats information from Exhibit 10-7, showing different numbers of workers and what they produce. The third column of the figure shows **marginal physical product**, which is the quantity of goods produced by the marginal worker. The fourth column shows the **marginal revenue product (MRP)**, which reveals how much revenue a firm could receive from hiring an additional worker and selling the output of that worker. The MRP is calculated by multiplying the marginal physical product by the market price of $6. A second calculation of marginal revenue product, this one based on a market price for birdhouses of $10, appears in the final column. The two different marginal revenue products, one based on a price for birdhouses of $6 and one based on a price of $10, are also shown in Exhibit 10-8. The marginal revenue product of hiring additional workers gradually declines because of diminishing marginal returns.

marginal physical product: The quantity of goods produced by an additional input (like an additional worker).

marginal revenue product (MRP): Reveals how much revenue a firm could receive from hiring an additional worker and selling the output of that worker.

When a profit-seeking, price-taking, perfectly competitive firm is thinking about the quantity of labor to hire, it will compare the input price with the marginal revenue product for that input. For example, say that the cost for Cheep Cheep of hiring a birdhouse maker is $100. At a market price of $6, Cheep Cheep will notice that hiring a third worker and a fourth worker will have a marginal revenue product of $120, but only cost $100. So it will clearly make sense to hire these workers. In fact, it makes sense to hire the fifth worker as well, since the marginal revenue product of that worker is $102 and thus still exceeds the wage. But at a market price for birdhouses of $6, it won't make sense to hire the sixth or seventh worker, because the marginal revenue product of hiring those workers will be less than $100.

A higher market price for the output of birdhouses will encourage more hiring. If the market price for birdhouses increased to $10, then Cheep Cheep will wish to hire a sixth worker, with a marginal revenue product of $110, but not a seventh worker, since the marginal revenue product of that final worker would only be $90. The optimal quantity of labor to hire will be where the price of the input is equal to the marginal revenue product of that input.

The concept of the marginal revenue product of labor hired explains why the demand curve for labor slopes down. When the wage is lower, more workers will have a marginal revenue product above that wage, so that firms will be willing to hire them. Conversely, when the wage is higher, fewer workers will have a marginal revenue product above that wage, so firms will demand a lower quantity of workers.

The derived demand approach and the marginal revenue product approach to figuring out the quantity of labor to hire are just two different ways of using the same basic

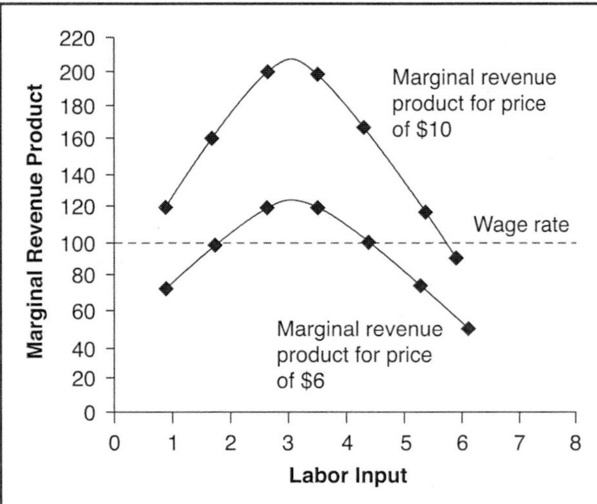

Labor	Output	Marginal Physical Product	Marginal Revenue Product (price $6)	Marginal Revenue Product (price $10)
0	0	—	—	
1	12	12	$72	$120
2	28	16	$96	$160
3	48	20	$120	$200
4	68	20	$120	$200
5	85	17	$102	$170
6	96	11	$66	$110
7	105	9	$54	$90

EXHIBIT 10-8 Marginal Revenue Product: The Cheep-Cheep Example Continues

The wage is shown as a horizontal line, with a cost of $100 for hiring a worker, because it does not vary according to how many workers the firm hires. Marginal revenue product first slopes up because of the increasing marginal returns at low levels of output in this example, and then slopes down because of diminishing marginal returns at higher levels of output. If a worker brings in more than enough marginal revenue to cover the wage of that worker, it will make sense to hire the worker. If the price of the birdhouse is $6, then the firm will hire five workers because the marginal revenue product of the fifth worker is $102. If the price rises to $10 per birdhouse, then the value of what workers produce increases, and the firm will hire six workers. Finally, if the wage rises—in the diagram, imagine the horizontal line at a higher level—the firm will hire fewer workers because fewer workers will have a high enough marginal revenue product to justify paying the higher wage.

information on production functions, input costs, and output prices. The two approaches should always obtain the same answer; in fact, the two methods can be used to check on each other.

Are Workers Paid as Much as They Deserve?

Many workers strongly suspect that they are not being paid as much as they deserve. Is this complaint nothing more than self-interested people who desire some additional income? Or is there reason to believe that in a competitive labor market, workers are systematically paid too little? The argument here suggests that workers are paid what they deserve in the specific sense that they are paid according to their marginal revenue product—that is, according to the value of what the marginal worker produces.

In the real economy, calculating the marginal revenue product may be nearly impossible for many workers. Imagine a company making refrigerators where workers perform many jobs: some work on the assembly line, some maintain and repair equipment, some do paperwork for paying workers and suppliers, some plan future investment in physical capital, some do sales and marketing, and some work on the shipping dock. How could any accountant disentangle exactly what each of these very different workers contributes to making a refrigerator?

However, even when firms cannot calculate marginal revenue product directly, the pressures of competition in the labor market will push pay toward the marginal revenue product of labor. After all, if a foolish employer consistently paid its workers more than the marginal revenue product of what the workers produced, then that employer would make losses, and such pay could not be sustained. On the other hand, if an employer tried to pay workers less than what they produce as measured by their marginal revenue product, then other employers will see an opportunity to hire away some of the marginal workers by offering them a modest increase over their current pay. With these competitive pressures in the labor market, wages are pushed in the direction of marginal revenue product. Of course, just as a market price is not always exactly at equilibrium, but only tending toward equilibrium, it will also be true that wages are not always exactly at the marginal revenue product, although they tend toward that level. Studies of labor markets within countries over time, and between countries, show that differences in how much workers are paid are clearly linked to the market value of what workers produce.

If workers find it difficult or costly to switch between employers, and firms know that workers may be unable or unwilling to move to other jobs, then employers will be able to pay those workers somewhat less than their marginal revenue product. For example, a worker in a rural area may have relatively few employment options that do not involve high monetary and emotional costs of moving. A recent immigrant may lack the information and the social network that would provide information and connections to other jobs. A society with widespread discrimination on the basis of race or gender may block people in certain groups from taking certain jobs. In any of these cases, employers may be able to pay certain workers less than the marginal revenue product of their labor.

Physical Capital Investment and the Hurdle Rate

In the long term, a perfectly competitive firm can adjust all of its inputs, including its investments in physical capital like buildings and machinery. Such investments in physical capital, by their nature, involve thinking about a rate of return over time; that is, the firm purchases the inputs of physical capital in the present and then uses them for production over a period of time in the future.

Consider a firm making plans for investments in physical capital. Managers from all over the company submit proposals. Each proposal includes either an estimate of the marginal revenue product of this capital investment—that is, how much additional revenue will this investment generate, or alternatively, by how much will this investment reduce the costs of the current level of output. Higher-level managers collect these proposals and check them over, estimating the rate of return that can be realistically expected from each proposal. The rates of return for a hypothetical list of 25 projects, ranked from top to bottom, are illustrated by the bar graph in Exhibit 10-9. In deciding which project to carry out, the profit-seeking firm will obviously prefer projects with high rates of return rather than projects with low rates of return (as long as the risk of the projects is similar). But to determine how many investment projects the firm should undertake, the managers of the firm must compare the rates of return to the cost of financial capital.

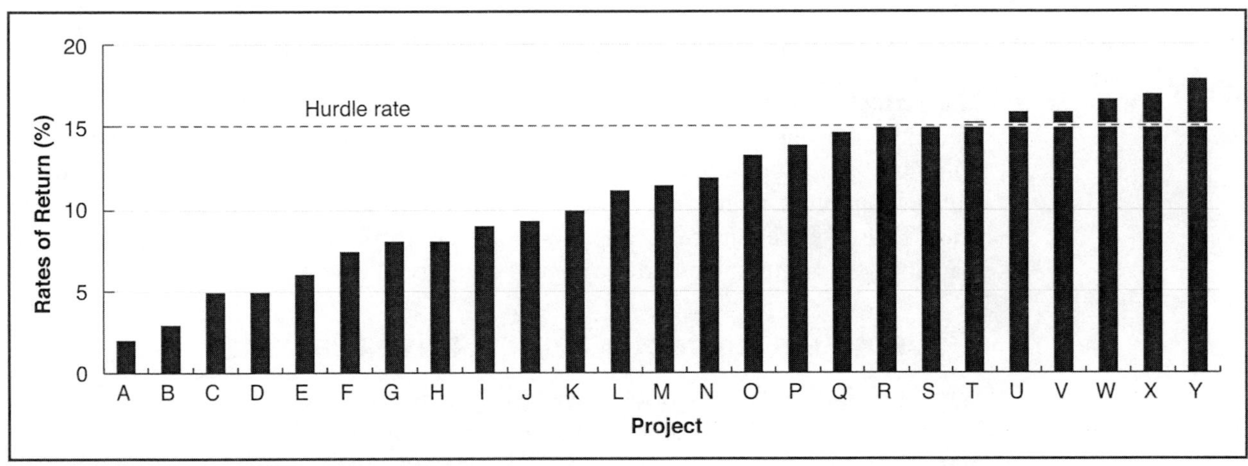

EXHIBIT 10-9 Considering Investment Projects

When a firm makes plans for investments in physical capital, it compares the projected rates of return on these investments with the cost of financial capital to the firm. Often, this comparison will use a hurdle rate as the rate of return that must be exceeded to make the project worth undertaking. In this example, projects A to S do not exceed the hurdle rate. A lower cost of capital will result in more investment projects being undertaken (imagine the horizontal hurdle rate line moving down, so that more projects cross the hurdle). Conversely, a higher cost of financial capital will result in fewer physical capital investment projects being undertaken.

Financial capital always comes at a cost. Sometimes, the firm must pay this cost directly; for example, the firm may borrow financial capital from a bank and thus need to pay an interest rate. However, even if the firm can use funds that it has earned from past profits, spending this money on an investment in physical capital still has an opportunity cost. After all, the firm's financial capital could have been invested in some other way that would have paid a rate of return. Thus, the cost of financial capital to the firm can be conceived of either as a rate of return or interest rate paid to others, or as an opportunity cost of a rate of return that was not received. The specific ways in which firms can raise money for investment—including reinvesting the profits that they earn or using bank loans, bonds, and stocks—will be discussed in Chapter 19.

Firms must also remember that any physical capital investment has some degree of risk. The business world is full of horror stories of factories that were constructed months or years late and cost much more than expected. In other cases, the costs may be estimated accurately, but the returns turn out to be lower than expected. When a company drills for oil, or decides to make a major investment in upgrading its computer systems, it can't be certain of the results in advance.

Firms often take risk into account by using a "hurdle rate," which is an interest rate that is somewhat higher than the actual cost of financial capital to the firm. The intuitive meaning of the hurdle rate is the rate of return that proposed investment projects must cross before being approved. Estimates of typical hurdle rates, based on studies of the investment decisions that firms make, are often about 5–8 percentage points higher than the actual cost of financial capital, whether it is measured as the borrowing interest rate or the opportunity cost of capital. This higher hurdle interest rate can be thought of as a risk premium; that is, it's an adjustment for the risks involved, and it gives the firm a margin for errors of bad luck and overly optimistic forecasts.

If a firm chooses a 15% hurdle rate for its physical capital investment, then such projects must pay an expected return of at least 15% to be worthwhile. A 15% rate of return is represented by the dashed line across Exhibit 10-9. If the cost of financial capital for the firm is higher, then fewer investment projects will make economic sense. Conversely, if the cost of financial capital declines, then a larger number of investment projects will make sense. This logic explains why the demand for financial capital is a downward-sloping curve; the downward slope means that a higher interest rate leads to a lower demand for financial capital because fewer physical capital investments will have expected rates of return that exceed the hurdle rate.

Physical Capital Investment and Long-Run Average Cost

In a perfectly competitive market, firms seek out the combination of variable inputs like labor and fixed inputs like physical capital investment that will allow them to produce at the minimum of the long-run average cost curve. If a firm does not produce at the lowest possible average cost, then firms with a lower cost of production will be able to sell at a lower price. Thus, the pressure of competition between firms will shape both the specific kinds of machinery and equipment and the overall quantity of investment in physical capital.

Efficiency in Perfectly Competitive Markets

When profit-maximizing firms in perfectly competitive markets combine with utility-maximizing consumers, something remarkable happens: the resulting quantities of outputs of goods and services demonstrate both productive and allocative efficiency (terms that were first introduced back in Chapter 2).

Productive efficiency means producing without waste, so that the choice is on the production possibility frontier. In the long run in a perfectly competitive market, because of the process of entry and exit, the price in the market is equal to the minimum of the long-run average cost curve. In other words, goods are being produced and sold at the lowest possible average cost. When the average cost of production is as low as possible, the economy will be operating on the production possibility frontier.

Allocative efficiency means that among the points on the production possibility frontier, the point that is chosen is socially preferred—at least in a particular and specific sense. In a perfectly competitive market, price will be equal to the marginal cost of production. Think about the price that is paid for a good as a measure of the social benefit received for that good; after all, the willingness to pay conveys what the good was worth to a buyer. Then think about the marginal cost of producing the good as representing not just the cost for the firm, but more broadly as the social cost of producing that good. When perfectly competitive firms follow the rule that profits are maximized by producing at the quantity where price is equal to marginal cost, they are thus ensuring that the social benefits received from producing a good, as reflected in the demand curve for a good, are in line with the social costs of production, as reflected in the supply curve for a good.

To explore what is meant by allocative efficiency, it is useful to walk through an example of what allocative *inefficiency* would imply. Begin by assuming that the market for ordinary television sets is perfectly competitive, and so P = MC. Now consider what it would mean if firms produced a lesser quantity of television sets. At a lesser quantity, marginal costs will not yet have increased as much, so that price will exceed marginal cost; that is, P > MC. In that situation, the benefit to society as a whole of producing additional goods, as measured by the willingness of consumers to pay for marginal units of a good, would be higher than the cost of the inputs of labor and physical capital needed to produce the marginal good. In other words, the gains to society as a whole from producing additional marginal units will be greater than the costs. Conversely, consider what it would mean if, compared to the level of output at the allocatively efficient choice when P = MC, firms produced a greater quantity of television sets. At a greater quantity, marginal costs of production will have increased so that P < MC. In that case, the marginal costs of producing additional television sets are greater than the benefit to society as measured by what people are willing to pay. For society as a whole, since the costs are outstripping the benefits, it will make sense to produce a lower quantity of such goods.

When perfectly competitive firms maximize their profits by producing the quantity where P = MC, they also assure that the benefits to consumers of what they are buying, as measured by the price they are willing to pay, is equal to the costs to society of producing the marginal units, as measured by the marginal costs the firm must pay—and thus that allocative efficiency holds.

The statements that a perfectly competitive market in the long run will feature both productive and allocative efficiency do need to be taken with a few grains of salt. Remember, economists are using the concept of "efficiency" in a particular and specific sense, not as a synonym for "desirable in every way." Perfect competition in the long run is a hypothetical extreme. In other competitive situations discussed in the next two chapters, like monopoly, monopolistic competition, and oligopoly, firms will not always produce at the minimum of average cost, nor will they always set price equal to marginal cost. Thus, these other competitive situations will not lead to productive and allocative efficiency. Moreover, real-world markets include many issues that are assumed away in the model of perfect competition, including pollution, inventions of new technology, poverty that may make some people unable to pay for basic necessities of life, government programs like national defense or education, discrimination in labor markets, and buyers and sellers who must deal with imperfect and unclear information. These issues are explored in later chapters of this book. However, the theoretical efficiency of perfect competition does provide a useful benchmark for comparing what issues arise from these real-world problems.

Conclusion

Extreme assumptions often provide a useful starting point for analysis. In a physics class, it may be useful to analyze gravity by assuming that a ball that is dropped from a great height experiences zero friction as it falls through the air. This assumption of zero friction is not literally true. But if the amount of friction from the air is relatively small compared to the pull of gravity, then assuming zero friction may not make much difference to the results. If friction is significant, then calculations for the effects of friction can be added, once the basic no-friction example is understood.

The assumption of perfect competition—that firms are perfect price takers, unable to raise their price by so much as a penny without losing all of their sales—is not literally true. But in a market with many competitors that have highly similar products, the assumption of perfect competition may provide a reasonable start for the analysis. In a highly competitive market—even if it is not strictly speaking perfectly competitive—firms will not lose all of their sales if they raise prices by a penny, but they might lose a large enough proportion of their sales to cripple the firm if they raise prices by 5%. In a highly competitive real-world market, not all firms will be producing at the absolute bottom of the average cost curve at all times—but the firms will still face considerable pressure to keep average costs as low as possible. Firms in a highly competitive market may earn profits in the short run, but the entry of new firms or the expansion of existing firms means that such profits will not persist in the long run. Truly perfect competition is a hypothetical extreme, but many real-world producers face highly competitive markets every day.

Key Concepts and Summary

1. A **perfectly competitive** firm is a price taker, which means that it must accept the prices at which its sell goods and the prices at which it purchases inputs as determined in the market. If a perfectly competitive firm attempts to charge even a tiny amount more than the market price, it will be unable to make any sales.
2. As a perfectly competitive firm produces a greater quantity of output, its **total revenue** steadily increases at a constant rate determined by the given market price.
3. Profits will be highest (or losses will be smallest) at the quantity of output where total revenues exceed total costs by the greatest amount (or where total revenues fall short of total costs by the smallest amount). Alternatively, profits will be highest at the quantity of output where **marginal revenue**, which is price for a perfectly competitive firm, is equal to marginal cost.
4. If the market price faced by a perfectly competitive firm is above average cost at the profit-maximizing quantity of output, then the firm is making profits. If the market price is below average cost at the profit-maximizing quantity of output, then the firm is making losses. If the market price is at average cost, at the profit-maximizing level of output, then the firm is making zero profits. The point where the marginal cost curve crosses the average cost curve, at the minimum of the average cost curve, is called the "zero-profit point."
5. The point where the marginal cost curve crosses the average variable cost curve is called the **shutdown point**. If the market price faced by a perfectly competitive firm is below average variable cost at the profit-maximizing quantity of output, then the firm should shut down operations immediately. If the market price faced by a perfectly competitive firm is above average variable cost, but below average cost, then the firm should continue producing in the short run, but exit in the long run.
6. In the long run, firms will respond to profits through a process of **entry**, where existing firms expand output and new firms enter the market. Conversely, firms will react to losses in the long run through a process of **exit**, in which existing firms reduce output or cease production altogether.
7. Through the process of entry in response to profits and exit in response to losses, the price level in a perfectly competitive market will move toward the zero-profit point, where the marginal cost curve crosses the AC curve, at the minimum of the average cost curve.
8. **Accounting profit** is measured by taking total revenues and subtracting expenditures. Economic profit is measured after taking total revenue, subtracting all expenditures, and also subtracting the opportunity cost of financial capital. Thus, zero **economic profit** actually means a normal accounting rate of profit.
9. A profit-maximizing firm will determine its optimal quantity of output and then hire the amount of the variable input, like labor, needed to produce that quantity of output.
10. The **marginal revenue product**, the value of what is produced by an additional worker, is calculated by taking the quantity of output produced by the marginal worker and multiplying it by the price of that output. A profit-maximizing firm will hire workers as long as the marginal revenue product of what they produce exceeds the wage, up to the point where the marginal revenue product is equal to the wage.
11. If an employer paid wages that were higher than marginal revenue product—that is, higher than the value of what workers produced—the employer would tend to make losses and such wages could not be continued. If one employer paid wages that were lower than

the marginal revenue product, then other employers would see a profit opportunity in hiring those workers and paying them more. If workers can move freely between comparable alternative jobs, the pressures of the labor market will tend to push wages toward marginal revenue product.

12. Firms will invest as long as the expected returns of the investment exceed the cost of capital, where the cost of capital typically includes a "hurdle rate" to take account of the risk involved.
13. When perfectly competitive firms produce at the minimum of the long-run average cost curve, the market will show productive efficiency, since they are producing at the lowest possible average cost. When perfectly competitive firms produce at the quantity where P = MC, the market will illustrate allocative efficiency, since each good is being produced up to the quantity where the amount that the good benefits society, as measured by the price people are willing to pay, is equal to the cost to society, as measured by the marginal cost of production.

Review Questions

1. How does a perfectly competitive firm decide what price to charge?
2. What prevents a perfectly competitive firm from seeking higher profits by increasing the price that it charges?
3. How does a perfectly competitive firm calculate total revenue?
4. Briefly explain the reason for the shape of a marginal revenue curve for a perfectly competitive firm.
5. What rule does a perfectly competitive firm apply to determine its profit-maximizing quantity of output?
6. How does the average cost curve help to show whether a firm is making profits or losses?
7. What two lines on a cost curve diagram intersect at the zero-profit point?
8. Should a firm shut down immediately if it is making losses?
9. How does the average variable cost curve help a firm know whether it should shut down immediately?
10. What two lines on a cost curve diagram intersect at the shutdown point?
11. Why does entry occur?
12. Why does exit occur?
13. Do entry and exit occur in the short run, the long run, both, or neither?
14. What price will a perfectly competitive firm end up charging in the long run? Why?
15. What's the difference between accounting profit and economic profit? Which one is higher?
16. Why is labor called a "derived demand"?
17. How can a perfectly competitive firm use derived demand to decide how much labor to hire?
18. How is the marginal revenue product of labor calculated?
19. How can a perfectly competitive firm use the marginal revenue product of labor to determine what quantity of labor to hire?
20. What is the "hurdle rate"?
21. How does a firm use the hurdle rate to decide which investments in physical capital to undertake?
22. Will a perfectly competitive industry display productive efficiency? Why or why not?
23. Will a perfectly competitive industry display allocative efficiency? Why or why not?

CHAPTER

11

Monopoly

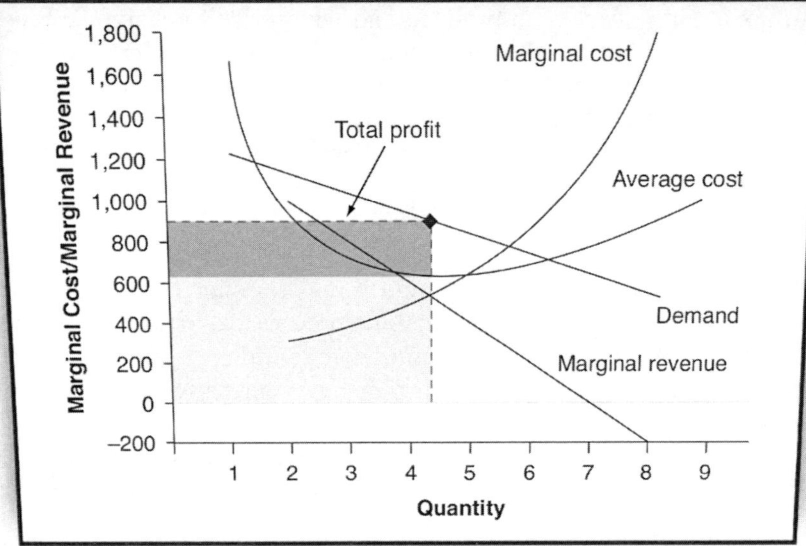

Chapter Outline

Barriers to Entry

Natural Monopoly

How a Profit-Maximizing Monopoly Chooses Output and Price

Conclusion

There is a widespread belief that top executives at firms are the strongest supporters of market competition, but this belief is far from the truth. Think about it this way: If you very much wanted to win an Olympic gold medal, would you rather be far better than everyone else, or locked in competition with many athletes just as good as you are—or even a little better? Similarly, if you'd like to attain a very high level of profits, would you rather manage a business with little or no competition, or struggle against many tough competitors who are trying to sell to your customers? Competition can benefit society as a whole because it encourages firms to try their hardest to please customers. But for individual firms, a lesser degree of competition can seem very attractive.

Thus, the dreams of business managers rarely take place in a world of perfect competition, with many firms selling identical products. Instead, top executives salivate over the idea of **imperfect competition**, which involves either a smaller number of competing firms, or products that aren't identical, or both. Imperfect competition comes in several flavors: monopoly, oligopoly, and monopolistic competition. In the case of **monopoly**, one firm produces all or nearly all of the output in a market. In the case of **monopolistic competition**, a large number of firms compete, but their products differ meaningfully from each other. In the case of **oligopoly**, a small number of firms—perhaps just two or three or four—sell all or nearly all of the output in a market. This chapter focuses on monopoly; the next chapter addresses the intermediate cases of monopolistic competition and oligopoly.

imperfect competition: Competition that does not fit the definition of perfect competition either because it involves a smaller number of firms or only one firm, or products that aren't identical.

monopoly: A firm that faces no competitors.

monopolistic competition: Many firms competing to sell similar but differentiated products.

oligopoly: When several large firms have all or most of the sales in an industry.

One of the most-publicized U.S. monopolies in the last two decades is the Microsoft Corporation, which sells (among other products) the Windows operating system for personal computers—that is, the background software that organizes and enables all the other programs on the computer. In the early 2000s, the Windows system ran on 90% or more of the most commonly sold type of personal computers. But most people deal with monopolies or near-monopolies every day. Google handles roughly 70% of all the Internet search requests in the United States. The U.S. Postal Service has a monopoly on the delivery of first-class mail. Most people have only one firm from which they can purchase electricity or garbage collection. Some new drugs are produced by only one pharmaceutical firm—and no close substitutes for that drug may exist.

This chapter begins with the ways in which monopolies may be protected from competition, including laws that prohibit competition, technological advantages, and certain configurations of demand and supply. The chapter then discusses how a monopoly will choose its profit-maximizing quantity to produce and what price to charge. While a monopoly must be concerned about whether consumers will purchase its products or spend their money on something altogether different, the monopolist need not worry about the actions of other competing firms. As a result, a monopoly is not a price-taker like a perfectly competitive firm, but instead exercises some power to choose its market price.

Barriers to Entry

barriers to entry: The legal, technological, or market forces that may discourage or prevent potential competitors from entering a market.

Barriers to entry are the legal, technological, or market forces that may discourage or prevent potential competitors from entering a market. In some cases, barriers to entry may lead to pure monopoly; in other cases, they may limit competition to a few oligopoly firms. Barriers to entry will block entry even if the firm or firms currently in the market are earning profits. Thus, in markets with barriers to entry, it is not true that abnormally high profits will attract the entry of new firms and that this entry of new firms will eventually cause the price to decline so that surviving firms earn only a normal level of profit in the long run.

Legal Restrictions

In some cases, the government erects barriers to entry by prohibiting or limiting competitors. Under U.S. law, no organization but the U.S. Post Office is legally allowed to deliver first-class mail. Many states or cities have laws or regulations that allow households a choice of only one electrical company, one water company, and one company to pick up the garbage.

deregulation: Removing government controls over setting prices and quantities in certain industries.

Government limitations on competition used to be even more common in the United States. For most of the twentieth century, only one phone company—AT&T—was legally allowed to provide local and long-distance service. From the 1930s up to the 1970s, federal regulations limited which destinations airlines could choose to fly to and what fares they could charge, another set of regulations limited the interest rates that banks could pay to depositors, and yet another set specified what trucking firms could charge customers. However, a wave of **deregulation**, starting in the late 1970s and running into the 1990s, eliminated or reduced U.S. government restrictions on the firms that could enter, the prices that could be charged, and the quantities that could be produced in many industries, including airlines, trucking, banking, telecommunications, electricity, and more. Around the world, from Europe to Latin America to Africa and Asia, many governments continue to control and limit competition in what those governments perceive to be key industries, including airlines, banks, steel companies, oil companies, telephone companies, and others.

Control of a Physical Resource

If a company can control a scarce physical resource, then other firms may find it difficult to compete. In the U.S. economy, one historical example of this pattern occurred when ALCOA—which stood for Aluminum Company of America—controlled most of the supply of bauxite, a key mineral used in making aluminum, back in the 1930s. Today, two well-known arrangements for controlling a physical resource involve oil and diamonds. The Organization for Petroleum Exporting Countries, commonly known as OPEC, includes many of the world's leading petroleum-exporting countries, including Saudi

Arabia and most of the Middle Eastern oil producers, along with Nigeria, Venezuela, and Indonesia. In one famous episode, from 1973–1975, OPEC more than doubled the price of oil, with dramatic effects on consumers of oil around the world. The majority of global diamond production is controlled by DeBeer's, a South African firm that controls over 10 prolific African diamond mines and also directs the Central Selling Organization, which controls a majority of the world's distribution and resale of rough diamonds.

Technological Superiority

Technological capabilities may also discourage competitors. The Windows operating system sold only by Microsoft is one example; it is technologically difficult, although not impossible, for other firms to produce an equivalent product. Attempts to gain a technological advantage are widespread. Pharmaceutical companies strive to invent new drugs that only they know how to make. Software companies strive to write distinctive new programs.

In some cases, technological superiority may combine with the law to create a barrier to entry. The Constitution of the United States specifies in Article I, Section 8: "The Congress shall have Power . . . To Promote the Progress of Science and Useful Arts, by securing for limited Times to Authors and Inventors the Exclusive Right to their Writings and Discoveries." Congress used this power to create the U.S. Patent and Trademark Office, as well as the U.S. Copyright Office. A **patent** gives the inventor the exclusive legal right to make, use, or sell the invention for a limited time; in the United States, exclusive patent rights last for 20 years.

A **trademark** is a word, name, symbol, or device that indicates the source of the goods, like the name Chiquita on bananas, the name Chevrolet on cars, or the Nike "swoosh" that appears on shoes and athletic gear. Roughly 800,000 trademarks are registered with the U.S. government. A firm can renew its trademarks over and over again, as long as it remains in active use.

A **copyright**, according the U.S. Copyright Office, "is a form of protection provided by the laws of the United States for 'original works of authorship' including literary, dramatic, musical, architectural, cartographic, choreographic, pantomimic, pictorial, graphic, sculptural, and audiovisual creations." No one can reproduce or display or perform a

patent: A government rule that gives the inventor the exclusive legal right to make, use, or sell the invention for a limited time.

trademark: A word, name, symbol, or device that indicates the source of the goods and can only be used by the firm that registered that trademark.

copyright: A form of legal protection to prevent copying for commercial purposes original works of authorship, including books and music.

Willy Wonka and Trade Secrets

Roald Dahl wrote a book in 1964 called *Charlie and the Chocolate Factory*, which has been made into a movie twice: the first time in a 1971 version starring Gene Wilder as the candy-maker Willy Wonka, and the second time in 2005 starring Johnny Depp. For economists, the story is about trying to steal candy industry trade secrets. Here's how Dahl tells it:

> "You see, Charlie, not so very long ago there used to be thousands of people working in Mr. Willy Wonka's factory. Then one day, all of a sudden, Mr. Wonka had to ask every single one of them to leave, to go home, never to come back."
>
> "But why?" asked Charlie.
>
> "Because of spies."
>
> "Spies?"
>
> "Yes. All the other chocolate makers, you see, had begun to grow jealous of the wonderful candies that Mr. Wonka was making, and they started sending in spies to steal his secret recipes. The spies took jobs in the Wonka factory, pretending they were ordinary workers, and while they were there, each one of them found out exactly how a certain special thing was made."

Dahl's story was rooted in common business practices of the candy industry during his childhood. The two biggest candy makers of that time, Cadbury and Rowntree, were famous for the number of spies they attempted to infiltrate into other companies. Other candy firms were known to hire detectives to investigate their own workers and to require outside contractors to be blindfolded when they entered the factory. Dahl went to school not far from the Cadbury headquarters, where he and fellow students were sometimes brought in as taste testers for new kinds of chocolate bars in plain foil wrappings.

copyrighted work without permission of the author. Copyright protection ordinarily lasts for the life of the author plus 70 years.

trade secrets: Methods of production kept secret by the producing firm.

intellectual property: The body of law including patents, trademarks, copyrights, and trade secret law that protects the right of inventors to produce and sell their inventions.

Roughly speaking, patent law covers inventions and copyright protects books, songs, and art. But in certain areas, like the invention of new software, it has been unclear whether patent or copyright protection should apply. There is also a body of law known as **trade secrets**. Even if a company does not have a patent on an invention, competing firms are not allowed to break into their factories and files and steal their secrets. One famous trade secret is the formula for Coca Cola, which is not protected under copyright or patent law, but is simply kept secret by the company.

Taken together, this combination of patents, trademarks, copyrights, and trade secret law is called **intellectual property** because it implies ownership over an idea or concept or image, not a physical piece of property like house or a car. Countries around the world have enacted laws to protect intellectual property, although the time periods and exact provisions of such laws vary across countries. There are ongoing negotiations, both through the World Intellectual Property Organization (WIPO) and through international treaties, to bring greater harmony to the intellectual property laws of different countries and to determine the extent to which patents and copyrights in one country will be respected in other countries.

Natural Monopoly

Economies of scale can combine with the size of the market to limit competition. (This theme was introduced in Chapter 9.) Exhibit 11-1 presents a long-run average cost curve for the airplane manufacturing industry. The long-run average cost curve shows economies of scale up to an output of 8,000 planes per year and a price of p_0, then constant

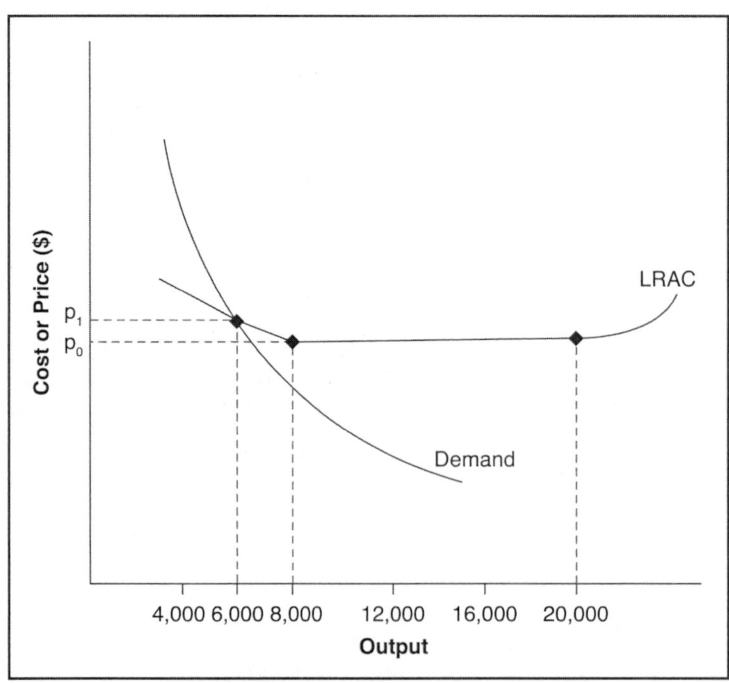

EXHIBIT 11-1 Economies of Scale and Natural Monopoly

In this market, the demand curve intersects the long-run average cost curve in the downward-sloping part of the LRAC curve. Imagine the situation where a monopoly is producing 6,000 units at a price of p_1. If a potential competitor tried to produce a smaller quantity, then its average costs would be too high to compete. If a potential competitor tried to produce a larger quantity, like 8,000 or 20,000, then it could produce at a lower average cost—but it could not sell the additional units because of a lack of demand in the market. Thus, a natural monopoly occurs when the quantity demanded is less than the minimum quantity it takes to be at the bottom of the long-run average cost curve.

returns to scale from 8,000 to 20,000 planes per year, and diseconomies of scale at a quantity of production greater than 20,000 planes per year. Now consider the market demand curve in the diagram, which intersects the long-run average cost curve at an output level of 6,000 planes per year and at a price p_1 which is higher than p_0. In this situation, the market has room for only one producer. If a second firm attempts to enter the market at a smaller size, say by producing a quantity of 4,000 planes, then its average costs will be higher than the existing firm, and it will be unable to compete. If the second firm attempts to enter the market at a larger size, like 8,000 planes per year, then it could produce at a lower average cost—but it couldn't sell all 8,000 planes that it produced because of insufficient demand in the market.

This situation, when economies of scale are large relative to the quantity demanded in the market, is called a **natural monopoly**. Natural monopolies often arise in industries where the marginal cost of adding an additional customer is very low, once the fixed costs of the overall system are in place. Once the main water pipes are laid through a neighborhood, the marginal cost of providing water service to another home is fairly low. Once electricity lines are installed through a neighborhood, the marginal cost of providing additional electrical service to one more home is very low. It would be costly and duplicative for a second water company to enter the market and invest in a whole second set of main water pipes, or for a second electricity company to enter the market and invest in a whole new set of electrical wires. These industries offer an example where, because of economies of scale, one producer could serve the entire market more efficiently than a number of smaller producers that would have needed to make duplicative physical capital investments. A natural monopoly can also arise in smaller local markets for products that are difficult to transport. For example, cement production exhibits economies of scale, and the quantity of cement demanded in a local area may not be much larger than what a single plant can produce. Moreover, the costs of transporting cement overland are high, and so a cement plant in an area without access to water transportation may be a natural monopoly.

natural monopoly: When the quantity demanded in the market is less than the quantity at the bottom of the long-run average cost curve.

Intimidating Potential Competition

Businesses have developed a number of schemes for creating barriers to entry by deterring potential competitors from entering the market. One method is known as **predatory pricing**, in which a firm uses the threat of sharp price cuts to discourage competition. Consider a large airline that provides most of the flights between two particular cities. A new, small start-up airline decides to offer service between these two cities. The large airline immediately slashes prices on this route to the bone, so that the new entrant can't make any money. After the new entrant has exited this market, the incumbent firm can raise prices again. After this pattern occurs once or twice, potential new entrants may decide that it isn't wise to try to compete. Small airlines often accuse larger airlines of predatory pricing: in the early 2000s, for example, ValuJet accused Delta of predatory pricing, Frontier accused United, and Reno Air accused Northwest. In late 2009, the American Booksellers Association, which represents independently owned and often smaller bookstores, accused Amazon, Wal-Mart, and Target of predatory pricing for selling new hardcover best-sellers at low prices.

predatory pricing: When an existing firm uses sharp but temporary price cuts to discourage new competition.

In some cases, large advertising budgets can also act as a way of discouraging the competition. If the only way to launch a successful new national cola drink is to spend more than the promotional budgets of Coca Cola and Pepsi Cola, not too many companies will try. A firmly established brand name can be difficult to dislodge.

Summing Up Barriers to Entry

The five categories of barriers to entry that have been discussed here are laws against entry and price changes, control of a physical resource, technological advantage, natural monopoly, and intimidating potential competitors. This list should not be viewed as exhaustive, since firms in many industries have proven to be highly creative in inventing business practices that discourage competition. When barriers to entry exist, perfect competition is no longer a reasonable description of how an industry works. When barriers to entry are high enough, monopoly can result.

How a Profit-Maximizing Monopoly Chooses Output and Price

Consider a monopoly firm, comfortably surrounded by barriers to entry so that it need not fear competition from other producers. How will this monopoly choose its profit-maximizing quantity of output, and what price will it charge? Profits for the monopolist, like any firm, will be equal to total revenues minus total costs. The pattern of costs for the monopoly can be analyzed within the same framework as the costs of a perfectly competitive firm—that is, by using total cost, fixed cost, variable cost, marginal cost, average cost, and average variable cost. However, because a monopoly faces no competition, its decision process will differ from that of a perfectly competitive firm.

Demand Curves Perceived by a Perfectly Competitive Firm and by a Monopoly

A perfectly competitive firm acts as a price taker, so its calculation of total revenue is made by taking the given market price and multiplying it by the quantity of output that the firm chooses. The demand curve *as it is perceived by a perfectly competitive firm* appears in Exhibit 11-2*a*. The flat perceived demand curve means that, from the price-taker viewpoint of a perfectly competitive firm, it could sell either a relatively low quantity like q_L or a relatively high quantity like q_H at the market price p*.

No monopolist, even one who is thoroughly protected by high barriers to entry from other competing firms, can require consumers to purchase its product. The demand curve for the monopolist's products *as it is perceived by a monopolist* is exactly the same as the market demand curve—because the monopolist is the only firm in the market. Because demand for most products is neither completely elastic nor completely inelastic, an in-between case is drawn in Exhibit 11-2*b*. The monopolist can either choose a point like

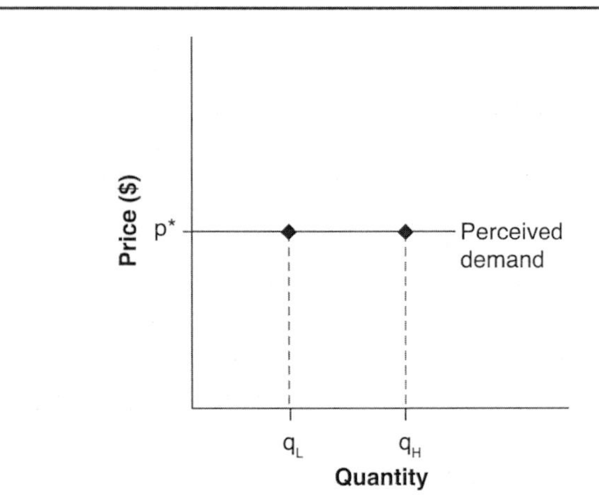

(a) Perceived demand curve by perfect competitor

Perceived demand for a perfect competitor. A perfectly competitive firm is a price-taker and thus perceives the demand curve that it faces to be flat. The flat shape means that the firm can sell either a low quantity q_L or a high quantity q_H at exactly the same price p*.

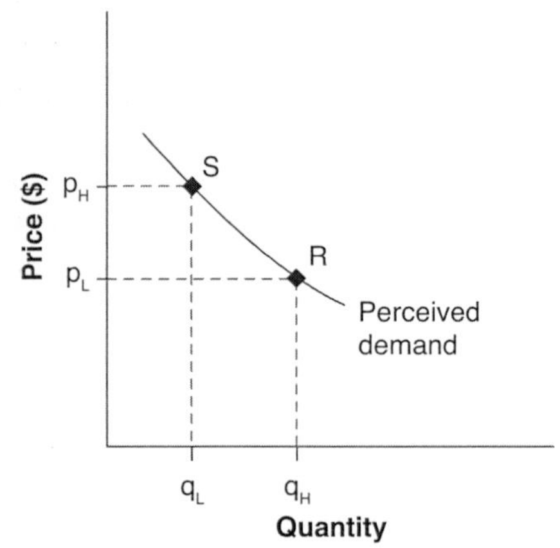

(b) Perceived demand curve by monopolist

Perceived demand for a monopolist. A monopolist is not a price-taker. It perceives the demand curve that it faces to be the same as the market demand curve, which for most goods is downward sloping. Thus, if the monopolist chooses a high level of output q_H, it can charge only a relatively low price p_L; conversely, if the monopolist chooses a low level of output q_L, it can then charge a higher price p_H. The monopolist can choose the combination of price and quantity that maximizes profits.

EXHIBIT 11-2 The Perceived Demand Curve for a Perfect Competitor and a Monopolist

R with a low price p_L and high quantity q_H, or a point like S with a high price p_H and a low quantity q_L, or some intermediate point. Setting the price too high will result in a low quantity sold and thus won't bring in much revenue. Conversely, setting the price too low may result in a high quantity sold, but because of the low price, it won't bring in much revenue either. The challenge of the monopolist is to strike a profit-maximizing balance between the price it charges and the quantity that it sells.

Total and Marginal Revenue for a Monopolist

Profits for a monopolist can be illustrated with a graph of total revenues and total costs, as shown with the example of the hypothetical HealthPill firm in Exhibit 11-3. The total cost curve has its typical shape; that is, total costs rise and grow steeper as output increases.

To calculate total revenue for a monopolist, start with the demand curve perceived by the monopolist. The table shows quantities along the demand curve, the price at each quantity demanded, and then calculates total revenue by multiplying price times quantity at each level of output. (In this example, the output is given as 1, 2, 3, 4, and the like, for the sake of simplicity. If you prefer a dash of greater realism, you can imagine that these output levels and the corresponding prices are measured per 1,000 or 10,000 pills.) As the exhibit illustrates, total revenue for a monopolist rises, flattens out, and then falls. In this example, total revenue is highest at a quantity of 6 or 7. Clearly, the total revenue for a monopolist is not a straight upward-sloping line, in the way that total revenue was for a perfectly competitive firm. The different total revenue pattern for a monopolist occurs because the quantity that a monopolist chooses to produce affects the market price, which was not true for a perfectly competitive firm. If the monopolist charges a very high price, then quantity demanded drops, and so total revenue is very low. If the monopolist charges a very low price, then even if quantity demanded is very high, total revenue won't add up to much. At some intermediate level, total revenue will be highest.

However, the monopolist is not seeking to maximize revenue, but instead to earn the highest possible profit. Profits are calculated in the final row of the table. In the HealthPill example in Exhibit 11-3, the highest profit will occur at the quantity where total revenue is the farthest above total cost. Of the choices given in the table, the highest profits occur at an output of 4, where profit is 900.

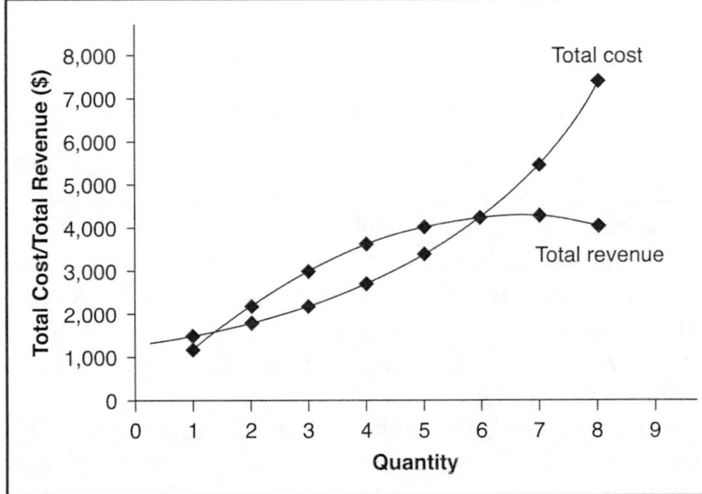

Quantity	Total Cost	Price	Total Revenue	Profit = Total Revenue – Total Cost
1	1,500	1,200	1,200	–300
2	1,800	1,100	2,200	400
3	2,200	1,000	3,000	800
4	2,700	900	3,600	900
5	3,300	800	4,000	700
6	4,200	700	4,200	0
7	5,400	600	4,200	–1,200
8	7,200	500	4,000	–3,200

EXHIBIT 11-3 Total Revenue and Total Cost for the HealthPill Monopoly

Total revenue for the monopoly firm called HealthPill first rises, then falls. Low levels of output bring in relatively little total revenue because the quantity is low. High levels of output bring in relatively less revenue because the high quantity pushes down the market price. The total cost curve is upward sloping. Profits will be highest at the quantity of output where total revenue is most above total cost; of the choices in the table, the highest profits happen at an output of 4. The profit-maximizing level of output is not the same as the revenue-maximizing level of output, which should make sense, because profits take costs into account and revenues don't.

What Is the Market?

A monopoly is a firm that sells all or nearly all of the goods and services in a given market. But what defines a "market"?

In a famous 1947 case, the federal government accused the DuPont company of having a monopoly in the cellophane market, pointing out that DuPont produced 75% of the cellophane in the United States. DuPont countered that even though it had 75% market share in cellophane, it produced less than 20% of the "flexible packaging materials," which includes all other moisture-proof papers, films, and foils. In 1956, after years of legal appeals, the U.S. Supreme Court held that the broader market definition was more appropriate, and the case against DuPont was dismissed.

Questions over how to define the market continue today. True, Microsoft in the 1990s had a dominant share of the software for computer operating systems, but in the total market for all computer software and services, including everything from games to scientific programs, the Microsoft share was only about 16% in 2000. The Greyhound bus company may have a near-monopoly on the market for intercity bus transportation, but it is only a small share of the market for intercity transportation if that market includes private cars, airplanes, and railroad service. DeBeer's has a monopoly in diamonds, but it is a much smaller share of the total market for precious gemstones and an even smaller share of the total market for jewelry. A small town in the country may have only one gas station: is this gas station a "monopoly" or does it compete with gas stations that might be five or ten or 50 miles away?

In general, if a firm produces a product without close substitutes, then the firm can be considered a monopoly producer in a single market, but if buyers have a range of similar—even if not identical—options available from other firms, then the firm is not a monopoly. But arguments over whether close substitutes are available can be controversial.

CLEARING IT UP

Perceived Demand and Market Demand

The demand curve as perceived by a perfectly competitive firm is not the overall market demand curve for that product. However, the firm's demand curve as perceived by a monopoly is the same as the market demand curve. The reason for the difference is that each perfectly competitive firm perceives the demand for its products in a market that includes many other firms; in effect, the demand curve perceived by a perfectly competitive firm is a tiny slice of the entire market demand curve. In contrast, a monopoly perceives demand for its product in a market where the monopoly is the only producer.

Marginal Revenue and Marginal Cost for a Monopolist

In the real world, a monopolist often does not have enough information to analyze its entire total revenues or total costs curves; after all, the firm doesn't know exactly what would happen if it was to alter production dramatically. But a monopoly often has fairly reliable information about how changing output by small or moderate amounts will affect its marginal revenues and marginal costs because it has had experience with such changes over time and because modest changes are easier to extrapolate from current experience. A monopolist can use information on marginal revenue and marginal cost to seek out the profit-maximizing combination of quantity and price.

The first four columns of Exhibit 11-4 use the numbers on total cost from the HealthPill example in the previous exhibit and calculate marginal cost and average cost. This monopoly faces a typical U-shaped average cost curve and upward-sloping marginal cost curve. The second three columns use the total revenue information from the previous exhibit and calculate marginal revenue. Notice that marginal revenue is zero at a quantity of 7 and turns negative at quantities higher than 7. It may seem counterintuitive that marginal revenue could ever be zero or negative: after all, doesn't an increase in quantity sold always mean more revenue? For a perfect competitor, each additional unit sold brought a positive marginal revenue because marginal revenue was equal to the given market

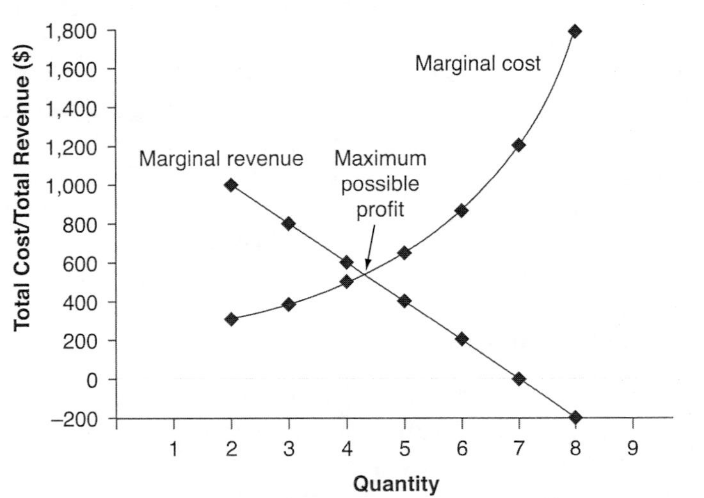

	Cost Information			Revenue Information		
Quantity	Total Cost	Marginal Cost	Average Cost	Price	Total Revenue	Marginal Revenue
1	1,500	–	1,500	1,200	1,200	–
2	1,800	300	900	1,100	2,200	1,000
3	2,200	400	733	1,000	3,000	800
4	2,700	500	675	900	3,600	600
5	3,300	600	660	800	4,000	400
6	4,200	900	700	700	4,200	200
7	5,400	1,200	771	600	4,200	0
8	7,200	1,800	900	500	4,000	–200

EXHIBIT 11-4 Marginal Revenue and Marginal Cost for the HealthPill Monopoly

For a monopoly like HealthPill, marginal revenue decreases as additional units are sold. The reason is that each additional unit sold causes a decrease in the price for all units. Marginal revenue can even be zero, as at an output of 7, or negative, as at an output of 8. The marginal cost curve is upward sloping. The profit-maximizing choice for the monopoly will be to produce at the quantity where marginal revenue is equal to marginal cost: that is, MR = MC. If the monopoly produces a lower quantity, then MR > MC at those levels of output, and the firm can make higher profits by expanding output. If the firm produces at a greater quantity, then MC > MR, and the firm can make higher profits by reducing its quantity of output.

price. But a monopolist can sell a larger quantity and see a decline in total revenue. When a monopolist increases sales by one unit, it gains some marginal revenue from selling that extra unit but also loses some marginal revenue because every other unit must now be sold at a lower price. As the quantity sold becomes higher, the drop in price affects a greater quantity of sales, eventually causing a situation where more sales cause marginal revenue to be negative.

A monopolist can determine its profit-maximizing price and quantity by analyzing the marginal revenue and marginal costs of producing an extra unit. If the marginal revenue exceeds the marginal cost, then the firm should produce the extra unit. For example, at an output of 2 in the example, marginal revenue is 1,000 and marginal cost is 300, so producing this unit will clearly add to overall profits. At an output of 4, marginal revenue is 600 and marginal cost is 500, so producing this unit still adds to overall profits. However, expanding output from 4 to 5 would involve a marginal revenue of 400 and a marginal cost of 600, so that fifth unit would actually reduce profits. Thus, the monopoly can tell from the marginal revenue and marginal cost that of the choices given in the table, the profit-maximizing level of output is 4.

Indeed, the monopoly could seek out the profit-maximizing level of output by increasing quantity by a small amount, calculating marginal revenue and marginal cost, and then either increasing output if marginal revenue exceeds marginal cost or reducing output if marginal cost exceeds marginal revenue. This incremental process works without any need to calculate total revenue and total cost. Thus, a profit-maximizing monopoly should follow the rule of producing up to the quantity where marginal revenue is equal to marginal cost— that is, MR = MC. A perfectly competitive firm will also find its profit-maximizing level of output where MR = MC. The key difference with a perfectly competitive firm is that in the case of perfect competition, marginal revenue is equal to price (MR = P), while for a monopolist, marginal revenue is not equal to the price, because changes in monopoly quantity of output affect the price.

Illustrating Monopoly Profits

It is straightforward to calculate profits if given numbers for total revenue and total cost. However, the size of monopoly profits can also be illustrated graphically with Exhibit 11-5, which takes the marginal cost and marginal revenue curves from the previous exhibit and adds an average cost curve and the monopolist's perceived demand curve. This diagram can also illustrate the three-step process where a monopolist: (1) selects the profit-maximizing quantity to produce; (2) decides what price to charge; and (3) determines total revenue, total cost, and profit.

Step 1: The Monopolist Determines Its Profit-Maximizing Level of Output

The firm can use the price and quantity combinations on the demand curve to calculate total revenue, and then based on total revenue, it can calculate its marginal revenue curve. The profit-maximizing quantity will occur where MR = MC—or at the last possible point before marginal costs start exceeding marginal revenue. In this example, MR = MC at an output slightly above 4.

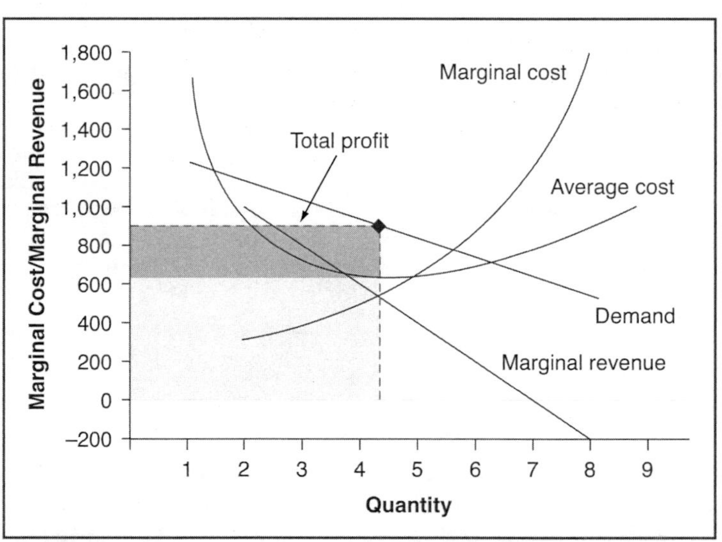

EXHIBIT 11-5 Illustrating Profits at the HealthPill Monopoly

This exhibit begins with the same marginal revenue and marginal cost curves from the HealthPill monopoly presented in Exhibit 11-4. It then adds an average cost curve and the demand curve faced by the monopolist. The HealthPill firm first chooses the quantity where MR = MC; in this example, 4 is the highest level of output before this occurs (although the intersection of MR and MC actually happens at a slightly higher level of output). The monopolist then decides what price to charge by looking at the demand curve it faces. The entire area of the shaded box (both dark and light shading), with quantity on the horizontal size and price on the vertical side, shows total revenue for the firm. Total costs for the firm are shown by the lighter-shaded area, which is quantity on the horizontal axis and average cost of production on the vertical axis. The large total revenue box minus the smaller total cost box leaves the darker-shaded area that shows total profits. Since the price charged is above average cost, the firm is earning positive profits.

CLEARING IT UP

Why Is a Monopolist's Marginal Revenue under the Demand Curve?

The marginal revenue curve for a monopolist always lies beneath the market demand curve. To understand why, think about increasing the quantity along the demand curve by one unit, so that you take one step down the demand curve to a slightly higher quantity but a slightly lower price. This step affects marginal revenue in two ways. First, it adds one additional unit sold at the new market price. Second, it means that all the previous units, which used to be sold at the higher price, now sell for less. Thus, the marginal revenue for a monopolist of selling an additional unit is equal to the price of that unit minus the reduction in price on all other units sold. For a monopolist, marginal revenue from expanding production is less than price—and the marginal revenue curve lies below the demand curve.

Step 2: The Monopolist Decides What Price to Charge

The monopolist will charge what the market is willing to pay. A dotted line drawn straight up from the profit-maximizing quantity to the demand curve shows the profit-maximizing price. This price is above the average cost curve, which shows that the firm is earning profits.

Step 3: Calculate Total Revenue, Total Cost, and Profit

Total revenue is the shaded box, including both lighter and darker shading, where the width of the box is the quantity being sold and the height is the price. The bottom part of the shaded box, which is shaded more lightly, shows total costs; that is, quantity on the horizontal axis multiplied by average cost on the vertical axis. The larger box of total revenues minus the smaller box of total costs will equal profits, which is shown by the darkly shaded box.

In a perfectly competitive market, the forces of entry would erode this profit in the long run. But a monopolist is protected by barriers to entry. In fact, one telltale sign of a possible monopoly is when a firm earns profits year after year, while doing more or less the same thing, without ever seeing those profits eroded by increased competition.

The Inefficiency of Monopoly

To understand why a monopoly is inefficient, it is useful to compare it with the benchmark model of perfect competition.

In perfect competition, the process of entry and exit means that eventually the market price is driven down to the price at the minimum of the average cost curve. Productive efficiency occurs when goods are being produced at the lowest possible average cost. However, a monopoly does not need to worry about entry, nor does it need to produce at the bottom of the average cost curve. As a result, a monopoly will not display productive efficiency.

The rule of profit maximization in a world of perfect competition was for each firm to produce the quantity of output where P = MC, where the price P is a measure of how much buyers value the good and the marginal cost MC is a measure of what marginal units cost society to produce. Following this rule assures allocative efficiency. If P > MC, then the benefit to society as measured by P is greater than the marginal cost to society MC of producing additional units, and a greater quantity should be produced. But in the case of monopoly, price is always greater than marginal cost at the profit-maximizing level of output, as can be seen by looking back at Exhibit 11-5. Thus, consumers will suffer from a monopoly because a lower quantity will be sold in the market, at a higher price, than would have been the case in a perfectly competitive market.

Productive and allocative efficiency in this discussion have referred to the quantity and price at a point in time. The problem of inefficiency for monopolies often runs even deeper than these issues and also involves incentives for efficiency over longer periods

Is a Diamond Monopoly Forever?

The DeBeer's diamond company is a South African firm that has organized a monopoly for selling diamonds around the world. The diamond monopoly works through a Central Selling Organization (CSO), which signs long-term exclusive contracts with diamond mines around the world to purchase all of their diamonds. It then groups the diamonds by size, brilliance, and other characteristics, and then sells them to diamond cutters and dealers. At its peak in the 1970s and 1980s, the CSO controlled about 85% of the world's diamonds. Thus, DeBeer's could control the quantity sold in the market and keep the price high.

But in the 1990s, a group of Australian diamond producers pulled out of the CSO. Diamonds were discovered in Canada at the Ekati mine. Diamond producers in Russia threatened to leave the CSO. Diamond production increased in Angola—organized in part by Russian and Australian firms. In the 2000s, the CSO controlled only about 40% of the world's diamond market.

What's next? DeBeer's will negotiate with other producers, pointing out that if the Central Selling Organization doesn't control the quantity produced, prices and profits will be lower for diamond producers as a group. However, the other producers may feel that they individually can earn higher profits by remaining outside the CSO. Instead of the "Diamonds are forever" ad campaign that DeBeer's started in the 1940s, which applied to all diamonds, different diamond producers will try to persuade consumers that there is something particularly special about the diamonds produced by their firm.

of time. There are counterbalancing incentives here. On one side, firms may strive for new inventions and new intellectual property because they want to become monopolies and earn high profits—at least for a few years until the competition catches up. In this way, monopolies may come to exist because of competitive pressures on firms. However, once a barrier to entry is in place, a monopoly that doesn't need to fear competition can just produce the same old products in the same old way—while still ringing up a healthy rate of profit. John Hicks, who won the Nobel Prize for economics in 1972, wrote back in 1935: "The best of all monopoly profits is a quiet life." He didn't mean the comment in a complimentary way. He meant that monopolies may bank their profits and slack off on trying to please their customers.

Until the early 1980s, for example, AT&T provided all of the local and long-distance phone service in the United States, along with manufacturing most of the phones. The old joke at the time was that you could have any color phone you wanted, as long as it was black. But in 1982, AT&T was split up by government litigation into a number of local phone companies, a long-distance phone company, and a phone equipment manufacturer. An explosion of innovation followed. Services like call waiting, caller ID, three-way calling, voicemail, mobile phones, and wireless connections to the Internet all became available. A wide range of payment plans was offered as well. It was no longer true that all phones were black; instead, phones came in a wild variety of shapes and colors. The end of the telephone monopoly helped to bring lower prices, a greater quantity of services, and also a wave of innovation aimed at attracting and pleasing customers.

Conclusion

A monopolist can analyze its costs with the same analytic tools as other firms: total cost, marginal cost, and average cost. Monopolists will often face the U-shaped average cost curve and upward-sloping marginal cost curve as shown in Exhibit 11-6. To maximize profits, Step 1 for the monopolist is to choose the quantity Q_1, where marginal costs and marginal revenues intersect. Step 2 is to sell that quantity at the price P_1, which is determined by point R on the demand curve. Step 3 is for the monopolist to determine its profits. As long as that monopoly price p_1 is above the average cost curve at the monopoly quantity Q_1, the monopoly is earning profits, shown by the shaded rectangle with its corners at P_1, R, S, and P_2. Moreover, if the monopolist is protected by sufficiently high barriers to entry, it can earn those profits forever, without fear of competitor firms that would be willing to sell at a lower price.

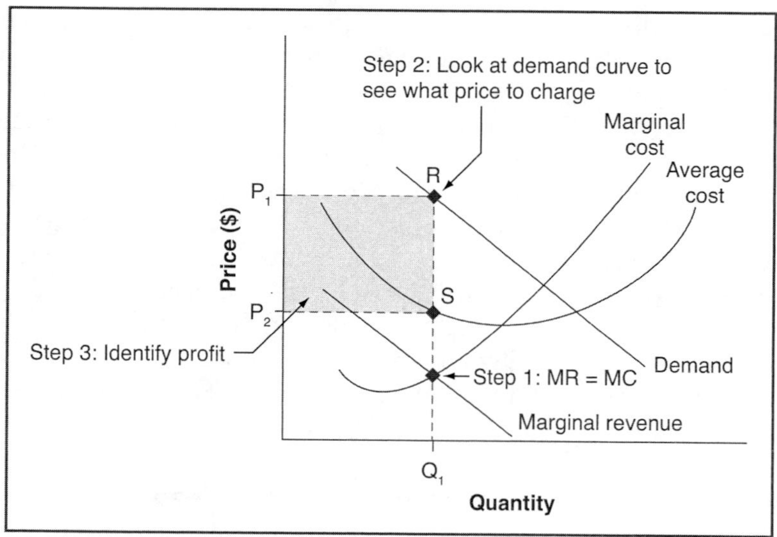

EXHIBIT 11-6 How a Profit-Maximizing Monopoly Decides

In Step 1, the monopoly chooses the profit-maximizing level of output Q_1, by choosing the quantity where MR = MC.
In Step 2, the monopoly decides how much to charge for output level Q_1 by drawing a line straight up from Q_1 to point R on its perceived demand curve. Thus, the monopoly will charge a price P_1.
In Step 3, the monopoly identifies its profit. Total revenue will be Q_1 multiplied by P_1. Total cost will be Q_1 multiplied by the average cost of producing Q_1, which is shown by point S on the average cost curve to be P_2. Profits will be the total revenue rectangle minus the total cost rectangle, shown by the shaded zone in the figure.

Chapter 13 will discuss how government policy may respond to monopolies that charge a higher price and produce a lower quantity than would a group of firms in a competitive industry. But before turning to the policy issues, Chapter 12 analyzes the profit-maximizing choices at two locations on the spectrum of competition between perfect competition and monopoly—that is, monopolistic competition and oligopoly.

Key Concepts and Summary

1. Perfect competition refers to an industry where many firms produce identical products. Conversely, **imperfect competition** refers to industries where either there are a small number of firms, or the firms don't sell an identical product, or both. There are three main varieties of imperfect competition: **monopoly**, which is the case of a single seller; **monopolistic competition**, where there are many sellers but their products are not identical; and **oligopoly**, which is the case of a small number of sellers.
2. **Barriers to entry** prevent or discourage competitors from entering the market. These barriers include legal restrictions on competition, control of a physical resource, technological superiority, economies of scale that lead to natural monopoly, and practices to intimidate the competition like **predatory pricing**.
3. **Intellectual property** refers to legally guaranteed ownership of an idea, rather than a physical item. The laws that protect intellectual property include **patents**, **trademarks**, **copyrights**, and **trade secrets**.
4. A **natural monopoly** arises when economies of scale persist over a large enough range of output that if one firm supplies the entire market, no second firm can enter without facing a cost disadvantage.
5. The demand curve perceived by a perfectly competitive firm is horizontal, which shows that such a firm is a price-taker, charging whatever price is determined in the market for the quantity that it sells. The demand curve perceived by a monopolist is the market demand curve, which is typically downward sloping. A monopolist is not a price-taker, because when it decides what quantity to produce, it also determines the market price.
6. For a monopolist, total revenue is relatively low at low quantities of output because not much is being sold if a very high price is charged. Total revenue is also relatively low at very high quantities of output because a very high quantity will sell only at a low price. Thus, as output of a monopolist rises, total revenue will start low, rise, and then decline.

7. The marginal revenue for a monopolist from selling additional units will decline. Each additional unit sold by a monopolist will push down the overall market price, and as more units are sold, this lower price applies to more and more units.
8. A monopolist can seek out the profit-maximizing quantity of output in two ways: it can choose the quantity where total revenue exceeds total cost by the highest amount, or it can choose the quantity where marginal revenue is equal to marginal cost.
9. The monopolist will select the profit-maximizing level of output where MR = MC and then charge the price for that quantity of output as determined by the market demand curve. If that price is above average cost, the monopolist earns positive profits.
10. Monopolists are not productively efficient, because they do not produce at the minimum of the average cost curve. Monopolists are not allocatively efficient, because they do not produce at the quantity where P = MC. As a result, monopolists produce less, at a higher average cost, and charge a higher price than would a combination of firms in a perfectly competitive industry. Monopolists also may lack incentives for innovation because they need not fear entry.

Review Questions

1. How is a monopoly industry different from an industry with perfect competition?
2. How is monopolistic competition different from perfect competition?
3. How is oligopoly different from perfect competition?
4. What is a barrier to entry? Give some examples.
5. What is predatory pricing?
6. How is intellectual property different from other property?
7. By what legal mechanisms is intellectual property protected?
8. In what sense is a natural monopoly "natural"?
9. How is the demand curve perceived by a perfectly competitive firm different from the demand curve perceived by a monopolist?
10. How does the demand curve perceived by a monopolist compare with the market demand curve?
11. Is a monopolist a price-taker? Explain briefly.
12. What is the usual shape of a total revenue curve for a monopolist? Why?
13. What is the usual shape of a marginal revenue curve for a monopolist? Why?
14. How can a monopolist identify the profit-maximizing level of output if it knows its total revenue and total cost curves?
15. How can a monopolist identify the profit-maximizing level of output if it knows its marginal revenue and marginal costs?
16. When a monopolist identifies its profit-maximizing quantity of output, how does it decide what price to charge?
17. Is a monopolist productively efficient? Why or why not?
18. Is a monopolist allocatively efficient? Why or why not?
19. How does the quantity produced and price charged by a monopolist compare to that of a perfectly competitive industry?

CHAPTER

12

Monopolistic Competition and Oligopoly

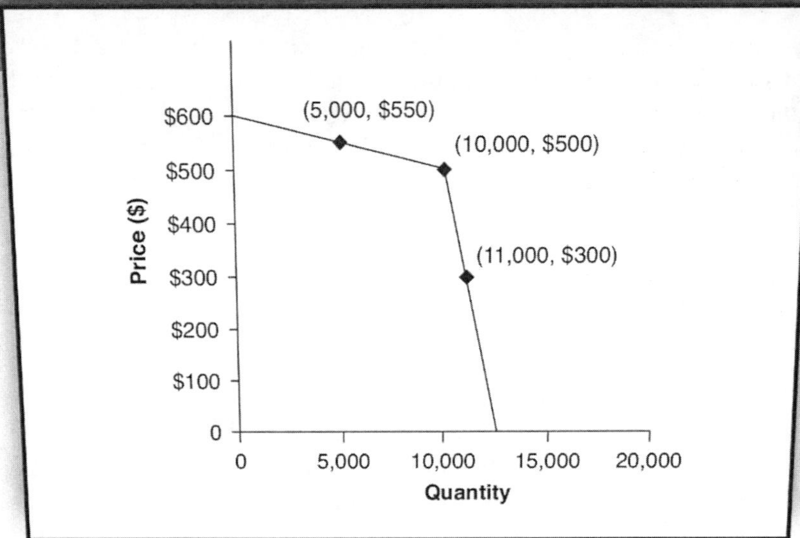

Chapter Outline

Perfect competition and monopoly stand at opposite ends of the spectrum of competition. A perfectly competitive market involves many firms selling identical products, who must all act as price-takers in the face of the competition. Monopoly arises when a single firm sells a product for which there are no close substitutes. But what about the in-between cases?

Many markets feature a large number of competing firms, but the products that they sell are not identical. In 2016, the Mall of America in Minnesota, the largest shopping mall in the United States, had 29 stores that sold women's "ready-to-wear" clothing (like Ann Taylor and Coldwater Creek), another 60 stores that sold clothing for both men and women (like Banana Republic, J. Crew, and Nordstrom's), plus 19 more stores that sold women's specialty clothing (like Motherhood Maternity and Victoria's Secret). These many clothing stores, competing in the same shopping mall to sell similar but not identical products, engage in what economists call monopolistic competition. Other markets feature a small number of competing firms, which is called an oligopoly. One example of an oligopoly is Boeing and Airbus, the two major firms in the world that manufacture large passenger aircraft. Another example is the Coca-Cola Company and PepsiCo, Incorporated, the two firms that dominate sales in the U.S. soft drink market.

This chapter begins with a discussion of how monopolistic competition arises and how monopolistically competitive firms will choose their profit-maximizing level of quantity and output. As the name "monopolistic competition" implies, a firm's decisions in this setting will in certain ways resemble monopoly and in other ways resemble perfect competition. Because a monopolistically competitive firm is not selling an identical product to other firms, it has a sort of mini-monopoly; for example, clothing stores in the Mall of America have a mini-monopoly on some of the specific styles of clothing that they sell. However, monopolistic competitors must also expect a process of entry and exit, like perfectly competitive firms, so they cannot earn higher-than-normal profits in the long run. The chapter then turns to a discussion of oligopoly firms, which face two conflicting temptations. On one side, oligopoly firms will wish to cooperate as if they were a single monopoly, to make their decisions about the price to charge and quantity to produce accordingly, and then to divide up the monopoly profits. On the other side, each oligopoly firm acting individually may seek to gain profits by expanding its levels of output and cutting prices. Thus, the behavior of oligopoly firms can also take on elements both of monopoly and of perfect competition.

Monopolistic Competition

monopolistic competition: Many firms competing to sell similar but differentiated products.

Monopolistic competition involves many firms competing against each other but selling products that are distinctive in some way. Examples include stores that sell different styles of clothing; restaurants or grocery stores that sell different kinds of food; and even products like golf balls or beer that may be at least somewhat similar in fact, but differ in public perception because of advertising and brand names. When products are distinctive, each firm has a mini-monopoly on its particular style or flavor or brand name. However, firms producing such products must also compete with other styles and flavors and brand names. The term "monopolistic competition" captures this mixture of mini-monopoly and tough competition.

Differentiated Products

differentiated products: Products that are distinctive in a particular way.

A firm can try to make its products different from those of its competitors in several ways: physical aspects of the product, location from which the product is sold, intangible aspects of the product, and perceptions of the product. Products that are distinctive in one of these ways are called **differentiated products**.

Physical aspects of a product include all the phrases you hear in advertisements: unbreakable bottle, nonstick surface, freezer-to-microwave, non-shrink, extra spicy, newly redesigned for your comfort, and many others. The location of a firm can also create a difference between producers. For example, a gas station located at a heavily traveled intersection can probably sell more gas because more cars drive by that corner. A supplier to an automobile manufacturer may find that it is an advantage to locate close to the car factory. Intangible aspects can differentiate a product, too, including a guarantee of satisfaction or money back, a reputation for high quality, services like free delivery, or offering a loan to purchase the product.

Golf Balls and Product Differentiation

The U.S. Golf Association runs a laboratory that tests 20,000 golf balls a year. There are strict rules for what makes a golf ball legal. The weight of a golf ball cannot exceed 1.620 ounces and its diameter cannot be less than 1.680 inches (which is 45.93 grams and 42.67 millimeters, in case you were wondering). The balls are also tested by being hit at different speeds. For example, the distance test involves having a mechanical golfer hit the ball with a titanium driver and a swing speed of 120 miles per hour. As the testing center explains: "The USGA system then uses an array of sensors that accurately measure the flight of a golf ball during a short, indoor trajectory from a ball launcher. From this flight data, a computer calculates the lift and drag forces that are generated by the speed, spin, and dimple pattern of the ball. . . . The distance limit is 317 yards."

Over 1,800 golf balls made by more than 100 companies meet the USGA standards. The balls do differ in various ways, like the pattern of dimples on the ball, the types of plastic used on the cover and in the cores, and so on. But since all balls need to conform to the USGA tests, they are much more alike than different.

However, retail sales of golf balls are about $500 million per year, which means that a lot of large companies have a powerful incentive to persuade players that golf balls are highly differentiated and that it makes a huge difference which one you choose. Sure, Tiger Woods can tell the difference. But for the average duffer who plays a few times a summer—and who loses a lot of golf balls in the woods and the lake and needs to buy new ones—most golf balls are pretty much indistinguishable.

Finally, product differentiation may occur in the minds of buyers. For example, many people can't tell the difference in taste between common varieties of beer or cigarettes if they are blindfolded, but because of past habits and advertising, they have strong preferences for certain brands. Advertising can play a role in shaping these intangible preferences.

The concept of differentiated products is closely related to the degree of variety that is available. If everyone in the economy wore only blue jeans, ate only white bread, and drank only tap water, then the markets for clothing, food, and drink would be much closer to perfectly competitive. The variety of styles, flavors, locations, and characteristics creates product differentiation and monopolistic competition.

Perceived Demand for a Monopolistic Competitor

A monopolistically competitive firm perceives a demand for its goods that is an intermediate case between monopoly and competition. Exhibit 12-1 offers a reminder that the demand curve as perceived by a perfectly competitive firm is flat because the perfectly competitive firm can sell any quantity it wishes at the prevailing market price. In contrast, the demand curve as perceived by a monopolist is the market demand curve, since a monopolist is the only firm in the market.

The demand curve as *perceived by a monopolistic competitor* is not flat, but rather downward sloping, which means that the monopolistic competitor can raise its price without losing all of its customers. However, the demand curve as perceived by the monopolistic competitor is flatter than the demand curve perceived by a monopolist. If a monopolist raises its price, some consumers will choose not to purchase its product—but they will then need to buy a completely different product. However, when a monopolistic competitor raises its price, some consumers will choose not to purchase the product at all, but others will choose to buy a similar product from another firm. If a monopolistic competitor raises its price, it will not lose as many customers as would a perfectly competitive firm, but it will lose more customers than would a monopoly that raised its prices.

At a glance, the demand curves faced by a monopoly and by a monopolistic competitor look similar—that is, they both slope down. But the underlying economic meaning of these perceived demand curves is different because a monopolist faces the market demand curve and a monopolistic competitor does not.

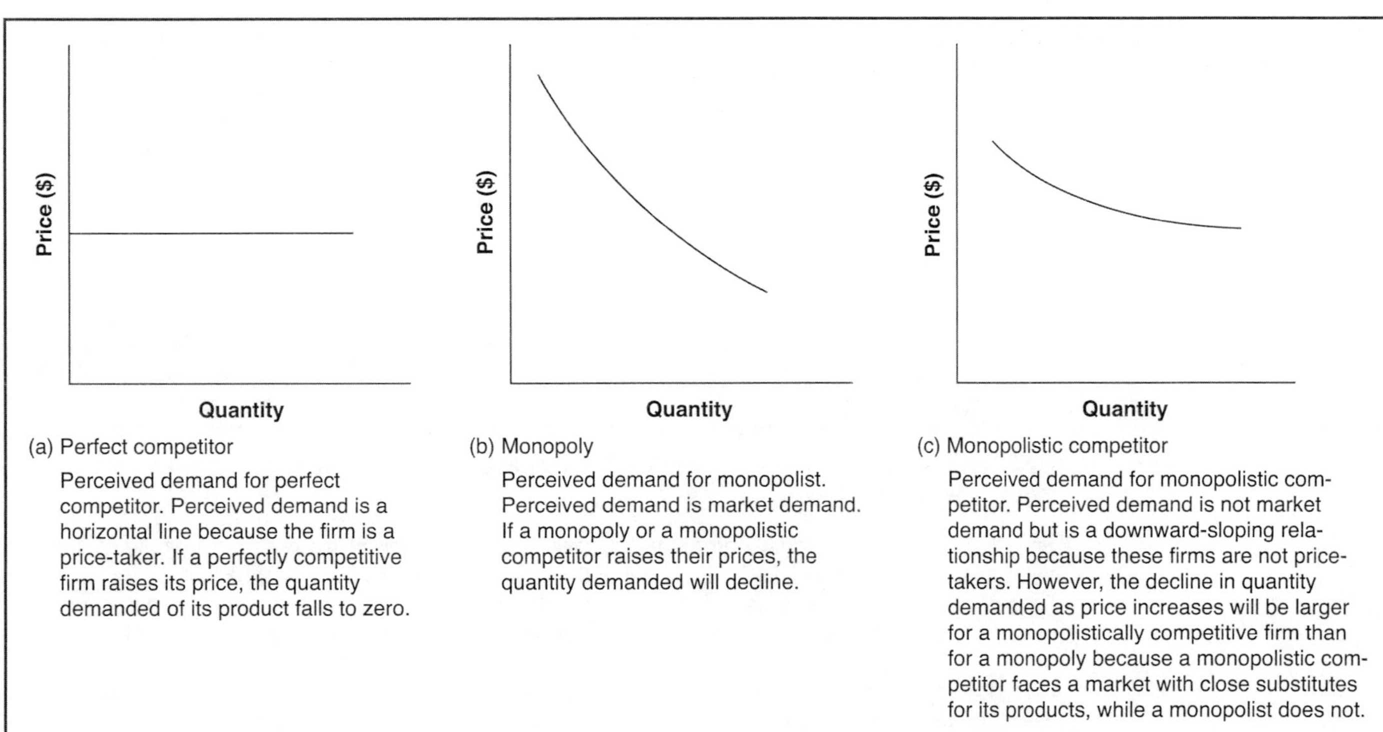

(a) Perfect competitor

Perceived demand for perfect competitor. Perceived demand is a horizontal line because the firm is a price-taker. If a perfectly competitive firm raises its price, the quantity demanded of its product falls to zero.

(b) Monopoly

Perceived demand for monopolist. Perceived demand is market demand. If a monopoly or a monopolistic competitor raises their prices, the quantity demanded will decline.

(c) Monopolistic competitor

Perceived demand for monopolistic competitor. Perceived demand is not market demand but is a downward-sloping relationship because these firms are not price-takers. However, the decline in quantity demanded as price increases will be larger for a monopolistically competitive firm than for a monopoly because a monopolistic competitor faces a market with close substitutes for its products, while a monopolist does not.

EXHIBIT 12-1 Perceived Demand for Firms in Different Competitive Settings

How a Monopolistic Competitor Chooses Price and Quantity

The monopolistically competitive firm decides on its profit-maximizing quantity and price in much the same way as a monopolist. A monopolistic competitor, like a monopolist, faces a downward-sloping demand curve, and so it will choose some combination of price and quantity along its perceived demand curve.

As an example of a profit-maximizing monopolistic competitor, consider the Authentic Chinese Pizza store, which serves pizza with cheese, sweet and sour sauce, and your choice of vegetables and meats. Although Authentic Chinese Pizza must compete against other pizza businesses and restaurants, it has a differentiated product. The firm's perceived demand curve is downward sloping, as shown in the first two columns of the table in Exhibit 12-2 and on the graph. The combinations of price and quantity at each point on the demand curve can be multiplied to calculate the total revenue that the firm would receive, which is shown in the third column. The fourth column, marginal revenue, is

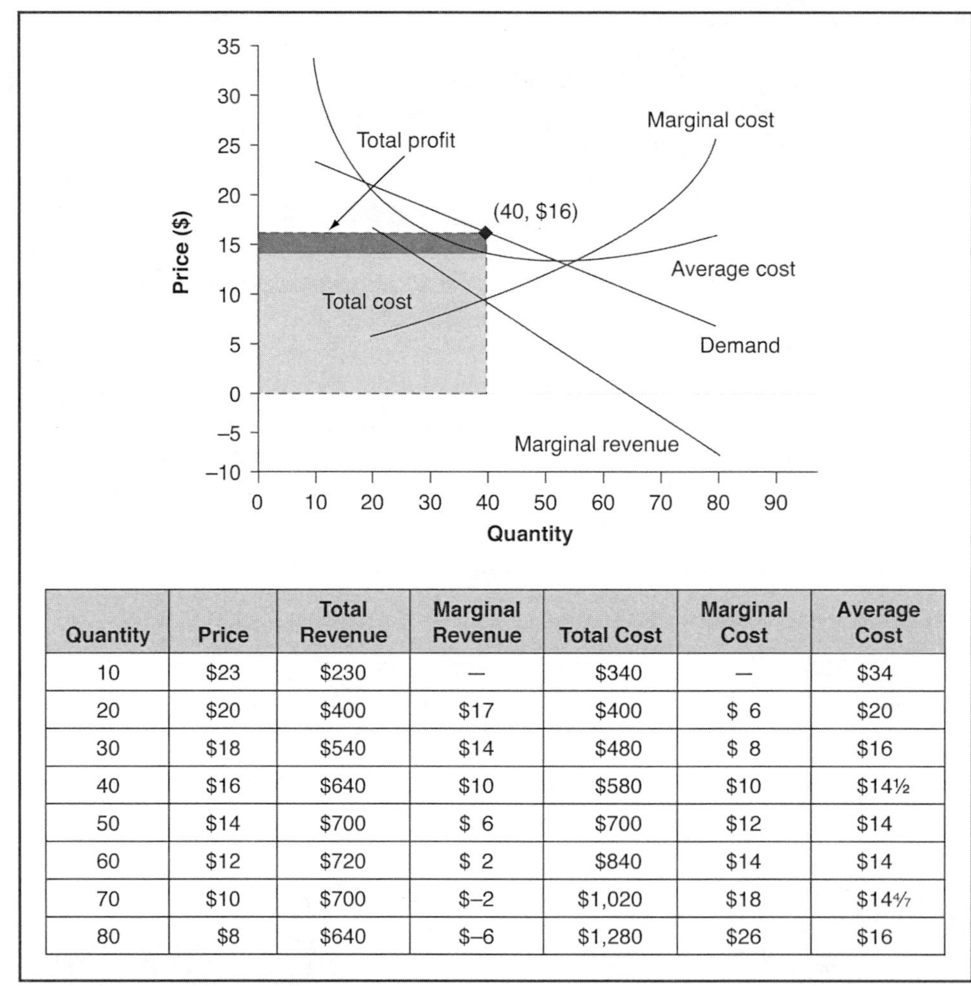

Quantity	Price	Total Revenue	Marginal Revenue	Total Cost	Marginal Cost	Average Cost
10	\$23	\$230	—	\$340	—	\$34
20	\$20	\$400	\$17	\$400	\$ 6	\$20
30	\$18	\$540	\$14	\$480	\$ 8	\$16
40	\$16	\$640	\$10	\$580	\$10	\$14½
50	\$14	\$700	\$ 6	\$700	\$12	\$14
60	\$12	\$720	\$ 2	\$840	\$14	\$14
70	\$10	\$700	\$–2	\$1,020	\$18	\$14 4/7
80	\$8	\$640	\$–6	\$1,280	\$26	\$16

EXHIBIT 12-2 How a Profit-Maximizing Monopolistic Competitor Decides What Price to Charge

Step 1: The monopolistically competitive firm determines the profit-maximizing quantity of output by applying the rule MR = MC. In this case, the profit-maximizing output is 40.
Step 2: The firm then decides how much to charge for this quantity by looking at its perceived demand curve. The vertical line up through a quantity of 40 hits the perceived demand curve at a price of \$16.
Step 3: The firm calculates total revenue, total cost, and profit. Total revenue is the rectangle with quantity on the horizontal axis and price on the vertical axis. Total cost is the rectangle with quantity on the horizontal axis and average cost on the vertical axis. Profit is total revenue of \$640 minus total cost of \$580, or \$60, which is the more darkly shaded area in the diagram.

calculated as the change in total revenue divided by the change in quantity. The final columns of the table show total cost, marginal cost, and average cost. As always, marginal cost is calculated by dividing the change in total cost by the change in quantity, while average cost is calculated by dividing total cost by quantity.

The process by which a monopolistic competitor chooses its profit-maximizing quantity and price resembles very closely how a monopoly makes these decisions, and can be summed up in the same three-step process in which the firm: (1) selects the profit-maximizing quantity to produce; (2) decides what price to charge; and (3) determines total revenue, total cost, and profit.

Step 1: The Monopolistic Competitor Determines Its Profit-Maximizing Level of Output

The Authentic Chinese Pizza company will determine the profit-maximizing quantity to produce by considering its marginal revenues and marginal costs. If the firm is producing at a quantity of output where marginal revenue exceeds marginal cost, then the firm should keep expanding production because each marginal unit is adding to profit by bringing in more revenue than its cost. In this way, the firm will produce up to the quantity where MR = MC. If the firm is producing at a quantity where marginal costs exceed marginal revenue, then each marginal unit is costing more than the revenue it brings in, and the firm will increase its profits by reducing the quantity of output. In this example, MR and MC intersect at a quantity of 40, which is the profit-maximizing level of output for the firm.

Step 2: The Monopolistic Competitor Decides What Price to Charge

When the firm has determined its profit-maximizing quantity of output, it can then look to its perceived demand curve to find out what it can charge for that quantity of output. In graphical terms, this process can be shown as a vertical line reaching up through the profit-maximizing quantity of 40 until it hits the firm's perceived demand curve. For Authentic Chinese Pizza, it should charge a price of $16 per pizza for a quantity of 40.

Step 3: Calculate Total Revenue, Total Cost, and Profit

At a quantity of 40, the price of $16 lies above the average cost curve, so the firm is making economic profits. From the table, at an output of 40, the firm's total revenue is $640 and its total cost are $580, so profits are $60. In Exhibit 12-2, the firm's total revenues are the rectangle with the quantity of 40 on the horizontal axis and the price of $16 on the vertical axis. The firm's total cost is the smaller rectangle with the same quantity of 40 on the horizontal axis but the average cost of $14.50 on the vertical axis. Profits are total revenues minus total costs, which is the shaded area above the average cost curve.

Although the process by which a monopolistic competitor makes decisions about quantity and price is similar to the way in which a monopolist makes such decisions, two differences are worth remembering. First, although both a monopolist and a monopolistic competitor face downward-sloping demand curves, the monopolist's perceived demand curve is the market demand curve, while the perceived demand curve for a monopolistic competitor is based on the extent of its product differentiation and how many competitors it faces. Second, a monopolist is surrounded by barriers to entry and need not fear entry, but a monopolistic competitor who earns profits must expect the entry of firms with similar, if differentiated, products.

Monopolistic Competitors and Entry

If one monopolistic competitor earns abnormally high profits, other firms will be tempted to enter the market. If one gas station is earning high profits, then it will be tempting for another gas station to open across the street or down the road—and perhaps the new gas station can also plan to sell coffee or have a carwash or some other attraction for potential customers. A successful restaurant with a unique barbecue sauce must be concerned that other restaurants will try to copy the sauce and offer their own unique recipes, too. A laundry detergent with a great reputation for quality must be concerned that competitors may seek to build their own reputations.

The entry of other firms into the same general market (like gas or restaurants or detergent) shifts the demand curve perceived by a monopolistically competitive firm. As more firms enter the market, the quantity demanded at a given price for any particular firm will decline, and the firm's perceived demand curve will shift to the left. As a firm's perceived demand curve shifts to the left, its marginal revenue curve will shift to the left, too. The shift in marginal revenue will change the profit-maximizing quantity that the firm chooses to produce, since marginal revenue will then equal marginal cost at a different point.

Exhibit 12-3*a* shows a situation where a monopolistic competitor was earning a profit with its original perceived demand curve D_0. The intersection of the marginal revenue curve MR_0 and marginal cost curve MC occurs at a quantity Q_0, which is associated on the demand curve at point T with price P_0. The combination of price P_0 and quantity Q_0 lies above the average cost curve, which shows that the firm is earning profits.

However, after entry occurred, the firm's perceived demand curve shifts to the left from D_0 to D_1, and the associated marginal revenue curve shifts from MR_0 to MR_1. The new quantity of profit-maximizing output is Q_1 because the intersection of the MR_1 and MC now occurs at point U. Moving vertically up from that quantity, the optimal price/quantity choice on the demand curve occurs at point V, where the firm's perceived demand curve touches the average cost curve. When price is equal to average cost, economic profits are zero. Thus, although a monopolistically competitive firm may earn abnormally high profits in the short term, the process of entry will drive those profits down to zero in the long run.

Exhibit 12-3*b* shows the reverse situation, where a monopolistically competitive firm is originally earning losses. The intersection of the original marginal revenue curve MR_0

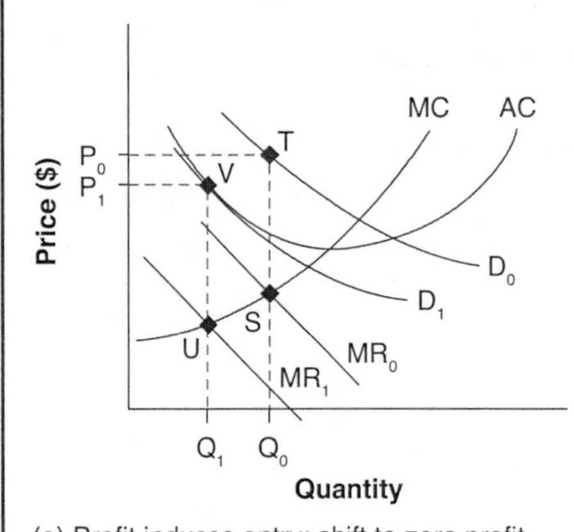

(a) Profit induces entry; shift to zero profit

The intersection of the original marginal revenue curve MR_0 and the marginal cost curve occurs at point S. Thus, the profit-maximizing quantity is Q_0, and the corresponding price on demand curve D_0 is P_0. The firm is earning a profit because price is above average cost. Profit encourages entry. As a result, the firm's perceived demand curve shifts from D_0 to D_1, and the marginal revenue curve shifts from MR_0 to MR_1. The new intersection of MR_1 and MC is at U. Now, the profit-maximizing quantity is Q_1, and the profit-maximizing price on demand curve D_1 is P_1. Point V sits right on the average cost curve, so because of entry, the firm is now earning zero profit.

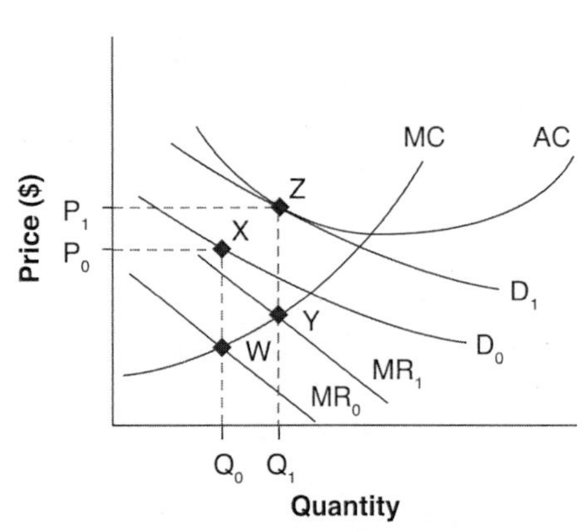

(b) Loss induces exit; shift to zero profit

The intersection of the original marginal revenue curve MR_0 and the marginal cost curve occurs at point W. Thus, the profit-maximizing quantity is Q_0, and the corresponding price on demand curve D_0 is P_0. The firm is suffering a loss because price is below average cost. Loss leads to exit. As a result, the firm's perceived demand curve shifts from D_0 to D_1, and its marginal revenue curve shifts from MR_0 to MR_1. The new intersection of MR_1 and MC is at Y. Now, the profit-maximizing quantity is Q_1, and the profit-maximizing price on demand curve D_1 is P_1. Point Z sits right on the average cost curve, so because of exit, the firm is now earning zero profit.

EXHIBIT 12-3 Monopolistic Competition, Entry, and Exit

CLEARING IT UP

Why Does a Shift in Perceived Demand Cause a Shift in Marginal Revenue?

The combinations of price and quantity at each point on a firm's perceived demand curve are used to calculate total revenue for each combination of price and quantity. This information on total revenue is then used to calculate marginal revenue, which is the change in total revenue divided by the change in quantity. A change in perceived demand will change total revenue at every quantity of output, and in turn, the change in total revenue will shift marginal revenue at each quantity of output. Thus, when entry occurs in a monopolistically competitive industry, the perceived demand curve for each firm will shift to the left because a smaller quantity will be demanded at any given price—and the marginal revenue curve will shift to the left as well. Conversely, exit causes the perceived demand curve for a monopolistically competitive firm to shift to the right, and the corresponding marginal revenue curve shifts right, too.

and the marginal cost curve MC occurs at point W, which represents a quantity of Q_0. The price associated with Q_0 at point X on the original demand curve D_0 is P_0. This price lies below the average cost curve, which shows that the firm is making losses. In the short run, firms may continue to produce, as long as the price covers their average variable costs (which for simplicity are not shown in this exhibit). But in the long run, some firms will exit. When exit occurs, the perceived demand curve for the remaining firms will shift to the right from D_0 to D_1 because at any given price, each of the remaining firms will be able to sell a larger quantity. The associated marginal revenue curve will shift from MR_0 to MR_1.The new intersection of MR_1 and MC occurs at point Y, which is at the quantity Q_1. The price P_1 associated with Q_1 on the firm's new perceived demand curve D_1 now sits right on the average cost curve at point Z. Through the process of exit, the monopolistically competitive firms remaining in the market are no longer earning losses, but instead are earning zero economic profits.

Monopolistic competitors can make a profit or loss in the short run, but in the long run, entry and exit will drive these firms toward a zero-profit outcome. However, the zero-profit outcome in monopolistic competition looks different from the zero-profit outcome in perfect competition in several ways relating both to efficiency and to variety in the market.

Monopolistic Competition and Efficiency

The long-term result of entry and exit in a perfectly competitive market is that all firms end up selling at the price level determined by the lowest point on the average cost curve. This outcome is why perfect competition displays productive efficiency; goods are being produced at the lowest possible average cost. However, in monopolistic competition, the end result of entry and exit is that firms end up with a price that lies on the downward-sloping portion of the average cost curve, not at the very bottom of the AC curve. Thus, monopolistic competition will not be productively efficient.

In a perfectly competitive market, each firm produces at a quantity where price is set equal to marginal cost, P = MC, both in the short run and in the long run. This outcome is why perfect competition displays allocative efficiency; the social benefits of additional production, as measured by the price that people are willing to pay, are in balance with the marginal costs to society of that production. But in a monopolistically competitive market, the rule for maximizing profit is to set MR = MC—and price is higher than marginal revenue, not equal to it. When P > MC, which is the outcome in a monopolistically competitive market, the benefits to society of providing additional quantity as measured by the price that people are willing to pay exceeds the marginal costs to society of producing those units. Thus, a monopolistically competitive industry will produce a lower quantity of a good and charge a higher price for it than would a perfectly competitive industry.

A monopolistically competitive industry does not display productive and allocative efficiency in either the short run, when firms are making profits and losses, or in the long run, when firms are earning zero profits.

Advertising and Monopolistic Competition

The U.S. economy was spending about $270 billion per year on advertising at the end of the first decade of the 2000s. Roughly one-seventh of this was newspaper advertising, one-quarter was television advertising, and one-fifth was direct mail. The rest was divided up between magazines, radio, telephone directory yellow pages, billboards, Internet ads, and some other miscellaneous sources. More than 400,000 workers held jobs in the advertising industry.

Advertising is all about explaining to people, or making people believe, that the products of one firm are differentiated from the products of another firm. In the framework of monopolistic competition, there are two ways to conceive of how advertising works: either advertising causes a firm's perceived demand curve to become more inelastic (i.e., it causes the perceived demand curve to become steeper), or advertising causes demand for the firm's product to increase (i.e., it causes the firm's perceived demand curve to shift to the right). In either case, a successful advertising campaign may allow a firm to sell either a greater quantity or to charge a higher price, or both, and thus increase its profits.

However, economists and business owners have also long suspected that much of the advertising may only offset other advertising. Famous economist A. C. Pigou wrote all the way back in 1920:

> It may happen that expenditures on advertisement made by competing monopolists [that is, what we now call monopolistic competitors] will simply neutralize one another, and leave the industrial position exactly as it would have been if neither had expended anything. For, clearly, if each of two rivals makes equal efforts to attract the favor of the public away from the other, the total result is the same as it would have been if neither had made any effort at all.

The Benefits of Variety and Product Differentiation

Even though monopolistic competition does not provide productive efficiency or allocative efficiency, it has benefits of its own. Product differentiation is based on variety and innovation. Many people would prefer to live in an economy with many kinds of clothes and foods and car styles, not a world of perfect competition where everyone will always wear blue jeans and white shirts, eat only spaghetti with plain red sauce, and drive an identical model of car. Many people would prefer to live in an economy where firms are struggling to figure out ways of attracting customers by methods like friendlier service, free delivery, guarantees of quality, variations on existing products, and a better shopping experience.

Economists have struggled, with only partial success, to address the question of whether a market-oriented economy produces the optimal amount of variety. Critics of market-oriented economies argue that society doesn't really need dozens of different athletic shoes or breakfast cereals or brands of deodorant. They argue that much of the cost of creating such a high degree of product differentiation, and then of advertising and marketing this differentiation, is socially wasteful—that is, most people would be just as happy with a smaller range of differentiated products produced and sold at a lower price. Defenders of a market-oriented economy respond that if people don't want to buy differentiated products or highly advertised brand names, no one is forcing them to do so. Moreover, they argue that consumers benefit substantially when firms seek short-term profits by providing differentiated products. This controversy may never be fully resolved, in part because deciding on the optimal amount of variety is very difficult, and in part because the two sides often place different values on what variety means for consumers.

Oligopoly

oligopoly: When a few large firms have all or most of the sales in an industry.

Oligopoly arises when a few large firms have all or most of the sales in an industry. Oligopolistic firms are like cats in a bag. They can either scratch each other to pieces or cuddle up and get comfortable with one another. If oligopolists compete hard against each other, the result may be that they end up acting very much like perfect competitors, driving down costs and leading to zero profits for all. But if oligopolists cooperate with each other, they may effectively act like a monopoly and succeed in pushing up prices and earning consistently high levels of profit. Analyzing the choices of oligopolistic firms about pricing and quantity produced involves thinking through these different choices.

Why Do Oligopolies Exist?

A combination of the barriers to entry that create monopolies and the product differentiation that characterizes monopolistic competition can create the setting for an oligopoly. For example, when a government grants a patent for an invention to one firm, it may create a monopoly. But when the government grants patents to, say, three different pharmaceutical companies that each has its own drug for reducing high blood pressure, those three firms may become an oligopoly.

Similarly, a natural monopoly will arise when the size of the firm that is needed to operate at the minimum of the long-run average cost curve is large compared to the quantity demanded in the market. In such a setting, the market only has room for one firm because no smaller firm can operate at a low enough average cost to compete, and no larger firm could sell what it produced, given the quantity demanded in the market. But quantity demanded in the market may also be, say, two or three times the quantity needed to produce at the minimum of the average cost curve—which means that the market would have room for only two or three oligopoly firms. Again, smaller firms would have higher average costs and be unable to compete, while larger firms would produce such a high quantity that they would not be able to sell it at a profitable price. This combination of economies of scale and market demand may explain the Boeing-Airbus oligopoly in making large passenger aircraft.

The product differentiation at the heart of monopolistic competition can also play a role in creating an oligopoly. For example, firms may reach at least a certain minimum size before they are able to spend enough on advertising and marketing to create a recognizable brand name. The problem in competing with, say, Coca-Cola or Pepsi is not that producing fizzy drinks is technologically difficult, but rather that creating a brand name and marketing effort to equal Coke or Pepsi is an enormous task.

Collusion or Competition?

When oligopoly firms in a certain market decide what quantity to produce and what price to charge, they face a temptation to act as if they were a monopoly. By acting together like a monopoly, oligopolistic firms could then hold down output, charge a higher price, and divide up the monopoly level of profit amongst themselves. When firms act together in this way to reduce output and keep prices high, it is called **collusion**. A group of firms that collude to produce the monopoly output and sell at the monopoly price is called a **cartel**. The desire of businesses to avoid competing with each other, so that they can instead raise the prices that they charge and earn higher profits, has been well-understood by economists for a long time. Adam Smith wrote in *The Wealth of Nations* way back in 1776: "People of the same trade seldom meet together, even for merriment and diversion, but the conversation ends in a conspiracy against the public, or in some contrivance to raise prices."

collusion: When firms act together to reduce output and keep prices high.

cartel: A group of firms that collude to produce the monopoly output and sell at the monopoly price.

But even when oligopolists recognize that they would benefit as a group by acting like a monopoly, each individual oligopoly faces a private temptation to produce just a slightly higher quantity and earn slightly higher profit—while still counting on the other oligopolists to hold down their production and keep prices high. If at least some oligopolists give in to this temptation and start producing more, then the market price will fall. Indeed, a small handful of oligopoly firms may end up competing so fiercely that they all end up earning zero profits—as if they were perfect competitors.

The Prisoner's Dilemma

game theory: A branch of mathematics often used by economists that analyzes situations in which players must make decisions and then receive payoffs.

To gain a deeper understanding of how oligopoly firms may either act together like a monopolist or compete with each other, economists use **game theory**, a branch of mathematics that analyzes situations in which players must make decisions and then receive payoffs. Game theory has found widespread applications in the social sciences, as well

		Prisoner B	
		Remain Silent (cooperate with other prisoner)	Confess (don't cooperate with other prisoner)
Prisoner A	Remain Silent (cooperate with other prisoner)	A gets 2 years, B gets 2 years	B gets 1 year, A gets 8 years
	Confess (don't cooperate with other prisoner)	A gets 1 year, B gets 8 years	A gets 5 years, B gets 5 years

EXHIBIT 12-4 The Prisoner's Dilemma Problem

as in business, law, and military strategy. The number of players, the range of choices available to them, the order in which they decide, the ways in which the players interact, the amount of the payoffs, and the amount of information available to the players can all differ from game to game.

prisoner's dilemma: A game in which if both players pursue their own self-interest, they both end up worse off than if they cooperate.

The **prisoner's dilemma**, a game in which the gains from cooperation are larger than the rewards from pursing self-interest, can be used to illustrate the possibilities for acting together faced by oligopolistic firms. Many games are named for a story that offers an intuitive understanding of the situation, and the story behind the prisoner's dilemma runs like this. Two prisoners are arrested. When they are taken to the police station, they refuse to say anything and are put in separate interrogation rooms. Eventually, a police officer enters the room where Prisoner A is being held and says: "You know what? Your partner in the other room is confessing. So your partner is going to get a light prison sentence of just one year, and because you're remaining silent, the judge is going to stick you with eight years in prison. Why don't you get smart? If you confess, too, we'll cut your jail time down to five years." Over in the next room, another police officer is giving exactly the same speech to Prisoner B. What the police officers don't say is that if both prisoners remain silent, the evidence against them is not especially strong, and the prisoners will end up with only two years in jail each.

The game theory situation facing the two prisoners is illustrated in Exhibit 12-4. To understand the prisoner's dilemma, first consider the choices from Prisoner A's point of view. If A believes that his partner B will confess, then A ought to confess, too, so as to not get stuck with the eight years in prison. But if A believes that B will not confess, then A will be tempted to act selfishly and confess, so as to serve only one year. The key point is that A has an incentive to confess, regardless of what choice B makes! B faces the same set of choices and thus will have an incentive to confess regardless of what choice A makes. The result is that if the prisoners each pursue their own self-interest, both will confess, and they will end up doing a total of 10 years of jail time between them.

But if the two prisoners had cooperated by both remaining silent, they would only have had to serve a total of four years of jail time between them. If the two prisoners can work out some way of cooperating so that neither one will confess, they will both be better off than if they each follow their own individual self-interest, which in this case leads straight into longer jail terms for both.

The Oligopoly Version of the Prisoner's Dilemma

duopoly: An oligopoly with only two firms.

The members of an oligopoly can face a prisoner's dilemma, too. If each of the oligopolists cooperates in holding down output, then high monopoly profits are possible. But each oligopolist must worry that while it is holding down output, other firms are pursuing their own self-interest by raising output and earning higher profits. Exhibit 12-5 shows the prisoner's dilemma for a two-firm oligopoly—known as a **duopoly.** If Firms A and

		Firm B	
		Holds Down Output (cooperates with other firm)	Increases Output (doesn't cooperate with other firm)
Firm A	Holds Down Output (cooperates with other firm)	A gets $1,000 B gets $1,000	B gets $200 A gets $1,500
	Increases Output (doesn't cooperate with other firm)	A gets $1,500 B gets $200	A gets $400 B gets $400

EXHIBIT 12-5 A Prisoner's Dilemma for Oligopolists

B both agree to hold down output, they are acting together as a monopoly and will each earn $1,000 in profits.

But can the two firms trust each other? Consider the situation of Firm A. If A thinks that B will cheat on their agreement and increase output, then A will increase output too, because for A the profit of $400 when both firms increase output (the bottom right-hand choice in the table) is better than a profit of only $200 if A keeps output low and B raises output (the upper right-hand choice in the table). But if A thinks that B will cooperate by holding down output, then A may seize the opportunity to earn higher profits by raising output. After all, if B is going to hold down output, then A can earn $1,500 in profits by expanding output (the bottom left-hand choice in the table) compared with only $1,000 by holding down output as well (the upper left-hand choice in the table). Thus, firm A

The Lysine Cartel: "Our Customers Are the Enemy"

Lysine, a $600-million-a-year industry, is an amino acid used by farmers as a feed additive to ensure the proper growth of swine and poultry. The primary U.S. producer of lysine is Archer Daniels Midland (ADM), but several other large European and Japanese firms are in this market. For a time in the first half of the 1990s, the world's major lysine producers met together in hotel conference rooms and decided together exactly how much each firm would sell and what it would charge. But the U.S. Federal Bureau of Investigation had learned of the cartel and bugged a number of their phone calls and meetings.

From FBI surveillance tapes, here's a comment that Terry Wilson, president of the corn processing division at ADM, made to the other lysine producers at a 1994 meeting in Mona, Hawaii:

> I wanna go back and I wanna say something very simple. If we're going to trust each other, okay, and if I'm assured that I'm gonna get 67,000 tons by the year's end, we're gonna sell it at the prices we agreed to. . . . The only thing we need to talk about there because we are gonna get manipulated by these God damn buyers—they can be smarter than us if we let them be smarter. . . . They [the customers] are not your friend. They are not my friend. And we gotta have 'em, but they are not my friends. You are my friend. I wanna be closer to you than I am to any customer. Cause you can make us . . . money. . . . And all I wanna to tell you again is let's—let's put the prices on the board. Let's all agree that's what we're gonna do and then walk out of here and do it.

The price of lysine doubled while the cartel was in effect. Confronted by the FBI tapes, Archer Daniels Midland pled guilty in 1996 and paid a fine of $100 million. A number of top executives, both at ADM and other firms, later paid fines of up to $350,000 and were sentenced to 24–30 months in prison.

In another one of the FBI recordings, the president of Archer Daniels Midland told an executive from another competing firm that ADM had a slogan that, in his words, had "penetrated the whole company." The company president stated the slogan this way: "Our competitors are our friends. Our customers are the enemy." That slogan could stand as the motto of cartels everywhere.

will reason that it makes sense to expand output if B holds down output and that it also makes sense to expand output if B raises output. Again, B faces a parallel set of decisions.

The result of this prisoner's dilemma is often that even though A and B could make the highest combined profits by cooperating in producing a lower level of output and acting like a monopolist, the two firms may well act in their own self-interest and end up in a situation where they both increase output and earn only $400 each in profits.

How to Enforce Cooperation

How can parties who find themselves in a prisoner's dilemma situation avoid the undesired outcome and cooperate with each other? The way out of a prisoner's dilemma is to find a way to penalize those who do not cooperate. For example, prisoners who confess to the police and cause others to be convicted may face verbal and physical abuse from other criminals. Given that one oligopoly can't physically beat up another oligopoly, firms that find themselves in a prisoner's dilemma may try to seek other alternatives to create pressure for members to keep output down and prices up.

Perhaps the easiest approach for colluding oligopolists, you might imagine, would be to sign a contract with each other that they will hold output low and keep prices high. But if a group of U.S. companies signed such a contract, it would be illegal. Certain international organizations, like the nations that are members of the Organization of Petroleum Exporting Countries (OPEC), have signed international agreements to act like a monopoly, hold down output, and keep prices high so that all of the countries can make high profits from oil exports. But such agreements are not legally enforceable. If Nigeria, for example, decides to start cutting prices and selling more oil, Saudi Arabia can't sue Nigeria in court and force it to stop.

kinked demand curve: A perceived demand curve that arises when competing oligopoly firms commit to match price cuts, but not price increases.

Because oligopolists cannot sign a legally enforceable contract to act like a monopoly, the firms may instead keep close tabs on what other firms are producing and charging. Alternatively, oligopolists may choose to act in a way that generates pressure on each firm to stick to its agreed quantity of output. For example, oligopolists may act in such a way that each firm perceives that it faces a **kinked demand curve**, as shown in Exhibit 12-6,

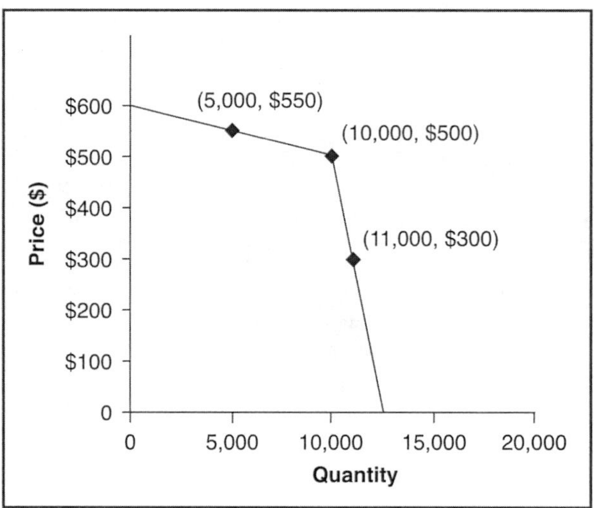

EXHIBIT 12-6 A Kinked Demand Curve

Consider a member firm in an oligopoly cartel that is supposed to produce a quantity of 10,000 and sell at a price of $500. The other members of the cartel can encourage this firm to honor its commitments by acting so that the firm perceives a kinked demand curve. If the oligopolist attempts to expand output and reduce price slightly, other firms also cut prices immediately—so if the firm expands output to 11,000, the price per unit falls dramatically, to $300. On the other side, if the oligopoly attempts to raise its price, other firms will not do so, so if the firm raises its price to $550, its sales decline sharply to 5,000. Thus, the members of a cartel can discipline each other to stick to the pre-agreed levels of quantity and price through a strategy of matching all price cuts but not matching any price increases.

which shows a perceived demand curve when competing oligopoly firms commit to match price cuts, but not price increases. Say that an oligopoly airline has agreed with the rest of a cartel to provide a quantity of 10,000 seats on the New York-to-Los Angeles route, at a price of $500. This choice is right at the kink in the firm's perceived demand curve. The reason that the firm perceives a kink in its demand curve is because of how the other oligopolists react to changes in prices. If the oligopoly decides to produce more and cut its price, other oligopolists will immediately match any price cuts—and therefore, a lower price brings very little increase in quantity sold. For example, if the firm cuts price to $300, it will only be able to sell 11,000 seats. However, if the airline seeks to raise prices, the other oligopolists will not raise their prices, and so the firm that raised prices will lose a considerable share of sales. For example, if the firm raises its price to $550, its sales drop to 5,000 seats sold. Thus, if oligopolists always match price cuts by other firms in the cartel, but don't match price increases, then none of the oligopolists will have any incentive to change prices. This strategy can work like a silent form of cooperation, in which the cartel successfully manages to hold down output, increase price, and share a monopoly level of profits even without any legally enforceable agreement.

Many real-world oligopolies, prodded by economic changes, legal and political pressures, and the egos of their top executives, go through episodes of cooperation and competition. If oligopolies could sustain cooperation with each other on output and pricing, they could earn profits as if they were a single monopoly. But each firm in an oligopoly has a self-interested incentive to produce more and grab a bigger share of the overall market, and when oligopoly firms start behaving in this way, the market outcome in terms of prices and quantity can be similar to that of a highly competitive market.

Conclusion

Competition has many faces. For example, perfect competition displays both productive and allocative efficiency; that is, products are produced at the lowest possible average cost, and the social benefits of products as measured by willingness to pay for them are balanced against the marginal cost of producing these products. But in the real world, perfect competition is rare. Firms in some industries are close to perfect competition, in the sense that they produce very similar products and must accept a market price as given. But very few markets for goods and services would meet the literal definition of perfect competition—that is, many firms selling near-identical products so that no firm can raise its price by even a penny.

Monopolistic competition among firms with differentiated products is probably the single most common form of competition in the U.S. economy. It provides useful incentives for innovation, as firms seek to earn profits in the short run, while entry assures that firms do not earn profits in the long run. However, monopolistically competitive firms do not produce at the lowest point on their average cost curves. In addition, the endless search to impress consumers through product differentiation provides greater variety, but it may also lead to excessive social expenses on advertising and marketing.

Oligopoly and monopoly are well-known, too. When oligopolies and monopolies result from patented innovations or from taking advantage of economies of scale to produce at low average cost, they may provide considerable benefit to consumers. But monopolies and oligopolies often try to earn sustained profits over long periods of time by holding down output and increasing price. They typically do not produce at the minimum of their average cost curves. Because they lack vibrant competition, even though oligopolies at least have some competitors, they may lack incentives to provide innovative products and high-quality service.

The task of public policy with regard to competition is to sort through these multiple realities, attempting to encourage firm behavior that is beneficial to the broader society and to discourage firm behavior that only adds to the profits of a few large companies with no corresponding benefit to consumers. The next chapter will discuss the delicate judgments that go into this task.

Key Concepts and Summary

1. **Monopolistic competition** refers to a market where many firms sell differentiated products. **Differentiated products** can arise from characteristics of the good or service, location from which the product is sold, intangible aspects of the product, and perceptions of the product.
2. The perceived demand curve for a monopolistically competitive firm is downward sloping, which shows that unlike a perfectly competitive firm with its flat perceived demand curve, a monopolistically competitive firm is not a price-taker, but rather chooses a combination of price and quantity. However, the perceived demand curve for a monopolistic competitor is flatter than the perceived demand curve for a monopolist because if a monopolistic competitor raises price, it will lose some customers to the competition, while a monopolist does not face any competition.
3. A profit-maximizing monopolistic competitor will seek out the quantity where marginal revenue is equal to marginal cost. The monopolistic competitor will produce that level of output and charge the price based on its perceived demand curve.
4. If the firms in a monopolistically competitive industry are earning economic profits, the industry will attract entry until profits are driven down to zero in the long run. If the firms in a monopolistically competitive industry are suffering losses, then the industry will experience exit until profits are driven up to zero in the long run.
5. A monopolistically competitive firm is not productively efficient, because it does not produce at the minimum of its average cost curve. A monopolistically competitive firm is not allocatively efficient, because it does not produce where $P = MC$, but instead produces where $P > MC$. Thus, a monopolistically competitive firm will tend to produce a lower quantity at a higher cost and to charge a higher price than a perfectly competitive firm.
6. Monopolistically competitive industries do offer benefits to consumers in the form of greater variety and incentives for improved products and services. There is some controversy over whether a market-oriented economy generates "too much" variety.
7. An **oligopoly** is a situation where a few firms sell most or all of the goods in a market.
8. Oligopolists would earn their highest profits if they could band together as a **cartel** and act like a monopolist by reducing output and raising price. But since each member of the oligopoly can benefit individually from expanding output, such collusion often breaks down—especially since explicit collusion is illegal.
9. The **prisoner's dilemma** is an example of **game theory**. It shows how, in certain situations, all sides can benefit from cooperative behavior rather than self-interested behavior. However, the challenge for parties is to encourage cooperative behavior.
10. Competition has many faces. Perfect competition has powerful incentives for efficiency, flexibility, and responsiveness. But the profits to be derived from imperfect competition encourage variety and innovation, whether in the form of monopolistic competition, monopoly, or oligopoly. Moreover, there may be cases like natural monopoly where a monopolist or an oligopoly can produce at a lower price than competition.

Review Questions

1. What are some of the ways a product can be differentiated?
2. What is the relationship between product differentiation and monopolistic competition?
3. How is the perceived demand curve for a monopolistically competitive firm different from the perceived demand curve for a perfectly competitive firm?
4. How is the perceived demand curve for a monopolistically competitive firm different from the perceived demand curve for a monopoly?
5. How does a monopolistic competitor choose its profit-maximizing quantity of output?
6. When a monopolistic competitor has chosen its profit-maximizing quantity of output, how does it determine what price to charge?
7. How can a monopolistic competitor tell whether the price it is charging will cause the firm to earn profits or losses?
8. If the firms in a monopolistically competitive market are earning economic profits in the short run, would

you expect them to continue doing so in the long run? Why?

9. If the firms in a monopolistically competitive market are earning losses in the short run, would you expect them to continue doing so in the long run? Why?
10. Is a monopolistically competitive firm productively efficient? Why or why not?
11. Is a monopolistically competitive firm allocatively efficient? Why or why not?
12. Explain how a monopolistically competitive industry may offer benefits of variety.
13. Will the firms in an oligopoly act more like a monopoly or more like competitors? Briefly explain.
14. What is a cartel?
15. What is collusion?
16. Does each individual in a prisoner's dilemma benefit more from cooperation or from pursuing self-interest? Explain briefly.
17. What is game theory?
18. Compare the advantages of perfect competition with those of monopolistic competition and oligopoly.

CHAPTER 13

Competition and Public Policy

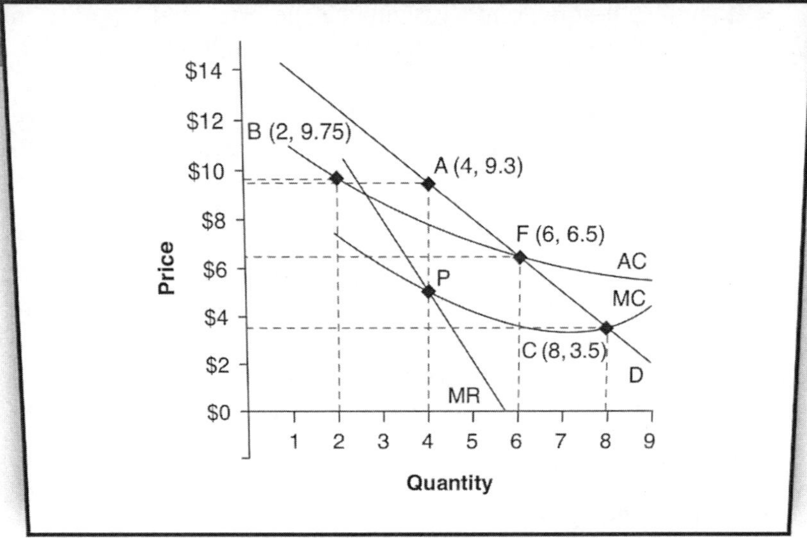

Chapter Outline

Corporate Mergers

Regulating Anticompetitive Behavior

When Breaking Up Is Hard to Do: Regulating Natural Monopolies

The Great Deregulation Experiment

Around the World: From Nationalization to Privatization

How much competition should society encourage? If an industry is perfectly competitive or monopolistically competitive, then the government has relatively little reason for concern about the extent of competition: after all, in these competitive settings, profits will lead firms to enter the market and losses will lead firms to exit, so the incentives for producing at low cost and coming up with new ways of pleasing customers are strong. But monopoly and oligopoly pose harder issues. On one side, the monopoly or oligopoly may have been created because a firm invented and patented a new product, or one or several large firms in an industry may be able to take advantage of economies of scale in a way that leads to lower production costs and potentially lower prices for consumers. On the other side, a monopoly or oligopoly may attempt to raise prices and reduce the quantity of output in a way that improves the firm's profits, but offers no corresponding benefits for consumers.

Government policy makers often must decide how to balance the potential benefits of corporate size against the potential benefits of competition. For example, in 2008, Delta Airlines merged with Northwest Airlines to create the largest airline in the world. Then in 2010, United Airlines purchased Continental Airlines, a transaction that (again) made United Airlines the largest airline in the world. In 2013, American Airlines merged with US Airways. Of course, the airlines argued that these mergers would benefit consumers, who would be able to purchase airline tickets at a lower price in a more coordinated and streamlined system of routes, because the newly created firm would be able to produce more efficiently, taking advantage of economies of scale and eliminating duplicative investments. However, a number of activist groups like the Consumer Travel Alliance expressed fears that the merger would reduce competition and lead to higher prices for consumers. Economists will spend years trying to determine whether these and other airline mergers helped consumers, hurt them, or didn't make much difference.

This chapter discusses public policy issues about competition. How can economists and governments analyze when mergers of companies like large airlines should be allowed and when they should be blocked? The government also plays a role in policing anticompetitive behavior other than mergers, like prohibiting certain kinds of contracts that might restrict competition. In the case of natural monopoly, however, trying to preserve competition probably won't work very well, and so government will often resort to regulation of price and/or quantity of output. In recent decades, there has been a global trend toward less government intervention in the price and output decisions of businesses. In the United States, for example, the government regulated the price and quantity in many industries during the twentieth century, but has removed many of those regulations since the late 1970s. Similarly, many governments around the world owned firms directly during much of the twentieth century. However, in recent decades, many countries have sold off many of those formerly government-owned firms to private ownership.

Corporate Mergers

merger: When two formerly separate firms combine to become a single firm; for practical purposes, often combined with acquisitions.

acquisition: When one firm purchases another; for practical purposes, often combined with mergers.

A corporate **merger** occurs when two formerly separate firms combine to become a single firm. When one firm purchases another, it is called an **acquisition**. An acquisition may appear different from a merger in that the newly purchased firm may continue to operate under its former company name. However, both mergers and acquisitions lead to two formerly separate firms being under common ownership, and so they are commonly grouped together.

Regulations for Approving Mergers

Since a merger combines two firms into one, it can reduce the extent of competition between firms. Therefore, when two U.S. firms announce a merger or acquisition where at least one of the firms is above a minimum size of sales (a set threshold that moves up gradually over time, and was at $78 million in 2016), or certain other conditions are met, they are required under law to notify the U.S. Federal Trade Commission (FTC). The left-hand panel of Exhibit 13-1 shows the number of mergers submitted for review to the FTC each year from 1999 to 2014. Mergers were very high in the late 1990s, diminished in the early 2000s, rebounded somewhat by around 2007, dipped during the grim economic times of 2008 and 2009, and then rebounded again. The right-hand panel of the exhibit shows the distribution of those mergers submitted for review in 2014 as measured by the size of the transaction. It's important to remember that this total leaves out many small mergers, which only need to be reported in certain limited circumstances. But about one-third of all reported merger and acquisition transactions in 2014 exceeded $500 million, while 14% exceeded $1 billion.

antitrust laws: Laws that give government the power to block certain mergers, and even in some cases to break up large firms into smaller ones.

The laws that give government the power to block certain mergers, and even in some cases to break up large firms into smaller ones, are called **antitrust laws**. Before a large merger happens, the antitrust regulators at the FTC and the U.S. Department of Justice can either allow the merger, prohibit it, or allow it if certain conditions are met. One common condition is that the merger will be allowed if the firm agrees to sell off certain parts. For example, in 2011, Google purchased ITA Software, which allowed people to search for airline flight schedules and fares. However, the government was concerned that a lack of competition in searching for airline prices might result. As a condition of making the purchase, Google was required to let other travel websites use the software in exchange for a licensing fee. In addition, Google was prohibited from entering into agreements with airlines that would limit airlines from sharing booking information with Google's competitors. Another requirement for the merger was that Google set up "firewall" restrictions to avoid unauthorized use of data gathered from customers. These additional conditions sought to preserve a greater degree of competition in the market for information about airline booking information—which in turn helps to encourage greater competition among airlines themselves.

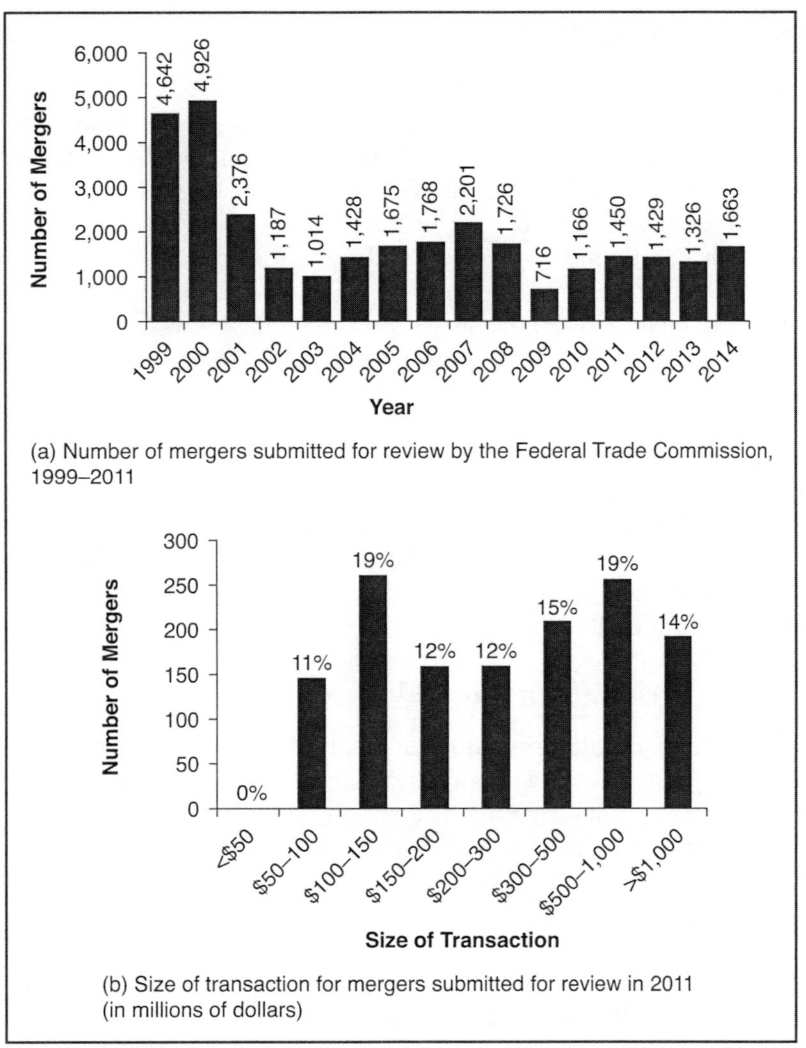

(a) Number of mergers submitted for review by the Federal Trade Commission, 1999–2011

(b) Size of transaction for mergers submitted for review in 2011 (in millions of dollars)

EXHIBIT 13-1 Mergers and Acquisitions: Number and Size

In the early 2000s, the number of mergers and acquisitions declined from the levels at the tail end of the 1990s, and has not yet recovered to those levels.

The government approves most proposed mergers. In a market-oriented economy, firms have the freedom to make their own choices. Private firms have the freedom to expand or reduce production; to set the price that they choose; to open new factories or sales facilities or to close them; to hire workers or to lay them off; and to start selling new products or to stop selling existing ones. If the owners want to acquire a firm or be acquired, or to merge with another firm, this decision is just one of many decisions that firms are free to make. Yes, the managers of private firms will make mistakes sometimes. They may close down a factory that, it later turns out, would have been profitable. They may start selling a product that loses money. A merger between two companies can sometimes lead to a clash of corporate personalities that makes both firms worse off. But the fundamental belief behind a market-oriented economy is that firms are in the best position to know if their actions will attract more customers or let them produce more efficiently.

Indeed, government regulators agree that most mergers are beneficial to consumers. As the Federal Trade Commission has noted on its website: "Most mergers actually benefit competition and consumers by allowing firms to operate more efficiently." But the FTC continues: "Some [mergers] are likely to lessen competition. That, in turn, can lead to higher prices, reduced availability of goods or services, lower quality of products, and less innovation. Indeed, some mergers create a concentrated market, while others enable a single firm to raise prices." Thus, the challenge for the antitrust regulators at the FTC and the U.S. Department of Justice is to figure out when a merger may hinder competition. This decision involves both numerical tools and some judgments that are more difficult to quantify.

The Four-Firm Concentration Ratio

four-firm concentration ratio: What percentage share of the total sales in the industry is accounted for by the largest four firms.

market share: The percentage share of total sales in the market.

The **four-firm concentration ratio**, which measures what share of the total sales in the industry are accounted for by the largest four firms, is one numerical way to measure the extent of competition in an industry. Say that the market for replacing broken automobile windshields in a certain city has 16 firms with the **market shares** shown in Exhibit 13-2, where the market share is each firm's proportion of total sales in that market. The four-firm concentration ratio is calculated by adding the market shares of the four largest firms: in this case, 16 + 10 + 8 + 6 = 40. This concentration ratio would not be considered especially high, because the largest four firms have less than half the market.

The concentration ratio approach can help to clarify some of the fuzziness over deciding when a merger might affect competition. For example, if two of the smallest firms in the hypothetical market for repairing automobile windshields merged, the four-firm concentration ratio would not change—which implies that there isn't much worry that the degree of competition in the market has notably diminished. However, if the top two firms merged, then the four-firm concentration ratio would become 46 (i.e., 26 + 8 + 6 + 6). While this concentration ratio is modestly higher, the four-firm concentration ratio would still be less than half, so such a proposed merger might barely raise an eyebrow among the antitrust regulators.

The Herfindahl-Hirschman Index

A four-firm concentration ratio is a simple tool, which may reveal only part of the story. For example, consider two industries that both have a four-firm concentration ratio of 80. However, in one industry five firms each control 20% of the market, while in the other industry, the top firm holds 77% of the market and all the other firms have 1% each. Although the four-firm concentration ratios are identical, it would be reasonable to worry more about the extent of competition in the second case—which is nearly a monopoly—than in the first.

Herfindahl-Hirschman Index (HHI): Take the market share of each firm in the industry, square each one, and add them.

Thus, another approach to measuring industry concentration that can distinguish between these two cases is called the **Herfindahl-Hirschman Index**. The HHI, as it is often called, is calculated by taking the market shares of every firm in the industry, squaring them, and adding them up to get a total. Exhibit 13-3 gives examples of an HHI calculation. For a monopoly with a market share of 100%, the HHI would reach a maximum value of 10,000. For an extremely competitive industry, with dozens or hundreds of extremely small competitors, the value of the HHI might drop as low as 100 or even less.

The HHI gives greater weight to large firms. Consider the example given a moment ago, comparing one industry where five firms each have 20% of the market with an industry where one firm has 77% and the other 23 firms have 1% each. The two industries have the same four-firm concentration ratio of 80. But the HHI for the first industry is $5(20^2) = 2{,}000$, while the HHI for the second industry is much higher at $77^2 + 23(1^2) = 5{,}952$. The near-monopolist in the second industry drives up the HHI measure of industrial concentration. Exhibit 13-4 gives some examples of the four-firm concentration ratio and the HHI in various U.S. industries in 2012.

EXHIBIT 13-2 Calculating Concentration Ratios from Market Shares

If the market shares in the market for replacing automobile windshields are:	
Smooth as Glass Repair Company	16% of the market
The Auto Glass Doctor Company	10% of the market
Your Car Shield Company	8% of the market
Seven firms that each have 6% of the market	42% of the market, combined
Eight firms that each have 3% of the market	24% of the market, combined
Then the four-firm concentration ratio is 16 + 10 + 8 + 6 = 40.	

The Birth of Antitrust Law

In the closing decades of the nineteenth century, many industries in the U.S. economy were dominated by a single firm that had most of the sales for the entire country. The table lists some of the firms at this time that had more than 70% of sales for the entire United States in their industry. Supporters of these large firms argued that they could take advantage of economies of scale and careful planning to provide consumers with products at low prices. However, critics pointed out that when competition was reduced, these firms were free to charge more and make permanently higher profits, and that without the goad of competition, it wasn't clear that they were as efficient or innovative as they could be.

In many cases these large firms were organized in the legal form of a "trust," in which a group of formerly independent firms were consolidated together by mergers and purchases, and a group of "trustees" then ran the companies as if they were a single firm. Thus, when the U.S. government passed the Sherman Act in 1890 to limit the power of these trusts, it was called an "antitrust" law. In an early demonstration of the law's power, the U.S. Supreme Court in 1911 upheld the government's right to break up Standard Oil, which had controlled about 90% of the country's oil refining, into 34 independent firms. In 1914, the Federal Trade Commission (FTC) was created to define more specifically what competition was unfair. In the twenty-first century, the FTC continues to work with attorneys from the U.S. Department of Justice to enforce antitrust laws.

Single Companies That Had More Than 70% of the Total U.S. Market about 1900

- American Can
- American Fork and Hoe
- American Hide and Leather
- American Ice
- American Locomotive
- American School Furniture
- American Window Glass
- American Writing Paper
- Corn Products
- DuPont
- Eastman Kodak
- International Harvester
- International Paper
- National Asphalt
- Otis Elevator
- Union Box Board and Paper
- United Shoe Machinery
- United States Envelope

EXHIBIT 13-3 Some Herfindahl-Hirschman Index Calculations

HHI for a monopoly	$100^2 = 10{,}000$
HHI for an industry with 100 firms that each have 1% of the market	$100(1^2) = 100$
HHI for the industry market share in Exhibit 13-2	$16^2 + 10^2 + 8^2 + 7(6^2) + 8(3^2) = 744$

EXHIBIT 13-4 Some Examples of Concentration Ratios and HHIs in the U.S. Economy, 2015

U.S. Industry	Largest Five Firms by Market Share	Four-Firm Ratio	HHI
Banking	JP Morgan Chase, Wells Fargo, Bank of America, Citigroup, US Bancorp	74	1,446
Automobiles	Nissan, General Motors, Ford, Honda, Toyota	57	1,095
Information technology services	International Business Machines, Accenture, Xerox, Visa, Cognizant	57	1,190
Airlines	Southwest, Delta, United, American, US Airways	63	1,107
Property and casualty insurance	State Farm, Liberty Mutual, Allstate, Berkshire Hathaway, Travelers	25	300

In the 1980s, the FTC followed guidelines that if a merger would result in an HHI of less than 1,000 for the industry, the FTC would probably approve it. If a merger would result in an HHI of more than 1,800, the FTC would probably challenge it. If a merger would result in an HHI between 1,000 and 1,800, then the FTC would scrutinize the plan and make a case-by-case decision. However, in the last few decades the antitrust enforcement authorities have moved away from relying as heavily on measures of concentration ratios and HHIs to determine whether a merger will be allowed, and instead carried out more case-by-case analysis of the extent of competition in different industries.

New Directions for Antitrust

Both the four-firm concentration ratio and the Herfindahl-Hirschman index share some weaknesses. First, they begin from the assumption that the "market" under discussion is well defined, and the only question is measuring how sales are divided in that market. Second, they are based on an implicit assumption that competitive conditions across industries are similar enough that a broad measure of concentration in the market is enough information, all by itself, to make a decision about the effects of a merger. In response to these two problems, the antitrust regulators have been changing their approach in the last decade or two.

Defining a market is often controversial. For example, Microsoft in the early 2000s had a dominant share of the software for computer operating systems. However, in the total market for all computer software and services, including everything from games to scientific programs, the Microsoft share was only about 16% in 2000. A narrowly defined market will tend to make concentration appear higher, while a broadly defined market will tend to make it appear smaller.

There are two especially important shifts in how markets are defined in recent decades: one involves technology, and the other involves globalization. With the vast improvement in communications technologies, including the development of the Internet, a consumer can order books or pet supplies from all over the country or the world. As a result, the degree of competition faced by many local retail businesses has increased. The same effect may operate even more strongly in markets for business supplies, where so-called "business-to-business" websites can allow buyers and suppliers from anywhere in the world to find each other.

The effect of globalization has changed the boundaries of markets as well. As recently as the 1970s, it was common for measurements of concentration ratios and HHIs to stop at national borders. Now, many industries find that their competition comes from the global market. A few decades ago, three companies—General Motors, Ford, and Chrysler—dominated the U.S. auto market. Now, these three firms make less than half of U.S. auto sales and face competition from such well-known car manufacturers as Toyota, Honda, Nissan, Volkswagen, Mitsubishi, and Mazda. When HHIs are calculated on a global perspective, concentration in most major industries—including cars—is lower than it was several decades ago.

Because attempting to define a particular market can be difficult and controversial, the Federal Trade Commission has begun to look less at market share and more at the data on actual competition between businesses. For example, Whole Foods Market and Wild Oats Market announced that they wished to merge in 2007. These were the two largest companies in the market that the government defined as "premium natural and organic supermarket chains." However, one could also argue that they were two relatively small companies in the broader market for all stores that sell groceries or specialty food products. Thus, rather than relying on a market definition, the government antitrust regulators looked at detailed evidence on profits and prices for specific stores in different cities, both before and after other competitive stores entered or exited. Based on that evidence, the Federal Trade Commission decided to block the merger. After two years of legal battles, the merger was eventually allowed in 2009 under the conditions that Whole Foods sell off the Wild Oats brand name and a number of individual stores—to preserve competition in certain local markets.

This new approach to antitrust regulation involves detailed analysis of specific markets and companies, instead of just counting the sales of firms in a market. Modern antitrust regulators often use statistical tools and real-world evidence to estimate the demand and supply curves faced by the firms that are proposing the merger. Next, they specify how competition occurs in this specific industry: some possibilities include competing to cut prices, to raise output, to build a brand name, through advertising, and to build a reputation for good service or high quality. With these pieces of the puzzle in place, it's then possible to build a statistical model that estimates the likely outcome for consumers if the two firms are allowed to merge. Of course, these models do require some subjective judgment, and so they can become the subject of legal disputes between the antitrust authorities and the companies that wish to merge.

Regulating Anticompetitive Behavior

The U.S. antitrust laws reach beyond blocking mergers that would reduce competition to include a wide array of anticompetitive practices. For example, it is illegal for competitors to collude together and make pricing and output decisions, as if they were a monopoly firm. The Federal Trade Commission and the U.S. Department of Justice have guidelines that forbid firms from agreeing to fix prices or output, rig bids, or share or divide markets by allocating customers, suppliers, territories, or lines of commerce. In the late 1990s, for example, the antitrust regulators prosecuted an international cartel of vitamin manufacturers, including the Swiss firm Hoffman-La Roche, the German firm BASF, and the French firm Rhone-Poulenc. These firms reached agreements on how much to produce, how much to charge, and which firm would sell to which customers. The high-priced vitamins were then bought by firms like General Mills, Kellogg, Purina-Mills, and Proctor and Gamble, which pushed up the prices of products for people and animals. Hoffman-La Roche, for example, pleaded guilty in May 1999 and agreed both to pay a fine of $500 million and to have at least one top executive serve four months of jail time.

Under the U.S. antitrust laws, monopoly itself is not illegal. If a firm has a monopoly because of a newly patented invention, for example, the law explicitly allows a firm to earn higher-than-normal profits for a time as a reward for innovation. If a firm achieves a large share of the market by producing a better product at a lower price, such behavior is not prohibited by antitrust law.

Antitrust law includes rules against **restrictive practices**—practices that do not involve outright agreements to raise price or to reduce the quantity produced, but that might have the effect of reducing competition. Antitrust cases involving restrictive practices are often controversial because they delve into specific contracts or agreements between firms that are allowed in some cases but not in others.

restrictive practices: Practices that reduce competition but that do not involve outright agreements between firms to raise price.

For example, if a product manufacturer is selling to a group of dealers who then sell to the general public, it is illegal for the manufacturer to demand a **minimum resale price maintenance agreement**, which would require the dealers to sell for at least a certain minimum price. A minimum price contract is illegal because it would restrict competition among dealers. However, the manufacturer is legally allowed to "suggest" minimum prices and to stop selling to dealers who regularly undercut the suggested price. If you think this rule sounds like a fairly subtle distinction, you're right.

minimum resale price maintenance agreement: An agreement that requires a dealer who buys from a manufacturer to sell for at least a certain minimum price.

An **exclusive dealing** agreement between a manufacturer and a dealer, which requires that the dealer sell only products from one manufacturer, can be legal or illegal. It is legal if the purpose of the contract is to encourage competition between dealers; for example, it is legal for the Ford Motor Company to sell its cars only to Ford dealers, for General Motors to sell only to GM dealers, and so on. However, exclusive deals may also limit competition. For example, if one large retailer obtained the exclusive rights to be the sole distributor of televisions, computers, and audio equipment made by a number of companies, then this exclusive contract would have an anticompetitive effect on other retailers.

exclusive dealing: An agreement that a dealer will sell only products from one manufacturer.

Tie-in sales refer to a situation where a customer is allowed to buy one product only if the customer also buys a second product. Tie-in sales may sometimes be illegal: for example, suppose that in order to purchase a popular CD, the store required that you also

tie-in sales: A situation where a customer is allowed to buy one product only if the customer also buys another product; also called "bundling."

bundling: A situation where a customer is allowed to buy one product only if the customer also buys another product; also called "tie-in sales."

predatory pricing: When an existing firm uses sharp but temporary price cuts to discourage new competition.

purchase two other CDs of your choice. However, in other cases, tie-in sales, or **bundling** as it is sometimes called because it wraps together several products, may be legal and even common. It is common for people to purchase season tickets to a sports team or a set of concerts so that they can be guaranteed tickets to the few contests or shows that are most popular and likely to sell out. Computer software may often bundle together a number of different programs, even when the buyer only actually wants a few of the programs.

Predatory pricing occurs when the existing firm (or firms) reacts to a new firm by dropping prices very low for a short time, until the new firm is driven out of the market, and then raising prices again. This pattern of pricing is aimed at deterring the entry of new firms into the market. But in practice, it can be hard to figure out when pricing should be considered predatory. Say that American Airlines is flying between two cities, and a new airline starts flying between the same two cities, at a lower price. If American Airlines cuts its price to match the new entrant, is this predatory pricing? Or is it just market competition at work? A commonly proposed rule is that if a firm is selling for less than its average variable cost—that is, at a price where it should be shutting down—then there is evidence for predatory pricing. But calculating in the real world what costs are variable and what costs are fixed is often not obvious, either.

The concept of restrictive practices is continually evolving, as firms seek out new ways to earn profits and government regulators define what is permissible and what is not. A situation where the law is evolving and changing is always somewhat troublesome, since laws are most useful and fair when firms know what they are in advance. In addition, since the law is open to interpretation, competitors who are losing out in the market can accuse successful firms of anticompetitive restrictive practices and try to win through government regulation what they have failed to accomplish in the market. Officials at the Federal Trade Commission and the Department of Justice are of course aware of these issues, but there is no easy way to address them.

When Breaking Up Is Hard to Do: Regulating Natural Monopolies

The case of natural monopoly poses a difficult challenge for competition policy because the structure of costs and demand seems to make competition unlikely or costly. A natural monopoly arises when average costs are declining over the range of production that satisfies market demand. As a result, one firm is able to supply the total quantity demanded in the market at lower cost than two or more firms—so splitting up the natural monopoly would raise the average cost of production and force customers to pay more.

Public utilities, the companies that have traditionally provided water and electrical service across much of the United States, are leading examples of natural monopoly. It would make little sense to argue that, say, a local water company should be broken up into several competing companies, each with its own separate set of pipes and water supplies. Installing four or five identical sets of pipes under a city, one for each water company, so that each household could choose its own provider of water, would be terribly costly. The same argument applies to the idea of having many competing companies for delivering electricity to homes, each with its own set of wires. Before the advent of wireless phones, the argument also applied to the idea of many different phone companies, each with its own set of phone wires running through the neighborhood.

The Choices in Regulating a Natural Monopoly

What is the appropriate competition policy for a natural monopoly? Exhibit 13-5 illustrates the case of natural monopoly, with a market demand curve that cuts through the downward-sloping portion of the average cost curve. Points A, B, C, and F illustrate four of the main choices for regulators.

The first possibility is to leave the natural monopoly alone. In this case, the monopoly will follow its usual approach to maximizing profits. It determines the quantity where

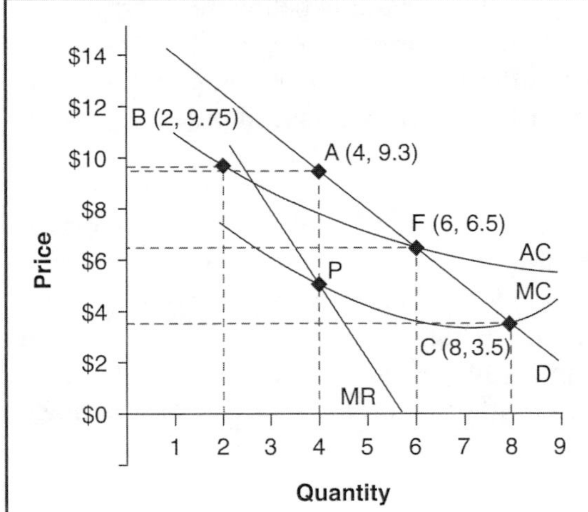

Quantity	Price	Total Revenue	Marginal Revenue	Total Cost	Marginal Cost	Average Cost
1	14.7	14.7	–	11	–	11
2	12.4	24.7	10	19.5	7.5	9.75
3	10.6	31.7	7	25.5	6	8.5
4	9.3	37.2	5.5	31	5.5	7.75
5	8	40	2.8	35	4	7
6	6.5	39	–1	39	4	6.5
7	5	35	–4	42	3	6
8	3.5	28	–7	45.5	3.5	5.7
9	2	18	–10	49.5	4	5.5

EXHIBIT 13-5 Regulatory Choices in Dealing with Natural Monopoly

A natural monopoly will maximize profits by producing at the quantity where MR = MC and by then looking to the market demand curve to see what price to charge for this quantity. This monopoly will produce at point A, with quantity of 4 and a price of 9.3. If antitrust regulators split this company exactly in half, then each half would produce at point B, with average costs of 9.75 and output of 2. Over time, these two firms might expand production, but with a downward-sloping AC curve, average costs for two smaller firms will always be higher than average costs for one large firm. The regulators might require the firm to produce where marginal cost crosses the market demand curve at point C. However, if the firm is required to produce at a quantity of 8 and sell at a price of 3.5, the firm will suffer losses because the price is below average cost for this quantity of output. The most likely choice is point F, where the firm is required to produce a quantity of 6 and charge a price of 6.5. Because price is equal to average cost, the firm is able to continue operating but does not make an abnormally high profit.

MR = MC, which happens at point P at a quantity of 4. The firm then looks to point A on the demand curve to find that it can charge a price of 9.3 for that profit-maximizing quantity. Since the price is above the average cost curve, the natural monopoly would earn economic profits.

A second outcome arises if antitrust authorities decide to divide the company, so that the new firms can compete with each other. As a simple example, imagine that the company is cut in half. Thus, instead of one large firm producing a quantity of 4, two half-size firms each produce a quantity of 2. Because of the declining average cost curve, the average cost of production for each of the half-size companies each producing 2, as shown at point B, would be 9.75, while the average cost of production for a larger firm producing 4 would only be 7.75. Thus, the economy would become less productively efficient, since the good is being produced at a higher average cost. In a situation with a downward-sloping average cost curve, two smaller firms will always have higher average costs of production than one larger firm for any quantity of total output. In addition, the antitrust authorities must worry that splitting the natural monopoly into pieces may be only the start of their problems. If one of the two firms grows larger than the other, it will have lower average costs and may be able to drive its competitor out of the market. Alternatively, two firms in a market may discover subtle ways of coordinating their behavior and keeping prices high. Either way, the result will not be the greater competition that was desired.

A third alternative is that regulators may decide to set prices and quantities produced for this industry. The regulators will try to choose a point along the market demand curve that benefits both consumers and the broader social interest. Point C illustrates one tempting choice: the regulator requires that the firm produce the quantity of output where marginal cost crosses the demand curve at an output of 8, and charge the price of 3.5, which is equal to marginal cost at that point. This rule is appealing because it requires price to be set equal to marginal cost, which is what would occur in a perfectly competitive market, and it would assure consumers a higher quantity and lower price than at the monopoly choice A. But attempting to bring about point C through force of regulation runs into a severe difficulty. At point C, with an output of 8, a price of 3.5 is below the average cost of production, which is 5.7, and so if the firm charges a price of 3.5, it will be suffering losses. Unless the regulators or the government offer the firm an ongoing public subsidy (which has obvious political problems of its own), the firm will lose money and need to go out of business.

Perhaps the most plausible option for the regulator is point F; that is, to set the price where AC crosses the demand curve at an output of 6 and a price of 6.5. This plan makes some sense at an intuitive level: let the natural monopoly charge enough to cover its average costs and earn a normal rate of profit, so that it can continue operating, but prevent the firm from raising prices and earning abnormally high monopoly profits, as it would at the monopoly choice A. Of course, determining this level of output and price with the political pressures, time constraints, and limited information of the real world is much harder than identifying the point on a graph.

Cost-Plus versus Price Cap Regulation

cost-plus regulation: When regulators permit a regulated firm to cover its costs and to make a normal level of profit.

price cap regulation: When the regulator sets a price that a firm cannot exceed over the next few years.

Indeed, regulators of public utilities for many decades followed the general approach of attempting to choose a point like F in Exhibit 13-5. They calculated the average cost of production for the water or electricity companies, including an adjustment for the normal rate of profit the firm should expect to earn, and set the price for consumers accordingly. This method was known as **cost-plus regulation**. But cost-plus regulation raises difficulties of its own. If producers are reimbursed for their costs, plus a bit more, then at a minimum, producers have less reason to be concerned with high costs—because they can just pass those costs along in higher prices. Worse, firms under cost-plus regulation even have an incentive to generate high costs by building huge factories or employing lots of staff because what they can charge is linked to the costs they incur.

Thus, in the 1980s and 1990s, some regulators of public utilities began to use **price cap regulation**, where regulators set a price that the firm can charge over the next few years. A common pattern was to require a price that declined slightly over time. If the firm can find ways of reducing its costs more quickly than the price caps, it can make a high level of profits. On the other hand, if the firm can't keep up with the price caps or suffers bad luck in the market, it may suffer losses. A few years down the road, the regulators will then set a new series of price caps based on the firm's recent performance.

Price cap regulation requires delicacy. It won't work well if the price regulators set the price cap unrealistically low. It may not work if the market changes dramatically so that the firm is doomed to incur losses no matter what it does—say, if energy prices rise dramatically on world markets, then a company selling natural gas or heating oil to homes may not be able to meet price caps that seemed reasonable a year or two ago. But if the regulators compare the prices with producers of the same good in other areas, they can in effect pressure a natural monopoly in one area to compete with the prices being charged in other areas. Moreover, the possibility of earning greater profits or experiencing losses—instead of having an average rate of profit locked in every year by cost-plus regulation—can provide the natural monopoly with incentives for efficiency and innovation.

Natural monopoly presents a situation where market competition is unlikely to take root, and so if consumers are not to suffer the high prices and restricted output of an unrestricted monopoly, government regulation will need to play a role. But in attempting to design a system of price cap regulation with flexibility and incentive, government regulators do not have an easy task, either.

The Great Deregulation Experiment

Governments have historically regulated the prices in a wide range of industries. In some cases, like water and electricity that have natural monopoly characteristics, there is some justification in economic theory for such regulation. But once politicians are given a basis to intervene in markets and to choose prices and quantities, it's hard to know where to stop.

Doubts about Regulation of Prices and Quantities

In the decades before wireless phones, when telephone technology required having a wire running to every home, it seemed plausible that telephone service had diminishing average costs and might need to be regulated like a natural monopoly. For most of the twentieth century, the national U.S. phone company was AT&T, and the company functioned as a regulated monopoly. A number of transportation-related industries may have declining marginal costs, in the sense that once a network of railroads or trucks or planes or buses was set up, the marginal cost of adding an extra passenger was low. Thus, for much of the twentieth century, the U.S. government had laws setting prices for the airline, railroad, bus, and trucking industries. Natural gas was shipped over pipelines, and since the fear of duplicate pipes could imply a natural monopoly, natural gas prices were regulated. In the United States until the late 1970s, banks were limited in the rate of interest they could pay to depositors. The argument was that if banks competed to pay higher rates of interest, they might also compete to make riskier loans, potentially imperiling the safety of the banking system.

However, by the 1970s, it became clear to policy makers of all political leanings that the widespread price regulation in all of these industries wasn't working especially well. The United States carried out a great policy experiment in **deregulation**, removing government controls over prices and quantities produced in airlines, railroads, trucking, intercity bus travel, natural gas, and bank interest rates.

deregulation: Removing government controls over setting prices and quantities in certain industries.

One difficulty with government price regulation is what economists call **regulatory capture**, in which the firms supposedly being regulated end up playing a large role in setting the regulations that they will follow. When the airline industry was being regulated, for example, the airline industry would suggest appointees to the regulatory board, attend every meeting of the board, send lobbyists to argue with the board, provide most of the

regulatory capture: When the firms supposedly being regulated end up playing a large role in setting the regulations that they will follow.

Airline Deregulation

In the early days of air travel, no airline could make a profit just by flying passengers. Airlines needed something else to carry. And so the first U.S. government regulation of the airline industry happened through the postal service, when in 1926 the postmaster general began giving airlines permission to fly certain routes based on the needs of mail delivery—and the airlines took some passengers along for the ride. In 1934, the postmaster general was charged by the antitrust authorities with colluding with the major airlines of that day to monopolize the nation's airways. In 1938, the Civil Aeronautics Board (CAB) was created to regulate airfares and routes instead. For 40 years, from 1938 to 1978, the CAB regulated the industry with a heavy hand. It approved all fares, controlled all entry and exit, and specified who could fly which routes. There was zero entry of new airlines on the main routes across the country for 40 years because the CAB didn't think it was necessary.

In 1978, the Airline Deregulation Act took the government out of the business of determining airfares and schedules. The new law shook up the industry. Famous old airlines like Pan American, Eastern, and Braniff went bankrupt and disappeared. Some new airlines like People Express were created—and then vanished.

But the greater competition from deregulation reduced airfares by about one-third over the next two decades, saving consumers billions of dollars a year. The average flight used to take off with just half its seats full; now it is two-thirds full, which is far more efficient. Airlines have also developed hub-and-spoke systems, where planes all fly into a central hub city at a certain time and then depart. As a result, one can fly between any of the spoke-cities with just one connection—and there is greater service to more cities than before deregulation. With lower fares and more service, the number of air passengers doubled from the late 1970s to the start of the 2000s—an increase that in turn doubled the number of jobs in the airline industry. Meanwhile, with the watchful oversight of government safety inspectors, commercial air travel has continued to get safer over time.

The U.S. airline industry is far from perfect: for example, a string of mergers in recent years has raised concerns over how competition might be affected. But it provides a better deal for consumers after deregulation than it did before.

information on which the board made decisions, and offer well-paid jobs to at least some of the people leaving the board. In comparison, consumers can easily end up not being very well represented by the regulators. The result of regulatory capture is that government price regulation can often become a way for existing competitors to act together to reduce output, keep prices high, and limit competition.

The Effects of Deregulation

Deregulation of airlines and other industries has been a mixed blessing. The greater pressure of competition led to entry and exit. When firms went bankrupt or contracted substantially in size, they laid off workers who had to find other jobs. Market competition is a full-contact sport.

But the bottom line is that after deregulation, firms in many industries found ways to make innovations in their management, operations, marketing, and technology. They offered more flexible arrangements to consumers and cut their costs substantially. For example, airline deregulation led to planes flying with two-thirds of the seats filled on average, compared to about half the seats filled before deregulation. In turn, fuller planes led to lower costs and to consumer prices that were one-third lower than they would otherwise have been. Since trucking prices were deregulated, trucks now drive many fewer empty miles, and the costs to shippers have fallen by 35%. When railroads were deregulated, they shut down a lot of track that was barely being used, and prices to shippers fell by 50%. Bottom line: by the start of the 2000s, the United States' great deregulation experiment of the 1970s and 1980s was saving consumers more than $50 billion per year in lower prices.

Frontiers of Deregulation

The overall success of the United States' great deregulation experiment in airlines, banking, trucking, and other industries has encouraged deregulators to push further and to think about injecting competition into industries where the arguments for deregulation are not as obvious. In the electricity and the telecommunications industry, for example, the challenge is to combine competition where possible with regulation where necessary.

Electricity had long been thought of as a natural monopoly. However, the argument that electricity is a natural monopoly focuses on the grid of wires that bring electricity to homes. It does not focus on how the electrical power is generated. Thus, a deregulation movement has grown up in which the electrical grid would continue to be publicly owned or regulated, but the business of producing electrical energy would become competitive. Since 1989, the United Kingdom has tried out various market arrangements for having electricity generators compete with each other. A number of U.S. states have also experimented with electricity deregulation, some with considerable success (Pennsylvania) and some with near-disastrous consequences (California). Many other states have been holding back on electricity deregulation, waiting to learn from the experience of the pioneers what methods work better or worse.

Another frontier for deregulation is the telecommunications industry. In 1982, the AT&T telephone monopoly that had served the United States for decades reached an agreement with the government antitrust lawyers to split itself up into several pieces: AT&T, which competed in the market for long-distance phone service; Bell Labs, the laboratory research arm and phone equipment maker, which later changed its name to Lucent Technologies; and seven local phone companies nicknamed the "Baby Bells" that each provided local phone service to a different geographic region of the United States. Since then, long-distance phone service has been a battleground for AT&T, Sprint, MCI, Worldcom, Internet firms that provide phone calls through a computer, and others. At least in theory, a variety of companies and technologies could provide local phone service, including existing regional "Baby Bell" phone companies, wireless phone companies, and cable TV companies that can use their cables to deliver phone service. In many areas, electricity or water companies own fiber optic cables that, at least in theory, could be used to provide phone service. In addition, the Internet is bringing a rising demand for high-speed computer connections, which can also carry telephone calls. As the degree of competition in telephone markets has risen, so has the level of innovation.

Deregulation does not eliminate all forms of government regulation. A deregulated airline industry, for example, still has government inspectors looking at airplane safety and counting the number of on-time departures. A deregulated banking system still has government bank inspectors seeking to make sure that banks are solvent and not taking crazy risks with depositor's money. A deregulated system of producing electricity still has government regulation of the electrical grid that delivers power. While deregulation expands the role of prices and incentives in production, market forces do rely on a foundation of laws and institutional arrangements to operate at their best.

Around the World: From Nationalization to Privatization

While the U.S. economy has had considerable experience with regulating the prices and output of various industries—airlines, water, electrical, telephones, trucking, and banking—**nationalization**, which is the outright ownership of firms by the government, has been relatively rare in the United States. However, other countries around the world have often had public ownership of a broad range of industries, including defense contracting, banking, airlines, energy production, and auto manufacturing. In many European countries in the 1990s, 8–10% of the economy consisted of government-owned production. In poorer countries of the world, including some nations in Latin America and Asia, the government-owned share of the economy was often larger, at perhaps 10–12%, and in Africa, the government-run share of the economy was often even higher.

nationalization: When government takes over ownership of firms.

Nationalization of an industry has many of the same problems as government regulation of prices charged and quantities produced. In theory, an industry is nationalized to serve the citizens of the country, but often it turns out that the nationalized industry can act as a monopoly, charging high prices and reducing the quantity of output. When nationalized industries suffer losses, they turn to taxpayers for a bailout. When a nationalized industry lacks competition, it also lacks incentives for productive efficiency and for innovation.

Thus, recent decades have seen a trend in which formerly government-owned firms are turned back into private companies. The early world leader in **privatization**, whereby a government-owned firm becomes privately owned, was the United Kingdom in the 1980s, under the leadership of Prime Minister Margaret Thatcher. Firms run by the British government constituted about 10% of Britain's economy in the mid-1970s, similar to the European average. But by the mid-1990s, after privatizing BritOil, British Steel, British Gas, British Telecom, British Aerospace, a national water company, a national electricity company, and others, government-run firms made up only about 2% of Britain's economy.

privatization: When a government-owned firm becomes privately owned.

After Britain led the way, a global wave of privatization followed in the 1990s and into the 2000s. More than 100 countries had privatization efforts in effect in the 2000s. Some of the most prominent cases have involved the shift of Russia and countries of Eastern Europe from communism to a more market-oriented society, but a great deal of privatization has also happened in Latin America and Western Europe. The main public argument for privatization often revolves around the amount of money it could raise for the government when the government sells off firms to private owners. But as economists are quick to point out, if Harriet the Homeowner sells her house, she doesn't get any richer. Instead of owning a house, which has a certain value, she now has money of that same value. Similarly, when the government sells a company, the government then has cash instead of a physical asset. The change in the form of the asset, from property to cash, doesn't make the government any richer. Instead, the deeper argument for privatization is that government regulators often aren't too good at quick reactions and innovation in an ever-changing marketplace, and that a private firm that can't rely on government bailouts will be exposed to incentives for efficiency and innovation.

Advocates of privatization often cite this motto: "Government should steer, not row." In other words, government should set the conditions and general direction of competition, but not try to micromanage the details of production. Although this motto is usually applied to privatization, it also conveys an appropriate government policy toward competition as a whole. All market-based economies operate against a background of laws and regulations, including laws about enforcing contracts, collecting taxes, and protecting health and the environment. The government competition policies discussed in this chapter—like blocking certain anticompetitive mergers, ending restrictive practices, imposing price cap regulation on natural monopolies, and deregulation—are not about eliminating government, but about shaping and reshaping the role of government to strengthen the incentives that come with a greater degree of competition.

Key Concepts and Summary

1. A corporate **merger** involves two private firms joining together. An **acquisition** refers to one firm buying another firm. In either case, two formerly independent firms become one firm.
2. **Antitrust laws** seek to ensure active competition in markets, sometimes by preventing large firms from forming through mergers and acquisitions, sometimes by regulating business practices that might restrict competition, and sometimes by breaking up large firms into smaller competitors.
3. A **four-firm concentration** ratio is one way of measuring the extent of competition in a market. It is calculated by adding the **market shares**—that is, the percentage of total sales—of the four largest firms in the market.
4. A **Herfindahl-Hirschman Index (HHI)** is another way of measuring the extent of competition in a market. It is calculated by taking the market shares of all firms in the market, squaring them, and then summing the total.
5. The forces of globalization and new communications and information technology have increased the level of competition faced by many firms by increasing the amount of competition from other regions and countries.
6. Because firms are blocked by antitrust authorities from openly colluding to form a cartel that will reduce output and raise prices, many antitrust cases involve **restrictive practices** that can reduce competition in certain circumstances, like **tie-in sales** (also called **bundling**) and **predatory pricing**.
7. In the case of a natural monopoly, market competition will not work well, and so rather than allowing an unregulated monopoly to raise price and reduce output, the government may wish to regulate price and/or output. Common examples of regulation are public utilities, the regulated firms that often provide electricity and water service.
8. **Cost-plus regulation** refers to government regulation of a firm that sets the price that a firm can charge over a period of time like a year by looking at the firm's accounting costs and then adding a normal rate of profit. **Price cap regulation** refers to government regulation of a firm where the government sets a price level several years in advance, and the firm can either make high profits by producing at lower costs or selling a higher quantity than expected, or suffer low profits or losses by producing at higher costs or selling a lower quantity than expected.
9. The U.S. economy experienced a wave of **deregulation** in the late 1970s and early 1980s, when a number of government regulations that had set prices and quantities produced in a number of industries were eliminated. There are current efforts to deregulate telecommunications and electricity—areas that were once thought to be natural monopolies.
10. **Regulatory capture** occurs when the industries being regulated end up having a strong influence over what regulations exist.
11. Privatization can increase the level of market competition and efficiency through the selling of previously **nationalized** assets to private owners. However, if privatization is to work well, it must provide incentives for a firm to be operated more efficiently, not just replace government ownership with an unregulated private monopoly.

Review Questions

1. What is a corporate merger? What is an acquisition?
2. What is the goal of antitrust policies?
3. How is a four-firm concentration ratio measured? What does a high measure mean about the extent of competition?
4. How is a Herfindahl-Hirschman Index measured? What does a low measure mean about the extent of competition?
5. Why can it be difficult to decide what a "market" is for purposes of measuring competition?
6. What is a minimum resale price maintenance agreement? How might it reduce competition, and when might it be acceptable?
7. What is exclusive dealing? How might it reduce competition, and when might it be acceptable?
8. What is a tie-in sale? How might it reduce competition, and when might it be acceptable?
9. What is predatory pricing? How might it reduce competition, and why might it be difficult to tell when it should be illegal?
10. If public utilities are a natural monopoly, what would be the danger in deregulating them?
11. If public utilities are a natural monopoly, what would be the danger in splitting them up into a number of separate competing firms?
12. What is cost-plus regulation?
13. What is price-cap regulation?
14. What is deregulation? Name some industries that have been deregulated in the United States.
15. What is regulatory capture?
16. Why does regulatory capture reduce the persuasiveness of the case for regulating industries for the benefit of consumers?
17. Who owns a nationalized firm?
18. Who owns a privatized firm?

Environmental Protection and Negative Externalities

CHAPTER 14

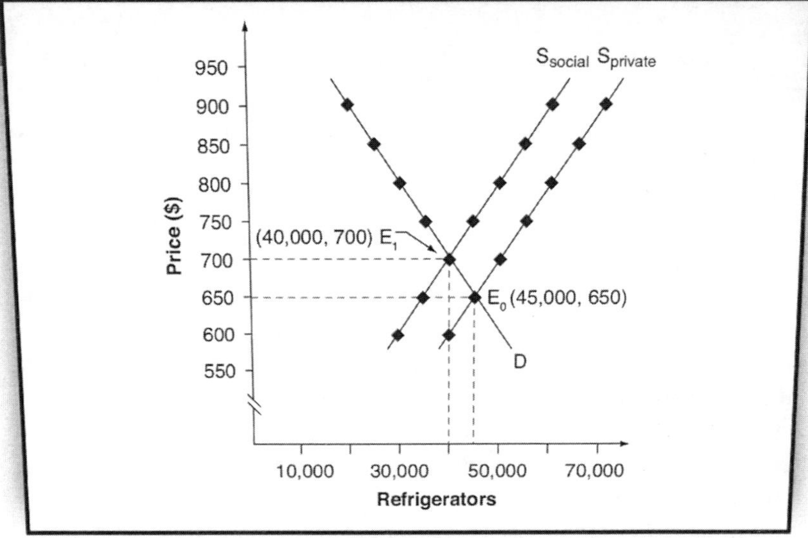

Chapter Outline

Economic output can injure the environment. Any firm that has ever dumped waste into a river or puffed harmful gases into the air serves as an example. The problem of pollution arises for every economy in the world, whether high-income or low-income, and whether primarily market-oriented or command-oriented. Indeed, countries with low incomes and command economies have often been more willing to sacrifice their environmental quality for some additional economic output than high-income, market-oriented economies like the United States and the nations of the European Union.

In the United States, the overall quality of the air and water has been steadily improving for several decades. Many people don't realize how bad the quality of America's water and air was not all that long ago. In 1969, the Cuyahoga River in Ohio was so polluted that it spontaneously burst into flame. At that time, air pollution was so bad that Chattanooga, Tennessee, was a city where (as one news story put it) the "death rate from tuberculosis was double that of the rest of Tennessee and triple that of the rest of the U.S., a city in which the filth in the air was so bad it melted nylon stockings off women's legs, in which executives kept supplies of clean white shirts in their offices so they could change when a shirt became too gray to be presentable, in which headlights were turned on at high noon because the sun was eclipsed by the gunk in the sky."

Since then, the United States has made genuine progress against a number of pollutants. Exhibit 14-1 shows emissions of five key air pollutants in 1970 and 2014. During this time, the U.S. population increased by one-third and the size of the U.S. economy more than doubled. However, emissions of certain key air pollutants declined substantially. Data for water pollution is harder to gather, since gathering and comparing data from rivers, streams, lakes, marshes, and ocean coastlines is a huge task, but there is strong evidence that water quality has improved in many ways. The number of people served by advanced wastewater treatment plants doubled between 1968 and the mid-1990s, but because the treatment plants became so much more effective, the quantity of

EXHIBIT 14-1 U.S. Air Pollution: 1970 and 2014

Emissions of pollutants are measured in millions of tons.

	1970 Emissions	2014 Emissions	Percentage Change from 1970 to 2014
Anthropogenic particulates	12.2	2.6	–79%
Sulfur dioxide	31.2	5	–84%
Nitrogen oxides	26.9	12.4	–54%
Volatile organic compounds	34.7	17.1	–51%
Carbon monoxide	204.0	67.8	–67%

waste emitted into the water after treatment decreased by about one-third. Fish, beavers, and blue herons have returned to the Cuyahoga River in Ohio, although health warnings remain about the safety of eating fish caught there.

Of course, many important environmental issues remain. Along with the continuing levels of air and water pollution, a list of important environmental issues would include hazardous waste disposal, destruction of wetlands and other habitats, the possibility that rising emissions of carbon dioxide and other "greenhouse gases" are leading to climate change, concerns over extinction of species, and other issues as well. But these remaining problems don't alter the encouraging news that substantial progress toward a cleaner environment has been made in a number of areas.

The environmental record of high-income market-oriented economies like the United States and Europe looks greener than much of the rest of the world. In the former Soviet Union, before it split into Russia, Ukraine, and many other countries in the early 1990s, the communist government officially owned and managed all firms. The Soviet economic planners often sacrificed environmental protection in their quest for economic growth. For example, the Aral Sea in the southwestern part of the former Soviet Union, in what is now the country of Kazakhstan, was literally drained to provide irrigation water for growing cotton, leaving behind a desert of toxic salts. The meltdown of the Chernobyl nuclear reactor in 1986, in what is now the independent country of Ukraine, led to the evacuation of over 200,000 people from a region covering 4,000 square kilometers. Unfortunately, the evacuation was not in time to prevent a soaring rate of radiation-related childhood cancers. In the industrial town of Norilsk, in the western part of Russia north of the Arctic Circle, a news report stated: "The snow turns black, the air is yellow with sulfur and over 60% of the population have serious respiratory problems." The legacy of air and water pollution across the former Soviet Union is appalling; in fact, it did much to weaken popular support for the communist system.

Around the world, the cities with the dirtiest air and water typically are in low-income countries in Africa and Asia. The air quality in many of these cities is so bad that for children who live there, breathing the air has the negative health equivalent of smoking two packs of cigarettes a day. Each year, diseases from contaminated water kill about 2 million children in poor countries. In sub-Saharan Africa, about one-fifth of urban residents and half of the rural population lack access to safe water.

Every country—whether it is high-income or low-income and whether its economy is market-oriented or command-oriented—will need to strike some balance between economic output and environmental quality. This chapter begins by discussing how firms may fail to take certain social costs, like pollution, into their planning if they do not need to pay these costs. Traditionally, policies for environmental protection have focused on setting limits for how much of each pollutant could be emitted. While this approach has had some success, economists have suggested a range of more flexible and market-oriented pollution-control policies that offer mechanisms for greater reductions of pollution at lower cost. The chapter then discusses some of the costs, benefits, and challenges facing U.S. and international pollution-control efforts.

Externalities

The principle that voluntary exchange benefits both parties is a fundamental building block of the economic way of thinking. But what happens when a voluntary exchange affects a third party who is neither the buyer nor the seller?

As an example, consider a concert producer who wants to build an outdoor arena that will host country music concerts a half-mile from your neighborhood. You will be able to hear these outdoor concerts while sitting on your back porch—or perhaps even in your dining room. In this case, the sellers and buyers of concert tickets may both be quite satisfied with their voluntary exchange, but you have no voice in their market transaction. The effect of a market exchange on a third party who is outside or "external" to the exchange is called an **externality**. Because externalities that occur in market transactions affect other parties beyond those involved in the transaction, they are sometimes called **spillovers**.

Externalities can be negative or positive. If you hate country music, then having it waft over your house every night would be a **negative externality**, a situation where a third party suffers from a market transaction by others. If you love country music, then a series of free concerts would be a **positive externality**, a situation where a third party benefits from a market transaction by others. In either case, your like or dislike of country music is not a factor that the market takes into account. This chapter focuses on negative externalities, with a particular emphasis on the issue of pollution. For example, being forced to listen to concerts that you don't want to hear in your own home might reasonably be called "noise pollution." The next chapter then discusses positive externalities, with an emphasis on examples involving technology.

externality: When a market exchange affects a third party who is outside or "external" to the exchange; sometimes called a "spillover."

spillover: When a market exchange affects a third party who is outside or "external" to the exchange; more formally called an externality.

negative externality: A situation where a third party, outside the transaction, suffers from a market transaction by others.

positive externality: A situation where a third party, outside the transaction, benefits from a market transaction by others.

Pollution as a Negative Externality

People suffer from pollution even when they were neither a buyer nor a producer of the product that led to the pollution being produced. Nonetheless, the social costs of pollution can be illustrated with a demand and supply diagram. Exhibit 14-2 shows demand and supply for manufacturing refrigerators. The demand curve D shows the quantity demanded at each price. The supply curve $S_{private}$ shows the quantity of refrigerators supplied at each

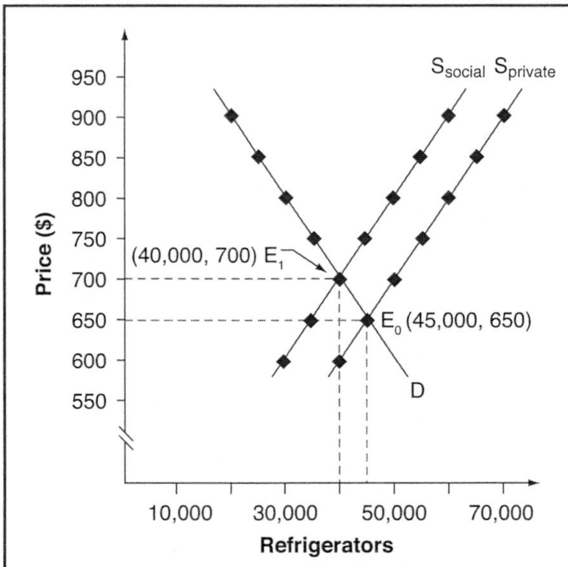

Price	Quantity Demanded	Quantity Supplied before Considering Pollution Cost	Quantity Supplied after Considering Pollution Cost
$600	50,000	40,000	30,000
$650	45,000	45,000	35,000
$700	40,000	50,000	40,000
$750	35,000	55,000	45,000
$800	30,000	60,000	50,000
$850	25,000	65,000	55,000
$900	20,000	70,000	60,000

EXHIBIT 14-2 Taking Social Costs into Account: A Supply Shift

If the firm takes only its private costs into account, then its supply curve will be $S_{private}$, and the market equilibrium will occur at E_0. Now imagine that the firm is required to take $100 of social costs of pollution into account each time it produces a refrigerator. Then the firm will need, for example, to receive $800 to produce the quantity of 50,000 that it used to be willing to produce for $700—and the firm's new supply curve will be S_{social}. The new equilibrium will occur at E_1. Taking the social costs of pollution into account results in a lower quantity of production and a lower quantity of pollution.

price if firms are is taking only their private costs into account and are allowed to emit pollution at zero cost. The market equilibrium E_0, where quantity supplied and quantity demanded are equal, is at a price of $650 and a quantity of 45,000.

However, as a by-product of the metals, plastics, chemicals, and energy that are used in manufacturing refrigerators, some pollution is created. Let's say that if these pollutants were emitted into the air and water, they would create costs of $100 per refrigerator produced. These costs might occur because of injuries to human health, property values, wildlife habitat, recreation possibilities, or in other ways. In a market with no anti-pollution restrictions, firms can receive one of their costs of production, the costs of disposing of certain wastes, absolutely free. But now imagine that firms that produce refrigerators must factor in these **social costs** of pollution—that is, the firms have to consider not only the costs of labor and materials making a refrigerator, but also the broader costs to society of injuries to health and other values caused by pollution.

social costs: Costs that include both the private costs incurred by firms and also costs incurred by third parties outside the production process, like costs of pollution.

Imagine that every time a firm produced a refrigerator, it had to pay an extra $100 to offset the social costs. As a result, the supply curve for producing refrigerators would shift back to the left to S_{social}. For example, if firms had been willing to produce 55,000 refrigerators at a price of $750 apiece, they would now need to receive $850 apiece before producing 55,000 refrigerators—to make up for the $100 charge for social costs. After this shift in the supply curve, the new equilibrium E_1 occurs at a price of $700 and a quantity of 40,000. As the quantity of refrigerators produced declines, so will the quantity of pollution.

Remember that the supply curve is based on choices about production that firms make while looking at their marginal costs, while the demand curve is based on the benefits that individuals perceive while maximizing utility. If no externalities existed, private costs would be the same as the costs to society as a whole, and private benefits would be the same as the benefits to society as a whole. Thus, if no externalities existed, the interaction of demand and supply would coordinate social costs and benefits. However, when the externality of pollution exists, the supply curve no longer represents all social costs. Because externalities represent a case where markets no longer consider all social costs, but only some of them, economists commonly refer to externalities as an example of **market failure**.

market failure: A situation in which the market on its own fails to allocate resources efficiently in a way that balances social costs and benefits; externalities are one example of a market failure.

A general lesson holds here. If firms were required to pay the social costs of pollution, they would produce fewer of the goods that lead to pollution and thus create less pollution—although the price of goods would probably also be higher. Let's now explore how governments might require firms to take into account the social costs of pollution.

Command-and-Control Regulation

When the United States started passing comprehensive environmental laws in the late 1960s and early 1970s, a typical law specified how much pollution could be emitted out of a smokestack or a drainpipe, and then imposed penalties if that limit was exceeded. In other cases, the laws required the installation of certain equipment—say, on automobile tailpipes or on smokestacks—to reduce pollution. These types of laws, which specify allowable quantities of pollution and may also detail which pollution-control technologies must be used, are called **command-and-control regulation**. In effect, command-and-control regulation requires that firms increase their costs by installing anti-pollution equipment, and firms are required to take the social costs of pollution into account in this way.

command-and-control regulation: Laws that specify allowable quantities of pollution and may also detail which pollution-control technologies must be used.

Command-and-control regulation has been highly successful in protecting and cleaning up the U.S. environment. In 1970, the Environmental Protection Agency (EPA) was created to oversee all environmental laws. In the same year, a Clean Air Act was passed to address air pollution. Just two years later, in 1972, legislators passed a far-reaching Clean Water Act. These command-and-control environmental laws of the early 1970s and their amendments and updates over time can take considerable credit for improvements in the quality of America's air and water in recent decades.

However, economists have pointed out three difficulties with command-and-control environmental regulation.

First, command-and-control regulation offers no incentive to improve the quality of the environment beyond the standard set by the law. Once the command-and-control regulation has been satisfied, zero incentive exists to do better.

Second, command-and-control regulation is inflexible. It usually requires the same standard for all potential polluters and often the same pollution-control technology as well. Thus, command-and-control regulation draws no distinctions between firms that would find it easy and inexpensive to meet the pollution standard—or to reduce pollution even further—and firms where it might be difficult and costly to meet the standard. When command-and-control regulation specifies that one particular pollution-control technology must be used, firms have no reason to rethink their production methods in fundamental ways that might reduce pollution by even greater amounts and at lower cost.

Third, command-and-control regulations are set by real-world legislators and bureaucrats, and so they are subject to compromises in the political process. For instance, existing firms often argue that stricter environmental standards should only apply to new firms that wish to start production, but not to existing firms. Real-world environmental laws are full of fine print, loopholes, and exceptions.

These arguments accept the goal of reducing pollution, but raise questions about whether command-and-control regulation is the best way to design policy tools for accomplishing that goal.

Market-Oriented Environmental Tools

Market-oriented environmental tools create incentives for firms to take the social costs of pollution into account, but then allow firms some flexibility in reacting to these incentives. The three main categories of market-oriented approaches to pollution control are pollution charges, marketable permits, and better-defined property rights. Each of these policy tools addresses the shortcomings of command-and-control regulation—albeit in different ways.

Market-Friendly Environmental Tool #1: Pollution Charges

A **pollution charge** is a tax imposed on the quantity of pollution that a firm emits. A pollution charge gives a profit-maximizing firm an incentive to figure out ways to reduce its emissions—as long as the marginal cost of reducing the emissions is less than the tax. For example, consider a small firm that emits 50 pounds per year of small particles, like soot, into the air. Particulate matter, as it is called, causes respiratory sickness and also raises cleaning bills for firms and individuals.

pollution charge: A tax imposed on the quantity of pollution that a firm emits; also called a "pollution tax."

Exhibit 14-3 illustrates the marginal costs that a firm faces in reducing pollution. Reducing particulate emissions by the first 10 pounds costs the firm $300, a reduction of the second 10 pounds would cost $500, the third 10 pounds would cost $900, the fourth 10 pounds would cost $1,500, and the fifth 10 pounds would cost $2,500. This pattern for the costs of reducing pollution is common, since the initial reductions in pollution can use the cheapest and easiest method, but additional reductions in pollution become more expensive.

Imagine the firm now faces a pollution tax of $1,000 for every 10 pounds of particulates emitted. The firm will decide to reduce pollutants by 30 pounds because the marginal cost of reducing pollution by this much is less than the pollution tax. However, the firm will continue to emit the remaining 20 pounds, and pay a pollution tax of $2,000, because it is cheaper for the firm to pay the pollution tax than it would be to eliminate this remaining amount of pollution. A higher pollution tax leads a firm to reduce emissions by more, while a lower pollution tax leads a firm to reduce emissions by less.

A firm that pays a pollution tax will have an incentive to figure out the least expensive technologies for reducing pollution. The firm will also have an incentive to search for additional ways of reducing pollution, since it must pay the pollution charge on any remaining emissions. Firms that can reduce pollution cheaply and easily will do so to

EXHIBIT 14-3 A Pollution Charge

If the pollution charge is set equal to $1,000, then the firm will have an incentive to reduce pollution by 30 pounds because the cost of these reductions would be less than the cost of paying the pollution charge. However, it would continue to emit pollution above this level. If the pollution charge is set higher, then the firm will have an incentive to reduce pollution further.

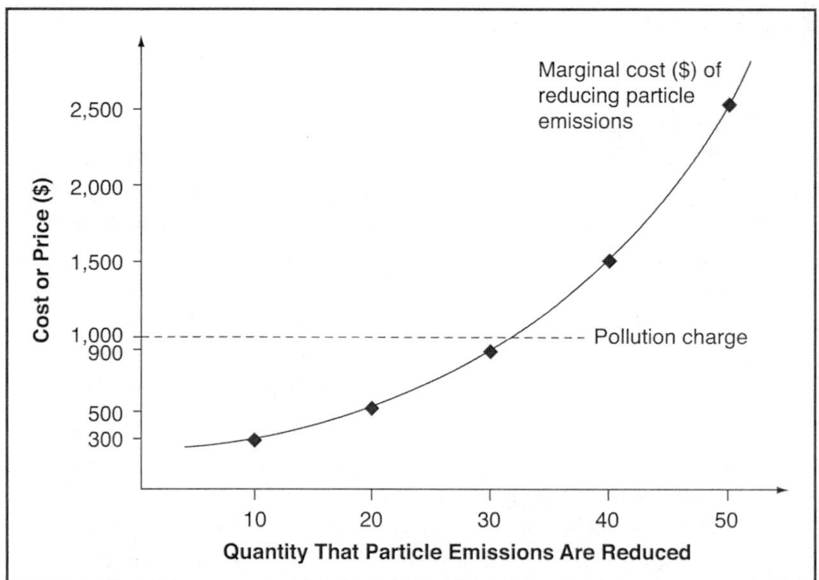

minimize their pollution taxes, while firms that have only a few costly ways of reducing pollution will end up paying the pollution tax instead. If the pollution tax applies to every source of pollution, then no special favoritism or loopholes are created for certain politically well-connected producers.

As an example of a pollution charge at the household level, consider two ways of charging for garbage collection. One method is to have a flat charge per household, no matter how much garbage a household produces. An alternative approach is to have several levels of charges, depending on how much garbage the household produces—and to offer lower or free charges for recyclable materials. Several thousand communities have implemented "pay as you throw" programs. When people have a financial incentive to put out less garbage and to increase recycling, they find ways of doing so.

A number of environmental policies resemble pollution charges, although they often don't travel under that name. For example, the federal government and many state governments impose taxes on gasoline, which can be viewed as a charge on the air pollution that is generated by cars. Indeed, petroleum taxes are far higher in most countries than in the United States, as shown in Exhibit 14-4. Similarly, the refundable charge of 5 or 10 cents that about a dozen states have for returning recyclable cans and bottles works like a pollution tax that provides an incentive to avoid littering or throwing bottles in the trash. Compared with command-and-control regulation, a pollution tax reduces pollution in a more flexible and cost-effective way.

EXHIBIT 14-4 Gasoline Prices and Taxes, 2016

	Before-Tax Price in U.S. Dollars per Gallon	After-Tax Consumer Price in U.S. Dollars per Gallon	Tax Rate (tax divided by before-tax price)
United States	$1.81	$2.26	25%
France	$1.96	$5.67	189%
Germany	$1.99	$5.69	186%
Italy	$1.99	$6.21	212%
United Kingdom	$1.79	$6.00	235%
Japan	$1.86	$4.12	121%
Canada	$2.00	$3.13	57%

Market-Friendly Environmental Tool #2: Marketable Permits

When a government establishes a **marketable permit** program, it must start by determining the overall quantity of a certain pollutant that will be allowed. Then, this quantity is divided up among the firms that emit that pollutant, with each firm receiving permits to emit a certain quantity of pollution. These permits to pollute could be auctioned to firms by the government, but in other cases, firms are simply given a permit, free of charge, that allows them in the current year to emit their current level of pollution. Now add two additional conditions. Imagine that these permits are designed to shrink the total emissions over time. For example, a permit may allow emitting 10 units of pollution one year, but only 9 units the next year, then 8 units the year after that, and so on down to some lower level. In addition, imagine that these are marketable permits, so that firms can buy and sell them.

marketable permit: A permit that allows a firm to emit a certain amount of pollution, where firms with more permits than pollution can sell the remaining permits to other firms.

To see how marketable permits can work to reduce pollution, consider the four firms listed in Exhibit 14-5. The current emissions of lead from each firm are shown, and at the start of the marketable permit program, each firm receives permits to allow this level of pollution. However, these permits are shrinkable, and next year the permits allow a firm to emit only half as much pollution. Let's say that in a year, Firm C finds it easy and cheap to reduce emissions from 600 tons of lead to 200 tons, which means that it has permits that it is not using to allow emitting 100 tons of lead. Firm B reduces its lead pollution from 400 tons to 200 tons, so it doesn't need to buy any permits, and it doesn't have any extra permits to sell. However, while Firm A can easily reduce pollution from 200 tons to 150 tons, it finds that it is cheaper to purchase permits from C rather than to reduce its own emissions to 100. Meanwhile, Firm D didn't even exist in the first period, so the only way it can start production is to purchase permits to emit 50 tons of lead. The total quantity of pollution will decline. But exactly which firms reduce pollution, and by how much, will be determined by the buying and selling of the marketable permits. With a system of marketable permits, the reduction in pollution will take place in the firms where it is least expensive to do so.

Marketable pollution permits have had several success stories in recent decades. In the early 1980s, the U.S. government decided to get the lead out of gasoline because medical studies showed that lead pollution in the air contributed to health problems like lower IQ and behavioral disorders in children and to high blood pressure in adults. In the 1970s, about three-quarters of all lead emissions came from burning leaded gasoline in car engines. In 1982, the EPA distributed tradable permits for lead at no cost to oil refineries. These permits were designed to phase down the permissible amount of lead over time until it was just 10% of its previous level. Oil refineries traded these permits with one another. By the end of the 1980s, lead emissions in the United States had fallen from about 50,000 tons a year in 1980 to less than 5,000 tons a year. Because of the flexibility of marketable permits in allowing the reduction in lead emissions to happen at the firms

EXHIBIT 14-5 How Marketable Permits Work

	Firm A	Firm B	Firm C	Firm D
Current emissions—permits distributed free for this amount	200 tons	400 tons	600 tons	0 tons
How much pollution will these permits allow in one year?	100 tons	200 tons	300 tons	0 tons
Actual emissions one year in the future	150 tons	200 tons	200 tons	50 tons
Buyer or seller of marketable permit?	Buys permits for 50 tons	Doesn't buy or sell permits	Sells permits for 100 tons	Buys permits for 50 tons

where it was cheapest to do so, the marketable permit program achieved the reduction in pollution at least 20% more cheaply than command-and-control regulation would have.

Another application of marketable permits occurred when the Clean Air Act was amended in 1990. The revised law sought to reduce sulfur dioxide emissions from electric power plants to half of the 1980 levels, out of concern that sulfur dioxide was causing "acid rain," which harms forests and buildings. In this case, the marketable permits were issued by the federal government free of charge to electricity-generating plants across the country, especially those that were burning coal (which produces sulfur dioxide). These permits were of the "shrinkable" type; that is, the amount of pollution allowed by a given permit declined with time. The plan went into effect in 1995. That year alone, emissions of sulfur dioxide fell from about 8 million tons in 1994 to just 5.3 million tons. Through the later 1990s, the cost of buying a permit to emit a ton of sulfur dioxide was about $100. Because of the flexibility of the marketable permit system, the reductions in sulfur emissions happened much faster than expected and cost millions of dollars a year less than a command-and-control approach.

Environmentalists have often tended to prefer marketable permits over pollution charges because the permits impose specific limits on the quantity of pollution—even if polluters are allowed to decide among themselves, through trading, which firms will actually emit that pollution. Also, some environmentalist groups have noticed that they can buy a marketable permit for pollution and then not use or re-sell it—thus directly reducing the amount of pollution that can be emitted. Marketable permits are a more efficient and flexible way than command-and-control regulation for society to allow a limited and declining amount of pollution to occur.

Market-Friendly Environmental Tool #3: Better-Defined Property Rights

A clarified and strengthened idea of property rights can also strike a balance between economic activity and pollution. Ronald Coase (1910–2013), who won the 1991 Nobel Prize in economics, once offered a vivid illustration of an externality: a railroad track running beside a farmer's field where the railroad locomotive sometimes gives off sparks and sets the field ablaze. Coase asked whose responsibility it was to address this spillover. Should the farmer be required to build a tall fence alongside the field to block the sparks? Should the railroad be required to put some gadget on the smokestack to reduce the number of sparks?

property rights: The legal rights of ownership on which others are not allowed to infringe without paying compensation.

Coase pointed out that this question could be viewed as one of **property rights**—that is, the legal rights of ownership on which others are not allowed to infringe without paying compensation. Does the farmer have a property right not to have a field burned? Does the railroad have a property right to run its own trains on its own tracks? From society's point of view, Coase observed, what matters is that that someone—either party!—should have a property right. If neither party has a property right, then the two sides may squabble endlessly, nothing will be done, and sparks will continue to set fields aflame. However, if either the farmer or the railroad has a well-defined legal responsibility, then that party will seek out and pay for the least costly method of reducing the risk that sparks will hit the fields. The property right determines whether the farmer or the railroad pays the bills.

The property rights approach to environmental issues often becomes highly relevant in cases involving endangered species. The U.S. government's endangered species list includes about 1,000 plants and animals, and about 90% of these species live on privately owned land. The protection of these endangered species requires careful thinking about incentives and property rights. The discovery of an endangered species on private land has often triggered an automatic reaction from the government to prohibit the landowner from using that land for any purpose that might disturb the imperiled creatures. Consider the incentives of that policy: If you admit to the government that you have an endangered species, the government effectively prohibits you from using your land! As a result, rumors abounded of landowners who followed a policy of "shoot, shovel, and shut up" when they found an endangered species on their land. Other landowners have deliberately

CLEARING IT UP

Environmental Policy Tools Come in Any Strength

Environmentalists sometimes fear that market-oriented environmental tools are an excuse to eliminate limits on pollution emissions and instead to allow more pollution. It's true that if pollution charges are set very low or if marketable permits don't shrink by very much, then market-oriented tools won't be effective in reducing pollution. But command-and-control environmental laws can also be written in ways full of loopholes or exemptions that don't reduce pollution by much either. The advantage of market-oriented environmental tools is not that they reduce pollution by more or less, but that because of their incentives and flexibility, they can achieve any desired reduction in pollution at a lower cost to society.

cut trees or managed land in a way that they knew would discourage endangered species from locating there.

A more productive policy would consider how to provide private landowners with an incentive to protect the endangered species that they find and to provide a habitat for additional endangered species. For example, the government might pay landowners who provide and maintain suitable habitat for endangered species, or the government might pay when the use of private land is restricted to protect an endangered species. Again, an environmental law built on incentives and flexibility offers greater promise than a command-and-control approach, which tries to oversee millions of acres of private land ownership.

Applying Market-Oriented Environmental Tools

Market-oriented environmental policies are a tool kit, and specific tools will work better in some situations than in others. For example, marketable permits work best when there are a few dozen or a few hundred parties who are highly interested in trading, as in the cases of the oil refineries trading lead permits or the electrical utilities trading sulfur dioxide permits. However, for cases in which millions of users are emitting small amounts of pollution and have no strong interest in trading—like emissions from car engines or garbage from soda cans—pollution charges will typically offer a better choice. Market-oriented environmental tools can also be combined. Marketable permits can be viewed as a form of improved property rights. Or the government could combine marketable permits with a pollution tax that would be charged on any emissions not covered by a permit.

Market-oriented environmental tools, like all forms of government regulation, need to be applied with care, judgment, and even a dash of creativity.

The Benefits and Costs of U.S. Environmental Laws

Government economists have estimated that U.S. firms may pay more than $200 billion per year to comply with federal environmental laws. That's big bucks. Is the money well spent?

Benefits and Costs of Clean Air and Clean Water

The benefits of a cleaner environment can be divided into four areas: (1) people may stay healthier and live longer; (2) certain industries that rely on clean air and water may benefit, like farming or fishing or tourism; (3) property values may be higher and costs of cleaning and corrosion lower; and (4) people may simply enjoy a cleaner environment, in a way that does not need to involve a market transaction. Some of these benefits are relatively easy to value in economic terms, like gains to tourism or farming. Others are harder to assign a monetary value, such as the value of clean air for someone with asthma. Still others seem nearly impossible to put a clear-cut monetary value on, such as the satisfaction you might receive from knowing that the air is clear over the Grand Canyon, even if you have never visited the Grand Canyon.

Ecotourism: Making Environmentalism Pay

The definition of "ecotourism" is a little vague. Does it mean sleeping on the ground, eating roots, and being sniffed by wild animals? Does it mean flying in a helicopter to shoot anesthetic darts at African wildlife? A little of both? The definition may be fuzzy, but tourists who hope to appreciate the ecology of their destination—"ecotourists"—are a big and growing business. The International Ecotourism Society estimates that international tourists interested in seeing nature or wildlife spend roughly $500 billion per year. In comparison, the total amount of foreign aid from all the wealthy countries of the world to the poorest countries is about $130 billion per year.

Realizing the attraction of ecotourism, the residents of low-income countries may come to see that preserving wildlife habitats is more lucrative than, say, chopping down forests or grazing livestock. In South Africa, Namibia, and Zimbabwe, for example, a substantial expansion of both rhinoceros and elephant populations is broadly credited to ecotourism, which has given local communities an economic interest in protecting them. Some of the leading ecotourism destinations include: Costa Rica and Panama in Central America, the Caribbean, Malaysia and other South Pacific destinations, New Zealand, the Serengeti in Tanzania, the Amazon rain forests, and the Galapagos Islands. In many of these countries, governments have enacted policies where revenues from ecotourism are shared with local communities, to give people in those local communities a kind of property right that encourages them to conserve their local environment.

Ecotourism needs careful management, so that the combination of eager tourists and local entrepreneurs doesn't destroy what the visitors are coming to see. But whatever one's qualms about certain kinds of ecotourism—like the occasional practice of rich tourists shooting elderly lions with high-powered rifles—it is worth remembering that the alternative is often that low-income people in poor countries will damage their local environment in their effort to survive.

Although estimates of environmental benefits should not be treated as precise, they can still be revealing. For example, a study by the Environmental Protection Agency looked at the costs and benefits of the Clean Air Act from 1970 to 1990. It found that total costs over that time period were roughly $500 billion—a huge amount. However, it also found that a middle-range estimate of the health and other benefits from cleaner air was $22 trillion—about 44 times higher than the costs! A similar study examined costs and benefits of the Clean Water Act and reported that the benefits from 1990 to 1995 exceeded the costs by $6.3 trillion. Cost-benefit estimates like these are always fair ground for dispute. However, when the estimated benefits are a large multiple of costs, then it seems unlikely that performing the calculations in slightly different ways would reverse the results.

Saying that overall benefits of environmental regulation have exceeded costs in the past, however, is very different from saying that every environmental regulation makes sense. For example, detailed studies suggest that the benefits of reducing air pollution largely come from reducing particulates and lead—but the costs of reducing other air pollutants may be comparable to or greater than the benefits. Just because some environmental regulations have had benefits much higher than costs does not prove that every individual regulation is a sensible idea.

Marginal Benefits and Marginal Costs

The patterns of marginal costs and benefits of environmental regulation help to explain why market-oriented environmental tools were mostly ignored by lawmakers in the 1960s and 1970s, but are now becoming more popular. Exhibit 14-6 illustrates the common situation. When the quantity of environmental protection is low so that pollution is extensive, like at quantity Q_A, then there are usually a lot of relatively cheap and easy ways to reduce pollution and the marginal benefits of doing so are quite high. However, as the extent of environmental protection increases, the cheap and easy ways of reducing pollution begin to dwindle, and more costly and innovative methods must be used. The marginal cost curve rises. Also as environmental protection increases, the biggest marginal benefits are achieved first, to be followed by smaller marginal benefits. Thus, as the quantity of

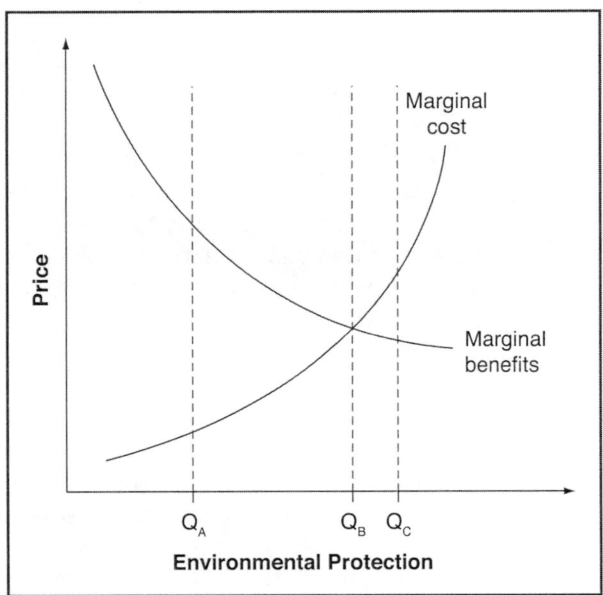

EXHIBIT 14-6 Marginal Costs and Marginal Benefits of Environmental Protection

The marginal costs of reducing pollution are generally rising because the least expensive and easiest reductions can be made first, leaving the more expensive steps for later. The marginal benefits of reducing pollution are generally declining because the steps that provide the greatest benefit can be taken first, and steps that provide less benefit can wait until later. When you are at a situation like the quantity of environmental protection Q_A, almost any step to reduce pollution will have marginal benefits greater than marginal costs. But as society draws closer to Q_B, it becomes more important to use market-oriented environment tools that hold down the costs of reducing pollution. After all, it's important to avoid environmental rules that would provide the quantity of environmental protection at Q_C, where marginal costs exceed marginal benefits.

environmental protection increases to, say, Q_B, the gap between marginal benefits and marginal costs narrows—and at some theoretical point shown as Q_C, the marginal costs will exceed the marginal benefits.

In the 1960s, before the pace of environmental protection picked up, U.S. environmental policy was probably at a choice like Q_A, where the air and water were so dirty that any policy tool, whether command-and-control or market-oriented, could accomplish a lot of good. But from our vantage point early in the twenty-first century, the United States has moved closer to a choice like Q_B, where the marginal benefits of environmental protection can often exceed the marginal costs, but the margin for error is smaller. It has become more important to target the specific kinds of pollution that are causing the greatest harms and to think about ways of using the market-oriented policy tools that offer the incentives and flexibility for firms to seek out ways of reducing pollution at the lowest possible cost.

The Unrealistic Goal of Zero Pollution

For some people, the economic way of looking at environmental problems makes sense in their heads, but not in their hearts. The head may appreciate the potential benefits of pollution charges, marketable permits, and better-defined property rights, but the heart keeps saying: "There's still too much pollution! None of these policy tools have reduced pollution to zero!"

The goal of reducing pollution to zero has a strong emotional appeal. Realistically, however, it doesn't make much sense. People exhale carbon dioxide and create bodily waste. The production of the foods we eat, the clothes we wear, and the cars we drive all cause pollution. Moreover, even if zero pollution serves as an important emotional goal,

What's a Life Worth?

In measuring the benefits of U.S. government environmental regulations (and other kinds of regulation, as well), a human life is often valued at approximately $9 million. Where does that number come from?

Economists value a human life based on studies of the value that people actually place on human lives in their own decisions. For example, some jobs have a higher probability of death than others, and these jobs typically pay more to compensate for the risk. Imagine that a certain job has an added risk of death of 1 in 10,000, but also pays an extra $900 per year. Thus, if 10,000 people take this job, then on average this group is being paid an extra $9 million (i.e., $900 multiplied by 10,000), even though one of them is expected to die on the job. A number of studies looking at jobs and wage levels have found an average cost per life roughly in the area of $9 million.

Government regulators use estimates like these when deciding what proposed rules are "reasonable," which inevitably means deciding which proposals have high enough benefits to justify their costs. The U.S. Department of Transportation, for example, when making decisions about what safety systems should be required in cars or airplanes, will only approve rules where the estimated cost per life saved is $9 million or less. The Environmental Protection Agency in some cases uses a similar rule for environmental regulations. Even resources spent on life-saving regulations create trade-offs. One study, by W. Kip Viscusi of Harvard University, estimated that when a regulation costs $50 million, it diverts enough spending in the rest of the economy from health care and safety expenditures that it costs a life. This finding suggests that any regulation that costs more than $50 million per life saved actually costs lives, rather than saving them.

it is certainly not going to happen in the next year or two. Protecting the environment is an ongoing task. Rather than arguing over whether the ultimate goal is zero pollution or a "reasonable" level of pollution, the immediate focus should be to tackle the environmental issues where the marginal benefits are greatest and the marginal costs are least.

International Environmental Issues

biodiversity: The full spectrum of animal and plant genetic material.

Many countries around the world have become more aware of the benefits of environmental protection. Yet even if most nations individually took steps to address their environmental issues, there are certain environmental problems that no nation acting alone can solve because the issues spill over national borders. One such issue is the risk that emissions of carbon dioxide and other gases are leading to a process of global warming. Another issue is the challenge of preserving **biodiversity**, which includes the full spectrum of animal and plant genetic material. No nation by itself can reduce emissions of carbon dioxide and other gases by enough to solve the problem of global warming, not without the cooperation of other nations. While a nation can protect biodiversity within its own borders, no nation acting alone can protect biodiversity around the world. Global warming and biodiversity are examples of international externalities or spillovers, where environmental effects arise across national borders.

Bringing the nations of the world to act together in addressing environmental issues that spill over national borders requires a difficult set of negotiations between countries with different income levels and different sets of priorities. If nations like China, India, Brazil, Mexico, and others develop their economies by burning vast amounts of fossil fuels or by stripping their forest and wildlife habitats, then the world's high-income countries acting alone will not be able to resolve the risks of greenhouse warming and reduced biodiversity. However, low- and middle-income countries, with some understandable exasperation, point out that high-income countries don't have much moral standing to lecture them on the necessities of putting environmental protection ahead of economic growth. After all, high-income countries have historically been the primary contributors to climate change and reduced biodiversity through their patterns of burning fossil fuels and paving and draining their own ecosystems. It's hard to tell people who are living in a low-income country, where adequate diet, health care, and education are lacking, that they should sacrifice an improved quality of life to worrying about the cleanliness of their environment.

Can high-income and low-income countries come together to address global environmental spillovers? Every few years, it seems, there is a much-hyped global conference chock-full of impassioned speeches, but the follow-up has been only so-so. If high-income countries want low-income countries to reduce their projected emissions of greenhouse gases and to protect the biodiversity of their environments, then the high-income countries will need to pay some of the costs. Perhaps some of these payments will happen through private markets; for example, some tourists from rich countries will pay handsomely to vacation near the natural treasures of low-income countries. Perhaps some of the transfer of resources can happen through making modern pollution-control technology available to poorer countries. However, more and more, the conversation in environmental circles has come to focus on systems of pollution taxes and marketable permits. For example, perhaps oil refineries in high-income countries would be required to reduce their emissions of carbon dioxide—but as an alternative, they could buy a permit to emit carbon dioxide from governments or companies in low-income countries. One can imagine a number of deals in which a company in a high-income country would agree to provide pollution-control or energy-efficiency equipment to producers in a low-income country, thus limiting emissions in that country, and receive in turn the right to emit carbon dioxide elsewhere.

The practical details of what such a system might look like and how it would operate across international borders are forbiddingly complex. But it seems highly unlikely that some form of world government will impose a detailed system of environmental command-and-control regulation around the world. As a result, a decentralized and market-oriented approach may be the only practical way to address international issues like global warming and biodiversity.

The Trade-off between Economic Output and Environmental Protection

The trade-off between economic output and the environment can be analyzed with a production possibility frontier like Exhibit 14-7. At one extreme, at a choice like P, a country would be selecting a high level of economic output but very little environmental protection. At the other extreme, at a choice like T, a country would be selecting a high level of environmental protection but little economic output. Efficiency suggests that the choice should be on the production possibility frontier.

Economists might well disagree with one another, just like members of the general public, when considering the choice between P, Q, R, S, and T in Exhibit 14-7, which all lie along the production possibility frontier. Countries with very low income levels, like those across much of Africa, may place a greater emphasis on economic output—which in turn helps to produce nutrition, shelter, health, education, and desirable consumer goods. Countries with higher income levels, where a greater share of people have access to the basic necessities of life, may be willing to place a relatively greater emphasis on environmental protection.

However, economists are united in their belief that an inefficient choice like M is undesirable. Rather than choice M, it would be possible for a nation to achieve either greater economic output with the same environmental protection, as at point Q, or greater environmental protection with the same level of output, as at point S. The problem with command-and-control environmental laws is that they tend to lead to a choice like M. Market-oriented environmental tools offer a mechanism for providing either the same environmental protection at lower cost or providing a greater degree of environmental protection for the same cost.

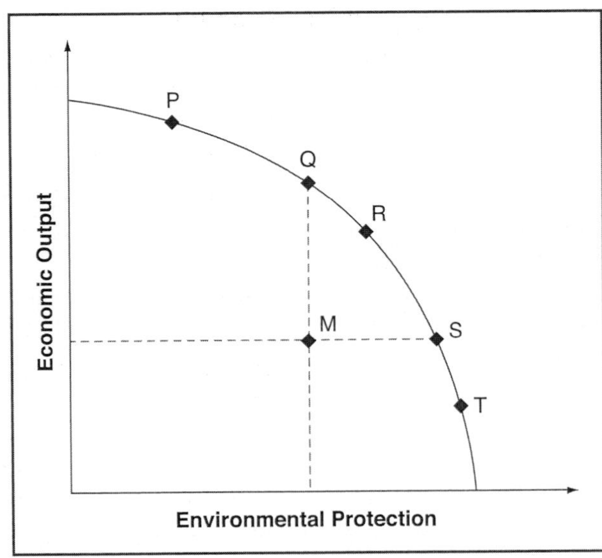

EXHIBIT 14-7 The Trade-off between Economic Output and Environmental Protection

Each society will have to weigh its own values and decide whether it prefers a choice like P with more economic output and less environmental protection, or a choice like T with more environmental protection and less economic output. But no matter what their preferences, all societies should wish to avoid choices like M, which are productively inefficient. A society at choice M could have either more economic output (like choice Q) or more environmental protection (like choice S) or more of both (like choice R). Market-oriented environmental policies help achieve environmental protection at lower cost and thus help to move from choices like M to choices on the production possibility frontier.

Key Concepts and Summary

1. Economic production can cause environmental damage. This trade-off arises for all countries, whether high-income or low-income, and whether their economies are market-oriented or command-oriented.
2. An **externality** occurs when an exchange between a buyer and seller has an impact on a third party who is not part of the exchange. An externality, which is sometimes also called a **spillover**, can have a negative or a positive impact on the third party.
3. If those parties imposing a **negative externality** on others had to take the broader social cost of their behavior into account, they would have an incentive to reduce the production of whatever is causing the negative externality.
4. **Command-and-control regulation** sets specific limits for pollution emissions and/or specific pollution-control technologies that must be used. Although such regulations have helped to protect the environment, they have three shortcomings: they provide no incentive to go beyond the limits they set, they offer limited flexibility in where and how pollution will be reduced, and they often have politically motivated loopholes.
5. Examples of market-oriented environmental policies include **pollution charges**, **marketable permits**, and better defined **property rights**. Market-oriented environmental policies use taxes, markets, and property rights so that those who impose negative externalities must face the social cost.
6. A strong case can be made that, taken as a whole, the benefits of U.S. environmental regulation have outweighed the costs. However, in certain individual cases, the costs may have outweighed the benefits.
7. As the extent of environment regulation increases, additional expenditures on environmental protection will probably have increasing marginal costs and decreasing marginal benefits. This pattern suggests that the flexibility and cost savings of market-oriented environmental policies will become more important.
8. Certain global environmental issues, like global warming and **biodiversity**, spill over national borders and will need to be addressed with some form of international agreement.
9. Based on their different income levels and political preferences, countries are likely to make different choices about allocative efficiency—that is, the choice between economic output and environmental protection along the production possibility frontier. However, all countries should prefer to make a choice that shows productive efficiency—that is, the choice is somewhere on the production possibility frontier rather than inside it.

Review Questions

1. What is an externality?
2. Give an example of a positive externality and an example of a negative externality.
3. In a market without environmental regulations, will the supply curve for a firm take into account private costs, social costs, both, or neither? Explain.
4. What is command-and-control environmental regulation?
5. What are the three problems that economists have noted with regard to command-and-control regulation?
6. What is a pollution charge, and what incentive does it provide for a firm to take social costs into account?
7. What is a marketable permit, and what incentive does it provide for a firm to take social costs into account?
8. What are better-defined property rights, and what incentive do they provide to take social costs into account?
9. As the extent of environmental protection expands, would you expect marginal costs of environmental protection to rise or fall? Why?
10. As the extent of environmental protection expands, would you expect the marginal benefits of environmental protection to rise or fall? Why?
11. In the trade-off between economic output and environmental protection, how many choices will be both productively efficient and allocatively efficient? Explain.

CHAPTER

15

Technology, Positive Externalities, and Public Goods

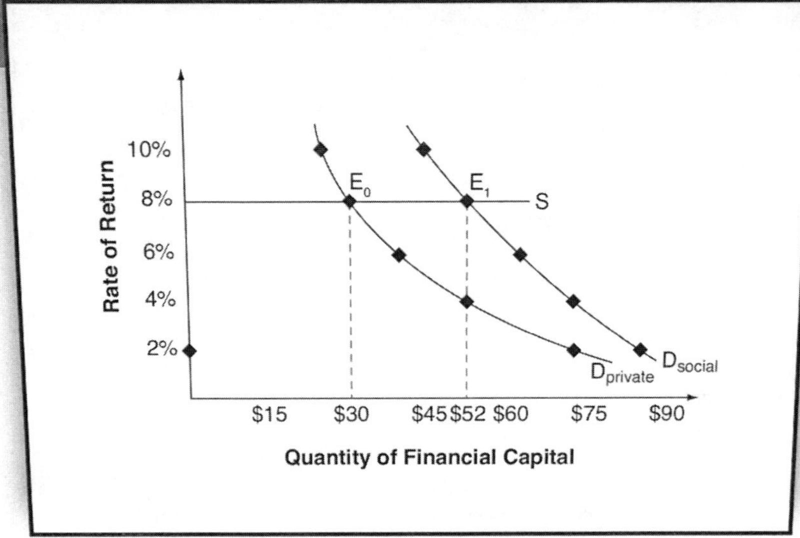

Chapter Outline

New technology changes how people live and work. Technology is the difference between horses and automobiles, between candles and electric lights, between fetching water in buckets and indoor plumbing, and between infection and antibiotics. The science fiction writer Arthur C. Clarke once said: "A sufficiently advanced technology is indistinguishable from magic." New technologies often appear magical—until we become accustomed to them and start taking them for granted.

A small sampling of the new technologies developed in the last two centuries are shown in the timeline in Exhibit 15-1. The variety of new inventions is remarkable. Some entries involve household products: the dishwasher, the coffee pot, roller skates, frozen food, video games. Some entries involve transportation: the steamboat, the gasoline-powered car, the airplane. Other entries are medical: spray medication, anesthesia, polio vaccine, antibiotics, and the artificial heart. Still other entries focus on communication: the telegraph, the telephone, radio, Internet communication.

Every invention has its own story of discovery and development, a story that often includes a parade of characters and firms over a period of years or decades. Consider the invention of the dishwasher by Josephine Cochrane in 1889. Cochrane was a wealthy woman living in Illinois who was concerned that her servants often chipped her family's fine china plates while washing them. She invented a machine where the plates sat in a wooden barrel while rollers turned them, and hot, soapy water could be pumped over them. Her invention won a grand prize at the 1893 Chicago World's Fair, but commercial success took longer. Cochrane's husband died, leaving her with few assets, and she started a company in the shed behind her house to make and sell her dishwashers. But at that time, soap for dishwashers was often expensive and of poor quality, so it often left a residue on the dishes. Moreover, a survey of women in the early twentieth century reported that they often found it enjoyable and relaxing to hand-wash dishes, so they weren't eager to purchase a

1794 Cotton Gin: Eli Whitney patents his machine to remove seeds from cotton.
1803 Medication Spray: Dr. Alan de Vilbiss of Toledo, Ohio, invents a device to spray medication into the mouth and nose.
1806 Coffee Pot: Benjamin Thompson, Count Rumford, invents a coffee pot with a metal sieve to strain away the grounds.
1807 Steamboat: The *Clermont*, invented by Robert Fulton, steams from New York City to Albany.
1809 Weaving Straw with Silk or Thread: Mary Dixon Kies becomes the first woman to receive a patent for her weaving process.
1831 Reaping Machine: The McCormick Reaper for cutting grain was not an economic success for several decades.
1833 Sewing Machine: Walter Hunt invents the sewing machine but does not patent his invention. Later, Isaac Singer becomes rich from a similar machine.
1834 Threshing Machine: John A. and Hiram Abial Pitts invent a machine that separates grain from chaff.
1840 Collapsible Metal Squeeze Tube for Artist's Paint: John Rand's invention is an immediate hit in Europe.
1842 Ether Anesthesia: Crawford Williamson Long performs the first operation (removal of a tumor) using ether-based anesthesia.
1844 Telegraph: Samuel Morse demonstrates his telegraph by sending a message to Baltimore from the chambers of the Supreme Court in Washington, DC.
1845 False Teeth: Claudius Ash's invention features porcelain teeth mounted with steel springs.
1859 Oil Well: Edwin Drake strikes oil at 69.5 feet below the earth's surface, and western Pennsylvania sees the world's first oil boom.
1863 Four-Wheeled Roller Skates: James Plimpton of Medford, Massachusetts, makes the first practical four-wheeled roller skate.
1867 Barbed Wire: Lucien B. Smith of Kent, Ohio, invents the product that will divide the American West.
1873 Typewriter: Christopher Latham Sholes sells a prototype to Remington and Sons, gunsmiths, who begin mass production.
1875 Electric Dental Drill: Be grateful to George F. Green of Kalamazoo, Michigan. Hey, it beats living with decayed teeth.
1876 Telephone: Alexander Graham Bell patents the telephone.
1879 Incandescent Light Bulb: Thomas Edison perfects an incandescent light bulb, which will see commercial use by 1881.
1882 Electric Fan: Dr. Schuyler Skaats Wheeler invents a two-bladed desk fan.
1889 Dishwasher: Josephine Cochrane of Shelbyville, Indiana, produces a practical dishwashing machine.
1892 Gasoline-Powered Car: Frank and Charles Duryea fabricate the first gasoline-powered automobile built in the U.S.
1901 Radio Over the Ocean: Guglielmo Marconi receives first trans-Atlantic radio transmission.
1902 Air Conditioning: Willis H. Carrier designs the first system to control temperature and humidity.
1903 Powered Airplane Flight: At Kitty Hawk, North Carolina, Orville and Wilbur Wright take a 12-second flight.
1908 Model T: Carmaker Henry Ford introduces his Model T automobile, which will be produced by an assembly line.
1920 First Commercial Radio Broadcast: AM station KDKA of Pittsburgh announces that Warren Harding has been elected president.
1926 Rocket Launch: Robert H. Goddard launches a liquid-fuel rocket to a height of 41 feet.
1929 Frozen Food: Clarence Birdseye offers his quick-frozen foods to the public.
1930 Scotch Tape: 3M introduces Scotch tape.
1932 Heart Defibrillator: Dr. William Bennett Kouwenhoven develops a device for jump-starting the heart with a burst of electricity.
1937 Chair Lift for Skiers: The Dollar Mountain ski resort in Sun Valley, Idaho, gets a chair lift.
1947 Transistor: William Shockley invents the transistor, the guts of the modern computer.
1948 Electric Guitar: Leo Fender debuts the first solid-bodied electric guitar.
1951 First Commercial Computer: Eckert and Mauchly Computer Co. of Philadelphia sells UNIVAC 1 to the U.S. Census Bureau.
1957 Polio Vaccine: Dr. Albert Sabin develops a polio vaccine.
1958 Satellite Space Exploration: The Soviet Union launches *Sputnik*. Three months later, the U.S. launches *Explorer I.*
1960 Laser: Theodore H. Maiman creates the first laser at Hughes Research Laboratories.
1960 Birth Control Pill: The Food and Drug Administration approves the birth control pill for sale.
1964 Operating System: IBM rolls out the OS/360, the first mass-produced computer operating system.
1970 Fiber Optics: Corning Glass announces a glass fiber that can transmit sound using pulses of light.
1972 Video Game: Nolan Bushnell invents Pong, one of the first mass-produced video games.
1974 Barcode: The first shipments of bar-coded products arrive in American stores.
1979 Cellular Phones: The first commercial cell phone system is started in Tokyo.
1981 Space Shuttle: NASA successfully launches—and lands—the first reusable space shuttle.
1982 Artificial Heart: Dr. Robert Jarvik implants a permanent artificial heart, which keeps Barney Clark alive for 112 days.
1982 First Genetically Engineered Product: Genentech gets permission to market human insulin produced through genetic engineering.
1984 The Mouse: Apple Computer introduces the mouse.
1990 Internet Programming Language Invented: Tim Berners-Lee invents HTTP and HTML.
1996 Cloning: "Dolly" is cloned from another sheep.
2000 Sequencing the Human Gene: The chemical bases of the human gene are listed in sequence.
2005 On-line Video Sharing: Steve Chen, Chad Hurley, and Jawed Karim invent YouTube.
2010 Driverless car: Google announces development of self-driving cars.

EXHIBIT 15-1 A Technology Timeline

dishwashing machine. Eventually, Cochrane's original company became the Kitchen Aid part of the Whirlpool Corporation in 1940. Today, about half of all U.S. households have a dishwasher.

Most inventions are motivated, at least in part, by a desire to earn a financial reward. This chapter begins by exploring the idea that an inventor typically receives only a fraction of the overall social benefit that an invention provides—with much of the benefit going to users of the invention or to other firms that can copy the idea behind the invention. Government has a variety of policies to increase the rate of return received by inventors, like granting patents and subsidizing research and development. However, the ultimate goal of such public policies is not to help inventors earn high returns, but to encourage a stream of inventions that will benefit society as a whole. The case of technology illustrates a broader problem that certain investments may be beneficial to society, but it may be difficult for private investors to earn a reasonable rate of return from these investments. The chapter concludes by discussing how a range of goods and services like police protection and highways share certain key characteristics with new technology, and that when these key characteristics exist, the government may need to encourage or coordinate production of the good or service, rather than leaving such investments up to incentives of the market.

The Incentives for Developing New Technology

Market competition and the invention of new technology, like quarreling relatives, have a complicated and unstable relationship. Market competition and technology sometimes support each other and sometimes oppose each other.

Market competition can provide an incentive for discovering new technology because a firm can earn higher profits by finding a way to produce existing products in cheaper ways or to create products with desirable characteristics. An innovative firm knows that it will usually have at least a temporary edge over its competitors and thus an ability to earn above-normal profits for a time before the competitors can catch up. Also, firms may innovate out of fear that if they aren't moving ahead, they will inevitably fall behind other competitors that are seeking out innovations.

However, in certain cases, market competition can also discourage new technology. Consider a pharmaceutical firm that is planning a research project to develop a new drug. On average, it can cost $800 million and take more than a decade to discover a new drug, to perform the necessary safety tests, and to bring the drug to market. If the research and development (R&D) effort fails—and every R&D project has some chance of failure—then the firm will suffer losses and could even be driven out of business. If the research and development project succeeds, then the firm's competitors may figure out ways of adapting and copying the underlying idea, but without having to pay the research and development costs themselves. As a result, the innovative company will bear the much higher costs of the R&D project and will enjoy at best only a small, temporary advantage over the competition—until the other firms copy its idea. Thus, a pharmaceutical firm might be willing to undertake certain research projects if the firm were guaranteed that if it succeeded, it could sell the new drug as a monopoly for at least a few years and earn sufficient profit to compensate for the costs of developing the new drug. But if that same firm must face market competition that can very quickly produce an identical product or a close substitute, the firm may decide against R&D projects of this sort.

Some Grumpy Inventors

Many inventors over the years have discovered that their inventions brought less of a return than they might have expected.

Eli Whitney (1765–1825) invented the cotton gin, a machine for separating seeds out of raw cotton. He received a patent on the cotton gin in 1794 and started a business to manufacture the machine. However, the machine was so wonderfully useful in the cotton-growing states of the American South that rather than paying for Whitney's gin, cotton planters built their own seed-separating devices with a few minor changes to Whitney's design. When Whitney sued in court for patent infringement, he found that the courts in southern states would not uphold his patent rights. Whitney never patented any of his other inventions and once wrote that "an invention can be so valuable as to be worthless to the inventor."

Thomas Edison (1847–1931) still holds the record for most patents granted to an individual. His first invention was an automatic vote counter, and despite the social benefits of such a machine in saving time, reducing error in vote counts, and preventing voter fraud, he could not find a government that wanted to buy it. After that experience, Edison vowed that he would work only on ideas for things that people would buy. Election controversies ever since then suggest that the market incentives have been inadequate to invent easy-to-use and accurate voting machines.

Gordon Gould (1920–2005) came up with the idea behind the laser in 1957; in fact, Gould had his research notebooks for November 1957 notarized so that he could prove when the idea had come to him. However, he put off applying for a patent, mistakenly believing that he needed to have a working laser before he could apply. By the time he did apply, other scientists had laser inventions of their own. A lengthy legal battle resulted, in which Gould had to spend $100,000 on lawyers before he eventually received a patent for the laser in 1977. But even though Gould received the patent, the laser seemed more like the work of a number of scientists working along intersecting and overlapping tracks, not the inspiration of a single person. The laser has had an enormous range of uses: manufacturing of compact discs, eye surgery tumor removal, precision measurement, navigational instruments, chemical research, printers, and as a cutting tool in textile and metalworking industries. Perhaps most of all, the laser has revolutionized telecommunications and computer networks by allowing so much more information to be carried over fiber-optic cable than could have been carried over old copper wires. Compared to the enormous social benefits of the laser, Gould received relatively little financial reward. Many of those other scientists who worked on the science leading up to lasers in the 1940s and 1950s, as well as the practical development of lasers since then, received no special benefit other than their usual salaries.

As these examples illustrate, inventors commonly receive only a portion of the total benefits of their inventions. A variety of studies done by economists have found that the original inventor often receives roughly one-third to one-half of the total economic benefits from innovations; other businesses and new-product users receive the rest of the benefits.

The Positive Externalities of New Technology

If a firm builds a factory or buys a piece of equipment, the firm will receive all of the economic benefits that result from such investments. However, when a firm invests in new technology, the private benefits that the firm receives are only a portion of the overall social benefits. In economic terms, positive externalities arise—a situation where a third party benefits from the spillover effects of a market transaction by others.

Consider the example of the Big Drug Company, which is planning its research and development budget for the next year. Economists working for Big Drug, together with scientists, have compiled a list of potential research and development projects and estimated the potential rates of return for each one. If the cost of financial capital is low, Big Drug will demand a large quantity of financial capital for research and development because many R&D projects are likely to exceed a low rate of return. However, as the cost of financial capital rises, the firm demands a lesser quantity of funding to invest in R&D, since fewer projects are likely to pay the higher rate of return. Big Drug's demand curve for financial capital to invest in R&D is shown by $D_{private}$ in Exhibit 15-2. For the sake of simplicity, say that Big Drug can borrow as much money as it wants at the prevailing market interest rate; thus, Big Drug perceives the supply curve S for financial capital as a horizontal line. At the equilibrium E_0, the quantity of financial capital that Big Drug will have invested in research and development is $30 million, and the interest rate prevailing in the market is 8%.

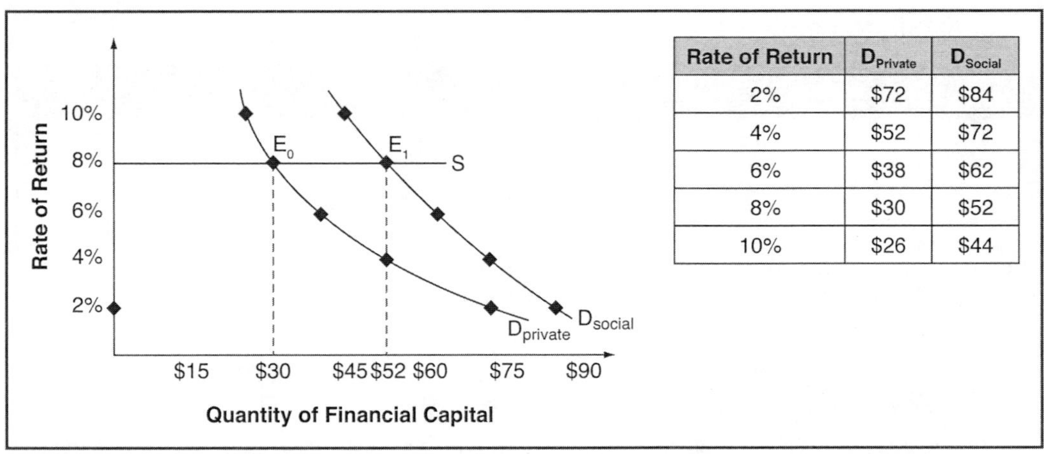

Rate of Return	$D_{Private}$	D_{Social}
2%	$72	$84
4%	$52	$72
6%	$38	$62
8%	$30	$52
10%	$26	$44

EXHIBIT 15-2 Positive Externalities and Technology

Big Drug faces a cost of financial capital of 8%. If the firm receives only the private benefits of investing in R&D, then its demand curve for financial capital is shown by D, and the equilibrium will occur at a quantity of $30. However, if the firm could also receive the social benefits of its investment in R&D, then its demand curve for financial capital would be D_{social}, and the equilibrium would be at a quantity of $52.

Big Drug's original demand for financial capital $D_{private}$ is based on the private rate of return received by the firm. However, every time Big Drug makes a new discovery, other pharmaceutical firms and health-care companies learn new lessons about how to treat certain medical conditions and become able to create their own improved (if not identical) products. Let's say that the economists at Big Drug calculated that the social rate of return on the investment would be twice as high—that is, a project that had a 4% private rate of return to Big Drug actually has an 8% social return. If Big Drug were able to gain this social return, its demand for financial capital would shift to the right to the new demand curve D_{social}. The new point of equilibrium E_1 will involve spending $52 million on research and development. Thus, if Big Drug could receive a greater share of the society's total benefits from its new pharmaceuticals, it would invest more in research and development. But if Big Drug is receiving only 50 cents of each dollar of social benefit that its innovations create, then the firm won't spend as much on creating new products as it would if it received a greater share of the total social benefit that it is creating.

Contrasting Positive Externalities and Negative Externalities

Exhibit 15-3 summarizes the parallels and contrasts between negative and positive externalities. For a negative externality, the private costs of an action are less than the costs imposed on society as a whole, and so private actors have an incentive to carry out activities, like emitting pollution, at a level that is greater than society as a whole desires. For a positive externality, the private benefits of an action are less than the social benefits, and so private actors lack an incentive to carry out activities, like innovation that leads to new technology, to the extent that society as a whole desires.

Although technology may be the most prominent example of a positive externality, it is far from the only one. For example, being vaccinated against disease is not only a protection for the individual, but it has the positive spillover of protecting those who might otherwise have been infected by that individual. Education clearly benefits the person who receives it, but a society where most people have a good level of education provides positive externalities for all. When a number of homes in a neighborhood are modernized, updated, and restored, not only does it increase the value of those homes, but the value of other properties in the neighborhood may increase as well. It's also possible, instead of talking about the connection between pollution and negative externalities, to flip-flop the terminology and instead talk about the connection from antipollution equipment to positive externalities. Just as too much pollution exists because firms do

EXHIBIT 15-3 Positive and Negative Externalities: Parallels and Contrasts

	Negative Externality	Positive Externality
A prominent example	Pollution	Technology
Market doesn't take into account . . .	Harms incurred by third parties	Benefits received by third parties
. . . so that as a result	Too much of the negative externality is provided	Too little of the positive externality is provided
General solution	Require those who produce the negative externality to take social costs into account	Assist those who provide the positive externality to receive a greater share of the social benefits
Specific solutions	Regulations, pollution taxes, marketable permits, better-defined property rights	Government R&D spending, tax incentives for private R&D spending, intellectual property protection, allowing business cooperation on R&D

not take negative externalities like pollution into account, one can argue that too little anti-pollution equipment is installed because firms do not take into account the positive externalities of doing so.

The last row of Exhibit 15-3 points out that the appropriate response of public policy to a negative externality like pollution is to find ways so that the social costs of the negative externality are taken into account in economic decisions. Conversely, the appropriate public policy response to a positive externality, like new technology, is to help the party creating the positive externality to receive a greater share of the social benefits. Practical proposals for reacting to the positive externalities of technology are discussed in the next section.

How to Raise the Rate of Return for Innovators

A number of different mechanisms can increase the rate of return earned by inventors of new technology: intellectual property rights, government assistance with the costs of research and development, even cooperative research ventures between companies. Let us explore these policies in turn.

Intellectual Property Rights

intellectual property: The body of law including patents, trademarks, copyrights, and trade secret law that protects the right of inventors to produce and sell their inventions.

Intellectual property rights include patents, which give the inventor the exclusive legal right to make, use, or sell the invention for a limited time, and copyright laws, which give the author an exclusive legal right over works of literature, music, movies, and pictures. These topics were introduced in Chapters 11–13 in the discussions of monopoly, oligopoly, and imperfect competition. For example, if a pharmaceutical firm has a patent on a new drug, then no other firm can manufacture or sell that drug unless the firm with the patent grants permission. Without a patent, the pharmaceutical firm would have to face entry and competition for any successful products, and thus it could earn no more than a normal rate of profit. But with a patent, a firm is able to earn monopoly profits on its product—which offers an incentive for research and development to take place. Exhibit 15-4 illustrates how the number of patent applications filed with the U.S. Patent and Trademark Office and the number of patents granted have changed since the 1980s. Intellectual property rights do provide a method for increasing the rate of return for inventors, but there are a number of reasons to doubt whether patents provide fully appropriate and sufficient incentives for innovation.

First, the economic studies that show that inventors receive only one-third to one-half of the total economic value of their inventions were all calculated in countries that already

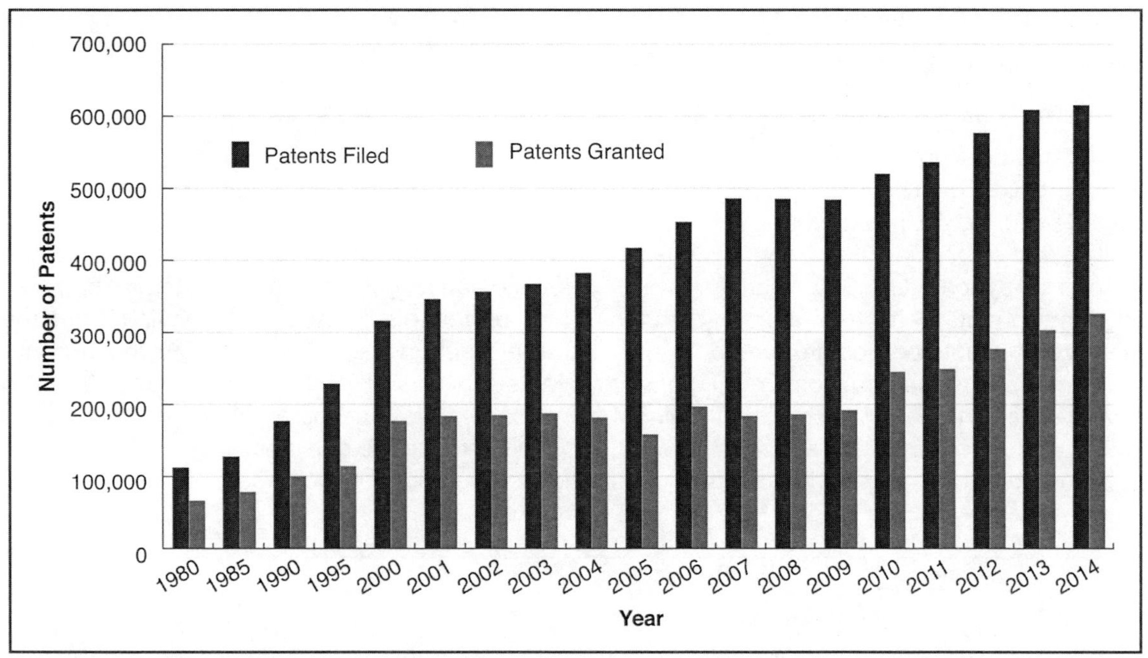

EXHIBIT 15-4 Patents Filed and Granted

The number of applications filed for patents increased substantially from the mid-1990s into the first half of the 2000s. The number of patents granted increased in the late 1990s, rose less quickly in the mid-2000s, and then seemed to increase again in the last few years.

had patents. Thus, even with patents in place, inventors of new technology are receiving only a slice of the social value of their inventions.

Second, in a fast-moving high-technology industry like biotechnology or semiconductor design, patents may be largely irrelevant. When technology is advancing so quickly, even a patent from, say, two years ago may be outdated because no firm is relying on that technology any longer. In these cases, the market forces firms to innovate as fast as they can just to keep up with others.

Third, not every new idea can be protected with a patent or a copyright. For example, a new way of organizing a factory, or a new way of training employees, or a new combination of product features may not be an "invention" in the sense that patent law uses the term. Moreover, a patent cannot cover the new ideas that it spurs others to create.

Fourth, patents and copyrights offer an incentive for research and development because they offer a temporary monopoly, which in turn allows charging a higher price for a reduced level of output. But if an alternative policy could encourage both invention and competition instead of invention and monopoly, consumers would benefit from the lower price and greater quantity sold.

Fifth, patents may sometimes cover too much or be granted too easily. In the early 1970s, Xerox had received over 1,700 patents on various elements of the photocopy machine. Every time Xerox improved the photocopier, it received a patent on the improvement. In the early 1970s, the U.S. government charged Xerox with abusing the patent process by using this potentially everlasting stream of patents to block the entry of other firms into the photocopier market. In 1975, while not admitting that it had done anything wrong, Xerox agreed to allow other companies to use its patents, to drop all of its lawsuits against other companies for violating its patents, and to provide competitors with access to certain future patents. A flood of new competition followed. Xerox's market share fell from about 95 percent of the U.S. photocopier market in the early 1970s to less than half by 1980.

Sixth, the 20-year time period for a patent is somewhat arbitrary. Ideally, a patent should cover a long enough period of time for the inventor to earn a hearty return, but not so long that it allows the inventor to charge a high monopoly price permanently. The 20-year time period for patents may be too long in some cases and not long enough in

Protecting Mickey Mouse

All patents and copyrights are scheduled to end someday, and in 2003, copyright protection for Mickey Mouse was scheduled to run out. In theory, anyone would be able to copy old Mickey Mouse cartoons or draw and sell new ones. But in 1998, Congress passed the Sonny Bono Copyright Term Extension Act. It extended copyright from 50 to 70 years after an author's death and, for works produced "for hire" and owned by firms, from 75 to 95 years after publication. Along with protecting Mickey for another 20 years, the copyright extension also affected about 400,000 books, movies, and songs, including books by Ernest Hemingway and songs by George Gershwin.

The act was not politically controversial; it passed the U.S. Senate with a unanimous vote. But copyright had already extended 50 years after the death of the author, and it seems highly unlikely that an additional 20 years after death will provide an incentive for additional creative work. Congress voted to lengthen copyright protection because of lobbying from the firms that are continuing to benefit from these copyrighted works—the way Disney benefits from Mickey Mouse. But copyrights (and patents) were never supposed to be forever, and the social interest might have been better served by allowing broad public access to these classic works.

others. For example, in the 1980s it was noted by pharmaceutical companies that for certain drugs, which are first patented and then need to go through years of testing before they can be broadly marketed, the typical term of a patent might result in only a few years of actual sales. Consequently, in 1984, Congress passed the Drug Price Competition and Patent Term Restoration Act to extend the patent life of brand-name drugs for five years, to make up for time lost between the original patent and the health and safety testing.

Patents serve a useful function in providing incentives for inventors. But patents are imperfect and blunt tools that usually protect only part of the value of an invention. Patents may also be granted or denied for unclear reasons; after all, many of the examiners who decide whether a patent will be granted are young lawyers who often leave the patent office after a few years for better-paying jobs in industry. Alternative methods of improving the rate of return for inventors of new technology are desirable as well.

Government Spending on Research and Development

If the private sector does not have sufficient incentive to carry out research and development, one possible response is for the government to fund such work directly. Government provides direct financial support for research and development, which is done at colleges and universities, nonprofit research entities, and sometimes private firms, as well as at government-run laboratories.

The first column of Exhibit 15-5 shows the sources of U.S. spending on research and development; about three-fifths of R&D is funded by industry and about one-third by the federal government. The second column shows where the R&D is actually performed; about two-thirds of R&D is done by industry and about one-eighth by universities and colleges. When the government pays directly for a share of an R&D project, it reduces the costs of innovation for firms.

Since the 1960s, R&D spending has grown at roughly the same rate as the overall U.S. economy. However, in the 1960s the federal government paid for about two-thirds of the nation's R&D. Thus, over time, the U.S. economy has come to rely much more heavily on industry-funded R&D. The federal government has tried to focus its direct R&D spending on areas where private firms are not as active. Of the more than $400 billion spent on R&D in 2011, $75 billion (roughly one-fifth) was classified as **basic research**. Basic research is defined as the search for fundamental scientific breakthroughs that may offer commercial applications only in the distant future. The remainder of R&D is **applied research**, which is often focused on a particular product that promises an economic payoff in the short term or the medium term. The federal government funds about half of the nation's basic R&D, much of it carried out at colleges and universities.

basic research: Research on fundamental scientific breakthroughs that may offer commercial applications only in the distant future.

applied research: Research focused on a particular product that promises an economic payoff in the short or medium term.

EXHIBIT 15-5 U.S. Research and Development Expenditures, 2011

Sources of R&D Funding		Where R&D Was Performed	
Federal government	$125 billion	Federal government	$49 billion
Industry	$267 billion	Industry	$294 billion
Universities/colleges	$12 billion	Universities/colleges	$62 billion
Nonprofits	$15 billion	Nonprofits	$17 billion
Nonfederal government	$3 billion		
Total	*$422 billion*	*Total*	*$422 billion*

Tax Breaks for Research and Development

One difficulty with direct government support of R&D is that it inevitably involves government decisions about which projects are worthy. In a political setting, the scientific question of whether research is worthwhile can easily become entangled with considerations like the location of the congressional district in which the research funding is being spent. A complementary approach to supporting R&D that does not involve the government's close scrutiny of particular R&D projects is to give firms a reduction in their taxes depending on how much research and development they do. Tax breaks to encourage R&D spending reduced the tax that would otherwise have been paid by corporations by about $10 billion in 2016, according to the U.S. Department of the Treasury.

Cooperative Research and Development

Another tool for increasing the returns to innovation was enacted by the National Cooperative Research and Production Act of 1993, which allowed companies to form jointly funded R&D institutions. When companies work together, they share the expenses of R&D and share any discoveries that result. Such joint agencies offer a way for firms to share the risks of R&D as well as the benefits, rather than facing the risk that one winner-take-all innovator will get the patent and lock up the market. Before this law passed, antitrust authorities might have challenged such joint research efforts, but the new 1993 law removed that threat.

A Balancing Act

Because new technology brings positive externalities, there is a case for some sort of government action to support the development of new technology. However, each of the policies discussed here involves some balancing of interests. Patents can serve a useful role in providing incentives for inventors, but they also create temporary monopolies, they may be granted too slowly in some cases and too easily in others, and even at their best, they allow the inventor to receive only a fraction of the social benefit of the invention. Government spending on research and development produces technology that is broadly available for firms to use, but it costs money to taxpayers and can sometimes be directed more for political than for scientific or economic reasons. Allowing firms to collaborate on research and development may help hold down costs, but it may also lead to a situation where firms strive less hard for new technology, since they know that any new technology will be shared anyway. Thus, while the general case for government action to support technology and innovation is a strong one, the enactment of such programs through the political system can be controversial.

Public Goods

Even though new technology creates positive externalities, so that perhaps one-third or one-half of the social benefit of new inventions spills over to others, the inventor still receives some private return from new technology. But what about a situation where the positive externalities are so extensive that the private firm producing a certain product could not expect to receive any of the social benefit at all? This kind of good is called a public good. Public goods include many items that are typically supplied to a considerable extent by government, like national defense and basic research. Let's begin by defining the characteristics of a public good. We'll then discuss why these characteristics make it difficult for private firms to supply public goods and how government may step in to address the issue.

The Definition of a Public Good

To understand the defining characteristics of a public good, first consider an ordinary private good, like a piece of pizza. A piece of pizza can be bought and sold fairly easily because it is a separate and identifiable item. However, public goods are not separate and identifiable in this way.

public good: A good that is nonexcludable and nonrivalrous and thus is difficult for market producers to sell to individual consumers.

nonexcludable: When it is costly or impossible to exclude someone from using the good, and thus it is hard to charge for it.

nonrivalrous: A good where, when one person uses the good, others can also use it.

Instead, **public goods** have two defining characteristics: they are nonexcludable and nonrivalrous. The first characteristic, that a public good is **nonexcludable**, means that it is costly or impossible to exclude someone from using the good. If Larry buys a private good like a piece of pizza, then he can exclude others like Lorna from eating that pizza. But if national defense is being provided, then it includes everyone. Even if you strongly disagree with America's defense policies or with the level of defense spending, the national defense still protects you. You can't choose to be unprotected, and national defense can't protect everyone else and exclude you.

The second main characteristic of a public good, that it is **nonrivalrous**, means that when one person uses the public good, another can also use it. With a private good like pizza, if Max is eating the pizza, then Michelle cannot also eat it; that is, the two people are rivals in consumption. But with a public good like national defense, Max's consumption of national defense doesn't reduce the amount left for Michelle, so they are nonrivalrous in this area.

Knowledge and information often display the two key characteristics of a public good. Thomas Jefferson expressed the notion that ideas are at least nonrivalrous, and perhaps nonexcludable as well, in elegant language: "If nature has made any one thing less susceptible than all others of exclusive property, it is the action of the thinking power called an idea. . . . No one possesses the less, because every other possess the whole of it. He, who receives an idea from me, receives instruction himself without lessening mine; as he who lights his taper [that is, his candle] at mine, receives light without darkening me."

Ideas discovered as a result of basic scientific research are certainly nonrivalrous; when Percival uses these ideas, it does not reduce Polly's use of them. Ideas stemming from basic research are also nonexcludable, at least to some extent, because once they are known, then understanding of the scientific situation is altered. A knowledge-based public good for which economists have a particularly warm spot in their hearts is the collection and publication of economic statistics. Again, this information is nonrivalrous: Quentin's knowing the rate at which the economy has grown doesn't prevent Quintessa from knowing the same information. Such knowledge is also nonexcludable in the sense that once the information is out there—perhaps in a news report about how the economy is growing—it would be very difficult to prevent that information from spreading.

A number of other government services are referred to as public goods even if they are not completely nonexcludable and nonrivalrous. For instance, fire and police protection are not easily excludable. It wouldn't be easy to provide fire and police service so that some people in a neighborhood would be protected from the burning and burglary of their property, while others would not be protected at all. Protecting some necessarily means protecting others, too. Police and fire protection are also in some ways nonrivalrous; Oliver's protection from crime or fire doesn't mean that Oleanna is less protected (except perhaps in the extreme case where all the fire or police personnel are busy in one area and can't respond anywhere else).

The Tragedy of the Commons

The historical meaning of a commons is a piece of pasture land that is open to anyone who wishes to graze cattle upon it. However, the term has come to apply to any area that is open to all, like a city park. In a famous 1968 article, a professor of ecology named Garrett Hardin (1915–2003) described a scenario called the tragedy of the commons, in which the utility-maximizing behavior of individuals ruins the commons for all.

Hardin imagined a pasture that is open to many herdsmen, each with their own herd of cattle. A herdsman benefits from adding cows, but too many cows will lead to overgrazing and even to ruining the commons. The problem is that when a herdsman adds a cow, the herdsman personally receives all of the gain, but when that cow contributes to overgrazing and injures the commons, the loss is suffered by all of the herdsmen as a group—so any individual herdsman suffers only a small fraction of the loss. Hardin wrote: "Therein is the tragedy. Each man is locked into a system that compels him to increase his herd without limit—in a world that is limited. Ruin is the destination toward which all men rush, each pursuing his own best interest in a society that believes in the freedom of the commons. Freedom in a commons brings ruin to all."

This tragedy of the commons can arise in any situation where benefits are primarily received by one party, while the costs are spread out over many parties. For example, clean air can be regarded as a commons, where firms that pollute air can gain higher profits, but firms that pay for anti-pollution equipment provide a benefit to others. A commons can be regarded as a public good, where it is difficult to exclude anyone from use (nonexcludability) and where many parties can use the resource simultaneously (nonrivalrous).

The historical commons was often protected, at least for a time, by social rules that limited how many cattle a herdsman could graze. Avoiding a tragedy of the commons with the environment will require its own set of rules that limit how the common resource can be used.

The Free Rider Problem

Competitive markets made up of a number of different firms and buyers may find it difficult to produce public goods. If a good or service is nonexcludable, like national defense, so that it is impossible or very costly to exclude people from using this good or service, then how can a firm charge people for it? If a good is nonrivalrous, then there is zero marginal cost to adding an additional user, a fact that seems to imply that if businesses compete against each other, the price will keep dropping all the way down to zero. But if businesses can't earn much or any revenue by selling a product, then they will lack an incentive to provide such a good.

When individuals make decisions about buying a public good, a **free rider** problem can arise, in which people have an incentive to let others pay for the public good and then to "free ride" on the purchases of others. The free rider problem can be expressed in terms of the prisoner's dilemma game, which we first discussed as a representation of oligopoly in Chapter 12.

free rider: Those who want others to pay for the public good and then plan to use the good themselves; if many people act as free riders, the public good may never be provided.

Say that two people are thinking about contributing to a public good: Rachel and Samuel. When either of them contributes to a public good such as a local fire department, their personal cost of doing so is 4, and the social benefit of that person's contribution is 6. Thus, the investment is a good idea for society as a whole. But the problem is that while Rachel and Samuel pay for the entire cost of their contribution to the public good, they receive only half of the benefit because the benefit of the public good is divided equally among the members of society. This sets up the prisoner's dilemma illustrated in Exhibit 15-6.

If neither Rachel nor Samuel contributes to the public good, then there are no costs and no benefits of the public good. If one person contributes and the other does not, then the contributor pays 4 but receives benefits of 3 (i.e., half of 6), while the noncontributing free rider also receives benefits of 3. Finally, if both parties contribute, then the total social contribution to the public good is 8 and the total payoff is 12, so each individual has a payoff of 2.

The difficulty with the prisoner's dilemma arises as each person thinks through his or her strategic choices. Rachel reasons in this way: If Samuel does not contribute, then I

		Samuel: Contribute	Samuel: Don't Contribute
Rachel	Contribute	A pays 4, gets 6, +2 B pays 4, gets 6, +2	A pays 4, gets 3, –1 B pays 0, gets 3, +3
Rachel	Don't Contribute	A pays 0, gets 3, +3 B pays 4, gets 3, –1	A pays 0, gets 0 B pays 0, gets 0

EXHIBIT 15-6 Contributing to a Public Good as a Prisoner's Dilemma

would be a fool to contribute. However, if Samuel does contribute, then I can come out ahead by not contributing. Both ways, I should choose not to contribute, and instead hope that I can be a free rider who uses the public good paid for by Samuel. Samuel reasons the same way about Rachel. But when both people reason in that way, the public good never gets built, and there is no movement to the option where everyone cooperates that is actually best for all parties.

The free rider problem becomes greater if the concept of the prisoner's dilemma is expanded to include many people, not just two of them. For example, say that 10,000 people are asked to pay $100 in taxes apiece to finance a new road. Each person will reason as follows: This new road costs me personally $100, but the actual benefits from my $100 are divided by all 10,000 people, so my personal $100 only brings me 1 cent (i.e., $100 divided by 10,000) in benefits. If I act as a free rider and refuse to contribute to the road, the road will still be built, I can still drive on the road (because it is nonexcludable and nonrivalrous), and I can save my $100 for something I want to buy for myself. But if everyone reasons this way and acts as a free rider, then no money is collected and the road never gets built.

Why Are People Living Longer?

One of the most remarkable changes in the standard of living in the last several centuries is that people are living longer. Back in the Stone Age, thousands of years ago, human life expectancies are believed to have been in the range of 20–30 years. By 1900, average life expectancy in the United States at birth was 47 years. By the start of the twenty-first century, U.S. life expectancy was 77 years. Thus, most of the gains in life expectancy in the history of the human race happened in the twentieth century.

The rise in life expectancy stems from three primary factors. First, systems for providing clean water and disposing of human waste late in the nineteenth and into the twentieth century helped to prevent the transmission of many diseases. Second, changes in public behavior have advanced health. Early in the twentieth century, for example, people learned the importance of boiling bottles and milk, washing their hands, and protecting food from flies. More recent behavioral changes include reducing the number of people who smoke tobacco and precautions to limit sexually transmitted diseases. Third, medicine has played a role. Immunizations for diphtheria, cholera, pertussis, tuberculosis, tetanus, and yellow fever were developed between 1890 and 1930. Penicillin, discovered in 1941, led to a series of other antibiotic drugs for bringing infectious diseases under control. In recent decades, drugs that reduce the risks of high blood pressure have had a dramatic effect in extending lives.

These advances in public health have all been closely linked to positive externalities and public goods. Public health officials taught hygienic practices to mothers in the early 1900s and encouraged less smoking in the late 1900s. Many medical discoveries came out of government- or university-funded research in the twentieth century. Patents and intellectual property rights provided an additional incentive for private inventors. The reason for requiring immunizations, phrased in economic terms, is that it prevents spillovers of illness to others—as well as helping the person immunized. Many of the public sanitation systems and storm sewers were funded by government because they have the key traits of public goods.

The Role of Government in Paying for Public Goods

The key insight in paying for public goods is to find a way of assuring that everyone will make a contribution. There must be a method for preventing too many free riders. For example, if people come together through the political process and agree to pay taxes and make group decisions about the quantity of public goods, they can defeat the free rider problem by requiring through the law that people contribute to public goods. Or some roads can become toll roads, which means that they can exclude users who do not pay to drive on them.

However, government purchases and charges are not the only way to provide public goods. Markets can in some cases produce public goods. For example, think about radio. It is nonexcludable because once the radio signal is being broadcast, it would be highly difficult to stop someone from receiving it. It is nonrivalrous, since one person listening to the signal does not prevent others from listening as well. Because of these features, it is practically impossible to charge listeners directly for listening to conventional radio broadcasts. However, radio found a way to collect revenue by selling advertising, which is an indirect way of "charging" listeners by taking up some of their time, and satellite radio manages to charge a regular subscription fee. Some public goods will also have a mixture of public provision at no charge along with fees for some purposes, like a public city park that is free to use, but where the government charges a fee for parking your car, for reserving certain picnic grounds, and for food sold at a refreshment stand.

In other cases, social pressures and personal appeals can be used, rather than the force of law, to reduce the number of free riders and to collect resources for the public good. For example, neighbors sometimes form an association to carry out beautification projects or to patrol their area after dark to discourage crime. In low-income countries, farmers in a region may come together to work on a large irrigation project that will benefit everyone and where social pressure strongly encourages all farmers to participate. Many fundraising efforts, including raising money for local charities and for the endowments of colleges and universities, also can be viewed as an attempt to use social pressure to discourage free riding and to serve the outcome that will produce a public benefit.

Positive Externalities and Public Goods

Positive externalities and public goods are closely related concepts. With regard to both positive externalities and public goods, private firms or individuals may fail to make an expenditure or investment that would produce broad social benefits because the private benefits of such expenditure will be substantially less than the social benefits. In such cases, the challenge for society is to assure that such socially beneficial expenditures are made, whether through direct government spending or by providing appropriate incentives for individuals and firms.

Key Concepts and Summary

1. The pressure of market competition can provide producers with incentives to develop and distribute new technologies. However, if new inventions can easily be copied by others, then the original inventor may not be able to earn a higher-than-usual rate of return, in which case innovators would have a reduced incentive to invest in new technologies.
2. New technology often has positive externalities; that is, there are often spillovers from the invention of new technology that benefit firms other than the inventor. The social benefit of an invention, once these spillovers are taken into account, typically exceeds the private benefit to the inventor. If inventors could receive a greater share of the broader social benefits for their behavior, they would have a greater incentive to seek out new inventions.
3. Government has a variety of policy tools for increasing the rate of return for new technology and encouraging

its development: direct government funding of R&D, tax incentives for R&D, protection of **intellectual property**, letting companies work jointly on R&D, and helping to finance the spread of available technology.

4. Public policy with regard to technology must often strike a balance. For example, patents provide an incentive for inventors, but they should be limited to genuinely new inventions and not extend forever. Government spending on R&D must be balanced against other government spending priorities.
5. A **public good** has two key characteristics: it is **nonexcludable** and **nonrivalrous**. Nonexcludable means that it is costly or impossible for one user to exclude others from using the good. Nonrivalrous means that when one person uses the good, it does not prevent others from using it.
6. Markets often have a difficult time producing public goods because **free riders** will attempt to use the public good without making a contribution to paying for it. The free rider problem can be overcome through measures to ensure that users of the public good pay for it. Such measures include government actions, social pressures, and specific situations where markets have discovered a way to collect payments.

Review Questions

1. Explain how competition in markets can often provide incentives for the invention of new technology.
2. Using the ideas of social benefit and private benefit, explain the concept of a positive externality.
3. Why does new technology have positive externalities?
4. Why might a competitive market tend to provide too few incentives for the development of new technology?
5. What can government do to encourage the development of new technology?
6. What are the two key characteristics of public goods?
7. Name two public goods, and explain why they are public goods.
8. What is the free rider problem?
9. How can the free rider problem be overcome?

CHAPTER

16

Poverty and Economic Inequality

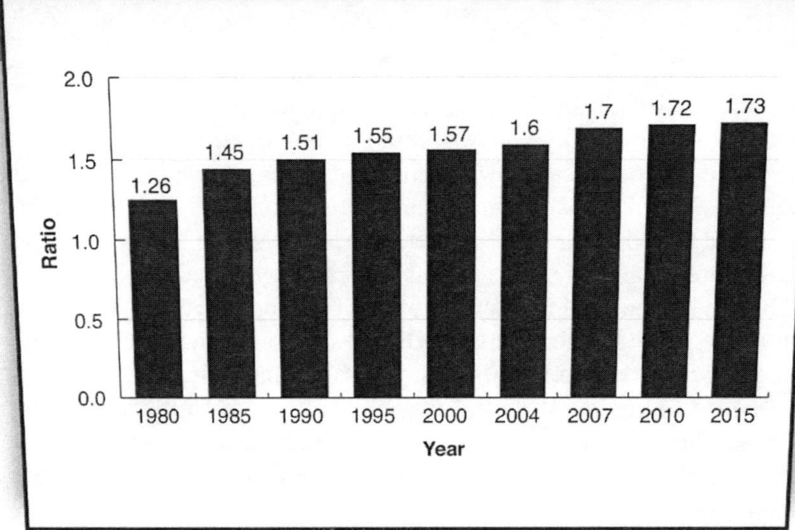

Chapter Outline

Drawing the Poverty Line

The Poverty Trap

The Safety Net

Measuring Income Inequality

Causes of Growing Income Inequality

Government Policies to Reduce Income Inequality

The Trade-off between Incentives and Income Equality

The labor markets that determine what workers are paid don't take into account how much income a family needs to afford necessities like food, shelter, clothing, and health care. Market forces don't worry about what happens to families when a major local employer goes out of business. Market forces don't contemplate whether those who are earning higher incomes should pay an even higher share of taxes.

However, labor markets do create considerable inequalities of income. In 2014, the median American family had income of $53,567 (the median is the level at which half of all families had more than that level and half had less). However, top executives at many companies earned much more. Also in 2014, for example, David Zaslav of Discovery Communications received total compensation of $156 million. The point here is not to pick on Zaslav or to pick on corporate executives—certain athletes, entertainers, and others have extremely high incomes, too. But the amounts are still amazing. Zaslov's $156 million was equal to the combined income of about 2,900 typical families.

At the other extreme, about 9.5 million U.S. families were classified by the federal government as being below the poverty line in 2014. Think about the practical aspects for a family of three—perhaps a single mother with two children—attempting to pay for the basics of life on perhaps $15,000 per year. After paying rent, health care, clothing, and transportation, such a family might have $6,000 to spend each year on food. Spread over 365 days per year, the food budget for the entire family would be about $17 per day. Most cities have upscale restaurants where $17 will buy you an appetizer for one.

Such comparisons of high and low incomes raise issues of economic inequality and poverty. While these two issues are often mentioned in the same breath, they are not the same.

Poverty is measured by the number of people who fall below a certain level of income—called the **poverty line**—that defines the income needed for a basic standard of living. Economic **inequality** compares the share of the total income

poverty: Falling below a certain level of income needed for a basic standard of living.

poverty line: The specific amount of income needed for a basic standard of living.

inequality: When one group receives a higher share of total income or wealth than others.

(or wealth) in society that is received by different groups; for example, comparing the share of income received by the top 10% to the share of income received by the bottom 10%. This chapter first explores the issues of poverty in detail: how the U.S. government defines poverty, the trade-offs between assisting the poor without discouraging work, and how U.S. antipoverty programs work. The chapter then moves to a discussion of inequality: how economists measure inequality, why inequality has changed in recent decades, the range of possible government policies to reduce inequality, and the danger of a trade-off that too great a reduction in inequality may reduce incentives for producing output.

Drawing the Poverty Line

In the United States, the official definition of the poverty line traces back to a single person: Mollie Orshansky. In 1963, Orshansky was working for the Social Security Administration, where she published an article called "Children of the Poor" in a highly useful and dry-as-dust publication called the *Social Security Bulletin*. Orshansky's idea was to define a poverty line based on the cost of a healthy diet. Her previous job had been at the U.S. Department of Agriculture, where she had worked in an agency called the Bureau of Home Economics and Human Nutrition, and one task of this bureau had been to calculate the cost of a nutritionally adequate diet fora family. Orshansky found evidence that the average family spent one-third of its income on food. Thus, she proposed that the poverty line be the amount needed to buy a nutritionally adequate diet, given the size of the family, multiplied by three. The current U.S. poverty line is essentially the same as the Orshansky poverty line, although the dollar amounts are adjusted each year to represent the same buying power over time.

The current U.S. poverty lines, based on family size, appear in Exhibit 16-1. Exhibit 16-2 shows the U.S. poverty rate over time; that is, the percentage of the population below the poverty rate in any given year. The poverty rate declined through the 1960s, rose in the early 1980s and early 1990s, dropped a bit in the mid-1990s, and then rose sharply. Exhibit 16-3 compares poverty rates for different groups in 2011. Poverty rates are relatively low for whites, for the elderly, for the well educated, and for male-headed households.

EXHIBIT 16-1 The U.S. Poverty Line in 2015

If a family, given its size, had less than the amount of income shown in the table, then it was considered officially "poor" or "in poverty."

Size of Family Unit	Poverty-Line Income Threshold
One person (unrelated individual)	$12,085
Under 65	$12,331
65 years and over	$11,367
Two people	$15,397
Householder under 65	$15,953
Householder 65 years and over	$14,343
Three people	$18,872
Four people	$24,259
Five people	$28,729
Six people	$32,512
Seven people	$36,971
Eight people	$41,017
Nine people or more	$49,079

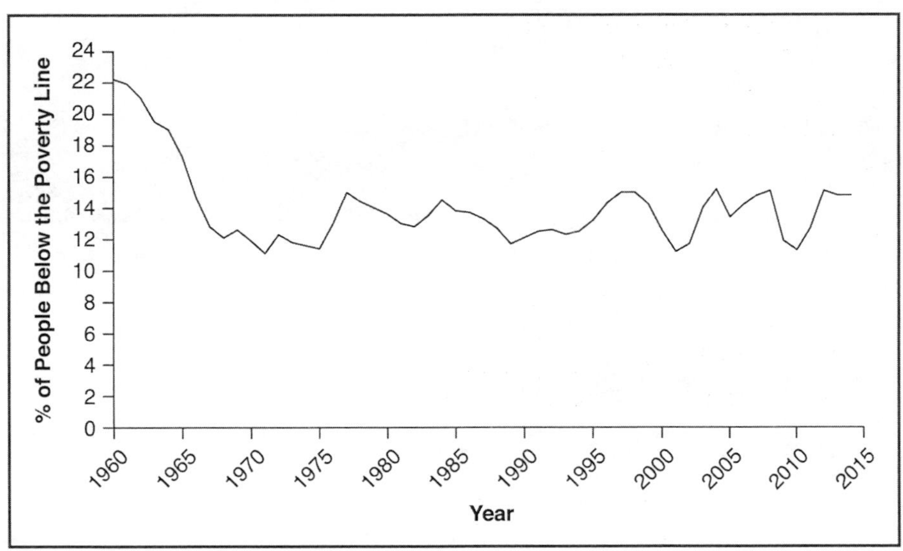

EXHIBIT 16-2 The U.S. Poverty Rate since 1960

The poverty rate fell dramatically during the 1960s, but it has fluctuated within a fairly narrow band since the late 1970s.

EXHIBIT 16-3 Poverty Rates by Group, 2011

Poverty rates are lower for men than for women, lower for whites than for blacks or Hispanics, and lower for those of prime working age than for those earlier in life.

Group	Poverty Rate
Females	16.1%
Males	13.4%
White	12.7%
Black	26.2%
Hispanic	23.6%
Under age 18	21.1%
Ages 18–64	13.5%
Ages 65 and older	10.0%

The concept of a poverty line raises many tricky questions. In a vast country like the United States, should the same national poverty line apply in all states? After all, the median household income varies considerably across states, and prices of some basic goods like housing are quite different between states. The poverty line is based on cash income, which means it doesn't take into account government programs that provide assistance to the poor in a non-cash form, like Medicaid that provides health insurance to the poor or Supplemental Nutrition Assistance Program benefits that can be exchanged for food in grocery stores. Should the poverty line be adjusted to take the value of such programs into account? (These programs and other welfare programs will be discussed in detail later in this chapter.) Perhaps rather than just updating Molly Orshansky's poverty line from the early 1960s, the concept of what poverty means in the twenty-first century should be rethought from scratch?

Government statisticians at the U.S. Census Bureau have ongoing research programs to address questions like these. But any poverty line will be somewhat arbitrary, and it is useful to have a poverty line whose basic definition doesn't change much over time. If Congress voted every few years to redefine what poverty means, then it would be difficult to compare poverty rates over time. After all, would a lower poverty rate mean that the definition had been changed, or that people were actually better off?

Poverty in Low-Income Countries

The World Bank sets two poverty lines that it applies to low-income countries around the world. One poverty line is set at an income of $1.90/day per person; the other is at $3.10/day. By comparison, the U.S. poverty line of $18,872 annually for a family of three works out to $17.23 per person per day. Clearly, many people around the world are far poorer than Americans. China and India both have more than a billion people, and Nigeria is the most populous country in Africa. In all three of those countries, a substantial share of the population subsists in dire poverty on less than $3.10/day. Indeed, more than a third of the world lives on less than $3.10 a day, and about 80% of the world lives on less than $10/day.

Country	Share of Population below $1.90/Day	Share of Population below $3.10/Day
Brazil (2013)	4.9%	9.1%
China (2010)	11.2%	27.2%
India (2011)	21.3%	58.0%
Mexico (2012)	2.7%	10.3%
Nigeria (2009)	53.5%	76.5%

The Poverty Trap

A conflict lies at the heart of assisting the poor. When people are provided with food, shelter, health care, income, and other necessities, such assistance may reduce their incentives to work. For example, consider a program to fight poverty that works in this reasonable-sounding manner: the government provides assistance to the poor, but as the poor earn income to support themselves, the government reduces the level of assistance it provides. With such a program, every time a poor person earns $100, the person also loses $100 in government support. As a result of such a program, the person will experience no net gain to working. Economists call this problem the **poverty trap**.

poverty trap: When antipoverty programs are set up so that government benefits decline substantially as people earn more income—and as a result, working provides little financial gain.

For a concrete example of the poverty trap, consider the situation faced by a single mother with two children, as illustrated in Exhibit 16-4. First consider the labor-leisure budget constraint faced by this family in a situation without government assistance to

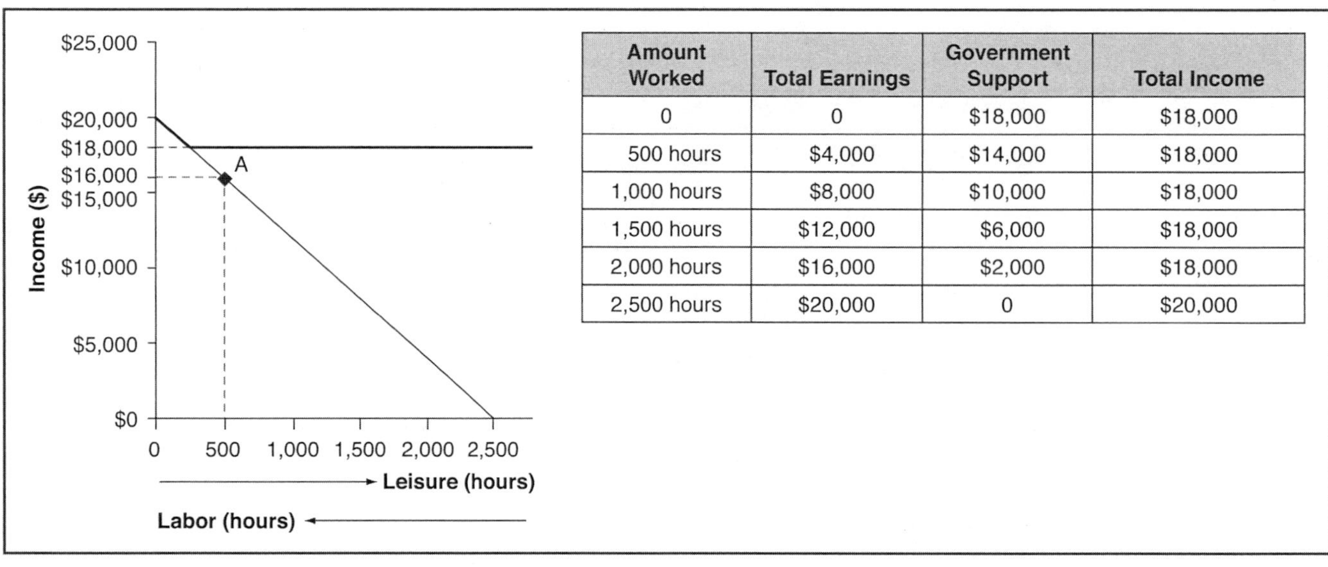

Amount Worked	Total Earnings	Government Support	Total Income
0	0	$18,000	$18,000
500 hours	$4,000	$14,000	$18,000
1,000 hours	$8,000	$10,000	$18,000
1,500 hours	$12,000	$6,000	$18,000
2,000 hours	$16,000	$2,000	$18,000
2,500 hours	$20,000	0	$20,000

EXHIBIT 16-4 The Poverty Trap in Action

The original choice is 500 hours of leisure, 2,000 hours of work at point A, and income of $16,000. With a guaranteed income of $18,000, this family would receive $18,000 whether it provides zero hours of work or 2,000 hours of work. Only if the family provides, say, 2,300 hours of work does its income rise above the guaranteed level of $18,000—and even then, the marginal gain to income from working many hours is small.

the poor. Assume that the mother can earn a wage of $8 per hour. By working 40 hours a week, 50 weeks a year, let's say that her utility-maximizing choice is to work a total of 2,000 hours per year and earn $16,000. Now suppose that a government antipoverty program is created that guarantees every family with a single mother and two children $18,000 in income. With this program, each time the mother earns $1,000, the government will deduct $1,000 of its support.

The new budget line, with the antipoverty program in place, is the heavy line that is flat at $18,000 and rising at the far left of the budget line. If the mother doesn't work at all, she receives $18,000, all from the government. If she works full time, giving up 40 hours per week with her children, she still ends up with $18,000 at the end of the year. Only if she works, say, 2,300 hours in the year—which is an average of 44 hours per week for 50 weeks a year—does household income rise to $18,400. But even in this case, all of her year's work means that household income rises by only $400 over the income she would receive if she did not work at all.

Clearly, this kind of government antipoverty program creates a powerful incentive not to work. Indeed, the poverty trap is even stronger than this simplified example shows because a working mother will have extra expenses like transportation and child care that a nonworking mother will not face—making the economic gains from working even smaller. Of course, those who don't work fail to build up job experience and contacts, which makes working in the future even less attractive.

The bite of the poverty trap can be reduced by designing the antipoverty program so that instead of reducing government payments by $1 for every $1 earned, payments are reduced by some smaller amount. Exhibit 16-5 illustrates a government program that guarantees $18,000 in income, even for those who do not work at all, but then reduces this amount by 50 cents for each $1 earned. The new, higher budget line in the figure shows that with this program in place, additional hours of work will bring some economic gain. However, this type of program raises some issues as well. First, even if it does not

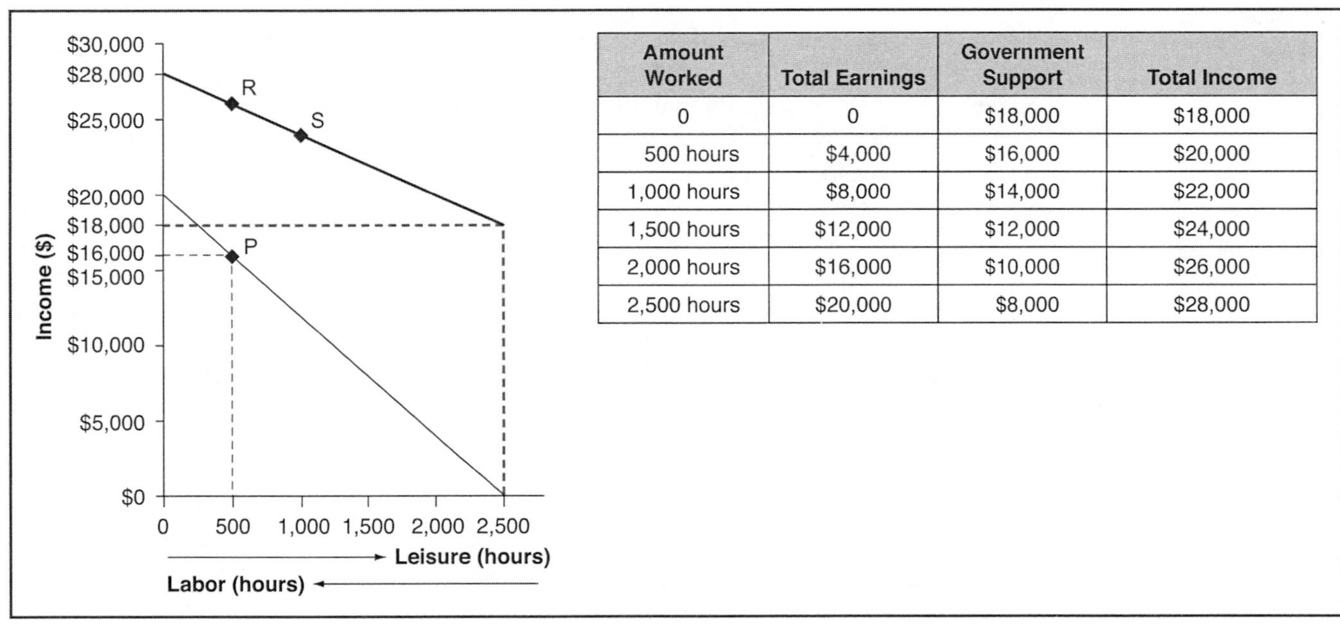

Amount Worked	Total Earnings	Government Support	Total Income
0	0	$18,000	$18,000
500 hours	$4,000	$16,000	$20,000
1,000 hours	$8,000	$14,000	$22,000
1,500 hours	$12,000	$12,000	$24,000
2,000 hours	$16,000	$10,000	$26,000
2,500 hours	$20,000	$8,000	$28,000

EXHIBIT 16-5 Loosening the Poverty Trap: Reducing Government Assistance by 50 Cents for Every $1 Earned

On the original labor-leisure opportunity set, the lower budget set in the figure, the preferred choice P is 500 hours of leisure and $16,000 of income. Then the government created an antipoverty program that guarantees $18,000 in income even to those who work zero hours. In addition, every $1 earned leads to phasing out 50 cents of benefits. This program leads to the higher budget set shown in the diagram. The hope is that low-income workers will find that this program provides incentives to work the same or more hours, despite receiving income assistance. However, it is possible that the recipients will choose a point on the new budget set like S, with less work, more leisure, and greater income, or a point like R, with the same work and greater income.

eliminate the incentive to work by reducing government payments by $1 for every $1 earned, enacting such a program may still reduce the incentive to work. For example, at least some people who would be working 2,000 hours per year without this program might decide to work fewer hours but still end up with more income—that is, their choice on the new budget line would be like S, above and to the right of the original choice P. Of course, others may choose a point like R, which involves the same amount of work as P, or even a point to the left of R that involves more work. The second major issue is that when the government phases out its support payments more slowly, the antipoverty program costs the government more money. Still, it may be preferable in the long run to spend more money on a program that retains a greater incentive to work, rather than spending less money on a program that nearly eliminates any gains from working.

The next section will consider a variety of U.S. government support programs that are focused specifically on the poor, including welfare, Medicaid, the earned income tax credit, the Supplemental Nutrition Assistance Program, and more. Although these programs vary from state to state, it is generally a true statement that in many states from the 1960s into the 1990s, if poor people worked, their level of income barely rose—or did not rise at all—after the reduction in government support payments was factored in. One major issue with rethinking antipoverty programs in the last decade or two is to find ways to combine assistance for the poor with incentives to work—and to declaw the poverty trap.

The Safety Net

The U.S. government has implemented a number of programs to assist those below the poverty line and those who have incomes just above the poverty line, who are referred to as the **near-poor**. As a group, such programs are nicknamed the **safety net**, in recognition of the fact that they offer some protection for those who find themselves without jobs or income.

near-poor: Those who have incomes just above the poverty line.

safety net: Nickname for the group of government programs that provide assistance to the poor and the near-poor.

Temporary Assistance for Needy Families

From the Great Depression of the 1930s until 1996, the most visible U.S. antipoverty program was Aid to Families with Dependent Children (AFDC), which provided cash payments to mothers with children who were below the poverty line. This program was often just called "welfare." In 1996, Congress passed and President Bill Clinton signed into law the Personal Responsibility and Work Opportunity Reconciliation Act, more commonly called the welfare reform act. The new law replaced AFDC with Temporary Assistance for Needy Families (TANF).

TANF brought several dramatic changes in how welfare operated. Under the old AFDC program, states set the level of welfare benefits that they would pay to the poor, and the federal government guaranteed to chip in some money as well. Thus, the federal government's welfare spending would rise or fall depending on the number of poor people and on how each state set its own welfare contribution. Under TANF, however, the federal government gives a fixed amount of money to each state. The state can then use the money for almost any program with an antipoverty component: for example, the state might use the money to give cash to poor families, or to reduce teenage pregnancy, or even to raise the high school graduation rate. However, the federal government imposes two key requirements. First, if states are to keep receiving the TANF grants, they must impose work requirements so that most of those receiving TANF benefits are working (or attending school). Second, no one can receive TANF benefits with federal money for more than a total of five years over his or her lifetime. The old AFDC program had no such work requirements or time limits.

TANF attempts avoid the poverty trap by requiring that welfare recipients work and by limiting the length of time they can receive benefits. In its first few years, the program was quite successful. The number of families receiving payments in 1995, the last year of AFDC, was 4.8 million. By 2002, the number of families receiving payments under TANF was 2.0 million—a decline of more than half.

TANF benefits to poor families vary considerably across states; for example, in 2014 the highest monthly payment in California to a single mother with two children was $670, while in Mississippi the highest monthly payment to that family was $170. Total spending on TANF was $32 billion in 2014, split about evenly between the federal and state governments.

Earned Income Tax Credit (EITC)

The *earned income tax credit (EITC)* is a method of assisting the working poor through the tax system. For every $1 in earned income, a family with children receives a tax refund. The amount of the tax break increases with the amount of income earned, up to a point. In 2016, for example, a single parent with two children would have received a tax refund of 40 cents for every dollar earned up to an income level of $13,931—for a total tax refund of $5,572. The earned income credit has often been popular with both economists and the general public because of the way it effectively increases the payment received for work.

What about the danger of the poverty trap that every additional $1 earned will reduce government support payments by close to $1? To minimize this problem, the earned income credit is phased out slowly. For a single-parent family with two children in 2016, the credit is not reduced at all (but neither is it increased) as earnings rise from $13,931 to $18,190. Then, for every $1 earned above $18,190, the amount received from the credit is reduced by 21 cents, until the credit phases out completely at an income level of $44,648.

In recent years, the EITC has become the single most expensive government program for providing income assistance to the poor and near-poor, costing about $69 billion in 2015. In 2015, the EITC provided benefits to about 27 million families and individuals, and on average is worth about $2,400 per family with children. One reason that the welfare reform bill of 1996 worked as well as it did in the years just after its passage is that the EITC was greatly expanded in the late 1980s and again in the early 1990s, which increased the returns to work for low-income Americans.

Supplemental Nutrition Assistance Program

The Supplemental Nutrition Assistance Program (SNAP) is a federally funded program started in 1964 to assist poor people in buying food. Recipients used to receive this assistance in the form of coupons known as "food stamps." But now people receive SNAP benefits monthly through an Electronic Benefit Transfer card that can be used to buy food in grocery stores. The amount of benefits for which a household is eligible varies by income, number of children, and other factors, but in general, households are expected to spend about 30% of their own income on food, and if 30% of their income is not enough to purchase a nutritionally adequate diet, then those households are eligible for SNAP.

SNAP contributes to the poverty trap. For every $100 earned, the government assumes that a family can spend $30 more on food and thus reduces eligibility for SNAP by $30. This decreased benefit is not a complete disincentive to work, but combined with how other programs reduce benefits as income increases, it doesn't help. However, SNAP does try to address the poverty trap with its own set of work requirements and time limits for recipients.

Why provide assistance that must be spent on food, rather than just giving cash to SNAP recipients? Part of the political support for SNAP comes from a belief that since the benefits must be spent on food, they can't be "wasted" on other forms of consumption. But from an economic point of view, this belief seems wrong-headed. After all, say that a poor family is spending $2,500 per year on food, and then it starts receiving $1,000 per year in SNAP benefits. The family might react by spending $3,500 per year on food (own income plus government benefits), or it might react by continuing to spend $2,500 per year on food but use the $1,000 in SNAP benefits to free up $1,000 that can now be spent on other goods. Thus, it is reasonable to think of SNAP as an alternative method, along with TANF and the earned income tax credit, of transferring income to the working poor.

Indeed, anyone eligible for TANF is also eligible for SNAP, although states can expand eligibility for SNAP benefits if they wish to do so. In some states where TANF welfare spending is relatively low, a poor family may receive more in support from SNAP than from TANF. In 2015, about 46 million people received SNAP benefits at an annual cost of about $74 billion. The average monthly benefit was about $126 per person per month—thus, a qualifying mother with two children might receive $4,536 per year in SNAP benefits.

Medicaid

Medicaid is a federal-state joint program enacted in 1965 that provides medical insurance for certain (not all) low-income people, including the near-poor as well as those below the poverty line, and focusing on low-income families with children, the low-income elderly, and the disabled. About one-third of Medicaid spending is for low-income mothers with children; an increasing share of the program funding in recent years has gone to pay for nursing home costs for the elderly poor. States must provide a basic level of benefits under Medicaid, but they are free to provide higher levels if they wish.

In the past, a common problem has been that many low-paying jobs pay enough so that a family could lose its eligibility for Medicaid, yet the job doesn't offer health insurance benefits either. Thus, a poor parent considering such a job might choose not to work rather than to lose health insurance for his or her children. In this way, health insurance can become a part of the poverty trap. Many states recognized this problem in the 1980s and 1990s and expanded their Medicaid coverage to include not just the poor but also the near-poor earning up to 135% or even 185% of the poverty line. Some states also guaranteed that children would not lose coverage if their parents worked. These expanded guarantees cost money to the government, of course, but they also helped to encourage those on welfare to enter the labor force.

Medicaid spending totaled $496 billion in federal and state spending in 2014, which is roughly triple the total combined spending of TANF, the earned income tax credit, and SNAP benefits. About 70 million people were eligible for Medicaid in 2015.

Other Safety Net Programs

The safety net includes a number of other programs: government-subsidized school lunches and breakfasts for children from low-income families; the Special Supplemental Food Program for Women, Infants, and Children (WIC), which provides food assistance for pregnant women and newborns; the Low Income Home Energy Assistance Program, which provides help with home heating bills; housing assistance, which helps pay the rent; and Supplemental Security Income, which provides cash support for the elderly poor.

There is no straightforward answer to the problem of ensuring that the poor have a decent standard of living while also providing incentives to work. TANF tries to use work requirements and time limits. The earned income credit attempts to increase the incentives for work. Medicaid has been expanded to be widely available to the near-poor as well as the poor. But with all of these programs, and SNAP benefits as well, there comes a point where, as families earn more money, their government support payments are reduced, which inevitably reduces the incentives for the poor and near-poor to work. The poverty trap can be loosened, but it cannot be abolished.

Measuring Income Inequality

Economic inequality involves comparing those with high incomes, middle incomes, and low incomes—not just looking at those below or near the poverty line. In turn, measuring income inequality means dividing up the population into various groups and then comparing the groups, a task that can be carried out in several ways.

EXHIBIT 16-6 Share of Aggregate Income Received by Each Fifth and Top 5% of Households, 1967–2014

The share of income received by the top quintile has grown since the late 1970s. Much of this increase in the share of income going to the top fifth can be traced to an increase in the share of income going to those at the very top of the income distribution, as shown by the rising share going to the top 5% in the final column.

Year	Lowest Quintile	Second Quintile	Third Quintile	Fourth Quintile	Highest Quintile	Top 5%
1967	5.4	12.2	17.5	23.5	41.4	16.4
1970	5.4	12.2	17.6	23.8	40.9	15.6
1975	5.6	11.9	17.7	24.2	40.7	14.9
1980	5.3	11.6	17.6	24.4	41.1	14.6
1985	4.8	11.0	16.9	24.3	43.1	16.1
1990	4.6	10.8	16.6	23.8	44.3	17.4
1995	4.4	10.1	15.8	23.2	46.5	20.0
2000	4.3	9.8	15.4	22.7	47.7	21.1
2005	4.0	9.6	15.3	22.9	48.1	21.1
2010	3.8	9.4	15.4	23.5	47.9	20.0
2014	3.6	9.2	15.1	23.2	48.9	20.8

Income Distribution by Quintiles

One common way of measuring income inequality is to rank all households by income, from lowest to highest, and then to divide all households into five groups with equal numbers of people—known as **quintiles**. This calculation allows measuring inequality by comparing what share of the total income is earned by each quintile.

quintiles: Dividing a group into fifths, a method often used to look at distribution of income.

U.S. income distribution by quintile appears in Exhibit 16-6. In 2005, for example, the bottom quintile of the income distribution received 3.4% of income; the second quintile received 8.6%; the third quintile, 14.6%; the fourth quintile, 23.0%; and the top quintile, 50.4%. The final column of the table shows what share of income went to households in the top 5% of the income distribution: specifically, 22.2% in 2005. Over time, from the late 1960s to the early 1980s, the top fifth of the income distribution typically received between 43–44% of all income. However, the share of income that the top fifth received then began to rise. Using the quintile measure, income inequality has increased in recent decades.

CLEARING IT UP

Separating Poverty and Income Inequality

Poverty can change even when inequality does not move at all. Imagine, for example, a situation in which income for everyone in the population declines by 10%. Poverty would rise, since a greater share of the population would now fall below the poverty line income level. However, inequality would be the same because everyone suffered the same proportional loss. Conversely, a general rise in income levels over time would keep inequality the same, but reduce poverty.

It's also possible for economic inequality to change without affecting the poverty rate. Imagine a situation in which a large number of people who already have high incomes increase their incomes by even more. Inequality would rise as a result—but the number of people below the poverty line would remain unchanged.

It can also be useful to divide the income distribution in ways other than quintiles— for example, into tenths or even into percentiles (i.e., hundredths). A more detailed breakdown can provide additional insights. For example, the last column of Exhibit 16-6 shows the income received by the top 5% of the income distribution. From 1980 to 2014 the share of income going to the top fifth increased by more than 7 percentage points (from 41.1% in 1980 to 48.9% in 2014). Over this same time, the share of income going to the top 5% increased by more than 6 percentage points (from 14.6% in 1980 to 20.8% in 2014). Thus, the increased share of income going to the top fifth is mostly accounted for by the increased share of income going to the top 5% of the income distribution.

Lorenz Curve

Lorenz curve: A graph that shows the share of population on the horizontal axis and the cumulative percentage of total income received on the vertical axis.

The data on income inequality can be presented in various ways. For example, you could draw a bar graph that showed the share of income going to each fifth of the income distribution. Exhibit 16-7 presents an alternative way of showing inequality data. The **Lorenz curve** shows the share of population on the horizontal axis and the *cumulative* percentage of total income received on the vertical axis.

Every Lorenz curve diagram begins with a line sloping up at a 45-degree angle, shown as a dashed line in Exhibit 16-7. The points along this line show what perfect equality of the income distribution looks like. It would mean, for example, that the bottom 20% of the income distribution has 20% of the total income, the bottom 40% has 40% of total income, and so on. The other lines in Exhibit 16-7 reflect actual U.S. data on inequality for 1980 and 2014. The trick in graphing a Lorenz curve is that you must transform the *shares* of income for each specific quintile, which are shown in the first column of numbers in the table, into *cumulative* income, shown in the second column of numbers. For example, the bottom 40% of the cumulative income distribution will be the sum of the first and second quintiles; the bottom 60% of the cumulative income distribution will be the sum of the first, second, and third quintiles, and so on. The final entry in the cumulative income column needs to be 100% because, by definition, 100% of the population receives 100% of the income.

In a Lorenz curve diagram, a more unequal distribution of income will loop further down and away from the 45-degree line, while a more equal distribution of income will cuddle closer to the 45-degree line. The greater inequality of the U.S. income distribution between 1980 and 2014 is illustrated in Exhibit 16-7 because the Lorenz curve for 2014 is farther from the 45-degree line than the Lorenz curve for 1980. The Lorenz curve is

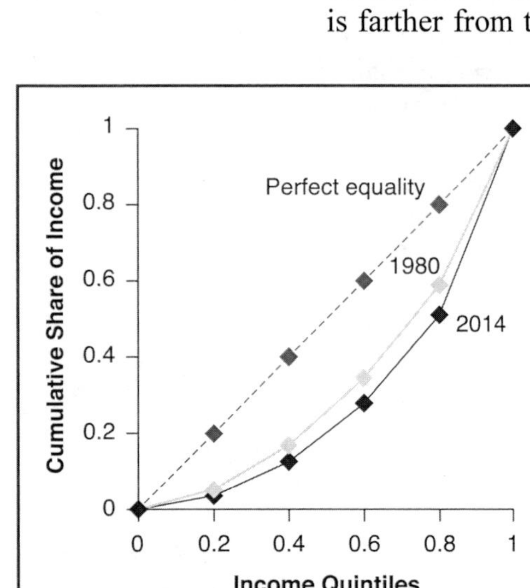

Income Category	Share of Income in 1980	Cumulative Share of Income in 1980	Share of Income in 2014	Cumulative Share of Income in 2014
First quintile	5.3	5.3	3.6	3.6
Second quintile	11.6	16.9	9.2	12.8
Third quintile	17.6	34.5	15.1	27.9
Fourth quintile	24.4	58.9	23.2	51.1
Fifth quintile	41.1	100	48.9	100

EXHIBIT 16-7 Lorenz Curve

A Lorenz curve graphs the cumulative shares of income received by everyone up to a certain quintile. The income distribution in 1980 was closer to the perfect equality line than the income distribution in 2014—that is, the U.S. income distribution has become more unequal over time.

Economic Inequality around the World

The U.S. economy has a relatively high degree of income inequality by global standards. As the table shows, based on a variety of national surveys done for a selection of recent years (and adjusted to make the measures comparable), the U.S. economy has greater inequality than Germany (along with most western European countries). The region of the world with the highest level of income inequality is Latin America; this is illustrated in the numbers for Brazil and Mexico. The level of inequality in the United States is lower than in some of the low-income countries of the world, like Nigeria. However, not all poor countries have highly unequal income distributions; India provides a counterexample.

Country	Survey Year	First Quintile	Second Quintile	Third Quintile	Fourth Quintile	Fifth Quintile
United States	2014	3.6%	9.2%	15.1%	23.2%	48.9%
Germany	2011	8.4%	13.1%	17.2%	22.7%	38.6%
Brazil	2013	3.3%	7.6%	12.4%	19.3%	57.4%
Mexico	2012	4.9%	8.8%	12.8%	19.5%	54.1%
China	2010	4.7%	9.7%	15.3%	23.3%	47.1%
India	2011	8.2%	11.8%	15.2%	20.5%	44.2%
Russia	2012	5.9%	10.1%	14.5%	21.2%	48.3%
Nigeria	2010	4.4%	8.3%	13.0%	20.3%	54.0%

a useful way of presenting the quintile data that provides an image of all of the quintile data at once.

Causes of Growing Income Inequality

Why did inequality of household income increase in the United States in recent decades? Indeed, a trend toward greater income inequality has occurred in many countries around the world, although the effect has been more powerful in the U.S. economy. Economists have focused their explanations for the increasing inequality of income on two factors that changed more or less continually from the 1970s into the 2000s. One set of explanations focuses on the changing shape of American households; the other focuses on greater inequality of wages.

The Changing Composition of American Households

In 1970, 41% of married women were in the labor force, but by 2014, 58% of married women were in the labor force. One result of this trend is that more households have two people earning income. Moreover, it has become more common for one high earner to marry another high earner. A few decades ago, the common pattern featured a man with relatively high earnings, such as an executive or a doctor, marrying a woman who didn't earn as much, like a secretary or a nurse. Often, the woman would leave paid employment, at least for a few years, to raise a family. However, now doctors are marrying doctors and executives are marrying executives, and mothers with high-powered careers are often returning to work while their children are quite young. This pattern of households with two high-earners tends to increase the proportion of high-earning households.

Even as two-earner couples have increased, so have single-parent households. In 1970, 10.8% of all U.S. families were headed by single mothers; by 2014, about 19% of all families were headed by single mothers. The poverty rate among single-parent households tends to be relatively high.

These changes in family structure, including the growth of single-parent families who tend to be near the lower end of the income distribution and the growth of two-career high-earner couples near the top end of the income distribution, account for roughly half of the rise in income inequality across households in recent decades.

A Shift in the Distribution of Wages

Another factor behind the rise in U.S. income inequality is that earnings have become less equal since the late 1970s. In particular, the earnings received by high-skilled labor relative to low-skilled labor have increased. One way to measure this change is to take the earnings of workers with at least a four-year college bachelor's degree (including those who went on and completed an advanced degree) and divide them by the earnings of workers with only a high school degree. The result is illustrated in Exhibit 16-8, which shows that those in the 25–34 age bracket with college degrees earned about 1.2 times as much as high school graduates in 1980, but now earn about 1.7 times as much.

Economists use the demand and supply model to reason through the most likely causes of this shift. In recent decades, the supply of U.S. workers with college degrees has increased substantially; for example, 840,000 four-year bachelor's degrees were conferred on Americans in 1970; in the 2015–2016 academic year, 1.8 million such degrees were conferred—more than double. In Exhibit 16-9, this shift in supply to the right from S_0 to S_1 should result in a lower equilibrium wage for high-skilled labor. Thus, the increase in the price of high-skilled labor must be explained by a greater demand for high-skilled labor, like the movement from D_0 to D_1. Evidently, combining both the increase in supply and in demand has resulted in a shift from E_0 to E_1, and a resulting higher wage.

What factors would cause the demand for high-skilled labor to rise? One plausible explanation is that while the explosion in new information and communications technologies over the last several decades has helped many workers to become more productive, the benefits have been especially great for many high-skilled workers like top business managers, lawyers, consultants, design professionals, and others. The new communication and information technologies have also helped to encourage globalization, the remarkable increase in international trade over the last few decades, by making it more possible to learn about and coordinate economic interactions all around the world. In turn, the rise of globalization has opened up greater opportunities for high-skilled workers to sell their services around the world. Of course, a supply and demand analysis can also be applied to low- and medium-skilled labor. As U.S. education levels have risen in recent

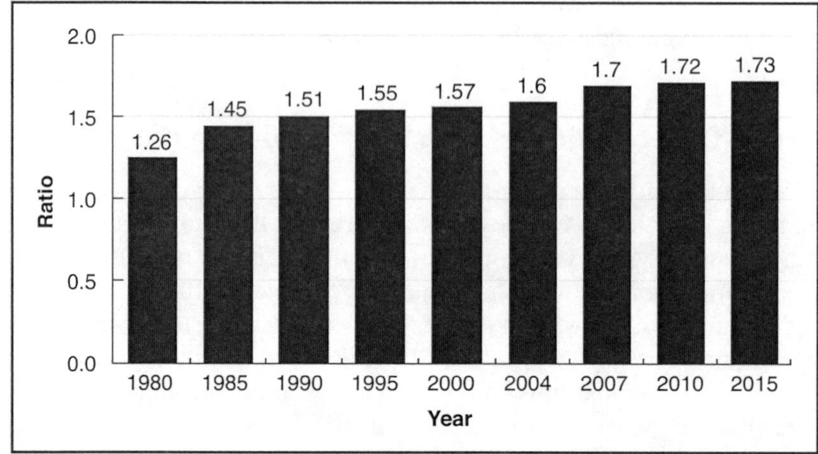

EXHIBIT 16-8 Ratio of Median Earnings for Full-Time Workers, Ages 25–34, with a Bachelor's Degree or More to Those with Only a High School Diploma or Equivalent

The returns to skill have increased in the last few decades, in the sense that the additional wages gained from having a college degree, over having only a high school diploma, have increased.

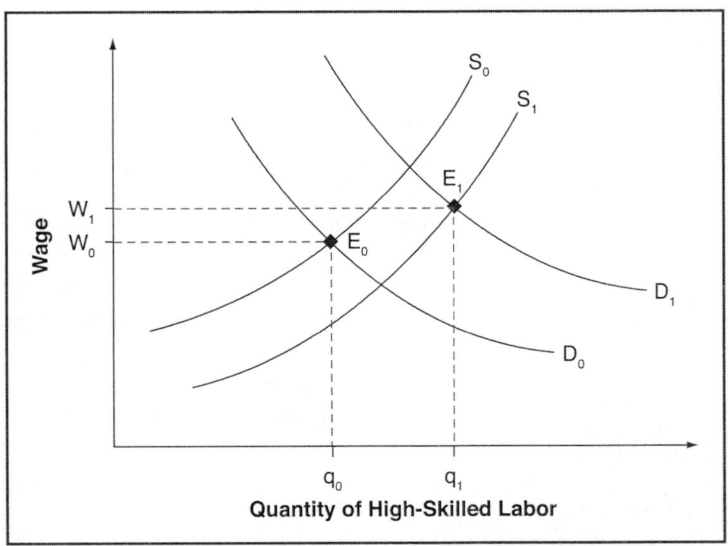

EXHIBIT 16-9 Why Would Wages Rise for High-Skilled Labor?

The proportion of workers attending college has increased in recent decades, so the supply curve for high-skilled labor has shifted to the right from S_0 to S_1. If the demand for high-skilled labor had remained at D_0, then this shift in supply would have led to lower wages for high-skilled labor. But the relative wages for high-skilled labor have increased even with the shift in supply of such labor to the right. The explanation must lie in a shift to the right in demand for high-skilled labor from D_0 to D_1. The figure shows how a combination of the shift in supply from S_0 to S_1 and the shift in demand from D_0 to D_1 led to both an increase in the quantity of high-skilled labor hired and also to a rise in the wage for such labor from W_0 to W_1.

decades, the supply of low-skilled labor has fallen. But new technology has reduced the demand for certain types of low- and medium-skilled labor even faster. In some industries, automation or robots can replace low-skilled labor. Meanwhile, globalization has increased competitive pressures for medium- and lower-skilled U.S. workers, who may now find their employers competing with firms from lower-wage economies from Latin America to Asia and Africa. This shift in labor demand has been strong enough to reduce job prospects and hold down wages for many low- and medium-skill workers.

Government Policies to Reduce Income Inequality

No society should expect or desire complete equality of income at a given point in time, for a number of reasons. First, most workers receive relatively low earnings in their first few jobs, higher earnings as they reach middle age, and then lower earnings after retirement. Thus, a society with people of varying ages will have a certain amount of income inequality. Second, people's preferences and desires differ. Some are willing to work long hours to have income for large houses, fast cars and computers, luxury vacations, and the ability to support children and grandchildren. Others will work fewer hours and instead use their time for reading books, listening to music, and cooking meals to eat with their family. Third, people can be lucky or unlucky. Some people will take a job with a company that grows by leaps and bounds, or will be born with traits that help make it possible for them to be a professional athlete or model, or will win the lottery. Others may take a job with a company that goes broke, or their unique personal traits may not bring any special reward in the labor market. Finally, any economic system with incentives for acquiring skill, working hard, and inventing new goods and services will result in some inequality.

But even if some degree of economic inequality is expected at any point in time, how much inequality should there be? Some decades ago, an economist named Henry Simons (1889–1946) tried to find an objective, scientific way to determine how much inequality was appropriate. After a great deal of thought, he decided that the question had no answer

Wealth Inequality

Income is a flow of money received, often measured on a monthly or an annual basis; wealth is the total amount stored up. A retired person, for example, may have relatively little income in a given year, other than a pension or Social Security. However, if that person has saved and invested over time, the person's accumulated wealth can be substantial. Wealth is the sum of value of all assets, including money in bank accounts, financial investments, a pension fund, and value of a home. However, in calculating wealth, all debts must be subtracted, such as debt owed on a home mortgage and on credit cards.

The wealth distribution is more unequal than the income distribution, because differences in income can accumulate over time to make even larger differences in wealth. However, the degree of inequality in the wealth distribution can be measured with the same tools that we use to measure the inequality in the income distribution, like quintile measurements. Data on wealth in U.S. households is collected every three years in the Survey of Consumer Finance. A study based on this data found that in 2013, the top 3% of the wealth distribution had more wealth than the bottom 90% of the wealth distribution; that is, the top 1% held 54% of all wealth in the U.S. economy in 2013, while the bottom 90% of the wealth distribution held a total of 25% of all wealth.

and wrote that arguments against inequality ultimately depend on "the ethical or aesthetic judgment that the prevailing distribution of wealth and income reveals a degree (and/or kind) of inequality which is distinctly evil or unlovely."

But even if economics cannot answer the question of how much inequality is "evil or unlovely," economists can still play an important role in spelling out policy options and trade-offs. If a society decides to reduce the level of economic inequality, it has three main sets of tools that it might use: redistribution from those with high incomes to those with low incomes; trying to assure that a ladder of opportunity is widely available; and a tax on inheritances. Let's consider these in turn.

Redistribution

redistribution: Taking income from those with higher incomes and providing income to those with lower incomes.

Redistribution means taking income from those with higher incomes and providing income to those with lower incomes. Earlier in this chapter, we considered some of the key government policies that provide support for the poor: the welfare program TANF, the earned income tax credit, the Supplemental Nutrition Assistance Program, and Medicaid. If a reduction in inequality seemed socially desirable, these programs could receive additional funding.

These programs are paid for through the federal income tax, which is designed in such a way that the rich pay considerably more in income taxes than the poor. Exhibit 16-10 shows data from individual income tax returns in 2011. The top 1%, which had an average income of $1,413,100 per year in pre-tax income, paid 20.3% of their total income in income taxes, and 29% of their total income in all federal taxes combined. This top 1% paid 35.4% of all income taxes and 24% of total federal taxes. Meanwhile, the bottom two quintiles actually paid negative income taxes on average because of provisions like the earned income credit that provide income to many of these families. News stories occasionally report on a high-income person who has managed to pay very little in taxes, but while such individual cases exist, the typical pattern is that people with higher incomes pay a higher average share of their income to federal income taxes.

Of course, the fact that some degree of redistribution occurs now through the federal income tax and government antipoverty programs doesn't settle the questions of how much redistribution is appropriate and whether more redistribution should occur.

The Ladder of Opportunity

Economic inequality is perhaps most troubling when it is not the result of effort or talent, but instead is determined by the circumstances under which a child grows up. One child

EXHIBIT 16-10 Tax Rates and Share of Taxes Paid: 2011

Columns 2 and 3 show the average pre-tax and post-tax income for that quintile, or for the top 5% and 1% of the income distribution. The effective income tax rate in column 4 is the average share of income paid in federal income taxes. The effective tax rate for all federal taxes in column 5 includes non-income taxes like the payroll taxes that fund Social Security and Medicare, as well as federal alcohol and gasoline taxes. For example, the top 1% of the income distribution paid 20.3% of its income in individual income taxes and 29% of its income in total federal taxes. The share paid of income tax liabilities appears in column 6, while the share paid of total federal taxes is shown in column 7. For example, the top quintile paid 88% of all income taxes and 68.7% of all federal taxes in 2011.

Income category	Average Pre-tax Income	Average Post-tax Income	Effective Income Tax Rate	Effective Tax Rate All Federal Taxes	Share Paid of All Income Tax Liabilities	Share Paid of All Total Federal Taxes
Lowest quintile	$24,600	$24,100	–7.5%	1.9%	–4.7%	0.6%
Second quintile	$45,300	$42,100	n1.3%	7.0%	–1.5%	3.8%
Third quintile	$66,400	$59,000	2.4%	11.2%	4.0%	8.9%
Fourth quintile	$97,500	$82,600	5.8%	15.2%	14.2%	17.6%
Fifth quintile	$245,700	$188,200	14.2%	23.4%	88.0%	68.7%
Top 5%	$299,000	$226,400	15.6%	24.3%	23.6%	17.4%
Top 1%	$1,453,100	$1,031,900	20.3%	29.0%	35.4%	24.0%

attends a well-run grade school and high school and heads on to college, while parents help out by supporting education and other interests; paying for college, a first car, and a first house; and offering work connections that lead to internships and jobs. Another child attends a poorly run grade school, barely makes it through a low-quality high school, doesn't go to college, and lacks family and peer support. These two children may be similar in their underlying talents and in the effort they put forth, but their economic outcomes are likely to be quite different.

Public policy can attempt to build a ladder of opportunities so that, even though all children will never come from identical families and attend identical schools, each child has a reasonable opportunity to attain an economic niche in society based on his or her interests, desires, talents, and efforts. Opportunity-oriented policies begin with focus on children: for example, programs for improved day care; enrichment programs for preschoolers; improved public schools; after-school and community activities; and internships and apprenticeships to connect teenagers to the job market. At the college and university level, the ladder of opportunity might involve widespread loans and grants for those in financial need, along with public support for a range of institutions from two-year community colleges to large research universities. For adults, the ladder of opportunity might involve opportunities for retraining and acquiring new skills, as well as actively prohibiting discrimination in job markets and housing on the basis of race, gender, age, and disability.

The United States has often been called a land of opportunity. Although the general idea of a ladder of opportunity for all citizens continues to exert a powerful attraction, specifics are often controversial. One problem is that some of the policies to create more opportunity could be highly costly to taxpayers—for example, the costs would be very high if the government offered to pay for several years of preschool, to increase funding for all students from kindergarten through 12th grade, and also to help pay for college for every student. Moreover, the success of many of these proposals may depend less on the level of spending than on how the projects are managed and directed. For example, improving the quality of public schools is easy to say, but hard to achieve. Government training for adults seems to work well in some programs but not in others. Society can experiment with a wide variety of proposals for building a ladder of opportunity, especially for those who otherwise seem likely to start their lives in a disadvantaged position. But such policy experiments need to be carried out in a spirit of open-mindedness, because some will succeed while others will not show positive results or will cost too much to enact on a widespread basis.

Inheritance Taxes

If wealthy parents can give large gifts and inheritances to their children, then economic inequality may persist across generations. How much wealth should rich people be able to pass on to their children? On the one hand, it seems self-evident that people who have worked hard all their lives and saved up a substantial nest egg should be able to give their money and possessions to their children and grandchildren if they wish. In particular, it would seem un-American if children were unable to inherit a family business or a family home. On the other hand, many Americans are far more comfortable with inequality resulting from high-income people who earned their money by starting innovative new companies than they are with inequality resulting from high-income people who have inherited money from rich parents.

estate tax: A tax imposed on the value of an inheritance.

The United States does have an **estate tax**—that is, a tax imposed on the value of an inheritance—which suggests a willingness to limit how much wealth can be passed on as an inheritance. However, in 2016 the estate tax applied only to those leaving inheritances of more than $55.45million and thus applies to only a tiny percentage of the population who have very high levels of wealth. The estate tax collects less than 1% of federal tax revenues. Even for the small minority who are subject to the estate tax, a good tax lawyer or a savvy estate planner can often figure out ways to minimize what must be paid.

As a matter of practical politics, there seems to be relatively little support for a substantial increase in redistribution by taxing either the income or the inheritances of those with high incomes and wealth. In contrast, an opportunity agenda remains relatively popular. For example, the expansions of the earned income credit and of Medicaid to cover near-poor families can be viewed as attempts to strengthen the rungs on the ladder of opportunity, as can various proposals to improve education. The ultimate test will be whether detailed studies show that these policies are working reasonably well.

The Trade-off between Incentives and Income Equality

Government policies to reduce poverty or to encourage economic equality, if carried to extremes, can injure incentives for economic output. The poverty trap, for example, defines a situation where guaranteeing a certain level of income can eliminate or reduce the incentive to work at a low-paid job. Extremely high taxes on the rich would at some point be likely to discourage work and entrepreneurship. Thus, it is common to draw the trade-off between economic output and equality as shown in Exhibit 16-11*a*. In this formulation, if society wishes a high level of economic output like point A, it must also accept a high degree of inequality; conversely, if society wants a high level of equality like point B, it must accept a lower level of economic output because of reduced incentives for production.

But this view of the trade-off between economic output and equality may be too pessimistic, and Exhibit 16-11*b* presents an alternate vision. Here, the trade-off between economic output and equality first slopes up, in the vicinity of choice C, suggesting that certain programs might increase both output and economic equality. For example, the policy of providing free public education has an element of redistribution, since the value of the public schooling received by children of low-income families is clearly higher than what low-income families pay in taxes. But a well-educated population is also an enormously powerful factor in providing the skilled workers of tomorrow and helping the economy to grow and expand. In this case, equality and economic growth may complement each other. Moreover, policies to diminish inequality and soften the hardship of poverty may sustain political support for a market economy. After all, if society does not make at least some efforts toward reducing inequality and poverty, the alternative might

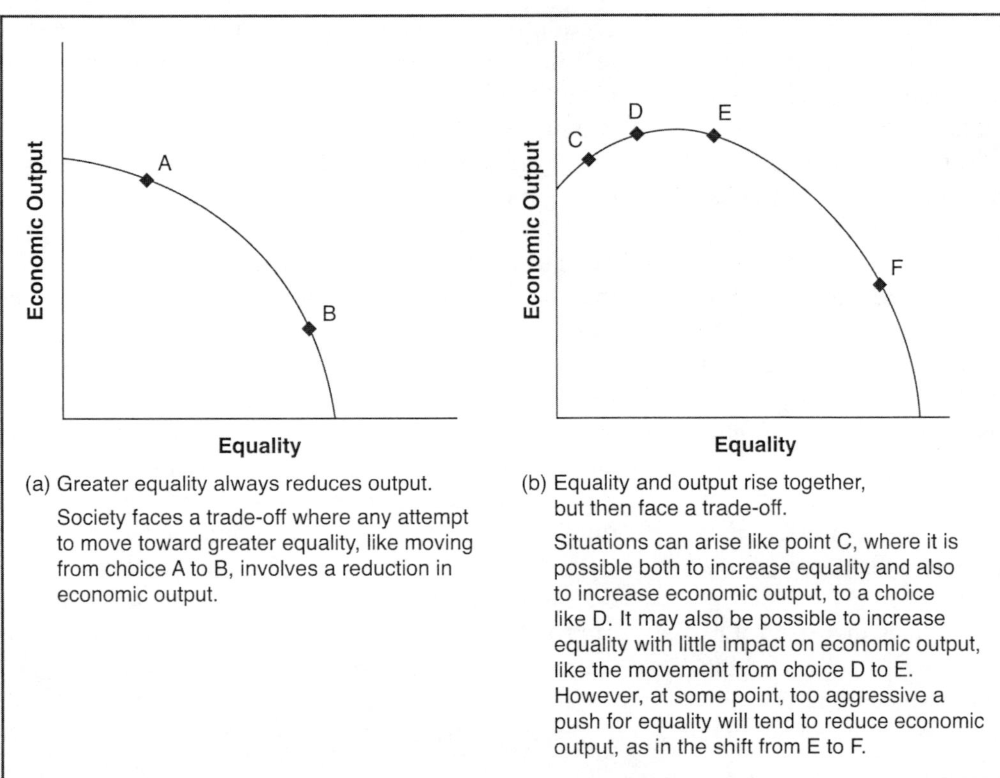

(a) Greater equality always reduces output.

Society faces a trade-off where any attempt to move toward greater equality, like moving from choice A to B, involves a reduction in economic output.

(b) Equality and output rise together, but then face a trade-off.

Situations can arise like point C, where it is possible both to increase equality and also to increase economic output, to a choice like D. It may also be possible to increase equality with little impact on economic output, like the movement from choice D to E. However, at some point, too aggressive a push for equality will tend to reduce economic output, as in the shift from E to F.

EXHIBIT 16-11 The Trade-off between Incentives and Economic Equality

be that fearful citizens would rebel against market forces. For example, citizens might seek economic security by demanding that their legislators pass laws that would forbid employers from ever laying off workers or reducing wages, or laws that would impose price floors and price ceilings and shut off international trade. From this viewpoint, policies to reduce inequality may help economic output by building social support for allowing markets to operate.

The trade-off in Exhibit 16-11*b* then flattens out in the area between points D and E, which reflects the pattern that there are a number of economies that provide roughly similar levels of income to their citizens—the United States, Canada, the nations of the European Union, Japan, Australia—but these countries have different levels of inequality. This pattern suggests that countries in this range could choose a greater or a lesser degree of inequality without much impact on economic output. Only if these countries push for a much higher level of equality, like at point F, will they experience the diminished incentives that lead to lower levels of economic output. In this view, while a danger always exists that an agenda to reduce poverty or inequality can be poorly designed or pushed too far, it is also possible to discover and design policies that improve equality and do not injure incentives for economic output by very much—or even improve such incentives.

Key Concepts and Summary

1. Labor markets will determine wages according to demand and supply, which can lead to very low incomes for some people and very high incomes for others.
2. **Poverty** and economic **inequality** are not the same thing. Poverty applies to the condition of people who cannot afford the necessities of life. Economic inequality refers to the disparity between those with higher and lower incomes.
3. The poverty rate is what percentage of the population lives below the **poverty line**, which is determined by the amount of income that it takes to purchase the necessities of life. Choosing a poverty line will always be somewhat controversial. The near-poor are those with low incomes who are just above the poverty line.
4. A **poverty trap** occurs when government-support payments for the poor decline as the poor earn more income. As a result, the poor do not end up with much more income when they work because the loss of government support largely or completely offsets any income that is earned by working. The bite of the

poverty trap can be reduced by phasing out government benefits more slowly, as well as by imposing requirements for work as a condition of receiving benefits and a time limit on benefits.

5. The groups of government programs that assist the poor are called the **safety net**. In the United States, prominent safety net programs include Temporary Assistance to Needy Families (TANF), the earned income credit (EIC), Medicaid, and the Supplemental Nutrition Assistance Program.
6. Measuring inequality involves making comparisons across the entire distribution of income, not just the poor. One way of doing this is to divide the population into groups, like **quintiles**, and then calculate what share of income is received by each group. An alternative approach is to draw **Lorenz curves**, which compare the cumulative income actually received to a perfectly equal distribution of income.
7. Income inequality in the United States increased substantially from the late 1970s or early 1980s into the 2000s. The two most common explanation cited by economists are changes in the structure of households that have led to more two-earner couples and single-parent families, and the effect of new information and communications technology on wages.
8. There are a number of plausible reasons for a degree of income inequality: for example, differences in age, differences in preferences, a need for incentives, year-to-year fluctuations, and luck. However, inequality that is rising, or that is passed between generations, can create social and political tensions.
9. Policies that can affect the level of economic inequality include **redistribution** between rich and poor, making it easier for people to climb the ladder of opportunity, and **estate taxes**, which are taxes on inheritances.
10. Pushing too aggressively for economic equality can run the risk of decreasing economic incentives. However, a moderate push for economic equality can increase economic output, both through methods like improved education and by building a base of political support for market forces.

Review Questions

1. What is the difference between poverty and income inequality?
2. How is the poverty rate calculated?
3. What is the poverty line?
4. Who are the near-poor?
5. How does the poverty trap discourage people from working?
6. How can the effect of the poverty trap be reduced?
7. What is the safety net?
8. Briefly explain the differences between TANF, the earned income tax credit, the Supplemental Nutrition Assistance Program, and Medicaid.
9. Who is included in the top income quintile?
10. What is measured on the two axes of a Lorenz curve?
11. How has the inequality of income changed in the U.S. economy since the late 1970s?
12. What are some reasons why a certain degree of inequality of income would be expected in a market economy?
13. What are the main reasons economists give for the increase in inequality of incomes?
14. Name some public policies that can reduce the level of economic inequality.
15. Describe how a push for economic equality might reduce incentives to work and produce output. Then describe how a push for economic inequality might not have such effects.

CHAPTER

17

Issues in Labor Markets: Unions, Discrimination, Immigration

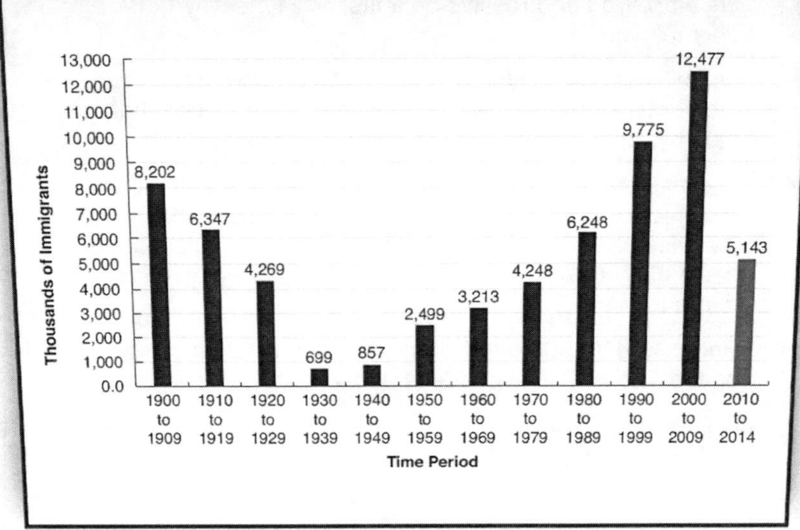

Chapter Outline

A worker without a job will feel considerable stress; after all, there are bills to pay and mouths to feed. But most employers have a number of employees. If a company fires a worker or delays hiring a worker, the company as a whole is unlikely to experience any noticeable rise or fall in profits. Thus, when a worker or job applicant is bargaining with an employer, the individual is often at a disadvantage because the worker needs the job more than the employer needs that particular worker. John Bates Clark (1847–1938), often named as the first great American economist, wrote in 1907: "In the making of the wage contract the individual laborer is always at a disadvantage. He has something which he is obliged to sell and which his employer is not obliged to take, since he [that is, the employer] can reject individual men with impunity."

A number of laws have been passed to create greater balance in negotiations between workers and employers. For example, there are laws setting minimum hourly wages, limiting the hours that employers can require (at least before they pay overtime rates), prohibiting child labor, regulating health and safety conditions in the workplace, and preventing discrimination on the basis of race, ethnicity, gender, and age. Laws have also been enacted to require that employers provide family leave, that employers give advance notice of layoffs, that workers have unemployment insurance, and to limit the number of immigrant workers from other countries. Exhibit 17-1 lists some prominent U.S. workplace protection laws. Many of the laws listed in the table were only the start of labor market regulations in these areas and have been followed over time by other related laws, regulations, and court rulings. Many of these laws are discussed at other places in this book: for example, Chapter 5 considered minimum wage laws as an example of a price floor.

This chapter will focus on three aspects of workplace protection. The first section discusses labor unions, in which workers join together and negotiate as a group for wages, benefits, and other conditions of employment with the firm.

EXHIBIT 17-1 Prominent U.S. Workplace Protection Laws

National Labor-Management Relations Act of 1935 (the "Wagner Act")	Establishes procedures for establishing a union that firms are obligated to follow, and sets up the National Labor Relations Board for deciding disputes
Social Security Act of 1935	Under Title III, establishes a state-run system of unemployment insurance, in which workers pay into a state fund when they are employed and receive benefits for a time when they are unemployed
Fair Labor Standards Act of 1938	Establishes the minimum wage, limits on child labor, and rules requiring payment of overtime pay for those in jobs that are paid by the hour and exceed 40 hours per week
Taft-Hartley Act of 1947	Allows states to decide whether all workers at a firm can be required to join a union as a condition of employment, and in the case of a disruptive union strike, permits the president to declare a "cooling-off period" during which workers have to return to work
Civil Rights Act of 1964	Under Title VII of the Act prohibits discrimination in employment on the basis of race, gender, national origin, or religion
Occupational Health and Safety Act of 1970	Creates the Occupational Safety and Health Administration (OSHA), which protects workers from physical harm in the workplace
Employee Retirement and Income Security Act of 1974	Regulates employee pension rules and benefits
Immigration Reform and Control Act of 1986	Prohibits hiring of illegal immigrants, requires employers to ask for proof of citizenship, protects rights of legal immigrants
Worker Adjustment and Retraining Notification Act of 1988	Requires employers with more than 100 employees to provide written notice 60 days before plant closings or large layoffs
Americans with Disabilities Act of 1990	Prohibits discrimination against those with disabilities and requires reasonable accommodations for them on the job
Family and Medical Leave Act of 1993	Allows employees to take up to 12 weeks of unpaid leave per year for family reasons, including birth or family illness
Pension Protection Act of 2006	Penalizes firms for underfunding their pension plans and gives employees more information about their pension accounts

The second section discusses the economics of discrimination against women or minority groups in the labor market. What effect has such discrimination had on wages and other work conditions? Finally, the chapter moves to a discussion of immigration, which in economic terms can be viewed as a situation where the supply of labor is extended to include workers who arrive from outside the country.

Labor Unions

labor union: An organization of workers that negotiates with employers as a group over wages and working conditions.

collective bargaining: Negotiations between unions and a firm or firms.

A **labor union** is an organization of workers that negotiates with employers as a group over wages and working conditions. A labor union seeks to change the balance of negotiations between employers and workers by forcing employers to deal with workers collectively, rather than as individuals. Thus, negotiations between unions and firms are sometimes called **collective bargaining**. Labor unions can be controversial. Supporters of labor unions view them as the workers' primary line of defense against efforts by profit-seeking firms to hold down wages. Critics of labor unions view them as having a tendency to grab as much as they can in the short term, even if it injures workers in

EXHIBIT 17-2 Which American Workers Belong to Unions in 2015?

- 11.5% of U.S. male workers belong to unions; 10.6% of female workers do.
- 10.8% of white workers, 13.6% of black workers, and 9.4% of Hispanic workers belong to unions.
- 12.2% of full-time workers and 5.9% of part-time workers are union members.
- 4.4% of workers ages 16–24 belong to unions, as do 9.7% of workers ages 25–34, 12.3% of workers ages 35–44, 13.6% of workers ages 45–54, 14.3% of workers ages 55–64, and 9.5% of workers ages 65 and older.
- Occupations in which relatively high percentages of workers belong to unions are government (35.2% belong to a union); transportation and utilities (19.3%); natural resources, construction, and maintenance (15%); and production, transportation, and material moving (14.2%).
- Occupations that have relatively low percentages of unionized workers are agricultural workers (1.2%), financial services (1.3%), professional and business services (2.5%), leisure and hospitality (3.1%), and wholesale and retail trade (4.6%).

EXHIBIT 17-3 The Five Largest American Unions in 2014

Union	Membership
National Education Association	2,963,000
Service Employees International Union	1,893,000
American Federation of State, County, and Municipal Employees	1,337,000
International Brotherhood of Teamsters	1,305,000
United Food and Commercial Workers International Union	1,274,000

the long run by driving firms into bankruptcy or by blocking the new technologies and production methods that lead to economic growth. Let's start here with some facts about union membership in the United States.

Facts about Union Membership and Pay

About 11% of all U.S. workers belong to unions. As Exhibit 17-2 shows, the percentage of workers belonging to a union is higher for men than women, higher for blacks than for whites or Hispanics, higher for people in the 45–64 age range, and higher among workers in government and manufacturing than workers in agriculture or service-oriented jobs. Exhibit 17-3 provides a list of the five largest U.S. labor unions and their membership.

In terms of pay and number of jobs, U.S. unions offer a good news/bad news story. The good news for unions is that their members earn about 20% more than nonunion members, even after adjusting for factors such as years of work experience and education level. The bad news for unions is that the share of U.S. workers who belong to a labor union has been steadily declining for 50 years, as shown in Exhibit 17-4. About one-quarter of all U.S. workers belonged to a union in the mid-1950s, but only 11% of U.S. workers are union members today. If you leave out workers employed by the government (which includes teachers in public schools), only 6.7% of the workers employed by private firms now belong to a union. The next section analyzes the higher pay for unions, and the following section analyzes declining union membership levels, two issues that will allow us to discuss many aspects of how unions work.

Higher Wages for Union Workers

Why might union workers receive higher pay? What are the limits on how much higher pay they can receive? To analyze these questions, let's consider a situation where, because

EXHIBIT 17-4 Percentage of Wage and Salary Workers Who Are Union Members

The share of wage and salary workers who belong to unions rose sharply in the 1930s and 1940s, but has tailed off since then to about 11% of all workers.

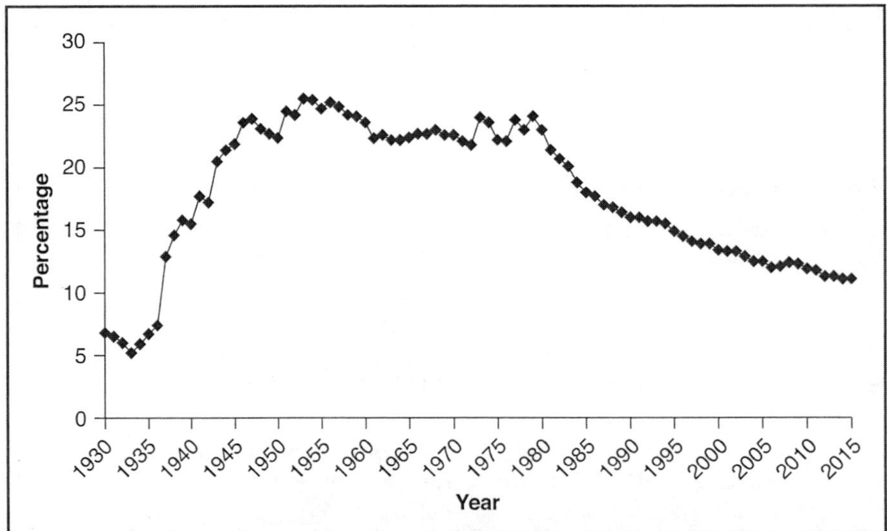

of some combination of laws that requires bargaining with unions and existing labor contracts, all firms in an industry must negotiate with a single union, and no firm is allowed to hire nonunion labor. If no labor union existed in this market, then equilibrium E in the labor market would occur at the intersection of the demand for labor D and the supply of labor S in Exhibit 17-5. But the union can threaten that unless firms agree to the wages they demand, the workers will strike. As a result, the labor union manages to achieve through negotiations with the firms a union wage of w_u for its members, above what the equilibrium wage would otherwise have been.

This labor market situation resembles what a monopoly firm does in selling a product, but in this case it is a union acting as a "monopoly" in selling labor to firms. At the higher union wage w_u, the firms in this industry will hire less labor than they would have hired in equilibrium. Moreover, an excess supply of workers will wish to take union jobs, but firms will not be hiring for such jobs.

From the union point of view, those workers who receive higher wages are better off. However, notice that the quantity of workers q_d hired at the union wage w_u is less than the quantity q_e that would have been hired at the original equilibrium wage. A sensible union must recognize that when it pushes up the wage, it also reduces the incentive of firms to hire. This situation doesn't necessarily mean that union workers are fired. Instead, it may be that when union workers move on to other jobs or retire, their jobs aren't always replaced. Or perhaps when a firm expands production, it expands employment somewhat less with a higher union wage than it would have done with the lower equilibrium wage.

EXHIBIT 17-5 Union Wage Negotiations

Without a union, the equilibrium at E would have involved the wage w_e and the quantity of labor q_e. However, the union is able to use its bargaining power to raise the wage to w_u. The result is an excess supply of labor for union jobs; that is, a quantity of workers q_s would like to work for a union firm at the wage w_u, but the firms will only demand a quantity of workers q_d at that wage.

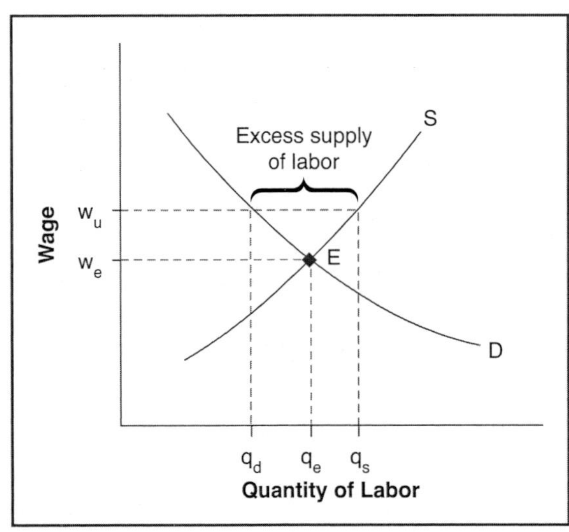

Or perhaps firms decide to purchase certain inputs from nonunion producers, rather than producing them with their own highly paid unionized workers.

From the firms' point of view, the key question is whether the higher wage of union workers is matched with higher productivity. If so, then the firm can afford to pay the higher union wages; if not, then the higher union wage will cause lower profits or losses for the firm. Union workers might have higher productivity than nonunion workers for a number of reasons. For example, union workers tend to stay longer at a given job, a trend that reduces the employer's costs for training and hiring and leads to workers with more years of experience. Many unions also offer job training, which can raise productivity.

In addition, firms that are confronted with union demands for higher wages may choose their production methods so that they use more physical capital and less labor. Exhibit 17-6 provides an example. Assume that a firm can produce a home exercise cycling machine with three different combinations of labor and machines. Say that labor is paid \$16/hour and machines cost \$200 each. Then the total cost of producing a home exercise cycle will be lowest if the firm adopts the technology of 50 hours of labor and one machine, as the table shows. Now suppose that a union negotiates a wage of \$20/hour. In this case, the firm is indifferent between the total cost of the three technologies, but it might prefer to use more machines and to hire fewer union workers. (After all, machines never threaten to strike.) In the final column of the table, the wage has risen to \$24/hour. In this case, the incentives of the firm are clearly to use the technology that involves hiring 30 workers and using three machines. If management responds to union demands for higher wages by investing more in machinery, then union workers can be more productive because they are working with more or better physical capital equipment than the typical nonunion worker.

The willingness of unions to adopt new technology has been questioned. In some cases, unions have discouraged the use of labor-saving physical capital equipment—out of the reasonable fear that new machinery would reduce the number of union jobs. For example, in 2002, the union representing longshoremen who unload ships and the firms that operate shipping companies and port facilities experienced a work stoppage that shut down the ports on the western coast of the United States. A key issue in the dispute was the desire of the shipping companies and port operators to use handheld scanners for record-keeping and computer-operated cabs for loading and unloading ships, while the union opposed these changes.

On the other side, unions have sometimes proved quite willing to adopt new technologies. In the 1950s and 1960s, to cite one prominent example, the United Mineworkers Union demanded that companies install labor-saving machinery in the mines. The mineworker's union realized that the new machines would reduce the number of jobs in the mines over time, but the union leaders also knew that jobs could only pay higher wages if the workers became more productive, and mechanization was a necessary step to that greater productivity. In fact, union workers may in some cases be more willing to accept new technology than nonunion workers because the union workers believe that the union will negotiate to protect their jobs and wages, while nonunion workers may have a greater fear that the new technology will replace their job. Overall, it is hard to make a definitive

EXHIBIT 17-6 Three Production Function Choices to Make a Home Exercise Cycling Machine

Hours of Labor	Number of Machines	Labor		
		\$16/hour	*\$20/hour*	*\$24/hr*
30	3	480 + 600 = 1,080	600 + 600 = 1,200	720 + 600 = 1,320
40	2	640 + 400 = 1,040	800 + 400 = 1,200	960 + 400 = 1,360
50	1	800 + 200 = 1,000	1,000 + 200 = 1,200	1,200 + 200 = 1,400

When the Ports Closed

A dispute ignited in 2002 between the Pacific Maritime Association, which represents 80 shipping companies and operators of shipping terminals, and the International Longshore and Warehouse Union, which represents 10,500 workers at 29 ports from San Diego to Seattle on the West Coast of the United States.

The previous contract between management and the union had expired. In the new contract, the port operators and shipping companies wanted to introduce new technologies like optical scanners, so that less information would need to be entered by hand as cargo moved on and off ships. Management also wanted to use computerized crane cabs to speed up and cut the costs of loading and unloading of ships. Finally, management also wanted to hold down the costs of pensions and health care benefits. The union would only agree to accept the new technologies—which would have reduced the number of union jobs by several hundred—if certain other jobs at the ports became part of the union, like previously nonunion jobs that involved planning where shipping containers will be placed within ships. Moreover, the union wanted to maintain and increase wages and benefits.

The negotiations turned nasty. Port operators accused the longshoremen of deliberately working slowly and responded by shutting down the ports for 10 days. The port closings affected several hundred ships and by some estimates were costing the U.S. economy $1 billion per day.

On October 9, 2002, President George W. Bush invoked the Labor Management Relations Act of 1947—commonly known as the "Taft-Hartley law." One provision of the Act allows the president to ask a court to end a work stoppage and require firms and workers to get back to work for 80 days. This "cooling-off period," as it is called, both seeks to limit the economic damage that a work stoppage can cause to the rest of the economy, and also to create some time for labor negotiations to proceed without the work stoppage looming over the talks. Bush's action was the 36th time that Taft-Hartley had been invoked by a U.S. president to create a cooling-off period.

Federal mediators were called in, and the two sides agreed to a deal in November 2002. The ultimate agreement allowed the new technologies, but also kept wages, health, and pension benefits high for workers. In the past, presidential use of the Taft-Hartley law has sometimes made labor negotiations more bitter and argumentative, but in this case, it seems to have smoothed the road to an agreement.

case that union workers as a group are always either more or less welcoming to new technology than are nonunion workers.

Perhaps the strongest evidence that union workers are more productive is that in many markets where firms with union labor compete with firms that have nonunion labor, profits don't appear to be lower for the firms with union labor. At least in some cases, although not in all, the higher productivity of union workers does compensate for their higher wages.

The Decline in U.S. Union Membership

Economists have offered a number of possible explanations for why the proportion of U.S. workers belonging to unions has declined so dramatically since the early 1950s: (1) the shift from manufacturing to service industries; (2) the force of globalization and increased competition from foreign producers; (3) a reduced desire for unions because of the workplace protection laws now in place; and (4) a U.S. legal environment that makes it relatively more difficult for unions to organize workers and expand their membership. Let's consider these four explanations in turn.

A first possible explanation for the decline in the share of U.S. workers belonging to unions involves the patterns of job growth in the manufacturing and service sectors of the economy, shown in Exhibit 17-7. The U.S. economy had about 15 million manufacturing jobs in 1960. This total rose a bit to 19 million by the late 1970s and had declined to 12 million by 2015. Meanwhile, the number of jobs in service industries and in government combined rose from 35 million in 1960 to about 120 million by 2015. Because unions were historically stronger in manufacturing than in service industries, the growth in jobs wasn't happening where the unions were. Several of the biggest unions in the country are made up of government workers, including the American Federation of State,

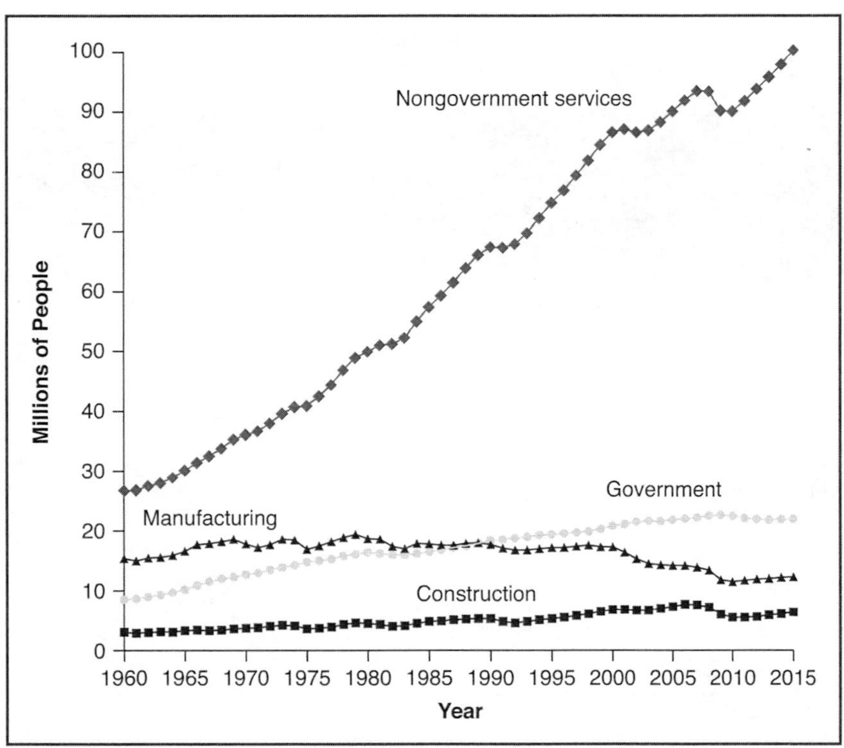

EXHIBIT 17-7 The Growth of Service Jobs

Jobs in services have increased dramatically in the last few decades. Jobs in government have increased modestly. Jobs in manufacturing have not changed much, although they have trended down in recent years.

County, and Municipal Employees (AFSCME); the Service Employees Union; and the National Education Association (whose memberships were listed earlier in Exhibit 17-3). But outside of government employees, unions have not had great success organizing the service sector.

A second explanation for the decline in the share of unionized workers focuses on patterns of international trade. Starting in the 1960s, U.S. carmakers and steelmakers faced increasing competition from Japanese and European manufacturers. As sales of imported cars, steel, and other products increased, union membership in these industries declined. For example, membership in the United Autoworkers union was 975,000 in 1985 but had fallen to 710,000 by 2000. In contrast, unions have performed relatively well at organizing public-sector workers, who are not threatened by import competition. By 2015, 35% of government workers belonged to unions. However, import competition can't be the entire story. Again, union membership has stayed very low in service industries, although many service industries like real estate or banking experience little import competition.

A third possible reason for the decline of unions focuses on how modern workers seek to address their problems. Instead of forming a union, workers often call upon their elected representatives to pass laws about work conditions, overtime, parental leave, regulation of pensions, and other issues like those addressed by the workplace protection laws in Exhibit 17-1. Unions offered political support for many of these laws aimed at protecting workers, but in an ironic twist, those laws then made many workers feel less need for unions.

These first three reasons for the decline of unions are all somewhat plausible, but they share a common problem. Most other developed economies have experienced similar economic and political trends, like the shift from manufacturing to services, globalization, and increasing government social benefits and regulation of the workplace. Yet in other countries, the share of the population belonging to unions is very high by U.S. standards. Exhibit 17-8 shows the proportion of workers in a number of the world's high-income economies who belong to unions. The share of American workers belonging to unions is near the bottom, along with France and Spain. However, in many countries, the wages of many workers who do not officially belong to a union are still determined by collective bargaining between unions and firms. The last column shows "union coverage," defined as those workers whose wages are largely determined by a union negotiation even if the

EXHIBIT 17-8 International Comparisons of Union Membership and Coverage in 2013

Country	Union Density: Percentage of Workers Belonging to a Union	Union Coverage: Percentage of Workers Whose Wages Are Determined by Union Bargaining
Austria	27.8%	98.0%
France	7.7%	98.0%
Germany	18.1%	57.6%
Japan	17.8%	17.1%
Netherlands	17.8%	84.8%
Spain	16.9%	77.6%
Sweden	67.7%	89.0%
United Kingdom	25.8%	29.5%
United States	10.8%	11.9%

workers don't officially belong to the union. In the United States, union membership is almost identical to union coverage. But in a number of other countries, unions effectively determine the wages of many workers who don't actually belong to the union.

These international differences in union membership suggest a fourth reason for the decline of union membership in the United States: perhaps U.S. laws are less friendly to the formation of unions than such laws in other countries. The close connection between union membership and a friendly legal environment is apparent in the history of U.S. unions. The great rise in union membership in the 1930s followed the passage of the National Labor-Management Relations Act of 1935, which specified that workers had a right to organize unions and that management had to give them a fair chance to do so. The U.S. government strongly encouraged unions to be formed in the early 1940s from a belief that unions would help to coordinate the all-out production efforts needed during World War II. However, after World War II came the passage of the Taft-Hartley Act of 1947, which gave states the power to allow workers to opt out of the union in their workplace if they so desired. This law made the legal climate less encouraging for unions, and union membership levels soon started declining.

The procedures for forming a union differ substantially from country to country. For example, in the United States, when a group of workers wish to form a union, they announce this fact and an election date is set when the employees at a firm will vote in a secret ballot on whether to form a union. Supporters of the union lobby for a "yes" vote, and the management of the firm often hires consultants to lobby for a "no" vote. In Canada, by contrast, a union is formed when a sufficient proportion of workers (usually about 60%) sign an official card saying that they want a union. There is no separate "election date." The management of Canadian firms is limited by law in its ability to lobby against the union. In short, forming unions is easier in Canada—and in many other countries—than in the United States. Thus, the declining share of workers belonging to unions may be because U.S. laws are less friendly to the formation of unions than laws of other countries.

Concluding Thoughts about the Economics of Unions

The economic analysis of unions, as is true of many issues, doesn't end up with blanket conclusions that they are automatically good or bad. Instead, economic insights are often phrased as "if . . . then. . . ." If unions push up wages, then employers will seek out ways of hiring fewer union workers. If unions block new technology, go on strike repeatedly, or negotiate so aggressively for higher wages that they injure the long-term health of firms, then they may be economically harmful. However, if unions help workers to feel more secure, be better trained and more flexible, and communicate better with management, then unions may be economically beneficial. There is little evidence that countries with high union membership tend to suffer economic damage as a result, nor that the reduction in U.S. union membership over time has brought broad benefits or costs for the U.S. economy as a whole. The study of unions and their economic effects needs to focus on specific situations, not on generalities. Economists are less interested in judging unions than they are in analyzing and understanding their patterns of pay and employment.

Employment Discrimination

Discrimination involves acting on the belief that members of a certain group have lesser ability solely because of a factor like their race, gender, or religion. Discrimination can arise in social circumstances, and also in goods, labor, and financial capital markets. Discrimination in goods markets would occur when a woman ends up paying a higher price at a car dealership than a man would have paid, or when a realtor steers a Hispanic family away from buying a home in a certain neighborhood. Discrimination in financial capital markets would arise if a bank is willing to make a loan to a white family with certain economic characteristics, but would deny the loan to a black family with those same economic characteristics. The focus here will be on race and gender discrimination in labor markets, which arises if workers with the same skill levels—say, as measured by education, experience, and expertise—receive different pay..

Earnings Gaps by Race and Gender

A possible signal of labor market discrimination is when one group is paid less than another. Exhibit 17-9 shows the average wages of black workers as a fraction of the average wage of white workers and the average wages of women workers as a fraction of the average wage of male workers. The gap between the earnings of women and men has declined since about 1980. Overall, the gap between the earnings of blacks and whites has overall declined a little since the late 1970s, but not by a large amount. In both gender and race, a substantial earnings gap remains.

But an earnings gap, in and of itself, does not prove that discrimination is occurring in the labor market. Instead, gender discrimination in the labor market means that women are paid less than men *given comparable levels of education, experience, and expertise.* Similarly, racial discrimination in the labor market exists when blacks are paid less than whites *with comparable levels of education, experience, and expertise.* Let's consider some evidence on such differences.

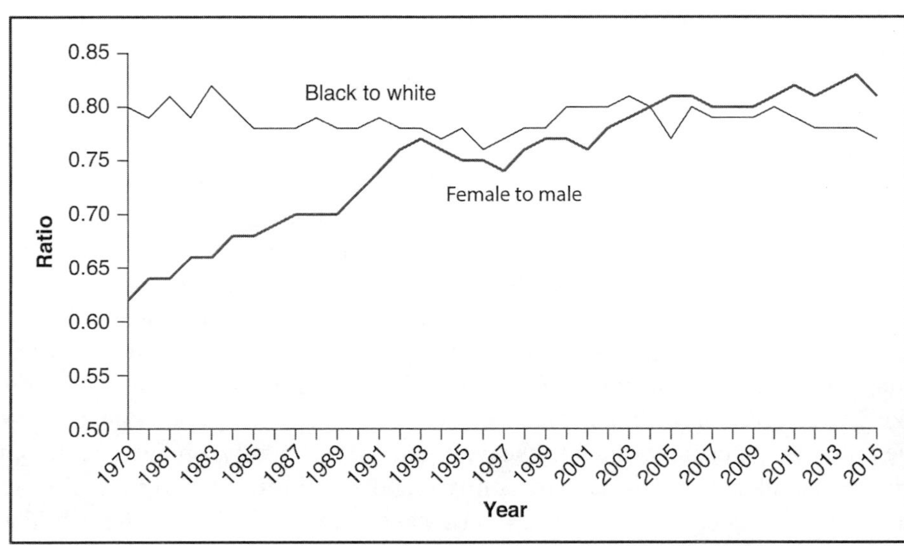

EXHIBIT 17-9 Wage Ratios by Sex and Race

Overall, the ratio of wages for black and white workers has declined a little since the late 1970s. The ratio of wages for female and male workers rose substantially since the 1980s and has continued to rise since then. In both cases, a gap remains between the average wages of black and white workers and between the average wages of female and male workers.

The U.S. Supreme Court Declares Women Workers Unequal

In 1903, the state of Oregon passed a law stating that no woman would be allowed to work more than ten hours in a day. In a 1905 case, the U.S. Supreme Court held that a law limiting male workers to a 10-hour day and a 60-hour week was unconstitutional because it was "an unreasonable, unnecessary, and arbitrary interference with the right and liberty of the individual" to make contracts with an employer. But in *Muller v. State of Oregon*, the U.S. Supreme Court ruled in 1908 that such a law was acceptable if it applied only to women. Using language that today would be laughable, the Supreme Court wrote:

> That woman's physical structure and the performance of maternal functions place her at a disadvantage in the struggle for subsistence is obvious. . . . [B]y abundant testimony of the medical fraternity continuance for a long time on her feet at work, repeating this from day to day, tends to injurious effects upon the body, and as healthy mothers are essential to vigorous offspring, the physical well-being of woman becomes an object of public interest and care in order to preserve the strength and vigor of the race.
>
> Still again, history discloses the fact that woman has always been dependent upon man. . . . Even though all restrictions on political, personal and contractual rights were taken away, and she stood, so far as statutes are concerned, upon an absolutely equal plane with him, it would still be true that she is so constituted that she will rest upon and look to him for protection; that her physical structure and a proper discharge of her maternal functions—having in view not merely her own health, but the well-being of the race—justify legislation to protect her from the greed as well as the passion of man. The limitations which this statute places upon her contractual powers, upon her right to agree with her employer as to the time she shall labor, are not imposed solely for her benefit, but also largely for the benefit of all. Many words cannot make this plainer. The two sexes differ in structure of body, in the functions to be performed by each, in the amount of physical strength, in the capacity for long-continued labor, particularly when done standing, the influence of vigorous health upon the future well-being of the race, the self-reliance which enables one to assert full rights, and in the capacity to maintain the struggle for subsistence. This difference justifies a difference in legislation and upholds that which is designed to compensate for some of the burdens which rest upon her.

Investigating the Female/Male Earnings Gap

Labor market discrimination against women was open and legal for much of the twentieth century. For example, in the 1950s, newspaper help-wanted advertisements were often split into separate sections for men and for women. Social customs also discouraged women, especially married women, from working. Indeed, many firms and local school boards had explicit "marriage bar" rules until the 1950s that single women would be fired if they married and that married women would not be hired. In 1960, 35% of adult women held jobs, while 79% of adult men did.

But as a result of changes in law and culture, women began to enter the paid workforce in substantial numbers. In 2014, 57% of adult women held jobs while 69% of adult men did. Moreover, women began to ratchet up their education levels. In 1971, 43% of undergraduate college degrees went to women; by 2013, women received 62% of bachelor's degrees. In 1970, women received 5.4% of the degrees from law schools and 8.4% of the degrees from medical schools. By 2013, women were receiving 48% of the medical degrees, and 47% of the law degrees. Concerns remain about the extent to which women have not yet assumed a substantial share of the positions at the top of the largest companies or in the U.S. Congress. But the job market experience and education levels of women workers have expanded very substantially in recent decades.

However, even in the twenty-first century, U.S. women are likely to bear a disproportionately large share of household responsibilities. A mother of young children is more likely to drop out of the labor force for several years or work on a reduced schedule than is the father. As a result, women in their 30s and 40s are likely, on average, to have less job experience than men. Because of family responsibilities, women may also have a more difficult time focusing their energy on a career. In the United States, childless women with the same education and experience levels as men are typically paid comparably. However, women with families and children are typically paid about 10–15% less than other women of similar education and work experience. (Meanwhile, married men earn about 10–15% *more* than single men with comparable education and work experience.)

Thus, in the 1960s and 1970s, women who had not previously worked in the paid labor force started taking such jobs in large numbers, encouraged by changes in both social customs and law. At first, this trend led to large numbers of women in the labor market with relatively little job experience because they had just started recently, so the earnings gap between men and women barely budged. But by the 1980s, women workers had increased their educational levels and had built up their job experience, and the earnings gap began to close. The remaining gap in earnings seems to be largely explained by the fact that women continue to shoulder a larger share of family responsibilities, and thus have less work experience. The different patterns of family responsibilities might reasonably be called "discrimination," but it is primarily rooted in America's social patterns of discrimination that involve the roles that fathers and mothers play in child-rearing, rather than discrimination by employers in hiring and salary decisions.

Investigating the Black/White Earnings Gap

Blacks experienced open labor market discrimination during much of the twentieth century. Until the passage of the Civil Rights Act of 1964, it was legal in many states to refuse to hire a black worker, regardless of the credentials or experience of that worker. Moreover, blacks were often denied access to educational opportunities, which in turn meant that a disproportionate share of blacks had lower levels of qualifications for many jobs. A number of economic studies have shown that the 1964 Act is partially responsible for the narrowing of the gap in black/white earnings in the late 1960s and into the 1970s; for example, the ratio of total earnings of black male workers to white male workers rose dramatically from 0.62 in 1964 to 0.72 by 1975.

However, the earnings gap between black and white workers has moved up and down without changing dramatically since the 1980s. The remaining gap seems related both to continuing differences in education levels and to the presence of discrimination. Exhibit 17-10 shows that the percentage of blacks who complete a four-year college degree remains substantially lower than the percentage of whites. Both whites and blacks have higher levels of educational attainment than Hispanics but lower than those of Asians. The lower average levels of education for black workers surely explain part of the earnings gap. In fact, black women who have the same levels of education and experience as white women receive on average about the same level of pay. However, black men with the same levels of education and experience as white men are paid 12–15% less than white men, an outcome that suggests the possibility of continuing discrimination.

The lower levels of education for black workers can also be a result of discrimination—although it may be social discrimination, rather than direct discrimination by employers in the labor market. For example, if discrimination in housing markets causes low-income black families to live clustered together in certain neighborhoods, then the public schools that serve these neighborhoods may be overwhelmed with students who need additional help. When blacks were effectively barred from many high-paying jobs, getting additional education could have seemed somewhat pointless because the educational degrees were

EXHIBIT 17-10 Educational Attainment by Race and Ethnicity in 2015

Whites are more likely than blacks or Hispanics to complete college. However, Asians are more likely than whites to complete college.

	White	Hispanic	Black	Asian
Completed four years of high school or more	93.3	66.7	87.0	89.0
Completed four years of college or more	36.2	15.5	22.5	53.9

Audit Studies of Discrimination

Some of the most persuasive evidence that outright prejudicial discrimination continues in the U.S. economy comes from *audit studies*, in which pairs of people of different genders or races are assigned made-up characters with essentially identical economic characteristics, like income level and job experience. They receive training in how to respond to interview questions so that they will respond in the same ways. Then the pairs of individuals—perhaps one black and one white, or one male and one female—are sent out to apply for the same job, to buy a comparable house or car, or apply for a bank loan for the same amount of money. The results of these studies are disquieting.

A 1989 Housing Discrimination Study carried out audit studies over 20 metropolitan areas and found that blacks and Hispanics were often shown fewer places to buy and rent, were quoted higher prices, and were simply not shown certain available dwellings in mainly white neighborhoods. Similarly, in a 1997 audit study done in San Antonio, a Hispanic woman and a white woman who had been assigned very similar jobs and incomes applied for the same two-bedroom apartment. The Hispanic women was quoted a rent of $670/month with a $200 security deposit, while a white female was quoted a rent of $616/month and a $100 security deposit.

In a 2004 study, fictional resumes were sent to employers in Boston and Chicago, some with white-sounding names and some with black-sounding names. About 10% of the white-sounding names got a callback based on their resume, compared with 6% for the black-sounding names. The study also found that improved credentials, such as increased years of education and job experience, have less of an effect on callback rates for black-sounding names than for white-sounding names.

In the United States of the twenty-first century, nondiscrimination may be the ideal, but audit studies continue to demonstrate that it is not always the reality.

not likely to pay off. Even when labor market discrimination has been legally abolished, it can take some time to establish a tradition of valuing education highly. In these ways, a legacy of past discrimination may contribute to an attitude that blacks will have a difficult time succeeding in academic subjects. In any case, the impact of social discrimination in labor markets is more complicated than seeking to punish a few bigoted employers.

Competitive Markets and Discrimination

Gary Becker (1930–2014), who won the Nobel Prize in economics in 1992, was one of the first to analyze discrimination in economic terms. Becker pointed out that while competitive markets can allow some employers to practice discrimination, they can also provide profit-seeking firms with incentives not to discriminate. For example, if a business located in an area with a large minority population refuses to sell to minorities, it will cut into its own profits. If some businesses run by bigoted employers refuse to pay women and/or minorities a wage based on their productivity, then other profit-seeking employers can hire these workers, pay them a little more, and make a profit. Overall, if the owners of a business care more about the color of money than about the color of skin, they will have an incentive to make buying and selling and hiring and promotion decisions strictly based on economic factors.

The power of markets to offer at least a degree of freedom to oppressed groups should not be underestimated. In many countries, cohesive minority groups like Jews and emigrant Chinese have managed to carve out a space for themselves through their economic activities, despite legal and social discrimination against them. Many immigrants, including those who come to the United States, have taken advantage of economic freedom to make new lives for themselves. However, history teaches that market forces alone are unlikely to eliminate discrimination. After all, discrimination against African-Americans persisted in the market-oriented U.S. economy during the century between President Abraham Lincoln's Emancipation Proclamation that freed the slaves in 1863 and the passage of the Civil Rights Act of 1964—and has continued since then, too.

Gary Becker also sought to explain why market forces may not always reduce discrimination. Discriminatory impulses can emerge at a number of levels: among managers, among workers, and among customers. Consider the situation of a manager who is not personally prejudiced, but has many workers or customers who are prejudiced. If that manager treats minority groups or women fairly, the manager may find it hurts the morale of prejudiced co-workers or drives away prejudiced customers. In such a situation, a policy of nondiscrimination could reduce the firm's profits. After all, a business firm is part of society, and a firm that does not follow the social norms is likely to suffer. Market forces alone are unlikely to overwhelm strong social attitudes about discrimination.

Public Policies to Reduce Discrimination

A first public policy step against discrimination in the labor market is to make it illegal. For example, the Equal Pay Act of 1963 said that men and women who do equal work at a company must be paid the same. The Civil Rights Act of 1964 prohibits employment discrimination based on race, color, religion, sex, or national origin. The Age Discrimination in Employment Act of 1967 prohibits discrimination on the basis of age against individuals who are 40 years of age or older. The Civil Rights Act of 1991 provides monetary damages in cases of intentional employment discrimination. But passing a law is only part of the answer, since discrimination by prejudiced employers may be less important than broader social patterns.

In the case of the earnings gap between men and women, probably the single largest remaining cause is the differences in family responsibilities assumed by mothers and fathers. Sweden, for example, offers nearly a year of parental leave from work after the birth of a child, and child care is almost entirely paid for by tax dollars rather than by parents. By U.S. standards, these policies may seem extreme. However, without shifts in attitudes by men and women about home and child responsibilities, the U.S. labor market is likely to continue showing a wage gap between men and women.

In the case of the earnings gap between blacks and whites (and also between Hispanics and whites), probably the single largest step at this point in U.S. history would be to reduce the gap in educational achievement. Part of the answer involves finding ways to improve the performance of schools, which is a controversial topic in itself. But in addition, the education gap won't close unless black and Hispanic families and peer groups strengthen their culture of support for educational achievement.

Affirmative action is the name given to active efforts to improve the job opportunities or outcomes of minority groups or women. Affirmative action in its limited and not especially controversial form means making an effort to reach out to a broader range of minority candidates for jobs. In its more aggressive and controversial form, affirmative action might require businesses to set specific numerical targets or quotas for the percentages of minorities and women that the firms will hire and promote. Those who favor numerical goals argue that without hard results, the affirmative action will be more talk than action. Those opposed to numerical targets question how numerical goals are set. Surely, they say, it is not reasonable that every employer, for every job, in every area of the economy, should hire a statistical cross-section of the U.S. population. The critics also point out that numerical targets can cause resentment and backlash among other workers, who may be quick to assume that the successes of minorities and women are due to affirmative action policies rather than merit. The affirmative action controversy seems likely to continue simmering.

affirmative action: Active efforts to improve the job opportunities or outcomes of minority groups or women.

An Increasingly Diverse Workforce

Racial and ethnic diversity is on the rise in the U.S. population and work force. Exhibit 17-11 shows that while white Americans composed 69.4% of the population in 2000, the U.S. Bureau of the Census projects that whites will be less than half of the U.S. population by 2060. The proportion of U.S. citizens who are of Hispanic and Asian background will rise substantially. Moreover, the women who entered the workforce in the 1970s and 1980s and since then are moving up the promotion ladders within their organizations.

Fortune-telling isn't economics, but it still can be clarifying to speculate about the future. Optimists argue that the growing proportions of minority workers and highly

EXHIBIT 17-11 Projected Changes in Racial and Ethnic Diversity of U.S. Population

	2000	2014	2060
White alone (not Hispanic)	69.4%	62.2%	43.6%
Black alone	12.7%	13.2%	14.3%
Hispanic alone	12.6%	17.4%	28.6%
Asian alone	3.8%	5.4%	9.3%
All other races	2.5%	2.5%	3.1%

experienced and educated women will knock over remaining discriminatory barriers. The economy will benefit as an increasing proportion of workers from traditionally disadvantaged groups have a greater opportunity to fulfill their potential. Pessimists worry that the social tensions between men and women, and between ethnic groups, will rise and that workers will be less productive as a result. Anti-discrimination policy at its best seeks to help society move toward the more optimistic outcome.

Immigration

Most Americans would be outraged if a law prevented them from moving to another city or another state. But when the conversation turns to crossing national borders, and other people arriving in the United States, laws preventing such movement often seem more reasonable. Some of the tensions over immigration stem from worries over how it might affect a country's culture, including differences in language, and patterns of family, authority, or gender relationships. Economics doesn't have much to say about such cultural issues. But some of the worries about immigration have to do with its effects on wages and income levels, and how it affects government taxes and spending. On those topics, economists have insights and research to offer.

Historical Patterns of Immigration

Supporters and opponents of immigration look at the same data and see different patterns. Those who express concern about immigration levels to the United States point to Exhibit 17-12, which shows total inflows of immigrants decade by decade through the twentieth century. Clearly, the level of immigration has been high and rising in recent years, about as many as the towering levels of the early twentieth century. However, those who are less worried about immigration point out that the high immigration levels of the early twentieth century happened when total population was much lower. Because the U.S. population roughly tripled during the twentieth century, the seemingly high levels of immigration in the 1990s and 2000s would look relatively smaller if they were divided by the existing population at the time.

Where have the immigrants come from? Immigrants from Europe were more than 90% of the total in the first decade of the twentieth century, but less than 20% of the total by the end of the century. At the start of the 2000s, about half of U.S. immigration was coming from the rest of the Americas, especially Mexico, and about a quarter from various countries in Asia. By 2014, 42% of U.S. immigration was coming from Asia (including China and India) and 39% from the rest of North or South America.

Economic Effects of Immigration

A surge of immigration can affect the economy in a number of different ways. Here, we will consider how immigrants might benefit the rest of the economy, how they might affect wage levels, and how they might affect government spending at the federal and local level.

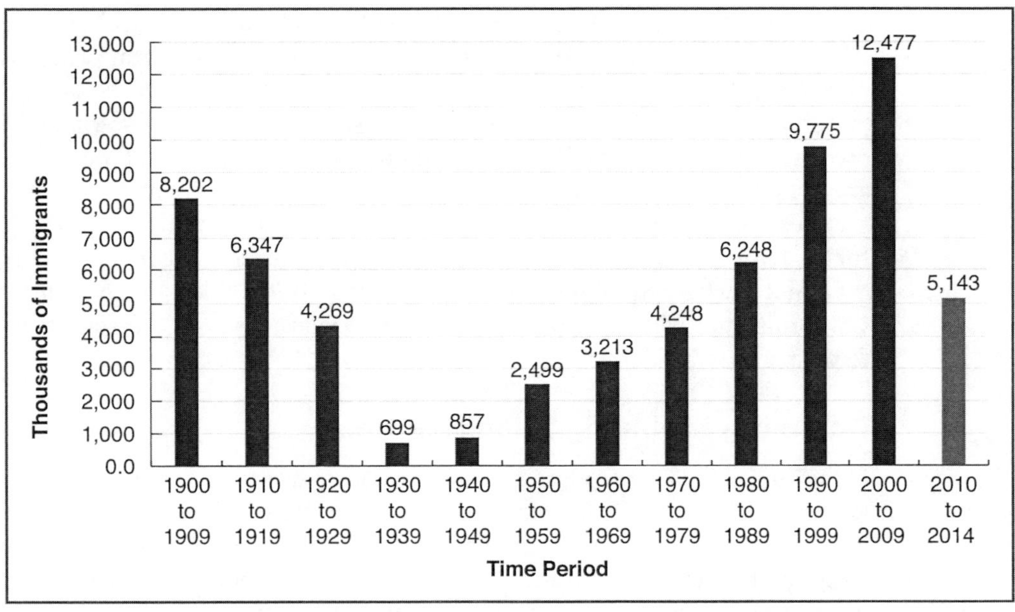

EXHIBIT 17-12 Immigration since 1900

The number of immigrants each decade declined in the middle of the twentieth century but has been at higher levels in recent decades.

To understand the economic consequences of immigration, consider the following scenario. Imagine that the immigrants entering the United States looked exactly like the existing U.S. population in terms of the range of ages, education, skill levels, family size, occupations, and so on. How would immigration of this type affect the rest of the U.S. economy? Immigrants themselves would be much better off because their standard of living would be higher in the United States. However, the pre-existing population would not be much benefited or harmed by this type of immigration. The reason is that the range of jobs performed, income earned, taxes paid, and public services needed would not be much affected by this kind of immigration. It would be as if the population was a little larger but had the same overall mix of characteristics.

Now consider the reality of recent immigration to the United States. Immigrants are *not* identical to the rest of the U.S. population. About one-third of immigrants over the age of 25 lack a high school degree. As a result, many of the recent immigrants end up in jobs like restaurant and hotel work, lawn care, and janitorial work. This kind of immigration represents a shift to the right in the supply of unskilled labor for a number of jobs, which will lead to lower wages for these jobs. The middle- and upper-income households that purchase the services of these unskilled workers will benefit from these lower wages. However, low-skilled U.S. workers who must compete with low-skilled immigrants for jobs will tend to suffer from immigration. A study commissioned some years ago by the prestigious and nonpartisan National Academy of Sciences estimated these gains and losses from immigration and found that, overall, immigration brings gains to the U.S. economy of $10 billion per year. In your checking account, that's a lot of money; in the context of the $15 trillion U.S. economy, $10 billion is less than one-tenth of 1%, which is barely noticeable.

The difficult policy questions about immigration are not so much about the overall gains to the rest of the economy, which seem to be real but small in the context of the U.S. economy, as they are about the disruptive effects of immigration in producing those gains. One disruptive effect, as just noted, is that immigration weighted toward low-skill workers tends to reduce wages for domestic low-skill workers. The effects on wages of low-skill workers are not large—perhaps in the range of decline of about 1%, and some studies find no effect at all—but any policy that provides gains to those with higher incomes and may impose costs on those with lower incomes deserves to be looked at twice, or even three times.

Another disruptive effect affects the budgets of state and local government. Many of the costs imposed by immigrants are costs that arise in state-run programs, like the cost of public schooling and of welfare benefits. However, many of the taxes that immigrants pay are federal taxes like income taxes and Social Security taxes. Many immigrants don't own property, so they don't pay property taxes, which are one of the main sources of state and local tax revenue. A number of studies have found that when all taxes paid and public services consumed are taken into account, the average immigrant brings an overall gain for the federal budget, but an overall cost for the state and local budget. In certain areas of the country where immigrants are highly concentrated, like some major cities in southern California, and parts of Texas along the Mexican border, these state and local costs can feel especially burdensome.

Proposals for Immigration Reform

In the 1990s, the U.S. Congress established a bipartisan U.S. Commission on Immigration Reform (CIR) to report to Congress on immigration policy. The commission was chaired by Barbara Jordan, a former member of the House of Representatives from Texas, and is often referred to as the "Jordan Commission." The commission issued several reports in the mid-1990s on a wide variety of immigration issues. Several of its recommendations were aimed at addressing the issues of the costs that immigration imposes on low-skill workers and on state and local governments.

For example, the Jordan Commission proposed reducing overall levels of immigration and refocusing U.S. immigration policy to give priority to immigrants with a higher level of skills. In the labor market, focusing on high-skilled immigrants would help prevent any negative effects on the wages of low-skilled workers. For government budgets, higher-skilled workers find jobs more quickly, earn higher wages, and pay more in taxes. Several other immigration-friendly countries, notably Canada and Australia, have immigration systems where those with high levels of education or job skills have a much better chance of obtaining permission to immigrate. Another proposal from the Jordan Commission was that the federal government could recognize that certain local governments are having their finances sorely tested by new immigrant arrivals, and that the national government could pick up some of the tab, too.

If the United States decided to reduce immigration substantially, the economic losses would be small relative to the overall economy. If the United States decided to increase immigration substantially, the U.S. economy certainly is large enough to afford some additional assistance to low-wage workers or to local governments that might be adversely affected by immigration. But whether immigration levels are increased, decreased, or left the same, the quality of the debate over immigration policy would be improved by an explicit recognition of who receives economic benefits from immigration and who bears its costs.

Conclusion

Many of the arguments about workplace protection are conducted in terms of claims about human rights and justice. The freedom of workers to organize into a union is often considered a basic human right, as is the right to be free of discrimination on the basis of race or sex. Arguments in favor of immigration often invoke the image of the Statue of Liberty welcoming newcomers to the United States.

Economic analysis steers away from these philosophical arguments and insists on digging down to specifics. The laws governing unions, and the unions themselves, can operate in many different ways. Addressing earnings gaps in the labor market may begin with laws against labor market discrimination, but must also consider patterns of social discrimination. Immigration is not a public policy question that can be addressed with a yes or a no, but instead requires arguments about how many and which people will be allowed to enter. Since the big philosophical questions are important, economic analysis will not provide a definitive answer to questions involved in workplace protection. But economic analysis can nonetheless illuminate the trade-offs involved in any specific policy choice.

Key Concepts and Summary

1. Employers have an advantage in bargaining with employees because it's usually easier for an employer to replace or do without a single employee than it is for an employee to find another job or be unemployed.
2. A **labor union** is an organization of workers that negotiates as a group with employers over compensation and work conditions.
3. Union workers in the United States are paid more on average than other workers with comparable education and experience. Thus, either union workers must be more productive to match this higher pay, or the higher pay will lead employers to find ways of hiring fewer union workers than they otherwise would.
4. American union membership has been falling for decades. Some possible reasons include the shift of jobs to service industries, greater competition from globalization, the passage of worker-friendly legislation, and U.S. laws that are less favorable to organizing unions.
5. Discrimination occurs in a labor market when workers with the same economic characteristics like education, experience, and skill are paid different amounts because of race, gender, religion, age, or disability status.
6. In the United States, female workers on average earn less than male workers, and black workers on average earn less than white workers. There is controversy over the extent to which these earnings gaps can be explained by discrimination or by differences in factors like education and job experience.
7. Free markets can allow discrimination to occur, but the threat of a loss of sales or a loss of productive workers can also create incentives for a firm not to discriminate.
8. A range of public policies can be used to reduce earnings gaps between men and women or between white and other racial/ethnic groups: requiring equal pay for equal work, attaining more equal educational outcomes, providing greater support for mothers in the workforce, and **affirmative action**.
9. The recent level of U.S. immigration is at a historically high level if measured in absolute numbers, but appears somewhat lower if measured as a share of population.
10. The overall gains to the U.S. economy from immigration are real but relatively small. However, immigration also causes effects like slightly lower wages for low-skill workers and budget problems for certain state and local governments.

Review Questions

1. Why do employers have a natural advantage in bargaining with employees?
2. Why can't employers use their bargaining advantage over workers to push wages very close to zero?
3. What is a labor union?
4. How does the presence of a labor union change the negotiation that occurs between employers and workers?
5. Would you expect labor unions to lead to higher or lower pay for their workers? A higher or lower quantity of workers hired by those employers? Explain briefly.
6. What is the long-term trend in American union membership?
7. Describe how the earnings gap between men and women has evolved in recent decades.
8. Describe how the earnings gap between blacks and whites has evolved in recent decades.
9. Does a gap between the average earnings of men and women, or between whites and blacks, prove that employers are discriminating in the labor market? Explain briefly.
10. Will a free market tend to encourage or discourage discrimination? Explain briefly.
11. What policies, when used together with antidiscrimination laws, might help to reduce the earnings gap between men and women or between white and black workers?
12. What is affirmative action in the labor market?
13. Have levels of immigration to the United States been relatively high or low in recent years?
14. How would you expect immigration by primarily low-skill workers to affect American low-skilled workers?

CHAPTER

18

Information, Risk, and Insurance

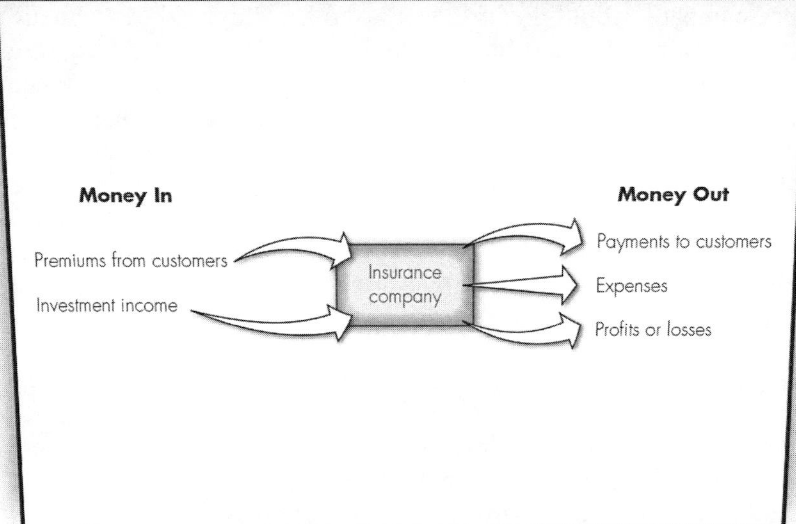

Chapter Outline

Every purchase is based on a belief about the satisfaction that will be provided by the good or service. In turn, these beliefs are based on the information that the buyer has available. But for many products, the information available to the buyer and the seller is imperfect or unclear, which can either make buyers regret past purchases or avoid making future ones.

Consider a purchase that many people make at important times in their lives: buying expensive jewelry. Most buyers face a situation of imperfect information when they buy gemstones.

The U.S. Federal Trade Commission warns on its website that many gemstones are treated or enhanced, for example: "heating can lighten, darken, or change the color of some gemstones, or improve a stone's clarity"; "irradiation can add color to colored diamonds, certain other gemstones, and pearls"; "Impregnating some gemstones with colorless oils, wax, or resins hides a variety of imperfections"; "fracture filling hides cracks in gemstones through an injection of colorless plastic or glass"; "diffusion treatment adds color to the surface . . . the center of the stone remains colorless"; "dying adds color and improves color uniformity in some gemstones and pearls"; "bleaching lightens and whitens some gemstones, including jade and pearls." Such treatments can sometimes alter the stone in undesirable ways. For example, emeralds often have internal flaws, and so they are often soaked in clear oil or an epoxy resin to hide the flaws and to deepen and clarify the color. But clear oil can leak out over time, and epoxy resin can discolor with age or heat. Many gemstones, such as rubies and sapphires, are heated in a furnace to improve their color and transparency, but one result is that the stones become more brittle, and thus the sharp edges of the stones can become scratched more easily. Diamond, topaz, and tourmaline are often irradiated to enhance their colors. The general rule is that all treatments to gemstones should be disclosed, along with the consequences of the treatments for the appearance and value of the stone—but either because the seller is dishonest or just doesn't know, such disclosure often doesn't happen.

This chapter discusses how imperfect information affects markets. The first major section of the chapter discusses how imperfect information affects markets for goods, labor, and financial capital. When buyers have imperfect information about a good, such as a gemstone, for example, sellers will be tempted to mislead buyers about quality. But if a buyer cannot have at least some confidence in the quality of what is being purchased, then buyers will be reluctant or unwilling to purchase such products. Thus, buyers and sellers will try to create mechanisms to bridge this information gap. The second part of the chapter discusses insurance markets, which also face problems of imperfect information. For example, a car insurance company would prefer to sell insurance only to those who are unlikely to have auto accidents, but it's hard for the firm to identify those perfectly safe drivers. Conversely, buyers of car insurance would like to persuade the auto insurance company that they are safe drivers and should pay only a low price for insurance, even when the particular driver is inexperienced, careless, or worse. If insurance markets cannot find ways to grapple with these problems of imperfect information, then even people who have low or average risks of making claims may be unable to purchase insurance. The next chapter will focus on financial markets, such as the markets for stocks and bonds, where the problems of imperfect information can be especially vivid. Imperfect information cannot be eliminated, but it can often be managed.

The Problem of Imperfect Information

imperfect information: A situation where the buyer or the seller, or both, are uncertain about the qualities of what is being bought and sold.

Many economic transactions are made in a situation of **imperfect information**, where either the buyer or the seller, or both, are less than 100% certain about the qualities of what is being bought and sold. Let's begin here with some examples of how imperfect information complicates transactions in goods, labor, and financial capital markets. The presence of imperfect information can easily cause a decline in prices or quantities of products sold. However, buyers and sellers also have incentives to create mechanisms that will allow them to make mutually beneficial transactions even in the face of imperfect information.

"Lemons" and Other Examples of Imperfect Information

Consider Marvin, who is trying to decide whether to buy a used car. Let's assume that Marvin is truly clueless about what happens inside a car's engine. He's willing to do some background research, like reading *Consumer Reports* or checking websites that offer information about makes and models of used cars and what they should cost. He might pay a mechanic to inspect the car. But even after devoting some money and time to collecting information, Marvin still can't be absolutely, positively sure that the car he is buying is a good value. He knows that he might buy the car, drive it home, and use it for a few weeks before discovering that the car is a "lemon," which is slang for an item (especially a car) that does not live up to expectations.

Imagine that Marvin, worried about getting stuck with a lemon, shops for used cars and finds two that appear very similar. One car costs just about what he expects this make and model to cost, while the other costs only half as much. Which car should Marvin buy? (Pause for a moment. If you were Marvin, which car would *you* buy?)

If Marvin were choosing in a world of perfect information, the answer would be simple. If he had perfect information to reveal that the two cars are equal in quality, he would buy the cheaper car. But Marvin is making a decision in a world of imperfect information, and so he must worry that the far-cheaper car is so much less expensive for a reason—that is, it is a lemon that the seller is trying to unload. With this concern in mind, Marvin's decision is no longer simple. Marvin might figure that the safer choice is to buy the used car that is selling for the expected price, even though it looks identical to him and costs more than the alternative, because he is fearful of getting stuck with a lemon and spending months in repair shops. Alternatively, Marvin might also decide that the half-price car has a low enough price to be worth the risk that it is a lemon. In either case, the presence of imperfect information complicates Marvin's decision and may even discourage him from buying at all.

Similar problems with imperfect information arise in labor and financial capital markets. Consider Greta, who is applying for a job. Her potential employer, like the used car buyer, is concerned about ending up with a lemon—in this case, a poor-quality employee rather than a car that breaks down frequently. The employer will collect information about Greta's academic and work history. In the end, however, a degree of uncertainty will inevitably remain with regard to Greta's abilities. Will she be a competent worker, or will she be a lemon? After all, resumes never tell the whole story. If the potential employer doesn't feel as if Greta has communicated enough information to show that she will be a good employee, then Greta may receive only an offer with a low salary—or no job offer may be extended at all.

Imagine a small business, Shorty's Trucking and Hauling, that wants to borrow some money from a local bank to buy a new truck and expand its business. The bank must worry over whether the loan will be a lemon—that is, whether the loan will be repaid on time. The bank will ask Shorty to fill out forms about his business: sales, profits, customers. The bank will also check Shorty's past record: has he repaid previous loans on time? But even if Shorty's Trucking and Hauling appears to be a profitable business that has repaid loans in the past, information about whether it will be able to repay in the future remains imperfect. Unless the bank is sufficiently persuaded, Shorty will not receive a loan.

How Imperfect Information Can Affect Equilibrium Price and Quantity

The presence of imperfect information can discourage both buyers and sellers from participating in the market. Buyers may become reluctant to participate because they can't be confident of purchasing a high-quality product. They will only pay a low price, if they are willing to buy at all. Sellers of high-quality or medium-quality goods may become reluctant to participate because they know that it will be difficult to demonstrate the quality of their goods to buyers—and because buyers can't perceive which goods have higher quality, they will be unwilling to pay a higher price for such goods.

A market with few buyers and few sellers is sometimes referred to as "thin"; by contrast, a market with many buyers and sellers is called a "thick" market. When imperfect information is severe and buyers and sellers are discouraged from participating, markets may become extremely thin as a relatively small number of buyers and sellers attempt to communicate enough information that they can agree on a price.

When Price Mixes with Imperfect Information about Quality

A buyer confronted with imperfect information will often believe that the price being charged reveals something about the quality of the product. For example, a buyer may assume that a gemstone or a used car that costs more must be of higher quality, even though the buyer is not expert enough to know why. Think of the expensive restaurant where the food *must* be good because it is so expensive, or the shop where the clothes *must* be stylish because they cost so much, or the gallery where the art *must* be great because it costs so much. If you are hiring a lawyer, you might assume that a lawyer who charges $400 per hour must be better than a lawyer who charges $150 per hour. If you have imperfect information, it's logical to make such connections between price and quantity: after all, you reason, even if I don't know much about used cars, some other buyers have more information, and the car dealer or the restaurant or the lawyer couldn't expect to charge more unless their goods and services were of higher quality.

But when buyers use the market price to draw inferences about the quality of products, then markets may have trouble reaching an equilibrium price and quantity. Imagine a situation where a used car dealer has a lot full of used cars that don't seem to be selling, and so the dealer decides to cut the prices of the cars to sell a greater quantity. In a market with imperfect information, many buyers may assume that the lower prices imply low-quality cars. As a result, the lower prices may not attract more customers. Conversely, a dealer who raises prices may find that customers assume that the higher prices mean that cars are of higher quality; as a result of raising prices, the dealer might sell more cars.

The idea that higher prices might cause a greater quantity demanded and that lower prices might cause a lower quantity demanded runs exactly counter to the basic model of demand and supply. These contrary effects will reach some natural limits. At some point, if the price is jacked up sky-high, the quantity demanded will surely decline. Conversely, if the price becomes dirt-cheap, at some point it will make sense for buyers to take a chance on low quality. In addition, information eventually becomes more widely known. An overpriced restaurant that charges more than the quality of its food is worth to many buyers won't last forever. But at least for a time, imperfect information can lead to a situation where, even if sellers are faced with a situation of excess supply, they will decide not to cut prices because they know that buyers reacting to imperfect information will not react by purchasing a higher quantity.

Mechanisms to Reduce the Risk of Imperfect Information

If you were selling a good like emeralds or used cars where imperfect information is likely to be a problem, how could you reassure possible buyers? (If you were buying a good where imperfect information is a problem, what would it take to reassure you?) Buyers and sellers in goods, labor, and financial capital markets have a long list of mechanisms to provide such reassurance: guarantees, warrantees, service contracts, and reputation in goods markets; occupational licenses and certification in labor markets; and cosigners and collateral in capital markets. Let's consider these in turn.

money-back guarantee: A promise that the buyer's money will be refunded under certain conditions, like if the product doesn't work or sometimes even if the buyer decides to return the product.

warranty: A promise to fix or replace the good, at least for a certain period of time.

service contract: The buyer pays an extra amount and the seller agrees to fix anything that goes wrong for a set time period.

In the goods market, the seller of a good might offer a **money-back guarantee**, an agreement that functions as a promise of quality. This strategy may be especially important for a company that sells goods through mail-order catalogs or over the web, whose customers can't see the actual products, because it encourages people to buy something even if they aren't certain they want to keep it.

Sellers may offer a **warranty**, which is a promise to fix or replace the good, at least for a certain period of time. The seller may also offer a buyer a chance to buy a **service contract**, where the buyer pays an extra amount and the seller agrees to fix anything that goes wrong for a set time period. Service contracts often cover large purchases like cars and appliances, but they are also offered as part of buying a home—that is, if anything in the house breaks down in the first year, the seller will fix it at no additional charge.

Guarantees, warranties, and service contracts are examples of explicit reassurance that sellers provide. In many cases, firms also offer unstated guarantees. For example, some movie theaters might refund the cost of a ticket to a customer who walks out complaining

Money-Back Guarantees and Imperfect Information

One way to reassure a buyer who is facing a situation of imperfect information is to offer a money-back guarantee. Many firms offer such guarantees for a few weeks or months. But L.L. Bean, a company based in Freeport, Maine, that sells outdoor wear and equipment, has offered a complete money-back guarantee since the firm was founded in 1912. Anything you have bought from L.L. Bean can always be returned, no matter how many years later or what condition the product is in, for a full money-back guarantee.

A story at the firm is that when the company's founder first decided to start a company in 1911, he stitched together some waterproof shoe rubbers to leather shoe tops, and sold them as hunting shoes. He guaranteed satisfaction. But the stitching came apart, and out of the first batch of 100 pairs that were sold, 90 pairs were returned. L.L. Bean took out a bank loan, repaired all of the shoes, and replaced them. The L.L. Bean reputation for customer satisfaction began to spread.

L.L. Bean has very few bricks-and-mortar stores. Instead, most of its sales are made by mail, telephone, or web-based orders. For this kind of firm, imperfect information may be an especially difficult problem because customers can't see and touch what they are buying. A combination of a money-back guarantee and a reputation for quality can help a mail-order firm to flourish.

about the show. Likewise, while many restaurants do not advertise a money-back guarantee or exchange policies, many restaurants allow customers to exchange one dish for another, or if a customer is dissatisfied with a meal, the restaurant will take the charge for the meal off of the customer's bill. (Helpful hint: If you devour a meal first and then complain about it afterward, it is less likely that you will receive a replacement or a refund.)

The reason behind these policies is that if a firm hopes to attract repeat customers, who in turn will recommend the business to others, it must be concerned about establishing a good reputation. When buyers know that a firm is concerned about its reputation, they are less likely to worry about receiving a poor-quality product. For example, a well-established grocery store with a good reputation can often charge a higher price than a temporary stand at a local farmer's market, where the buyer may never see the seller again.

Sellers in the labor market—that is, people looking for work—provide information through resumes, recommendations, school transcripts, and examples of their work. Another method of providing reassurance about quality in the labor market involves **occupational licenses**, which are licenses issued by government agencies, which mean that a worker has completed a certain type of education or passed a certain test. Some of the professionals who must hold a license are teachers, nurses, engineers, accountants, and lawyers. In addition, most states require a license to work as a barber, an embalmer, a dietitian, a massage therapist, a hearing aid dealer, a counselor, an insurance agent, and a real estate broker. Some other jobs require a license in only one state. Minnesota requires a state license to be a field archeologist; North Dakota has a state license for bait retailers. In Louisiana, a state license is needed to be a "stress analyst," and California requires a state license to be a furniture upholsterer. About one-fifth of U.S. workers have jobs that require occupational licenses.

occupational licenses: Licenses issued by government agencies that mean that a worker has completed a certain type of education or passed a certain test.

On the buyer's side of the labor market, a standard precaution against hiring a "lemon" of an employee is to specify that the first few months of employment are officially a trial period, and that the worker can be let go for any reason or no reason after that time. Sometimes workers also receive lower pay during this trial period.

Advertising and Imperfect Information

Many advertisements seem full of imperfect information—at least by what they imply. Driving a certain car, or drinking a particular soda, or wearing a certain shoe are all unlikely to bring fashionable friends and fun automatically, if at all. The government rules on advertising, enforced by the Federal Trade Commission, allow advertising to contain a certain amount of exaggeration about the general delight of using a product. But they also demand that if a claim is presented as a fact, it must be true.

A classic case of legally deceptive advertising from the 1950s occurred when Colgate-Palmolive created a television ad that claimed to show Rapid Shave shaving cream being spread on sandpaper, and then the sand was shaved off the sandpaper. But what the TV ad showed was sand sprinkled on Plexiglas—without glue—and then scraped aside by the razor.

In the 1960s, in magazine ads for Campbell's vegetable soup, the company was having problems getting an appetizing picture of the soup because the vegetables kept sinking. So they filled a bowl with marbles and poured the soup over the top, so that the bowl appeared to be crammed with vegetables.

In the late 1980s, the Volvo company filmed a TV ad that showed a monster truck driving over cars, crunching their roofs—all except for the Volvo, which did not crush. However, the FTC found in 1991 that the roof of the Volvo had been reinforced with an extra steel framework, while the roof supports on the other car brands had been cut.

The Wonder Bread company ran TV ads featuring "Professor Wonder," who said that because Wonder Bread contained extra calcium, it would help children's minds work better and improve their memory. The FTC objected, and in 2002 the company agreed to stop running the ads.

In short, factual claims about what products can do are checked to some extent by the Federal Trade Commission. But language and images that are exaggerated or ambiguous but not actually false are allowed in advertising. An old Latin saying applies when watching advertisements: *Caveat emptor*—that is, "let the buyer beware."

In the financial capital market, before a bank makes a loan, it tries to collect relevant information by having a prospective borrower fill out forms regarding the sources of income and by doing a credit check on the individual's past borrowing. Another approach is to require a **cosigner** on a loan—that is, another person or firm that legally pledges to repay some or all of the money if the original borrower does not do so. Yet another approach is to require **collateral**, which is something valuable—often property or equipment—that the bank would have a right to seize and sell if the loan is not repaid.

cosigner: On a loan, another person or firm that legally pledges to repay some or all of the money if the original borrower does not do so.

collateral: Something valuable—often property or equipment—that a lender would have a right to seize and sell if the loan is not repaid.

Buyers of goods and services cannot possibly become experts in evaluating the quality of gemstones, used cars, lawyers, and everything else they buy. Employers and lenders cannot be perfect fortune-tellers about whether possible workers will turn out well or potential borrowers will repay loans on time. But these mechanisms can reduce the risk associated with imperfect information by enough so that the buyer and seller are willing to proceed.

Insurance and Imperfect Information

An **insurance** system works like this: a group of people all make regular payments, called **premiums**, and then those members of the group who suffer a specified bad experience receive payments from this pool of money. Many people have several kinds of insurance: health insurance that pays when they receive medical care, car insurance that pays in the case of an auto accident, house or renter's insurance that pays if possessions are stolen or damaged by fire, and life insurance for their family if they die. Exhibit 18-1 lists a set of insurance markets.

insurance: A group of people who face a risk of a certain bad experience all make regular payments, and those members of the group who actually suffer a bad experience receive payments.

premiums: Payments made to an insurance company.

All insurance involves imperfect information in both an obvious way and in a deeper way. At an obvious level, future events can't be predicted with certainty. For example, it cannot be known with certainty who will have a car accident, or become ill, or die, or have their home robbed in the next year. But imperfect information also applies to estimating the risk that something will happen to any individual. It's difficult for an insurance company to estimate the risk that, say, a particular 20-year-old male driver from New York City will have an accident, because even within that group, some drivers will drive more safely than others. Thus, adverse events occur out of a combination of people's characteristics and choices that make the risks higher or lower, and then the good or bad luck of what actually happens.

How Insurance Works

A simplified example of automobile insurance might work this way. Suppose that a group of 100 drivers can be divided into three groups. In a given year, 60 of those people have

EXHIBIT 18-1 Some Insurance Markets

Type of Insurance	Who Pays for It?	It Pays Out When . . .
Health insurance	Employers and individuals	Medical expenses are incurred.
Life insurance	Employers and individuals	Policyholder dies.
Auto insurance	Individuals	Car is damaged or stolen, or causes damage to others.
Property and homeowner's insurance	Homeowners and renters	Dwelling is damaged or burglarized.
Liability insurance	Firms and individuals	An injury occurs for which you are partly responsible.
Malpractice insurance	Doctors, lawyers, and other professionals	A poor quality of service is provided that causes harm to others.

only a few door dings or chipped paint, which costs $100 each. Another 30 of the drivers have medium-sized accidents that cost an average of $1,000 in damages, and 10 of the drivers have large accidents that cost $15,000 in damages. For the moment, let's imagine that at the beginning of any year, there is no way of identifying which drivers are low risk, medium risk, or high risk. The total damage incurred by car accidents in this group of 100 drivers will be $186,000 (that is, [60 × $100] + [30 × $1,000] + [10 × $15,000]). If each of the 100 drivers pays a premium of $1,860 each year, the insurance company will collect the $186,000 that is needed to cover the costs of the accidents that occur.

Insurance companies have one major source of income other than insurance premiums and one additional set of costs other than benefits payouts, as Exhibit 18-2 shows. The other additional source of income is investment income, which the insurance company receives from investing premiums that it has received in the past. Insurance companies need to plan ahead for the possibility of major disasters. The U.S. government's National Climatic Data Center found that from 2000 to 2015, the United States experienced 113 weather-related disasters that caused at least $1 billion in damages. For example, Hurricane Katrina caused $153 billion in damages and 1,833 deaths in Louisiana, Mississippi, and nearby states in 2005, while Superstorm Sandy caused $67 billion in damages and 159 deaths in 2012. Thus, insurance companies typically build up reserves, which are funds not paid out as insurance claims in the current year, so that they will have funds to pay off losses when costly disasters do occur. In the meantime, the insurance company receives a rate of return from making financial investments with these reserves.

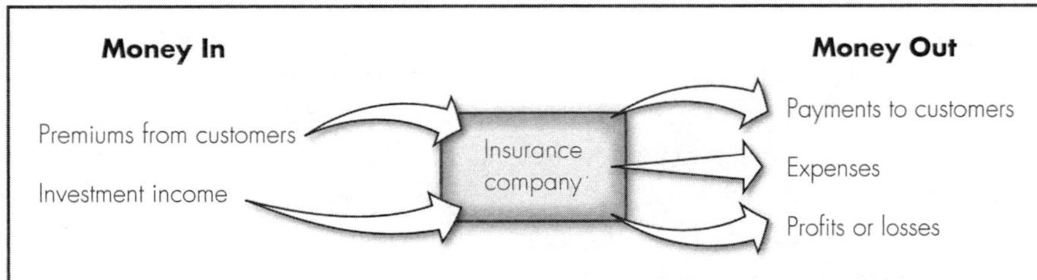

EXHIBIT 18-2 An Insurance Company: What Comes In, What Goes Out

Government and Social Insurance

Federal and state governments run a number of insurance programs. Some of the programs look much like private insurance, in the sense that the members of a group make steady payments into a fund, and those in the group who suffer an adverse experience receive payments. Other programs protect against risk, but without an explicit fund being set up. Here are some examples.

- *Unemployment insurance:* Workers in every state have a small amount deducted from their paychecks for unemployment insurance, which goes into a fund that is used to pay benefits to workers for a period of time, usually six months, after they lose their jobs.
- *Pension insurance:* Employers that offer pensions to their retired employees are required by law to pay a small fraction of what they are setting aside for pensions to the Pension Benefit Guarantee Corporation, which is used to pay at least some pension benefits to workers if a company goes bankrupt and cannot pay the pensions it has promised.
- *Deposit insurance:* Banks are required by law to pay a small fraction of their deposits to the Federal Deposit Insurance Corporation, which goes into a fund that is used to pay depositors the value of their bank deposits up to $250,000 if the bank should go bankrupt.
- *Workman's compensation insurance:* Employers are required by law to pay a small percentage of the salaries that they pay into funds, typically run at the state level, that are used to compensate benefits to workers who suffer an injury on the job.
- *Retirement insurance:* All workers contribute a percentage of their income into Social Security and into Medicare, which then provides income and health-care benefits to the elderly. Social Security and Medicare are not literally "insurance" in the sense that those currently contributing to the fund are not eligible for benefits. But they function like insurance in the sense that regular payments are made into the programs today in exchange for benefits to be received in the case of a later event—either becoming old or becoming sick when old. Such programs are sometimes called "social insurance."

The major additional costs to insurance companies, other than the payment of claims, are the costs of running a business: the administrative costs of hiring workers, administering accounts, and processing insurance claims. For most insurance companies most of the time, the insurance premiums coming in and the claims payments going out are much larger than the amounts earned by investing money or the administrative costs.

Thus, while factors like investment income earned on reserves, administrative costs, and groups with different risks complicate the overall picture, a fundamental law of insurance must hold true: What the average person pays into insurance over time must be very similar to what the average person gets out, with relatively minor variations caused by the investment income of the insurance company and the costs of running the system.

Risk Groups and Actuarial Fairness

risk group: A group that shares roughly the same risks of an adverse event occurring.

Not all of those who purchase insurance face the same risks. Some people may be more likely, because of genetics or personal habits, to fall sick with certain diseases. Some people may live in an area where car theft or home robbery is more likely than others. Some drivers are safer than others. A **risk group** can be defined as a group that shares roughly the same risks of an adverse event occurring.

Insurance companies often classify people into risk groups and charge lower premiums to those with lower risks. If people are not separated into risk groups, then those with low risk must pay equal premiums as those with high risk. In the simple example of how car insurance works given earlier, 60 drivers had very low damage of $100 each, 30 drivers had medium-sized accidents that cost $1,000 each, and 10 of the drivers had large accidents that cost $15,000. If all 100 of these drivers pay the same $1,860, then those with low damages are in effect paying for those with high damages.

If it is possible to classify drivers according to risk group, then each group can be charged according to its expected losses. For example, the insurance company might charge the 60 drivers who seem safest of all $100 apiece, which is the average value of the damages they cause. Then the intermediate group could pay $1,000 apiece and the high-cost group $15,000 each. When the level of insurance premiums that someone pays is equal to the amount that an average person in that risk group would collect in insurance payments, the level of insurance is said to be "actuarially fair."

Classifying people into risk groups can be controversial. For example, if someone had a major auto accident last year, should that person be classified as a high-risk driver who is likely to have similar accidents in the future, or as a low-risk driver who was just extremely unlucky? The driver is likely to claim to be low risk, and thus someone who should be in a risk group with those who pay low insurance premiums in the future. The insurance company is likely to believe that, on average, having a major accident is a signal of being a high-risk driver, and thus try to charge this driver higher insurance premiums. The next two sections discuss the two major problems of imperfect information in insurance markets—called moral hazard and adverse selection. Both problems arise from attempts to categorize those purchasing insurance into risk groups.

The Moral Hazard Problem

moral hazard: When people have insurance against a certain event, they are less likely to guard against that event occurring.

The **moral hazard** problem arises because when people have insurance against a certain event, they are less likely to guard against that event occurring. For example, if you have health insurance that covers the cost of visiting the doctor, you are more likely to make a doctor's appointment every time you feel an ache or a sniffle. If you have car insurance, you will worry less about driving or parking your car in ways that make it more likely to get dented. In short, the presence of insurance against an event makes that event more likely to occur.

The word "moral" at the start of "moral hazard" may seem to imply that adjusting one's behavior to the presence of insurance is dishonest or wrong, but this conclusion is only sometimes true. The most extreme cases of moral hazard are those of outright insurance fraud; say, someone lies to the police that jewelry was stolen from their home and claims reimbursement from the insurance company, or someone puts a dent in their own car, claims that an accident occurred, and gets a new paint job when the car is repaired. But in other cases, the moral issue of moral hazard is more subtle. If you are applying for health insurance, and you know that your family has a rare genetic disorder that makes a certain disease more likely, are you morally required to tell the insurance company? Even though you know that the insurance company is likely to react by charging you a higher premium or refusing to sell you health insurance at all? In still other cases, moral hazard is about the level of protection that one takes against risk. A business without insurance might install absolute top-level security and fire sprinkler systems to guard against theft and fire. After buying insurance, that same business might only install a minimum level of security and fire sprinkler systems.

Moral hazard cannot be eliminated, but insurance companies have some ways of reducing its effect. Investigations to prevent insurance fraud are one way of reducing the extreme cases of moral hazard. Insurance companies can also monitor certain kinds of behavior; to return to the example of a moment ago, they might offer a business a lower rate on property insurance if the business installs a top-level security and fire sprinkler system and has those systems inspected once a year.

Another method to reduce moral hazard is to require the injured party to pay a share of the costs. For example, insurance policies often have **deductibles**, which is an amount that the insurance policyholders must pay out of their own pocket before the insurance coverage kicks in. For example, auto insurance might pay for all losses greater than $500. Health insurance policies often have a **copayment**, in which the policyholder must pay a small amount; for example, a person might have to pay $20 for each doctor visit, and the insurance company would cover the rest. Another method of cost-sharing is **coinsurance**, which means that the insurance company covers a certain percentage of the cost. For example, insurance might pay for 80% of the costs of repairing a home after a fire, but the homeowner would pay the other 20%.

deductible: An amount that the insurance policyholders must pay out of their own pocket before the insurance coverage pays anything.

copayment: When an insurance policyholder must pay a small amount for each service, before insurance covers the rest.

coinsurance: When an insurance policyholder pays a percentage of a loss, and the insurance company pays the remaining cost.

All of these forms of cost-sharing discourage moral hazard because people know that that they will have to pay something out of their own pocket when they make an insurance claim. The effect can be powerful. One prominent study found that when people face moderate deductibles and copayments for their health insurance, they consume about one-third less medical care than people who have complete insurance and don't pay anything out of pocket—presumably because deductibles and copayments reduce the level of moral hazard. However, those who consumed less health care didn't seem to have any difference in health status.

A final way of reducing moral hazard, which is especially applicable to health care, is to focus on the incentives of providers of health care, rather than consumers. Traditionally, most health care in the United States has been provided on a **fee-for-service** basis, which means that medical care providers are paid for the services they provide, and are paid more if they provide additional services. However, in the last decade or so, the structure of health-care provision has shifted to an emphasis on **health maintenance organizations (HMOs)**, in which health care is provided by an organization that receives a fixed amount per person enrolled in the plan—regardless of how many services are provided. In this case, a patient with insurance has an incentive to demand more care, but the health-care provider, which is receiving only a fixed payment, has an incentive to reduce the moral hazard problem by limiting the quantity of care provided— as long as it won't lead to worse health problems and higher costs later. Today, many doctors are paid with some combination of managed care and fee for service; that is, a flat amount per patient, but with additional payments for the treatment of certain health conditions.

fee-for-service: When medical care providers are paid according to the services they provide.

health maintenance organization (HMO): An organization that provides health care and is paid a fixed amount per person enrolled in the plan—regardless of how many services are provided.

Imperfect information is the cause of the moral hazard problem. If an insurance company had perfect information on risk, it could simply raise its premiums every time an insured party engaged in riskier behavior. However, an insurance company cannot monitor all the risks that people take all the time, and so even with various checks and cost-sharing, moral hazard will remain a problem.

The Adverse Selection Problem

adverse selection: The problem that arises when one party knows more about the quality of the good than the other, and as a result, the party with less knowledge must worry about ending up at a disadvantage.

Adverse selection arises when one party knows more about the quality of the good than the other, and as a result, the party with less knowledge must worry about ending up at a disadvantage. The problem of lemons in used car markets, discussed earlier in this chapter, is an adverse selection problem. In that case, a buyer of a used car typically has less information than the seller, and must be concerned about paying for a car of high or medium quality but ending up with a lemon. In the case of insurance, adverse selection arises because the buyers of insurance have more information about whether they are high risk or low risk than the insurance company does. For example, someone purchasing health insurance or life insurance probably knows more about their family's health history than an insurer can reasonably find out even with a costly investigation; someone purchasing car insurance may know that they are a high-risk driver who hasn't yet had a major accident—but it's hard for the insurance company to collect information about how people actually drive.

To understand how adverse selection can strangle an insurance market, return again to the situation of 100 drivers who are buying auto insurance, where 60 drivers have very low damages of $100 each, 30 drivers have medium-sized accidents that cost $1,000 each, and 10 of the drivers have large accidents that cost $15,000. Imagine that while the insurance company knows the overall size of the losses, it cannot identify the high-risk, medium-risk and low-risk drivers. However, the drivers themselves know their risk groups. Imagine that the insurance company sets the price of insurance at $1,860 per year, to cover the average loss. The result is that those with low risks of only $100 will decide not to buy insurance; after all, it makes no sense for them to pay $1,860 per year when they are only going to experience losses of $100. Those with medium risks of a $1,000 accident won't buy insurance either. So the insurance company ends up selling insurance for $1,860 to high risks who will average $15,000 in claims apiece—and losing a lot of money.

Thus, the problem of adverse selection in insurance markets is that if insurance companies cannot differentiate those with low and high risks, and tries to charge an insurance premium that averages together those with low risks and those with high risks, then those with low risks will avoid buying insurance and the company will be left with only the high risks—like those who are more likely to have health problems or car accidents. If the insurance company tries to raise its premiums to cover the losses of those with high risks, then those with low or medium risks will be even more discouraged from buying insurance. Rather than face such a situation of adverse selection, the insurance company may decide not to sell insurance in this market at all. If an insurance market is to exist, then one of two things must happen. First, the insurance company might find some way of separating insurance buyers into risk groups with some degree of accuracy and charging them accordingly, which in practice often means that the insurance company tries not to sell insurance to those who may pose high risks. Or second, those with low risks must be required to buy insurance, even if they have to pay more than the actuarially fair amount for their risk group. The notion that people can be required to purchase insurance raises the issue of government laws and regulations that influence the insurance industry.

Government Regulation of Insurance

The U.S. insurance industry has traditionally been regulated at the state level; indeed, since 1871 there has been a National Association of Insurance Commissioners that brings together these state regulators to exchange information and strategies. Since the passage of the Patient Protection and Affordable Care Act signed into law by President Barack Obama in 2010, health insurance has had a heavier dose of federal regulation. All insurance regulators typically attempt to accomplish two things: to keep the price of insurance low and to make sure that everyone has insurance. But these goals can conflict with each other and also can easily become entangled in politics.

U.S. Health Care in an International Context

The United States is the only high-income country in the world where most health insurance is paid for and provided by private firms. Greater government involvement in the provision of health insurance can be thought of as a way of addressing moral hazard and adverse selection problems.

The moral hazard problem with health insurance is that when people have insurance, they will demand higher quantities of health care. In the United States, private health-care insurance tends to encourage an ever-greater demand for health-care services that health-care providers are happy to fulfill. U.S. health expenditures were $3 trillion in 2014, or over 18% of the entire U.S. economy that year. The table shows that on a per-person basis, U.S. health-care spending towers above other countries.

The adverse selection problem in health insurance is that insurance companies fear that when they sell insurance, those with low risks will decide not to buy and the firm will end up selling insurance only to those with high risks. In the U.S. health insurance market, the main way of solving this adverse selection problem is that health insurance is often sold through groups based on place of employment. From an insurance company's point of view, selling insurance through an employer mixes together a group of people—some with high risks of future health problems and some with lower risks—and thus reduces the insurance firm's fear of attracting only those who have high risks. However, many small companies do not provide health insurance to their employees, and many lower-paying jobs do not include health insurance. Even after all U.S. government programs that provide health insurance for the elderly and the poor and the expanded health insurance coverage resulting from the Patient Protection and Affordable Care Act of 2010 are taken into account, roughly 30 million Americans lacked health insurance coverage in 2015. Despite the very high costs of the U.S. health-care system, the United States doesn't do better than other high-income countries on basic measures of health like longer life expectancies and lower rates of infant mortality, as shown in the table. The relatively modest U.S. health statistics shouldn't be blamed on the U.S. health-care industry. Many studies have shown that a country's health is not directly connected to its spending on medical care but is instead more closely related to diet, exercise, and genetic factors. But this fact only emphasizes further that the United States is spending very large amounts on medical care with little obvious health gain.

At its best, the largely private U.S. system of health insurance and health-care delivery provides an extraordinarily high quality of care, along with generating a seemingly endless parade of life-saving innovations. But the system also struggles to control its high costs and to provide basic medical care to all. Other countries have lower costs and more equal access, but they often struggle to provide rapid access to health care and to offer the near-miracles of the most up-to-date medical care. The challenge is a health-care system that strikes the right balance between quality, access, and cost.

Country	Health-Care Spending per Person (in 2013)	Life Expectancy at Birth in Years (in 2013)		Chance of Dying before Age 5, per 1,000 (in 2015)	
		Male	*Female*	*Male*	*Female*
United States	$9,146	77	81	7	6
Germany	$5,006	79	83	4	3
France	$4,864	79	85	4	4
Canada	$5,718	79	84	5	5
Japan	$3,966	80	87	3	3
United Kingdom	$3,598	79	83	4	4

If insurance premiums are set at actuarially fair levels, so that people end up paying an amount that accurately reflects their risk group, certain people will end up paying a lot. For example, if health insurance companies were trying to cover people who already have a chronic disease like AIDS, or who were elderly, they would charge these groups very high premiums for health insurance because their expected health-care costs are quite high. Women in the age bracket 18–44 consume, on average, about 65% more in health-care spending than men. Young male drivers have more car accidents than young female drivers; for example, among drivers aged 20 and younger, more than twice as many men as women are involved in fatal accidents. Thus, actuarially fair insurance would tend to charge young men much more for car insurance than young women. Because people in high-risk groups would find themselves charged so heavily for insurance, they might choose not to buy insurance at all.

Insurance regulators have sometimes reacted by passing rules that attempt to set low premiums for insurance. But over time, the fundamental law of insurance must hold: the average amount received by individuals must equal the average amount paid in premiums. When rules are passed to keep premiums low, insurance companies try to avoid insuring high-risk or even medium-risk parties or find ways to limit the amount of coverage provided by the insurance policies. If a legislature passes strict rules requiring insurance companies to sell to everyone at low prices, the insurance companies always have the option of withdrawing from doing business in that state. For example, the insurance regulators in New Jersey are well known for attempting to keep auto insurance premiums low, and more than 20 different insurance companies stopped doing business in the state in the late 1990s and early 2000s. Similarly, in 2009, State Farm announced that it was withdrawing from selling property insurance in Florida.

In short, government regulators can't force companies to charge low prices and provide high levels of insurance coverage—and thus take losses—for a sustained period of time. If insurance premiums are going to be set below the actuarially fair level for a certain group, some other group will have to pay to make up the difference. There are two other groups who can make up the difference: taxpayers or other buyers of insurance.

In some industries, the U.S. government has apparently decided free markets will not provide insurance at an affordable price, and so the government will pay for it directly. For example, private health insurance doesn't work well for the poor because their incomes are too low to afford it. Thus, the U.S. government together with the states runs the Medicaid program, which provides insurance to those with low incomes. Private health insurance also doesn't work well for the elderly because their average health-care costs can be very high. Thus, the U.S. government started the Medicare program, which finances health insurance for those over age 65. Other government-funded health-care programs are aimed at children in families with relatively low incomes and at military veterans.

Another common government intervention in insurance markets is to require that everyone buy certain kinds of insurance. For example, most states legally require car owners to buy auto insurance. Likewise, when a bank loans someone money to buy a home, the person is typically required to have homeowner's insurance, which protects against fire and other physical damage (like hailstorms) to the home. The Patient Protection and Affordable Care Act of 2010 contained an "individual mandate" requiring that people either obtain health insurance or pay a fine, but the provision was so controversial that it may be little enforced and thus have little effect. A legal requirement that everyone must buy insurance means that insurance companies don't need to worry that those with low risks will avoid buying insurance. Since insurance companies don't need to fear adverse selection, they can set their prices based on an average for the market, and those with lower risks will to some extent end up subsidizing those with higher risks. However, even when laws are passed requiring people to purchase insurance, insurance companies cannot be compelled to sell insurance to everyone who asks—at least not at low cost. Thus, insurance companies will still try to avoid selling insurance to those with high risks whenever possible.

Even the government cannot violate the fundamental law of insurance: that average payments going into an insurance fund must equal average payments coming out. Nor can government pass laws that make the problems of moral hazard and adverse selection disappear. But the government can make political decisions that certain groups should have insurance, even though the private market would not otherwise provide that insurance, and then the government can impose the costs of that decision on taxpayers or on other buyers of insurance.

Conclusion

The government has a wide variety of laws that seek to reduce the problem of imperfect information in markets. For example, the government requires that processed food products list their ingredients in order of importance on the outside of the package. Restaurants and workplaces are subject to government safety inspections, which reduce the imperfect information of diners about what is happening in the kitchen. Many states also have laws against fraud and deceptive or high-pressure sales tactics. These laws about providing information then combine with magazines like *Consumer Reports* or websites that discuss and compare products. Buyers and sellers have a number of ways of reducing the risks of imperfect information, too: for example, stores can offer warranties, money-back guarantees, and their reputation. Through the combined results of these factors, imperfect information can often be minimized enough that buyers and sellers can make mutually beneficial trades.

But in some markets for goods and services—like insurance markets—the problems of incomplete information are more difficult to resolve. The problems erupt into public view over issues of price and availability of insurance. For example, in 2015 auto insurance on average cost about $850 per year in Ohio and Iowa, but about $2,000 per year in Montana and Michigan—which makes auto insurance a political issue in those states. The medical-care costs of a severe accident or extensive illness can easily run into tens of thousands of dollars, which is more than most people can pay; yet tens of millions of Americans lack either private or government-provided health insurance. In these cases, economists can diagnose the problems of how moral hazard can drive up costs by encouraging those with insurance to demand more services, and how adverse selection can cause insurance companies to avoid offering insurance to many individuals. But addressing those problems will require political decisions about who receives how much insurance and who will pay the costs.

Key Concepts and Summary

1. Many economic transactions are made in a situation of **imperfect information**, where either the buyer or the seller or both are less than 100% certain about the qualities of what is being bought and sold. When information about the quality of products is highly imperfect, it may be difficult for a market to exist.
2. A "lemon" is the name given to a product that turns out, after the purchase, to have low quality. When the seller has more accurate information about the quality of the product than the buyer, the buyer will be hesitant to buy, out of fear of purchasing a lemon.
3. Markets have many ways to deal with imperfect information. In goods markets, buyers facing imperfect information about products may turn to guidebooks or product reviews, **money-back guarantees**, **warranties**, **service contracts**, and reputation. In labor markets, employers facing imperfect information about potential employees may turn to resumes, recommendations, **occupational licenses** for certain jobs, and employment for trial periods. In capital markets, lenders facing imperfect information about borrowers may require detailed loan applications and credit checks, **cosigners**, and **collateral**.
4. **Insurance** is a way of sharing risk. A group of people pay premiums for insurance against some unpleasant event, and those in the group who actually experience the unpleasant event then receive some compensation.
5. The fundamental law of insurance is that what the average person pays in over time must be very similar to what the average person gets out. In an actuarially

fair insurance policy, the premiums that a person pays to the insurance company are the same as the average amount of benefits for a person in that **risk group**.

6. **Moral hazard** arises in insurance markets because those who are insured against a risk will have less reason to take steps to avoid the costs from that risk.
7. Many insurance policies have **deductibles**, **copayments**, or **coinsurance**. A deductible is the maximum amount that the policyholder must pay out-of-pocket before the insurance company pays the rest of the bill. A copayment is a flat fee that an insurance policyholder must pay before receiving services. Coinsurance requires the policyholder to pay a certain percentage of costs. Deductibles, copayments, and coinsurance reduce moral hazard by requiring the insured party to bear some of the costs before collecting insurance benefits.
8. In a **fee-for-service** health financing system, medical care providers are reimbursed according to the cost of services they provide. An alternative method of organizing health care is through **health maintenance organizations (HMOs)**, where medical care providers are reimbursed according to the number of patients they handle, and it is up to the providers to allocate resources between patients who receive more or fewer health-care services.
9. **Adverse selection** arises in insurance markets when insurance buyers know more about the risks they face than does the insurance company. As a result, the insurance company runs the risk that low-risk parties will avoid its insurance because it is too costly for them, while high-risk parties will embrace it because it looks like a good deal to them.

Review Questions

1. Why might it be difficult for a buyer and seller to agree on a price when imperfect information exists?
2. What do economists (and used-car dealers) mean by a "lemon"?
3. What are some of the ways a seller of goods might reassure a possible buyer who is faced with imperfect information?
4. What are some of the ways a seller of labor (that is, someone looking for a job) might reassure a possible employer who is faced with imperfect information?
5. What are some of the ways that someone looking for a loan might reassure a bank that is faced with imperfect information about whether the loan will be repaid?
6. What is an insurance premium?
7. In an insurance system, would you expect each person to receive in benefits pretty much what they pay in premiums? Or is it just that the average benefits paid will equal the average premiums paid?
8. What is an actuarially fair insurance policy?
9. What is the problem of moral hazard?
10. How can moral hazard lead to insurance being more costly than was expected?
11. Define deductibles, copayments, and coinsurance.
12. How can deductibles, copayments, and coinsurance reduce moral hazard?
13. What is the key difference between a fee-for-service health-care system and a system based on health maintenance organizations?
14. What is adverse selection?
15. How might adverse selection make it difficult for an insurance market to operate?

Financial Markets

CHAPTER

19

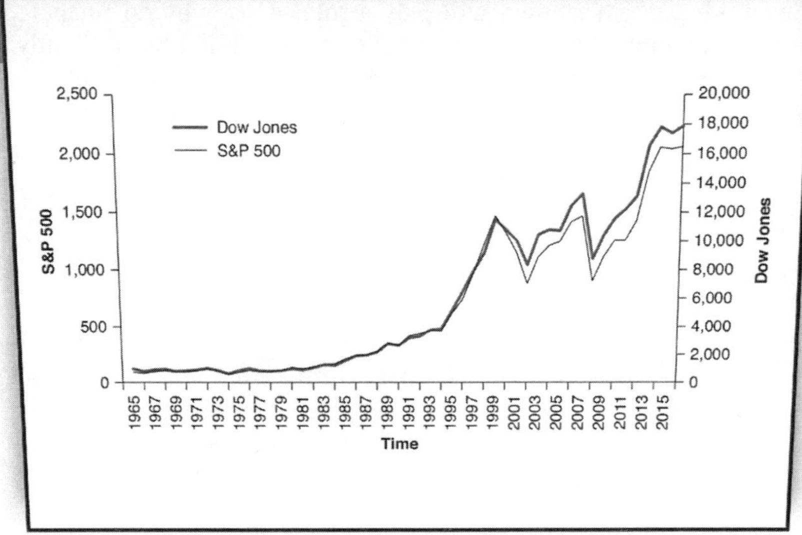

Chapter Outline

Firms need financial capital to make real physical capital investments. For example, U.S. firms invested $2.3 trillion in new equipment and structures in 2016, hoping that these investments would bring higher profits in the years ahead. But many firms, from huge companies like General Motors to a start-up firm writing computer software, don't have the financial resources within the firm to make all of the desired investments. These firms need financial capital from outside investors, and the firms are willing to pay a rate of return for that financial capital. On the other side of the financial capital market, suppliers of financial capital, like households, wish to invest their savings in a way that will provide a rate of return. But individuals cannot take the few thousand dollars that they save in any given year, write a letter to General Motors or some other firm, and negotiate to invest their money with that firm. Financial capital markets bridge this gap: that is, they find ways to take the inflow of funds from many separate suppliers of financial capital and transform it into the funds desired by demanders of financial capital. Such financial markets discussed in this chapter include stocks, bonds, bank loans, and other financial investments.

Movements in financial markets have powerful consequences for both demanders and suppliers of capital. For example, consider the Dow Jones Industrial Average (DJIA), one widely reported measure of the stock market. In 2002 and 2003, the DJIA was at about 9,000. By July 2007, the DJIA had peaked at 13,900—an increase of more than 50%. In July 2009, the DJIA had fallen all the way to 8,100. The stocks that households held in mid-2007 had lost about $6 trillion in value by early 2009. By April 2016, the DJIA had risen to above 18,000, considerably above the peak in July 2007. This kind of roller coaster ride forces households that have financial investments in the stock market to rethink major life decisions like whether to retire, or whether to buy a house, or what sort of college or university is affordable.

This chapter describes and investigates financial markets. It begins on the demand side of financial capital markets, discussing how firms raise the money they need for investments through mechanisms like venture capital, reinvesting the firm's previously earned profits, bank loans, bonds, and stocks. The perspective then shifts to consider how these financial investments appear to suppliers of capital, such as the households that are saving money. Households have a range of financial investment options: bank accounts, certificates of deposit, bonds, stocks, mutual funds, housing, and even tangible assets like gold. In choosing among these alternatives, the expected rate of return, risk, and liquidity of each kind of investment will play a role. Also, why do financial markets—and specifically stock markets—undergo periods of boom and bust? Finally, the chapter investigates two methods for becoming rich: a quick and easy and unreliable method and a method that is slower and more difficult but that over a lifetime can work quite well.

How Businesses Raise Financial Capital

Firms often make decisions that involve spending money in the present and expecting to earn profits in the future. Examples include when a firm buys a machine that will last 10 years, or builds a new plant that will last for 30 years, or starts a research and development project that won't pay off in the immediate future. Firms can raise the financial capital that they need to pay for such projects in four main ways: early-stage investors, reinvesting profits, borrowing through banks or bonds, and selling stock. When a business chooses its sources of financial capital, it is also choosing how it will need to pay a rate of return.

Early-Stage Financial Capital

Firms that are just beginning often have an idea or a prototype for a product or service to sell, but they may have few customers, or even no customers at all, and thus are not earning profits. Such firms face a difficult problem when it comes to raising financial capital: that is, how can a firm that has not yet demonstrated any ability to earn profits pay a rate of return to financial investors?

Early-stage investors provide financial capital in exchange for part-ownership of the firm. For many small businesses, the original source of money is the owner of the business. For example, people who decide to start a restaurant or a gas station might cover the costs of starting the business by dipping into their own bank account or by borrowing money (perhaps using their homes as collateral). Alternatively, many cities have a network of well-to-do individuals known as "angel investors," who decide to put their own money into small new companies at an early stage of development, in exchange for owning some portion of the firm.

venture capital: Financial investments in new companies that are still relatively small in size but that have potential to grow substantially.

Venture capital firms make financial investments in new companies that are still relatively small in size but that have potential to grow substantially. These firms gather money from a variety of individual or institutional investors, including banks, institutions like college endowments, insurance companies that hold financial reserves, and corporate pension funds. Venture capital firms do more than just supply money to small start-up firms. They also provide advice to the firm on potential products, customers, and key employees. Typically, a venture capital fund invests in a number of firms, and then investors in that fund receive returns according to how the fund as a whole performs.

The amount of money invested in venture capital fluctuates substantially from year to year: as one example, venture capital firms invested $54 billion in 2015. All early-stage investors realize that the majority of small start-up businesses will never hit it big; indeed, many of them will go out of business within a few months or years. But they also know that getting in on the ground floor of a few huge successes like Google or Amazon can make up for a lot of failures.

Profits as a Source of Financial Capital

If firms are earning profits, then they can choose to reinvest some of these profits in equipment, structures, and research and development. In 2015, total corporate profits were about $2.0 trillion, although after firms paid taxes, the remaining profits were $1.5 trillion. For many established companies, reinvesting their own profits is one primary source of financial capital.

From a firm's point of view, profits have one big shortcoming as a source of financial capital: they may not provide financial capital when the firm needs it. For example, small companies and firms just getting started may find themselves in a situation where they have numerous attractive investment opportunities, but few current profits. Even large firms can experience a year or two of earning low profits or even suffering losses, but unless the firm can find a steady and reliable source of financial capital so that it can continue making real investments in its tough times, the firm may not survive until better times arrive. Thus, firms often find themselves in situations where they desire other methods, in addition to the profits they earn, to raise financial capital for real investment.

Borrowing: Banks and Bonds

When a firm has a record of at least earning significant revenues, and better still of earning profits, the firm can then make a credible promise to pay interest, and so it becomes possible for the firm to borrow money. Firms have two main methods of borrowing: banks and bonds.

A bank loan for a firm works in much the same way as a loan for an individual who is buying a car or a house. The firm borrows an amount of money and then promises to repay it, including some rate of interest, over a predetermined period of time. In some cases, for an especially big loan, several banks will join together to make the loan. If the firm fails to make its loan payments, the bank (or banks) can often take the firm to court and require the firm to sell buildings or equipment that the firm owns to make the loan payments.

A **bond** is a financial contract through which a borrower agrees to repay the amount that was borrowed and also a rate of interest over a period of time in the future. **Corporate bonds** are issued by firms, but bonds are also issued by various levels of government. For example, **municipal bonds** are issued by cities, state bonds by U.S. states, and **Treasury bonds** by the federal government through the U.S. Department of the Treasury. A bond specifies an amount that will be borrowed, the interest rate that will be paid, and the time until repayment. For example, a large company might issue bonds for $10 million, where the firm would promise to make interest payments at an annual rate of 8%, or $800,000 per year, and then after 10 years the firm would repay the $10 million that it originally borrowed. When a firm issues bonds, the total amount that is borrowed is divided up; for example, when a firm seeks to borrow $50 million by issuing bonds, it might actually issue 10,000 bonds that each involves borrowing $5,000. In this way, an individual financial investor could in effect loan the firm $5,000, or any multiple of that amount the investor desires. Those who own bonds and receive the interest payments are called **bondholders**. If a firm issues bonds and fails to make the promised interest payments, the bondholders can take the firm to court and require the firm to pay, even if the firm needs to raise the money by selling buildings or equipment that it owns.

bond: A financial contract through which a borrower like a corporation, a city or state, or the federal government agrees to repay the amount that was borrowed and also a rate of interest over a period of time in the future.

corporate bonds: Bonds issued by firms that wish to borrow.

municipal bonds: Bonds issued by cities that wish to borrow.

Treasury bonds: Bonds issued by the federal government through the U.S. Department of the Treasury.

bondholders: Those who own bonds and receive the interest payments.

Bank borrowing often works better for relatively small firms, where the bank can get to know the firm extremely well—often because the bank can monitor a firm's sales and expenses quite accurately by looking at the deposits and withdrawals that the firm makes. Relatively large and well-known firms often issue bonds instead. U.S. corporations issued $1.5 trillion in corporate bonds in 2015. Some of these bonds were to raise new financial capital that would pay for real investment; other bonds were used to raise financial capital to pay off old bonds or to buy other firms. However, the idea that banks are usually for relatively smaller loans and bonds are for larger loans is not an ironclad rule; sometimes, groups of banks coordinate to make large loans, and sometimes, relatively small and lesser-known firms issue bonds.

Corporate Stock and Public Firms

stock: A claim on partial ownership of a firm.

shares: The stock of a firm is divided into individual shares.

shareholders: Those who own at least some stock in a firm.

Stock represents ownership of a firm; that is, a person who owns 100% of a company's stock by definition owns the entire company. The stock of a company is divided into **shares**. Corporate giants like IBM, AT&T, Ford, General Electric, Microsoft, Merck, and Exxon all have millions of shares of stock. Those who own some shares of stock in a company are called **shareholders**. In most large and well-known firms, no individual owns a majority of the shares of the stock. Instead, large numbers of shareholders—even those who hold thousands of shares—each have only a small slice of the overall ownership of the firm. When a company is owned by a large number of shareholders, there are three questions to answer: (1) How and when does the company get money from the sale of its stock? (2) What rate of return does the company promise to pay when it sells stock? (3) Who makes decisions in a company owned by a large number of shareholders? Let's consider these questions in turn.

initial public offering (IPO): When a firm first sells shares of stock to outside investors.

A firm receives money from the sale of its stock only when the company sells its own stock to the public. A firm's first sale of stock to the public is called an **initial public offering (IPO)**. The IPO is important for two reasons. First, the IPO or later stock offerings provide the funds to repay the early-stage investors, like the angel investors and the venture capital firms. For example, a venture capital firm may have provided funding in exchange for 40% ownership of the firm. When the firm sells stock, the venture capital firm sells its part-ownership of the firm to the public. A second reason for the importance of the IPO is that it provides a source of financial capital to the company for a substantial expansion of its operations.

But most of the time when corporate stock is bought or sold, the firm receives no financial capital at all. If you buy shares of stock in General Motors, you almost certainly buy them from the current owner of those shares, and General Motors doesn't receive any of your money. This pattern shouldn't seem particularly odd. After all, if you buy a house, the current owner gets your money, not the original owner of the land or the house. Similarly, when you buy shares of stock, you are buying a small slice of ownership of the firm from the existing owner—and the firm that originally issued the stock is not a part of this transaction.

dividend: A direct payment from a firm to its shareholders.

capital gain: A financial gain from buying an asset, like a share of stock or a house, and later selling it at a higher price.

When a firm decides to issue stock, it must recognize that investors will expect to receive a rate of return. That rate of return can come in two forms. A firm can make a direct payment to its shareholders, called a **dividend**. Alternatively, a financial investor might buy a share of stock in Wal-Mart for $45 and then later sell that share of stock to someone else for $60, for a gain of $15. The increase in the value of the stock (or of any asset) between when it is bought and when it is sold is called a **capital gain**. The factors that determine whether the price of a stock will rise and thus provide a capital gain to investors will be discussed later in this chapter. Here, focusing on the firm's point of view as it raises financial capital, notice that dividends are paid directly by the firm to the shareholder out of any profits the firm has earned; thus, dividends are usually paid by well-established firms that earn a steady stream of profits, while new and young firms often pay no dividend at all. When one financial investor sells shares of stock to another, it does not involve any direct payment to or from the firm; instead, it is only a payment between two financial investors.

Who makes the decisions about when a firm will issue stock, or pay dividends, or re-invest profits? To understand the answers to these questions, it's useful to separate firms into two groups: private and public.

private company: A firm owned by the people who run it on a day-to-day basis.

A **private company** is owned by the people who run it on a day-to-day basis. Private companies can either be run by individuals, in which case they are called *sole proprietorships*, or they can be run by a group, in which case they are *partnerships*. A small law firm run by one person, even if it employs some other lawyers, would be a sole proprietorship. However, a larger law firm may be owned jointly by its partners. In

2012, the U.S. economy had about 23 million sole proprietorships and 3.4 million partnerships. Most private companies are relatively small, but there are exceptions. Some large private companies, with tens of billions of dollars in annual sales, include the farm products dealer Cargill, the Mars candy company, and the Bechtel engineering and construction firm.

When a firm decides to sell stock, which in turn can be bought and sold by financial investors, it is then called a **public company**. Shareholders own a public company. Because the shareholders are a very broad group, often consisting of thousands or even millions of investors, they vote for a board of directors, who in turn hire top executives to run the firm on a day-to-day basis. The more shares of stock a shareholder owns, the more votes that shareholder is entitled to cast for the company's board of directors. In turn, this board of directors hires the top managers who run the company on a day-to-day basis, like the chief executive officer (CEO). In theory, the board of directors helps to make sure that the firm is run in the interests of the true owners—that is, the shareholders. However, conflicts often arise in which the top executives who run the firm have a strong voice in choosing the candidates who will be on their board of directors. After all, few shareholders are knowledgeable enough or have enough of a personal incentive to spend energy and money nominating alternative members of the board. Many corporate scandals raise the question of whether a firm was being run for the personal benefit of top executives or in the broader interests of shareholders as a group.

public company: A firm that has sold stock to the public, which in turn can be bought and sold by investors.

How Firms Choose between Sources of Financial Capital

There are clear patterns in how businesses raise financial capital. These patterns can be explained in terms of imperfect information, which as discussed in the previous chapter is a situation where buyers and sellers in a market do not both have full and equal information. Those who are actually running a firm day-to-day will almost always have more information about whether the firm is likely to earn profits in the future than outside investors who provide financial capital.

Any young start-up firm is a risk; indeed, some start-up firms are only a little more than an idea on paper. The firm's founders inevitably have better information about how hard they are willing to work, and whether the firm is likely to succeed, than anyone else does. When the founders of the firm put their own money into the firm, they demonstrate a belief in its prospects. At this early stage, angel investors and venture capitalists who support the firm try to overcome the imperfect information, at least in part, by knowing the managers and their business plan personally and by giving them advice.

As a firm becomes at least somewhat established and its strategy appears likely to lead to profits in the not-too-distant future, knowing the individual managers and their business plans on a personal basis becomes less important, because information has become more widely available regarding the company's products, revenues, costs, and profits. As a result, other outside investors who don't know the managers personally, like bondholders and shareholders, become willing to provide financial capital to the firm.

At this point, a firm must often choose between borrowing financial capital using banks or bonds, which means agreeing to pay a certain rate of interest, or instead raising financial capital by issuing share of stock, which only requires that the firm consider paying dividends to shareholders—although it is not required to do so.

If you owned a small firm that had become somewhat established, but you needed a surge of financial capital to carry out a major expansion, would you prefer to raise the funds through borrowing or by issuing stock? The great disadvantage of borrowing money rather than issuing stock is that when you have borrowed money, you need to make the scheduled interest payments, but when you have issued stock, you only need to think about whether to pay dividends. The great advantage of borrowing money rather than issuing stock is that stock involves selling off ownership of your company and becoming responsible to a board of directors, whereas if you borrow money and make the interest payments, you can still own and run your firm without outside control—and keep any profits it makes for yourself.

These trade-offs suggest that a firm will prefer to issue stock under two situations. One situation is that of a small and growing firm that would prefer to receive a large chunk of financial capital in the present, but not pay out any returns for a few years, until it becomes firmly established. In this situation, selling stock to the public can make sense for both the firm and for financial investors. The other situation where a firm prefers to issue stock is less cheerful; perhaps those running the firm aren't making profits *and aren't confident that they can make profits in the future, either*. Thus, they would rather receive financial capital by issuing stock because they don't believe that the firm will be able to make future interest payments.

Potential shareholders with imperfect information about the firm may have a hard time looking at a firm that is issuing stock and deciding whether the firm is issuing stock because its growth prospects are so good, or because its growth prospects are so poor. However, financial investors often follow this logic: if an established firm is trying to sell stock, a wary investor is likely to presume that the firm might have tried to get a loan for the project, but failed. Thus, financial investors often assume that if a well-established firm is trying to sell additional stock, it was already turned down for a loan by banks and

Corporate Governance and the Enron Story

On December 31, 2000, stock in Enron—a company that bought and sold natural gas and electricity, among other goods—was priced at $83. The stock price had risen 87% in 2000, following a 56% rise in 1999 and a 37% rise in 1998. Enron was rated the most innovative large company in America in *Fortune* magazine's survey of Most Admired Companies for its web-based markets and its strategies with long-term contracts. By December 2, 2001, less than one year later, Enron had filed for bankruptcy and several legal investigations had started into accusations that some of the firm's financial records were highly misleading or even fraudulent. How can a company go from being a role model to having its top executives threatened with jail in less than a year? What safeguards were supposed to be in place—but failed?

Corporate governance is the name that economists give to the institutions that are supposed to watch over top executives in companies owned by shareholders. In the case of Enron, corporate governance didn't perform well, misled by a toxic combination of wild over-optimism and shady management.

The board of directors, who are elected by the shareholders, are the first line of oversight for top executives. However, members of the board are often hand-picked by top executives, so their independence can be questioned. Also, board members may not have the time or information to provide close oversight. Being a board member is a part-time job that often consists of a few meetings a year, where information is provided by the top executives themselves.

A second institution of corporate governance is the auditing firm hired to go over the financial records of the company and certify that everything looks reasonable. The auditors for Enron were from the Arthur Andersen company. In 2000, Andersen earned $52 million in fees from Enron, which may have created an incentive not to risk offending top management.

A third institution of corporate governance is outside investors, especially large shareholders like those who invest large mutual funds or pension funds. They should buy or sell stock based on their own views about the health of the company. Such large investors owned about 60% of the total Enron stock late in 2000. But they continued holding 60% of Enron stock right up to October 2001, many months after it had become clear that something was deeply wrong at the firm.

Other contributors to corporate governance include the stock market analysts who give advice to financial investors, government financial regulators, journalists who write for the business press, and even employees of the firm itself, who should speak up or seek employment elsewhere if they know that their employer is doing something illegal or unethical. But with a few exceptions (for example, *Fortune* magazine published a prominent story in March 2001 asking if Enron's stock price was headed for a fall), these watchdogs did not bark.

In response to the situation of Enron and other firms, Congress passed the Sarbanes-Oxley Act of 2002. The act imposed a number of new rules on the institutions of corporate governance, including boards of directors, auditors, and stock market analysts, along with a new government accounting oversight board. But the top executives of firms have strong incentives to report high profits, and others have strong incentives not to upset or anger top executives. Given these basic realities, it remains uncertain whether the new rules will provide substantial benefit.

bond investors—and so buying stock to finance the firm probably isn't such a good idea. Thus, because of the dynamics created by imperfect information, young companies often find it easier to sell stock, while established firms often raise financial capital by borrowing from banks and bond markets.

How Households Supply Financial Capital

The ways in which firms would prefer to raise funds are only half the story of financial markets. The other half is what those households who supply funds desire and how they perceive the available choices. Thus, the focus of the discussion now shifts from firms on the demand side of financial capital markets to households on the supply side of those markets. The mechanisms for saving available to households can be divided into several categories: deposits in bank accounts, bonds, stocks, mutual funds, and housing and other tangible assets like owning gold. For each of these investments, households will think about three factors: the expected rate of return it will pay, the risk that the return will be much lower or higher than expected, and the **liquidity** of the investment, which refers to how easy it is to sell a financial investment when desired.

liquidity: How easy it is to sell an asset when desired.

Bank Accounts

An "intermediary" is one who stands between two other parties; for example, a person who arranges a blind date between two other people is one kind of intermediary. In financial capital markets, banks are an example of a **financial intermediary**—that is, an institution that operates between a saver who deposits money in a bank and a borrower who receives a loan from that bank. But when a bank serves as a financial intermediary, unlike the situation with a couple on a blind date, the saver and the borrower never meet each other. In fact, it isn't even possible to make direct connections between those who deposit money in banks and those who borrow from banks, because all funds deposited end up in one big pool, which is then loaned out. Exhibit 19-1 illustrates the position of banks as a financial intermediary, with a pattern of deposits flowing into a bank and loans flowing out, and then repayment of the loans flowing back to the bank, with interest payments for the original savers.

financial intermediary: An institution, like a bank, that receives money from savers and provides funds to borrowers.

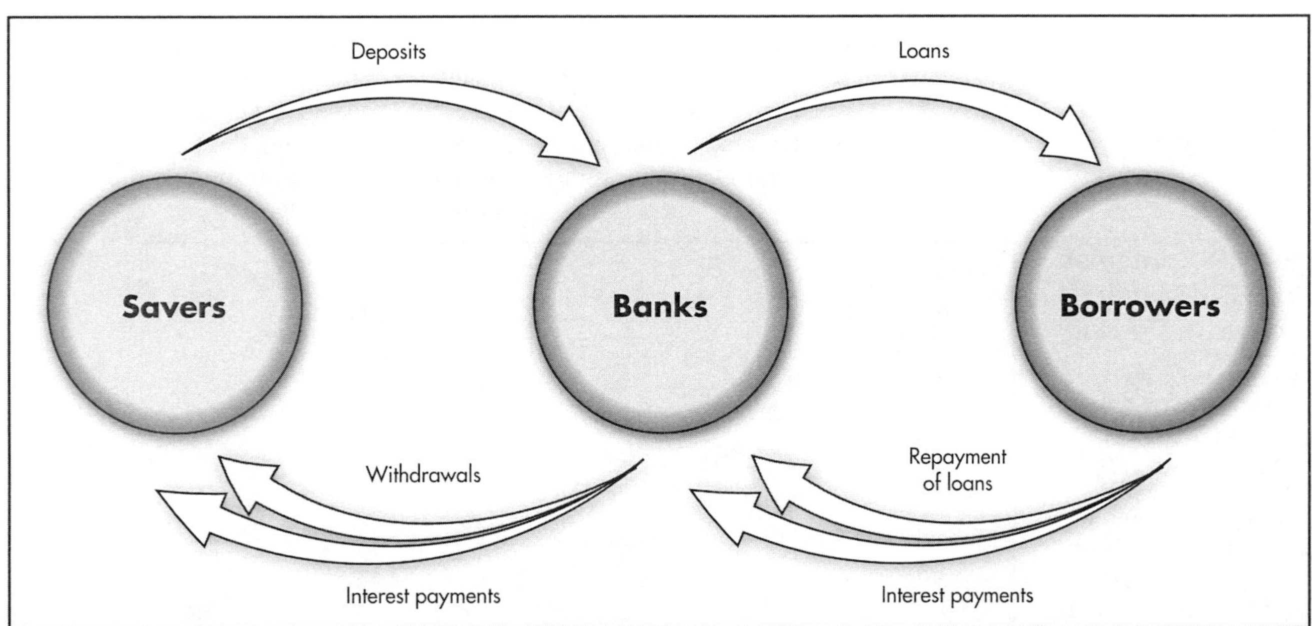

EXHIBIT 19-1 Banks as Financial Intermediaries

Banks are a financial intermediary because they stand between savers and borrowers. Savers place deposits with banks, and then receive interest payments and withdraw money. Borrowers receive loans from banks and repay the loans with interest.

CLEARING IT UP

Expected Rate of Return, Risk, and Actual Rate of Return

The expected rate of return refers to an average over a period of time usually measured in years or even decades. High risk refers to the fact that a wide range of actual outcomes are reasonably possible. Thus, a low-risk investment will have actual returns that are fairly close to its expected rate of return year after year. A high-risk investment will have actual returns that are much higher than the expected rate of return in some months or years and much lower than the expected rate of return in other months or years.

checking account: A bank account that typically pays little or no interest, but that gives easy access to your money, either by writing a check or by using a debit card.

debit card: A card that lets you make purchases, where the cost is immediately deducted from your checking account.

savings account: A bank account that pays an interest rate, but withdrawing the money typically requires you to make a trip to the bank or an automatic teller machine.

certificate of deposit (CD): A mechanism for a saver to deposit funds at a bank and promise to leave them at the bank for a time, in exchange for a higher rate of interest.

Banks offer a range of accounts to serve different needs. A **checking account** typically pays little or no interest, but it facilitates transactions by giving you easy access to your money, either by writing a check or by using a **debit card** (i.e., a card that works like a credit card, except that purchases are immediately deducted from your checking account rather than being billed separately through a credit card company). A **savings account** typically pays some interest rate, but withdrawing the money typically requires you to make a trip to the bank or an automatic teller machine. The lines between checking and savings accounts have blurred in the last few decades, as many banks offer checking accounts that will pay an interest rate similar to a savings account if you keep a certain minimum amount in the account, or conversely, offer savings accounts that allow you to write at least a few checks per month.

Another way to deposit savings at a bank is to use a **certificate of deposit (CD)**. With a CD, as it is commonly called, you agree to deposit a certain amount of money, often measured in hundreds or thousands of dollars, in the account for a stated period of time, typically ranging from a few months to several years. In exchange, the bank agrees to pay a higher interest rate than for a regular savings account. While you can withdraw the money before the allotted time, as the advertisements for CDs always warn, there is "a substantial penalty for early withdrawal." Exhibit 19-2 shows the annual rate of interest paid in a six-month CD since 1990. The interest rates paid by savings accounts are typically a little lower than the CD rate because financial investors need to receive a slightly higher rate of interest as compensation for promising to leave their deposits untouched for a period of time in a CD, and thus giving up some liquidity.

The great advantages of bank accounts are that financial investors have very easy access to their money, and also that money in bank accounts is extremely safe. In part, this safety arises because a bank account offers more security than keeping a few thousand dollars in the toe of a sock in your underwear drawer. In addition, the federal government established the Federal Deposit Insurance Corporation (FDIC) to protect the savings of

EXHIBIT 19-2 Interest Rates on Six-Month Certificates of Deposit

The interest rate on six-month certificates of deposit has fluctuated over time. It was about 6% per year during the 1990s, then dropped to just over 1% in the early 2000s. It bounced back to a little above 5% in 2006 and 2007 before diving to 1% and less in recent years.

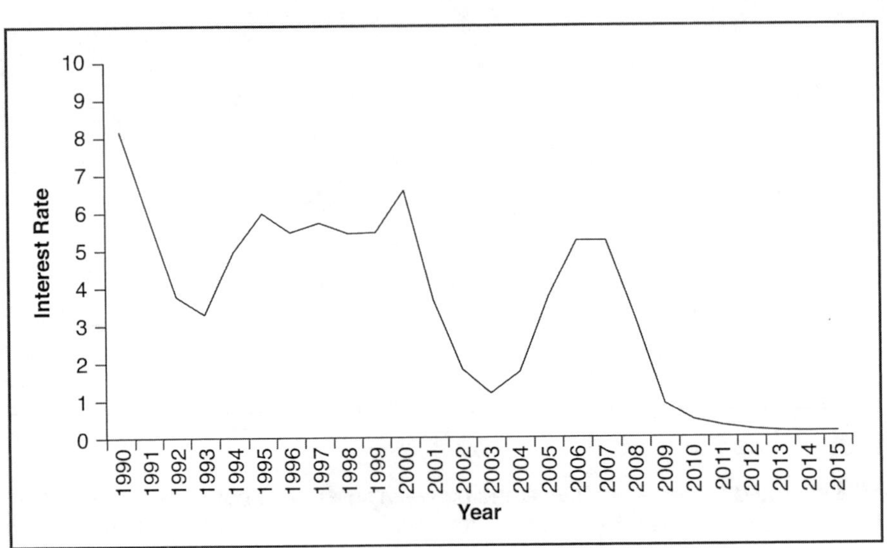

the average person. Every bank is required by law to pay a fee to the FDIC, based on the size of its deposits. Then, if a bank should happen to go bankrupt and not be able to repay depositors their money, the FDIC provides insurance, guaranteeing that all customers will receive their deposits back up to $250,000.

The bottom line on bank accounts looks like this: Rate of return—very low; Risk—very low; Liquidity—very high.

Bonds

An investor who buys a bond expects to receive a rate of return. However, bonds vary in the rates of return that they offer, according to the riskiness of the borrower. An interest rate can always be divided up into three components (as explained in Chapter 2): compensation for delaying consumption, an adjustment for an inflationary rise in the overall level of prices, and a risk premium that takes the borrower's riskiness into account. The U.S. government is considered to be an extremely safe borrower, so when the U.S. government issues Treasury bonds, it can pay a relatively low rate of interest. Firms that appear to be safe borrowers, perhaps because of their sheer size or because they have consistently earned profits over time, will still pay a higher interest rate than the U.S. government. Firms that appear to be riskier borrowers, perhaps because they are still growing or their businesses appear shaky, will pay the highest interest rates when they issue bonds. Bonds that offer high interest rates to compensate for their relatively high chance of default are sometimes called **junk bonds**. A number of today's well-known firms issued junk bonds back in the 1980s when they were starting to grow up, including Turner Broadcasting and Microsoft.

junk bonds: Bonds that offer relatively high interest rates to compensate for their relatively high chance of default.

A bond issued by the U.S. government or a large corporation may seem to be relatively low risk: after all, the issuer of the bond has promised to make certain payments over time, and except for rare cases of bankruptcy, these payments will be made. If the issuer of a corporate bond fails to make the payments that it owes to its bondholders, the bondholders can require that the company declare bankruptcy, sell off its assets, and pay them as much as it can. Even in the case of junk bonds, a wise investor can reduce the risk by purchasing bonds from a wide range of different companies, since even if a few firms go broke and don't pay, they aren't *all* likely to go bankrupt.

However, bonds present a different risk because even though the payments made by a typical bond do not change, interest rates in the economy do change. For example, imagine that you decide to buy a $1,000 bond that pays an annual interest rate of 8%. However, soon after you buy the bond, equilibrium interest rates rise in the financial capital market, so that now similar companies are paying an annual rate of 11% when they issue bonds. Thus, anyone who buys a bond in the present can receive annual payments of $110 per year, but since your bond was issued at an interest rate of 8%, you have tied up $1,000 and are receiving payments of only $80 per year. In the meaningful sense of opportunity cost, you are missing out on the higher payments that you could have received. (The Appendix to this chapter discusses specific calculations for how a change in interest rates will alter the value of a bond.)

The **bond yield** measures the rate of return that a bond is expected to pay at the time of purchase. Bonds are not only bought at the time they are issued, but they are also bought and sold during their lifetimes. When buying a bond that has been around for a few years, investors should know that the interest rate printed on a bond is often not the same as the bond yield. For example, consider a $1,000 bond that makes payments of $80 per year, based on an interest rate of 8%. However, the interest rates prevailing in the economy have now risen to 12%. What would you pay for this bond when it has one year left to run? The expected payments from the bond one year from now are $1080 because in the bond's last year, the issuer of the bond will make the final year of interest payments and then also repay the original $1000. Given that interest rates in this example are now 12%, you know that you could invest $964 in an alternative investment and receive $1080 a year from now; that is, $964[1 + 0.12] = $1080. Therefore, you will not pay more than $964 for the original $1,000 bond. Even though the annual payments of that bond were

bond yield: The rate of return that a bond is expected to pay at the time of purchase.

EXHIBIT 19-3 Interest Rates for Corporate Bonds and 10-Year U.S. Treasury Bonds

The interest rates for corporate bonds and U.S. Treasury bonds (officially "notes") rise and fall together, depending on conditions for borrowers and lenders in financial markets for borrowing. But the corporate bonds always must pay a higher interest rate, to make up for the higher risk that they have of defaulting compared with the U.S. government.

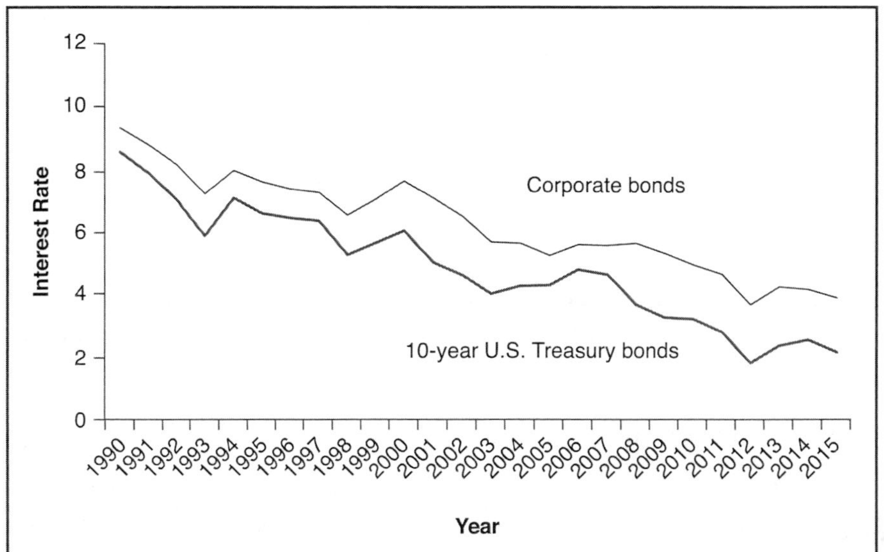

originally based on an 8% interest rate, the bond cannot be sold unless its payoff reflects the currently prevailing interest rate. When interest rates rise, bonds previously issued at lower interest rates will sell for less than face value. Conversely, when interest rates fall, bonds previously issued at higher interest rates will sell for more than face value.

Exhibit 19-3 shows bond yield for two kinds of bonds: 10-year Treasury bonds (which are officially called "notes") and corporate bonds issued by firms that have been given an Aaa rating as relatively safe borrowers by Moody's, an independent firm that publishes such ratings. Corporate bonds pay a higher interest rate because firms are riskier borrowers than the federal government. But the rates tend to rise and fall together. Treasury bonds typically pay more than bank accounts, and corporate bonds typically pay a higher interest rate than Treasury bonds.

The bottom line for bonds: Rate of return—low to moderate, depending on the risk of the borrower; Risk—low to moderate, depending on whether interest rates in the economy change substantially after the bond is issued; Liquidity—moderate, because the bond needs to be sold before the investor regains access to cash.

Stocks

The rate of return on a financial investment in a share of stock can come in two forms: as dividends paid by the firm and as a capital gain achieved by selling the stock for more than you paid. The range of possible returns from buying stock is mind-bending. Firms can decide to pay dividends or not. A stock price can rise to a multiple of its original price or sink all the way to zero. For example, Netflix, a company that specializes in on-demand video and streaming media, saw its stock price rise by 134% in 2015. Conversely, Chesapeake Energy, a company that specializes in oil and gas exploration and production, saw its stock price fall by 77% in 2015. The reasons why stock prices fall and rise so abruptly will be discussed in a moment.

But first, there are a number of different ways of measuring the overall performance of the stock market, based on averaging the stock prices of different subsets of companies. Perhaps the best-known measure of the stock markets is the Dow Jones Industrial Average, mentioned at the start of this chapter, which is based on the stock prices of 30 large U.S. companies. Another gauge of stock market performance, the Standard and Poor's 500, follows the stock prices of the 500 largest U.S. companies. The Wilshire 5000 tracks the stock prices of essentially all U.S. companies that have stock that the public can buy and sell. Other measures of stock markets focus on *where* stocks are traded. For example, the New York Stock Exchange monitors the performance of stocks that are traded on that exchange in New York City. The NASDAQ stock market includes about 3,100 stocks,

EXHIBIT 19-4 Some Measures of Stock Markets

Measure of the Stock Market	Comments
Dow Jones Industrial Average (DJIA) http://indexes.dowjones.com	Based on 30 large companies from a diverse set of representative industries, chosen by analysts at Dow Jones and Company, owners of the *Wall Street Journal*. Goes back to 1896.
Standard and Poor's 500 http://www.standardandpoors.com	Based on 500 large U.S. firms, chosen by analysts at Standard & Poor's to represent the economy as a whole.
Wilshire 5000 http://www.wilshire.com	Includes essentially all U.S. companies with stock ownership. Despite the name, this index includes about 7,000 firms.
New York Stock Exchange http://www.nyse.com	The oldest and largest U.S. stock market, dating back to 1792. It trades stocks for 2,800 companies of all sizes. It is located at 18 Broad St. in New York City.
NASDAQ http://www.nasdaq.com	Founded in 1971 as an electronic stock market, allowing people to buy or sell from many physical locations. It has about 3,100 companies.
Some Prominent Foreign Stock Exchanges	
FTSE http://www.ftse.com	Includes the 100 largest companies on the London Stock Exchange. Pronounced "footsie." Originally stood for Financial Time Stock Exchange.
Nikkei http://www.nni.nikkei.co.jp	*Nikkei* stands for *Nihon Keizai Shimbun*, which translates as the *Japan Economic Journal*, a major business newspaper in Japan. Index includes the 225 largest and most actively traded stocks on the Tokyo Stock Exchange.
DAX http://www.exchange.de	Tracks 30 of the largest companies on the Frankfurt, Germany stock exchange. DAX is an abbreviation for Deutscher Aktien Index.

with something of a concentration on technology stocks. Exhibit 19-4 lists some of the most commonly cited measures of U.S. and international stock markets.

The trend in the stock market is generally up over time, but with some large dips along the way. Exhibit 19-5 shows the path of the Standard & Poor's 500 index (which is measured on the left-hand vertical axis) and the Dow Jones Index (which is measured on the right-hand vertical axis). Broad measures of the stock market, like these two, tend to move together. When looking at graphs of the overall stock market like these, the numbers on the vertical axis are produced by formulas that don't have an easy intuitive explanation. However, when the Dow Jones average rises from 5,000 to 10,000, you know that the average price of the stocks in that index has (roughly) doubled. Thus, Exhibit 19-5 shows that stock prices didn't rise much in the 1970s, but then started a steady climb in the 1980s. From 2000 to 2012, stock prices bounced up and down but ended up at about the same level, preceding a sharp rise in 2013 and 2014.

Exhibit 19-6 shows the total annual rate of return that an investor would have received from buying the stocks in the S&P 500 index over recent decades. The total return here includes both dividends paid by these companies and also capital gains arising from increases in the value of the stock. (For technical reasons related to how the numbers are calculated, the dividends and capital gains don't add exactly to the total return.) From the 1950s up to the 1980s, the average firm paid annual dividends equal to about 4% of the value of its stock. But since the 1990s, dividends have dropped and now often provide

EXHIBIT 19-5 The Dow Jones Industrial Index and the Standard & Poor's 500, 1965–2015

Stock prices rose dramatically from the 1980s up to about 2000. From 2000 to 2012, stock prices bounced up and down but then rose in 2013 and 2014.

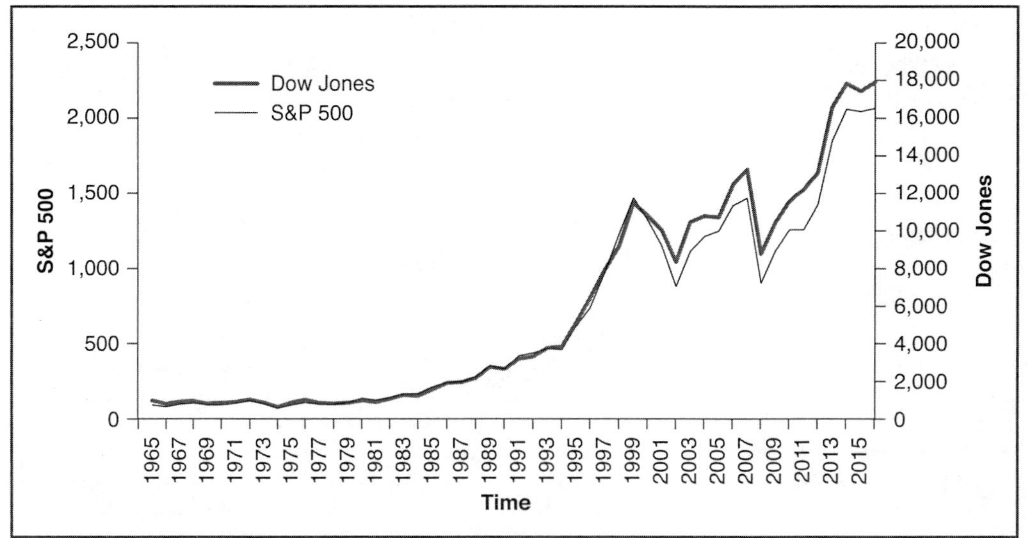

EXHIBIT 19-6 Annual Returns on Stocks: 1950–2015

Period	Total Annual Return (%)	Capital Gains (%)	Dividends (%)
1950–1959	19.25	14.26	4.99
1960–1969	7.78	4.53	3.25
1970–1979	5.88	1.68	4.20
1980–1989	17.55	13.15	4.40
1990–1999	18.21	15.70	2.51
2000	–9.10	–10.10	1.00
2001	–11.89	–13.21	1.32
2002	–22.10	–23.75	1.65
2003	28.68	26.86	1.82
2004	10.88	9.15	1.73
2005	4.91	3.06	1.85
2006	15.80	13.89	1.91
2007	5.49	3.60	1.89
2008	–37.00	–38.88	1.88
2009	23.45	21.47	1.98
2010	12.78	10.99	1.79
2011	0.00	–2.06	2.06
2012	13.41	11.30	2.11
2013	32.15	30.21	1.94
2014	13.52	11.60	1.92
2015	1.36	–0.75	2.11

a return closer to 1–2%. In the 1960s and 1970s, capital gains from owning stock were (very) roughly the same as dividends. But in the 1980s and 1990s, capital gains were far higher than dividends. In the 2000s, dividends remained low, and while stock prices fluctuated, they have remained low.

The overall pattern is that stocks as a group have provided a high rate of return over extended periods of time, but this return comes with risks. Individual companies can rise and fall substantially, both over short time periods and over the long run. During extended periods of time like the 1970s or the first decade of the 2000s, the overall return on the stock market can be quite modest. The stock market can sometimes fall sharply, as it did from 2000–2002 and in 2008. To understand why stocks are so risky, it's useful to consider the two basic motivations for buying and selling of stocks: fundamentals trading and momentum trading.

The value of the stock of a firm is ultimately determined by the future profits the firm is expected to earn. To understand why this statement must hold true, imagine that you purchase 100% of the shares of stock of a company, so that you become the sole owner. Being the sole owner means that, along with the power to run the firm, any profits the firm earns in the future belong to you. Thus, what you are willing to pay for all of the stock in the firm will depend on what it is worth to you to receive all of the future profits from the firm. The same lesson holds true, on a smaller scale, for investors who buy only a few shares of stock in a firm.

Fundamentals trading involves buying or selling stock based on estimates of the future expected profits of the firm. Say that you believe the future profits of the firm are currently worth $10 million, and the firm has 1 million shares of stock. Then you will believe that the fundamental value of the stock should be $10 a share. If the current market value of the stock is less than $10, you will want to purchase the stock. If the current market value of the stock is more than $10, you will want to sell the stock. Those who believe that the stock is overvalued, relative to the fundamental value of its future expected profits, will sell their shares to those who believe that the stock is undervalued. Of course, the firm's profits may turn out much higher or much lower than expected. If the firm's future profits turn out to be far above common expectations, then shareholders can recognize extremely large capital gains. If the firm's future profits turn out to be nonexistent, the price of the firm's stock can fall all the way to zero. Thus, one reason for the riskiness of stocks is because the future is uncertain, and shareholders are not guaranteed any dividends or other payments from the firm.

fundamentals trading: Buying or selling stock based on estimates of the future expected profits.

The risks of fundamentals trading are magnified by the second main motivation for stock market trading: **Momentum trading** refers to buying stock because the price seems to be rising, or selling stock because the price seems to be falling. In other words, momentum trading follows the trends, regardless of whether they match some notion of long-run fundamental value. The idea of momentum trading has been around a long time. The eighteenth century French author and philosopher Voltaire (1694–1778) once wrote: "If you see a Swiss banker jump out of a window, follow him—there is surely money to be made." The problem with momentum trading is that it creates unsustainable outcomes. When momentum traders expect a firm's stock price to rise, they buy that stock, but their own increased demand for stock also causes the stock's price to rise, thus encouraging other momentum traders to purchase still more stock, which drives the stock price still higher. Conversely, when momentum traders expect a firm's stock price to fall, they sell that stock, but as they sell their own stock, they also cause the stock's price to fall further, thus encouraging other momentum traders to sell still more stock. The result of momentum trading can be a stock market that soars or collapses based on the momentum of financial investors, without much change in the value of the fundamental value of the firm as determined by expected future profits. But momentum cannot last forever. Eventually, the future profits or losses start to occur. Stock prices gradually struggle back toward the fundamental levels that are justified by actual expectations of future profits.

momentum trading: Buying or selling stock by following the current trend; that is, buying when the price seems to be rising, or selling stock because the price seems to be falling.

One piece of evidence for the existence of a substantial number of momentum traders is that stock can move sharply in ways that are hard to explain as a result of fundamental factors. On October 19, 1987, for example, U.S. stock market prices fell 23% in a single day. From March 2000 to September 2001, the NASDAQ stock index, which includes many technology-oriented companies, dropped by 67%. In Japan stock prices sank by more than half from 1990 to 1992, and they have stayed roughly at that lower level ever since. In Thailand, stock prices toppled by more than half from February to September 1998. Over three weeks from September to October 2008, the U.S. stock market fell 26%. In these cases of market crashes, and many others like them, it seems implausible that fundamental factors about expectations of future profits shifted so dramatically that all the stocks in the market suddenly were worth so much less. Instead, it seems likelier that the self-fulfilling prophecy of momentum trading pushed the value of stocks above a price that could be justified by fundamental factors, but at some point as time passed and firms actually earned profits or made losses, stock prices dropped back toward their fundamental values. These episodes in which momentum trading pushes stock prices far above or below their fundamental values can last for years.

Bottom line on investing in individual stocks: Rate of return—High on average over lengthy periods of time; Risk—High, especially in the short run; Liquidity—Moderate, since stock does need to be sold to turn gains into spendable money.

Mutual Funds

diversification: Investing in a wide range of companies, to reduce the level of risk.

mutual funds: A fund that buys a range of stocks or bonds from different companies, thus allowing an investor an easy way to diversify.

index fund: A mutual fund that seeks only to mimic the overall performance of the market.

Buying stock or bonds issued by a single company is always somewhat risky. An individual firm may find itself buffeted by unfavorable supply and demand conditions or hurt by unlucky or unwise managerial decisions. Thus, a standard recommendation for financial investors, already hinted at in the earlier discussion, is **diversification**, which means buying stocks or bonds from a wide range of companies. A saver who diversifies is following the old proverb: "Don't put all your eggs in one basket." In any broad group of companies, some firms will do better than expected and some will do worse—but that random variation will have a tendency to cancel out, so the result will be the average for the group.

To simplify the process of buying a diversified group of stocks, companies offer **mutual funds**, which are funds that buy a range of stocks or bonds from different companies. The financial investor buys shares of the mutual fund and then receives a return based on how the fund as a whole performs. Roughly half of U.S. households have a financial investment in a mutual fund—including many people who have their retirement savings or pension money invested in this way.

Mutual funds can be focused in certain areas; for example, one mutual fund might invest only in stock of companies based in Indonesia, or only in bonds issued by large manufacturing companies, or only in stock of biotechnology companies. At the other end of the spectrum, a mutual fund might be quite broad; at the extreme, some mutual funds own a tiny share of every firm in the stock market, and thus the value of the mutual fund will fluctuate with the average of the overall stock market. A mutual fund that seeks only to mimic the overall performance of the market is called an **index fund**.

Diversification can offset some of the risks of individual stocks rising or falling. But even investors who buy an indexed mutual fund, designed to mimic some measure of the broad stock market like the Standard and Poor's 500, had better buckle their seatbelts against some ups and downs, like those the stock market experienced in the first decade of the 2000s.

Housing and Other Tangible Assets

equity: The monetary value a homeowner would have after selling the house and repaying any outstanding bank loans used to buy the house.

Households can also seek a rate of return by purchasing tangible assets, especially housing. About two-thirds of U.S. households own their own home. An owner's **equity** in a house is the monetary value the owner would have after selling the house and repaying any outstanding bank loans used to buy the house. For example, imagine that you buy a house for $200,000, paying 10% of the price as a down payment and taking out a bank loan for the remaining $180,000. Over time, you pay off some of your bank loan, so that only $100,000 remains, and the value of the house on the market rises to $250,000. At that point, your equity in the home is the value of the home minus the value of the loan outstanding, which is $150,000. For many middle-class Americans, their home equity is their single greatest financial asset. The total value of all home equity held by U.S. households was about $12 trillion in 2015.

Investment in a house is tangibly different from bank accounts, stocks, and bonds because a house offers both a financial and a non-financial return. If you buy a house to live in, part of the return on your investment occurs from your consumption of "housing services"—that is, having a place to live. (Of course, if you buy a home and rent it out, you receive rental payments for the housing services you provide, which would offer a financial return.) But buying a house to live in also offers the possibility of a capital gain from selling the house in the future for more than you paid for it.

In the second half of the twentieth century, housing prices averaged over the United States as a whole rose every year. However, the possible capital gains from rising housing prices are riskier than these national price averages reveal. Certain regions of the U.S. and certain metropolitan areas saw falls in housing prices. In the first decade of the 2000s, housing prices for the country as a whole first rose rapidly for several years, and then the median housing price for the United States as a whole fell almost 10% in 2008 and declined further in 2009 before rising again in the following years.

Investors can also put money into other tangible assets. For example, financial markets make it possible to invest in gold, silver, and other precious metals, or in duller commodities like sugar, cocoa, coffee, orange juice, oil, and natural gas. The return on these investments derives from the saver's hope of buying low, selling high, and receiving a capital gain. Investing in, say, gold or coffee offers relatively little in the way of nonfinancial benefits to the user (unless the investor likes to caress gold or gaze upon a warehouse full of coffee). Indeed, typically investors in these commodities never even see

Boom and Bust in the U.S. Housing Market

The price of an average U.S. home took off from 2003 to 2005, rising at more than 10% per year. No serious analyst believed that this rate of price growth rate was sustainable; after all, if housing prices grew at, say, 11% per year over time, the average price of a home would more than double every seven years. However, many serious analysts at the time saw no reason for deep concern. After all, housing prices often change in fits and starts, like all prices, and a price surge for a few years is often followed by prices that are flat or even declining a bit as local markets adjust.

The sharp rise in housing prices was driven by a high level of demand for housing. Interest rates were low, so people were encouraged to borrow money to buy a house. Banks became much more flexible in their lending, making what were called "subprime" loans. Banks loaned money with low or sometimes no down-payment. They sometimes offered loans with very low interest payments for the first two years but then much higher payments after that; the idea was that housing prices would keep rising, so the borrower would just refinance the mortgage two years in the future, and thus wouldn't ever have to make the higher payments. Some banks even offered so-called NINJA loans, which meant a loan given even though the borrower had No Income, No Job or Assets.

In retrospect, a number of these loans seem foolhardy. But many borrowers figured that as long as housing prices kept rising, it made sense to buy. Many lenders used a process called "securitizing," in which they sold their mortgages to financial companies that put all the mortgages into a big pool, creating large financial securities, and then re-sold these mortgage-backed securities to investors. In this way, the lenders felt that they had protected themselves against the risk of the mortgages not being repaid. Bank and financial regulators watched this process unfold, but saw no reason at the time to intervene.

When housing prices turned down, many households who had borrowed when prices were high found that what they owed the bank was more than their home was worth. Many banks believed that they had diversified by selling their individual loans and instead buying securities based on mortgage loans from all over the country. After all, back in 2005, banks knew that the average price of a house had not declined at any time since the Great Depression of the 1930s. But these securities based on mortgage loans turned out to be far riskier than expected. The bust in housing prices weakened the finances of both banks and households, and thus helped bring on the Great Recession of 2007–2009.

the physical goods; instead, they sign a contract that takes ownership of a certain quantity of these commodities, which are stored in a warehouse someplace, and later they sell the ownership to someone else. As one example, from 1981 to 2005, the price of gold generally fluctuated between about $300 and $500 per ounce, but then rose sharply to over $1,700 per ounce in late 2012, before falling back to $1,300 per ounce by mid-2016.

A final area of tangible assets are "collectibles" like paintings, fine wine, jewelry, antiques, or even baseball cards. Most collectibles provide returns both in the form of services or of a potentially higher selling price in the future. You can use paintings by hanging them on the wall, jewelry by wearing it, baseball cards by displaying them. You can also hope to sell them someday for more than you paid for them. However, the evidence on prices of collectibles, while scanty, is that while they may go through periods where prices skyrocket for a time, you should not expect to make a higher-than-average rate of return over a sustained period of time from investing in this way.

The bottom line on investing in tangible assets: Rate of return—Moderate, especially if you can receive nonfinancial benefits from, say, living in the house; Risk—Moderate for housing or high if you buy gold or baseball cards; Liquidity—Low, because it often takes considerable time and energy to sell a house or a piece of fine art and turn your capital gain into cash.

The Trade-offs between Return and Risk

The discussion of financial investments has emphasized the expected rate of return, the risk, and the liquidity of each investment. Exhibit 19-7 summarizes these characteristics.

The household investment choices listed here display a trade-off between the expected return and the degree of risk involved. Bank accounts have very low risk and very low returns; bonds have higher risk but higher returns; and stocks are riskiest of all but pay still higher returns. In effect, the higher average return compensates for the higher degree of risk. If risky assets like stocks did not also offer a higher average return, then few investors would desire them.

This trade-off between return and risk complicates the task of any financial investor: Is it better to invest safely for a low expected return, or to take a risk and go for the possibility of a higher return? Ultimately, investor choices about risk and return will be based on personal preferences. However, it is often useful to examine risk and return in the context of different time frames. The high returns of stock market investments refer to a high average return that can be expected over a period of several years or decades. The high risk of such investments refers to the fact that in shorter time frames, from months to a few years, the rate of return may fluctuate a great deal. Thus, a person near retirement age, who already owns a house, may prefer reduced risk and certainty about retirement income. For young workers, just starting to make a reasonable income, it may make sense

EXHIBIT 19-7 Key Characteristics for Financial Investors

Financial Investment	Return	Risk	Liquidity
Checking account	Very low	Very little	Very high
Savings account	Low	Very little	High
Certificate of deposit	Low to medium	Very little	Medium
Stocks	High	Medium to high	Medium
Bonds	Medium	Low to medium	Medium
Mutual funds	Medium to high	Medium to high	Medium-high
Housing	Medium	Medium	Low
Gold	Medium	High	Low
Collectibles	Low to medium	High	Low

to put most of their savings for retirement in stocks. Stocks are risky in the short term, to be sure, but when the worker can look forward to several decades during which bounces of the stock market up and down can even out, stocks will typically pay a substantially higher return over that extended period than will bonds or bank accounts. Thus, trade-offs between risk and return must be considered in the context of where the investor is in life.

How to Become Rich

Getting rich may seem straightforward enough. Figure out what companies are going to grow and earn high profits in the future, if you are a fundamental trader, or figure out what companies are going to become popular for everyone else to buy, if you are a momentum trader. Those companies are the ones that will pay high dividends or whose stock price will climb in the future. Then, buy stock in those companies. Presto! Multiply your money! Why isn't this path to riches as easy as it sounds? This section first discusses the problems with picking stocks and then discusses a more reliable but undeniably duller method of accumulating personal wealth.

Why It's Hard to Get Rich Quick: The Random Walk Theory

The chief problem with attempting to buy stock in companies that will have higher prices in the future is that many other financial investors are trying to do the same thing. Thus, in attempting to get rich in the stock market, it is no help to identify a company that is going to earn high profits if many other investors have already reached the same conclusion about the company, because the stock price will already be high, based on the commonly expected high level of future profits.

The idea that stock prices are based on expectations about the future has a powerful and unexpected implication. If expectations determine stock price, then *shifts* in expectations will determine *shifts* in the stock price. Thus, what matters for predicting whether the stock price of a company will do well in the future is not whether the company will actually earn profits in the future. Instead, one must find a company that is widely believed at present to have poor prospects, but that will actually turn out to be a shining star. Brigades of stock market analysts and individual investors are carrying out such research 24 hours a day.

The fundamental problem with predicting future stock winners is that by definition, no one can predict the future news that alters expectations about profits. Because stock prices will shift in response to unpredictable future news, these prices will tend to follow what mathematicians call a "random walk with a trend." The *random walk* part means that on any given day, stock prices are just as likely to rise as to fall. *With a trend* means that over time, the upward steps tend to be larger than the downward steps, so stocks do gradually climb.

If stocks follow a random walk, then not even financial professionals will be able to choose stocks that will beat the average consistently. While some investment advisers are better-than-average in any given year, and some even succeed for a number of years in a row, the majority of financial investors do not outguess the market. If one looks back over time, it is typically true that one-half or two-thirds of the mutual funds that attempted to pick stocks that would rise more than the market average actually ended up doing worse than the market average. For the average investor who reads the business pages of the newspaper over a cup of coffee in the morning, the odds of doing better than full-time professionals is not very good at all. Trying to pick the stocks that will gain a great deal in the future is a risky and unlikely way for the average investor to become rich.

Getting Rich the Slow, Boring Way

Many U.S. citizens can accumulate a large amount of wealth during their lifetime, if they make two key choices. The first choice is to complete additional education and training. In 2014, the median earnings for full-time workers age 25 and over who had only a high school degree were $40,930; for those with a two-year associate degree, median earnings were $51,110, and for those with a four-year bachelor's degree (but no further professional degrees), median annual earnings were $68,160. Learning is not only good for you, but it pays off financially, too.

The second key choice is to start saving money early in life and to give the power of compound interest a chance. Imagine that at age 25, you save $3,000 and sock that money into an account that you don't touch. In the long run, it's not unreasonable to assume a 5% real annual rate of return (i.e., 5% above the rate of inflation) on money invested in a well-diversified stock portfolio. After 40 years, using the formula for compound interest introduced in Chapter 2, the original $3,000 investment will have multiplied nearly fifteenfold:

$$\$3,000(1 + .05)^{40} = \$21,120$$

Of course, having $21,120 doesn't make you a millionaire. But notice that this tidy sum is the result of saving $3,000 exactly once. Saving that amount every year for several decades—and saving more as income rises—will multiply the total considerably. This type of wealth won't rival the riches of Microsoft chief executive officer Bill Gates or legendary investor Warren Buffett, but remember that only half of Americans have any money in mutual funds at all. Accumulating hundreds of thousands of dollars by retirement is a perfectly achievable goal for a well-educated person who starts saving early in life—and that amount of accumulated wealth will put you at or near the top 10% of all American households.

Getting additional education and saving money early in life obviously won't make you rich overnight. Additional education typically means putting off earning income and living like a student for more years. Saving money often require choices like driving an older or less fancy car, living in a smaller apartment or buying a smaller house, and making other day-to-day sacrifices. For most people, the trade-offs for achieving substantial personal wealth will require effort, patience, and sacrifice.

How Capital Markets Transform Financial Flows

Financial capital markets have the power to repackage money as it moves from those who supply financial capital to those who demand it. Banks accept checking account deposits, bundle them together, and turn them into long-term loans to companies. Individual firms sell shares of stock and issue bonds to raise capital. Firms make and sell an astonishing array of goods and services, but an investor can receive a return on the company's decisions by buying stock in a company. Stocks and bonds are sold and resold by financial investors to each other. Venture capitalists and angel investors search for promising small companies. Mutual funds combine the stocks and bonds—and thus, indirectly, the products and investments—of many different companies.

This chapter has discussed the basics mechanisms of financial markets, but a more advanced course in economics or finance will consider more sophisticated tools. For example, stocks and bonds come in many varieties. There is *nonvoting stock* where the holder can buy and sell the stock, but not vote for the board of directors. Some bonds make their payments based on interest rates that vary according to inflation or some other factor, rather than fixed interest rates. Other bonds make all of the interest payments in one lump sum when the bond comes due, not on a year-by-year basis. Some stocks give shareholders an option to convert them into bonds; some bonds give bondholders an option to convert them into stocks. In the "options market," a financial investor buys not the stock or bond itself but rather an option to buy the stock or bond at a predetermined price if the price rises in the future, or an option to sell the stock if the price falls.

But the fundamentals of financial capital markets remain the same. Firms are trying to raise financial capital, and households are looking for a desirable combination of rate of return, risk, and liquidity. Financial markets are society's mechanisms for bringing together these forces of demand and supply.

Key Concepts and Summary

1. Companies can raise early-stage financial capital in several ways: from their managers' personal savings and from private investors like angel investors and **venture capital** firms.
2. For many firms, reinvesting their own previously earned profits is a substantial source of financial capital for investment. However, reinvesting profits will not work well for firms that have limited profits.
3. As companies become more established, with a record of earning profits, it becomes possible for them to borrow money, either from banks or by issuing bonds, because the lenders can have some confidence that they will be repaid.
4. A **bond** is a financial contract through which a borrower agrees to repay the amount that was borrowed A bond specifies an amount that will be borrowed, the amounts that will be repaid over time based on the interest rate when the bond is issued, and the time until repayment. **Corporate bonds** are issued by firms; **municipal bonds** are issued by cities, state bonds by U.S. states, and **Treasury bonds** by the federal government through the U.S. Department of the Treasury.
5. **Stock** represents ownership of a firm; that is, a person who owns 100% of a company's stock by definition owns the entire company. The stock of a company is divided into **shares**. A firm receives financial capital when it sells stock to the public. A company's first sale of stock to the public is called the **initial public offering (IPO)**. However, a firm does not receive any funds when one **shareholder** sells stock in the firm to another shareholder.
6. The rate of return on stock is received in two forms. Firms can make direct cash payments to shareholders called **dividends**. In addition, a shareholder might buy shares of stock at a lower price and sell them at a higher price, which is called a **capital gain**.
7. A **private company** is owned by the people who run it on a day-to-day basis. A private company owned and run by an individual is called a **sole proprietorship**, while a firm owned and run by a group is called a **partnership**. When a firm decides to sell stock that can be bought and sold by financial investors, then the firm is owned by its shareholders—who in turn elect a board of directors to hire top day-to-day management—and is called a **public company**.
8. All investments can be categorized according to three key characteristics: average expected return, degree of risk, and liquidity. To get a higher rate of return, an investor must typically accept either more risk or less liquidity.
9. Banks are an example of a **financial intermediary**, an institution that operates to coordinate supply and demand in the financial capital market. A bank, for example, receives money from suppliers of financial capital and provides loans to demanders of financial capital.
10. Banks offer a range of accounts, including **checking accounts**, **savings accounts**, and **certificates of deposit**. Under the federal program of **deposit insurance**, banks purchase insurance against the risk of a bank failure.
11. A typical bond promises the financial investor a series of payments over time, based on the interest rate at the time the bond is issued, and then repayment of what was borrowed. Bonds that offer a high rate of return but also a relatively high chance of defaulting on the payments are called junk bonds.
12. The **bond yield** is the rate of return that a bond promises to pay at the time of purchase. Even when bonds make payments based on a fixed rate of interest, they are somewhat risky, because if interest rates rise for the economy as a whole, an investor who owns bonds issued at lower interest rates is now locked into the low rate and suffers a loss.
13. The price of a company's stock will be determined by expectations of future profits. There are two main motivations for purchasing stock. **Fundamentals trading** involves buying or selling stock based on estimates of the future expected profits of the firm. **Momentum trading** involves buying stock because the price is rising or selling stock because the price is falling, without regard for long-term fundamental value. Momentum trading may lead to sharp rises and falls in stock prices.
14. Investing in any individual firm is somewhat risky, so investors are wise to practice **diversification**, which means investing in a range of companies.
15. A **mutual fund** purchases an array of stocks and/or bonds. An investor in the mutual fund then receives a return depending on the overall performance of the investments made by the fund as a whole. A mutual fund that seeks to imitate the overall behavior of the stock market is called an **index fund**.
16. Housing and other tangible assets can also be regarded as forms of financial investment, which pay a rate of return in the form of capital gains. Housing can also offer a nonfinancial return—specifically, you can live in it.
17. Changes in the price of a stock depend on changes in expectations about future profits. Because changes

in expectations are largely unpredictable, movements in stock prices will tend to be a "random walk." It is difficult, even for financial professionals, to predict changes in future expectations and thus to choose the stocks whose price is going to rise in the future.

18. Most Americans can accumulate considerable financial wealth if they follow two rules: complete significant additional education and training after graduating from high school, and start saving money early in life.

Review Questions

1. What are the most common ways for start-up firms to raise financial capital?
2. Why can't firms just use their own profits for financial capital, with no need for outside investors?
3. Why are banks more willing to lend to well-established firms?
4. What is a bond? What is a junk bond?
5. What does a share of stock represent?
6. When do firms receive money from the sale of stock in their firm, and when do they not receive money?
7. What is a dividend?
8. What is a capital gain?
9. What's the difference between a private company and a public company?
10. How do the shareholders who own a company choose the actual managers of the company?
11. What are the three main concerns of a financial investor?
12. Why are banks called "financial intermediaries"?
13. Name several different kinds of bank accounts. How are they different?
14. Why are bonds somewhat risky to buy, even though they make predetermined payments based on a fixed rate of interest?
15. What's the difference between fundamentals trading and momentum trading?
16. Why should a financial investor care about diversification?
17. What is a mutual fund?
18. What is an index fund?
19. How is buying a house to live in a type of financial investment?
20. Why is it hard to forecast future movements in stock prices?

CHAPTER

20

Public Choice

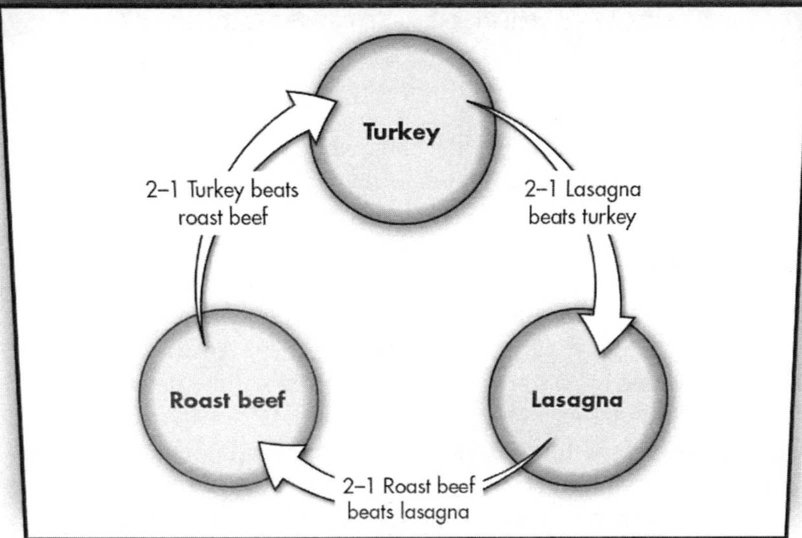

Chapter Outline

Democratic governments are supposed to be, as President Abraham Lincoln famously said in his 1863 Gettysburg Address, "of the people, by the people, and for the people." But can democratic governments be relied on to enact sensible economic policies? After all, democratic government reacts to voters, not to analyses of demand and supply curves. The main focus of an economics course is, naturally enough, to analyze the characteristics of markets and purely economic institutions. But political institutions also play a role in allocating the scarce resources of society, and economists have played an active role along with other social scientists in analyzing how such political institutions work.

The previous nine chapters of this book have discussed situations in which market forces can sometimes lead to undesirable results: monopoly, imperfect competition, and antitrust policy (Chapters 11–13); negative externalities like pollution (Chapter 14); positive externalities and public goods like research and development (Chapter 15); poverty and inequality of incomes (Chapter 16); worker protection from employers, as in the case of discrimination (Chapter 17); failures to provide insurance and other issues related to imperfect information (Chapter 18); and financial markets that may go from boom to bust (Chapter 19). Many of these discussions suggested the possibility that government economic policies could be aimed at addressing these issues.

But just as markets can face issues and problems that lead to undesirable outcomes, a democratic system of government can also make mistakes, either by enacting policies that don't benefit society as a whole or by failing to enact policies that would have benefited society as a whole. This chapter discusses some practical difficulties of democracy from an economic point of view in which the actors in the political system are presumed to follow their own self-interest. For example, many voters don't vote, which obviously raises questions about whether a democratic system will reflect everyone's interests. Benefits or costs of government action are sometimes concentrated on small groups, who in some cases may organize together and have a disproportionately large effect on politics and in other cases may fail to organize and end up neglected. Legislators who worry about support from voters of their district may focus on local spending projects for their own district, without sufficient concern for whether this spending is in the interest of the nation as a whole. When more than two choices exist, the principle that the majority of voters should decide may not always make logical sense because situations can arise where it becomes literally impossible to decide what the "majority" prefers. Finally, government may be slower than private firms to correct its mistakes because government agencies do not face competition or a threat of new entry. Let's consider these factors in turn.

When Voters Don't Participate

In U.S. presidential elections over the last few decades, about 55–65% of voting-age citizens actually vote. In congressional elections when there is no presidential race, or in local elections, the turnout is typically lower, often less than half of the eligible voters. In other countries, the share of adults who vote is often higher than in the United States. For example, in national elections since the 1980s in Germany, Spain, and France, about 75–80% of those of voting age cast ballots. But even this total falls well short of 100%. Some countries have laws that require voting, among them Australia, Belgium, Italy, Greece, Turkey, Singapore, and most Latin American nations. At the time the United States was founded, voting was mandatory in Virginia, Maryland, Delaware, and Georgia. But even if the law can require people to vote, no law can require that each voter cast an informed or a thoughtful vote. Moreover, in the United States and in most countries around the world, the freedom to vote has typically meant the freedom *not* to vote, as well.

Why don't people vote? Perhaps they don't much care who wins, or they are uninformed about who is running, or they don't believe that their vote will matter. Indeed, these reasons are probably tied together, since people who don't believe their votes matter won't bother to become informed and won't much care who wins. Economists have suggested reasons why a utility-maximizing person might rationally decide not to vote or not to become informed about the election. While a few elections in very small towns may be decided by a single vote, in most elections of any size, the margin of victory is measured in hundreds, thousands, or even millions of votes. A rational voter will recognize that one vote is extremely unlikely to make a difference. This theory of **rational ignorance** holds that people won't bother incurring the costs of becoming informed and voting because they know that their vote won't be decisive in the election.

rational ignorance: The theory that rational people won't bother incurring the costs of becoming informed and voting because they know that their vote won't be decisive in the election.

In a 1957 work, *An Economic Theory of Democracy*, the economist Anthony Downs stated the problem this way: "It seems probable that for a great many citizens in a democracy, rational behavior excludes any investment whatever in political information per se. No matter how significant a difference between parties is revealed to the rational citizen by his free information, or how uncertain he is about which party to support, he realizes that his vote has almost no chance of influencing the outcome. . . . He will not even utilize all the free information available, since assimilating it takes time." In his classic 1948 novel *Walden II*, the psychologist B. F. Skinner puts the issue even more succinctly via one of his characters, who states: "The chance that one man's vote will decide the issue in a national election . . . is less than the chance that he will be killed on his way to the polls."

While many Americans don't bother to vote in presidential elections, more than half do. What is the motivation of those who do vote? Research on voting behavior has shown that people who, on average, are more settled or more "connected" to society tend to vote more frequently. For example, married people vote more than single people. Those with a job vote more than the unemployed. Those who have lived longer in a neighborhood are more likely to vote than newcomers. Those who report that they know their neighbors and talk to them are more likely to vote than more socially isolated people. Those with a higher income and level of education are also more likely to vote. These factors suggest that political actions are likely to focus more on the interests of married, employed, well-educated people with at least a middle-class level of income than of other groups.

Does the United States Spend Too Much Money on Elections?

In the 2012 elections for president, Congress, and a raft of state and local offices, a total of about $7 billion was spent on the election campaigns, including advertising, fundraising, travel, and staff. Many people worry that politicians spend too much of their time raising money and thus end up entangled with special interests. They would prefer a system that restricts what candidates can spend, perhaps in exchange for limited public campaign financing or TV advertising time that would be free to the candidates.

But how much spending on campaigns is too much? In the U.S. economy, which exceeded $15 trillion in 2012, the $7 billion spent on political campaigns is about 1/20 of 1% of the overall economy.

Total government spending in 2012, including federal and state government, totaled about $5.5 trillion, so the cost of choosing the people who would determine how this money would be spent cost about 1/8 of 1% of government spending.

In the context of the enormous U.S. economy, $7 billion isn't as much money as it sounds. For example, consumers in the U.S. economy spend about $2 billion per year on toothpaste. In 2012, Procter and Gamble spent $4.8 billion on advertising, and General Motors spent $3.1 billion. Americans spend about $22 billion per year on pet food—three times as much as was spent on the 2012 election.

Whatever we believe about whether candidates and their parties spend too much or too little on elections, the U.S. Supreme Court has placed limits on how government can limit campaign spending. In a 1976 decision, *Buckley vs. Valeo*, the Supreme Court emphasized that the first amendment to the U.S. Constitution specifies freedom of speech. The federal government and states can offer candidates a voluntary deal in which government makes some public financing available to candidates, but only if the candidates agree to abide by certain spending limits. Of course, candidates can also voluntarily agree to set certain spending limits if they wish to do so. But government cannot forbid people or organizations from raising and spending money that is above these limits if they choose to do so. There is an ongoing political and legal battle over what rules will govern campaign-related spending by groups that are not explicitly connected with a particular candidate.

For example, those who vote may tend to be more supportive of financial assistance for the two-year and four-year colleges that they expect their children to attend than they are of medical care or public school education aimed at families of the poor and unemployed.

A number of proposals have been offered to encourage greater voter turnout: making it easier to register to vote, keeping the polls open for more hours, or even moving election day to a weekend when more people don't need to worry about jobs or school commitments. In general, it has become easier to vote in the United States over recent decades. However, these changes do not seem to have caused a long-term upward trend in the number of people voting. After all, casting an informed vote will always impose some costs of time and energy. It's not clear how to strengthen people's feeling of connectedness to society in a way that will lead to a substantial increase in voter turnout. But otherwise, politicians elected by the votes of 60% or less of the population may not enact economic policy in the best interests of 100% of the population.

Special-Interest Politics

Many political issues are of intense interest to a relatively small group. For example, many Americans don't much care where the tires for their car were made. But in September 2009, President Obama enacted a tariff on tires imported from China, which would increase the import price of Chinese tires by 35 percent in its first year, 30 percent in the second year, and 25 percent in the third year. Interestingly, the U.S. companies that make tires did not favor this step because most of them also import tires from China and other countries. However, the United Steelworkers union, which had seen jobs making tires fall by 5,000 over the previous five years, lobbied fiercely for the tariffs to be enacted.

Special-interest groups are groups that are numerically small but quite well organized. A focused special-interest group can pressure legislators to enact public policies that do not benefit social surplus. For example, imagine an environmental rule to reduce air pollution

special-interest groups: Groups that are numerically small but well organized and thus exert a disproportionate effect on political outcomes.

that will cost 10 large companies $8 million each, for a total cost of $80 million. The social benefits from enacting this rule provide an average of $10 for every person in the United States, so the benefits are about $3 trillion. But even though the benefits are far higher than the costs for society as a whole, the 10 companies are likely to lobby much more fiercely to avoid $8 million in costs than the average person is to argue for $10 worth of benefits.

As this example suggests, the problem of special interests in politics can be related to an issue raised back in Chapter 14 about economic policy with respect to negative externalities and pollution—the problem called "regulatory capture." In any government office where fine print is being written—laws and regulations about how much corporations will pay in taxes, or rules for safety in the workplace, or how to satisfy environmental regulations—you can bet that the specific industry affected has lobbyists who study every word and every comma. They talk with the legislators who are writing the legislation and suggest alternative wording. They contribute to the campaigns of legislators on the key committees—and may even offer those legislators high-paying jobs after they have left office. As a result, it often turns out that those who are being regulated can exercise considerable influence over the regulators. The idea of special interests takes this insight one step further and points out that when legislation is being considered and enacted, it can also be strongly affected by the groups that are most heavily involved in lobbying the politicians.

A democratic political system does offer some hope that neither an overemphasized and well-organized special-interest group nor an underemphasized and unorganized minority group will last forever. Special interests may develop a close relationship with one political party, and so their ability to influence legislation rises and falls as that party moves in or out of power. A special interest may even hurt a political party if it appears to a number of voters that the relationship is too cozy. In a close election, a small group that has been underemphasized in the past may find that it can tip the election one way or another—and so that group will suddenly receive considerable attention. Democratic institutions produce an ebb and flow of political parties and interests, and thus offer both opportunities for special interests and ways of counterbalancing those interests over time.

Identifiable Winners, Anonymous Losers

A number of economic policies involve gains where the beneficiaries are easily identifiable, but some or all of the costs are spread over those who are more anonymous. A democratic political system probably has a bias toward those who are identifiable.

For example, policies that impose price controls—like rent control—may look as if they benefit renters and only impose costs on landlords. But when landlords decide to contract or not to expand the number of rental units available, then a number of people who would have liked to rent an apartment end up living somewhere else because when they looked for rental apartments, none were available. These would-be renters have experienced a cost of rent control, but it's hard to identify who they are.

Similarly, policies that block imports will benefit the firms that would have competed with those imports—and workers at those firms—who are likely to be quite visible. On the other hand, consumers who would have preferred to purchase the imported products, and thus who bear some costs of the protectionist policy, are much less visible.

Specific tax breaks or spending programs can also fit this pattern of identifiable winners, with the costs of paying for these policies imposed on those who are hard to identify. Special interests are more likely to form from a group that is easily identifiable, rather than from a group where some of those who suffered may not even recognize that they are bearing costs.

Pork Barrels and Logrolling

pork-barrel spending: Spending that benefits mainly a single political district.

Politicians have an incentive to assure that government money is spent in their home state or district, where it will benefit their constituents in a direct and obvious way. Thus, when legislators are negotiating over whether to support a piece of legislation, a common request is to include **pork-barrel spending**, which is defined as legislation that benefits mainly a single political district. Pork-barrel spending can be thought of as another case where democracy is challenged by concentrated benefits and widely dispersed costs: the benefits of pork-barrel spending are obvious and direct to local voters, while the costs are spread over the entire country.

U.S. Senator Robert C. Byrd of West Virginia, who was originally elected to the Senate in 1958 and had set the record for the longest-serving member by the time of his death in 2010, was widely regarded as one of the masters of pork-barrel politics, directing a steady stream of federal funds to his home state. A journalist once compiled a list of structures in West Virginia at least partly funded by the government and named after Byrd: "the Robert C. Byrd Highway, the Robert C. Byrd Locks and Dam, the Robert C. Byrd Institute, the Robert C. Byrd Life Long Learning Center, the Robert C. Byrd Honors Scholarship Program, the Robert C. Byrd Green Bank Telescope, the Robert C. Byrd Institute for Advanced Flexible Manufacturing, the Robert C. Byrd Federal Courthouse, the Robert C. Byrd Health Sciences Center, the Robert C. Byrd Academic and Technology Center, the Robert C. Byrd United Technical Center, the Robert C. Byrd Federal Building, the Robert C. Byrd Drive, the Robert C. Byrd Hilltop Office Complex, the Robert C. Byrd Library, the Robert C. Byrd Learning Resource Center, the Robert C. Byrd Rural Health Center." Moreover, this list doesn't include government-funded projects in West Virginia that were not named after Byrd. Of course, it would be necessary to analyze each of these expenditures in detail to figure out whether they should be treated as pork-barrel spending or whether they provide widespread benefits that reach beyond West Virginia. But at least some of them certainly smell like pork. The amount spent on individual pork-barrel projects is small, but many small projects can add up to a substantial total.

Pork-barrel spending can be encouraged by **logrolling** on the part of politicians, which refers to a situation where a group of legislators all agree to vote for a package of otherwise unrelated laws that they individually favor. For example, if one member of Congress suggests building a new bridge or hospital in that member's own congressional district, the other members might oppose it. But if 51% of the legislators come together, they can pass a bill that includes a bridge or hospital for every one of their districts. For example, the U.S. government has typically spread out its spending on military bases and weapons programs to congressional districts all across the country, in part to help create a situation where many members of Congress would be encouraged to vote in support of defense spending.

logrolling: When a group of legislators all agree to vote for a package of otherwise unrelated laws that they individually favor.

The Law and Economics Movement

A few decades ago, most lawyers and judges knew relatively little about economics. Conventional wisdom said that law was about legislation, rights and wrongs, and justice, while economics was an altogether different subject. But in the last few decades, the "law and economics movement" has tightened the connections between the two fields.

One place for close connections between law and economics lay in the area of antitrust law and enforcement. Issues of measuring the level of competition in a market and determining whether a firm is engaging in legal or illegal restrictive practices (as addressed in Chapter 12) are issues in which economists have many useful insights. In high-profile cases involving the conduct of large firms, economists have helped to analyze the issues.

But the law and economics movement goes much deeper. As one example, an economics framework can provide a ready interpretation in legal cases about liability, where one side is sued for causing harm to the other side. For example, scooters went through a wave of popularity about a decade ago, and the number of scooter-related injuries requiring an emergency room visit rose from 43,500 in 2000 to 99,800 in 2001—along with 10 deaths. Should society encourage lawsuits against those who make scooters in response to this data? Should laws be passed about scooter safety? Or should it just be accepted that some scooter-related accidents will occur? Moreover, economics can analyze how to address liability issues in terms of whether they provide the appropriate incentives to reduce injuries in the future.

Most legal rules don't just settle past disputes, but create incentives for future behavior that economics is well-suited to analyze. Most law schools now have at least a few faculty members who are both lawyers and Ph.D. economists, and require students to study at least basic economics.

Voting Cycles

Democracy is sometimes summed up (and oversimplified) in two words: "Majority rule." But when voters face three or more choices, then voting may not always be a useful way of determining what the majority prefers.

As one example, consider an election in a state where 60% of the population is liberal and 40% is conservative. If there are only two candidates, one from each side, and if similar proportions of liberals and conservatives vote, then the liberal will win. But what if the election includes two liberal candidates and only one conservative? It is possible that the liberal vote will split and victory will go to the minority party. In this case, the outcome does not reflect the majority's preference. In the French national elections of 2002, for example, the two leading candidates were expected to be Jacques Chirac and Lionel Jospin. But French elections happen in two rounds: a preliminary round that reduces the candidates to the top two and then a runoff round between those top two. In the preliminary round, the vote splintered: Chirac led with 19% of the vote, and Jospin received 16%. However, a candidate named Jean-Marie Le Pen received 17% of the vote and sneaked into the runoff ahead of Jospin. The other 48% of the vote was split between 13 other candidates. This outcome made international headlines because Le Pen had been frequently criticized for extreme nationalist views that sometimes seemed to cross the line into intolerance or racism. In the runoff, the supporters of other candidates united behind Chirac, who beat Le Pen by a majority of 82% to 18%. But Jospin might have beaten Chirac in a runoff, if voting had not been so splintered in the preliminary round.

In some cases with three or more options, it is not even clear how to define what the majority opinion might be. Step aside from politics for a moment and think about a choice facing three families—the Abbotts, the Burnses, and the Costellos—who are planning to celebrate New Year's Day together. They agree to vote on the menu, choosing from three entrees, and they agree that the majority vote wins. With three families, it seems reasonable that one choice of entree will get a 2–1 majority.

But what if their vote ends up looking like the choices in Exhibit 20-1? Clearly, the three families disagree on their first choice. But the problem goes even deeper. Instead of looking at all three choices at once, compare them two at a time. In a vote of turkey vs. beef, turkey wins by 2–1. In a vote of beef vs. lasagna, beef wins 2–1. If turkey beats beef, and beef beats lasagna, then it might seem only logical that turkey must also beat lasagna. However, with the preferences shown, lasagna is preferred to turkey by a 2–1 vote, as well. But if lasagna is preferred to turkey, and turkey beats beef, then surely it must be that lasagna also beats beef? Actually, no. Beef beats lasagna.

voting cycle: When a majority prefers A over B, B over C, and C over A.

The situation where Choice A is preferred by a majority over Choice B, Choice B is preferred by a majority over Choice C, and Choice C is preferred by a majority over Choice A is called a **voting cycle**. It's easy to imagine sets of government choices—say, perhaps the choice between increased defense spending, increased government spending on health care, and a tax cut—where a voting cycle could occur. When a voting cycle does occur, the result will be determined by the order in which choices are presented and voted on, not by majority rule, because every choice is both preferred to some alternative and also not preferred to another alternative.

Where Is Government's Self-Correcting Mechanism?

When a firm produces a product that no one wants to buy or produces at a higher cost than its competitors, the firm is likely to suffer losses, and if the firm cannot change its ways, it will go out of business altogether. This self-correcting mechanism of the private economy can have harsh effects in some cases on workers or on local economies, but it also puts pressure on firms for good performance.

Government agencies, on the other hand, do not sell their products in a market or face direct competitors. If the U.S. Department of Education or the U.S. Department of Defense is doing a poor job, citizens cannot purchase their services from another provider and drive the existing government agencies into bankruptcy. If you are upset that the

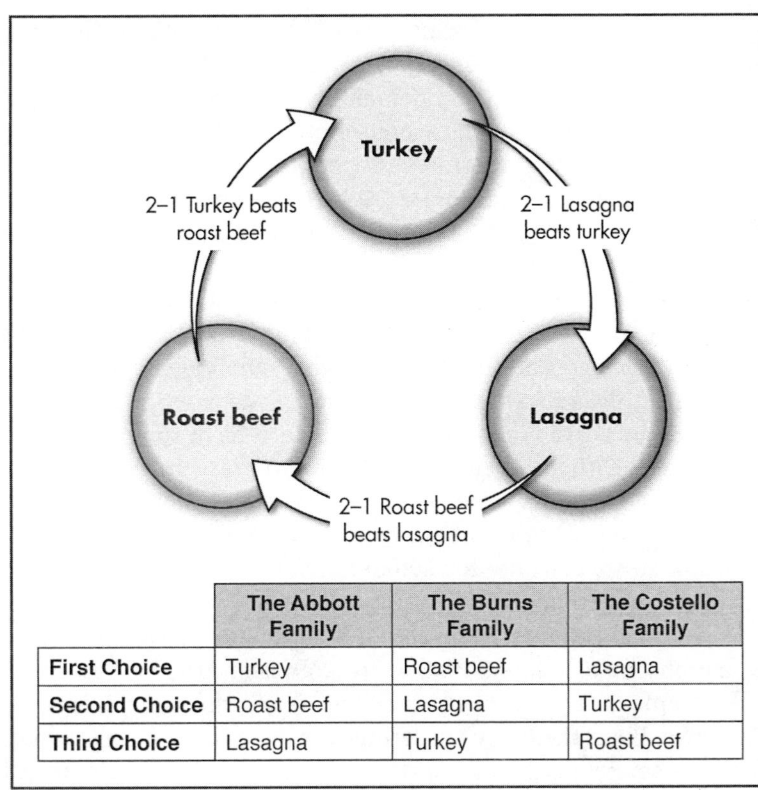

	The Abbott Family	The Burns Family	The Costello Family
First Choice	Turkey	Roast beef	Lasagna
Second Choice	Roast beef	Lasagna	Turkey
Third Choice	Lasagna	Turkey	Roast beef

EXHIBIT 20-1 A Voting Cycle

Given these choices, voting will struggle to produce a majority outcome. Turkey is favored over roast beef by 2–1, and roast beef is favored over lasagna by 2–1. If turkey beats roast beef and roast beef beats lasagna, then it might seem that turkey must beat lasagna, too. But given these preferences, lasagna is favored over turkey by 2–1.

Internal Revenue Service is slow in sending you a tax refund or seems unable to answer your questions, you can't decide to pay your income taxes through a different organization. Of course, elected politicians can assign new leaders to government agencies and instruct them to reorganize or to emphasize a different mission. But the pressure that government faces to make changes in its bureaucracy to seek greater efficiency and customer responsiveness is much milder than the threat of being put out of business altogether.

This insight suggests that when government provides goods or services directly, it might be expected to do so with less efficiency than private firms—except in certain cases where the government agency may compete directly with private firms. At the local level, for example, services like garbage collection can be provided by government directly, by private firms under contract to the government, or by a mix of government employees competing with private firms.

A Balanced View of Markets and Government

The British statesman Sir Winston Churchill (1874–1965) once wrote: "No one pretends that democracy is perfect or all-wise. Indeed, it has been said that democracy is the worst form of government except for all of the other forms which have been tried from time to time." In that spirit, the theme of this discussion is certainly not that democratic government should be abandoned. But a practical student of public policy needs to recognize that in some cases, like the case of well-organized special interests or pork-barrel legislation, a democratic government may seek to enact economically unwise projects or programs. In other cases, by placing a low priority on the problems of those who are not well organized or who are less likely to vote, the government may fail to act when it could do some good. In these and other cases, there is no automatic reason to believe that government will necessarily make economically sensible choices.

"The true test of a first-rate mind is the ability to hold two contradictory ideas at the same time," wrote the American author F. Scott Fitzgerald (1896–1940). At this point in your study of microeconomics, you should be able to go one better than Fitzgerald and to hold three somewhat contradictory ideas about the interrelationship between markets and government in your mind at the same time.

First, markets are extraordinarily useful and flexible institutions through which society can allocate its scarce resources. This idea was introduced with the subjects of international trade in Chapter 3, and demand and supply in Chapter 4, and reinforced in all the subsequent discussions of how households and firms make decisions.

Second, markets may sometimes produce unwanted results. A short list of the conditions where markets produce unwanted results would include monopoly and other issues of imperfect competition, pollution, poverty and inequality of incomes, discrimination, and failures to provide insurance.

Third, while government may play a useful role in addressing the problems of markets, government action is also imperfect. Economists readily admit that in those settings like monopoly or negative externalities, a *potential* role exists for government intervention. However, in the real world, it isn't enough to point out that government action might *potentially* be a good idea. Instead, you must have some confidence that the government is likely to identify and carry out the appropriate public policy. To make sensible judgments about economic policy, you must see the strengths and weaknesses of both markets and government. Don't idealize or demonize either unregulated markets or government actions. Instead, consider the actual strengths and weaknesses of real-world markets and real-world governments.

These three insights often do not lead to simple or obvious political conclusions. As the famous British economist, Joan Robinson (1903–1983), wrote some decades ago: "[E]conomic theory, in itself, preaches no doctrines and cannot establish any universally valid laws. It is a method of ordering ideas and formulating questions." The study of economics is neither politically conservative, nor moderate, nor liberal. There are economists who are Democrats, Republicans, libertarians, socialists, and every other political group you can name. Of course, conservatives may tend to emphasize the virtues of markets and the limitations of government, while liberals may tend to emphasize the shortcomings of markets and the need for government programs. But such differences only illustrate that the language and terminology of economics is not limited to one set of political beliefs, but can be used by all.

Key Concepts and Summary

1. The theory of **rational ignorance** holds that voters will recognize that their single vote is extremely unlikely to influence the outcome of an election, and they will thus choose to remain uninformed about issues and not to vote. This theory helps to explain why voter turnout is so low in the United States.
2. Special-interest politics arises when a relatively small group, called a **special-interest group**, each of whose members has a large interest in a political outcome, devotes a lot of time and energy to lobbying for the group's preferred choice. Meanwhile, the large majority, each of whose members has only a small interest in this issue, pays no attention.
3. **Pork-barrel spending** is defined as legislation where the benefits are concentrated on a single district while the costs are spread widely over the country. **Logrolling** refers to a situation where two or more legislators agree to vote for each other's legislation, which can then encourage pork-barrel spending in many districts.
4. Majority votes can run into difficulties when more than three choices exist. A **voting cycle** occurs when in a situation with at least three choices, choice A is preferred by a majority vote to choice B, choice B is preferred by a majority vote to choice C, and choice C is preferred by a majority vote to choice A. In such a situation, it is impossible even to define what the majority prefers. Another difficulty arises when the vote is so divided that a no choice receives a majority.
5. A practical approach to microeconomic policy will need to take a realistic view of the specific strengths and weaknesses of markets and the specific strengths and weaknesses of government, rather than making the easy, wrong assumption that either markets or government are always beneficial or always harmful.

Review Questions

1. How does rational ignorance discourage voting?
2. How can a small special-interest group win, since the benefits flow only to a small group, under a situation of majority voting?
3. How can pork-barrel spending occur, since it benefits only a small group, in a situation of majority voting?
4. Why does a voting cycle make it impossible to decide on a majority-approved choice?

CHAPTER

21

The Macroeconomic Perspective

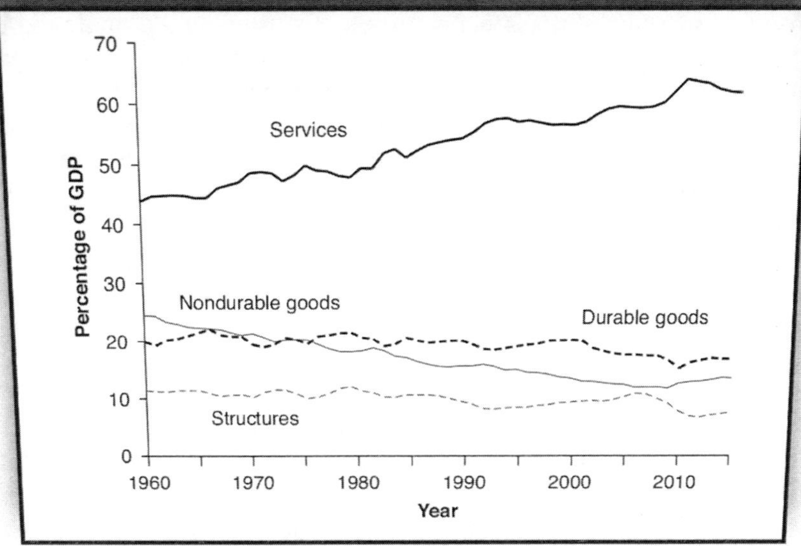

Chapter Outline

Macroeconomics and microeconomics are two different perspectives on the subject of economics, but what seems sensible from a microeconomic point of view can have unexpected or counterproductive results at the macroeconomic level. For example, imagine that you are sitting at an event with a large audience, like a live concert or a basketball game. A few people decide that they want a better view, so they stand up. However, when these people stand up, they block the view for some other people, so that the others need to stand up as well if they want to see. Eventually, nearly everyone is standing up, and as a result, no one can see much better than before. The individually rational decision of some individuals at the micro level—stand up to see better—ended up being self-defeating at the macro level.

Or consider the case of a farmer who finds out that the long-range weather forecast predicts an especially fine growing season. The farmer decides to plant extra land to take advantage of the fine weather. However, if all farmers see the same forecast, and all decide to plant extra, then the result will be a shift out to the right of the supply curve that depresses the equilibrium market price for all farmers. In this case, the microeconomic rational behavior of individual farmers who are seeking higher profits ends up with an outcome—lower prices—that none of them desired.

Finally, consider the case of a country in which many foreign individuals and firms are making financial investments. A rumor circulates that the economy of this country may be weakening and that some of its leading companies may go bankrupt. The foreign investors become worried. They start selling their assets in the country and refusing to make any new investments. But when many foreign investors react in this way, the country's economy actually does become much weaker from a lack of loans and financial investment capital, and many leading companies go bankrupt as a result. Again, individually rational, cautious decisions by investors—in this case, reducing the amount invested in the country—leads to a self-fulfilling prophecy that their investments turn out poorly.

These stories have a common theme: Individually rational motivations help economic agents coordinate their behavior in some ways, but in certain cases, they can also lead to undesired outcomes. In such cases, society may wish to create other coordinating mechanisms. In the case of people in a crowd trying to see better, for example, the coordinating mechanism is often social pressure: that is, the group accepts that people will stand up in moments of excitement, but if someone stands at other times, then others in the audience might yell at that person to sit down. In macroeconomic settings, government may in certain situations be able to play a coordinating role to avoid unwanted outcomes.

This chapter begins the discussion of macroeconomics by focusing on the single most common measure of the size of the macroeconomy: gross domestic product or GDP. Since the macroeconomy involves all the buying and selling transactions that occur, GDP can be measured in two ways: by looking at the overall demand for goods and services, or by looking at what is produced. The chapter will compare GDP across countries, examine patterns of GDP in the long run and the short run, and discuss the extent to which GDP captures the broader concept of a society's standard of living.

The chapters that follow will first discuss macroeconomic goals, then frameworks for analysis, and finally policy tools. Exhibit 21-1 illustrates the structure. In thinking about the overall health of a macroeconomy, it is useful to consider four goals. *Economic growth*, which can be approximated by the growth of gross domestic product, ultimately determines the prevailing standard of living in a country. *Unemployment*, the situation in which people want to work but can't find a job, is not only potentially devastating for individuals and families, but in addition, society as a whole loses the value of the output that could have been produced if the unemployed had found a job. *Inflation* refers to a rise in the overall level of prices. For example, if many people face a situation where the prices that they pay for food, shelter, and health care are rising much faster than the wages they receive for their labor, there will be widespread unhappiness. Finally, a sustainable *balance of trade* refers to the flows of goods and financial capital back and forth between countries. Although the gains from trade in the global economy can produce economic gains for all nations, trade imbalances can also be a source of macroeconomic disruption and instability. One or more of these statistics are in the news almost every day. The next four chapters—from Chapters 22–25—will explore and explain these four goals.

None of these macroeconomic goals is straightforward to analyze from a microeconomic perspective. For example, microeconomic analysis of supply and demand can explain why equilibrium quantity might increase in a single market for a good or a service, but it does not offer a simple method for explaining overall growth in the entire economy. Microeconomic analysis can explain why a firm or an industry might hire more or fewer workers, but it does not offer a simple method for explaining why many firms might become unwilling to hire at the same time, thus creating the macroeconomic problem of unemployment. Microeconomic analysis can explain why the price might rise or fall for a particular product, but it doesn't offer any simple way of discussing why most prices might all rise by roughly the same amount at the same time in a process of inflation. Finally, microeconomic analysis can explain why a firm might have success selling

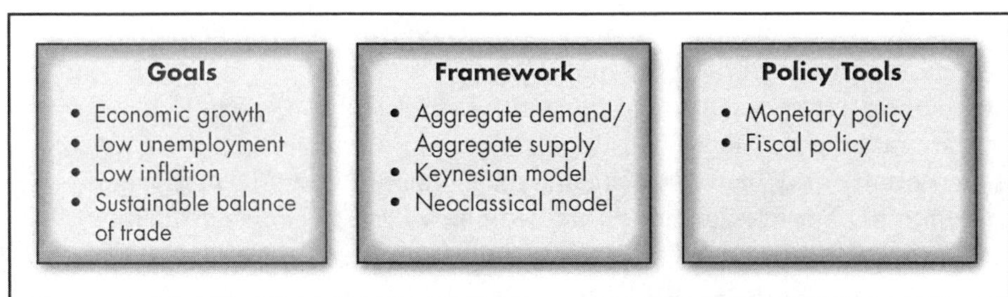

EXHIBIT 21-1 Macroeconomic Goals, Framework, and Policies

The discussion of macroeconomics in the chapters that follow will discuss four goals of macroeconomics, present several analytical frameworks for thinking about how these goals may interact and conflict, and finally, discuss two broad sets of macroeconomic policies.

its goods abroad and why consumers might want to buy goods from abroad, but it offers no easy framework for discussing the implications of the overall balance of exports and imports—that is, the balance of trade.

Several different analytical frameworks exist for thinking about how these four macroeconomic goals relate to each other, and how pursuing one goal may in some cases or over the short run or the long run involve trade-offs with other goals. These frameworks have names like "aggregate supply and aggregate demand models," "sticky price Keynesian models," and "flexible price neoclassical models." At this point, these names are just empty words, but they will be explained in Chapters 26–28.

With the goals and frameworks in mind, the stage is set to discuss how the macroeconomic policy tools available to government, working through the analytical frameworks, will affect the ultimate policy goals. *Monetary policy* includes policies that affect money, banking, interest rates, and exchange rates, and these policies are discussed in Chapters 29–31.

Fiscal policy means policies that involve government taxes or spending, and applications of fiscal policy are discussed in Chapters 32–33. Chapter 34, the final chapter of the macroeconomics section, offers overall lessons of macroeconomics in a global context.

Measuring the Size of the Economy: Gross Domestic Product

The size of a nation's overall economy is typically measured by its **gross domestic product** or **GDP**, which is the value of the output of all goods and services produced within a country. The measurement of GDP thus involves counting up millions of different goods and services—cars, haircuts, computers, steel, bananas, college educations, and everything else—and summing them into a total value. As a conceptual matter, this task is straightforward: take the quantity of everything produced, multiply it by the price for which everything was sold, and add up the total. In 2019, the U.S. GDP totaled nearly $18 trillion.

gross domestic product (GDP): The value of the output of all goods and services produced within a country.

Each of the market transactions that enters into GDP must involve both a buyer and a seller. Thus, the GDP of an economy can be measured either by the total of what is demanded in the economy, or by the total of what is produced in the economy.

GDP Measured by Components of Demand

GDP as measured by demand is commonly divided into five parts: consumption, investment, government, exports, and imports. Exhibit 21-2 shows how these five factors add up to the GDP in 2015. Exhibit 21-3*a* shows the levels of consumption, investment, and government consumption over time, expressed as a percentage of GDP, while Exhibit 21-3*b* shows the levels of exports and imports as a percentage of GDP over time. A few patterns about each of these components are worth noticing.

Consumption (*C*) by households is the largest component of GDP, accounting for about two-thirds of the GDP in any year. However, consumption is a gentle elephant: when viewed over time, it doesn't jump around too much.

EXHIBIT 21-2 Components of GDP in 2015: From the Demand Side

	Components of GDP on the Demand Side (in trillions of dollars)	Percentage of Total
Consumption	$12.2	68%
Investment	$3.1	17%
Government	$3.2	18%
Exports	$2.2	12%
Imports	$–2.8	–16%
Total	*$17.9*	*100%*

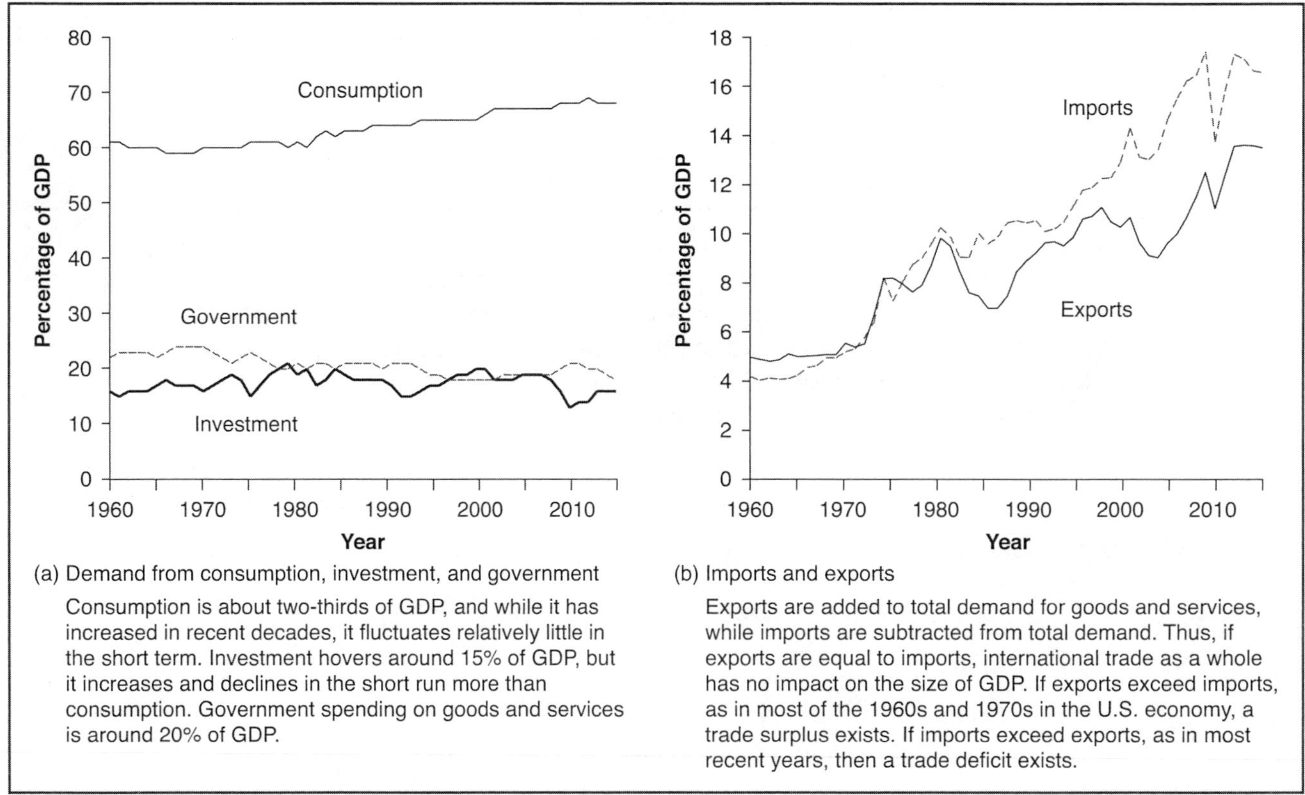

(a) Demand from consumption, investment, and government

Consumption is about two-thirds of GDP, and while it has increased in recent decades, it fluctuates relatively little in the short term. Investment hovers around 15% of GDP, but it increases and declines in the short run more than consumption. Government spending on goods and services is around 20% of GDP.

(b) Imports and exports

Exports are added to total demand for goods and services, while imports are subtracted from total demand. Thus, if exports are equal to imports, international trade as a whole has no impact on the size of GDP. If exports exceed imports, as in most of the 1960s and 1970s in the U.S. economy, a trade surplus exists. If imports exceed exports, as in most recent years, then a trade deficit exists.

EXHIBIT 21-3 Components of GDP on the Demand Side

Investment (*I*) by businesses refers to real purchases of physical plant and equipment by businesses. Investment demand is far smaller than consumption demand, typically accounting for only about 15–20% of GDP. However, it moves up and down more noticeably than consumption. Investment is a cat in a bag: it jumps around unexpectedly.

Government (*G*) demand in the United States appears relatively small, at about 20% of GDP. This proportion may seem too low. Indeed, government in the United States (including the federal, state, and local levels) collects about one-third of GDP in taxes. However, much of that money is passed directly to citizens, through programs like Social Security, welfare payments to the poor, or interest payments on past government borrowing. In these cases, the money that passes through government hands is counted as part of consumption. The only part of government spending counted in demand is—returning to the basic definition of GDP—government purchases of goods or services produced in the economy. Examples would include when the government buys a new fighter jet or when it pays workers who deliver government services.

When thinking about the demand for domestically produced goods in a global economy, it is important to count demand for *exports* (*X*)—that is, domestically made goods that are sold abroad. However, if one is going to add in the extra demand generated by foreign buyers, one must also subtract out *imports* (*M*)—that is, goods produced in other countries that are purchased in this country. The gap between exports and imports is called the **trade balance.** If a country's exports are larger than its imports, then a country is said to have a **trade surplus**. In the United States, exports typically exceeded imports in the 1960s and 1970s, as shown in Exhibit 21-3*b*. But since the early 1980s, imports have typically exceeded exports, and so the United States has experienced a **trade deficit** in most years. Indeed, the trade deficit grew quite large in the late 1990s and in the mid-2000s. Exhibit 21-3 also shows that imports and exports as a share of GDP have both generally been on an upward trend in recent decades, illustrating the process of globalization. If exports and imports are equal, then foreign trade has no effect on the total GDP of the econ-

trade balance: Gap between exports and imports.

trade surplus: When exports exceed imports.

trade deficit: When imports exceed exports.

How Statisticians Measure GDP

Economists have an old, sad joke that there are two things you never want to watch being made: sausages and economic statistics. The joke comes to mind in considering the task of the government economists at the Bureau of Economic Analysis (BEA), within the U.S. Department of Commerce, who piece together estimates of GDP from a variety of sources.

Analysts use a variety of data sources to estimate what is produced for consumers. Once every five years, in the second and seventh year of each decade, the Bureau of the Census carries out a detailed census of businesses throughout the United States. In between, the Census Bureau carries out a monthly survey of retail sales. These figures are adjusted with foreign trade data, to account for exports that are produced in the United States and sold abroad and for imports that are produced abroad and sold in the United States. Once every 10 years, the Census Bureau does a comprehensive survey of housing and residential finance. For investment, the Census Bureau does a monthly survey of construction and an annual survey of expenditures on physical capital equipment.

For what is purchased by the federal government, the statisticians rely on the U.S. Department of the Treasury. An annual Census of Governments gathers information on state and local governments. Because a lot of government spending at all levels involves hiring people to provide services, a large portion of government spending can also be tracked through payroll records collected by state governments and by the Social Security Administration.

With regard to foreign trade, the Census Bureau compiles a monthly record of all import and export documents. Additional surveys cover transportation and travel, and adjustment needs to be made for financial services that are produced in the United States for foreign customers.

Many other sources contribute to the estimates of GDP. Information on energy comes from the U.S. Department of Transportation and Department of Energy. Information on health care is collected by the Health Care Financing Administration. Surveys of landlords collect data about rent. The Department of Agriculture collects statistics on farming.

All of these bits and pieces of information arrive in different forms, at different time intervals. The Bureau of Economic Analysis melds them together to produce estimates of GDP on a quarterly basis (i.e., every three months). These estimates are then updated and revised. The "advance" estimate of GDP for a certain quarter is released one month after a quarter. The "preliminary" estimate comes out one month after that. The "final" estimate is published one month later, but it isn't actually final. In July, roughly, updated estimates for the previous calendar year are released. Then, once every five years, after the results of the latest detailed five-year business census have been processed, the BEA revises all of the past estimates of GDP according to the newest methods and data, going all the way back to 1929.

When you read newspaper reports of recent GDP announcements, be aware that the "advance," "preliminary," and "final" announcements of quarterly GDP during a year usually don't change much. However, the annual revisions released each summer can be substantial—enough to make GDP growth appear quite different than the quarterly reports released earlier that year.

omy. However, even if exports and imports are balanced overall, foreign trade might still have powerful effects on particular industries and workers by causing nations to shift workers and physical capital investment toward specializing in one industry rather than another.

Based on these five components of demand, GDP can be measured as:

$$\text{GDP} = \text{Consumption} + \text{Investment} + \text{Government} + \text{Trade balance}$$

$$\text{GDP} = C + I + G + (X - M).$$

Remember this definition. It will prove important for analyzing connections in the macroeconomy and for thinking about macroeconomic policy tools.

durable goods: Long-lasting goods like cars and refrigerators.

nondurable goods: Short-lived goods like food and clothing.

inventories: Goods that have been produced, but not yet been sold.

GDP Measured by What Is Produced

Everything that is purchased with components of demand must also be produced. Exhibit 21-4 breaks down what is produced into five categories: **durable goods**, **nondurable goods**, services, structures, and the change in **inventories**. Before going into detail about these categories, notice that total GDP measured according to what is produced is

EXHIBIT 21-4 Components of GDP on the Supply Side in 2015

	Components of GDP on the Supply Side (in trillions of dollars)	Percentage of Total
Goods		
Durable Goods	$3.0	16.8%
Nondurable Goods	$2.5	14.0%
Services	$11.0	61.4%
Structures	$1.4	7.8%
Change in Inventories	>$0.1	>0.1%
Total	*$17.9*	*100%*

exactly the same as the GDP measured by looking at the five components of demand. Since every market transaction must have both a buyer and a seller, GDP must be the same whether measured by what is demanded or what is produced. Exhibit 21-5 shows these components of what is produced, expressed as a percentage of GDP, since 1960. Again, a few patterns stand out.

In thinking about what is produced in the economy, many non-economists immediately focus on solid, long-lasting goods, like cars and computers. But by far the largest part of GDP is services, rather than goods. Moreover, services have been a growing share of GDP over time. A detailed breakdown of the leading service industries would include health care, education, law, and financial services. It has been decades since most of the U.S. economy involved making solid objects. Instead, the most common jobs in a modern economy involve a worker looking at pieces of paper or a computer screen, making phone calls, or communicating with co-workers, customers, or suppliers.

Even within the overall category of goods, long-lasting durable goods like cars and refrigerators are about the same share of the economy as short-lived nondurable goods like food and clothing. The category of structures includes everything from homes, to

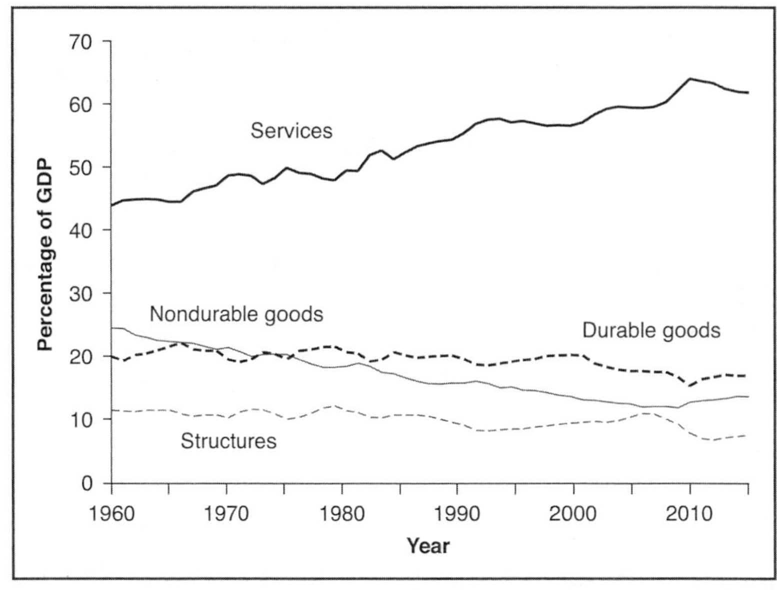

EXHIBIT 21-5 Components of Supply

Services are the largest single component of aggregate supply, representing roughly two-thirds of GDP. Nondurable goods used to be larger than durable goods, but in recent years, both categories are about 13-15% of GDP. Structures hover under 10% of GDP. The change in inventories, the final component of aggregate supply, is not shown here; it is typically much less than 1% of GDP.

office buildings, shopping malls, and factories. Inventories is a small category that refers to the goods that have been produced by one business but have not yet been sold to consumers, and are still sitting in warehouses and on shelves. The amount of inventories sitting on shelves will tend to decline if business is better than expected, or to rise if business is worse than expected.

The Problem of Double Counting

One danger for the statisticians who calculate GDP is to avoid the mistake of **double counting**, in which output is counted two or more times as it travels through the stages of production. This problem arises because in an economy with a division of labor, most products must work through an interconnected network of producers. For example, imagine what would happen if the government statisticians who calculate GDP first counted the value of mining iron ore, and then counted the value of the steel that used that iron ore, and then counted the value of the car that used that steel. In this example, the value of the original iron ore would have been counted three times—once at each stage of production.

double counting: A potential mistake to be avoided in measuring GDP, in which output is counted two or more times as it travels through the stages of production.

To avoid this problem, which could overstate the size of the economy considerably, government statisticians count just the **final goods and services** in the chain of production that are sold for consumption, investment, government, and trade purposes. This need to avoid double counting (or triple counting, or worse) explains why neither method of measuring GDP—what is demanded or what is produced—includes the many **intermediate goods and services** that businesses provide to other businesses. The value of what businesses provide to other businesses is captured in the final products at the end of the production chain. Similarly, the value of people's work is included in the price of the goods and services that are eventually produced.

final goods and services: Output used directly for consumption, investment, government, and trade purposes; contrast with "intermediate goods."

intermediate goods and services: Output provided to other businesses at an intermediate stage of production, not for final users; contrast with "final goods and services."

The concept of GDP is fairly straightforward: it's just the value of all final goods and services bought and sold in the economy. But in a decentralized, market-oriented economy, actually calculating the $18 trillion U.S. GDP—along with how it is changing every few months—is a full-time job for a brigade of government statisticians.

Comparing GDP among Countries

When comparing the GDP of different countries, two issues immediately arise. First, the GDP of a country is measured in its own currency: the United States uses the U.S. dollar; Canada, the Canadian dollar; most countries of western Europe, the euro; Japan, the yen; Mexico, the peso; and so on. Thus, comparing GDP between two countries requires converting from one currency to another. A second problem is that countries have very different population sizes. For instance, the United States has a much larger economy than Mexico or Canada, but it also has roughly three times as many people as Mexico and nine times as many people as Canada. Thus, comparing GDP across countries requires a way of adjusting for different currencies and for different population levels.

Converting Currencies with Exchange Rates

To compare the GDP of two different countries with different currencies, it is necessary to use an **exchange rate**, which is the rate at which one currency exchanges for another. Exchange rates can be expressed either as the units of country A currency that need to be traded for a single unit of country B currency, or units of country B currency that need to be traded for a single unit of country A currency. For example, the exchange rate between the Mexican peso and the U.S. dollar can be expressed either as approximately 13 Mexican pesos per 1 U.S. dollar; or to put it the other way, it takes 1/13 of a U.S. dollar (about 8 cents) to buy a peso. It is equally accurate to express the exchange rate in either way, so you can choose whichever measure is more convenient.

exchange rate: The rate at which one currency exchanges for another.

Exchange rates are published each day in the "Business" section of major newspapers and are available at banks and many websites. An illustrative list of exchange rates from early 2016 appears in Exhibit 21-6. Each exchange rate is expressed in two ways: the foreign currency per one U.S. dollar, and the amount in U.S. dollars to buy a unit of

Cousins of GDP

In the world of economic statistics, too much is never enough. There are several different but closely related ways of measuring the size of the economy other than GDP.

One of the closest cousins of GDP is GNP, or gross national product. GDP includes only what is produced by labor and capital located within a country's borders. However, GNP adds what is produced by a nation's labor and capital that are located in the rest of the world, and subtracts out any payments sent home to other countries by foreign labor and capital located in the home country. In other words, GNP is based more on production of citizens and firms from a country, wherever they are located, and GDP is based on what happens within the geographic boundaries of a certain country. For the United States, the gap between GDP and GNP is relatively small—in recent years, only about 0.2%. But for small nations, which may have a substantial share of their population working abroad and sending money back home, the difference can be significant.

Gross national income, or GNI, is calculated not by looking at the value of output sold, but instead by measuring the value of the income generated by selling output. In theory, GDP should equal GNI. However, the two calculations use different data sources, which have different time lags and measurement errors, and so they don't quite match. The U.S. Bureau of Economic Analysis now publishes both GDP and GNI, along with an average of the two.

For practical purposes, it isn't vital to memorize these definitions. However, it is important to be aware that these differences exist and to know what statistic you are looking at so that you don't accidentally compare, say, GDP in one year or for one country with GNP or GNI in another year or another country.

EXHIBIT 21-6 Examples of Exchange Rates in Early 2016

Country (currency)	Currency per U.S. Dollar	U.S. Dollar Equivalent
Brazil (real)	4.017	0.249
China (yuan)	6.555	0.153
Egypt (pound)	7.831	0.128
Euro	0.912	1.089
India (rupee)	68.24	0.015
Japan (yen)	112.21	0.009
Mexico (peso)	18.157	0.055
Nigeria (naira)	199.25	0.005
South Africa (rand)	15.881	0.063
United Kingdom (pound)	0.718	1.393
United States (dollar)	1.000	1.000

foreign currency. These two measures are reciprocals; in mathematical terms, multiplying the currency per U.S. dollar exchange rate times the U.S. dollars per foreign currency exchange rate will always equal 1.

Using the exchange rate to convert GDP from one currency to another is straightforward. Say that the task is to compare Japan's GDP of 500 trillion yen with the U.S. GDP of \$18 trillion. The exchange rate is 110 yen = \$1. (These numbers are roughly realistic, but rounded off to simplify the calculations.) To convert Japan's GDP into U.S. dollars, multiply:

$$\text{Japan's GDP in yen} \times \frac{\$}{\text{yen}} = \text{exchange rate}$$

$$500 \text{ trillion yen} \times \frac{\$1}{110 \text{ yen}} = \$4.545 \text{ trillion}$$

CLEARING IT UP

Write Out the Exchange Rate Units

The most common mistake that students make when using exchange rates to convert between currencies is to put the exchange rate upside down: for example, they might use U.S. dollars per euro when they meant to use euros per U.S. dollar. To avoid this error, write out the currency units when doing these calculations. Then, you will notice that the currency units that you are converting away from cancel out in the numerator and denominator of the multiplication calculation, as shown in the conversion of U.S. and Japanese GDP in the text, leaving behind the currency units into which you are converting.

EXHIBIT 21-7 Exchange Rates and Gross Domestic Product (GDP)

The second column shows the size of each country's GDP, as measured by the World Bank in billions of units of its own currency in 2014. The third column shows the exchange rate, measured in terms of how many units of domestic currency to each U.S. dollar. The fourth column takes the GDP in the nation's own currency, multiplies by 1/exchange rate in the third column, and thus calculates the country's GDP in U.S. dollars.

Country	GDP in Domestic Currency (in billions)	Currency per U.S. Dollar	GDP (in billions of U.S. dollars)
Brazil	5,521 reals	4.017	$1,374
China	63,613 yuan	6.555	$9,705
Egypt	1,997 pounds	7.831	$255
Germany	2,915 euros	0.912	$3,197
India	125,412 rupees	68.24	$1,838
Japan	487,500 yen	112.21	$ 4,345
Mexico	17,209 pesos	18.157	$948
Nigeria	90,136 nairas	199.25	$452
South Africa	3,796 rands	15.881	$239
United Kingdom	1,816 pounds	0.718	$2,530
United States	17,419 dollars	1.00	$17,419

Of course, it is equally possible to convert the U.S. GDP into yen:

$$\text{U.S. GDP in \$} \times \frac{\text{yen}}{\$} = \text{U.S. GDP in yen}$$

$$\$18 \text{ trillion} \times \frac{110 \text{ yen}}{\$1} = 1{,}980 \text{ trillion yen}$$

In either case, after converting to a common currency, GDP in the United States is more than triple that of GDP in Japan.

To compare the size of several economies, you must convert all of the different measures of GDP into a common currency. The second column of Exhibit 21-7 shows the size of each country's GDP, measured in billions of units of its own currency. The third column shows the exchange rate, measured in U.S. dollars per unit of foreign currency. The fourth column takes the GDP in each country's own currency, multiplies by 1/exchange rate in the third column, and thus expresses the GDP for each country in U.S. dollars.

Converting to Per Capita GDP

The U.S. economy has the largest GDP in the world when economies are compared by converting their GDPs using the market exchange rate. But the United States is also a

EXHIBIT 21-8 Per Capita GDP in 2014

Country (currency)	GDP (in billions of U.S. dollars)	Population (in millions)	Per Capita GDP (U.S. dollars)
Brazil (real)	$1,374	206	$6,672
China (yuan)	$9,705	1,364	$7,115
Egypt (pound)	$255	89	$2,866
Euro	$3,197	80	$39,962
India (rupee)	$1,838	1295	$1,419
Japan (yen)	$4,345	127	$34,209
Mexico (peso)	$948	125	$7,583
Nigeria (naira)	$452	177	$2,556
South Africa (rand)	$239	54	$4,427
United Kingdom (pound)	$2,530	64	$39,529
United States (dollar)	$17,419	318	$54,777

populous country; in fact, it is the third-largest country by population in the world, although well behind China and India. So is the U.S. economy larger than most other countries just because the United States has more people than most other countries or because the U.S. economy is actually larger on a per-person basis? This question can be answered by calculating a country's **per capita GDP**; that is, the GDP divided by the population.

per capita GDP: GDP divided by the population.

The second column of Exhibit 21-8 lists the GDP of the same selection of countries that appeared in the previous two exhibits, showing their GDP in 2014 as converted into U.S. dollars. The third column gives the population for each country. The fourth column lists the per capita GDP, which is calculated by dividing the second column by the third.

Exhibit 21-8 illustrates that a country with a small population can have a smaller GDP but a larger per capita GDP than a country with a larger population. For example, the GDP of China is much larger than that of Mexico, but the per capita GDP of Mexico is larger than that of China. Looking ahead, economic growth in China will probably cause China to have the largest overall economy in the world—while still having a much lower per capita GDP than the United States. After all, because China has about four times as many people as the United States, its per capita GDP only needs to be more than one-fourth as large as the U.S. per capita GDP for China's total GDP to exceed that of the United States.

The high-income nations of the world—including the United States and Canada, the western European countries, and Japan—typically have per capita GDP in the range of $20,000 to $50,000. Middle-income countries, which include much of Latin America, Eastern Europe, and some countries in East Asia, have per capita GDP in the range of $6,000 to $12,000. The low-income countries in the world, many of them located in Africa and Asia, often have per capita GDP of less than $2,000 per year, and in some cases, even less than $1,000 per year.

The Pattern of GDP over Time

For most high-income countries of the world, the long-term pattern of GDP looks generally similar. GDP rises gradually over time, but the road can be bumpy.

Exhibit 21-9 illustrates this general pattern with data on U.S. GDP and per capita GDP. These GDP data are presented after adjusting for inflation. As the discussion of inflation in Chapter 24 will explore in detail, GDP can rise either because a greater quantity of goods and services are being produced, or because the prices of goods and services are higher as a result of inflation. By stripping out the effects of inflation, the remaining

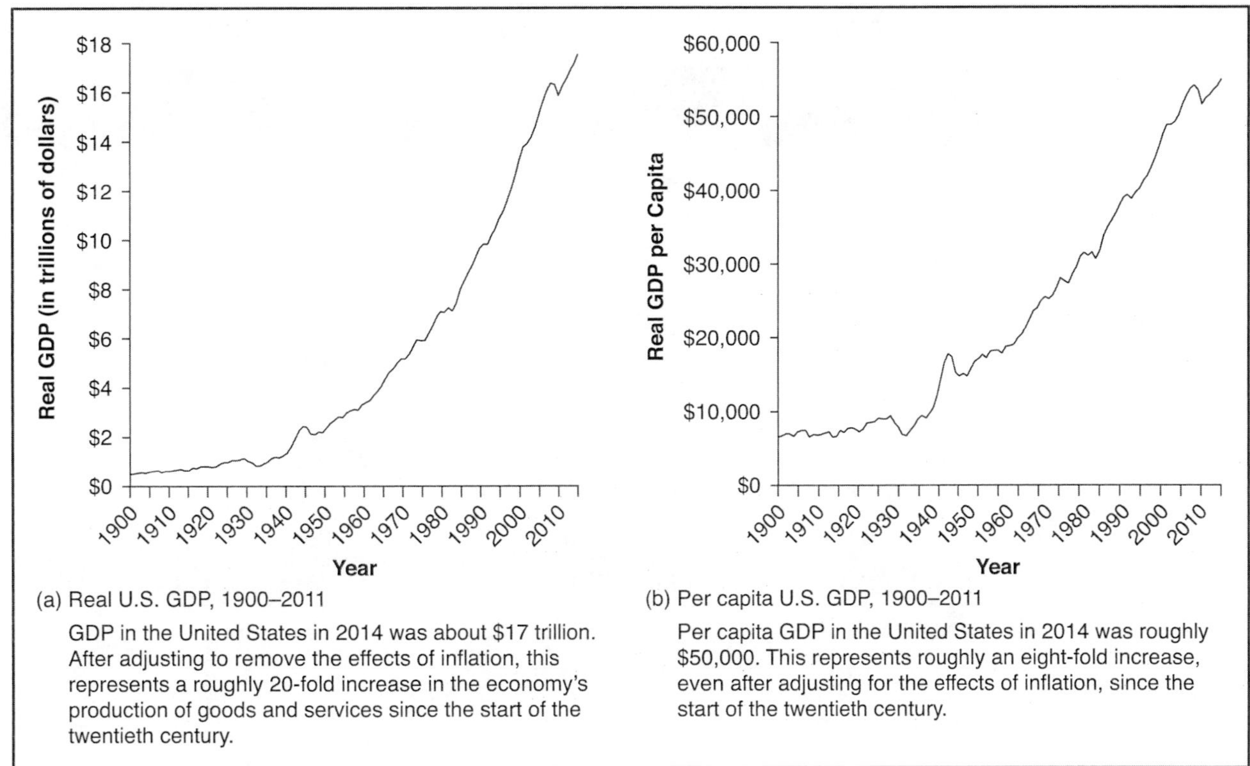

(a) Real U.S. GDP, 1900–2011

GDP in the United States in 2014 was about $17 trillion. After adjusting to remove the effects of inflation, this represents a roughly 20-fold increase in the economy's production of goods and services since the start of the twentieth century.

(b) Per capita U.S. GDP, 1900–2011

Per capita GDP in the United States in 2014 was roughly $50,000. This represents roughly an eight-fold increase, even after adjusting for the effects of inflation, since the start of the twentieth century.

EXHIBIT 21-9 U.S. GDP, 1900–2014

rise in GDP shown in the exhibits represents only an increase in the quantity of goods and services produced. Chapter 24 will also discuss how this adjustment for inflation is performed.

Exhibit 21-9*a* shows the pattern of total U.S. GDP since 1900. The generally upward long-term path of GDP has been regularly interrupted by short-term declines in GDP. A significant decline in national output is called a **recession**. An especially lengthy and deep recession is called a **depression**. The severe drop in GDP that occurred during the Great Depression of the 1930s is clearly visible, as is the Great Recession of 2007–2009. The most significant human problem associated with recessions (and their larger, uglier cousins, depressions) is that a slowdown in production means that many firms will need to hire fewer people or even fire some of the workers that they have. Losing a job imposes painful financial and personal costs on workers, and often on their extended family as well. In addition, even those who keep their jobs are likely to find that wage raises are scanty at best—or they may even be asked to take pay cuts. Exhibit 21-9*b* shows the corresponding rise in per capita GDP (again adjusted for inflation). Even though the U.S. population nearly quadrupled over the twentieth century, GDP on a per capita basis has multiplied eight-fold since 1900. The per capita growth rate of GDP during the twentieth century averaged about 2% per year.

recession: A significant decline in national output.

depression: An especially lengthy and deep decline in output.

Exhibit 21-10 lists the pattern of recessions and expansions in the U.S. economy since 1900. The highest point of the economy, before the recession begins, is called the **peak**; conversely, the lowest point of a recession, before a recovery begins, is called the **trough**. Thus, a recession lasts from peak to trough, and an economic upswing runs from trough to peak. The movement of the economy from peak to trough and trough to peak is called the **business cycle**. It is intriguing to notice that the three longest trough-to-peak expansions of the twentieth century have happened since 1960. As of mid-2016, the most recent recession started in December 2007 and ended in June 2009.

peak: During the business cycle, the highest point of output before a recession begins.

trough: During the business cycle, the lowest point of output in a recession, before a recovery begins.

business cycle: The relatively short-term movement of the economy in and out of recession.

These patterns of GDP growth suggest that the health of the macroeconomy, as measured by the pattern of GDP over time, poses two main issues: economic growth and recessions. The time frame for worrying about economic growth is over the long term;

EXHIBIT 21-10 Dates of U.S. Business Cycles since 1900

Trough	Peak	Months of Contraction	Months of Expansion
December 1900	September 1902	—	21
August 1904	May 1907	23	33
June 1908	January 1910	13	19
January 1912	January 1913	24	12
December 1914	August 1918	23	44
March 1919	January 1920	7	10
July 1921	May 1923	18	22
July 1924	October 1926	14	27
November 1927	August 1929	23	21
March 1933	May 1937	43	50
June 1938	February 1945	13	80
October 1945	November 1948	8	37
October 1949	July 1953	11	45
May 1954	August 1957	10	39
April 1958	April 1960	8	24
February 1961	December 1969	10	106
November 1970	November 1973	11	36
March 1975	January 1980	16	58
July 1980	July 1981	6	12
November 1982	July 1990	16	92
March 1991	March 2001	8	120
November 2001	December 2007	8	73
June 2009	—	18	—

the time frame for worrying about recessions is the short term. This long-term/short-term approach to thinking about GDP will play a central role in macroeconomic analysis.

How Well Does GDP Measure the Well-Being of Society?

The level of per capita GDP clearly captures some element of what is meant by the phrase "standard of living." Most of the international migration in the world, for example, involves people who are moving from countries with relatively low per capita GDP to countries with relatively high per capita GDP. Similarly, it is not common to find many people in a high-income country who choose to deny themselves the benefits of electricity, plumbing, modern medicine, automobile and plane travel, and choose instead to live only with the income levels and technologies that were available 50 or 100 years ago in high-income countries—or with the technologies that are still in common use in low-income countries.

However, "standard of living" is a broader term than GDP. GDP focuses on production that is bought and sold in markets. Standard of living includes all elements that affect people's happiness, whether they are bought and sold in the market or not. To illuminate the gap between GDP and standard of living, it's useful to spell out some things that GDP does not cover that are clearly relevant to standard of living.

Some Differences between GDP and Standard of Living

GDP includes spending on recreation and travel, but it does not cover leisure time. Clearly, however, there is a substantial difference between an economy that is large because people work long hours, and an economy that grows because people work the same number of hours but are more productive with their time. For example, the per capita GDP of the U.S. economy is larger than the per capita GDP of Germany, as was shown in Exhibit 21-8, but it's also true that the average U.S. worker works several hundred hours more per year more than the average German worker. The calculation of GDP doesn't take the German worker's extra weeks of vacation into account.

GDP includes what is spent on environmental protection, health care, and education, but it does not include actual levels of environmental cleanliness, health, and learning. Thus, GDP includes the cost of buying pollution-control equipment, but it does not address whether the air and water are actually cleaner or dirtier. GDP includes spending on medical care, but does not address whether life expectancy or infant mortality have risen or fallen. Similarly, it counts spending on education, but doesn't address directly how much of the population can read, write, or do basic mathematics.

GDP includes production that is exchanged in the market, but it does not cover production that is not exchanged in the market. For example, hiring someone to mow your lawn or clean your house is conceptually part of GDP, but doing these tasks yourself is not part of GDP. One remarkable change in the U.S. economy in recent decades is the increased number of women in the labor market. As of 1970, only about 42% of women participated in the paid labor force. In 2015, more than 55% of women participated in the paid labor force. As women have entered the labor force, many of the services that they used to produce in the non-market economy, like food preparation and child care, have shifted to some extent into the market economy, which makes the GDP appear larger even if more services are not actually being consumed.

GDP includes newly produced goods and services, but does not count the buying and selling of previously existing assets. For example, a house built this year is counted in GDP, but a house built in the past that is sold this year is not part of GDP—because nothing new was produced this year. Although the price of the old house is not part of GDP, the amount paid to a realtor for the service of assisting with the transaction is counted in this year's GDP.

GDP has nothing to say about the level of inequality in society. Per capita GDP is an average. When per capita GDP rises by 5%, it could mean that everyone in the society has risen by 5%, or that some groups have risen by more while others have risen by less—or even declined. GDP has nothing in particular to say about the amount of variety available. If a family buys 100 loaves of bread in a year, GDP doesn't care whether they are all white bread, or whether the family can choose from wheat, rye, pumpernickel, and many others—it just looks at whether the total amount spent on bread is the same.

GDP has nothing much to say about what technology and products are available. The standard of living in, say, 1950 or 1900 wasn't affected only by how much money people had—it was also affected by what they could buy. No matter how much money you had in 1950, you could not buy a portable phone, let alone a smart-phone.

In certain cases, it isn't clear that a rise in GDP is even a good thing. If a city is wrecked by a hurricane and then experiences a surge of rebuilding construction activity, it would be peculiar to claim that the destruction of the hurricane was therefore economically beneficial. If people are led by a rising fear of crime to pay for installation of bars and burglar alarms on all their windows, it is hard to believe that this increase in GDP has made them better off. Some people would argue that sales of certain goods, like pornography or extremely violent movies, do not represent a gain to society's standard of living.

The Human Development Index

Economists have long recognized that GDP is not a complete measure of social well-being. In 1990, an economist named Mahbud ul Haq at the United Nations Development Programme (UNDP) decided to do something about it. The UNDP began publishing an annual Human Development Report. Each year, along with a discussion of economic and social issues affecting low-income countries, the report includes a Human Development Index (HDI), which ranks countries in three broad areas: health, as measured by life expectancy; education, as measured by years of schooling; and material standard of living, as measured by per capita GDP.

By blending per capita GDP with measures of health and education, countries with good levels of health and education may rank higher in the Human Development Index than other countries that have greater per capita GDP. For example, in the rankings for 2014, the U.S. per capita GDP was 25% higher than that of Australia. However, life expectancy in Australia was three years greater than in the United States, and expected years of schooling was three years higher for Australians than for Americans. Thus, in the HDI rankings, Australia ranked above the United States.

To choose another example, the per capita GDP of China is about 30% above that of Sri Lanka. However, Sri Lanka leads China both in life expectancy and in expected years of schooling, and given the formula used for computing the HDI rankings, Sri Lanka is ranked ahead of China.

The HDI rankings are controversial. Are these factors, measured in these specific ways, the right ones to include? What about making additional adjustments for gender or racial equality, the level of poverty, or environmental quality? Are the three factors weighted properly, or is, say, years of schooling getting too much weight and per capita GDP too little weight? The UNDP readily acknowledges: "The concept of human development is much deeper and richer than what can be captured in any composite or even by a detailed set of statistical indicators."

Does a Rise in GDP Overstate or Understate the Rise in the Standard of Living?

The fact that per capita GDP does not fully capture the broader idea of standard of living has led to a concern that the increases in GDP over time are illusory. It is at least theoretically possible that while the measured GDP is rising, the standard of living could be falling if human health, environmental cleanliness, and other factors that aren't included in GDP are worsening. Fortunately, this fear appears to be overstated.

In some ways, the rise in GDP *understates* the actual rise in the standard of living. For example, the typical workweek for a U.S. worker has fallen over the last century from about 60 hours per week to less than 40 hours per week. Life expectancy and health have risen dramatically, and so has the average level of education. Since 1970, the air and water in the United States have generally (with some exceptions) been getting cleaner. New technologies have been developed for many functions, including entertainment, travel, information, and health. A much wider variety of basic products like food and clothing is available today than several decades ago. Because GDP does not capture leisure, health, a cleaner environment, the possibilities created by new technology, or an increase in variety, the actual rise in the standard of living for Americans in recent decades has exceeded the rise in GDP.

On the other side, inequality of incomes and levels of traffic congestion and certain emissions, such as greenhouse gases, are higher in the United States now than they were in the 1960s. Moreover, a substantial number of services that used to be provided, primarily by women, in the non-market economy are now part of the market economy that is counted by GDP. By ignoring these factors, GDP would tend to overstate the true rise in the standard of living.

The positive factors ignored by GDP are probably larger than the negative factors ignored by GDP, in which case GDP over time would understate the true rise in the standard of living. But that judgment can be a controversial one.

GDP Is Rough, but Useful

It would be foolish and blinkered to believe that a high level of GDP should be the only goal of macroeconomic policy or government policy more broadly. But even though GDP does not measure broader standard of living with any precision, it still reveals something important about the standard of living. In most countries, a significantly higher per capita GDP occurs hand in hand with other improvements in everyday life along many dimensions like education, health, and environmental protection.

No single number can capture all the elements of a term as broad as "standard of living." Per capita GDP has real limitations, which must always be kept in mind. Nonetheless, per capita GDP is a reasonable, rough-and-ready measure of the standard of living.

Conclusion

There is sometimes a tendency to speak as if certain parts of the economy deserve more emphasis than others: for example, that high-technology industries are more important to the economy than established industries like making paper, or service jobs in areas like tourism. Even within the high-tech industries, certain hot new firms—perhaps those involved in cloud computing or biotechnology—are sometimes claimed to be more important than older established firms.

This desire to treat certain industries like favorite children is typically misguided because an economy is not like a country's Olympic team. In the Olympics, a country can celebrate if a few of its top athletes perform well. In the Olympics, it doesn't matter if the rest of the people in the country, who are at home watching the games on television, are lazy and out of shape. But in an economy, every business counts. For an economy as a whole, it doesn't work especially well to have a few wonderful, world-class companies, while the rest of the economy is flabby and inefficient. After all, people work everywhere in the economy and buy goods from everywhere in the economy. Everyone throughout the economy needs good products, good jobs, good pay, and a generally rising standard of living.

Key Concepts and Summary

1. In a number of cases, behavior that seems rational at the microeconomic level for individuals and firms can end up leading to unexpected or even counterproductive outcomes at the macroeconomic level.
2. The size of a nation's economy is commonly measured by its **gross domestic product** or **GDP**, which measures the value of the output of all goods and services produced within the country. GDP is measured by taking the quantities of all goods and services produced, multiplying them by their prices, and summing the total.
3. Since GDP measures what is bought and sold in the economy, it can be measured either by the sum of what is demanded in the economy or what is produced. Demand can be divided into consumption, investment, government, exports, and imports. What is produced in the economy can be divided into **durable goods, nondurable goods**, services, structures, and **inventories**.
4. To avoid **double counting**, GDP counts only final output of goods and services, not the production of intermediate goods or the value of labor in the chain of production.
5. In comparing GDP figures among countries, it is necessary to convert to a common currency using **exchange rates** and to divide by population to calculate **per capita GDP**.
6. In the long term, the key issue concerning GDP is real per capita growth. In the short run, the key issue concerning GDP is shortening or reducing the size of **recessions** and **depressions**—or avoiding them completely.
7. GDP is an indicator of a society's standard of living, but it is only a rough indicator. GDP does not directly take account of leisure, environmental quality, levels of health and education, activities conducted outside the market, changes in inequality of income, increases in variety, increases in technology, or the (positive or negative) value that society may place on certain types of output.

Review Questions

1. What are the main components of measuring GDP with what is demanded?
2. What are the main components of measuring GDP with what is produced?
3. Would you usually expect GDP as measured by what is demanded to be greater than GDP as measured by what is supplied, or the reverse?
4. Why is double counting a danger when measuring GDP?
5. What are the two main difficulties that arise in comparing the GDP of different countries?
6. What are the typical patterns of GDP for a high-income economy like the United States in the long run and the short run?
7. List some of the reasons why GDP should not be considered a precise measure of the standard of living in a country.

CHAPTER

22

Economic Growth

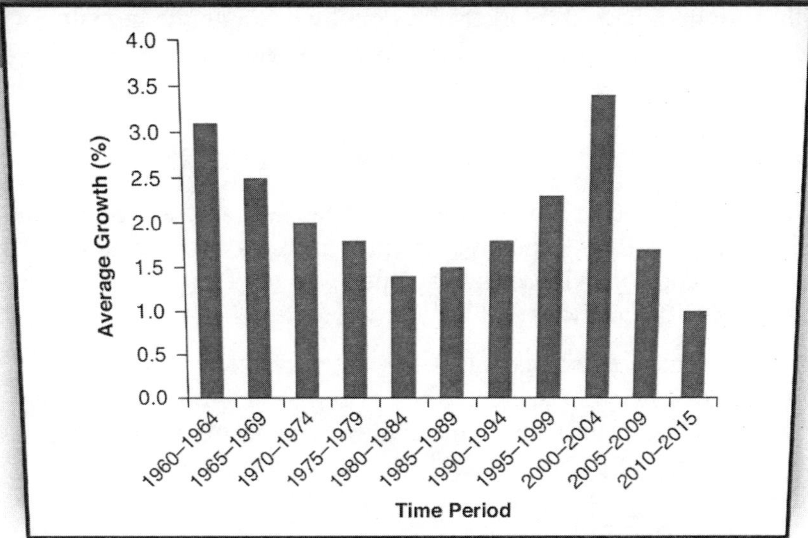

Chapter Outline

Every country worries about economic growth. In the United States and other high-income countries, will economic growth continue to provide the same remarkable gains in standard of living that it has in the last century? Can middle-income countries like Brazil, Egypt, Malaysia, and South Africa catch up to the higher-income countries, or must they remain in the second tier of per capita income? Of the world's population of 7 billion people, about 2 billion are scraping by on incomes of less than $3 per day. Can the world's poor be lifted from their fearful poverty? As economist Robert E. Lucas Jr., the 1995 Nobel laureate in economics, once noted: "The consequences for human welfare involved in questions like these are simply staggering: Once one starts to think about them, it is hard to think about anything else."

Dramatic movements in a nation's standard of living are possible. After the Korean War in the late 1950s, the Republic of Korea, often referred to as South Korea, was one of the poorest economies in the world, along with low-income countries of Africa and south Asia. Most South Koreans worked in peasant agriculture. Per capita GDP was perhaps $200 per year. But from the 1960s to the early twenty-first century, a time period well within the lifetime and memory of a single adult, the economy of South Korea blossomed. Over these four decades, per capita GDP increased by more than 6% per year. Per capita GDP for the Republic of Korea now exceeds $27,000, which places South Korea among the high-income countries of the world, near nations like Italy and Spain. Measured by total GDP, South Korea ranked as the world's thirteenth-largest economy overall in 2015—slightly larger than the economy of Canada. This transformation for a nation of 50 million people is extraordinary.

South Korea is a standout example, but it is not the only case of rapid and sustained economic growth. Other nations of east Asia, like Thailand and Indonesia, have seen very rapid growth as well. The economy of China has grown enormously since market-oriented economic reforms were enacted around 1980. In a longer historical perspective, per capita GDP in high-income economies like the United States has grown dramatically as well, as the U.S. economy has been transformed from primarily rural and agricultural economies to a modern economy based on services, manufacturing, and technology.

This chapter begins with a brief overview of patterns of economic growth around the world in the last two centuries. It then discusses the power of even seemingly low levels of economic growth to transform living standards over time, the key macroeconomic ingredients for growth, and the link from worker productivity to economic growth. The discussion concludes by examining the prospects for countries with lower levels of per capita GDP to catch up to the high-income countries.

The Relatively Recent Arrival of Economic Growth

Economic growth is a relatively recent experience for the human race: it didn't really gain momentum until about 1800. Before then, while kings and conquerors could afford some extravagances, the standard of living of average people hadn't changed much for centuries. The famous economist John Maynard Keynes wrote in 1930:

> From the earliest times of which we have record—back, say, to two thousand years before Christ—down to the beginning of the eighteenth century, there was no very great change in the life of the average man living in the civilized centers of the earth. Ups and downs certainly. Visitations of plague, famine, and war. Golden intervals. But no progressive, violent change.

Industrial Revolution: The widespread use of power-driven machinery and the economic and social changes that occurred in the first half of the 1800s.

But progressive, powerful economic change started in the late eighteenth and early nineteenth centuries, first in Great Britain, and soon spreading to the United States, Germany, and other countries. The **Industrial Revolution** arrived—a term that refers to the widespread use of power-driven machinery and the economic and social changes that resulted in the first half of the 1800s. Ingenious machines—the steam engine, the power loom, the locomotive, and others—performed tasks that would have taken vast numbers of workers. The jobs for ordinary people working with these machines were often dirty and dangerous by modern standards, but their alternative jobs for that time in peasant agriculture and small-village industry were often dirty and dangerous, too. The new jobs of the Industrial Revolution typically offered higher pay and chance for social mobility. A self-reinforcing cycle began: new inventions and investments created profits, profits provided funds and incentives for new investment and invention, and the investments and inventions provided opportunities for further profits. Slowly, a group of national economies in Europe and North America emerged from centuries of economic stagnation and lifted off. During the last two centuries, the average rate of growth of per capita GDP in the leading industrialized countries has averaged about 2% per year.

A growth rate of just 2% per year might seem too slow to explain the phenomenal changes in the standard of living over the last two centuries. But never forget that seemingly low rates of growth, compounded over time, can have mighty results. Thus, if a country's per capita GDP starts at a level of 100, and then grows for 200 years at 2%, its per capita GDP at the end of that period will be:

$$100\ (1 + .02)^{200} = 5{,}248$$

In other words, a 2% annual growth rate continued over 200 years means that per capita GDP will rise by a multiple of more than 52!

The Industrial Revolution led to a widening of the inequality between nations as some economies took flight, while others, like many of those in Africa or Asia, remained close to a subsistence standard of living. However, by the middle of the twentieth century, some countries had shown that catching up was possible. Japan's economic growth took off in the 1960s and 1970s, with a growth rate of real per capita GDP averaging 11% per year during those decades. Certain countries in Latin America experienced a boom in economic growth in the 1960s as well: in Brazil, for example, per capita GDP expanded by an average annual rate of 9% from 1968 to 1973. In the 1970s, some economies in east Asia zoomed as well, including South Korea, Thailand, and Taiwan. In these countries, growth rates of 11–12% per year in per capita GDP were not uncommon. More recently, the economy of China, with its population of 1.3 billion people, grew at a per capita rate of 9% per year from 1984 into the first decade of the 2000s. India, with a population of 1.1 billion, showed promising signs of economic growth in the 1990s, with growth in per capita GDP of about 4% per year during the 1990s and climbing toward 7–8% per year in the 2000s.

These waves of catch-up economic growth have not touched all shores. In certain African countries like Malawi, Niger, and Somalia , for example, per capita GDP in 2015 was still well below $1,000, not all that much higher than it was in the nineteenth century and for centuries before that. But in thinking about the overall situation of low-income people around the world, the good economic news from China (population: 1.3 billion) and India (population: 1.2 billion) is nonetheless astounding and heartening.

Economic growth in the last two centuries has made a striking change in the human condition. Richard Easterlin, an economist at the University of Southern California, wrote in 2000:

> By many measures, a revolution in the human condition is sweeping the world. Most people today are better fed, clothed, and housed than their predecessors two centuries ago. They are healthier, live longer, and are better educated. Women's lives are less centered on reproduction and political democracy has gained a foothold. Although western Europe and its offshoots have been the leaders of this advance, most of the less developed nations have joined in during the 20th century, with the newly emerging nations of sub-Saharan Africa the latest to participate. Although the picture is not one of universal progress, it is the greatest advance in the human condition of the world's population ever achieved in such a brief span of time.

Worker Productivity and Economic Growth

Per capita GDP offers one measure of economic prosperity; that is, taking the total output of goods and services in an economy—the GDP—and dividing by the population. A useful alternative measure is to start with GDP and divide by the number of workers in an economy or by the number of hours that are worked. The value of what is produced per worker, or per hour worked, is called **productivity**.

productivity: The value of what is produced per worker or per hour worked.

An economy's rate of productivity growth is closely linked to the growth rate of its per capita GDP, although the two aren't identical. For example, if the percentage of the population who hold jobs in an economy increases, per capita GDP will increase but the productivity of individual workers need not be affected. But over the long term, the only way that per capita GDP can grow continually is if the productivity of the average worker rises.

A common measure of U.S. productivity is output per hour in the business sector. This measure excludes government workers, because their output is not sold in the market and so their productivity is hard to measure, and farming, which accounts for only a relatively small share of the U.S. economy. Exhibit 22-1 shows that the amount produced by a U.S. worker in an hour averaged about $73 in 2015, about triple what an average worker produced per hour in 1960. Exhibit 22-2 shows average annual rates of productivity growth averaged over five-year periods since 1960. U.S. productivity growth was fairly strong in the 1960s but then dropped lower in the 1970s and 1980s before rising again in the second half of the 1990s, especially the first half of the 2000s, and then dropping again. In general, strong rates of productivity growth over these five-year intervals are about 3% per year, whereas weak rates of productivity growth are 1.0–1.5% per year.

Productivity growth is also closely linked to the average level of wages received by workers. Over time, the amount that firms are willing to pay workers will depend on the

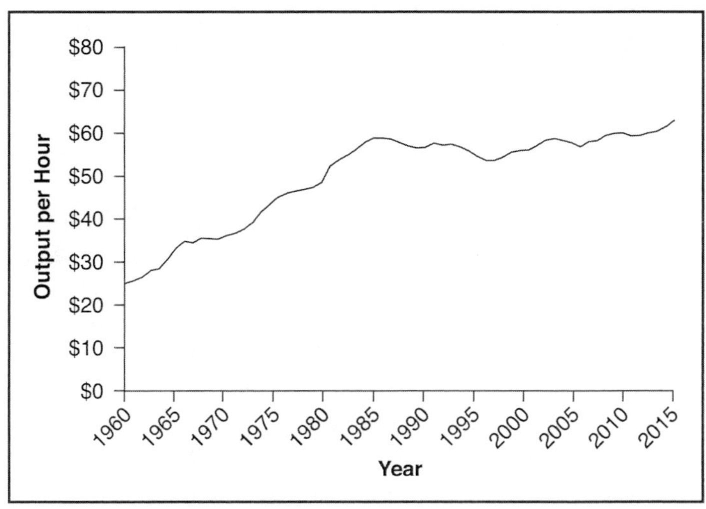

EXHIBIT 22-1 Output per Hour Worked in the U.S. Economy, 1960–2015

Output per hour worked is a measure of worker productivity. In the U.S. economy, worker productivity rose more quickly in the 1960s than during the 1970s, and it rose more quickly during the mid-1990s than in recent years. However, these growth rate differences are only a few percentage points per year, so you have to look carefully to see them in the upward slope of the figure. The average U.S. worker produced nearly $73 per hour in 2015. The output-per-hour numbers have been adjusted to remove the effects of price inflation.

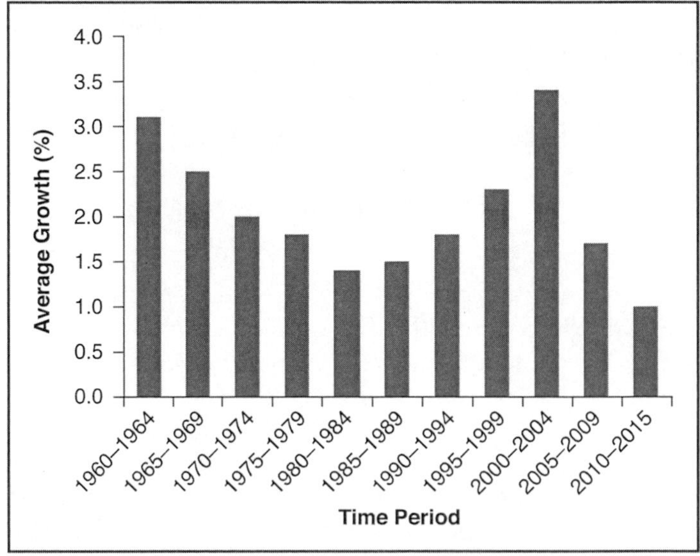

EXHIBIT 22-2 Annual Rate of Productivity Growth in Output per Hour Worked: Five-Year Averages

U.S. growth in worker productivity was very high in the early 1960s, then declined to lower levels in the 1970s and the 1980s. The late 1990s and early 2000s saw a productivity rebound, but then productivity sagged again.

value of the output that those workers produce. If a few employers tried to pay their workers less than what those workers produced, then those workers would receive job offers with higher wages from other profit-seeking employers. If a few employers mistakenly paid their workers more than what those workers produced, the employers would soon end up making losses, and would either have to reduce wages or go out of business. Over the long run, productivity per hour is the most important determinant of the average wage level in any economy.

EXHIBIT 22-3 Growth of GDP over Different Time Horizons

At time zero, GDP = 100. Apply the formula: GDP at starting date × (1 + growth rate of GDP)^{years} = GDP at end date			
	Time Period		
Growth Rate	***10 Years***	***25 Years***	***50 Years***
1%	110	128	164
3%	134	209	438
5%	163	338	1,147
8%	216	685	4,690

The Power of Sustained Economic Growth

Even small changes in the rate of economic growth, when compounded over long periods of time, make an enormous difference in the standard of living. Consider Exhibit 22-3, in which the rows of the table show several different rates of growth in per capita GDP and the columns show different periods of time. Assume for simplicity that an economy starts with a per capita GDP of 100. The table then applies the formula

$$\text{GDP at starting date} \times (1 + \text{growth rate of GDP})^{\text{years}} = \text{GDP at end date}$$

to calculate what GDP will be at the given growth rate at the future time. For example, an economy that starts with a GDP of 100 and grows at 3% per year will reach a GDP of 209 after 25 years; that is, $100 \times (1.03)^{25} = 209$.

The slowest rate of per capita GDP growth in the table, just 1% per year, is similar to what the United States experienced during its weakest years of productivity growth. The second highest rate, 3% per year, is close to what the U.S. economy experienced during the strong economy of the late 1990s and into the 2000s. The higher rates of per capita growth, 5% or 8% per year, represent the experience of rapid growth in economies like Japan, Korea, and China.

Exhibit 22-3 teaches that even a few percentage points of difference in economic growth rates will have a profound effect if sustained and compounded over time. For example, an economy growing at a 1% annual rate over 50 years will see its per capita GDP rise by a total of 64%, from 100 to 164 in this example. However, a country growing at a 5% annual rate will see (almost) this same amount of growth—from 100 to 163—over just 10 years. Rapid rates of economic growth can be transforming. At an 8% rate of growth, young adults starting at age 20 would see the average standard of living in their

CLEARING IT UP

Compound Growth Rates and Compound Interest Rates

The formula for growth rates of GDP over different periods of time, as used in Exhibit 22-3, is exactly the same as the formula for how a given amount of financial savings grows at a certain interest rate over time, as presented back in Chapter 2. Both formulas have the same ingredients: an original starting amount, in one case GDP and in the other case an amount of financial saving; a percentage increase over time, in one case the growth rate of GDP and in the other case an interest rate; and an amount of time over which this effect happens. Just as compound interest means earning interest on past interest, which causes the total amount of financial savings to grow dramatically over time, a compound rate of economic growth means that the rate of growth is being multiplied by a base that includes past GDP growth, which can cause an economy to grow dramatically over time.

country more than double by the time they had reached age 30 and grow nearly seven-fold by the time they had reached age 45.

production function: The process of a firm turning economic inputs like labor, machinery, and raw materials into outputs like goods and services used by consumers.

aggregate production function: The process of an economy as a whole turning economic inputs like labor, machinery, and raw materials into outputs like goods and services used by consumers.

physical capital: The plant and equipment used by firms in production.

human capital: The skills and education of workers.

technology: All the ways in which a certain level of capital investment can produce a greater quantity or higher quality, as well as different and altogether new products.

The Aggregate Production Function

To analyze the sources of economic growth, whether measured by per capita GDP or by worker productivity, it is useful to think about a **production function**, which is a process of turning economic inputs like labor, machinery, and raw materials into outputs like goods and services used by consumers. A microeconomic production function would describe the inputs and outputs of a firm, or perhaps an industry. In macroeconomics, the connection from inputs to outputs for the entire economy is called an **aggregate production function.**

Components of the Aggregate Production Function

Exhibit 22-4 presents two aggregate production functions. In the first production function (Exhibit 22-4*a*), the output is GDP. The inputs are population, human capital, physical capital, and technology.

The category of population is reasonably self-explanatory: more population usually means more workers, who can then produce additional output. The category of **physical capital** includes the plant and equipment used by firms. **Human capital** is the name that economists give the skills and education of workers. As the phrase "human capital" implies, economists make a useful analogy between the intangible skills of workers and the physical capital of the economy. In both cases, investments pay off in longer-term productivity in the future.

The category of **technology** is the joker in the deck. When most people think of new technology, inventions like the laser, the transistor, or some new wonder drug come to

EXHIBIT 22-4
Aggregate Production Functions

An aggregate production function shows what goes into producing the output for an overall economy.
(a) This aggregate production function has GDP as its output.
(b) This aggregate production function uses GDP per capita, which because it is calculated on a per-person basis, means that the "population" input is already figured into the other factors and doesn't need to be listed separately.

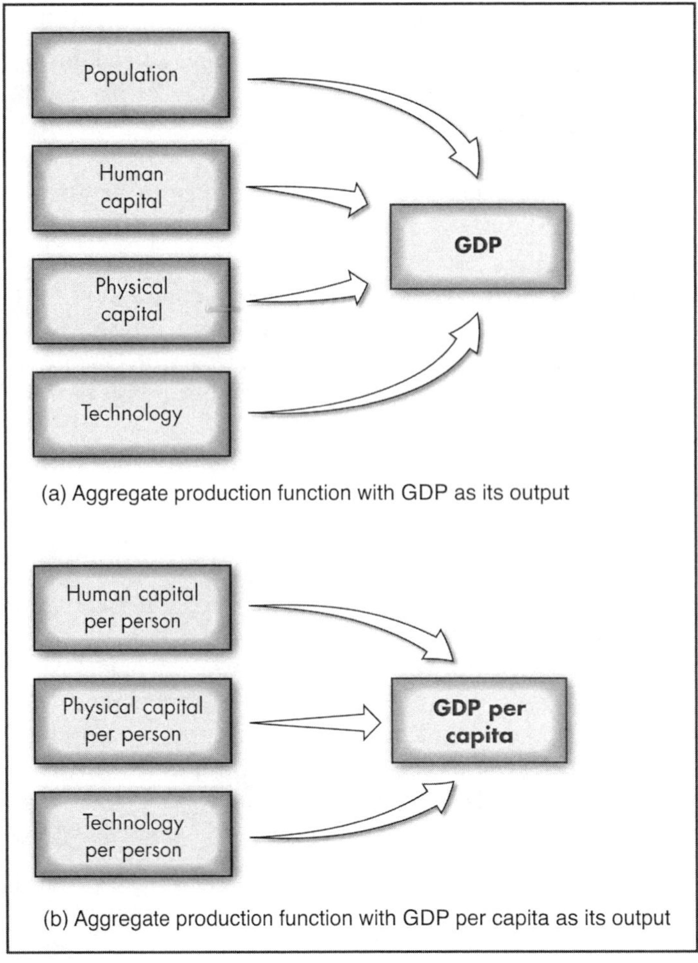

(a) Aggregate production function with GDP as its output

(b) Aggregate production function with GDP per capita as its output

mind. Such prominent inventions are included in the category of technology, but much more is included as well. The economy is full of small new technologies: the bleach that cleans clothes a little whiter, the phone that shrinks a little smaller, the improved design of a car tire that grabs the road better, the computer monitor that tilts at a slightly more comfortable angle. Added together, the vast number of ongoing small changes like these may be every bit as important as the relatively few major technological inventions. But technology, as economists use the term, includes still more. It includes new ways of organizing work, like the invention of the assembly line, as well as new methods for assuring better quality of output in factories. In short, technology comprises all the advances by which people figure out how to make a certain level of capital investment produce a greater quantity or higher quality, as well as different and altogether new products.

When discussing economic growth, it is often useful to focus on per capita GDP, to avoid studying changes in the size of GDP that represent only having more people in the economy. Using per capita GDP also makes it easier to compare countries with smaller numbers of people, like Belgium or Uruguay or Zimbabwe, with countries that have larger populations, like the United States or Russia or Nigeria.

For this purpose, divide everything in the first aggregate production function in Exhibit 22-4*a* by the population. This creates a revised aggregate production function where the output is per capita GDP (i.e., GDP divided by population) and the inputs are the average level of human capital per person, the average level of physical capital per person, and the level of technology per person—see Exhibit 22-4*b*. In effect, any growth that occurs because of a rise in population is divided out.

When society has an increasing level of capital per person, it is called **capital deepening**. The idea of capital deepening can apply both to additional human capital per worker and to additional physical capital per worker.

capital deepening: When an economy has a higher average level of physical and/or human capital per person.

Exhibit 22-5 illustrates the human capital deepening for U.S. workers by showing that the proportion of the U.S. population with a high school and a college degree is rising. As recently as 1970, for example, only about half of U.S. adults had at least a high school degree; now, almost 90% of adults have a high school degree. The idea of human capital deepening also applies to the years of experience that workers have, but the average experience level of U.S. workers hasn't changed much in recent decades. Thus, the key dimension for deepening human capital in the U.S. economy focuses more on additional education and training than on a higher average level of work experience.

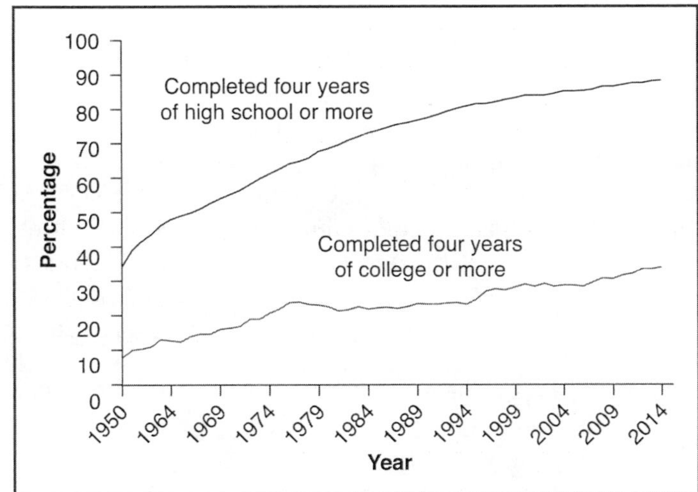

EXHIBIT 22-5 Human Capital Deepening in the U.S. Economy: Education Level of Those Age 25 and Older

Rising levels of education show the deepening of human capital in the U.S. economy. Notice that even today, relatively few American adults have completed a four-year college degree. There is clearly room for additional deepening of human capital to occur.

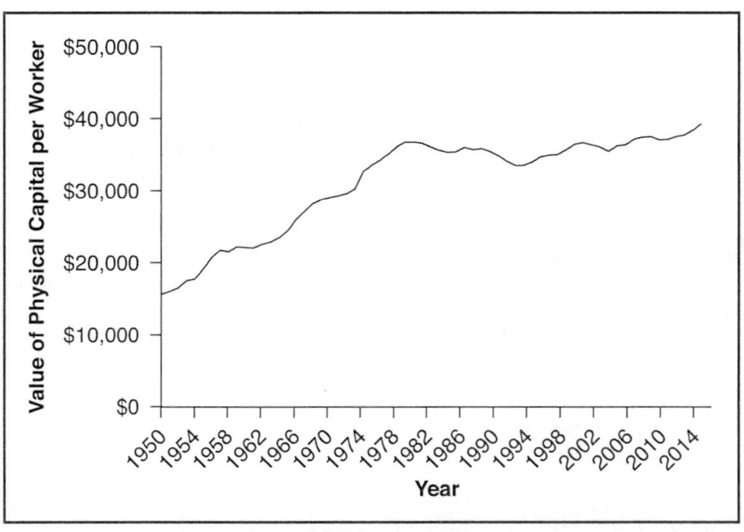

EXHIBIT 22-6 Physical Capital per Worker in the United States, 1950–2014

The value of the physical capital, measured by plant and equipment, used by the average worker in the U.S. economy has risen over the decades. The increase leveled off in the 1970s and 1980s, which were not, coincidentally, times of slower-than-usual growth in worker productivity. There was a renewed increase in physical capital per worker in the late 1990s, followed by another flattening in recent years. (The numbers in the graph are adjusted to remove the effect of price inflation.)

Physical capital deepening in the U.S. economy is shown in Exhibit 22-6, which shows that the rise in the average amount of physical capital per worker has risen substantially over time. The average U.S. worker in the late 2000s was working with physical capital worth three times as much as the average worker of the early 1950s—although physical capital per worker has not been rising as rapidly in recent years.

Not only does the current U.S. economy have better-educated workers with more physical capital than it did several decades ago, but these workers can use more advanced technologies. Growth in technology is impossible to measure with a simple line on a graph, but evidence that we live in an age of technological marvels is all around us: discoveries in genetics, in the structure of particles, the wireless Internet, and other inventions too numerous to count. The U.S. Patent and Trademark Office has typically been issuing more than 150,000 patents annually in recent years.

This recipe for economic growth and worker productivity—a mix of human capital, physical capital, and technology—applies beyond the border of the U.S. economy. South Korea's economy, for example, achieved universal enrollment in primary school (the equivalent of kindergarten through sixth grade in the United States) in 1965, when Korea's per capita GDP was still near its rock-bottom low. By the late 1980s, Korea had achieved almost universal secondary school education (the equivalent of a high school education in the United States). With regard to physical capital, Korea's rate of investment had been about 15% of GDP at the start of the 1960s, but doubled to 30–35% of GDP by the late 1960s and early 1970s. With regard to technology, South Korean students went to universities and colleges around the world to get scientific and technical training, and South Korean firms reached out to learn from and form partnerships with foreign firms that could offer them technological insights. These factors combined to foster South Korea's high rate of economic growth.

Growth Accounting Studies

Since the late 1950s, economists have performed "growth accounting" studies to calculate what specific portion of economic growth is accounted for by deepening of physical capital, deepening of human capital, and technology. The usual approach of these studies is to estimate how much of per capita economic growth can be attributed to growth in physical capital and human capital, which can be measured at least roughly, and then to attribute whatever residual increase in output that can't be explained by these factors to growth in technology. The exact numerical estimates differ from study to study and from country to country, depending on how researchers measured these three main factors and the time horizon used. But for studies of the U.S. economy, three lessons commonly emerge from these growth accounting studies.

First, technology is typically the most important contributor to U.S. economic growth. Growth in human capital and physical capital often explain only half or less than half of the economic growth that occurs. New ways of doing things and new products are tremendously important to economic growth.

Second, while investment in physical capital is essential to growth in worker productivity and per capita GDP, building human capital is at least as important as physical capital. Economic growth is not just a matter of more machines and buildings. One vivid example of the power of human capital and technological knowledge occurred in Europe in the years after World War II. During the war, a large share of Europe's physical capital—factories, roads, vehicles—was destroyed. However, the powerful combination of skilled workers and technological knowledge, working within a market-oriented economic framework, rebuilt Europe's productive capacity to an even higher level within less than two decades.

A third lesson is that these three factors of human capital, physical capital, and technology work together. Workers with a higher level of education and skills are often better at coming up with new technological innovations. These technological innovations are often ideas that cannot increase production until they become a part of new investment in physical capital. New machines that embody technological innovations often require additional training, which builds skills of workers further. If the recipe for economic growth is to succeed, an economy needs all the ingredients of the aggregate production function.

A Healthy Climate for Economic Growth

The sources of economic growth—technology, human capital, and physical capital—need to combine within a healthy economic climate. At the microeconomic level, a healthy economic climate will have a market orientation because the rewards that are available in

Girls' Education and Economic Growth in Low-Income Countries

In the low-income countries of the world, in the early 2000s, about 110 million children between the ages of 6–11 were not in school—and about two-thirds of them were girls. In Bangladesh, for example, the illiteracy rate for those aged 15–24 was 61% for females, compared to 40% for males. In Egypt, for this age group, illiteracy was 38% for females and 24% for males. Cambodia had 59% illiteracy for females and 25% for males. Nigeria had 18% illiteracy for females in the 15–24 age bracket and 11% for males.

Whenever any child does not receive a basic education, it is both a human and an economic loss. In low-income countries, wages typically increase by an average of 10 to 20 percent with each additional year of education. But there is some intriguing evidence that helping girls in low-income countries to close the education gap with boys may be especially important because of the social role that many of the girls will play as mothers and homemakers.

Girls in low-income countries who receive more education tend to grow up to have fewer, healthier, better-educated children. Their children are more likely to be better nourished and to receive basic health care like immunizations.

Economic research on women in low-income economies backs up these findings. When 20 women get one additional year of schooling, as a group they will on average have one less child. When 1,000 women get one additional year of schooling, on average 1–2 fewer women from that group will die in childbirth. When a woman stays in school an additional year, that factor alone means that on average, each of her children will spend an additional half-year in school.

Of course, these benefits should be combined with the benefits of education that apply to both genders, like more productive workers, broader personal horizons, and greater control over one's life.

a market provide incentives to encourage economic growth. Workers have an incentive to acquire additional human capital because in a market-oriented economy, the additional education and skills will pay off in higher wages. Firms have an incentive to make investments in physical capital and in training their workers because they expect to earn higher profits as a result. Both individuals and firms look for new technologies because small inventions can make your work easier or improve your products, and major inventions can be worth a fortune. This market orientation of healthy economies typically reaches beyond national borders and includes openness to international trade.

A general orientation toward markets doesn't rule out some important roles for government. Government often plays a role in setting up and funding the education system, especially at the primary and secondary level. Government regulations and taxes can favor savings and investment, or discourage them. Governments can administer laws in a fair and impartial way, or they can offer favoritism and patronage that encourage businesses to try to make money by lobbying government ministers, rather than by providing goods and services that consumers desire. Governments can encourage international trade, or surrender to protectionism. Governments can play a key role in overseeing the safety of banks and the financial system, in enforcing contracts, and in supporting infrastructure projects like roads and electricity generators. Governments can support scientific research and technical training that helps to create and spread new technologies, or not. Governments can protect the ability of inventors to profit from their inventions, or not. Governments also have a role to play in preventing the economy from sinking deep into recession or inflation, either of which can create a situation where individuals and firms are under such great stress from dismal macroeconomic conditions that they have little chance to plan the investments and discoveries that lead to economic growth.

Thus, the full recipe for growth in per capita GDP and worker productivity would include human capital deepening, physical capital deepening, and technological gains, operating in a market-oriented economy with supportive government policies.

Future Economic Convergence?

convergence: When economies with low per capita incomes are growing faster than economies with high per capita incomes.

Some low-income and middle-income economies around the world have shown a pattern of **convergence**, in which their economies grow faster than those of high-income countries. GDP increased by an average rate of 2.7% per year in the 1990s and 2.3% per year from 2000–2008 in the high-income countries of the world, which includes the United States, Canada, the countries of the European Union, Japan, Australia, and New Zealand.

Exhibit 22-7 lists seven countries of the world that belong to an informal "fast-growth club:" specifically, these countries averaged GDP growth (after adjusting for inflation) of at least 5% per year in both the time periods from 1990–2000 and from 2001–2014. Since economic growth in these countries has been exceeding the average of the world's high-income economies, the economies of these countries have been converging with the high-income countries. The second part of Exhibit 22-7 lists the "slow-growth club," which consists of countries that averaged GDP growth of 2% per year or less (after adjusting for inflation) during both time periods. The final portion of the exhibit shows GDP growth rates for the countries of the world divided by income.

Each of the countries in Exhibit 22-7 has its own unique story of investments in human and physical capital, technological gains, market forces, government policies, and even lucky events. But an overall pattern of convergence over the last two decades is clear. The low-income and middle-income countries have GDP growth faster than the high-income countries. More specifically, two prominent members of the fast-growth club are China and India, which between them have nearly 40% of the world's population. Some prominent members of the slow-growth club are high-income countries like France, Italy, and Japan. Will this pattern of economic convergence persist into future decades? This question is controversial among economists. Here are some of the main arguments on both sides.

EXHIBIT 22-7 Economic Growth around the World

Country	Average Growth Rate of GDP	
	1990–2000	2001–2014
Fast-Growth Club (5% or more per year in both time periods)		
Cambodia	7.5%	7.8%
China	9.8%	9.8%
India	5.6%	7.2%
Lao PDR	6.2%	7.4%
Mozambique	5.1%	7.9%
Uganda	6.5%	6.9%
Vietnam	7.4%	6.4%
Slow-Growth Club (2% or less per year in both time periods)		
Central African Republic	0.9%	2.0%
France	2.0%	1.1%
Haiti	0.0%	1.2%
Italy	1.6%	0.1%
Jamaica	2.0%	0.7%
Japan	1.5%	0.8%
Switzerland	1.3%	1.8%
World Overview		
High income	2.7%	1.7%
Middle income	3.7%	5.9%
Low income	2.8%	5.6%

Arguments Favoring Convergence

Several arguments suggest that low-income countries might have an advantage achieving greater worker productivity and economic growth in the future.

A first argument is based on diminishing marginal returns. Even though deepening human and physical capital will tend to increase per capita GDP, the law of diminishing returns suggests that as an economy increases its human and physical capital, the marginal gains to economic growth will diminish. For example, raising the average education level of the population by two years, from a tenth-grade level to a high school degree (while holding all other inputs constant), would produce a certain increase in output. An additional two-year increase, so that the average person had a two-year college degree, would increase output further, but the marginal gain would be smaller. Yet another additional two-year increase in the level of education, so that the average person would have a four-year college bachelor's degree, would increase output still further, but the marginal increase would again be smaller. A similar lesson holds for physical capital. If the quantity of physical capital available to the average worker increases, for example, from $5,000 to $10,000 (again, while holding all other inputs constant), it will increase the level of output. An additional increase from $10,000 to $15,000 will increase output further, but the marginal increase will be smaller.

A few decades ago, countries like China and India had very low levels of human capital and physical capital; as a result, an investment in capital deepening should have had a

The Challenges of Africa's Geography and Climate for Economic Growth

Many of the poorest countries of the world are in sub-Saharan Africa, where the average per capita GDP in 2015 was about $1,500. There are many reasons for poor economic performance, but some economic research has suggested that Africa's economic growth may have been limited by its geography and climate.

In many parts of the world, water transportation by river and ocean has helped to link together economies, but this doesn't work well for Africa. Other continents have major river systems that can be navigated by ocean-going vessels: like the Mississippi in North America, the Amazon in South America, the Rhine in Europe, or the Yangtze in Asia. But major rivers in Africa like the Nile, the Niger, the Congo, and the Zambezi have a number of steep waterfalls. Small boats might be transported around such waterfalls, but not large vessels. Moreover, Africa has a relatively straight coastline and thus relatively few natural ports with access to the ocean. Western Europe has one-eighth the land area of Africa, but its winding coastline is actually 50 percent longer.

As a result, in low-income countries in the world outside of Africa, more than half of the population lives within 60 miles of a sea or river. But in Africa, only one-fifth of the population lives within 60 miles of a sea or river.

Much of Africa has poor soil quality and little rain, which makes the challenges of agriculture different and more difficult than in other regions.

Africa is more tropical than any other region of the world; specifically, 93% of the land area of Africa is between the tropic of Cancer (an imaginary line drawn around the world at a latitude of 23.5 degrees north of the equator) and the tropic of Capricorn (an imaginary line drawn around the world at a latitude of 23.5 degrees south of the equator).

A tropical climate poses many challenges for economic growth. Many technologies that are developed for climates like the United States or Europe, like those for agriculture and construction, don't transfer well to tropical climates. Certain plant, animal, and human diseases that would be killed off or weakened by winter, like the malaria carried by mosquitoes, seem to thrive in a tropical climate. Moreover, Africa's tropical location means that it is a long way from the world's major markets in North America and Europe.

None of these arguments prove that Africa's economies cannot grow; indeed, a number of African countries have shown encouraging progress toward faster growth in the last decade or so. Nor do these arguments disprove the general recipe for economic growth of investments in human capital, physical capital, and technology, operating in a market-oriented environment. But they do suggest that the nations of Africa face some distinctive economic challenges and will have to discover their own unique path to economic growth.

larger marginal effect in those countries than it would have had in high-income countries, where levels of human and physical capital are already relatively high. This factor should give low-income economies a chance for converging economic growth.

A second argument is that low-income countries may find it easier to improve their technologies than high-income countries. The reason is high-income countries must continually invent new technologies, whereas low-income countries can often find ways of applying technology that had already been invented and is well understood. An economist named Alexander Gerschenkron (1904–1978) gave this phenomenon a memorable name—"the advantages of backwardness." Of course, he didn't literally mean that it was an advantage to have a lower standard of living. But he was pointing out that a country that is behind has some extra potential for catching up.

Finally, optimists argue that lower-income countries can observe the experience of those countries that have grown more quickly and can learn from it. Moreover, once the people of a country begin to enjoy the benefits of an increased standard of living, they may be more likely to build and support the market-friendly institutions that will help provide this standard of living.

Arguments That Convergence Is Neither Inevitable Nor Likely

If the growth of an economy depended only on the deepening of human capital and physical capital, then the growth rate of that economy would be expected to slow down over the

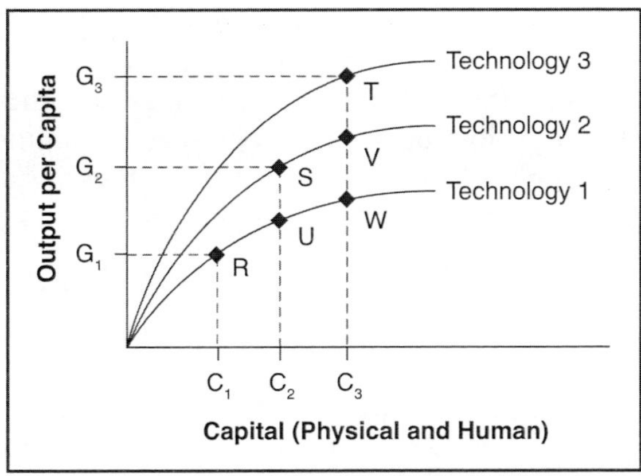

EXHIBIT 22-8 Capital Deepening and New Technology

Imagine the economy starts at point *R*, with the level of physical and human capital C_1 and the GDP per capita at G_1. If the economy relies only on capital deepening, while remaining at the technology level shown by the Technology 1 line, then it would face diminishing marginal returns as it moved from point *R* to point *U* to point *W*. However, now imagine that capital deepening is combined with improvements in technology. Then, as capital deepens from C_1 to C_2, technology improves from Technology 1 to Technology 2, and the economy moves from *R* to *S*. Similarly, as capital deepens from C_2 to C_3, technology increases from Technology 2 to Technology 3, and the economy moves from *S* to *T*. With improvements in technology, there is no longer any reason that economic growth must necessarily slow down.

long run as these inputs run into diminishing marginal returns. However, there is another crucial factor in the aggregate production function: technology.

The development of new technology can provide a way for an economy to sidestep the diminishing marginal returns of capital deepening. Exhibit 22-8 shows how. The horizontal axis of the figure measures the amount of capital deepening, which on this figure is an overall measure that includes deepening of both physical and human capital. The amount of human and physical capital per worker increases as you move from left to right from C_1 to C_2 to C_3. The vertical axis of the diagram measures per capita output. Start by considering the lowest line in this diagram, labeled Technology 1. Along this aggregate production function, the level of technology is being held constant, so the line shows only the relationship between capital deepening and output. As capital deepens from C_1 to C_2 to C_3 and the economy moves from *R* to *U* to *W*, per capita output does increase—but the way in which the line starts out steeper on the left but then flattens as it moves to the right shows the diminishing marginal returns, as additional marginal amounts of capital deepening increase output by ever-smaller amounts. The shape of the aggregate production line Technology 1 shows how the ability of capital deepening by itself to generate sustained economic growth is limited, since diminishing returns will eventually set in.

Now bring improvements in technology into the picture. Improved technology means that, with a given set of inputs, more output is possible. The production function labeled Technology 1 is based on one level of technology, but Technology 2 is based on an improved level of technology, so for every level of capital deepening on the horizontal axis, it produces a higher level of output on the vertical axis. In turn, production function Technology 3 represents a still higher level of technology, so that for every level of inputs on the horizontal axis, it produces a higher level of output on the vertical axis than either of the other two aggregate production functions.

Most healthy, growing economies are both deepening their human and physical capital and increasing technology at the same time. As a result, the economy can move from a choice like point *R* on the Technology 1 aggregate production function to a point like *S* on Technology 2 and a point like *T* on the still-higher aggregate production function Technology 3. With the combination of technology and capital deepening, the rise in per capita GDP in high-income countries does not need to fade away because of diminishing returns. The gains from technology can offset the diminishing returns involved with capital deepening, in part because the ideas of new technology can often be widely applied at a marginal cost that is very low or even zero. A specific additional machine or an additional year of education must be used by a specific worker or group of workers. But a new technology or invention can be used by many workers across the economy at very little marginal cost.

But will technological improvements themselves run into diminishing returns over time? That is, will it become continually harder and more costly to discover new technological improvements? Measuring technological progress is inherently difficult, so there is controversy among economists over this point. Some argue that the gains from the previous big wave of innovations in the first part of the twentieth century—that is, the spread of electric power, the internal combustion engine, petrochemicals, and telephones—was bigger than the current wave of innovation based on computing power, information and communication technology, and their many applications. Others argue that the productivity enhancements from web-based technologies are only just barely getting under way, and the economy is also just beginning to exploit other discoveries, such as biotechnology and material science. Of course, the answer to this controversy will gradually become apparent over time. The argument that it is easier for a low-income country to copy and to adapt existing technology than it is for a high-income country to invent new technology isn't necessarily true either. A society's performance when it comes to adapting and using new technology isn't automatic; it is the result of whether the economic, educational, and public policy institutions of the country are supportive. In theory, perhaps, low-income countries have many opportunities to copy and adapt technology, but if they lack the appropriate supportive economic institutions, the theoretical possibility that backwardness might have certain advantages is of little practical relevance.

The Slowness of Convergence

Although economic convergence between the high-income countries and the rest of the world seems possible and even likely, it will proceed only slowly. Consider, for example, one country that starts off with a per capita GDP of $40,000, which would roughly represent a typical high-income country today, and another country that starts out at $4,000, which is roughly the level in lower-middle-income countries like Indonesia, Guatemala, and Egypt. Say that the high-income country chugs along at a 2% annual growth rate of per capita GDP, while the poorer country grows at the aggressive rate of 7% per year. After 30 years, per capita GDP in the rich country will be $72,450 (i.e., $\$40,000 \times (1 + .02)^{30}$), while in the poor country it will be $30,450 (i.e., $\$4,000 \times (1 + .07)^{30}$). Convergence has occurred; the rich country used to be 10 times as wealthy as the poor one, and now it is only about 2.4 times as wealthy. But even after 30 consecutive years of very rapid growth, people in the low-income country are still likely to feel quite poor compared to people in the rich country. Moreover, as the poor country catches up, its opportunities for catch-up growth are reduced, and its growth rate may slow down somewhat.

The slowness of convergence illustrates again that small differences in annual rates of economic growth accumulate to huge differences over time. The high-income countries have been building up their advantage in standard of living over decades—more than a century in some cases. Even in an optimistic scenario, it will take decades for the low-income countries of the world to catch up significantly.

Key Concepts and Summary

1. Since the **Industrial Revolution** of the nineteenth century, a process of economic growth began in which the world's leading economies—mostly those in Western Europe and North America—expanded per capita GDP at an average rate of about 2% per year. In the last half century, countries like Japan, Korea, and China have shown potential for catch-up growth at higher rates, which has helped them to converge with the leading economies.
2. **Productivity** can be measured as the level of GDP per worker or GDP per hour. The rate of productivity growth is the primary determinant of its rate of long-term economic growth.
3. Over decades and generations, seemingly small differences of a few percentage points in the annual rate of economic growth make an enormous difference in per capita GDP.
4. An **aggregate production function** specifies how certain inputs in the economy, like human capital, physical capital, and technology, lead to the output measured as per capita GDP.
5. **Capital deepening** refers to a greater amount of capital per worker. It can apply to a greater amount of **human capital** per worker, in the form of higher education or skills, or to a greater amount of **physical capital** per worker.
6. **Technology**, in its economic meaning, refers broadly to all new methods of production, which include major scientific inventions but also small inventions and even better forms of management or company organization.
7. The recipe for growth in per capita GDP is to improve human capital, physical capital, and technology, in a market-oriented environment with supportive public policies and institutions.
8. **Convergence** refers to the issue of when, or if, countries with lower levels of per capita GDP will catch up to countries with higher levels of per capita GDP.
9. Because high-income economies will run into diminishing marginal returns on their investments in human capital and physical capital, and because high-income economies must continually invent new technologies, lower-income economies have a chance for convergent growth. However, many high-income economies have developed economic and political institutions that provide a healthy economic climate for an ongoing stream of technological innovations. The ongoing stream of technological innovations can counterbalance diminishing returns to investments in human and physical capital.

Review Questions

1. What was the Industrial Revolution?
2. How is per capita GDP calculated differently from worker productivity?
3. How do gains in worker productivity lead to gains in per capita GDP?
4. How much should a nation be concerned if its rate of economic growth is just 2% slower than other nations?
5. What is an aggregate production function? Describe one.
6. What is capital deepening?
7. What do economists mean when they refer to improvements in technology?
8. What is the overall recipe for growth in per capita GDP or worker productivity?
9. For a high-income economy like the United States, what elements of the aggregate production function are most important in bringing about growth in per capita GDP?
10. What do economists mean by convergence?
11. List some arguments for and against the likelihood of convergence.

Unemployment

CHAPTER

23

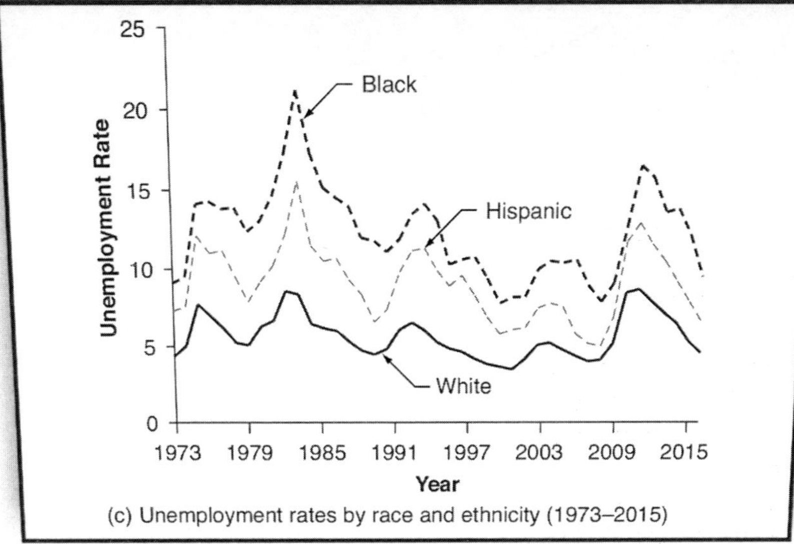

(c) Unemployment rates by race and ethnicity (1973–2015)

Chapter Outline

Unemployment is typically described in newspaper or television reports as a percentage; for example, from April 2016 to May 2016, U.S. unemployment declined from 5.0% to 4.7%. At a glance, the month-to-month changes in the unemployment rate percentages may seem small. But remember that the U.S. economy includes more than 150 million adults who either have jobs or are looking for them. A rise or fall of just 0.1% in the unemployment rate of 150 million potential workers translates into 150,000 people, which is roughly the total population of a city like Syracuse, New York; Brownsville, Texas; or Pasadena, California. Large movements in the unemployment rate, like the fall in the unemployment rate from 10% in October 2009 to 6% in September 2014, represent millions of people who were able to find jobs—and millions more who don't have one. Unemployment can be a terrible and wrenching life experience—like a bone-breaking automobile accident or a messy divorce—whose consequences can be fully understood only by someone who has experienced it personally. For unemployed individuals and their families, there is the day-to-day financial stress of not knowing where the next paycheck is coming from. There are painful adjustments, like watching your savings account dwindle, selling your car, or moving to a less expensive place. Even when the unemployed person finds a new job, it may pay less than the previous one. For many people, their job is one important part of their sense of self. When unemployment separates people from the workforce, it can affect family relationships and mental and physical health.

The human costs of unemployment alone would justify making a low level of unemployment an important priority for public policy. But the costs of unemployment also include economic costs to the broader society. When millions of unemployed but willing workers cannot find jobs, an economic resource is going unused. An economy with high unemployment is like a company operating with a functional but unused factory. The opportunity cost of unemployment is the output that could have been produced by the unemployed workers. One way in which this opportunity cost becomes apparent is through its effect on government budgets. Employed workers pay their share of taxes; unemployed workers often collect government support checks.

This chapter will discuss how to define and calculate unemployment rates. It will consider the patterns of unemployment over time, for the U.S. economy as a whole, for some different groups in the U.S. economy, and for other countries. We'll then consider an economic explanation for unemployment and how it explains the patterns of unemployment and suggests public policies for reducing unemployment.

Unemployment and the Labor Force

Unemployment may seem an obvious concept. President Calvin Coolidge, who was known in his time as Silent Cal for the brevity of his comments, once reportedly said: "When people are out of work, unemployment results." But when a concept runs into reality, it can get complicated.

In or Out of the Labor Force?

Should everyone without a job be counted as unemployed? Of course not. Children, for example, should not be counted as unemployed. Surely, the elderly who voluntarily left employment some years ago and are enjoying a happy retirement shouldn't be counted as unemployed. Many full-time college students have only a part-time job, or no job at all, but it seems inappropriate to count them as suffering the pains of unemployment. Some people are not working because they are ill, or on vacation, or on parental leave. Some people line up a new job and then take a month or two of vacation after leaving the previous job and before starting the new job; surely, they aren't suffering from unemployment in any meaningful sense of the word. In some marriages, one parent stays home with the children and the other holds a paying job; if the stay-at-home spouse is happy with that role and not looking for work, it would seem perverse to refer to this person as "unemployed."

These examples raise a common underlying theme. The adult population isn't just divided into employed and unemployed. A third group exists: people who don't have a job, and for some reason—retirement, looking after children, taking a voluntary break before a new job—aren't interested in having a job either. Economists refer to this third group of those who are not working and not looking for work as **out of the labor force**.

out of the labor force: Those who do not have a job and are not looking for a job.

The U.S. unemployment rate, which is based on a monthly survey carried out by the U.S. Bureau of the Census, asks a series of questions to divide up the adult population into employed, unemployed, or not in the labor force. To be classified as unemployed, a person must be without a job, currently available to work, and actively looking for work in the previous four weeks. Thus, a person who doesn't have a job but who is not currently available to work or has not actively looked for work in the last four weeks is counted as out of the labor force.

Calculating the Unemployment Rate

Exhibit 23-1 shows the three-way division of the over-16 adult population. In January 2016, 63% of the adult population was "in the labor force"—that is, either employed or without a job but looking for work. Those in the labor force can be divided into the employed and the unemployed. The **unemployment rate** is not the percentage of the total adult population without jobs, but rather the percentage of adults who are in the labor force but who do not have jobs:

unemployment rate: The percentage of adults who are in the labor force and thus seeking jobs, but who do not have jobs.

$$\text{Unemployment rate} = \frac{\text{Unemployed people}}{\text{Total labor force}}$$

In this example, the unemployment rate can be calculated as 7.8 million unemployed people divided by 158.3 million people in the labor force, which works out to a 4.9% rate of unemployment.

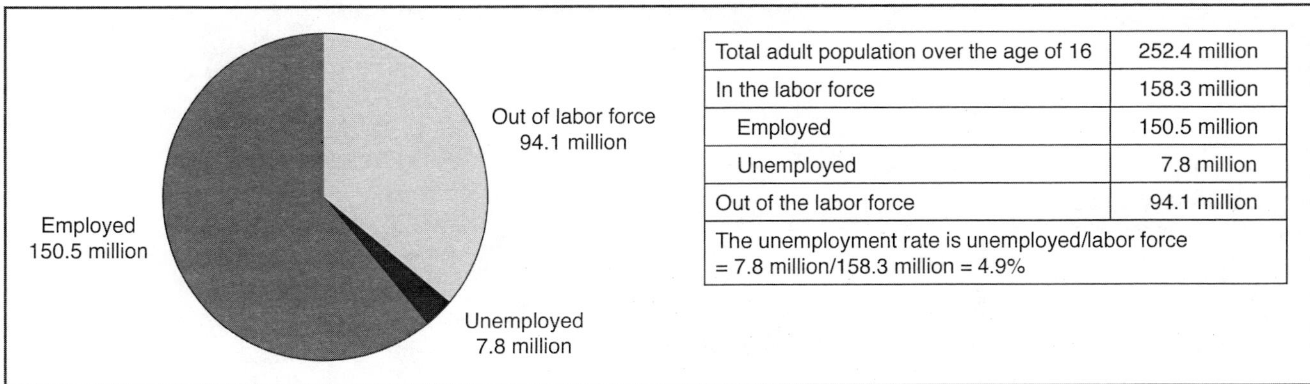

Total adult population over the age of 16	252.4 million
In the labor force	158.3 million
Employed	150.5 million
Unemployed	7.8 million
Out of the labor force	94.1 million
The unemployment rate is unemployed/labor force = 7.8 million/158.3 million = 4.9%	

EXHIBIT 23-1 Employed, Unemployed, Out of the Labor Force Distribution of Adult Population (age 16 and older), January 2016

Controversies over Measuring Unemployment

There is always controversy, gently simmering, over how best to draw the lines between unemployment and being out of the labor force. For example, what about people who don't have jobs and would be available to work, but have gotten discouraged at the lack of available jobs in their area and stopped looking? Such people, and their families, may be suffering the pains of unemployment. But the survey counts them as out of the labor force because they aren't actively looking for work. Other people may tell the Census Bureau that they are ready to work and looking for a job, but really, truly, they aren't that eager to work and aren't looking very hard. They are counted as unemployed, although they might more accurately be classified as out of the labor force. Still other people may have a job, perhaps doing something like yard work, child care, or cleaning houses, but aren't reporting the income earned to the tax authorities. They may report being unemployed when they are actually working.

Although the unemployment rate gets most of the public and media attention, economic researchers at the Bureau of Labor Statistics publish a wide array of surveys and reports that try to measure these kinds of issues and to develop a more nuanced and complete view of the labor market. It's not exactly a hot news flash that economic statistics are imperfect. But imperfect measures like the unemployment rate can still be quite informative, when interpreted knowledgeably and sensibly.

U.S. Unemployment Statistics

The unemployment rate announced by the U.S. Bureau of Labor Statistics each month is based on the Current Population Survey (CPS), which has been carried out every month since 1940. Great care is taken to make this survey representative of the country as a whole. The country is first divided into 3,137 counties or cities, and then these divisions are grouped into 1,973 geographic areas. The U.S. Bureau of the Census then selects 729 of these areas to survey. The 729 areas are then divided into "enumeration districts" of about 300 households each, and each "enumeration district" is divided into clusters of about four dwelling units. Every month, 1,500 Census Bureau employees call about 15,000 of the four-household clusters, for a total of 60,000 households. Households are interviewed for four consecutive months, then rotated out of the survey for eight months, and then interviewed again for the same four months the following year, before leaving the sample permanently.

Based on this survey, unemployment rates are calculated by state, industry, urban and rural areas, gender, age, race or ethnicity, and level of education. A wide variety of other data is available, too. For example, how long have people been unemployed? Did they become unemployed because they quit, or were laid off, or their employer went out of business? Is the unemployed person the only wage earner in the family? The Current Population Survey is a treasure trove of information about employment and unemployment.

EXHIBIT 23-2 The U.S. Unemployment Rate, 1948–2016

The U.S. unemployment rate moves up and down as the economy moves in and out of recessions. But over time, the unemployment rate seems to return to a range of 4% to 6%. There does not seem to be a long-term trend toward the U.S. unemployment rate moving generally higher or generally lower.

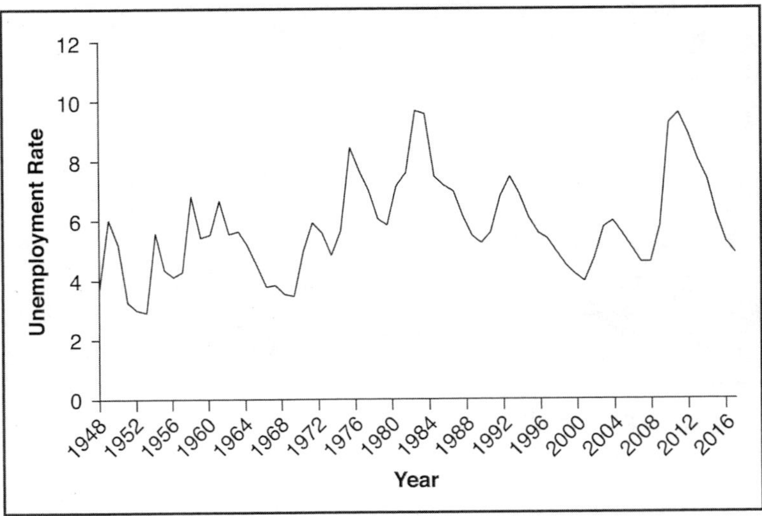

Patterns of Unemployment

The unemployment rate can be viewed from different angles: as a measure of the labor market situation in the overall U.S. economy, as a perspective on the labor market experiences of different groups, and in an international context.

The Historical U.S. Unemployment Rate

Exhibit 23-2 shows the historical pattern of U.S. unemployment since 1948. Several patterns stand out.

1. Unemployment rates do fluctuate over time. During the deep recessions of the early 1980s and of 2007–2009, unemployment reached roughly 10%. For comparison, during the Great Depression of the 1930s, the unemployment rate reached more than 25% of the labor force.
2. Unemployment rates in the late 1990s, the mid-2000s, and in 2015–2016 were low by historical standards at 5% or less. The previous time unemployment had been less than 5% for three consecutive years was three decades earlier, from 1968 to 1970.
3. The unemployment rate never falls all the way to zero. Indeed, it never seems to get below 3%—and it stays that low only for very short periods.
4. The timing of rises and falls in unemployment matches fairly well with the timing of upswings and downswings in the overall economy. During periods of recession and depression, unemployment is high. During periods of economic growth, unemployment tends to be lower.
5. No significant upward or downward trend in unemployment rates is apparent. This point is especially worth noting because the U.S. population nearly quadrupled from 76 million in 1900 to about 320 million by 2015. Moreover, a higher proportion of U.S. adults are now in the paid workforce because women have entered the paid labor force in significant numbers in recent decades. Women composed 18% of the paid workforce in 1900 and half of the paid workforce in 2010. But despite the increased number of workers, as well as other economic events like globalization and the continuous invention of new technologies, the economy has provided jobs without causing any long-term upward or downward trend in unemployment rates.

Unemployment Rates by Group

Unemployment is not distributed evenly across the U.S. population. Exhibit 23-3 shows unemployment rates broken down in various ways: by gender, age, and race/ethnicity.

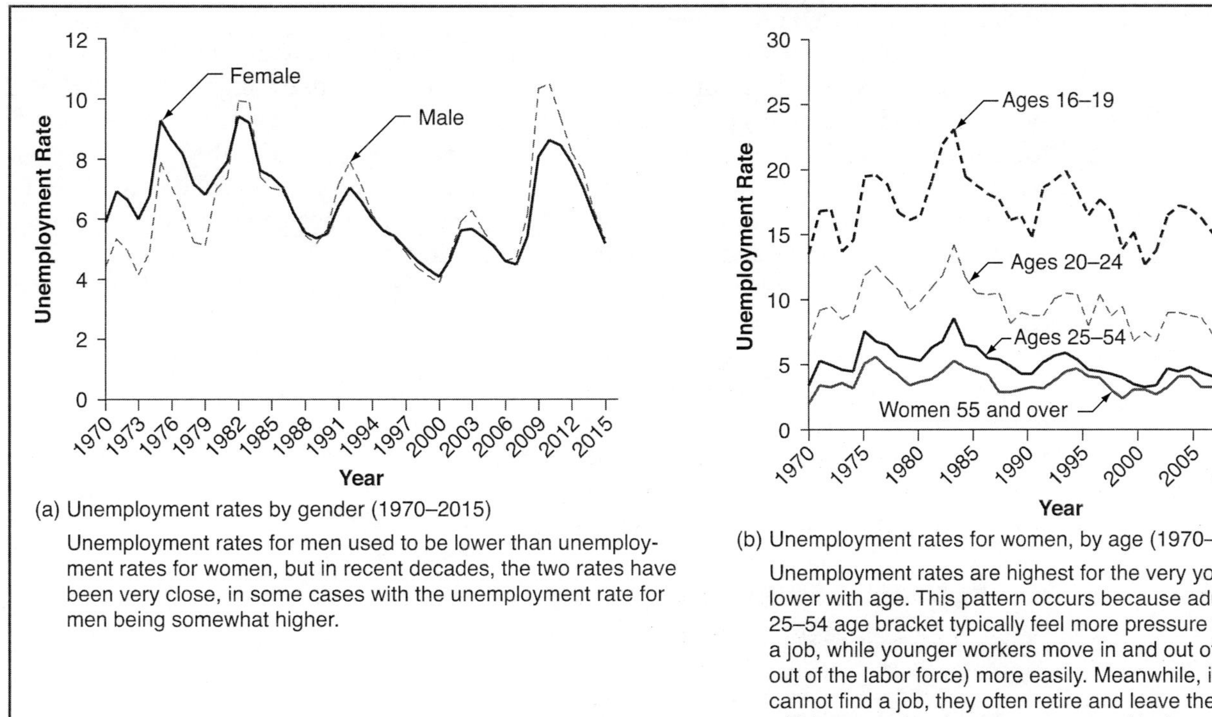

(a) Unemployment rates by gender (1970–2015)

Unemployment rates for men used to be lower than unemployment rates for women, but in recent decades, the two rates have been very close, in some cases with the unemployment rate for men being somewhat higher.

(b) Unemployment rates for women, by age (1970–2015)

Unemployment rates are highest for the very young and become lower with age. This pattern occurs because adult workers in the 25–54 age bracket typically feel more pressure to find or to keep a job, while younger workers move in and out of jobs (and in and out of the labor force) more easily. Meanwhile, if older workers cannot find a job, they often retire and leave the labor force—which means that they are not counted in the unemployment statistics.

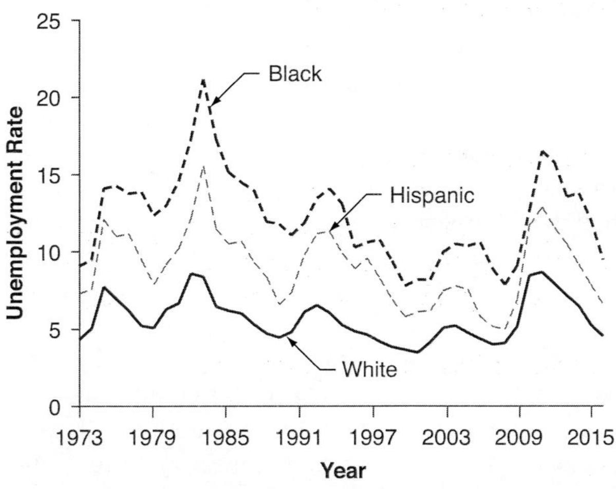

(c) Unemployment rates by race and ethnicity (1973–2015)

Although unemployment rates for all groups tend to rise and fall together, the unemployment rate for whites has been lower than the unemployment rate for blacks and Hispanics in recent decades.

EXHIBIT 23-3 Unemployment Rate

The unemployment rate for women had historically tended to be higher than the unemployment rate for men, perhaps reflecting the historical pattern than many women were seen as "secondary" earners. By about 1980, however, the unemployment rate for women was essentially the same as that for men, as shown in Exhibit 23-3*a*. During the recession of 2007–2009, the unemployment rate climbed higher for men than for women.

Younger workers tend to have higher unemployment, while middle-aged workers tend to have lower unemployment, probably because the middle-aged workers feel the responsibility of needing to have a job more heavily. Elderly workers have extremely low rates of unemployment because those who do not have jobs often exit the labor force by retiring, and thus are not counted in the unemployment statistics. Exhibit 23-3*b* shows unemployment rates for women divided by age; the pattern for men is similar.

The unemployment rate for African-Americans is substantially higher than the rate for other racial or ethnic groups, a fact that surely reflects to some extent a pattern of discrimination that has constrained blacks' labor market opportunities. However, the gaps between unemployment rates for whites, blacks, and Hispanics diminished in the 1990s, as shown in Exhibit 23-3*c*. In fact, unemployment rates for blacks and Hispanics were at the lowest levels in several decades during the mid-2000s.

Finally, those with less education typically suffer higher unemployment. In calendar year 2015, for example, the unemployment rate for those with a college degree was 2.8%; for those with some college but not a four-year degree, the unemployment rate was 5.0%; and for those without a high school diploma, the unemployment rate was 8.0%. This pattern may arise because additional education offers better connections to the labor market, or it may occur because the labor market opportunities for low-skilled workers are less attractive than the opportunities for the more highly skilled because of lower pay, and so low-skilled workers are less motivated to find jobs.

International Unemployment Comparisons

From an international perspective, the U.S. unemployment rate historically has looked a little better than the rate for many other high-income countries. Exhibit 23-4 compares unemployment rates for 1991, 1996, 2001, 2006, 2008, 2010, and 2014 for several high-income countries. However, the recession from 2007–2009 pushed U.S. unemployment rates higher than many of these other comparison countries.

Cross-country comparisons of unemployment rates need to be treated with care because each country has slightly different survey tools for measuring unemployment and also different labor markets. For example, Japan's unemployment rates appear quite low, but Japan's economy has been mired in slow growth and recession since the late 1980s, and Japan's unemployment rate probably paints too rosy a picture of its labor market. In Japan, workers who lose their jobs are often quick to exit the labor force and not look for a new job, in which case they are not counted as unemployed. In addition, Japanese firms are often quite reluctant to fire workers, and so some Japanese firms have substantial numbers of workers who are on reduced hours or officially employed, but doing very little. This Japanese pattern is perhaps best viewed as an unusual method for society to provide support for the unemployed, rather than a sign of a healthy economy.

Comparing unemployment rates in the United States and other high-income economies with unemployment rates in Latin America, Africa, and Asia is very difficult. One reason is that the statistical agencies in many poorer countries lack the resources and technical capabilities of the U.S. Bureau of Labor Statistics. But a more difficult problem with international comparisons is that in many low-income countries, most workers aren't

EXHIBIT 23-4 International Comparisons of Unemployment Rates

Country	1991	1996	2001	2006	2008	2010	2014
United States	6.8%	5.4%	4.8%	4.4%	5.8%	9.6%	6.2%
Canada	9.8%	8.8%	6.4%	6.2%	5.4%	7.1%	6.9%
Japan	2.1%	3.4%	5.1%	4.5%	4.1%	4.8%	3.7%
France	9.5%	12.5%	8.7%	10.1%	7.5%	9.5%	9.9%
Germany	5.6%	9.0%	8.9%	9.8%	7.6%	7.1%	5.0%
Italy	6.9%	11.7%	9.6%	7.8%	6.9%	8.5%	12.5%
Sweden	3.1%	9.9%	5.0%	5.2%	6.0%	8.3%	8.0%
United Kingdom	8.8%	8.1%	5.1%	5.5%	5.7%	7.9%	6.3%

involved in the labor market through an employer who pays them regularly. Instead, workers in these poor countries are engaged in short-term work, subsistence activities, and barter. Moreover, the effect of unemployment is very different in high-income and low-income countries. Unemployed workers in the developed economies have access to various government programs like unemployment insurance, welfare, and food stamps, while such programs may barely exist in poorer countries. Although unemployment is a serious problem in many low-income countries, it manifests itself in a different way than in high-income countries.

Why Unemployment Is a Puzzle for Economists

From the standpoint of the supply-and-demand model, unemployment presents a puzzle. In a supply-and-demand model of a labor market with flexible wages the labor market should move toward an equilibrium wage and quantity. At the equilibrium wage w_e, the equilibrium quantity q_e of labor supplied by workers should be equal to the quantity of labor demanded by employers. So where does unemployment occur in this model?

Looking for Unemployment with Flexible Wages

One possibility is that some of the people being counted as unemployed are actually on the upper-right portion of the supply curve of labor, above the equilibrium, in the circled area in Exhibit 23-5. That is, they would be willing to work if the wage were higher, but at the equilibrium wage, they aren't willing to work. The U.S. government economic statisticians may count some of these people as unemployed if they say that they are ready and looking for work, but in fact these people aren't willing to take a job for the wages that they are being offered in the labor market.

Probably a few people are unemployed because of unrealistic expectations about wages, but they certainly don't represent the majority of the unemployed. Instead, unemployed people often have friends or acquaintances of similar skill levels who are employed, and

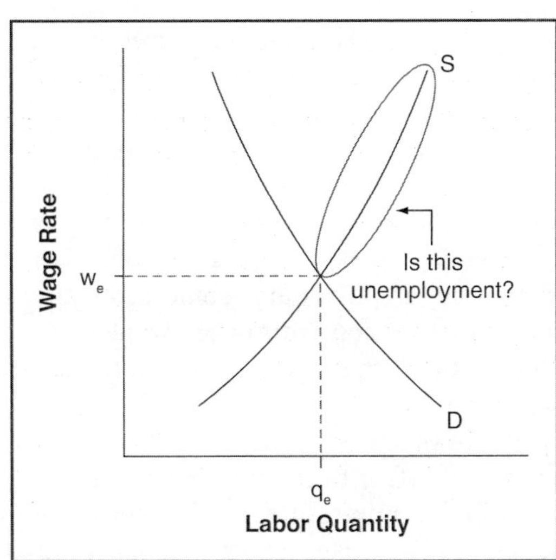

EXHIBIT 23-5 The Puzzle of Unemployment and Equilibrium in the Labor Market

In a labor market with flexible wages, the equilibrium will occur at the intersection of the supply curve S and the demand curve D, at wage w_e and quantity q_e. So how does unemployment enter the picture? One possible answer is that the unemployed are people who want to supply labor but are not willing to do so at the equilibrium wage. These people are represented by the circled part of the supply curve. While there are probably some people in this category, this doesn't seem to convey what is meant by unemployment. For most unemployed people, the problem is not that they are demanding higher wages than others of their skill level are receiving. Instead, the problem is that they can't find someone who is hiring and willing to pay the wage that others of their skill level are receiving.

the unemployed would be willing to work at the jobs and wages similar to what is being received by those people. But the employers of their friends and acquaintances don't seem to be hiring.

To economists, this kind of unemployment is something of a riddle. The definition of market equilibrium is that at the equilibrium wage, the quantity of labor demanded by employers will equal the quantity supplied. The supply and demand model can explain why wages will adjust up and down, and why the quantity of labor employed will rise and fall. But unemployment typically represents a situation in which people are willing to work at the market wage appropriate to their skills and experience, but still have trouble finding an employer to hire them. How can this situation occur?

Why Wages Might Be Sticky Downward

If a model with flexible wages does not describe unemployment very well—because it predicts that anyone willing to work at the going wage can always find a job—then it may prove useful to consider economic models in which wages are not flexible or adjust only very slowly. In particular, even though wage increases may occur with relative ease, wage decreases are few and far between.

One set of reasons why wages may be "sticky downward," as economists put it, involves economic laws and institutions. For low-skilled workers being paid the minimum wage, it is illegal to reduce their wages. For union workers operating under a multi-year contract with a company, wage cuts might violate the contract and create a labor dispute or a strike. However, minimum wages and union contracts aren't a sufficient reason why wages would be sticky downward for the U.S. economy as a whole. After all, out of the 150 million or so workers in the U.S. economy, less than 2% are paid the minimum wage. Similarly, only about 12% of American wage and salary workers are represented by a labor union. In other high-income countries, more workers may have their wages determined by unions, or the minimum wage may be set at a level that applies to a larger share of workers. But for the United States, these two factors combined affect only about one-seventh of the labor force.

Thus, economists looking for reasons why wages might be sticky downwards have focused on factors that may characterize most labor relationships in the economy, not just a few. A number of different theories have been proposed, but they share a common tone.

One argument is that even employees who are not union members often work under an **implicit contract**, which is that the employer will try to keep wages from falling when the economy is weak or the business is having trouble, and the employee will not expect huge salary increases when the economy or the business is strong. This wage-setting behavior acts like a form of insurance: the employee has some protection against wage declines in bad times, but pays for that protection with lower wages in good times. Clearly, this sort of implicit contract means that firms will be hesitant to cut wages, lest workers feel betrayed and work less hard or even leave the firm.

implicit contract: An unwritten agreement in the labor market that the employer will try to keep wages from falling when the economy is weak or the business is having trouble, and the employee will not expect huge salary increases when the economy or the business is strong.

efficiency wage theory: The theory that the productivity of workers, either individually or as a group, will increase if they are paid more.

Efficiency wage theory argues that the productivity of workers will increase if they are paid more, and so employers will often find it worthwhile to pay their employees somewhat more than market conditions might dictate. One reason why employees who are paid better are more productive is that they recognize that if they were to lose their current jobs, they would probably suffer a decline in salary at an alternative job. As a result, they will be motivated to work harder and to stay with the current employer. In addition, employers know that it is costly and time-consuming to hire and train new employees, so they would prefer to pay workers a little extra now rather than to lose them and have to hire and train new workers. Thus, by avoiding wage cuts, the employer minimizes costs of training and hiring new workers, and reaps the benefits of well-motivated employees.

The *adverse selection of wage cuts* argument points out that if an employer reacts to poor business conditions by reducing wages for all workers, then the best workers, with the best employment alternatives at other firms, are the most likely to leave, and the least-attractive workers, with fewer employment alternatives, are more likely to stay. Consequently, firms are more likely to choose which workers should depart, through layoffs and firings, rather than trimming wages across the board. Sometimes companies that are going through tough times can persuade workers to take a pay cut for the short term and still retain most of the firm's workers. But these stories are notable because they are so uncommon. It is far more typical for companies to lay off some workers, rather than to cut wages for everyone.

The **insider-outsider model** of the labor force argues that those already working for firms are "insiders," while new employees, at least for a time, are "outsiders." A firm depends on its insiders to grease the wheels of the organization, to be familiar with routine procedures, to train new employees, and so on. However, cutting wages will alienate the insiders and damage the firm's productivity and prospects.

insider-outsider model: A model that divides workers into "insiders" already working for the firm who know the procedures and "outsiders" who are recent or prospective hires.

Finally, the *relative wage coordination argument* points out that even if most workers were hypothetically willing to see a decline in their own wages in bad economic times *as long as everyone else also experiences such a decline*, there is no obvious way for a decentralized economy to implement such a plan. Instead, workers confronted with the possibility of a wage cut will worry that other workers will not have such a wage cut, and so a wage cut means being worse off both in absolute terms and relative to others. As a result, workers fight hard against wage cuts.

These theories of why wages tend not to move downward differ in their logic and their implications, and figuring out the strengths and weaknesses of each theory is an ongoing subject of research. But for present purposes, their common element is what matters. The value of labor is determined, at least in part, by the motivation and morale of employees, and employers must pay attention to these factors. Employees are different—some are more productive than others—and employers want to retain the better workers. In addition, employers know that there are costs of hiring and training, and so they want to avoid excessive turnover of their labor force. All of these reasons tend to imply that wages will decline only very slowly, if at all, even when the economy or a business is having tough times. When wages are inflexible and unlikely to fall, then either short-run or long-run unemployment can result.

The Short Run: Cyclical Unemployment

Let's make the plausible assumption that wages have an element of stickiness to them—in particular, that wages are sticky about moving downward. Let's also make the plausible assumption that in the short run from a few months to a few years, the quantity of hours that the average person is willing to work for a given wage doesn't change much, so the labor supply curve doesn't shift much. In addition, make the standard *ceteris paribus* assumption that there is no substantial short-term change in the age structure of the labor force, the institutions and laws affecting the labor market, or other possibly relevant factors.

One primary determinant of the demand for labor from firms is how they perceive the state of the macroeconomy. If firms believe that business is expanding, then at any given wage, they will desire to hire a greater quantity of labor, and the labor demand curve shifts to the right. Conversely, if firms perceive that the economy is slowing down or entering a recession, then they will wish to hire a lower quantity of labor at any given wage, and the labor demand curve will shift to the left.

The interaction between shifts in labor demand and wages that are sticky downward are illustrated in Exhibit 23-6. Exhibit 23-6*a* illustrates the situation in which the demand for labor shifts to the right from D_0 to D_1. In this case, the equilibrium wage rises from w_0 to w_1, and the equilibrium quantity of labor hired increases from q_0 to q_1. It doesn't hurt employee morale at all for wages to rise! However, Exhibit 23-6*b* shows the situation in which the demand for labor shifts to the left, from D_0 to D_1, as it would tend to do in a recession. Because wages are sticky downward, they do not adjust toward what would have been the new equilibrium wage w_1, at least not in the short run. Instead, after the shift in the labor demand curve, the same quantity of workers is willing to work at that wage as before; however, the quantity of workers demanded at that wage has declined from the original equilibrium q_0 to q_2. The gap between the original equilibrium quantity

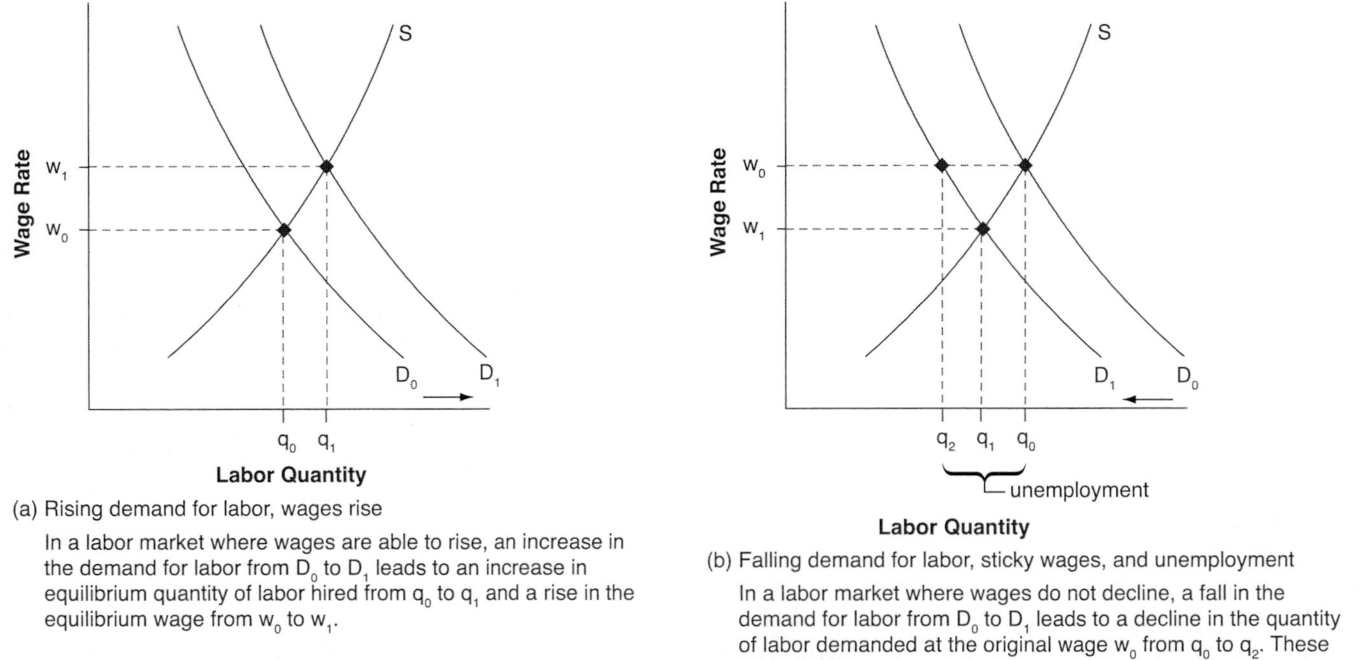

(a) Rising demand for labor, wages rise

In a labor market where wages are able to rise, an increase in the demand for labor from D_0 to D_1 leads to an increase in equilibrium quantity of labor hired from q_0 to q_1 and a rise in the equilibrium wage from w_0 to w_1.

(b) Falling demand for labor, sticky wages, and unemployment

In a labor market where wages do not decline, a fall in the demand for labor from D_0 to D_1 leads to a decline in the quantity of labor demanded at the original wage w_0 from q_0 to q_2. These workers will want to work at the prevailing wage w_0, but won't be able to find jobs.

EXHIBIT 23-6 Rising Wage and Low Unemployment/Where Is the Unemployment in Supply and Demand?

q_0 and the new quantity demanded of labor q_2 represents workers who would be willing to work at the going wage but can't find jobs. The gap represents the economic meaning of unemployment.

This analysis helps to explain the connection noted earlier, that unemployment tends to rise in recessions and to decline during expansions. The overall state of the economy shifts the labor demand curve, and combined with wages that are sticky downwards, unemployment changes. The rise in unemployment that occurs because of a recession is known as **cyclical unemployment** because it is closely tied to the business cycle.

cyclical unemployment: Unemployment closely tied to the business cycle, like higher unemployment during a recession.

The Long Run: The Natural Rate of Unemployment

Cyclical unemployment explains why unemployment rises during a recession and falls during an economic expansion. But what explains the remaining level of unemployment even in good economic times? Even when the U.S. economy is growing strongly, the unemployment rate only rarely dips as low as 4%. Moreover, the discussion earlier in this chapter pointed out that unemployment rates in many European countries like Italy, France, and Germany have often been remarkably high at various times in the last few decades. Why does some level of unemployment persist even when economies are growing strongly? Why are unemployment rates continually higher in certain economies, through good economic years and bad? Economists have a term to describe the remaining level of unemployment that occurs even when the economy is healthy: it is called the **natural rate of unemployment.**

natural rate of unemployment: The unemployment rate that would exist in a growing and healthy economy from the combination of economic, social, and political factors that exist at a time.

The natural rate of unemployment is not "natural" in the sense that water freezes at zero degrees Celsius or boils at 100 degrees Celsius. It is not a physical and unchanging law of nature. Instead, it is only the "natural" rate because it is the unemployment rate that would result from the combination of economic, social, and political factors that exist at a time—not including recession. These forces include the usual pattern of companies expanding and contracting their workforces in a dynamic economy, social and economic forces that affect the labor market, or public policies that affect either the eagerness of people to work or the willingness of businesses to hire. Let's discuss these factors in more detail.

Frictional Unemployment

In a market economy, some companies are always going broke for a variety of reasons: old technology, poor management, good management that happened to make bad decisions, shifts in tastes of consumers so that less of the firm's product is desired, a large customer who went broke, or tough domestic or foreign competitors. Conversely, other companies will be doing very well for just the opposite reasons and looking to hire more employees. In a perfect world, all of those who lost jobs would immediately find new ones. But in the real world, it takes time to find out about new jobs, to interview and figure out if the new job is a good match, perhaps to sell a house and buy another. The unemployment that occurs in the meantime, as workers move between jobs, is called **frictional unemployment.**

frictional unemployment: Unemployment that occurs as workers move between jobs.

In the mid-2000s, before the recession of 2007–2009 hit, it was nevertheless true that about 7% of U.S. workers saw their jobs disappear in any three-month period. But in periods of economic growth, these destroyed jobs are counterbalanced for the economy as a whole by a larger number of jobs created. In 2016, for example, there were typically about 7.5 million unemployed people at any given time in the U.S. economy. Even though about 60% of those unemployed people found a job in 14 weeks or less, the unemployment rate didn't change much during the year because those who found new jobs were largely offset by others who lost jobs.

Of course, it would be preferable if all of the people who were losing jobs could immediately and easily move into the new jobs being created, but in the real world, that isn't possible. Someone who is laid off by a textile mill in South Carolina can't turn around and immediately become a computer programmer in California. Instead, the adjustment process happens in ripples. Some people find new jobs near their old ones, while others find that they must move to new locations. Some people can do a very similar job with a different company, while others must start new career paths. Some people may be near retirement and decide to look only for part-time work, while others want an employer that offers a fruitful long-term career path. The frictional unemployment that results from people moving between jobs in a dynamic economy may account for 1–2 percentage points of total unemployment.

The level of frictional unemployment will depend to some extent on how willing people are to move to new areas to find jobs—which in turn may depend on history and culture. The extent of frictional unemployment will also depend on how easy it is for workers to learn about alternative jobs, which may reflect the ease of communications about job prospects in the economy.

Frictional unemployment and the natural rate of unemployment also seem to depend on the age distribution of the population. Exhibit 23-3*b* showed that unemployment rates are typically lower for people between about 25–54 years of age than they are for those who are either younger or older. "Prime-age workers," as those in the 25–54 age bracket are sometimes called, are typically at a place in their lives when they want very much to have a job and income arriving at all times. But some proportion of those who are under 30 may still be trying out jobs and life options and some proportion of those over 55 are eyeing retirement. In both cases, the relatively young or old tend to worry less about unemployment than those in-between, and their periods of frictional unemployment may be longer as a result. Thus, a society with a relatively high proportion of relatively young or old workers will tend to have a higher unemployment rate than a society with a higher proportion of its workers in middle age.

Productivity Shifts and the Natural Rate of Unemployment

Unexpected shifts in productivity can have a powerful effect on the natural rate of unemployment. Over time, the level of wages in an economy will be determined by the productivity of workers. After all, if a business paid workers more than could be justified by their productivity, the business would ultimately lose money and go bankrupt. Conversely, if a business tries to pay workers less than their productivity, then in a competitive market economy, other businesses will find it worthwhile to hire away those workers and pay them more.

However, adjustments of wages to productivity levels will not happen quickly or smoothly. Wages are typically reviewed only once or twice a year. In many modern jobs, it's difficult to measure productivity at the individual level. For example, how precisely would one measure the quantity produced by an accountant who is one of many people working in the tax department of a large corporation? Because productivity is difficult to observe, wages increases are often determined based on recent experience with productivity; if productivity has been rising at, say, 2% per year, then wages rise at that level as well. However, when productivity changes unexpectedly, it can affect the natural rate of unemployment for a time.

The U.S. economy in the 1970s and 1990s provides two vivid examples of this process. In the 1970s, productivity growth slowed down unexpectedly (as discussed in the previous chapter). For example, output per hour of U.S. workers in the business sector increased at an annual rate of 3.3% per year from 1960 to 1973, but only 0.8% from 1973 to 1982. Exhibit 23-7*a* illustrates the situation where the demand for labor—that is, the quantity of labor that business is willing to hire at any given wage—has been shifting out a little each year because of rising productivity, from D_0 to D_1 to D_2. As a result, equilibrium wages have been rising each year from w_0 to w_1 to w_2. But when productivity unexpectedly slows down, the pattern of wage increases does not adjust right away. Wages keep rising each year from w_2 to w_3 to w_4. But the demand for labor is no longer shifting up. As a result, a gap opens where the quantity of labor supplied at wage level w_4 is greater than the quantity demanded. The natural rate of unemployment rises; indeed, in the aftermath of this unexpectedly low productivity in the 1970s, the national unemployment rate did not fall below 7% from 1980 until 1987. Over time, the rise in wages will adjust to match the slower gains in productivity, and the unemployment rate will ease back down. But this process may take years.

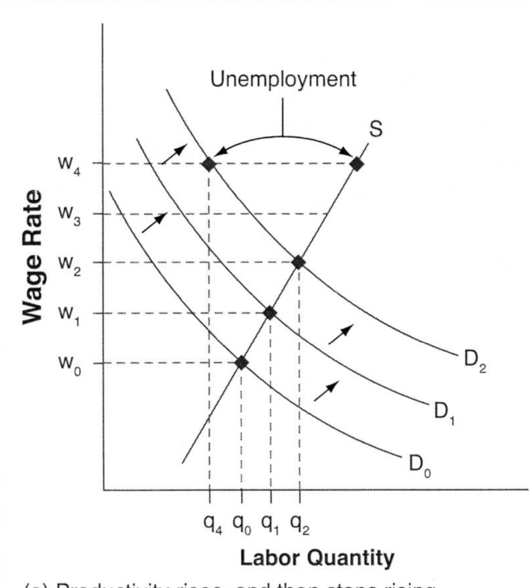

(a) Productivity rises, and then stops rising

Productivity is rising for a time, increasing the demand for labor from D_0 to D_1, and then from D_1 to D_2. Employers and workers become used to the pattern of wage increases, from w_0 to w_1, and from w_1 to w_2. Then productivity suddenly stops increasing. However, the expectations of employers and workers for wage increases don't shift immediately, so wages keep rising as before, from w_2 to w_3, and from w_3 to w_4. But the demand for labor has not increased, and so at wage w_4, unemployment exists where the quantity supplied of labor exceeds the quantity demanded.

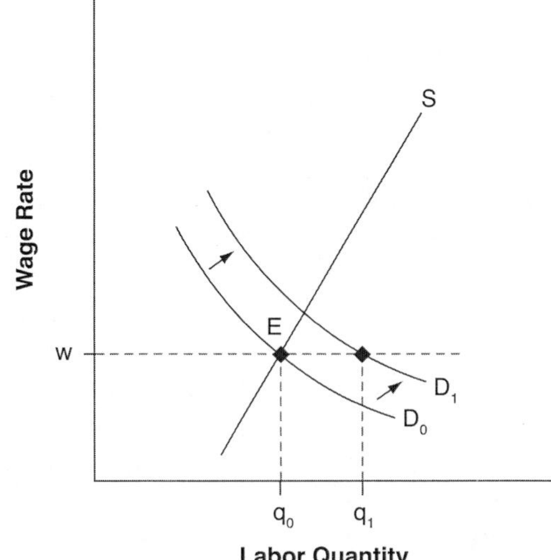

(b) Productivity doesn't change, and then rises

Now imagine that the rate of productivity increase has been zero for a time, so employers and workers have come to accept the equilibrium wage level w. But then productivity increases unexpectedly, shifting demand for labor from D_0 to D_1. At the wage w, this means that the quantity demanded of labor exceeds the quantity supplied, and with job offers extremely plentiful, the unemployment rate in this situation will be very low.

EXHIBIT 23-7 Unexpected Productivity Changes and Unemployment

The late 1990s provide an opposite example: instead of the surprise decline in productivity in the 1970s, productivity unexpectedly rose in the mid-1990s. The annual growth rate of real output per hour of labor increased from 1.7% from 1980 to 1995, to an annual rate of 2.6% from 1995–2001. Let's simplify the situation a bit, so that the economic lesson of the story is easier to see graphically, and say that productivity had not been increasing at all in earlier years, so the intersection of the labor market was at point E in Exhibit 23-7*b*, where the demand curve for labor D_0 intersects the supply curve for labor. As a result, real wages were not increasing. Now productivity jumps upward, which shifts the demand for labor out to the right, from D_0 to D_1, but at least for a time, wages are still being set according to the earlier expectations of no productivity growth, so wages do not rise. The result is that at the prevailing wage level w, the quantity of labor demanded q_D will for a time exceed the quantity of labor supplied q_S, and unemployment will be very low—actually below the natural level of unemployment for a time. This pattern of unexpectedly high productivity helps to explain why the unemployment rate stayed below 4.5%—quite a low level by historical standards—from 1998 until after the U.S. economy entered a recession in 2001.

Average levels of unemployment will tend to be somewhat higher when productivity is unexpectedly low and, conversely, will tend to be somewhat lower when productivity is unexpectedly high. But over time, wages do eventually adjust to reflect productivity levels.

Public Policy and the Natural Rate of Unemployment

Public policy can also have a powerful effect on the natural rate of unemployment. On the supply side of the labor market, public policies to assist the unemployed can affect how eager people are to find work. For example, if a worker who loses a job is guaranteed a hearty package of unemployment insurance, welfare benefits, food stamps, and government medical benefits, then the opportunity cost of being unemployed is lower and that worker will be less eager to seek a new job. What seems to matter most is not just the generosity of these benefits, but how long such benefits last. A society that provides generous help for the unemployed that phases out after, say, six months, may provide less of an incentive for unemployment than a society that provides less generous help that lasts for several years. Conversely, government assistance for job search or retraining can in some cases encourage people back to work sooner.

On the demand side of the labor market, government rules and social institutions can affect the willingness of firms to hire. For example, if government makes it hard for businesses to start up or expand, by wrapping new businesses in bureaucratic red tape, then businesses will be less enthusiastic about hiring. Government regulations can make it harder to start a business by requiring that a new business obtain many permits and pay many fees, or by restricting the types and quality of products that can be sold. Other government regulations like zoning laws may limit where business can be done, or whether businesses are allowed to be open during evenings or on Sundays. Whatever defenses may be offered for such laws in terms of social value—like the value some Christians place on not working on Sunday—these kinds of restrictions impose a barrier between some willing workers and other willing employers, and thus contribute to a higher natural rate of unemployment. Similarly, if government makes it difficult to fire or lay off workers, businesses may react by trying not to hire more workers than strictly necessary—since laying these workers off would be costly and difficult. High minimum wages may discourage businesses from hiring low-skill workers. Government rules may encourage and support powerful unions, which can then push up wages for union workers, but at a cost of discouraging businesses from hiring union workers.

The Natural Rate of Unemployment in Recent Years

The natural rate of unemployment includes all the factors influencing demand for labor and supply of labor, whether these factors are determined by the characteristics of the

How U.S. Unemployment Insurance Works

Unemployment insurance is a joint federal–state program, established by federal law in 1935. The federal government sets minimum standards for the program, but most of the administration is done by state governments.

The funding for the program is a federal tax collected from employers. The federal government requires that the tax be collected on the first $7,000 in wages paid to each worker; however, states can choose to collect the tax on a higher amount if they wish, and 41 states have set a higher limit. States can choose the length of time that benefits will be paid, although most states limit unemployment benefits to 26 weeks—with extensions often occurring in times of especially high unemployment. The fund is then used to pay benefits to those who become unemployed. Average unemployment benefits are equal to about one-third of the wage earned by the person in their previous job, but the level of unemployment benefits varies considerably across states.

Average Weekly Unemployment Benefits by State in 2014

Some states that pay, on average, less than $260/week		Some states that pay, on average, more than $340/week	
Alabama	$209	Colorado	$357
Alaska	$251	Hawaii	$429
Arizona	$223	Massachusetts	$433
Florida	$137	Minnesota	$386
Louisiana	$210	New Jersey	$409
Mississippi	$196	Pennsylvania	$370
South Carolina	$247	Rhode Island	$347
		Washington	$387

population, or of employers, or of public policy—all the relevant factors except recession, which is covered by the idea of cyclical unemployment. The underlying economic, social, and political factors that determine the natural rate of unemployment can change over time, which means that the natural rate of unemployment can change over time, too.

Estimates by economists of the natural rate of unemployment in the U.S. economy in the 2000s have often fallen in the range of 4.5 to 5.5%. Back in the 1980s, estimates of the natural rate of unemployment were commonly in the range of 6.0 to 6.5%. For a number of reasons, economists believe that the natural rate of unemployment in the U.S. economy declined from the 1980s to the 1990s into the 2000s.

1. The Internet has provided a remarkable new tool through which job seekers can find out about jobs at different companies and can send resumes and cover letters to possible employers with relative ease. An Internet search is far easier than trying to find a list of local employers and then hunting up phone numbers for all of their human resources departments, requesting a list of jobs and application forms, and so on.
2. The growth of the temporary worker industry has probably helped to reduce the natural rate of unemployment. In the early 1980s, only about 0.5% of all workers held jobs through temp agencies; by 2015, the proportion was 2.4%. Temp agencies can provide jobs for workers while they are looking for permanent work. They can also serve as a clearinghouse, helping workers find out about jobs with certain employers and getting a tryout with the employer. For many workers, a temp job is a stepping-stone to a permanent job that they might not have heard about or gotten any other way, so the growth of temp jobs will tend to reduce frictional unemployment, too.

3. The aging of the "baby boom generation"—that especially large generation of Americans born between 1946 and 1963—meant that the proportion of young workers in the economy was relatively high in the 1970s, as the boomers entered the labor market, but is relatively low today. As noted earlier, middle-aged workers are far more likely to keep steady jobs than younger workers, a factor that tends to reduce the natural rate of unemployment.

The combined result of these factors is that the natural rate of unemployment was on average lower in the 1990s and the early 2000s than in the 1980s. For example, from 1980 to 1986 the unemployment rate did not fall below 7%—despite rapid economic growth from 1983 to 1986. From 1990 up to 2007, the unemployment rate exceeded 7% in only one year—the recession year of 1992 when cyclical unemployment pushed the unemployment rate to 7.5%. The Great Recession of 2007 to 2009 pushed monthly unemployment rates above 10% in late 2009. But even at that time, the Congressional Budget Office was forecasting that unemployment rates would fall back to about 5% by 2016, which is what happened.

The Natural Rate of Unemployment in Europe

By the standards of other high-income economies, the natural rate of unemployment in the U.S. economy appears relatively low. Through good economic years and bad, many European economies had unemployment rates hovering near 10%, or even higher, from the 1970s up to the 2000s. European rates of unemployment have been higher not because recessions in Europe have been deeper, but rather because the conditions underlying supply and demand for labor have been different in Europe, in a way that has created a created a much higher natural rate of unemployment.

Many European countries have a combination of generous welfare and unemployment benefits, together with nests of rules that impose additional costs on businesses when they hire. In addition, many European countries have laws that require firms to give workers months of notice before laying them off and to provide substantial severance or retraining packages after laying them off. The legally required notice before laying off a worker can be more than three months in Spain, Germany, Denmark, and Belgium, and the legally required severance package can be as high as a year's salary or more in Austria, Spain, Portugal, Italy, and Greece. Such laws will surely discourage laying off or firing current workers. But when companies know that it will be difficult to fire or lay off workers, they also become hesitant about hiring in the first place.

Of course, economists and policy makers in European countries are well aware of these issues, and in recent years, countries like Germany, Sweden, and Netherlands have made concerted efforts to redesign various laws and rules so that they would be less likely to increase unemployment.

A Preview of Policies to Fight Unemployment

Later chapters will provide a detailed discussion of how to fight unemployment, when these policies can be discussed in the context of the full array of macroeconomic goals and frameworks for analysis. But even at this preliminary stage, it is useful to preview the main themes concerning policies to fight unemployment.

The remedy for unemployment will depend on the diagnosis. Cyclical unemployment is a short-term problem, caused because the economy is in a recession. Thus, the preferred solution will be to avoid or minimize recessions. As later chapters will discuss, this policy can be enacted by stimulating the overall buying power in the economy, so that firms perceive that sales and profits are possible, which makes them eager to hire.

Dealing with the natural rate of unemployment is trickier. There isn't much to be done about the fact that in a market-oriented economy, firms will hire and fire workers. Nor is there much to be done about how the evolving age structure of the economy, or unexpected shifts in productivity, will affect the natural rate of unemployment for a time.

However, government policy can affect the natural rate of unemployment that will persist in an economy even when GDP is growing. When a government enacts policies that will affect workers or employers, it must examine how these policies will affect the information and incentives that employees and employers have to seek each other out. For example, the government may also have a role to play in helping some of the unemployed with job searches. The design of government programs that offer assistance to unemployed workers and protections to employed workers may need to be rethought so that they will not unduly discourage the supply of labor. Similarly, rules that make it difficult for businesses to begin or to expand may need to be redesigned so that they will not unduly discourage the demand for labor. The message is not that all laws affecting labor markets should be repealed, but only that when such laws are enacted, a society that cares about unemployment will need to consider the trade-offs involved.

Key Concepts and Summary

1. Unemployment imposes high costs. Unemployed individuals suffer from loss of income and from stress. An economy with high unemployment suffers an opportunity cost of unused resources.
2. The adult population can be divided into those in the labor force and those **out of the labor force**. In turn, those in the labor force are divided into employed and unemployed. A person without a job must be willing and able to work and actively looking for work to be counted as unemployed; otherwise, a person without a job is counted as being out of the labor force.
3. The **unemployment rate** is defined as the number of unemployed persons divided by the number of persons in the labor force (not the overall adult population).
4. The U.S. unemployment rate rises during recessions and depressions, but falls back to the range of 4–6% when the economy is strong. The unemployment rate never falls to zero.
5. Despite enormous growth in the size of the U.S. population and labor force in the twentieth century, along with other major trends like globalization and new technology, the unemployment rate shows no long-term rising trend.
6. Unemployment rates differ by group: higher for African-Americans and Hispanics than for whites; higher for less educated than more educated; higher for the young than the middle-aged. Women's unemployment rates used to be higher than men's, but in recent years, men's and women's unemployment rates have been very similar.
7. In recent years, unemployment rates in the United States have compared favorably with unemployment rates in most other high-income economies.
8. In a labor market with flexible wages, unemployment is a puzzle, since wages will adjust in such a market so that quantity demanded of labor always equals the quantity supplied of labor at the equilibrium wage.
9. Many theories have been proposed for why wages might not be flexible, but instead may adjust only in a "sticky" way, especially when it comes to downward adjustments: **implicit contracts**, **efficiency wage theory**, adverse selection of wage cuts, **insider-outsider model**, and relative wage coordination.
10. **Cyclical unemployment** rises and falls with the business cycle.
11. The **natural rate of unemployment** is the rate of unemployment that would be caused by the economic, social, and political forces in the economy *even when the economy is not in a recession.* These factors include the **frictional unemployment** that occurs when people are put out of work for a time by the shifts of a dynamic and changing economy and any laws concerning conditions of hiring and firing that have the undesired side effect of discouraging job formation.

Review Questions

1. What does it mean to be in or out of the labor force?
2. How is the unemployment rate calculated?
3. Are all adults who do not hold jobs counted as unemployed?
4. Over the long term of decades, has the U.S. unemployment rate generally trended up, trended down, or remained at basically the same level?
5. Whose unemployment rates are commonly higher in the U.S. economy: Whites or nonwhites? The young or the middle-aged? College graduates or high school graduates?
6. Are U.S. unemployment rates typically higher, lower, or about the same as unemployment rates in other high-income countries?

7. Why is unemployment considered a puzzle in a labor market with flexible wages?
8. Name and explain some of the reasons why wages are likely to be sticky, especially in downward adjustments.
9. When would you expect cyclical unemployment to be rising? Falling?
10. What forces create the natural rate of unemployment for an economy?
11. Would you expect the natural rate of unemployment to be roughly the same in different countries?
12. Would you expect the natural rate of unemployment to remain the same within one country over the long run of several decades?
13. What is frictional unemployment?

CHAPTER 24

Inflation

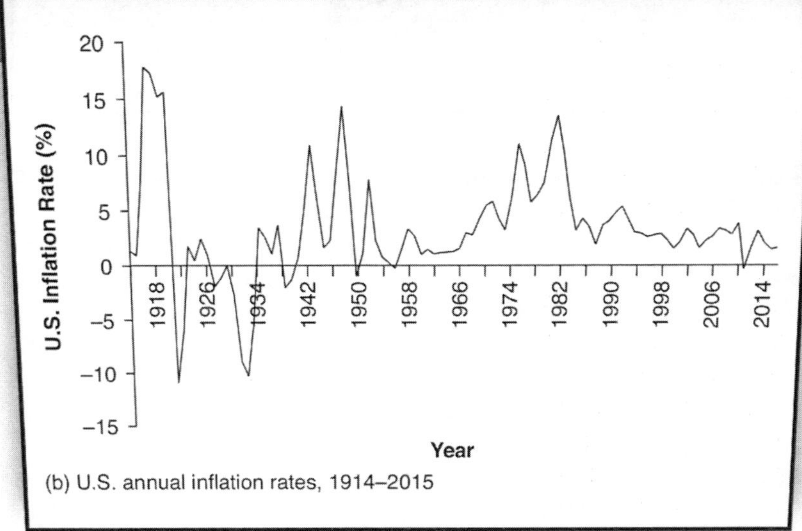

(b) U.S. annual inflation rates, 1914–2015

Chapter Outline

- Combining Prices to Measure the Inflation Rate
- Inflation Experiences
- Inflation around the World
- Adjusting Nominal Values to Real Values
- The Dislocations of Inflation
- Indexing and Its Limitations
- A Preview of Policy Discussions of Inflation

Inflation refers to a general and ongoing rise in the level of prices in an economy. This definition includes two ways in which inflation differs from the rises and falls in prices that happen in microeconomic markets. The first difference is that price changes in the microeconomic supply-and-demand model referred to a price in a particular market, like cars or oranges or phone service. While inflation does not mean that every single price in the economy rises by the same amount, it does imply that pressure for price increases reaches across most markets, not just one. The second difference is that price increases in the supply-and-demand model were one-time events, representing a shift from a previous equilibrium to a new one. While one occasionally sees references to inflation over short time periods, the term typically implies an ongoing rise in prices. If inflation happened for one year and then stopped—well, then it wouldn't be inflation any more.

inflation: A general and ongoing rise in the level of prices in an economy.

The presence of inflation is revealed when people remember back a few decades to when everything seemed to cost so much less and reminisce about how you could buy three gallons of gasoline for a dollar and then go see a discounted afternoon movie for another dollar. Exhibit 24-1 compares some prices of common goods in 1970 and 2014. Of course, the average prices shown in this table may not reflect the prices where you live. For example, the price of gasoline varies across states, depending on state-level regulations, the location of oil refineries, and transportation costs. In addition, certain products have evolved over recent decades. A new car, all loaded up with antipollution equipment, safety gear, computerized engine controls, and many other technological advances, is a more advanced machine than a car in 1970. But put detailed issues like these to one side for the moment, and look at the overall pattern. The primary reason behind these price rises in Exhibit 24-1—and all the price rises throughout the economy—isn't specific to the market for cars or gasoline or movie tickets. Instead, it's part of a general inflationary rise in the level of all prices. In 2014, $1 had about the same purchasing power in

EXHIBIT 24-1 Price Comparisons: 1970 and circa 2014

	1970	2012
Pound of ground beef	66 cents	$3.89
Pound of butter	87 cents	$3.37
Movie ticket	$1.55	$8.17
New car	$3,000	$32,709
Gallon of gasoline	36 cents	$3.37
Average hourly wage for a manufacturing worker	$3.23	$20.50

overall terms of goods and services as 16 cents did back in 1970 because of the amount of inflation over that time.

Moreover, the power of inflation doesn't just affect goods and services, but wages and income levels, too. The last row of Exhibit 24-1 shows that the average hourly wage for a manufacturing worker increased more than six-fold from 1970 to 2014. Sure, the average worker today is better educated and more productive than the average worker in 1970—but not five times more productive! Sure, per capita GDP increased substantially from 1970 to 2014, but is the average person in the U.S. economy really nine times better off in just 44 years? It doesn't seem plausible.

This chapter begins by showing how to combine prices of specific goods and services to create a measure of inflation. It discusses the historical and recent experience of inflation both in the United States and in other countries. Earlier chapters have sometimes included a note under an exhibit or a parenthetical reminder in the text saying that the numbers had been adjusted for inflation. In this chapter, it's time to show how to use inflation statistics to adjust other economic variables, so that you can calculate how much of, say, the rise in GDP over different periods of time can be attributed to an actual increase in the production of goods and services and how much should be attributed to the fact that prices for everything have risen. Inflation has consequences for many people and firms throughout the economy, in their roles as lenders and borrowers, wage earners, taxpayers, and consumers. The chapter concludes with a discussion of some imperfections and biases in the inflation statistics, and a preview of policies that will be discussed in later chapters for fighting inflation.

Combining Prices to Measure the Inflation Rate

A modern economy has millions of goods and services whose prices are continually quivering in the breezes of supply and demand. How can all of these shifts in price be boiled down to a single inflation rate? As with many problems in economic measurement, the conceptual answer is reasonably straightforward, but practical difficulties arise in applying the concept.

The Changing Price of a Basket of Goods

basket of goods and services: A hypothetical group of different items, with specified quantities of each one, used as a basis for calculating how the price level changes over time.

To calculate the rate of inflation, economists begin with the concept of a **basket of goods and services**, consisting of specified quantities of different items. Then inflation can be calculated in terms of how the overall cost of buying the basket of goods changes over time.

In thinking about how to combine individual price changes into an overall inflation rate, many people find that their first impulse is to calculate the average of the price changes of many goods. But such a calculation could easily be misleading, because some price increases matter more than others. Changes in the prices of goods for which people spend a larger share of their incomes will matter more than changes in the prices of goods for which people spend a smaller share of their incomes. An increase of 10% in the rental rate on apartments matters more to most people than whether the price of carrots rises by

EXHIBIT 24-2 A College Student's Price Index

Items	Quantity	(Year 1)		(Year 2)		(Year 3)		(Year 4)	
		Price	*Amount Spent*	*Price*	*Amount Spent*	*Price*	*Amount Spent*	*Price*	*Amount Spent*
Hamburgers	20	$3.00	$60.00	$3.20	$64.00	$3.10	$62.00	$3.50	$70.00
Aspirin	1	$10.00	$10.00	$10.00	$10.00	$10.00	$10.00	$10.00	$10.00
Movies	5	$6.00	$30.00	$6.50	$32.50	$7.00	$35.00	$7.50	$37.50
Total			$100.00		$106.50		$107.00		$117.50

10%. To construct an overall measure that captures inflation in the prices of many different items and also gives greater weight to the items on which people spend more money, economists consider the total cost of purchasing a basket of goods and services, where the basket will include quantities of the goods and services being purchased that reflect what people actually buy.

Consider the simple basket of goods with only three items, represented in Exhibit 24-2. Say that in any given month, a college student spends money on 20 hamburgers, 1 bottle of aspirin, and 5 movies. Prices for these items over four years are given in the table. Prices of some goods in the basket may rise while others fall. In this example, the price of aspirin doesn't change over the four years, while movies increase in price and hamburgers bounce up and down. Each year, the cost of buying the given basket of goods at the prices prevailing at that time is shown.

To calculate the annual rate of inflation in this example, find the percentage change in the cost of purchasing the overall basket of goods between the time periods. The general equation for percentage changes between two years, whether in the context of inflation or in any other calculation, is:

$$\frac{(\text{Level in new year} - \text{level in original year})}{(\text{level in original year})} \times 100 = \text{percentage change}$$

From year 1 to year 2, the total cost of purchasing the basket of goods in Exhibit 24-2 rises from $100 to $106.50. Therefore, the percentage change over this time—the inflation rate—is:

$$\frac{(106.50 - 100)}{100} \times 100 = 6.5\%$$

From year 2 to year 3, the overall change in the cost of purchasing the basket rises from $106.50 to $107. Thus, the inflation rate over this time, again calculated by the percentage change, is approximately:

$$\frac{(107 - 106.50)}{106.50} \times 100 = 0.5\%$$

This calculation of the change in the total cost of purchasing a basket of goods takes into account how much is spent on each good. Hamburgers are the lowest-priced good in this example, and aspirin is the highest-priced. But if an individual buys a greater quantity of a low-priced good, then it makes sense that changes in the price of that good should have a larger effect on the buying power of that person's money. The larger effect of hamburgers on inflation shows up in the "amount spent" column, where in all four years hamburgers are the largest item within total spending.

Index Numbers

The numerical results of a calculation based on a basket of goods can get a little messy. The simplified example in Exhibit 24-2 has only three goods, and the prices are in easy dollar amounts, not numbers like 79 cents or \$124.99. If the list of products was much longer, and more realistic prices were used, the total quantity spent over a year might be some messy-looking number like \$17,147.51 or \$27,654.92.

index number: When one arbitrary year is chosen to equal 100, and then values in all other years are set proportionately equal to that base year.

To simplify the task of interpreting the price levels for more realistic and complex baskets of goods, the price level in each period is typically not reported as a dollar amount for buying the basket of goods but rather as an **index number**. Index numbers work like this: Arbitrarily choose one year to be the base year, and in the base year, set the index equal to 100. In the example above, say that time period 3 is chosen as the base year, and so the total amount of spending in that year—\$107—is set equal to 100. Then, the total amount of spending for all other years is expressed in proportion to the level in the base year. The formula for the calculation is:

$$\frac{\text{Total amount spent in base year}}{\text{Index number in base year, always 100}} = \frac{\text{Total amount spent in other year}}{\text{Index number in other year}}$$

Thus, if period 3 is the base period, then the index number for period 1 would be:

$$\frac{107}{100} = \frac{100}{x} \qquad x = 93.4$$

Calculations for the other index numbers, based on the example presented in Exhibit 24-2 are shown in Exhibit 24-3. Because the index numbers are calculated so that they are in exactly the same proportion as the total dollar cost of purchasing the basket of goods, the inflation rate can be calculated based on the index numbers, using the percentage change formula. Thus, the inflation rate from period 1 to period 2 would be

$$\frac{(99.5 - 93.4)}{93.4} \times 100 = 6.5\%,$$

which is the same answer that was derived when measuring inflation based on the dollar cost of the basket of goods at different times.

The two graphs in Exhibit 24-4 illustrate the change in the price level over time. In Exhibit 24-4*a*, two lines are plotted: one is based on the dollar values taken from Exhibit 24-2; the other is based on the index numbers just calculated. Notice that the shape of the line is exactly the same in either case because the index numbers are constructed to reflect exactly the same pattern as the dollar figures. One line lies above the other only because the index was set up so that \$107 in spending during year 3 is equal to an index number of 100.

EXHIBIT 24-3 Calculating Index Numbers

	Total Spending	Index Number	Inflation Rate Since Previous Period
Year 1	\$100	$\frac{107}{100} = \frac{100}{x}$ $x = 93.4$	—
Year 2	\$106.50	$\frac{107}{100} = \frac{106.50}{x}$ $x = 99.5$	$\frac{(99.5 - 93.4)}{93.4} \times 100 = 6.5\%$
Year 3	\$107	100 (chosen arbitrarily)	$\frac{(100 - 99.5)}{99.5} \times 100 = 0.5\%$
Year 4	\$117.50	$\frac{107}{100} = \frac{117.50}{x}$ $x = 109.8$	$\frac{(109.8 - 100)}{100} \times 100 = 9.8\%$

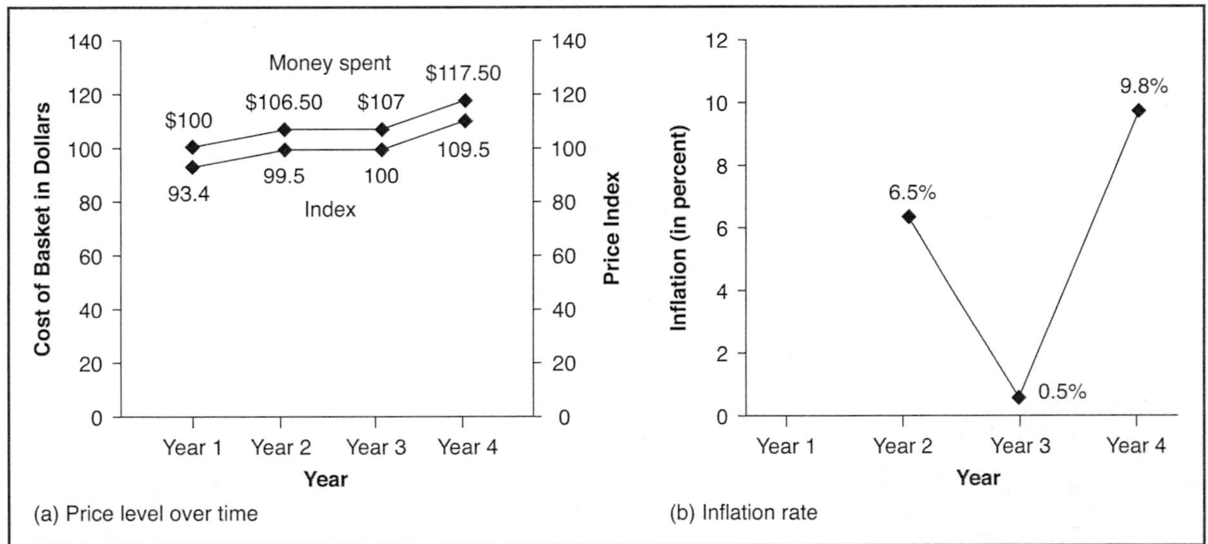

EXHIBIT 24-4 Using Price Levels and Index Numbers to Calculate Inflation Rates

In panel (a) on the left, the left-hand axis shows the cost of purchasing the college student's basket of goods as measured in dollars. The right-hand axis shows the cost of purchasing the basket of goods after converting to an index number. The two lines move in exactly the same way, since after all, the index numbers were calculated in such a way as to mirror exactly the dollar numbers. As a result, the percentage change in the price level from one year to the next, whether the price level is measured in terms of money or as a price index, will produce the same inflation rate, shown in panel (b) on the right.

Exhibit 24-4*b* shows the rate of inflation in periods 2, 3, and 4. It's not possible to calculate an inflation rate for period 1, because the price level in the previous time period isn't provided. The inflation rate will be exactly the same whether it is calculated based on the dollar spending totals in Exhibit 24-2 or on the index numbers in Exhibit 24-3.

If the inflation rate is the same whether it is based on dollar values or index numbers, then why bother with the index numbers? The advantage is that indexing allows easier eyeballing of the inflation numbers. If you glance at two index numbers like 107 and 110, you know automatically that the rate of inflation between the two years is about 3%. By contrast, imagine that the price levels were expressed in absolute dollars of a large basket of goods, so that when you looked at the data, the numbers were $19,493.62 and $20,009.32. Most people find it difficult to eyeball those kinds of numbers and say that it's a change of about 3%. However, the two numbers expressed in absolute dollars are exactly in the same proportion of 107 to 110 as the previous example.

Two final points about index numbers are worth remembering. First, index numbers have no dollar signs or other units attached to them. Although index numbers can be used to calculate a percentage inflation rate, the index numbers themselves do not have percentage signs on them. Index numbers just mirror the proportions found in other data. They transform the other data so that the data are easier to work with.

Second, the choice of a base year for the index number—that is, the year that is automatically set equal to 100—is arbitrary. In the official inflation statistics, it is common to use one base year for a few years, and then to update it, so that the base year of 100 is relatively close to the present and eyeballing the recent data is easier. But any base year that is chosen for the index numbers will result in exactly the same inflation rate. To see this in the previous example, imagine that year 1, when total spending was $100 was also chosen as the base year, and given an index number of 100. At a glance, you can see that the index numbers would now exactly match the dollar figures, the inflation rate in the first period would be 6.5%, and so on.

Measuring Changes in the Cost of Living

The most commonly cited measure of inflation in the United States is the **Consumer Price Index (CPI)**. The CPI is calculated by government statisticians at the U.S. Bureau of

Consumer Price Index (CPI): A measure of inflation calculated by U.S. government statisticians based on the price level from a basket of goods and services that represents the purchases of the average consumer.

Inflation in Massachusetts in 1780

In 1780, the state of Massachusetts wanted to encourage soldiers to sign up to fight in the Revolutionary War. However, the value of the new U.S. currency was unstable and inflation was high, so prospective soldiers worried that even if they survived the fighting, their pay could end up being worth almost nothing. How could the government address their worries?

In one of the first known examples of using a basket of goods to calculate inflation for public policy purposes, Massachusetts legislators devised their own way of calculating the inflation rate. They decreed that soldiers would be paid "in the then current Money of the State, in a greater or lesser Sum, according as Five Bushels of Corn, Sixty-eight Pounds and four-seventh Parts of a Pound of Beef, Ten Pounds of Sheep Wool, and Sixteen Pounds of Sole Leather shall then cost, more or less than One Hundred and Thirty Pounds of Current Money." In other words, soldiers would be paid 130 pounds in real value, adjusted for inflation in the price of the four goods.

The uneven and strange-sounding units—five bushels, 68 4/7 pounds, ten pounds, and 16 pounds—were chosen so that the overall amount spent on each good would be the same at the start of the calculation.

The Massachusetts legislature appointed county agents to collect price data every month. However, many of the Massachusetts agents had trouble doing the calculations, and others didn't collect data at all. Then, the central administrators seem to have taken what price data did exist and understated the actual level of price increases reported by the agents. After all, the state administrators knew that finding a high rate of inflation would have cost Massachusetts more money when the time came to pay the soldiers.

Labor Statistics (BLS) based on the price level of a basket of goods and services that represents the purchases of the average consumer. However, during the last two decades, the statisticians at the Bureau of Labor Statistics have paid considerable attention to a subtle problem: measuring how the total cost of buying a fixed basket of goods has evolved over time is conceptually not quite the same as measuring a change in the cost of living, which represents how much it costs for people to feel that their consumption provides an equal level of satisfaction or utility.

To understand the distinction, imagine that over the past 10 years, the cost of purchasing a fixed basket of goods increased by 25% and your salary also increased by 25%. Has your personal standard of living held constant? If you don't necessarily purchase the same identical fixed basket of goods every year, then an inflation calculation based on the cost of a fixed basket of goods may be a misleading measure of how your cost of living has changed. Two problems arise: substitution bias and quality/new goods bias.

When the price of a good rises, consumers tend to purchase less of it and to seek out substitutes instead. Conversely, as the price of a good falls, people will tend to purchase more of it. This pattern implies that goods with generally rising prices should tend over time to become less important in the basket of goods used to calculate inflation, while goods with falling prices should tend to become more important. However, a fixed and unchanging basket of goods assumes that consumers are locked into buying exactly the same goods, regardless of price changes. Thus, **substitution bias** is that the rise in the price of a fixed basket of goods over time tends to overstate the rise in a consumer's true cost of living because it doesn't take into account that the person can substitute between goods according to changes in their relative prices.

substitution bias: An inflation rate calculated using a fixed basket of goods over time tends to overstate the true rise in the cost of living because it doesn't take into account that the person can substitute away from goods whose prices rise a lot.

CLEARING IT UP

Don't Just Subtract Index Numbers

When a price index moves from, say, 107 to 110, the rate of inflation is not *exactly* 3%. Remember, the inflation rate is not derived by subtracting the index numbers, but rather through the percentage-change calculation. The precise inflation rate as the price index moves from 107 to 110 is calculated as $(110 - 107)/107 \times 100 = 2.8\%$. When the base year is fairly close to 100, a quick subtraction is not a terrible shortcut to calculating the inflation rate—but when precision matters down to tenths of a percent, it's not a precise way to proceed.

The other major problem in using a fixed basket of goods as the basis for calculating inflation is how to deal with the arrival of improved versions of older goods or altogether new goods. Consider the problem that arises if a cereal is improved by adding 12 essential vitamins and minerals—and also if a box of the cereal costs 5% more. It would clearly be misleading to count the entire resulting higher price as inflation, because the new price is being charged for a product of higher (or at least different) quality. Ideally, one would like to know how much of the higher price is due to the quality change, and how much of it is just a higher price, but even the producer may not know. This problem occurs all the time because quality changes and price changes typically happen together.

A new product can be thought of as an extreme improvement in quality—from something that didn't exist to something that does. However, the basket of goods that was fixed in the past obviously doesn't include new goods created since then. The bundle of goods used in the Consumer Price Index is revised and updated over time, and so new products are gradually included. But the process takes some time. For example, room air conditioners were widely sold in the early 1950s, but were not introduced into the basket of goods behind the Consumer Price Index until 1964. The VCR and personal computer were available in the late 1970s and widely sold by the early 1980s, but didn't enter the CPI basket of goods until 1987. By 1996, there were more than 40 million cellular phone subscribers in the United States—but cell phones weren't yet part of the CPI basket of goods. The parade of inventions has continued, with the CPI inevitably lagging a few years behind.

The arrival of new goods creates problems with respect to the accuracy of measuring inflation. The reason that people buy new goods, presumably, is that the new goods offer better value for money than existing goods. Thus, if the price index leaves out new goods, it overlooks one of the ways in which the cost of living is improving. In addition, the price of a new good is often higher when it is first introduced and then declines over time. If the new good isn't included in the CPI for some years until its price has already fallen, the CPI may miss counting this price decline altogether. Taking these arguments together, the **quality/new goods bias** is that the rise in the price of a fixed basket of goods over time tends to overstate the rise in a consumer's true cost of living because it doesn't take into account how improvements in the quality of existing goods or the invention of new goods improves the standard of living.

quality/new goods bias: Inflation calculated using a fixed basket of goods over time tends to overstate the true rise in cost of living because it doesn't take into account improvements in the quality of existing goods or the invention of new goods.

Practical Solutions for the Substitution and the Quality/New Goods Biases

By the early 2000s, the Bureau of Labor Statistics was using alternative mathematical methods for calculating the Consumer Price Index, more complicated than just adding up the cost of a fixed basket of goods, to allow for some substitution between goods. It was also updating the basket of goods behind the CPI more frequently, so that new and improved goods were included more rapidly. For certain products, the BLS was carrying out studies to try to measure the quality improvement; for example, an economic study can try to adjust for changes in speed, memory, screen size, and other characteristics of computers and then calculate the change in price after these changes in the product are taken into account. But these adjustments are inevitably imperfect, and exactly how to make such these adjustments is often a source of controversy between professional economists.

As a result of these adjustments in how the inflation rate is calculated, the effects of substitution bias and quality/new goods bias have been reduced. At present, the rise in the CPI probably overstates the true rise in inflation by only about 0.5% per year. Over one or a few years, this isn't much, but over a period of decade or two, even half of a percent per year compounds to a significant amount.

When measuring inflation (and other economic statistics, too), a trade-off arises between simplicity and interpretation. If the inflation rate is calculated with a basket of goods that is fixed and unchanging, then the calculation of an inflation rate is straightforward, but the problems of substitution bias and quality/new goods bias will arise.

How U.S. Government Statisticians Measure the Consumer Price Index

When the U.S. Bureau of Labor Statistics (BLS) calculates the Consumer Price Index, a first task is to decide upon a basket of goods that is representative for the purchases of the average household. This is done by using the Consumer Expenditure Survey, a national survey of about 7,000 households, which provides detailed information on spending habits. Consumer expenditures are broken up into eight major groups, shown below, which in turn are broken up into more than 200 individual item categories, some of which also appear in the list.

For each of the 200 individual expenditure items, the BLS chooses several hundred very specific examples of that item and looks at the prices of those examples. Thus, in figuring out the "breakfast cereal" item under the overall category of "Foods and beverages," the BLS picks several hundred examples of breakfast cereal: one example might be the price of a 24-oz. box of a particular brand of cereal sold at a particular store. The specific products and sizes and stores chosen are statistically selected to reflect what people buy and where they shop. The basket of goods in the Consumer Price Index thus consists of about 80,000 products; that is, several hundred specific products in over 200 broad-item categories. About one-quarter of these 80,000 specific products are rotated out of the sample each year and replaced with a different set of products.

The next step is to collect data on prices. Data collectors visit or call about 23,000 stores in 87 urban areas all over the United States every month to collect prices on these 80,000 specific products. A survey of 50,000 landlords or tenants is also carried out to collect information about rents.

The Consumer Price Index is then calculated by taking the 80,000 prices of individual products and combining them, using weights determined by the quantities of these products that people buy and allowing for factors like substitution between goods and quality improvements, into price indexes for the 200 or so overall items. Then, the price indexes for the 200 items are combined into an overall Consumer Price Index.

The Eight Major Categories in the Consumer Price Index

1. Food and beverages (breakfast cereal, milk, coffee, chicken, wine, full-service meals, and snacks)
2. Housing (renter's cost of housing, homeowner's cost of housing, fuel oil, bedroom furniture)
3. Apparel (men's shirts and sweaters, women's dresses, jewelry)
4. Transportation (new vehicles, airline fares, gasoline, motor vehicle insurance)
5. Medical care (prescription drugs and medical supplies, physicians' services, eyeglasses and eye care, hospital services)
6. Recreation (televisions, cable television, pets and pet products, sports equipment, admissions)
7. Education and communication (college tuition, postage, telephone services, computer software and accessories)
8. Other goods and services (tobacco and smoking products, haircuts and other personal services, funeral expenses)

However, when the basket of goods is allowed to shift and evolve to reflect substitution toward lower relative prices, quality improvements, and new goods, the technical details of calculating the inflation rate grow more complex.

Alternative Price Indexes: PPI, GDP Deflator, and More

The basket of goods behind the Consumer Price Index represents an average hypothetical U.S. consumer, which is to say that it doesn't exactly capture anyone's personal experience. When the task is to calculate an average level of inflation, this approach works fine. But what if one is concerned about inflation experienced by a certain group, like the elderly, or the poor, or single-parent families with children, or Hispanic-Americans? In specific situations, a price index based on the buying power of the average consumer may not be appropriate.

This problem has a straightforward solution. If the Consumer Price Index doesn't serve the desired purpose, then invent another index, based on a basket of goods appropriate for the group of interest. Indeed, the Bureau of Labor Statistics publishes a number of experimental price indexes: some for particular groups like the elderly or the poor, some for different geographic areas, some for certain broad categories of goods like food or housing.

The BLS also calculates several price indexes that are not based on baskets of consumer goods. For example, the **Producer Price Index** is based on prices paid for supplies and inputs by producers of goods and services. It can be broken down into price indexes for different industries, commodities, and stages of processing (like finished goods, intermediate goods, crude materials for further processing, and so on). There is an **International Price Index** based on the prices of merchandise that is exported or imported. An **Employment Cost Index** measures wage inflation in the labor market. The **GDP deflator** is a price index that includes all the components of GDP (i.e., consumption plus investment plus government plus exports minus imports).

Producer Price Index: A measure of inflation based on the prices paid for supplies and inputs by producers of goods and services.

International Price Index: A measure of inflation based on the prices of merchandise that is exported or imported.

Employment Cost Index: A measure of inflation based on the wage paid in the labor market.

GDP deflator: A measure of inflation based on all the components of GDP.

What's the best measure of inflation? As the U.S. Bureau of Labor Statistics says: "The 'best' measure of inflation for a given application depends on the intended use of the data."

Inflation Experiences

In the last two decades, inflation has been relatively low in the U.S. economy, with the Consumer Price Index typically rising 2–4% per year. But looking back over the twentieth century, waves of inflation have sometimes occurred at double-digit rates.

Historical Inflation in the U.S. Economy

Exhibit 24-5*a* shows the level of prices in the Consumer Price Index stretching back to 1913. In this case, the base year when the CPI is set to equal 100 is set for the average level of prices that existed from 1982 to 1984. Exhibit 24-5*b* shows the annual percentage changes in the CPI over time, which is the inflation rate. These two graphs, showing the price level as expressed by the CPI and the annual inflation rate derived from those price levels, are analogous to the two graphs of Exhibit 24-4 showing the price level for the college student's price index and the inflation rate derived from that calculation.

The first two waves of inflation are easy to characterize in historical terms: they are right after World War I and World War II. However, there are also two periods of severe negative inflation—called **deflation**—in the early decades of the twentieth century: one following the deep recession of 1920–21 and the other during the Great Depression of the 1930s. (Given that inflation is a time when the buying power of money in terms of goods and services is reduced, deflation will be a time when the buying power of money in terms of goods and services increases.) For the period from 1900 to about 1960, the major inflations and deflations nearly balanced each other out, so the average annual rate of inflation over these years was only about 1% per year. A third wave of more severe inflation arrived in the 1970s and departed in the early 1980s.

deflation: Negative inflation.

Times of recession or depression often seem to be times when inflation is decreasing, as in the recession of 1920–1921, the Great Depression, the recession of 1980–1982, and the Great Recession in 2009. Conversely, the rate of inflation often (but not always) seems to start rising when the economy is growing very strongly, like right after wartime or the 1960s. The previous chapter noted that recessions are typically accompanied by higher levels of unemployment. The frameworks for macroeconomic analysis that will be developed in later chapters will need to explain why recession often accompanies higher unemployment and lower inflation, while rapid economic growth often brings lower unemployment but higher inflation.

Inflation around the World

Patterns of inflation vary around the world. Many industrialized countries, not just the United States, had relatively high inflation rates in the 1970s; for example, in 1975, Japan's inflation rate was 11% and the inflation rate for the United Kingdom was 24%. In the 1980s, inflation rates came down in the United States and in Europe and have largely stayed down.

Countries with controlled economies in the 1970s, like the Soviet Union and China, historically had very low rates of officially measured inflation—because prices were

EXHIBIT 24-5 U.S. Price Level and Inflation Rates since 1913

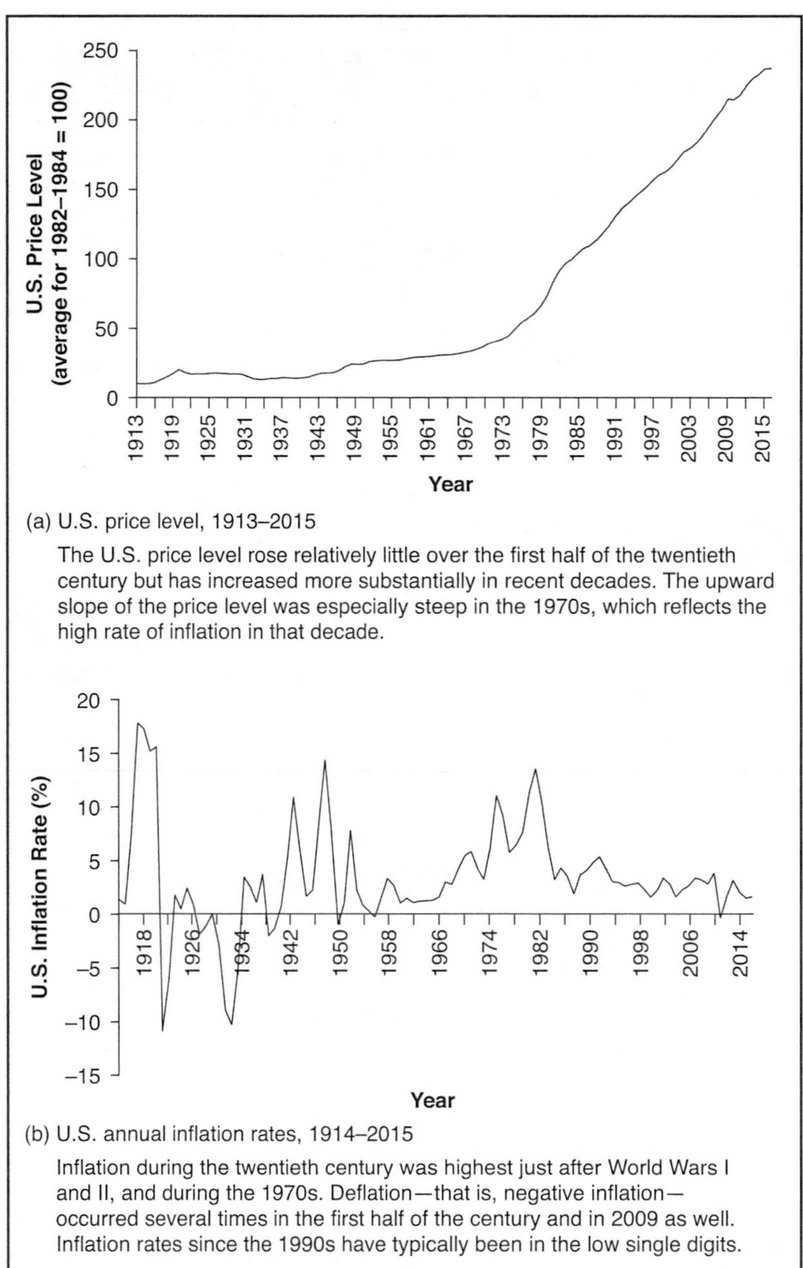

(a) U.S. price level, 1913–2015

The U.S. price level rose relatively little over the first half of the twentieth century but has increased more substantially in recent decades. The upward slope of the price level was especially steep in the 1970s, which reflects the high rate of inflation in that decade.

(b) U.S. annual inflation rates, 1914–2015

Inflation during the twentieth century was highest just after World Wars I and II, and during the 1970s. Deflation—that is, negative inflation—occurred several times in the first half of the century and in 2009 as well. Inflation rates since the 1990s have typically been in the low single digits.

forbidden to rise by law! However, these countries also had perpetual shortages of goods, since forbidding prices to rise acts like a price ceiling and creates a situation where quantity demanded often exceeds quantity supplied. As Russia and China made a transition toward more market-oriented economies, they also experienced outbursts of inflation, although the statistics for these economies should be regarded as somewhat shakier. Inflation in China averaged about 10% for much of the 1980s and early 1990s, although it has dropped since then. Russia experienced **hyperinflation**—that is, extremely high rates of inflation—of 2500% per year back in the early 1990s, although in the last few years Russia's consumer price inflation has typically been in the range of 8–15% per year.

hyperinflation: Extremely high rates of inflation.

Many countries in Latin America experienced raging hyperinflation during the 1980s and early 1990s, with inflation rates often well above 100% per year. In 1990, for example, both Brazil and Argentina saw annual inflation climb above 2000%. Certain countries in Africa experienced extremely high rates of inflation, sometimes bordering on hyperinflation, in the 1990s. Nigeria, the most populous country in Africa, had an inflation rate of 75% in 1995.

In the early 2000s, the problem of inflation appears to have diminished for most countries, at least in comparison to the worst times of recent decades. In recent years, two of the most extreme examples of inflation have been in Zimbabwe and Venezuela. During Zimbabwe's inflation from about 2007 to 2009, at one point the government was issuing bills with a face value of $100 trillion (in Zimbabwean dollars)—that is, the bills had $100,000,000,000,000 written on the front, but they were almost worthless. In Venezuela in 2015, the rate of inflation soared above 700%. In many countries, the memory of double-digit, triple-digit, and even quadruple-digit inflation is not very far in the past.

Adjusting Nominal Values to Real Values

Looking at economic statistics without considering inflation is like looking through a pair of binoculars and trying to guess how close something is: unless you know how strong the lenses are, you can't guess the distance very accurately. Similarly, if you don't know the rate of inflation, it is difficult to figure out if a rise in GDP is due mainly to a rise in the overall level of prices or to a change in quantities of goods produced. The **nominal value** of any economic statistic refers to the number that is actually announced at that time, while the **real value** refers to the statistic after it has been adjusted for inflation.

nominal value: The economic statistic actually announced at that time, not adjusted for inflation; contrast with real value.

real value: An economic statistic after it has been adjusted for inflation; contrast with nominal value.

Nominal to Real GDP

The second column in Exhibit 24-6 gives the U.S. GDP at five-year intervals since 1960 in nominal dollars; that is, in the dollars prevailing in each stated year. The third column gives the price level over that time measured by the GDP deflator, which is the measure of inflation based on a basket of goods that includes everything in GDP (using a base year of 2005 for when the index number is set equal to 100).

If an unwary analyst compared nominal GDP in 1960 to nominal GDP in 1990, it might appear that GDP had risen by a factor of eleven over this time (i.e., GDP of $5,803 billion in 1990 divided by GDP of $527 billion in 1960). But this calculation would be highly misleading. As the GDP deflator shows, the price level in 1990 was almost four times higher than in 1960 (the deflator for 1990 was 72 vs. a level of 19 in 1960). Clearly, much of the apparent growth in nominal GDP was due to inflation, not an actual change in real economic activity.

To adjust nominal GDP into real terms, you need to factor out the inflation that has occurred. After all, the dollars used to measure nominal GDP in 1960 are worth more

EXHIBIT 24-6 Nominal Values and Price Indexes

Year	Nominal GDP (billions of dollars)	GDP Deflator (2005 = 100)
1960	$527	19
1965	$720	20
1970	$1,040	24
1975	$1,638	34
1980	$2,788	48
1985	$4,213	62
1990	$5,803	72
1995	$7,415	82
2000	$9,952	89
2005	$12,623	100
2010	$14,527	111
2014	$17,615	115

CLEARING IT UP

Tips for Converting Nominal Annual Values to Real

When converting nominal annual values into real values, here are three tips.

1. Make sure that you convert all nominal figures into a single common year.
2. Be sure that you don't get the numerator and the denominator in the price index expression turned upside down.
3. When you have calculated an answer, apply your common sense. If you are working forward in time during a period of inflation, then the nominal number should grow when converted to real dollars. If you are working backward in time during a period of inflation, the nominal number should shrink. If your answer offends common sense, look back to the first two tips to see what you might have done wrong.

than the inflated dollars of 1990—and the price index tells exactly how much more. To calculate the real gain in GDP from 1960 to 1990, we can measure the nominal 1960 GDP in 1990 dollars, using the price index for the two different years:

$$\text{1960 GDP in 1960 dollars} \times \frac{\text{price level in 1990}}{\text{price level in 1960}} = \text{1960 GDP in 1990 dollars}$$

$$\$527 \text{ billion} \times \frac{72}{19} = \$1{,}997 \text{ billion}$$

To find the percentage change from the 1960 GDP in 1990 dollars to the 1990 GDP, also measured in 1990 dollars, calculate:

$$\frac{\text{(1990 GDP in 1990 dollars} - \text{1960 GDP in 1990 dollars)}}{\text{1960 GDP in 1990 \$}} \times 100 = \%\text{ change}$$

$$\frac{(5{,}803 - 1{,}997)}{1{,}997} \times 100 = 190\% \text{ growth in real GDP from 1960 to 1990}$$

The calculation also works in reverse. Convert the nominal 1990 GDP into 1960 dollars.

$$\text{1990 GDP in 1990 dollars} \times \frac{\text{price level in 1960}}{\text{price level in 1990}} = \text{1990 GDP in 1960 dollars}$$

$$\$5{,}803 \text{ billion} \times \frac{19}{72} = \$1{,}531 \text{ billion}$$

Then calculate the percentage change, and the answer is exactly the same 190%.

Any change in nominal dollar amounts over time—the price of a gallon of gasoline, wages, the buying power of a pension—can be adjusted for inflation in this way. Exhibit 24-7 shows the nominal GDP since 1960 and the real GDP over that time. Because 2009 is the base year, the nominal and real values are exactly the same in that year. However, over time, the rise in nominal GDP looks much larger than the rise in real GDP (i.e., the nominal GDP line rises more steeply than the real GDP line) because the rise in nominal GDP is exaggerated by the presence of inflation, especially in the 1970s.

Nominal to Real Interest Rates

Adjusting from nominal to real terms affects interest rates, too. Any interest rate can be divided into three components (as discussed in Chapter 2): the time value of money, the inflation rate, and the risk that a particular loan will not be repaid in full. No lender would be willing to lend without believing that the amount repaid will offer compensation for all three elements. The **real interest rate** is defined as the nominal rate of interest with inflation subtracted:

real interest rate: The rate of interest with inflation subtracted.

$$\text{Real interest rate} = \text{Nominal interest rate} - \text{Inflation rate.}$$

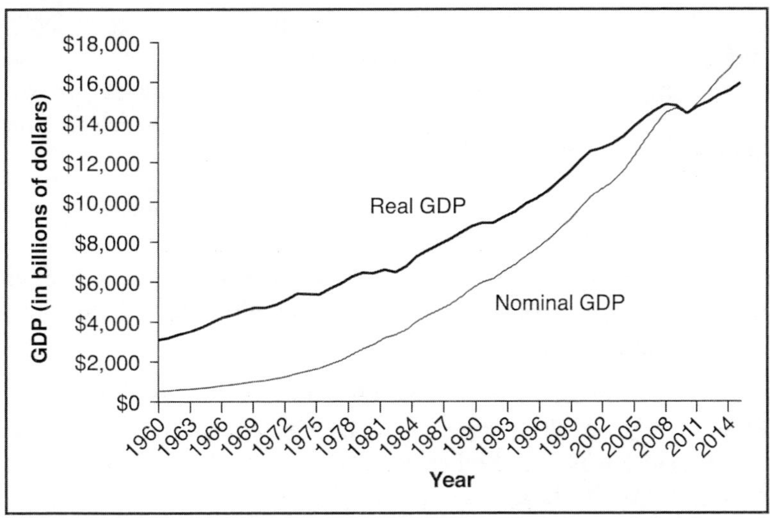

EXHIBIT 24-7 Nominal and Real GDP, 1960–2014

The lighter line measures GDP in nominal dollars. The darker line measures GDP in real dollars, where all dollar values have been converted to 2009 dollars. Since real GDP is expressed in 2009 dollars, the two lines cross in 2009. However, real GDP will appear higher than nominal GDP in the years before in 2005 because dollars were worth less in 2009 than in previous years. Conversely, real GDP will appear lower in the years after 2009 because dollars were worth more in 2009 than in later years.

The real interest rate represents how much in additional buying power a lender or investor receives, or alternatively, how much a borrower or supplier of capital has to pay. Consider a person who takes out a home mortgage, borrowing money to buy a house, at a nominal fixed rate of 8%. From the lender's point of view, say that out of the 8% nominal interest that is paid, 3 percentage points is accounted for by the expected lower value of inflated dollars in the future. Thus, the borrower and the lender enter into the loan expecting that the real rate of interest paid will be 5%. However, if inflation is lower than both parties expected, the actual real rate of interest will be higher than expected; conversely, if inflation is consistently higher than expected, the real rate of interest will be lower than expected.

Looking only at nominal interest rates can be very misleading. For example, in the early 1970s it was common for people to take out a 30-year mortgage to buy a home at a nominal interest rate of about 7%. However, there were two periods during the 1970s, first in 1974–1975 and then in 1979–1981, when inflation rose above 10% per year. If you had borrowed at 7% per year, you were actually facing a negative real interest rate in those years. Conversely, people who borrowed to purchase a home in the early 1980s might have taken out a 30-year home mortgage at a 13% rate of interest. A nominal interest rate of 13% can look reasonable if you are expecting annual rates of inflation to be 10% or higher. But by 1985 or so, annual inflation rates had fallen to 2–3%, and so the real interest rate turned out to be very high. In recent years, the rate of inflation has been low and fairly steady, so nominal and real interest rates have not fluctuated as much.

The real rate of interest is what ultimately matters. Receiving 200% nominal interest every year can be a bad deal—if the inflation rate is 250% per year. It would be better to get a 4% nominal return in a country with only 2% inflation!

The Dislocations of Inflation

Economists usually oppose high inflation, but they oppose it in a milder way than many non-economists. Robert Shiller, an economist at Yale University, carried out several surveys during the 1990s about attitudes toward inflation. One of his questions asked, "Do you agree that preventing high inflation is an important national priority, as important as preventing drug abuse or preventing deterioration in the quality of our schools?" Answers were on a scale of 1–5, where 1 meant "Fully agree" and 5 meant "Completely disagree." For the U.S. population as a whole, 52% answered "Fully agree" that preventing high inflation was highly important, and just 4% said "Completely disagree." However, among professional economists, only 18% answered "Fully agree," while the same percentage of 18% answered "Completely disagree."

The Land of Funny Money

What are the economic dislocations and problems caused by inflation, and why do economists often regard them with less concern than the general public? Consider a very short story: "The Land of Funny Money."

> One morning, everyone in the Land of Funny Money awakened to find that everything denominated in money was 20% larger. The change was completely unexpected. Every price in every store was 20% higher. Paychecks were 20% higher. The amount of money, everywhere from wallets to savings accounts, was 20% larger. This overnight inflation of prices made newspaper headlines everywhere in the Land of Funny Money. But the headlines quickly disappeared, as people realized that in terms of what they could actually buy with their incomes, this inflation had no economic impact. Everyone's pay could still buy exactly the same set of goods as it did before. Everyone's savings were still sufficient to buy exactly the same car or vacation or retirement that they could have bought before. Equal levels of inflation in all wages and prices ended up not mattering much at all.

When the people in Shiller's surveys (and similar follow-up surveys) explained their concerns about inflation, one typical reason was that they feared that as prices rose, they wouldn't be able to afford to buy as much. In other words, people were worried because they did not live in a place like the Land of Funny Money, where all prices and wages rose simultaneously. Instead, here on planet Earth, prices might rise while wages do not, or wages may rise more slowly than prices. If all prices, wages, and interest rates adjusted automatically and immediately with inflation, as in the Land of Funny Money, then no one's purchasing power or profits or real loan payments would change. However, if other economic variables do not move exactly in synch with inflation, or if they adjust for inflation only after a time lag, then inflation can cause three types of problems: unintended redistributions of purchasing power, blurred price signals, and difficulties in long-term planning.

Unintended Redistributions of Purchasing Power

Inflation can cause redistributions of purchasing power that hurt some and help others.

People who are hurt by inflation include those who are holding a lot of cash, whether it is in a safe deposit box or in a cardboard box under the bed. When inflation happens, the buying power of cash is diminished. But cash is only an example of a more general problem: anyone who has financial assets invested in a way that the nominal return doesn't keep up with inflation will tend to suffer from inflation. For example, if a person has money in a bank account that pays 4% interest, but inflation rises to 5%, then the real rate of return for the money invested in that bank account is negative 1%.

The problem of an attractive nominal interest rate being transformed into a disappointing real interest rate can be worsened by taxes. The U.S. income tax is charged on the nominal interest received in dollar terms, without an adjustment for inflation. Thus, a person who invests $10,000 and receives a 5% nominal rate of interest is taxed on the $500 received—no matter whether the inflation rate is 0% or 5% or 10%. If inflation is 0%, then the real interest rate is 5% and all $500 is a gain in buying power. But if inflation is 5%, then the real interest rate is zero and the person had no real gain—but owes income tax on the nominal gain anyway. If inflation is 10%, then the real interest rate is *negative* 5%, and the person is actually falling behind in buying, but would still owe taxes on the $500 in nominal gains.

CLEARING IT UP

Yet Again, Compound Growth Rates

The mathematical formula for the effect of how a certain percentage rate of inflation will cause the price level to increase over time is exactly the same formula in mathematical terms as two formulas you have already seen in earlier chapters: the formula for how a certain percentage interest rate will cause an amount of savings to increase over time from Chapter 2 and the formula for how a certain percentage rate of economic growth causes GDP to rise over time, as discussed in Chapter 22. In all three cases, seemingly low percentage rates of change can have large effects when compounded over long periods of time.

Inflation can cause unintended redistributions for wage earners, too. Wages do typically creep up with inflation over time, eventually. The last row of Exhibit 24-1 at the start of this chapter showed that average hourly wage in the U.S. economy increased from $3.23 in 1970 to $20.50 in 2014, which is an increase by a factor of more than five. Over that time period, the Consumer Price Index increased by a similar amount. However, increases in wages may lag behind inflation for a year or two, since wage adjustments are often somewhat sticky and occur only once or twice a year. Moreover, the extent to which wages keep up with inflation creates insecurity for workers and may involve painful, prolonged conflicts between employers and employees.

One sizeable group of people has often received a large share of their income in a form that doesn't increase over time: retirees who receive a private company pension. Most pensions have traditionally been set as a fixed nominal dollar amount per year at retirement. Even if inflation is low, the combination of inflation and a fixed income can create a substantial problem over time. A person who retires on a fixed income at age 65 will find that losing just 1–2% of buying power per year to inflation compounds to a considerable loss of buying power after a decade or two. If the price index for the consumption of a retiree is set at 100 at age 65 but rises 2% per year, then in 20 years that price level will reach:

$$100\,(1 + .02)^{20} = 149$$

It will now take $149 to purchase the same basket of goods that sold for $100 dollars at the beginning of the time period, and retirees living on a fixed dollar income will find that their standard of living has substantially eroded. Of course, if inflation is higher than the moderate level of 2%, the problem will be worse.

However, ordinary people can sometimes benefit from the unintended redistributions of inflation, too. Consider someone who borrows $10,000 to buy a car at a fixed interest rate of 9%. If inflation is 3% at the time the loan is made, then the loan must be repaid at a real interest rate of 6%. But if inflation rises to, say, 9%, then the real interest rate on the loan is zero! In this case, the borrower's benefit from inflation is the lender's loss. A borrower paying a fixed interest rate, who benefits from inflation, is just the flip side of an investor receiving a fixed interest rate, who suffers from inflation. The lesson is that when interest rates are fixed, rises in the rate of inflation tend to penalize suppliers of financial capital, who end up being repaid in dollars that are worth less because of inflation, while demanders of financial capital end up better off because they can repay their loans in dollars that are worth less than originally expected.

The unintended redistributions of buying power caused by inflation may have a broader effect on society. America's generally widespread acceptance of market forces rests on a perception that people's actions have a reasonable connection to market outcomes. But when inflation causes a retiree who built up a pension or invested at a fixed interest rate to suffer, while someone who borrowed at a fixed interest rate benefits from inflation by being able to repay at a lower real interest rate, it's hard to believe that this outcome was deserved in any way. Similarly, when homeowners benefit from inflation because the price of their homes rises, while renters suffer because they are paying higher rent,

German Hyperinflation and Hitler's Rise to Power

Germany suffered an intense hyperinflation of its currency, the Mark, in the years after World War I, which helped create the climate of social turmoil that Adolf Hitler took advantage of in his rise to power. Robert Shiller of Yale University describes the connection:

> A fact that is probably little known to young people today, even in Germany, is that the final collapse of the Mark in 1923, the time when the Mark's inflation reaches astronomical levels (inflation of 35,974.9% in November 1923 alone, for an annual rate that month of $4.69 \times 10^{28}\%$), came in the same month as did Hitler's Beer Hall Putsch, his Nazi Party's armed attempt to overthrow the German government. This failed putsch resulted in Hitler's imprisonment, at which time he wrote his book *Mein Kampf*, setting forth an inspirational plan for Germany's future, suggesting plans for world domination. . . .
>
> Most people in Germany today probably do not clearly remember these events; this lack of attention to it may be because its memory is blurred by the more dramatic events that succeeded it (the Nazi seizure of power and World War II). However, to someone living through these historical events in sequence . . . [the putsch] may have been remembered as vivid evidence of the potential effects of inflation.

it's hard to see any useful incentive effects. One of the reasons that inflation is so disliked by the general public is a sense that it makes economic rewards and penalties more arbitrary—and therefore likely to be perceived as unfair.

Blurred Price Signals

Prices are the messengers in a market economy, conveying information about conditions of demand and supply. Inflation blurs those price messages. Inflation means that price signals are perceived more vaguely, like a radio program received with a lot of static. If the static becomes severe, it's hard to tell what's happening.

In Israel, when inflation accelerated to an annual rate of 500% in 1985, some stores stopped posting prices directly on items, since they would have had to put new labels on the items or shelves every few days to reflect inflation. Instead, a shopper just took items from a shelf and went up to the checkout register to find out the prices for that day. Obviously, this situation makes comparing prices and shopping for the best deal rather difficult. When the levels and changes of prices become uncertain, businesses and individuals find it harder to react to economic signals. In a world where inflation is at a high rate, but bouncing up and down to some extent, does a higher price of a good mean that inflation has risen, or that supply of that good has decreased, or that demand for that good has increased? Should a buyer of the good take the higher prices as an economic hint to start substituting other products—or have the prices of the substitutes risen by an equal amount? Should a seller of the good take a higher price as a reason to increase production—or is the higher price only a sign of a general inflation in which the prices of all inputs to production are rising as well? The true story will presumably become clear over time, but at a given moment, who can say? High and variable inflation means that the incentives in the economy to adjust in response to changes in prices are weaker. Markets will adjust toward their equilibrium prices and quantities more erratically, and many individual markets will experience a greater chance of surpluses and shortages.

Problems of Long-Term Planning

Inflation can make long-term planning difficult. In discussing unintended redistributions, we considered the case of someone trying to plan for retirement with a pension that is fixed in nominal terms and a high rate of inflation. But similar problems arise for all people trying to save for retirement, who must consider what their money will really buy several decades in the future when the rate of future inflation cannot be known with certainty.

Inflation, especially at moderate or high levels, will pose substantial planning problems for businesses, too. A firm can make money from inflation—for example, by paying bills and wages as late as possible so that it can pay in inflated dollars, while collecting revenues as soon as possible. A firm can also suffer losses from inflation, as in the case of a retail business that gets stuck holding too much cash, only to see the value of that cash eroded by inflation. But when a business spends its time focusing on how to profit by inflation, or at least on how to avoid suffering from it, an inevitable trade-off strikes: less time is spent on improving products and services or on figuring out how to make existing products and services more cheaply. An economy with high inflation rewards businesses that have found clever ways of profiting from inflation, which are not necessarily the businesses that excel at productivity, innovation, or quality of service.

In the short term, low or moderate levels of inflation may not pose an overwhelming difficulty for business planning because costs of doing business and sales revenues may rise at similar rates. But if inflation varies substantially over the short or medium term, then it may make sense for businesses to stick to shorter-term strategies. The evidence as to whether relatively low rates of inflation reduce productivity is controversial among economists. There is some evidence that if inflation can be held to moderate levels of less than, say, 30% per year, it need not prevent a nation's real economy from growing at a healthy pace. For some countries that have experienced hyperinflation of several thousand percent per year, an annual inflation rate of 20–30% may feel nearly the same as zero! However, several economists have pointed to the suggestive fact that when U.S. inflation heated up in the early 1970s, U.S. growth in productivity slowed, and when inflation slowed down in the 1980s, productivity edged up again not long thereafter.

Some Benefits of Inflation?

Although the economic effects of substantial inflation are primarily negative, two countervailing points are worth noting. First, the effect of inflation will differ considerably according to whether it is creeping up slowly at 0–2% per year, galloping along at 10–20% per year, or racing to the point of hyperinflation at, say, 40% per *month*. Hyperinflation can rip an economy and a society apart. But an annual inflation rate of 2% or 3% or 4% is a long way from a national crisis.

Second, an argument is sometimes made that low rates of inflation may help the economy by making wages in labor markets more flexible. The discussion of unemployment in the previous chapter pointed out that wages tend to be sticky in their downward movements and that unemployment can result. A little inflation could nibble away at real wages, and thus help real wages to decline if necessary. In this way, even if a moderate or high rate of inflation may act as sand in the gears of the economy, perhaps a low rate of inflation serves as oil for the gears of the labor market. This argument is controversial. A full analysis would have to take all the effects of inflation into account. But it does offer another reason to believe that, all things considered, very low rates of inflation may offer much reason for concern.

Indexing and Its Limitations

When a price, wage, or interest rate is adjusted automatically with inflation, it is said to be **indexed**. An indexed payment rises according to the index number that measures inflation. A wide array of indexing arrangements is observed in private markets and government programs. Since the negative effects of inflation depend in large part on having inflation unexpectedly affect one part of the economy but not another—say, increasing the prices that people pay but not the wages that workers receive—indexing will take some of the sting out of inflation.

indexed: When a price, wage, or interest rate is adjusted automatically for inflation.

Indexing in Private Markets

cost-of-living adjustments (COLAs): A contractual provision that wage increases will keep up with inflation.

In the 1970s and 1980s, labor unions commonly negotiated wage contracts that had **cost-of-living adjustments**—known as **COLAs**—that guaranteed that their wages would keep up with inflation. These contracts were sometimes written as, say, COLA plus 3%. Thus, if inflation was 5%, the wage increase would automatically be 8%, but if inflation rose to 9%, the wage increase would automatically be 12%. COLAs are a form of indexing applied to wages.

adjustable rate mortgage (ARM): A loan used to purchase a home in which the interest rate varies with the rate of inflation.

Loans often have built-in inflation adjustments, too, so that if the inflation rate rises by 2%, then the interest rate charged on the loan rises 2% as well. An **adjustable rate mortgage**, a kind of loan used to purchase a home in which the interest rate varies with the rate of inflation, is referred to as an **ARM**. Often, a borrower will be able receive a lower interest rate at the start of the loan if borrowing with an ARM, compared to a fixed-rate loan. The reason is that with an ARM, the lender is protected against the risk that higher inflation will reduce the real loan payments, and so the risk premium part of the interest rate can be correspondingly lower.

A number of ongoing or long-term business contracts also have provisions that prices will be adjusted automatically according to inflation. Sellers like such contracts because they are not locked into a low nominal selling price if inflation turns out higher than expected; buyers like such contracts because they are not locked into a high buying price if inflation turns out to be lower than expected. A contract with automatic adjustments for inflation in effect agrees on a real price to be paid, rather than a nominal price.

Indexing in Government Programs

Many government programs are indexed to inflation. The U.S. income tax code is designed so that as a person's income rises above certain levels, the tax rate on the marginal income earned rises as well; this is what is meant by the expression "move into a higher tax bracket." For example, according to the basic tax tables from the Internal Revenue Service, in 2016 a single person owed 10% of all income from $0 to $9,275; 15% of all income from $9,275 to $37,650; 25% of all income from $37,650 to $91.150; 28% of all income from $91,150 to $190,150; 33% of all income from $190,150 to $413,350; 35% of income from $413,350 to $415,050; and 39.6% of all income above $415,050. Because of the many other provisions in the rest of the tax code, the taxes owed by any individual cannot be exactly determined based on these income levels and tax rates, but they illustrate the theme that tax rates rise as the marginal dollar of income rises. Until the late 1970s, if nominal wages increased along with inflation, people were moved into higher tax brackets and owed a higher proportion of their income in taxes, even though their real income had not risen! This "bracket creep," as it was called, was eliminated by law in 1981. Now, the income levels where higher tax rates kick in are indexed to rise automatically with inflation.

The Social Security program offers two examples of indexing. Since the passage of the Social Security Indexing Act of 1972, the level of Social Security benefits increases each year along with the Consumer Price Index. Also, Social Security is funded by payroll taxes, which are imposed on the income earned up to a certain amount—$118,500 in 2016. This level of income is adjusted upwards each year according to the rate of inflation, so that the indexed rise in the benefit level is accompanied by an indexed increase in the Social Security tax base.

As yet another example of a government program affected by indexing, in 1996 the U.S. government began offering indexed bonds. Bonds are means by which the U.S. government (and many private-sector companies as well) borrows money; that is, investors buy the bonds, and then the government repays the money with interest. Traditionally, government bonds have paid a fixed rate of interest. This policy gave a government that had borrowed an incentive to encourage inflation because it could then repay its past borrowing in inflated dollars at a lower real interest rate. But indexed bonds promise to pay a certain real rate of interest above whatever inflation rate occurs. In the case of, say, a retiree trying to plan for the long term, indexed bonds that guarantee a rate of return higher than inflation—no matter the level of inflation—can be a very comforting investment.

Might Indexing Reduce Concern over Inflation?

Indexing may seem like an obviously useful step. After all, when individuals, firms, and government programs are indexed against inflation, then people can worry less about the arbitrary redistributions and other effects of inflation.

However, some of the fiercest opponents of inflation express grave concern about indexing. They point out that indexing is always partial. Not every employer will provide COLAs for workers. Not all companies can assume that costs and revenues will rise in lockstep with the general rates of inflation. Not all interest rates for borrowers and savers will change to match inflation exactly. But as partial inflation indexing spreads, the political opposition to inflation may diminish. After all, older people whose Social Security benefits are protected against inflation, or banks that have loaned their money with adjustable rate loans, no longer have as much reason to care whether inflation heats up. In a world where some people are indexed against inflation and some are not, financially savvy businesses and investors may seek out ways to be protected against inflation, while the financially unsophisticated and small businesses may suffer from it most heavily.

A Preview of Policy Discussions of Inflation

This chapter has focused on how inflation is measured, historical experience with inflation, how to adjust nominal variables into real ones, how inflation affects the economy, and how indexing works. The causes of inflation have barely been hinted at, and government policies to deal with inflation have not been addressed at all. These issues will be taken up in depth in later chapters. However, it is useful to offer a preview here.

The cause of inflation can be summed up in one sentence: too many dollars chasing too few goods. The great surges of inflation early in the twentieth century came after wars, which are a time when government spending is very high, but consumers have little to buy because production is focused on the war effort. Governments also commonly impose price controls during wartime. But after the war, the price controls end and pent-up buying power surges, driving up inflation. On the other hand, if too few dollars are chasing too many goods, then inflation will decline or even turn into deflation. Therefore, slowdowns in economic activity, as in major recessions and the Great Depression, are typically associated with a reduction in inflation or even outright deflation. The policy implications are clear. If inflation is to be avoided, the amount of purchasing power in the economy must grow at roughly the same rate as the production of goods. Macroeconomic policies that the government can make to affect the amount of purchasing power—through taxes, spending, and regulation of interest rates and credit—can thus cause inflation to rise or can reduce inflation to lower levels.

Key Concepts and Summary

1. The price level is measured by using a **basket of goods and services** and calculating how the total cost of buying that basket of goods will increase over time. The price level is often expressed in terms of **index numbers**, which transform the cost of buying the basket of goods and services into a series of numbers in the same proportion to each other, but with an arbitrary base year of 100.
2. The rate of **inflation** is measured as the percentage change between price levels over time.
3. Measuring price levels with a fixed basket of goods will always have two problems: the **substitution bias**, by which a fixed basket of goods does not allow for buying more of what is relatively less expensive and less of what is relatively more expensive; and the **quality/new goods bias**, by which a fixed basket cannot take into account improvements in quality and the advent of new goods. These problems can be reduced in degree—for example, by allowing the basket of goods to evolve over time—but they cannot be totally eliminated.
4. The most commonly cited measure of inflation is the **Consumer Price Index (CPI)**, which is based on a basket of goods representing what the typical consumer buys.
5. Different measures of inflation are based on different baskets of goods. The **GDP deflator** is based on a basket of goods representing everything in GDP. The

Producer Price Index is based on a basket of goods representing supplies and inputs bought by producers of goods and services.

6. In the U.S. economy, the annual inflation rate in the last two decades has typically been around 2–4%. The periods of highest inflation in the United States in the twentieth century occurred during the years after World Wars I and II, and in the 1970s. The period of lowest inflation—actually, with **deflation**—was the Great Depression of the 1930s.
7. The **nominal value** of an economic statistic is the commonly announced value. The **real value** is the value after adjusting for changes in inflation.
8. To convert nominal economic data from several different years into real, inflation-adjusted data, the starting point is to choose arbitrarily a base year and then use a price index to convert the measurements so that they are measured in the money prevailing in the base year. The formula is:

$$\begin{array}{l}\text{Nominal economic variable}\\ \text{measured in currency from}\\ \text{the original year}\end{array} \times \frac{\text{Price index in base year}}{\text{Price index in original year}} = \begin{array}{l}\text{Economic variable}\\ \text{measured in currency}\\ \text{from the base year}\end{array}$$

9. The **real interest rate** is the nominal interest rate minus the rate of inflation.
10. Unexpected inflation will tend to hurt those whose money received, in terms of wages and interest payments, does not rise with inflation. In contrast, inflation can help those who owe money that can be repaid in less valuable, inflated dollars.
11. Low rates of inflation have relatively little economic impact over the short term. But over the medium and the long term, even low rates of inflation can complicate future planning. High rates of inflation can muddle price signals in the short term and prevent market forces from operating efficiently, and can vastly complicate long-term savings and investment decisions.
12. A payment is said to be **indexed** if it is automatically adjusted for inflation. Examples of indexing in the private sector include wage contracts with **cost-of-living adjustments (COLAs)** and loan agreements like **adjustable rate mortgages (ARMs)**. Examples of indexing in the public sector include tax brackets and Social Security payments.

Review Questions

1. How is a basket of goods used to measure the price level?
2. Why are index numbers used to measure the price level?
3. What's the difference between the price level and the rate of inflation?
4. Why does "substitution bias" arise if the inflation rate is calculated based on a fixed basket of goods?
5. Why does the "quality/new goods bias" arise if the inflation rate is calculated based on a fixed basket of goods?
6. What's the difference between the following measures of inflation: the Consumer Price Index, the Producer Price Index, and the GDP deflator?
7. What has been a typical range of inflation in the U.S. economy in the last decade or so?
8. Over the last century, during what periods was the U.S. inflation rate highest and lowest?
9. What is deflation?
10. What's the difference between a series of economic data over time measured in nominal terms versus the same data series over time measured in real terms?
11. How do you convert a series of nominal economic data over time to real terms?
12. How do you convert a nominal interest rate to a real interest rate?
13. Identify several parties likely to be helped and hurt by inflation.
14. What is indexing?
15. Name several forms of indexing in the private and public sector.

The Balance of Trade

CHAPTER

25

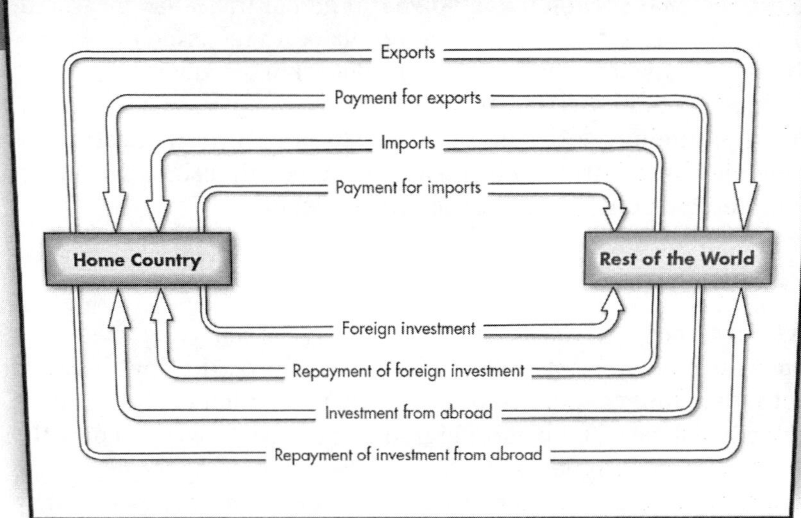

Chapter Outline

The **balance of trade** refers to the gap, if any, between a nation's **exports**, or what its producers sell abroad, and a nation's **imports**, or the foreign-made products and services purchased by households and businesses. If exports exceed imports, the economy is said to have a **trade surplus**. If imports exceed exports, the economy is said to have a **trade deficit**. If exports and imports are equal, then trade is balanced. But what happens when trade is out of balance and large trade surpluses or deficits exist?

Germany, for example, has experienced substantial trade surpluses in recent decades, in which exports have greatly exceeded imports. In 2015, Germany exported $1,331 billion of goods and services and imported $1,056 billion, for a trade surplus of $275 billion. In contrast, the U.S. economy in recent decades has experienced large trade deficits, in which imports have considerably exceeded exports. In 2015, U.S. imports of goods and services were $2,764 billion while exports were $2,223 billion, so that for the U.S. economy, imports exceeded exports by a sizeable $541 billion.

A series of macroeconomic events triggered by unbalanced trade has led some economies into deep recessions. The typical sequence of events begins with large trade deficits. At some point, foreign investors became pessimistic about the economy and moved their money to other countries, and as a result, the economy tumbled into deep recession. Mexico suffered through this sequence of events in 1995. A number of countries in East Asia—like Thailand, South Korea, Malaysia, and Indonesia—came down with the same economic illness in 1997–98. In the late 1990s and into the early 2000s, Russia and Argentina had the same experience. So did Greece around 2010. What are the connections between imbalances of trade in goods and services and the flows of international financial capital that have set off these economic avalanches?

The starting point for this chapter is to define the balance of trade in more detail and to sketch some patterns of trade balances both in the United States and around the world. The discussion then turns to examining the intimate

balance of trade: The gap, if any, between a nation's exports and imports.

exports: Goods and services that are produced domestically and sold in another country.

imports: Goods and services produced abroad and then sold domestically.

trade surplus: When exports exceed imports.

trade deficit: When imports exceed exports.

connection between international flows of goods and services and international flows of financial capital, which to economists are really just two sides of the same coin. Some perhaps surprising conclusions emerge from this discussion. It is often assumed that trade surpluses like those in Germany must be a positive sign for an economy, while trade deficits like those in the United States must be harmful. But as it turns out, both trade surpluses and deficits can be either beneficial or harmful for an economy in certain circumstances. Moreover, it is often presumed that an economy with a larger involvement in foreign trade is more likely to suffer a larger trade imbalance. However, it turns out that the extent to which a national economy is involved in global trade—as measured, say, by exports as a share of GDP—is not very strongly related to the issue of whether the economy has a substantial trade imbalance, nor to the underlying economic meaning of trade imbalances. As in the previous chapters on the macroeconomic goals of growth, unemployment, and inflation, the focus of this chapter is to lay a firm foundation for understanding what trade imbalances are, and then later chapters will discuss the underlying causes and macroeconomic policy responses in greater detail.

Measuring Trade Balances

A few decades ago, it was common to measure flows of trade by amounts of goods—that is, the solid, physical items that were transported by ships or trucks or airplanes between countries. The balance of trade measured by comparing exports and imports of goods is called the **merchandise trade balance**. But in most high-income economies, including the United States, goods make up less than half of GDP, while services compose more than half. The last two decades have seen a surge in international trade in services, powered by technological advances in telecommunications and computers that have made it possible for work in customer service, finance, law, advertising, management consulting, software, product design, and other areas to be performed in one country and sold in another. Most global trade still takes the form of goods, rather than services, and the merchandise trade balance is still announced by the government and reported in the media. Old habits are hard to break. But economists typically rely on a broader measure of international trade that includes goods, services, and other factors like international flows of income and foreign aid. This broad measure of the trade is called the **current account balance**.

merchandise trade balance: The balance of trade looking only at goods.

current account balance: A broad measure of the balance of trade that includes trade in goods and services, as well as international flows of income and foreign aid.

How the U.S. Government Collects Trade Statistics

Statistics on the balance of trade are compiled by the Bureau of Economic Analysis (BEA) within the U.S. Department of Commerce, using a variety of different sources.

Importers and exporters of merchandise must file monthly documents with the Census Bureau, which provides the basic data for merchandise trade. To measure international trade in services—which can happen over a telephone line or computer network without any physical goods being shipped—the BEA carries out a set of surveys. Another set of BEA surveys tracks investment flows, and there are even specific surveys to collect travel information from U.S. residents visiting Canada and Mexico. For measuring unilateral transfers, the BEA has access to official U.S. government spending on aid, and then also carries out a survey of charitable organizations that make foreign donations.

This information on international flows of goods and capital is then cross-checked against other available data. For example, the Census Bureau also collects data from the shipping industry, which can be used to check the data on trade in goods. All companies involved in international flows of capital—including banks and financial investments like stocks—must file reports, which are ultimately compiled by the U.S. Department of the Treasury. Information on foreign trade can also be cross-checked by looking at data collected by other countries on their foreign trade with the United States, and also at the data collected by various international organizations. Take these data sources, stir carefully, and you have the U.S. balance of trade statistics.

EXHIBIT 25-1 Components of the U.S. Current Account Balance, 2015 (measured in billions of dollars)

	Exports	Imports	Balance
Goods	$1,513	$2,273	–$760
Services	$710	$491	$219
Income payments	$783	$592	$191
Unilateral transfers	$133	$267	–$134
Current account balance	$3,139	$3,623	–$484

Components of the U.S. Current Account Balance

Exhibit 25-1 breaks down the four main components of the U.S. current account balance for 2015. The first line shows the merchandise trade balance—that is, exports and imports of goods. Because imports exceed exports, the balance in the final column is negative, showing a merchandise trade deficit.

The second row provides data on trade in services. In services, the U.S. economy is running a surplus. Although the level of trade in services is still relatively small compared to trade in goods, the importance of services in trade has expanded substantially over the last few decades. For example, U.S. exports of services were equal to nearly one-half of U.S. exports of goods in 2015, compared to one-fifth back in 1980.

The third component of the current account balance, labeled "income payments," refers to returns received by U.S. financial investors on their foreign investments, and payments made by parties in the U.S. economy to foreign investors who have invested their funds here. The reason for including these returns on foreign investment in the overall measure of trade, along with goods and services, is that from an economic perspective, financial investment is just as much an economic transaction as shipments of cars or wheat or oil: it's just trade that is happening in the financial capital market. A return on investment is a payment for letting someone else use your financial capital. A payment made from a U.S. company to a foreign investor, in which money flows from the U.S. economy to another country, is fundamentally the same thing as a payment made for a service provided from another country, except that in this case, the "service" consists of providing financial capital. Conversely, a payment made by a foreign firm to a U.S. investor, in which money flows from the foreign country to the U.S. economy, looks in economic terms just like an export of a service. The U.S. economy was running a moderate surplus in "income payments" in 2015.

The final category of the current account balance is "unilateral transfers," which can be thought of as payments made by government, private charities, or individuals in which money is sent abroad without any direct good or service being received. For example, economic or military assistance from the U.S. government to other countries fits into this category, as does spending by charities to address poverty or social inequalities abroad. When an individual in the U.S. sends money overseas, as in the case of a worker from another country who sends money back home, it is also counted in this category. The current account balance treats these unilateral payments like imports because they also involve a stream of payments leaving the country. For the U.S. economy, unilateral transfers are almost always negative—that is, transfer payments for economic and military assistance flow out from the United States to other countries, rather than the reverse. But this pattern doesn't always hold. In 1991, for example, when the United States led an international coalition against Saddam Hussein's Iraq in the Gulf War, many other nations agreed that they would make payments to the United States to offset the U.S. war expenses. These payments were large enough that in 1991, the overall U.S. balance on unilateral transfers was a positive $10 billion.

Merchandise trade remains the biggest single factor in the overall balance of trade. But trade in services is growing rapidly, and for a complete picture, the other two elements in the current account balance of payments shouldn't be neglected.

Trade Balances in Historical and International Context

The history of the U.S. current account balance in recent decades is presented in several different ways in Exhibit 25-2. Exhibit 25-2*a* shows the current account balance and the merchandise trade balance in nominal dollar terms—that is, in the dollar values that would have been announced in each year. Exhibit 25-2*b* shows the current account balance and merchandise account balance yet again, this time with the figures presented as a share of the GDP for that year. By dividing the trade deficit in each year by GDP in that year, Exhibit 25-2*b* factors out both inflation and growth in the real economy.

By either measure, the general pattern of the U.S. balance of trade is clear. From the 1960s into the 1970s, the U.S. economy had mostly small trade surpluses—that is, the graphs of Exhibit 25-2 show positive numbers. However, starting in the 1980s, the trade deficit increased rapidly, and after a tiny trade surplus in 1991, the current account trade deficit got even larger in the late 1990s and into the mid-2000s. However, the trade deficit declined in 2009 after the recession had taken hold.

Exhibit 25-3 shows the U.S. trade picture in 2014 compared with some other economies from around the world. While the U.S. economy has consistently run trade deficits in recent years, Japan and many European nations, among them France and Italy, have consistently run trade surpluses. Some of the other countries listed include Brazil, the largest economy in Latin America; Nigeria, the largest economy in Africa; and China, India, and Korea. The second column of the exhibit offers one measure of the globalization of an economy: specifically, exports of goods and services as a percentage of GDP. The third column shows the trade balance. Most of the time, most countries have trade surpluses or deficits that are less than 5% of GDP, with occasional exceptions in some years.

All the trade deficits and trade surpluses of all the nations in the world must to sum to zero. Exports for one country are always imports for another country, and vice versa. In this sense, global trade, by definition, is always in perfect balance.

The Intimate Connection between Trade Balances and Flows of Financial Capital

The terminology of trade "deficits" and "surpluses" and "balance" can sometime be a barrier to understanding. Isn't "balance" a good thing? If not "balance," then isn't a "sur-

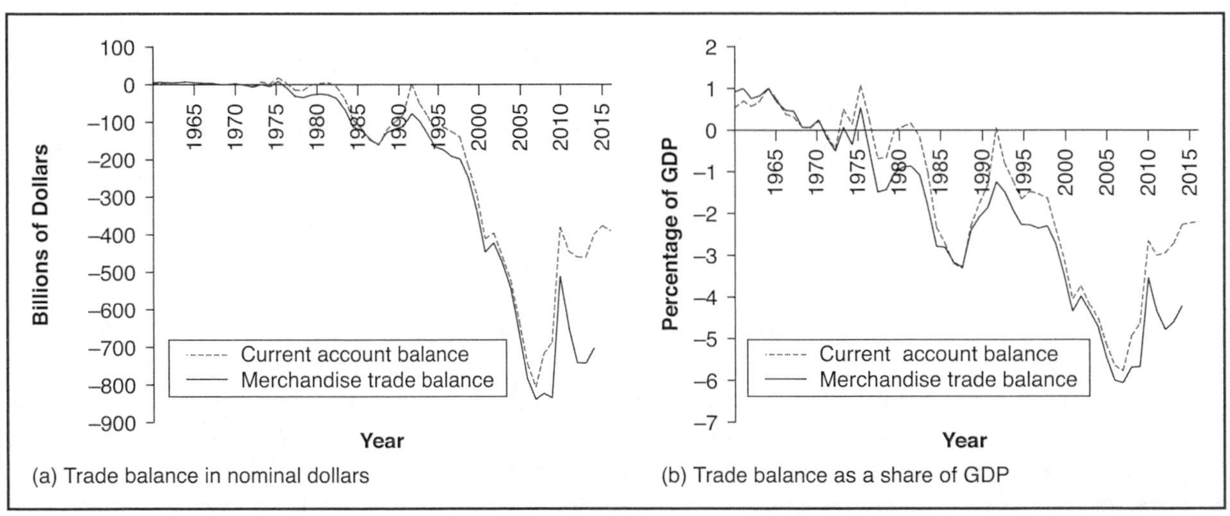

(a) Trade balance in nominal dollars

(b) Trade balance as a share of GDP

EXHIBIT 25-2 Current Account Balance and Merchandise Trade Balance, 1960–2015

EXHIBIT 25-3 Level and Balance of Trade in 2014 (as a percentage of GDP)

	Exports of Goods and Services	Current Account Balance
United States	13.5%	–2.2%
Japan	16.2%	0.5%
Germany	45.7%	7.5%
United Kingdom	28.4%	–5.8%
Canada	31.6%	–2.1%
Sweden	44.5%	7.8%
Korea, Rep.	50.6%	6.3%
Mexico	32.4%	–2.0%
Brazil	11.5%	–4.4%
China	22.6%	1.9%
India	23.2%	–1.5%
Nigeria	18.4%	4.4%
World	30.4%	0%

plus" better than a "deficit"? In some settings, these quick judgments are true enough. But in the case of trade imbalances, these preconceptions must be stripped away. As economists see it, trade surpluses can be either good or bad, depending on circumstances, and trade deficits can be good or bad, too. The challenge is to avoid being hypnotized by the terminology, and instead understand the economic meaning of the trade balance and how international flows of goods and services are interconnected with international flows of financial capital. This section will illustrate the intimate connection between trade balances and flows of financial capital in two ways: a parable of trade between Robinson Crusoe and Friday, and a circular flow diagram representing flows of trade and payments.

The Parable of Robinson Crusoe and Friday

To understand how economists view trade deficits and surpluses, consider a parable based on the story of Robinson Crusoe. Robinson, as you may remember from the classic novel by Daniel Defoe first published in 1719, was shipwrecked on a desert island. After living alone for some time, Robinson is joined by a second person, whom he names Friday. Think about the balance of trade in a two-person economy like that of Robinson and Friday.

Robinson and Friday trade goods and services with each other. Perhaps Robinson catches fish and trades them to Friday for coconuts. Or Friday weaves a hat out of tree fronds and trades it to Robinson for help in carrying water. For a period of time, each individual trade is self-contained and complete. Because each trade is voluntary, both Robinson and Friday must feel that they are receiving fair value for what they are giving. As a result, each person's exports are always equal to his imports, and trade is always in balance between the two men. Neither person experiences a trade deficit or a trade surplus.

However, one day Robinson approaches Friday with a proposition. Robinson wants to dig ditches for an irrigation system for his garden, but he knows that if he starts this project, he won't have much time left to fish and gather coconuts to feed himself each day. He proposes that Friday supply him with a certain number of fish and coconuts for several months, and then after that time, he promises to repay Friday out of the extra produce that he will be able to grow in his irrigated garden. If Friday accepts this offer, then a trade imbalance comes into being. For several months, Friday will have a trade surplus: that is, he is exporting to Robinson more than he is importing. More precisely, he is giving Robinson fish and coconuts, and at least for the moment, he is receiving nothing in return. Conversely, Robinson will have a trade deficit for a time, because he is importing more from Friday than he is exporting.

This parable raises several useful issues in thinking about what a trade deficit and a trade surplus really mean in economic terms.

The first issue raised by this story of Robinson and Friday is: Is it better to have a trade surplus or a trade deficit? The answer, as in any voluntary market interaction, is that if both parties agree to the transaction, then they may both be better off. Over time, if Robinson's irrigated garden is a success, it is certainly possible that both Robinson and Friday can benefit from this agreement.

A second issue raised by the parable is: What can go wrong? Robinson's proposal to Friday introduces an element of uncertainty. Friday is in effect making a loan of fish and coconuts to Robinson, and Friday's happiness with this arrangement will depend on whether that loan is repaid as planned, in full and on time. Perhaps Robinson spends several months loafing and never builds the irrigation system. Or perhaps Robinson has been too optimistic about how much he will be able to grow with the new irrigation system, which instead turns out not to be very productive. Perhaps after building the irrigation system, Robinson decides that he doesn't want to repay Friday as much as previously agreed. Any of these developments will prompt a new round of negotiations between Friday and Robinson. Friday's attitude toward these renegotiations is likely to be shaped by why the repayment failed. If Robinson worked very hard and the irrigation system just didn't increase production as intended, Friday may have some sympathy. But if Robinson loafed, or if he just refuses to pay, Friday may become peeved. Whenever money is borrowed for an investment project and the project goes bad, a negotiation takes place between the borrower and the lender as to how much of the original loan will be repaid. Such negotiations are often full of accusations and anger.

A third issue raised by the parable of Robinson and Friday is that an intimate relationship exists between a trade deficit and international borrowing, and between a trade surplus and international lending. The size of Friday's trade surplus is exactly how much he is lending to Robinson. The size of Robinson's trade deficit is exactly how much he is borrowing from Friday. Indeed, to economists, a trade surplus literally means the same thing as an outflow of financial capital, and a trade deficit literally means the same thing as an inflow of financial capital. This last insight is worth exploring in greater detail.

The Balance of Trade as the Balance of Payments

The connection between trade balances and international flows of financial capital is so close that the balance of trade is sometimes described as the "balance of payments." Each category of the current account balance involves a corresponding flow of payments between a given country and the rest of the world economy.

Exhibit 25-4 shows with a circular flow diagram how flows of goods and services are counterbalanced by flows of payments back and forth between one country—the United States in this example—and the rest of the world. The top line shows U.S. exports of goods and services, with the second line showing that these exports involve financial payments flowing from purchasers in other countries back to the U.S. economy. The third line then shows U.S. imports of goods, services, and investment capital, with the fourth line showing a counterbalancing flow of payments leaving the home economy and headed to the rest of the world. The bottom four lines of Exhibit 25-4 show flows of financial investment running to and from the home country to the rest of the world, and then rates of return and repayments for these financial investments running in the other direction. Unilateral transfers aren't shown in this exhibit, but they shouldn't be forgotten.

If the current account balance is equal to zero, then the financial payments flowing in and out of the country will also be equal. Since inflows and outflows of international

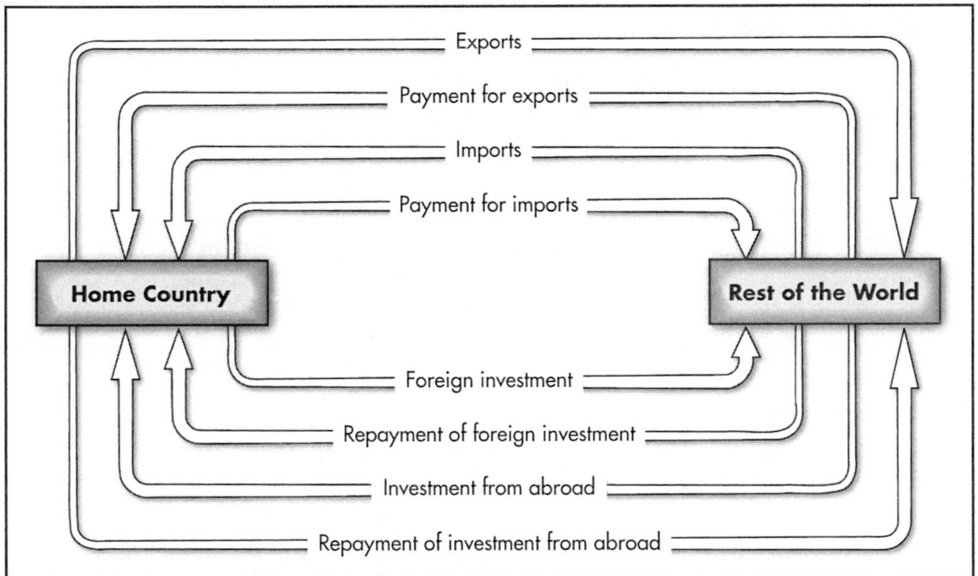

EXHIBIT 25-4 Flow of Investment Goods and Capital

Each element of the current account balance involves a flow of financial payments between countries. The top line shows exports of goods and services leaving the home country; the second line shows the flow of payments received by the home country for those exports. The third line shows imports received by the home country; the fourth line shows the payments sent abroad by the home country in exchange for these imports. The bottom four lines all show flows of financial capital—either financial investment received from abroad or repayment of that investment.

payments match in a country with a trade balance of zero, such a country is not an overall or a net investor in other countries.

A current account trade deficit means that, after taking all the flows of payments from goods, services, and income together, a larger flow of payments has left a nation's economy than has entered it. So a logical question arises—what happened to those extra payments? The answer is that a trade deficit represents an overall or net inflow of financial investment capital arriving from foreign investors. Indeed, a deficit in the current account balance is exactly equal to the overall or net inflow of foreign capital from abroad. Conversely, if the current account balance is positive, then the flow of payments out of a country must be larger than the flow of payments into a country. Just like the parable of Robinson and Friday, the lesson is that a trade surplus means an overall outflow of financial investment capital, as domestic investors put their funds abroad, while the deficit in the current account balance is exactly equal to the overall or net inflow of foreign investment capital from abroad.

It's important to recognize that an inflow and outflow of foreign capital does not necessarily refer to a debt that governments owe to other governments, although government debt may be part of the picture. Instead, these international flows of financial capital refer to all of the ways in which private investors in one country may invest in another country, by buying real estate, companies, and financial investments like stocks and bonds. The international flow of financial capital is not so much one large tide of payments as it is a million different rivers and streams all flowing in different directions.

The National Saving and Investment Identity

The close connection between trade balances and international flows of savings and investments leads to the macroeconomic way of thinking about trade balances. This approach views trade balances—and their associated flows of financial capital—in the context of the overall levels of savings and financial investment in the economy.

The National Saving and Investment Identity

national saving and investment identity: For any country, the quantity of financial capital supplied at any given time by savings must equal the quantity of financial capital demanded for purposes of making investments.

An "identity" is a term lifted from mathematics that refers to a statement that is always true, by definition. For example, the statement that GDP = C + I + G + X – M is an identity, because it is true according to the definition of GDP. The **national saving and investment identity** provides a useful way to understand the determinants of the trade balance. In a nation's financial capital market, the quantity of financial capital supplied at any given time must equal the quantity of capital financial demanded for purposes of making investments.

There are two main sources for the supply of capital in the U.S. economy in recent years: savings by individuals and firms, called S, and the inflow of financial capital from foreign investors, which is equal to the trade deficit M – X, or imports minus exports. There are also two main sources of demand for financial capital in the U.S. economy: private-sector investment, I, and government borrowing, where the government needs to borrow when government spending, G, is higher than the taxes collected, T. This national saving and investment identity can be expressed in algebraic terms:

$$\text{Supply of financial capital} = \text{Demand for financial capital}$$

$$S + (M - X) = I + (G - T)$$

Again, in this equation, S is private savings, T is taxes, G is government spending, M is imports, X is exports, and I is investment. This relationship is true as a matter of definition because, for the macroeconomy, the quantity supplied of financial capital must be equal to the quantity demanded.

However, certain components of the national saving and investment identity can switch between the supply side and the demand side. Some countries, like the United States in most years since the 1970s, have budget deficits, which means that the amount that government is spending is more than it collects in taxes, and so the government needs to borrow funds. In this case, the government term would be G – T, showing that spending is larger than taxes, and the government would be a demander of financial capital on the left-hand side of the equation (i.e., a borrower), not a supplier of financial capital on the right-hand side. However, if the government runs a budget surplus so that the taxes exceed spending, as the U.S. government did from 1998 to 2001, then the government is in that year contributing to the supply of financial capital, and (T – G) would appear on the saving side of the national saving and investment identity.

Similarly, if a national economy runs a trade surplus, then instead of the trade sector providing an inflow and supply of financial capital, as it does for an economy with a trade deficit, the trade sector will involve an outflow of financial capital to other countries. A trade surplus means that the domestic financial capital is being demanded from within a country to be invested in other countries. When a trade surplus exists, X – M would move to the "demand for financial capital" side of the national saving and investment identity.

Clearly, the national saving and investment identity must be thought through anew each time it is written out. The fundamental notion that total quantity of financial capital demanded equals total quantity of financial capital supplied must always remain true. Domestic savings will always appear as part of the supply of financial capital, and domestic investment will always appear as part of the demand for financial capital. However, the government and trade balance elements of the equation can move back and forth as either suppliers or demanders of financial capital, depending on whether government budgets and the trade balance are in surplus or deficit.

Domestic Savings and Investment Determine the Trade Balance

One insight from the national saving and investment identity is that a nation's balance of trade is determined by that nation's own levels of domestic savings and domestic investment. To understand this point, rearrange the identity to put the balance of trade all by itself on one side of the equation. Consider first the situation with a trade deficit, and then the situation with a trade surplus.

In the case of a trade deficit, the national saving and investment identity can be rewritten as:

Trade deficit = Domestic investment – Private domestic savings – Government savings

$$(M - X) = I - S - (T - G)$$

In this case, domestic investment is higher than domestic savings, including both private and government savings. The only way that domestic investment can exceed domestic savings is if capital is flowing into a country from abroad. After all, that extra financial capital for investment has to come from someplace.

Now consider a trade *surplus* from the standpoint of the national saving and investment identity:

Trade surplus = Private domestic savings + Public savings – Domestic investment

$$(X - M) = S + (G - T) - I$$

In this case, the trade surplus is a situation where domestic savings (both private and public) is higher than domestic investment. That extra financial capital needs to go someplace, and if it is not being used in the domestic economy, then it must be flowing out to the rest of the world economy.

This connection from domestic savings and investment to the trade balance explains why economists view the balance of trade as a fundamentally macroeconomic phenomenon. As the national saving and investment identity shows, the trade balance isn't determined by the performance of certain sectors of an economy, like cars or steel. Nor is the trade balance determined by whether the nation's trade laws and regulations encourage free trade or protectionism.

Exploring Trade Balances One Factor at a Time

The national saving and investment identity also provides a framework for thinking about what will cause trade deficits to rise or fall. Begin with the version of the identity that has domestic savings and investment on the left and the trade deficit on the right:

Domestic investment – Private domestic savings – Public domestic savings = Trade deficit

$$I - S - (T - G) = (M - X)$$

Now consider the factors on the left-hand side of the equation one at a time, while holding the other factors constant.

As a first example, assume that the level of domestic investment in a country rises, while the level of private and public savings remains unchanged. The result is shown in the first row of Exhibit 25-5 under the equation. Since the equality of the national saving and investment identity must continue to hold—it is, after all, an identity that must be true by definition—the rise in domestic investment will mean a higher trade deficit. This situation occurred in the U.S. economy in the late 1990s. Because of the surge of new information and communications technologies that became available, business investment increased substantially. A fall in private savings during this time and a rise in government savings more or less offset each other. As a result, the financial capital to fund that

EXHIBIT 25-5 Causes of a Changing Trade Balance

Domestic Investment	–	Private Domestic Savings	–	Public Domestic Savings	=	Trade Deficit
I	–	S	–	(T – G)	=	(M – X)
Up		No change		No change		Then M – X must rise
No change		Up		No change		Then M – X must fall
No change		No change		Down		Then M – X must rise

business investment came from abroad, which is one reason for the very high U.S. trade deficits of the late 1990s and early 2000s.

As a second scenario, assume that the level of domestic savings rises, while the level of domestic investment and private savings remains unchanged. In this case, the trade deficit would decline. As domestic savings rises, there would be less need for foreign financial capital to meet investment needs. For this reason, a policy proposal often made for reducing the U.S. trade deficit is to increase private savings—although exactly how to increase the overall rate of savings has proven controversial.

As a third scenario, imagine that the government budget deficit increased dramatically, while domestic investment and private savings remained unchanged. This scenario occurred in the U.S. economy in the mid-1980s. The federal budget deficit increased from $79 billion in 1981 to $221 billion in 1986—an increase in the demand for financial capital of $142 billion. The current account balance collapsed from a surplus of $5 billion in 1981 to a deficit of $147 billion in 1986—an increase in the supply of financial capital from abroad of $152 billion. The two numbers don't match exactly, since in the real world, private savings and investment didn't remain fixed. But the connection at that time is clear: a sharp increase in government borrowing increased the U.S. economy's demand for financial capital, and that increase was primarily supplied by foreign investors through the trade deficit.

How Short-Term Movements in the Business Cycle Can Affect the Trade Balance

In the short run, trade imbalances can be affected by whether an economy is in a recession or an upswing. A recession tends to make a trade deficit smaller, or a trade surplus larger, while a period of strong economic growth tends to make a trade deficit larger, or a trade surplus smaller.

As an example, notice that the U.S. trade deficit became much smaller in size around 2009. One primary reason for this change is that during the recession, as the U.S. economy slowed down, it purchased fewer of all goods, including fewer imports from abroad. However, buying power abroad was less affected by the U.S. recession, and so U.S. exports didn't fall by as much.

Conversely, in the mid-2000s, when the U.S. trade deficit became very large, a contributing short-term reason was that the U.S. economy was growing. As a result, there was lots of aggressive buying in the U.S. economy, including the buying of imports. Thus, a rapidly growing domestic economy is often accompanied by a trade deficit (or a much lower trade surplus), while a slowing or recessionary domestic economy is accompanied by a trade surplus (or a much lower trade deficit).

When the trade deficit rises, it necessarily means a greater net inflow of foreign financial capital. The national saving and investment identity teaches that the rest of the economy can absorb this inflow of foreign financial capital in several different ways. For example, the additional inflow of financial capital from abroad could be offset by reduced private savings, leaving domestic investment and public savings unchanged. Alternatively, the inflow of foreign financial capital could result in higher domestic investment, leaving private and public savings unchanged. Yet another possibility is that the inflow of foreign financial capital could be absorbed by greater government borrowing, leaving domestic savings and investment unchanged. The national saving and investment identity doesn't specify which of these scenarios, alone or in combination, will occur—only that one of them must occur.

When Are Trade Deficits and Surpluses Beneficial or Harmful?

Because flows of trade always involve flows of financial payments, flows of international trade are actually the same subject as flows of international financial capital. The question of whether trade deficits or surpluses are good or bad for an economy is, in economic terms, exactly the same question as whether it is a good idea for an economy to rely on net inflows of financial capital from abroad or to make net investments of financial capital abroad. Conventional wisdom often holds that borrowing money is foolhardy and that a prudent country, like a prudent person, should always rely on its own resources. But while it is certainly possible to borrow too much—as anyone with an overloaded credit card can testify—borrowing at certain times can also make sound economic sense. For both individuals and countries, there is no economic merit in a policy of abstaining from participation in financial capital markets.

It makes economic sense to borrow when you are buying something with a long-run payoff—that is, when you are making an investment. For this reason, it can make economic sense to borrow for a college education because the education will typically allow you to earn higher wages, and so to repay the loan and still come out ahead. It can also make sense for a business to borrow to purchase a machine that will last 10 years, as long as the machine will increase output and profits by more than enough to repay the loan. Similarly, it can make economic sense for a national economy to borrow from abroad, as long as the money is wisely invested in ways that will tend to raise the nation's economic growth over time. Then, it will be possible for the national economy to repay the borrowed money over time and still end up better off than before.

One vivid example of a country that borrowed heavily from abroad, invested wisely, and did perfectly well is the United States during the nineteenth century. The United States ran a trade deficit in 40 of the 45 years from 1831 to 1875, which meant that it was importing capital from abroad over that time. However, that financial capital was by and large invested in projects like railroads that brought substantial economic payoffs. A more recent example along these lines is the experience of South Korea, which had trade deficits during much of the 1970s—and thus was an importer of capital over that time. However, South Korea also had high rates of investment in physical plant and equipment, and its economy grew rapidly. From the mid-1980s into the mid-1990s, South Korea often had trade surpluses—that is, it was repaying its past borrowing by sending capital abroad.

On the other side, some countries have run large trade deficits, borrowed heavily in global capital markets, and ended up in all kinds of trouble. Two sorts of trouble are worth examining.

First, a borrower nation can find itself in a bind if the incoming funds from abroad are not invested in a way that leads to increased productivity. Several of the large economies of Latin America, including Mexico and Brazil, ran large trade deficits and borrowed heavily from abroad in the 1970s, but the inflow of financial capital did not boost productivity sufficiently, which meant that these countries faced enormous troubles in repaying when economic conditions shifted during the 1980s. Similarly, it appears that a number of African nations that borrowed foreign funds in the 1970s and 1980s did not invest in productive economic assets. As a result, several of those countries later faced large interest payments, with no economic growth to show for the borrowed funds.

A second problem is what happens if the foreign money flows in—and then suddenly flows out again. This scenario was raised at the start of this chapter. In the mid-1990s, a number of countries in East Asia—Thailand, Indonesia, Malaysia, and South Korea—ran large trade deficits and imported capital from abroad. However, in 1997 and 1998 many foreign investors became concerned about the health of these economies and fled for the exits. The extremely rapid departure of that foreign capital staggered the banking systems and economies of these countries, plunging them into deep recession. We will investigate and discuss the links between international capital flows, banks, and recession in Chapter 31.

Nor is there any guarantee that running a trade surplus will bring robust economic health. For example, Germany and Japan ran substantial trade surpluses for most of the last three decades. But regardless of their persistent trade surpluses, both countries have nonetheless experienced occasional recessions, and Japan in particular has experienced weak economic growth in recent decades.

Are Trade Deficits Always Harmful? The Case of Nineteenth-Century America

For most of the nineteenth century, U.S. imports exceeded exports and the U.S. economy had a trade deficit. Yet the string of trade deficits didn't hold back the U.S. economy at all; instead, the trade deficits mildly contributed to the strong economic growth that gave the U.S. economy the highest per capita GDP in the world by around 1900.

The U.S. trade deficits meant that the U.S. economy was receiving a net inflow of foreign capital from abroad. Much of that foreign capital flowed into two areas of investment—railroads and public infrastructure like roads, water systems, and schools—which were important to helping the growth of the U.S. economy.

The effect of foreign investment capital on assisting the U.S. economy shouldn't be overstated. In most years the foreign financial capital represented no more than 6–10% of the funds used for overall physical investment in the U.S. economy. Nonetheless, the U.S. trade deficit and the accompanying investment funds from abroad were clearly a help, not a hindrance, to the U.S. economy in the nineteenth century.

The sheer size and persistence of the U.S. trade deficits and inflows of foreign capital since the 1980s are legitimate causes for concern. The huge U.S. economy will not be destabilized by an outflow of international capital as easily as, say, the comparatively tiny economies of Thailand and Indonesia were in 1997–1998. But even an economy that is not knocked down can still be shaken. American policy makers should certainly be paying attention to those cases where a pattern of extensive and sustained current account deficits and foreign borrowing has gone badly—if only as a precautionary measure.

The Difference between Level of Trade and the Trade Balance

A nation's *level* of trade may at first sound like much the same issue as the *balance* of trade, but these two issues are actually quite separate. It is perfectly possible for a country to have a very high level of trade—say, measured by its exports of goods and services as a percentage of its GDP—while it also has a near balance between exports and imports. It is also possible for a country's trade to be a relatively low percentage of GDP, relative to global averages, but for the imbalance between its exports and its imports to be quite large. This general theme was emphasized earlier in Exhibit 25-3, which offered some illustrative figures on trade levels and balances.

Three factors strongly influence a nation's level of trade: the size of its economy, its geographic location, and its history of trade. Large economies like the United States can do much of their trading internally, while smaller economies like Sweden have less ability

Are Trade Surpluses Always Beneficial? Japan since the 1990s

Perhaps no economy around the world has been better known for its trade surpluses than Japan. Since 1990, the size of these surpluses has often been near \$100 billion per year. When Japan's economy was growing vigorously in the 1960s and 1970s, its large trade surpluses were often described, especially by non-economists, as either a cause or a result of its robust economic health.

But from a standpoint of economic growth, Japan's economy has been teetering in and out of recession since 1990, with real GDP growth averaging only about 1% per year since the early 1990s, and an unemployment rate that has been creeping higher. Clearly, a whopping trade surplus is no guarantee of economic good health.

Instead, Japan's trade surplus reflects that Japan has a very high rate of domestic savings, more than the Japanese economy can invest domestically, and so the extra funds are invested abroad. In Japan's slow economy, the growth of consumption is relatively low, which also means that consumption of imports is relatively low. Thus, Japan's exports continually exceed its imports, leaving the trade surplus continually high.

Are Trade Surpluses Always Beneficial? The Case of Colonial India

India was formally under British rule from 1858 to 1947. During that time, India consistently had trade surpluses with Great Britain, typically equal to 1–2% of India's GDP per year. Anyone who believes that trade surpluses are a sign of economic strength and dominance while trade deficits are a sign of economic weakness must find this pattern odd, since it would mean that colonial India was successfully dominating and exploiting Great Britain for almost a century—which seems highly unlikely.

Instead, India's trade surpluses with Great Britain meant that each year, there was an overall flow of financial capital from India to Great Britain. In India, this flow of financial capital was heavily criticized as the "drain," and eliminating the drain of financial capital was viewed as one of the many reasons why colonial India would benefit from achieving independence from Great Britain. Of course, if Britain's colonial rule over India had involved a net flow of financial capital from Britain to India, then India would have experienced a string of trade deficits.

to provide what they want internally and thus tend to have higher ratios of exports and imports to GDP. Nations that are geographically nearby tend to trade more, since costs of transportation and communication are lower. Moreover, some nations have long and established patterns of international trade, while others do not. Thus, a relatively small economy like Sweden, with many nearby trading partners across Europe and a long history of foreign trade, has a high level of trade. Brazil and India, which are fairly large economies that have often sought to inhibit trade in recent decades, have lower levels of trade. The United States and Japan are extremely large economies that have comparatively few nearby trading partners. Both countries actually have quite low levels of trade by world standards. The ratio of exports to GDP in either the United States or in Japan is about half of the world average.

The balance of trade is a separate issue from the level of trade. The United States has a low level of trade but had substantial trade deficits for most years from the mid-1980s into the 2000s. Japan has a low level of trade by world standards but has typically shown large trade surpluses in recent decades. Nations like Germany and the United Kingdom have medium to high levels of trade by world standards, but Germany had a trade surplus in 2015, while the United Kingdom had a trade deficit. Sweden had a high level of trade and a large trade surplus in 2015, while Brazil had a low level of trade and a large trade deficit that same year.

In short, it is quite possible for nations with a relatively low level of trade, expressed as a percentage of GDP, to have relatively large trade deficits. It is also quite possible for nations with a near balance between exports and imports to worry about the consequences of high levels of trade. There is no inconsistency in believing that a high level of trade is potentially beneficial to an economy, because of the way it allows nations to play to their comparative advantages, but at the same time being concerned about macroeconomic instability that might be caused by a long-term pattern of unwisely large trade deficits.

Final Thoughts about Trade Balances

Trade deficits can be either a good or bad sign for an economy, depending on the economic situation, and the same is true of trade surpluses. Even a trade balance of zero—which just means that a nation is neither a net borrower nor lender in the international economy—can be either a good or bad sign. The fundamental economic question is not whether a nation's economy is borrowing or lending at all, but whether the particular borrowing or lending in the particular economic conditions of that country makes sense.

It's interesting to reflect on how public attitudes toward trade deficits and surpluses might change if we could somehow change the labels that people and the news media affix to these occurrences. If a trade deficit was called "attracting foreign financial capital"—which accurately describes what a trade deficit means—then trade deficits might look more pleasant. Conversely, if a trade surplus were called "shipping financial capital abroad"—which accurately captures what a trade surplus does—then trade surpluses might look less attractive. Either way, the key to understanding trade balances is to understand the relationships between flows of trade and flows of international payments, and what these relationships imply about the causes, benefits, and risks of different kinds of trade balances. The first step along this journey of understanding is to move beyond knee-jerk reactions to terms like "trade surplus," "trade balance," and "trade deficit."

Key Concepts and Summary

1. A nation has a **trade surplus** if **exports** exceed **imports**, and a **trade deficit** if imports exceed exports.
2. The **merchandise trade balance** measures only imports and exports of goods. The **current account balance** includes trade in goods, services, payments on foreign investments, and unilateral transfers.
3. The U.S. economy ran modest current account trade surpluses for most years from the 1950s to the 1970s. It developed large trade surpluses in the early 1980s, swung back to a tiny trade surplus in 1991, and then had even larger trade deficits in the late 1990s and early 2000s.
4. A trade deficit necessarily means a net inflow of financial capital from abroad, while a trade surplus necessarily means a net outflow of financial capital from an economy to other countries.
5. The **national saving and investment identity** is based on the relationship that the total quantity of financial capital supplied from all sources must equal the total quantity of financial capital demanded from all sources. If S is private savings, T is taxes, G is government spending, M is imports, X is exports, and I is investment, then for an economy with a current account deficit and a budget deficit:

Supply of financial capital = Demand for financial capital

$$S + (M - X) = I + (T - G)$$

6. A recession tends to increase the trade balance (meaning a higher trade surplus or lower trade deficit), while economic boom will tend to decrease the trade balance (meaning a lower trade surplus or a larger trade deficit).
7. Trade surpluses are no guarantee of economic health, and trade deficits are no guarantee of economic weakness. Either trade deficits or trade surpluses can work out well or poorly, depending on whether the corresponding flows of financial capital are wisely invested.
8. Small economies that have nearby trading partners and a history of international trade will tend to have higher levels of trade. Larger economies with few nearby trading partners and a limited history of international trade will tend to have lower levels of trade.
9. The level of trade, where trade is expressed as a share of GDP, is different from the trade balance. Nations with high levels of trade can have small trade imbalances, while nations with lower levels of trade can have larger trade imbalances.

Review Questions

1. If imports exceed exports, is it a trade deficit or a trade surplus? What about if exports exceed imports?
2. What is included in the current account balance?
3. In recent decades, has the U.S. trade balance usually been in deficit, surplus, or near balance?
4. Does a trade surplus mean an overall inflow of financial capital to an economy, or an overall outflow of financial capital? What about a trade deficit?
5. What are the two main sides of the national saving and investment identity?
6. What are the main components of the national saving and investment identity?
7. What determines whether the trade balance and the government budget will represent supply of financial capital or demand for financial capital?
8. Will the trade deficit tend to be higher or lower in a recession? What about during an economic upswing?
9. When is a trade deficit likely to work out well for an economy? When is it likely to work out poorly?
10. Does a trade surplus help to guarantee strong economic growth?
11. What three factors will determine whether a nation has a higher or lower share of trade relative to its GDP?
12. Will nations that are more involved in foreign trade tend to have higher trade imbalances, lower trade imbalances, or is the pattern unpredictable?

PART CHAPTER

26

The Aggregate Supply–Aggregate Demand Model

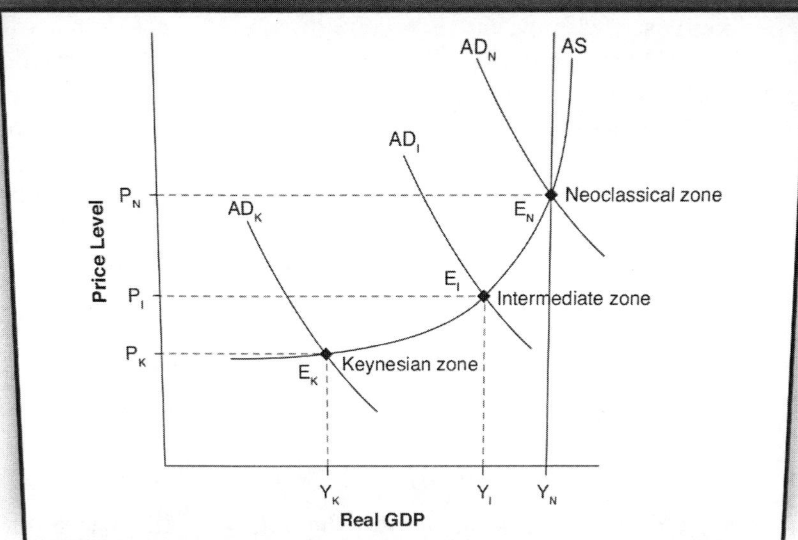

Chapter Outline

Having goals is helpful when they provide a sense of direction. However, having four separate goals can cause confusion when it is impossible to reach all of the goals at the same time. For example, it is impossible to accomplish simultaneously the four goals of being in Los Angeles, London, Beijing, and Rio de Janeiro. But if the four goals are to visit the Statue of Liberty, the Empire State Building, the New York Stock Exchange, and a Broadway show, then all four goals can be accomplished with a single trip to New York City. Are the four goals of macroeconomics—growth, low unemployment, low inflation, and a sustainable balance of trade—like trying to visit four different cities in a single day, in the sense that it is impossible to achieve all four at the same time? Or is it possible for an economy to attain (at least roughly) several or all of its macroeconomic goals at the same time?

U.S. economic experience during the last decade or so hints that some macroeconomic goals can be accomplished together, whereas others may involve trade-offs. U.S. macroeconomic performance during the past 10 or so years has been dominated by what is often called the Great Recession of 2007–2009 and its aftermath. Prior to the global recession, real gross domestic product (GDP) rose at about 3% per year from 2004 to 2006. But real GDP growth then slowed in 2007, and it was near zero in 2008 and *negative* 2.8% in 2009 before rebounding to annual growth rates of about 1.5–2.5% in the years that followed. The unemployment rate was 5% or lower throughout 2006–2007, but it then climbed as the recession took hold, peaking at 10% in late 2009 before gradually declining back to 5% by late 2015. Inflation as measured by the Consumer Price Index had been fairly low before the Great Recession: for example, inflation rates were in the 2–4% range during 2006–2007. But inflation rates then fell lower, declining to negative levels throughout most of 2009 and again early in 2015, then reaching 1% per year in 2016. The current account deficit had roughly doubled from $400 billion in 2001 to more than $800 billion in 2006 before returning to the range of $400 billion to $500 billion per year from 2014 to 2016.

Macroeconomic analysis investigates the patterns of these macroeconomic goals and the connections between them. How is the rate of economic growth connected to rises and falls in the unemployment rate? Is there a reason why unemployment and inflation seem to move in opposite directions, as exemplified by lower unemployment and higher inflation in the mid-2000s, then higher unemployment and lower inflation in 2009? Why did the current account deficit rise so high but then show steady decline since 2009? What explains the pattern of these macroeconomic variables in the years since the recession ended in 2009?

To analyze questions like these, we must move beyond discussing the four macroeconomic goals one at a time and begin building economic models that will capture the relationships and interconnections between them. The next three chapters take up this task. This chapter introduces the macroeconomic model of aggregate supply and aggregate demand, how they reach a macroeconomic equilibrium, and how shifts in aggregate demand or aggregate supply will affect that equilibrium. It also relates the model of aggregate supply and aggregate demand to the four goals of economic growth, low unemployment, low inflation, and a sustainable balance of trade, thus offering a framework for thinking about many of the connections and trade-offs between these goals. Chapter 27 will then discuss this model with an emphasis on the short run in which aggregate demand plays a crucial role, while Chapter 28 will discuss the model with an emphasis on the long run in which aggregate supply plays a crucial role.

Macroeconomic Perspectives on Demand and Supply

The gross domestic product (GDP), which is the sum of the values of all final goods and services produced in the economy, can be measured in several ways, as discussed in Chapter 21. One approach looked at what final goods and services were supplied in the economy, and divided them up into durable and nondurable goods, services, and construction (with an adjustment for inventories that build up or decline each year). An alternative method measured GDP through the five components of demand for these goods and services: consumption, investment, government, exports, and imports. The total amount demanded must equal the total amount supplied because nothing can be sold unless something is being bought at the same time. However, macroeconomists over the last two centuries have often divided into two groups: those who argued that supply was the most important determinant of the size of the macroeconomy, while demand just tagged along, and those who argued that demand was the most important factor in the size of the macroeconomy, while supply just tagged along.

Say's Law and the Macroeconomics of Supply

Say's Law: "Supply creates its own demand."

Those economists who emphasize the role of supply in the macroeconomy often refer to the work of a famous French economist of the early nineteenth century named Jean-Baptiste Say (1767–1832). **Say's Law** is: "Supply creates its own demand." As a matter of historical accuracy, it seems clear that Say never actually wrote down this law and that the law oversimplifies his beliefs, but the law lives on as a useful shorthand for summarizing a point of view.

neoclassical economists: Economists who generally emphasize the importance of aggregate supply in determining the size of the macroeconomy over the long run.

The intuition behind Say's Law is that each time a good or service is produced and sold, it represents income that is earned for someone: a worker, a manager, an owner, or those who are workers, managers, and owners at firms that supply inputs down the chain of production. The forces of supply and demand in individual markets will cause prices to rise and fall. But the bottom line remains that every sale represents income to someone, and so, Say's Law argues, a given value of supply must create an equivalent value of demand somewhere else in the economy. Because Jean-Baptiste Say, Adam Smith, and other economists writing around the turn of the nineteenth century who discussed this view were known as "classical" economists, modern economists who generally subscribe to the Say's law view on the importance of supply for determining the size of the macroeconomy are called **neoclassical economists**.

But if supply always creates exactly enough demand at the macroeconomic level, then (as Say himself recognized) it's hard to understand why periods of recession and high unemployment should ever occur. To be sure, even if total supply always creates an equal amount of total demand, the economy could still experience a situation of some firms earning profits while other firms suffer losses. Nevertheless, a recession is not a situation where all business failures are exactly counterbalanced by an offsetting number of successes. A recession is a situation in which the economy as a whole is shrinking in size, business failures outnumber the remaining success stories, and many firms end up suffering losses and laying off workers.

Say's law that supply creates its own demand does seem a good approximation for the long run of the economy. Over periods of some years or decades, as the productive power of an economy to supply goods and services increases, total demand in the economy grows as well at roughly the same pace. However, over shorter time horizons of a few months or even years, recessions or even depressions occur in which firms, as a group, seem to face a lack of demand for their products.

Keynes' Law and the Macroeconomics of Demand

The alternative to Say's Law, with its emphasis on supply, can be named **Keynes' Law**: "Demand creates its own supply." As a matter of historical accuracy, just as Jean-Baptiste Say never wrote down anything as simpleminded as Say's Law, John Maynard Keynes never wrote down Keynes' Law, but the law is a useful simplification that conveys a certain point of view.

Keynes' Law: "Demand creates its own supply."

When Keynes was writing his great work *The General Theory of Employment, Interest, and Money* during the Great Depression of the 1930s, he pointed out that during the Depression, the capacity of the economy to supply goods and services had not changed much. U.S. unemployment rates soared higher than 20% from 1933–35, but the number of possible workers had not increased or decreased much. Factories were closed and shuttered, but machinery and equipment had not disappeared. Technologies that had been invented in the 1920s were not disinvented and forgotten in the 1930s. Thus, Keynes argued that the Great Depression—and many ordinary recessions as well—were not caused by a drop in the ability of the economy to supply goods as measured by labor, physical capital, or technology. Keynes argued the economy often produced less than its full potential, not because it was technically impossible to produce more with the existing workers and machines, but because of a lack of demand for the economy as a whole led to inadequate incentives for firms to produce. At such times, he argued, the level of GDP in the economy was thus not primarily determined by the potential of what the economy could supply, but rather by the amount of total demand.

Keynes' Law seems to apply fairly well in the short run of a few months to a few years, when many firms experience either a drop in demand for their output during a recession or so much demand that they have trouble producing enough during an economic boom. However, demand cannot tell the whole macroeconomic story, either. After all, if demand was all that mattered at the macroeconomic level, then the government could make the economy as large as it wanted just by pumping up total demand through a large increase in the government spending (G) component or by legislating large tax cuts to push up the consumption (C) component. But economies do face genuine limits to how much they can produce, limits determined by the quantity of labor, physical capital, technology, and the institutional and market structures that bring these factors of production together. These constraints on what an economy can supply at the macroeconomic level do not disappear just because of an increase in demand.

Combining Supply and Demand in Macroeconomics

Two insights emerge from this overview of Say's Law with its emphasis on macroeconomic supply and Keynes' Law with its emphasis on macroeconomic demand. The first conclusion, which is not exactly a news flash, is that an economic approach that focuses only on the supply side or only on the demand side can only be partially successful. Both supply and demand need to be taken into account. The second conclusion is that because Keynes' law applies more accurately in the short run and Say's law applies more accurately in the long run, the trade-offs and connections between the four goals of macroeconomics may be different in the short run and the long run.

Building a Model of Aggregate Supply and Aggregate Demand

The discussion of macroeconomic supply and demand to this point has focused on them as quantities; for example, in using them to measure GDP. However, to build a useful macroeconomic model, we need to build a model that shows what determines total supply or total demand for the economy, and how total demand and total supply interact at the macroeconomic level. This model is called the aggregate supply–aggregate demand model. This section will explain aggregate supply, aggregate demand, and the equilibrium between them. The following sections will discuss the causes of shifts in aggregate supply and aggregate demand.

The Aggregate Supply Curve and Potential GDP

Firms make decisions about what quantity to supply based on the profits that they expect to earn. Profits, in turn, are also determined by the price of the outputs that the firm sells and by the price of the inputs like labor or supplies that the firm needs to buy. The **aggregate supply (AS)** curve shows the total quantity that firms choose to produce and sell at each different price level for output.

aggregate supply (AS): The relationship between the total quantity that firms choose to produce and sell and the price level for output, holding the price of inputs fixed.

Exhibit 26-1 shows an aggregate supply curve. Let us walk through the elements of the diagram one at a time: the horizontal and vertical axes, the aggregate supply curve itself, and the meaning of the potential GDP vertical line.

The horizontal axis of the diagram shows real GDP—that is, the level of GDP adjusted for inflation. The vertical axis shows the price level. Remember that the price level is different from the inflation rate. Visualize the price level as an index number, like that measured by the Consumer Price Index or the GDP deflator, while the inflation rate is the percentage change between price levels over time.

The accompanying table beside the exhibit gives an illustrative set of numbers that define the shape of an aggregate supply or AS curve. As the price level rises, the aggregate quantity of goods and services supplied rises as well. Why? The price level shown on the vertical axis represents prices for final goods or outputs bought in the economy—like

EXHIBIT 26-1 The Aggregate Supply Curve

Aggregate supply (AS) slopes up because, as the price level for outputs increases, with the price of inputs remaining fixed, firms have an incentive to produce more and to earn higher profits. The potential GDP line shows the maximum that the economy can produce with full employment of workers and physical capital.

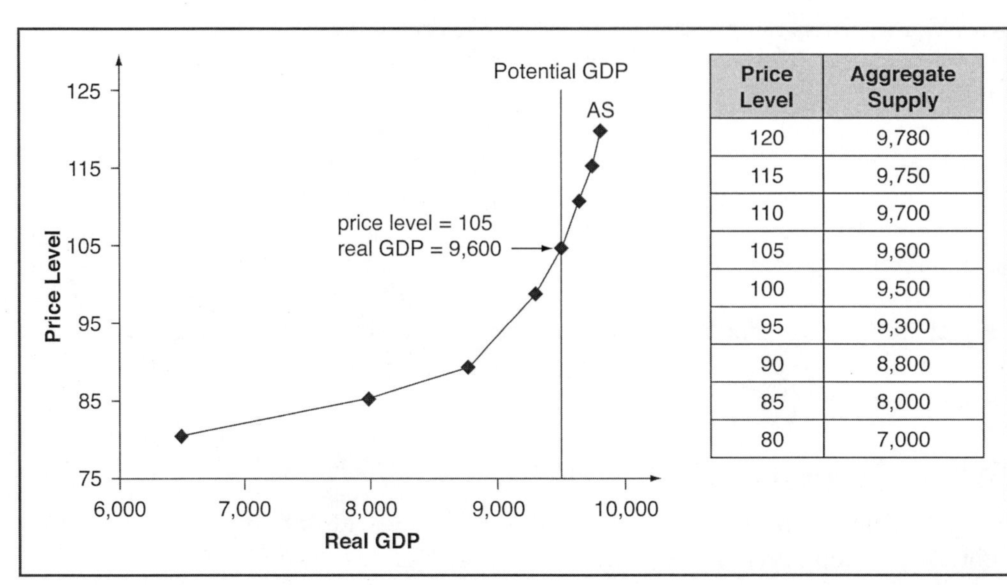

Price Level	Aggregate Supply
120	9,780
115	9,750
110	9,700
105	9,600
100	9,500
95	9,300
90	8,800
85	8,000
80	7,000

CLEARING IT UP

Why Does AS Cross Potential GDP?

The aggregate supply curve is typically drawn to cross the potential GDP line. This shape may seem puzzling: How can an economy produce at an output level which is higher than its "potential" or "full employment" GDP? The economic intuition here is that if prices for outputs were high enough, producers would make fanatical efforts to produce: all workers would be on double-overtime, all machines would run 24 hours a day, seven days a week. Such hyper-intense production would go beyond using potential labor and physical capital resources fully, to using them in a way that is not sustainable in the long term. Thus, it is indeed possible for production to sprint above potential GDP, but only in the short run.

the GDP deflator or the Consumer Price Index—not the price level for intermediate goods and services that are inputs to production. Thus, the AS curve describes how suppliers will react to a higher price level for final outputs of goods and services, *while holding the prices of inputs like labor and energy constant*. If firms across the economy face a situation where the price level of what they produce and sell is rising, but their costs of production are not rising, then the lure of higher profits will induce firms to expand production.

The slope of an AS curve changes from nearly flat at its far left to nearly vertical at its far right. At the far left of the aggregate supply curve, the level of output in the economy is far below **potential GDP**, which is defined as the maximum quantity that an economy can produce given its existing levels of labor, physical capital, and technology, in the context of its existing market and legal institutions. At these relatively low levels of output, levels of unemployment are high, and many factories are running only part-time, or have closed their doors. In this situation, a relatively small increase in the prices of the outputs that businesses sell—while making the ceteris paribus assumption of no rise in input prices—can encourage a considerable surge in the quantity of aggregate supply because so many workers and factories are ready to swing into production.

potential GDP: The maximum quantity that an economy can produce given its existing levels of labor, physical capital, technology, and institutions.

As the quantity produced increases, however, certain firms and industries will start running into limits: perhaps nearly all of the expert workers in a certain industry will have jobs, or factories in certain geographic areas or industries will be running at full speed. In the intermediate area of the AS curve, a higher price level for outputs continues to encourage a greater quantity—but as the increasingly steep upward slope of the aggregate supply curve shows, the increase in quantity in response to a given rise in the price level won't be quite as large.

At the far right, the aggregate supply curve becomes nearly vertical. At this quantity, higher prices for outputs cannot encourage additional output, because even if firms desire to expand output, the inputs of labor and machinery in the economy are fully employed. In this example, the vertical line in the exhibit shows that potential GDP occurs at a total output of 9,500. When an economy is operating at its potential GDP, machines and factories are running at capacity, and the unemployment rate is relatively low at the natural rate of unemployment. For this reason, potential GDP is sometimes also called **full-employment GDP**.

full employment GDP: Another name for potential GDP, when the economy is producing at its potential and unemployment is at the natural rate of unemployment.

The Aggregate Demand Curve

The total amount of demand in an economy is determined by a number of factors, but one of them is the price level of what is being purchased. The **aggregate demand (AD)** curve shows the total quantity of goods and services that will be demanded at each price level. The AD curve includes all five parts of demand: consumption, investment, government spending, exports, and imports.

aggregate demand (AD): The relationship between the total quantity of goods and services demanded and the price level for output.

Exhibit 26-2 presents an aggregate demand (AD) curve. Just like the aggregate supply curve, the horizontal axis shows real GDP and the vertical axis shows the price level. The AD curve slopes down, which means that increases in the price level of outputs lead to

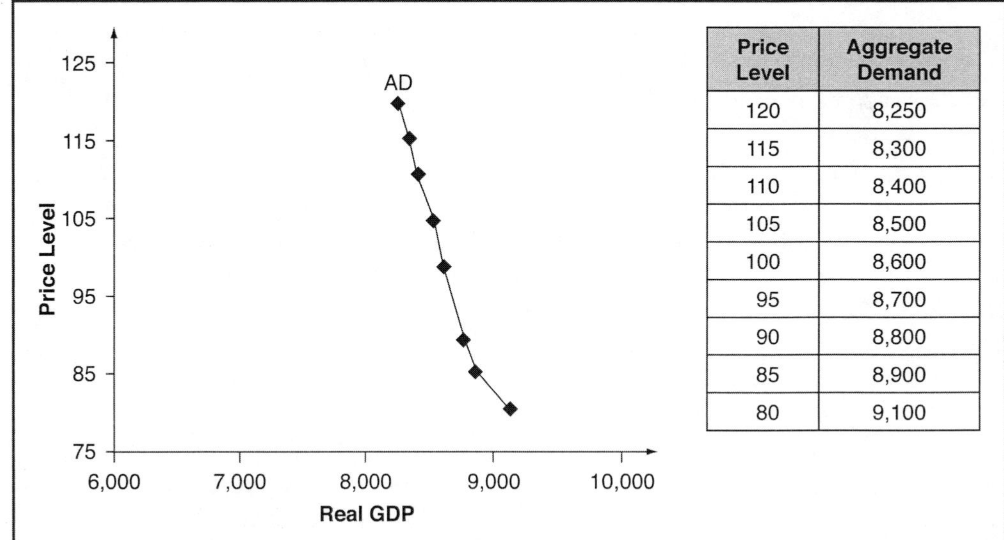

Price Level	Aggregate Demand
120	8,250
115	8,300
110	8,400
105	8,500
100	8,600
95	8,700
90	8,800
85	8,900
80	9,100

EXHIBIT 26-2 The Aggregate Demand Curve

Aggregate demand (AD) slopes down, showing that as the price level rises, the quantity of aggregate demand declines.

a lower quantity of aggregate demand. The reasons behind this shape are related to how changes in the price level affect the different components of aggregate demand: C + I + G + X − M.

The *wealth effect* holds that as the price level increases, the buying power of wealth that people have stored up in bank accounts and cash will diminish, eaten away to some extent by inflation. Because a rise in the price level reduces people's wealth, consumption will fall as the price level rises.

The *interest rate effect* suggests that as prices for outputs rise, it will be necessary for people making purchases to have more money or credit. This additional demand for money and credit will push interest rates higher. In turn, higher interest rates mean less borrowing by businesses for investment purposes and less borrowing by households for homes and cars—and thus a reduction in consumption and investment.

The *foreign price effect* points out that if prices rise in the United States while remaining fixed in other countries, then goods in the United States will be relatively more expensive compared to goods in the rest of the world. U.S. exports will be relatively more expensive, and the quantity of exports sold will fall. U.S. imports from abroad will be relatively cheaper, so the quantity of imports will rise. Thus, a higher domestic price level, relative to price levels in other countries, will be associated with a lower GDP.

Truth be told, all three of these effects are controversial among economists, in part because they seem fairly small. For this reason, the aggregate demand curve in Exhibit 26-2 slopes downward fairly steeply; the steep slope indicates that a higher price level for final outputs reduces aggregate demand for all three of these reasons, but that the change in the quantity of aggregate demand as a result of changes in price level is not very large.

Equilibrium in the Aggregate Supply–Aggregate Demand Model

The intersection of the aggregate supply and aggregate demand curves will determine equilibrium, which will involve a combination of the real GDP and the price level in the economy. At a relatively low price level for output, firms have little incentive to produce, although consumers would be willing to demand a high quantity. As the price level for outputs rises, the quantity of aggregate supply rises and the quantity of aggregate demand falls until the equilibrium point is reached.

Exhibit 26-3 combines the AS curve from Exhibit 26-1 and the AD curve from Exhibit 26-2 and places them both on a single diagram. In this example, the equilibrium point occurs at point E, at a price level of 90 and an output level of 8,800. The equilibrium level can also be read off the table directly, even if there was no figure to look at; equilibrium is the price level where the real GDP of aggregate supply equals the real GDP of

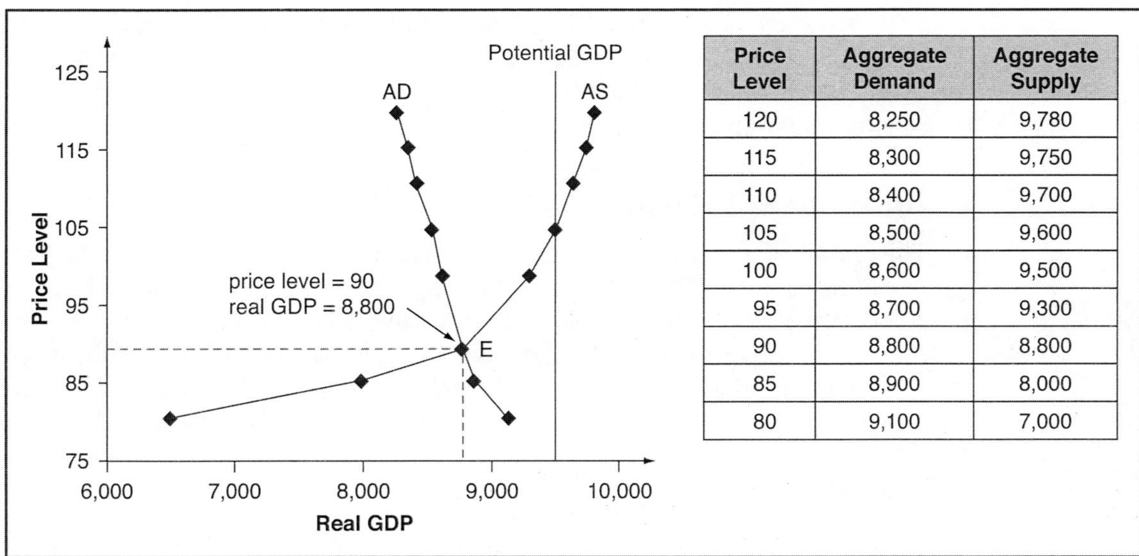

Price Level	Aggregate Demand	Aggregate Supply
120	8,250	9,780
115	8,300	9,750
110	8,400	9,700
105	8,500	9,600
100	8,600	9,500
95	8,700	9,300
90	8,800	8,800
85	8,900	8,000
80	9,100	7,000

EXHIBIT 26-3 Aggregate Supply and Aggregate Demand

The equilibrium, where the quantity of aggregate supply (AS) and aggregate demand (AD) are equal, occurs at a price level of 90 and an output level of 8,800. In this example, the equilibrium occurs at a quantity of output that is below potential GDP.

aggregate demand. In this example, the equilibrium point is below the level of potential GDP, which in this example is at an output of 9,600.

AS and AD Are Macro, Not Micro

Confusion sometimes arises between the aggregate supply and aggregate demand model and the microeconomic analysis of demand and supply in particular markets for goods, services, labor, and capital. However, mixing up the macroeconomics of aggregate supply and aggregate demand with the microeconomics of individual markets leads only to confusion. These diagrams have a superficial resemblance, but they also have many underlying differences.

For example, the vertical and horizontal axes have distinctly different meanings in macroeconomic and microeconomic diagrams. The vertical axis of a microeconomic demand and supply diagram expresses a price (or wage or rate of return) for an individual market. In contrast, the vertical axis of an aggregate supply and aggregate demand diagram expresses the level of a price index like the Consumer Price Index or the GDP deflator—combining a wide array of prices from across the economy. The horizontal axis of a microeconomic supply and demand curve measures the quantity of a particular good or service, or the quantity of labor or financial capital. In contrast, the horizontal axis of the aggregate demand and aggregate supply diagram measures GDP, which is the sum of all of the final goods and services produced in the economy, not the quantity in a specific market.

In addition, the economic reasons for the shapes of the curves in the macroeconomic model are different from the reasons behind the shapes of the curves in microeconomic models. Supply curves for markets for individual goods and services, for example, don't have any shape or level that represents full employment for an economy. Demand curves for individual goods or services slope down primarily because of the existence of substitute goods, not the wealth effects, interest rate effects, and foreign price effects associated with aggregate demand curves. The slopes of individual supply and demand curves can have a variety of different slopes, depending on the extent to which quantity demanded and quantity supplied react to price in that specific market, but the slopes of the AS and AD curves are much the same in every diagram (although as we shall see in later chapters, short-run and long-run perspectives will emphasize different parts of the AS curve).

In short, just because the AS–AD diagram has two lines that cross, do not assume that it is the same as every other diagram where two lines cross. The intuitions and meanings of the macro and micro diagrams are only distant cousins from different branches of the economics family tree.

Shifts in Aggregate Supply

The original equilibrium in the AS–AD diagram will shift to a new equilibrium if the AS or AD curve shifts. When the aggregate supply curve shifts to the right, then at every price level, a greater quantity is produced. When the AS curve shifts to the left, then at every price level, a lower quantity is produced. This section discusses two of the most important factors that can lead to shifts in the AS curve: productivity growth and input prices. The following section itemizes some factors that cause the AD curve to shift.

How Productivity Growth Shifts the AS Curve

In the long term, the most important factor shifting the AS curve is productivity growth. Historically, the real growth in per capita GDP in an advanced economy like the United States has averaged about 2–3% per year, but productivity growth has been faster during certain extended periods like the 1960s and the late 1990s and early 2000s, or slower during periods like the 1970s. A higher level of productivity shifts the AS curve to the right, because with improved productivity, firms can now produce a greater quantity at every given price level for output. Exhibit 26-4*a* shows an outward shift in productivity over two time periods. The AS curve shifts out from AS_0 to AS_1 to AS_2, reflecting the rise in potential GDP in this economy, and the equilibrium shifts from E_0 to E_1 to E_2.

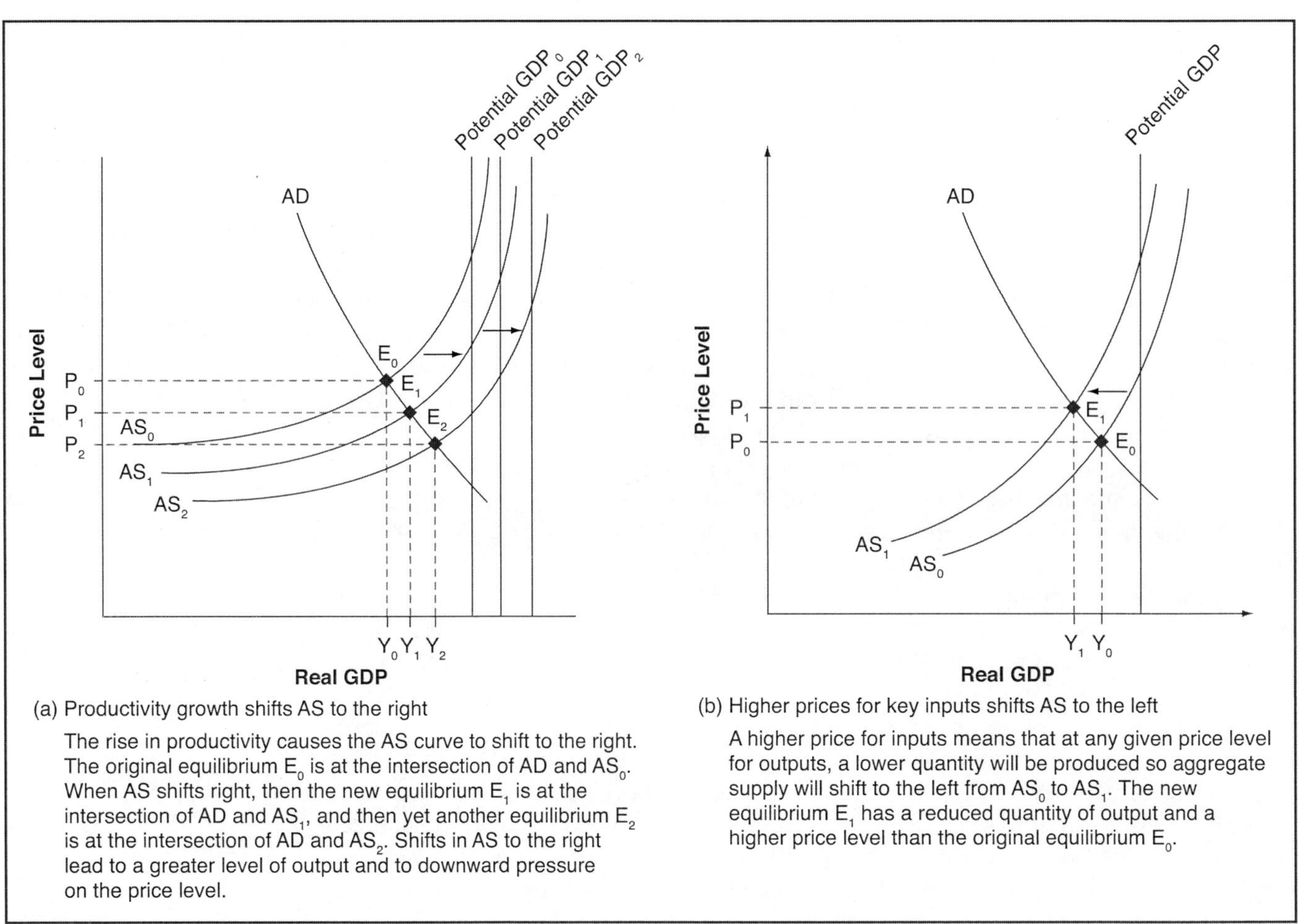

(a) Productivity growth shifts AS to the right

The rise in productivity causes the AS curve to shift to the right. The original equilibrium E_0 is at the intersection of AD and AS_0. When AS shifts right, then the new equilibrium E_1 is at the intersection of AD and AS_1, and then yet another equilibrium E_2 is at the intersection of AD and AS_2. Shifts in AS to the right lead to a greater level of output and to downward pressure on the price level.

(b) Higher prices for key inputs shifts AS to the left

A higher price for inputs means that at any given price level for outputs, a lower quantity will be produced so aggregate supply will shift to the left from AS_0 to AS_1. The new equilibrium E_1 has a reduced quantity of output and a higher price level than the original equilibrium E_0.

EXHIBIT 26-4 Shifts in Aggregate Supply

A shift in the AS curve to the right will result in a greater quantity of macroeconomic output and downward pressure on the price level, if aggregate demand remains unchanged. However, if this shift in AS results from gains in productivity growth, which are typically measured in terms of a few percentage points per year, the effect will be relatively small over a few months or even a few years.

How Changes in Input Prices Shift the AS Curve

Higher prices for inputs that are widely used across the entire economy can have a macroeconomic impact on aggregate supply. Examples of such widely used inputs include wages and energy products. Increases in the price of such inputs will cause the AS curve shift to the left, which means that at each given price level for outputs, a higher price for inputs will discourage production because it will reduce the possibilities for earning profits. Exhibit 26-4*b* shows the aggregate supply curve shifting to the left from AS_0 to AS_1, causing the equilibrium to move from E_0 to E_1. The movement from the original equilibrium of E_0 to the new equilibrium of E_1 will bring a nasty set of effects: reduced GDP or recession, higher unemployment because the economy is now further away from potential GDP, and an inflationary higher price level as well. For example, the U.S. economy

Oil Price Shocks and Recessions

In the last three decades, the U.S. economy has experienced several recessions in which higher oil prices were one of the causes. In the 1973–75 recession, the members of the Organization of Petroleum Exporting Countries (OPEC), who produce much of the world's oil supply, acted together to reduce supply and raise the price of oil. The members of OPEC are Algeria, Libya, Nigeria, Indonesia, Iran, Iraq, Kuwait, Qatar, Saudi Arabia, United Arab Emirates, and Venezuela.

Just before the two back-to-back recessions from 1980–82, oil prices rose following hostilities between Iran and the United States, which significantly reduced the supply of oil.

In 1990, the supply of oil declined and prices rose after Iraq, under Saddam Hussein, invaded Kuwait, igniting a war, just before the recession of 1991–92.

In 1999, global demand for oil first plummeted and prices fell when economies in East Asia experienced a deep recession in 1997–98, and then demand for oil surged and prices increased when these economies recovered more quickly than expected, not too long before the recession of 2001.

In late 2007 and the first half of 2008, oil prices surged when world demand especially in China continued to increase rapidly, and several oil exporting countries suffered production setbacks, just as the recession that started in 2007 was gaining force.

In all five cases, the rise in the price of oil—a key imported economic input—contributed to a shift of the AS curve to the left. The table offers some illustrative data. Each recession is different, of course, and oil prices are only one of the factors at work. But the common pattern of higher oil prices, recession, higher unemployment, and (often but not always) higher inflation is unmistakable.

Date of Recessions	Change in Real Price of Crude Oil per Barrel	Unemployment Rate	Inflation Rate
November 1973 to March 1975	Up 62% from 1973–1974	4.9% in 1973; 8.5% in 1975	3.2% in 1973; 11% in 1974
January 1980 to July 1980 and July 1981 to November 1982	Up 173% from 1978–1981	5.9% in 1979; 9.7% in 1982	6.5% in 1977; 13.5% in 1980
July 1990 to March 1991	Up 48% from 1988–1990	5.3% in 1989; 7.5% in 1992	1.9% in 1986; 5.4% in 1990
March 2001 to November 2001	Up 137% from 1998–2000	4.0% in 2000; 5.8% in 2002	1.6% in 1998; 3.4% in 2000
December 2007 to June 2009	Up 125% from 2007–2008	4.6% in 2007; 9.3% in 2009	2.8% in 2007; –0.4% in 2009

experienced recessions in 1974–75, 1980–82, and 1990–91, 2001, and 2007–2009 that were each preceded or accompanied by a rise in the key input of oil prices. In the 1970s, this pattern of a shift to the left in AS leading to a stagnant economy with high unemployment and inflation was nicknamed **stagflation**.

stagflation: When an economy experiences stagnant growth and high inflation at the same time.

Conversely, a decline in the price of a key input like oil will shift the AS curve to the right, providing an incentive for more to be produced at every given price level for outputs. From spring 2015 to summer 2015, for example, the average price of crude oil fell by almost half, from \$100 a barrel to \$40 a barrel. The plummeting price of oil led to a situation like that presented earlier in Exhibit 26-4*a*, where the outward shift of AS to the right helped the economy to expand, unemployment to fall, and inflation to decline.

Along with energy prices, two other key inputs that may shift the AS curve are the cost of labor, or wages, and the cost of imported goods that are used as inputs for other products. In these cases as well, the lesson is that lower prices for inputs cause AS to shift to the right, while higher prices cause it to shift back to the left.

Shifts in Aggregate Demand

The components of aggregate demand spending are consumption (C), investment (I), government (G), and exports (X) minus imports (M). A shift of the AD curve to the right means that a change occurred in at least one of these components of aggregate demand so that a greater quantity would be demanded at every price level. A shift of the AD curve to the left means that in at least one of these components of demand, a change occurred so that a lesser quantity would be demanded at every price level. The next chapter will discuss the components of aggregate demand and the factors that affect them one by one. Here, the discussion will sketch two broad categories that could cause AD curves to shift: changes in the behavior of consumers and firms, and changes in government tax and spending policy.

How Changes by Consumers and Firms Can Affect AD

When consumers feel more confident about the future of the economy, they tend to consume more. If business confidence is high, then firms tend to invest more, believing that the future payoff to those investments will be substantial. Conversely, if consumer or business confidence drops, then consumption and investment decline.

A number of organizations carry out surveys of consumers and businesses to gauge their level of confidence over time, including the University of Michigan Survey of Consumers and surveys done by the Conference Board, a business-funded research organization. The Organisation for Economic Co-operation and Development (OECD), a Paris-based think-tank with the world's high-income countries as members, collects data for these countries. Such survey measures are of course imprecise. But they can suggest when confidence is rising or falling or when it is relatively high or low compared to the past.

Because a rise in confidence is associated with higher consumption and investment demand, it will lead to an outward shift in the AD curve, and a move of the equilibrium from E_0 to E_1 to a higher quantity of output and a higher price level, as shown in Exhibit 26-5*a*. Consumer and business confidence often reflect macroeconomic realities; for example, confidence is usually high when the economy is growing briskly and low during a recession. However, economic confidence can sometimes rise or fall for reasons that do not have a close connection to the immediate economy, like a risk of war, election results, foreign policy events, or a pessimistic prediction about the future by a prominent public figure.

U.S. presidents, for example, must be careful in their public pronouncements about the economy. If they offer economic pessimism, they risk provoking a decline in confidence that reduces consumption and investment and shifts AD to the left, and in a self-fulfilling prophecy, contributes to causing the recession that the president warned against in the first place. A shift of AD to the left, and the corresponding movement of the equilibrium from E_0 to E_1 to a lower quantity of output and a lower price level, is shown in Exhibit 26-5*b*.

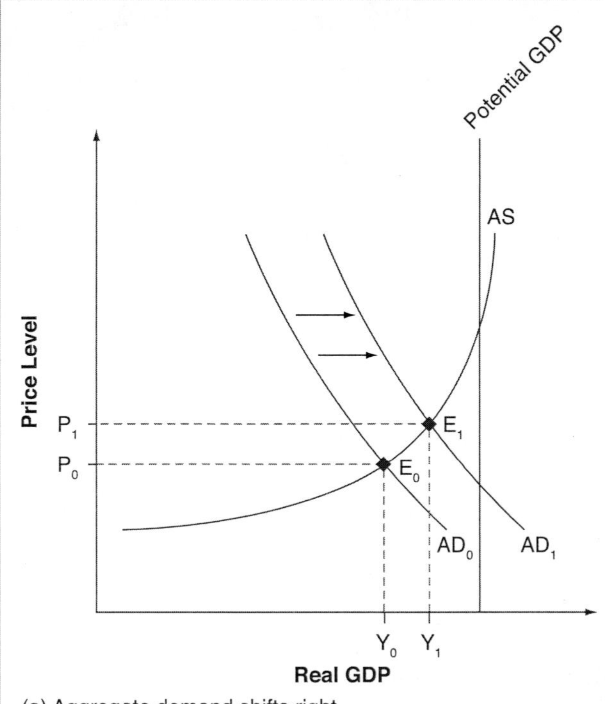

(a) Aggregate demand shifts right

An increase in consumer confidence or business confidence can shift AD to the right, from AD_0 to AD_1. When AD shifts to the right, the new equilibrium E_1 will have a higher quantity of output and also a higher price level compared with the original equilibrium E_0. In this example, the new equilibrium E_1 is also closer to potential GDP. An increase in government spending or a cut in taxes that leads to a rise in consumer spending can also shift AD to the right.

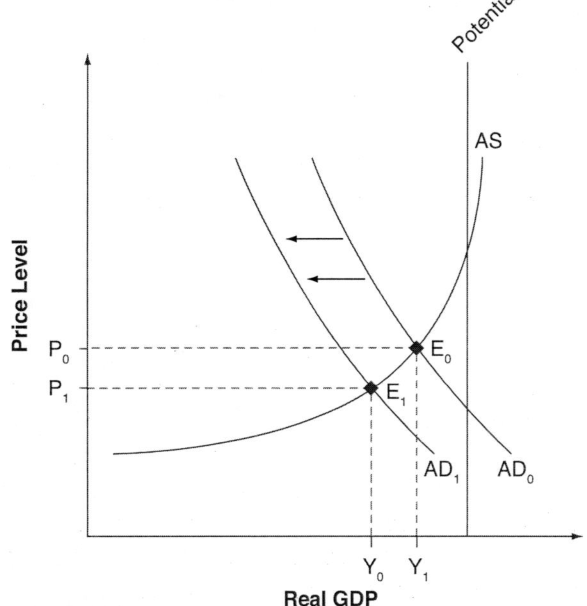

(b) Aggregate demand shifts left

A decrease in consumer confidence or business confidence can shift AD to the left, from AD_0 to AD_1. When AD shifts to the left, the new equilibrium E_1 will have a lower quantity of output and also a lower price level compared with the original equilibrium E_0. In this example, the new equilibrium E_1 is also farther below potential GDP. A decrease in government spending or higher taxes that leads to a fall in consumer spending can also shift AD to the left.

EXHIBIT 26-5 Shifts in Aggregate Demand

Do Economists Favor Tax Cuts or Oppose Them?

One of the most fundamental divisions in American politics over the last few decades has been between those who believe that the government should cut taxes substantially and those who disagree. Ronald Reagan rode into the presidency in 1980 partly because of his promise, soon carried out, to enact a substantial tax cut. George Bush lost his bid for reelection against Bill Clinton in 1992 partly because he supported a tax increase after promising in 1988: "Read my lips! No new taxes!" In the 2000 presidential election, both George W. Bush and Al Gore advocated substantial tax cuts and Bush succeeded in pushing a package of tax cuts through Congress early in 2001. Barack Obama cut taxes early in his first term but then pushed back against Republicans who wanted additional or extended tax cuts. Disputes over tax cuts often ignite at the state and local level as well.

What side are economists on? Do they support broad tax cuts or oppose them? The answer, unsatisfying to zealots on both sides, is that it depends.

One issue is whether the tax cuts are accompanied by equally large government spending cuts. Economists differ, as does any broad cross-section of the public, on how large government spending should be and what programs might be cut back.

A second issue, more relevant to the discussion in this chapter, concerns how close the economy is to the full employment level of output. In a recession, when the intersection of the AD and AS curves is far below the full employment level, tax cuts can make sense as a way of shifting AD to the right. However, when the economy is already doing extremely well, tax cuts may shift AD so far to the right that as to generate inflationary pressures, with little gain to GDP. With the AS–AD framework in mind, many economists have little difficulty believing that the Reagan tax cuts of 1981, which took effect just after two serious recessions, were beneficial economic policy. Similarly, the Bush tax cuts of 2001 and the Obama tax cuts of 2009 were enacted during recessions. However, some of the same economists who favor tax cuts in time of recession would be much more dubious about identical tax cuts at a time the economy is performing well and cyclical unemployment is low.

How Government Macroeconomic Policy Choices Can Shift AD

Government spending is one component of AD. Thus, higher government spending will cause AD to shift to the right, as in Exhibit 26-5*a*, while lower government spending will cause AD to shift to the left, as in Exhibit 26-5*b*. For example, from 2008 to 2009, U.S. government spending increased from 20.2% to 24.4% of GDP. From 2012 to 2013, U.S. government spending fell from 22.1% to 20.9% of GDP. If changes of a percentage point of GDP seem small to you, remember that because GDP was roughly $18 trillion in 2016, a seemingly small change of 1.0% of GDP in annual spending is equal to more than $180 billion.

Tax policy can affect consumption and investment, too. Tax cuts for individuals will tend to increase consumption demand, while tax increases will tend to diminish it. Tax policy can also pump up investment demand by offering lower tax rates for corporations or tax reductions that benefit specific kinds of investment. Shifting C or I will shift in the AD curve as a whole.

During a recession, when unemployment is high and many businesses are suffering low profits or losses, the U.S. Congress often passes tax cuts. During the recessions of 2001 and 2007–2009, for example, tax cuts were enacted into law. At such times, the political rhetoric often focuses on how people going through hard times need relief from taxes. But the aggregate supply and aggregate demand framework offers a complementary rationale, as illustrated in Exhibit 26-6. The original equilibrium during a recession is at point E_0, relatively far from the full employment level of output. The tax cut, by increasing consumption, shifts the AD curve to the right. At the new equilibrium E_1, real GDP rises and unemployment falls, and because in this diagram the economy has not yet reached its potential or full employment level of GDP, any rise in the price level remains muted.

The use of government spending and tax cuts can be a useful tool to affect aggregate demand, and it will be discussed in greater detail in Chapters 32 and 33. But other policy tools can shift the aggregate demand curve as well. For example, as will be discussed in Chapters 29–31, the government can affect interest rates and the availability of credit through the ways in which it affects interest rates. Higher interest rates will tend to discourage borrowing, and thus reduce both household consumption on big-ticket items

EXHIBIT 26-6
Recession and Full Employment in the AS–AD Model

Whether the economy is in a recession is illustrated in the AS–AD model by how close the equilibrium is to the potential GDP line. In this example, the level of output Y_0 at the equilibrium E_0 is relatively far from the potential GDP line, so it can represent an economy in recession, well below the full employment level of GDP. In contrast, the level of output Y_1 at the equilibrium E_1 is relatively close to potential GDP, and so it would represent an economy with a lower unemployment rate.

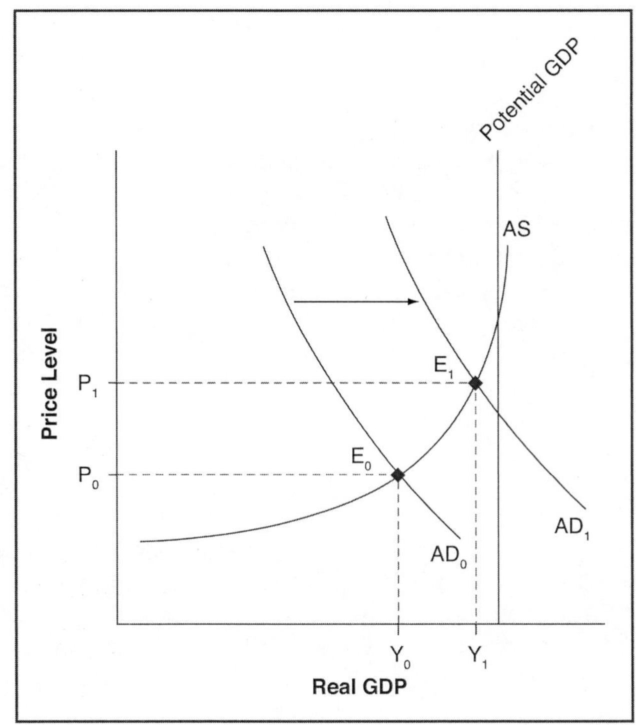

like houses and cars, and investment by business. Conversely, lower interest rates will stimulate consumption and investment demand. Interest rates can also affect exchange rates, which in turn will have effects on the export and import components of aggregate demand.

But spelling out the details of these alternative policies and how they affect the components of aggregate demand can wait for later chapters. Here, the key lesson is that a shift of the aggregate demand curve to the right leads to a greater quantity of output and to upward pressure on the price level. Conversely, a shift of aggregate demand to the left leads to a lower quantity of output and a lower price level. However, whether these changes in output and price level are relatively large or relatively small, and how the change in equilibrium relates to potential GDP, depends on whether the shift in the AD curve is happening in the relatively flat or relatively steep portion of the AS curve.

How the AS–AD Model Combines Growth, Unemployment, Inflation, and the Balance of Trade

The AS–AD model can convey a number of interlocking relationships between the four macroeconomic goals of growth, unemployment, inflation, and trade balances. Moreover, the AS–AD framework is flexible enough to accommodate both the Keynes' Law approach that focuses on aggregate demand and the short run, while also including the Say's Law approach that focuses on aggregate supply and the long run. These advantages are considerable. But every model is a simplified version of the deeper reality, and in the context of the AS–AD model, the four macroeconomic goals arise in ways that are sometimes indirect or incomplete. Let's consider how the AS–AD model illustrates the four macroeconomic goals of growth, low unemployment, low inflation, and a sustainable balance of trade.

Growth and Recession in the AS–AD Diagram

In the AS–AD model, long-run economic growth due to productivity increases over time will be represented by a gradual shift to the right of aggregate supply. The dashed vertical line representing potential GDP (or the "full employment level of GDP") will gradually shift to the right over time as well. A pattern of economic growth over three years, with the AS curve shifting slightly out to the right each year, was shown earlier in Exhibit 26-4*a*. However, the factors that determine the speed of this long-term economic growth rate—like investment in physical and human capital, technology, and whether an economy can take advantage of catch-up growth—do not appear directly in the AS–AD diagram.

In the short run, GDP falls and rises in every economy, as the economy dips into recession or expands out of recession. Recessions are illustrated in the AS–AD diagram when the equilibrium level of real GDP is substantially below potential GDP, as occurred at the equilibrium point E_0 in Exhibit 26-6. On the other hand, in years of resurgent economic growth the equilibrium will typically be close to potential GDP, as shown at equilibrium point E_1 in that earlier exhibit.

Unemployment in the AS–AD Diagram

Two types of unemployment were described in Chapter 23. Cyclical unemployment bounces up and down according to the short-run movements of GDP. Over the long run in the United States, the unemployment rate typically hovers around 5% (give or take 0.5 percentage points), when the economy is healthy. In many of the national economies across Europe, the rate of unemployment in recent decades has only dropped to about 8–10%, even in a good economic year. This baseline level of unemployment that occurs year-in, year-out is determined by how well the structures of market and government institutions in the economy lead to a matching of workers and employers in the labor market; it is called the natural rate of unemployment. Potential GDP can imply different unemployment rates in different economies, depending on the natural rate of unemployment for that economy.

In the AS–AD diagram, cyclical unemployment is shown by how close the economy is to the potential or full employment level of GDP. Returning to Exhibit 26-6, relatively low cyclical unemployment for an economy occurs when the level of output is close to potential GDP, as in the equilibrium point E_1; conversely, high cyclical unemployment arises when the output is substantially to the left of potential GDP on the AS–AD diagram during a recession, as at the equilibrium point E_0. The factors that determine the natural rate of unemployment are not shown separately in the AS–AD model, although they are implicitly part of what determines potential GDP or full employment GDP in a given economy.

Inflationary Pressures in the AS–AD Diagram

Inflation fluctuates in the short run. Higher inflation rates have typically occurred either during or just after economic booms: for example, the biggest spurts of inflation in the U.S. economy during the twentieth century followed the wartime booms of World War I and World War II. Conversely, rates of inflation decline during recessions. As an extreme example, inflation actually became negative—a situation called "deflation"—during the Great Depression. For example, during the relatively short recession of 2001, the rate of inflation declined from 3.4% in 2000 to 1.6% in 2002; during the deep recession of 2007–2009, the rate of inflation declined from 3.8% in 2008 to –0.4% in 2009. Some countries have experienced bouts of high inflation that lasted for years. But in the U.S. economy since the mid-1980s, inflation does not seem to have any long-term trend to be substantially higher or lower; instead, it has fluctuated mostly in a range of 0–5%.

The AS–AD framework implies two ways that inflationary pressures may arise. One possible trigger is if aggregate demand continues to shift to the right when the economy is already at or near potential GDP and full employment, thus pushing the macroeconomic equilibrium into the steep portion of the AS curve. In Exhibit 26-7*a*, there is a shift of aggregate demand to the right; the new equilibrium E_1 is clearly at a higher price level than the original equilibrium E_0. In this situation, the aggregate demand in the economy has soared so high that firms in the economy are not capable of producing additional goods because labor and physical capital are fully employed, and so additional increases in aggregate demand can only result in a rise in the price level.

An alternative source of inflationary pressures can occur due to a rise in input prices that affects many or most firms across the economy—perhaps an important input to production like oil or wages—causes the aggregate supply curve to shift back to the left. In Exhibit 26-7*b*, the shift of the AS curve back to the left also increases the price level from P_0 at the original equilibrium E_0 to a higher price level of P_1 at the new equilibrium E_1. In effect, the rise in input prices ends up, after the final output is produced and sold, being passed along in the form of a higher price level for outputs.

The AS–AD diagram shows only a one-time shift in the price level. Thus, it does not directly address the question of what would cause inflation either to vanish after a year or to sustain itself for several years. There are two explanations for why inflation may be persistent over time. One way that continual inflationary price increases can occur is if the government continually attempts to stimulate aggregate demand in a way that keeps pushing the AD curve when it is already in the steep portion of the AS curve. A second possibility is that if inflation has been occurring for several years, a certain level of inflation may come to be expected. For example, if consumers, workers, and businesses all expect prices and wages to rise by a certain amount, then these expected rises in the price level can become built into the annual increases of prices, wages, and interest rates of the economy. These two reasons are interrelated, because if a government fosters a macroeconomic environment with inflationary pressures, then people will grow to expect inflation. However, the AS–AD diagram does not show these patterns of ongoing or expected inflation in a direct way.

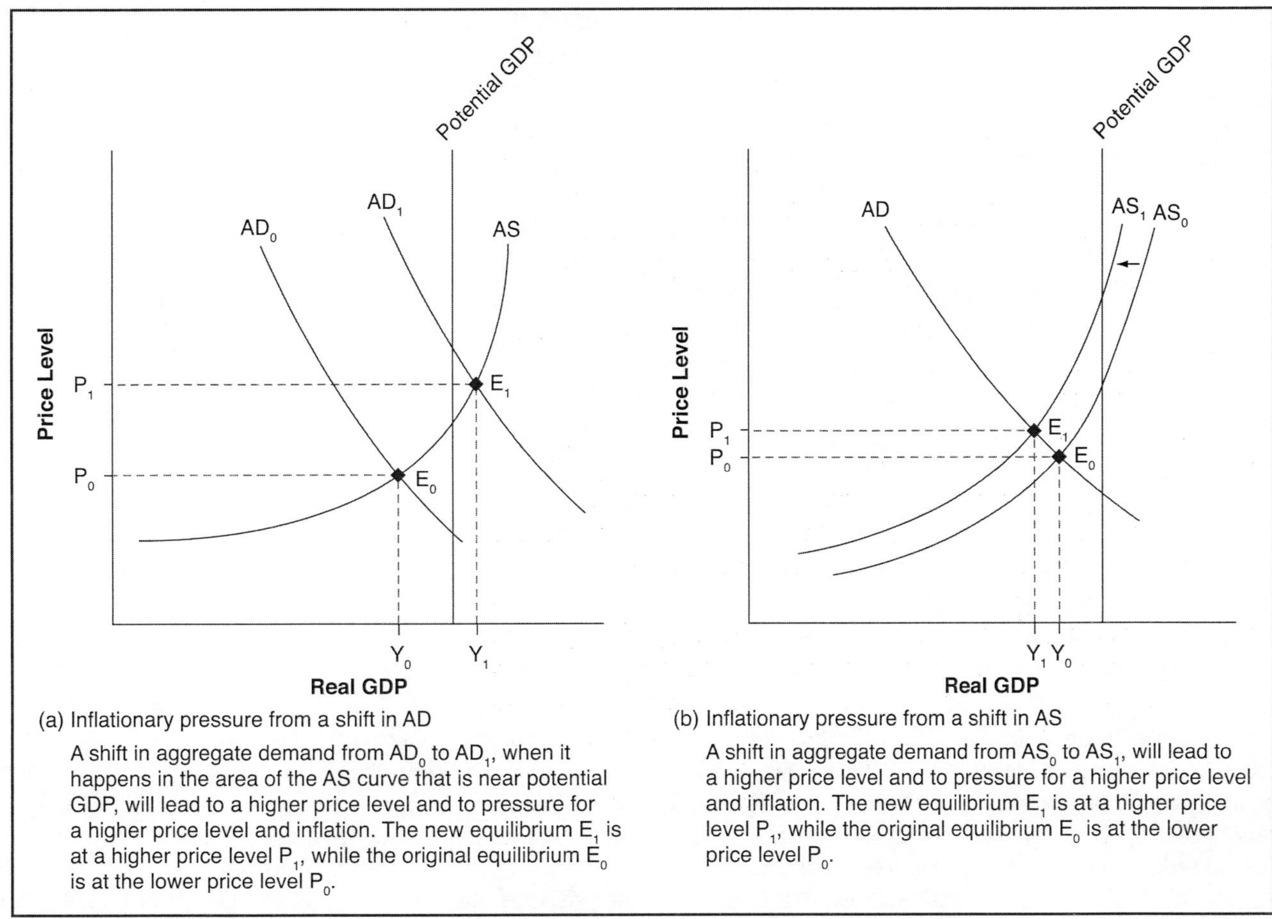

(a) Inflationary pressure from a shift in AD

A shift in aggregate demand from AD_0 to AD_1, when it happens in the area of the AS curve that is near potential GDP, will lead to a higher price level and to pressure for a higher price level and inflation. The new equilibrium E_1 is at a higher price level P_1, while the original equilibrium E_0 is at the lower price level P_0.

(b) Inflationary pressure from a shift in AS

A shift in aggregate demand from AS_0 to AS_1, will lead to a higher price level and to pressure for a higher price level and inflation. The new equilibrium E_1 is at a higher price level P_1, while the original equilibrium E_0 is at the lower price level P_0.

EXHIBIT 26-7 Sources of Inflationary Pressure in the AD–AS Model

The Balance of Trade and the AS–AD Diagram

The balance of trade does not appear in the AS–AD diagram in a direct way. The current account balance is determined by the combination of exports, imports, savings, investment, and flows of financial capital between countries, as explained in Chapter 25.

In some cases, movements in the balance of trade will shift the aggregate demand or aggregate supply curves. As one example, if the economies of major U.S. trading partners like Germany and Canada grow relatively fast, then those economies are likely to purchase a larger quantity of U.S. exports, and thus raise aggregate demand for U.S. products. If the economies of U.S. trading partners grow relatively slowly, however, U.S. exports and aggregate demand are likely to diminish. Of course, a higher level of exports will tend to increase a trade surplus, or reduce a trade deficit. As another example, many imports are used as inputs to production of goods produced in the United States. When the price of imported oil increases sharply, the AS curve shifts to the left. In addition, the higher price of imports leads to a larger trade deficit, or a reduced trade surplus.

In other cases, movements in AD or AS that arise from other causes will also affect the balance of trade. For example, when a nation's economy is growing rapidly, more of everything tends to be bought—including imports. As a result, a rapidly growing economy often experiences a trade deficit or a reduced trade surplus. Conversely, when an economy is staggering in recession, less of everything is being purchased, including imports, which typically means a smaller trade deficit or a larger trade surplus. As another example, consider the situation where an economy experiences a boom in investment, shifting AD to the right, which is financed by an inflow of financial capital from abroad. The AD curve will shift to the right, as a result of the surge in the investment component

Aggregate Supply and Aggregate Demand

Macroeconomics takes an overall view of the economy, which means that it needs to juggle some different concepts. For example, start with the four macroeconomic goals of growth, low inflation, low unemployment, and a sustainable balance of trade. Aggregate demand has five elements: consumption, investment, government spending, exports and imports. Aggregate supply reveals how businesses throughout the economy will react to a higher price level for outputs. Finally, a wide array of economic events and policy decisions can affect aggregate demand and aggregate supply, including government tax and spending decisions; consumer and business confidence; changes in prices of key inputs like oil; and technology that brings higher levels of productivity.

The aggregate supply–aggregate demand model is one of the fundamental diagrams in this course (like the budget constraint diagram introduced in Chapter 2 and the supply and demand diagram introduced in Chapter 4) because it provides an overall framework for bringing these factors together in one diagram, shown here. Indeed, some version of the AS–AD model will appear in every chapter in the rest of this book. On an AS–AD diagram, the horizontal axis of the diagram measures real GDP. The vertical axis of the diagram measures the price level. The intersection of aggregate demand and aggregate supply determines the level of output and the price level in the economy. Movements of either AD or AS then lead to a new macroeconomic equilibrium with changes in the GDP and the price level.

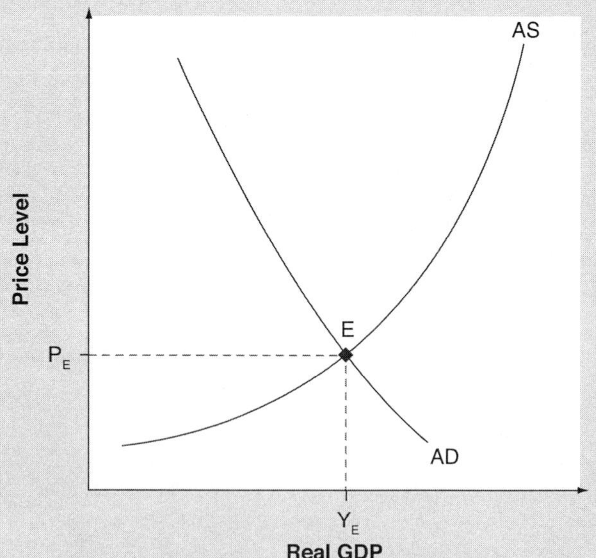

In the model of aggregate demand and aggregate supply, the intersection of the AD and AS curves determines an equilibrium price level P_E and an equilibrium quantity level Y_E. Economic changes that alter consumption, investment, government spending, and exports or imports will move aggregate demand. Shifts in the productivity or the prices of key inputs to production will shift aggregate supply. Movements in AD or AS will lead to a new equilibrium quantity of output and also for inflationary pressures for change in the price level. In these ways, the AD–AS diagram serves as a fundamental diagram for organizing macroeconomic analysis.

of aggregate demand, and the current account balance will decline (or the current account deficit will fall further) as a result of the greater inflow of financial capital.

The graphical presentation of the AS–AD model contains no specific point or gap or line that shows the size or change in the trade balance. But exports, imports, and the impacts of international financial flows can either cause shifts in either the AD or AS curves, or can be the result of such shifts.

Keynes' Law and Say's Law in the AS–AD Model

The AS–AD model can be used to illustrate both Keynes' Law that demand creates its own supply and of Say's Law that supply creates its own demand. Consider the three zones of the AS curve as identified in Exhibit 26-8: the Keynesian zone, the neoclassical zone, and the intermediate zone.

Focus first on the *Keynesian zone*, that portion of the AS curve on the far left which is relatively flat. If the AD curve crosses this portion of the AS curve at an equilibrium point like E_K, then certain statements about the economic situation will follow. In the Keynesian zone, the equilibrium level of real GDP is far below potential GDP, the economy is in recession, and cyclical unemployment is high. If aggregate demand shifted to the right or left in the Keynesian zone, it will determine the resulting level of output (and thus unemployment). However, inflationary price pressure is not much of a worry in the Keynesian zone, since the price level does not vary much in this zone.

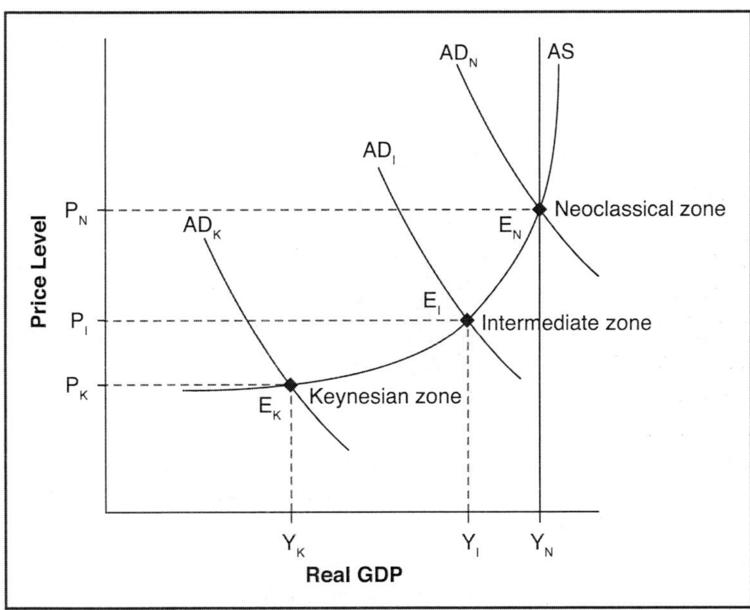

EXHIBIT 26-8 Keynes, Neoclassical, and Intermediate Zones in the Aggregate Supply Curve

Near the equilibrium E_K, in the Keynesian zone at the far left of the AS curve, small shifts in AD either to the right or the left will affect the output level Y_K, but will not much affect the price level. In the Keynesian zone, AD largely determines the quantity of output. Near the equilibrium E_N, in the neoclassical zone at the far right of the AS curve, small shifts in AD either to the right or the left will have relatively little effect on the output level Y_N, but instead will have a greater effect on the price level. In the neoclassical zone, the near-vertical AS curve close to the level of potential GDP largely determines the quantity of output. In the intermediate zone around equilibrium E_I, movement in AD to the right will increase both the output level and the price level, while a movement in AD to the left would decrease both the output level and the price level.

Now focus your attention on the *neoclassical zone* of the AS curve, which is the near-vertical portion on the right-hand side. If the AD curve crosses this portion of the AS curve at an equilibrium point like E_N where output is at or near potential GDP, then the size of potential GDP pretty much determines the level of output in the economy. Since the equilibrium is near potential GDP, cyclical unemployment is low in this economy, although structural unemployment may remain an issue. In the neoclassical zone, shifts of aggregate demand to the right or the left have little effect on the level of output or employment. The only way to increase the size of the real GDP in the neoclassical zone is for AS to shift to the right. However, shifts in AD in the neoclassical zone will create pressures to change the price level.

Finally, consider the intermediate portion of the AS curve in Exhibit 26-8. If the AD curve crosses this portion of the AS curve at an equilibrium point like E_I, then one might expect unemployment and inflation to move in opposing directions. For instance, a shift of AD to the right will move output closer to potential GDP and thus reduce unemployment, but will also lead to a higher price level and upward pressure on inflation. Conversely, a shift of AD to the left will move output further from potential GDP and raise unemployment, but will also lead to a lower price level and downward pressure on inflation.

This approach of dividing the AS curve into different zones works is a diagnostic test that can be applied to an economy, like a doctor checking a patient for symptoms. First figure out what zone the economy is in, and then the economic issues, trade-offs, and policy choices will be clarified. Some economists believe that the economy is strongly predisposed to be in one zone or another. Thus, hard-line Keynesian economists believe that economies are in the Keynesian zone most of the time, and so they view the neoclassical zone as a theoretical abstraction. Conversely, hard-line neoclassical economists argue that economies are in the neoclassical zone most of the time and that the Keynesian zone is a distraction. The next two chapters should help to clarify the underpinnings and consequences of these contrasting views of the macroeconomy.

Key Concepts and Summary

1. **Neoclassical economists** emphasize **Say's Law**, which holds that supply creates its own demand. Keynesian economists emphasize **Keynes' Law**, which holds that demand creates its own supply. Many mainstream economists take a Keynesian perspective, emphasizing the importance of aggregate demand, for the short run and a neoclassical perspective, emphasizing the importance of aggregate supply, for the long run.
2. The upward-sloping **aggregate supply (AS)** curve shows the relationship between the price level for outputs and the level of output. Aggregate supply slopes up because when the price level for outputs increases, while the price level of inputs remains fixed, then the opportunity for additional profits encourages more production.
3. The aggregate supply curve is near-horizontal on the left and near-vertical on the right. This shape occurs because when the level of output is relatively low, there are a large number of available workers, machinery, and factories available, so a relatively small increase in the price level for outputs can easily encourage a large increase in output. However, when the level of output is relatively high, and the available workers and facilities are fully employed, then an increase in the price level for outputs cannot encourage much additional output.
4. A vertical line near the right-hand side of the AS curve shows the level of **potential GDP**, which is the maximum level of output that the economy can produce with its existing levels of workers, physical capital, technology, and economic institutions.
5. The downward-sloping **aggregate demand (AD)** curve shows the relationship between the price level for outputs and the quantity of aggregate demand in the economy. It slopes down because of: (a) the wealth effect, which means that a higher price level leads to lower real wealth, which reduces the level of consumption; (b) the interest rate effect, which holds that a higher price level will mean a greater demand for money, which will tend to drive up interest rates and reduce investment spending; and (c) the foreign price effect, which holds that a rise in the price level will make domestic goods relatively more expensive, discouraging exports and encouraging imports.
6. The aggregate supply–aggregate demand (AS–AD) diagram shows how AS and AD interact with each other. The intersection of the AD and AS curve shows the equilibrium output and price level in the economy. Movements of either AS or AD will result in a different equilibrium output and price level.
7. The aggregate supply curve will shift out to the right as productivity increases. It will shift back to the left as the price of key inputs rises, and will shift out to the right if the price of key inputs falls.
8. If the AS curve shifts back to the left, the combination of lower output, higher unemployment, and higher inflation called **stagflation** occurs. If AS shifts out to the right, a combination of lower inflation, higher output, and lower unemployment is possible.
9. The AD curve will shift out as the components of aggregate demand—C, I, G, and X – M—rise. It will shift back to the left as these components fall. These factors can change because of different personal choices, like those resulting from consumer or business confidence, or from policy choices like changes in government spending and taxes.
10. If the AD curve shifts to the right, then the equilibrium quantity of output and the price level will rise. If the AD curve shifts to the left, then the equilibrium quantity of output and the price level will fall. Whether equilibrium output changes relatively more than the price level or whether the price level changes relatively more than output is determined by where the AD curve intersects with the AS curve.
11. The AS–AD diagram superficially resembles the microeconomic supply and demand diagram on the surface, but in reality, what is on the horizontal and vertical axes and the underlying economic reasons for the shapes of the curves are very different.
12. Long-term economic growth is illustrated in the AS–AD framework by a gradual shift of the aggregate supply curve to the right. A recession is illustrated when the intersection of AD and AS is substantially below potential GDP, while an expanding economy is illustrated when the intersection of AS and AD is near potential GDP.
13. Cyclical unemployment is relatively large in the AS–AD framework when the equilibrium is substantially below potential GDP. Cyclical unemployment is small in the AS–AD framework when the equilibrium is near potential GDP. The natural rate of unemployment as determined by the labor market institutions of the economy is built into what is meant by potential GDP, but does not otherwise appear in an AS–AD diagram.
14. Pressures for inflation to rise or fall are shown in the AS–AD framework when the movement from one equilibrium to another causes the price level to rise or to fall.
15. The balance of trade does not appear directly in the AS–AD diagram, but it appears indirectly in several ways. Increases in exports or declines in imports can cause shifts in AD. Changes in the price of key imported inputs to production, like oil, can cause shifts in AS.

16. The AS curve can be divided into three zones. The Keynesian zone occurs at the left of the AS curve where it is fairly flat, so movements in AD will affect output, but have little effect on the price level. The neoclassical zone occurs at the right of the AS curve where it is fairly vertical, and so movements in AD will affect the price level, but have little impact on output. The intermediate zone in the middle of the AS curve is upward-sloping, so a rise in AD will cause higher output and price level, while a fall in AD will lead to a lower output and price level.

Review Questions

1. State Say's law.
2. State Keynes' law.
3. Do neoclassical economists believe in Keynes' law or Say's law?
4. Does Say's law apply more accurately in the long run or the short run? What about Keynes' law?
5. What is on the horizontal axis of the AS–AD diagram? What is on the vertical axis?
6. What is the economic reason why the AS curve slopes up?
7. What is the economic reason why the AD curve slopes down?
8. Briefly explain the reason for the near-horizontal shape of the AS curve on its far left.
9. Briefly explain the reason for the near-vertical shape of the AS curve on its far right.
10. What is potential GDP?
11. Name some factors that could cause the AS curve to shift, and say whether they would shift AS to the right or to the left.
12. Name some factors that could cause AD to shift, and say whether they would shift AS to the right or to the left.
13. Will the shift of AD to the right tend to make the equilibrium quantity and price level higher or lower? What about a shift of AD to the left?
14. Will the shift of AS to the right tend to make the equilibrium quantity and price level higher or lower? What about a shift of AS to the left?
15. What is stagflation?
16. How are the axes of an AS–AD diagram different from the axes for a microeconomic supply and demand diagram for a typical good?
17. How does the economic meaning behind an upward-sloping AS curve differ from that of an upward-sloping microeconomic supply curve for a good?
18. How does the economic meaning behind a downward-sloping AD curve differ from that of a downward-sloping microeconomic demand curve for a good?
19. How is long-term growth illustrated in an AS–AD model?
20. How is recession illustrated in an AS–AD model?
21. How is cyclical unemployment illustrated in an AS–AD model?
22. How is the natural rate of unemployment illustrated in an AS–AD model?
23. How are pressure inflationary price increases shown in an AS–AD model?
24. What are some of the ways in which exports and imports can affect the AS–AD model?
25. What is the Keynesian zone of the AS curve? How much is the price level likely to change in the Keynesian zone?
26. What is the neoclassical zone of the AS curve? How much is the output level likely to change in the neoclassical zone?
27. What is the intermediate zone of the AS curve? Will a rise in output be accompanied by a rise or a fall in the price level in this zone?

The Keynesian Perspective

CHAPTER

27

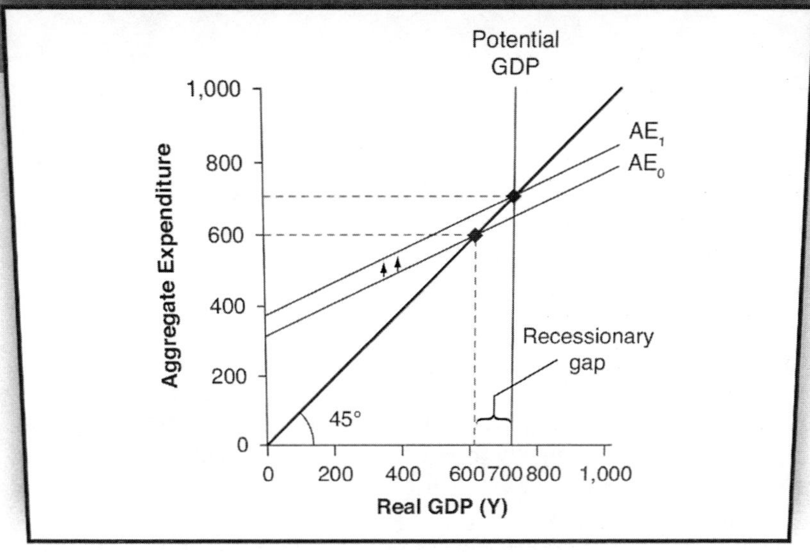

Chapter Outline

An argument is sometimes made that an occasional recession should not cause too much concern because it will soon be over, and in the meantime, tough economic times can create a powerful incentive for firms to become more productive lest they be driven into bankruptcy. Perhaps the most compelling criticism of the argument that recessions should be viewed without overmuch concern came from the great economist John Maynard Keynes. Soon after the steep recession of 1920–1921, Keynes wrote:

> Now "in the long run" this [idea that recessions are part of a process of long-term economic growth] is probably true. . . . But this long run is a misleading guide to current affairs. *In the long run* we are all dead. Economists set themselves too easy, too useless a task if in tempestuous seasons they can only tell us that when the storm is long past the ocean is flat again.

The worst U.S. economic storm of the twentieth century was the Great Depression of the 1930s. Over several years, the U.S. GDP plummeted by 30%. Unemployment rocketed from 3.2% in 1929 to 24.9% in 1933, and even as late as 1939, unemployment still hovered above 17%. So few dollars were chasing so many goods that deflation resulted, with the price level falling by 24% from 1929 to 1933. (In a situation of deflation, if you have money to spend, every dollar *increases* substantially in purchasing power.) The human misery of the Depression was even worse than these grim statistics imply. Up to a million Americans were homeless. Hunger and malnutrition were widespread. In the early 1930s, comparatively few government social programs existed. Millions of people had literally no way to make a living—no way to feed or shelter themselves or their families.

Yet in the early years of the Great Depression, many well-known economists did not perceive anything fundamentally wrong with the economy. After all, the 1920s had seen several recessions: from January 1920 to July 1921, from May 1923 to July 1924, and from October 1926 to November 1927.

Even including these recessions, real GDP had risen at a healthy annual average rate of 2.6% per year from 1919 to 1928. Thus, some economists argued that recessions every few years were part of the process of a growing economy. However, other economists focused, like Keynes, on the human costs of suffering through a recession every few years. More recently, the U.S. economy suffered a recession starting in December 2007, and the number of unemployed Americans rose from 6.8 million in May 2007 to 15.4 million in October 2009. It would not have been helpful for those additional 8.6 million unemployed workers to tell them that their joblessness was just part of a process of long-term growth.

This chapter begins with a Keynesian diagnosis of causes of recession and then discusses the components of aggregate demand—consumption, investment, government spending, exports, and imports. The discussion will use the model of aggregate supply and aggregate demand to show how recessions occur and can be counteracted. This Keynesian model implies trade-offs between unemployment and inflation. The discussion then presents a macroeconomic model called the expenditure-output model. Finally, the chapter addresses the question of whether Keynesian economics should be viewed as opposing or complementary to a market-oriented economy.

The Building Blocks of Keynesian Analysis

Keynesian economics focuses on explaining why recessions and depressions occur and offers a policy prescription for minimizing their effects. Not all of what is now called "Keynesian economics" can be found in an exact form in the writings of John Maynard Keynes because these ideas have evolved over time. However, the Keynesian view of recession is based on two key building blocks. First, aggregate demand is not always automatically high enough to provide firms with an incentive to hire enough workers to reach full employment. Second, the macroeconomy may adjust only slowly to shifts in aggregate demand because of stickiness of wages and prices. Let's consider these two claims in turn, and then see how they are represented in the model of aggregate supply and aggregate demand.

The Importance of Aggregate Demand in Recessions

The Keynesian diagnosis of recession argues that a shift in aggregate demand is usually a more likely explanation of recession than a shift in aggregate supply. After all, even during the Great Depression, the physical capacity of the economy to supply goods did not alter much. No flood or earthquake or other natural disaster ruined factories in 1929 or 1930. No outbreak of disease decimated the ranks of workers. No key input price, like the price of oil, soared on world markets. The U.S. economy in 1933 had just about the same factories, workers, and state of technology as it had four years earlier in 1929—and yet the economy shrunk dramatically. Indeed, most recessions are not accompanied by destruction of machinery and equipment on the supply side of the economy. It seems more plausible that they are caused by shifts of aggregate demand.

As Keynes recognized, the events of the Depression contradicted Say's law that "supply creates its own demand." Instead, Keynes argued, an economy has periods when its potential GDP changes little, but aggregate demand falls by a lot. One likely cause is that the demand for physical investment spending by firms can shift quickly. When firms are pessimistic or uncertain about the economic future, they postpone investment projects. When businesses become more optimistic, they may have a backlog of projects in mind that they can start up all at once. Thus, the investment component of aggregate demand is likely to surge and decline rapidly.

More recent analysis in a Keynesian spirit has also emphasized how a country's ailing financial system—especially if its banks are performing poorly—can drag down the economy. As the U.S. economy staggered into Depression during the early 1930s, many businesses and households were unable to repay their loans, and banks went bankrupt as a result. Of the 24,000 U.S. banks in operation in 1929, only 14,400 remained in 1933.

When so many banks went out of business, the availability of loans diminished for firms seeking to invest and for households seeking to buy a home or car. Thus, the reduction in aggregate demand injured the banking system, making the reduction in aggregate demand even worse, creating a vicious cycle of worsening depression. The U.S. recession from 2007–2009 was also worsened by a weakened banking system.

Wage and Price Stickiness

The Keynesian diagnosis of recession is based on the stickiness of wages. If markets throughout the economy all had flexible and continually adjusting prices, then a shift in aggregate demand would result in changes in prices and wages, but not in any additional unemployment. To put it another way, if all prices and wages were flexible and continually adjusting, the economy would always head for its natural rate of unemployment, as discussed in Chapter 23.

Keynes emphasized one particular reason why wages were sticky: the *coordination argument*. The coordination argument points out that even if most people would be willing—at least hypothetically—to see a decline in their own wages in bad economic times *as long as everyone else also experienced such a decline*, a market-oriented economy has no obvious way to implement a plan of coordinated wage reductions. The discussion of unemployment in Chapter 23 proposed a number of reasons why wages might be sticky downwards, most of which come down to the argument that businesses avoid wage cuts because they may in one way or another depress morale and hurt the productivity of the existing workers.

Some modern economists have argued in a Keynesian spirit that along with wages, other prices may be sticky, too. Many firms don't change their prices every day or even every month. For example, many companies publish sales catalogs every six months or every year, instead of announcing that the prices may change on any given day. When a firm considers changing prices, it must consider two sets of costs. First, changing prices uses company resources: managers must analyze the competition and market demand and decide what the new prices will be, sales materials must be updated, billing records will change, and product labels and price labels must be redone. Second, frequent price

The Slow Speed of Price Adjustments

Probably few companies anywhere in the world know more about inflation and pricing strategies than the business magazine *Fortune*. But consider how the cover price of *Fortune* has changed over time. In May 1970, the cover price was raised $1.50 to $2.00. The price increases since 1970 are shown in the first column of the table. The second column shows the Consumer Price Index for those years (using a base period where the average price level from 1982–84 was set equal to 100), and the third column converts the nominal cover price into real 2016 dollars.

Clearly, *Fortune* used to be a lot more expensive in 1970, measured in real dollars. During the high inflation of the 1970s, the magazine allowed its real price to fall. Throughout the 1980s and 1990s, then, *Fortune*'s pricing strategy seemed to be to wait until the price level had increased about 10–15%—and the real price of the magazine had been eroded by that amount—before bumping up the nominal price to roughly the same real level. In the 2000s, the strategy seems to have been to keep the cover price at the same level while allowing the real price to fall.

	Cover Price	CPI	Real Price (in 2016 dollars)
May 1970	$2.00	38.8	$12.31
January 1980	$2.50	82.4	$7.24
May 1982	$3.00	96.5	$7.42
May 1985	$3.50	107.6	$7.77
April 1990	$3.95	130.7	$7.20
May 1994	$4.50	148.2	$7.25
October 1997	$4.95	160.5	$7.36
May 2001	$4.99	177.1	$6.72
April 2016	$4.99	238.9	$4.99

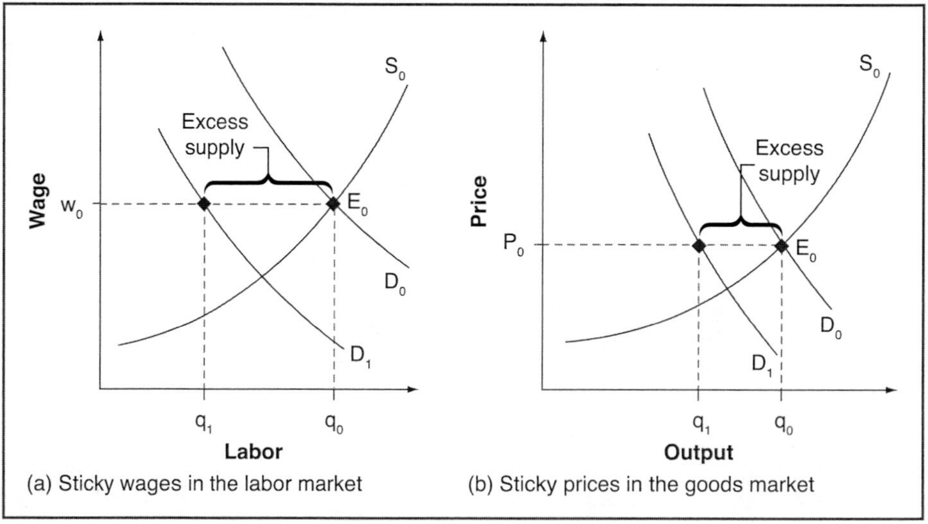

EXHIBIT 27-1 Sticky Prices and Falling Demand in the Labor and Goods Market

In both *a* and *b*, demand shifts left from D_0 to D_1. However, the wage in *a* and the price in *b* do not decline. In *a*, the quantity demanded of labor at the original wage w_0, but the new demand curve for labor D_1, will be q_1. In *b*, the quantity demanded of goods at the original price P_0 but the new demand curve D_1 will be q_1. An excess supply of labor will exist, called unemployment. An excess supply of goods will also exist, where the quantity demanded is substantially less than the quantity supplied. Thus, sticky wages and sticky prices combined with a drop in demand bring about unemployment and recession.

menu costs: The costs that firms face in changing prices.

changes may leave customers confused or angry—especially if they find out that a product now costs more than expected. These costs of changing prices are called **menu costs**—like the costs of printing up a new set of menus with different prices in a restaurant. Prices do respond to forces of supply and demand, but from a macroeconomic perspective, the process of changing all prices throughout the economy takes time.

To understand the effect of sticky wages and prices in the economy, consider Exhibit 27-1. Exhibit 27-1*a* illustrates the overall labor market, while Exhibit 27-1*b* illustrates a market for goods and services. The original equilibrium E_0 in each market occurs at the intersection of demand curve D_0 and supply curve S_0. When aggregate demand declines, the demand for labor shifts to the left to D_1 in Exhibit 27-1*a* and the demand for goods shifts to the left to D_1 in Exhibit 27-1*b*. However, because of sticky wages and prices, the wage for a time remains at its original wage level w_0 and the price remains at its original level p_0. As a result, a situation of excess supply—where the quantity supplied exceeds the quantity demanded at the existing wage or price—exists in markets for both labor and goods, and q_1 is less than q_0 in both Exhibit 27-1*a* and Exhibit 27-1*b*. When many labor markets and many goods markets all across the economy find themselves in this position, the economy is in a recession: that is, firms cannot sell what they wish to produce at the existing market price and don't wish to hire all workers who are willing to work at the existing market wage.

The Two Keynesian Assumptions in the AS–AD Model

These two Keynesian assumptions—the importance of aggregate demand in causing recession and the stickiness of wages and prices—are illustrated by the AS–AD diagram in Exhibit 27-2. The original equilibrium of this economy occurs where the aggregate demand function AD_0 intersects with AS. Since this intersection occurs well below the full employment level, this economy is suffering a recession and high cyclical unemployment.

This description of the recession encompasses the two key building blocks of Keynesian economics. The importance of aggregate demand is illustrated because the output of the economy is being determined by the fact that AD_0 is far to the left of AD_1 and thus far from where the AS curve is near-vertical in the vicinity of potential GDP. The importance

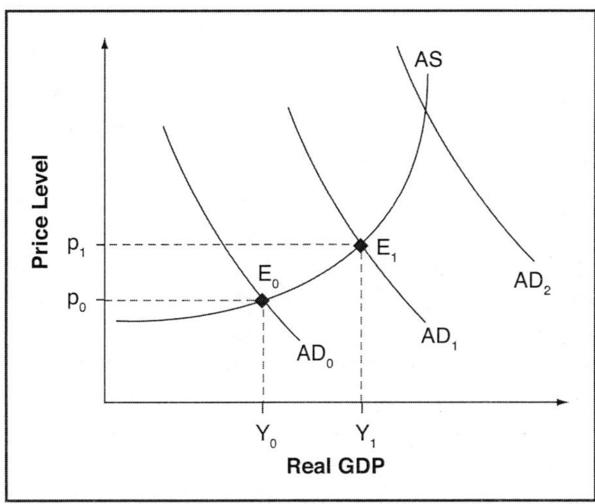

EXHIBIT 27-2 A Keynesian Perspective on Recession

The equilibrium E_0 illustrates the two key assumptions behind Keynesian economics. The importance of aggregate demand is shown because this equilibrium is a recession which has occurred because aggregate demand is at AD_0 instead of AD_1. The importance of sticky wages and prices is shown because the economic logic of the AS curve is built on the assumption of fixed prices for inputs, like wages, and because the intersection E_0 occurs in the relatively flat portion of the AS curve where the price level for outputs does not change by much.

of sticky wages and prices is illustrated because the aggregate supply curve is built on an assumption that the prices of inputs like wages are being held constant—so the AS curve assumes sticky wages. Because the shift of aggregate demand happens primarily in the flatter portion of the AS curve, to the left of the potential GDP level of output, it has little impact on the price level—which fits well with the notion that prices are sticky and don't alter by much. Thus, the AS–AD model is well designed to explain how the combination of a fall in demand and sticky wages and prices can bring about a recession.

The Components of Aggregate Demand

What economic events or policies might cause aggregate demand to shift to the left, away from the potential GDP level of output? Conversely, what economic events or policies could cause AD to shift to the right? This section investigates the Keynesian approach by considering in turn each of the components of aggregate demand—consumption, investment, government, exports and imports.

What Causes Consumption to Shift?

Consumption is the largest component of aggregate demand. If consumption increases at every given price level, then the aggregate demand curve will shift to the right. If consumption declines, then the AD curve will shift to the left.

For most people, the single most powerful determinant of how much they consume is how much income they have in their take-home pay, after the government subtracts taxes. This insight suggests two factors that affect consumption: income and taxes. Higher incomes or tax cuts will tend to lead to more consumption and cause AD to shift out to the right. Lower incomes or tax increases will cause AD to shift to the left.

But in thinking about how much to consume in the present, people will also think about their *expectations about future incomes*. An economic theory known as the **permanent income hypothesis** suggests that when individuals think about how much to consume, they won't look just at the current paycheck but will look into the future, too, and calculate their expected "permanent income" over their lifetime. An implication of the permanent income hypothesis is that if people believe that their income is especially high this year, and is likely to be lower in the future, then they are likely to save more in the present.

permanent income hypothesis: When individuals think about how much to consume, they look into the future and consider how much income they expect to earn in their lifetime.

Conversely, if people think that their income is especially low this year, but will rise in the future, then they may not worry about saving much at all in the present. The permanent income hypothesis also implies that a temporary tax cut, which increases take-home income for only one year, will have a much smaller impact on current consumption than a permanent tax cut, which is expected to increase take-home income for many years.

Choices about whether to save or borrow in the present will also be influenced by the interest rate. For a borrower, the interest rate is the price that is paid for borrowing; for a saver, the interest rate is the price that is received for saving. Lower real interest rates will tend to encourage consumer borrowing for purchases of big-ticket items like cars or refrigerators and cause AD to shift to the right. Conversely, higher real interest rates will tend to discourage purchases on credit and thus shift AD to the left.

Finally, a variety of other factors combine to determine how much people save, including personal preferences and wealth. If household preferences about saving shift in a way that encourages consumption rather than saving, then AD would shift out to the right. When households experience a rise in wealth, then they may be willing to consume a higher share of their income and to save less. When the U.S. stock market rose dramatically in the late 1990s, for example, U.S. rates of saving declined, probably in part because people felt that their wealth had increased and there was less need to save. On the other side, when the U.S. stock market declined about 40% from March 2008 to March 2009, as the recession took hold and many people felt far greater uncertainty about their economic future, rates of saving increased while consumption declined.

What Causes Investment to Shift?

When a firm makes an investment in physical assets, like plants or equipment, or in intangible assets, like skills or a research and development project, it is spending in the present in the expectation that the future will bring a worthwhile rate of return. When a firm plans its investment demand, it calculates an expected rate of return—that is, the percentage return that the firm expects to receive over time, after all the costs of the investment are taken into account. If firms believe that they can make a high expected return, they will be more eager to invest.

The expected rate of return depends on several factors. One consideration is the range of investment opportunities open to the firm. The creation of new technologies, for example, may offer investment opportunities with a high expected rate of return. Another key factor is that if the economy appears likely to grow in the next few years, then businesses will perceive a growing market for their products, and their higher degree of business confidence will encourage investment. In the second half of the 1990s, the U.S. economy experienced both a wave of new information and communications technologies, like the Internet and vastly improved mobile phones, while also having a long period of sustained economic growth sometimes called the "dot-com boom." For both reasons, U.S. investment levels surged at this time from 18% of GDP in 1994 to 21% of GDP in 2000. However, a recession started in the U.S. economy in 2001, and many firms came to believe that the returns from investing in new computers was not as high as they had thought, so U.S. investment levels quickly sank back to 18% of GDP by 2002.

When considering the expected rate of gains from investment opportunities, firms need to take into account not only the direct costs of investments—like buying a new piece of machinery—but also an opportunity cost that involves the interest rate. When a firm borrows funds to make an investment in physical plant or equipment, this opportunity cost is readily apparent in the interest payments that the firm has to make. But even if a firm doesn't need to borrow money for a certain investment—perhaps because it is earning enough profits to finance its investment using its own internal funds—the firm could have chosen to invest those profits and receive interest payments. The interest payments that could have been received, but are not, because of the decision to invest profits in new plant and equipment, are also an opportunity cost of the investment decision. In either case, a higher real interest rate discourages a firm from investing in tangible or intangible capital by raising its cost.

Developments in the rest of the economy or in public policy can also affect the expected rate of return on investment. For example, if the price of energy declines, then investments that use energy as an input will have a higher expected rate of return. If government offers special incentives through the tax code for investment, then investment will look more attractive; conversely, if government removes special investment incentives from the tax code, or increases other business taxes, then investment will look less attractive.

Firms often have some flexibility about when to invest. It's easy to postpone or scale back physical investment decisions for a time if economic conditions are unfavorable, and it's often possible to accelerate or increase investments if economic conditions appear more favorable. Thus, investment often happens in waves, surging and then ebbing. A decline in investment would shift AD back and to the left, and unless it was offset by other portions of aggregate demand, a recession could result.

What Causes Government Demand to Shift?

Governments make decisions for political reasons, which in turn can depend on the philosophy of those who are in power. A government presiding over an economy with a low level of GDP may decide that there is too little tax revenue to justify much government spending, or alternatively, it may decide that the economy is in desperate need of government programs and higher spending. Conversely, a government with a high level of GDP may decide that in a high-income country, people can afford a high level of government services, or it may decide that in a high-income country, most people should be responsible for purchasing their own goods and services and so the government services and government spending should be low. In any given year, a government can decide to run a budget surplus—that is, to collect more in taxes than it spends—or to run a budget deficit—that is, to spend more than it collects in taxes. Whatever its political justification, an increase in the government spending component of demand will cause AD to shift to the right, while a decline in government spending demand will cause AD to shift to the left. These policy decisions about taxes and spending will be taken up in more detail in Chapters 32 and 33.

What Causes Exports and Imports to Shift?

Two sets of factors can cause shifts in export and import demand: changes in relative growth rates between countries and changes in relative prices between countries. The level of demand for a nation's exports tends to be most heavily affected by what is happening in the economies of the other countries that would be purchasing those exports. For example, if major importers of American-made products like Canada, Japan, and Germany have recessions, exports of U.S. producers to those countries are likely to decline. Conversely, the quantity of a nation's imports is directly affected by the amount of income in the domestic economy: more income will cause a higher level of imports.

One implication of thinking about exports and imports in this way is that the trade deficit in an economy will tend to arise (or an existing trade surplus will shrink) when an economy is growing strongly, while a trade surplus will tend to arise (or an existing trade deficit will shrink) when an economy is stagnant or shrinking. A more rapidly growing domestic economy draws in more imports, but it does not affect exports (which are determined by what happens in other countries), thus reducing the balance of trade. Conversely, a domestic recession will reduce imports, along with all other consumption, but will not much affect exports, thus increasing the balance of trade. For example, the U.S. economy ran very large trade deficits in the mid-2000s during a period of sustained growth, but the trade deficit fell by about half when the recession took full hold in 2009.

Exports and imports can also be affected by relative prices of goods in domestic and international markets. If U.S. goods are relatively cheaper compared with goods made in other places, perhaps because a group of U.S. producers has mastered certain productivity breakthroughs, then U.S. exports are likely to rise. But if U.S. goods become relatively more expensive, perhaps because a change in exchange rate between the U.S. dollar and

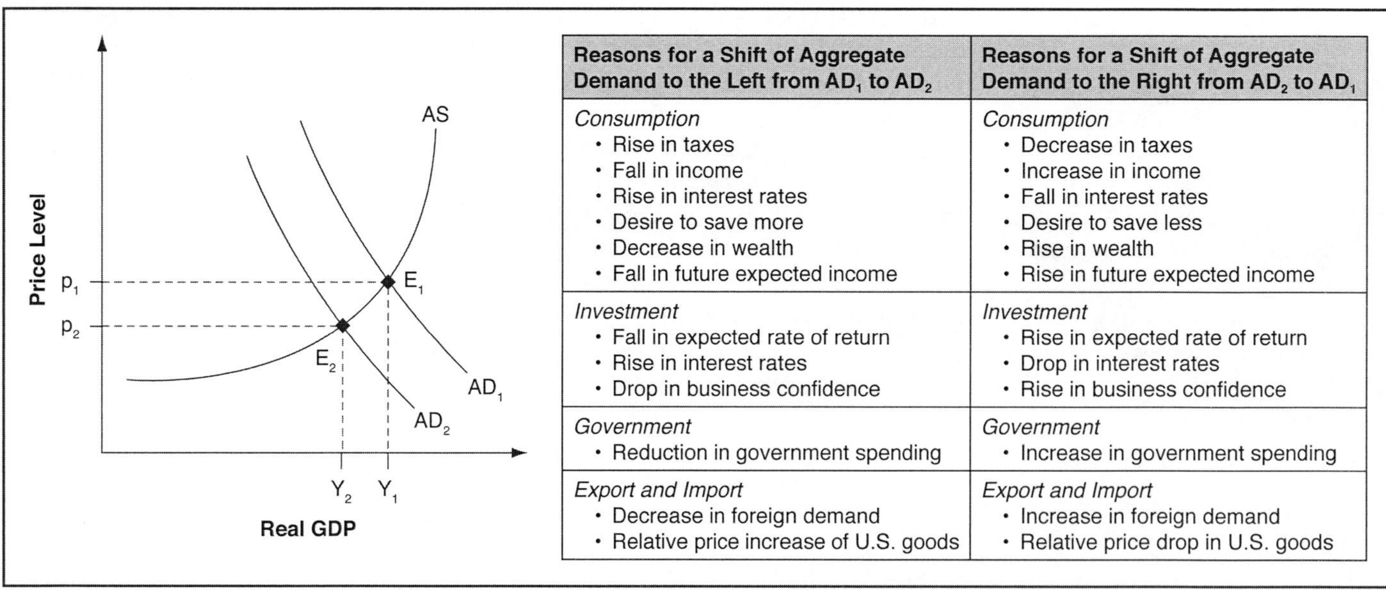

Reasons for a Shift of Aggregate Demand to the Left from AD_1 to AD_2	Reasons for a Shift of Aggregate Demand to the Right from AD_2 to AD_1
Consumption • Rise in taxes • Fall in income • Rise in interest rates • Desire to save more • Decrease in wealth • Fall in future expected income	*Consumption* • Decrease in taxes • Increase in income • Fall in interest rates • Desire to save less • Rise in wealth • Rise in future expected income
Investment • Fall in expected rate of return • Rise in interest rates • Drop in business confidence	*Investment* • Rise in expected rate of return • Drop in interest rates • Rise in business confidence
Government • Reduction in government spending	*Government* • Increase in government spending
Export and Import • Decrease in foreign demand • Relative price increase of U.S. goods	*Export and Import* • Increase in foreign demand • Relative price drop in U.S. goods

EXHIBIT 27-3 Reasons for Shifts in the Components of Aggregate Demand

other currencies has pushed up the price of inputs to production in the United States, then exports from U.S. producers are likely to decline. Chapter 31 will discuss exchange rates in more detail.

Exhibit 27-3 summarizes the reasons given in this section for why the aggregate demand curve might shift to the left, from AD_1 to AD_2, or alternatively to the right, from AD_2 to AD_1. Many of the reasons involve economic events, like changes in preference for saving, or the rate of growth in other economies that purchase exports. But some of the factors that shift aggregate demand can be affected by government policy.

The Phillips Curve

The Keynesian economic framework is based on an assumption that prices and wages are sticky and do not adjust rapidly. This assumption made some sense during the Great Depression, when Keynes was writing, and more generally during any recession when the intersection of AD and AS is below the potential GDP level of output. However, do prices still remain sticky when an economy is not in recession, but instead is near or even above its potential GDP?

The Discovery of the Phillips Curve

In the 1950s, a New Zealand economist named A.W. Phillips was studying the Keynesian analytical framework at the London School of Economics. He noticed that when the economy is in a recession, with real GDP well below potential GDP and high unemployment, the Keynesian theory implies that pressures for inflationary increases in the price level also tend to be low. However, when the level of output is at or even pushing beyond potential GDP, so that unemployment is low, Keynesian theory implies that the economy is at greater risk of inflationary pressures.

Exhibit 27-4 illustrates how during a recession, a move of aggregate demand from AD_1 to AD_2 barely shifts the equilibrium price level at all. However, if the economy is already near potential GDP at AD_3, then a move to AD_4 will increase the price level. When the level of output lies in the flatter part of the AS curve, far below potential GDP, then an increase in aggregate demand can easily encourage more firms to produce more. However, when an economy is already near potential GDP, it becomes increasingly difficult for an additional rise of aggregate demand to bring forth more supply—because the factories and workers in the economy are near full employment already. In this situation, the rise in aggregate demand begins to translate into a higher price level, rather than more output.

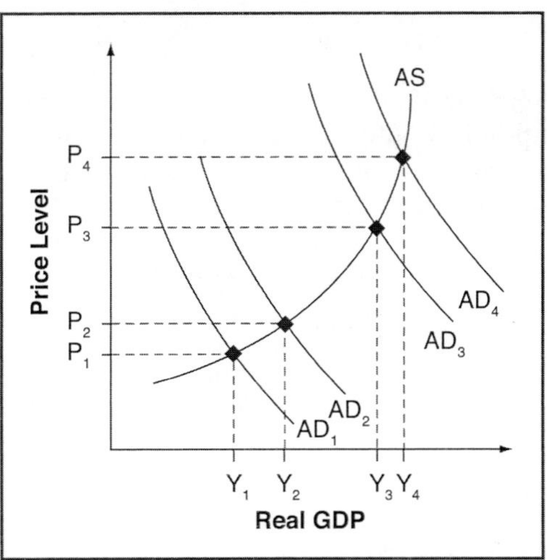

EXHIBIT 27-4 When Shifts in Aggregate Demand Increase the Price Level

A shift of aggregate demand to the right from AD_1 to AD_2 leads to a relatively small increase in the price level from P_1 to P_2, but a relatively large increase in real GDP from Y_1 to Y_2. When unemployment is relatively high, the inflationary increase in the price level is small. However, a similar shift of aggregate demand to the right from AD_3 to AD_4 leads to a relatively large increase in the price level from P_3 to P_4, and only a relatively small increase in real GDP from Y_3 to Y_4. When unemployment is relatively low, because the equilibrium is occurring in the near-vertical portion of the AS curve, close to potential GDP, then the pressure for inflationary price increases can be larger. This pattern suggests a trade-off: when unemployment is high, inflation may be low; and when unemployment is low, inflation may be high.

EXHIBIT 27-5 A Keynesian Phillips Curve Trade-off between Unemployment and Inflation

A Phillips curve illustrates a trade-off between the unemployment rate and the inflation rate; if one is higher, the other must be lower. For example, point A illustrates an inflation rate of 5% and an unemployment rate of 4%. If the government attempts to reduce inflation to 2%, then it will experience a rise in unemployment to 7%, as shown at point B.

Phillips went searching in the historical data to see if these theoretical predictions held true: Is inflation high when unemployment is low, and vice versa? Phillips graphed annual British data over 60 years, with unemployment rates on the horizontal axis and the rise in wages (as a measure of inflation) on the vertical axis. He found that the British data over this period of time did indeed trace out a downward-sloping curve, which became known as a **Phillips curve**. Exhibit 27-5 shows a theoretical Phillips curve. In this example, society must choose between a point like A, with 4% unemployment and 5% inflation, and a point like B, with 7% unemployment and 2% inflation.

Phillips curve: The trade-off between unemployment and inflation.

The Instability of the Phillips Curve

American economists began graphing unemployment and inflation data to see if the Phillips curve relationship held in the U.S. economy as well. Exhibit 27-6*a* is based on U.S. unemployment and inflation data for the years 1960–69. Over this time, the U.S. economy seemed first to move down a Phillips curve, then back up toward the middle.

EXHIBIT 27-6 The Evolution of the Keynesian Phillips Curve

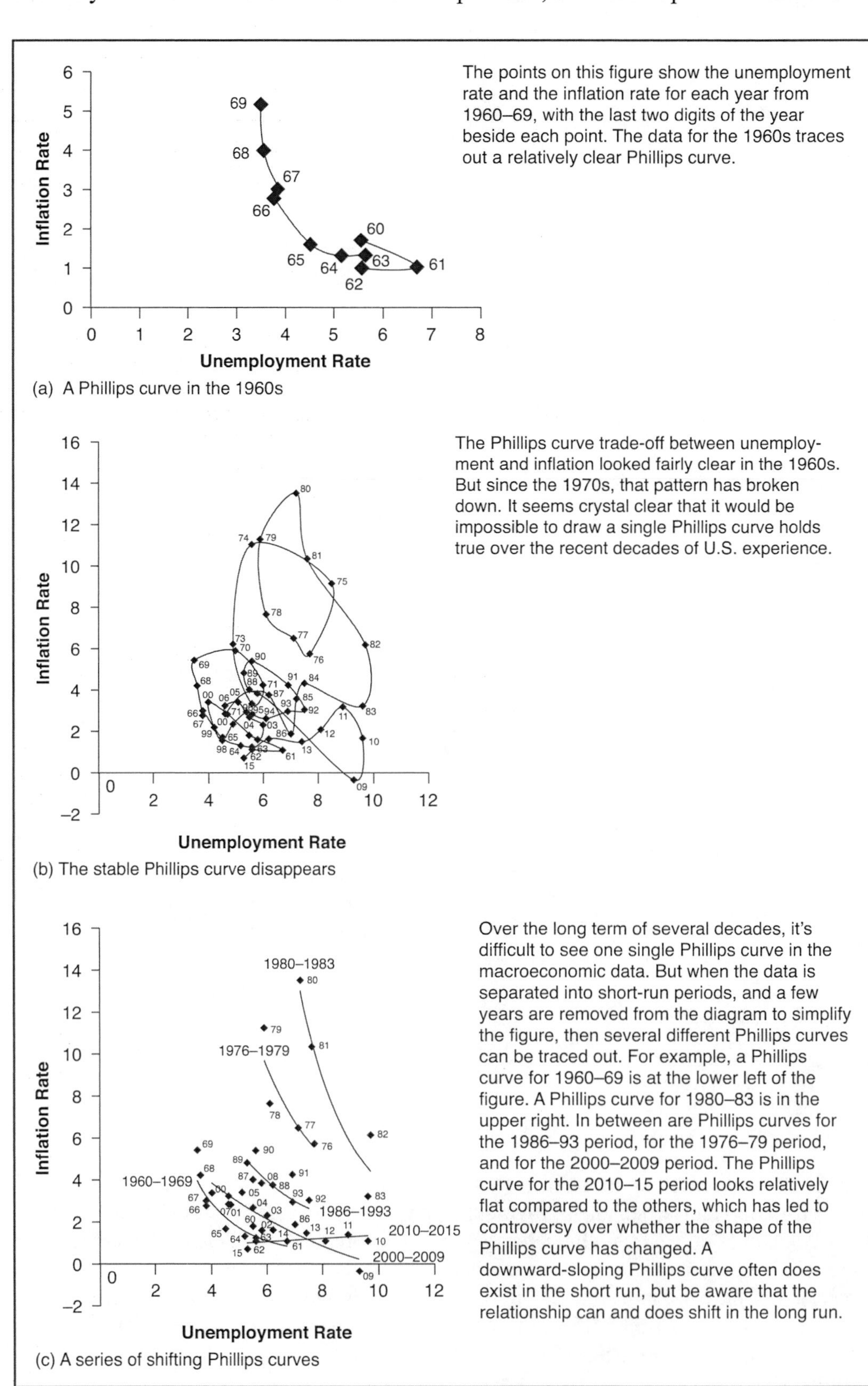

With the image of the Phillips curve in mind, macroeconomists in the 1960s sometimes discussed the optimal point on the Phillips curve. The extremes of the Phillips curve—high unemployment or high inflation—were both undesirable. But in the middle ground, which point should be favored?

But by the 1970s, this debate became obsolete. Instead of a trade-off between unemployment and inflation, several deep recessions occurred in which unemployment and inflation rose *at the same time*. The U.S. economy experienced this pattern in the deep recession from 1973–75, and again in the back-to-back recessions from 1980–82. For example, the U.S. unemployment rate rose from 4.9% in 1973 to 8.5% by 1975, while inflation was rising from 3.2% in 1972 to 11% in 1974. The unemployment rate rose from 5.8% in 1979 to 9.7% in 1982, while inflation had risen from 7.6% in 1978 to 13.5% in 1980. Exhibit 27-6*b* graphs the data on U.S. unemployment and inflation from 1960–2015. It is clearly impossible to draw a single smooth curve through this forest of data points. Many nations around the world saw similar increases in unemployment and inflation. This pattern was known as **stagflation**—an unhealthy combination of a stagnating economy with high inflation.

stagflation: When an economy experiences stagnant growth and high inflation at the same time.

Critics of a Phillips curve will sometimes point to a diagram like Exhibit 27-6*b* and argue that the Phillips curve doesn't exist, but that argument goes too far. Consider again the patterns of U.S. unemployment and inflation as portrayed in Exhibit 27-6*c*. The diagram shows six Phillips curves for the U.S. economy: one based on the years 1960–69; one based on the years 1980–83; three middle ones based on the years 1976–79, 1986–93, and 2000–2009; and a relatively flat Phillips curve near the bottom for the years from 2010–15. The diagram shows that a Phillips curve trade-off between unemployment and inflation does hold for periods of several years, but then the Phillips curve itself can shift. This idea that a Phillips curve can shift over time is quite reasonable. After all, the original Phillips curve was based on a short-term Keynesian model, which looked at movements in aggregate demand in an economy where aggregate supply was not moving and prices did not adjust rapidly. Aggregate supply had been relatively stable in the 1960s, so the Phillips curve looked relatively stable. But then aggregate supply shifted to the left in 1974–75 and again in 1979–80, driven in part by higher prices for the key economic input of imported oil. These shifts in the AS curve led to shifts in the Phillips curve as shown in Exhibit 27-6*c*. Thus, a downward-sloping Phillips curve should be interpreted as valid for short-run periods of several years, but over longer periods when aggregate supply shifts, the downward-sloping Phillips curve can shift so that unemployment and inflation are both higher (as in the 1970s and early 1980s) or both lower (as in the early 1990s or first decade of the 2000s).

Keynesian Policy for Fighting Unemployment and Inflation

Keynesian macroeconomics was born in the Great Depression, when the main concern was how to fight recession. Keynes argued that the solution to a recession would include policies to shift the aggregate demand curve to the right, like tax cuts for consumers and businesses to stimulate consumption and investment, or direct increases in government spending. For example, if aggregate demand was originally at AD_R in Exhibit 27-7, so that the economy was in recession, the appropriate policy would be for government to shift aggregate demand to the right from AD_R to AD_F, where the economy would be at potential GDP and full employment. Keynes noted that while it would be nice if government could spend additional money on housing, roads, and other amenities, he also argued that if the government couldn't agree on how to spend money in practical ways, then it could spend in impractical ways. For example, Keynes suggested building monuments, like a modern equivalent of the Egyptian pyramids. He proposed that the government could bury money underground, and let mining companies get started to dig the money up again. These suggestions were slightly tongue-in-cheek, but their purpose was to emphasize that a Great Depression is no time to quibble over the specifics of government spending programs and tax cuts when the goal should be to pump up aggregate demand by enough to lift the economy to potential GDP.

EXHIBIT 27-7 Fighting Recession and Inflation with Keynesian Policy

If an economy is in recession, with an equilibrium at E_R, then the Keynesian response would be to enact a policy to shift aggregate demand to the right from AD_R toward AD_F. If an economy is experiencing inflationary pressures with an equilibrium at E_I, then the Keynesian response would be to enact a policy response to shift aggregate demand to the left from AD_I toward AD_F.

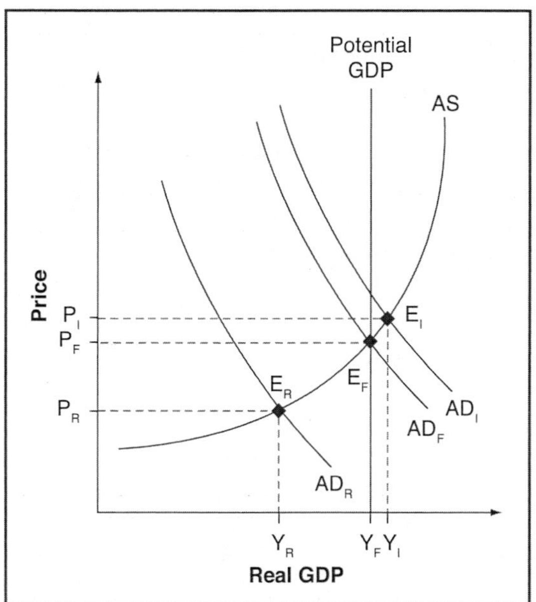

The other side of Keynesian policy occurs when the economy is operating at or even above potential GDP. In this situation, unemployment is low, but inflationary rises in the price level are a concern. The Keynesian response would be to use tax increases or government spending cuts to shift AD to the left. The result would be downward pressure on the price level, but very little reduction in output or very little rise in unemployment. If aggregate demand was originally at AD_I in Exhibit 27-7, so that the economy was experiencing inflationary rises in the price level, the appropriate policy would be for government to shift aggregate demand to the left from AD_I toward AD_F, which reduces the pressure for a higher price level while the economy remains at full employment.

In the Keynesian economic model, too little aggregate demand brings unemployment and too much brings inflation. Thus, you can think of Keynesian economics as pursuing a "Goldilocks" level of aggregate demand: not too much, not too little, but looking for what is just right.

The Expenditure-Output Model

The fundamental ideas of Keynesian economics were developed before the AS–AD model was popularized. For decades, Keynesian economics was typically explained with a different model, known as the expenditure-output approach. (Some classes will choose to skip this discussion of the "Keynesian cross" model and move straight to the closing section of this chapter, which can be done without loss of continuity.) This approach is strongly rooted in the fundamental assumptions of Keynesian economics: it focuses on the total amount of expenditure or demand in the economy, with no explicit mention of aggregate supply or of the price level (although as you will see, it is possible to draw some inferences about aggregate supply and price levels based on the diagram). This laser-like focus on expenditures in the economy has a payoff. It allows a closer analysis of how shifts in demand or spending affect the rest of the economy; for example, it shows how a tax cut or spending increase of a certain amount, like \$10 billion, can have more than \$10 billion worth of impact on equilibrium GDP.

expenditure-output model: A macroeconomic model in which equilibrium output occurs where the total or aggregate expenditures in the economy are equal to the amount produced; also called the "Keynesian cross model."

The Axes of the Expenditure-Output Diagram

The **expenditure-output model**, sometimes also called the "Keynesian cross diagram," determines the equilibrium level of real GDP by the point where the total or aggregate expenditures in the economy are equal to the amount produced in the economy. Thus, the axes of the Keynesian cross diagram as presented in Exhibit 27-8 show real GDP on the

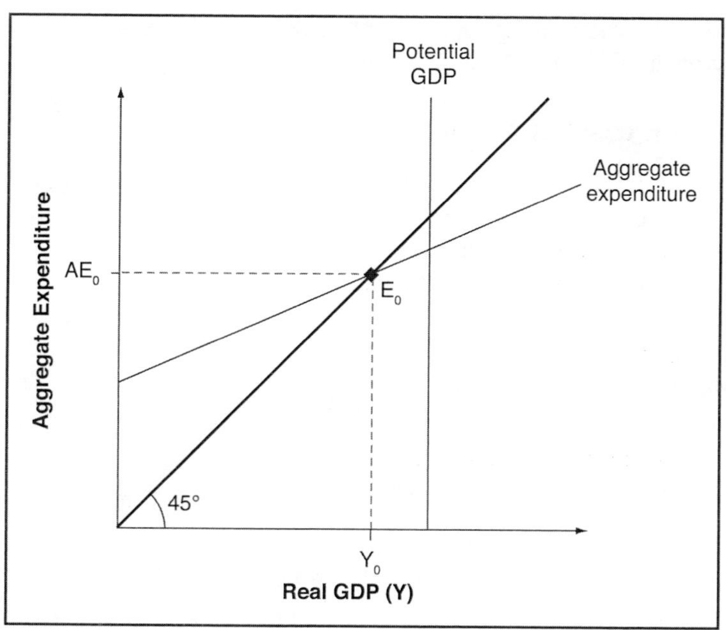

EXHIBIT 27-8 The Expenditure-Output Diagram

The aggregate expenditure-output model, sometimes called the Keynesian cross diagram, has aggregate expenditures on the vertical axis and real GDP as a measure of output on the horizontal axis. A vertical line shows potential GDP or full employment GDP. The 45° line shows all points where aggregate expenditures and output are equal. The aggregate expenditure schedule shows how total spending or aggregate expenditure increases as output or real GDP rises. The intersection of the aggregate expenditure schedule and the 45° line will be the equilibrium. Equilibrium occurs at E_0, where aggregate expenditure AE_0 is equal to the output level Y_0.

horizontal axis as a measure of output and aggregate expenditures on the vertical axis as a measure of spending.

Remember that GDP can be thought of in several equivalent ways: it measures both the value of spending on final goods and also the value of the production of final goods. All sales of the final goods and services that make up GDP will eventually end up as income for workers, for managers, and for investors and owners of firms. The sum of all the income received for contributing resources to GDP is called **national income (Y)**. At some points in the discussion that follows, it will be useful to refer to real GDP as "national income." Both of these axes are measured in real (inflation-adjusted) terms.

national income (Y): The sum of all income received for producing GDP.

The Potential GDP Line and the 45-degree Line

The Keynesian cross diagram illustrated in Figure 27-8 contains two lines that serve as conceptual guideposts to orient the discussion. The first conceptual line is a vertical line shows the level of potential GDP. Potential GDP means the same thing here that it means in the AS–AD diagrams: it refers to the quantity of output that the economy can produce with full employment of its labor and physical capital.

The second conceptual line on the Keynesian cross diagram is the 45-degree line, which starts at the origin and reaches up and to the right. A line that stretches up at a 45-degree angle represents the set of points (1, 1), (2, 2), (3, 3) and so on, where the measurement on the vertical axis is equal to the measurement on the horizontal axis. In this diagram, the 45-degree line shows the set of points where the level of aggregate expenditure in the economy, measured on the vertical axis, is equal to the level of output or national income in the economy, measured by GDP on the horizontal axis. When the macroeconomy is in equilibrium, it must be true that the aggregate expenditures in the economy are equal to the real GDP—because by definition, GDP is the measure of what is spent on final sales of goods and services in the economy. Thus, the equilibrium calculated with a Keynesian cross diagram will always end up where aggregate expenditure and output are equal—which will only occur along the 45-degree line.

The Aggregate Expenditure Schedule

The final ingredient of the Keynesian cross or expenditure-output diagram is the aggregate expenditure schedule, which will show the total expenditures in the economy for each level of real GDP. The next section will explain the aggregate expenditure schedule in detail. But first, notice that the intersection of the aggregate expenditure line with the 45-degree line—at point E_0 in Exhibit 27-8—will show the equilibrium for the economy because it is the point where aggregate expenditure is equal to output. After developing an understanding of what the aggregate expenditures schedule means in the next section, we'll return to this equilibrium and how to interpret it.

Building the Aggregate Expenditure Schedule

The aggregate expenditure schedule shows, either in the form of a table or on a graph, how aggregate expenditures in the economy rise as real GDP or national income rises. Thus, in thinking about the components of the aggregate expenditure line—consumption, investment, government spending, exports and imports—the key question is how expenditures in each category will adjust as national income rises.

Consumption as a Function of National Income

How do consumption expenditures increase as national income rises? People can do two things with their income: consume it or save it. (For the moment, let's ignore the need to pay taxes with some of it.) Each person who receives an additional dollar faces this choice. The **marginal propensity to consume**, or **MPC**, is the share of the additional dollar a person decides to consume. The **marginal propensity to save**, or **MPS**, is the share of the additional dollar a person decides to save. It must always hold true that

marginal propensity to consume (MPC): The share of an additional dollar of income that goes to consumption.

marginal propensity to save (MPS): The share of an additional dollar that goes to saving.

$$MPC + MPS = 1$$

For example, if the marginal propensity to consume out of the marginal amount of income earned is .9, then the marginal propensity to save is .1.

With this relationship in mind, consider the relationship among income, consumption, and savings shown in Exhibit 27-9. An assumption commonly made in this model is that even if income were zero, people would have to consume *something*. In this example, consumption would be 600 even if income were zero. In this example, the MPC is .8 and the MPS is .2, Thus, when income increases by 1,000, consumption rises by 800 and savings rises by 200. At an income of 4,000, for example, total consumption will be the 600 that would be consumed even without any income, plus 4,000 multiplied by the marginal propensity to consume of .8, or 3,200, for a total of 3,800. The total amount of consumption and saving must always add up to the total amount of income. (Exactly how

CLEARING IT UP

Does a Fixed MPC Make Sense?

Students sometimes question whether a fixed marginal propensity to consume makes sense. "After all," they say, "a low-income household can't afford to save much and a high-income household can afford to save a lot, so surely the MPC is higher for a low-income household than a high-income one?" It is true that high-income households typically save a higher proportion of their income than low-income households. But the macroeconomic perspective on consumption and saving considers the overall economy, taking all different kinds of households together. From a macroeconomic perspective, using one MPC to represent an overall average for the economy is a reasonable, if rough, approximation.

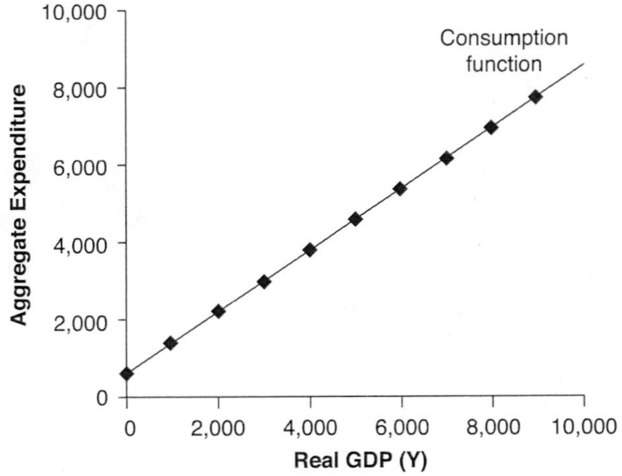

Income	Consumption	Savings
0	600	–600
1,000	1,400	–400
2,000	2,200	–200
3,000	3,000	0
4,000	3,800	200
5,000	4,600	400
6,000	5,400	600
7,000	6,200	800
8,000	7,000	1,000
9,000	7,800	1,200

EXHIBIT 27-9 The Consumption Function

In the expenditure-output model, how does consumption increase with the level of national income? Output on the horizontal axis is conceptually the same as national income, since the value of all final output that is produced and sold must be income to someone, somewhere in the economy. At a national income level of zero, 600 are consumed. Then, each time income rises by 1,000, consumption rises by 800, because in this example, the marginal propensity to consume is .8. The pattern of consumption shown in the table is plotted on the diagram. To calculate consumption, multiply the income level by .8, for the marginal propensity to consume, and add 600, for the amount that would be consumed even if income was zero. Consumption plus savings must be equal to income.

a situation of zero income and negative savings would work in practice is not important, because even low-income societies are not literally at zero income, so the point is hypothetical.) This relationship between income and consumption, illustrated in the figure beside the table, is called the **consumption function.**

consumption function: The relationship between income and expenditures on consumption.

However, a number of factors other than income can also cause the entire consumption function to shift. These factors were summarized in the earlier discussion of consumption, and listed in Exhibit 27-3. When the consumption function moves, it can shift in two ways: either the entire consumption function can move up or down in a parallel manner, or the slope of the consumption function can shift so that it becomes steeper or flatter. For example, if a tax cut leads consumers to spend more, but doesn't affect their marginal propensity to consume, it would cause an upward shift to a new consumption function that is parallel to the original one. However, a change in household preferences for saving that reduced the marginal propensity to save would cause the slope of the consumption function to become steeper: that is, if the savings rate is lower, then every increase in income leads to a larger rise in consumption.

Investment as a Function of National Income

Investment decisions are forward-looking, based on expected rates of return. Precisely because investment decisions depend primarily on perceptions about future economic conditions, they do not depend primarily on the level of GDP in the current year. Thus, on a Keynesian cross diagram, the investment function can be drawn as a horizontal line, at a fixed level of expenditure. Exhibit 27-10 shows an investment function where the level of investment is, for the sake of concreteness, set at the specific level of 500. Just as a consumption function shows the relationship between consumption levels and real GDP (or national income), the investment function shows the relationship between investment levels and real GDP.

The appearance of the investment function as a horizontal line does *not* mean that the level of investment never moves. The horizontal line for investment means only that in the context of this two-dimensional diagram, the level of investment on the vertical aggregate expenditure axis does not vary according to the current level of real GDP on the

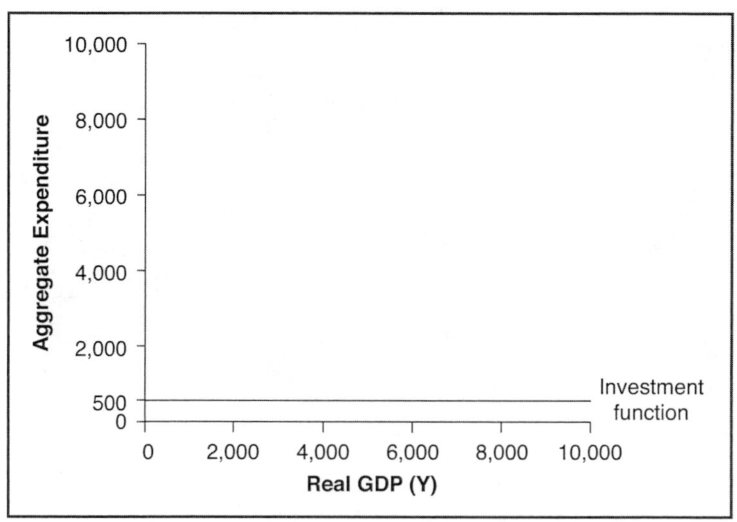

EXHIBIT 27-10 The Investment Function

The investment function is drawn as a flat line because investment is based on expectations about the future, and so it doesn't change with the level of current national income. In this example, investment expenditures are at a level of 500. However, changes in factors like technological opportunities, expectations about near-term economic growth, and real interest rates would all cause the investment function to shift up or down.

horizontal axis. However, all the other factors that vary investment—new technological opportunities, expectations about near-term economic growth, real interest rates, the price of key inputs, and tax incentives for investment—can cause the horizontal investment function to shift up or down.

Government Spending and Taxes as a Function of National Income

In the Keynesian cross model, government spending appears as a horizontal line, as in Exhibit 27-11 where government spending is set at a level of 1,300. As in the case of investment spending, this horizontal line does not mean that government spending is

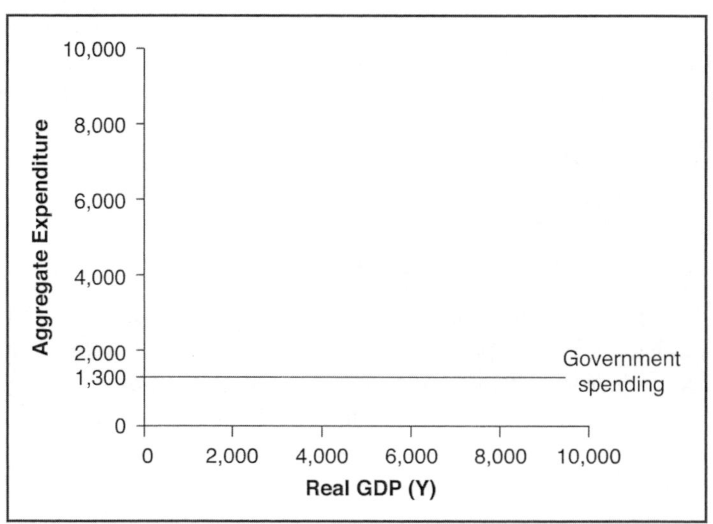

EXHIBIT 27-11 The Government Spending Function

The level of government spending is determined by political factors, not by the level of real GDP in a given year. Thus, government spending is drawn as a horizontal line. In this example, government spending is at a level of 1,300. Political decisions to increase government spending will cause this horizontal line to shift up, while political decisions to reduce spending would cause it to shift down.

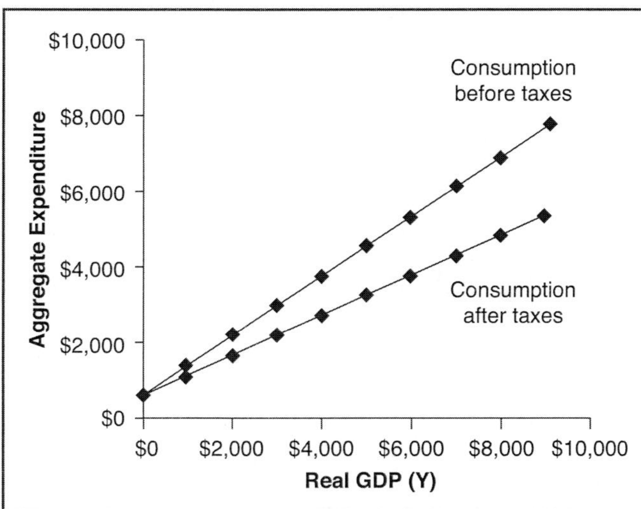

Income	Taxes	After-Tax Income	Consumption	Savings
0	0	0	600	–600
1,000	300	700	1,160	–460
2,000	600	1,400	1,720	–320
3,000	900	2,100	2,280	–180
4,000	1,200	2,800	2,840	–40
5,000	1,500	3,500	3,400	100
6,000	1,800	4,200	3,960	240
7,000	2,100	4,900	4,520	380
8,000	2,400	5,600	5,080	520
9,000	2,700	6,300	5,640	660

EXHIBIT 27-12 The Consumption Function before and after Taxes

The upper line repeats the consumption function from Exhibit 27-9. The lower line shows the consumption function if taxes must first be paid on income, and then consumption is based on after-tax income. The first column of the table shows income. The second column shows taxes, which in this example are 30% of income. The third column takes income and subtracts taxes to calculate after-tax income. The fourth column calculates consumption based on after-tax income, by multiplying after-tax income by the MPC of .8 and adding 600. The final column calculates saving, given that consumption plus saving plus taxes must equal income. When taxes are included, each additional rise of income results in a smaller increase in consumption, which is why the consumption function with taxes included is flatter than when taxes are not included. In this example, taxes are .3 of income, MPC is .8 of after-tax income, and MPS is .2 of after-tax income.

unchanging. It means only that government spending changes for political reasons, rather than shifting in a predictable way with the current size of the real GDP shown on the horizontal axis.

The situation of taxes is different because taxes often rise or fall with the size of the economy. For example, income taxes are based on the level of income earned and sales taxes are based on the amount of sales made, and both income and sales tend to be higher when the economy is growing and lower when the economy is in a recession. For the purposes of constructing the basic Keynesian cross model, it is helpful to view taxes as a proportionate share of GDP. (Specific taxes will be discussed in more detail in Chapter 32.) In the United States, for example, taking federal, state, and local taxes together, government typically collects about 30–35% of income as taxes.

Exhibit 27-12 revises the earlier table on the consumption function so that it takes taxes into account. The first column shows national income. The second column calculates taxes, which in this example are set at a rate of 30%, or .3. The third column shows after-tax income; that is, total income minus taxes. The fourth column then calculates consumption in the same manner as before; multiply after-tax income by .8, representing the marginal propensity to consume, and then add 600, for the amount that would be consumed even if income was zero. When taxes are included, each additional dollar of income results in a smaller increase in consumption—because some of that income is now paid as taxes. For this reason, the consumption function with taxes included is flatter than the consumption function without taxes.

Exports and Imports as a Function of National Income

The export function, which shows how exports change with the level of a country's own real GDP, is drawn as a horizontal line, as in the example in Exhibit 27-13*a* where exports are drawn at a level of 840. Again, as in the case of investment spending and government spending, drawing the export function as horizontal does not imply that exports never change. It just means that they don't change because of what is on the horizontal axis—that is, a country's own level of domestic production—and instead are shaped by the level

EXHIBIT 27-13 The Export and Import Functions

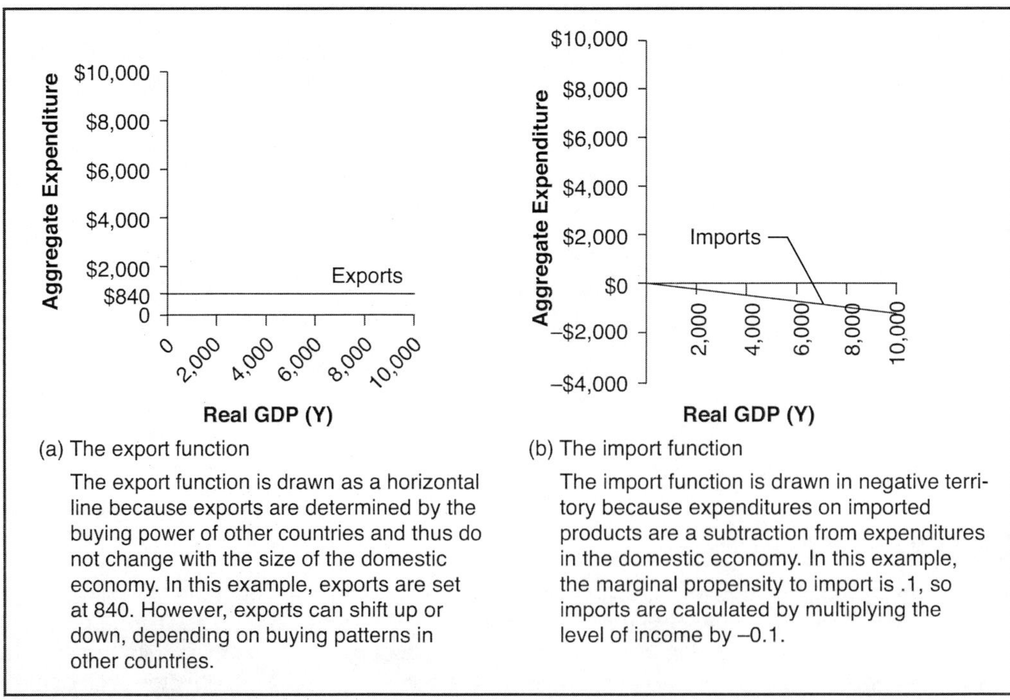

(a) The export function

The export function is drawn as a horizontal line because exports are determined by the buying power of other countries and thus do not change with the size of the domestic economy. In this example, exports are set at 840. However, exports can shift up or down, depending on buying patterns in other countries.

(b) The import function

The import function is drawn in negative territory because expenditures on imported products are a subtraction from expenditures in the domestic economy. In this example, the marginal propensity to import is .1, so imports are calculated by multiplying the level of income by –0.1.

of aggregate demand in other countries. More demand for exports from other countries would cause the export function to shift up; less demand for exports from other countries would cause it to shift down.

marginal propensity to import (MPI): The share of an additional dollar of income that goes to imports.

Imports are drawn in the Keynesian cross diagram as a downward-sloping line, with the downward slope determined by the **marginal propensity to import**, or **MPI**, out of national income. In Exhibit 27-13*b*, the marginal propensity to import is .1. Thus, if real GDP is 5,000, imports are 500; if national income is 6,000, imports are 600, and so on. The import function is drawn as downward sloping and negative because it represents a subtraction from the aggregate expenditures in the domestic economy. A change in the marginal propensity to import, perhaps as a result of changes in preferences or because of a change in relative prices of imported goods, would alter the slope of the import function.

Building the Combined Aggregate Expenditure Function

All the components of aggregate demand—consumption, investment, government spending, and the trade balance—are now in place to build the Keynesian cross diagram. Exhibit 27-14 builds up an aggregate expenditure function, based on the numerical illustrations of C, I, G, X, and M that have been used throughout this section. The first three columns under Exhibit 27-14 are lifted from the earlier Exhibit 27-12, which showed how to bring taxes into the consumption function. The first column is real GDP or national income, which is what appears on the horizontal axis of the income-expenditure diagram. The second column calculates after-tax income, based on the assumption in this case that 30% of real GDP is collected in taxes. The third column is based on an MPC of .8, so that as after-tax income rises by 700 from one row to the next, consumption rises by 560 (700 × .8) from one row to the next. Investment, government spending, and exports do not change with the level of current national income. In the previous discussion, investment was 500, government spending was 1,300, and exports were 840, for a total of 2,640. This total is shown in the fourth column. Imports are .1 of real GDP in this example, and the level of imports is calculated in the fifth column. The final column, aggregate expenditures, sums up C + I + G + X – M. This aggregate expenditure line is illustrated in Exhibit 27-14.

The aggregate expenditure function is conceptually formed by stacking on top of each other the consumption function (with taxes included), the investment function, the government spending function, the export function, and the import function. The point at which the aggregate expenditure function intersects the vertical axis will be determined

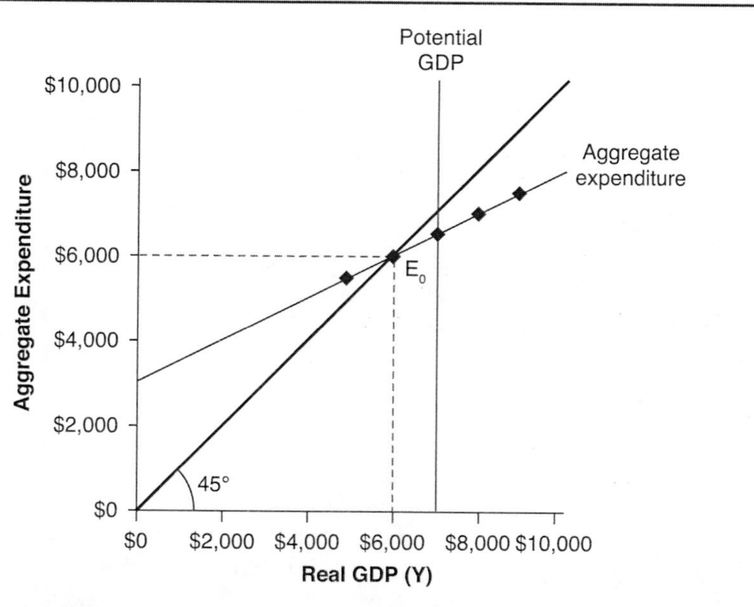

National Income	After-Tax Income	Consumption	Government Spending + Investment + Exports	Imports	Aggregate Expenditure
$3,000	$2,100	$2,280	$2,640	$300	$4,570
$4,000	$2,800	$2,840	$2,640	$400	$5,080
$5,000	$3,500	$3,400	$2,640	$500	$5,540
$6,000	$4,200	$3,960	$2,640	$600	$6,000
$7,000	$4,900	$4,520	$2,640	$700	$6,460
$8,000	$5,600	$5,080	$2,640	$800	$6,920
$9,000	$6,300	$5,640	$2,640	$900	$7,380

EXHIBIT 27-14 A Keynesian Cross Diagram

The table starts with national income on the left, and then shows after-tax consumption, government spending, investment, exports, and imports, which combine to form aggregate expenditure. On the graph, each combination of national income and aggregate expenditure is graphed. The equilibrium occurs where aggregate expenditure is equal to national income; on the graph, this occurs where the aggregate expenditure schedule crosses the 45° line, at a level of $6,000. Potential GDP in this example is $7,000, so the equilibrium is occurring at a level of output or real GDP below the potential GDP level.

by the levels of investment, government, and export expenditures—which do not vary with national income. The upward slope of the aggregate expenditure function will be determined by the marginal propensity to save, the tax rate, and the marginal propensity to import. A higher marginal propensity to save, a higher tax rate, and a higher marginal propensity to import will all make the slope of the aggregate expenditure function flatter—because out of any extra income, more is going to savings or taxes or imports and less to spending on domestic goods and services.

The equilibrium occurs where national income is equal to aggregate expenditure, which is shown on the graph as the point where the aggregate expenditure schedule crosses the 45° line. In this example, the equilibrium occurs at 6,000. This equilibrium can also be read off the table under the figure; it's the level of national income where aggregate expenditure is equal to national income.

Equilibrium in the Keynesian Cross Model

With the aggregate expenditure line in place, the next step is to relate it to the two other elements of the Keynesian cross diagram. Thus, the first subsection interprets the intersection of the aggregate expenditure function and the 45° line, while the next subsection relates this point of intersection to the potential GDP line.

Where Equilibrium Occurs

The point where the aggregate expenditure line that is constructed from C + I + G + X – M crosses the 45-degree line will be the equilibrium for the economy. It is the only point on the aggregate expenditure line where the total amount being spent on aggregate demand

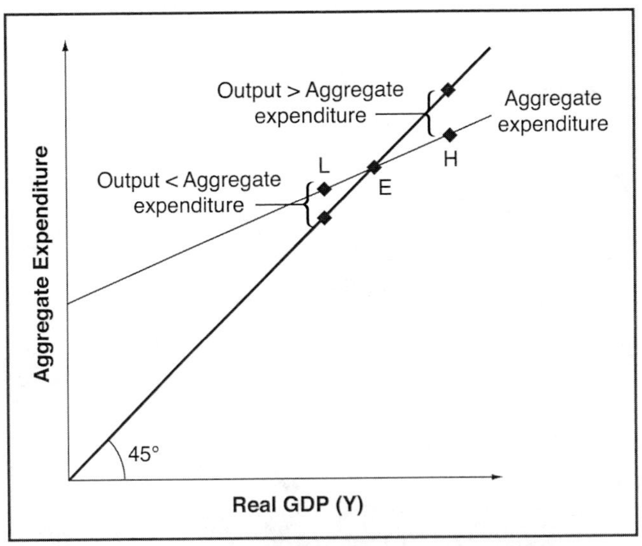

EXHIBIT 27-15 Equilibrium in the Keynesian Cross Diagram

If output was above the equilibrium level, at H, then the real output is greater than the aggregate expenditure in the economy. This pattern cannot hold in the long term because it would mean that goods are produced but piling up unsold. If output was below the equilibrium level at L, then aggregate expenditure would be greater than output. This pattern cannot hold in the long run, either, because it would mean that spending exceeds the number of goods being produced. Only point E can be an equilibrium, where output or national income and aggregate expenditure are equal. The equilibrium E must lie on the 45° line, which is the set of points where national income and aggregate expenditure are equal to each other.

is in balance with the total level of production. In Exhibit 27-14, this point of equilibrium E happens at 6,000, which can be read off the table or seen in the figure.

The meaning of "equilibrium" remains the same; that is, equilibrium is a point of balance where no incentive exists to shift away from that outcome. To understand why the point of intersection between the aggregate expenditure function and the 45-degree line is a macroeconomic equilibrium, consider what would happen if an economy found itself to the right of the equilibrium point E, say point H in Exhibit 27-15 where output is higher than the equilibrium. At point H, the level of aggregate expenditure is below the 45-degree line, so that the level of aggregate expenditure in the economy is less than the level of output. As a result, at point H output is piling up unsold—not a sustainable state of affairs in the long run.

Conversely, consider the situation where the level of output is at point L, where real output is lower than the equilibrium. In that case, the level of aggregate demand in the economy is above the 45-degree line, indicating that the level of aggregate expenditure in the economy is greater than the level of output. When the level of aggregate demand has emptied the store shelves, it cannot be sustained in the long run, either. Thus, the equilibrium must be the point where the amount produced and the amount spent are in balance, at the intersection of the aggregate expenditure function and the 45-degree line.

Recessionary and Inflationary Gaps

In the Keynesian cross diagram, if the aggregate expenditure line intersects the 45-degree line at the level of potential GDP, then the economy is in sound shape. There is no recession, and unemployment is low. But there's no guarantee that the equilibrium will occur at the potential GDP level of output. The equilibrium might be either higher or lower.

For example, Exhibit 27-16*a* illustrates a situation where the aggregate expenditure line intersects the 45-degree line at point E_0, which is a real GDP of 6,000, which is below the potential GDP of 7,000. In this situation, the level of aggregate expenditure is too low for GDP to reach its full employment level, and unemployment will occur. The distance

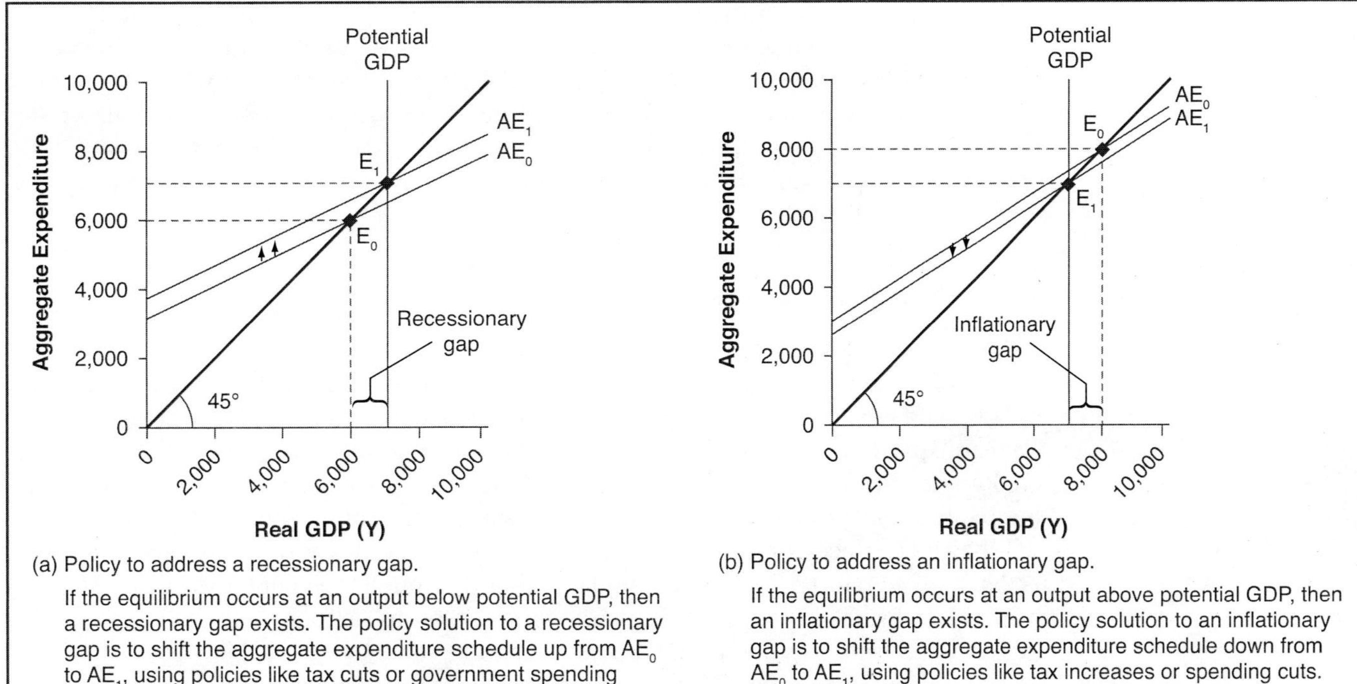

(a) Policy to address a recessionary gap.

If the equilibrium occurs at an output below potential GDP, then a recessionary gap exists. The policy solution to a recessionary gap is to shift the aggregate expenditure schedule up from AE$_0$ to AE$_1$, using policies like tax cuts or government spending increases. Then the new equilibrium E$_1$ occurs at potential GDP.

(b) Policy to address an inflationary gap.

If the equilibrium occurs at an output above potential GDP, then an inflationary gap exists. The policy solution to an inflationary gap is to shift the aggregate expenditure schedule down from AE$_0$ to AE$_1$, using policies like tax increases or spending cuts. Then, the new equilibrium E$_1$ occurs at potential GDP.

EXHIBIT 27-16 Addressing Recessionary and Inflationary Gaps

between an output level like E$_0$ that is below potential GDP and the level of potential GDP is called a **recessionary gap.** Because the equilibrium level of real GDP is so low, firms will not wish to hire the full employment number of workers. Unemployment will be high.

recessionary gap: The gap in output between an economy in recession and potential GDP.

What might cause a recessionary gap? Anything that shifts the aggregate expenditure line down is a potential cause of recession, including a decline in consumption, a rise in savings, a fall in investment, a drop in government spending or a rise in taxes, or a fall in exports or a rise in imports. Moreover, an economy that is at equilibrium with a recessionary gap may just stay there and suffer high unemployment for a long time; remember, the meaning of equilibrium is that there is no particular adjustment of prices or quantities in the economy to chase the recession away.

The appropriate response to a recessionary gap is for the government to reduce taxes or increase spending so that the aggregate expenditure function shifts up from AE$_0$ to AE$_1$. When this shift occurs, the new equilibrium E$_1$ now occurs at potential GDP as shown in Exhibit 27-16*a*.

Conversely, Exhibit 27-16*b* shows a situation where the aggregate expenditure schedule AE$_0$ intersects the 45-degree line above potential GDP. The gap between the level of real GDP at the equilibrium E$_0$ and potential GDP is called an **inflationary gap**. The inflationary gap also requires a bit of interpreting. After all, a naïve reading of the Keynesian cross figure might suggest that if the aggregate expenditure function is just pushed up high enough, real GDP can be as large as desired—even doubling or tripling the potential GDP level of the economy! This implication is clearly wrong. An economy faces some supply-side limits on how much it can produce at a given time with its existing quantities of workers, physical and human capital, technology, and market institutions.

inflationary gap: The gap between real GDP and potential GDP, when the level of output is above the level of potential GDP.

The inflationary gap should be interpreted not as a literal prediction of how large real GDP will be, but as a statement of how much extra aggregate expenditure is in the economy beyond what is needed to reach potential GDP. An inflationary gap suggests that because the economy can't produce enough goods and services to absorb this level of aggregate expenditures, the spending will instead cause an inflationary increase in the price level. In this way, even though changes in the price level do not appear explicitly in the Keynesian cross equation, the notion of inflation is implicit in the concept of the inflationary gap.

The appropriate Keynesian response to an inflationary gap is shown in Exhibit 27-16*b*. The original intersection of aggregate expenditure line AE_0 and the 45-degree line occurs at 8,000, which is above the level of potential GDP at 7,000. If AE_0 shifts down to AE_1, so that the new equilibrium is at E_1, then the economy will be at potential GDP without pressures for inflationary price increases. The government can achieve a downward shift in aggregate expenditure by increasing taxes on consumers or firms, or by reducing government expenditures.

The Multiplier Effect

The Keynesian policy prescription has one final twist. Assume that for a certain economy, the intersection of the aggregate expenditure function and the 45-degree line is at a GDP of 700, while the level of potential GDP for this economy is 800. By how much does government spending need to be increased so that the economy reaches the full employment GDP? The obvious answer might seem to be 800 – 700 = 100, so raise government spending by 100. But that answer is incorrect. A change of 100 in government expenditures will have an effect of more than 100 on the equilibrium level of real GDP. The reason is that a change in aggregate expenditures circles through the economy: households buy from firms, firms pay workers and suppliers, workers and suppliers buy goods from other firms, those firms pay their workers and suppliers, and so on. In this way, the original change in aggregate expenditures is actually spent more than once.

How Does the Multiplier Work?

multiplier effect: How a given change in expenditure cycles repeatedly through the economy, and thus has a larger final impact than the initial change.

The process in which an original increase in aggregate expenditure cycles repeatedly through the economy and thus has a larger result is called the **multiplier effect**. To understand how the multiplier effect works, return to the example in which the current equilibrium in the Keynesian cross diagram is a real GDP of 700 but the government, seeking to raise the equilibrium to a potential GDP of 800, increases government spending by 100. When the government first spends 100, it does indeed add 100 to aggregate expenditures—but this increase is only the first step. When the government increases spending by 100, someone in the economy receives that spending and can treat it as income. Assume that those who receive this income pay 30% in taxes, save 10% of after-tax income, spend 10% of total income on imports, and then spend the rest on domestically produced goods and services. As shown in the calculations in Exhibit 27-17, out of the original 100 in government spending in the first round, 53 is then cycled back into purchases of domestically produced goods and services in the spent second round. Moreover, a pattern begins. The 53 that was cycled back into additional expenditures is also income to someone, somewhere in the economy. Those who receive that income also pay 30% in taxes, save 10% of after-tax income, and spend 10% of total income on imports, as shown in Exhibit 27-18, so that an additional 28.09 (i.e., 0.53 × 53) is spent in the third round. The people who receive that income then pay taxes, save, and buy imports, and the amount spent in the fourth round is 14.8877 (i.e., .53 × 28.09).

Thus, over the first four rounds of aggregate expenditures, the impact of the original increase in government spending of 100 creates a rise in aggregate expenditures of 100 + 53 + 28.09 + 14.8877 = 195.9777. Exhibit 27-17 shows these total aggregate expenditures after these first four rounds, and then the figure shows the total aggregate expenditures after 30 rounds. The additional boost to aggregate expenditures is shrinking in each round of consumption. After about 10 rounds, the additional increments are very small indeed—nearly invisible to the naked eye. After 30 rounds, the additional increments in each round are so small that they have no practical consequence. After 30 periods, the cumulative value of the initial boost in aggregate expenditure is approximately 213. Thus, the government spending increase of 100 eventually, after many cycles, produced an increase of 213 in aggregate expenditure and real GDP. The definition of the multiplier is:

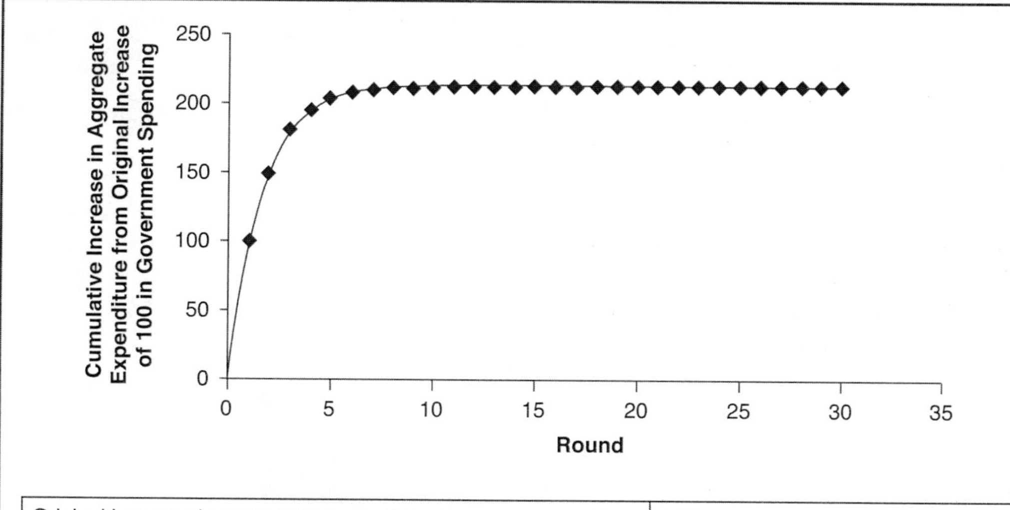

Original increase in aggregate expenditure from government spending	100
Which is income to people throughout the economy: Pay 30% in taxes. Save 10% of after-tax income. Spend 10% of income on imports. Second-round increase of . . .	70 – 7 – 10 = 53
Which is 53 of income to people through the economy: Pay 30% in taxes. Save 10% of after-tax income. Spend 10% of income on imports. Third-round increase of . . .	37.1 – 3.71 – 5.3 = 28.09
Which is 28.09 of income to people through the economy: Pay 30% in taxes. Save 10% of after-tax income. Spend 10% of income on imports. Fourth-round increase of . . .	19.663 – 1.96633 – 2.809 = 14.8877

EXHIBIT 27-17 The Multiplier Effect

An original increase of government spending of 100 causes a rise in aggregate expenditure of 100. But that 100 is income to others in the economy, and after they save, pay taxes, and buy imports, they spend 53 of that 100 in a second round. In turn, that 53 is income to others. Thus, the original government spending of 100 is multiplied by these cycles of spending, but the impact of each successive cycle gets smaller and smaller. Given the numbers in this example, the original government spending increase of 100 raises aggregate expenditure by 213; therefore, the multiplier in this example is 213/100 = 2.13.

$$\text{Multiplier} = \frac{\text{Total increase in aggregate expenditures}}{\text{Original increase in expenditures}}$$

In this example, the **multiplier** is 213/100 = 2.13.

multiplier: Total increase in aggregate expenditures divided by the original increase in expenditures.

Calculating the Multiplier

Fortunately for everyone who isn't carrying around a computer with a spreadsheet program to project the impact of an original increase in expenditures over 20 or 50 or 100 cycles of spending, there is a formula for calculating the multiplier. The formula begins by calculating what fraction F of expenditures is recycled at each stage. To calculate this fraction, start off with a marginal dollar of income, and then adjust for how much money that flows into taxes, savings, and imports and thus doesn't become expenditures in the next round. In the example just presented, 30% of a marginal dollar goes to taxes, 10% of the after-tax income goes to savings, and 10% of income goes to imports. Thus, the relevant calculation looks like this:

$$\text{Fraction of expenditures recycled} = 1 - \text{What goes into taxes} - \text{What goes into savings} - \text{What goes into imports}$$

$$F = (1 - .3) - .1(1 - .3) - .1$$

$$F = .7 - .07 - .1 = .53$$

Given this fraction F, the equation for the multiplier (which is derived algebraically in the box) is:

$$\text{Multiplier} = \frac{1}{1 - F}$$

EXHIBIT 27-18 The Multiplier Effect in an Expenditure-Output Model

The power of the multiplier effect is that an increase in expenditure has a larger increase on the equilibrium output. The increase in expenditure is the vertical increase from AE_0 to AE_1. However, the increase in equilibrium output, shown on the horizontal axis, is clearly larger.

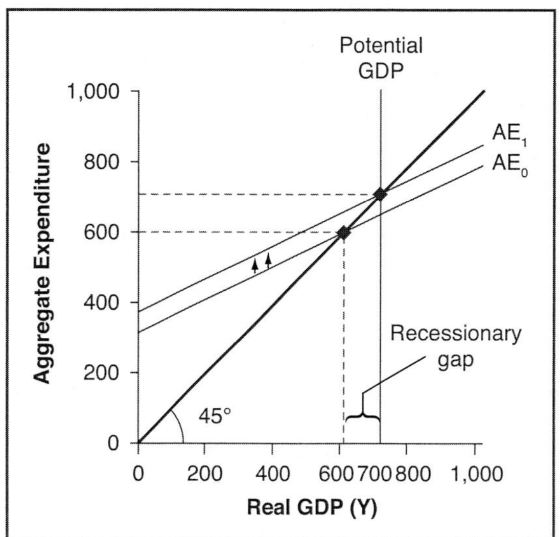

If F = .53, then the multiplier would be 1/(1 – .53) = 1/.47 = 2.13. Thus, an original increase in expenditures of 100, when multiplied by 2.13, will lead to an increase in aggregate expenditure of 213. Not coincidentally, this result is exactly what was calculated in Exhibit 27-18 after many rounds of expenditures cycling through the economy.

The size of the multiplier is determined by what proportion of the marginal dollar of income goes into taxes, saving, and imports. These three factors are known as "leakages," because they determine how much demand "leaks out" in each round of the multiplier effect. If the leakages are relatively small, then each successive rounds of the multiplier effect will have larger amounts of demand, and the multiplier will be high. Conversely, if the leakages are relatively large, then any initial change in demand will diminish more

Deriving the Multiplier Formula

Say that the original change in aggregate expenditures is N. The fractional amount of how much expenditure is cycled back into the economy in the next stage—determined by tax rates, savings, and imports—is F. Then, the total aggregate expenditure T that is triggered by the original change N as it cycles through the economy will be

$$N + NF^1 + NF^2 + NF^3 + NF^4 + \dots = T$$

If the N term is factored out, then the formula for the total expenditure T can be rewritten as

$$N(1 + F^1 + F^2 + F^3 + F^4 + \dots) = T$$

The term in the parentheses is equal to the multiplier; it's the amount by which the original change in aggregate expenditures N is multiplied to get the change in equilibrium output T. Set the multiplier equal to M:

$$M = 1 + F^1 + F^2 + F^3 + F^4 + \dots$$

This multiplier is an "infinite geometric series," a term you may have heard in a mathematics class. We want to express the multiplier in a simpler form that doesn't involve an infinite series. To accomplish this, we'll use a computational trick. Multiply both sides of the multiplier formula by F.

$$FM = F(1 + F^1 + F^2 + F^3 + F^4 + \dots)$$
$$FM = F^1 + F^2 + F^3 + F^4 + \dots$$

Then take the original equation for the multiplier and subtract the equation for the multiplier multiplied by F; that is, subtract the left-hand side of one equation from the other and the right-hand side of one equation from the other. In this calculation, the infinite series portion of one equation subtracts from the infinite series portion of the other equation and disappears, leaving only a value of 1 behind. Then manipulate the algebra so that the multiplier M is alone on the left-hand side.

$$M - FM = (1 + F^1 + F^2 + F^3 + F^4 + \dots) - (F^1 + F^2 + F^3 + F^4 + \dots) = 1$$
$$M - FM = 1$$
$$M(1 - F) = 1$$
$$M = 1/(1 - F)$$

This formula is the multiplier equation used in the text.

quickly in the second, third, and later rounds, and the multiplier will be small. Changes in the size of the leakages—a change in the marginal propensity to save, the tax rate, or the marginal propensity to import—will change the size of the multiplier.

Calculating Keynesian Policy Interventions

Now return yet again to the original question of this section: What if the intersection of the aggregate expenditure function and the 45-degree line in a Keynesian cross diagram was happening at 700, but potential GDP were 800. How much should government spending be increased to produce a total increase in real GDP of 100? If the goal is to increase aggregate demand by 100, and the multiplier is 2.13, then the increase in government spending that would be necessary to achieve that goal would be 100/2.13 = 47. That is, an increase in government spending of approximately 47, when combined with a multiplier of 2.13 (which is, remember, based on the specific assumptions about tax, saving, and import rates), produces an overall increase in real GDP of 100.

The multiplier does not just affect government spending, but applies to any change in the economy. Say that business confidence declines and investment falls off, or that the economy of a leading trading partner slows down so that export sales decline. These changes will reduce aggregate expenditures, and then will have an even larger effect on real GDP because of the multiplier effect.

The multiplier effect is also visible on the Keynesian cross diagram. Exhibit 27-18 shows the example we have been discussing: a recessionary gap with an equilibrium of 600, potential GDP of 700, the slope of the aggregate expenditure function AE_0 determined by the assumptions that taxes are .3 of income, savings are .1 of after-tax income, and imports are .1 of before-tax income. At AE_1, the aggregate expenditure function is

Using the Multiplier to Analyze the Local Economic Impact of Professional Sports

What effect does a professional sports team have on a local economy? The multiplier can be used to gain insight into this issue. Most professional athletes and owners of sports teams are rich enough to owe a lot of taxes, so let's say that 40% of any marginal income they earn is paid in taxes. Because athletes are often high earners with short careers, let's assume that they save one-third of their after-tax income. However, many professional athletes don't live year-round in the city in which they play, so let's say that one-half of the money that they do spend is spent outside the local area.

Now consider the impact of money spent at local entertainment venues other than professional sports. While the owners of these other businesses may be comfortably middle-income, few of them are in the economic stratosphere of professional athletes. Because their incomes are lower, so are their taxes; say that they pay only 35% of their marginal income in taxes. They don't have the same ability, or need, to save as much as professional athletes, so let's assume their MPC is just 0.8. Finally, because more of them live locally, they will spend a higher proportion of their income on local goods—say, 65%.

If these general assumptions hold true, then money spent on professional sports will have less local economic impact than money spent on other forms of entertainment. For professional athletes, out of a dollar earned, 40% goes to taxes, leaving 60 cents. Of that 60 cents, one-third is saved, leaving 40 cents, and half is spent outside the area, leaving 20 cents. Only 20 cents of each dollar is cycled into the local economy in the first round. For locally owned entertainment, out of a dollar earned, 35 cents goes to taxes, leaving 65 cents. Of the rest, .2 is saved, leaving 52 cents, and of that amount, 65% is spent in the local area, so that 33.8 cents of each dollar of income is recycled into the local economy.

Now make the plausible assumption that within their household budgets, people have a fixed amount to spend on entertainment. If this assumption holds true, then money spent attending professional sports events is money that was not spent on other entertainment options in a given metropolitan area. Since the multiplier is lower for professional sports than for other local entertainment options, the arrival of professional sports to a city would reallocate entertainment spending in a way that causes the local economy to shrink, rather than to grow.

moved up to reach potential GDP. Now compare the vertical shift upwards in the aggregate expenditure function, which is 47, with the horizontal shift outward in real GDP, which is 100 (as these numbers were calculated earlier). The rise in real GDP is more than double the rise in the aggregate expenditure function. (Similarly, if you look back at Exhibit 27-16, you will see that the vertical movements in the aggregate expenditure functions are smaller than the change in equilibrium output that is produced on the horizontal axis. Again, this is the multiplier effect at work.) In this way, the power of the multiplier is apparent in the income-expenditure graph, as well as in the arithmetic calculation.

Multiplier Trade-offs: Stability vs. the Power of Macroeconomic Policy

Is an economy healthier with a high multiplier or a low one? With a high multiplier, any change in aggregate demand will tend to be substantially magnified, and so the economy will be more unstable. With a low multiplier, by contrast, changes in aggregate demand will not be multiplied much, so the economy will tend to be more stable.

However, with a low multiplier, government policy changes in taxes or spending will tend to have less effect on the equilibrium level of real output. With a higher multiplier, government policies to raise or reduce aggregate expenditures will have a larger effect. Thus, a low multiplier means a more stable economy, but also weaker government macroeconomic policy, while a high multiplier means a more volatile economy, but also an economy in which government macroeconomic policy is more powerful.

Is Keynesian Economics Pro-Market or Anti-Market?

Ever since the birth of Keynesian economics in the 1930s, controversy has simmered over the extent to which government should play an active role in managing the economy. In the aftermath of the human devastation and misery of the Great Depression, many people—including many economists—lost their confidence in a market-oriented economic system. Some supporters of Keynesian economics advocated a high degree of government planning in all parts of the economy.

However, John Maynard Keynes himself was careful to separate the issue of aggregate demand from the issue of how well individual markets worked. He argued that individual markets for goods and services were appropriate and useful, but that sometimes that level of aggregate demand was just too low. For example, Keynes argued that when 10 million people are willing and able to work, but one million of them are unemployed, individual markets may be doing a perfectly good job of allocating the efforts of the 9 million workers—the problem is that insufficient aggregate demand exists to support jobs for all 10 million. Thus, Keynes believed that while government should assure that overall level of aggregate demand is sufficient for an economy to reach full employment, this task did not imply that the government should attempt to set prices and wages throughout the economy, nor to take over and manage large corporations or entire industries directly.

Even if one accepts the Keynesian economic theory, a number of practical questions remain. In the real world, can government economists identify potential GDP accurately? Is a desired increase in aggregate demand better accomplished by a tax cut or by an increase in government spending? Given the inevitable delays and uncertainties as policies are enacted into law, is it reasonable to expect that the government can implement Keynesian economics? Can fixing a recession really be just as simple as pumping up aggregate demand? Chapters 32–33 on government tax and spending policy will probe these practical issues. The Keynesian approach, with its focus on aggregate demand and sticky prices, has proved useful in understanding how the economy fluctuates in the short run and why recessions and cyclical unemployment occur. In the next chapter, we'll consider some of the shortcomings of the Keynesian approach and why it is not especially well-suited for long-run macroeconomic analysis.

Key Concepts and Summary

1. Keynesian economics is based on two main ideas: a) aggregate demand is more likely than aggregate supply to be the primary cause of a short-run economic event like a recession because aggregate supply usually moves slowly; b) wages and prices can be sticky, and so in an economic downturn unemployment can result.
2. **Menu costs** are the costs of changing prices. They include the internal costs a business faces in changing prices in terms of labeling, record keeping, accounting, and also the costs of communicating the price change to (possibly unhappy) customers.
3. The aggregate demand curve will shift based on movements in consumption, investment, government spending or taxes, exports, and imports. Consumption will change for a number of reasons, including movements in income, taxes, expectations about future incomes, and changes in wealth levels. Investment will change in response to its expected rate of return, which in turn is shaped by the real interest rate, the creation of new technologies, expectations about future economic growth, the price of key inputs, and tax incentives for investment. Government spending and taxes are determined by political considerations. Exports and imports change according to relative growth rates and prices between two economies.
4. A **Phillips curve** shows the trade-off between unemployment and inflation in an economy. From a Keynesian viewpoint, the Phillips curve should slope down so that higher unemployment means lower inflation, and vice versa. However, a downward-sloping Phillips curve is a short-term relationship that may shift after a few years.
5. Keynesian macroeconomic policy suggests that aggregate demand should be increased (shifted to the right) when the economy is in recession, and decreased (shifted to the left) when the economy faces a situation of high inflation.
6. The **expenditure-output model** or "Keynesian cross diagram" shows how the level of aggregate expenditure (on the vertical axis) varies with the level of economic output (shown on the horizontal axis). Since the value of all macroeconomic output also represents income to someone somewhere else in the economy, the horizontal axis can also be interpreted as **national income (Y)**. The equilibrium in the diagram will occur where the aggregate expenditure line crosses the 45-degree line, which represents the set of points where aggregate expenditure in the economy is equal to output (or national income). Equilibrium in a Keynesian cross diagram can happen at potential GDP, or below or above that level.
7. The **consumption function** shows the upward-sloping relationship between national income and consumption. The **marginal propensity to consume (MPC)** is the amount consumed out of an additional dollar of income. A higher marginal propensity to consume means a steeper consumption function; a lower marginal propensity to consume means a flatter consumption function. The **marginal propensity to save (MPS)** is the amount saved out of an additional dollar of income. It is necessarily true that MPC + MPS = 1.
8. The investment function is drawn as a flat line, showing that investment in the current year doesn't change with regard to the current level of national income. However, the investment function will move up and down based on the expected rate of return in the future.
9. Government spending is drawn as a horizontal line in the Keynesian cross diagram because its level is determined by political considerations, not by the current level of income in the economy. Taxes in the basic Keynesian cross model are taken into account by adjusting the consumption function.
10. The export function is drawn as a horizontal line in the Keynesian cross diagram because exports don't change as a result of changes in domestic income, but they move as a result of changes in foreign income, as well as changes in exchange rates. The import function is drawn as a downward-sloping line because imports rise with national income, but imports are a subtraction from aggregate demand. Thus, a higher level of imports means a lower level of expenditure on domestic goods. The **marginal propensity to import (MPI)** can be changed by movements in exchange rates.
11. In a Keynesian cross diagram, the equilibrium may be at a level below potential GDP, which is called a **recessionary gap**, or at a level above potential GDP, which is called an **inflationary gap**.
12. The **multiplier effect** describes how the impact of an original change in aggregate demand is multiplied as it cycles repeatedly through the economy. The size of the **multiplier** is determined by three leakages: spending on savings, taxes, and imports. The multiplier is defined as:

$$\text{Multiplier} = \frac{\text{Total increase in aggregate expenditures}}{\text{Original increase in expenditures}}$$

13. An economy with a lower multiplier is more stable—it is less affected either by economic events or by government policy than an economy with a higher multiplier.
14. The Keynesian macroeconomic prescription for adjusting aggregate demand higher or lower, as needed, need not imply that the government should be passing laws or regulations that set prices and quantities in microeconomic markets.

Review Questions

1. From a Keynesian point of view, which is more likely to cause a recession: aggregate demand or aggregate supply?
2. Why do sticky wages and prices increase the impact of an economic downturn on unemployment and recession?
3. What do economists mean by "menu costs"?
4. Name some economic events, not related to government policy, which could cause aggregate demand to shift.
5. Name some government policies that could cause aggregate demand to shift.
6. What trade-off is shown by a Phillips curve?
7. Would you expect to see long-run data trace out a stable downward-sloping Phillips curve?
8. What is the Keynesian prescription for recession? For inflation?
9. What is on the axes of an expenditure-output diagram?
10. What does the 45-degree line show?
11. What determines the slope of a consumption function?
12. What is the marginal propensity to consume, and how is it related to the marginal propensity to save?
13. Why are the investment function, the government spending function, and the export function all drawn as flat lines?
14. Why does the import function slope down? What is the marginal propensity to import?
15. What are the components on which the aggregate expenditure function is based?
16. Is the equilibrium in a Keynesian cross diagram usually expected to be at or near potential GDP?
17. What is an inflationary gap? A recessionary gap?
18. What is the multiplier effect?
19. Why are savings, taxes, and imports referred to as "leakages" in calculating the multiplier effect?
20. Will an economy with a high multiplier be more stable or less stable than an economy with a low multiplier in response to changes in the economy or in government policy?

CHAPTER

28

The Neoclassical Perspective

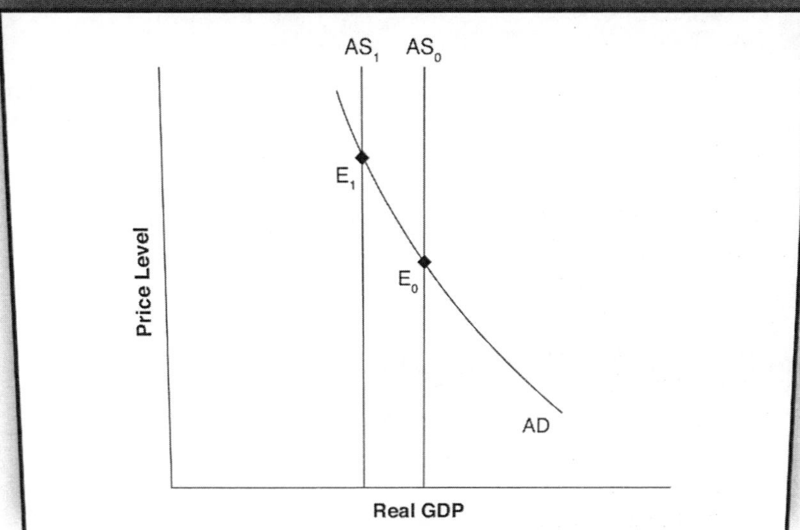

Chapter Outline

In Chicago, Illinois, the highest recorded temperature was 105° in July 1995, while the lowest recorded temperature was 27° below zero in January 1958. Understanding why these extreme weather patterns occurred would be interesting. But if you wanted to understand the typical weather pattern in Chicago, instead of focusing on one-time extremes, you need to look at the entire pattern of data over time.

A similar lesson applies to the study of macroeconomics. It's interesting to study extreme situations, like the Great Depression of the 1930s or what many have called the Great Recession of 2007–2009. But if you want to understand the typical patterns, you need to look at the long term. Consider the unemployment rate. Since 1955, the highest annual unemployment rate was 9.7% in 1982, and the lowest was 3.5% in 1969. But even as the U.S. unemployment rate rose during recessions and declined during periods of sustained growth, it kept returning to the general neighborhood of 5.0–5.5%. For example, in 1960, the unemployment rate was 5.5%. In 1973, the unemployment rate was 4.9%. In 1979, the unemployment rate was 5.8%. In 1989, the unemployment rate was 5.3%. In 1996, the unemployment rate was 5.6%. In 2004, the unemployment rate was 5.5%. In mid-2016, the unemployment rate was about 5.0%. When the nonpartisan Congressional Budget Office makes long-range economic forecasts, it assumes that the unemployment rate will return to 5.0%. From a long-run perspective, the economy seems to keep adjusting back to a roughly similar level of unemployment.

The neoclassical perspective on macroeconomics emphasizes that in the long run, the economy seems to rebound back to its potential GDP and its natural rate of unemployment. This chapter begins with two building blocks of neoclassical economics: (1) in the long run, the size of the economy is determined by potential GDP; and (2) in the long run, wages and prices will adjust in a flexible manner. A neoclassical version of the aggregate supply and aggregate demand model can illustrate these building blocks. If the neoclassical assumptions hold true—and some controversy exists over the extent to which they hold true—certain policy implications follow: for example, the government should focus more on long-term growth and on controlling inflation than on worrying about recession or cyclical unemployment. The overall theme is not that Keynesian economics is "wrong" while neoclassical economics is "right," nor vice versa, but rather that the two approaches complement each other, with Keynesian economics tending to be more useful for analyzing the macroeconomic short run and neoclassical economics more useful for the long run.

The Building Blocks of Neoclassical Analysis

Neoclassical economics argues that over time the economy adjusts back to its potential GDP level of output. The neoclassical approach is based on two key building blocks. First, over the long term, the expansion of potential GDP due to economic growth will determine the size of the economy. Second, even if the Keynesian assumption of price and wage stickiness is reasonable in the short run, over the longer run levels of prices and wages will adjust in a flexible manner. Let's consider these two claims in turn, and how they can be embodied in the aggregate supply–aggregate demand model.

The Importance of Potential GDP in the Long Run

Over the long run, the level of potential GDP determines the size of real GDP. For example, the U.S. GDP was approximately 25 times larger in 2000 than it was in 1900.

The reasons for this phenomenal change are based in how the productive power of labor, physical capital, and technological capabilities have expanded. The U.S. population rose by a factor of 3.6 in the twentieth century, from 76 million in 1900 to 275 million by 2000. The human capital of modern workers was far higher, too, because the education and skills of workers have risen dramatically. In 1900 only about one-eighth of the U.S. population had completed high school and just one person in 40 had completed a four-year college degree. By 2000, more than four-fifths of Americans had a high school degree and one out of four had a four-year college degree as well. The average amount of physical capital per worker has grown dramatically, but even more important, the technology available to modern workers is extraordinarily better than a century ago: cars, airplanes, electrical machinery, telephones, computers, chemical and biological advances, materials science, health care—the list of technological advances could run on and on. Horse-drawn plows were effective tools for farmers back in 1900, but a plow made of high-strength, low-weight materials mounted on the front of a powerful tractor, and combined with modern seeds, fertilizer, irrigation, and computerized knowledge of soils types, crop possibilities, and weather, is a truly remarkable combination of technologies. The number of bushels of corn that a U.S. farmer could grow on an acre of land was roughly six times higher in 2000 than it was in 1900.

Put these factors together—more workers, higher skill levels, larger amounts of physical capital per worker, and amazingly better technology—and potential GDP for the U.S. economy has clearly increased a great deal since 1900. Sure, in certain years the economy may fall below its potential GDP, perhaps because of a Keynesian lack of aggregate demand. From 2007 to 2009, the U.S. economy tumbled into recession. At other times, like in the late 1990s, the economy runs at potential GDP—or even slightly ahead—for a time. One line in Exhibit 28-1 shows the actual data for the increase in nominal GDP since 1960. The slightly smoother line shows the potential GDP since 1960 as estimated by the nonpartisan Congressional Budget Office. During periods of recession, like 1980–82, 1990–91, and 2007–2009, and often during the years immediately after recessions, actual GDP is below its potential. In the red-hot economy of the late 1990s, however, actual GDP was above its potential for a time. Most economic recessions and upswings are times when the economy is 1–3% below or above potential GDP. Clearly, short-run fluctuations around potential GDP do exist, but over the long run, the upward trend of potential GDP determines the size of the economy.

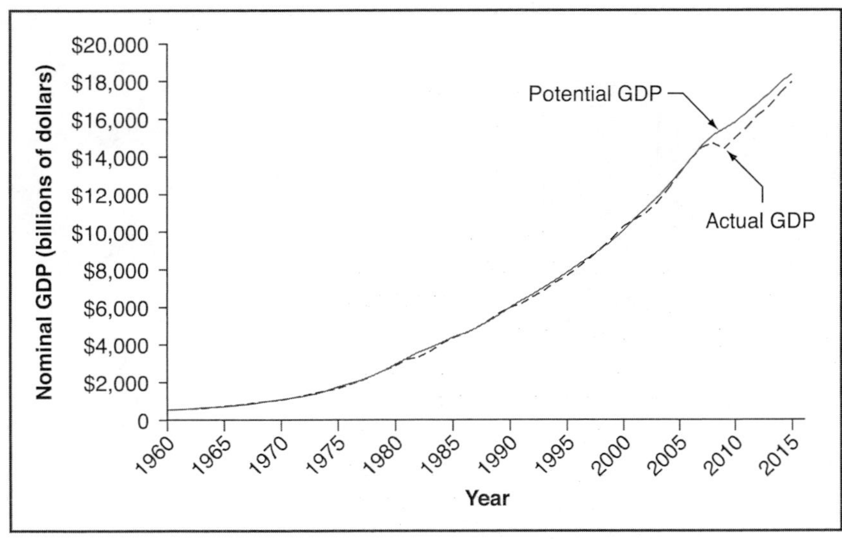

EXHIBIT 28-1 Potential and Actual GDP (in nominal dollars)

Actual GDP falls below potential GDP during and after recessions, like the recessions of 1980 and 1981–82, 1990–91, 2001, and 2007–2009—and may remain below potential GDP for at time as the economy begins to grow again. In other cases, actual GDP can be above potential GDP for a time, as occurred during the late 1990s.

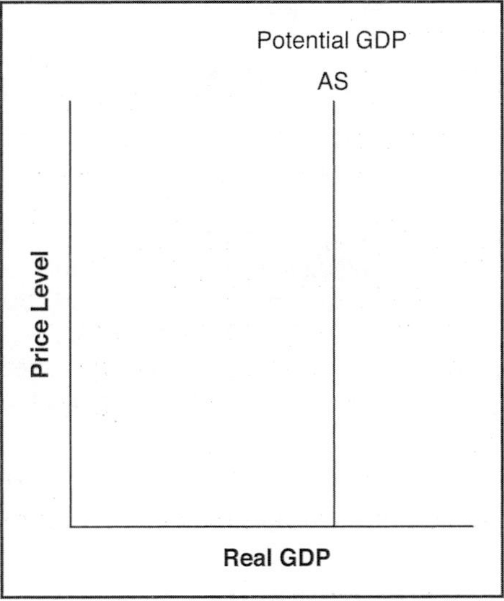

EXHIBIT 28-2 A Vertical AS Curve

In the neoclassical model, the aggregate supply curve is drawn as a vertical line at the level of potential GDP. If AS is vertical, then it determines the level of real output, no matter where the aggregate demand curve is drawn. Over time, the AS curve shifts to the right as productivity increases and potential GDP expands.

In the neoclassical version of the model of aggregate supply and aggregate demand, potential GDP is shown as a vertical line. Neoclassical economists who focus on potential GDP as the primary determinant of real GDP argue that the aggregate supply curve should look the same as potential GDP—that is, the aggregate supply curve is a vertical line drawn at the level of potential GDP, as shown in Exhibit 28-2. A vertical AS curve means that the level of aggregate supply (or potential GDP) will determine the real GDP of the economy, regardless of the level of aggregate demand. Over time, economic growth shifts potential GDP and the vertical AS curve gradually to the right.

The Role of Flexible Prices

How does the macroeconomy adjust back to its level of potential GDP in the long run? What if aggregate demand increases or decreases? The neoclassical view of how the macroeconomy adjusts is based on the insight that even if wages and prices are sticky in the short run, they can be flexible over time. To understand the neoclassical view of how the macroeconomy works, let's follow the connections from the short-run to the long-run situation.

The aggregate demand and aggregate supply diagram shown in Exhibit 28-3 shows two aggregate supply curves. The original aggregate supply curve AS_0 is a short-run or Keynesian AS curve. The vertical aggregate supply curve AS_N is the long-run or neoclassical AS curve, which is located at potential GDP. The original aggregate demand curve,

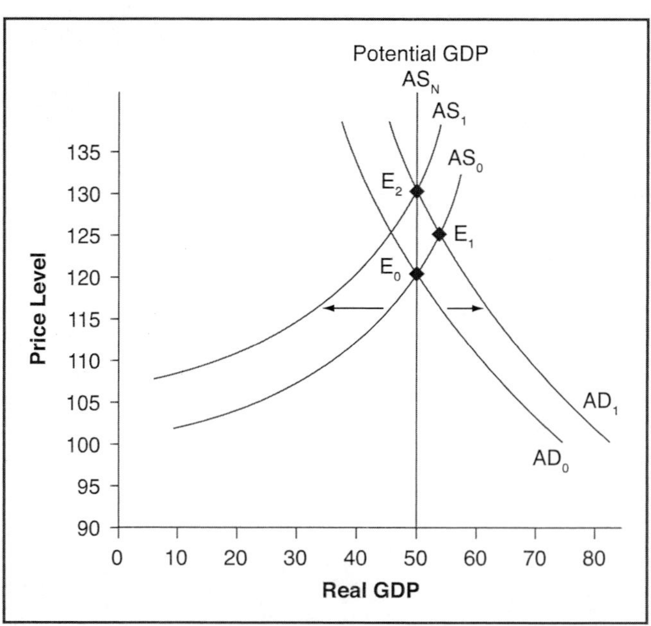

EXHIBIT 28-3 The Rebound to Potential GDP after AD Increases

The original equilibrium E_0, at an output level of 50 and a price level of 120, happens at the intersection of the aggregate demand curve AD_0 and the short-run aggregate supply curve AS_0. The output at E_0 is equal to potential GDP. Aggregate demand shifts right from AD_0 to AD_1. The new equilibrium is E_1, with a higher output level of 55 and an inflationary increase in the price level to 125. With unemployment rates unsustainably low, wages are bid up by eager employers. Higher wages are an economy-wide increase in the price of a key input, which shifts short-run aggregate supply to the left from AS_0 to AS_1. The new equilibrium E_2 is at the same original level of output, 50, but at a higher price level of 130. Thus, the long-run aggregate supply curve AS_N, which is vertical at the level of potential GDP, determines the level of real GDP in this economy in the long run.

labeled AD_0, is drawn so that the original equilibrium occurs at point E_0, at which point the economy is producing at its potential GDP.

Now imagine that some economic event boosts aggregate demand: perhaps a surge of export sales or a rise in business confidence that leads to more investment, or perhaps a policy decision like higher government spending or a tax cut that leads to additional aggregate demand. The short-run Keynesian analysis is that the rise in aggregate demand will shift the aggregate demand curve out to the right from AD_0 to AD_1, leading to a new equilibrium at point E_1 with higher output, lower unemployment, and pressure for an inflationary rise in the price level.

But in the long-run neoclassical analysis, the chain of economic consequences is just beginning. As economic output rises above potential GDP, the level of unemployment falls. Eager employers are trying to bid workers away from other companies and to encourage their current workers to exert more effort and to put in longer hours. This high demand for labor will drive up wages. Most workers have their salaries reviewed only once or twice a year, and so it will take time before the higher wages filter through the economy. But as wages do rise, it will mean a leftward shift in the short-run Keynesian aggregate supply curve back to AS_1 because the price of a major input to production has increased. The economy moves to a new equilibrium E_2. The new equilibrium has the same level of real GDP as did the original equilibrium E_0. However, an inflationary increase in the price level has occurred in the meantime.

This description of the short-run shift from E_0 to E_1 and the long-run shift from E_1 to E_2 is a step-by-step way of making a simple point: the economy can't sustain production above its potential GDP in the long run. An economy may produce above its level of potential GDP in the short run, under pressure from a surge in aggregate demand. But over the long run, that surge in aggregate demand ends up as an increase in the price level, not as a rise in output.

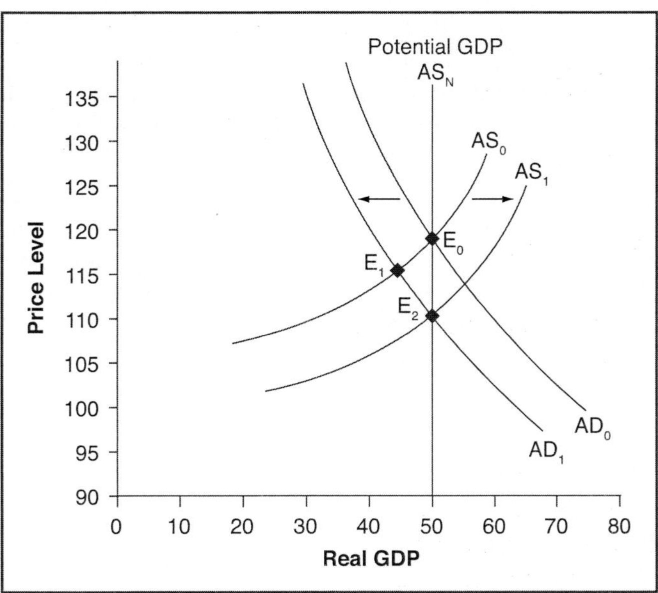

EXHIBIT 28-4 A Rebound Back to Potential GDP from a Shift to the Left in Aggregate Demand

The original equilibrium E_0, at an output level of 50 and a price level of 120, happens at the intersection of the aggregate demand curve AD_0 and the short-run aggregate supply curve AS0. The output at E_0 is equal to potential GDP. Aggregate demand shifts left from AD_0 to AD_1. The new equilibrium is E_1, with a higher output level of 45 and downward pressure on the price level of 115. But with high unemployment rates, wages are held down. Lower wages are an economy-wide decrease in the price of a key input, which shifts short-run aggregate supply to the right from AS_0 to AS_1. The new equilibrium E_2 is at the same original level of output, 50, but at a lower price level of 110. Thus, the long-run aggregate supply curve AS_N, which is vertical at the level of potential GDP, ultimately determines the real GDP of this economy.

The rebound of the economy back to potential GDP also works in response to a shift to the left in aggregate demand. Exhibit 28-4 again starts with two aggregate supply curves, with AS_0 showing the original short-run Keynesian AS curve and AS_N showing the vertical long-run neoclassical aggregate supply curve. A decrease in aggregate demand—say, because of a decline in consumer confidence that leads to less consumption and more saving—causes the original aggregate demand curve AD_0 to shift back to AD_1. The shift from the original equilibrium E_0 to the new equilibrium E_1 results in a decline in output. As output falls below potential GDP, unemployment rises.

Again, from the neoclassical perspective, this short-run scenario is only the beginning of the chain of events. The higher level of unemployment means more workers looking for jobs. As a result, employers can hold down on pay increases—or perhaps even replace some of their higher-paid workers with unemployed people willing to accept a lower wage. As wages stagnate or fall, this decline in the price of a key input means that the short-run Keynesian aggregate supply curve shifts to the right from its original AS_0 to AS_1. The overall impact in the long run, as the macroeconomic equilibrium shifts from E_0 to E_1 to E_2, is that the level of output returns to potential GDP, where it started. But there is downward pressure on the price level—or at least pressure for a lower level of inflation.

Thus, in the neoclassical view, changes in aggregate demand can have only a short-run effect on output and on unemployment. In the long run, when wages and prices are flexible, potential GDP and aggregate supply determine the size of real GDP.

How Fast Is the Speed of Macroeconomic Adjustment?

How long does it take for wage and prices to adjust, and for the economy to rebound back to its potential GDP? This subject has been highly contentious. Keynesian economists argue that if the adjustment from recession to potential GDP takes a very long time, then neoclassical theory may be more hypothetical than practical. In the immortal words of John Maynard Keynes quoted in the previous chapter, "In the long run we are all dead." Neoclassical economists respond that even if the adjustment takes as long as, say, ten years—and it may happen in five years or less—then it becomes of central importance in understanding the economy.

rational expectations: The theory that people form the most accurate possible expectations about the future that they can, using all information available to them.

One subset of neoclassical economists holds that the adjustment of wages and prices in the macroeconomy might be quite rapid indeed. The theory of **rational expectations** holds that people form the most accurate possible expectations about the future that they can, using all information available to them. In an economy where most people have rational expectations, economic adjustments may happen very quickly.

To understand how rational expectations may affect the speed of price adjustments, think about a situation in the real estate market. Imagine that several events are announced that seem likely to push up the value of homes in the neighborhood. For example, perhaps a local employer announces that it is going to hire many more people or the city announces that it is going to build a local park or a library in that neighborhood. The theory of rational expectations points out that even though none of the changes will happen immediately, home prices in the neighborhood will rise immediately because the expectation that homes will be worth more in the future will lead buyers to be willing to pay more for homes in the present. The amount of the immediate increase in home prices will depend on how likely it seems that the announcements about the future will actually happen and on how distant the local jobs and neighborhood improvements are in the future. The key point is that because of rational expectations, prices do not wait on events, but adjust immediately.

At a macroeconomic level, the theory of rational expectations points out that if the aggregate supply curve is vertical over time, then people should rationally expect this pattern. When a shift in aggregate demand occurs, people and businesses with rational expectations will know that its impact on output and employment will only be temporary, while its impact on the price level will be permanent. If firms and workers perceive the outcome of the process in advance, and if all firms and workers know that everyone else is perceiving the process in the same way, then they have no incentive to go through an extended series of short-run scenarios, like a firm first hiring more people when aggregate demand shifts out and then firing those same people when aggregate supply shifts back. Instead, everyone will recognize where this process is heading—toward a change in the price level—and then will act on that expectation. In this scenario, the expected long-run

Do You, and Everyone around You, Have Rational Expectations?

Here's a social experiment to reveal both your rationality and your expectations about the rationality of others. You and everyone else in a group of people are asked to choose a number between 0 and 100. The winner is whoever makes a guess that is closest to one-half of the average of all the numbers chosen. What number should you pick? Think about it for a moment.

You might begin by reasoning that if the guesses of the other parties are distributed randomly over the interval from 0 to 100, then the average of the other guesses will be 50, and therefore you should guess 25. But if everyone reasons in this way, then everyone will guess 25, and so you should guess 12 or 13. But if everyone follows the logic of this reasoning, then everyone will guess 12 or 13 as well, so you should guess 6. But if everyone else follows this logic, then everyone will guess 6, and you should guess 3. You can see where this train of logic is headed. If everyone is fully rational, and everyone expects everyone else to be fully rational, then everyone should guess zero. A group of economists who call themselves "experimental economists" organize games like this and see how people respond. When the game is first played, guesses of about 25 are common. As the game is then repeated, the guesses sink lower and lower. However, very few people ever guess zero.

These results suggest several conclusions. People are not fully rational in their expectations, and they do not expect others to be fully rational, either. However, when people repeat a situation several times, they do learn and adapt their behavior in the direction of greater rationality.

change in the price level may happen very quickly, without a drawn-out zigzag of output and employment first moving one way and then the other.

The theory that people and firms have rational expectations can be a useful simplification, but as a statement about how people and businesses actually behave, the assumption seems too strong. After all, many people and firms are not especially well informed either about what is happening in the economy or about how the economy works. It is probably more realistic to believe that people and firms act with **adaptive expectations**: they look at past experience and gradually adapt their beliefs and behavior as circumstances change, but are not perfect synthesizers of information and accurate predictors of the future in the sense of rational expectations theory. If most people and businesses have some form of adaptive expectations, then the adjustment from the short run and long run will be traced out in incremental steps that occur over time.

adaptive expectations: The theory that people look at past experience and gradually adapt their beliefs and behavior as circumstances change.

The empirical evidence on the speed of macroeconomic adjustment of prices and wages is not clear-cut. Indeed, the speed of macroeconomic adjustment probably varies among different countries and time periods. But a reasonable guess is that the initial short-run effect of a shift in aggregate demand might last 2–5 years, before the adjustments in wages and prices cause the economy to adjust back to potential GDP. Thus, one might think of the short run for applying Keynesian analysis as time periods less than 2–5 years, and the long run for applying neoclassical analysis as longer than five years. For practical purposes, this guideline is frustratingly imprecise, but when analyzing a complex social mechanism like an economy as it evolves over time, some imprecision seems unavoidable.

Policy Implications of the Neoclassical Perspective

The neoclassical school of macroeconomics argues that the economy has a self-correcting tendency to move back to potential GDP. If one accepts this theory, then it has implications for how to view the main problems of the macroeconomy. For example, fighting recession seems relatively less important, while encouraging long-term growth seems more important. For similar reasons, fighting cyclical unemployment seems relatively less important, while fighting inflation seems more important. Let's consider these choices in turn, along with their implications for the shape of the Phillips curve trade-off between unemployment and inflation.

Data on Inflation Expectations

Expectations about inflation may seem like a highly theoretical concept, but in fact, data do exist on this subject.

Joseph Livingston, a financial journalist for the *Philadelphia Inquirer*, started a twice-a-year survey of economists about their expectations of inflation in 1946. After Livingston's death in 1969, the survey was continued by the Federal Reserve Bank of Philadelphia. The Institute of Survey Research at the University of Michigan started carrying out a survey of inflation expectations of 500 random households in 1948. Finally, the American Statistical Association together with a private organization called the National Bureau of Economic Research started carrying out a survey of professional economic forecasters that included expectations about inflation in 1968.

Economic research can then compare these expectations to the actual inflation that occurred, but the results are mixed. Expectations do not seem to be purely adaptive and based on past experience of inflation; instead, people are clearly looking ahead. In fact, the average forecast of households is roughly as accurate as the average forecasts of the professionals. However, expectations do not seem to be perfectly rational forecasts of the future, either, because people often repeat past errors. For example, all parties have a tendency to overestimate future inflation when inflation is currently low and to underestimate future inflation when inflation is currently high. However, the forecasts of economists have become more accurate in the last few decades. Economists are actively researching how expectations of inflation and other economic variables are formed and changed.

Fighting Recession or Encouraging Long-Term Growth?

Late in 2007, the U.S. economy entered a severe recession. Real GDP declined through the middle of 2009. Most Keynesian economists would probably focus on the immediate recession. But neoclassical economists might well emphasize that the economy will rebound out of the recession and begin growing again. From the neoclassical point of view, perhaps a more important question is the growth rate of long-term productivity, which determines the rate at which potential GDP expands. As measured by growth in output per hour in the business sector, productivity growth was very strong from 1998–2003, growing at an annual rate of 3.6%. However, productivity growth averaged ½% per year from 2004–2008. After bounding up and down during the Great Recession, it bounced up to about 3% per year in 2009 and 2010 and then slumped to an average rate of 0.5% from 2011–2015. From a neoclassical perspective, the key question of the next few years is whether productivity growth will return to the high levels of the late 1990s and early 2000s or whether it will remain at the slower rates of 2011–2015. Neoclassical economists are often skeptical of the government's ability to manipulate aggregate demand skillfully and in a timely manner, as Keynesian economics recommends. Instead, neoclassical economists are likely to focus their attention on the underpinnings of long-run productivity growth: namely, an economy's investments in human capital, physical capital, and technology, operating together in a market-oriented environment that rewards innovation.

Fighting Unemployment or Inflation?

In the neoclassical model, the level of real GDP is determined by potential GDP, which is illustrated with a vertical aggregate supply curve. Unemployment can be divided into two categories, as explained in Chapter 23: cyclical unemployment and the natural rate of unemployment. Cyclical unemployment is created when the economy is producing below potential GDP, giving potential employers less incentive to hire. When the economy is producing at potential GDP, cyclical unemployment will be zero. Historical evidence shows that the unemployment rate never falls to 0%, not even when the economy is producing at or even slightly above potential GDP. The unemployment rate that is created by the dynamic forces of supply and demand in the labor market, even when the economy is at potential GDP, is called the natural rate of unemployment.

The neoclassical view of unemployment tends to focus attention away from the problem of cyclical unemployment—that is, unemployment caused by recession—while putting more attention on the issue of the rates of unemployment that prevail even when the economy is operating at potential GDP. To put it another way, the neoclassical view of unemployment tends to focus on how public policy might be adjusted to reduce the natural rate of unemployment. Such policy changes might involve redesigning unemployment and welfare programs so that they still support those in need, but also offer greater encouragement for job-hunting. It might involve redesigning business rules with an eye to whether they are unintentionally discouraging businesses from taking on new employees. It might involve building institutions to improve the flow of information about jobs and the mobility of workers, to help bring together workers and employers more quickly.

Neoclassical economists will not tend to see aggregate demand as a useful tool for reducing unemployment; after all, if economic output is determined by a vertical aggregate supply curve, then aggregate demand has no effect on unemployment. Instead, neoclassical economists believe that aggregate demand should be allowed to expand only to match the gradual shifts of aggregate supply to the right—keeping the price level much the same and inflationary pressures low.

If aggregate demand rises rapidly in the neoclassical model, it leads only to inflationary pressures. Exhibit 28-5 shows a vertical long-run AS curve and three different levels of aggregate demand, rising from AD_0 to AD_1 to AD_2. As the macroeconomic equilibrium rises from E_0 to E_1 and E_2, the price level rises. But real GDP does not budge. The rate of unemployment, which adjusts to its natural rate, does not budge, either Conversely,

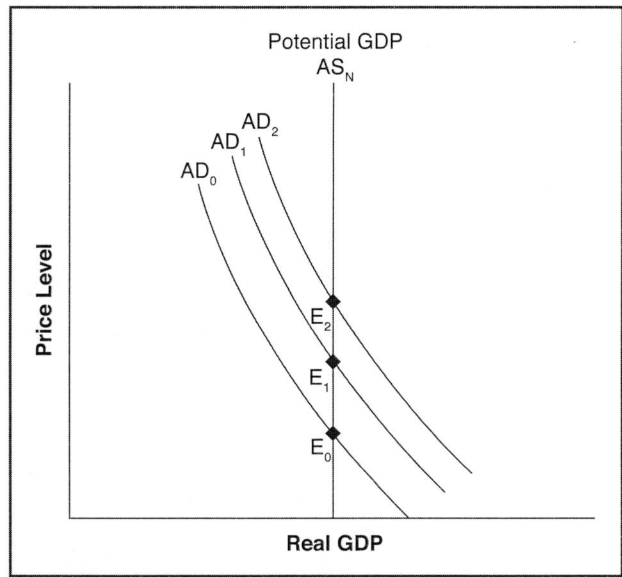

EXHIBIT 28-5 How Aggregate Demand Determines the Price Level in the Long Run

As aggregate demand shifts to the right from AD_0 to AD_1 to AD_2, real GDP in this economy and the level of unemployment do not change. However, there is inflationary pressure for a higher price level as the equilibrium changes from E_0 to E_1 to E_2.

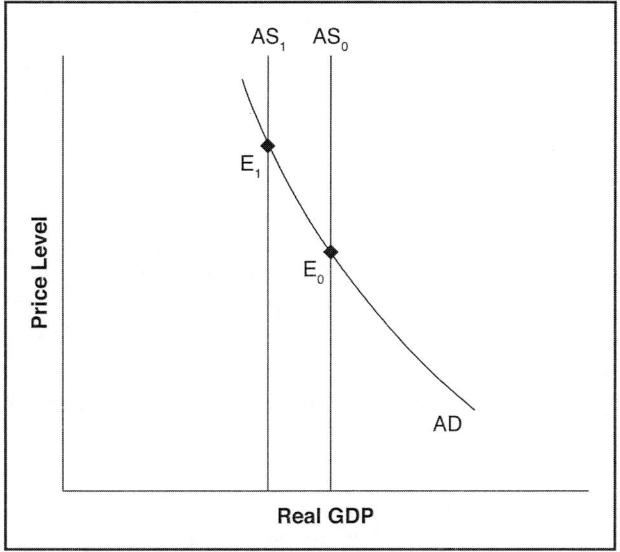

EXHIBIT 28-6 How a Shift to the Left in AS Can Push Up the Price Level

A shift in aggregate supply to the left from AS_0 to AS_1 causes inflationary pressure for a higher price level as the equilibrium shifts from E_0 to E_1.

reducing inflation has no long-term costs, either. Think about Exhibit 28-5 in reverse, as the aggregate demand curve shifts from AD_2 to AD_1 to AD_0, and the equilibrium moves from E_2 to E_1 to E_0. During this process, the price level falls, but neither real GDP nor the natural rate of unemployment is changed.

A shift to the left in aggregate supply can also push up the price level. Exhibit 28-6 shows a shift to the left of a vertical aggregate supply, which might result from an increase in prices of key inputs, like oil or wages. It can also result from a breakdown of key market institutions, like banks, which could prevent the economy from operating as smoothly as it had before. A shift back to the left of AS means that potential GDP has fallen, and perhaps conditions of the labor market have shifted in such a way such that the natural rate of unemployment is higher as well. But at the new AS curve, it remains true that aggregate supply determines the level of output, while changes in aggregate demand will determine the price level.

The Neoclassical Phillips Curve Trade-off

A neoclassical long-run aggregate supply curve will imply a vertical shape for the Phillips curve trade-off between inflation and unemployment. Exhibit 28-7*a* shows the vertical AS curve, with three different levels of aggregate demand resulting in three different

EXHIBIT 28-7 From a Long-Run AS Curve to a Long-Run Phillips Curve

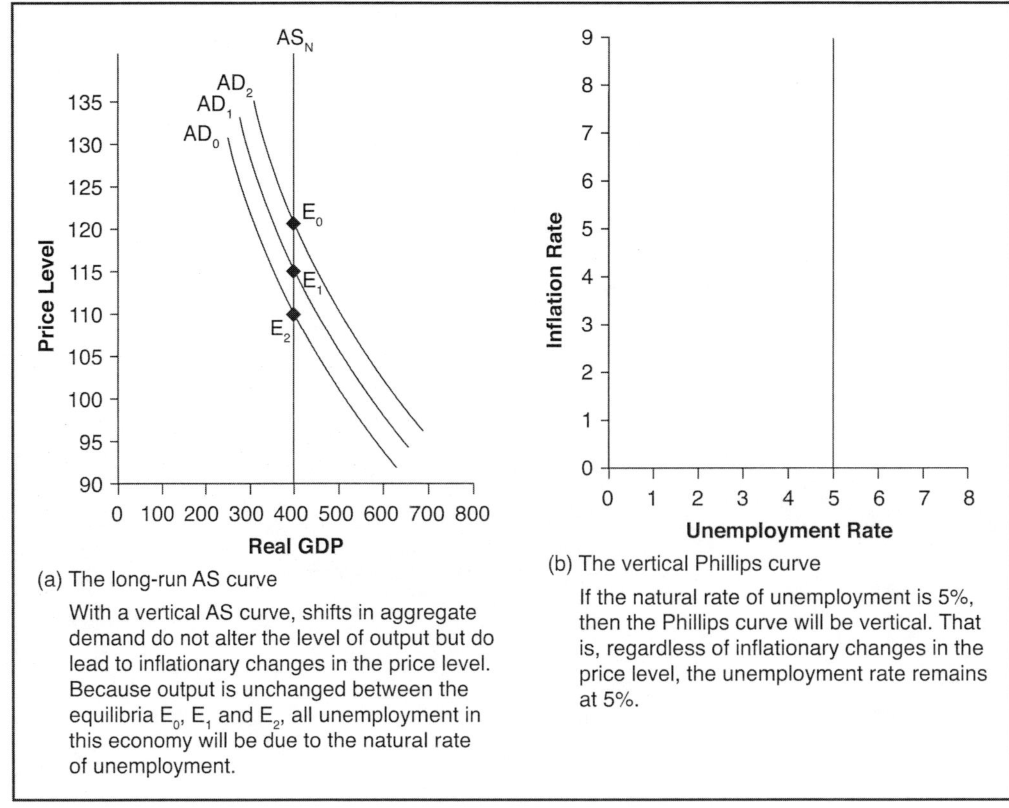

(a) The long-run AS curve

With a vertical AS curve, shifts in aggregate demand do not alter the level of output but do lead to inflationary changes in the price level. Because output is unchanged between the equilibria E_0, E_1 and E_2, all unemployment in this economy will be due to the natural rate of unemployment.

(b) The vertical Phillips curve

If the natural rate of unemployment is 5%, then the Phillips curve will be vertical. That is, regardless of inflationary changes in the price level, the unemployment rate remains at 5%.

equilibria at three different price levels. At every point along that vertical AS curve, potential GDP and the rate of unemployment remains the same. Assume that in this economy, the natural rate of unemployment when the economy is producing at potential GDP is 5%. As a result, the long-run Phillips curve relationship shown in Exhibit 28-7*b* is a vertical line, rising up from 5% unemployment, at any level of inflation.

The unemployment rate on the long-run Phillips curve will be the natural rate of unemployment. A small inflationary increase in the price level from AD_0 to AD_1 will have the same natural rate of unemployment as a larger inflationary increase in the price level from AD_0 to AD_2. The macroeconomic equilibrium along the vertical aggregate supply curve can occur at a variety of different price levels, and the natural rate of unemployment can be consistent with all different rates of inflation. The great economist Milton Friedman (1912–2006) summed up the neoclassical view of the long-term Phillips curve trade-off in a 1967 speech: "[T]here is always a temporary trade-off between inflation and unemployment; there is no permanent trade-off."

In the Keynesian perspective, the primary focus is on adjusting the level of aggregate demand in relationship to an upward-sloping aggregate supply curve; in particular, AD should be adjusted so that the economy produces at its potential GDP, not so low that cyclical unemployment results and not so high that inflation results. In the neoclassical perspective, aggregate supply will determine output at potential GDP, unemployment is determined by the natural rate of unemployment churned out by the forces of supply and demand in the labor market, and shifts in aggregate demand are the primary determinant of changes in the price level.

Macroeconomists Riding Two Horses

When a circus performer stands up on two horses, with a foot on each one, much of the excitement for the viewer resides in contemplating the gap between the two. As modern macroeconomists ride into the future with one foot on the short-term Keynesian perspective and the other foot on the long-term neoclassical perspective, the balancing act may appear to be an uncomfortable one, but there doesn't seem to be any way to avoid it. Each approach, Keynesian and neoclassical, has its strengths and weaknesses.

The short-term Keynesian model, built on the importance of aggregate demand as a cause of business cycles and a degree of wage and price rigidity, does a sound job of explaining many recessions and why cyclical unemployment rises and falls. However, Keynesian economics does a less good job of capturing the reality that the economy does usually seem to revert to a natural rate of unemployment over time. By focusing on the short-run adjustments of aggregate demand, Keynesian economics creates some danger of overlooking the long-term causes of economic growth or the natural rate of unemployment that exists even when the economy is producing at potential GDP.

The neoclassical model, with its emphasis on aggregate supply, focuses on the underlying determinants of output and employment in markets, and thus tends to put more emphasis on economic growth and how labor markets work. However, the neoclassical view is not especially helpful in explaining why unemployment moves up and down over short time horizons of a few years. Nor is the neoclassical model especially helpful when the economy is mired in an especially deep and long-lasting recession, like the Great Depression. Keynesian economics tends to view inflation as a price that might sometimes be paid for lower unemployment; neoclassical economics tends to view inflation as a cost that offers no offsetting gains in terms of lower unemployment.

The Keynesian and neoclassical approaches differ in their views of government macroeconomic policy, too. Keynesian macroeconomic policy requires some optimism about the ability of the government to recognize a situation of too little or too much aggregate demand, and to adjust aggregate demand accordingly with the right level of changes in taxes or spending, all enacted in a timely fashion. Conversely, even when neoclassical economists admit that a Keynesian increase in aggregate demand might in theory help to avoid a recession, they often argue it is unlikely to work well in practice. After all, neoclassical economists argue, it takes government statisticians months to produce even preliminary estimates of GDP so that politicians know whether a recession is occurring—and those preliminary estimates may be revised substantially later. Moreover, the political process can take more months to enact a tax cut or a spending increase; the amount of those tax or spending changes will be determined as much by political considerations as economic ones; and then the economy will take still more months to put changes in aggregate demand into effect through spending and production.

But macroeconomics cannot be summed up as an argument between one group of economists who are pure Keynesians and another group who are pure neoclassicals. Instead, many economists believe that all of these statements are true—it's just that the Keynesian statements are more relevant in the short run and the neoclassical statements in the long run. Robert Solow, the Nobel laureate in economics in 1987, described the dual approach in this way: "At short time scales, I think, something sort of 'Keynesian' is a good approximation, and surely better than anything straight 'neoclassical.' At very long time scales, the interesting questions are best studied in a neoclassical framework, and attention to the Keynesian side of things would be a minor distraction. At the five-to-ten-year time scale, we have to piece things together as best we can, and look for a hybrid model that will do the job."

Many modern macroeconomists spend considerable time and energy trying to construct models that blend the most attractive aspects of the Keynesian and neoclassical approaches. It's possible to construct a somewhat complex mathematical model where aggregate demand and sticky wages and prices matter in the short run, but wages, prices and aggregate supply adjust in the long run. However, creating an overall model that encompasses both short-term Keynesian and long-term neoclassical models is not easy. Even if one of these hybrid models eventually becomes well accepted in the economics profession, it will probably still feel like riding two separate horses, but now with a double-saddle arrangement linking them together more closely, so that the rider is not quite so precarious.

Key Comments and Summary

1. Neoclassical economics argues that in the long run, the economy will adjust back to its potential GDP level of output through flexible price levels.
2. In the neoclassical view, potential GDP and the natural rate of unemployment are determined in the long run by market forces. Thus, the neoclassical perspective views the long-run AS curve as vertical.
3. A **rational expectations** perspective argues that people have excellent information about economic events and how the economy works, and that as a result, price and other economic adjustments will happen very quickly. **Adaptive expectations** is a milder theory in which people have limited information about economic information and how the economy works, and so price and other economic adjustments can be slow.
4. Neoclassical economists tend to put relatively more emphasis on long-term growth than on fighting recession, because they believe that recessions will fade in a few years and long-term growth will ultimately determine the standard of living.
5. Neoclassical economists tend to focus more on reducing the natural rate of unemployment caused by economic institutions and government policies than the cyclical rate of unemployment caused by recession.
6. Neoclassical economists see no social benefit to inflation. With an upward-sloping Keynesian AS curve, inflation can arise because an economy is approaching full employment. But with a vertical long-run neoclassical AS curve, inflation does not accompany any rise in output.
7. If aggregate supply is vertical, then aggregate demand does not affect the quantity of output. Instead, aggregate demand can only cause inflationary changes in the price level.
8. A vertical aggregate supply curve, where the quantity of output is consistent with many different price levels, also implies a vertical Phillips curve.
9. Many mainstream economists take a Keynesian perspective, assuming sticky wages and prices and emphasizing the power of aggregate demand, for purposes of short-run analysis and a neoclassical perspective, assuming adjustment of wages and prices and emphasizing the power of long-run supply, for purposes of long-run analysis.

Review Questions

1. Does neoclassical economics focus on the long term or the short term?
2. Does neoclassical economics view prices and wages as sticky or flexible?
3. What shape is the long-run aggregate supply curve?
4. What is the difference between rational expectations and adaptive expectations?
5. Do neoclassical economists tend to focus more on economic growth or on recessions? Explain briefly.
6. Do neoclassical economists tend to focus more on cyclical unemployment or on inflation? Explain briefly.
7. Do neoclassical economists see a value in tolerating a little more inflation if it brings additional economic output?
8. If aggregate supply is vertical, what role does aggregate demand play in determining output? In determining the price level?
9. What is the shape of the neoclassical long-run Phillips curve?

PART CHAPTER

29

Money and Banks

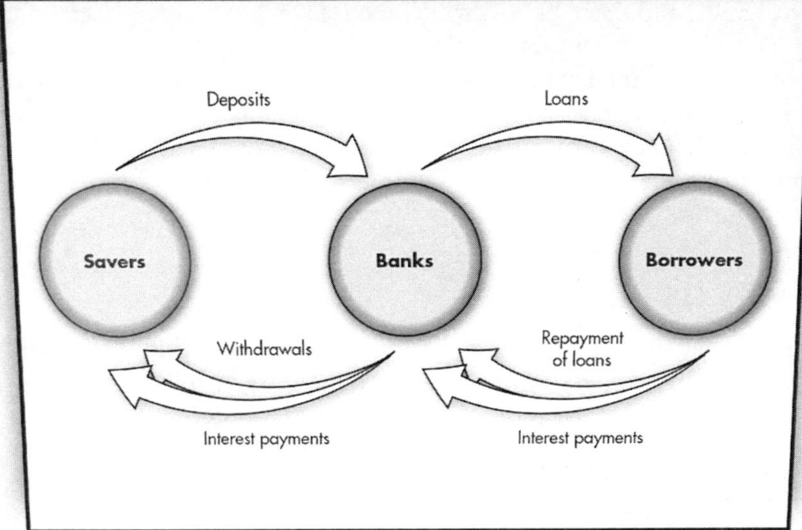

Chapter Outline

Money is not an end in itself. You can't eat dollar bills or wear your bank account. Ultimately, the usefulness of money rests in exchanging it for goods or services. As the American writer and humorist Ambrose Bierce (1842–1914) wrote in 1911, money is a "blessing that is of no advantage to us excepting when we part with it."

Here's a trivia question: In the history of the world, what item was used for money over the broadest geographic area and the longest period of time? The answer isn't gold or silver, or any precious metal. It's the cowrie, a mollusk shell found mainly off the Maldive Islands in the Indian Ocean. Cowries served as money as early as 700 B.C. in China. By the 1500s, they were in widespread use across India and Africa. For several centuries after that, cowries were used in markets including southern Europe, western Africa, India, and China for a wide range of purchases: everything from buying lunch or a ferry ride to paying for a shipload of silk or rice. Cowries were still acceptable as a way of paying taxes in certain African nations in the early twentieth century.

What made cowries work so well as money? First, they are extremely durable and last a century or more. As one writer put it, they can be "poured, sacked, shoveled, hoarded in heaps" while remaining "clean, dainty, stainless, polished, and milk-white." Second, parties could use cowries either by counting shells of a certain size, or—for large purchases—by measuring the weight or volume of the total shells to be exchanged. Third, it was impossible to counterfeit a cowrie shell, but gold or silver coins could be counterfeited by making copies with cheaper metals. Finally, in the heyday of cowrie money from the 1500s into the 1800s, the collection of cowries was tightly controlled, first by the Portuguese and later by the Dutch and the English. As a result, the supply of cowries was allowed to grow quickly enough to serve the needs of commerce, but not so quickly that they were no longer scarce.

The discussion of money and banking in this chapter begins a new main section in the study of macroeconomics. At this point, you should have firmly in mind the four main goals of macroeconomics: economic growth, low unemployment, low inflation, and a sustainable balance of trade. You should also understand Keynesian and neoclassical frameworks for macroeconomic analysis and how these frameworks can be embodied in the aggregate demand–aggregate supply (AD–AS) model. With the goals and frameworks for macroeconomic analysis in mind, the final step is to discuss the two main categories of macroeconomic policy: monetary policy, which focuses on money, banking and lending, and interest rates; and fiscal policy, which focuses on government spending, taxes, and borrowing. This chapter discusses what economists mean by money, and how money is closely interrelated with the banking system. Chapter 30 discusses how central banks, such as the U.S. Federal Reserve, can affect the money supply and the conditions for lending in the economy. Chapter 31 discusses the international dimensions of money, including the economic and policy factors that determine exchange rates between the money from different countries.

Defining Money by Its Functions

Money is what people in a society regularly use when purchasing or selling goods and services, and thus money must be widely accepted by both buyers and sellers. This concept of money is intentionally flexible, because money has taken a wide variety of forms in different cultures. Money has been made of gold, silver, and paper. Native Americans and early American settlers used strings of beads called wampum as money. In the islands of Fiji in the southern Pacific Ocean, islanders once exchanged the teeth of the sperm whale as money. People have used cattle as money over the centuries; in certain areas of Russia, horses were the main form of money well into the twentieth century, with sheep and lambskins used for small change. Metal forms of money have included not only coins, but metal anklets and bracelets have been used as a type of wearable money, especially in western Africa. In prisons and prisoner-of-war camps in the twentieth century, cigarettes have sometimes served as money. Modern examples of money include U.S. dollars, European euros, the Chinese yuan, India's rupee, Japanese yen, Nigerian naira, Brazilian reals, Polish zlotys, and the coins and bills of every country.

Barter and the Double Coincidence of Wants

To understand the usefulness of money, consider the inconvenience of exchange without money.

barter: Trading one good or service for another directly, without using money.

double coincidence of wants: A situation in which both of two people each wants some good or service that the other person can provide.

Barter—literally trading one good or service for another—is a completely inadequate mechanism for trying to coordinate the trades in a modern advanced economy. In an economy without money, an exchange between two people would involve a **double coincidence of wants**, a situation in which both of two people each wants some good or service that the other person can provide. For example, if an accountant wants a pair of shoes, this accountant must find someone who has a pair of shoes in the correct size and who is willing to exchange the shoes for some hours of accounting services. Such a trade is likely to be difficult to arrange. Think about the complexity of such trades in a modern economy, with its extensive division of labor that involves thousands upon thousands of different jobs and goods.

Money greases the social machinery of exchange. In an economy with money, an accountant doesn't need to seek out people who sell shoes and find out if they want to exchange them for a few hours of accounting services. Instead, the accountant works for a company and receives money wages, which can then be used to purchase shoes or other goods. Employers don't need to pay their workers in apartments, food, or clothing; instead, employers pay money. People don't need to save for their retirement by piling up canned food in their basements; they save money in the bank instead. Money is a marvelous invention that makes possible the division of labor and other complex economic activities.

Mademoiselle Zelie's Problems with Barter

In 1875, famous British economist William Stanley Jevons (1835–1882) wrote a book called *Money and the Mechanics of Exchange*, in which he illustrated the problems of barter with the following example:

> Some years since, Mademoiselle Zelie, a singer of the Theatre Lyrique at Paris, made a professional tour around the world, and gave a concert in the Society Islands. In exchange for an air from *Norma* and a few other songs, she was to receive a third part of the receipts. When counted, her share was found to consist of three pigs, twenty-three turkeys, forty-four chickens, five thousand cocoanuts, besides considerable quantities of bananas, lemons, and oranges. At the Halle in Paris, as the prima donna remarks in her lively letter, printed by M. Wolowski, this amount of livestock and vegetables might have brought four thousand francs, which would have been good remuneration for five songs. In the Society Islands, however, pieces of money were very scarce; and as Mademoiselle could not consume any considerable portion of the receipts herself, it became necessary in the meantime to feed the pigs and poultry with the fruit. . . .
>
> In modern civilized society the inconveniences of the primitive method of exchange are wholly unknown, and might almost seem to be imaginary. Accustomed as we are to the use of money, we are unconscious of the inestimable benefits which it confers upon us; and only when we recur to altogether different states of society can we realize the difficulties which arise in its absence.

Three Functions for Money

Economists have identified three specific functions of money. First, money serves as a **medium of exchange**, which means that money must be very widely accepted as a method of payment in the markets for goods, labor, and financial capital. U.S. paper money, for example, carries the statement: "THIS NOTE IS LEGAL TENDER FOR ALL DEBTS, PUBLIC AND PRIVATE." In other words, if you owe a debt, then legally speaking, you can pay that debt with currency.

medium of exchange: Whatever is widely accepted as a method of payment.

Second, money serves as a **unit of account**, which means that it is the ruler by which other values are measured. Without money, you would have to carry around a list of all the possible opportunity costs in your head: for example, a loaf of bread will have an opportunity cost of 10 minutes of work or a rental movie. Money acts as a common denominator, an accounting method that simplifies thinking about trade-offs. At a supermarket, the unit of account function of money allows the cashier to add the values of many individual items into a single value. A common unit of account allows government statisticians to add up the value of cars, haircuts, Internet service providers and all other goods and services into a single money value to calculate GDP.

unit of account: The common way in which market values are measured in an economy.

Third, money serves as a **store of value**; that is, when you receive money, you know that you don't need to spend it immediately because it will still hold its value the next day, or the next year. Holding money is a much easier and less wasteful way of storing value than trying to purchase physical goods, such as apples or refrigerators, storing those goods, and then trying to exchange them in the future. This function of money does not require that money is a *perfect* store of value. In an economy with inflation, money loses some buying power each year, but it remains money.

store of value: Something that serves as a way of preserving economic value that can be spent or consumed in the future.

Money needs to serve all three of these functions: medium of exchange, unit of account, and store of value. Serving only one of these functions is not enough. For example, a house may serve as a store of value, in the sense that it can be sold later. But houses do not serve as mediums of exchange or units of account, and so they are not money.

money: Whatever serves society in three functions: medium of exchange, unit of account, and store of value.

Measuring Money: Currency, M1, and M2

Cash in your pocket certainly serves as a medium of exchange, unit of account, and a store of value. But what about checks or credit cards? Are they money, too? Rather than trying to state a single way of measuring money, economists offer a series of ever-broader definitions of money.

currency: Coins and paper bills.

demand deposits: Deposits in banks that are available by making a cash withdrawal or writing a check.

M1: A narrow definition of the money supply that includes currency, traveler's checks, and checking accounts in banks.

M2: A definition of the money supply that includes everything in M1, but also adds savings deposits, money market funds, and certificates of deposit.

savings deposits: Bank accounts where you can't withdraw money by writing a check, but can withdraw the money at a bank—or can transfer it easily to a checking account.

money market funds: Where the deposits of many investors are pooled together and invested in a safe way like short-term government bonds.

certificate of deposit (CD): A mechanism for a saver to deposit funds at a bank and promise to leave them at the bank for a time, in exchange for a higher rate of interest.

time deposits: Accounts that the depositor has committed to leaving in the bank for a certain period of time, in exchange for a higher rate of interest; also called certificates of deposit.

Money certainly includes **currency**, the coins and bills that circulate in an economy. Closely related to currency are two items that you can use, in most circumstances, almost as easily as cash. One of them is *traveler's checks*, which you purchase from a bank or financial company, sign, and then redeem with an additional signature when you want to spend them. Traveler's checks have the advantage of being accepted almost as widely as currency, and, if they are lost or stolen, the company that issued them will replace them. Cash offers no such protection. The other item closely related to currency is personal checks, also known to economists as **demand deposits**, because they are deposits in banks that are available by making a cash withdrawal or writing a check. These three items together—currency, traveler's checks, and checking accounts in banks—make up the definition of money known as **M1**.

A broader definition of money, known as **M2**, includes everything in M1, but also adds the bank accounts on which money can be withdrawn fairly easily, but not as easily as with personal checks. For example, M2 includes **savings deposits** in banks, which are bank accounts on which you can't write a check directly, but you can easily withdraw the money at an automatic teller machine or bank. Many banks and other financial institutions offer a chance to invest in **money market funds**, where the deposits of many individual investors are pooled together and invested in a safe way like short-term government bonds. Another ingredient of M2 are the relatively small (i.e., less than about $100,000) **certificates of deposit** or **time deposits**, which are accounts that the depositor has committed to leaving in the bank for a certain period of time, ranging from a few months to a few years, in exchange for a higher interest rate. In short, these ingredients of M2 are money that you can withdraw and spend, but with a greater effort than the items in M1.

Exhibit 29-1 should help in visualizing the relationship between M1 and M2. Note that M1 is nested in M2. At the end of 2015, M1 was $3,077 billion, while M2 was $12,330 billion. For comparison, the size of the U.S. GDP in 2015 was nearly $18 trillion.

The lines between separating M1 and M2 can become a little blurry. Sometimes elements of M1 are not treated alike; for example, some businesses won't accept personal checks for large amounts, but will accept traveler's checks or cash. Changes in banking practices and technology have made the savings accounts in M2 more similar to the checking accounts in M1. For example, some savings accounts will allow depositors to write checks, use automatic teller machines, and pay bills over the Internet, which has made it easier to access savings accounts. As with many other economic terms and statistics, the important point is to know the strengths and limitations of the various definitions of money, not to believe that such definitions are as clear-cut to economists as, say, the definition of nitrogen is to chemists.

Where does "plastic money" like credit cards fit into this picture? When you make a purchase with a credit card, the credit card company immediately transfers money from

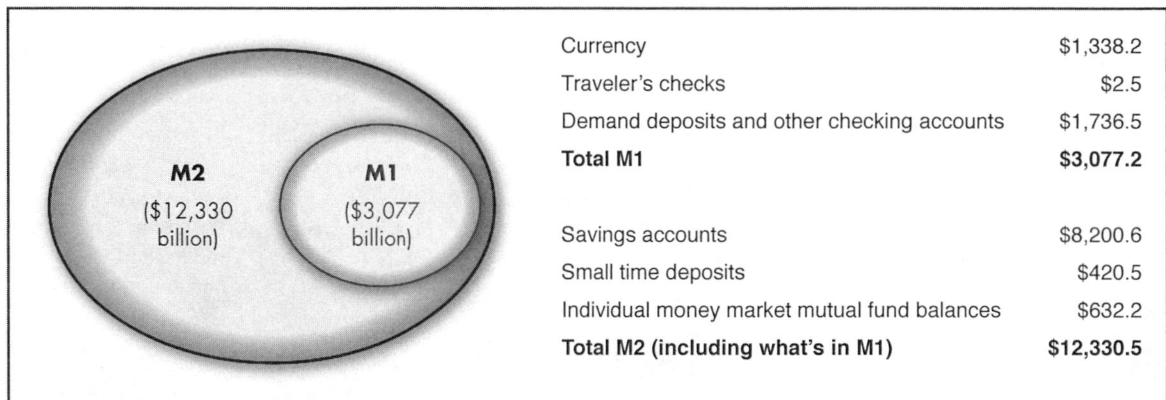

Currency	$1,338.2
Traveler's checks	$2.5
Demand deposits and other checking accounts	$1,736.5
Total M1	**$3,077.2**
Savings accounts	$8,200.6
Small time deposits	$420.5
Individual money market mutual fund balances	$632.2
Total M2 (including what's in M1)	**$12,330.5**

EXHIBIT 29-1 Defining Money with M1 and M2

The money stock has several definitions, ranging from narrow to broad. M1 is mainly currency and checking accounts. M2 is everything in M1, plus savings accounts, small time deposits, and money market funds. The totals are for December 2015.

The Case of the Missing Currency

Here is a puzzle. The Federal Reserve reported that about $1.3 trillion in currency—that is, paper money and coins—was in circulation in 2015. Dividing the total currency by roughly 240 million U.S. adults 18 or older works out to an average of approximately $5,400 in currency for every man and woman.

This average seems ridiculously high. Survey results suggest that the average holdings of currency for each adult are more like $350—and that number takes into account well-off people who hold large amounts of cash in safes and safety deposit boxes. If 240 million adults are each holding $350, then total holdings of U.S. currency by individuals is about $84 billion. Businesses traditionally hold about 3% of all currency, or about $39 billion. After all, most businesses try not to hold currency, but instead quickly get money to the bank where it can earn some interest.

So if households and firms together hold about $123 billion in currency, where is the other $1 trillion or so? No one is quite sure. There are three possible answers: it may be held by children; as part of the unmeasured "underground" economy; or by foreigners. Even if one believes that teenage buying power is important to certain sectors of the economy, and that underground, unreported businesses are everywhere, it is very hard to believe that these two components are larger than the uses of money by adults and legal businesses. As a result, it seems likely that hundreds of billions of dollars of U.S. currency is circulating in the hands of foreigners. Indeed, almost all of the recent growth of U.S. currency has been an expansion in the number of $100 bills in circulation, which are not often used for everyday transactions in the U.S. economy.

When a country's own currency is plagued with uncertainty, perhaps because of a high inflation rate, people in that country may start carrying out transactions and saving money using U.S. dollars. But in the middle- and low-income countries of the world, the average families are too poor to account for hundreds of billions of dollars of U.S. currency. Thus, a plausible explanation is that most U.S. currency—especially in large denominations like $100 bills—is facilitating criminal behavior such as the illegal drug trade, human trafficking and smuggling, terrorism, and bribery.

its checking account to the seller, and at the end of the month, the credit card company sends you a bill for what you have charged that month. Until you pay the credit card bill, you have effectively borrowed money from the credit card company, although typically no interest is charged on the loan if you pay your credit card bill on time. When you make a purchase with a *debit card*, another kind of plastic money, the funds are transferred directly and immediately from your bank account to the seller. With a *smart card*, you can store a certain value of money on the card and then use the card to make purchases. Some "smart cards" used for specific purposes, like long-distance phone calls or making purchases at a campus bookstore and cafeteria, aren't really all that smart, because they can only be used for certain purchases or in certain places. However, in the Netherlands, millions of smart cards that are good for small purchases in many stores have been in circulation since the late 1990s. In some situations, people can make purchases using their smart-phones. In short, credit cards, debit cards, smart cards, and smart-phones are different ways to move money when a purchase is made. But having more credit cards or debit cards or paying by smart-phone doesn't change the quantity of money in the economy, any more than having more checks printed increases the amount of money in your checking account.

One key message underlying this discussion of M1 and M2 is that money in a modern economy is not just paper bills and coins; instead, money is closely linked to bank accounts. Indeed, the macroeconomic policies concerning money are largely conducted through the banking system. The next section explains how banks function and how a nation's banking system has the power to create money.

How Banks Work

An old-time bank robber named Willie Sutton (1901–1980) was once asked why he robbed banks. He answered: "That's where the money is." From the perspective of modern economists, Sutton is both right and wrong. He is wrong because the overwhelming majority of money in the economy is not in the form of currency sitting in vaults or drawers at banks, waiting for a robber to appear. Most money is in the form of bank accounts, which exist only as electronic records on computers. From a broader perspective, however, the bank robber was more right than he may have known. Banking is intimately tied up with money and consequently, with the broader economy.

Banks make it far easier for a complex economy to carry out the extraordinary range of transactions that occur in goods, labor, and financial capital markets. Imagine for a moment what the economy would be like if all payments had to be made in cash. When shopping for a large purchase or going on vacation you might need to carry hundreds of dollars in a pocket or purse. Even small businesses would need stockpiles of cash to pay workers and to purchase supplies. In a world where large quantities of cash are common, burglars and pickpockets would be rampant. But along with making transactions much safer and easier, banks play a key role in the saving and borrowing that takes place in financial capital markets.

Banks as Financial Intermediaries

financial intermediary: An institution that operates between a saver with financial assets to invest and an entity who will receive those assets and pay a rate of return.

An "intermediary" is one who stands between two other parties; for example, a person who arranges a blind date between two friends is one kind of intermediary. Banks are a **financial intermediary**—that is, an institution that operates between a saver who deposits money in a bank and a borrower who receives a loan from that bank. But when a bank serves as a financial intermediary, unlike the situation with a couple on a blind date, the saver and the borrower never meet. All the funds deposited are mingled in one big pool, which is then loaned out. Exhibit 29-2 illustrates the position of banks as financial intermediaries, with deposits flowing into a bank and loans flowing out. Of course, when banks make loans to firms, the banks will try to funnel financial capital to healthy businesses that have good prospects for repaying the loans, not to firms that are suffering losses and may be unable to repay.

A bank receives revenue from two sources: interest payments to the bank from those who have received bank loans, and other fees and charges imposed by the bank. Conversely, banks have four main categories of expenses: interest payments to depositors; loans that are not repaid; operating costs of employees, office space and equipment; and taxes. Exhibit 29-3 shows the combined statistics for revenues and expenses for the roughly 7,000 U.S. banks and savings institutions. The U.S. banking industry as a whole earned $79 billion in accounting profits in 2010. Of course, just because the overall banking industry earned a profit doesn't mean that every individual bank did so.

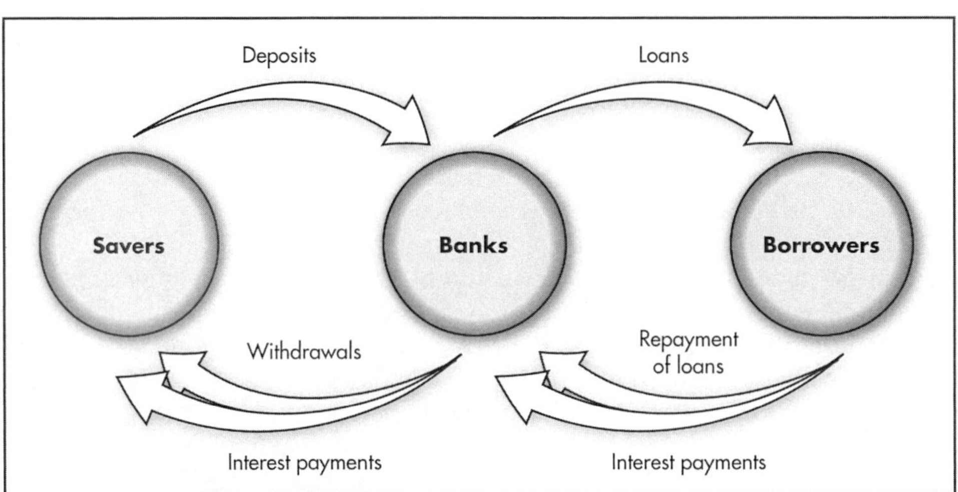

EXHIBIT 29-2 Banks as Financial Intermediaries

Banks act as financial intermediaries because they stand between savers and borrowers. Savers place deposits with banks, and then receive interest payments and withdraw money. Borrowers receive loans from banks, and repay the loans with interest. In turn, banks return money to savers in the form of withdrawals, which also include interest payments from banks to savers.

Banks, Savings and Loans, and Credit Unions

Banks have a couple of close cousins: *savings institutions* and *credit unions*. Banks, as explained in the text, receive deposits from individuals and businesses and make loans with the money.

Savings institutions are also sometimes called "savings and loans" or "thrifts." They also take loans and make deposits. However, from the 1930s until the 1980s, federal law limited how much interest savings institutions were allowed to pay to depositors. They were also required to make most of their loans in the form of housing-related loans, either to home buyers or to real-estate developers and builders.

A *credit union* is a nonprofit financial institution that its members own and run. Members of each credit union decide who is eligible to be a member. Usually, potential members would be everyone in a certain community, or groups of employees, or members of a certain organization. The credit union accepts deposits from members and focuses on making loans back to its members. While there are more credit unions than banks and more banks than savings and loans, the total assets of credit unions are relatively small.

In 2015, the U.S. economy had 5,300 banks, 400 thrifts, and 6,090 credit unions. The banks and savings and loans tend to be roughly the same size. In 2015, on average, these institutions held $2.9 billion in assets each. Credit unions are much smaller. In 2014, they averaged about $180 million in assets each.

EXHIBIT 29-3 Revenues, Expenses, and Profits for the U.S. Banking Industry in 2014

Total Revenues		Total Costs	
Interest income	$469 billion	Interest payments	$47 billion
Other income (fees and charges)	$246 billion	Cost of loans that are not repaid	$29 billion
		Operating expenses (salaries, office space, equipment)	$421 billion
		Taxes	$67 billion
Total revenues	$715 billion	Total costs	$564 billion
Accounting profits = Total revenues – Total costs = $151 billion			

A Bank's Balance Sheet

Banks calculate their profits at the end of each quarter or year. But banks also evaluate their financial condition by comparing their **assets**, which are defined as items of value owned by the firm, with their **liabilities**, which are any amounts or debts owed by the firm. A **balance sheet** is an accounting tool that lists assets and liabilities. Exhibit 29-4 illustrates a hypothetical balance sheet for the Safe and Secure Bank. Because of the two-column format of the balance sheet, with the T-shape formed by the vertical line down the middle and the horizontal line under "Assets" and "Liabilities," it is sometimes called a **T-account**.

assets: Items of value owned by a firm or an individual.

liabilities: Any amounts or debts owed by a firm or an individual.

balance sheet: An accounting tool that lists assets and liabilities.

T-account: A balance sheet with two-column format, with the T-shape formed by the vertical line down the middle and the horizontal line under the column headings for "Assets" and "Liabilities."

When bank customers deposit money into a checking account, savings account, or a certificate of deposit, the bank views these deposits as liabilities. After all, the bank owes these deposits to its customers, when the customers wish to withdraw their money. The Safe and Secure Bank holds $10 million in deposits.

Loans are the first category of bank assets shown in Exhibit 29-4. Say that a family takes out a 30-year mortgage loan to purchase a house, which means that the borrower will repay the loan over the next 30 years. This loan is clearly an asset from the bank's perspective because the borrower has a legal obligation to make payments to the bank over time. But in practical terms, how can the value of the mortgage loan that is being paid over 30 years be measured in the present? One way of measuring the value of something—whether a loan or anything else—is by estimating what another party in the market is willing to pay for it. Many banks issue home loans, and charge various handling and processing fees for doing so, but then sell the loans to other banks or financial institutions

EXHIBIT 29-4 A Balance Sheet for the Safe and Secure Bank

The "T" in a T-account separates the assets of a firm on the left from its liabilities on the right. All firms use (much more complex) T-accounts. But for a bank, the assets are the financial instruments that either the bank is holding—its reserves—or those instruments where other parties owe money to the bank—like loans made by the bank and bonds purchased by the bank. Liabilities are what the bank owes to others: specifically, the bank owes any deposits made in the bank to those who have made them. The net worth of the bank is the total assets minus total liabilities. For a healthy business, net worth will be positive. For a bankrupt firm, net worth will be negative.

Assets		**Liabilities**	
Loans	$5 million	Deposits	$10 million
Bonds	$4 million		
Reserves	$2 million		

Net worth = Assets – Liabilities
$1 million = $11 million – $10 million

who collect the loan payments. The market where loans are made to borrowers is called the *primary loan market*, while the market in which these loans are bought and sold by financial institutions is the *secondary loan market*.

One key factor that affects what financial institutions are willing to pay for a loan, when they buy it in the secondary loan market, is the perceived riskiness of the loan: that is, given the characteristics of the borrower like income level and whether the local economy is performing strongly, what proportion of loans of this type will be repaid? The greater the risk that a loan will not be repaid, the less that any financial institution will pay to acquire the loan. Another key factor is to compare the interest rate charged on the original loan with the current interest rate in the economy. If the original loan made at some point in the past requires the borrower to pay a low interest rate, but current interest rates are relatively high, then a financial institution will pay less to acquire the loan. In contrast, if the original loan requires the borrower to pay a high interest rate, while current interest rates are relatively low, then a financial institution will pay more to acquire the loan. For the Safe and Secure Bank in this example, the total value of its loans if they were sold to other financial institutions in the secondary market is $5 million.

bond: A financial contract through which a borrower like a corporation, a city or state, or the federal government agrees to repay the amount that was borrowed and also a rate of interest over a period of time in the future.

The second category of bank asset is **bonds**, which are a contract that works this way: when someone buys a bond, the party that issued the bond receives money in the present and promises to repay with interest in the future. Bonds are a common mechanism for borrowing, used not only by the federal government but also by state governments, private companies, and nonprofit organizations. A bank takes some of the money it has received in deposits and uses the money to buy bonds—typically bonds issued by the

CLEARING IT UP

Is a Bank Account a "Liability"?

The way in which a bank views its "assets" and "liabilities" may seem backward at first. How can a bank account be a liability? However, banks look at assets and liabilities in the opposite way from individuals. As a bank customer, you consider your bank deposit as an asset, while if you borrow money from a bank, you view it as a liability. But from the bank's point of view, it owes the bank deposit to you, which makes the deposit a liability, and the bank plans to receive loan payments from you, which makes the loan an asset to the bank. So when drawing up a list of bank assets and liabilities, think as if you are managing a bank!

government. Government bonds are low-risk because the government is virtually certain to pay off the bond, albeit at a low rate of interest. These bonds are an asset for banks in the same way that loans are an asset; that is, the bank will receive a stream of payments in the future. The Safe and Secure Bank holds bonds with a total value of $4 million.

The final entry under assets is **reserves**, which is money that the bank keeps on hand, and that is not loaned out or invested in bonds—and thus might not lead to interest payments. The Safe and Secure Bank is holding $2 million in reserves. Government regulators typically set minimum reserve levels that banks must hold, but banks can also hold additional reserves if they wish. The next chapter will explain how these reserves provide a policy tool that governments can use to influence bank behavior.

reserves: Funds that a bank keeps on hand and that are not loaned out or invested in bonds.

The **net worth** of a bank is defined as its total assets minus its total liabilities. For the Safe and Secure Bank shown in Exhibit 29-4, net worth is equal to $1 million; that is, $11 million in assets minus $10 million in liabilities. For a financially healthy bank, the net worth will be positive. If a bank has negative net worth, and depositors tried to withdraw their money, the bank would not be able to give all depositors their money.

net worth: Total assets minus total liabilities.

How Banks Go Bankrupt

A bank that is bankrupt will have a negative net worth; that is, its assets will be worth less than its liabilities. How can this happen? The balance sheet helps to explain.

A well-run bank will assume that a small percentage of borrowers do not repay their loans on time, or at all, and factor these missing payments into its planning. Remember, the calculations of the expenses of banks every year includes a factor for loans that are not repaid, and the value of a bank's loans on its balance sheet assumes a certain level of riskiness because some loans will not be repaid. But even if a bank expects a certain number of loan defaults, it will suffer if the number of loan defaults is much greater than expected, as can happen during a recession. For example, if the Safe and Secure Bank in Exhibit 29-4 experienced a wave of unexpected defaults, so that its loans declined in value from $5 million to $3 million, then the assets of the Safe and Secure Bank would decline so that the bank had negative net worth.

The risk of an unexpectedly high level of loan defaults can be especially difficult for banks because of a bank's liabilities, namely the deposits of its customers, can be withdrawn quickly, while many of the bank's assets like loans and bonds will only be repaid over years or even decades. This **asset-liability time mismatch**—a bank's liabilities can be withdrawn in the short term while its assets are repaid in the long term—can cause severe problems for a bank. For example, imagine a bank that has loaned a substantial amount of money at a certain interest rate, but then sees interest rates rise substantially. The bank can find itself in a precarious situation. If it doesn't raise the interest rate it pays to depositors, then deposits will flow to other institutions that offer the higher interest rates that are now prevailing. However, if the bank raises the interest rates that it pays to depositors, it may end up in a situation where it is paying a higher interest rate to depositors than it is collecting from those past loans that were made at lower interest rates. Clearly, the bank can't survive in the long term if it is paying out more in interest to depositors than it is receiving from borrowers.

asset-liability time mismatch: A bank's liabilities can be withdrawn in the short term while its assets are repaid in the long term.

How can banks protect themselves against an unexpectedly high rate of loan defaults and against the risk of an asset-liability time mismatch? One strategy is for a bank to **diversify** its loans, which means lending to a variety of customers. For example, suppose a bank specialized in lending to a niche market—say, making a high proportion of its loans to construction companies that build offices in one downtown area. If that one area suffers an unexpected economic downturn, the bank will suffer large losses. However, if a bank loans both to consumers who are buying homes and cars and also to a wide range of firms in many industries and geographic areas, the bank is less exposed to risk. When a bank diversifies its loans, those categories of borrowers who have an unexpectedly large number of defaults will tend to be balanced out, according to random chance, by other borrowers who have an unexpectedly low number of defaults. Thus, diversification of

diversify: Making loans or investments with a variety of firms, to reduce the risk of being adversely affected by events at one or a few firms.

Securitized Subprime Loans and the Financial Crisis of 2007–2009

Many banks make mortgage loans so that people can buy a home, but then don't keep the loans on their books as an asset. Instead, the bank sells the loan. These loans are commonly "securitized," which means that they are bundled together into a financial security, which is sold to investors. Investors in these mortgage-backed securities receive a rate of return based on the payments that people make on all the mortgages that stand behind the security.

Securitization offers certain advantages. If a bank makes most of its loans in a local area, then the bank may be financially vulnerable if the local economy declines, so that many people are unable to make their payments. But if a bank sells its local loans, and then buys a mortgage-backed security based on home loans in many parts of the country, it can avoid being exposed to local financial risks. (In the simple example in the text, banks just own "bonds." In reality, banks can own a number of financial instruments, as long as these financial investments are safe enough to satisfy the government bank regulators.) From the standpoint of a local home buyer, securitization offers the benefit that a local bank doesn't need to have lots of extra funds to make a loan, because the bank is only planning to hold that loan for a short time, before selling the loan so that it can be pooled into a financial security.

But securitization also offers one potentially large disadvantage. If a bank is going to hold a mortgage loan as an asset, the bank has an incentive to scrutinize the borrower carefully to ensure that the loan is likely to be repaid. However, a bank that is going to sell the loan may be less careful in making the loan in the first place. The bank will be more willing to make what are called "subprime loans," which are loans which have characteristics like low or zero down-payment, little scrutiny of whether the borrower has a reliable income, and sometimes low payments for the next year or two that will be followed by much higher payments after that. Some subprime loans made in the mid-2000s were later dubbed NINJA loans: that is, loans made even though the borrower had demonstrated No Income, No Job, or Assets.

These subprime loans were typically sold and turned into financial securities—but with a twist. The idea was that if losses occurred on these mortgage-backed securities, certain investors would agree to take the first, say, 5% of such losses. Other investors would agree to take, say, the next 5% of losses. By this approach, still other investors would not need to take any losses unless these mortgage-backed financial securities lost 25% or 30% or more of their total value. These complex securities, along with other economic factors, encouraged a large expansion of subprime loans in the mid-2000s.

The economic stage was now set for a banking crisis. Banks thought they were buying only ultra-safe securities, because even though the securities were ultimately backed by risky subprime mortgages, the banks only invested in the part of those securities where they were protected from small or moderate levels of losses. But as housing prices fell after 2007, and the deepening recession made it harder for many people to make their mortgage payments, many banks found that their mortgage-backed financial assets could end up being worth much less than they had expected—and so the banks were staring bankruptcy in the face.

loans can help banks to keep a positive net worth. However, if a widespread recession occurs that touches many industries and geographic areas, diversification won't help.

Along with diversifying their loans, banks have several other strategies to reduce the risk of an unexpectedly large number of loan defaults. For example, banks can sell some of the loans they make in the secondary loan market, as described earlier, and instead hold a greater share of assets in the form of government bonds or reserves. Nevertheless, in a lengthy recession, most banks will see their net worth decline because a higher share of loans will not be repaid in tough economic times.

How Banks Create Money

Banks and money are intertwined. It's not just that most money is in the form of bank accounts. In addition, the banking system can literally create money through the process of making loans. This section describes how banks create money.

The Story of System Bank

Let's start with a hypothetical example. The people in an economy have $10 million in money, and they all deposit all of their money in a single bank, called System Bank. Sys-

EXHIBIT 29-5 System Bank's Balance Sheet, 100% Reserves

A bank with 100% reserves would hold all of its deposits as reserves, and not make any loans.

Assets		Liabilities	
Reserves	$10 million	Deposits	$10 million

tem Bank starts off with a simple business plan: It keeps the depositor's money safe by holding all money in the form of reserves. The T-account balance sheet for System Bank with 100% reserves is shown in Exhibit 29-5. Obviously, System Bank can't afford to pay interest to depositors because it isn't earning any interest by making loans. In this form, System Bank is basically just a big piggy bank for keeping money safe.

However, the owners of System Bank notice that from month to month, the inflows of deposits from some people are pretty much counterbalanced by the withdrawals of others. Thus, in some months the deposits and reserves of System Bank grow a little higher than $10 million, and sometimes they fall a little below $10 million, but there is always at least $9.5 million in the bank. So the owners of System Bank come up with a new business plan. They will hold reserves of only 10%, rather than 100%, and they will loan out the remaining $9 million. By loaning out the $9 million and charging interest, they reason, they will be able to make interest payments to depositors. Instead of becoming just a storage place for deposits, System Bank can become a financial intermediary between savers and borrowers.

This change in business plan alters System Bank's balance sheet, as shown in Exhibit 29-6. In this economy, remember, people either deposit all of their money in System Bank, or they buy something from a firm that deposits the money in the firm's account at System Bank. So the total deposits in this economy—that is, the liabilities for System Bank—now total $19 million; that is, the original $10 million in deposits plus the additional $9 million in deposits resulting from the loans. The assets of System Bank also total $19 million. Although the bank loaned out $9 million, thus reducing its original reserves from $10 million to $1 million, the bank also received $9 million in additional deposits to put back into reserves, raising its reserves back to the original $10 million. In addition, System Bank now has $9 million in loan assets.

Before discussing further the situation of System Bank, pause for a moment and notice a remarkable fact: when System Bank decided to stop holding all money in reserves and

EXHIBIT 29-6 System Bank's Balance Sheet: 10% Reserves, One Round of Loans

Imagine that System Bank starts with the situation in Exhibit 29-5, but then decides to hold only 10% of its original $10 million in deposits as reserves and to loan out the remaining $9 million. However, since System Bank is the only bank in this economy, the $9 million that is loaned out also ends up being deposited in the bank by the recipients of the loan. Thus, bank deposits rise from the original $10 million to $19 million. With deposits of $19 million and loans of $9 million, the remaining reserves are still $10 million.

Assets		Liabilities	
Loans	$9 million	Deposits	$19 million
Reserves	$10 million		

instead to hold only a portion in reserves and loan out the rest, the quantity of money in the economy expanded. By making loans, System Bank created money.

Of course, the assumption that an economy has only one bank is a gross oversimplification, but the banking system as a whole will work to create money, just like in the example of System Bank. When banks start making loans, and people and firms start redepositing the loans in other bank accounts, money is created in the economy. System Bank uses the metaphor of a single bank for the entire economy to describe the process of money creation for the banking system as a whole.

The Money Multiplier

The owners of System Bank now notice another intriguing fact. They had originally decided that holding reserves equal to 10% of deposits was a sufficient margin for safety, to assure that System Bank would have enough cash on hand for those who are withdrawing money. But after making one round of loans, System Bank has $19 million in deposits. If the bank wishes to hold 10% of that amount in reserves, it needs to hold only $1.9 million in reserves. But if System Bank has $10 million in reserves, and wishes to hold only $1.9 million in reserves, then the bank can make a second round of loans, this time of $8.1 million.

Again, those people who receive the loans either deposit the money in System Bank themselves, or spend the money with a business that deposits the money in System Bank. The new balance sheet of System Bank appears in Exhibit 29-7. The liabilities of System Bank—that is, its deposits—now total $27.1 million, which is the previous $19 million in deposits plus $8.1 million. The total loans of the bank are now $17.1 million; that is, the $9 million in loans from the first round plus $8.1 million in loans from the second round. Finally, the reserves of the bank remain at $10 million. System Bank loaned out $8.1 million of its reserves, but it also received deposits of $8.1 million, which it is holding in its reserves.

But now System Bank is holding $27.1 million in deposits, and for a 10% margin of safety, it wishes to hold only $2.71 million in reserves. Since the bank is holding $10 million in reserves, it can now make a third round of loans, this time of $10 million – $2.71 million = $7.29 million. A pattern is forming here. System Bank is making cycle after cycle of loans, but each cycle is less than the previous one.

Exactly how much money will exist in this economy as System Bank (or the banking system) makes all of these successive rounds of loans? The original quantity of money in this economy was $10 million. In the first round of lending, System Bank kept 10%

EXHIBIT 29-7 System Bank's Balance Sheet: 10% Reserves, Second Round of Loans

Imagine that System Bank starts off with the situation in Exhibit 29-6, but still wishes to hold only 10% of its deposits as reserves. Thus, starting with $19 million in deposits, it wishes to hold $1.9 million in reserves. Since the bank currently has $10 million in reserves, it can loan out $8.1 million. Total loans increase from $9 million to $17.1 million. However, since System Bank is the only bank in this economy, the $8.1 million that is loaned out also ends up being deposited in the bank by the recipients of the loan. Thus, bank deposits rise from $19 million to $27.1 million. With deposits of $27.1 million and loans of $17.1 million, the remaining reserves are still at $10 million.

Assets		Liabilities	
Loans	$17.1 million	Deposits	$27.1 million
Reserves	$10 million		

of that $10 million in reserves and loaned out the remaining $9 million, which then came back to the bank in the form of deposits. In the second round of lending, System Bank kept 10% of that additional $9 million in reserve, and loaned out the remaining $8.1 million. In a third round, System Bank would keep 10% of that $8.1 million in reserve, and loan out the remaining $7.29 million. These rounds of lending will continue through a fourth, fifth, and sixth round, and indeed many more rounds. Each round of lending will create additional money, but the marginal additions become smaller and smaller.

Fortunately, a formula exists for calculating the total of these many rounds of lending in a banking system. If the **reserve ratio** is the proportion of deposits that the bank wished to hold in reserves, then the formula is:

reserve ratio: The proportion of deposits that the bank holds in the form of reserves.

$$\text{Total quantity of money} = \text{Original quantity of reserves} \times \frac{1}{\text{Reserve ratio}}$$

$$= \$10 \text{ million} \times \frac{1}{0.1}$$

$$= \$10 \text{ million} \times 10 = \$100 \text{ million}$$

Thus, in this example, the total quantity of money generated in this economy after all rounds of lending are completed will be $100 million. The **money multiplier** is equal to the total money in the economy divided by the original quantity of money. The formula to calculate the money multiplier is 1/reserve ratio. In this example, the reserve ratio is 10% or 0.1, and the money multiplier is 10. The money multiplier also shows how much the total supply of money in the economy would be altered if the original quantity of reserves was increased or decreased by $1.

money multiplier: Total money in the economy divided by the original quantity of money, or change in the total money in the economy divided by a change in the original quantity of money.

Cautions about the Money Multiplier

The money multiplier will depend on the proportion of reserves that banks choose to hold. System Bank chose to hold reserves equal to 10% of deposits, leading to a money multiplier of 10. But if System Bank had chosen to hold reserves of 20% of deposits, then the money multiplier would fall to 5. Banks may decide to vary how much they hold in reserves for two reasons: macroeconomic conditions and government rules. When an economy is in recession, banks are likely to hold a higher proportion of reserves because they fear that loans are less likely to be repaid when the economy is slow. The government may also raise or lower the required reserves held by banks.

The process of how banks create money shows how the quantity of money in an economy is closely linked to the quantity of lending or credit in the economy. Indeed, all of the money in the economy, except for the original reserves, is a result of bank loans that are redeposited and loaned out, again and again.

The additional creation of money in this economy isn't making anyone rich. Sure, the total quantity of bank deposits gets larger as the money multiplier operates, but so does the total quantity of loans. If you borrow $5,000 and put the money in your bank account, you haven't made yourself any richer, because the money in your bank account is exactly equal to the money you owe. The money multiplier reflects an increase in lending and borrowing in the economy, but lending and borrowing by themselves don't mean that real goods and services have been produced.

Finally, the money multiplier depends on people redepositing the money that they receive in the banking system. If people instead store their cash in safe-deposit boxes or in shoeboxes hidden in their closets, then banks cannot recirculate the money in the form of loans. Indeed, governments have an incentive to assure that bank deposits are safe because if people worry that they may lose their bank deposits, they may start holding more money in cash, instead of depositing it in banks, and the quantity of loans in an economy will decline. In countries with a high degree of economic or political instability, economists sometimes refer to "mattress savings," by which they mean money that people are hiding in their homes because they don't trust banks. When mattress savings in an economy are substantial, then banks cannot lend out those funds and the money multiplier cannot operate as effectively, the overall quantity of money and loans in such an economy will therefore be reduced.

Conclusion

Money and banks are marvelous social inventions that help a modern economy to function. Compared with the alternative of barter, money makes market exchanges vastly easier in goods, labor, and financial markets. Banking makes money still more effective in facilitating exchanges in goods and labor markets. Moreover, the process of banks making loans in financial capital markets is intimately tied to the creation of money.

But the extraordinary economic gains that are possible through money and banking also suggest some possible corresponding dangers. If banks aren't working well, it sets off a decline in convenience and safety of transactions throughout the economy. If the banks are under financial stress because of a widespread decline in the value of their assets, loans may become far less available, which can deal a crushing blow to sectors of the economy that depend on borrowed money like business investment, home construction, and car manufacturing. Given the macroeconomic dangers of a malfunctioning banking system, the next chapter will discuss government policies for controlling the money supply and for keeping the banking system safe.

Key Concepts and Summary

1. **Money** is what people in a society regularly use when purchasing or selling goods and services.
2. If money were not available, people would need to **barter** with each other, meaning that each person would need to identify others with whom they have a **double coincidence of wants**—that is, each party has a specific good or service that the other desires.
3. Money serves three functions: a **medium of exchange**, a **unit of account**, and as a **store of value**.
4. Money is measured with several definitions: **M1** includes **currency**, traveler's checks, and money in checking accounts (**demand deposits**). **M2** includes all of M1, plus **savings deposits**, small **time deposits** like **certificates of deposit**, and **money market funds**.
5. Banks facilitate the use of money for transactions in the economy, since people and firms can use bank accounts when selling or buying goods and services, when paying a worker or being paid, and when saving money or receiving a loan. In the financial capital market, banks are **financial intermediaries**; that is, they operate between savers who supply financial capital and borrowers who demand loans.
6. A **balance sheet** (sometimes called a **T-account**) is an accounting tool which lists assets in one column and **liabilities** in another column. The liabilities of a bank are its deposits. The assets of a bank include its loans, its ownership of bonds, and its **reserves** (which are not loaned out). The **net worth** of a bank is calculated by subtracting the bank's liabilities from its assets.
7. Banks run a risk of negative net worth if the value of their assets declines. The value of assets can decline because of an unexpectedly high number of defaults on loans, or if interest rates rise and the bank suffers an **asset-liability time mismatch** in which the bank is receiving a low rate of interest on its long-term loans but must pay the currently higher market rate of interest to attract depositors. Banks can protect themselves against these risks by choosing to **diversify** their loans or to hold a greater proportion of their assets in bonds and reserves.
8. If banks hold only a fraction of their deposits as reserves, then the process of banks lending money, those loans being redeposited in banks, and the banks making additional loans will create money in the economy.
9. The **money multiplier** is defined as the quantity of money that the banking system can generate from each $1 of bank reserves. The formula for calculating the multiplier is 1/reserve ratio, where the **reserve ratio** is the fraction of deposits that the bank wishes to hold as reserves.
10. The quantity of money in an economy and the quantity of credit for loans are inextricably intertwined. Much of the money in an economy is created by the network of banks making loans, people making deposits, and banks making more loans.

Review Questions

1. What are the three functions served by money?
2. How does the existence of money simplify the process of buying and selling?
3. What is the double coincidence of wants?
4. Define M1 and M2.
5. Why is a bank called a financial intermediary?
6. How do banks help money to work better as a medium of exchange?
7. What does a balance sheet show?
8. What are the assets of a bank? What are its liabilities?
9. How do you calculate the net worth of a bank?
10. How can a bank end up with negative net worth?
11. What is the asset-liability time mismatch that all banks face?
12. What is the risk if a bank does not diversify its loans?
13. How do banks create money?
14. What is the formula for the money multiplier?

CHAPTER

30

Monetary Policy and Bank Regulation

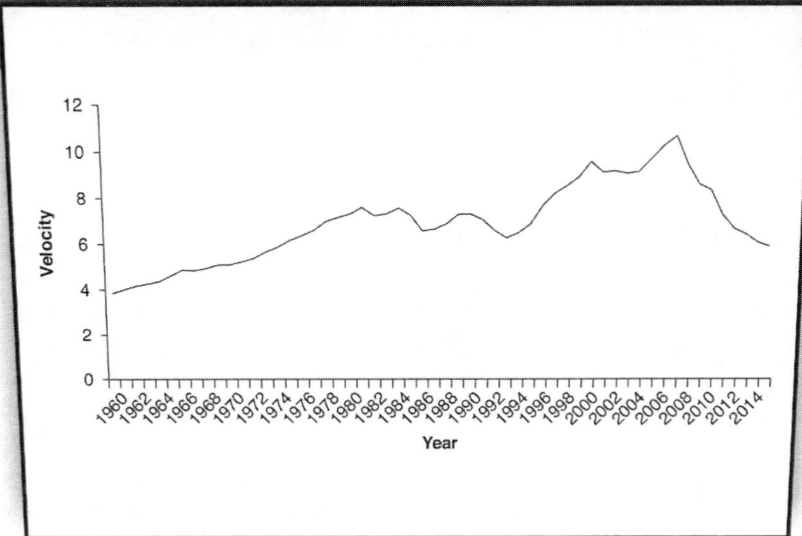

Chapter Outline

Money, loans, and banks are all tied together. Money is held in bank accounts. A banking system creates money when loans made by one bank are deposited and thus counted as money in other banks. When interlocking system of money, loans, and banks works well, economic transactions are made smoothly in goods and labor markets and savers are connected with borrowers. But if the money and banking system doesn't operate smoothly, the economy can tumble into recession.

The government of every country has public policies that attempt to assure that the system of money, loans, and banking functions well. But these policies don't always work perfectly, and the result can either be recession or inflation. This chapter begins by discussing the policies that can affect the quantity of money in the economy. These monetary policy decisions are made by an institution called a central bank. In the United States, the central bank is called the Federal Reserve. In making decisions about the money supply, a central bank decides to raise or lower interest rates, and in this way, to affect some goals of macroeconomic policy like keeping unemployment and inflation low. Another set of policies related to the money and banking system involves reinforcing the stability of a nation's banking system with a combination of protections for bank depositors and regular government inspections of the balance sheets of banks. In the U.S. economy, these policies to assure stability of the banking system involve both the Federal Reserve and several other regulatory institutions within the U.S. Department of the Treasury.

Monetary Policy and the Central Bank

Monetary policy involves altering the quantity of money—and thus the quantity of lending—in the economy. The **central bank** is the institution designed to control the quantity of money in the economy and also to oversee the safety and stability of the banking system. This section introduces the U.S. Federal

monetary policy: Policy that involves altering the quantity of money and thus affecting the level of interest rates and the extent of borrowing.

central bank: An institution to conduct monetary policy and regulate the banking system.

Reserve and some other examples of central banks, while the next section discusses how central banks conduct monetary policy.

The Federal Reserve

The most important task of a central bank is to determine the quantity of money in the economy. Article I, Section 8 of the U.S. Constitution gives Congress the power "to coin money" and "to regulate the value thereof." As part of the 1913 legislation that created the Federal Reserve, Congress delegated these powers to the Fed.

The Federal Reserve is a peculiar organization because it mixes government appointees with representation from private-sector banks. The Federal Reserve at the national level is run by a Board of Governors, which consists of seven members who the President of the United States appoints and the U.S. Senate must confirm. Board of Governor appointments are for 14-year terms and they are arranged so that one term expires January 31 of every even-numbered year. A person may serve only one full term on the Board of Governors. However, the 14-year terms are so long that board members often leave before their term is completed. If a person is appointed to fill out the remainder of someone else's term, that person can still be appointed to an additional full 14-year term. One member of the Board of Governors is designated as the chair. Janet Yellen started a 14-year term on the Board of Governors in 2010 and then was appointed to a 4-year term as chair of the Board of Governors starting in 2014. The Federal Reserve System consists of 12 districts, which are headquartered in the cities shown in Exhibit 30-1. The president of each regional Fed bank is chosen by a nine-member Board of Directors, which includes six representatives elected by commercial banks in each district and three representatives chosen by the Board of Governors. In turn, on certain key policymaking committees, as explained later in the chapter, members of the Board of Governors are combined with presidents of the regional Fed banks.

Other Tasks and Funding of Central Banks

Along with its glamorous task of conducting monetary policy, the Federal Reserve has a number of everyday responsibilities. For example, a central bank must ensure that enough currency and coins are circulating through the financial system to meet public demands.

EXHIBIT 30-1 The 12 Federal Reserve Districts

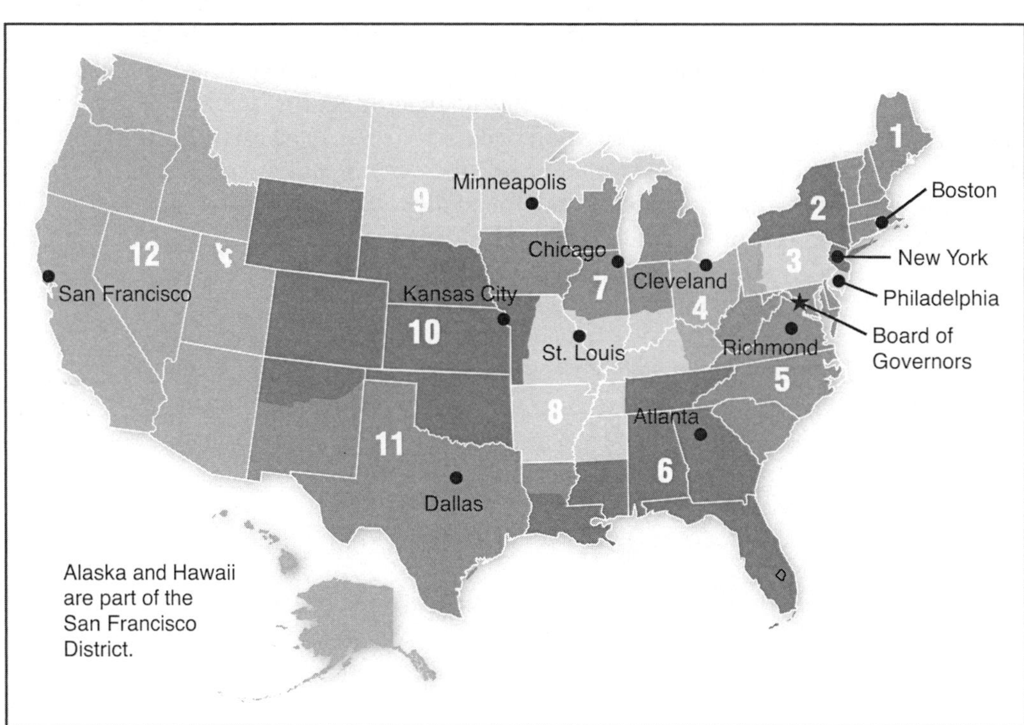

Thus, each year the Federal Reserve increases the amount of currency available in banks around the end-of-December shopping season and reduces it again in January.

The Federal Reserve is also responsible for assuring that banks are in compliance with a wide variety of consumer protection laws. For example, banks are forbidden from discriminating on the basis of age, race, sex, or marital status. Banks are also required to disclose information about the loans they make for buying houses and how those loans are distributed geographically, as well as by sex and race of the loan applicants. Banks are required to disclose certain information to customers about interest rates and fees, but also required to protect the privacy of bank customers unless government authorities follow specific procedures. Most banks are examined on these matters about every 18 months, although those with a poor record of past performance are examined more frequently.

The Fed is also responsible for check processing. When you write a check, say, to buy a pizza, the pizza restaurant deposits the check in its bank. Then, the physical check (or an image of that actual check) needs to be returned to your bank. The Fed contracts out a substantial amount of this work of collecting, sorting, and transmitting checks to private firms. In addition, money needs to be transferred from your bank account to the account of the pizza restaurant. The Fed acts as a bank for the banks and transfers funds as needed between banks to reflect the flows of checks.

The Federal Reserve is financially self-supporting. The Fed holds reserves from member banks, and uses that money to purchase government bonds, which then pay interest to the Fed. The Fed also makes some money from charging banks about 2 cents per check for helping to send checks back from the bank that receives the check to the bank on which the check was written. If the Fed has extra money left over after paying its expenses, it goes to the U.S. Treasury. Typically, about 90% of the total money received by the Federal Reserve—most of it in the form of interest payments on U.S. government bonds—is returned to the U.S. government. Thus, even though the Federal Reserve is self-supporting, it is only allowed to keep enough money to cover its funding needs.

Each currency is managed by a different central bank. These central banks share the common task of determining the money supply for their currencies. Thus, a European Central Bank determines the quantity of euros, the Bank of Japan determines the quantity of the Japanese yen, and the Bank of England determines the quantity of the British pound.

Money at the Millennium

As January 1, 2000, approached, fears abounded of a great computer crash. One fear was that certain computer software might not be able to handle the change from 1999 to 2000. Another concern was that a hidden computer virus that had already spread secretly to many computers might be triggered by the change in date. No one knew quite how seriously to take the threat. But U.S. firms spent roughly $150 billion to protect themselves against Y2K, as the change to the year 2000 was called.

With regard to the nation's banking system, the fear was that people might make especially large cash withdrawals in the days leading up to January 1. If credit card networks and check-clearing systems failed to function after Y2K, then people might flock to banks for even larger cash withdrawals. At worst, a financial panic could set in. Thus, by October 1, 1999, the Fed announced that it had stockpiled $200 billion in cash in Federal Reserve banks and commercial banks all around the country.

After New Year's Day in the year 2000, a number of minor computer mishaps occurred. For example, the U.S. government lost touch with a set of spy satellites for four days. A number of airports experienced short-term glitches in the computers that run their air traffic control systems. Seven nuclear power plants experienced problems with their computer systems. About 4,000 small businesses found that their systems for processing credit cards didn't work.

In the banking system, people's demand for currency did surge right around January 1, 2000, but the increase was only about $20 billion—far less than the Fed had on hand. By the end of January, that extra $20 billion in cash had been deposited back into the banking system. In the end, January 1, 2000, brought only some minor computer hitches. But for the Fed, having extra currency on hand, just in case, was a relatively cheap form of insurance against the risk that something might have gone terribly wrong.

In some nations, almost all of the bank supervision and regulation happens through the central bank. In other nations, like the United States, bank supervision and regulation are shared with other government agencies.

How a Central Bank Affects the Money Supply

The Great Recession that rocked the world economy in 2007–2009 led to dramatic changes in how banks around the world conduct monetary policy. Before 2007, a central bank was generally thought to have three traditional tools to affect the quantity of money and credit in the economy: open market operations, reserve requirements, and the discount rate. In discussing how these three tools work, it's useful to think of the central bank as a "bank for banks"—that is, each private-sector bank has its own account at the central bank. However, during the recession of 2007–2009, these three traditional tools proved too weak, and so central banks around the world turned to an innovative set of monetary policies that includes quantitative easing and forward guidance. In December 2015, the Federal Reserve began to use a brand-new method of monetary policy: specifically, it began to use the interest rate that it pays on the reserves that banks hold at the Fed as a policy tool. Let's discuss the three traditional monetary tools, why they became ineffective, and how the newfangled monetary policy tools work.

Within the Federal Reserve, the 12-member Federal Open Market Committee (FOMC) is responsible for making decisions about the conduct of monetary policy. The FOMC includes the seven members of the Fed's Board of Governors who are appointed by the president. It also includes five voting members who are drawn from the 12 regional Federal Reserve Banks—although all of the regional bank presidents typically attend the meetings and participate in the discussions of the FOMC. Thus, while the Board of Governors members hold a majority on the FOMC, the representatives of banks from different regions participate in the decision making, too. The FOMC typically meets every six weeks. The FOMC tries to act by consensus; however, the chair of the Fed has traditionally played a powerful role in defining and shaping that consensus.

Open Market Operations

open market operations: The central bank buying or selling bonds to influence the quantity of money and the level of interest rates.

For several decades leading up to 2009, **open market operations** were the most common Federal Reserve policy tool. This mechanism for conducting monetary policy involved the central bank buying or selling U.S. Treasury bonds in such a way as to influence the quantity of money and the level of interest rates. To understand how open market operations affect the money supply, consider the balance sheet of Happy Bank shown in Exhibit 30-2. Exhibit 30-2*a* shows that Happy Bank starts with \$460 million in assets, divided among reserves, bonds and loans, and \$400 million in liabilities in the form of deposits, with a net worth of \$60 million. Now the central bank purchases \$20 million in bonds from Happy Bank, so that the bond holdings of Happy Bank fall by \$20 million and the bank's reserves rise by \$20 million, as shown in Exhibit 30-2*b*. However, Happy Bank only wants to hold \$40 million in reserves (the quantity of reserves that it started with in Exhibit 30-2*a*), so the bank now decides to loan out the extra \$20 million in reserves, and its loans rise by \$20 million as shown in Exhibit 30-2*c*. The open market operation by the central bank causes Happy Bank to make loans instead of holding its assets in the form of government bonds, which expands the money supply. As the new loans are deposited in banks throughout the economy, these banks will in turn loan out some of the deposits they receive, triggering the money multiplier discussed in the previous chapter.

Where did the Federal Reserve get the \$20 million that it used to purchase the bonds? A central bank has the power to create money. In practical terms, the Federal Reserve would write a check to Happy Bank, so that Happy Bank can have that money credited to its bank account at the Federal Reserve. To be blunt about it, the Federal Reserve created the money to purchase the bonds out of thin air—or with a few clicks on some computer keys.

Open market operations can also reduce the quantity of money and loans in an economy. Exhibit 30-3*a* shows the balance sheet of Happy Bank before the central bank sells

EXHIBIT 30-2 Tracing an Open Market Operation through the Happy Bank's Balance Sheets

Assets		Liabilities	
Loans	300	Deposits	400
Reserves	40		
Bonds	120		

Net worth is 60

(a) The original balance sheet of Happy Bank.

Assets		Liabilities	
Loans	300	Deposits	400
Reserves	40 + 20 = 60		
Bonds	120 – 20 = 100		

Net worth is 60

(b) The central bank buys 20 in bonds from Happy Bank; Happy Bank receives money, and the central bank gets bonds.

Assets		Liabilities	
Loans	300 + 20 = 320	Deposits	400
Reserves	60 – 20 = 40		
Bonds	100		

Net worth is 60

(c) Happy Bank now has more reserves than it wants, so will lend out extra assets. Notice that total assets, total liabilities, and net worth of the bank don't change. All that changes is that because of the open market operation, the bank now holds its assets in a different form.

bonds in the open market. When Happy Bank purchases $30 million in bonds, Happy Bank sends $30 million of its reserves to the central bank, but now holds an additional $30 million in bonds, as shown in Exhibit 30-3*b*. However, Happy Bank wants to hold $40 million in reserves, as in Exhibit 30-3*a*, so it will adjust down the quantity of its loans by $30 million, to bring its reserves back to the desired level, as shown in Exhibit 30-3*c*. In practical terms, a bank can easily reduce its quantity of loans. At any given time, a bank is receiving payments on loans that it made previously and also making new loans. If the bank just slows down or briefly halts making new loans, and instead adds those funds to its reserves, then its overall quantity of loans will decrease. A decrease in the quantity of loans also means fewer deposits in other banks, and other banks reducing their lending as well, as the money multiplier discussed in the previous chapter takes effect.

As mentioned earlier, open market operations were the most commonly used tool of monetary policy in the United States and in most countries for several decades up through 2009. For example, the Federal Reserve announced 78 separate open market operations

EXHIBIT 30-3 An Open Market Operation to Contract the Money Supply

Assets		Liabilities	
Loans	300	Deposits	400
Reserves	40		
Bonds	120		

Net worth is 60

(a) Balance sheet of Happy Bank at start.

Assets		Liabilities	
Loans	300	Deposits	400
Reserves	40 – 30 = 10		
Bonds	120 + 30 = 150		

Net worth is 60

(b) The central bank sells 30 in bonds to Happy Bank. Happy Bank receives the bonds, and the central bank gets money from the reserves of Happy Bank.

Assets		Liabilities	
Loans	300 – 30 = 270	Deposits	400
Reserves	10 + 30 = 40		
Bonds	150		

Net worth is 60

(c) Happy Bank now has less reserves than it wants, so it will build up its reserves by making fewer loans, which decreases the money supply. Because of the open market operation, Happy Bank now holds its assets in a different form—that is, more bonds and fewer loans—which decreases the money supply.

from 1990 to 2009. When the Federal Reserve carried out these open market operations, it announced in advance what effect it wished to have on one particular interest rate—the **federal funds rate**, which is the rate at which banks and certain large financial institutions borrow from and lend to each other when they need a short-term source of funds. These loans are made without collateral, but they are considered to be very low-risk loans because of the size and (presumed) stability of the financial institutions involved.

federal funds interest rate: The interest rate at which banks and other major financial institutions borrow from and lend to each other for short-term loans without collateral.

For example, an overnight loan might occur when a bank needs money to meet its legal reserve requirement and borrows the money from another bank. By selling and buying U.S. government bonds through open market operations, the Federal Reserve can move the federal funds interest rate that banks charge each other higher or lower.

Of course, financial capital markets display a wide range of interest rates, representing borrowers with different risk premiums and loans that are to be repaid over different periods of time. In general, when the federal funds rate drops, other interest rates drop, too, and when the federal funds rate rises, other interest rates rise. But a fall or rise of 1 percentage point in the federal funds rate—which, remember, is for borrowing overnight—will typically have an effect of less than 1 percentage point on a 30-year loan to purchase

CLEARING IT UP

Does Selling or Buying Bonds Increase the Money Supply?

Should a central bank buy bonds or sell bonds to increase the money supply? To avoid confusion, keep track of whether money is flowing in or out of the central bank. When a central bank buys bonds, money is flowing out of the central bank to individual banks in the economy, and thus increasing the money supply in the broader economy. When a central bank sells bonds, then money from individual banks in the economy is flowing into the central bank—reducing the quantity of money in the economy.

a house or a 3-year loan to purchase a car. Monetary policy can push the entire spectrum of interest rates higher or lower, but the specific interest rates are set by the forces of supply and demand in those specific markets for lending and borrowing.

Reserve Requirements

A second traditional method of conducting monetary policy is for the central bank to raise or lower the **reserve requirement**, which is the proportion of its deposits that a bank is legally required to deposit with the central bank. If banks are required to hold a greater amount in reserves, they have less money available to lend out. If banks are allowed to hold a smaller amount in reserves, they will have a greater amount of money available to lend out.

reserve requirement: The proportion of its deposits that a bank is legally required to deposit with the central bank.

In mid-2016, the Federal Reserve required banks to hold reserves equal to 0% of the first \$15.2 million in deposits, then to hold reserves equal to 3% of the deposits from \$15.2 million up to \$110.2 million in deposits, and 10% of any amount above \$110.2 million. Small changes in the reserve requirements are made almost every year, but changes in reserve requirements that have a large effect on bank reserves are rare.

The Discount Rate

A third traditional method for conducting monetary policy is to raise or lower the **discount rate**, which is the interest rate charged by the central bank when it makes loans to commercial banks. If a bank finds that it is not holding enough in reserves to meet the reserve requirements, it needs to borrow at least for the short term from the central bank. If the central bank raises the discount rate, then banks will hold a higher level of reserves to reduce the chance of needing to borrow at that higher interest rate. When banks hold these higher reserves, it reduces the money supply in the economy as a whole. If the central bank lowers the discount rate it charges to banks, then banks will be less concerned about the prospect of needing a short-term loan to fill out their reserves. In turn, the bank will be more willing to lend aggressively, which will increase the money supply.

discount rate: The interest rate charged by the central bank when it makes loans to commercial banks.

As it turns out, the Federal Reserve has traditionally loaned relatively little money at the discount rate. Before a bank borrows from the Federal Reserve to fill out its needed reserves, the bank is expected to first borrow from other available sources, like other banks. When banks ended up turning to the Federal Reserve for a discount rate loan, it was often taken as a sign that the bank was in financial trouble, and no other bank was willing to lend to it. Given that most banks borrowed little at the discount rate, changing the discount rate up or down has little impact on their behavior. Consequently, altering the discount rate is a relatively weak tool of monetary policy.

Quantitative Easing

The most powerful and commonly used of the three traditional tools of monetary policy—open market operations—worked by expanding or contracting the money supply in a way that influenced the federal funds interest rate, and thus other interest rates as well. But in late 2008, as the U.S. economy struggled with recession, the Federal Reserve had already reduced the federal funds interest rate to nearly zero. With the recession still ongoing, the

Fed decided to take innovative and nontraditional steps to expand the quantity of money and credit.

quantitative easing: A central bank policy of expanding the supply of lending and credit by direct large-scale purchase of government and private financial assets.

The policy of **quantitative easing** involves the Federal Reserve making large-scale purchases of financial assets. By mid-2016, the Fed held roughly $2.4 trillion in U.S. Treasury securities and $1.7 trillion in private-sector financial securities that were backed by mortgage loans. In these cases, the Fed expanded the supply of money and credit in the economy by creating a greater quantity of the money and credit outright.

The quantitative easing policy fundamentally changed the financial sheet of the Federal Reserve. Exhibit 30-4 shows a simplified version of the actual balance sheet of the Federal Reserve back in August 2007, when concerns about the possibility of a financial crisis first began to percolate, and what had happened by July 2016. In August 2007, the main asset held by the Fed was financial securities, mainly bonds issued by the U.S. Treasury. The main liability of the Fed was the outstanding U.S. currency. In particular, notice that back in 2007, reserve balances held by U.S. banks at the Fed were a relatively low $14 billion, only a little more than was legally required. Now compare the Fed balance sheet in mid-2016. As a result of the policy of quantitative easing, the total assets and liabilities of the Fed had more than quintupled. In July 2016, the Fed held $4.2 trillion in financial securities, mainly U.S. Treasury bonds and private-sector mortgage-backed securities, which it had purchased as part of the quantitative easing policy. But on the liabilities side of its balance sheet, reserve balances had climbed to $2.3 trillion. Banks were now holding vast quantities of excess reserves, more than 20 times as much as legally required.

Most of the major central banks around the world have used quantitative easing policies in the last few years. A substantial number of economic studies have found that by expanding the supply of credit, such policies help to reduce interest rates: for example, a common finding is that when the central bank purchases long-term bonds equivalent to 10% of that country's GDP, the rate of return on those bonds falls by about 0.5%. In mid-2016, the Federal Reserve had purchased bonds equal to about 25% of the GDP of the U.S. economy.

The quantitative easing policies adopted by the Federal Reserve (and by other central banks around the world) were usually thought of as temporary measures at the time they were adopted. In 2016, the Federal Reserve policy was that it was not planning to purchase any additional securities. These financial securities are government or private-sector bonds that pay off over a certain period of time, such as 10 years or 30 years, and so if the Fed does not purchase any additional securities, its stock of existing securities will gradually diminish over time. But the future direction of quantitative easing policies is controversial, both in the United States and around the world. Some would prefer to see quantitative easing held stable or gradually reduced. A typical concern is that even if quantitative easing is needed when the target federal funds interest rate is pushed to nearly 0% in a deep recession, in more usual times, financial markets will operate better—in the

EXHIBIT 30-4 The Evolution of the Federal Reserve Balance Sheet (in billions of dollars)

Balance sheet on August 8, 2007				*Balance sheet on July 27, 2016*			
Assets		**Liabilities**		**Assets**		**Liabilities**	
Securities	$791	Reserve Balances	$ 14	Securities	$4,226	Reserve Balances	$2,332
Other Assets	$ 78	Currency	$777	Other Assets	$ 238	Currency	$1,417
		Other	$ 45			Other	$ 675
		Capital	$ 33			Capital	$ 40
Total	**$869**	**Total**	**$869**	**Total**	**$4,464**	**Total**	**$4,464**

sense that they will, on average, produce more accurate assessments of risks and interest rates—if the Federal Reserve is not stepping in to purchase assets worth trillions of dollars. However, others have suggested that quantitative easing could be expanded to having the central bank print money to add to the supply of lending in other parts of the economy, such as loans to small businesses.

Adjusting Interest Rates on Bank Reserves

U.S. banks are now holding more than $2 trillion in reserves with the Federal Reserve, which, as shown earlier in Exhibit 30-4, is a dramatic change from a decade ago. As a result, the Federal Reserve announced in September 2014 that when the time came for it to raise interest rates, it was planning to use a new policy tool: adjusting the rate of interest that it pays to banks on the reserves that banks are holding at the Fed. The Fed uses the policy tool of adjusting the interest rate paid on bank reserves to affect the federal funds interest rate—that is, the same interest rate it used to target with open market operations.

The basic principle is straightforward. Imagine that you are running a bank, and another bank asks for a short-term loan. If the Federal Reserve is paying your bank an interest rate of 0.5% on its reserves, you will not be willing to lend to that other bank for an interest rate of less than the 0.5% you are receiving on your reserves. If the Fed raises the interest rate that it pays on bank reserves to 1.0%, you won't be willing to lend to that other bank for an interest rate of less than 1.0%. Thus, when the Federal Reserve adjusts the interest rate that it will pay on bank reserves, it will affect supply in the federal funds market for short-term loans between large financial institutions.

However, the market for lending and borrowing at the federal funds interest rate has evolved in recent years, in a way that makes the use of this policy tool more complicated. A decade or more in the past, the federal funds market primarily involved short-term lending by banks to other banks. However, given that banks are already holding enormous quantities of reserves, their need for short-term borrowing has been greatly reduced. (After all, if a bank needs a quick source of short-term funds, it can usually just draw on its reserves held at the Federal Reserve, without a need to borrow.) But the federal funds market also involves borrowing and lending by financial institutions other than banks. For example, it includes bank holding companies and foreign banking organizations, which are companies that own banks but also carry out other nonbank financial transactions. The borrowers and lenders in the federal funds market also include certain government-sponsored enterprises that seek to support the home mortgage industry. The Federal Home Loan Bank Board is a system of regional banks that lend money to over 7,000 member banks so that the member banks have funds to make mortgage loans. Two other agencies commonly known as Fannie Mae and Freddie Mac—and more formally named the Federal National Mortgage Association and the Federal Home Loan Mortgage Corporation—help banks in packaging their home mortgages into financial securities that can then be resold to investors.

However, although the Federal Reserve pays interest on the reserves held by banks, these interest payments are not available to the other players in the federal funds market. Thus, these other financial institutions will typically be willing to lend in the federal funds market at a slightly lower interest rate than whatever rate the Federal Reserve is paying to banks. Of course, the Federal Reserve is aware of this. The Fed sets a "target zone" for the federal funds interest rate, and it sets the interest rate that it pays on excess bank reserves at the top of this target zone. Near the end of 2016, for example, the Fed's target for the federal funds interest rate was 0.25%–0.5%, and so the interest rate on reserves was set at 0.5%.

Looking ahead in late 2016, the Federal Reserve is planning to use the interest rate on bank reserves as its main tool of monetary policy. For example, if the Fed raises the interest rate it pays on bank reserves, there will be less supply of funds by banks to the federal funds market, and interest rates in that market should also rise. Conversely, if the Fed lowers the interest rate that it pays on bank reserves, this step will increase supply to the federal funds market, and reduce the federal funds interest rate. As explained earlier, the notion is that increases or decreases in the federal funds interest rate will then lead to shifts in the same direction (if not always of the same size) in other interest rates across the economy. But the Fed used the policy tool of adjusting interest rates paid on bank reserves for the first time in December 2015, and at that time, it involved only a very small rise in the federal funds interest rate from a target zone of 0%–0.25% up to a target of 0.25%–0.5%. How well this tool works in practice—and whether or how much it needs to be supplemented with other Federal Reserve policy actions—remains to be seen.

Forward Guidance

forward guidance: A central bank policy of announcing its expectations for the course of the economy and monetary policy, and in this way affecting current interest rates and lending by affecting the expectations of lenders and borrowers.

Even when the Federal Reserve reduced interest rates to low levels during the Great Recession in 2008, potential borrowers in financial markets still had to consider the risk that interest might rise in the future. To address this concern, the Federal Reserve and other central banks around the world have engaged in a policy of **forward guidance**, which involves announcing that interest rates are going to remain low for a certain period of time into the future. For example, following the December 2012 meeting of the FOMC, it was announced that the Fed anticipated keeping interest rates near zero as long as the unemployment rate remained above 6.5% and as long as inflation projected a year or two into the future did not seem likely to exceed 2.5%.

When deciding to lend or to borrow, one must inevitably form expectations about the future: for example, what real interest rates, inflation rates, and nominal interest rates are likely to be. Forward guidance seeks to influence current interest rates by affecting those expectations about the future. Of course, forward guidance by a central bank only works to the extent that participants in financial markets believe that the central bank will actually follow its announced plans. When the Federal Reserve announced in 2012 that it would keep interest rates near zero until unemployment fell below 6.5%, it seemed to be implying that it would at that point raise interest rates. However, when the unemployment rate fell below 6.5% in April 2014, the Fed did not actually act to raise the federal funds interest rate until December 2015.

Back before the Great Recession, a central bank that wished to increase the quantity of money and lending in the economy would typically buy bonds in an open market operation, although it also had the option of reducing the reserve requirement and lowering the discount rate. At present, a central bank that wishes to increase the quantity of money and lending would engage in quantitative easing, or reduce the interest rate that it is paying on bank reserves, or offer forward guidance about its expected economic outlook and intended future policy actions that would encourage more lending. Conversely, a central bank that desires to restrain the growth of money and lending in the economy would use these tools in the opposite way. A decade ago, before the Great Recession, that central bank would sell bonds in an open market operation, raise the reserve requirement, or raise the discount rate. At present, that central bank would reverse its past practices of quantitative easing, raise the interest rate that it pays on reserves, or alter its forward guidance in a way that would discourage additional lending.

Monetary Policy and Economic Outcomes

expansionary monetary policy: A monetary policy that increases the supply of money and the quantity of loans; also called a "loose" monetary policy.

contractionary monetary policy: A monetary policy that reduces the supply of money and loans; also called a "tight" monetary policy.

A monetary policy that expands the quantity of money and loans is known as an **expansionary monetary policy** or a "loose" monetary policy. Conversely, a monetary policy which reduces the amount of money and loans in the economy is a **contractionary monetary policy** or a "tight" monetary policy. This section will discuss how expansionary and contractionary monetary policies affect interest rates and aggregate demand, and thus how such policies will affect macroeconomic goals like unemployment and inflation.

The Effect of Monetary Policy on Interest Rates

Consider the market for loanable bank funds, shown in Exhibit 30-5. The original equilibrium E_0 occurs at an interest rate of 8% and a quantity of funds loaned and borrowed

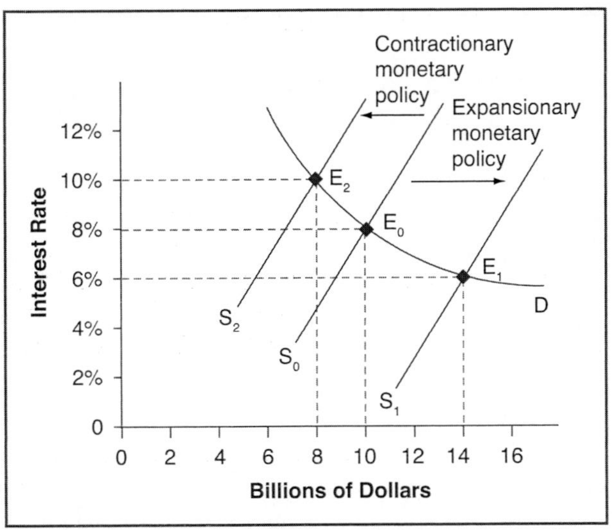

EXHIBIT 30-5 Monetary Policy and Interest Rates

The original equilibrium occurs at E_0. An expansionary monetary policy will shift the supply of loanable funds to the right from the original supply curve S_0 to the new supply curve S_1 and to a new equilibrium of E_1, reducing the interest rate from 8% to 6%. A contractionary monetary policy will shift the supply of loanable funds to the left from the original supply curve S_0 to the new supply S_2, and raise the interest rate from 8% to 10%.

of $10 billion. An expansionary monetary policy will shift the supply of loanable funds to the right from the original supply curve S_0 to S_1, leading to an equilibrium E_1 with a lower interest rate of 6% and a quantity of funds loaned of $14 billion. Conversely, a contractionary monetary policy will shift the supply of loanable funds to the left from the original supply curve S_0 to S_2, leading to an equilibrium E_2 with a higher interest rate of 10% and a quantity of funds loaned of $8 billion.

When describing the monetary policy actions taken by a central bank, it's common to hear that the central bank "raised interest rates" or "lowered interest rates." Such statements are potentially misleading if they are taken to imply that the central bank is a dictator that can force banks to charge a certain interest rate. Instead, the central bank alters the quantity of money and credit in a way that affects the supply curve in the market for loanable funds, and in that way, it can move the interest rate higher or lower.

The Effect of Monetary Policy on Aggregate Demand

Monetary policy affects interest rates and the available quantity of loanable funds, which in turn affects several components of aggregate demand. Tight or contractionary monetary policy that leads to higher interest rates and a reduced quantity of loanable funds will reduce two components of aggregate demand. Business investment will decline because it is less attractive for firms to borrow money, and even firms that have money will notice that with higher interest rates, it is relatively more attractive to put those funds in a financial investment than to make an investment in physical capital. In addition, higher interest rates will discourage consumer borrowing for big-ticket items like houses and cars. Conversely, loose or expansionary monetary policy that leads to lower interest rates and a higher quantity of loanable funds will tend to increase business investment and consumer borrowing for big-ticket items.

If the economy is suffering a recession and high unemployment, with output below potential GDP, loose monetary policy can help the economy return to potential GDP. Exhibit 30-6*a* illustrates this situation. This example uses a short-run upward-sloping Keynesian aggregate supply curve AS. The original equilibrium during a recession of E_R occurs at an output level of 600. An expansionary monetary policy will reduce interest rates and stimulate investment and consumption spending, causing the original aggregate

EXHIBIT 30-6
Expansionary or Contractionary Monetary Policy

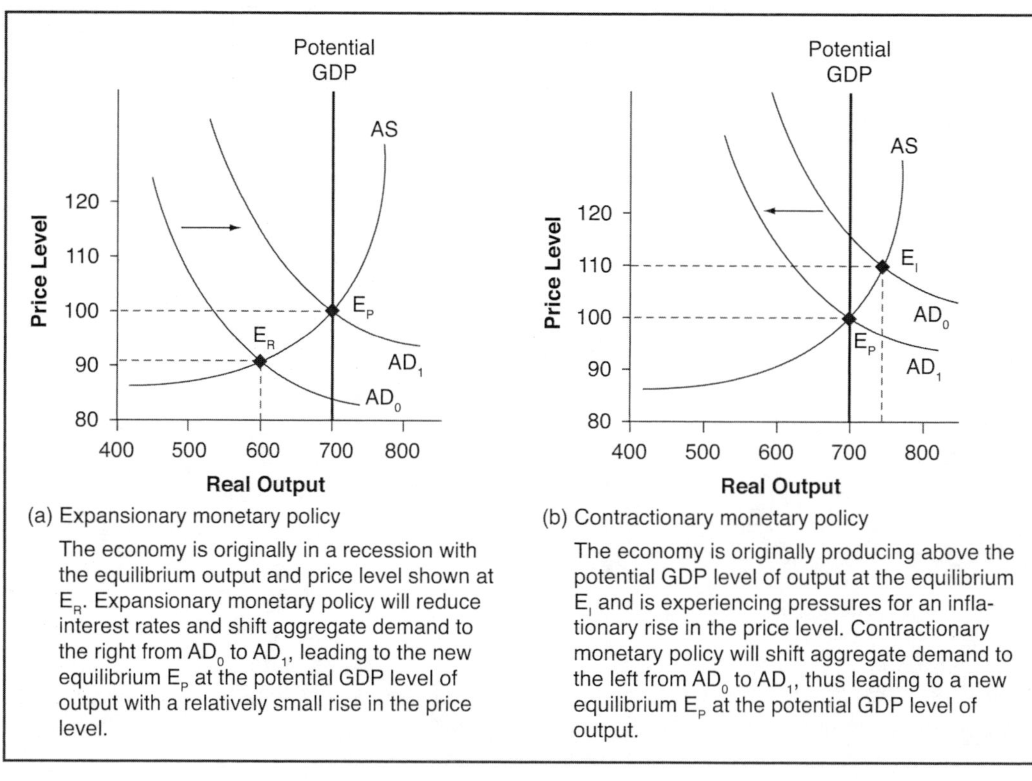

(a) Expansionary monetary policy

The economy is originally in a recession with the equilibrium output and price level shown at E_R. Expansionary monetary policy will reduce interest rates and shift aggregate demand to the right from AD_0 to AD_1, leading to the new equilibrium E_P at the potential GDP level of output with a relatively small rise in the price level.

(b) Contractionary monetary policy

The economy is originally producing above the potential GDP level of output at the equilibrium E_I and is experiencing pressures for an inflationary rise in the price level. Contractionary monetary policy will shift aggregate demand to the left from AD_0 to AD_1, thus leading to a new equilibrium E_P at the potential GDP level of output.

demand curve AD_0 to shift right to AD_1, so that the new equilibrium E_P occurs at the potential GDP level of 700.

Conversely, if an economy is producing at a quantity of output above its potential GDP, a tight or contractionary monetary policy can reduce the inflationary pressures for a rising price level. In Exhibit 30-6*b*, the original equilibrium E_I occurs at an output of 750, which is above potential GDP. A contractionary monetary policy will raise interest rates, discourage borrowing for investment and consumption spending, and cause the original demand curve AD_0 to shift left to AD_1, so that the new equilibrium E_P occurs at the potential GDP level of 700.

countercyclical: Moving in the opposite direction of the business cycle of economic downturns and upswings.

These examples suggest that monetary policy should be **countercyclical**; that is, it should act to counterbalance the business cycles of economic downturns and upswings. Monetary policy should be loosened when a recession has caused unemployment to increase and tightened when inflation threatens. Of course, countercylical policy does pose a danger of overreaction. If loose monetary policy seeking to end a recession goes too far, it may push aggregate demand so far to the right that it triggers inflation. If tight monetary policy seeking to reduce inflation goes too far, it may push aggregate demand so far to the left that a recession begins. Exhibit 30-7 summarizes the chain of effects that connect loose and tight monetary policy to changes in output and the price level.

What the Federal Reserve Has Done

For the period from the mid-1970s up through the end of 2007, Federal Reserve monetary policy can largely be summed up by looking at how it targeted the federal funds interest rate using open market operations. But in the Great Recession of 2007–2009, Fed policy began to use creative policies of quantitative easing and forward guidance. In 2015, it began to use the interest rate that the Fed pays banks on their excess reserves as a policy tool.

Of course, telling the story of the U.S. economy since 1975 in terms of Federal Reserve actions leaves out many other macroeconomic factors that were influencing unemployment, recession, economic growth, and inflation over this time. But the nine episodes quickly sketched here also demonstrate that when telling the story of a macroeconomy, the central bank must be treated as one of the leading characters. Indeed, the single per-

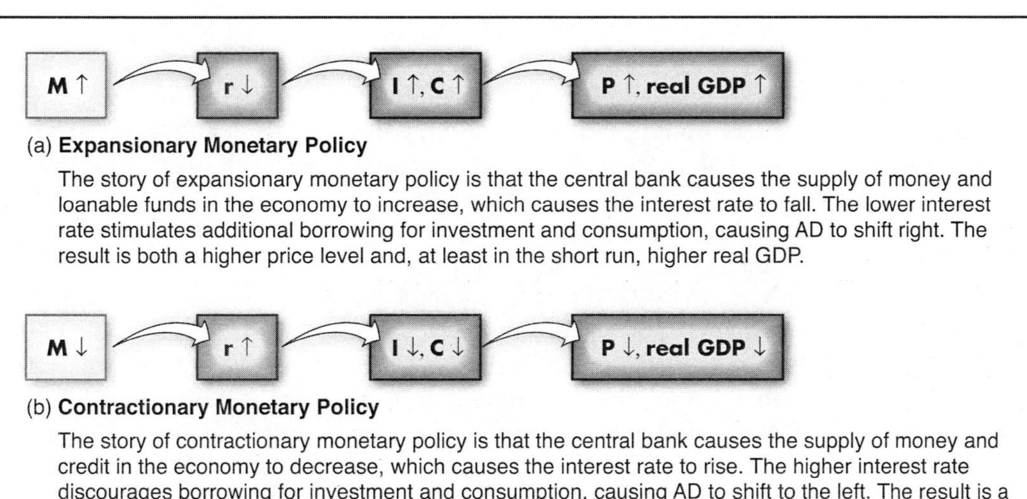

EXHIBIT 30-7 The Pathways of Monetary Policy

son with the greatest power to influence the U.S. economy is probably the chairman of the Federal Reserve, who has considerable power over the monetary policies of the Fed, rather than the President of the United States, who can only act through laws that must first be passed by Congress.

Exhibit 30-8 shows how the Federal Reserve has carried out monetary policy by targeting the federal funds interest rate in the last few decades. The graph shows the federal funds interest rate (remember, this interest rate is set through open market operations), the unemployment rate, and the inflation rate since 1975. Different episodes of monetary policy during this period are indicated on the exhibit.

Consider *Episode 1* in the late 1970s. The rate of inflation was very high, exceeding 10% in 1979 and 1980, so the Fed used a tight monetary policy to raise interest rates, with the federal funds rate rising from 5.5% in 1977 to 16.4% in 1981. By 1983, inflation was down to 3.2%, but aggregate demand contracted sharply enough that back-to-back recessions occurred in 1980 and in 1981–82, and the unemployment rate rose from 5.8% in 1979 to 9.7% in 1982.

In *Episode 2*, when the Federal Reserve was persuaded in the early 1980s that inflation was declining, the Fed began slashing interest rates to reduce unemployment. The federal funds interest rate fell from 16.4% in 1981 to 6.8% in 1986. By 1986 or so, inflation had fallen to about 2% and the unemployment rate had come down to 7%, and was still falling.

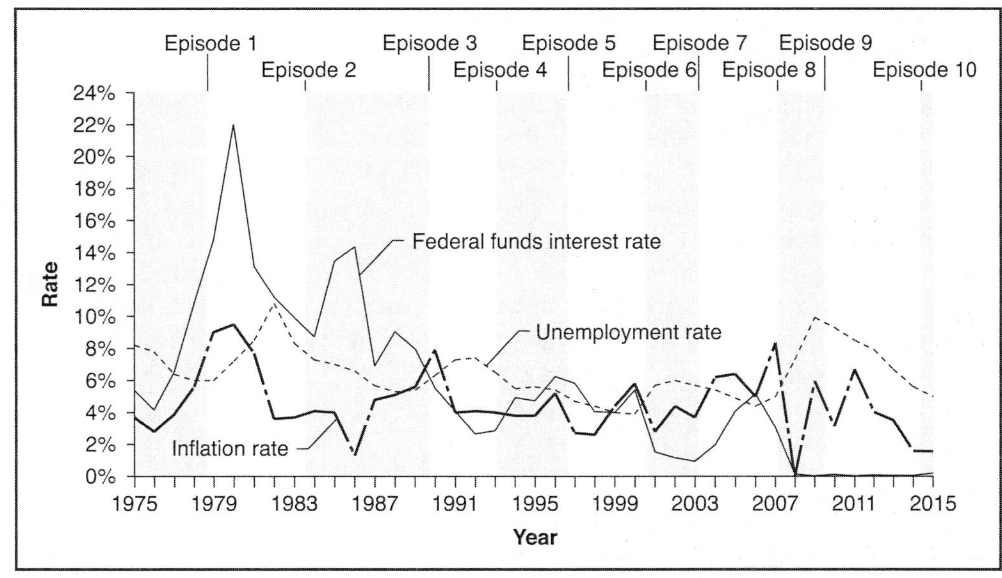

EXHIBIT 30-8 Monetary Policy, Unemployment, and Inflation

Through the episodes shown here, the Federal Reserve typically reacted to higher inflation with a contractionary monetary policy and a higher interest rate, and reacted to higher unemployment with an expansionary monetary policy and a lower interest rate.

However, during *Episode 3* in the late 1980s, inflation appeared to be creeping up again, rising from 2% in 1986 up toward 5% by 1989. In response, the Fed used contractionary monetary policy to raise the federal funds rates from 6.6% in 1987 to 9.2% in 1989. The tighter monetary policy stopped inflation, which fell from above 5% in 1990 to under 3% in 1992, but it also helped to cause the recession of 1990–91, and the unemployment rate rose from 5.3% in 1989 to 7.5% by 1992.

In *Episode 4* in the early 1990s, when the Fed was confident that inflation was back under control, it then reduced interest rates, with the federal funds interest rate falling from 8.1% in 1990 to 3.5% in 1992. As the economy expanded, the unemployment rate declined from 7.5% in 1992 to less than 5% by 1997.

In *Episode 5*, the Fed perceived a risk of inflation in 1994 and raised the federal funds rate from 3% in 1993 to 5.8% in 1995. Inflation didn't rise, and the period of economic growth during the 1990s continued. The federal funds rate changed little for several years.

In *Episode 6*, in 1999 and 2000, the Fed was concerned that inflation seemed to be creeping up from 1.6% in 1998 to 3.4% by 2000, and so it raised the federal funds interest rate from 4.6% in December 1998 to 6.5% in June 2000. By early 2001, inflation was declining again, headed for a rate of just 1.6% in 2002, but a recession occurred in 2001 and the unemployment rate rose from 4.0% in 2000 to 5.8% in 2002.

In *Episode 7*, the Federal Reserve conducted a loose monetary policy and slashed the federal funds rate from 6.2% in 2000 to just 1.7% in 2002. The recession ended, but just as it had taken some years for unemployment rates to decline after the recessions of the early 1980s and the early 1990s, unemployment rates were slow to decline in the early 2000s.

In *Episode 8*, the federal funds interest rate bottomed out at about 1% in late 2003 and early 2004. The unemployment rate had stayed low and declining, but inflation had perked up just a bit, and so the Federal Reserve began to raise the federal funds rate until it reached 5% by 2007.

In *Episode 9*, as the Great Recession took hold in 2008, the Federal Reserve was quick to slash interest rates, taking them down to 2% in 2008 and to nearly 0% in 2009. But when the Fed had taken interest rates down to near-zero by December 2008, the economy was still deep in recession. Open market operations could not make the interest rate turn negative! Thus, the Federal Reserve turned to the alternative policies of quantitative easing, greatly expanding the direct loans that it made and also creating money to purchase some financial securities directly, as well as becoming more active and explicit in forward guidance.

In *Episode 10*, starting in December 2015, monetary policy is being conducted with a combination of quantitative easing (although this is currently being slowly phased out by the Federal Reserve), forward guidance, and the new policy tool of adjusting the interest rate paid on bank reserves held at the Fed.

Pitfalls for Monetary Policy

Monetary policy may seem straightforward. If the economy is in a recession, substantially below potential GDP, then the central bank should raise the supply of money and credit. In the old days before 2008, this was typically done with open market operations. Since then, the usual monetary policy tools are quantitative easing, forward guidance, and adjusting the interest rate paid to banks on their reserves held at the central bank. If the economy is producing in overdrive above potential GDP and/or experiencing high inflation, then the central bank should use these same tools in reverse to limit the growth of money and credit and to raise interest rates. However, in the real world, matters are more complicated than they may at first appear.

Long and Variable Time Lags

Monetary policy affects the economy only after a time lag that is typically long and of variable length. Remember, monetary policy involves a chain of events: the central bank must perceive a situation in the economy, hold a meeting, and make a decision to react by tightening or loosening monetary policy. The change in monetary policy must percolate through the banking system, changing the quantity of loans and affecting interest rates. When interest rates change, businesses must change their investment levels and consumers must change their borrowing patterns when purchasing homes or cars. Then it takes time for these changes to filter through the rest of the economy.

As a result of this chain of events, monetary policy has little effect in the immediate future; instead, its primary effects are felt perhaps 1–3 years in the future. Monetary policy is like steering a car down a twisting, turning road, where you can see the road behind you, but you have to turn the steering wheel to match the curves you cannot yet see that are ahead. For example, when a central bank decides to loosen monetary policy, it must consider the possibility that by the time the policy actually takes effect in 1–3 years, it will wish it had actually decided to tighten or to take no action at all. The reality of long and variable time lags doesn't mean that a central bank should refuse to make decisions—after all, refusing to make a decision is, in itself, a decision. But it does mean that central banks should be humble about taking action because of the risk that their actions can create as much or more economic instability as they resolve.

Excess Reserves

Banks are legally required to hold a minimum level of reserves, but no rule prohibits them from holding additional **excess reserves** above the legally mandated limit. For example, during a recession banks may be hesitant to lend because they fear that when the economy is contracting, a high proportion of loan applicants become less likely to repay their loans. Since the Great Recession, U.S. banks have been holding extremely large quantities of excess reserves; as shown earlier in Figure 30-3, bank reserves rose from $14 billion in 2007, which was roughly equal to the required amount at that time, to more than $2.3 trillion in 2016.

excess reserves: Reserves that banks hold above the legally mandated limit.

When many banks are choosing to hold excess reserves, expansionary monetary policy may not work as well. For example, consider an economy in the throes of a recession, with output substantially below potential GDP. The central bank diagnoses the situation and decides to use expansionary monetary policy, with the hope of causing an expansion of the quantity of lending and borrowing to stimulate the economy. But there's an old proverb that says, "You can lead a horse to water, but you can't make him drink." If banks prefer to hold excess reserves above the legally required level, the central bank can't force individual banks to make loans. Similarly, sensible businesses and consumers may be reluctant to borrow substantial amounts of money when an economy is experiencing slow growth or is in an outright recession because they recognize that firms' sales and employees' jobs are more uncertain at such times, and they don't want to face the unrelenting need to make interest payments. The result is that when banks are holding excess reserves, it can be harder for an expansionary monetary policy to have an effect on either the price level or the real GDP.

Japan experienced this situation in the 1990s and early 2000s. Japan's economy entered a period of very slow growth, dipping in and out of recession, in the early 1990s. By February 1999, the Bank of Japan had lowered the equivalent of its federal funds rate to 0% and kept it there most of the time through 2003. Moreover, in the two years from March 2001 to March 2003, the Bank of Japan also expanded the money supply of the country by about 50%—an enormous increase. But even this highly expansionary monetary policy had no substantial effect on stimulating aggregate demand. Japan's economy continued to experience extremely slow growth into the mid-2000s.

The problem of excess reserves has much less of an effect on contractionary policy. Central bankers have an old saying that monetary policy can be like pulling and pushing on a string: when the central bank pulls on the string and uses contractionary monetary policy, it can definitely raise interest rates and reduce aggregate demand. However, when the central bank tries to push on the string of expansionary monetary policy, the string may sometimes just fold up limp and have little effect because banks decide not to loan out their excess reserves. This analogy shouldn't be taken too literally—expansionary

Should Monetary Policy Decisions Be Made More Democratically?

Should monetary policy be conducted by a nation's Congress or legislature made up of elected representatives? Or should it be conducted by a politically appointed central bank that is more independent of voters? Here are some of the arguments made by each side.

The Case for Greater Democratic Control of Monetary Policy

Elected representatives conduct fiscal policy by passing tax and spending bills. They could handle monetary policy in the same way. Sure, they will sometimes make mistakes, but in a democracy, it's better to have mistakes made by elected officials accountable to voters than by political appointees. After all, the people appointed to the top governing positions at the Federal Reserve—and to most central banks around the world—are typically bankers and economists. They aren't representatives of borrowers like small businesses or farmers, or representatives of labor unions. Central banks might not be so quick to raise interest rates if they had to pay more attention to firms and people in the real economy.

The Case for an Independent Central Bank

America's judicial system is governed by judges who are presidential appointees. These judges interpret the laws made by elected officials. Few people believe that the legislature should vote on legal cases, and many of the same arguments apply to the central bank. Because the central bank has some insulation from day-to-day politics, its members can take a nonpartisan look at specific economic situations and make tough, immediate decisions when necessary. The idea of giving a legislature the ability to create money and hand out loans is likely to end up badly, sooner or later. Also, a central bank, acting according to the laws passed by elected officials, can respond far more quickly than a legislature. For example, the U.S. budget takes months to debate, pass, and be signed into law, but monetary policy decisions can be made much more rapidly. Day-to-day democratic control of monetary policy is impractical and seems likely to lead to an overly expansionary monetary policy and higher inflation.

Who Wins This Debate?

This debate isn't going away. The most common trend in the 2000s has been that countries around the world are moving toward writing rules for the central bank to follow and then leaving it up to the central bank to achieve that goal, rather than moving toward greater day-to-day democratic control of the central bank.

monetary policy usually does have real effects, after that inconveniently long and variable lag. But there are also times, like Japan's economy in the late 1990s and early 2000s and the U.S. economy after the end of the Great Recession in 2009 when expansionary monetary policy has been insufficient to give a substantial lift-off to a sluggish recovery after a deep recession.

Unpredictable Movements of Velocity

velocity: The speed with which money circulates through the economy, calculated as the nominal GDP divided by a measure of the size of the money supply.

Velocity is a term that economists use to describe how quickly money circulates through the economy. The velocity of money in a year is defined as:

$$\text{Velocity} = \frac{\text{nominal GDP}}{\text{money supply}}.$$

In 2012, for example, M1 was $2.3 trillion and nominal GDP was $15.7 trillion, so the velocity of M1 was $15.7 trillion/$2.3 trillion = 6.8. A higher velocity of money means that the average dollar circulates more times in a year; a lower velocity means that the average dollar circulates fewer times in a year. Velocity can also be measured using other definitions of the money supply, like M2.

Changes in velocity can cause problems for monetary policy. To understand why, rewrite the definition of velocity so that the money supply is on the left-hand side of the equation. That is,

$$\text{Money supply} \times \text{Velocity} = \text{Nominal GDP}$$

basic quantity equation of money: Money supply × Velocity = Nominal GDP.

This equation is sometimes called the **basic quantity equation of money**, but as you can see, it's just the definition of velocity written in a different form. This equation must hold true, by definition.

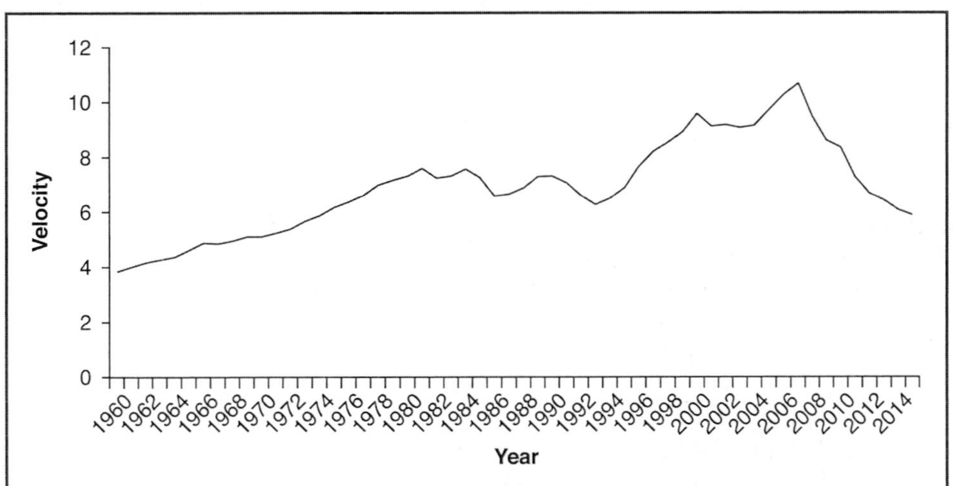

EXHIBIT 30-9 Velocity

Velocity is the nominal GDP divided by the money supply for a given year. Different measures of velocity can be calculated by using different measures of the money supply. Velocity as calculated by using M1 has lacked a steady trend since the 1980s, instead bouncing up and down and then falling in recent years

If velocity is constant over time, then a certain percentage rise in the money supply on the left-hand side of the basic quantity equation of money will inevitably lead to the same percentage rise in nominal GDP—although this change could happen through an increase in inflation, or an increase in real GDP, or some combination of the two. If velocity is changing over time but in a constant and predictable way, then changes in the money supply will continue to have a predictable effect on nominal GDP. But if velocity changes unpredictably over time, then the effect of changes in the money supply on nominal GDP becomes unpredictable.

The actual velocity of money in the U.S. economy as measured by using M1, the most common definition of the money supply, is illustrated in Exhibit 30-9. From 1960 up to about 1980, velocity appears fairly predictable; that is, it is increasing at a fairly constant rate. In the early 1980s, however, velocity as calculated with M1 becomes more variable, and velocity has fallen substantially since the end of the Great Recession in 2009. Economists suspect that some of the changes in velocity are related to innovations in banking and finance which have changed how money is used in making economic transactions: for example, the growth of electronic payments; a rise in personal borrowing and credit card usage; and accounts that make it easier for people to hold money in savings accounts, where it is counted as M2, right up to the moment that they want to write a check on the money and transfer it to M1. But at least so far, it has proven difficult to draw clear links between these kinds of factors and the specific up-and-down fluctuations in velocity.

In the 1970s, when velocity as measured by M1 seemed reasonably predictable, a number of economists, led by Nobel laureate Milton Friedman (1912–2006), argued that the best monetary policy was for the central bank to increase the money supply slowly and steadily over time. These economists argued that with the long and variable lags of monetary policy, and the political pressures on central bankers, central bank monetary policies were as likely to have undesirable as to have desirable effects. Thus, these economists believed that the monetary policy should seek steady growth in the money supply of 3% per year. They argued that a steady rate of monetary growth would be correct over longer time periods, since it would roughly match the growth of the real economy. In addition, they argued that giving the central bank less discretion to conduct monetary policy would prevent an overly activist central bank from becoming a source of economic instability and uncertainty. In this spirit, Friedman wrote in 1967: "The first and most important lesson that history teaches about what monetary policy can do—and it is a lesson of the most profound importance—is that monetary policy can prevent money itself from being a major source of economic disturbance."

But as the velocity of M1 began to fluctuate in the 1980s, having the money supply grow at a predetermined and unchanging rate seemed less desirable, because as the quantity theory of money shows, the combination of constant growth in the money supply and fluctuating velocity would cause nominal GDP to rise and fall in unpredictable ways. The

Episodes of Deflation

Deflation occurs when the rate of inflation is negative; that is, instead of money having less purchasing power over time, as occurs with inflation, money is worth more. Having money be worth more may not sound so bad! But when deflation interacts with interest rates, it can cause recessions that are difficult for monetary policy to address.

Remember that the real interest rate is the nominal interest rate minus the rate of inflation. If the nominal interest rate is 7% and the rate of inflation is 3%, then the borrower is effectively paying a 4% real interest rate. But if the nominal interest rate is 7% and there is *deflation* of 2%, then the real interest rate is actually 9%. In this way, an unexpected deflation raises the real interest payments for borrowers. It can lead to a situation where an unexpectedly high number of loans are not repaid and banks find that their net worth is decreasing or negative. When banks are suffering losses, they become less able and eager to make new loans. Aggregate demand declines, which can lead to recession.

Then comes the double-whammy: After causing a recession, deflation can make it difficult for monetary policy to work. Say that the central bank uses expansionary monetary policy to reduce the nominal interest rate all the way to zero—but the economy has 5% deflation. As a result, the real interest rate is 5%, and because it is difficult for a central bank to make the nominal interest rate negative, expansionary policy can't reduce the real interest rate further.

In the U.S. economy during the early 1930s, deflation was 6.7% per year from 1930–33, which caused many borrowers to default on their loans and many banks to end up bankrupt, which in turn contributed substantially to the Great Depression. But not all episodes of deflation end in Depression. Japan experienced deflation of slightly less than 1% per year from 1999–2002, and while Japan's economy was mired in slow growth, it did grow by about 0.9% per year over this period. Indeed, there is at least one historical example of deflation coexisting with rapid growth. The U.S. economy experienced deflation of about 1.1% per year over the quarter-century from 1876–1900, but real GDP also expanded at a rapid clip of 4% per year over this time, despite some occasional severe recessions.

The central bank should be on guard against deflation, and if necessary use expansionary monetary policy to prevent any long-lasting or extreme deflation from occurring. But except in severe cases like the Great Depression, deflation does not guarantee economic disaster.

jumpiness of velocity in the 1980s and since then caused many central banks to focus less on the rate at which the quantity of money in the economy was increasing, and instead to set monetary policy by reacting to whether the economy was experiencing or in danger of higher inflation or unemployment.

Is Unemployment or Inflation More Important?

If you were to survey central bankers around the world and ask them what they believe should be the primary task of monetary policy, the traditional answer in recent decades would have been to emphasize fighting inflation. Most central bankers believe that the neoclassical model of economics accurately represents the economy over the medium and long term. Remember that in the neoclassical model of the economy, the aggregate supply curve is drawn as a vertical line at the level of potential GDP, as shown in Exhibit 30-10. In the neoclassical model, the level of potential GDP (and the natural rate of unemployment that exists when the economy is producing at potential GDP) is determined by real economic factors. If the original level of aggregate demand is AD_0, then an expansionary monetary policy that shifts aggregate demand to AD_1 only creates an inflationary increase in the price level, but it does not alter GDP or unemployment. From this perspective, all that monetary policy can do is to lead to low inflation or high inflation—and low inflation provides a better climate for a healthy and growing economy. After all, low inflation means that businesses making investments can focus on real economic issues, not on figuring out ways to protecting themselves from the costs and risks of inflation. In this way, a consistent pattern of low inflation can even be seen as contributing to long-term growth.

inflation-targeting: A rule that the central bank is required to focus only on keeping inflation low.

This vision of focusing monetary policy on a low rate of inflation is so attractive that many countries have rewritten their central banking laws since in the 1990s to have their bank practice **inflation-targeting**, which means that the central bank is legally required to

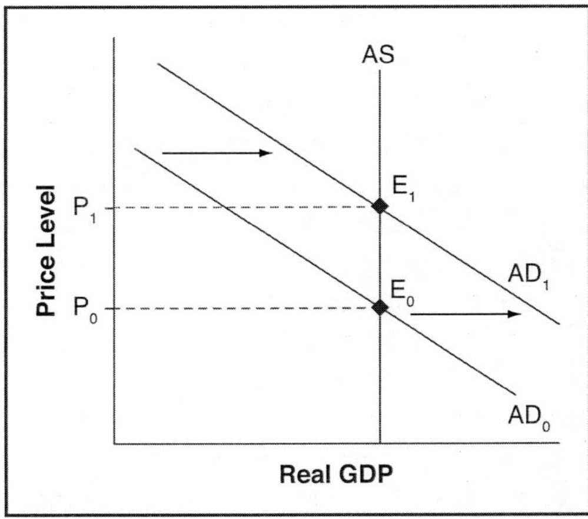

EXHIBIT 30-10 Monetary Policy in a Neoclassical Model

In a neoclassical view, monetary policy affects only the price level, not the level of output in the economy. For example, an expansionary monetary policy causes aggregate demand to shift from the original AD_0 to AD_1. However, the adjustment of the economy from the original equilibrium E_0 to the new equilibrium E_1 represents an inflationary increase in the price level from P_0 to P_1, but has no effect in the long run on output or the unemployment rate. In fact, no shift in AD will affect the equilibrium quantity of output in this model.

focus only on keeping inflation low. By 2013, central banks in 26 countries from all over the world faced a legal requirement to target the inflation rate, including Austria, Brazil, Canada, Israel, Korea, Mexico, New Zealand, Spain, Sweden, Thailand, and the United Kingdom. The legislation establishing the European Central Bank, which controls the quantity of euros, sets "price stability" as its primary goal, which it defines as an inflation rate of 2% per year or less. However, the Federal Reserve in the United States does not practice inflation-targeting. Instead, the law governing the Federal Reserve requires it to take both unemployment and inflation into account.

Economists have not reached a consensus on whether a central bank should be required to focus only on inflation or should have greater discretion. For those who subscribe to the inflation-targeting philosophy, the fear is that when politicians who are worried about slow economic growth and unemployment will constantly pressure the central bank to conduct a loose monetary policy—even if the economy is already producing at potential GDP. In some countries, the central bank may lack the political power to resist such pressures, with the result of higher inflation but no long-term reduction in unemployment. The U.S. Federal Reserve has a tradition of independence, but central banks in other countries may be under greater political pressure. Or in another scenario, central bankers may be tempted to tinker continually with the interest rate, pushing it up and down from month to month in a way that creates uncertainty and risk in the economy. However, inflation-targeting has its risks, too. A central bank that focuses only on inflation will not use expansionary monetary policy to fight a recession. In the early 2000s, for example, unemployment rates rose in many European countries, but the European Central Bank focused only on keeping inflation rates low, not on whether it might have been wise to run a more expansionary monetary policy.

For all of these reasons—long and variable lags, excess reserves, unstable velocity, and controversy over economic goals—monetary policy in the real world is often difficult. But the basic message remains that central banks can affect aggregate demand through the conduct of monetary policy, and in that way influence macroeconomic outcomes.

Should the Central Bank Tackle Asset Bubbles and Leverage Cycles?

One long-standing concern about having the central bank focus on inflation and unemployment is that it may be overlooking certain other economic problems that are looming in the future. For example, in the late 1990s during what was known as the "dot-com" boom, the U.S. stock market as measured by the Dow Jones Industrial Index, which includes 30 very large companies from across the U.S. economy, nearly tripled in value from 1994 to 2000. The NASDAQ index, which includes many smaller technology companies, increased in value by a multiple of five from 1994 to 2000. These rates of increase were clearly not sustainable. Indeed, stock values as measured by the Dow Jones were almost 20% lower in 2009 than they had been in 2000. Stock values in the NASDAQ index were 50% lower in 2009 than they had been in 2000. The drop-off in stock market values contributed to the recession of 2001 and the higher unemployment that followed.

A similar story can be told about housing prices in the mid-2000s. During what came to be known as the "housing bubble" from 2003 to 2006, housing prices increased at double-digit annual rates, which were clearly not sustainable. When the price of housing fell in 2007 and 2008, many banks and households found that their assets were worth less than they expected, which contributed to the recession that started in 2007.

At a broader level, some economists worry about a "leverage cycle," where "leverage" is a term used by financial economists to mean "borrowing." When economic times are good, banks and the financial sector are eager to lend, and people and firms are eager to borrow. Remember that the amount of money and credit in an economy is determined by a money multiplier—a process of loans being made, money being deposited, and more loans being made. In good economic times, this surge of lending exaggerates the episode of economic growth. It can even be part of what lead prices of certain assets—like stock prices or housing prices—to rise at unsustainably high annual rates for several years. At some point, when economic times turn bad, then banks and the financial sector become much less willing to lend, and credit becomes expensive or unavailable to many potential borrowers. The sharp reduction in credit, perhaps combined with the deflating prices of a dot-com stock price bubble or a housing bubble, makes the economic downturn worse than it would otherwise be.

Thus, some economists have suggested that the central bank should not just look at economic growth, inflation, and unemployment rates, but should also keep an eye on asset prices and leverage cycles. Such proposals are controversial. If a central bank had announced in 1997 that stock prices were rising "too fast" or in 2004 that housing prices were rising "too fast," and then taken action to hold down price increases, many people and their elected political representatives would have been outraged. Neither the Federal Reserve nor any other central banks want the responsibility of deciding when stock prices and housing prices are too high, too low, or just right. But as further research explores how asset price bubbles and leverage cycles can affect an economy, central banks may need to think about whether they should conduct monetary policy—or the bank regulatory policies discussed in the next section—in a way that would seek to moderate these effects.

Bank Regulation

The safety and stability of a nation's banking system is a matter of macroeconomic concern. If banks falter at their tasks of collecting deposits and making loans, the effect can be similar to a contractionary monetary policy enacted by the central bank: that is, a lower quantity of loans, a reduction in aggregate demand, and a recession. This section begins by discussing two scenarios in which weaknesses in the banking system have caused macroeconomic harm: (1) when households lose confidence in banks and rush to withdraw their money; and (2) when a large proportion of the banks in an economy have extremely low or negative net worth and decide not to make many loans. The discussion then turns to three government policies for assuring safe and stable banking systems: (1) the provision of deposit insurance to reassure households that their bank deposits are safe; (2) examining the financial records of banks to ensure that they have positive net worth; and (3) making emergency short-term loans to financial institutions in times of financial chaos.

Bank Runs

Back in the nineteenth century and during the first few decades of the twentieth century, putting your money in a bank could be nerve-wracking. Imagine that the net worth of your bank became negative, so that the bank's assets weren't enough to cover its liabilities. In this situation, whoever withdrew their deposits first received all of their money, and those who didn't rush to the bank quickly enough lost their money. This scenario, in which depositors raced to the bank to withdraw their deposits for fear that otherwise they would be lost, is called a **bank run**. The drama of bank runs has even entered the plot of some well-known movies. In *Mary Poppins*, the little boy Michael wants his tuppence back, and when someone overhears that the bank director played by Dick Van Dyke won't give back his money, a comic bank run results. In *It's a Wonderful Life*, the bank manager played by Jimmy Stewart faces a mob of worried bank depositors who want to withdraw their money, but manages to allay their fears by allowing some of them to withdraw a portion of their deposits—using the money from his own pocket that was supposed to pay for his honeymoon.

bank run: When depositors race to the bank to withdraw their deposits for fear that otherwise they would be lost.

The risk of bank runs created instability in the banking system. Even a rumor that a bank might experience negative net worth could trigger a bank run, and in a bank run, even healthy banks could be destroyed. Because a bank loans out most of the money it receives, and because it keeps only limited reserves on hand, a bank run of any size would quickly drain any of the bank's available cash. When the bank had no cash remaining, it only intensified the fears of remaining depositors that they could lose their money. Moreover, a bank run at one bank often triggered a chain reaction of runs on other banks. In the late nineteenth and early twentieth century, bank runs were typically not the original cause of a recession—but bank runs could make a recession much worse.

A Weakened Banking Sector

In a nation with many banks, the failure of any one bank probably won't affect the macroeconomy much. But if many banks are simultaneously close to failing, and as a result the bank system substantially reduces the quantity of loans, the result can be slow growth or recession.

Japan's economy offers a vivid connection from insolvent banks to a weak economy over the last decade or so. Japanese banks (unlike U.S. banks) are allowed to hold some of their assets in the form of real estate and company stock. But from late 1989 to late 1992, real estate and stock prices in Japan fell, on average, by about 60%. Many Japanese banks suffered a dramatic decline in the value of their assets and faced negative net worth. As a result, Japan's banks became extremely reluctant to make loans. This is one reason why Japan's economy was sleepwalking from the early 1990s and into the 2000s, dipping in and out of recession with an average real growth rate of less than 1% per year.

The U.S. economy during the Great Recession of 2007–2009 also experienced the link from a weakened financial sector to an economic slowdown. Over 160 U.S. banks failed in 2008 and 2009; many others were on the verge of failing. Again, a cycle can begin in which a weakened economy means that fewer people repay their loans, thus weakening many banks; then banks that are financially weak become reluctant to lend, which makes the economy weaker.

Given the macroeconomic dangers from an unstable banking system, government laws and regulations have sought to reassure households that their bank deposits are safe and also to supervise banks to make sure that their balance sheets show positive net worth and a moderate level of risk. The following sections describe the government policies to address these goals.

Deposit Insurance

deposit insurance: An insurance system that makes sure depositors in a bank do not lose their money, even if the bank goes bankrupt.

Deposit insurance is an insurance system that makes sure depositors in a bank do not lose their money, even if the bank goes bankrupt. About 70 countries around the world, including all of the major economies, have deposit insurance programs. In the United States, the Federal Deposit Insurance Corporation (FDIC) is responsible for deposit insurance. Banks pay an insurance premium to the FDIC. The insurance premium is based on the bank's level of deposits, and then adjusted according to the riskiness of a bank's financial situation. In 2015, for example, a fairly safe bank with a high net worth might have paid 9 cents in insurance premiums for every $100 in bank deposits, whereas a risky bank with very low net worth might have paid 45 cents for every $100 in bank deposits. Bank examiners from the FDIC evaluate the balance sheets of banks, looking at the value of assets and liabilities, to determine the level of riskiness. The FDIC provides deposit insurance for about 5,300 banks. Even if a bank has negative net worth and the executives of the bank lose their jobs, the government guarantees that depositors will receive their money up to $250,000, which is enough for almost all individuals, although not for some businesses.

Since the United States enacted deposit insurance in the 1930s, no one has lost any of their insured deposits. Bank runs no longer happen at insured banks. But in the case of a severe financial crisis, when the government has not previously collected enough in deposit insurance premiums to cover the costs, the costs to the government of ensuring that people do not lose the funds deposited in insured bank accounts can be quite large: often 5%, 10%, and more of one year's GDP for that country.

Bank Supervision

Several government agencies also check the balance sheets of banks to make sure they have positive net worth and are not taking too high a level of risk. Within the U.S. Department of the Treasury, the Office of the Comptroller of the Currency has a national staff of bank examiners who conduct on-site reviews of about 1,700 of the largest national banks. The bank examiners also review any foreign banks that have branches in the United States. The National Credit Union Administration (NCUA) supervises credit unions, which are nonprofit banks owned and run by their members. There are about 6,100 credit unions in the U.S. economy, but the typical credit union is small compared to most banks. The Federal Reserve also has some responsibility for supervising financial institutions. For example, there are firms that own banks and other businesses called "bank holding companies." While other regulators like the Office of the Comptroller of the Currency supervises the banks, the Federal Reserve supervises the holding companies.

When the supervision of banks (and bank-like institutions such as savings and loans and credit unions) works well, most banks will remain financially healthy most of the time. If the bank supervisors find that a bank has low or negative net worth, or is making too high a proportion of risky loans, they can require that the bank change its behavior—or in extreme cases even force the bank to be closed or sold to a financially healthy bank.

But bank supervision can run into both practical and political questions. The practical question is that measuring the value of a bank's assets is not always straightforward. As discussed in the previous chapter, a bank's assets are its loans, and the value of these assets depends on estimates about the risk that these loans will not be repaid. These issues can become even more complex when a bank makes loans to banks or firms in other countries, or arranges financial deals that are much more complex than a basic loan. The political question arises because the decision by a bank supervisor to require a bank to close or to change its financial investments is often controversial, and the bank supervisor often comes under political pressure from the owners of the bank and the local politicians where the bank is located to shut up and back off. For example, many observers have pointed out that Japan's banks were in deep financial trouble through most of the 1990s, but little was done about it. A similar unwillingness to confront problems with struggling banks often occurs in many countries.

In the United States, laws were passed in the 1990s requiring that bank supervisors make their findings open and public, and that they act as soon as a problem is identified. But as many U.S. banks were staggered by the recession of 2007–2009, critics of the bank regulators asked pointed questions about why the regulators hadn't foreseen the financial shakiness of the banks earlier, before such large losses had a chance to accumulate. One goal of the Wall Street Reform and Consumer Protection Act of 2010, commonly known as the Dodd-Frank act, was to assure that financial weaknesses of banks were recognized and resolved more effectively.

One substantial change in the regulation of banks and other financial institutions in recent years is an emphasis on what is called **macroprudential policy**. Much bank regulation can be thought of as assuring that individual banks act in a prudent manner (thus the name "prudential policy"). But macroprudential policy is not focused on individual banks or financial institutions; instead, it watches for indications that certain financial assets may be exhibiting bubble-like price behavior and then adjusts regulations to reduce the risk of financial instability. One reason that central banks can focus their monetary policies on the dual issues of output and inflation is that they can use macroprudential regulatory policies as a tool for dealing with financial instability and asset bubbles.

macroprudential policy: The bank and financial regulatory policies that are not aimed at a specific company but instead at reducing the risk of financial instability for the macroeconomy as a whole.

Lender of Last Resort

When a panic spreads in financial markets, a situation can arise in which a financial institution needs a short-term emergency loan. In the old days of bank runs, for example, a healthy bank could have positive net worth, but not enough cash on hand so that a flock of depositors could withdraw their money. In such cases, the central bank can step in as a **lender of last resort**, which involves providing short-term emergency loans when a financial crisis occurs. For banks, the central bank acting as a lender of last resort helps to reinforce the effect of deposit insurance and thus to reassure bank customers that they won't lose their money. But the lender of last resort task can come up in other financial crises. During the panic of the stock market crash in 1987, when the value of U.S. stocks fell by 25% in a single day, the Federal Reserve made a number of short-term emergency

lender of last resort: An institution that provides short-term emergency loans in conditions of financial crisis.

The Emancipation of U.S. Banks

During the Great Depression of the 1930s, the banking system crashed along with the economy. Politicians at that time believed the solution was to pass the Glass-Steagall Act of 1933, which restricted the types of business in which banks could become involved. For example, the Glass-Steagall Act restricted banks to making loans only to businesses and individuals. Banks were not allowed to own companies, own stock in companies, sell stock, or offer other financial products such as insurance. A few years earlier, the McFadden Act of 1927 had placed geographic limits on banks, prohibiting such institutions from establishing branches across state lines. Many state laws also restricted the number of branches that a bank could have per state.

The idea behind these restrictions was that if banks were limited in what they could do, they were less likely to get into financial trouble. But as economists pointed out, such legislation limited banks' ability to diversify their risks, and in that way made it *more* likely that they would be financially shaky, rather than less likely. Banks in other high-income countries around the world did not face these kinds of restrictions.

In the 1990s, banking laws began to change. In 1994, the Riegle-Neal Act allowed banks to set up as many branches as they wished, both within states and across state lines. In 1999, the Gramm-Leach-Bliley Act allowed banks to set up overall companies ("financial holding companies") that contained banks within them, as well as insurance companies and companies that market stocks and bonds. However, unlike the situation in any other high-income economies, except for Japan, U.S. banks are still prohibited from owning commercial businesses, and commercial businesses are prohibited from owning banks. Some in the banking industry would like to eliminate these restrictions, too.

But in the aftermath of the 2007–2009 recession, there was a widespread sense that many U.S. banks had borrowed and loaned unwisely. The Wall Street Reform and Consumer Protection Act of 2010, commonly known as the Dodd-Frank act, called upon financial regulators to write several hundred new regulations to limit the risks that financial institutions could take and to ensure that if the remaining risks went badly, private sector investors would be more likely to bear the costs than taxpayers. These rules will not involve returning to the restrictive banking laws of the 1930s, but banks and other financial institutions will clearly face significant new restrictions and oversight on their risk-taking.

loans so that the financial system could keep functioning. When fears were expressed late in 1999 that bank computers might malfunction on January 1, 2000, the Federal Reserve loudly announced that if any problems occurred, it was standing by to act as a lender of last resort until the problems were sorted out. During the recession of 2007–2009, the Federal Reserve established a number of agencies to make short-term loans to several different kinds of financial institutions to assist them through the crisis and then shut down these agencies when their task was completed.

Summary

Overall, bank regulation in the United States is coordinated by the Federal Financial Institutions Examination Council (FFIEC), which in turn draws its membership from the agencies mentioned in this section: the Federal Reserve System, the Federal Deposit Insurance Corporation (FDIC), the National Credit Union Administration (NCUA), the Office of the Comptroller of the Currency (OCC), and the Consumer Financial Protection Bureau (CFPB), as well as representatives of several state-level financial regulators. The task of the FFIEC is to assure that this alphabet soup of bank regulators all communicate with each other and use similar standards when evaluating the riskiness of banks.

The failure of a single bank can be treated like any other business failure. Yet if many banks fail, it can reduce aggregate demand in a way that can bring on or deepen a recession. The combination of deposit insurance, bank supervision, and lender of last resort policies help to prevent weaknesses in the banking system from causing recessions.

Conclusion

Through expansionary monetary policy, a central bank can reduce interest rates and increase the quantity of loans, increase aggregate demand to the right, and help a recession-stricken economy return to potential GDP. Through contractionary monetary policy, a central bank can raise interest rates and decrease the quantity of loans, shift aggregate demand to the left, and reduce inflation. The appropriate timing and direction of monetary policy isn't always clear because of issues like long and variable lags, banks that hold excess reserves, movements in velocity, and disagreements over whether reducing inflation or unemployment should take higher priority. Moreover, in the long run the neoclassical model shows that economic output and unemployment are determined by real factors in markets, while monetary policy determines only the inflation rate. But during the ups and downs of the business cycle, when recessions and inflations occur, monetary policy can play some role in stabilizing the swings of the economy.

The discussion in this chapter has focused on domestic monetary policy; that is, the view of monetary policy within an economy. The next chapter explores the international dimension of monetary policy, and how monetary policy becomes involved with exchange rates and international flows of financial capital.

Key Concepts and Summary

1. The most prominent task of a **central bank** is to conduct **monetary policy**, which involves controlling the quantity of money (and loans) in the economy. Some prominent central banks around the world include the U.S. Federal Reserve, the European Central Bank, the Bank of Japan, and the Bank of England.
2. A central bank has three traditional tools to conduct monetary policy: **open market operations**, which involves buying and selling government bonds with banks; **reserve requirements**, which determine what level of reserves a bank is legally required to hold; and **discount rates**, which is the interest rate at which a central bank makes loans to individual banks.
3. Central banks have three nontraditional tools to conduct monetary policy: **quantitative easing**, which involves large-scale purchase of government and

private-sector financial assets; **forward guidance**, which involves announcing the intended path of monetary policy in advance; and paying interest on bank reserves held at the central bank.

4. A loose or **expansionary monetary policy** raises the quantity of money and credit above what it otherwise would have been and reduces interest rates.
5. A **contractionary monetary policy**, also called a tight monetary policy, reduces the quantity of money and credit below what it otherwise would have been and raises interest rates, seeking to hold down inflation. An expansionary monetary policy, also called a loose monetary policy, seeks to boost aggregate demand, and thus to counter recession.
6. Monetary policy is inevitably imprecise, for a number of reasons: (a) the effects occur only after long and variable lags; (b) if banks decide to hold **excess reserves**, monetary policy cannot force them to lend; and (c) **velocity** may shift in unpredictable ways.
7. The **basic quantity equation of money** is MV = PQ, where M is the money supply, V is the velocity of money, P is the price level, and Q is the real output of the economy.
8. Some central banks like the European Central Bank practice **inflation-targeting**, which means that the only goal of the central bank is to keep inflation within a low target range. Other central banks like the U.S. Federal Reserve are free to focus on either reducing inflation or stimulating an economy that is in recession, whichever goal seems most important at the time.
9. A **bank run** occurs when there are rumors (possibly true, possibly false) that a bank is at financial risk of having negative net worth. As a result, depositors rush to the bank to withdraw their money and put it someplace safer. Even false rumors, if they cause a bank run, can force a healthy bank to lose its deposits and be forced to close.
10. **Deposit insurance** guarantees bank depositors that even if the bank has negative net worth, their deposits will be protected. In the United States, the Federal Deposit Insurance Corporation (FDIC) collects deposit insurance premiums from banks and guarantees bank deposits up to $100,000.
11. Bank supervision involves inspecting the balance sheets of banks to make sure that they have positive net worth and that their assets are not too risky. In the United States, the Office of the Comptroller of the Currency (OCC) is responsible for supervising banks, and the National Credit Union Administration (NCUA) is responsible for inspecting credit unions. The FDIC and the Federal Reserve also play a role in bank supervision. These agencies coordinate their efforts through the Federal Financial Institutions Examination Council (FFIEC).
12. **Macroprudential policy** is the set of financial regulatory policies that are not focused on the safety or security of any particular financial institutions but instead seek to reduce the risk of financial instability for the economy as a whole.
13. When a central bank acts as a **lender of last resort**, it makes short-term loans available in situations of severe financial panic or stress.

Review Questions

1. How is a central bank different from a typical commercial bank?
2. List the three traditional tools that a central bank has for controlling the money supply.
3. Explain how to use an open market operation to expand the money supply.
4. Explain how to use the reserve requirement to expand the money supply.
5. Explain how to use the discount rate to expand the money supply.
6. Explain how to use quantitative easing to expand the money supply.
7. Explain how to use forward guidance to affect credit and lending in the economy.
8. Explain how to use interest paid on bank reserves to affect credit and lending in the economy.
9. How do the following types of monetary policy affect the quantity of money: expansionary or contractionary?
10. How do the following types of monetary policy affect interest rates: tight or loose?
11. How do the following types of monetary policy affect aggregate demand: expansionary, tight, contractionary, and loose?
12. Which kind of monetary policy would you expect in response to high inflation: expansionary or contractionary? Why?
13. Which kind of monetary policy would you expect in response to recession: expansionary or contractionary? Why?
14. How might each of the following factors complicate the implementation of monetary policy: long and variable lags, excess reserves, and movements in velocity?
15. Define the velocity of the money supply.
16. What is the basic quantity equation of money?
17. How does a monetary policy of inflation targeting work?

18. How is bank regulation linked to the conduct of monetary policy?
19. What is a bank run?
20. In a program of deposit insurance as it is operated in the United States, what is being insured and who pays the insurance premiums?
21. In government programs of bank supervision, what is being supervised?
22. What is the purpose of macroprudential policy?
23. What is the lender of last resort?
24. Name and briefly describe the responsibilities of each of the following agencies: FFIEC, FDIC, NCUA, and OCC.

CHAPTER

31

Exchange Rates and International Capital Flows

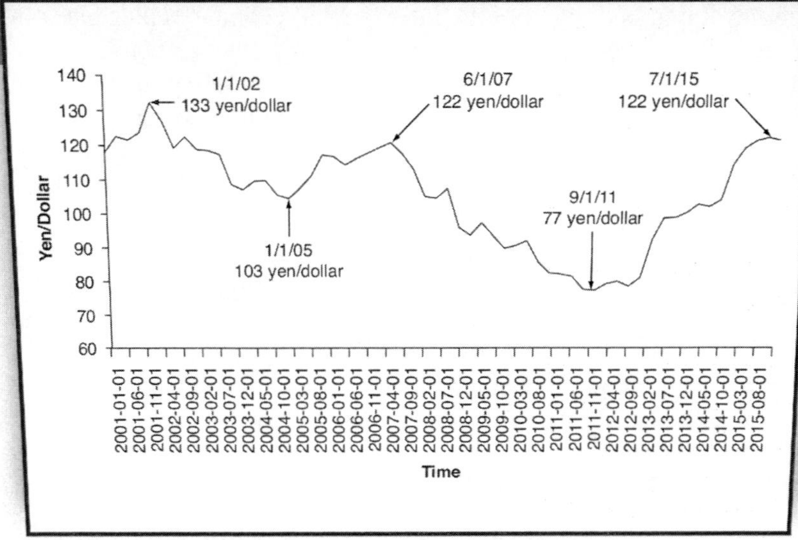

Chapter Outline

How the Foreign Exchange Market Works

Demand and Supply Shifts in Foreign Exchange Markets

Macroeconomic Effects of Exchange Rates

Exchange Rate Policies

Conclusion

The world has over 160 different currencies, from the Afghanistan afghani and the Albanian lek all the way through the alphabet to the Yemeni rial and the Zambian kwacha. For international economic transactions, households or firms will wish to exchange one currency for another. Perhaps the need for exchanging currencies will come from a German firm that exports products to Russia, but then wishes to exchange the Russian rubles it has earned for euros, so that the firm can pay its workers and suppliers in Germany. Perhaps it will be a South African firm that wishes to purchase a mining operation in Angola, but to make the purchase, it must convert South African rand to Angolan kwanza. Perhaps it will be an American tourist visiting China, who wishes to convert U.S. dollars to Chinese yuan to pay the hotel bill.

Exchange rates can sometimes move very swiftly. For example, one euro was worth about $1.20 in U.S. currency in July 2012, $1.40 per euro in March 2014, and $1.10 per euro in March 2015. For firms engaged in international buying, selling, lending, and borrowing, these kinds of swings in exchange rates can have an enormous effect on profits.

This chapter discusses the international dimension of money, which involves conversions from one currency to another at an exchange rate. Exchange rates are nothing more than a price—that is, the price of one currency in terms of another currency—and so they can be analyzed with the tools of demand and supply. The first main section of this chapter begins with an overview of foreign exchange markets: their size, their main participants, and the vocabulary for discussing movements of exchange rates. The next section uses demand and supply graphs to analyze some main factors that cause shifts in exchange rates. A final section then brings the central bank and monetary policy back into the picture. Each country must decide whether to allow its exchange rate to be determined in the market, or whether the central bank should intervene in the exchange rate market. All of the choices for exchange rate policy involve distinctive trade-offs and risks.

How the Foreign Exchange Market Works

dollarize: When a country that is not the United States uses the U.S. dollar as its currency.

foreign exchange market: The market in which people buy one currency while using another currency.

Most countries have different currencies, but not all. Sometimes small economies use the currency of an economically larger neighbor. For example, Ecuador, El Salvador, and Panama have decided to **dollarize**—that is, to use the U.S. dollar as their currency. Sometimes nations share a common currency. A large-scale example of a common currency is the decision by 19 European nations—including some very large economies such as France, Germany, and Italy—to replace their former currencies with the euro. However, with these exceptions duly noted, most of the international economy takes place in a situation of multiple national currencies, and people and firms need to convert from one currency to another when selling, buying, hiring, borrowing, traveling, or investing across national borders. The market in which people or firms use one currency to purchase another currency is called the **foreign exchange market**.

You have encountered the basic concept of exchange rates in earlier chapters. Chapter 21, for example, discussed how exchange rates are used to compare GDP statistics from countries where GDP is measured in different currencies. But these earlier examples took the actual exchange rate as given, as if it were a fact of nature. In reality, the exchange rate is a price—the price of one currency expressed in terms of units of another currency. The key framework for analyzing prices, whether in this course, any other economics course, or in public policy and business examples, or on any planet in the solar system, or in any galaxy in the universe, is the operation of supply and demand in markets.

The Extraordinary Size of the Foreign Exchange Markets

The quantities traded in foreign exchange markets are breathtaking. A survey done in 2013 by the Bank of International Settlements, an international organization for banks and the financial industry, found that $5.3 trillion *per day* was traded on foreign exchange markets.

Exhibit 31-1 shows the currencies most commonly traded on foreign exchange markets. The foreign exchange market is dominated by the U.S. dollar, the currencies used by nations in Western Europe (the euro, the British pound, and the Swiss franc), and the Japanese yen.

Demanders and Suppliers of Currency in Foreign Exchange Markets

In foreign exchange markets, demand and supply become closely interrelated because a person or firm who demands one currency must at the same time supply another

EXHIBIT 31-1 Currencies Traded Most on Foreign Exchange Markets in 2013

Currency	Shares of Foreign Exchange Market Transactions
U.S. dollar	43.5%
Euro	16.7%
Japanese yen	11.5%
British pound	5.9%
Australian dollar	4.3%
Swiss franc	2.6%
Canadian dollar	2.3%
Swedish krona	0.9%
Hong Kong dollar	0.7%
All other	11.6%

currency—and vice versa. To get an intuitive sense of how demand and supply operate in foreign exchange markets, it's useful to consider four groups of people or firms who participate in the market: (1) firms that are involved in international trade of goods and services; (2) tourists visiting other countries; (3) international investors buying ownership (or part-ownership) of a foreign firm; (4) international investors making financial investment that don't involve ownership. Let's consider these categories in turn.

Firms that buy and sell on international markets find that their costs for workers, suppliers, and investors are measured in the currency of the nation where their production occurs, but their revenues from sales are measured in the currency of the different nation where their sales happened. Thus, a Chinese firm exporting abroad will earn some other currency—say, U.S. dollars—but will need Chinese yuan to pay the workers, suppliers, and investors who are based in China. In the foreign exchange markets, this firm will be a supplier of U.S. dollars and a demander of Chinese yuan.

International tourists will supply their home currency to receive the currency of the country they are visiting. For example, an American tourist who is visiting China will both supply U.S. dollars into the foreign exchange market and demand Chinese yuan.

Financial investments that cross international boundaries, and thus require exchanging currency, are often divided into two categories. **Foreign direct investment** refers to purchases of firms in another country that involve taking a management responsibility; for example, in 2013 the Japanese firm SoftBank bought the U.S. telecommunications company Sprint Nextel for $21 billion. To make this purchase of a U.S. firm, Soft Bank would have to supply yen (the currency of Japan) to the foreign exchange market and demand U.S. dollars.

foreign direct investment: Purchases of firms in another country that involve taking a management responsibility.

The other kind of international financial investment, **portfolio investment**, involves a purely financial investment that doesn't involve any management responsibility. An example would be a U.S. financial investor who purchased bonds issued by the government of the United Kingdom, or deposited money in a British bank. In order to make such investments, the American investor would supply U.S. dollars in the foreign exchange market and demand British pounds.

portfolio investment: An investment in another country that is purely financial and doesn't involve any management responsibility.

Portfolio investment is often linked to expectations about how exchange rates will shift. For example, consider a U.S. financial investor who is considering purchasing bonds issued in the United Kingdom. For simplicity, ignore any interest paid by the bond (which will be small in the short run anyway) and focus on exchange rates. Say that a British pound is currently worth $1.50 in U.S. currency. However, the investor believes that in a month, the British pound will be worth $1.60 in U.S. currency. Thus, as Exhibit 31-2*a* shows, this investor would change $24,000 for 16,000 British pounds. In a month, if the pound is indeed worth $1.60, then the portfolio investor can trade back to U.S. dollars at the new exchange rate, and have $25,600—a nice profit. A portfolio investor who believes that the foreign exchange rate for the pound will work in the opposite direction can also invest accordingly. Say that an investor expects that the pound, now worth $1.50 in U.S. currency, will decline to $1.40. Then, as shown in Exhibit 31-2*b*, that investor could start off with 20,000 pounds (borrowing the money if necessary), convert it to $30,000 in U.S. currency, wait a month, and then convert back to approximately 21,428 British pounds—again making a nice profit. Of course, this kind of investing comes without guarantees, and an investor will suffer losses if the exchange rates do not move as predicted.

Many portfolio investment decisions are not as simple as betting that the value of the currency will change in one direction or the other. Instead, they involve firms trying to protect themselves from movements in exchange rates. Imagine that you are running a U.S. firm that is exporting to France. You have signed a contract to deliver certain products and will receive 1 million euros a year from now. But you don't know how much this contract will be worth in U.S. dollars because the dollar/euro exchange rate can fluctuate in the next year. Let's say you want to know for sure what the contract will be worth, and not take a risk that the euro will be worth less in U.S. dollars than it currently is. You can **hedge**, which means using a financial transaction to protect yourself against risk. Specifically, you can sign a financial contract and pay a fee that guarantees you a certain

hedge: Using a financial transaction as protection against risk.

EXHIBIT 31-2 A Portfolio Investor Trying to Benefit from Exchange Rate Movements

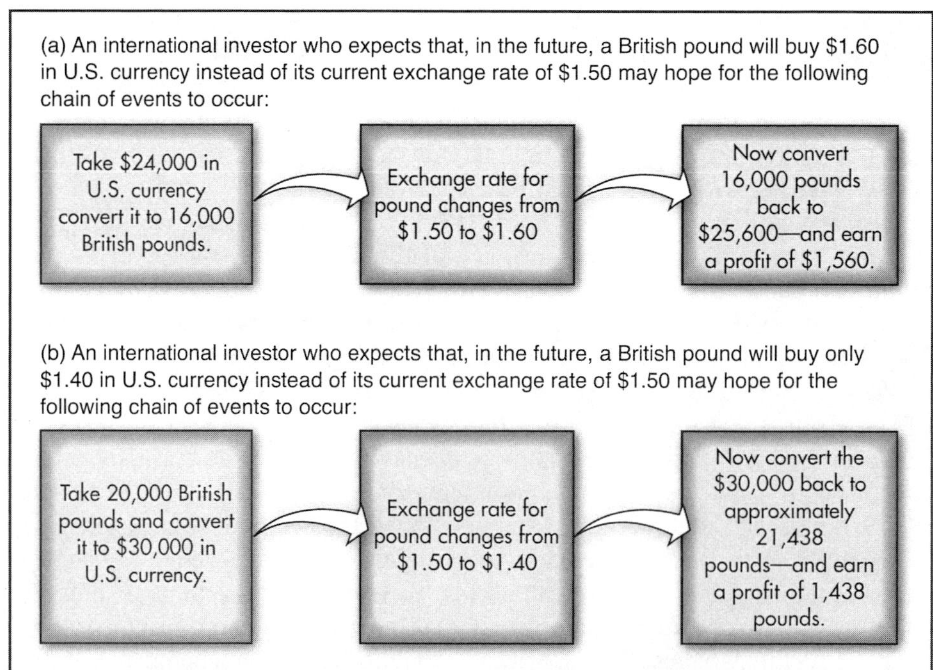

exchange rate one year from now—regardless of what the market exchange rate is at that time. Now, it's possible that the euro will be worth more in dollars a year from now, your hedging contract will be unnecessary, and you will have paid a fee for nothing. But if the value of the euro in dollars declines, then you are protected by the hedge. Financial contracts like hedging, where parties wish to be protected against exchange rate movements, also commonly lead to a further series of portfolio investments because the firm that is receiving a fee to provide the hedge will undertake further transactions to protect itself against the risks of exchange rate movements, too.

Both foreign direct investment and portfolio investment involve an investor who supplies domestic currency and demands a foreign currency. However, purely financial portfolio investment often has a short-run focus, while foreign direct investment usually involves at least partial ownership and managerial responsibility, and thus tends to have a more long-run focus. As a practical matter, portfolio investments can be withdrawn from a country much more quickly than foreign direct investments. A U.S. portfolio investor who wants to buy or sell bonds issued by the government of the United Kingdom can do so with a phone call or a few clicks of a computer key. However, a U.S. firm that wants to buy or sell a company that manufactures automobile parts in the United Kingdom will find that planning and carrying out the transaction takes at least a few weeks, and perhaps even many months. Portfolio investments are often made based on beliefs about how exchange rates or rates of return are likely to move in the near future; in contrast, foreign direct investments, like ownership of a foreign firm, is usually made with a longer-term horizon in mind. Exhibit 31-3 summarizes the main categories of demanders and suppliers of currency.

Participants in the Exchange Rate Market

The foreign exchange market does not involve the ultimate suppliers and demanders of foreign exchange literally seeking each other out. If Martina decides to leave her home in Venezuela and take a trip in the United States, she doesn't need to find a U.S. citizen who is planning to take a vacation in Venezuela and arrange a person-to-person currency trade. Instead, the foreign exchange market works through financial institutions, and it operates on several levels.

Most people and firms who are exchanging a substantial quantity of currency go to a bank, and most banks provide foreign exchange as a service to customers. However, behind the scenes these banks then turn to a smaller number of financial firms known as

EXHIBIT 31-3 The Demand and Supply Line-Ups in Foreign Exchange Markets

Demand for the U.S. Dollar Comes from . . .	Supply of the U.S. Dollar Comes from . . .
A U.S. exporting firm that earned foreign currency and is trying to pay U.S.-based expenses	A foreign firm that has sold imported goods in the United States, earned U.S. dollars, and is trying to pay expenses incurred in its home country
Foreign tourists visiting the United States	U.S. tourists leaving to visit other countries
Foreign investors who wish to make direct investments in the U.S. economy	U.S. investors who want to make foreign direct investments in other countries
Foreign investors who wish to make portfolio investments in the U.S. economy	U.S. investors who want to make portfolio investments in other countries

"dealers," who are actively involved in large quantities of foreign exchange trading. Most foreign exchange dealers are banks, so this behind-the-scenes market is sometimes called the "interbank market," although a few insurance companies and other kinds of financial firms are involved. Trades between foreign exchange dealers can be very large, involving hundreds of millions of dollars. In the world economy, roughly 2,000 firms are foreign exchange dealers. The U.S. economy has less than 100 total foreign exchange dealers, but the largest 12 or so dealers carried out more than half of the total transactions. The foreign exchange market has no central location, although the major dealers keep a close watch on each other at all times.

The foreign exchange market is huge not because of the demands of tourists, firms, or even foreign direct investment, but instead because of portfolio investment and the actions of interlocking foreign exchange dealers. International tourism is a very large industry, involving $1.5 trillion in spending in 2015. Global exports are about 25% of global GDP; say, about $20 trillion per year. Foreign direct investment totaled about $1.2 trillion in 2015. But these quantities are dwarfed by the $5.3 trillion *per day* being traded in foreign exchange markets. Most transactions in the foreign exchange market are for portfolio investment—relatively short-term movements of financial capital between currencies—and by the actions of the large foreign exchange dealers as they constantly buy and sell with each other.

Strengthening and Weakening Currency

When the prices of most goods and services change, the price is said to "rise" or "fall." For exchange rates, the terminology is different. When the exchange rate for a currency rises, so that the currency exchanges for more of other currencies, it is referred to as **appreciating** or "strengthening." When the exchange rate for a currency falls, so that a currency trades for less of other currencies, it is referred to as **depreciating** or "weakening."

appreciating: When a currency is worth more in terms of other currencies; also called "strengthening."

depreciating: When a currency is worth less in terms of other currencies; also called "weakening."

To illustrate the use of these terms, consider the exchange rate between the U.S. dollar and the Canadian dollar since 1980 shown in Exhibit 31-4. The vertical axis in Exhibit 31-4*a* shows the price of $1 in U.S. currency, measured in terms of Canadian currency. Clearly, exchange rates can move up and down substantially. A U.S. dollar traded for $1.17 Canadian in 1980. The U.S. dollar appreciated or strengthened to $1.40 Canadian in 1986, depreciated or weakened to $1.15 Canadian in 1991, and then appreciated or strengthened to $1.60 Canadian by early in 2002, fell to roughly $1.00 Canadian in 2009, and then had a sharp spike up and decline in 2009 and 2010, and then rose back to about $1.40 Canadian by 2016. The units in which exchange rates are measured can be confusing because the exchange rate of the U.S. dollar is being measured using a different currency—the Canadian dollar. But exchange rates always measure the price of one unit of currency by using a different currency.

In looking at the exchange rate between two currencies, the appreciation or strengthening of one currency must mean the depreciation or weakening of the other. Exhibit 31-4*b* shows the exchange rate for the Canadian dollar, measured in terms of U.S. dollars. The

EXHIBIT 31-4
Strengthen or Appreciate vs. Weaken or Depreciate

Exchange rates move up and down substantially, even between close neighbors like the United States and Canada. Exhibit 31-4*a* is a mirror image of Exhibit 31-4*b*: that is, any appreciation of one currency must mean depreciation of the other currency, and vice versa.

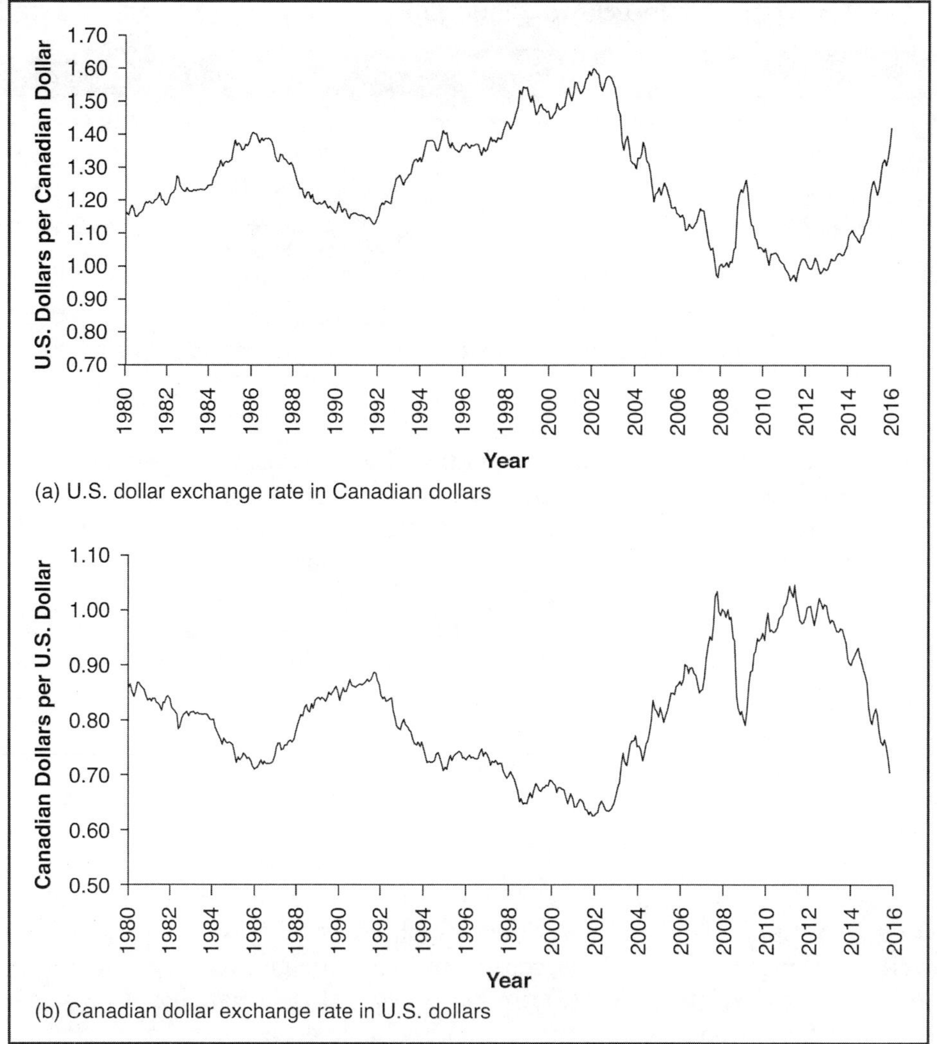

(a) U.S. dollar exchange rate in Canadian dollars

(b) Canadian dollar exchange rate in U.S. dollars

exchange rate of the U.S. dollar measured in Canadian dollars shown in Exhibit 31-4*a* is a perfect mirror image with the exchange rate of the Canadian dollar measured in U.S. dollars shown in Exhibit 31-4*b*. A fall in the Canada $/U.S. $ ratio means a rise in the U.S. $/Canada $ ratio, and vice versa.

With the price of a typical good or service, it's clear that higher prices benefit sellers and hurt buyers, while lower prices benefit buyers and hurt sellers. In the case of exchange rates, where the buyers and sellers are not always intuitively obvious, it's useful to trace through how different participants in the market will be affected by a stronger or weaker currency. Consider, for example, the impact of a stronger U.S. dollar on six different groups of economic actors as shown in Exhibit 31-5: (1) U.S. exporters selling abroad; (2) foreign exporters (that is, firms selling imports in the U.S. economy); (3) U.S. tourists abroad; (4) foreign tourists visiting the United States; (5) U.S. investors (either foreign direct investment or portfolio investment) considering opportunities in other countries; (6) and foreign investors considering opportunities in the U.S. economy.

For a U.S. firm selling abroad, a stronger U.S. dollar is a curse. A strong U.S. dollar means that foreign currencies are correspondingly weak. When this exporting firm earns foreign currencies through its export sales, and then converts them back to U.S. dollars to pay workers, suppliers, and investors, the stronger dollar means that the foreign currency buys fewer U.S. dollars than would have been expected if the currency had not strengthened, and that the firm's profits (as measured in dollars) fall. As a result, the firm may choose to reduce its exports, or it may raise its selling price, which will also tend to reduce its exports. In this way, a stronger currency reduces a country's exports.

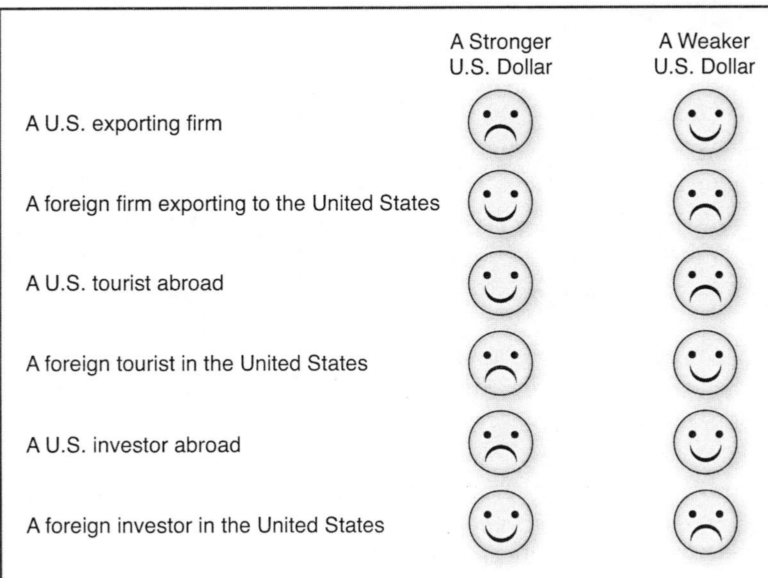

EXHIBIT 31-5 How Do Exchange Rate Movements Affect Each Group?

Conversely, for a foreign firm selling in the U.S. economy, a stronger dollar is a blessing. Each dollar earned through export sales, when traded back into the home currency of the exporting firm, will now buy more of the home currency than expected before the dollar had strengthened. As a result, the stronger dollar means that the importing firm will earn higher profits than expected before the dollar had strengthened. The firm will seek to expand its sales in the U.S. economy, or it may reduce prices, which will also lead to expanded sales. In this way, a stronger U.S. dollar means that consumers will purchase more from foreign producers, expanding the country's level of imports.

For a U.S. tourist abroad, who is exchanging U.S. dollars for foreign currency as necessary, a stronger U.S. dollar is a benefit. The tourist receives more foreign currency for each U.S. dollar, and consequently the cost of the trip in U.S. dollars is lower. When a country's currency is strong, it's a good time for citizens of that country to tour abroad. For example, imagine a U.S. tourist who has saved up $5,000 for a trip to Russia. At the end of January 2015, $1 bought 70 Russian rubles, so the tourist had 350,000 rubles to spend. Months later in May 2015, $1 bought only 50 rubles, so the tourist had 250,000 rubles to spend. By January 2016, $1 bought 80 rubles, so the tourist had 400,000 rubles to spend. During the period from early 2015 into early 2016, the beginning of 2016 clearly represented the best financial deal for U.S. tourists who were visiting Russia. For foreign visitors to the United States, the opposite pattern holds true. A relatively stronger U.S. dollar means that their own currencies are relatively weaker, so that as they shift from their own currency to U.S. dollars, they have fewer U.S. dollars than previously. When a country's currency is strong, it's not an especially good time for foreign tourists to visit.

A stronger dollar injures the prospects of a U.S. financial investor who has already invested money in another country. A U.S. financial investor abroad must first convert U.S. dollars to a foreign currency, invest in a foreign country, and then later convert that foreign currency back to U.S. dollars. If in the meantime the U.S. dollar becomes stronger and the foreign currency becomes weaker, then when the investor converts back to U.S. dollars, the rate of return on that investment will be less than originally expected at the time it was made.

However, a stronger U.S. dollar boosts the returns of a foreign investor putting money into a U.S. investment. That foreign investor converts from their home currency to U.S. dollars and seeks a U.S. investment, while later planning to switch back to their home currency. If, in the meantime, the dollar grows stronger, then when the time comes to convert from U.S. dollars back to the foreign currency, the investor will receive more foreign currency than expected at the time the original investment was made.

CLEARING IT UP

A Stronger Currency Isn't Necessarily Better, Just Different

One common misunderstanding about exchange rates is that a "stronger" or "appreciating" currency must be better than a "weaker" or "depreciating" currency. After all, isn't it obvious that "strong" is better than "weak"? But don't let the terminology confuse you. When a currency becomes stronger, so that it purchases more of other currencies, it benefits some in the economy and injures others.

The preceding paragraphs all focus on the case where the U.S. dollar becomes stronger. The corresponding happy or unhappy economic reactions are illustrated in the first column of Exhibit 31-5. As an exercise, describe in your own words the reasons for the reactions to a weaker dollar, illustrated by the reactions in the second column of the exhibit. Think through these connections for another currency, like how American firms, consumers, and investors might feel if the Mexican peso rose or fell.

At this point, you should have a good sense of who many of the players are in the foreign exchange market: firms involved in international trade, tourists, international financial investors, banks, and foreign exchange dealers. The next section shows how the tools of demand and supply can be used in foreign exchange markets to explain the underlying causes of stronger and weaker currencies.

Demand and Supply Shifts in Foreign Exchange Markets

The foreign exchange market involves firms, households, and investors who demand and supply currencies coming together through their banks and the key foreign exchange dealers. Exhibit 31-6*a* offers a hypothetical example for the exchange rate between the U.S. dollar and the Mexican peso. The vertical axis shows the exchange rate for U.S. dollars, which in this case is measured in pesos. The horizontal axis shows the quantity of U.S. dollars being traded in the foreign exchange market each day. The demand curve D for U.S. dollars intersects with the supply curve S of U.S. dollars at the equilibrium point E, which is an exchange rate of 10 pesos per dollar and a total volume of $8.5 billion.

Exhibit 31-6*b* presents the same demand and supply information from the perspective of the Mexican peso. The vertical axis shows the exchange rate for Mexican pesos, which is measured in U.S. dollars. The horizontal axis shows the quantity of Mexican

EXHIBIT 31-6 Demand and Supply for the U.S. Dollar and Mexican Peso Exchange Rate

In both graphs, the equilibrium exchange rate occurs at point E, at the intersection of the demand curve D and the supply curve S.

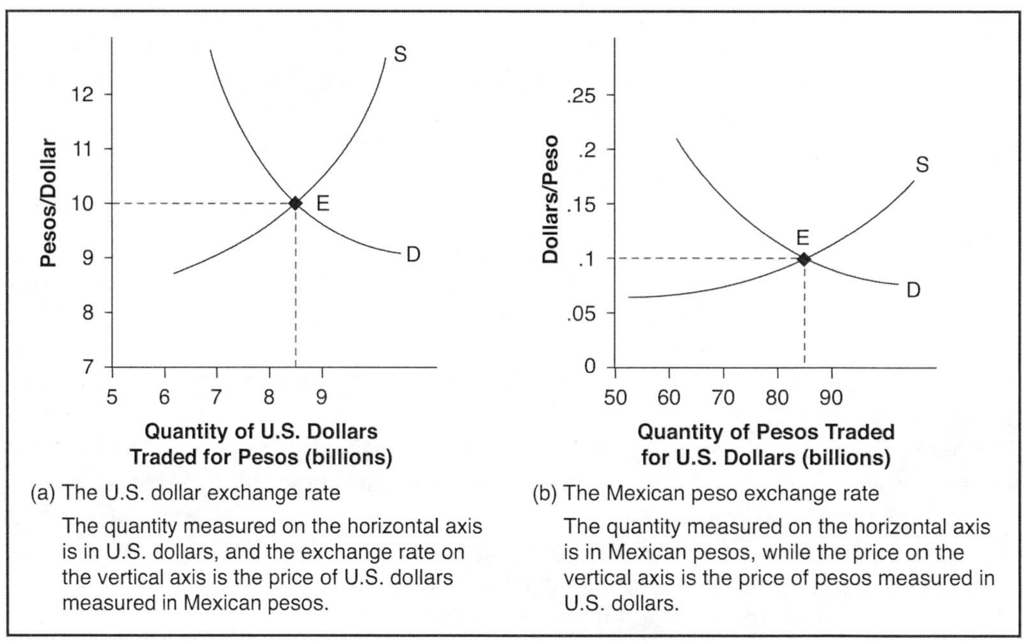

(a) The U.S. dollar exchange rate

The quantity measured on the horizontal axis is in U.S. dollars, and the exchange rate on the vertical axis is the price of U.S. dollars measured in Mexican pesos.

(b) The Mexican peso exchange rate

The quantity measured on the horizontal axis is in Mexican pesos, while the price on the vertical axis is the price of pesos measured in U.S. dollars.

pesos traded in the foreign exchange market. The demand curve D for Mexican pesos intersects with the supply curve S of Mexican pesos at the equilibrium point E, which is an exchange rate of 10 cents in U.S. currency for each Mexican peso and a total volume of 85 billion pesos. In the actual foreign exchange market, almost all of the trading for Mexican pesos is done for U.S. dollars. What factors would cause the demand or supply to shift, thus leading to a change in the equilibrium exchange rate?

Expectations about Future Exchange Rates

One reason to demand a currency on the foreign exchange market is the belief that the value of the currency is about to increase. One reason to supply a currency—that is, sell it on the foreign exchange market—is the expectation that the value of the currency is about to decline. For example, imagine that a leading business newspaper, like the *Wall Street Journal* or the *Financial Times*, runs an article predicting that the Mexican peso will appreciate in value. The likely effects of such an article are illustrated in Exhibit 31-7. Demand for the Mexican peso shifts to the right from D_0 to D_1, as investors become eager to purchase pesos. Conversely, the supply of pesos shifts to the left from S_0 to S_1 because investors will be less willing to give them up. The result is that the equilibrium exchange rate rises from 10 cents/peso to 12 cents/peso and the equilibrium exchange rate rises from 85 billion to 90 billion pesos as the equilibrium moves from E_0 to E_1.

Exhibit 31-7 also illustrates some peculiar traits of supply and demand diagrams in the foreign exchange market. In contrast to all of the other cases of supply and demand you have considered, in the foreign exchange market, supply and demand typically both move at the same time. Groups of participants in the foreign exchange market like firms and investors include some who are buyers and some who are sellers. An expectation of a future shift in the exchange rate affects both buyers and sellers—that is, it affects both demand and supply for a currency. The shifts in demand and supply curves both cause the exchange rate to shift in the same direction; in this example, they both make the peso exchange rate stronger. However, the shifts in demand and supply work in opposing directions on the quantity traded. In this example, the rising demand for pesos is causing the quantity to rise while the falling supply of pesos is causing quantity to fall. In this specific example, the result is a higher quantity. But in other cases, the result could be that quantity remains unchanged or declines.

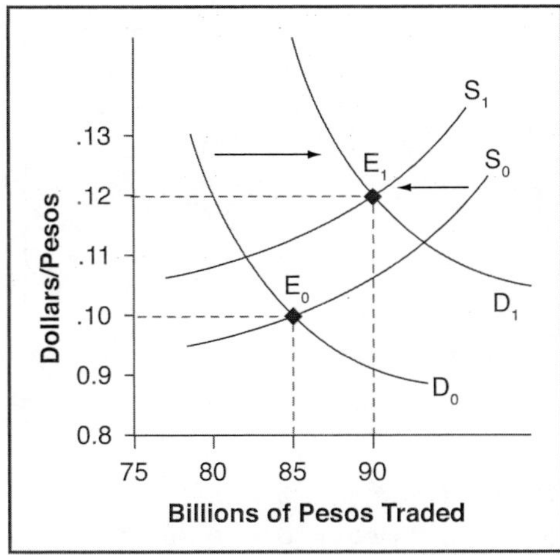

EXHIBIT 31-7 Exchange Rate Market for Mexican Peso Reacts to Expectations about Future Exchange Rates

An announcement that the peso exchange rate is likely to strengthen in the future will lead to greater demand for the peso in the present from investors who wish to benefit from the appreciation. Similarly, it will make investors less likely to supply pesos to the foreign exchange market. Both the shift of demand to the right and the shift of supply to the left cause an immediate appreciation in the exchange rate.

This example also helps to explain why exchange rates often move quite substantially in a short period of a few weeks or months. When investors expect a country's currency to strengthen in the future, they buy the currency and cause it to appreciate immediately. The appreciation of the currency can lead other investors to believe that future appreciation is likely—and thus lead to even further appreciation. Similarly, a fear that a currency *might* weaken quickly leads to an *actual* weakening of the currency, which often reinforces the belief that the currency is going to weaken further. Thus, beliefs about the future path of exchange rates can be self-reinforcing, at least for a time, and a large share of the trading in foreign exchange markets involves dealers trying to outguess each other on what direction exchange rates will move next.

Differences across Countries in Rates of Return

The motivation for investment, whether domestic or foreign, is to earn a return. If rates of return in a country look relatively high, then that country will tend to attract funds from abroad. Conversely, if rates of return in a country look relatively low, then funds will tend to flee to other economies. Changes in the expected rate of return will shift demand and supply for a currency. For example, imagine that interest rates rise in the United States as compared with Mexico. Thus, financial investments in the United States promise a higher return than they previously did. As a result, more investors will demand U.S. dollars so that they can buy interest bearing assets and more will be willing to supply U.S. dollars to foreign exchange markets. Demand for the U.S. dollar will shift to the right from D_0 to D_1 and supply will shift to the left from S_0 to S_1, as shown in Exhibit 31-8. The new equilibrium E_1 will occur at an exchange rate of 9 pesos/ dollar and the same quantity of \$8.5 billion. Thus, a higher interest rate or rate of return relative to other countries leads a nation's currency to appreciate or strengthen, and a lower interest rate relative to other countries leads a nation's currency to depreciate or weaken. Since a nation's central bank can use monetary policy to affect its interest rates, a central bank can also cause changes in exchange rates—a connection that will be discussed in more detail later in this chapter.

Relative Inflation

If a country experiences a relatively high inflation rate compared with other economies, then the buying power of its currency is eroding, which will tend to discourage anyone

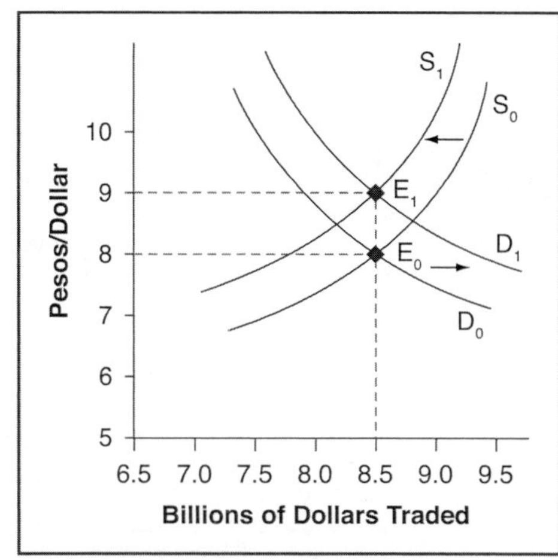

EXHIBIT 31-8 Exchange Rate Market for U.S. Dollars Reacts to Higher Interest Rates

A higher rate of return for U.S. dollar makes holding dollars more attractive. Thus, the demand for dollars in the foreign exchange market shifts to the right from D_0 to D_1, while the supply of dollars shifts to the left from S_0 to S_1. The new equilibrium E_1 has a stronger exchange rate than the original equilibrium E_0, but in this example, the equilibrium quantity traded does not change.

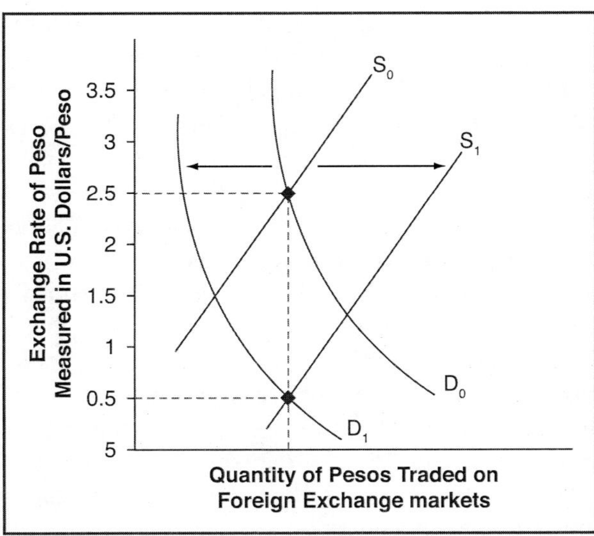

EXHIBIT 31-9 Exchange Rate Markets React to Higher Inflation

If a currency is experiencing relatively high inflation, then its buying power is decreasing and international investors will be less eager to hold it. Thus, a rise in inflation in the Mexican peso would lead demand to shift from D_0 to D_1, and supply to increase from S_0 to S_1. Both movements in demand and supply would cause the currency to depreciate. The effect on the quantity traded is drawn here as a decrease, but in truth it could be an increase or no change, depending on the actual movements of demand and supply.

from wanting to acquire or to hold the currency. Exhibit 31-9 shows an example based on an episode for the Mexican peso. Back in 1986–87, Mexico experienced an inflation rate of over 200%. Not surprisingly, as inflation dramatically decreased the purchasing power of the peso in Mexico, the exchange rate value of the peso declined as well. As shown in Exhibit 31-9, demand for the peso on foreign exchange markets decreased from D_0 to D_1, while supply of the peso increased from S_0 to S_1. The equilibrium exchange rate fell from \$2.50 per peso at the original equilibrium E_0 to \$0.50 per peso at the new equilibrium E_1. In this example, the quantity of pesos traded on foreign exchange markets remained the same, even as the exchange rate shifted.

Purchasing Power Parity

Over the long term, exchange rates must bear some relationship to the buying power of the currency in terms of goods that are internationally traded. If at a certain exchange rate it was much cheaper to buy internationally traded goods—such as oil, steel, computers, and cars—in one country than in another country, businesses would start buying in the cheap country, selling in other countries, and pocketing the profits. For example, if a U.S. dollar is worth $1.40 in Canadian currency, then a car that sells for $20,000 in the United States should sell for $28,000 in Canada. If the price of cars in Canada was much lower than $28,000, then at least some U.S. car-buyers would convert their U.S. dollars to Canadian dollars and buy their cars in Canada. If the price of cars was much higher than $28,000 in this example, then at least some Canadian buyers would convert their Canadian dollars to U.S. dollars and come south of the border to purchase their cars. This process of buying and selling goods across international borders may occur slowly, but over time, it will force prices and exchange rates to align so that the price of internationally traded goods is similar in all countries.

The exchange rate that equalizes the prices of internationally traded goods across countries is called the **purchasing power parity** or **PPP** exchange rate. A group of economists at the International Comparison Program, run by the World Bank, estimates the PPP exchange rate for all countries, based on detailed studies of the prices and qualities of internationally tradable goods.

purchasing power parity (PPP): The exchange rate that equalizes the prices of internationally traded goods across countries.

The purchasing power parity exchange rate serves two main functions. First, PPP exchange rates can be useful for making comparisons between countries. Imagine that you are preparing a table showing the size of GDP in many countries in several recent years, and for ease of comparison, you are converting all the values into U.S. dollars. When you insert the value for Japan, you need to use a yen/dollar exchange rate. But should you use the market exchange rate or the PPP exchange rate? Market exchange rates bounce around. In summer 2008, the exchange rate was 108 yen/dollar, but in late 2009 the U.S. dollar exchange rate versus the yen was 90 yen/dollar. For simplicity, say that Japan's GDP was 500 trillion yen in both 2008 and 2009. But if you use the market exchange rates, then Japan's GDP will be $4.6 trillion in 2008 (that is, 500 trillion yen/(108 yen/ dollar)) and $5.5 trillion in 2009 (that is, 500 trillion yen/(90 yen/dollar)). Of course, it's not true that Japan's economy increased enormously in 2009—in fact, Japan had a recession like much of the rest of the world. The misleading appearance of a booming Japanese economy occurs only because of using the market exchange rate, which often has short-run rises and falls. However, PPP exchange rates stay fairly constant from day to day or week to week, and change only modestly, if at all, from year to year. Thus, PPP exchange rates are often used for international comparisons of GDP and other economic statistics.

Second, over a period of years, exchange rates do tend to move in the general direction of the PPP exchange rate. It's true that in the short run and medium run, as exchange rates adjust to relative inflation rates, rates of return, and to expectations about how interest rates and inflation will shift, the exchange rates will often move away from the PPP exchange rate for a time. But there is some value in knowing in which direction the exchange rate is more likely to shift over the long run.

Macroeconomic Effects of Exchange Rates

A central bank will be concerned about the exchange rate for three reasons: (1) Movements in the exchange rate will affect the quantity of aggregate demand in an economy; (2) Frequent substantial fluctuations in the exchange rate can disrupt international trade and cause problems in a nation's banking system; (3) The exchange rate may contribute to an unsustainable balance of trade and large inflows of international financial capital, which can set the economy up for a deep recession if international investors decide to move their money to another country. Let's discuss these scenarios in turn. Then, the next section will consider a range of exchange rate policies.

Exchange Rates, Aggregate Demand, and Aggregate Supply

Foreign trade in goods and services typically involves incurring the costs of production in one currency while receiving revenues from sales in another currency. As a result, movements in exchange rates can have a powerful effect on incentives to export and import, and thus on aggregate demand in the economy as a whole.

For example, in 1999 when the euro first became a currency, its value measured in U.S. currency was $1.06/euro. By the middle of 2001, the euro had fallen (and the U.S. dollar had correspondingly strengthened) to 87 cents/euro. Consider the situation of a French firm that each year incurs 10 million euros in costs, and sold its products in the United States for $10 million. In 1999, when this firm converted $10 million back to euros at the exchange rate of $1.06/euro (that is, $10 million × [1 euro/$1.06]), it had 9.4 million euros, and suffered a loss. In 2001, when this same firm converted $10 million back to euros at the exchange rate of 87 cents/euro (that is, $10 million × 1 euro/[87 cents]), it had 11.5 million euros and a substantial profit. This example shows how a weaker euro encourages exports by the French firm, because it makes the costs of production in the domestic currency lower relative to the sales revenues earned in another country. From the point of view of the U.S. economy, the example also shows how a stronger U.S. dollar encouraged imports.

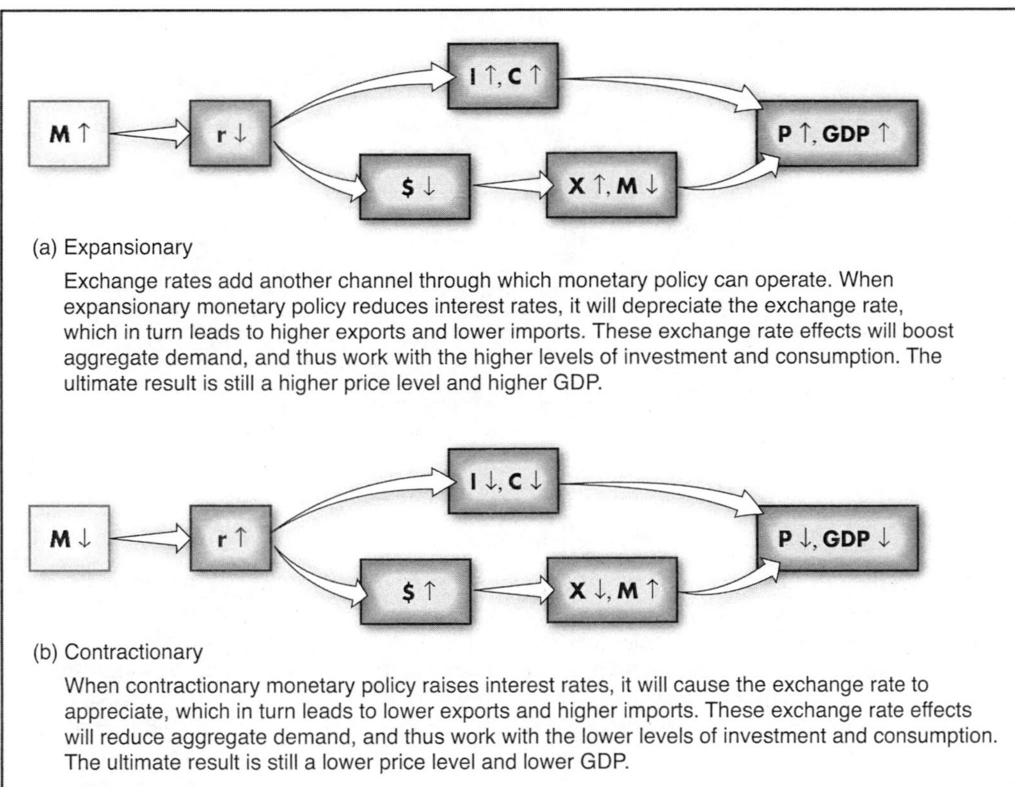

(a) Expansionary

Exchange rates add another channel through which monetary policy can operate. When expansionary monetary policy reduces interest rates, it will depreciate the exchange rate, which in turn leads to higher exports and lower imports. These exchange rate effects will boost aggregate demand, and thus work with the higher levels of investment and consumption. The ultimate result is still a higher price level and higher GDP.

(b) Contractionary

When contractionary monetary policy raises interest rates, it will cause the exchange rate to appreciate, which in turn leads to lower exports and higher imports. These exchange rate effects will reduce aggregate demand, and thus work with the lower levels of investment and consumption. The ultimate result is still a lower price level and lower GDP.

EXHIBIT 31-10
Monetary Policy with Exchange Rate Effects

From a macroeconomic point of view, increases in exports add to aggregate demand, while increases in imports subtract from aggregate demand. Thus, a weaker currency should stimulate aggregate demand. In fact, bringing exchange rates into the picture provides another economic pathway to explain how monetary policy works, as shown in Exhibit 31-10*a*. Expansionary monetary policy lowers interest rates, and increases demand for investment and consumer borrowing, which shifts aggregate demand to the right. However, the lower interest rates will also weaken the exchange rate, which makes exports more attractive and imports less attractive. These factors will cause aggregate demand to rise as well. Exhibit 31-10*b* shows how exchange rates can also reinforce the effects of contractionary monetary policy in reducing aggregate demand. A tight monetary policy raises interest rates, which reduces investment, consumption, and aggregate demand in the domestic economy. In addition, the higher interest rates also strengthen the exchange rate, which decreases aggregate demand further by stimulating imports and reducing exports. Thus, exchange rate adjustments make monetary policy more powerful in affecting aggregate demand.

However, while monetary policy can help an economy that is suffering a recession to move toward the potential output level of GDP, it does not increase the level of potential GDP. This lesson continues to apply when exchange rates are added to the picture. In the aggregate demand-aggregate supply diagram in Exhibit 31-11, the original equilibrium of the aggregate demand curve AD_0 and the short-run aggregate supply curve AS_0 occurs at equilibrium E_0, with an output of 700 and a price level of 95. The central bank uses expansionary monetary policy to increase the supply of money and loans, reduce interest rates, and shift aggregate demand from AD_0 to AD_1. With a short-run upward-sloping AS_0 curve, the equilibrium shifts from E_0 to E_1, as output rises to 740 and the price level rises to 100. This shift includes both the effect of expansionary monetary policy on domestic investment and also the effect through exchange rates on exports and imports.

However, let's say that the potential GDP level of output for this economy is 720. A long-run neoclassical AS curve would thus be a vertical line at this quantity of output. When a country has a weaker exchange rate, all imported inputs to production become

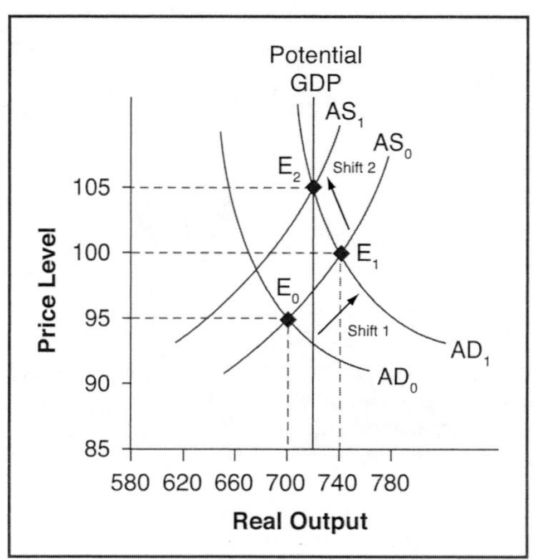

EXHIBIT 31-11 How a Weaker Exchange Rate Affects Inflation and Output

Why can't a nation expand its economy by depreciating its currency? After all, a weaker currency will stimulate exports and reduce imports, and thus cause aggregate demand to shift to the right from AD_0 to AD_1, and from the original equilibrium E_0 to E_1. But a weaker currency also affects aggregate supply. When the currency depreciates, then all inputs to production imported from other countries become more expensive (which is why imports fall, after all). The increase in costs of goods and services causes the original aggregate supply curve AS_0 to shift to the left to AS_1. The resulting equilibrium E_2 at the intersection of AD_1 and AS_1 will definitely have a higher price level than the original equilibrium E_0. However, the change in GDP is unlikely to be very large; it may be a little larger or a little smaller, but the effects of AS and AD on the quantity of output are shifting in opposite directions, and in the long term the economy ends up producing at potential GDP.

relatively more expensive (which is why the quantity of imports decreases). A higher cost for a wide range of inputs shifts the short-run aggregate supply curve to the left from AS_0 to AS_1, for the same reasons that a hike in the price of imported oil shifts an AS curve to the left. At the resulting equilibrium, E_2, the price level has risen to 105, while the equilibrium quantity has fallen 720.

Upon reflection, the idea that a weaker currency leads to higher inflation, both from the effects of aggregate demand shifting to the right and aggregate supply shifting to the left, should make intuitive sense. After all, a weaker exchange rate means that a nation's currency has less buying power in other nations with different currencies—and inflation also means that a currency has less buying power. Thus, exchange rates can help monetary policy to be more powerful in affecting aggregate demand in the short run, but cannot avoid the reality that national output is determined by potential GDP in the long run.

Fluctuations in Exchange Rates

Exchange rates can fluctuate a great deal in the short run. Exhibit 31-4 earlier showed that even two well-developed neighboring economies like the United States and Canada can see significant movements in exchange rates over a few years. Short-term exchange rate fluctuations for less-developed economies like India and Brazil can potentially be even greater. For firms that depend on export sales, or firms that rely on imported inputs to production, or even purely domestic firms that compete with firms tied into international trade—which in many countries adds up to half or more of a nation's GDP—sharp movements in exchange rates can lead to dramatic changes in profits and losses. Thus, a central bank may desire to keep exchange rates from moving too much as part of providing a stable business climate, where firms can focus on productivity and innovation, not on reacting to exchange rate fluctuations.

One of the most economically destructive effects of exchange rate fluctuations can happen through the banking system. Most international loans are measured in a few large

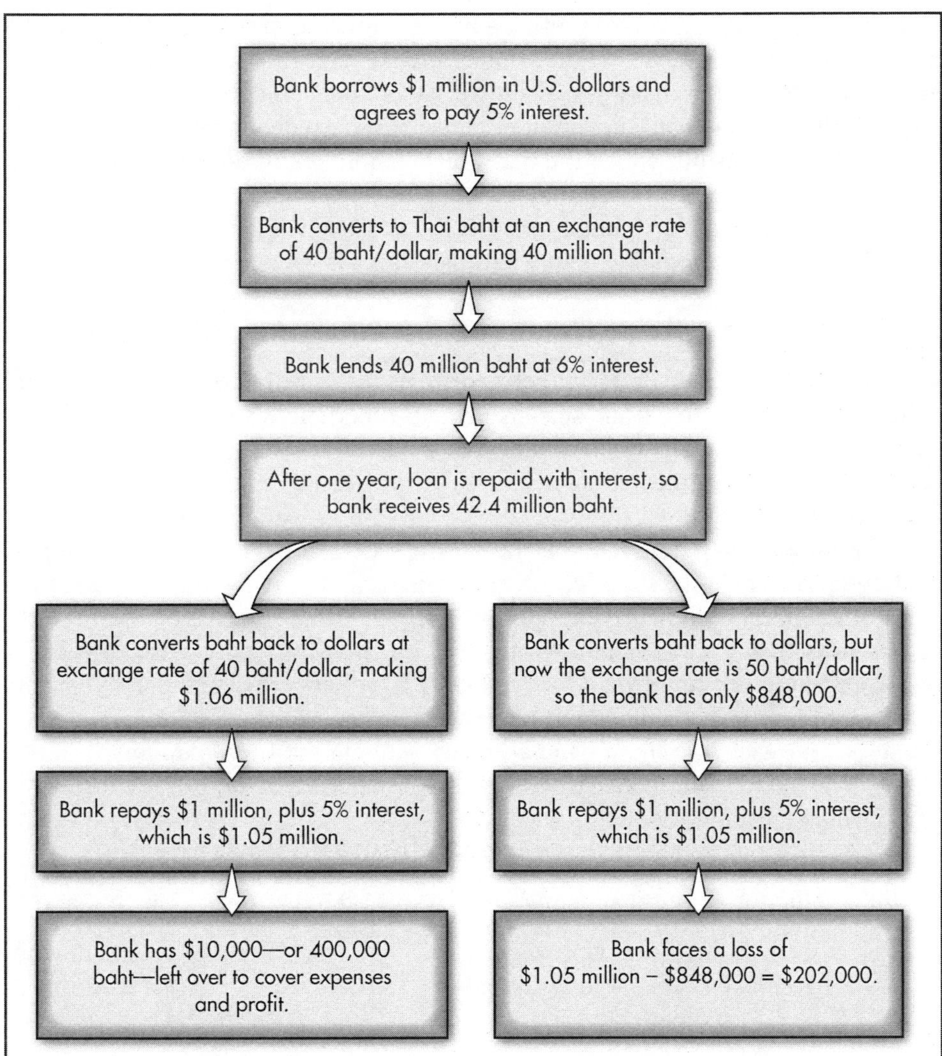

EXHIBIT 31-12
International Borrowing

The scenario of international borrowing that ends on the left is a success story, but the scenario that ends on the right shows what happens when the exchange rate weakens.

currencies, like U.S. dollars, European euros, and Japanese yen. In countries that do not use these currencies, banks often borrow funds in the currencies of other countries, like U.S. dollars, but then lend in their own domestic currency. The left-hand chain of events in Exhibit 31-12 shows how this pattern of international borrowing can work. A bank in Thailand borrows $1 million in U.S. dollars. Then the bank converts the dollars to its domestic currency—in the case of Thailand, the currency is the baht—at a rate of 40 baht/dollar. The bank then lends the baht to a firm in Thailand. The business repays the loan in baht, and the bank converts it back to U.S. dollars to pay off its original U.S. dollar loan.

This process of borrowing in a foreign currency and lending in a domestic currency can work just fine, as long as the exchange rate doesn't shift. But if the dollar strengthens and the baht weakens, a problem arises. The right-hand chain of events in Exhibit 31-12 illustrates what happens when the baht unexpectedly weakens from 40 baht/dollar to 50 baht/dollar. The Thai firm still repays the loan in full to the bank. But because of the shift in the exchange rate, the bank cannot repay its loan in U.S. dollars. (Of course, if the exchange rate had changed in the other direction, making the Thai currency stronger, the bank could have realized an unexpectedly large profit.)

In 1997–98, countries across eastern Asia like Thailand, Korea, Malaysia, and Indonesia experienced a sharp depreciation of their currencies, often 50% or more. These countries had been experiencing substantial inflows of foreign investment capital, with bank lending increasing 20–30% per year through the mid-1990s. When their exchange rates depreciated, the banking systems in these countries were bankrupt. As noted at the start of this chapter, Argentina experienced a similar chain of events in 2002. When the

Argentine peso depreciated, Argentina's banks found themselves unable to pay back what they had borrowed in U.S. dollars. Banks play a vital role in any economy in facilitating transactions and in making loans to firms and consumers. When most of a country's largest banks become bankrupt simultaneously, a sharp decline in aggregate demand and a deep recession results. Since the main responsibilities of a central bank are to control the money supply and to assure that the banking system is stable, a central bank must be concerned about whether a large and unexpected exchange rate depreciation will drive most of the country's existing banks into bankruptcy.

Exchange Rates, Trade Balances, and International Capital Flows

An economy with a trade deficit experiences a net inflow of international financial capital, while an economy with a trade surplus always experiences a net outflow of international capital. This connection was explained in Chapter 25. The exchange rate can help to explain these linkages further—and also explain why movements in exchange rates, trade balances, and international flows of capital sometimes lead to macroeconomic disaster.

In the foreign exchange market, the quantity demanded of a currency in equilibrium must equal the quantity supplied of that currency. In the foreign exchange market for U.S. dollars, U.S. dollars are supplied by foreign firms who have sold imported goods and services to the U.S. economy and by U.S. investors who wish to make financial investments in other countries. Conversely, U.S. dollars are demanded by U.S. firms that have earned foreign currencies and now wish to trade back to U.S. dollars, and by foreign investors who wish to make financial investments in the U.S. economy. (For simplicity, let's include the tourism industry here as part of exports and imports.) Thus, the following relationships must hold:

$$\begin{array}{c}\text{Quantity supplied of U.S. dollars}\\ \text{in the foreign exchange market}\end{array} = \begin{array}{c}\text{Quantity demanded of U.S. dollars}\\ \text{in the foreign exchange market}\end{array}$$

$$\text{Imports} + \begin{array}{c}\text{U.S. investors who wish}\\ \text{to make financial investments}\\ \text{in other countries}\end{array} = \text{Exports} + \begin{array}{c}\text{Foreign investors who wish}\\ \text{to make financial investments}\\ \text{in the U.S. economy}\end{array}$$

When a trade deficit exists, then imports exceed exports. If the quantity demanded is to equal the quantity supplied in foreign exchange markets, then it must also be true that international financial investment entering the U.S. economy is larger than international financial investment leaving the U.S. economy. Thus, a trade deficit always and inevitably means a net inflow of international financial capital. When a trade surplus exists, and exports exceed imports, then it must also be true that international financial investment entering the U.S. economy is smaller than international financial investment leaving the U.S. economy. A trade surplus always and inevitably means a net outflow of international financial capital. When the balance of trade in goods and services is zero, then the inflows and outflows of international financial capital must be equal. Exhibit 31-13 summarizes the three scenarios of trade deficit, trade balance, and trade surplus, and how they are connected to net flows of international financial capital.

There is no reason that each national economy should have a trade balance of zero. In fact, any time there is a net inflow or outflow of financial capital across international borders, that economy will also have an imbalance of trade. If low-income countries around the world succeed in their goal of attracting net investment from high-income economies, they will also necessarily experience trade deficits.

A stronger or appreciating currency is typically associated with a larger trade deficit. To understand why, imagine that the economy of Argentina starts with balanced trade in goods and services. Say that the exchange rate at the equilibrium E_0 is \$1.20 U.S. dollar per peso and the equilibrium quantity is \$2 billion per day, as shown in Exhibit 31-14. Now imagine that Argentina's economy appears to be growing in a healthy way, so that U.S. and other international investors want to make financial investments in Argentina. The demand for the pesos in the foreign exchange market increases from D_0 to D_1, and the

EXHIBIT 31-13 Trade Balances and International Financial Flows

Scenario 1	Scenario 2	Scenario 3
Trade Deficit	***Trade Balance***	***Trade Surplus***
Imports greater than exports	Imports equal to exports	Exports greater than imports
The value of U.S. dollars earned by foreign producers who sell goods and services in the United States is greater than the value of foreign currencies earned by U.S. producers selling abroad.	The value of U.S. dollars earned by foreign producers who sell goods and services in the United States is equal to the value of foreign currencies earned by U.S. producers selling abroad.	The value of U.S. dollars earned by foreign producers who sell goods and services in the U.S. economy is less than the value of foreign currencies earned by U.S. producers selling abroad.
Inflow of international financial capital greater than outflow of financial capital	Inflow of financial capital equal to outflow of financial capital	Outflow of financial capital to other economies greater than inflow of financial capital

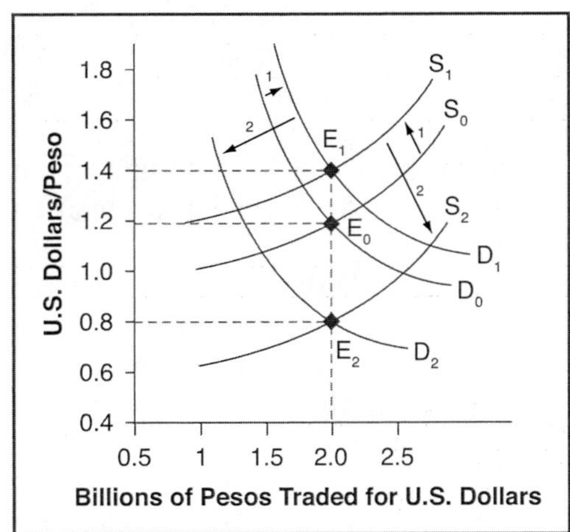

EXHIBIT 31-14 From Appreciation to Depreciation

The exchange rate starts at E_0. The local economy grows and attracts an inflow of international financial capital. Demand for the currency on foreign exchange markets increases from D_0 to D_1, supply falls from S_0 to S_1, and the currency appreciates from $1.20/peso at E_0 to $1.40/ peso at E_1. But at some point, the enthusiasm of foreign investors for this economy diminishes. As international financial investors move funds to other countries, and as the depreciation causes even more disenchantment with this currency, the supply of this currency on foreign exchange markets shifts to the right from S_1 to S_2, and demand for the currency shifts to the left from D_1 to D_2. Eventually, the exchange rate has fallen from $1.40 at E_1 to $0.80 at E_2. This sharp decline in exchange rates can stagger firms involved in international trade, the banking system, and the macroeconomy.

supply of U.S. dollars decreases from S_0 to S_1. At the new equilibrium E_1, the equilibrium quantity in the market remains the same but the exchange rate has risen to $1.40/peso. This higher exchange rate will discourage exports from Argentina and encourage imports. Thus, the exchange rate provides a connection through which an economy that experiences a rise in net capital inflows will also have a trade deficit.

But a dangerous macroeconomic scenario has repeated itself a number of times in recent years: a nation's economy appears to have good prospects for future growth, and so it attracts inflows of international financial capital leading to a stronger currency. Indeed, many low-income and middle-income countries hope to experience a steady inflow of foreign financial investment, which not only brings funds for physical capital investment, but is often accompanied by management expertise, international business contacts, and improved training for local workers. However, at some point, the economic growth of the country suffered an inevitable hiccup, from one cause or another. The hiccup need not be large—only large enough to make international investors fear that the country's exchange rate is likely to weaken. This fear causes some international investors to withdraw their short-term portfolio investments in the country. But as foreign investors sell their financial investments in the country, they increase the supply of that country's currency on foreign exchange markets and reduce their demand for the currency, thus causing the currency to fall. A self-fulfilling prophecy has occurred: expectations that the currency would fall led to an immediate decline. The falling currency led to expectations of a further decline, which led to more financial investment fleeing the country and more downward pressure on the currency. By the time this avalanche has ended, the supply of currency in Exhibit 31-14 increases from S_0 to S_1 and the demand for that currency falls from D_0 to D_1. The new equilibrium E_2 has the same quantity, but now the exchange rate is only 80 cents per peso.

A sharp decline in the exchange rate will reduce the trade deficit (or increase a trade surplus) by benefiting exporters and making imports more expensive. But severe problems can arise in the banking system. At various times in the late 1990s and early 2000s, banks in Mexico and Thailand and Russia and Argentina had borrowed extensively in U.S. dollars and loaned in their local currencies. When the local currencies depreciated, the banks could not repay their international loans. As entire banking systems went bankrupt, the national economies plummeted. GDP fell by 10%, 20%, and more within a year or two. The risk of these extremely severe recessions means that central banks must be concerned that an inflow of financial capital will turn into an outflow, leading to a sharp decline in exchange rates that cripples the financial sector of the economy and leads to deep recession.

The U.S. economy has experienced fairly large trade deficits in the 2000s: for example, in 2006 the current account trade balance for the U.S. economy was a deficit 5.7% of GDP, although in more recent years it has typically been in the range of 2–3% of GDP. Nonetheless, the U.S. economy is clearly less vulnerable to a sharp downturn in the exchange rate of its currency than many other countries. One protection is that the U.S. dollar is so widely held—as shown in Exhibit 31-1 earlier, it makes up almost half of all exchange rate trading. It's possible for international markets to flee small currencies like those of Argentina or Thailand, but it's harder to flee the U.S. dollar. Also, U.S. banks typically have both liabilities and assets in U.S. dollars, so they would not be crippled by a fall in the dollar exchange rate like the banks in Argentina or Thailand. Still, a sharp decline in the value of the U.S. dollar would increase aggregate demand by raising exports and reducing imports. It would also shift aggregate supply to the left by raising the price of imported goods and services throughout the U.S. economy. If the Federal Reserve attempted to fight the resulting inflationary pressures with a contractionary monetary policy, a recession might result. Even the mighty U.S. economy is not invulnerable to pressures from the globalized economy.

Summing Up Public Policy and Exchange Rates

Every nation would prefer a stable exchange rate to facilitate international trade and reduce the degree of risk and uncertainty in the economy. However, a nation may sometimes want a weaker exchange rate to stimulate aggregate demand and reduce a recession, or a stronger exchange rate to fight inflation. Any country must also be concerned that rapid movements from a weak to a strong exchange rate may cripple its export industries, while rapid movements from a strong to a weak exchange rate can cripple its banking sector. In short, every choice of an exchange rate—whether it should be stronger or weaker, or fixed or changing—represents potential trade-offs. The next section discusses the range of policy choices that a country can make about its exchange rate.

Exchange Rate Policies

Exchange rate policies come in a range of different forms listed in Exhibit 31-15: let the foreign exchange market determine the exchange rate; let the market set the value of the

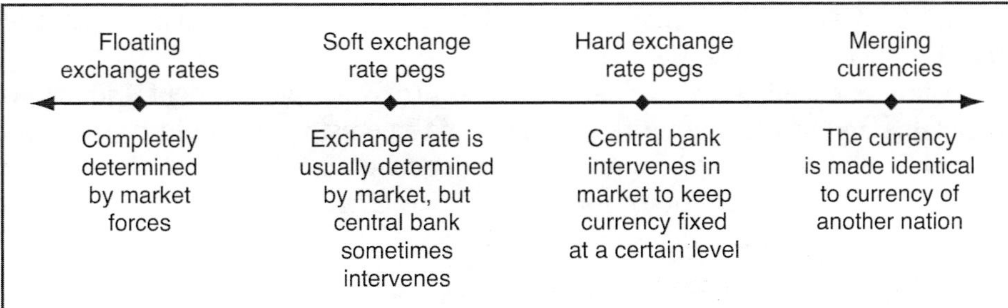

EXHIBIT 31-15 A Spectrum of Exchange Rate Policies

exchange rate most of the time, but have the central bank sometimes intervene to prevent fluctuations that seem too large; have the central bank guarantee a specific exchange rate; or share a currency with other countries. Let's discuss each type of exchange rate policy and its trade-offs in turn.

Floating Exchange Rates

A policy which allows the foreign exchange market to set exchange rates is referred to as a **floating exchange rate.** The U.S. dollar is a floating exchange rate, as are currencies of about 40% of the countries in the world economy. The major concern with this policy is that exchange rates can move a great deal in a short time.

floating exchange rate: When a country lets the value of its currency be determined in the exchange rate market.

Consider the U.S. exchange rate expressed in terms of another fairly stable currency, the Japanese yen, as shown in Exhibit 31-16. On January 1, 2002, the exchange rate was 133 yen/dollar. In January 2005, it was 103 yen/dollar. By June 2007, it was 122 yen/dollar, and by September 2011, it had fallen to 77 yen/dollar, before rising back up to about 120 yen/dollar in 2016. As investor sentiment swings back and forth, driving exchange rates up and down, exporters, importers, and banks involved in international lending are all affected. At worst, large movements in exchange rates can drive companies into bankruptcy or trigger a nationwide banking collapse. But even in the moderate case of the yen/dollar exchange rate, these movements back and forth impose stress on both economies as firms must alter their export and import plans to take the new exchange rates into account. Especially in smaller economies where international trade is a relatively large share of GDP, exchange rate movements can rattle their economies.

However, the movements of floating exchange rates have advantages, too. After all, prices of goods and services rise and fall throughout a market economy, as demand and supply shift. If an economy experiences strong inflows or outflows of international financial capital, or has relatively high inflation, or if it experiences strong productivity growth

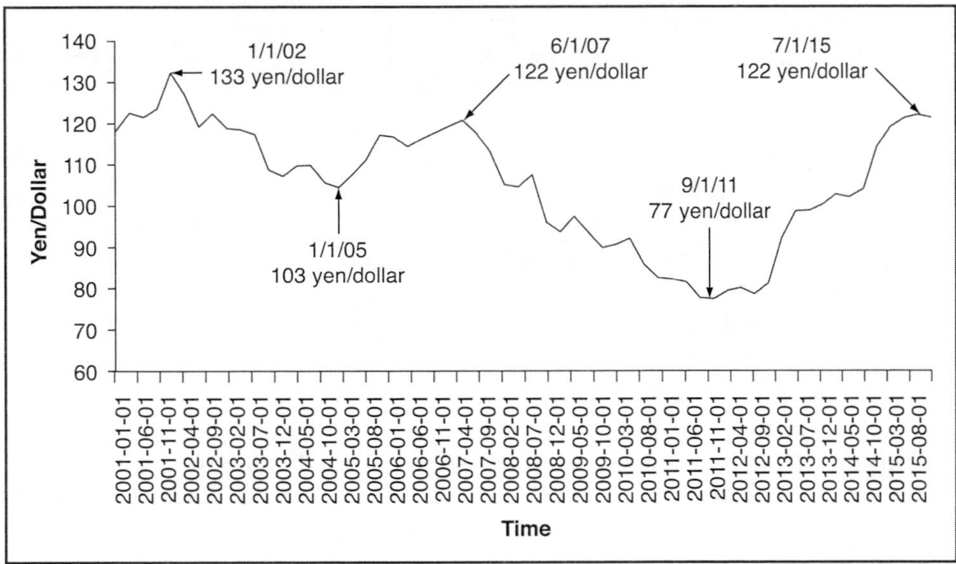

EXHIBIT 31-16 U.S. Dollar Exchange Rate in Japanese Yen

Even relatively stable exchange rates can vary a fair amount. The exchange rate for the U.S. dollar, measured in Japanese yen, fell about 30% from the start of 2002 to the start of 2005, rose back by mid-2007, dropped by late 2011, and then rebounded somewhat by 2016.

so that purchasing power changes relative to other economies, then it makes economic sense for the exchange rate to shift as well.

Floating exchange rate advocates often argue that if government policies were more predictable and stable, then inflation rates and interest rates would be more predictable and stable, and so exchange rates would bounce around less, too. The great economist Milton Friedman (1912–2006), for example, wrote a defense of floating exchange rates in 1961 in his book *Capitalism and Freedom*:

> Being in favor of floating exchange rates does not mean being in favor of unstable exchange rates. When we support a free price system [for goods and services] at home, this does not imply that we favor a system in which prices fluctuate wildly up and down. What we want is a system in which prices are free to fluctuate but in which the forces determining them are sufficiently stable so that in fact prices move within moderate ranges. This is equally true in a system of floating exchange rates. The ultimate objective is a world in which exchange rates, while free to vary, are, in fact, highly stable because basic economic policies and conditions are stable.

Thus, advocates of floating exchange rates admit that, yes, exchange rates may sometimes fluctuate. But they point out that if a central bank focuses on preventing either high inflation or deep recession, with low and reasonably steady interest rates, then exchange rates will have less reason to vary.

Using Soft Pegs and Hard Pegs

soft peg: An exchange rate policy where the government usually allows the exchange rate to be set by the market, but in some cases, especially if the exchange rate seems to be moving rapidly in one direction, the central bank will intervene.

hard peg: An exchange rate policy in which the central bank sets a fixed and unchanging value for the exchange rate.

When a government intervenes in the foreign exchange market so that the exchange rate of its currency is different from what the market would have produced, it is said to have established a "peg" for its currency. A **soft peg** is the name for an exchange rate policy where the government usually allows the exchange rate to be set by the market, but in some cases, especially if the exchange rate seems to be moving rapidly in one direction, the central bank will intervene in the market. With a **hard peg** exchange rate policy, the central bank sets a fixed value for the exchange rate, which it intends to change only rarely. This section explains how a central bank can implement soft peg and hard peg policies, while the next section discusses the trade-offs and costs of these policies.

Suppose that the market exchange rate for the Brazilian currency, the real, would be 35 cents/real with a daily quantity of 15 billion real traded in the market, as shown at the equilibrium E_0 in Exhibit 31-17*a* and Exhibit 31-17*b*. However, the government of Brazil decides that the exchange rate should be 30 cents/real, as shown in Exhibit 31-17*a*. Perhaps Brazil sets this lower exchange rate to benefit its export industries; perhaps it is an attempt to stimulate aggregate demand by stimulating exports; perhaps Brazil believes that the current market exchange rate is higher than the long-term purchasing power parity value of the real, so it is minimizing fluctuations in the real by keeping it at this lower rate; perhaps the target exchange rate was set sometime in the past, and is now being maintained for the sake of stability. Whatever the reason, if Brazil's central bank wishes to keep the exchange rate below the market level, it must face the reality that at this weaker exchange rate of 30 cents/real, the quantity demanded of its currency at 17 billion reals is greater than the quantity supplied of 13 billion reals in the foreign exchange market.

The Brazilian central bank could weaken its exchange rate below what would otherwise be the market-determined level in two ways. One approach is to use an expansionary monetary policy that leads to lower interest rates. In foreign exchange markets, the lower interest rates will reduce demand and increase supply of the real and lead to depreciation. Alternatively, Brazil's central bank could trade directly in the foreign exchange market. The central bank can expand the money supply by creating reals, use the reals to purchase foreign currencies, and avoid selling any of its own currency. In this way, it can fill the gap between quantity demanded and quantity supplied of its currency.

Exhibit 31-17*b* shows the opposite situation. Here, the Brazilian government desires a stronger exchange rate of 40 cents/real than the market rate of 35 cents/real. Perhaps Brazil desires the stronger currency to reduce aggregate demand and to fight inflation, or

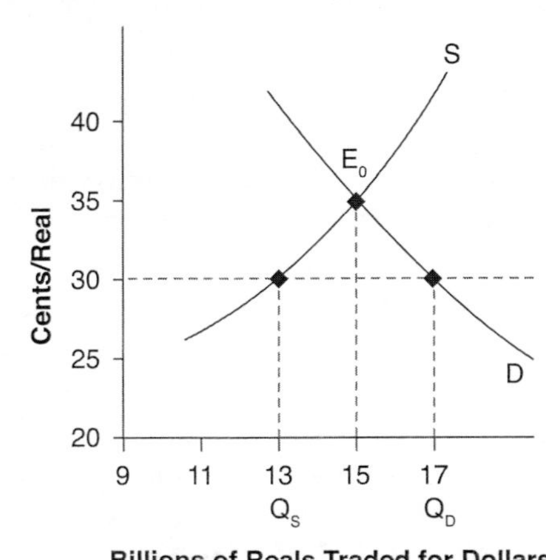

Billions of Reals Traded for Dollars

(a) Pegging an exchange rate below equilibrium

If an exchange rate is pegged below what would otherwise be the equilibrium, then the quantity demanded of the currency will exceed the quantity supplied. The central bank can fill this gap in two ways. One approach would be an expansionary monetary policy to reduce interest rates, which will reduce demand for the currency in foreign exchange markets and increase supply. Alternatively, the central bank could create money and supply it directly in the foreign exchange market.

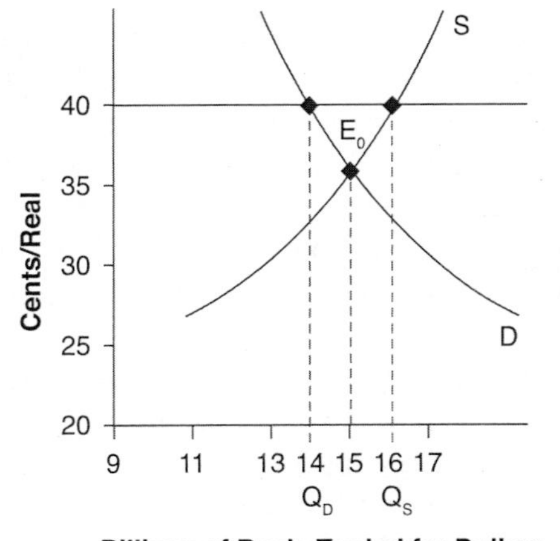

Billions of Reals Traded for Dollars

(b) Pegging an exchange rate above equilibrium

If an exchange rate is pegged above what would otherwise be the equilibrium, then the quantity supplied of the currency exceeds the quantity demanded. The central bank can create this situation with a contractionary monetary policy to raise interest rates, and thus to increase demand for its currency and reduce supply of its currency in foreign exchange markets. Alternatively, the central bank can use its reserves of foreign currency to purchase its own currency on foreign exchange markets and thus to increase demand directly.

EXHIBIT 31-17
Pegging an Exchange Rate

perhaps Brazil believes that current market exchange rate is temporarily lower than the long-term rate. But whatever the reason, at the higher desired exchange rate, the quantity supplied of 16 billion reals exceeds the quantity demanded of 14 billion reals.

Brazil's central bank can use a contractionary monetary policy to raise interest rates, which will increase demand and reduce supply of the currency on foreign exchange markets, and lead to an appreciation. Alternatively, Brazil's central bank can trade directly in the foreign exchange market. In this case, with an excess supply of its own currency in foreign exchange markets, the central bank must use reserves of foreign currency, like U.S. dollars, to demand its own currency and thus cause an appreciation of its exchange rate.

Both a soft peg and a hard peg policy require that the central bank intervene in the foreign exchange market. However, a hard peg policy attempts to preserve a fixed exchange rate. A soft peg policy typically allows the exchange rate to move up and down by relatively small amounts in the short run of several months or a year, and to move by larger amounts over time, but seeks to avoid extreme short-term fluctuations.

Trade-offs of Soft Pegs and Hard Pegs

When a country decides to alter the market exchange rate, it faces a number of trade-offs. If it uses monetary policy to alter the exchange rate, it then cannot at the same time use monetary policy to address issues of inflation or recession. If it uses direct purchases and sales of foreign currencies in exchange rates, then it must face the issue of how it will handle its reserves of foreign currency. Finally, a pegged exchange rate can even create additional movements of the exchange rate; for example, even the possibility of government intervention in exchange rate markets will lead to rumors about whether and when the government will intervene, and dealers in the foreign exchange market will react to those rumors. Let's consider these issues in turn.

A first concern with pegged exchange rate policies is that they imply that a country's monetary policy is no longer focused on controlling inflation or shortening recessions, but now must also take the exchange rate into account. For example, when a country pegs its exchange rate, it will sometimes face economic situations where it would like to have an expansionary monetary policy to fight recession—but it cannot do so because that policy would depreciate its exchange rate and break its hard peg. With a soft peg exchange rate policy, the central bank can sometimes ignore the exchange rate and focus on domestic inflation or recession—but in other cases the central bank may ignore inflation or recession and instead focus on its soft peg exchange rate. With a hard peg policy, domestic monetary policy is effectively no longer determined by domestic inflation or unemployment, but only by what monetary policy is needed to keep the exchange rate at the hard peg.

A second issue arises when a central bank intervenes directly in the exchange rate market. If a central bank ends up in a situation where it is perpetually creating and selling its own currency on foreign exchange markets, it will be buying the currency of other countries, like U.S. dollars or euros, to hold as reserves. Holding large reserves of other currencies has an opportunity cost, and central banks will not wish to boost such reserves without limit. Also, a central bank that causes a large increase in the supply of money is also risking an inflationary surge in aggregate demand. Conversely, when a central bank wishes to buy its own currency, it can do so by using its reserves of international currency like the U.S. dollar or the euro. But if the central bank runs out of such reserves, it can no longer use this method to strengthen its currency. Thus, buying foreign currencies in exchange rate markets can be expensive and inflationary, while selling foreign currencies can only work until a central bank runs out of reserves.

A third issue is that when a government pegs its exchange rate, it may unintentionally create another reason for additional fluctuation. With a soft peg policy, foreign exchange dealers and international investors react to every rumor about how or when the central bank is likely to intervene to influence the exchange rate, and as they react to rumors the exchange rate will shift up and down. Thus, even though the goal of a soft peg policy is to reduce short-term fluctuations of the exchange rate, the existence of the policy—when anticipated in the foreign exchange market—may sometimes increase short-term fluctu-

Capital Controls and Tobin Taxes

Some countries like Chile and Malaysia have sought to reduce movements in exchange rates by limiting inflows and outflows of international financial capital. This policy can be enacted either through targeted taxes or by regulations.

Taxes on international capital flows are sometimes known as "Tobin taxes," named after James Tobin, the 1981 Nobel laureate in economics who proposed such a tax in a 1972 lecture. For example, a government might tax all foreign exchange transactions, or attempt to tax short-term portfolio investment while exempting long-term foreign direct investment. Countries can also use regulation either to forbid certain kinds of foreign investment in the first place or to make it difficult for international financial investors to withdraw their funds from a country.

The goal of such policies is to reduce international capital flows, especially short-term portfolio flows, in the hope that doing so will reduce the chance of large movements in exchange rates that can bring macroeconomic disaster.

But proposals to limit international financial flows have some practical difficulties. Taxes are imposed by national governments, not international ones. If one government imposes a Tobin tax on exchange rate transactions carried out within its territory, the exchange rate market might easily be operated by a firm based someplace like the Grand Caymans, an island nation in the Caribbean well-known for allowing some financial wheeling and dealing. In an interconnected global economy, if goods and services are allowed to flow across national borders, then payments need to flow across borders, too. It is very difficult—close to impossible—for a nation to allow only the flows of payments that relate to goods and services, while clamping down or taxing other flows of financial capital. If a nation participates in international trade, it must also participate in international capital movements.

Finally, countries all over the world, especially low-income countries, are crying out for foreign investment to help develop their economies. Policies that discourage international financial investment may prevent some possible harm, but they may also rule out potentially substantial economic benefits as well.

ations of the exchange rate as international investors try to anticipate how and when the central bank will act.

A hard peg exchange rate policy will not allow short-term fluctuations in the exchange rate. But if the government first announces a hard peg but later changes its mind—for example, perhaps the government becomes unwilling to keep interest rates high or to hold high levels of foreign exchange reserves—then the result of abandoning a hard peg could be a dramatic shift in the exchange rate.

In the mid-2000s, about one-third of the countries in the world used a soft peg approach and about one-quarter used a hard peg approach. The general trend since the 1990s has been to shift away from a soft peg approach in favor of either floating rates or a hard peg. The concern is that a successful soft peg policy may for a time lead to very little variation in exchange rates, so that firms and banks in the economy begin to act as if a hard peg exists. When the exchange rate does move, the effects are especially painful because firms and banks haven't planned and hedged against a possible change. Thus, the argument went, it is better either to be clear that the exchange rate is always flexible, or that it is fixed, but choosing an in-between soft peg option may end up being worst of all.

A Single Currency

A final approach to exchange rate policy is for a nation to choose a common currency shared with one or more nations. A single currency approach eliminates foreign exchange risk altogether. Just as no one worries about exchange rate movements when buying and selling between New York and California, Europeans know that the value of the euro will be the same in Germany and France and other European nations that have adopted the euro.

However, a single currency also poses problems. Like a hard peg, a single currency means that a nation has given up altogether on domestic monetary policy, and instead has put its interest rate policies in other hands. When Ecuador uses the U.S. dollar as its currency, it has no voice in whether the Federal Reserve raises or lowers interest rates. The European Central Bank that determines monetary policy for the euro has representatives from all the euro nations. However, from the standpoint of, say, Portugal, there will be times when the decisions of the European Central Bank about monetary policy do not match the decisions that would have been made by a Portuguese central bank. In recent years, the 19 European countries in the euro zone have faced difficult economic challenges in devising a one-size-fits-all monetary policy. Some countries using the euro, like Greece and Spain, have faced financial crises and high unemployment, and thus wanted the European Central Bank to loosen monetary policies and make active use of it lender-of-last-resort functions. However, other countries using the euro, like Germany, perceived their economies as fairly healthy and thus tended to favor alternative monetary policies.

The lines between these four different exchange rate policies can blend into each other. For example, a soft peg exchange rate policy in which the government almost never acts to intervene in the exchange rate market will look a great deal like a floating exchange rate. Conversely, a soft peg policy in which the government intervenes often to keep the exchange rate near a specific level will look a lot like a hard peg. A decision to merge currencies with another country is, in effect, a decision to have a permanently fixed exchange rate with those countries, which is like a very hard exchange rate peg. The range of exchange rates policy choices, with their advantages and disadvantages, are summarized in Exhibit 31-18.

Conclusion

Global macroeconomics would be easier to study and understand if the whole world had one currency and one central bank. The exchange rates between many different currencies complicate the picture. If exchange rates are set solely by financial markets, they will fluctuate substantially as short-term portfolio investors try to anticipate tomorrow's news. If the government attempts to intervene in exchange rate markets through soft pegs or hard pegs, it gives up at least some of the power to use monetary policy to focus on

EXHIBIT 31-18 Trade-offs of Exchange Rate Policies

	Floating Exchange Rates	Soft Peg	Hard Peg	Merging Currencies
Large short-run fluctuations in exchange rates?	Often a lot in the short term	Maybe less in the short run, but still large changes over time	None, unless a change in the fixed rate	None
Large long-term fluctuations in exchange rates?	Can often happen	Can often happen	Can't happen unless hard peg changes	Can't happen
Power of central bank to conduct countercyclical monetary policy	Flexible exchange rates make monetary policy stronger	Some power, although conflicts may arise between exchange rate policy and countercyclical policy	Very little; central bank must keep exchange rate fixed	None; nation doesn't have its own currency
Costs of holding foreign exchange reserves	Don't need to hold reserves	Hold moderate reserves that rise and fall over time	Hold large reserves	No need to hold reserves
Risk of being stuck with an exchange rate that causes a large trade imbalance and very high inflows or outflows of financial capital	A floating rate adjusts often	A soft peg will adjust over the medium term, if not the short term	A hard peg may become stuck over time either far above or below the market level	A merged currency cannot adjust

domestic inflations and recessions, and it risks causing even greater fluctuations in foreign exchange markets. There is no consensus among economists about which exchange rate policies are best: floating, soft peg, hard peg, or merged currencies. The choice depends both on how well a nation's central bank can implement a specific exchange rate policy and on how well a nation's firms and banks can adapt to different exchange rate policies. A national economy that does a fairly good job at achieving the four main economic goals of growth, low inflation, low unemployment, and a sustainable balance of trade will probably do just fine the vast majority of the time with any exchange rate policy; conversely, no exchange rate policy is likely to save an economy that consistently fails at achieving these goals.

Key Concepts and Summary

1. The **foreign exchange market** is the market in which people and firms exchange one currency to purchase another currency.
2. On the demand side of the foreign exchange market for the trading of U.S. dollars are U.S. export firms seeking to convert their earnings in foreign currency back into U.S. dollars; foreign tourists in the United States; and foreign investors seeking to make financial investments in the U.S. economy. On the supply side of the foreign exchange market for the trading of U.S. dollars are foreign firms that have sold imports in the U.S. economy and are seeking to convert their earnings back to their home currency; U.S. tourists abroad; and U.S. investors seeking to make financial investments in foreign economies.
3. When currency A can buy more of currency B, then currency A has strengthened or **appreciated** relative to B. When currency A can buy less of currency B, then currency A has weakened or **depreciated** relative to B. If currency A strengthens or appreciates relative to currency B, then currency B must necessarily weaken or depreciate with regard to currency A. A stronger currency benefits those who are buying with that currency and injures those who are selling. A weaker currency injures those, like importers, who are buying with that currency and benefits those who are selling with it, like exporters.
4. In the extreme short run, ranging from a few minutes to a few weeks, exchange rates are influenced by speculators who are trying to invest in currencies that will

grow stronger, and to sell currencies that will grow weaker. Such speculation can create a self-fulfilling prophecy, at least for a time, where an expected appreciation leads to a stronger currency and vice versa.

5. In the relatively short run, exchange rate markets are influenced by differences in rates of return. Countries with relatively high real rates of return (for example, high interest rates) will tend to experience stronger currencies as they attract money from abroad, while countries with relatively low rates of return will tend to experience weaker exchange rates as investors convert to other currencies.
6. In the medium run of a few months or a few years, exchange rate markets are influenced by inflation rates. Countries with relatively high inflation will tend to experience less demand for their currency than countries with lower inflation, and thus currency depreciation.
7. Over long periods of many years, exchange rates tend to adjust toward the **purchasing power parity (PPP)** rate, which is the exchange rate such that the prices of internationally tradable goods in different countries, when converted at the PPP exchange rate to a common currency, are similar in all economies.
8. A central bank will be concerned about the exchange rate for several reasons. Exchange rates will affect imports and exports, and thus affect aggregate demand in the economy. Fluctuations in exchange rates may cause difficulties for many firms, but especially banks. The exchange rate may accompany unsustainable flows of international financial capital.
9. In a **floating exchange rate** policy, a country's exchange rate is determined in the foreign exchange market. In a **soft peg** exchange rate policy, a country's exchange rate is usually determined in the foreign exchange market, but the government sometimes intervenes to strengthen or weaken the exchange rate. In a **hard peg** exchange rate policy, the government chooses an exchange rate.
10. A central bank can intervene in exchange markets in two ways. It can raise or lower interest rates to make the currency stronger or weaker. Or it can directly purchase or sell its currency in foreign exchange markets.
11. All exchange rate policies face trade-offs. A hard peg exchange rate policy will reduce exchange rate fluctuations, but means that a country must focus its monetary policy on the exchange rate, not on fighting recession or controlling inflation. When a nation merges its currency with another nation, it gives up on nationally-oriented monetary policy altogether. A soft peg exchange rate may create additional volatility as exchange rate markets try to anticipate when and how the government will intervene. A flexible exchange rate policy allows monetary policy to focus on inflation and unemployment, and allows the exchange rate to change with inflation and rates of return, but also raises a risk that exchange rates may sometimes make large and abrupt movements.
12. The spectrum of exchange rate policies includes: (a) a floating exchange rate, (b) exchange rate zones, (c) a pegged exchange rate, and (d) a single currency.

Review Questions

1. What is the foreign exchange market?
2. Describe some buyers and some sellers in the market for U.S. dollars.
3. What's the difference between foreign direct investment and portfolio investment?
4. What does it mean to hedge a financial transaction?
5. What does it mean to say that a currency appreciates? Depreciates? Becomes stronger? Becomes weaker?
6. Does an expectation of a stronger exchange rate in the future affect the exchange rate in the present? If so, how?
7. Does a higher rate of return in a nation's economy, other things being equal, affect the exchange rate of its currency? If so, how?
8. Does a higher inflation rate in an economy, other things being equal, affect the exchange rate of its currency? If so, how?
9. What is the purchasing power parity exchange rate?
10. What are some of the reasons a central bank is likely to care, at least to some extent, about the exchange rate?
11. How can an unexpected fall in exchange rates injure the financial health of a nation's banks?
12. What's the difference between a floating exchange rate, a soft peg, a hard peg, and dollarization?
13. List some advantages and disadvantages of the different exchange rate policies.

CHAPTER 32

Government Budgets and Fiscal Policy

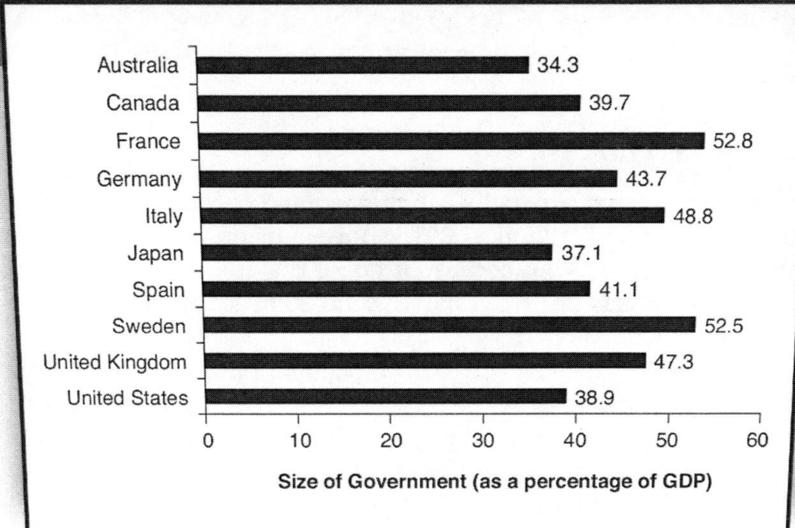

Chapter Outline

An Overview of Government Spending

An Overview of Taxation

Federal Deficits and Debt

Using Fiscal Policy to Affect Recession, Unemployment and Inflation

Automatic Stabilizers

Practical Problems with Discretionary Fiscal Policy

Requiring a Balanced Budget?

Conclusion

All levels of government—federal, state and local—have budgets that show how much money the government expects to have available to spend and how the government plans to spend it. However, budgets can shift dramatically within a few years, as policy decisions and unexpected events shake up earlier tax and spending plans.

For example, during Barack Obama's first term as president of the United States in 2009, the U.S. government experienced its largest budget deficits, relative to the size of gross domestic product (GDP), since the mammoth borrowing used to finance World War II. During the years from 2009 to 2012, the federal budget deficits were 9.8%, 8.7%, 8.5%, and 6.8% of GDP, respectively. To what extent was this series of humongous budget deficits a result of the recession the U.S. economy experienced starting in late 2007, before Obama's term of office began? To what extent was this series of deficits caused by tax cuts and spending increases seeking to stimulate consumption and thus shorten the length of the recession? How will the effects of short-term deficits in the aftermath of a steep recession differ from the effects of long-term and sustained deficits?

The previous three chapters discussed monetary policy, while this chapter and the next will discuss the other main channel of macroeconomic policy—government fiscal policies of taxes and spending. The discussion will focus on the macroeconomics of government budgets, not the microeconomics; for example, this chapter will focus on how government taxes and spending taken as a whole affect aggregate demand for the economy as a whole, not on the merits of specific taxes or spending programs. This chapter begins with an overview of U.S. government spending and taxes. It then discusses fiscal policy from a short-run perspective; that is, how government might use tax and spending policies to address issues of recession, unemployment, and inflation; how periods of recession and growth affect government budgets; and the merits of proposals that the government should seek a perfect balance between taxes and spending—a balanced budget—each and every year.

An Overview of Government Spending

fiscal policy: Economic policies that involve government spending and taxes.

The "fisc," an old-fashioned word that appears in dictionaries but seldom in print anymore, is defined as a nation's treasury, the department of government that handles the inflow of taxes and the outflow of spending. **Fiscal policies** are the set of policies relating to government spending, taxation, and borrowing. Both words, *fisc* and *fiscal*, stem from the Latin word *fiscus*, which can mean "treasury" or, more descriptively, "basket," as in an imaginary basket in which inflows of money are gathered and from which outflows are distributed. This section presents an overview of government spending in the United States; the next section provides an overview of government taxes; and the following section discusses budget deficits and debt.

Total U.S. Government Spending

Federal spending in nominal dollars has grown by a multiple of more than 42 since 1960, from $92 billion in 1960 to almost $4 trillion in 2015. But comparing nominal dollars between two years can be highly deceiving because it doesn't take into account either inflation or how the real economy has grown. A more useful comparison is to examine government spending as a percentage of GDP.

The top line in Exhibit 32-1 shows the level of federal spending since 1960, expressed as a share of GDP. Despite a widespread sense among many Americans that the federal government has been growing steadily larger, the graph shows that this perception is incorrect. Federal spending has hovered in the range of 18–22% of GDP during most of the time since 1960. The other lines in Exhibit 32-1 show some major categories of federal spending: national defense, Social Security, health programs, and interest payments. National defense spending as a share of GDP has generally declined since the 1960s, although there were some upward bumps in the 1980s buildup under President Ronald Reagan and in the aftermath of the terrorist attacks on September 11, 2001.

Although defense spending as a share of GDP has sagged overall during recent decades, spending in other areas has risen. Spending on Social Security payments for the elderly has grown substantially during the last few decades. Government spending on health care has also increased. The two main federal health care programs are Medicare, which pays for health care to the elderly, and Medicaid, in which the federal government pays some of the bill for health care to those with low incomes (part of the Medicaid program is also funded by state governments).

EXHIBIT 32-1 Federal Spending, 1960–2015

Since 1960, total federal spending has mostly ranged from about 18–22% of GDP in recent decades. The share being spent on national defense has generally declined, while the share spent on Social Security and on health care expenses (mainly Medicare and Medicaid) has increased.

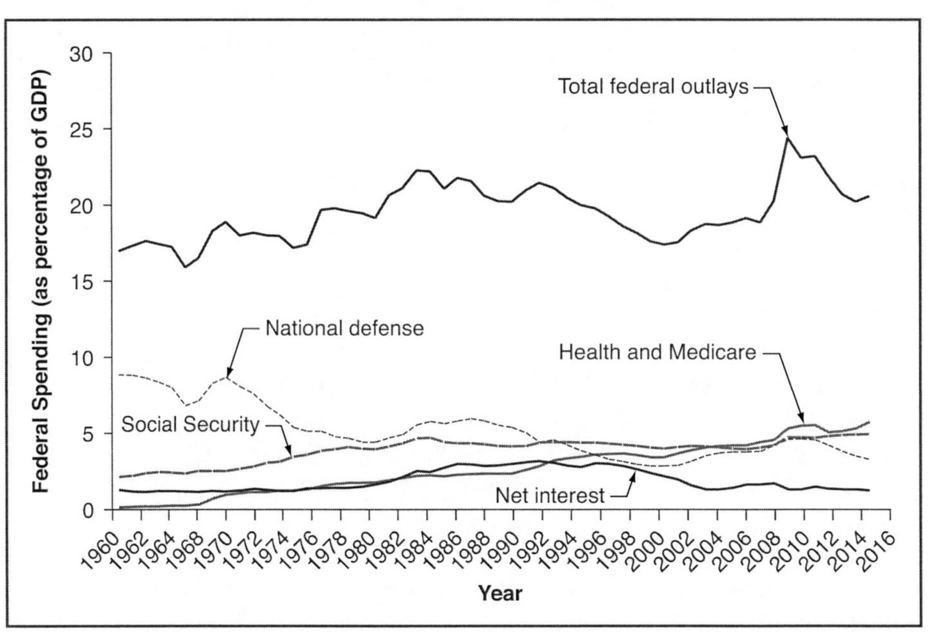

Interest payments are a final main category of government spending shown in Exhibit 32-1. When the government receives more in taxes than it spends in a year, it runs a **budget surplus**. Conversely, when the federal government spends more than it collects in taxes in a given year, it runs a **budget deficit**. If government spending and taxes are equal, it is said to have a **balanced budget**. The government borrows funds to cover its budget deficits by issuing Treasury bonds, thus borrowing from the public and promising to repay with interest in the future. The U.S. government ran budget deficits, and thus borrowed money, every year but one from 1961 to 1997, had budget surpluses from 1998 to 2001, and then returned to budget deficits. The interest payments on past federal government borrowing were typically 1–2% of GDP in the 1960s and 1970s, but then climbed above 3% of GDP in the 1980s and stayed there until the late 1990s. However, the government was able to repay some of its past borrowing by running surpluses from 1998–2001, and with help from low interest rates, interest payments had fallen to under 2% of GDP in recent years. We'll investigate the patterns of government borrowing and debt in more detail later in this chapter.

budget surplus: When the government receives more in taxes than it spends in a year.

budget deficit: When the federal government spends more than it collects in taxes in a given year.

balanced budget: When government spending and taxes are equal.

These four categories—national defense, Social Security, health care, and interest payments—account for roughly 70% of all federal spending, as Exhibit 32-2 shows. The remaining 30% or so wedge of the pie chart covers all other categories of federal

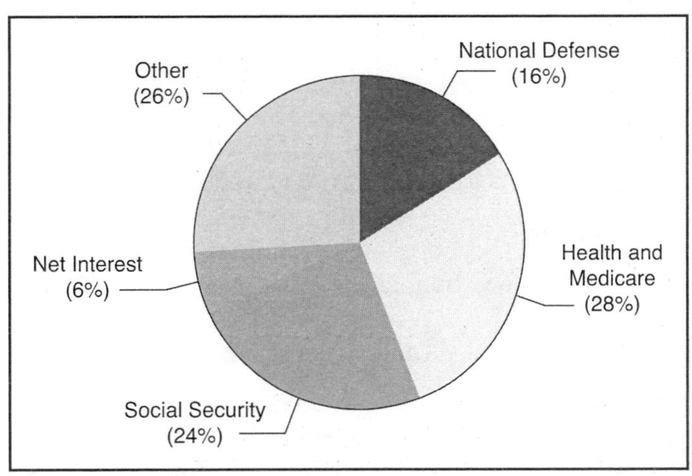

EXHIBIT 32-2 Slices of Federal Spending, 2015

Roughly 70% of U.S. government spending in recent years has gone to four major areas: national defense, Social Security, health care, and interest payments on past borrowing. This leaves about 30% of federal spending for all other functions of the U.S. government.

U.S. Government Spending in the Twentieth Century

Although the spending levels of the U.S. federal government haven't changed much in the last 50 years, they rose quite a bit earlier in the twentieth century. In 1900, the federal government spent only about 2–3% of GDP each year. But federal spending spiked upward sharply during World War I and World War II because during the wars, the U.S. government purchased large quantities of supplies and weapons and paid large numbers of soldiers, and also became very active in organizing industry to promote the war efforts. Although federal spending declined substantially after each war, it never quite returned to the prewar levels. Instead, Americans seemed to become more comfortable after each war with their government collecting higher levels of taxes and providing a more extensive array of programs.

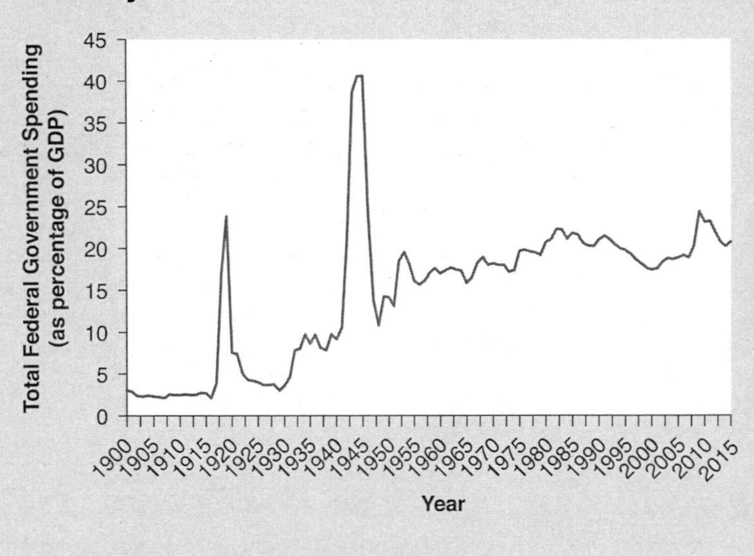

government spending: international affairs, science and technology, natural resources and the environment, transportation, housing, education, income support for the poor, community and regional development, law enforcement and the judicial system, and the administrative costs of running the government.

Keeping Federal Budget Numbers in Perspective

When you're listening to some of the perennial arguments over specific federal spending programs, it's useful to keep the overall size of the federal budget in mind. For example, there has been controversy for many years concerning the National Endowment for the Arts (NEA). Supporters argue that the government has an important role to play in supporting the arts. Detractors insist that much of what is supported is "art" only in a loose sense of the word, and that even if state and local governments want to support the arts for their local residents, the federal government has little reason to do so. Whatever side one takes in this dispute, it's worth remembering that the total NEA budget in 2016 was around $150 million. Maybe the NEA is a good idea; maybe it's a waste of money. Either way, in the overall federal budget, $150 million is less than one-hundredth of 1% of total federal spending.

Similarly, many people believe that foreign aid accounts for a large portion of federal spending; according to one poll a few years ago, the average U.S. citizen thinks that foreign aid accounts for about one-fourth of the entire federal budget. However, the foreign aid budget in the first decade of the 2000s has been roughly 1% of federal spending. Again, foreign aid may be a good idea or a bad idea, and 1% of the federal budget is certainly worth more attention than the $150 million for the NEA. But in the context of nearly $4 trillion in federal spending in 2016, either eliminating foreign aid or doubling it wouldn't make a huge difference to the overall picture. Moreover, a certain amount of that foreign aid has more to do with foreign policy—such as trying to encourage peace and stability in the Middle East—than with financial aid to poor countries.

State and Local Government Spending

Although federal government spending often gets most of the media attention, the spending of state and local government is substantial, too, at about $3.4 trillion in 2013. Exhibit 32-3 shows that state and local government spending as a share of GDP has

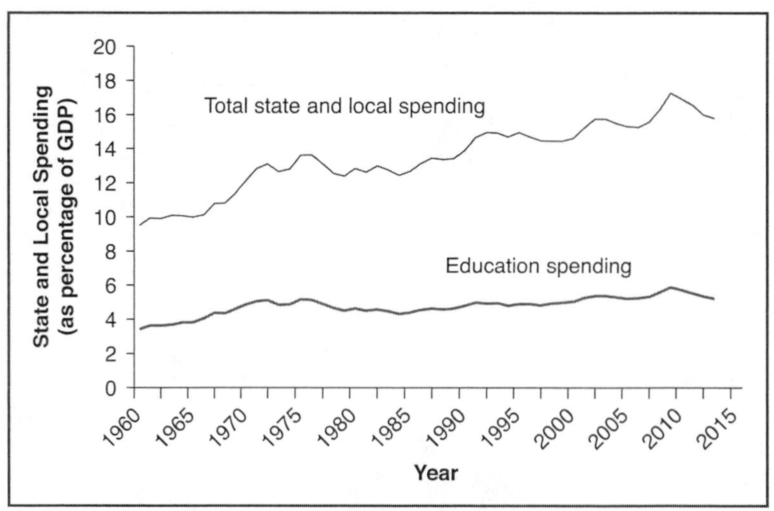

EXHIBIT 32-3 State and Local Spending, 1960–2013

Spending by state and local government increased from about 10% of GDP in the early 1960s to about 16% of GDP in more recent years. The single biggest spending item of state and local government is education spending, including both K–12 spending and support for public colleges and universities, which has been about 5–6% of GDP in recent decades.

increased during the last four decades from about 10% of GDP to about 16% of GDP. The single biggest item on the tab of state and local spending is education, which accounts for about one-third of the total. The rest covers programs like highways, libraries, hospitals and health care, parks, and police and fire protection.

U.S. presidential candidates often run for office pledging to improve the public schools or to get tough on crime. But in the U.S. system of government, these tasks are primarily the responsibilities of state and local governments, not the federal government. Indeed, in the fiscal year from 2012–2013, state and local government spent about $900 billion on education, including K–12 education and college and university education—a total that exceeds either the federal defense budget or federal spending on Social Security. A politician who earnestly wants hands-on responsibility for reforming education or reducing crime might do better to run for mayor of a large city or for state governor rather than for president of the United States.

An Overview of Taxation

Just as many Americans think that federal spending has grown considerably, many also believe that taxes have increased substantially. The top line of Exhibit 32-4 shows total federal taxes as a share of GDP since 1960. Although the line rises and falls, it typically remains within the range of 17–20% of GDP.

Exhibit 32-4 also shows the patterns of taxation for the main categories of taxes levied by the federal government: personal income taxes, payroll taxes, corporate income taxes, and excise taxes. When most people think of taxes levied by the federal government, the first tax that comes to mind is the **individual income tax** that is due on April 15 (or the first business day after). The personal income tax is the largest single source of federal government revenue, but it still represents less than half of federal tax money. The personal income tax collects 8–10% of GDP in most years—although it was well below this level in 2009. The second largest source of federal revenue is the **payroll tax**, which provides funds for Social Security and Medicare. Payroll taxes have increased steadily over time. Together, the personal income tax and the payroll tax have accounted for about 85% of federal tax revenues in recent years.

Although the personal income tax accounts for more total revenue than the payroll tax, over half of the households in the country pay more in payroll taxes than in income taxes. The reason is that income tax is a **progressive tax**, which means that it collects a greater share of income from those with high incomes than from those with lower incomes. The income tax works this way: The first dollars of income earned are not subject to the income

individual income tax: A tax based on the income of all forms received by individuals.

payroll tax: A tax based on the pay received from employers; the taxes provide funds for Social Security and Medicare.

progressive tax: A tax that collects a greater share of income from those with high incomes than from those with lower incomes.

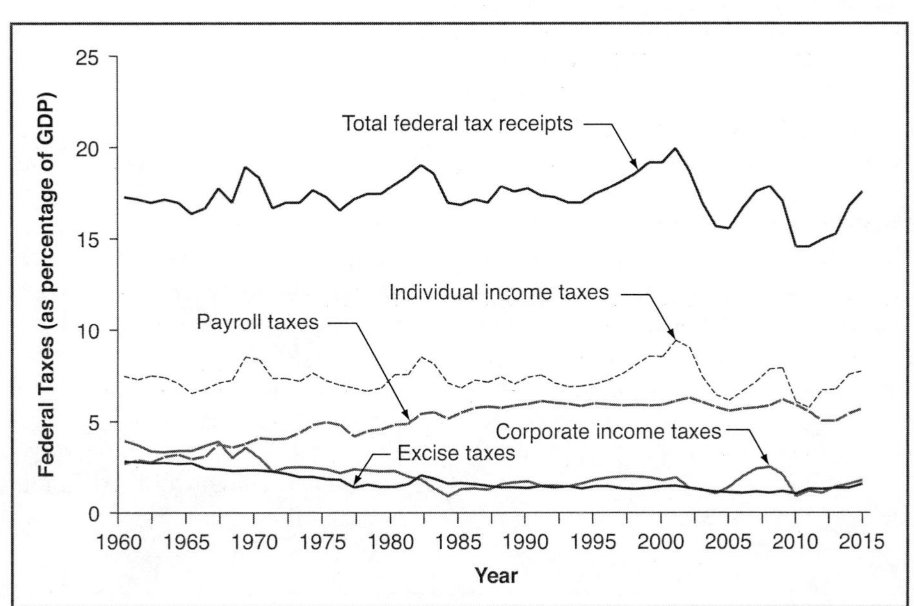

EXHIBIT 32-4 Federal Taxes, 1960–2015

Federal taxes have been about 17–20% of GDP during most periods in recent decades. The primary sources of federal taxes are individual income taxes and the payroll taxes that finance Social Security and Medicare. Corporation income taxes, excise taxes, and other taxes provide smaller shares of revenue.

tax. This amount that is exempt from taxation is determined by the size of the family and is adjusted each year. For example, a single person in 2016 paid no taxes on the first $9,275 in income earned. However, this person then paid 15% on any additional amount earned from $9,275 to $37,650; 25% of income earned from $37,650 up to $91,150; 28% of any income earned above that level and up to $190,150; 33% of any income above that level and up to $413,350; and 39.6% of income earned above that level. Of course, income taxes are much more complex than this simple example. Taxes vary with marital status, family size, and many other features. But the key lesson here is that the federal income tax is designed so that high-income citizens pay a larger share of income in taxes. In 2014, for example, the top 20% of taxpayers paid 84% of total federal income taxes collected.

The payroll taxes that support Social Security and Medicare are designed in a different way. The payroll taxes for Social Security are currently imposed at a rate of 12.4% up to a certain earnings limit, set at $118,500 in 2016. This limit rises in step with the average increase in wages across the economy. The payroll taxes that support the part of Medicare that pays for hospitalization for the elderly is imposed at a rate of 2.9% of all income earned, with no upper ceiling. In both cases, the taxes are technically collected half from employee paychecks and half from employers. However, as economists are quick to point out, the employer's half of the taxes is probably passed along to the employees in the form

The Complexity of Individual Income Taxes

The basic income tax calculation is straightforward. Figure out how much income you received, remembering to include all wage or salary income, as well as income from any other source like interest payments. Figure out whether you're married and count your children. Then look in a table how much you owe in taxes. But some tax calculations can get far more complex. As two economists noted a few years ago: "Although length is not necessarily synonymous with complexity, the U.S. income tax code now has more than 700 times as many words as the U.S. Constitution." The complications arise in several main areas.

Deductions

A deduction is an amount that you are allowed to subtract ("deduct") from your income before figuring out how much you owe in taxes. The trick here is to compare the standard deduction, which was $12,600 for a married couple filing a joint tax return in 2016, with specific deductions allowed by Congress. Everyone can take the standard deduction automatically. If the deductions allowed by law that apply to a person's taxes are higher than the standard deduction, then it makes sense to list, or "itemize," the other deductions. Some common deductions in the tax code include interest paid on a home mortgage, charitable contributions, state and local taxes, and costly medical procedures, and certain other expenses. About 30% of taxpayers itemize deductions on their returns, while the rest take the standard deduction.

Tax Credits

A tax credit is an amount you are allowed to subtract directly from the amount of taxes owed (unlike a deduction, which is subtracted from the income on which you owe taxes). Certain tax credits for the working poor are designed so that even if people do not owe income taxes (because their income is so low), the amount of the tax credit will still be paid to people as a tax "refund."

Establishing When Taxpayers Become Employers

If you hire a nanny to look after children, or any employee who works for you regularly and earns more than $1,000 per quarter, then you become an employer and are treated as a business by the state and national governments. You are now an employer, and must fill out a whole new set of forms. If you are self-employed, then your taxes must show both revenues and business-related costs. Your tax will be based on the income left over.

Simplification Is Difficult

It's easy to plead for a simpler tax code, but difficult to achieve it. Many parts of the tax code have some justification—it's just that when they are all combined together, the result is exceedingly complex. Tax lawyers and accountants are always trying to find loopholes in the tax code that can reduce the taxes owed. Legislators are always tinkering with the tax code, closing up some loopholes, but opening others for favored groups. Everyone is willing to eliminate deductions or tax credits used by others, but unwilling to eliminate the ones they use themselves. Substantial simplification of the tax code is politically quite difficult.

CLEARING IT UP

The Deficit Is Not the Debt

The difference between the deficit and the debt lies in the time frame. The government deficit (or surplus) refers to what happens each year. The government debt is accumulated over time; it is the sum of all past deficits and surpluses. Similarly, if you borrow $10,000 per year for each of four years of college, you might say that your annual deficit was $10,000, but your accumulated debt over the four years is $40,000.

of lower wages. The Medicare payroll tax is a **proportional tax**; that is, a flat percentage of all income earned. The Social Security payroll tax is proportional up to the earnings limit, but above that level of income it becomes a **regressive tax**, meaning that people with higher incomes pay a smaller share of their income in tax. As a result, income taxes are paid mainly by the relatively small number of those with incomes of six-figures and higher, while payroll taxes are paid mainly by the larger number of five-figure earners.

The third-largest source of federal tax revenue shown in Exhibit 32-4 is the **corporate income tax**—and the common name for corporate income is "profits." Over time, corporate income tax receipts have declined as a share of GDP, from about 4% of GDP in the 1960s to 1–2% of GDP in the first decade of the 2000s. The federal government has a few other, smaller sources of revenue. The federal government imposes **excise taxes**—that is, taxes on a particular good—on gasoline, tobacco, and alcohol. As a share of GDP, the amount collected by these taxes has also declined over time, from about 2% of GDP in the 1960s to roughly 0.5% of GDP by 2010. The government also imposes an **estate and gift tax** on people who pass large amounts of assets to the next generation—either after death or during life in the form of gifts. These estate and gift taxes collected about 0.2% of GDP in the first decade of the 2000s. By a quirk of legislation, the estate and gift tax was repealed just for 2010, but then reinstated in 2011. Other federal taxes, which are also relatively small in magnitude, include tariffs collected on imported goods, and charges for inspections of goods entering the country.

proportional tax: A tax that is a flat percentage of income earned, regardless of level of income.

regressive tax: A tax in which people with higher incomes pay a smaller share of their income in tax.

corporate income tax: A tax imposed on corporate profits.

excise taxes: A tax on a specific good—on gasoline, tobacco, and alcohol.

estate and gift tax: A tax on people who pass assets to the next generation—either after death or during life in the form of gifts.

State and Local Taxes

At the state and local level, taxes have been rising as a share of GDP over the last few decades as Exhibit 32-5 illustrates. The main revenue sources for state and local governments are sales taxes and property taxes, but many state and local governments also levy personal and corporate income taxes, as well as imposing a wide variety of fees and charges. The specific sources of tax revenue vary widely across state and local

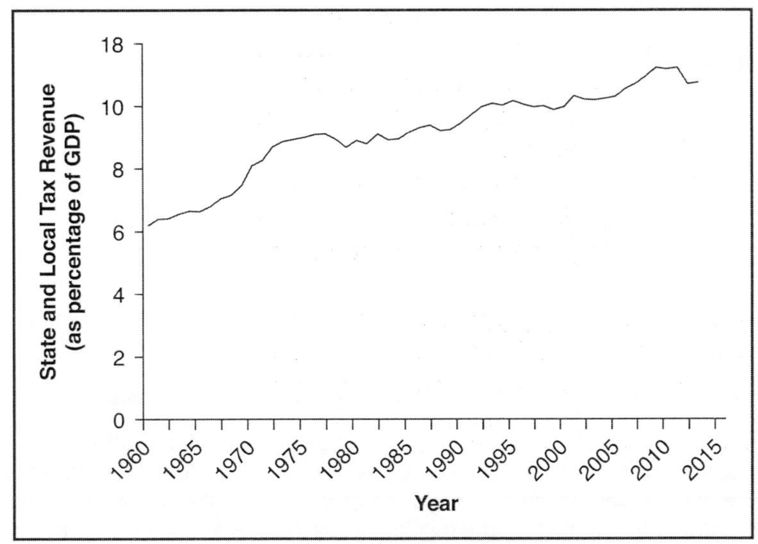

EXHIBIT 32-5 State and Local Tax Revenue as a Share of GDP, 1960–2013

State and local tax revenues have increased modestly over time.

governments. The careful reader will notice that the amount collected by state and local governments in tax revenues is not nearly high enough to cover the level of state and local spending described earlier. The main explanation for this gap is that the federal government provides substantial funding to state and local programs.

Federal Deficits and Debt

The federal budget picture turned a somersault in the 1990s and first decade of the 2000s, from large deficits in the early 1990s to surpluses in the late 1990s and then back to deficits for the first decade of the 2000s. Exhibit 32-6 shows the pattern of annual federal budget deficits and surpluses all the way back to 1930 as a share of GDP. When the line is above the horizontal axis in positive territory, the budget is in surplus; when the line is below the horizontal axis in negative territory, a budget deficit occurred. Clearly, the biggest deficits as a share of GDP during this time were incurred to finance the fighting of World War II. Deficits were also large during the 1980s and early 1990s, and most recently during the recession of 2007–2009 and its aftermath.

Debt/GDP Ratio

government debt: The total accumulated amount that the government has borrowed and not yet paid back over time.

Another useful way to view the budget deficit is through the prism of accumulated debt rather than annual deficits. **Government debt** refers to the total amount that the government has borrowed over time; in contrast, the budget deficit or the budget surplus refers to how much has been borrowed in one particular year. Exhibit 32-7 shows the ratio of debt/GDP since 1940. Until the 1970s, the debt/GDP ratio revealed a fairly clear pattern of federal borrowing. The government ran up large deficits and raised the debt/ GDP ratio in World War II, but from the 1950s to the 1970s, the government ran either budget surpluses or relatively small deficits, and so the debt/GDP ratio drifted down. Large deficits in the 1980s and early 1990s caused the debt/GDP ratio to rise sharply. When budget surpluses arrived from 1998 to 2001, the debt/GDP ratio declined substantially. The budget deficits starting in 2002 then tugged the debt/GDP ratio higher—with a more substantial rise when the recession took hold in 2008 and during the years after the recession.

The Path from Deficits to Surpluses to Deficits

Why did the budget deficits suddenly turn to surpluses from 1998 to 2001? And why did the surpluses return to deficits in 2002? Why did the deficit become so large in 2009?

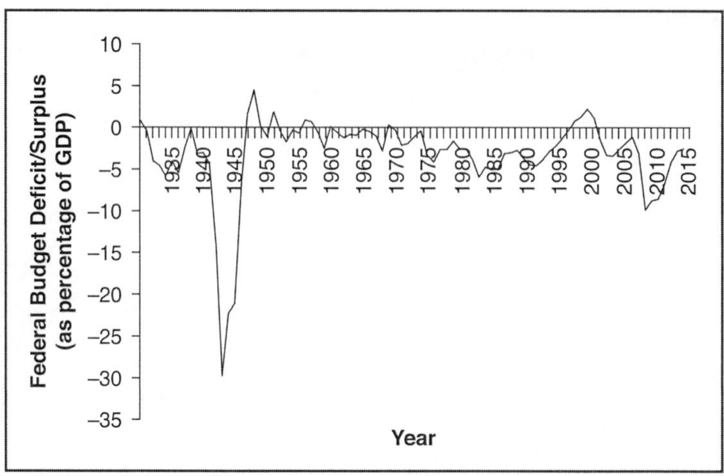

EXHIBIT 32-6 Pattern of Federal Budget Deficits and Surpluses, 1930–2015

The federal government had huge budget deficits during World War II. Budget deficits were also relatively large during the Great Depression of the 1930s and during the 1980s and early 1990s. The budget was briefly in surplus in the late 1990s, before heading into deficit again in the first decade of the 2000s—and especially deep deficits during the recession of 2007–2009 and its aftermath.

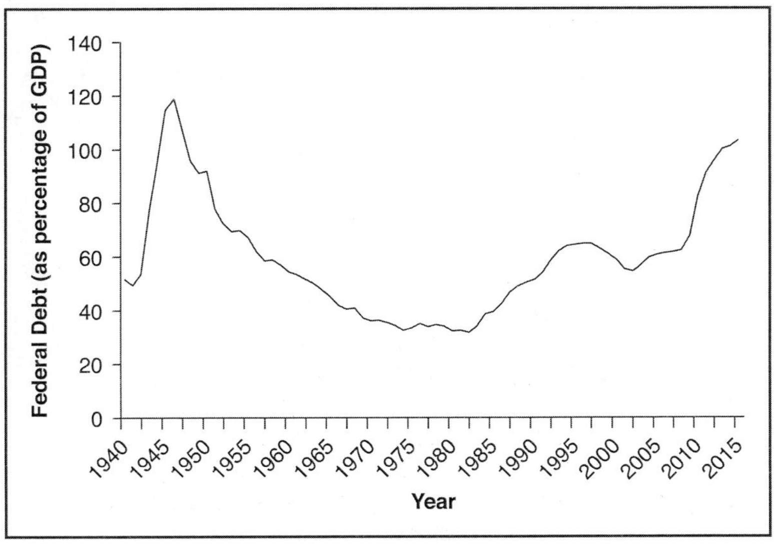

EXHIBIT 32-7 Federal Debt as a Percentage of GDP, 1940–2015

Federal debt is the sum of annual budget deficits and surpluses. Debt increases when deficits are large, like during World Wars I and II and during the 1980s and early 1990s. However, annual deficits do not always mean that the debt/GDP ratio is rising. During the 1960s and 1970s, the government often ran small deficits, but since the debt was growing more slowly than the economy, the debt/GDP ratio was declining over this time. In the 2007–2009 recession and its aftermath, the debt/ GDP ratio rose sharply.

The Size of U.S. Government in International Perspective

When comparing the size of U.S. government to the governments of other high-income countries, it is conventional to look at all levels of government combined; in the case of the United States, that means combining federal, state, and local government. The reason is that some countries have a larger role for the national government, while others have a larger role for regional, provincial, state, city, or local governments. Rather than trying to adjust for these differences, it is easier to compare overall levels of total government spending. The bar chart shows United States has a substantially smaller sector for government spending than do most European countries.

Why is the level of U.S. government spending relatively low compared to many other countries? One reason is that most other countries have government-run health care sectors, while in the United States, a large share of health care spending happens in the private sector—although about half of all U.S. health care spending, like the Medicare and Medicaid spending mentioned earlier, is in the government sector. Ultimately, the reason for the difference is that people in other high-income countries, acting through their own democratic institutions, prefer to see a greater share of society's resources allocated by political decisions rather than by market forces.

Government Expenditures as a Percentage of GDP, 2013

U.S. government spending (combining federal, state, and local levels) as a share of GDP is lower than in many European countries.

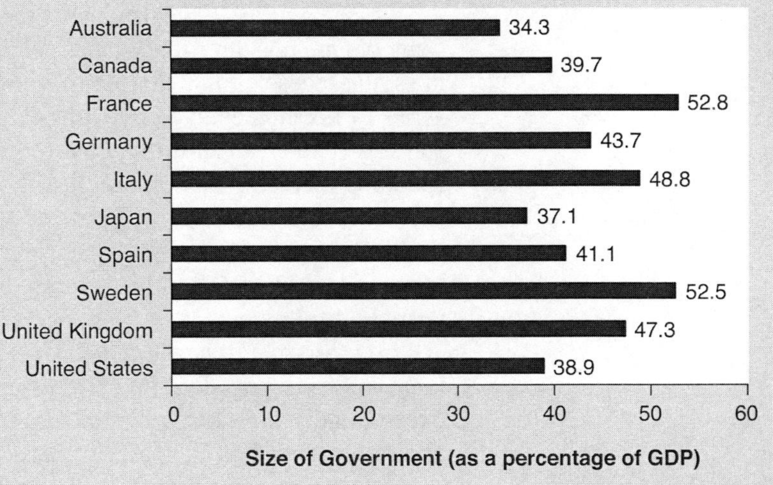

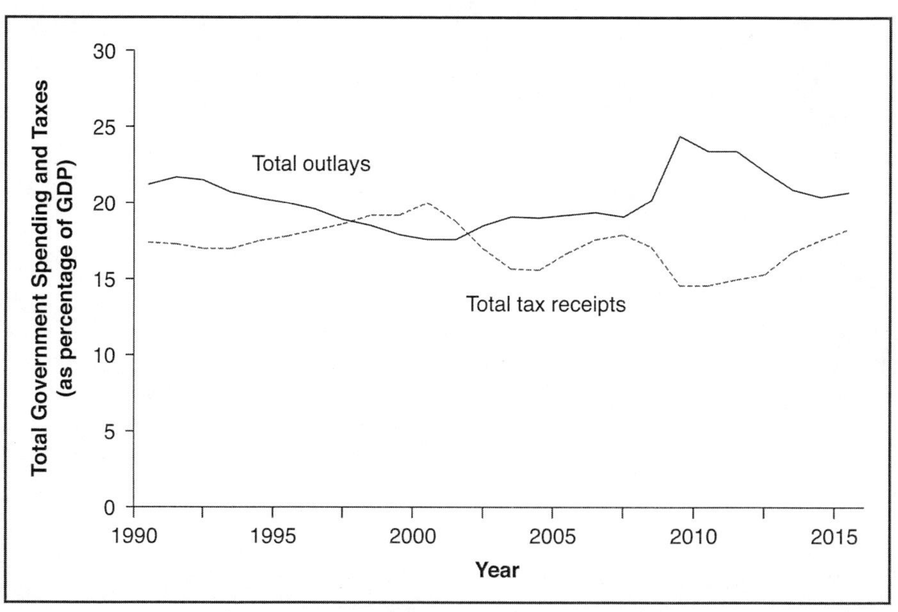

EXHIBIT 32-8 Total Government Spending and Taxes as a Share of GDP, 1990–2015

When government spending exceeds taxes, the gap is the budget deficit. When taxes exceed spending, the gap is a budget surplus. Thus, the 1990s saw a decline in government spending and a rise in tax receipts that led to a budget surplus from 1998–2001, and then a fall in tax receipts and a rise in spending that caused a return to budget deficits starting in 2002. The recessionary period starting in late 2007 saw higher spending and lower taxes, combining to create large deficits starting in 2009. In the last few years, both spending and taxes have moved back toward their more usual levels.

Exhibit 32-8 suggests some answers. The exhibit combines the earlier information on total federal spending and taxes in a single graph, but focuses on the federal budget since 1990.

Government spending as a share of GDP declined steadily through the 1990s. The biggest single reason was that defense spending declined from 5.2% of GDP in 1990 to 3.0% of GDP in 2000, but interest payments by the federal government also fell by about 1.0% of GDP.

However, federal taxes increased substantially in the later 1990s, jumping from 18.1% of GDP in 1994 to 20.8% of GDP in 2000. Powerful economic growth in the late 1990s fueled the boom in taxes. Personal income taxes rise as income goes up; payroll taxes rise as jobs and payrolls go up; corporate income taxes rise as profits go up. This sharp increase in tax revenues was largely unexpected even by experienced budget analysts, and so these budget surpluses came as a surprise.

But in the early 2000s, many of these factors started running in reverse. Tax revenues sagged. One reason is that just as economic growth in the late 1990s pumped up tax revenues, the recession that started in March 2001 pulled down revenues. Another reason is a series of tax cuts enacted by Congress and signed into law by President George W. Bush starting in 2001. In addition, government spending increased because of a combination of spending increases on defense, health care, education, Social Security, and providing support to people who were suffering economically during the recession and the slow growth that followed. Deficits returned. When the severe recession hit in late 2007, spending climbed and taxes fell to historically unusual levels, resulting in enormous deficits in the years that followed.

Longer-term forecasts of the U.S. budget, a decade or more into the future, predict large and growing deficits. The primary reason traces back to the "baby boom"—the exceptionally high birthrates that began in 1946, right after World War II, and lasted for about two decades. Starting in 2010, the front edge of the baby boom generation will begin to reach age 65, and in the following two decades, the proportion of Americans

The Aging of America and the Long-Term Budget Outlook

In 1946, just one American in 13 was over age 65. By 2000, it was one in eight. By 2030, one American in five will be over age 65. Two enormous U.S. federal programs focus on the elderly—Social Security and Medicare. The growing numbers of elderly Americans will increase spending on these programs. The current payroll tax levied on workers, which support all of Social Security and the hospitalization insurance part of Medicare, won't be enough to cover the expected costs.

None of the possible reactions to the expected growth of these programs for the elderly is very attractive. Spending on these programs could be cut. Taxes could be raised to fund these programs. Other programs could be cut instead. Or the government could run very large budget deficits and borrow the money to finance these programs. Some proposals also suggest moving Social Security and Medicare from systems in which workers pay for retirees toward programs that set up accounts where workers save money over their lifetime and then draw it out after retirement. Whatever the merits of such plans, they don't solve the problem that Social Security and Medicare are not sustainable as currently constructed.

Long-term projections from the Congressional Budget Office in 2015 are that Medicare and Social Security spending combined will rise from 10.1% of GDP in 2015 to 14.2% of GDP by 2040. If this rise in spending occurs, then some mix of three changes must occur: (1) taxes will need to be increased substantially to finance it; (2) other spending will need to be cut substantially; or (3) the U.S. government will need to run large budget deficits for decades. None of these options is especially attractive.

The United States is not alone in this problem. Indeed, the problems of providing the promised level of retirement and health benefits to a growing proportion of elderly with a falling proportion of workers is even more severe in many European nations and in Japan. Addressing the question of how to pay promised levels of benefits to the elderly will be a difficult public policy challenge for many high-income nations in the twenty-first century.

over the age of 65 will increase substantially. The current level of the payroll taxes that support Social Security and Medicare will fall well short of the projected expenses of these programs; thus, the forecast is for large budget deficits. A decision either to collect more revenue to support these programs or to decrease their benefit levels would alter this long-term forecast.

With the broad shape of fiscal policy in mind, let's shift attention to how fiscal policy might be used to affect business cycle fluctuations that lead to unemployment or inflation. Conversely, how will business cycle fluctuations like recession affect budget deficits? How do economists evaluate proposed policies that would require a balanced budget—that is, for government spending and taxes to be equal each year? Chapter 33 will then look at how fiscal policy and government borrowing will affect national saving—and thus affect economic growth and trade imbalances.

Using Fiscal Policy to Affect Recession, Unemployment, and Inflation

A healthy economy follows a long-term trend of economic growth, but also experiences occasional recessions. Exhibit 32-9 illustrates the process by using an aggregate demand/ aggregate supply diagram. The original equilibrium occurs at E_0, the intersection of aggregate demand curve AD_0 and aggregate supply curve AS_0, at an output level of 200 and a price level of 90. One year later, aggregate supply has shifted to the right to AS_1 in the process of long-term economic growth, and aggregate demand has also shifted to the right to AD_1, keeping the economy operating at the new level of potential GDP. The new equilibrium E_1 is an output level of 206 and a price level of 92. One more year later, aggregate supply has again shifted to the right, now to AS_2, and aggregate demand shifts right as well to AD_2. Now the equilibrium is E_2, with an output level of 212 and a price level of 94. In short, the figure shows an economy that is growing steadily year to year, producing at its potential GDP each year, with only small inflationary increases in the price level.

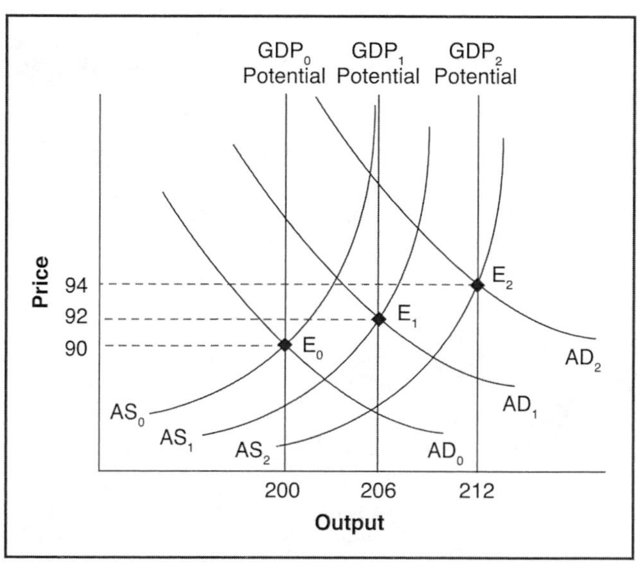

EXHIBIT 32-9 A Healthy, Growing Economy

In this well-functioning economy, each year aggregate supply and aggregate demand shift to the right so that the economy proceeds from equilibrium E_0 to E_1 to E_2. Each year, the economy produces at potential GDP with only a small inflationary increase in the price level. But if aggregate demand does not smoothly shift to the right and match increases in aggregate supply, either recession or inflation can develop.

But aggregate demand and aggregate supply do not always dance neatly together. Aggregate demand may fail to increase smoothly along with aggregate supply, or aggregate demand may even shift left, for a number of possible causes: households become hesitant about consuming; firms decide against investing as much; or perhaps the demand from other countries for exports diminishes. For example, investment by private firms in physical capital in the U.S. economy boomed during the late 1990s, rising from 14.1% of GDP in 1993 to 17.2% of GDP in 2000, before falling back to 15.2% of GDP by 2002. Conversely, if shifts in aggregate demand run ahead of increases in aggregate supply, then the inflationary increases in the price level will result. When aggregate demand and aggregate supply fall out of step, the business cycles of economic recessions and upswings are the result.

The previous discussion of monetary policy taught that a central bank can use its powers over the banking system to engage in countercyclical—or "against the business cycle"—policy. If recession threatens, the central bank uses an expansionary monetary policy to increase the quantity of loans, reduce interest rates, and shift aggregate demand to the right. If inflation threatens, the central bank uses contractionary monetary policy to reduce the quantity of loans, raise interest rates, and shift aggregate demand to the left. Fiscal policy is another macroeconomic policy tool for adjusting aggregate demand by using either government spending or taxation policy.

Expansionary Fiscal Policy

expansionary monetary policy: A monetary policy that increases the supply of money and the quantity of loans; also called a "loose" monetary policy.

contractionary fiscal policy: When fiscal policy decreases the level of aggregate demand, either through cuts in government spending or increases in taxes.

Expansionary fiscal policy increases the level of aggregate demand, through either increases in government spending or reductions in taxes. **Contractionary fiscal policy** decreases the level of aggregate demand, either through cuts in government spending or increases in taxes. The aggregate demand/aggregate supply model is useful in judging whether expansionary or contractionary fiscal policy is appropriate.

Consider first the situation in Exhibit 32-10, which is similar to the U.S. economy during the recession in 2009. The intersection of aggregate demand AD_0 and aggregate supply AS_0 is occurring below the level of potential GDP. At the equilibrium E_0, a recession occurs and unemployment rises. (The figure uses the upward-sloping AS curve associated with a Keynesian economic approach, rather than the vertical AS curve associated

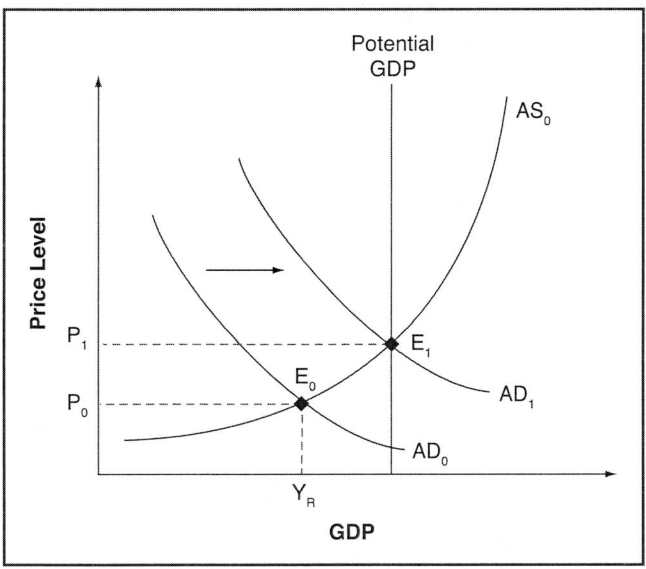

EXHIBIT 32-10 Expansionary Fiscal Policy

The original equilibrium E_0 represents a recession, occurring at a quantity of output Y_R below potential GDP. However, a shift of aggregate demand from AD_0 to AD_1, enacted through an expansionary fiscal policy that combines some mixture of spending increases and tax cuts, can move the economy to a new equilibrium output of E_1 at the level of potential GDP. Since the economy was originally producing below potential GDP, any inflationary increase in the price level from P_0 to P_1 that results from this expansionary fiscal policy should be relatively small.

with a neoclassical approach; this is because our focus here is on macroeconomic policy over the short-run business cycle rather than over the long run.) In this case, expansionary fiscal policy can shift aggregate demand to AD_1, closer to the full-employment level of output. There is relatively little danger that this increase in aggregate demand will increase inflation—although if the AD curve were pushed too far to the right, pressures for a higher rate of inflation could arise.

Should the government use tax cuts or spending increases, or a mix of the two, to carry out its expansionary fiscal policy? After the recession of 2007–2009, U.S. government spending rose from 19.6% of GDP in 2007 to 24.6% of GDP in 2009, while taxes declined from 18.5% of GDP in 2007 to 14.8% of GDP in 2009. The choice between whether to use tax or spending tools often has a political tinge. As a general statement, conservatives and Republicans prefer to see expansionary fiscal policy carried out by tax cuts, while liberals and Democrats prefer that expansionary fiscal policy be implemented through spending increases. This ambiguity over which policy tool to use can be frustrating to those who want to categorize economics as "liberal" or "conservative," or who want to use economic models to argue against their political opponents. But the AD–AS model can be readily used both by advocates of smaller government, who seek to reduce taxes and government spending, and also by advocates of bigger government, who seek to raise taxes and government spending. Economic studies of specific taxing and spending programs can help to inform decisions about whether taxes or spending should be changed, and in what ways. But ultimately, decisions about whether to use tax or spending mechanisms to implement macroeconomic policy are in large part a political decision, rather than a purely economic one.

Contractionary Fiscal Policy

Fiscal policy can also contribute to pushing aggregate demand beyond potential GDP in a way that leads to inflation. For example, in the terribly mismanaged economy of Zimbabwe, the government budget deficit was 40% of GDP in 2010, after a long string of similarly enormous deficits. Not coincidentally, inflation in Zimbabwe was so high that it was hard to measure with any precision: for a period in early 2009, the value of the Zimbabwe

EXHIBIT 32-11
A Contractionary Fiscal Policy

The economy starts at the equilibrium quantity of output E_0, which is above potential GDP and thus cannot be sustained in the long run. Instead, the extremely high level of aggregate demand will generate inflationary increases in the price level. A contractionary fiscal policy can shift aggregate demand from AD_0 to AD_1, thus leading to a new equilibrium output E_1, which occurs at potential GDP.

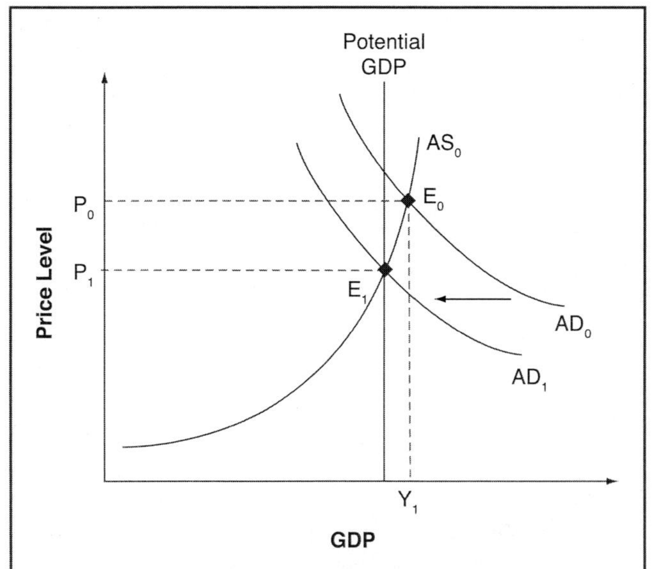

dollar was falling by about half against the U.S. dollar roughly *every two days*. As shown in Exhibit 32-11, a very large budget deficit was pushing up aggregate demand, so that the intersection of aggregate demand AD_0 and aggregate supply AS_0 occurs at equilibrium E_0, which is a level output above potential GDP. In this situation, contractionary fiscal policy involving spending cuts or tax increases can help to reduce the upward pressure on the price level by shifting aggregate demand to the left to AD_1 and causing the new equilibrium E_1 to be at potential GDP.

Again, the AD/AS model does not dictate how this contractionary fiscal policy is to be carried out. Some may prefer spending cuts; others may prefer tax increases; still others may say that it depends on the specific situation. The model only argues that aggregate demand needs to be reduced in this situation.

Automatic Stabilizers

discretionary fiscal policy: When the government passes a new law that explicitly changes overall tax or spending levels.

automatic stabilizers: Tax and spending rules that have the effect of increasing aggregate demand when the economy slows down and restraining aggregate demand when the economy speeds up, without any additional change in legislation.

The quantities of government spending and taxes can change for two broad sets of reasons. The first type of decision, called **discretionary fiscal policy**, occurs when the government passes a new law that explicitly changes tax or spending levels. A second type of taxing and spending changes happens because of laws that are already in place. For example, an economy that grows more rapidly will increase household incomes and firm profits, and thus lead to higher tax revenues, even if the existing tax laws don't change at all. These changes in tax and spending levels that happen without any specific change in law are called **automatic stabilizers** because, without the government passing any new laws, they have the effect of stimulating aggregate demand in a recession and holding down aggregate demand in a potentially inflationary boom.

Counterbalancing Recession and Boom

Consider first the situation where aggregate demand has risen sharply, and during this economic boom the equilibrium is occurring at a level of output above potential GDP so that inflationary increases in the price level are occurring. The policy prescription in this setting would be a dose of contractionary fiscal policy, implemented through either higher taxes or lower spending. To some extent, *both* of these changes happen automatically. On the tax side, a rise in aggregate demand means that workers and firms throughout the economy earn more income. Because taxes are based on personal income and corporate profits, a rise in aggregate demand automatically increases tax payments. On the spending side, stronger aggregate demand typically means lower unemployment and fewer layoffs, and so there is less need for government spending on unemployment benefits, welfare, Medicaid, and other programs in the social safety net.

The process works in reverse, too. If aggregate demand were to fall sharply so that a recession occurs, then the prescription would be for expansionary fiscal policy—some mix of tax cuts and spending increases. The lower level of aggregate demand and higher unemployment will tend to pull down personal incomes and corporate profits, an effect that will reduce the amount of taxes owed automatically. Higher unemployment and a weaker economy should lead to increased government spending on unemployment benefits, welfare, and other similar domestic programs. Thus, the automatic stabilizers react to a weakening of aggregate demand with expansionary fiscal policy and react to a strengthening of aggregate demand with contractionary fiscal policy, just as the AS–AD analysis suggests.

The very large budget deficits during and immediately after the Great Recession of 2007–2009 were produced by a combination of automatic stabilizers and discretionary fiscal policy. The severe U.S. recession starting in late 2007 meant less tax-generating economic activity, which triggered the automatic stabilizers that reduce taxes. Also, both President Bush in 2008 and President Obama in 2009 signed additional tax cuts into law. On the spending side, President Obama with bipartisan support signed a fiscal stimulus package of spending increases into effect early in 2009. Most economists, even those who are concerned about a possible pattern of persistently large budget deficits, are much less concerned or even quite supportive of larger budget deficits in the short run of a few years during and immediately after a recession.

A glance back at economic history provides a second illustration of the power of automatic stabilizers. Remember that the length of economic upswings between recessions has become longer in the U.S. economy in recent decades (as discussed in Chapter 21). The four longest economic booms of the twentieth century happened in the 1960s, the 1980s, the 1991–2001 period, and the slow-but-steady recovery after the end of the Great Recession in June 2009. One reason why the economy has tipped into recession less frequently in recent decades is that the size of government spending and taxes has increased in the second half of the twentieth century. Thus, the automatic stabilizing effects from spending and taxes are now larger than they were in the first half of the twentieth century. Around 1900, for example, federal spending was only about 2% of GDP. In 1929, just before the Great Depression hit, government spending was still just 4% of GDP. In those earlier times, the smaller size of government made automatic stabilizers far less powerful than in the last few decades, when government spending often hovers at 20% of GDP or more.

Automatic stabilizers are implemented quickly. Lower income means that a lower quantity of taxes is withheld from paychecks right away. Higher unemployment or poverty means that government spending in those areas rises as quickly as people apply for benefits. While the automatic stabilizers offset part of the shifts in aggregate demand, they do not offset all or even most of it. Nonetheless, automatic stabilizers, like shock absorbers in a car, can be useful because they reduce the impact of the worst bumps, even if they don't eliminate the bumps altogether.

Practical Problems with Discretionary Fiscal Policy

In the early 1960s, when the Keynesian economic framework had been developed and was fairly well understood by many economists, the economics profession had a few years of extreme (and unaccustomed) cheerfulness. Many leading economists believed that the problem of the business cycle, and the swings between cyclical unemployment and inflation, were a thing of the past. On the cover of its December 31, 1965, issue, *Time* magazine ran a picture of John Maynard Keynes, and the story inside identified Keynesian theories as "the prime influence on the world's economies." Policymakers have "used Keynesian principles not only to avoid the violent [business] cycles of prewar days but to produce phenomenal economic growth and to achieve remarkably stable prices," reported the article.

But this happy consensus didn't last. The U.S. economy suffered one recession from December 1969 to November 1970, a deeper recession from November 1973 to March 1975, and then double-dip recessions from January to June 1980 and from July 1981 to

November 1982. At various times, inflation and unemployment both soared. Clearly, the problems of macroeconomic policy had not been solved! As economists began to consider what had gone wrong, they identified a number of issues that make discretionary fiscal policy more difficult than it had seemed in the rosy optimism of the mid-1960s.

Long and Variable Time Lags

Monetary policy can be changed several times each year, but fiscal policy is much slower to be enacted. Imagine that the economy starts to slow down. It often takes some months before the economic statistics signal clearly that a downturn has started, and a few months more to confirm that it is truly a recession and not just a one- or two-month blip. Policymakers become aware of the problem and propose fiscal policy bills. The bills go into various congressional committees for hearings, negotiations, votes, and then, if passed, eventually for the president's signature. Many fiscal policy bills about spending or taxes propose changes that would start in the next budget year or would be phased in gradually over time.

Moreover, the exact level of fiscal policy to be implemented is never completely clear. Should the budget deficit be increased by 0.5% of GDP? By 1% of GDP? By 2% of GDP? In an AS–AD diagram, it's straightforward to sketch an aggregate demand curve shifting to the potential GDP level of output. But in the real world, the actual level of potential output is known only roughly, not precisely, and exactly how a spending cut or tax increase will affect aggregate demand is always somewhat controversial.

Thus, it can take many months or even more than a year to begin an expansionary fiscal policy after a recession started—and even then, uncertainty will remain over exactly how much to expand or contract taxes and spending. When politicians attempt to use countercyclical fiscal policy to fight recession or inflation, they run the risk of responding to the macroeconomic situation of two or three years ago, in a way that may be wrong for the economy at that time. George P. Schultz, a professor of economics who also had an illustrious political career as Secretary of Labor and also Director of the Office of Management and Budget during the Nixon administration, and as Secretary of State during the Reagan administration, once wrote: "While the economist is accustomed to the concept of lags, the politician likes instant results. The tension comes because, as I have seen on many occasions, the economist's lag is the politician's nightmare."

Temporary and Permanent Fiscal Policy

A temporary tax cut or spending increase will explicitly last only for a year or two, and then revert back to its original level. A permanent tax cut or spending increase is expected to stay in place for the foreseeable future. The effect of temporary and permanent fiscal policies on aggregate demand can be very different. Consider how you would react if the government announced a tax cut that would last one year, and then be repealed, in comparison with how you would react if the government announced a permanent tax cut. Most people and firms will react more strongly to a permanent policy change than a temporary one.

This fact creates an unavoidable difficulty for countercyclical fiscal policy. The appropriate policy may be to have an expansionary fiscal policy with large budget deficits during a recession, and then a contractionary fiscal policy with budget surpluses when the economy is growing well. But if both of these policies are explicitly temporary, they will have a less powerful effect than a permanent policy.

Coordinating Fiscal and Monetary Policy

Because fiscal policy affects the quantity that the government borrows in financial capital markets, it doesn't only affect aggregate demand—it also affects interest rates. In Exhibit 32-12, the original equilibrium E_0 in the financial capital market occurs at a quantity of $800 billion and an interest rate of 6%. However, an increase in government budget

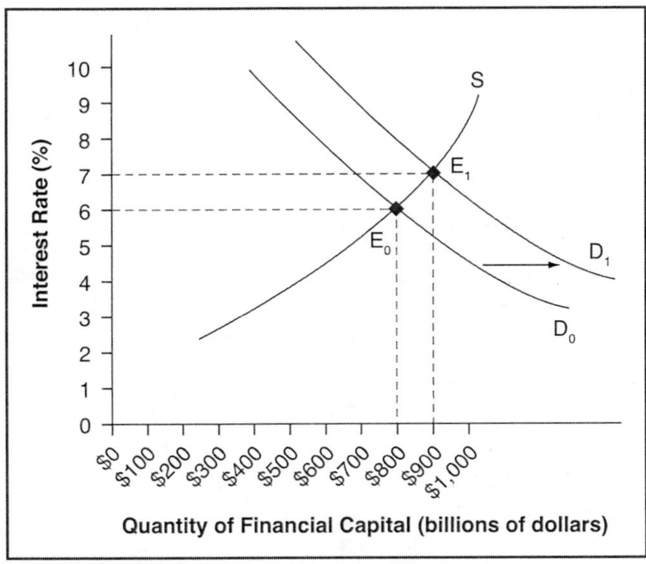

EXHIBIT 32-12 Fiscal Policy and Interest Rates

When a government borrows money in the financial capital market, it causes a shift in the demand for financial capital from D_0 to D_1. As the equilibrium moves from E_0 to E_1, the equilibrium interest rate rises from 6% to 7% in this example. In this way, an expansionary fiscal policy that is intended to shift aggregate demand to the right can also lead to a higher interest rate, which has the effect of shifting aggregate demand to the left. The impact of the higher interest rate can be reduced if fiscal and monetary policy work together.

deficits shifts the demand for financial capital from D_0 to D_1. The new equilibrium E_1 occurs at a quantity of $900 billion and an interest rate of 7%. (If the federal government is running surpluses, then it is acting as a supplier in financial capital markets. A lower budget surplus will shift the supply of financial capital to the left, also leading to a higher interest rate.) A consensus estimate based on a number of studies using historical data is that a sustained increase in budget deficits (or a fall in budget surplus) by 1% of GDP will cause an increase of 0.5–1.0% in the long-term interest rate.

A problem arises here. An expansionary fiscal policy, with tax cuts or spending increases, is intended to increase aggregate demand. But if an expansionary fiscal policy also causes higher interest rates, then firms and households are discouraged from borrowing and spending (as occurs with tight monetary policy), thus reducing aggregate demand. Even if the direct effect of expansionary fiscal policy on increasing demand is not totally offset by lower aggregate demand from higher interest rates, fiscal policy can end up being less powerful than was originally expected.

The broader lesson is that fiscal and monetary policy should be coordinated. If expansionary fiscal policy is to work well, then the central bank needs to prevent interest rates from rising. Conversely, monetary policy can also help to ensure that contractionary fiscal policy doesn't lead to a recession.

Structural Economic Change Takes Time

When an economy recovers from a recession, it does not usually revert back to its exact earlier shape. Instead, the internal structure of the economy evolves and changes, and this process can take time. For example, much of the economic growth of the mid-2000s was involved in the sectors of construction (especially of housing) and finance. However, when housing prices started falling in 2007 and the resulting financial crunch led into recession (as discussed in Chapter 30), both of these sectors contracted. The manufacturing sector of the U.S. economy has been losing jobs in recent years as well, under pressure from technological change and foreign competition. Many of the people thrown out of work from these sectors in the recession of 2007–2009 will never return to the same jobs in the same sectors of the economy; instead, the economy will need to grow in new and different directions. Fiscal policy can increase overall demand, but the process of structural economic change—the expansion of a new set of industries and the movement of workers to those industries—inevitably takes time.

The Limitations of Potential GDP and the Natural Rate of Unemployment

Fiscal policy can help an economy that is producing below its potential GDP to expand aggregate demand so that it produces closer to potential GDP. But fiscal policy cannot help an economy produce at an output level above potential GDP. Similarly, expansionary fiscal policy can help in reducing the cyclical unemployment that is associated with recession. But it cannot help in reducing the natural rate of unemployment that exists as a result of the incentives for hiring and working in the economy.

Educating Politicians

A final problem for discretionary fiscal policy arises out of the difficulties of explaining to politicians how a countercyclical fiscal policy that runs against the tide of the business cycle should work. Politicians often have a gut-level belief that when the economy and tax revenues slow down, it's time to hunker down, pinch pennies, and trim expenses. Countercyclical policy, however, says that when the economy has slowed down, it's time for the government to go on a spree, raising spending and cutting taxes. Conversely, when economic times are good and tax revenues are rolling in, politicians often feel that it's prime time for tax cuts and new spending. But countercyclical policy says that this economic boom should be an appropriate time for keeping taxes high and restraining spending.

Politicians tend to prefer expansionary fiscal policy over contractionary policy. There is rarely a shortage of proposals for tax cuts and spending increases, especially during recessions. However, politicians are less willing to hear the message that in good economic times, they should propose tax increases and spending limits. During the economic upswing of the late 1990s and early 2000s, for example, the U.S. GDP grew rapidly. Estimates from respected government economic forecasters like the nonpartisan Congressional Budget Office and the Office of Management and Budget (which is run by the White House) stated that the GDP was above potential GDP, and that unemployment rates were unsustainably low. However, no mainstream politician took the lead in saying that the booming economic times might be an appropriate time for spending cuts or tax increases.

Summing Up Discretionary Fiscal Policy

Expansionary fiscal policy can help to end recessions, and contractionary fiscal policy can help to reduce inflation. But given the uncertainties over interest rate effects, time lags, temporary and permanent policies, and the uncertainties of political behavior, many economists and knowledgeable policymakers have argued that discretionary fiscal policy is a blunt instrument, more like a club than a scalpel. It still makes sense to use it in extreme economic situations like an especially deep or long recession. But for milder situations, it often seems preferable to let fiscal policy work through the automatic stabilizers and then focus on monetary policy to steer short-term countercyclical policy.

Requiring a Balanced Budget?

For many decades, going back to the 1930s, proposals have been put forward to require that the U.S. government balance its budget every year. In 1995, a proposed constitutional amendment that would require a balanced budget passed the U.S. House of Representatives by a wide margin and failed in the U.S. Senate by a single vote.

Most economists view the proposals for a perpetually balanced budget with bemusement. After all, in the short term, economists would expect the budget deficits and surpluses to fluctuate up and down with the economy and the automatic stabilizers. Economic recessions should automatically lead to larger budget deficits or smaller budget surpluses, while economic booms lead to smaller deficits or larger surpluses. A requirement that the budget be balanced each and every year would prevent these automatic stabilizers from working and thus would worsen the severity of economic fluctuations.

Some supporters of the balanced budget amendment like to argue that since households must balance their own budgets, the government should do so, too. But this analogy between household and government behavior is badly flawed. Most households do not balance their budgets every year. In some years, households borrow money to buy houses or cars or to pay for medical expenses or college tuition. In other years, they repay loans and save money in retirement accounts. After retirement, households withdraw and spend those savings. Also, the government is not a household for many reasons, one of which is that the government has macroeconomic responsibilities. The argument of Keynesian macroeconomic policy is that the government needs to lean against the wind, spending when times are hard and saving when times are good, for the sake of the overall economy.

There is also no particular reason to expect a government budget to be balanced in the medium term of a few years. For example, a government may decide that by running large budget deficits, it can make crucial long-term investments in human capital and physical infrastructure that will build the long-term productivity of a country. These decisions may work out well or poorly, but they are not inevitably irrational. Such policies of ongoing government budget deficits may persist for decades. As the U.S. experience from the end of World War II up to about 1980 shows, it is perfectly possible to run budget deficits almost every year for decades, but as long as the percentage increases in debt are smaller than the percentage growth of GDP, then debt/GDP ratio will decline at the same time.

Nothing in this argument should be taken as a claim that budget deficits are always a wise policy. In the short run, a government that runs extremely large budget deficits can shift aggregate demand to the right so violently that it causes severe inflation. Governments may borrow for foolish or impractical reasons. The next chapter will discuss how large budget deficits, by reducing national saving, can in certain cases reduce economic growth and even contribute to international financial crises. But a requirement that the budget be balanced in each calendar year is a misguided overreaction to the fear that in some cases, budget deficits can grow too large.

Conclusion

The relationship between government fiscal policy and the macroeconomy goes in both directions. The sheer size of government spending and taxes mean that they play an important role in a nation's macroeconomy. Fiscal policy affects aggregate demand in a number of ways: for example, through government spending and through the impact of taxes on consumption and investment. Conversely, automatic stabilizers exist because the levels of government spending and taxes are affected by a country's macroeconomic performance. This chapter has focused on fiscal policy in the context of recession, cyclical unemployment, inflation, and short-run business cycles. The next chapter focuses on how government spending and taxes affect national savings and thus have an impact on long-run economic growth as well as the trade balance and international flows of financial capital.

Key Concepts and Summary

1. **Fiscal policy** is the set of policies that relate to government spending, taxation, and borrowing.
2. In recent decades, the level of federal government spending and taxes, expressed as a share of GDP, has not changed much, typically fluctuating between about 18 to 22% of GDP. However, the level of state spending and taxes, as a share of GDP, has risen by more than 40% over the last four decades.
3. The four main areas of federal spending are national defense, Social Security, health care, and interest payments, which together account for about 70% of all federal spending.

4. When a government spends more than it collects in taxes, it is said to have a **budget deficit**. When a government collects more in taxes than it spends, it is said to have a **budget surplus**. If government spending and taxes are equal, it is said to have a **balanced budget**.
5. The two main federal taxes are **individual income taxes** and **payroll taxes** that provide funds for Social Security and Medicare. These taxes together account for more than 80% of federal revenues. Other federal taxes include the **corporate income tax**; excise taxes on alcohol, gasoline, and tobacco; and the **estate and gift tax**.
6. A **progressive tax** is one, like the federal income tax, where those with higher incomes pay a higher share of income in taxes than those with lower incomes. A **proportional tax** is one, like the payroll tax for Medicare, where everyone pays the same share of income in taxes regardless of income level, like the payroll tax for Medicare. A **regressive tax** is one, like the payroll tax that supports Social Security, where those with high income pay a lower share of income in taxes than those with lower incomes.
7. For most of the twentieth century, the U.S. government took on debt during wartime and then paid down that debt slowly in peacetime. However, the U.S. government took on quite substantial debts in peacetime in the 1980 and early 1990s, before a brief period of budget surpluses from 1998 to 2001, followed by a return to annual budget deficits since 2002, with very large deficits in the recession of 2008 and 2009.
8. A budget deficit or budget surplus is measured annually. **Total government debt** is the sum of budget deficits and budget surpluses over time.
9. **Expansionary fiscal policy** increases the level of aggregate demand, either through increases in government spending or through reductions in taxes. Expansionary fiscal policy is most appropriate when an economy is in recession and producing below its potential GDP. **Contractionary fiscal policy** decreases the level of aggregate demand, either through cuts in government spending or increases in taxes. Contractionary fiscal policy is most appropriate when an economy is producing above its potential GDP.
10. Fiscal policy is conducted both through **discretionary fiscal policy**, which occurs when the government enacts taxation or spending changes in response to economic events, or through **automatic stabilizers**, which are taxing and spending mechanisms that by their design shift in response to economic events without any further legislation.
11. Discretionary fiscal policy faces some practical difficulties: (a) expansionary fiscal policy can raise interest rates, which tends to reduce the expansionary impact of the policy; (b) there are long and variable time lags in enacting fiscal policy and waiting for it to have an effect; (c) the impact of temporary fiscal policy is smaller than the impact of permanent fiscal policy; (d) fiscal policy cannot push economic output above the potential GDP level of output; (e) it may be hard to persuade politicians of the merits of countercyclical fiscal policy.
12. Laws requiring a balanced budget every year would inhibit both automatic stabilizers and discretionary fiscal policy, as well as long-term uses of fiscal policy to increase national saving or to invest in a nation's future.

Review Questions

1. What is fiscal policy?
2. Do spending and taxes of the U.S. federal government generally have an upward or a downward trend in the last few decades?
3. What are the main categories of U.S. federal government spending?
4. What's the difference between a budget deficit, a balanced budget, and a budget surplus?
5. Have spending and taxes by state and local governments in the United States had a generally upward or downward trend in the last few decades?
6. What are the main categories of U.S. federal government taxes?
7. What's the difference between a progressive tax, a proportional tax, and a regressive tax?
8. What has been the general pattern of U.S. budget deficits in recent decades?
9. What's the difference between a budget deficit and the government debt?
10. What's the difference between expansionary fiscal policy and contractionary fiscal policy?
11. Under what general macroeconomic circumstances might a government use expansionary fiscal policy? Contractionary fiscal policy?
12. What's the difference between discretionary fiscal policy and automatic stabilizers?
13. Why do automatic stabilizers function "automatically"?
14. What are some practical weaknesses of discretionary fiscal policy?
15. What are some of the arguments for and against a requirement that the federal government budget be balanced every year?

Government Borrowing and National Savings

CHAPTER

33

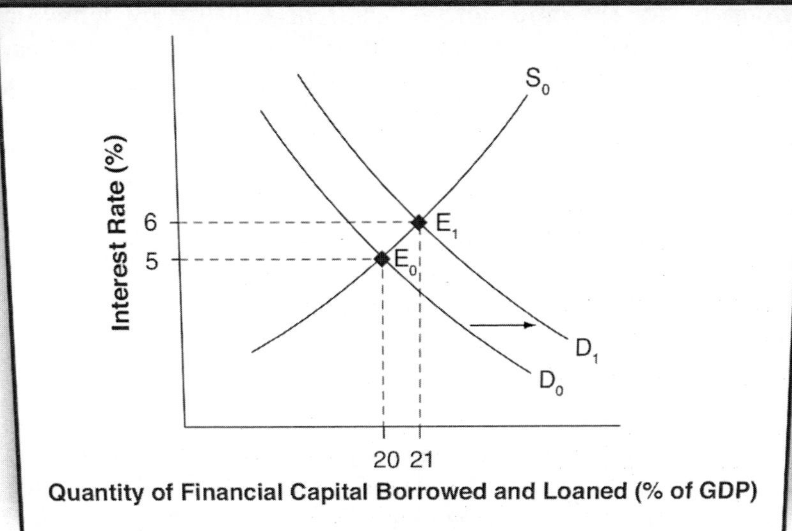

Chapter Outline

When a government spends more than it collects in taxes and runs a budget deficit, it needs to borrow. When government borrowing becomes especially large and sustained, it can reduce the financial capital available to private-sector firms, as well as leading to trade imbalances and even financial crises.

The previous chapter introduced the concepts of deficits and debt, and how a government could use fiscal policy during the short-run of the business cycle to address recession or inflation. This chapter begins by building upon the national savings and investment identity, first introduced in Chapter 25, to show how government borrowing affects physical capital investment levels of firms and trade balances. A prolonged period of budget deficits may lead to lower economic growth, in part because the funds borrowed by the government to fund its budget deficits are typically no longer available for investment. Moreover, a sustained pattern of large budget deficits can lead to disruptive economic patterns of high inflation, substantial inflows of financial capital from abroad, plummeting exchange rates, and heavy strains on a country's banking and financial system.

How Government Borrowing Affects Investment and the Trade Balance

When governments increase their borrowing in financial capital markets, there are three possible sources for the funds from a macroeconomic point of view: (1) households might save more; (2) private firms might borrow less; and (3) the funds might come outside the country, from foreign financial investors. Let's begin with a review of why one of these three options must occur, and then explore how interest rates and exchange rates can help to explain these connections.

The National Saving and Investment Identity

The national saving and investment identity, first introduced in Chapter 25, provides a framework for showing the relationships between the sources of demand and supply in financial capital markets. The identity begins with a statement that must always hold true: the quantity of financial capital supplied in the market must equal the quantity of financial capital demanded. The U.S. economy has two main sources for financial capital: private savings S from households and firms inside the U.S. economy; and the inflow of foreign financial investment from abroad. The inflow of savings from abroad is by definition equal to the trade deficit, as explained in Chapter 25, so this inflow of foreign investment capital can be written as imports M minus exports X. There are also two main sources of demand for financial capital: private sector investment I and government borrowing. Government borrowing in any given year is equal to the budget deficit, and thus can be written as the difference between government spending G and taxes T. Thus, in algebraic terms, the national savings and investment identity can be written like this:

$$\text{Quantity supplied of financial capital} = \text{Quantity demanded of financial capital}$$

$$\text{Private savings} + \begin{matrix}\text{Inflow of}\\ \text{foreign savings}\end{matrix} = \text{Private investment} + \begin{matrix}\text{Government}\\ \text{budget deficit}\end{matrix}$$

$$S + (M - X) = I + (G - T)$$

A change in any part of the national saving and investment identity *must* be accompanied by offsetting changes in at least one other part of the equation because the equality of quantity supplied and quantity demanded must continue to hold true. Thus, if the government budget deficit changes, then either private saving or investment or the trade balance or some combination of the three *must* change as well. Exhibit 33-1 lists the possible effects.

What about Budget Surpluses and Trade Surpluses?

The national saving and investment identity must always hold true because the quantity supplied and quantity demanded in the financial capital market must always be equal by definition. However, the formula will look somewhat different if the government budget is in deficit rather than surplus or if the balance of trade is in surplus rather than deficit. For example, from 1998 to 2001, the U.S. government had budget surpluses, although the economy was still experiencing trade deficits. When the government was running budget surpluses, it was acting as a saver rather than a borrower, and supplying financial capital rather than demanding it. As a result, the national saving and investment identity during this time would be more properly written:

$$\text{Quantity supplied of financial capital} = \text{Quantity demanded of financial capital}$$

$$\text{Private savings} + \text{Trade deficit} + \text{Government surplus} = \text{Private investment}$$

$$S + (M - X) + (T - G) = I$$

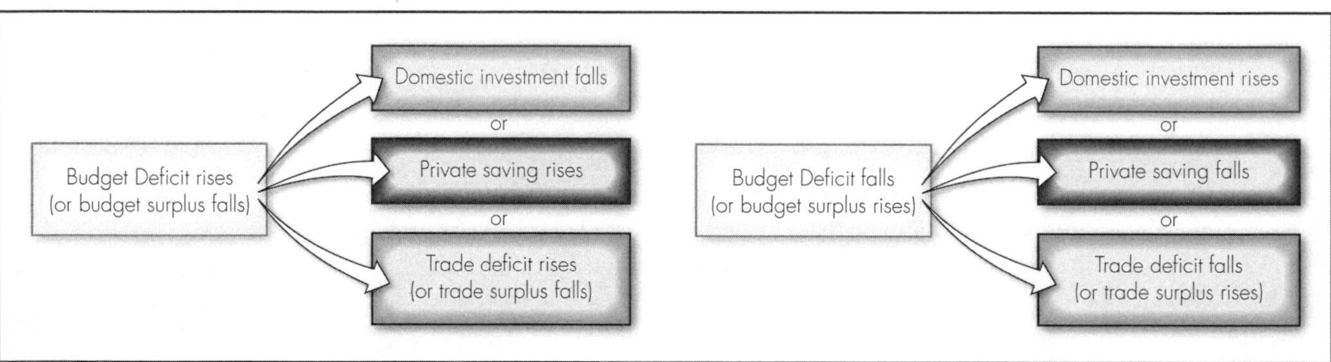

EXHIBIT 33-1 Effects of Change in Budget Surplus or Deficit

Notice that this expression is mathematically the same as the earlier version of the national saving and investment identity, except that (T– G) has been added to each side. Instead of a government deficit appearing in the equation as part of the quantity demanded of financial capital, now the budget surplus appears as part of the quantity supplied of financial capital.

During the 1960s, the U.S. government was often running a budget deficit but the economy was typically running trade surpluses. Since a trade surplus means that an economy is experiencing a net outflow of financial capital, the national saving and investment identity would be written:

Quantity supplied of financial capital = Quantity demanded of financial capital demand

Private savings = Private investment + Government budget deficit + Trade surplus

$$S = I + (G - T) + (X - M)$$

Instead of the balance of trade representing part of the supply of financial capital, which occurs with a trade deficit, a trade surplus represents an outflow of financial capital leaving the domestic economy and being invested elsewhere in the world.

The moral of this parade of equations is that the national saving and investment identity is always true, but when you write these relationships it is important to engage your brain and think about what is on the supply side and the demand side of the financial capital market before your pencil moves into gear. In the circumstances of the U.S. government during the second decade of the 2000s, a rise in the budget deficit must cause one of three possible effects: a fall in domestic investment, a rise in private savings, or a rise in the trade deficit. The following sections discuss each of these possible effects in more detail.

Fiscal Policy, Investment, and Economic Growth

The underpinnings of economic growth are investments in physical capital, human capital, and technology, all set in an economic environment where firms and individuals can react to the incentives provided by well-functioning markets and flexible prices. Government borrowing can reduce the financial capital available for private firms to invest in physical capital. But government spending can also encourage certain elements of long-term growth. Examples include government spending on publicly owned physical capital like roads or water systems, on education that creates human capital, or on research and development that creates new technology.

Crowding Out Physical Capital Investment

A larger budget deficit will increase demand for financial capital. If private saving and the trade balance remain the same, then less financial capital will be available for private investment in physical capital. When government borrowing soaks up available financial capital and leaves less for private investment in physical capital, the result is known as **crowding out.**

crowding out: When government borrowing soaks up available financial capital and leaves less for private investment in physical capital.

To understand the potential impact of crowding out, consider the situation of the U.S. economy before the exceptional circumstances of the recession that started in late 2007. In 2005, for example, the budget deficit was roughly 4% of GDP. The unemployment rate in 2005 was about 5%, so there was no countercyclical reason to be running a loose or expansionary fiscal policy in 2005. Private investment by firms in the U.S. economy has hovered in the range of 14–18% of GDP in recent decades. However, in any given year, roughly half of U.S. investment in physical capital just replaces machinery and equipment that has worn out or become technologically obsolete. Thus, only about half of total investment in physical capital represents an increase for the total quantity of physical capital in the economy. With this adjustment in mind, investment in new physical capital in any year is about 7–9% of GDP. In this situation, even U.S. budget deficits in the range of 4% of GDP can potentially crowd out a substantial share of the new investment spending in the U.S. economy. Conversely, a smaller budget deficit (or an increased budget surplus) would increase the pool of financial capital available for private investment.

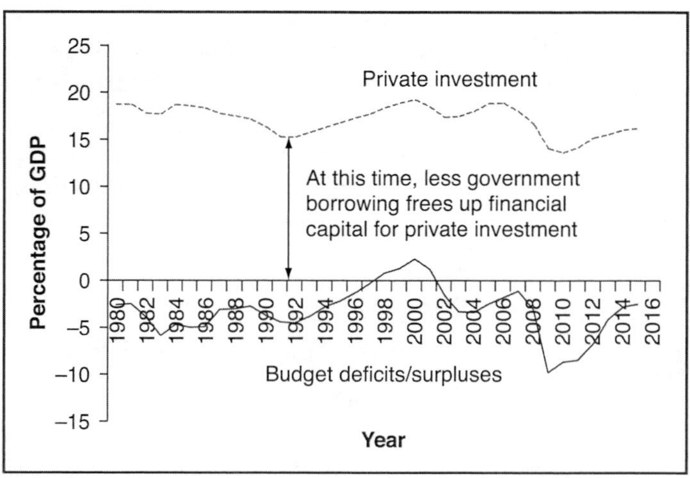

EXHIBIT 33-2 U.S. Budget Deficits/Surpluses and Private Investment

The connection from government borrowing to private investment in physical capital is not a precise one. After all, private savings and flows of international capital also play a role. But government borrowing and private investment have generally risen and fallen together during the last two decades For example, the mid- to late 1990s show a pattern in which reduced government borrowing helped to reduce crowding out so that more funds were available for private investment.

The patterns of U.S. budget deficits and private investment since 1980 are shown in Exhibit 33-2. If greater government deficits lead to less private investment in physical capital, while reduced government deficits or budget surpluses lead to more investment in physical capital, then these two lines should move up and down at roughly the same time. For example, in the mid-1990s when federal deficits were falling and then turning to surpluses, more funds were available for private investments, which rose at that time.

This argument does not claim that a government's budget deficits will exactly shadow its national rate of private investment: after all, as the national saving and income identity shows, private saving and inflows of foreign financial investment must also be taken into account. In the mid-1980s, for example, government budget deficits increase substantially without a corresponding drop-off in private investment. In 2009 and the years immediately afterward, investment drops off primarily because during the recession, firms lack both the funds and the incentive to invest—not because budget deficits increased. However, government borrowing can clearly have an effect in crowding out private investment in physical capital, while a reduction in government borrowing can offer private investment a chance to expand.

The Interest Rate Connection

A government that is borrowing substantial amounts will have an effect on financial capital markets. In Exhibit 33-3, the original equilibrium E_0 where the demand curve D_0 for borrowing financial capital intersects with the supply curve S_0 for lending financial capital at an interest rate of 5% and an equilibrium quantity equal to 20% of GDP. However, the government budget deficit increases and the demand curve for financial capital shifts from D_0 to D_1. The new equilibrium E_1 occurs at an interest rate of 6% and an equilibrium quantity of borrowing and lending of 21% of GDP.

A survey of economic studies on the connection between government borrowing and interest rates in the U.S. economy using historical data suggests that an increase of 1% in the budget deficit will lead to a rise in interest rates of between 0.5 and 1.0%, other factors held equal. In turn, a higher interest rate tends to discourage firms from making physical capital investments. Thus, one reason that government budget deficits crowd out private investment is because of the increase in interest rates.

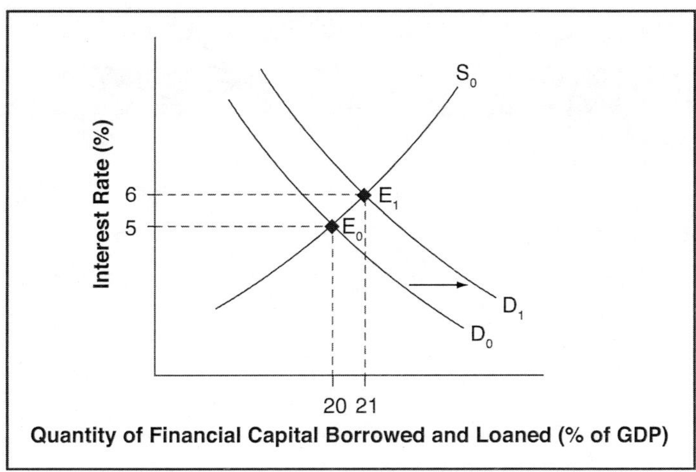

EXHIBIT 33-3 Budget Deficits and Interest Rates

In the financial capital market, an increase in government borrowing can shift the demand curve for borrowing financial capital to the right from D_0 to D_1. As the equilibrium interest rate shifts from E_0 to E_1, the interest rate rises from 5% to 6% in this example. The higher interest rate is one economic mechanism by which government borrowing can crowd out private investment.

At this point, you may wonder about the Federal Reserve. After all, can't the Federal Reserve use expansionary monetary policy to reduce interest rates, or in this case, to prevent interest rates from rising? This useful question emphasizes the importance of considering how fiscal and monetary policies work in relation to each other. Imagine a central bank faced with a government that is running large budget deficits, thus causing an increase in interest rates and crowding out private investment. If the budget deficits are increasing aggregate demand when the economy is already producing near potential GDP such that that an inflationary increase in price level is threatened, then the central bank may react with a contractionary monetary policy. In this situation, the higher interest rates from the government borrowing would be made even higher by contractionary monetary policy, and the government borrowing might crowd out a great deal of private investment. On the other hand, if the budget deficits are increasing aggregate demand when the economy is producing substantially less than potential GDP, then an inflationary increase in the price level is not much of a danger and the central bank might react with expansionary monetary policy. In this situation, any higher interest rates from government borrowing would be largely offset by the lower interest rates from expansionary monetary policy, and little crowding out of private investment would occur.

However, even a central bank cannot erase the overall message of the national savings and investment identity. If government borrowing rises, then private investment must fall, or private saving must rise, or the trade deficit must fall. By reacting with contractionary or expansionary monetary policy, the central bank can only help to determine which of these outcomes is likely to occur.

Public Investment in Physical Capital

Government can invest in physical capital directly: roads and bridges; water supply and sewers; seaports and airports; schools and hospitals; plants that generate electricity like hydroelectric dams, nuclear power, or windmills; telecommunications facilities; and weapons used by the military. Exhibit 33-4 shows the total value of the physical capital that was owned by federal, state, and local governments in the United States in 2014. Physical capital related to the military or to residences where people live is left out of this table because the focus here is on public investments that have a direct effect on raising output in the private sector. Still, the tally reaches a remarkable total of almost \$10 trillion in publicly-owned physical capital. About 90% of the physical capital in the table is owned by state and local governments, not by the federal government.

EXHIBIT 33-4 Nonmilitary, Nonresidential Public Physical Capital in 2014

Type of Public Physical Capital	Value in 2014
Highways and streets	$3,314 billion
Water supply and sewer systems	$1,299 billion
Schools, hospitals, police, and fire	$2,805 billion
Conservation and development structures	$346 billion
Transportation and power	$1,042 billion
Equipment and software	$1,082 billion
Total	**$9,888 billion**

Public physical capital investment of this sort can increase the output and productivity of the economy. After all, an economy with reliable roads and electricity will be able to produce more. But it is hard to draw a general lesson about how much government investment in physical capital will benefit the economy because government responds to political incentives as well as to economic incentives. When a firm makes an investment in physical capital it is subject to the discipline of the market: if the firm doesn't receive a positive return on its investment, the firm may lose money or even go out of business. However, legislatures don't have to worry much about going broke. In some cases, lawmakers might make investments in physical capital as a way of spending money in the districts of key politicians. Unnecessary roads or office buildings may be built. Even if a project is useful and necessary, it might be done in a way that is excessively costly as a favor to local construction contractors or unions of construction workers who make campaign contributions to politicians. Managing public investment so that it is done in a cost-effective way can be difficult because the discipline imposed by political decisions is different than the discipline imposed by market competition.

If a government decides to finance an investment in public physical capital with higher taxes or lower government spending in other areas, it need not worry that it is crowding out private investment. However, if a government decides to finance an investment in public physical capital by borrowing, it may end up increasing the quantity of public physical capital at the cost of crowding out investment in private physical capital.

Public Investment in Human Capital

In most countries, the government plays a large role in society's investment in human capital through the education system. In 2013, in the high-income countries of the world, public spending on education is 5.4% of GDP; in the middle-income countries, it is 4.8% of GDP; in the low-income countries, it is 4.2% of GDP. A highly educated and skilled workforce contributes to a higher rate of economic growth, and especially for the low-income nations of the world, an additional investment in human capital seems likely to increase productivity and growth.

But for United States, tough questions have been raised about how much increases in government spending on education will improve the actual level of education achieved. Among economists, discussions of education reform often begin with some uncomfortable facts. As shown in Exhibit 33-5, spending per student for kindergarten through grade 12 (K–12) has increased substantially in real dollars; for example, real (that is, adjusted for inflation) education spending per student more than doubled from about $5,000 per student in 1970 to more than $11,000 per student in recent years. However, as measured by standardized tests like the SAT, the level of student academic achievement has barely budged in recent decades. Indeed, on international tests, the U.S. students lag behind students from many other countries. (Of course, test scores are an imperfect measure of education for a variety of reasons. But it would be difficult to argue that all the problems of the U.S. education system are due to mismeasurement!)

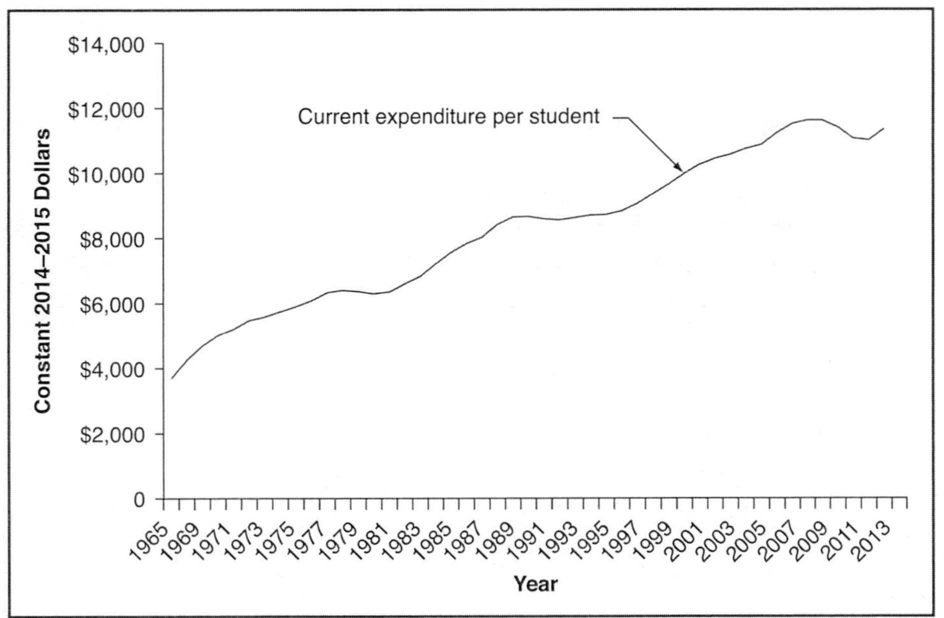

EXHIBIT 33-5 Higher Education Spending per Student

Despite higher spending per student, as shown in the figure, educational achievement as measured by test scores has been largely stagnant since 1970.

The fact that increased financial resources per student has not brought more substantial and measurable gains in student performance has led some education experts to question whether the problems of education may be due to the incentive structure of education, not just the resources spent on education. U.S. states have implemented many different proposals: rewarding schools financially when students make exceptional gains, and threatening to close schools where students are not making sufficient gains; requiring testing of students at various grades, including tests as a requirement for high school graduation; requiring additional teacher training; allowing students a greater degree of choice between public schools, to put pressure on weak schools to perform better; and allowing teachers and parents to start new schools, sometimes called charter schools, to compete with existing schools. The most controversial proposals have called for giving students a voucher that they could use at any state-accredited school, public or private, and to let families choose where their children attend. Economists and other social science researchers continually attempt to evaluate and propose adjustments to such programs.

In 2001, Congress passed and President George W. Bush signed into law the No Child Left Behind Act. The act requires all states to test children in grades 3–8, to publish the results, to intervene in schools where inadequate progress is occurring, and to assure that a growing share of teachers are highly qualified in the specific subjects they are teaching. In 2015, Congress passed and President Barack Obama signed into law the Every Student Succeeds Act, which gave states additional flexibility in setting educational standards and evaluating school performance. As states react to this law, additional data should become available about what methods for improving education work best.

Other government programs seek to increase human capital either before or after the K–12 education system. Programs for early childhood education, like the federal Head Start program, are directed at families where the parents may have limited educational and financial resources. Early preschool education does not seem to lead to a long-lasting increase scores on standardized tests, but there is evidence that it can make students more attached to school, more motivated to persevere and avoid dropping out of school, and thus ultimately more likely to get better jobs later in life.

Government also offers substantial support for universities and colleges. One of the traditional strengths of the U.S. education system has been the relatively high proportion of students who go on to additional education after the high school level. However, in the last few decades many nations across the world have dramatically increased the proportion of students attending a college or university, and the U.S economy now ranks in the middle of pack among high-income economies in the share of students who go on to additional education after high school. Of course, American colleges and universities could teach more effectively if high school graduates were better prepared to take full advantage of a college-level education.

Not all spending on educational human capital needs to happen through the government: for example, many college students in the United States pay a substantial share of the cost of their education. But if low-income countries of the world are going to experience a widespread increase in their education levels for grade-school children, government spending seems likely to play a substantial role. For the U.S. economy, and for other high-income countries, the primary focus at this time seems to be more on how to get a bigger return from existing spending on education and how to improve the performance of the average high school graduate, rather than on advocating dramatic increases in education spending.

How Fiscal Policy Can Improve Technology

Research and development (R&D) efforts are the lifeblood of new technology. But U.S. levels of R&D spending have been between 2.1% and 2.8% of GDP since the 1960s, and have shown no particular increases in recent decades. For comparison, U.S. R&D in 2013, at 2.7% of GDP, was essentially the same as Germany's R&D effort of 2.9% of GDP but behind Japan's R&D spending of 3.5% of GDP. Also, about one-fifth of U.S. R&D spending goes to defense and space-oriented research, a much greater share than in Japan and Germany. Although this defense-oriented R&D spending may sometimes eventually produce consumer-oriented spin-offs, R&D that is aimed at producing new weapons is less likely to benefit the civilian economy than direct civilian R&D spending.

Fiscal policy can encourage R&D using either direct spending or tax policy. Government could spend more on the R&D that is carried out in government laboratories, as well as expanding federal R&D grants to universities and colleges, nonprofit organizations, and the private sector. In the mid-1960s, the U.S. federal government paid for about two-thirds of the nation's R&D. By 2013, however, the federal share of R&D spending had fallen to about one-fourth—that is, $127 billion from the federal government out of total R&D spending of $4546 billion. Fiscal policy can also support R&D through tax incentives, which allow firms to reduce their tax bill as they increase spending on research and development.

Summary of Fiscal Policy, Investment, and Economic Growth

Investment in physical capital, human capital, and new technology is essential for long-term economic growth. In a market-oriented economy, private firms will undertake most of the investment in physical capital, and fiscal policy should seek to avoid a long series of outsized budget deficits that might crowd out such investment. Governments can invest directly in publicly-owned physical capital and in educational human capital, and can encourage R&D both by direct spending and by incentives for the private sector. A high rate of investment is not enough to guarantee the process of economic growth, which also benefits from a non-recessionary, low-inflation, market-oriented economy with an innovative and flexible business sector. Moreover, the effects of many growth-oriented policies will only be seen very gradually over time, as students are better educated, physical capital investments are made, and new technologies are invented and implemented. But with these limitations duly noted, greater investment will typically produce a higher rate of economic growth.

Will Private Saving Offset Government Borrowing?

A change in government budgets may affect private saving. Imagine that people observe government budgets and adjust their savings accordingly. For example, whenever the government runs a budget deficit, people might reason: "Well, a higher budget deficit means that I'm just going to owe more taxes in the future to pay off all that government borrowing, so I'll start saving now." If the government runs budget surpluses, people might reason: "With these budget surpluses (or lower budget deficits), interest rates are

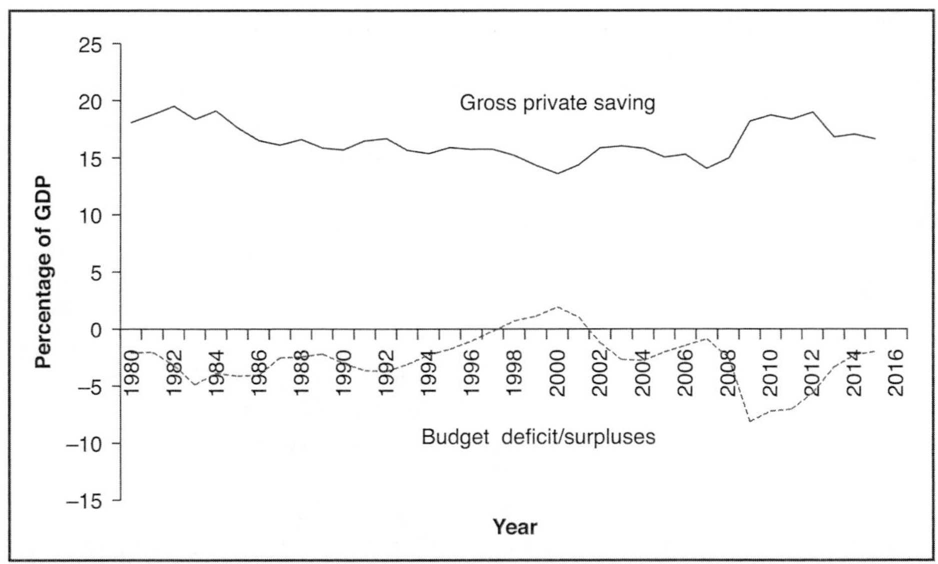

EXHIBIT 33-6 U.S. Budget Deficits and Private Savings

The theory of Ricardian neutrality suggests that any increase in government borrowing will be offset by additional private saving, while any decrease in government borrowing will be offset by reduced private saving. At some times, this theory holds true; for example, in the 1990s, the reduction in government borrowing was accompanied by a fall in private savings, and in 2008–2009, a rise in government borrowing was accompanied by a rise in private saving. However, such offsets are typically only partial and sometimes do not occur at all.

falling, so that saving is less attractive. Moreover, with a budget surplus the country will be able to afford a tax cut sometime in the future. I won't bother saving as much now."

The theory that rational private households might shift their saving to offset government saving or borrowing is known as **Ricardian equivalence** because the idea has intellectual roots in the writings of the early-nineteenth-century economist David Ricardo (1772–1823). If Ricardian equivalence holds completely true, then in the national saving and investment identity, any change in budget deficits or budget surpluses would be completely offset by a corresponding change in private saving. As a result, changes in government borrowing would have no effect at all on either physical capital investment or trade balances.

Ricardian equivalence: The theory that rational private households might shift their saving to offset government saving or borrowing.

In practice, the private sector only sometimes and partially adjusts its savings behavior to offset government budget deficits and surpluses. Exhibit 33-6 shows the patterns of U.S. government budget deficits and surpluses and the rate of private saving—which includes saving by both households and firms—since 1980. The connection between the two is not at all obvious. In the mid-1980s, for example, government budget deficits were quite large, but there is no corresponding surge of private saving. However, when budget deficits turn to surpluses in the late 1990s, there is a simultaneous decline in private saving. When budget deficits get very large in 2008 and 2009, on the other hand, there is some sign of a rise in saving. Several studies based on U.S. and international experience suggest that, on average, and with a lot of variation around the average, when government borrowing increases by $1, private saving rises, on average, by about 30 cents.

Thus, private saving does increase to some extent when governments run large budget deficits, and private saving falls when governments reduce deficits or run large budget surpluses. However, the offsetting effects of private saving compared to government borrowing are much less than one-to-one. In addition, this effect can vary a great deal from country to country, from time to time, and over the short run and the long run.

Fiscal Policy and the Trade Balance

Government budget balances can affect the trade balance. When government borrowing increases, one possible source of funding is an inflow of foreign financial investment. As

Chapter 25 discussed, a net inflow of foreign financial investment always accompanies a trade deficit, while a net outflow of financial investment always accompanies a trade surplus. One way to understand the connection from budget deficits to trade deficits is that when government creates a budget deficit with some combination of tax cuts or spending increases, it will increase aggregate demand in the economy, and some of that increase in aggregate demand will result in a higher level of imports. A higher level of imports, with exports remaining fixed, will cause a larger trade deficit.

Twin Deficits?

In the mid-1980s, it was common to hear economists and even newspaper articles refer to the "twin deficits," as the budget deficit and trade deficit both grew substantially. Exhibit 33-7 shows the pattern. The federal budget deficit went from 2.6% of GDP in 1981 to 5.1% of GDP in 1985—a drop of 2.5% of GDP. Over that time, the trade deficit moved from 0.5% in 1981 to 2.9% in 1985—a drop of 2.4% of GDP. In the mid-1980s, the considerable increase in government borrowing was filled with an inflow of foreign investment capital, so the government budget deficit and the trade deficit moved together.

Of course, no one should expect the budget deficit and trade deficit to move in lockstep because the other parts of the national saving and investment identity—investment and private savings—will often change as well. In the late 1990s, for example, the government budget balance turned from deficit to surplus, but the trade deficit remained large and growing. During this time, the inflow of foreign financial investment was supporting a surge of physical capital investment by U.S. firms. In the first half of the 2000s, the budget and trade deficits again increased together, but in 2009, the budget deficit increased while the trade deficit declined. The budget deficit and the trade deficit are related to each other, but they are more like cousins than twins.

Fiscal Policy and Exchange Rates

Exchange rates can also help to explain why budget deficits are linked to trade deficits. Exhibit 33-8 shows a situation using the exchange rate for the U.S. dollar, measured in

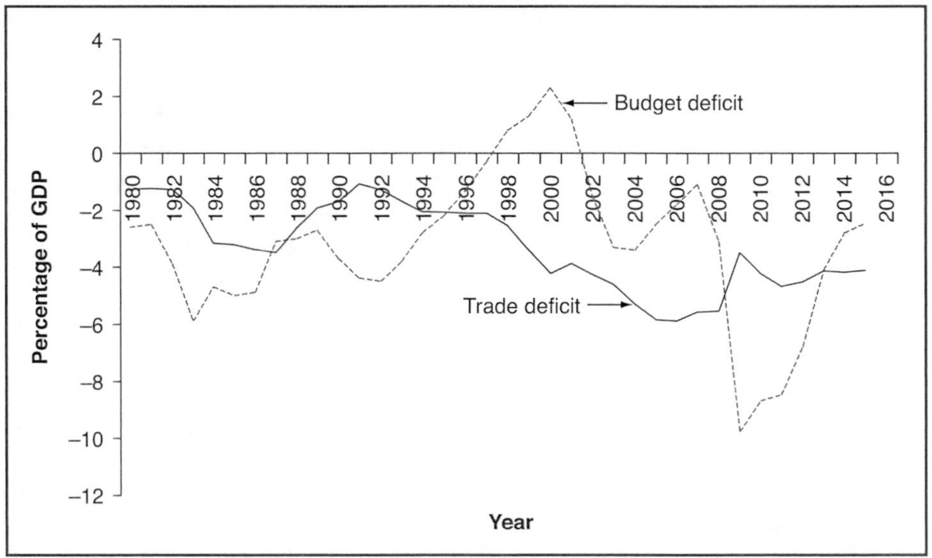

EXHIBIT 33-7 U.S. Budget Deficits and Trade Deficits

In the 1980s, the budget deficit and the trade deficit both declined at the same time, leading to much discussion of the "twin deficits." However, since then, the deficits have stopped being twins. The trade deficit grew smaller in the early 1990s as the budget deficit increased, and then the trade deficit grew larger in the late 1990s as the budget deficit turned into a surplus. In the first half of the 2000s, both budget and trade deficits increased. But for a few years starting in 2009, the trade deficit declined as the budget deficit increased.

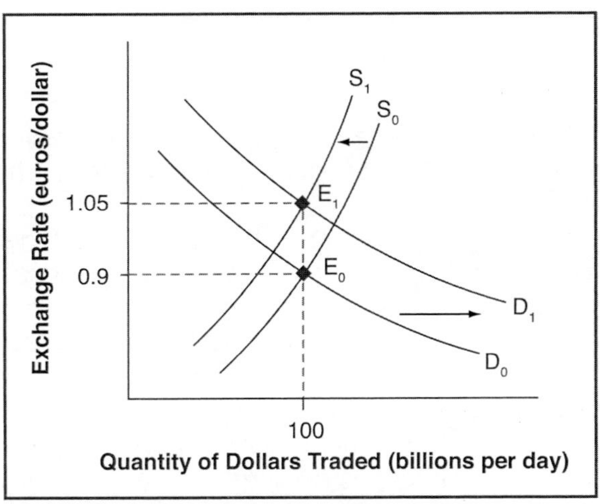

EXHIBIT 33-8 Budget Deficits and Exchange Rates

Imagine that the U.S. government increases its borrowing and the funds come from European financial investors. To purchase U.S. government bonds, those European investors will need to demand more U.S. dollars on foreign exchange markets, causing the demand for U.S. dollars to shift to the right from D_0 to D_1. European financial investors as a group will also be less likely to supply U.S. dollars to the foreign exchange markets, causing supply of U.S. dollars to shift from S_0 to S_1. The equilibrium exchange rate strengthens from 0.9 euro/dollar at E_0 to 1.05 euros/dollar at E_1.

euros. At the original equilibrium E_0, where the demand for U.S. dollars D_0 intersects with the supply of U.S. dollars S_0 on the foreign exchange market, the exchange rate is .9 euros per U.S. dollar and the equilibrium quantity traded in the market is $200 billion per day (which was roughly the quantity of dollar-euro trading in exchange rate markets in the mid-2000s). But then the U.S. budget deficit rises, and foreign financial investment provides the source of funds for that budget deficit. International financial investors as a group will demand more U.S. dollars on foreign exchange markets to purchase the U.S. government bonds, and they will supply fewer of the U.S. dollars that they already hold in these markets. Demand for U.S. dollars on the foreign exchange market shifts from D_0 to D_1 and the supply of U.S. dollars falls from S_0 to S_1. At the new equilibrium E_1, the exchange rate has appreciated to 1.05 euros per dollar, while in this example the quantity traded remains the same.

A stronger exchange rate, of course, makes it more difficult for exporters to sell their goods abroad while making imports cheaper, so a trade deficit (or a reduced trade surplus) results. Thus, a budget deficit can easily result in an inflow of foreign financial capital, a stronger exchange rate, and a trade deficit.

You can also imagine this appreciation of the exchange rate as being driven by interest rates. As explained earlier in Exhibit 33-3, a budget deficit increases demand in markets for domestic financial capital, raising the domestic interest rate. A higher interest rate will attract an inflow of foreign financial capital, appreciate the exchange rate, and lead to a larger trade deficit (or reduced trade surplus). The connections between inflows of foreign investment capital, interest rates, and exchange rates are all just different ways of drawing the same economic connections: A larger budget deficit can result in a larger trade deficit, although the connection should not be expected to be one to one.

From Budget Deficits to International Economic Crisis

The economic story of how an outflow of international financial capital can cause a deep recession was laid out step by step in Chapter 31. When international financial investors decide to withdraw their funds from a country like Turkey, they increase the supply of the Turkish lira and reduce the demand for lira, depreciating the lira exchange rate. But when firms and the government in a country like Turkey borrow money in international

The Risks of Chronic Large Deficits

If a government runs large budget deficits for a sustained period of time, what can go wrong? Eventually, the ratio of government debt/GDP grows high enough that both domestic and foreign lenders become concerned that the government will not be able to repay. At that point, some combination of the following effects is likely to happen.

The interest rate that the government must pay in order to continue its borrowing will start to increase to offset the additional risk perceived by investors, so that the cost of financing debt rises as well.

As the costs of borrowing rise, the government will face enormous financial pressure to take dramatic steps to reduce its budget deficits through spending cuts and tax increases. These steps will be politically painful, and they will also have a contractionary effect on aggregate demand in the economy.

High levels of government debt are often entangled with a private sector financial crisis. In some cases, the government responds to a financial crisis in the banking sector by offering guarantees to bank depositors and investors—thus turning the banking crisis into a government debt crisis. In other cases, banks and other financial firms are holding large amounts of government debt, and when the debt of an overborrowed government begins to look too risky, then the assets held by banks and other financial firms may no longer be secure.

A government with very a high debt/GDP level will be strongly tempted to allow a surge of inflation. After all, if the government has borrowed at a fixed interest rate of, say, 5%, and it lets inflation rise above that 5%, then it will effectively be able to repay its debt at a negative real interest rate.

What is the danger level of debt where these sorts of changes take effect? This central question doesn't have a definitive answer. A large economy in which the government can borrow mostly from its own domestic savings, such as Japan, can sustain a very high debt/GDP ratio that probably would not work for a smaller economy, such as Greece, where the government depends on inflows of international financial capital when it borrows. In the U.S. economy, the non-partisan Congressional Budget Office has predicted for years that as the U.S. population continues to age and if health-care costs continue to grow faster than the economy as a whole, even the mighty U.S. economy could face a troublingly high debt/GDP ratio 20–30 years in the future.

financial markets, they typically do so in stages. First, banks in Turkey borrow in a widely used currency like U.S. dollars or euros, then convert those U.S. dollars to lira, and then lend the money to borrowers in Turkey. If the value of the lira exchange rate depreciates, then Turkey's banks will find it impossible to repay the international loans that are in U.S. dollars or euros. The combination of less foreign investment capital and banks that are bankrupt can sharply reduce aggregate demand that causes a deep recession. Many countries around the world have experienced this kind of recession in recent years: along with Turkey in 2002, this general pattern was followed by Mexico in 1995, Thailand and countries across East Asia in 1997–98, Russia in 1998, Argentina in 2002, and Greece starting around 2010.

In many of these countries, large government budget deficits played a role in setting the stage for the financial crisis. A moderate increase in a budget deficit that leads to a moderate increase in a trade deficit and a moderate appreciation of the exchange rate is not necessarily a cause for concern. But beyond some point that is hard to define in advance, a series of large budget deficits can become a cause for concern among international investors.

One reason for concern is that extremely large budget deficits mean that aggregate demand may shift so far to the right as to cause high inflation. The example of Turkey at the beginning of this chapter is a situation where very large budget deficits brought inflation rates well into double digits. In addition, very large budget deficits at some point begin to raise a fear that the borrowing will not be repaid. In the last 175 years, the government of Turkey has been unable to pay its debts and defaulted on its loans six times. Brazil's government has been unable to pay its debts and defaulted on its loans seven times; Venezuela, nine times; and Argentina, five times. The government of Greece received several bailouts before officially defaulting on its debts in 2015. The risk of high inflation or a default on repaying international loans will worry international financial investors, since both factors imply that the rate of return on their investments in that country may end up lower than expected. If international financial investors start withdrawing the funds from a country rapidly, the scenario of less investment, a depreciated exchange rate, widespread bank failure, and deep recession can occur.

Using Fiscal Policy to Address Trade Imbalances

If a nation is experiencing the inflow of foreign investment capital associated with a trade deficit because foreign investors are making long-term direct investments in firms, there may be no substantial reason for concern. After all, many low-income nations around the world would welcome direct investment by multinational firms that ties them more closely into the global networks of production and distribution of goods and services. In this case, the inflows of foreign investment capital and the trade deficit are attracted by the opportunities for a good rate of return on private sector investment in an economy.

However, governments should beware a sustained pattern of high budget deficits and high trade deficits. The danger arises in particular when the inflow of foreign investment capital is not funding long-term physical capital investment by firms, but instead is short-term portfolio investment in government bonds. When inflows of foreign financial investment reach high levels, foreign financial investors will be on the alert for any reason to fear that the country's exchange rate may decline or the government may be unable to repay what it has borrowed on time. Just as a few falling rocks can trigger an avalanche, a relatively small piece of bad news about an economy can trigger an enormous outflow of short-term financial capital. Reducing a nation's budget deficit will not always be a successful method of reducing its trade deficit because other elements of the national saving and investment identity like private saving or investment may change instead. But in those cases when the budget deficit is the main cause of the trade deficit, governments should take steps to reduce their budget deficits, lest they make their economy vulnerable to a rapid outflow of international financial capital that could bring a deep recession.

Conclusion

Nothing in this chapter should be taken to suggest that government budgets should be balanced or in surplus every year, regardless of whether an economy is in recession. A government need not fear annual budget deficits, or even a sustained pattern of budget deficits, as long as its overall debt/GDP ratio is not continually increasing. After all, just as firms borrow to make investments in physical capital, governments might reasonably borrow to make investments in publicly owned physical capital, in the education system that builds human capital, and in the research and development that creates the technologies of the future.

But although a wise government may sometimes run budget deficits, it will also take care that its borrowing does not grow ever-larger for a sustained period of time. Government budget deficits involve borrowing in financial capital markets, and when deficits are large for a sustained period of time, high levels of government borrowing can cause severe economic problems. The previous chapter discussed the danger that if high levels of government spending or tax cuts cause large budget deficits, the resulting increase in aggregate demand can cause inflationary increases in the price level. Within the domestic economy, high levels of government borrowing can drive up interest rates and crowd out financial capital that would otherwise have been available to private firms. If government borrowing is being financed mainly with an inflow of foreign investment capital, the economy can become vulnerable to exchange rate depreciation and a deep recession if those foreign investors decide to stop providing financial capital. The economic costs of a sustained pattern of overly large budget deficits can be very high.

Key Concepts and Summary

1. A change in any part of the national saving and investment identity points out that if the government budget deficit changes, then either saving, private investment in physical capital or the trade balance—or some combination of the three—*must* change as well.
2. Economic growth comes from a combination of investment in physical capital, human capital, and technology. Government borrowing can **crowd out** private sector investment in physical capital, but fiscal policy can also increase investment in publicly owned physical capital, human capital (education) and research and development.
3. Possible methods for improving education and society's investment in human capital include spending more money on teachers and other educational resources and reorganizing the education system to provide greater incentives for success.
4. Methods for increasing research and development spending to generate new technology include direct government spending on R&D and tax incentives for business to conduct additional R&D.
5. The theory of **Ricardian equivalence** holds that changes in government borrowing or saving will be offset by changes in private saving. Thus, higher budget deficits will be offset by greater private saving, while larger budget surpluses would be offset by greater private borrowing. If the theory holds true, then changes in government borrowing or saving would have no effect on private investment in physical capital or on the trade balance. However, empirical evidence suggests that the theory holds true only partially.
6. If the funding for a larger budget deficit comes from international financial investors, then a budget deficit may be accompanied by a trade deficit. In some countries, this pattern of "twin deficits" has set the stage for international financial investors first to send their funds to a country and cause an appreciation of its exchange rate and then to pull their funds out and cause a depreciation of the exchange rate and a financial crisis as well.
7. The government need not balance its budget every year. However, a sustained pattern of large budget deficits over time risks causing several negative macroeconomic outcomes: a shift to the right in aggregate demand that causes an inflationary increase in the price level; crowding out private investment in physical capital in a way that slows down economic growth; and creating a dependence on inflows of international portfolio investment that can sometimes turn into outflows of foreign financial investment that can be injurious to a macroeconomy.

Review Questions

1. Based on the national saving and investment identity, what are the three ways the macroeconomy might react to greater government budget deficits?
2. How would you expect larger budget deficits to affect private-sector investment in physical capital? Why?
3. What are some of the ways that fiscal policy might encourage economic growth?
4. What are some fiscal policies for improving society's level of human capital?
5. What are some fiscal policies of improving the technologies that the economy will have to draw upon in the future?
6. What is the theory of Ricardian equivalence?
7. Under what conditions will a larger budget deficit cause a trade deficit?

CHAPTER

34

Macroeconomic Policy around the World

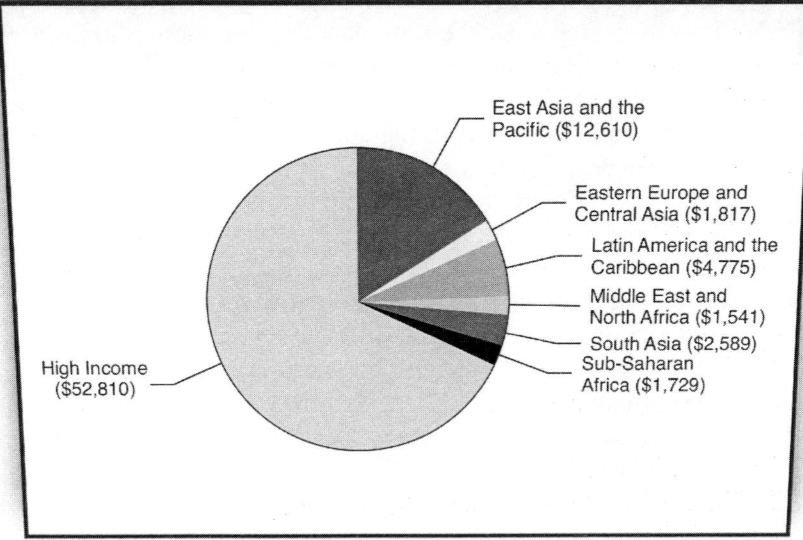

Chapter Outline

- The Diversity of Countries and Economies across the World
- Economic Growth
- Lower Unemployment
- Policies for Lower Inflation
- Policies for a Sustainable Balance of Trade
- Final Thoughts on Economics and Market Institutions

Given the extraordinary differences across the economies of all the countries of the world, can the same macroeconomic analysis possibly apply to all of them? For example, China had an estimated population of nearly 1.4 billion people in 2015, a per capita GDP of about $8,000, and a fast-growing economy over the previous several decades. The United States had a population of about 320 million, less than one-fourth that of China, but had a per capita GDP of about $55,000 in 2015, according to statistics from the World Bank. Although inflation in the U.S. economy has been quite low in recent years, the U.S. economy in the mid-2000s had several years in which its budget deficit and trade deficit exceeded 4% of GDP. Venezuela has a population of 30 million, less than one-tenth of the U.S. population. Its per capita GDP was about $15,000 in 2015, but inflation in Venezuela was at an annual rate of 700% for some months in mid-2015.

Despite the obvious and enormous differences across the more than 200 countries of the world, the general structure of macroeconomic analysis can be applied in China, the United States, Venezuela, and other countries as well. Of course, every economy has its own distinctive characteristics, and thus may well require macroeconomic policies aimed at its own specific issues. Nevertheless, the four goals of macroeconomic policy—growth in standard of living, low unemployment, low inflation, and a sustainable balance of trade—are universal. The macroeconomic frameworks of analysis, including a short-run Keynesian perspective that focuses on fluctuations in aggregate demand and a long-term neoclassical perspective that focuses on economic growth and gradual increases in potential GDP, are useful in the analysis of any economy. The macroeconomic toolkit of monetary policy and fiscal policy is available to every country. This chapter begins with a discussion of the diversity of the economies in the world. It then discusses how countries around the world can seek to address the four macroeconomic goals, using the Keynesian and neoclassical frameworks for analysis and the tools of monetary and fiscal policy.

The Diversity of Countries and Economies across the World

The national economies that make up the global economy are remarkably diverse. The GDP of Spain, for example, with its population of approximately 47 million, is larger than the total GDP of all the nations of sub-Saharan Africa, which have a combined population of 875 million.

Exhibit 34-1 presents a snapshot view of the world GDP and population in 2014, in which the world is divided into seven regions. The differences across these regions are remarkable. For example, per capita GDP for the 525 million people living in Latin America and the Caribbean region is approximately six times larger than the per capita GDP of the 2.7 billion people living in South Asia and sub-Saharan Africa. In turn, the people in the high-income nations of the world, including the United States, western Europe, and Japan, have a per capita GDP that is more than quadruple that of the people of Latin America. The high-income economies of the world have about 18% of the world's population, but they produce and consume about 70% of the world's GDP.

Such comparisons between regions of the world are admittedly rough. After all, per capita GDP does not capture the standard of living in a precise way. Many other factors have a large impact, like health, education, human rights, crime and personal safety, cleanliness of environment, and others. Exhibit 34-2 shows a few selected measures of health and education: the death rate for children under age five, life expectancy, and illiteracy rates. These measures also reveal very wide differences in the standard of living across the regions of the world.

EXHIBIT 34-1 Global Comparisons of GDP and Population in 2014

	GDP (in billions of dollars)	Population (in millions)	Per Capita GDP
East Asia and the Pacific	$12,610	2,021	$6,156
Eastern Europe and Central Asia	$1,817	264	$6,892
Latin America and the Caribbean	$4,775	525	$8,990
Middle East and North Africa	$1,541	357	$4,722
South Asia	$2,589	1,721	$1,496
Sub-Saharan Africa	$1,729	973	$1,638
High income	$52,810	1,399	$38,274

EXHIBIT 34-2 Other Measures of Standard of Living circa 2014

	Death Rate for Population under Age 5 in 2014 (per 1,000 live births)	Life Expectancy at Birth in 2013 (in years)	Adult Literacy Rate circa 2010
East Asia and the Pacific	18	74	95%
Eastern Europe and Central Asia	21	72	98%
Latin America and the Caribbean	19	74	92%
Middle East and North Africa	25	72	78%
South Asia	53	68	67%
Sub-Saharan Africa	83	58	60%
High income	7	79	99%

Yet the differences in economic statistics and other measures of well-being, substantial though they are, do not fully capture the enormous differences among countries that also shape their economic situation. Countries have geographic differences: some have extensive coastlines, some are landlocked; some have large rivers that have been a path of commerce for centuries, others have mountains that have been a barrier to trade; some have deserts, some have rain forests. Countries have considerable differences in the age distribution of the population. Many high-income nations are approaching a situation by 2020 or so in which the elderly will form a much larger share of the population; most low-income countries still have a higher proportion of youth and young adults, but by about 2050, the elderly populations in these low-income countries are expected to boom as well. Countries have differences in industry structure. In the high-income economies of the world, only about 1.5% of GDP comes from agriculture; the average for the rest of the world is 10%. Countries have strong differences in degree of urbanization: in the high income countries of the world, along with the regions of Latin America and eastern Europe/Central Asia, about 60–70% of people live in urban areas. In East Asia, sub-Saharan Africa, and South Asia, only about 40–50% of the population lives in urban areas. Countries have strong differences in economic institutions: some nations have economies that are extremely market-oriented, while other nations have command economies. Some nations are open to international trade, while others use tariffs and import quotas to limit the impact of trade. Some nations are torn by long-standing armed conflicts; other nations are largely at peace. There are differences in political institutions, religious, and social institutions as well.

No nation intentionally aims for a low standard of living, high rates of unemployment and inflation, or an unsustainable trade imbalance. However, nations will differ in their priorities and in the situations in which they find themselves, and so their policy choices can reasonably vary, too. The next sections will discuss how nations around the world, from high-income to low-income, approach the four macroeconomic goals of economic growth, low unemployment, low inflation, and a sustainable balance of trade.

Economic Growth

Economic growth is built on a foundation of productivity improvements. In turn, productivity improvements are the result of improvements in human capital, physical capital, and technology, interacting in a market-driven economy. But in the pursuit of economic growth, some countries and regions are starting from a higher level than others, as illustrated by the differences in per capita GDP presented earlier in Exhibit 34-1. In thinking about how nations around the world should pursue the goal of raising their standard of living, it's useful to divide the nations of the world into three groups: (1) technology leaders, which includes high-income countries like the United States, Canada, Japan, and western Europe; (2) converging countries, which have shown some ability, even if not always sustained, to catch up to the technology leaders; and (3) the technologically disconnected, a group representing perhaps a third of the world's population, which has lagged behind economically.

Growth Policies for the Technological Leaders

For the high-income countries, the problem of economic growth is to push continually for a more educated workforce that can create, invest in, and apply new technologies. In effect, the goal of their growth-oriented public policy is to shift their aggregate supply curves to the right. Their main public policies targeted at achieving this goal are fiscal policies focused on investment, including investment in human capital, in technology, and in physical plant and equipment. These countries also recognize that economic growth works best in a stable and market-oriented economic climate, and they thus use monetary policy to keep inflation low and stable, to minimize the risk of exchange rate fluctuations, while also encouraging domestic and international competition.

However, in the second decade of the 2000s, many high-income countries have found themselves more focused on the short term than on the long term. The United States, the countries of the European Union, and Japan have all experienced a combination of financial crisis and deep recession, and the after-effects of the recession—like higher unemployment rates—then lingered for several years. Most of these governments took aggressive and in some cases controversial steps to cushion the pain of the recession and to attempt to jump-start their economies. But having run very large budget deficits as part of an expansionary fiscal policy to fight recession, they now find themselves needing to chart a politically unpleasant but economically necessary course toward some combination of lower spending and higher taxes over time. Similarly, many central banks ran highly expansionary monetary policies, with both near-zero interest rates and with unconventional quantitative easing monetary policies that involved having central banks make an array of loans and investments. There are a number of challenges in how to envision and enact monetary policy in the years ahead. As earlier chapters have discussed, macroeconomics needs to have both a short-run and a long-run focus. The challenge for many high-income countries in the next few years will be to extricate themselves from the aftermath of the 2007–2009 recession, along with the specific policies adopted in fighting that recession, while not neglecting their foundation for future long-term growth. After all, for the high income countries of the world, the combination of new technology, education, and physical capital investment has now been generating long-run economic growth since the Industrial Revolution of the early 1800s.

Growth Policies for the Converging Economies

The converging countries include China, India, many countries in the regions of East Asia and the Pacific, Latin America and the Caribbean, and eastern Europe. Firms and workers in these economies can often build upon or copy technologies and industries developed by the technology leaders. They can also find niches that they are well-suited to fill in the global networks of economic production.

The world's great economic success stories in the last few decades started back in the 1970s with that group of nations sometimes known as the east Asian "tigers": South Korea, Thailand, Malaysia, Indonesia, and Singapore. (The list of east Asian tigers also sometimes includes Hong Kong and Taiwan, although these are sometimes treated under international law as part of China, rather than as separate countries.) The economic growth of these east Asian tigers has been phenomenal, typically averaging 5.5% real per capita growth for several decades. In the 1980s, the economy of China began growing rapidly, often at annual rates of 7–10% per year. In the 1990s, the economy of India began growing rapidly, first at rates of about 5% per year, but then increasing in the first decade of the 2000s.

It's worth pausing a moment to marvel at these growth rates. If per capita GDP grows at, say, 6% per year, then applying the formula for compound growth rates—that is $(1 + .06)^{30}$—a nation's level of per capita GDP will rise by a multiple of almost 6 over 30 years. In a technological leader, chugging along with per capita growth rates of about 2% per year, multiplying per capita GDP by a factor of five would take about 80 years. In these fast-growing countries, the average standard of living rose by a factor of five in a time period less than an adult's working life—for instance, as a person ages from 25 to 55.

The underlying causes of these rapid growth rates are fairly clear. China and the east Asian tigers, in particular, have been among the highest savers in the world, often saving one-third or more of GDP, as compared to the roughly 20% of GDP, which would be a more typical saving rate in Latin America and Africa. These countries invested heavily in human capital, first building up primary-level education and then expanding secondary-level education, with a particular focus on encouraging the math and science skills that are useful in engineering and business. They made a concerted effort to seek out applicable technology, both by sending students and government commissions abroad to look at the most efficient industrial operations elsewhere and by opening up to foreign companies that wished to build plants in their countries. China and India in particular also allowed far greater freedom for market forces, both within their own domestic economies and also in encouraging their firms to participate in world markets. This combination of technology, human capital, and physical capital, combined with the incentives of a market-oriented economic context, proved an extremely powerful stimulant to growth.

Some of the economic policies of the governments of east Asia, China, India, and other fast-growing countries around the world have gone beyond providing a generally fertile climate for free markets and practiced more interventionist economic policies. Many of these converging countries have a legacy of government economic controls—for example, China, India, and the countries of eastern Europe that used to be part of the Soviet Union—that for political reasons can be dismantled only slowly over time. In many of these countries, the banking and financial sector is heavily regulated. The governments of these countries have also sometimes selected certain industries to receive low-interest loans or government subsidies. Such policies often raise the eyebrows of market-oriented economists, but economic policies should be evaluated on their actual effects, which can be positive or negative, not on the basis of the promises of their supporters or the theories of economists. The appropriate mixture between markets and government will not look the same for every country. But while government will play a different role across countries, all the converging economies have found that an increased dose of market-oriented incentives for firms and workers has been a critical ingredient in the recipe for faster growth.

Growth Policies for the Technologically Disconnected

Many of the technologically excluded areas of the world are in Africa, but pockets of disconnection are found in other areas as well: southern Mexico and certain tropical areas of central America and Brazil; interior portions of China far from the coastal trading areas; some of the central Asian nations that used to be part of the Soviet Union, like Mongolia. The level of poverty and human deprivation in these areas can be heartrending. The short answer to the question of what many people of these countries need is "almost everything." Thus, they need to invest in human capital, first by improving basic levels of education and health, and then building toward additional education and health services. They need banks and financial intermediaries to help mobilize domestic investment. They need economic and legal stability, along with market-oriented institutions, both to provide a fertile climate for domestic economic growth and to attract foreign investment. They need to find ways to participate in global trade and investment.

But even this vast agenda has something missing. After all, these countries are not just lagging behind, but they have shown little evidence of catching up, or even of being much connected to the rest of the world economy. Along with the general growth-oriented agenda, these countries need an improved infrastructure of communication and transportation, along with research into technology focused on their particular economic realities.

Connecting the economy of a region or country used to require transportation of goods: roads for wagons and trucks and ports for barges and ships. It still takes these kinds of transportation links, but in the modern economy, communications have become at least as important. If a company in Europe is thinking about relying on a supplier based in Africa, it must have the ability to communicate with that African firm to place orders, to check on delivery dates, to send engineering plans of what product is desired, to deal with billing, and all the other day-to-day issues of a modern firm. If communication isn't reliable, then the supplier is not viewed as reliable either—regardless of how hardworking the employees are or what high-quality goods or services they produce. In a growing number of industries, communications can provide a way of delivering the services themselves. For example, customer service calls can be answered and records updated from far-distant locations. Exhibit 34-3 compares the major regions of the world economy in some measures of transportation and communication: roads, telephones, and computers. Given that these disconnected areas have found it difficult or impossible to generate these sorts of investments for themselves, or to find foreign investors willing to put up the money, perhaps foreign aid will need to play in funding these sorts of projects.

A second main set of policies for the technologically disconnected is to recognize that these countries often face local technology issues. For example, in much of Africa,

EXHIBIT 34-3 Transportation and Communications

	Mobile Cellular Subscription per 100 People (2014)	Internet Users per 100 People (2014)	Percentage of Roads That Are Paved (2009)
East Asia and the Pacific	100	42	62%
Eastern Europe and Central Asia	113	48	86%
Latin America and the Caribbean	111	47	23%
Middle East and North Africa	101	32	79%
South Asia	75	16	54%
Sub-Saharan Africa	71	19	19%
High income	123	80	81%

annual rainfall is low and the soil is composed of a particular type of rock ("Basement Complex"), which is low in what agriculture specialists call "micronutrients." As a result, many of the high-yield plants and specific fertilizers developed for use in the United States or western Europe, or even for climates like India and Latin America, don't grow as well in Africa. Research and development focused on African agriculture might find ways for remarkable gains in output, but research applicable to U.S. and European farmers often won't provide as much benefit for African farmers.

Another important technology area for these countries involves health and medical research. For example, approximately 500 million cases of malaria occur each year, resulting in one million or more deaths a year. Almost all of these deaths are in low-income tropical areas of the world. If a fraction of the pharmaceutical research currently devoted to finding ways to reduce hair loss or increase sexual performance for middle-aged men in high-income economies could be directed to anti-malarial drugs, the gain to global human welfare could be very large. One economic study found that countries with intensive malaria had rates of economic growth that averaged 1.3% per year less than comparable countries without intensive malaria and that a 10% reduction in malaria, all by itself, could increase a country's economic growth rate by 0.3%. If the poorest people in the world could spend less time sick and more time learning and working, their economies could benefit considerably.

Although all countries desire economic growth, the focus of their policies is somewhat different. High-income technology leaders must find ways to generate and apply new technologies. Converging economies must improve their educational systems and seek out their niches in the global economy. The technologically disconnected need a full economic growth agenda: investment in private and public physical capital, education, applying existing technology, and finding new technologies that apply specifically to their situation.

Lower Unemployment

The causes of unemployment in high-income countries of the world can be categorized in two ways: either cyclical unemployment caused by the economy being in a recession, or the natural rate of unemployment caused by factors in labor markets like government regulations about conditions of hiring and starting businesses, which have discouraged employment.

Unemployment from a Recession

For unemployment caused by a recession, the Keynesian economic model points out that monetary and fiscal policy tools are available. The monetary policy prescription for dealing with recession is straightforward: run an expansionary monetary policy to increase the

The Debate over Foreign Aid

About $125 billion per year in foreign aid flows from the high-income countries of the world to the low-income ones. Relative to the size of their populations or economies, this is not a large amount for either donors or recipients. For low-income countries of the world, aid averages between 1–2% of their GDP, although the amount is larger in some countries and smaller in others. But even this relatively small amount has been highly controversial.

Supporters of additional foreign aid point to the extraordinary human suffering in the low- and middle-income countries of the world. They see opportunities all across Africa, Asia, and Latin America to set up health clinics and schools. They want to help with the task of building economic infrastructure: clean water, plumbing, electricity, and roads. Some also suggest helping start businesses to provide jobs and income in poor areas, by supporting all kinds of businesses from small farming and handcraft operations to factories that would make clothing or steel.

Opponents of increased aid don't quarrel with the goal of reducing human suffering, but they suggest that foreign aid has often proven a poor tool for advancing that goal. For example, what if a foreign aid donor gives money for a health program, and then the government of the recipient country cuts back its own spending on health care and instead spends that money on weapons used for attacking another country or persecuting a disfavored group in its own country? What if the aid donor tries to provide technology for helping farmers be more productive, but the government reacts to political pressure by urban food consumers by imposing price ceilings on farm products, so the farmers can't make a living anyway? Even worse, foreign aid has sometimes financed projects that turned out to be environmentally destructive and economically questionable, like dams across large rivers that required enormous forced resettlement of poor people, to produce electricity that the local economy couldn't use and most individuals couldn't afford.

Finally, if the government of a country creates a reasonably stable and market-oriented macroeconomic climate, then foreign investors will be likely to provide funds for many profitable activities. Conversely, if the government creates an unstable economic environment, foreign aid can't fix the problem. As a result, foreign aid is either redundant or ineffective.

Policymakers are now sadder and wiser about the limitations of foreign aid than they were a few decades ago. But wisdom need not mean cynicism. In targeted and specific cases, foreign aid can have a modest role to play in reducing the extreme levels of deprivation experienced by hundreds of millions of people around the world.

quantity of money and loans, drive down interest rates, and increase aggregate demand. In a recession, there is usually relatively little danger of inflation taking off, and so even a central bank that has fighting inflation as its top priority can usually justify some reduction in interest rates in a recession. With regard to fiscal policy, the automatic stabilizers embodied in fiscal policy should be allowed to work, even if this means larger budget deficits in time of recession. There is less agreement over whether, in addition to automatic stabilizers, governments in a recession should try to adopt discretionary fiscal policy of additional tax cuts or spending increases. In the case of the Great Recession from 2007–2009, the case for this kind of extra-aggressive expansionary fiscal policy is strong, but for a smaller recession, given the time lags of implementing fiscal policy, discretionary fiscal policy should be used with caution.

However, the aftermath of the 2007–2009 recession emphasizes that expansionary fiscal and monetary policy do not turn off a recession like flipping a switch turns off a lamp. Even after a recession is officially over, and positive growth has returned, it can take months—or even a few years—before private-sector firms believe fully that the economic climate is healthy enough so that they can expand their workforce.

The Natural Rate of Unemployment

Unemployment rates in the nations of Europe have typically been higher than in the United States. For example, in 2015, the U.S. unemployment rate was about 5.5%, compared with the average unemployment rate of 10.4% for the European countries that use the euro as a currency. The pattern of generally higher unemployment rates in Europe, which dates back to the 1970s, is typically attributed to the fact that European economies have a higher natural rate of unemployment because they have passed a greater number of rules and restrictions that have discouraged firms from hiring and unemployed workers from taking jobs. In recent years, difficulties related to the functioning of the euro across the countries of Europe have contributed to higher unemployment rates in some countries as well.

Addressing the natural rate of unemployment is straightforward in theory, but difficult in practice. Government can play a useful role in providing unemployment and welfare payments, passing rules about where and when businesses can operate, assuring that the workplace is safe, and so on. But these well-intended laws can in some cases become so intrusive that businesses decide to place limits on their hiring. For example, a law that imposes large costs on a business that tries to fire or lay off workers will mean that businesses try to avoid hiring in the first place. Laws that require employers to offer generous benefits to workers, like health insurance, child care, and vacation time, will make it more expensive to hire workers. Laws that offer generous and lengthy unemployment benefits or family leave will reduce the incentives of workers to find new jobs.

In recent decades, the world champion in restrictive labor laws in the last few decades was probably India. The government of India has gone through a number of economic reforms in the last decade or so to ease these laws. But looking back to the late 1990s, India had about 50 major labor laws. They required that employers did everything from providing pensions and health insurance, which isn't all that unusual, to running health clinics and subsidizing lunchrooms, which is less common. There were rules that any employer with more than 100 employees must notify the government of any change in job content or employee status, and in some industries, employees must agree before any changes were made. If a firm had more than 25 workers, it had to fill all job vacancies from a state list. If a firm had more than 100 workers, it needed government permission before firing anyone. It was also forbidden for a firm in India to react to these laws by declaring bankruptcy. Public sector jobs in India offered not only lifetime employment, but sometimes even a guarantee of a job after death, since an employee's job could be inherited by a relative. Little wonder, when faced with this blizzard of laws, that only about 3% of India's "official" economy was officially in private firms of more than 10 employees, since small firms are not affected by these laws. The attempts to get around these restrictions create weird categories, like people who are "working nonemployees," and then in turn create more laws to deal with these categories. India has made some attempts to scale back on these laws, but in 2007, over 90% of the workers in India still worked in the "informal" sector. Given these kinds of laws, it is little wonder that many firms in India have remained reluctant to hire anyone who might legally be treated as an official employee.

The challenge in addressing the natural rate of unemployment is to be both softhearted and hardheaded. Yes, workers deserve certain protections. But if those protections are implemented in a way that leads to a high natural rate of unemployment, then they need to be redesigned.

Undeveloped Labor Markets

The low-income and middle-income countries of this world face an employment issue that goes beyond unemployment as it is understood in the high-income economies of the world. A substantial number of workers in these economies provide many of their own needs by farming, fishing, or hunting. They barter and trade with others and may take a succession of short-term or one-day jobs, sometimes being paid with food or shelter, sometimes with money. They are not "unemployed" in the sense that term is used in the United States and Europe, but neither do they have an activity that utilizes their energies and talents appropriately, nor a regular wage-paying job.

The starting point of economic activity, as discussed back in Chapter 1, is the division of labor, in which workers specialize in certain tasks and trade the fruits of their labor with others. Workers who are not connected to a labor market are often unable to specialize very much. Because these workers are not "officially" employed, they are often not eligible for social benefits like unemployment insurance or old-age payments—if such payments are even available in their low-income economy. Helping these workers to become more connected to the labor market and the economy is an important policy goal. Indeed, recent research by development economists suggests that one of the key factors in raising people in low-income countries out of the worst kind of poverty is whether they can make a connection to a somewhat regular wage-paying job.

Policies for Lower Inflation

Here's a bold prediction of the sort that economists almost always live to regret making: among the high-income economies of the world, inflation isn't likely to be a severe problem in the foreseeable future. Yes, mild spurts of inflation may occur now and then. In the aftermath of the recession of 2007–2009, when governments around the world made aggressive use of expansionary fiscal and monetary policy, it's possible that inflation will eventually rise by a few percentage points for a few years. At some point in the future, aggregate demand may move ahead of potential GDP, perhaps fueled by overoptimistic lending by banks or a surge of export sales or a wave of government spending when the economy is already near full employment. At some times, the short-term aggregate supply curve will shift back to the left, creating inflationary pressures. One common cause is a sudden rise in input prices, perhaps from higher oil prices or because a nation's exchange rate suddenly weakens, driving up the price of all imported inputs to production at once.

But while inflationary pressures will sometimes arise in the short run, policymakers of the high-income economies appear to have learned some lessons about fighting inflation. First, whatever happens with aggregate supply and aggregate demand in the short run, monetary policy can be used to prevent inflation from becoming entrenched in the economy in the medium and long term. Second, there is no long-run gain to letting higher levels of inflation become established. As the neoclassical model points out, in the long run the potential output of the economy and its growth rate, along with its natural rate of unemployment, are determined by the underlying economic factors like levels of investment in human capital, physical capital, and technology, and by the incentives provided in markets. In fact, allowing inflation to become lasting and persistent poses undesirable risks and trade-offs. When inflation is high, businesses and individuals need to spend time and effort worrying about protecting themselves against inflation, rather than seeking out better ways to serve customers.

In short, the high-income economies appear to have both a political consensus to hold inflation low and the economic tools to do so. To be sure, disputes will continue over whether the central bank should use contractionary monetary policy to raise interest rates if the inflation rate is, say, 4% rather than 2% per year. But people who live in countries that have experienced hyperinflation at rates of 50% *per month* and more would laugh at the idea that inflation at rates of less than 5% a year is a devastating economic problem.

In a number of middle- and low-income economies around the world, inflation is far from a solved problem. In the early 2000s, Turkey experienced inflation of more than 50% per year for several years. From 2008–2010, Myanmar had inflation rates of 20–30% per year. Indonesia, Iran, Nigeria, and the Russian Federation all had double-digit inflation for most of the years from 2000–2010. From 2011–2014, the inflation rate of Sudan fluctuated between 20% and 40%. Argentina, Belarus, Ghana, and Ukraine all had double-digit inflation in 2014. Zimbabwe had hyperinflation, with inflation rates that went from more than 100% per year in the mid-2000s to a rate of several million percent in 2008. Venezuela had an inflation rate above 700% for a few months in mid-2015.

In these countries, the problem of high inflation generally arises from undisciplined macroeconomic policy. For example, a government may run an expansionary policy of huge and sustained budget deficits, which shift aggregate demand to the right so that output is beyond the potential GDP level, leading to inflationary increases in the price level. In some countries, the central bank is viewed as a mechanism for making loans to politically favored firms, without much regard to the effect on aggregate demand. Such policies can clearly lead to a sustained inflation.

But even when a small economy runs sensible fiscal and monetary policies, it can be vulnerable to inflation. One set of risks comes from global economic factors. For example, imagine a small economy that relies heavily on a few exported products, like coffee or copper. If the price of these goods should rise sharply on world markets, it will cause a flood of buying power for the local economy. Or imagine a small economy that becomes this year's popular destination for tourism, or for foreign investment. An amount of aggregate demand that is relatively small by the standards of the American or European economy can be a relatively large increase in consumer and investment spending in a small middle- or low-income economy. Yet another set of inflationary risks for a converging economy follow from the patterns of growth in that economy. If the GDP is growing quite briskly, at an annual rate of 6%, 8%, or even 10% per year, if aggregate demand jumps out ahead of aggregate supply, it may do so in a fairly dramatic fashion—much more dramatic than if the economy was only growing at the technological leader rate of 2% or so per year.

No country benefits from extremely high levels of inflation. However, a number of countries have managed to sustain solid levels of economic growth for sustained periods of time with levels of inflation that would sound high by recent U.S. standards, like 10–30% per year. In such economies, most contracts, wage levels, and interest rates are either indexed to inflation, or take place using the currency of another country, like the U.S. dollar or Europe's euro, to sidestep the problem of inflation. It is clearly possible—and perhaps sometimes necessary—for a converging economy to live with a degree of uncertainty over inflation that would be politically unacceptable in the high-income economies.

Policies for a Sustainable Balance of Trade

In the 1950s and 1960s, and even into the 1970s, openness to global flows of goods, services, and financial capital was often viewed in a negative light by low- and middle-income countries of the world. These countries feared that foreign trade would mean both economic losses as their economy was "exploited" by high-income trading partners and a loss of domestic political control to powerful business interests and multinational corporations.

These negative feelings about international trade have evolved. After all, the great economic success stories of recent years like Japan, the east Asian tiger economies, and China, and India, all took advantage of opportunities to sell in global markets. The economies of Europe thrive with high levels of trade. In the North American Free Trade Agreement, the United States, Canada, and Mexico pledged themselves to reduce trade barriers. Many countries have clearly learned that reducing barriers to trade is at least *potentially* beneficial to their economy. Indeed, many smaller economies of the world have learned an even tougher lesson: if they don't participate actively in world trade, they are unlikely to join the success stories among the converging economies. There are no examples in world history of small economies that remained apart from the global economy but still attained a high standard of living.

But although almost every country now claims that its goal is to participate in global trade, the possible negative consequences of trade have remained highly controversial in recent years. It is useful to divide up these possible negative consequences into issues involving trade of goods and services and issues involving flows of international capital. These issues are related, but not the same. An economy may have a high level of trade in goods and services relative to GDP, but if exports and imports are balanced, the net flow of foreign investment in and out of the economy will be zero. Conversely, an economy may have only a moderate level of trade relative to GDP, but find that it has a substantial current account trade imbalance. Thus, it is useful to consider the concerns over international trade of goods and services and international flows of financial capital separately.

Concerns over International Trade in Goods and Services

There is a long list of worries about foreign trade in goods and services: fear of job loss, environmental dangers, unfair labor practices, and many other concerns. These arguments were discussed at some length in Chapter 6, and there's no need to review the details here.

But in this final chapter, it's useful to remember the overall response of many economists to these issues about free trade in goods and services. There's an old saying: "Don't throw out the baby with the bathwater." In other words, when you're discarding stuff you don't want, be careful not to throw out something precious, too. Sure, international trade raises many public policy issues—in fact, many of the issues raised by the competitive forces of international trade are the same issues raised by competitive market forces in the domestic economy as well, as one state or region or company within a national economy competes against others. Of all of the arguments for limitations on trade, perhaps the most controversial one among economists is the infant industry argument; that is, subsidizing or protecting new industries for a time until they become established. Such policies have been used with some success at certain places and times, but in the world as a whole, support for key industries is far more often directed at long-established industries with substantial political power that are suffering losses and laying off workers, rather than potentially vibrant new industries that have yet to be established. If government is going to favor certain industries, it needs to do so in a way that is temporary and that orients those industries toward a future of market competition, rather than a future of unending government subsidies and trade protection.

Concerns over International Flows of Capital

The expected pattern of trade imbalances in the world economy is that high-income economies will run trade surpluses, which means they will experience a net outflow of capital to foreign destinations, while low- and middle-income economies will run trade deficits, which means that they will experience a net inflow of foreign capital. This pattern of international investing can benefit all sides. Investors in the high-income countries benefit because they can receive high returns on their investments, and also because they can diversify their investments so that they are at less risk of a downturn in their own domestic economy. The low-income economies that receive an inflow of capital presumably have potential for rapid catch-up economic growth, and they can use the inflow of international financial capital to help spur their physical capital investment. In addition, inflows of financial capital often come with management, technological expertise, and training.

But for the last couple of decades, this cheerful scenario faces two dark clouds. The first cloud is the large current account deficits in the U.S. economy. Instead of offering net financial investment abroad, the U.S. economy is soaking up financial investment from all over the world. These substantial U.S. trade deficits cannot grow forever. The question is whether they will be reduced gradually or with a bang. In the gradual scenario, U.S. exports could grow more rapidly than imports over a period of years, perhaps aided by a depreciation of the U.S. dollar. But the U.S. trade deficit could also be reduced with a bang. Here's one scenario: if foreign investors became less willing to hold U.S. dollar assets, the dollar exchange rate could weaken. As speculators see this process happening, they might rush to unload their dollar assets, which would drive the dollar down still further. A lower U.S. dollar would stimulate aggregate demand by making exports cheaper and imports more expensive. It would mean higher prices for imported inputs throughout the economy, shifting the short-term aggregate supply curve to the left. The result could involve considerable disruption for the U.S. economy. People sometimes talk as if the U.S. economy, with its great size, is invulnerable to this sort of pressure from international markets. But while it's tough to rock the $18 trillion U.S. economy, it's not impossible.

The second major issue is how the smaller economies of the world should deal with the possibility of sudden inflows and outflows of foreign financial capital. One vivid recent example of the potentially destructive forces of international capital movements occurred in the economies of the East Asian tigers in 1997–98. Thanks to their excellent growth performance over the last few decades, these economies had attracted considerable interest from foreign investors. But in the mid-1990s, foreign investment into these countries surged even further. Much of this money was funneled through banks that borrowed in

U.S. dollars and loaned in their national currencies. Bank lending surged at rates of 20% per year or more. This inflow of foreign capital meant that investment in these economies exceeded the level of domestic savings, so that current account deficits in these countries jumped into the range of 5–10% of GDP. But the surge in bank lending meant that many banks in these east Asian countries did not do an especially good job of screening out safe and unsafe borrowers. Many of the loans—as high as 10–15% of all loans in some of these countries—started to turn bad. Fearing losses, foreign investors started pulling their money out. As the foreign money left, the exchange rates of these countries crashed, often falling by 50% or more in a few months. The banks were stuck with a mismatch: even if the rest of their domestic loans were repaid, they could never pay back the U.S. dollars that they owed. The banking sector as a whole went bankrupt. The lack of credit and lending in the economy collapsed aggregate demand, bringing on a deep recession.

A similar scenario played itself out in several European countries in the last few years, including Greece, Spain, Ireland, and Portugal. As these countries joined the euro zone, they appeared to be much safer places for foreign investment capital, and they experienced a large inflow of international capital. Sometimes this inflow of foreign capital led to a construction boom and a bubble in housing prices; sometimes this inflow of foreign capital allowed very high government budget deficits. But these continuing inflows of foreign capital were not sustainable, and when they stopped, these countries experienced deep recessions and high unemployment.

If the flow and ebb of international capital markets can flip economies from the East Asian tigers to countries across Europe into recession, then it is no wonder that other middle- and low-income countries around the world are concerned. Thus, many nations are taking steps to reduce the risk that their economy will be injured if foreign financial capital takes flight, including having their central banks hold large reserves of foreign exchange and stepping up their regulation of domestic banks to avoid a wave of imprudent lending. The most controversial steps in this area involve countries should try to take steps to control or reduce the flows of foreign capital. If a country could discourage some of the inflow of speculative short-term capital, and instead only encourage investment capital that was committed for the medium term and the long term, then it could be at least somewhat less susceptible to swings in the sentiments of global investors.

How Much Economic Growth Is Enough?

In 1930, with the world economy slipping down into the Depression, the great economist John Maynard Keynes wrote a famous essay called "Economic Possibilities for Our Grandchildren," in which he fearlessly prophesied that with sustained economic growth, the "economic problem" of humanity would be solved in about 100 years because people will have pretty much all the goods and services that they want. Keynes wrote:

> If capital increases, say, 2 percent per annum, the capital equipment of the world will have increased by a half in 20 years, and seven and a half times in 100 years. Think of this in terms of material things—houses, transport, and the like. . . . I would predict that the standard of life in progressive countries one hundred years hence will be between four to eight times as high as it is to-day. There would be nothing surprising about this even in the light of our present knowledge. It would not be foolish to contemplate the possibility of a far greater progress still. . . . I draw the conclusion that, assuming no important wars and no important increase in population, the *economic problem* may be solved, or be at least within sight of solution, within a hundred years. . . . Thus for the first time since his creation man will be faced with his real, his permanent problem—how to use his freedom from pressing economic cares, how to occupy the leisure, which science and compound interest will have won for him, to live wisely and agreeably and well.

Keynes's prediction of economic growth rates of about 2% per year has (roughly) come true. Do you agree with his conclusion that by 2030, the economic problem will have been overcome, at least in certain parts of the world? Or will people's expectations and demands continue to rise over time?

If economies participate in the global trade of goods and services, they will also need to participate in international flows of financial payments and investments. These linkages can offer great benefits to an economy. But any nation that is experiencing a substantial and sustained pattern of trade deficits, along with the corresponding net inflow of international financial capital, has some reason for concern.

Final Thoughts on Economics and Market Institutions

The standard of living has increased dramatically for billions of people around the world in the last half century. Such increases have occurred not only in the technological leaders like the United States, Canada, the nations of Europe and Japan, but also in the east Asian tigers and in many nations of Latin America and eastern Europe.

In more recent years, some of the world's strongest growth rates have occurred where they are most needed, among some of the poorest people in the world. Both China and India have populations of well over 1 billion people each; together, these two countries have about one-third of the world's population. Many of their citizens were among the poorest people in the world for much of the 20th century. Starting in the late 1970s, although China remained officially a government-controlled command economy, the government began to allow a greater degree of economic freedom. For example, once Chinese farmers had grown the amount that they were required to grow under law, they were allowed to sell any extra they could produce at the market price. A variety of small manufacturing plants, many owned by townships and villages, were allowed to start. These modest steps toward a more market-oriented economy in the 1980s triggered an extraordinary wave of economic growth at annual rates of 7–8% per year for four decades.

India took a different path. For some decades after its independence in 1948, India's GDP seemed to grow in a solid but unexciting way, at about 3% per year. By the late 1980s, however, this rate of growth began to look less acceptable. Since it was very similar to the growth rates of high-income countries like the United States and Western Europe, India's 3% rate of growth was not helping its economy to catch up. Moreover, the experience of China, along with nations in East Asia like South Korea and Thailand, seemed to demonstrate a potential for considerably faster rates of growth. India had long had a heavily regulated economy, with detailed rules and regulations about hiring, starting businesses, selling, and every other detail of a market transaction. In the early 1990s, India began to eliminate and relax some of these rules and to allow additional freedom in the market. These moderate steps that have been taken encouraged India's GDP to increase by 5–7% per year since the early 1990s.

In both China and India, market-oriented economic reforms have brought economic gains to hundreds of millions of the poorest people in the world.

Other than the issue of economic growth, the other three main goals of macroeconomic policy—that is, low unemployment, low inflation, and a sustainable balance of trade—all involve situations in which, for some reason, the economy fails to coordinate the forces of supply and demand. In the case of cyclical unemployment, for example, aggregate demand falls behind aggregate supply. In the case of the natural rate of unemployment, government regulations create a situation where otherwise-willing employers become unwilling to hire otherwise-willing workers. Inflation is a situation in which aggregate demand outstrips aggregate supply, at least for a time, so that too much buying power is chasing too few goods. A trade imbalance is a situation where, because of a net inflow or outflow of foreign capital, domestic savings are not aligned with domestic investment. Each of these situations can create a range of easier or harder policy choices. But none of these macroeconomic problems are unanswerable or insoluble.

The importance of market economies and market institutions does not mean a one-size-fits-all economic policy. Economies come in a wide range of flavors. A U.S.-style market economy gives a comparatively free rein to business, with a relatively small government sector. A western European-style market economy has more rules and regulations for business, a larger government sector, a stronger labor union movement, and more efforts by government to impose higher taxes on the wealthy and offer higher benefits to the unemployed and poor. Countries like Canada and Australia tend to fall in between the U.S. and European models. Japan is a market-oriented economy with a relatively small government as measured by the size of GDP taken in taxes, but a relatively dense network of business and social connections that can limit the incentives for economic change. In some countries, fiscal policy involves more than half of GDP; in the United States and Japan, government taxes and spending are more like one-third of GDP. Some countries have a central bank that focuses on inflation; others on a mix of inflation and unemployment; still others on exchange rates.

Reasonable people can differ in the flavor of economic policy that they prefer. Economic wisdom is not limited to Republicans or Democrats in the United States, or to business or union leaders, or to the policies that are popular in Sweden or the United Kingdom or Japan. But among the high-income countries of the world, these differences of opinion all begin by agreeing that market forces will play a primary role in economic production, and the economic policy discussion that follows is about the appropriate set of laws and institutions to accompany the market.

Economists are sometimes accused of being joyless creatures who see every glass as half empty, with every choice as nothing but a trade-off. Economists are certainly no friends of public policy schemes that focus only on good intentions, while ignoring trade-offs and incentives. But from a different perspective, economists may be among the greatest optimists of all. Economists believe that it is possible for the division of labor, operating through the interconnected web of market transactions, to raise the standard of living for everyone in the world. Economists have a shared vision that as people come together in a market-oriented economy, acting as consumers, workers, managers, savers and investors, they have the possibility to make everyone who participates better off than they could otherwise be on their own. To be sure, a market-oriented economy must be watched with a wary eye. Economic growth doesn't just happen. Macroeconomic flows can become imbalanced, resulting in unemployment, inflation, and trade imbalances. But even with these issues noted, the coordinating power of the economy should also be watched with a marveling eye. The economy allows people acting as individuals to pool together their skills and desires in a decentralized way that is far beyond the planning or organizational capacity of any government or company or supercomputer, to create a vast system of social interaction that holds forth a great promise of improving the human condition.

Key Concepts and Summary

1. There are wide differences in standards of living in regions around the world, whether one measures by economic measures like per capita GDP or by education and health statistics.
2. The fundamentals of growth are the same in every country: that is, improvements in human capital, physical capital, and technology interacting in the context of a market-oriented economy. But countries that are high-income technology leaders will tend to focus more on developing and using new technology. Countries that are converging economies will focus more on increasing human capital and becoming more interconnected to the technology and markets in the global economy. Low-income, technologically disconnected countries have many needs, but they also face the challenge of becoming reliably connected to the rest of the global economy and finding the technologies that work best for them.
3. Cyclical unemployment can be addressed by expansionary fiscal and monetary policy. The natural rate of unemployment can be harder to deal with because it involves thinking carefully about the trade-offs involved in laws that affect employment and hiring.
4. Most high-income economies have learned that their central banks can control inflation in the medium- and the long-term. In addition, they have learned that inflation has no long-term benefits but potentially substantial long-term costs if it distracts businesses from focusing on real productivity gains. However, smaller economies around the world may face more volatile inflation because their smaller economies can be unsettled by international movements of capital and goods.
5. There are many legitimate concerns over possible negative consequences of free trade. Perhaps the single strongest response to these concerns is that there are

good ways to address the concerns without restricting trade and thus losing its benefits.

6. There are two major issues involving trade imbalances. One is what will happen with the large U.S. trade deficits, and whether they will come down gradually or with a rush. The other is whether smaller countries around the world should take some steps to limit flows of international capital, in the hope that they will not be quite so susceptible to economic whiplash from international financial capital flowing in and out of their economies.

Review Questions

1. What are some of the ways of comparing the standard of living in countries around the world?
2. What's the difference between a country that is a technology leader, a country that is a converging economy, and a country that is technologically disconnected?
3. What are the different policy tools for dealing with cyclical unemployment or the natural rate of unemployment?
4. In low-income countries, does it make sense to argue that most of the people without long-term jobs that pay regular wages are unemployed?
5. Is inflation likely to be a severe problem for at least some high-income economies in the near future?
6. Is inflation likely to be a problem for at least some low- and middle-income economies in the near future?
7. What are the major issues with regard to trade imbalances for the U.S. economy? For low- and middle-income countries?

Interpreting Graphs

APPENDIX CHAPTER

1

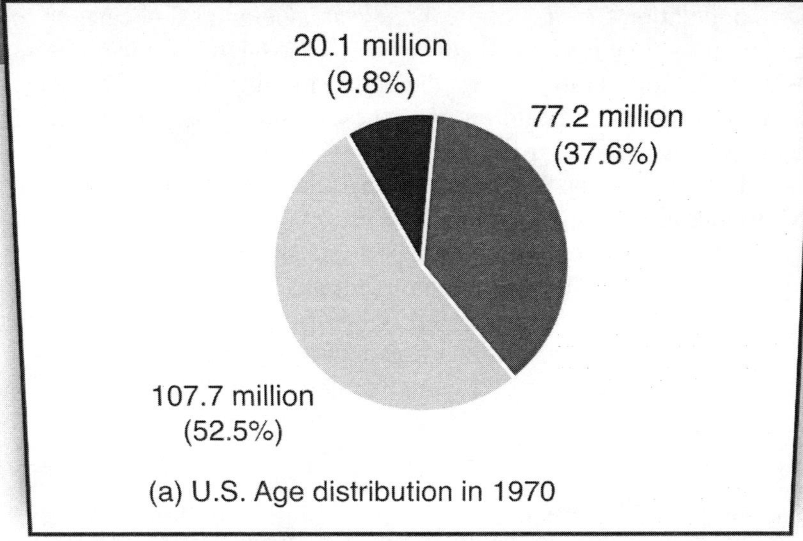

(a) U.S. Age distribution in 1970

Appendix Outline

Numerical data can be presented in two ways: digital or analogue. Digital presentation uses numbers. For example, a digital clock might report the time as 3:46:11 P.M.—that is, as 46 minutes and 11 seconds after three o'clock in the afternoon. An analogue presentation uses a physical image to convey the information. An analogue clock, with an hour hand, a minute hand, and a second hand, would report the time of 3:46:11 P.M. by showing the hour hand a little before the four on the clock face, the minute hand just past the nine, and the second hand just past the two. Which presentation is best—digital or analogue? It depends on the purpose. If you are timing a runner who is training for a five-mile cross-country race, then a digital clock that clearly displays seconds is most useful. If you are on your way to 4:00 doctor's appointment and you want to know if you will make it on time, a glance at an analogue clock tells you what you need to know.

Graphs are an analogue method of presenting numerical patterns. They condense detailed numerical information into a visual form in which relationships and numerical patterns can be perceived more easily. For example, which countries have larger or smaller populations? A careful reader could examine a long list of numbers representing the populations of many countries, but with over 200 nations in the world, searching through such a list would take concentration and time. Putting these same numbers on a graph can quickly reveal population patterns. Economists use graphs both for a compact and readable presentation of groups of numbers and for building an intuitive grasp of relationships and connections.

This appendix discusses the three graphs used in this book: *pie graphs*, *bar graphs*, and *line graphs*. It also provides warnings about how graphs can be manipulated to alter viewers' perceptions of the relationships in the data.

Pie Graphs

Pie graphs (sometimes called pie charts) are used to show how an overall total is divided into parts. A circle represents a group as a whole. The slices of this circular "pie" show the relative sizes of subgroups.

Exhibit 1-A1 shows how the U.S. population is divided among children, working-age adults, and the elderly in 1970, 2000, and projected for 2030. The information is first conveyed with numbers in a table, and then in three pie charts. The first column of the table shows the total U.S. population for each of the three years. Columns 2–4 categorize the total in terms of age groups—from birth to 18 years, from 19 to 64 years, and 65 years and above. In columns 2–4, the top number shows the actual number of people in each age category, while the percentage underneath, in parentheses, shows the percentage of the total population comprised by that age group.

The three pie graphs in Exhibit 1-A1 show that the share of the U.S. population 65 and over is growing. The pie graphs allow you to get a feel for the relative size of the different age groups from 1970 to 2000 to 2030, without requiring you to slog through the specific numbers and percentages in the table. Some common examples of how pie graphs are used include dividing the population into groups by age, income level, ethnicity, religion, occupation; dividing different firms into categories by size, industry, number of employees; and dividing up government spending or taxes into its main categories.

Bar Graphs

A *bar graph* uses the height of different bars to compare quantities. Exhibit 1-A2 provides a bar graph of the 12 most populous countries in the world. The height of the bars corresponds to the population of each country. In 2014, the world population was about 7.2 billion (that is, 7,200 million) people. Although it is widely known that China and India are the most populous countries in the world, seeing how the bars on the graph tower over the other countries helps illustrate the magnitude of the difference between the sizes of national populations.

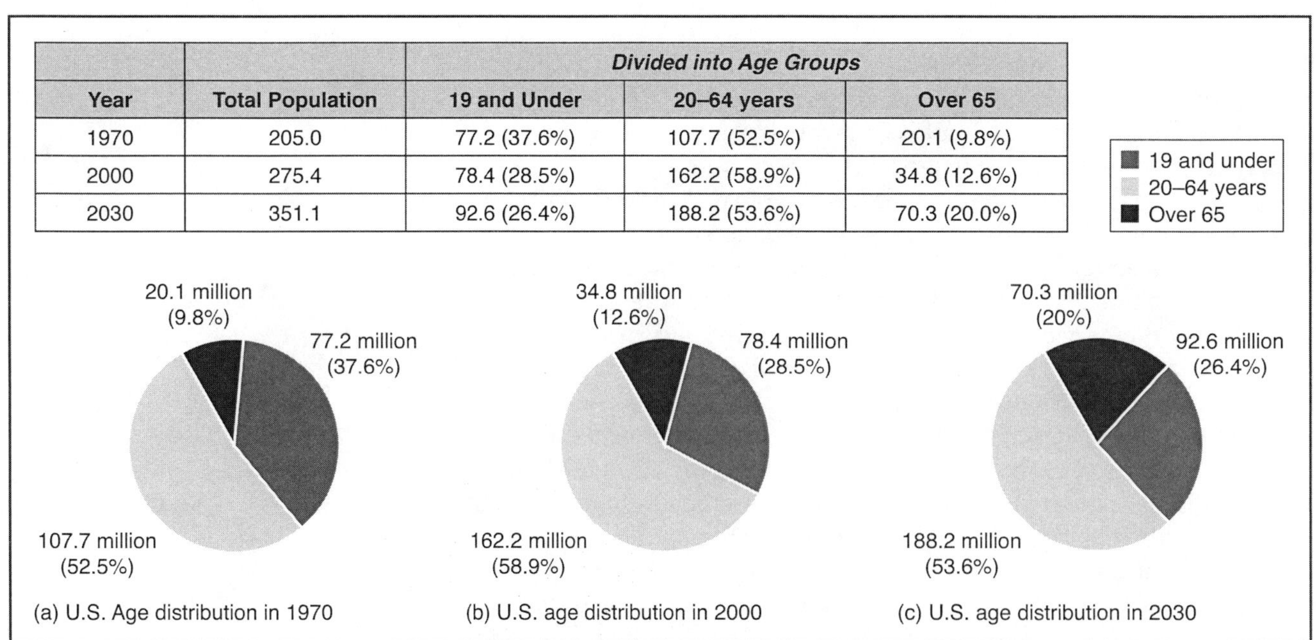

		Divided into Age Groups		
Year	Total Population	19 and Under	20–64 years	Over 65
1970	205.0	77.2 (37.6%)	107.7 (52.5%)	20.1 (9.8%)
2000	275.4	78.4 (28.5%)	162.2 (58.9%)	34.8 (12.6%)
2030	351.1	92.6 (26.4%)	188.2 (53.6%)	70.3 (20.0%)

EXHIBIT 1-A1 Pie Graphs of the U.S. Age Distribution (numbers in millions)

The first column shows the total U.S. population in 1970, 2000, and projected for 2030. The next three columns divide up that total into three age groups. The three pie graphs illustrate the division of total population into these three age groups for the three years.

Country	Population (in millions)
China	1,369
India	1,295
United States	319
Indonesia	254
Brazil	206
Pakistan	185
Bangladesh	159
Russia	143
Nigeria	177
Japan	127
Mexico	125
Philippines	99

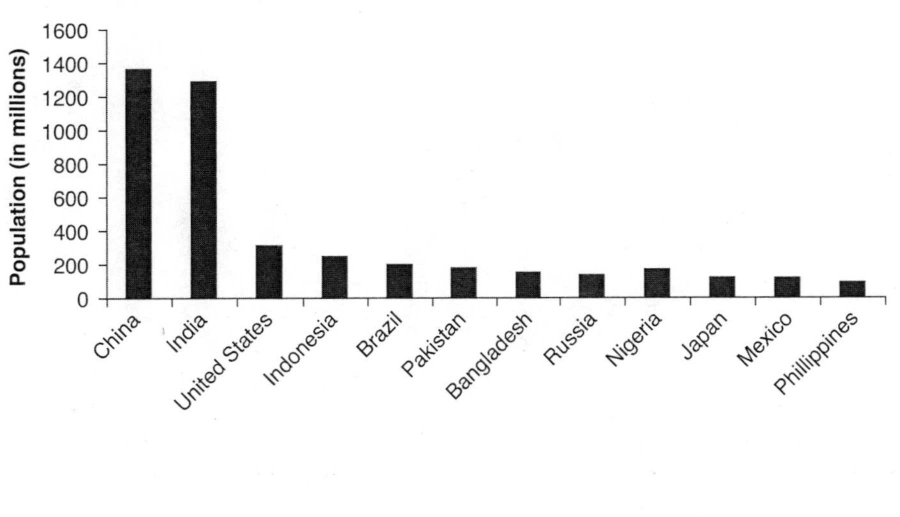

EXHIBIT 1-A2 Leading Countries of the World by Population, 2012 (in millions)

The table shows the 12 countries of the world with the largest population. The height of the bars in the bar graph shows the size of the population for each country.

Bar graphs can be subdivided in a way that reveals information similar to pie charts. Exhibit 1-A3 offers three bar graphs based on the information from Exhibit 1-A1 about the U.S. age distribution in 1970, 2000, and 2030. Exhibit 1-A3*a* shows three bars for each year, representing the total number of persons in each age bracket for each year. Exhibit 1-A3*b* shows just one bar for each year, but the different age groups are now shaded inside the bar. In Exhibit 1-A3*c*, still based on the same data, the vertical axis measures percentages rather than the number of persons. In this case, all three bar graphs are the same height, representing 100% of the population, with each bar divided according to the percentage of population in each age group. It is sometimes easier for the eyes of the reader to run across several bar graphs, comparing the shaded areas, rather than trying to compare several pie graphs.

Exhibits 1-A2 and 1-A3 show how the bars can represent countries or years, and how the vertical axis can represent a numerical or a percentage value. Bar graphs can also compare size, quantity, rates, distances, and other quantitative categories.

Line Graphs

To a mathematician or an economist, a "variable" is the name given to a quantity that may assume a range of values. Line graphs show a relationship between two variables: one measured on the horizontal axis and the other measured on the vertical axis.

Line Graphs with Two Variables

Exhibit 1-A4 shows the relationship between two variables: length and median weight for American baby boys and girls during the first three years of their life. (The "median" means that half of all babies weigh more than this and half weigh less.) The line graph measures length in inches on the horizontal axis and weight in pounds on the vertical axis. For example, point A on the figure shows that a boy who is 28 inches long will have a median weight of about 19 pounds. One line on the graph shows the length-weight relationship for boys and the other line shows the relationship for girls. This kind of graph is widely used by health care providers to check whether a child's physical development is roughly on track.

Exhibit 1-A5 presents another example of a line graph. In this case, the line graph shows how thin the air becomes when you climb a mountain. The horizontal axis of the

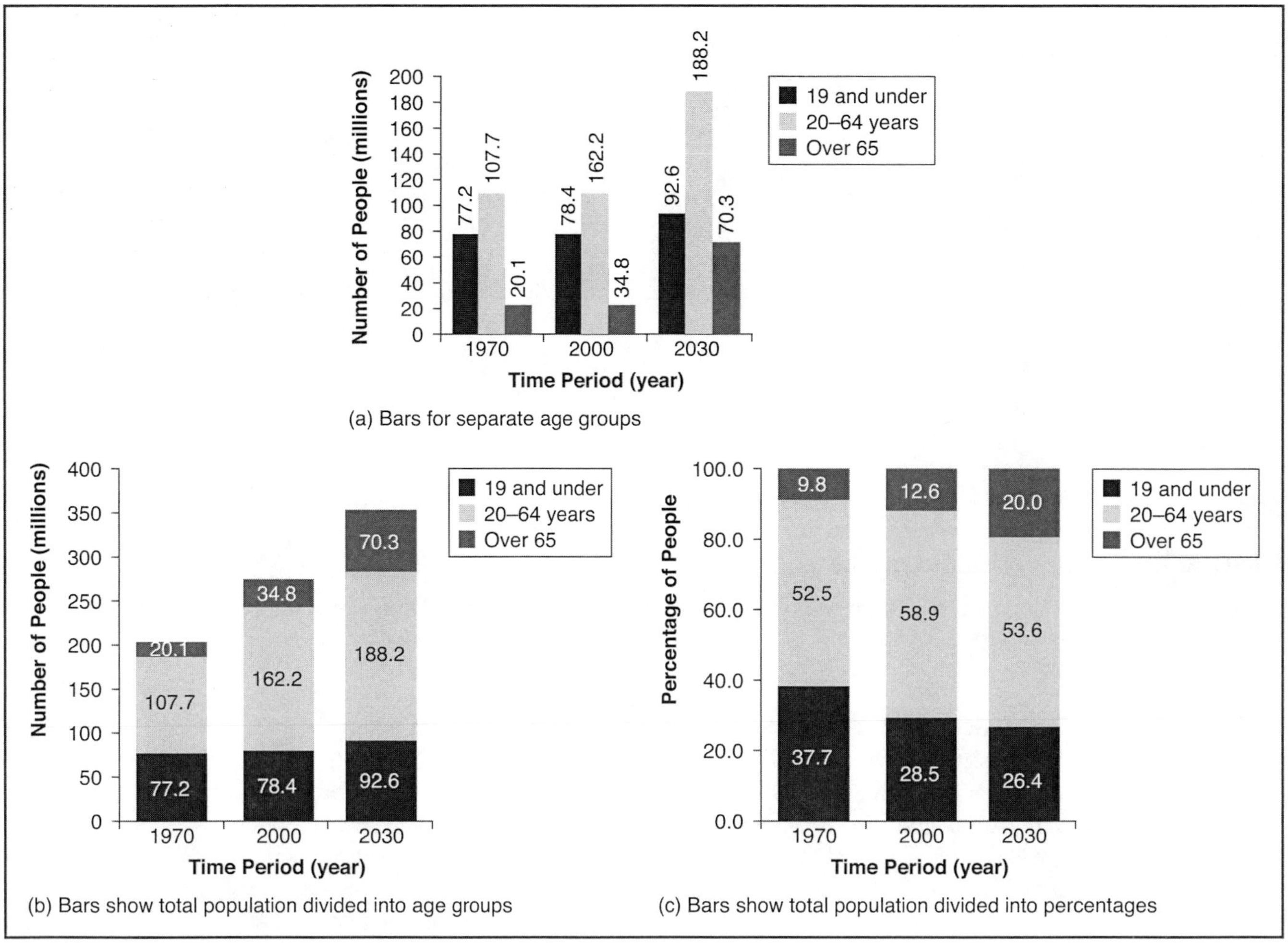

(a) Bars for separate age groups

(b) Bars show total population divided into age groups

(c) Bars show total population divided into percentages

EXHIBIT 1-A3 U.S. Population with Bar Graphs

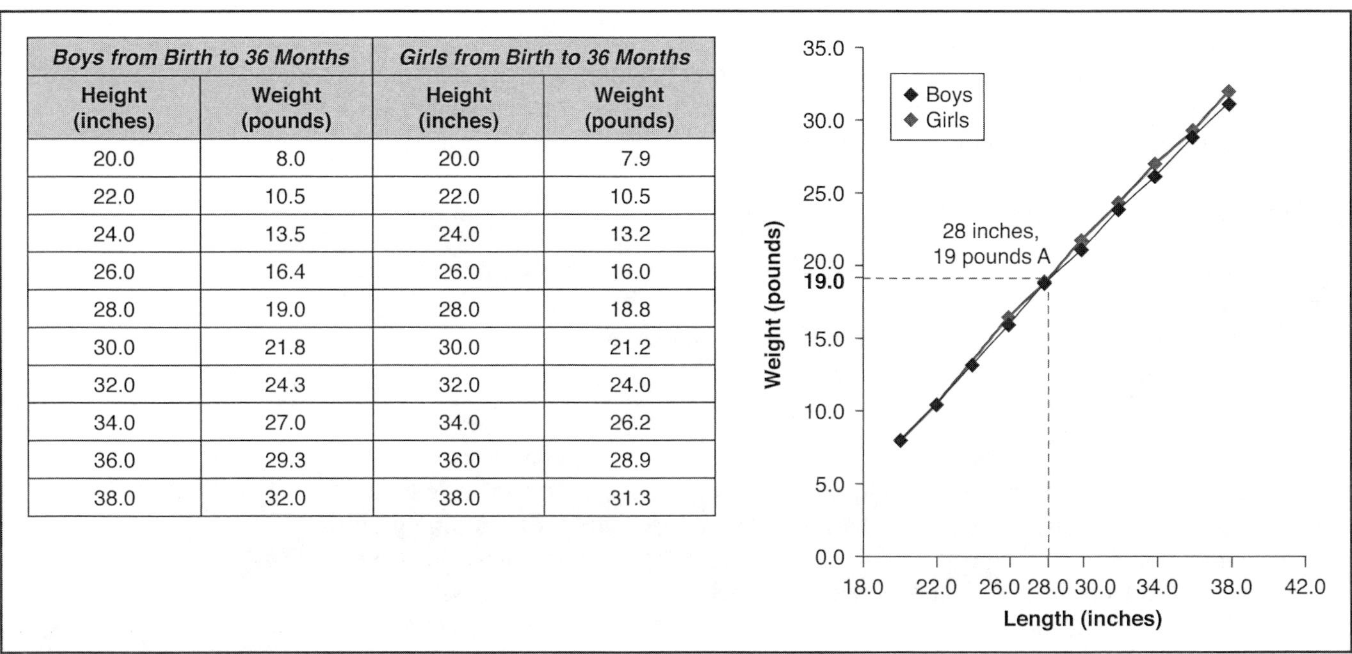

Boys from Birth to 36 Months		*Girls from Birth to 36 Months*	
Height (inches)	**Weight (pounds)**	**Height (inches)**	**Weight (pounds)**
20.0	8.0	20.0	7.9
22.0	10.5	22.0	10.5
24.0	13.5	24.0	13.2
26.0	16.4	26.0	16.0
28.0	19.0	28.0	18.8
30.0	21.8	30.0	21.2
32.0	24.3	32.0	24.0
34.0	27.0	34.0	26.2
36.0	29.3	36.0	28.9
38.0	32.0	38.0	31.3

EXHIBIT 1-A4 The Length-Weight Relationship for American Boys and Girls

The line graph shows the relationship between height and weight for boys and girls from birth to 36 months. Point A, for example, shows that a boy of 28 inches in height (measured on the horizontal axis) is typically 19 pounds in weight (measured on the vertical axis). These data apply only to children in the first three years of life.

Altitude (meters)	Air Density (kg/cubic meters)
0	1.200
500	1.093
1,000	0.831
1,500	0.678
2,000	0.569
2,500	0.484
3,000	0.415
3,500	0.357
4,000	0.307
4,500	0.231
5,000	0.182
5,500	0.142
6,000	0.100
6,500	0.085
7,000	0.066
7,500	0.051
8,000	0.041
8,500	0.025
9,000	0.022
9,500	0.019
10,000	0.014

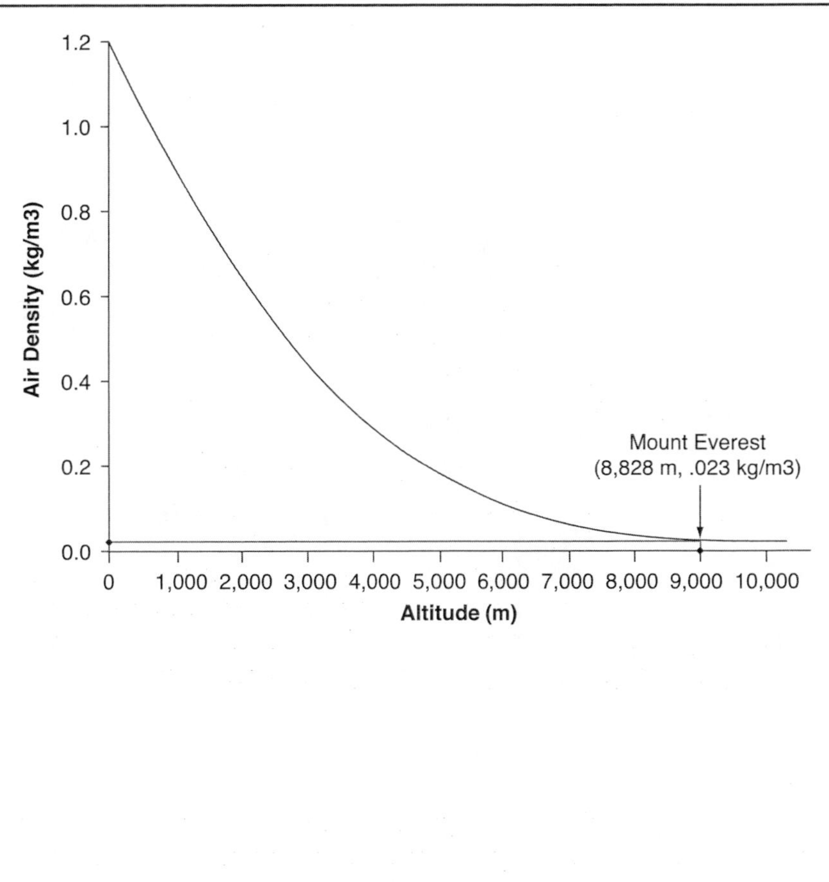

EXHIBIT 1-A5 Altitude-Air Density Relationship

This line graph shows the relationship between altitude, measured in meters above sea level, and air density, measured in kilograms of air per cubic meter. As altitude rises, air density declines. The point at the top of Mount Everest, shown in the diagram, has an altitude of approximately 8,828 meters above sea level (the horizontal axis) and air density of 0.23 kilograms per cubic meter (the vertical axis).

figure shows altitude, measured in meters above sea level. The vertical axis measures the density of the air at each altitude. Air density is measured by the weight of the air in a cubic meter of space (that is, a box measuring one meter in height, width, and depth). As the graph shows, air pressure is heaviest at ground level and becomes lighter as you climb. Exhibit 1-A5 shows that a cubic meter of air at an altitude of 500 meters weighs approximately 1 kilogram (about 2.2 pounds). However, as the altitude increases, air density decreases. A cubic meter of air at the top of Mount Everest, at about 8,828 meters, would weigh only .023 kilograms. The thin air at high altitudes explains why many mountain climbers need to breathe oxygen from tanks as they reach the top of a mountain.

The length-weight relationship and the altitude-air density relationships in these two exhibits represent averages. If you were to collect actual data on air pressure at different altitudes, the same altitude in different geographic locations will have slightly different air density, depending on factors like how far you are from the equator, the local weather conditions, and the humidity in the air. Similarly, in measuring the height and weight of children for the previous line graph, children of a particular height would have a range of different weights, some above average and some below. In the real world, this sort of variation in data is common. The task of a researcher is to organize that data in a way that helps to understand typical patterns. The study of statistics, especially when combined with computer statistics and spreadsheet programs, is a great help in organizing this kind of data, plotting line graphs, and looking for typical underlying relationships. For most economics and social science majors, a statistics course will be required at some point.

EXHIBIT 1-A6 U.S. Unemployment Rate, 1975–2015

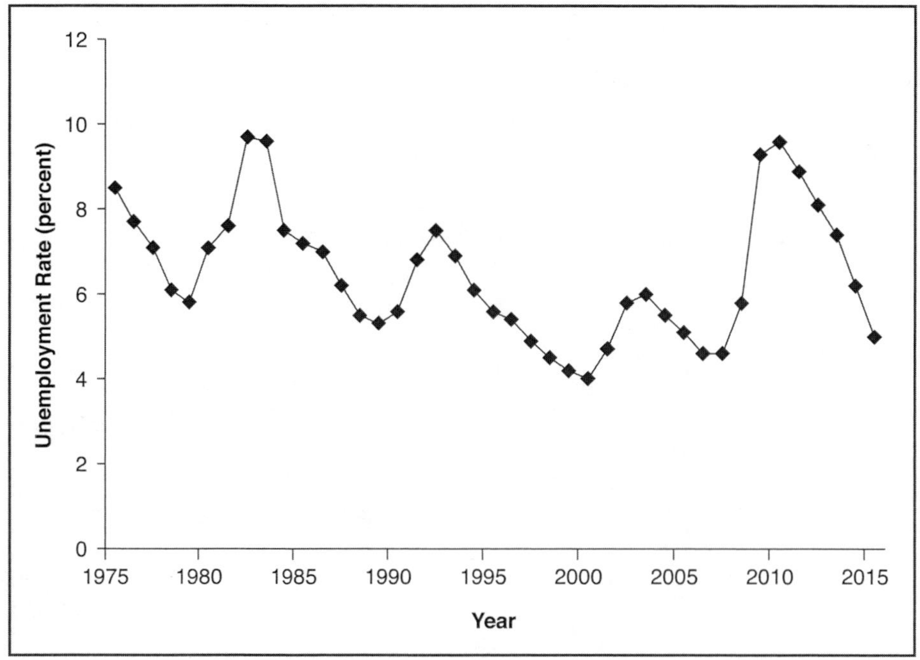

Time Series

One common line graph is called a time series, in which the horizontal axis shows time and the vertical axis displays another variable. Thus, a time series graph shows how a variable changes over time. Exhibit 1-A6 shows the unemployment rate in the United States since 1975, where unemployment is defined as the percentage of adults who want jobs and are looking for a job, but cannot find one. The points for the unemployment rate in each year are plotted on the graph, and a line then connects the points, showing how the unemployment rate has moved up and down since 1975. The line graph makes it easy to see, for example, that the highest unemployment rate during this time period was slightly less than 10% in the early 1980s, while the unemployment rate declined from the early 1990s to the end of the 1990s, before rising and then falling back in the early 2000s, rising sharply during the recession from 2007–2009, and dropping after the end of the recession.

Slope

In discussing the shape of line graphs, the concept of slope is often helpful. Slope is defined as "rise over run." More specifically, if y is the variable on the vertical axis, x is the variable on the horizontal axis, and the Greek letter delta Δ means "the change in," then the definitions of slope is:

$$\text{Slope} = \frac{\Delta y \text{ (rise)}}{\Delta x \text{ (run)}}$$

A *positive slope* means that as a line on the line graph moves from left to right, the line rises. The length-weight relationship in Exhibit 1-A4 has a positive slope. A negative slope means that as the line on the line graph moves from left to right, the line falls. The altitude-air density relationship in Exhibit 1-A5 has a *negative slope*. A slope of zero means that the line is flat—that is, zero rise over the run. Exhibit 1-A6 of the unemployment rate illustrates a common pattern of many line graphs: some segments where the slope is positive, other segments where the slope is negative, and still other segments where the slope is close to zero.

The slope of a straight line between two points can be calculated in numerical terms. To calculate slope, begin by designating one point as the "starting point" and the other point as the "end point" and then calculating the rise over run between these two points.

As an example, consider the slope of the air density graph between the points representing an altitude of 4,000 meters and an altitude of 6,000 meters:

Rise: Change in variable on vertical axis (end point minus original point)
$= .100 - .307 = -.207$

Run: Change in variable on horizontal axis (end point minus original point)
$= 6{,}000 - 4{,}000 = 2{,}000$

Thus, the slope of a straight line between these two points would be that from the altitude of 4,000 meters up to 6,000 meters, the density of the air decreases by approximately .1 kilograms/cubic meter for each of the next 1,000 meters.

Many graphs of data are not perfectly straight lines, at least not in all places, so that trying to draw a single straight line will not accurately capture the relationship between the two variables. For example, the true relationship between altitude and air density in Exhibit 1-A5 is a curve, not a straight line. However, you can draw a close approximation of a curved line by using a series of many short straight lines with different slopes. Thus, it is common to calculate the slope of a part of a curved line by choosing a starting point and an ending point that are quite close together, in which case the slope of the straight line between those two close points will offer a good approximation of the slope of the curved line between those two points. A straight line will have the same slope, regardless of what starting point and end point you choose; in contrast, a curved line will have different slopes depending on what starting point and end point you choose.

A higher positive slope means a steeper upward tilt to the line, while a smaller positive slope means a flatter upward tilt to the line. A negative slope that is larger in absolute value (that is, more negative) means a steeper downward tilt to the line. A slope of zero is a horizontal flat line. A vertical line has an infinite slope.

Slope of Straight Lines in Algebraic Terms

Straight lines can also be expressed as an algebraic formula, and when they are, the slope is easily visible in the formula. The algebraic equation for a straight line is

$$y = a + bx$$

where *x* and *y* are the variables, with *x* on the horizontal axis and *y* on the vertical axis, and *a* and *b* representing factors that determine the shape of the line. To see how this equation works, consider a numerical example:

$$y = 9 + 3x$$

In this equation for a specific line, the *a* term has been set equal to 9 and the *b* term has been set equal to 3. Exhibit 1-A7 shows this equation with a table and a graph. To construct

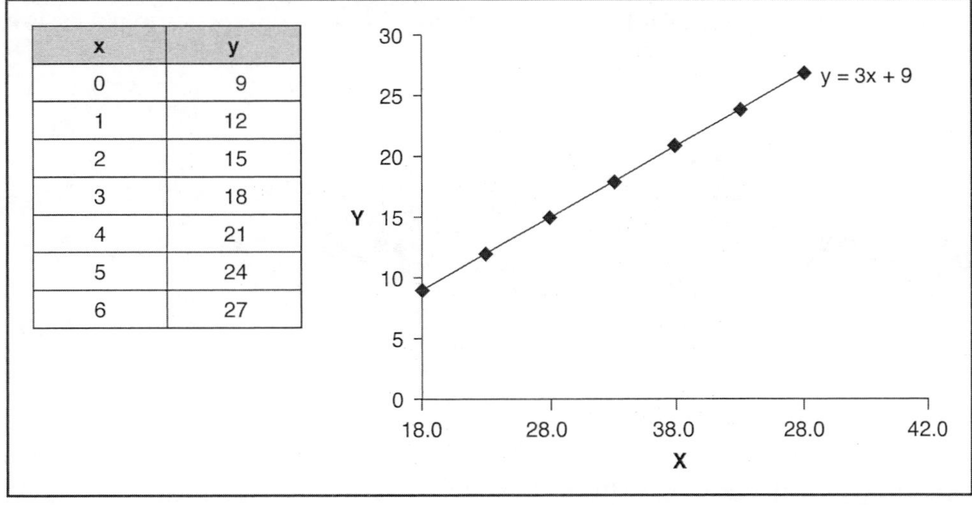

x	y
0	9
1	12
2	15
3	18
4	21
5	24
6	27

EXHIBIT 1-A7 Slope and the Algebra of Straight Lines

This line graph has *x* on the horizontal axis and *y* on the vertical axis. The *y*-intercept—that is, the point where the line intersects the *y*-axis—is 9. The slope of the line is 3; that is, there is a rise of 3 on the vertical axis for every increase of 1 on the horizontal axis. The slope is the same all along a straight line.

the table, just plug in a series of different values for x, and then calculate what value of y results. In the figure, these points are plotted and a line is drawn through them.

This example illustrates how the a and b terms in an equation for a straight line determine the shape of the line. The a term is called the *y-intercept*. The reason for this name is that if $x = 0$, then the a term will reveal where the line intercepts, or crosses, the vertical or y-axis. In this example, the line hits the vertical axis at 9. The b term in the equation for the line is the slope. Remember that slope is defined as rise over run; more specifically, the change in the vertical axis divided by the change in the horizontal axis. In this example, each time the x term increases by 1 (the run), the y term rises by 3. Thus, the slope of this line is 3. Specifying a y-intercept and a slope—that is, specifying a and b in the equation for a line—will identify a specific line. Although it is rare for real-world data points to arrange themselves as an exact straight line, it often turns out that a straight line can offer a reasonable approximation of actual data.

Comparing Line Graphs with Pie Charts and Bar Graphs

Now that you are familiar with pie graphs, bar graphs, and line graphs, how do you know which graph to use for your data? Pie graphs are often better than line graphs at showing how an overall group is divided. However, if a pie graph has too many slices, it can become difficult to interpret.

Bar graphs are especially useful when comparing quantities. For example, if you are studying the populations of different countries, as in Exhibit 1-A2, bar graphs can show the relationships between the population sizes of multiple countries. Not only can it show these relationships, but it can also show breakdowns of different groups within the population.

A line graph is often the most effective format for illustrating a relationship between two variables that are both changing. For example, time series graphs can show patterns as time changes, like the unemployment rate over time. Line graphs are widely used in economics to present continuous data about prices, wages, quantities bought and sold, the size of the economy, and other economic variables.

How Graphs Can Mislead

Graphs not only reveal patterns; they can also alter how patterns are perceived. To see some of the ways this can be done, consider the line graphs of Exhibit 1-A8. These graphs all illustrate the unemployment rate—but from different perspectives.

Imagine that you wanted a graph which gives an impression that the rise in unemployment in 2009 wasn't all that large, or all that extraordinary by historical standards. You might choose to present your data as in Exhibit 1-A8*a*. Exhibit 1-A8*a* shows the exact data presented earlier in Exhibit 1-A6, but stretches the horizontal axis out longer relative to the vertical axis. By spreading the graph wide and flat, the visual appearance is that the rise in unemployment isn't so large, and similar to some past rises in unemployment.

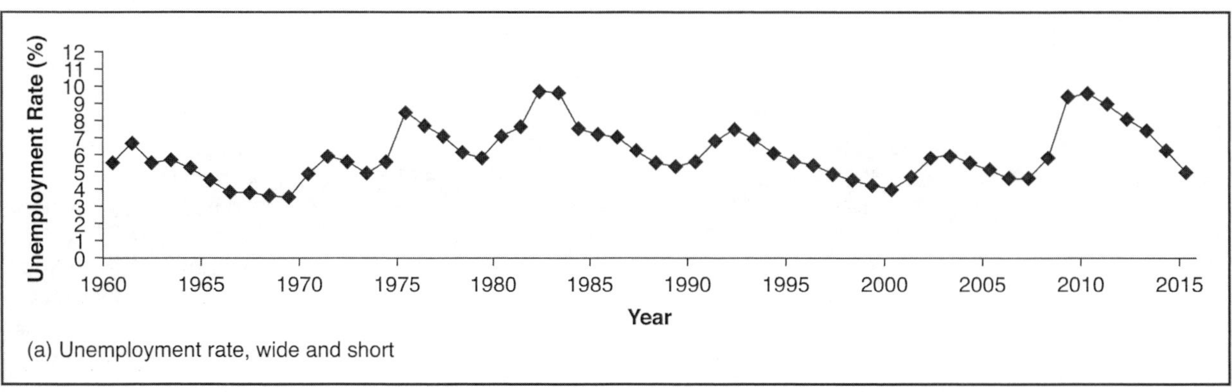

EXHIBIT 1-A8 Presenting Unemployment Rates in Different Ways, All of Them Accurate

Now imagine you wanted to emphasize how unemployment spiked substantially higher in 2009. In this case, using the same data, you can stretch the vertical axis out relative to the horizontal axis, as in Exhibit 1-A8*b*, which makes all rises and falls in unemployment appear sharper.

A similar effect can be accomplished without changing the length of the axes, but by changing the scale on the vertical axis. In Exhibit 1-A8*c*, the scale on the vertical axis runs from 0% to 30%, while in Exhibit 1-A8*d*, the vertical axis runs from 3% to 10%. Compared to Exhibit 1-A6, where the vertical scale runs from 0% to 12%, Exhibit 1-A8*c*

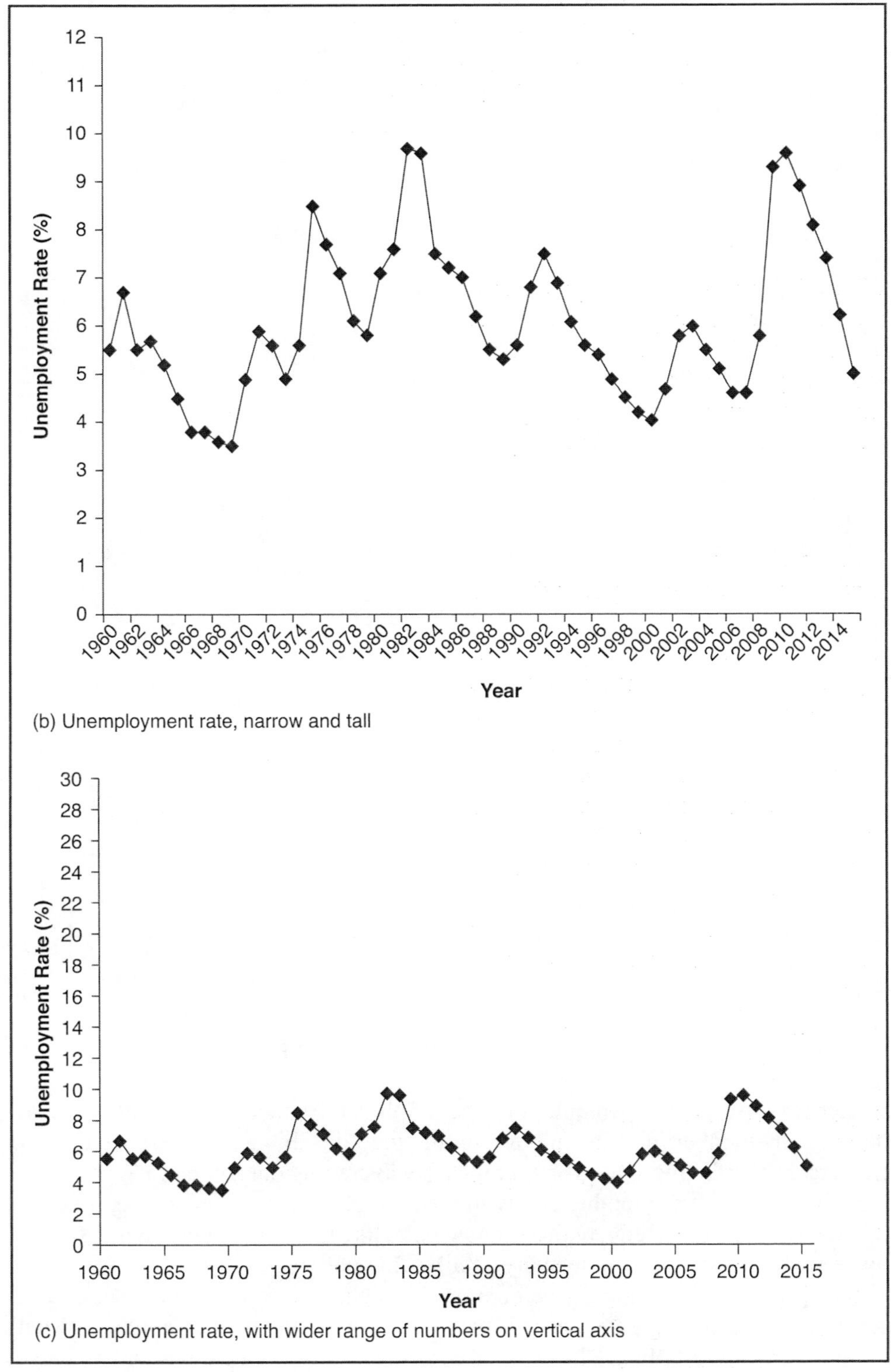

(b) Unemployment rate, narrow and tall

(c) Unemployment rate, with wider range of numbers on vertical axis

EXHIBIT 1-A8 *Continued*

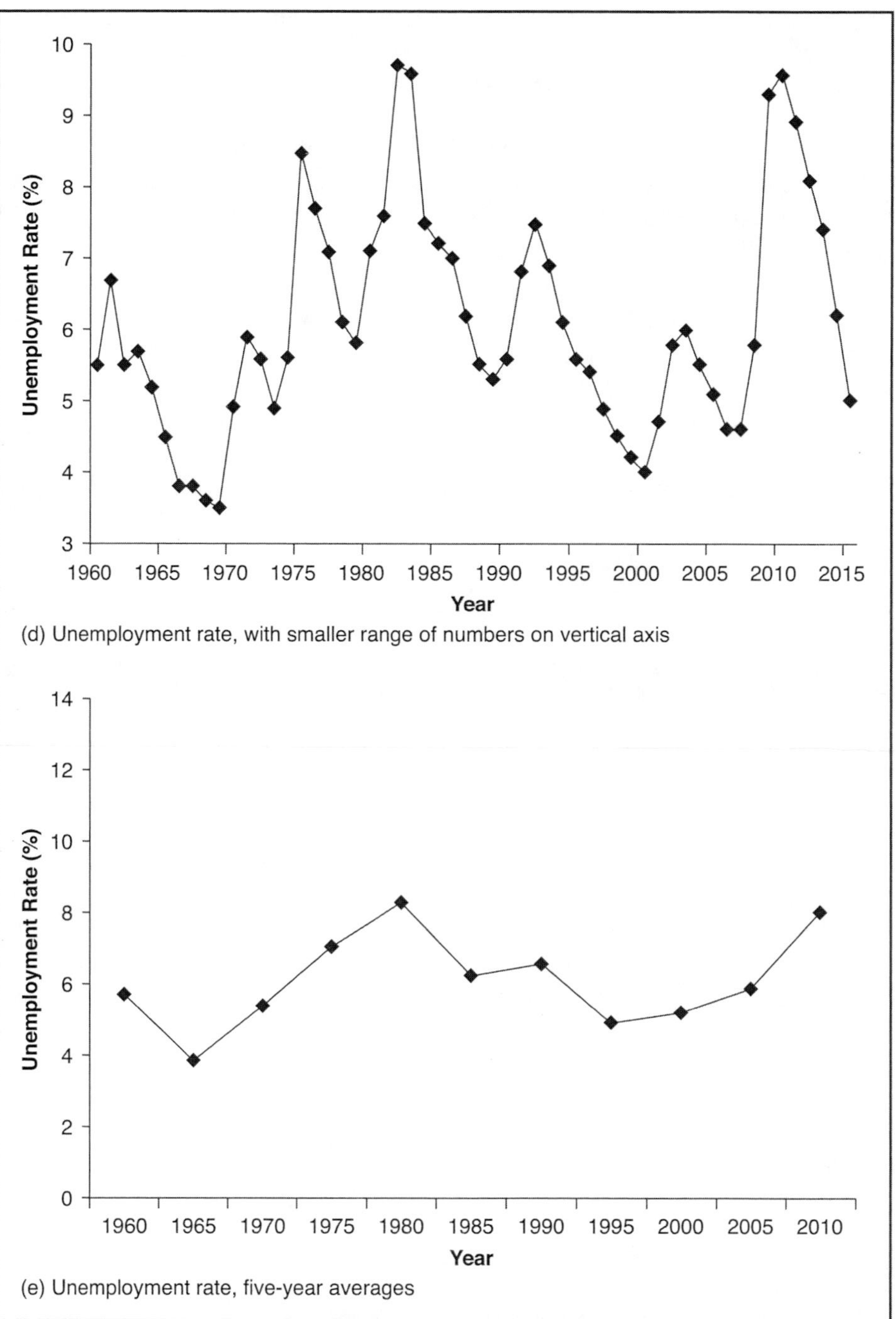

(d) Unemployment rate, with smaller range of numbers on vertical axis

(e) Unemployment rate, five-year averages

EXHIBIT 1-A8 *Continued*

makes the fluctuation in unemployment look smaller, while Exhibit 1-A8*d* makes it look larger.

Another way to alter the perception of the graph is to reduce the amount of variation by changing the number of points plotted on the graph. Exhibit 1-A8*e* shows the unemployment rate according to five-year averages. By averaging out some of the year-to-year changes, the line appears smoother and with fewer highs and lows. Of course, if you were to graph data that is more frequent than annual data, like monthly unemployment data, the unemployment rate would include many smaller fluctuations.

A final trick in manipulating the perception of graphical information is that, by choosing the starting and ending points carefully, you can influence the perception of whether the variable is rising or falling. The original data shows a general pattern with unemploy-

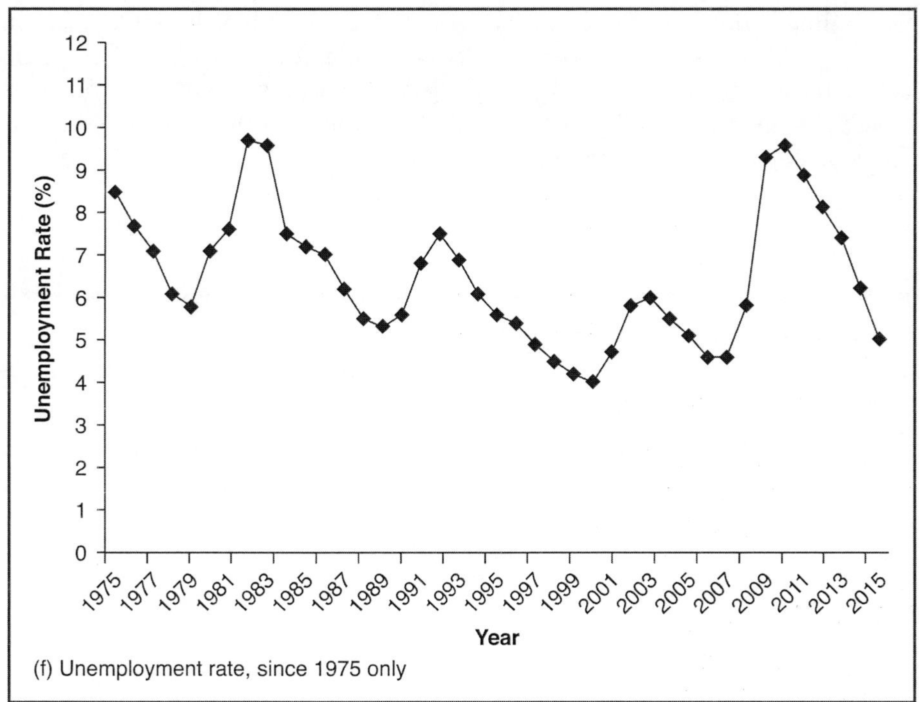

(f) Unemployment rate, since 1975 only

EXHIBIT 1-A8 *Continued*

ment low in the 1960s, but spiking up in the mid-1970s, early 1980s, early 1990s, early 2000s, and late 2000s. But Exhibit 1-A8*f* shows a graph that goes back only to 1975, which gives an impression that unemployment was more-or-less gradually falling over time until the 2009 recession pushed it back up to its "original" level—which is a plausible interpretation if one starts at the high point around 1975.

These kinds of tricks—or shall we just call them "choices about presentation"?— are not limited to line graphs. In a pie chart with many small slices and one large slice, someone must decide what categories should be used to produce these slices in the first place, thus making some slices appear bigger than others. If you are making a bar graph, you can make the vertical axis either taller or shorter, which will tend to make variations in the height of the bars appear more or less.

Being able to read graphs is an essential skill, both in economics and in life. But a graph is just one perspective or point of view, shaped by choices such as those discussed in this section. Don't always believe the first quick impression from a graph. View with caution.

Summary and Key Concepts

1. Graphs allow you to illustrate data graphically. They can illustrate patterns, comparisons, trends, and apportionment by condensing the numerical data and providing an intuitive sense of relationships in the data.
2. A *pie graph* shows how something is allotted, such as a sum of money or a group of people. The size of each slice of the pie is drawn to represent the corresponding percentage of the whole.
3. A *bar graph* uses the height of bars to show a relationship, where each bar represents a certain entity, like a country or a group of people. The bars on a bar graph can also be divided into segments to show subgroups.
4. A *line graph* shows the relationship between two variables: one is shown on the horizontal axis and one on the vertical axis.
5. Slope means "rise over run." The slope of the line on a line graph can be positive (upward-sloping), negative (downward-sloping), zero (flat), or infinite (vertical). The slope of a line on a graph may vary: for example, it may be positive in some segments, zero in other segments, and negative in other segments.
6. The algebraic equation for a line is $y = a + bx$, where x is the variable on the horizontal axis and y is the variable on the vertical axis, the a term is the *y-intercept*

and the b term is the slope. The slope of a line is the same at any point on the line.

7. Any graph is a single visual perspective on a subject. The impression it leaves will be based on many choices like what data or time frame is included, how data or groups are divided up, the relative size of vertical and horizontal axes, whether the scale used on a vertical starts at zero, and others. Thus, any graph should be regarded somewhat skeptically, remembering that the underlying relationship can be open to different interpretations.

Review Questions

1. Name three kinds of graphs and briefly state when it is most appropriate to use each type of graph.
2. What do the slices of a pie chart represent?
3. Why is a bar chart the best way to illustrate comparisons?
4. What is slope on a line graph?
5. How does the appearance of positive slope differ from negative slope and from zero slope?

APPENDIX CHAPTER

8

Indifference Curves

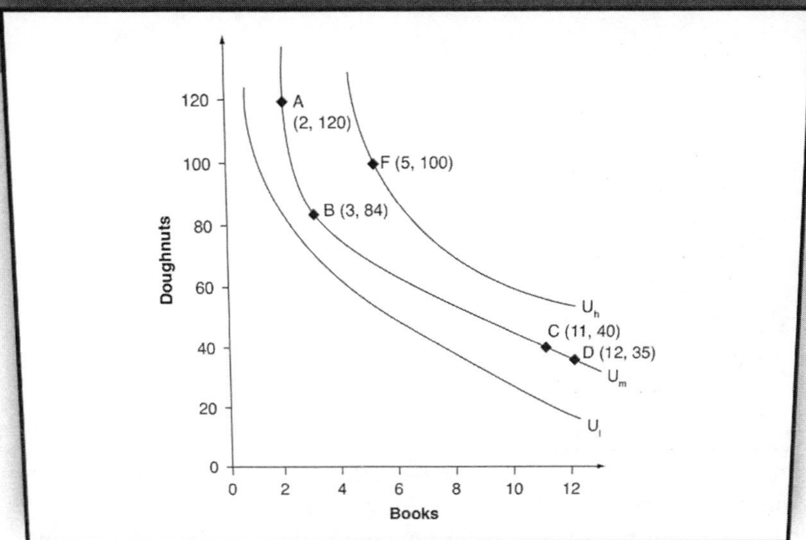

Appendix Outline

Economists use a vocabulary of maximizing utility to describe people's preferences. In Chapter 8, the level of utility that a person receives is described in numerical terms. This appendix presents an alternative approach to describing personal preferences, called indifference curves, which avoids any need for using numbers to measure utility. By setting aside the assumption of putting a numerical valuation on utility—an assumption that many students and economists find uncomfortably unrealistic—the indifference curve framework helps to clarify the logic of the underlying model.

What Is an Indifference Curve?

People can't place a numerical value on their level of satisfaction. However, they can and do identify what choices would give them more, or less, or the same amount of satisfaction. An indifference curve shows combinations of goods that provide an equal level of utility or satisfaction. For example, Exhibit 8-A1 presents three indifference curves that represent Lilly's preferences for the trade-offs that she faces in her two main relaxation activities: eating doughnuts and reading paperback books. Each indifference curve, U_L, U_M, and U_H, represents one level of utility. Let's first explore the meaning of one particular indifference curve, and then look at the indifference curves as a group.

The Shape of an Indifference Curve

The indifference curve U_M has four points labeled on it: A, B, C, and D. Since an indifference curve represents a set of choices that have the same level of utility, Lilly must receive an equal amount of utility, judged according to her personal preferences, from 2 books and 120 doughnuts (point A), from 3 books and 84 doughnuts (point B), from 11 books and 40 doughnuts (point C), or

EXHIBIT 8-A1 Lilly's Indifference Curves

Lilly would receive equal utility from all points on a given indifference curve. Any points on the highest indifference curve U_H, like F, provide greater utility than any points like A, B, C, and D on the middle indifference curve U_M. Similarly, any points on the middle indifference curve U_M provide greater utility than any points on the lowest indifference curve U_L.

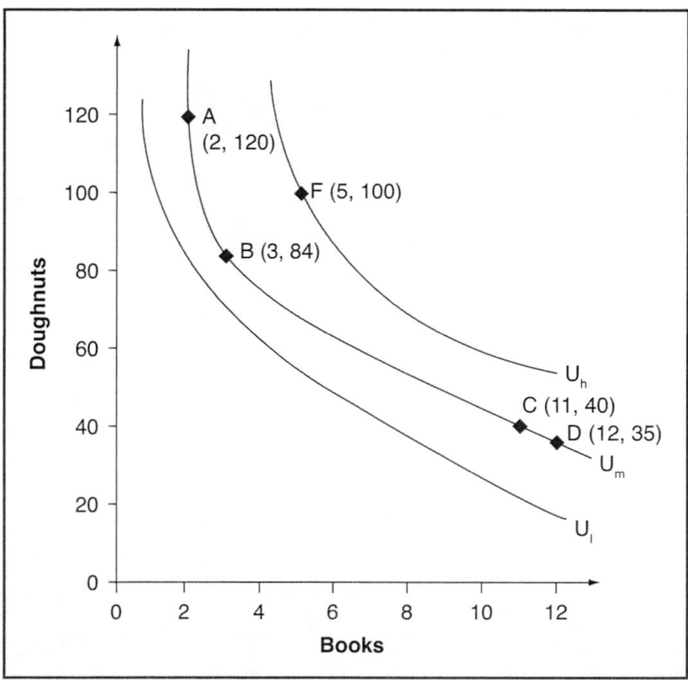

from 12 books and 35 doughnuts (point D). She would also receive the same utility from any of the unlabeled intermediate points along this indifference curve.

Indifference curves have a roughly similar shape in two ways: (1) they slope down; (2) they are steeper on the left and flatter on the right. The downward slope of the indifference curve means that as less of the good on the vertical axis (doughnuts) is consumed, if Lilly's utility is to remain the same, it will be necessary to have more consumption of the good on the vertical axis (in this case, books). For example, points A and B sit on the same indifference curve U_M, which means that they provide Lilly with the same level of utility. Thus, the marginal utility that Lilly would gain from, say, increasing her number of books from 2 to 3 must be equal to the marginal utility that she would lose if her number of doughnuts was cut from 120 to 84—so that her overall utility remains unchanged between points A and B. Indeed, the slope along an indifference curve is referred to as the *marginal rate of substitution*, which is the rate at which a person is willing to trade one good for another so that utility will remain the same.

Indifference curves like U_M are steeper on the left and flatter on the right. The reason behind this shape involves diminishing marginal utility—the notion that as a person consumes more of a good, the marginal utility from each additional unit becomes lower. Compare two different choices between points that all provide Lilly an equal amount of utility along the indifference curve U_M: the choice between A and B, and between C to D. In both choices, Lilly consumes one more book, but between A and B her consumption of doughnuts falls by 36 (from 120 to 84) and between C and D it falls by only 5 (from 40 to 35). The reason for this difference is that points A and C are different starting points, and thus have different implications for marginal utility. At point A, Lilly has few books and many doughnuts. Thus, her marginal utility from an extra book will be relatively high while the marginal utility of additional doughnuts is relatively low—so on the margin, it will take a relatively large number of doughnuts to offset the utility from the marginal book. At point C, however, Lilly has many books and few doughnuts. From this starting point, her marginal utility gained from extra books will be relatively low, while the marginal utility lost from additional doughnuts would be relatively high—so on the margin, it will take a relatively smaller number of doughnuts to offset the change of one marginal book. In short, the slope of the indifference curve changes because the marginal rate of substitution—that is, the quantity of one good that would be traded for the other good to keep utility constant—also changes, as a result of diminishing marginal utility of both goods.

The Field of Indifference Curves

Each indifference curve represents the choices that provide a single level of utility. Every level of utility will have its own indifference curve. Thus, Lilly's preferences will include an infinite number of indifference curves lying nestled together on the diagram—even though only three of the indifference curves representing three levels of utility appear on Exhibit 8-A1. In other words, an infinite number of indifference curves are not drawn on this diagram—but you should remember that they exist.

Higher indifference curves represent a greater level of utility than lower ones. In Exhibit 8-A1, indifference curve U_L can be thought of as a "low" level of utility, while U_M is a "medium" level of utility and U_H is a "high" level of utility. All of the choices on indifference curve U_H are preferred to all of the choices on indifference curve U_M, which in turn are preferred to all of the choices on U_L.

To understand why higher indifference curves are preferred to lower ones, compare point B on indifference curve U_M to point F on indifference curve U_H. Point F has greater consumption of both books (5 to 3) and doughnuts (100 to 84), so F is clearly preferable to point B. Given the definition of an indifference curve—that *all* the points on the curve have the same level of utility—if point F on indifference curve U_H is preferred to point B on indifference curve U_M, then it must be true that all points on indifference curve U_H have a higher level of utility than all points on U_M. More generally, for any point on a lower indifference curve, like U_L, you can identify a point on a higher indifference curve like U_M or U_H that has a higher consumption of both goods. Since one point on the higher indifference curve is preferred to one point on the lower curve, and since all the points on a given indifference curve have the same level of utility, it must be true that all points on higher indifference curves have greater utility than all points on lower indifference curves.

These arguments about the shapes of indifference curves and about higher or lower levels of utility do not require any numerical estimates of utility, either by the individual or by anyone else. They are only based on the assumptions that when people have less of one good, they need more of another good to make up for it if they are keeping the same level of utility, and that as people have more of a good, the marginal utility they receive from additional units of that good will diminish. Given these gentle assumptions, a field of indifference curves can be mapped out to describe the preferences of any individual.

The Individuality of Indifference Curves

Each person determines their own preferences and utility. Thus, while indifference curves have the same general shape—they slope down, and the slope is steeper on the left and flatter on the right—the specific shape of indifference curves can be different for every person. Exhibit 8-A1, for example, applies only to Lilly's preferences. Indifference curves for other people would travel through different points.

Utility-Maximizing with Indifference Curves

People seek the highest level of utility, which means that they wish to be on the highest possible indifference curve. However, people are limited by their budget constraints, which show what trade-offs are actually possible.

Maximizing Utility at the Highest Indifference Curve

Return to the situation of Lilly's choice between paperback books and doughnuts. Say that books cost \$6, doughnuts are 50 cents apiece, and that Lilly has \$60 to spend. This information provides the basis for the budget line shown in Exhibit 8-A2. Along with the budget line are shown the three indifference curves from Exhibit 8-A1. What is Lilly's utility-maximizing choice? Several possibilities are identified in the diagram.

The choice of F with 5 books and 100 doughnuts is highly desirable, since it is on the highest indifference curve U_H of those shown in the diagram. However, it isn't affordable

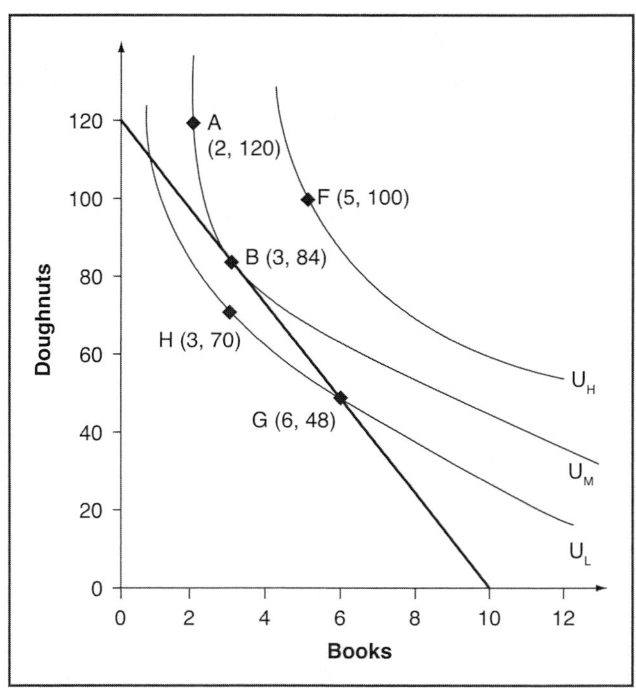

EXHIBIT 8-A2 Indifference Curves and a Budget Constraint

Lilly's preferences are shown by the indifference curves. Lilly's budget constraint, given the prices of books and doughnuts and her income, is shown by the straight line. Lilly's optimal choice will be point B, where the budget line is tangent to the indifference curve U_M. Lilly would have more utility at a point like F on the higher indifference curve U_H, but the budget line does not touch the higher indifference curve U_H at any point, so she cannot afford this choice. A choice like G is affordable to Lilly, but it lies on indifference curve U_L and thus provides less utility than choice B, which is on indifference curve U_M.

given Lilly's budget constraint. The choice of H with 3 books and 70 doughnuts on indifference curve U_L is a wasteful choice, since it is inside Lilly's budget set, and as a utility-maximizer, Lilly will always prefer a choice on the budget constraint itself. Choices B and G are both on the opportunity set. However, choice G of 6 books and 48 doughnuts is on lower indifference curve U_L than choice B of 3 books and 84 doughnuts, which is on the indifference curve U_M. If Lilly were to start at choice G, and then thought about whether the marginal utility she was deriving from doughnuts and books, she would decide that some additional doughnuts and fewer books would make her happier—which would cause her to move toward her preferred choice B. Given the combination of Lilly's personal preferences as identified by her indifference curves and Lilly's opportunity set, which is determined by prices and income, B will be her utility-maximizing choice.

The highest achievable indifference curve touches the opportunity set at a single point of tangency. Since an infinite number of indifference curves exist, even if only a few of them are drawn on any given diagram, there will always exist one indifference curve that touches the budget line at a single point of tangency. All higher indifference curves like U_H will be completely above the budget line, and although the choices on that indifference curve would provide higher utility, they aren't affordable given the budget set. All lower indifference curves, like U_L, will cross the budget line in two separate places. But when one indifference curve crosses the budget line in two places, there will be another, higher attainable indifference curve sitting above it that touches the budget line at only one point of tangency.

Changes in Income

A rise in income causes the budget constraint to shift to the right. In graphical terms, the new budget constraint will now be tangent to a higher indifference curve, representing

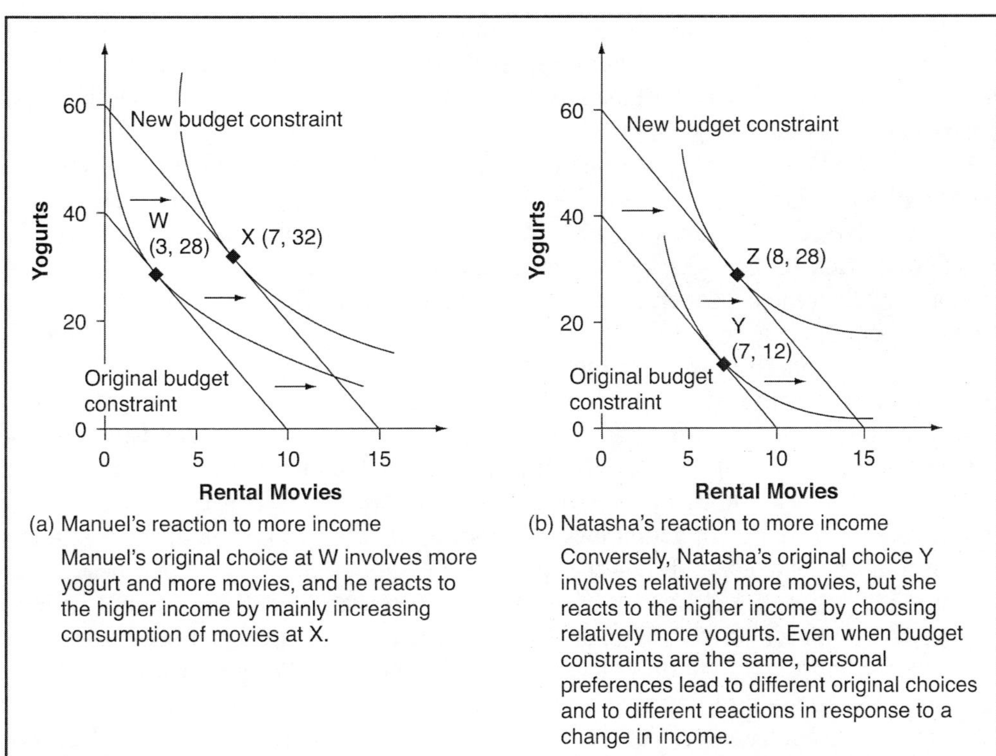

(a) Manuel's reaction to more income

Manuel's original choice at W involves more yogurt and more movies, and he reacts to the higher income by mainly increasing consumption of movies at X.

(b) Natasha's reaction to more income

Conversely, Natasha's original choice Y involves relatively more movies, but she reacts to the higher income by choosing relatively more yogurts. Even when budget constraints are the same, personal preferences lead to different original choices and to different reactions in response to a change in income.

EXHIBIT 8-A3

Manuel and Natasha originally face the same budget constraints; that is, same prices and same income. However, the indifference curves that illustrate their preferences are not the same.

a higher level of utility. A reduction in income will cause the budget constraint to shift to the left, which will cause it to be tangent to a lower indifference curve, representing a reduced level of utility. But if income rises by, say, 50%, exactly how much will a person alter consumption of books and doughnuts? Will consumption of both goods rise by 50%? Or the quantity of one good rises substantially, while the quantity of the other good rises only a little, or even declines?

Since personal preferences and the shape of indifference curves are different for each individual, the response to changes in income will be different, too. For example, consider the preferences of Manuel and Natasha in Exhibit 8-A3*a* and Exhibit 8-A3*b*. They each start with an identical income of $40, which they spend on yogurts that cost $1 and rental movies that cost $4. Thus, they face identical budget constraints. However, based on Manuel's preferences as revealed by his indifference curves, his utility-maximizing choice on the original budget set occurs where his opportunity set is tangent to the highest possible indifference curve at W, with 3 movies and 28 yogurts, while Natasha's utility-maximizing choice on the original budget set at Y will be 7 movies and 12 yogurts.

Now say that income rises to $60 for both Manuel and Natasha, so their budget constraints shift to the right. As shown in Exhibit 8-A3*a*, Manuel's new utility-maximizing choice at X will be 7 movies and 32 yogurts—that is, Manuel will choose to spend most of the extra income on movies. Natasha's new utility maximizing choice at Z will be 8 movies and 28 yogurts—that is, she will choose to spend most of the extra income on yogurt. In this way, the indifference curve approach allows for a range of possible responses. However, if both goods are normal goods, then the typical response to a higher level of income will be to purchase more of them—although exactly how much more is a matter of personal preference. If one of the goods is an inferior good, the response to a higher level of income will be to purchase less of it.

Responses to Price Changes: Substitution and Income Effects

A higher price for a good will cause the budget constraint to shift to the left, so that it is tangent to a lower indifference curve representing a reduced level of utility. Conversely, a lower price for a good will cause the opportunity set to shift to the right, so that it is tangent to a higher indifference curve representing an increased level of utility. Exactly how much a change in price will lead to the quantity demanded of each good will depend on personal preferences.

Anyone who faces a change in price will experience two interlinked motivations: a *substitution effect* and an *income effect*. The *substitution effect* is that when a good becomes more expensive, people seek out substitutes. If oranges become more expensive, fruit-lovers scale back on oranges and eat more apples or grapefruit or raisins. Conversely, when a good becomes cheaper, people substitute toward consuming more. If oranges get cheaper, people fire up their juicing machines and ease off on other fruits and foods. The *income effect* refers to how a change in the price of a good alters the effective buying power of one's income. If the price of a good that you have been buying falls, then in effect your buying power has risen—you are able to purchase more goods. Conversely, if the price of a good that you have been buying rises, then the buying power of a given amount of income is diminished. (One common confusion is that the "income effect" doesn't refer to a change in actual income. Instead, it refers to the situation in which the price of a good changes, and thus the quantities of goods that can be purchased with a fixed amount of income change. It might be more accurate to call the "income effect" a "buying power effect," but the "income effect" terminology has been used for decades, and it isn't going to change during this economics course.) Whenever a price changes, consumers feel the pull of both substitution and income effects at the same time.

Using indifference curves, you can illustrate the substitution and income effects on a graph. In Exhibit 8-A4, Ogden faces a choice between two goods: haircuts or personal pizzas. Haircuts cost $20, personal pizzas cost $6, and he has $120 to spend. The price of haircuts rises to $30. Ogden starts at choice A on the higher opportunity set and the

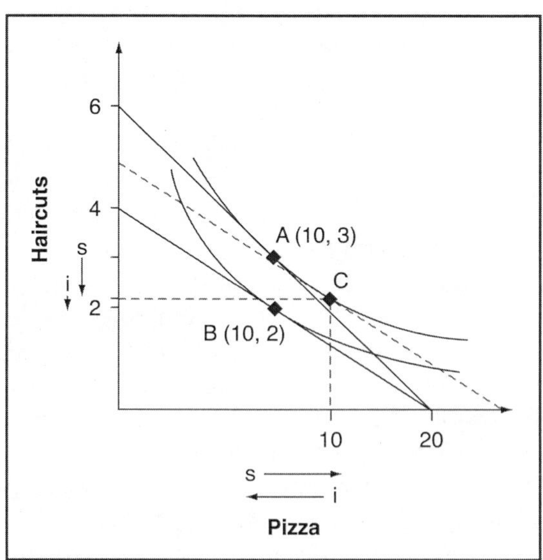

EXHIBIT 8-A4 Substitution and Income Effects

The original choice is A, the point of tangency between the original budget constraint and indifference curve. The new choice is B, the point of tangency between the new budget constraint and the lower indifference curve. Point C is the tangency between the dashed line, where the slope shows the new higher price of haircuts, and the original indifference curve. The substitution effect is the shift from A to C, which means getting fewer haircuts, which have become relatively more expensive, and more pizza, which is relatively less expensive. The income effect is the shift from C to B; that is, the reduction in buying power that causes a shift from the higher indifference curve to the lower indifference curve, with relative prices remaining unchanged. The income effect of lower buying power results in less consumed of both goods. Both substitution and income effects cause fewer haircuts to be consumed. For pizza, in this case, the substitution effect causing more pizza and income effect causing less pizza cancel out, leading to the same amount of pizza consumed.

higher indifference curve. After the price of pizza increases, he chooses B on the lower opportunity set and the lower indifference curve. Point B with 2 haircuts and 10 personal pizzas is immediately below point A with 3 haircuts and 10 personal pizzas, showing that Ogden reacted to a higher price of haircuts by cutting back only on haircuts, while leaving his consumption of pizza unchanged.

The dashed line in the diagram, and point C, are used to separate the substitution effect and the income effect. To understand their function, start by thinking about the substitution effect with this question: How would Ogden change his consumption if the relative prices of the two goods changed, but this change in relative prices did not affect his utility? The slope of the budget constraint is determined by the relative price of the two goods; thus, the slope of the original budget line is determined by the original relative prices, while the slope of the new budget line is determined by the new relative prices. With this thought in mind, the dashed line is a graphical tool inserted in a specific way: It is inserted so that it is parallel with the new budget constraint, so it reflects the new relative prices, but it is tangent to the original indifference curve, so it reflects the original level of utility or buying power.

Thus, the movement from the original choice A to point C is a substitution effect; it shows the choice that Ogden would make if relative prices shifted (as shown by the different slope between the original budget set and the dashed line) but if buying power did not shift (as shown by being tangent to the original indifference curve). The substitution effect will encourage people to shift away from the good that has become relatively more expensive—in Ogden's case, the haircuts on the vertical axis, and toward the good that has become relatively less expensive—in this case, the pizza on the vertical axis. The two arrows labeled with s for "substitution effect," one on each axis, show the direction of this movement.

The income effect is the movement from point C to B, which shows how Ogden reacts to a reduction in his buying power from the higher indifference curve to the lower indifference curve, but holding constant the relative prices (because the dashed line has the same slope as the new budget constraint). In this case where the price of one good increases, buying power is reduced, so the income effect means that consumption of both goods should fall (if they are both normal goods, which it is reasonable to assume unless there is reason to believe otherwise). The two arrows labeled with i for "income effect," one on each axis, show the direction of this income effect movement.

Now put the substitution and income effects together. When the price of pizza increased, Ogden consumed less of it, for two reasons shown in the exhibit: the substitution effect of the higher price led him to consume less, and the income effect of the higher price also led him to consume less. However, when the price of pizza increased, Ogden consumed the same quantity of haircuts. The substitution effect of a higher price for pizza meant that haircuts became relatively less expensive (compared to pizza), and this factor taken alone would have encouraged Ogden to consume more haircuts. However, the income effect of a higher price for pizza meant that he wished to consume less of both goods, and this factor taken alone would have encouraged Ogden to consume fewer haircuts. As shown in the exhibit, in this particular example the substitution effect and income effect on Ogden's consumption of haircuts are offsetting—so he ends up consuming the same quantity of haircuts after the price increase for pizza as before.

The size of these income and substitution effects will differ from person to person, depending on individual preferences. For example, if Ogden's substitution effect away from pizza and toward haircuts is especially strong, and outweighs the income effect, then a higher price for pizza might lead to increased consumption of haircuts. This case would be drawn on the graph so that the point of tangency between the new budget constraint and the relevant indifference curve occurred below point B and to the right. Conversely, if the substitution effect away from pizza and toward haircuts is not as strong, and the income effect on haircuts is relatively stronger, then Ogden will be more likely to react to the higher price of pizza by consuming less of both goods. In this case, his optimal choice after the price change will be above and to the left of choice B on the new budget constraint.

Although the substitution and income effects are often discussed as a sequence of events, it should be remembered that they are twin components of a single cause—a change in price. Although you can analyze them separately, the two effects are always proceeding hand in hand, happening at the same time.

Indifference Curves with Labor-Leisure and Intertemporal Choices

The concept of an indifference curve applies to trade-offs in any household choice, including the labor-leisure choice or the intertemporal choice between present and future consumption. In the labor-leisure choice, each indifference curve shows the combinations of leisure and income that provide a certain level of utility. In an intertemporal choice, each indifference curve shows the combinations of present and future consumption that provide a certain level of utility. The general shapes of the indifference curves—downward sloping, steeper on the left, and flatter on the right—also remain the same.

A Labor-Leisure Example

Petunia is working at a job that pays $12 per hour but she gets a raise to $20 per hour. After family responsibilities and sleep, she has 80 hours per week available for work or leisure. As shown in Exhibit 8-A5, the highest level of utility for Petunia on her original budget constraint is at choice A, where it is tangent to the lower indifference curve U_L. Point A has 30 hours of leisure and thus 50 hours per week of work, with income of $600 per week (that is, 50 hours of work times $12 per hour). Petunia then gets a raise to $20 per hour, which shifts her budget constraint to the right. Her new utility-maximizing choice occurs where the new budget constraint is tangent to the higher indifference curve U_L. At B, Petunia has 40 hours of leisure per week and works 40 hours, with income of $800 per week (that is, 40 hours of work times $20 per hour).

Substitution and income effects provide a vocabulary for discussing how Petunia reacts to a higher hourly wage. The dashed line serves as the tool for separating the two effects on the graph.

The substitution effect tells how Petunia would have changed her hours of work if her wage had risen, so that income was relatively cheaper to earn and leisure was relatively more expensive, but if she had remained at the same level of utility. The slope of the budget constraint in a labor-leisure diagram is determined by the wage rate. Thus, the dashed line is carefully inserted with the slope of the new opportunity set, reflecting the labor-leisure trade-off of the new wage rate, but tangent to the original indifference curve, showing the same level of utility or "buying power." The shift from original choice A to point C, which is the point of tangency between the original indifference curve and the dashed line, shows that because of the higher wage, Petunia will want to consume less leisure and more income. The s arrows on the horizontal and vertical axes of Exhibit 8-A5 show the substitution effect on leisure and on income.

The income effect is that the higher wage, by shifting the labor-leisure budget constraint to the right, makes it possible for Petunia to reach a higher level of utility. The income effect is the movement from point C to point B; that is, it shows how Petunia's behavior would change in response to a higher level of utility or "buying power," with the wage rate remaining the same (as shown by the dashed line being parallel to the new budget constraint). The income effect, encouraging Petunia to consume both more leisure and more income, is drawn with arrows on the horizontal and vertical axis of Exhibit 8-A5.

Putting these effects together, Petunia responds to the higher wage by moving from choice A to choice B. This movement involves choosing more income, both because the substitution effect of higher wages has made income relatively cheaper or easier to earn, and because the income effect of higher wages has made it possible to have more income and more leisure. Her movement from A to B also involves choosing more leisure because according to Petunia's preferences, the income effect that encourages choosing more leisure is stronger than the substitution effect that encourages choosing less leisure.

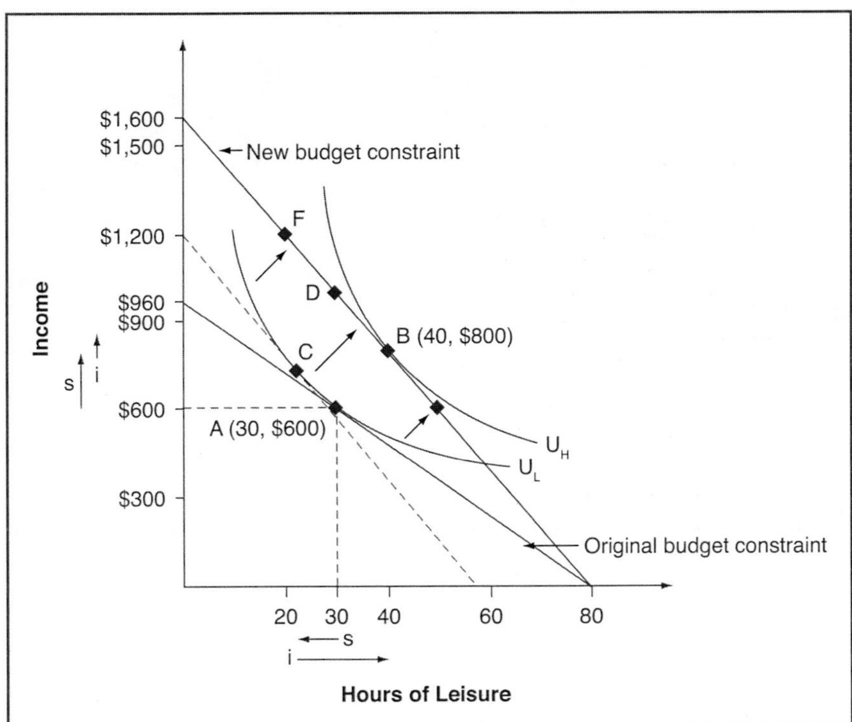

EXHIBIT 8-A5 Effects of a Change in Petunia's Wage

Petunia starts at choice A, the tangency between her original budget constraint and the lower indifference curve U_L. The wage increase shifts her budget constraint to the right, so that she can now choose B on indifference curve U_L. The substitution effect is the movement from A to C. It shows how Petunia would have changed her behavior if she had faced the new wage—which is represented by the dashed line having the same slope as the new budget line—but remained on the original indifference curve. In this case, the substitution effect would lead Petunia to choose less leisure, which is relatively more expensive, and more income, which is relatively cheaper to earn. The income effect is the movement from C to B. It shows how Petunia would change her behavior with the greater "buying power" of a higher wage, thus allowing a move to a higher indifference curve, but without a change in relative prices. The income effect in this example leads to greater consumption of both goods. Overall, in this example, income rises because of both substitution and income effects. However, leisure declines because of the substitution effect but increases because of the income effect—leading in Petunia's case to an overall increase in the quantity of leisure consumed.

But Exhibit 8-A5 represents only Petunia's preferences, and other people might make other choices. For example, a person whose substitution and income effects on leisure exactly counterbalanced each other would react to a higher wage with a choice like D, exactly above the original choice A, which means taking all of the benefit of the higher wages in the form of income while working the same number of hours. Yet another person, whose substitution effect on leisure outweighed the income effect, might react to a higher wage by making a choice like F, where the response to higher wages is to work more hours and earn much more income. To represent these different preferences, you could easily draw the indifference curve U_H to be tangent to the new budget constraint at D or F, rather than at B.

An Intertemporal Choice Example

Quentin has saved up $10,000. He is thinking about spending some or all of it on a vacation in the present, and then will save the rest for another big vacation five years from now. Over those five years, he expects to earn a total 80% rate of return. Exhibit 8-A6 shows Quentin's budget constraint and his indifference curves between present consumption and future consumption. The highest level of utility that Quentin can achieve at his original intertemporal budget constraint occurs at point A, where he is consuming $6,000,

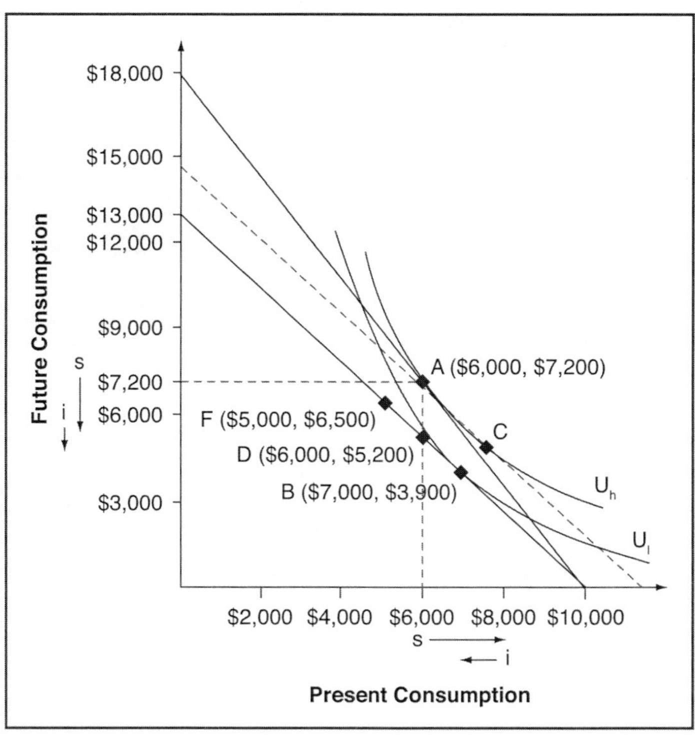

EXHIBIT 8-A6 Indifference Curve and an Intertemporal Budget Constraint

The original choice is A, at the tangency between the original budget constraint and the original indifference curve U_L. The dashed line is drawn parallel to the new budget set, so that its slope reflects the lower rate of return, but is tangent to the original indifference curve. The movement from A to C is the substitution effect: in this case, future consumption has become relatively more expensive, and present consumption has become relatively cheaper. The income effect is the shift from C to B; that is, the reduction in utility or "buying power" that causes a move to a lower indifference curve U_L, but with the relative price the same. It means less present and less future consumption. In the move from A to B, the substitution effect on present consumption is greater than the income effect, so the overall result is more present consumption. But notice that the lower indifference curve could have been drawn tangent to the lower budget constraint point D or point F, depending on personal preferences.

saving $4,000 for the future, and expecting with the accumulated interest to have $7,200 for future consumption (that is, $4,000 in current financial savings plus the 80% rate of return).

However, Quentin has just realized that his expected rate of return was unrealistically high. A more realistic expectation is that over five years he can earn a total return of 30%. In effect, his intertemporal budget constraint has pivoted to the left, so that his original utility-maximizing choice is no longer available. Will Quentin react to the lower rate of return by saving more, or less, or the same amount? Again, the language of substitution and income effects provides a framework for thinking about the motivations behind various choices. The dashed line, which is a graphical tool to separate the substitution and income effect, is carefully inserted with the same slope as the new opportunity set, so that it reflects the changed rate of return, but it is tangent to the original indifference curve, so that it shows no change in utility or "buying power."

The substitution effect tells how Quentin would have altered his consumption because the lower rate of return makes future consumption relatively more expensive and present consumption relatively cheaper. The movement from the original choice A to point C shows how Quentin substitutes toward more present consumption and less future consumption in response to the lower interest rate, with no change in utility. The substitution arrows on the horizontal and vertical axes of Exhibit 8-A6 show the direction of the substitution effect motivation. The substitution effect suggests that because of the lower interest rate, Quentin should consume more in the present and less in the future.

CLEARING IT UP

A Step-by-Step Guide to Sketching Substitution and Income Effects

If you are finding it a little tricky to sketch diagrams that show substitution and income effects so that the dashed line and the various points of tangency all come out correctly, it may be useful to follow this procedure.

Step 1: Begin with a budget constraint showing the choice between two goods, which this example will call "candy" and "movies." Choose a point A, which will be the optimal choice, where the indifference curve will be tangent—but it is often easier not to draw in the indifference curve just yet.

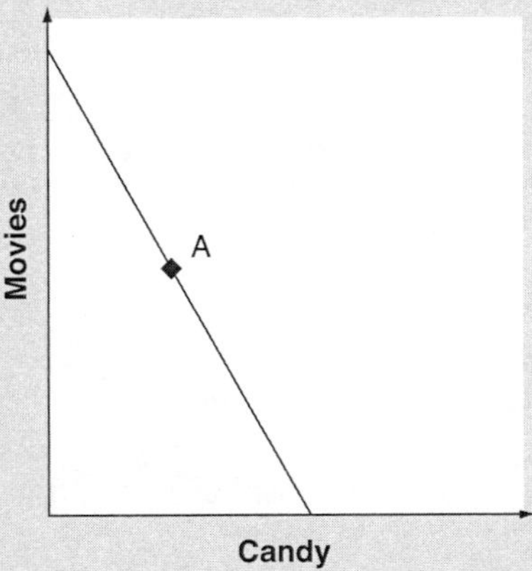

Draw the budget constraint. Insert optimal choice A.

Step 2: Now the price of movies changes: let's say that it rises. That shifts the budget set inward. You know that the higher price will push the decision-maker down to a lower level of utility, represented by a lower indifference curve. But at this stage, draw only the new budget set.

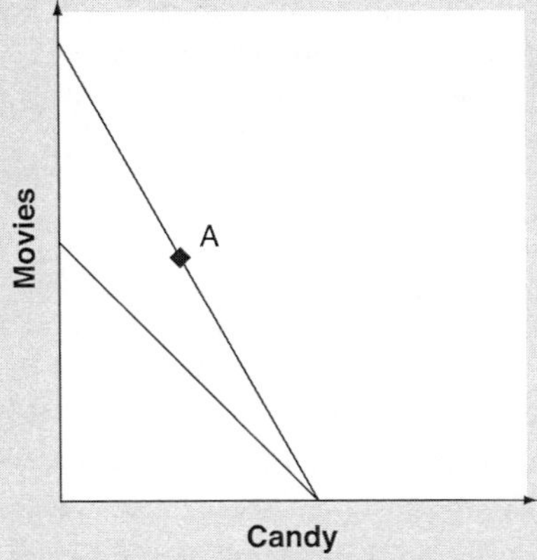

Draw the new budget constraint.

Step 3: The key tool in distinguishing between substitution and income effects is to insert a dashed line, parallel to the new budget line. This line is a graphical tool that allows you to distinguish between the two changes: (1) the effect on consumption of the two goods of the shift in prices—with the level of utility remaining unchanged—which is the substitution effect; and (2) the effect on consumption of the two goods of shifting from one indifference curve to the other—with relative prices staying unchanged—which is the income effect. The dashed line is inserted in this step. The trick is to have the dashed line travel close to the original choice A, but not directly through point A.

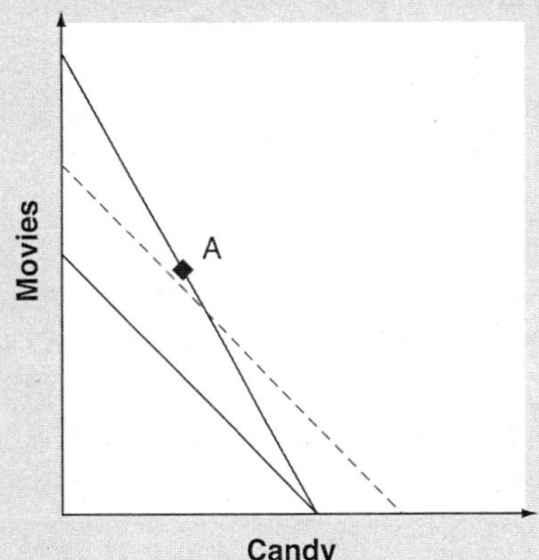

Draw in the dashed line, parallel to the new budget line, but crossing the original budget line near original choice A.

Step 4: Now draw the original indifference curve, so that it is tangent to both point A on the original budget line and to a point C on the dashed line. Many students find it easiest to first select the tangency point C where the original indifference curve touches the dashed line, and then to draw the original indifference curve through A and C. The substitution effect is illustrated by the movement along the original indifference curve as prices change but the level of utility holds constant, from A to C. As expected, the substitution effect leads to less consumed of the good that is relatively more expensive, as shown by the s-for-substitution arrow on the vertical axis, and more consumed of the good that is relatively less expensive, as shown by the s arrow on the horizontal axis.

CLEARING IT UP

A Step-by-Step Guide to Sketching Substitution and Income Effects *(Continued)*

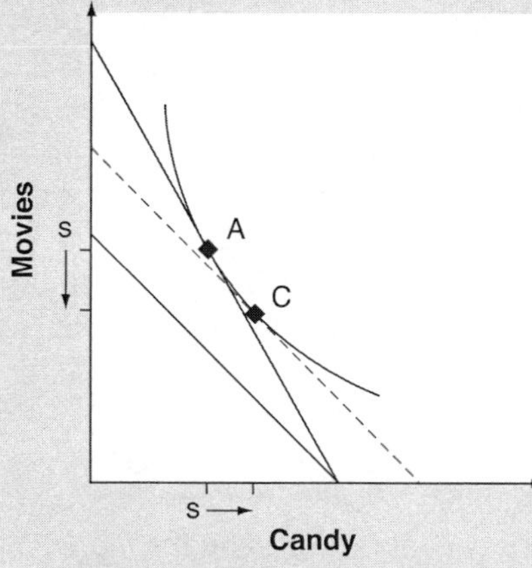

Draw in the original indifference curve, tangent both to the original choice A and to a point C on the dashed line. Identify the substitution effect.

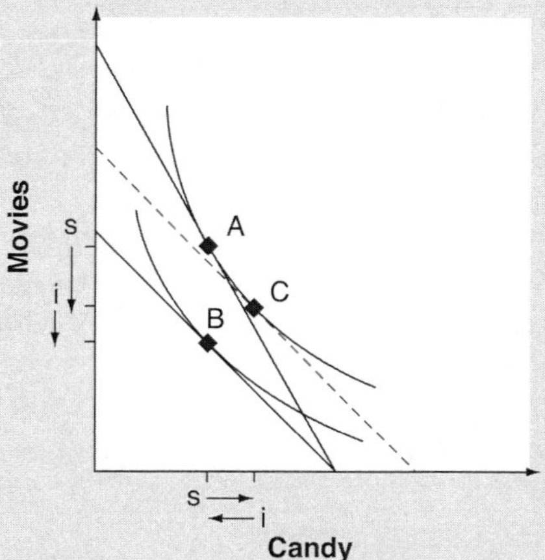

Identify new choice B on the new budget set, and draw the new indifference curve tangent to it. Think about whether B should be under A, or to the right or left of it, based on what the problem requires. The movement from C to B will be the income effect.

Step 5: With the substitution effect in place, now choose utility-maximizing point B on the new opportunity set. When you choose point B, think about whether you wish the substitution or the income effect to have a larger impact on the good on the horizontal axis. If you choose point B to be directly in a vertical line with point A (as is illustrated here), then the income effect will be exactly offsetting the substitution effect on the horizontal axis. If you insert point B so that it lies a little to the right of the original point A, then the substitution effect will exceed the income effect. If you insert point B so that it lies a little to the left of point A, then the income effect will exceed the substitution effect. The income effect is the movement from C to B, showing how choices shifted as a result of the decline in buying power and the movement between two levels of utility, with relative prices remaining the same. With normal goods, the negative income effect means less consumed of each good, as shown by the direction of the i-for-income-effect arrows on the vertical and horizontal axes.

In sketching substitution and income effect diagrams, you may wish to practice some of the following variations: (1) Price falls instead of rising; (2) The price change affects the good on either the vertical or the horizontal axis; (3) Sketch these diagrams so that the substitution effect exceeds the income effect; the income effect exceeds the substitution effect; and the two effects are equal.

One final note: The helpful dashed line can be drawn tangent to the new indifference curve, and parallel to the original budget line, rather than tangent to the original indifference curve and parallel to the new budget line. Some students find this approach more intuitively clear. But the answers you get about the direction and relative sizes of the substitution and income effects should be just the same.

Quentin also has an income effect motivation. The lower rate of return shifts the budget constraint to the left, which means that Quentin's utility or "buying power" is reduced. The income effect (assuming normal goods) encourages less of both present and future consumption. The impact of the income effect on reducing present and future consumption in this example is shown with i arrows on the horizontal and vertical axis of Exhibit 8-A6.

Taking both effects together, the substitution effect is encouraging Quentin toward more present and less future consumption because present consumption is relatively cheaper, while the income effect is encouraging him to less present and less future consumption because the lower interest rate is pushing him to a lower level of utility. For Quentin's personal preferences, the substitution effect is stronger so that overall, he reacts to the lower rate of return with more present consumption and less savings at choice B.

However, other people might have different preferences. They might react to a lower rate of return by choosing the same level of present consumption and savings at choice D, or by choosing less present consumption and more savings at a point like F. For these other sets of preferences, the income effect of a lower rate of return on present consumption would be relatively stronger, while the substitution effect would be relatively weaker.

Conclusion

Indifference curves provide an analytical tool for looking at all the choices that provide a single level of utility. They eliminate any need for placing numerical values on utility and help to illuminate the process of making utility-maximizing decisions. They also provide the basis for a more detailed investigation of the complementary motivations that arise in response to a change in a price, wage, or rate of return—namely, the substitution and income effects.

Key Concepts and Summary

1. An *indifference curve* is drawn on a budget constraint diagram that shows the tradeoffs between two goods. All points along a single indifference curve provide the same level of utility. Higher indifference curves represent higher levels of utility.
2. Indifference curves slope downward because, if utility is to remain the same at all points along the curve, a reduction in the quantity of the good on the vertical axis must be counterbalanced by an increase in the quantity of the good on the horizontal axis (or vice versa). Indifference curves are steeper on the far left and flatter on the far right, because of diminishing marginal utility.
3. The utility-maximizing choice along a budget constraint will be the point of tangency where the budget constraint touches an indifference curve at a single point.
4. A change in the price of any good has two effects: a *substitution effect* and an *income effect*. The substitution effect motivation encourages a utility-maximizer to buy less of what is relatively more expensive and more of what is relatively cheaper. The income effect motivation encourages a utility-maximizer to buy more of both goods if utility rises or less of both goods if utility falls (if they are both normal goods).
5. In a labor-leisure choice, every wage change has a substitution and an income effect. The substitution effect of a wage increase is to choose more income, since it is cheaper to earn, and less leisure, since its opportunity cost has increased. The income effect of a wage increase is to choose more of leisure and income, since they are both normal goods. The substitution and income effects of a wage decrease would reverse these directions.
6. In an intertemporal consumption choice, every interest rate change has a substitution and an income effect. The substitution effect of an interest rate increase is to choose more future consumption, since it is now cheaper to earn future consumption and less present consumption (more savings), since the opportunity cost of present consumption in terms of what is being given up in the future has increased. The income effect of an interest rate increase is to choose more of both present and future consumption, since they are both normal goods. The substitution and income effects of an interest rate decrease would reverse these directions.

Review Questions

1. What point is preferred along an indifference curve?
2. Why do indifference curves slope down?
3. Why are indifference curves steep on the left and flatter on the right?
4. How many indifference curves does a person have?
5. How can you tell which indifference curves represent higher or lower levels of utility?
6. What is a substitution effect?
7. What is an income effect?
8. Does the "income effect" involve a change in income? Explain.
9. Does a change in price have both an income effect and a substitution effect? Does a change in income have both an income effect and a substitution effect?
10. Would you expect in some cases to see only an income effect or only a substitution effect? Explain.
11. Which is larger, the income effect or the substitution effect?

CHAPTER APPENDIX

19

Present Discounted Value

Calculating Present Discounted Value of a Stock

Payments from Firm	Present Value
15 in present	15
20 in one year	$20/(1 + .15)^1 = 17.4$
25 in two years	$25/(1 + .15)^2 = 18.9$
Total	***51.3***

Appendix Outline

The prices of stocks and bonds depend on future events. The price of a bond depends on the future payments that the bond is expected to make, including both payments of interest and the repayment of the face value of the bond. The price of a stock depends on the expected future profits earned by the firm. The concept of a present discounted value (PDV), which is defined as the amount you should be willing to pay in the present for a stream of expected future payments, can be used to calculate appropriate prices for stocks and bonds. To place a present discounted value on a future payment, think about what amount of money you would need to have in the present to equal a certain amount in the future. This calculation will require an interest rate. For example, if the interest rate is 10%, then a payment of $110 a year from now will have a present discounted value of $100—that is, you could take $100 in the present and have $110 in the future. This appendix first shows how to apply the idea of present discounted value to a stock and then to a bond.

Applying Present Discounted Value to a Stock

Consider the case of Babble, Inc., a company that offers speaking lessons. For the sake of simplicity, say that the founder of Babble is 63 years old and plans to retire in two years, at which point the company will be disbanded. The company is selling 200 shares of stock and profits are expected to be $15 million right away, in the present, $20 million one year from now, and $25 million two years from now. All profits will be paid out as dividends to shareholders as they occur. Given this information, what will an investor pay for a share of stock in this company?

A financial investor thinking about what future payments are worth in the present will need to choose an interest rate. This interest rate will reflect the rate of return on other available financial investment opportunities, which is the opportunity cost of investing financial capital, and also a risk premium

EXHIBIT 19–A1 Calculating Present Discounted Value of a Stock

Payments from Firm	Present Value
15 in present	15
20 in one year	$20/(1 + .15)^1 = 17.4$
25 in two years	$25/(1 + .15)^2 = 18.9$
Total	***51.3***

(that is, using a higher interest rate than the rates available elsewhere if this investment appears especially risky). In this example, say that the financial investor decides that appropriate interest rate to value these future payments is 15%.

Exhibit 19-A1 shows how to calculate the present discounted value of the future profits. For each time period when a benefit is going to be received, apply the formula:

$$\text{Present discounted value} = \frac{(\text{Future value received } t \text{ years in the future})}{(1 + \text{Interest rate})^{\text{number of years } t}}$$

Then add up all the present values for the different time periods to get a final answer. The present value calculations ask what the amount in the future is worth in the present, given the 15% interest rate. Notice that a different PDV calculation needs to be done separately for amounts received at different times. Then divide the PDV of total profits by the number of shares, 200 in this case, and the price per share should be 51.3/200 = .2565, or about 25 cents per share.

Of course, in the real world expected profits are a best guess, not a hard piece of data. Deciding which interest rate to apply for discounting to the present can be tricky. One needs to take into account both potential capital gains from the future sale of the stock and also dividends that might be paid. Differences of opinion on these issues are exactly why some financial investors want to buy a stock that other people want to sell: they are more optimistic about its future prospects. But conceptually, it all comes down to what you are willing to pay in the present for a stream of benefits to be received in the future.

Applying Present Discounted Value to a Bond

A similar calculation works in the case of bonds. The chapter explains that if the interest rate falls after a bond is issued, so that the investor has locked in a higher rate, then that bond will sell for more than its face value. Conversely, if the interest rate rises after a bond is issued, then the investor is locked into a lower rate, and the bond will sell for less than its face value. The present value calculation sharpens this intuition.

Think about a simple two-year bond. It was issued for $3,000, at an interest rate of 8%. Thus, after the first year the bond pays interest of $240 ($3,000 × 8%). At the end of the second year, the bond pays $240 in interest, plus repaying the $3,000 in principle. Calculate how much this bond is worth in the present if the discount rate is 8%. Then recalculate if interest rates rise and the applicable discount rate is 11%. To carry out these calculations, look at the stream of payments being received from the bond in the future and figure out what they are worth in present discounted value terms. The calculations applying the present value formula are shown in Exhibit 19-A2.

The first calculation shows that the present value of a $3,000 bond, issued at 8%, is just $3,000. After all, that's how much money the borrower is receiving. The calculation confirms that the present value is the same for the lender. The bond is moving money around in time, from those willing to save in the present to those who want to borrow in the present, but the present value of what is received by the borrower is identical to the present value of what will be repaid to the lender.

The second calculation shows what happens if the interest rate rises from 8% to 11%. The actual dollar payments in the first column, as determined by the 8% interest rate,

EXHIBIT 19–A2 Computing the Present Discounted Value of a Bond

For the 8% Interest Rate	
Stream of Payments	*Present Value*
\$240 payment after one year	$240/(1 + .08)^1 = 222.2$
\$3,240 payment after second year	$3,240/(1 + .08)^2 = 2,777.8$
Total	***\$3,000***
For the 11% Interest Rate	
Stream of Payments	*Present Value*
\$240 payment after one year	$240/(1 + .11)^1 = 216.2$
\$3,240 payment after second year	$3,240/(1 + .11)^2 = 2,629.6$
Total	***\$2,845.8***

don't change. However, the present value of those payments, now discounted at a higher interest rate, is lower. Even though the future dollar payments that the bond is receiving have not changed, a person who tries to sell the bond will find that the value of the investment has fallen.

Again, real-world calculations are often more complex, in part because not only the interest rate prevailing in the market but also the riskiness of whether the borrower will repay the loan will change. But in any case, the price of a bond is always the present value of a stream of future expected payments.

Other Applications

Present discounted value is a widely used analytical tool outside the world of finance. Every time a business thinks about making a physical capital investment, it must compare a set of present costs of making that investment to the present discounted value of future benefits. When government thinks about a proposal to, say, add safety features to a highway, it must compare costs incurred in the present to benefits received in the future. Some academic disputes over environmental policies, like how much to reduce carbon dioxide emissions because of the risk that they will lead to a warming of global temperatures several decades in the future, turn on how one compares present costs of pollution control with long-run future benefits. Someone who wins the lottery and is scheduled to receive a string of payments over 30 years might be interested in knowing what the present discounted value is of those payments. Whenever a string of costs and benefits stretches from the present into different times in the future, present discounted value becomes an indispensable tool of analysis.

CHAPTER APPENDIX

27

An Algebraic Approach to the Expenditure-Output Model

Y = National income

Taxes = T = .25Y

C = Consumption = 400 + .85(Y – T)

I = 300

G = 200

X = 500

M = .1(Y – T)

Appendix Outline

In the expenditure-output or Keynesian cross model, the equilibrium occurs where the aggregate expenditure line AE line crosses the 45-degree line. Given algebraic equations for two lines, the point where they cross can be readily calculated. Imagine an economy with the following characteristics.

$$Y = \text{Real GDP or national income}$$

$$T = \text{Taxes} = .3Y$$

$$C = \text{Consumption} = 140 + .9(Y - T)$$

$$I = \text{Investment} = 400$$

$$G = \text{Government spending} = 800$$

$$X = \text{Exports} = 600$$

$$M = \text{Imports} = .15Y$$

The aggregate expenditure function in this case is:

$$AE = C + I + G + X - M$$

$$AE = 140 + .9(Y - T) + 400 + 800 + 600 - .15Y$$

The equation for the 45° line is the set of points where GDP or national income on the horizontal axis is equal to aggregate expenditure on the vertical axis. Thus, the equation for the 45-degree line is:

$$AE = Y.$$

The next step is to solve these two equations for Y (or AE, since they will be equal to each other).

$$Y = AE \quad AE = 140 + .9(Y - T) + 400 + 800 + 600 - .15Y$$

Substituting Y from the first equation into the AE in the second equation, and inserting the term .3Y for the tax rate T, produces an equation with only one variable, Y. The next step is to work through the algebra and solve for Y.

$$Y = 140 + .9(Y - .3Y) + 400 + 800 + 600 - .15Y.$$

$$Y - .63Y + .15Y = 1{,}940$$

$$.52Y = 1{,}940$$

$$Y = 3{,}730$$

This algebraic framework is flexible and useful in predicting how economic events and policy actions will affect real GDP. Say, for example, that because of changes in the relative prices of domestic and foreign goods, the marginal propensity to import falls to .1. Or say that because of a surge of business confidence, investment rises to 500. Simply plug the new numbers into the algebra, and you should be able to confirm that in the first case, the equilibrium output rises to 4,127 and in the second case rises to 3,923. Here's the calculation, when the marginal propensity to import has changed to .1.

$$Y = AE = 140 + .9(Y - .3Y) + 400 + 800 + 600 - .1Y.$$

$$Y - .63Y + .1Y = 1940$$

$$.47Y = 1940$$

$$Y = 4127$$

For investment rising to 500

$$Y = AE = 140 + .9(Y - .3Y) + 500 + 800 + 600 - .15Y.$$

Solving for Y means working through the algebra:

$$Y - .63Y + .15Y = 2{,}040$$

$$.52Y = 2{,}040$$

$$Y = 3{,}923$$

For issues of policy, the key questions would be how to adjust government spending levels or tax rates so that the equilibrium level of output is the full employment level. In this case, let the economic parameters be:

$$Y = \text{National income}$$

$$T = \text{Taxes} = .3Y$$

$$C = \text{Consumption} = 200 + .9(Y - T)$$

$$I = \text{Investment} = 600$$

$$G = \text{Government spending} = 1{,}000$$

$$X = \text{Exports} = 600$$

$$Y = \text{Imports} = .1(Y - T)$$

The equilibrium for this economy is:

$$Y = AE = 200 + .9(Y - .3Y) + 600 + 1000 + 600 - .1(Y - .3Y)$$

$$Y - .63Y + .07Y = 2{,}400$$

$$.44Y = 2{,}400$$

$$Y = 5{,}454$$

Let's assume that the full employment level of output is 6,000. What level of government spending would be necessary to reach that level? To answer this question, plug in 6,000 as equal to Y, but leave G as a variable, and solve for G. Thus:

$$6{,}000 = 200 + .9(6{,}000 - .3(6{,}000)) + 600 + G + 600 - .1(6{,}000 - .3(6{,}000))$$

Solving this problem is just arithmetic: G = 1,240. In other words, increasing government spending by 240, from its original level of 1,000 to 1,240, would raise output to the full employment level of GDP.

Indeed, the question of how much to increase government spending so that equilibrium output will rise from 5,454 to 6,000 can be answered without working through the algebra, just by using the multiplier formula. The multiplier equation in this case is $1/(1 - .56) = 2.27$. Thus, to raise output by 546 would require an increase in government spending of $546/2.27 = 240$, which is the same as the answer derived from the algebraic calculation.

This algebraic framework is highly flexible. For example, taxes can be treated as a total that is set by political considerations (like government spending) and not dependent on national income. Imports might be based on before-tax income, not after-tax income. For certain purposes, it may be helpful to analyze the economy without exports and imports. A more complicated approach could divide up consumption, investment, government, exports and imports into smaller categories, or to build in some variability in the rates of taxes, savings, and imports. A wise economist will shape the model to fit the specific question under investigation.

Question

1. An economy has the following characteristics:

$$Y = \text{National income}$$

$$\text{Taxes} = T = .25Y$$

$$C = \text{Consumption} = 400 + .85(Y - T)$$

$$I = 300$$

$$G = 200$$

$$X = 500$$

$$M = .1(Y - T)$$

Find the equilibrium for this economy. If potential GDP is 3,500, then what change in government spending is needed to achieve this level? Do this problem two ways. First, plug 3,500 into the equations and solve for G. Second, calculate the multiplier and figure it out that way.

Answer

1. Set up the calculation:

$$AE = 400 + .85(Y - T) + 300 + 200 + 500 - .1(Y - T)$$

$$AE = Y$$

$$Y = 400 + .85(Y - .25Y) + 300 + 200 + 500 - .1(Y - .25Y)$$

$$Y = 1{,}400 + .6375Y - .075Y$$

$$.4375Y = 1{,}400$$

$$Y = 3{,}200$$

If full employment is 3,500, then one approach is to plug in 3,500 for Y throughout the equation, but to leave G as a separate variable.

$$Y = 400 + .85(Y - .25Y) + 300 + G + 500 + .1(Y - .25Y)$$

$$3500 = 400 + .85(3{,}500 - .25(3{,}500)) + 300 + G + 500 - .1(3{,}500 - .25(3{,}500))$$

$$3{,}500 - 400 - 2{,}231.25 - 300 - 500 + 262.5 = G$$

G = 331.25, which is an increase of 131.25 from its original level of 200

Alternatively, the multiplier is that out of every dollar spent, .25 goes to taxes, leaving .75, and out of after-tax income, .15 goes to savings and .1 to imports. Because (.75)(.15) = .1125 and (.75)(.1) = .075, this means that out of every dollar spent, 1 – .25 – .1125 – .075 = .5625.

Thus, using the formula, the multiplier is 1/(1 – .5625) = 2.2837.

To increase equilibrium GDP by 300, it will take a boost of 300/2.2837, which again works out to 131.25.

Glossary

A

absolute advantage: When one nation can produce a product at lower cost relative to another nation.
accounting profit: Total revenues minus the firm's costs, without taking opportunity cost into account.
acquisition: When one firm purchases another; for practical purposes, often combined with mergers.
adaptive expectations: The theory that people look at past experience and gradually adapt their beliefs and behavior as circumstances change.
adjustable rate mortgage (ARM): A loan used to purchase a home in which the interest rate varies with the rate of inflation.
adverse selection: The problem that arises when one party knows more about the quality of the good than the other, and as a result, the party with less knowledge must worry about ending up at a disadvantage.
affirmative action: Active efforts to improve the job opportunities or outcomes of minority groups or women.
aggregate demand (AD): The relationship between the total quantity of goods and services demanded and the price level for output.
aggregate production function: The process of an economy as a whole turning economic inputs like labor, machinery, and raw materials into outputs like goods and services used by consumers.
aggregate supply (AS): The relationship between the total quantity that firms choose to produce and sell and the price level for output, holding the price of inputs fixed.
allocative efficiency: When the mix of goods being produced represents the allocation that society most desires.
anti-dumping laws: Laws that block imports sold below the cost of production and impose tariffs that would increase the price of these imports to reflect their cost of production.
antitrust laws: Laws that give government the power to block certain mergers, and even in some cases, to break up large firms into smaller ones.
applied research: Research focused on a particular product that promises an economic payoff in the short or medium term.
appreciating: When a currency is worth more in terms of other currencies; also called "strengthening."
asset-liability time mismatch: A bank's liabilities can be withdrawn in the short term while its assets are repaid in the long term.
assets: Items of value owned by a firm or an individual.
automatic stabilizers: Tax and spending rules that have the effect of increasing aggregate demand when the economy slows down and restraining aggregate demand when the economy speeds up, without any additional change in legislation.
average cost: Total cost divided by the quantity of output.
average variable cost: Variable cost divided by the quantity of output.

B

backward-bending supply curve for labor: The situation when high-wage people can earn so much that they respond to a still-higher wage by working fewer hours.
balance of trade: The gap, if any, between a nation's exports and imports.
balance sheet: An accounting tool that lists assets and liabilities.
balanced budget: When government spending and taxes are equal.
bank run: When depositors race to the bank to withdraw their deposits for fear that otherwise they would be lost.
barriers to entry: The legal, technological, or market forces that may discourage or prevent potential competitors from entering a market.
barter: Trading one good or service for another directly, without using money.
basic quantity equation of money: Money supply × Velocity = Nominal GDP.
basic research: Research on fundamental scientific breakthroughs that may offer commercial applications only in the distant future.
basket of goods and services: A hypothetical group of different items, with specified quantities of each one, used as a basis for calculating how the price level changes over time.
biodiversity: The full spectrum of animal and plant genetic material.
black market: An illegal market that breaks government rules on prices or sales.
bond: A financial contract through which a borrower like a corporation, a city or state, or the federal government agrees to repay the amount that was borrowed and also a rate of interest over a period of time in the future.
bond yield: The rate of return that a bond is expected to pay at the time of purchase.
bondholders: Those who own bonds and receive the interest payments.
budget constraint: A diagram that shows the possible choices.
budget deficit: When the federal government spends more than it collects in taxes in a given year.

budget surplus: When the government receives more in taxes than it spends in a year.
bundling: A situation where a customer is allowed to buy one product only if the customer also buys another product; also called "tie-in sales."
business cycle: The relatively short-term movement of the economy in and out of recession.

C

capital deepening: When an economy has a higher average level of physical and/or human capital per person.
capital gain: A financial gain from buying an asset, like a share of stock or a house, and later selling it at a higher price.
cartel: A group of firms that collude to produce the monopoly output and sell at the monopoly price.
central bank: An institution to conduct monetary policy and regulate the banking system.
certificates of deposit (CD): A mechanism for a saver to deposit funds at a bank and promise to leave them at the bank for a time, in exchange for a higher rate of interest.
***ceteris paribus*:** Other things being equal.
checking account: A bank account that typically pays little or no interest, but that gives easy access to your money, either by writing a check or by using a debit card.
circular flow diagram: A diagram that views the economy as consisting of households and firms interacting in a goods and services market, a labor market, and a financial capital market.
coinsurance: When an insurance policyholder pays a percentage of a loss, and the insurance company pays the remaining cost.
collateral: Something valuable—often property or equipment—that a lender would have a right to seize and sell if the loan is not repaid.
collective bargaining: Negotiations between unions and a firm or firms.
collusion: When firms act together to reduce output and keep prices high.
command economy: An economy in which the government either makes or strongly influences most economic decisions.
command-and-control regulation: Laws that specify allowable quantities of pollution and may also detail which pollution-control technologies must be used.
comparative advantage: The goods in which a nation has its greatest productivity advantage or its smallest productivity disadvantage; also, the goods that a nation can produce at a lower cost when measured in terms of opportunity cost.
complements: Goods that are often used together, so that a rise in the price of one good tends to decrease the quantity consumed of the other good, and vice versa.
compound interest: When interest payments in earlier periods are reinvested, so that in later time periods, the interest rate is paid on the total amount accumulated during previous years.
constant returns to scale: When expanding all inputs does not change the average cost of production.
Consumer Price Index (CPI): A measure of inflation calculated by U.S. government statisticians based on the price level from a basket of goods and services that represents the purchases of the average consumer.
consumer surplus: The benefit consumers receive from buying a good or service, measured by what the individuals would have been willing to pay minus the amount that they actually paid.
consumption function: The relationship between income and expenditures on consumption.
contractionary fiscal policy: When fiscal policy decreases the level of aggregate demand, either through cuts in government spending or increases in taxes.
contractionary monetary policy: A monetary policy that reduces the supply of money and loans; also called a "tight" monetary policy.
convergence: When economies with low per capita incomes are growing faster than economies with high per capita incomes.
copayment: When an insurance policyholder must pay a small amount for each service, before insurance covers the rest.
copyright: A form of legal protection to prevent copying for commercial purposes original works of authorship, including books and music.
corporate bonds: Bonds issued by firms that wish to borrow.
corporate income tax: A tax imposed on corporate profits.
cosigner: On a loan, another person or firm that legally pledges to repay some or all of the money if the original borrower does not do so.
cost-of-living adjustment (COLA): A contractual provision that wage increases will keep up with inflation.
cost-plus regulation: When regulators permit a regulated firm to cover its costs and to make a normal level of profit.
countercyclical: Moving in the opposite direction of the business cycle of economic downturns and upswings.
cross-price elasticity of demand: The percentage change in the quantity of good A that is demanded as a result of a percentage change in good B.
crowding out: When government borrowing soaks up available financial capital and leaves less for private investment in physical capital.
currency: Coins and paper bills.
current account balance: A broad measure of the balance of trade that includes trade in goods and services, as well as international flows of income and foreign aid.
cyclical unemployment: Unemployment closely tied to the business cycle, like higher unemployment during a recession.

D

deadweight loss: The loss in social surplus that occurs when a market produces an inefficient quantity.
debit card: A card that lets you make purchases, where the cost is immediately deducted from your checking account.
decreasing returns to scale: A situation in which as the quantity of output rises, the average cost of production rises.
deductible: An amount that the insurance policyholders must pay out of their own pocket before the insurance coverage pays anything.
deflation: Negative inflation.
demand: A relationship between price and the quantity demanded of a certain good or service.
demand curve: A line that shows the relationship between price and quantity demanded of a certain good or service on a

graph, with quantity on the horizontal axis and the price on the vertical axis.
demand deposits: Deposits in banks that are available by making a cash withdrawal or writing a check.
demand schedule: A table that shows a range of prices for a certain good or service and the quantity demanded at each price.
deposit insurance: An insurance system that makes sure depositors in a bank do not lose their money, even if the bank goes bankrupt.
depreciating: When a currency is worth less in terms of other currencies; also called "weakening."
depression: An especially lengthy and deep decline in output.
deregulation: Removing government controls over setting prices and quantities in certain industries.
differentiated products: Products that are distinctive in a particular way.
diminishing marginal returns: When the marginal gain in output diminishes as each additional unit of input is added.
diminishing marginal utility: The common pattern that each marginal unit of a good consumed provides less of an addition to utility than the previous unit.
discount rate: The interest rate charged by the central bank when it makes loans to commercial banks.
discretionary fiscal policy: When the government passes a new law that explicitly changes overall tax or spending levels.
diseconomies of scale: Another term for decreasing returns to scale.
diversification: Investing in a wide range of companies, to reduce the level of risk.
diversify: Making loans or investments with a variety of firms, to reduce the risk of being adversely affected by events at one or a few firms.
dividend: A direct payment from a firm to its shareholders.
division of labor: Dividing the work required to produce a good or service into tasks performed by different workers.
dollarize: When a country that is not the United States uses the U.S. dollar as its currency.
double coincidence of wants: A situation in which both of two people each wants some good or service that the other person can provide.
double counting: A potential mistake to be avoided in measuring GDP, in which output is counted two or more times as it travels through the stages of production.
dumping: Selling internationally traded goods below their cost of production.
duopoly: An oligopoly with only two firms.
durable goods: Long-lasting goods like cars and refrigerators.

E

economic profit: Total revenues minus all of the firm's costs, including opportunity costs.
economics: The study of the production, distribution, and consumption of goods and services.
economies of scale: When the average cost of producing each individual unit declines as total output increases.
economy: The social arrangements that determine what is produced, how it is produced, and for whom it is produced.
efficiency: When it is impossible to get more of something without experiencing a trade-off of less of something else.
efficiency wage theory: The theory that the productivity of workers, either individually or as a group, will increase if they are paid more.
elastic: The elasticity calculated from the appropriate formula has an absolute value greater than 1.
elasticity: How much a percentage change in quantity demanded or quantity supplied is affected by a percentage change in price.
elasticity of demand: The percentage change in quantity demanded divided by the percentage change in price.
elasticity of labor supply: The percentage change in hours worked divided by the percentage change in wages.
elasticity of savings: The percentage change in the quantity of savings divided by the percentage change in interest rates.
elasticity of supply: The percentage change in quantity supplied divided by the percentage change in price.
Employment Cost Index: A measure of inflation based on the wage paid in the labor market.
entry: The long-run process of firms beginning and expanding production when they see opportunity for profits.
equilibrium: The combination of price and quantity where there is no economic pressure from surpluses or shortages that would cause price or quantity to shift.
equilibrium price: The price where quantity demanded is equal to quantity supplied.
equilibrium quantity: The quantity at which quantity demanded and quantity supplied are equal at a certain price.
equity: The monetary value a homeowner would have after selling the house and repaying any outstanding bank loans used to buy the house.
estate and gift tax: A tax on people who pass assets to the next generation—either after death or during life in the form of gifts.
estate tax: A tax imposed on the value of an inheritance.
excess demand: At the existing price, the quantity demanded exceeds the quantity supplied; also called "shortage."
excess reserves: Reserves that banks hold above the legally mandated limit.
excess supply: When at the existing price, quantity supplied exceeds the quantity demanded; also called a "surplus."
exchange rate: The rate at which one currency exchanges for another.
excise taxes: A tax on a specific good—on gasoline, tobacco, and alcohol.
exclusive dealing: An agreement that a dealer will sell only products from one manufacturer.
exit: The long-run process of firms reducing production and shutting down because they expect losses.
expansionary fiscal policy: When fiscal policy increases the level of aggregate demand, through either increases in government spending or reductions in taxes.
expansionary monetary policy: A monetary policy that increases the supply of money and the quantity of loans; also called a "loose" monetary policy.
expenditure-output model: A macroeconomic model in which equilibrium output occurs where the total or aggregate

expenditures in the economy are equal to the amount produced; also called the "Keynesian cross model."

exports: Goods and services that are produced domestically and sold in another country.

externality: When a market exchange affects a third party who is outside or "external" to the exchange; sometimes called a "spillover."

F

federal funds interest rate: The interest rate at which banks and other major financial institutions borrow from and lend to each other for short-term loans without collateral.

fee-for-service: When medical care providers are paid according to the services they provide.

final goods and services: Output used directly for consumption, investment, government, and trade purposes; contrast with "intermediate goods."

financial capital market: The market in which those who save money provide financial capital and receive a rate of return from those who wish to raise money and pay a rate of return.

financial intermediary: An institution that operates between a saver with financial assets to invest and an entity who will receive those assets and pay a rate of return.

fiscal policy: Economic policies that involve government spending and taxation.

fixed costs: Expenditures that must be made before production starts and that do not change regardless of the level of production.

floating exchange rate: When a country lets the value of its currency be determined in the exchange rate market.

foreign direct investment: Purchases of firms in another country that involve taking a management responsibility.

foreign exchange market: The market in which people buy one currency while using another currency.

forward guidance: A central bank policy of announcing its expectations for the course of the economy and monetary policy, and in this way affecting current interest rates and lending by affecting the expectations of lenders and borrowers.

four-firm concentration ratio: What percentage share of the total sales in the industry is accounted for by the largest four firms.

free rider: Those who want others to pay for the public good and then plan to use the good themselves; if many people act as free riders, the public good may never be provided.

frictional unemployment: Unemployment that occurs as workers move between jobs.

full employment GDP: Another name for potential GDP, when the economy is producing at its potential and unemployment is at the natural rate of unemployment.

fundamentals trading: Buying or selling stock based on estimates of the future expected profits.

G

game theory: A branch of mathematics often used by economists that analyzes situations in which players must make decisions and then receive payoffs.

GDP deflator: A measure of inflation based on all the components of GDP.

Giffen good: The theoretical but unrealistic possibility that a higher price for a good could lead to a higher quantity demanded (or a lower price leads to a lesser quantity demanded).

globalization: The trend in which buying and selling in markets has increasingly crossed national borders.

goods and services market: A market in which firms are sellers of what they produce and households are buyers.

government debt: The total accumulated amount that the government has borrowed and not yet paid back over time.

gross domestic product (GDP): The value of the output of all goods and services produced within a country.

H

hard peg: An exchange rate policy in which the central bank sets a fixed and unchanging value for the exchange rate.

health maintenance organization (HMO): An organization that provides health care and is paid a fixed amount per person enrolled in the plan—regardless of how many services are provided.

hedge: Using a financial transaction as protection against risk.

Herfindahl-Hirschman Index (HHI): Take the market share of each firm in the industry, square each one, and add them.

human capital: The skills and education of workers.

hyperinflation: Extremely high rates of inflation.

I

imperfect competition: Competition that does not fit the definition of perfect competition either because it involves a smaller number of firms or only one firm, or products that aren't identical.

imperfect information: A situation where the buyer or the seller, or both, are uncertain about the qualities of what is being bought and sold.

implicit contract: An unwritten agreement in the labor market that the employer will try to keep wages from falling when the economy is weak or the business is having trouble, and the employee will not expect huge salary increases when the economy or the business is strong.

import quotas: Numerical limitations on the quantity of products that can be imported.

imports: Goods and services produced abroad and then sold domestically.

income effect: A change in price affects the buying power of income, with a higher price meaning that the buying power of income has been reduced, so that there is usually (with normal goods) an incentive to buy less of both goods, and a lower price meaning that the buying power of income has been increased, so that there is usually an incentive to buy more of both goods; always happens simultaneously with a substitution effect.

increasing returns to scale: When a larger-scale firm can produce at a lower cost than a smaller-scale firm; also called economies of scale.

index fund: A mutual fund that seeks only to mimic the overall performance of the market.

index number: When one arbitrary year is chosen to equal 100, and then values in all other years are set proportionately equal to that base year.

indexed: When a price, wage, or interest rate is adjusted automatically for inflation.

individual income tax: A tax based on the income of all forms received by individuals.
Industrial Revolution: The widespread use of power-driven machinery and the economic and social changes that occurred in the first half of the 1800s.
inelastic: The elasticity calculated from the appropriate formula has an absolute value less than 1.
inequality: When one group receives a higher share of total income or wealth than others.
infant industry argument: An argument to block imports for a short time, to give the infant industry time to mature, before eventually it starts competing on equal terms in the global economy.
inferior goods: Goods where the quantity demanded falls as income rises.
infinite elasticity: The extremely elastic situation where quantity changes by an infinite amount in response to even a tiny change in price.
inflation: A general and ongoing rise in the level of prices in an economy.
inflationary gap: The gap between real GDP and potential GDP, when the level of output is above the level of potential GDP.
inflation-targeting: A rule that the central bank is required to focus only on keeping inflation low.
initial public offering (IPO): When a firm first sells shares of stock to outside investors.
insider-outsider model: A model that divides workers into "insiders" already working for the firm who know the procedures and "outsiders" who are recent or prospective hires.
insurance: A group of people who face a risk of a certain bad experience all make regular payments, and those members of the group who actually suffer a bad experience receive payments.
intellectual property: The body of law including patents, trademarks, copyrights, and trade secret law that protects the right of inventors to produce and sell their inventions.
interest rate: A payment calculated as a percentage of the original amount saved or borrowed, and paid by the borrower to the saver.
intermediate goods and services: Output provided to other businesses at an intermediate stage of production, not for final users; contrast with "final goods and services."
International Price Index: A measure of inflation based on the prices of merchandise that is exported or imported.
intra-industry trade: International trade of goods within the same industry.
inventories: Goods that have been produced, but not yet been sold.

J

junk bonds: Bonds that offer relatively high interest rates to compensate for their relatively high chance of default.

K

Keynes' Law: "Demand creates its own supply."
kinked demand curve: A perceived demand curve that arises when competing oligopoly firms commit to match price cuts, but not price increases.

L

labor market: The market in which households sell their labor as workers to business firms or other employers.
labor union: An organization of workers that negotiates with employers as a group over wages and working conditions.
law of demand: The common relationship that a higher price leads to a lower quantity demanded of a certain good or service.
law of diminishing marginal utility: As a person receives more of a good, the marginal utility from each additional unit of the good is smaller than from the previous unit.
law of diminishing returns: As additional increments of resources are added to producing a good or service, the marginal benefit from those additional increments will decline.
law of supply: The common relationship that a higher price is associated with a greater quantity supplied.
lender of last resort: An institution that provides short-term emergency loans in conditions of financial crisis.
liabilities: Any amounts or debts owed by a firm or an individual.
life-cycle theory of savings: The common pattern that many people save little or borrow heavily early in life, save more in the middle of life, and then draw upon their accumulated savings later in life.
liquidity: How easy it is to sell an asset when desired.
logrolling: When a group of legislators all agree to vote for a package of otherwise unrelated laws that they individually favor.
Lorenz curve: A graph that shows the share of population on the horizontal axis and the cumulative percentage of total income received on the vertical axis.

M

M1: A narrow definition of the money supply that includes currency, traveler's checks, and checking accounts in banks.
M2: A definition of the money supply that includes everything in M1, but also adds savings deposits, money market funds, and certificates of deposit.
macroeconomics: The branch of economics that focuses on the economy as a whole, including issues like growth, unemployment, inflation, and the balance of trade.
macroprudential policy: The bank and financial regulatory policies that are not aimed at a specific company, but instead at reducing the risk of financial instability for the macroeconomy as a whole.
marginal analysis: Comparing the benefits and costs of choosing a little more or a little less of a good.
marginal cost: The additional cost of producing one more unit.
marginal physical product: The quantity of goods produced by an additional input (like an additional worker).
marginal propensity to consume (MPC): The share of an additional dollar of income that goes to consumption.
marginal propensity to import (MPI): The share of an additional dollar of income that goes to imports.
marginal propensity to save (MPS): The share of an additional dollar that goes to saving.
marginal revenue: The additional revenue gained from selling one more unit.

marginal revenue product (MRP): Reveals how much revenue a firm could receive from hiring an additional worker and selling the output of that worker.
marginal utility: The additional utility provided by one additional unit of consumption.
market: An institution that brings together buyers and sellers of goods or services.
market failure: A situation in which the market on its own fails to allocate resources efficiently in a way that balances social costs and benefits; externalities are one example of a market failure.
market share: The percentage share of total sales in the market.
marketable permit: A permit that allows a firm to emit a certain amount of pollution, where firms with more permits than pollution can sell the remaining permits to other firms.
market-oriented economy: An economy in which most economic decisions are made by buyers and sellers, who may be individuals or firms.
medium of exchange: Whatever is widely accepted as a method of payment.
menu costs: The costs that firms face in changing prices.
merchandise trade balance: The balance of trade looking only at goods.
merger: When two formerly separate firms combine to become a single firm; for practical purposes, often combined with acquisitions.
microeconomics: The branch of economics that focuses on actions of particular actors within the economy, like households, workers, and business firms.
minimum resale price maintenance agreement: An agreement that requires a dealer who buys from a manufacturer to sell for at least a certain minimum price.
minimum wage: A price floor that makes it illegal for an employer to pay employees less than a certain hourly rate.
model: A simplified representation of an object or situation that includes enough of the key features to be useful.
momentum trading: Buying or selling stock by following the current trend; that is, buying when the price seems to be rising, or selling stock because the price seems to be falling.
monetary policy: Policy that involves altering the quantity of money and thus affecting the level of interest rates and the extent of borrowing.
money: Whatever serves society in three functions: medium of exchange, unit of account, and store of value.
money market funds: Where the deposits of many investors are pooled together and invested in a safe way like short-term government bonds.
money multiplier: Total money in the economy divided by the original quantity of money, or change in the total money in the economy divided by a change in the original quantity of money.
money-back guarantee: A promise that the buyer's money will be refunded under certain conditions, like if the product doesn't work or sometimes even if the buyer decides to return the product.
monopolistic competition: Many firms competing to sell similar but differentiated products.
monopoly: A firm that faces no competitors.
moral hazard: When people have insurance against a certain event, they are less likely to guard against that event occurring.
multiplier: Total increase in aggregate expenditures divided by the original increase in expenditures.
multiplier effect: How a given change in expenditure cycles repeatedly through the economy, and thus has a larger final impact than the initial change.
municipal bonds: Bonds issued by cities that wish to borrow.
mutual funds: Funds that buy a range of stocks or bonds from different companies, thus allowing an investor an easy way to diversify.

N

national income (Y): The sum of all income received for producing GDP.
national saving and investment identity: For any country, the quantity of financial capital supplied at any given time by savings must equal the quantity of financial capital demanded for purposes of making investments.
nationalization: When government takes over ownership of firms.
natural monopoly: When the quantity demanded in the market is less than the quantity at the bottom of the long-run average cost curve.
natural rate of unemployment: The unemployment rate that would exist in a growing and healthy economy from the combination of economic, social, and political factors that exist at a time.
near-poor: Those who have incomes just above the poverty line.
negative externality: A situation where a third party, outside the transaction, suffers from a market transaction by others.
neoclassical economists: Economists who generally emphasize the importance of aggregate supply in determining the size of the macroeconomy over the long run.
net worth: Total assets minus total liabilities.
nominal value: The economic statistic actually announced at that time, not adjusted for inflation; contrast with real value.
nondurable goods: Short-lived goods like food and clothing.
nonexcludable: When it is costly or impossible to exclude someone from using the good, and thus hard to charge for it.
nonrivalrous: A good where, when one person uses the good, others can also use it.
nontariff barriers: All the other ways a nation can draw up rules, regulations, inspections, and paperwork to make it more costly or difficult to import products.
normal goods: Goods where the quantity demanded rises when income rises.
normative statements: Statements that describe how the world should be.

O

occupational licenses: Licenses issued by government agencies that mean that a worker has completed a certain type of education or passed a certain test.
oligopoly: When a few firms have all or nearly all of the sales in an industry.
open market operations: The central bank buying or selling bonds to influence the quantity of money and the level of interest rates.
opportunity cost: Whatever must be given up to obtain something that is desired.

opportunity set: Another name for the budget constraint.
out of the labor force: Those who do not have a job and are not looking for a job.

P

patent: A government rule that gives the inventor the exclusive legal right to make, use, or sell the invention for a limited time.
payroll tax: A tax based on the pay received from employers; the taxes provide funds for Social Security and Medicare.
peak: During the business cycle, the highest point of output before a recession begins.
per capita GDP: GDP divided by the population.
perfect competition: Each firm faces many competitors that sell identical products.
permanent income hypothesis: When individuals think about how much to consume, they look into the future and consider how much income they expect to earn in their lifetime.
Phillips curve: The trade-off between unemployment and inflation.
physical capital: The plant and equipment used by firms in production.
pollution charge: A tax imposed on the quantity of pollution that a firm emits; also called a "pollution tax."
pork-barrel spending: Spending that benefits mainly a single political district.
portfolio investment: An investment in another country that is purely financial and doesn't involve any management responsibility.
positive externality: A situation where a third party, outside the transaction, benefits from a market transaction by others.
positive statements: Statements that describe the world as it is.
potential GDP: The maximum quantity that an economy can produce given its existing levels of labor, physical capital, technology, and institutions.
poverty: Falling below a certain level of income needed for a basic standard of living.
poverty line: The specific amount of income needed for a basic standard of living.
poverty trap: When antipoverty programs are set up so that government benefits decline substantially as people earn more income—and as a result, working provides little financial gain.
predatory pricing: When an existing firm uses sharp but temporary price cuts to discourage new competition.
premiums: Payments made to an insurance company.
price cap regulation: When the regulator sets a price that a firm cannot exceed over the next few years.
price ceiling: A law that prevents a price from rising above a certain level.
price controls: Government laws to regulate prices.
price elasticity of demand: Same as elasticity of demand.
price elasticity of supply: Same as elasticity of supply.
price floor: A law that prevents a price from falling below a certain level.
price takers: Firms in a perfectly competitive market that must take the prevailing market price as given.
principal: The amount of an original financial investment, before any rate of return is paid.
prisoner's dilemma: A game in which if both players pursue their own self-interest, they both end up worse off than if they cooperate.
private company: A firm owned by the people who run it on a day-to-day basis.
privatization: When a government-owned firm becomes privately owned.
Producer Price Index: A measure of inflation based on the prices paid for supplies and inputs by producers of goods and services.
producer surplus: The benefit producers receive from selling a good or service, measured by the price the producer actually received minus the price the producer would have been willing to accept.
production function: The process of a firm turning economic inputs like labor, machinery, and raw materials into outputs like goods and services used by consumers.
production possibilities frontier: A diagram that shows the combinations of output that are possible for an economy to produce.
production technologies: Alternative methods of combining inputs to produce output.
productive efficiency: When it is impossible to produce more of one good without decreasing the quantity produced of another good.
productivity: What is produced per worker, or per hour worked.
progressive tax: A tax that collects a greater share of income from those with high incomes than from those with lower incomes.
property rights: The legal rights of ownership on which others are not allowed to infringe without paying compensation.
proportional tax: A tax that is a flat percentage of income earned, regardless of level of income.
protectionism: Government policies to reduce or block imports.
public company: A firm that has sold stock to the public, which in turn can be bought and sold by investors.
public good: A good that is nonexcludable and nonrivalrous, and thus is difficult for market producers to sell to individual consumers.
purchasing power parity (PPP): The exchange rate that equalizes the prices of internationally traded goods across countries.

Q

quality/new goods bias: Inflation calculated using a fixed basket of goods over time tends to overstate the true rise in cost of living because it doesn't take into account improvements in the quality of existing goods or the invention of new goods.
quantitative easing: A central bank policy of expanding the supply of lending and credit by direct large-scale purchase of government and private financial assets.
quantity demanded: The total number of units of a good or service purchased at a certain price.
quantity supplied: The total number of units of a good or service sold at a certain price.
quintiles: Dividing a group into fifths, a method often used to look at distribution of income.

R

race to the bottom: When production locates in countries with the lowest environmental (or other) standards, putting pressure on all countries to reduce their environmental standards.

rate of return: The payment in addition to the original investment from those who have received financial capital to those who provided it.
rational expectations: The theory that people form the most accurate possible expectations about the future that they can, using all information available to them.
rational ignorance: The theory that rational people won't bother incurring the costs of becoming informed and voting because they know that their vote won't be decisive in the election.
real interest rate: The rate of interest with inflation subtracted.
real value: An economic statistic after it has been adjusted for inflation; contrast with nominal value.
recession: A significant decline in national output.
recessionary gap: The gap in output between an economy in recession and potential GDP.
redistribution: Taking income from those with higher incomes and providing income to those with lower incomes.
regressive tax: A tax in which people with higher incomes pay a smaller share of their income in tax.
regulatory capture: When the firms supposedly being regulated end up playing a large role in setting the regulations that they will follow.
reserve ratio: The proportion of deposits that the bank holds in the form of reserves.
reserve requirement: The proportion of its deposits that a bank is legally required to deposit with the central bank.
reserves: Funds that a bank keeps on hand and that are not loaned out or invested in bonds.
restrictive practices: Practices that reduce competition but that do not involve outright agreements between firms to raise price.
Ricardian equivalence: The theory that rational private households might shift their saving to offset government saving or borrowing.
risk group: A group that shares roughly the same risks of an adverse event occurring.
risk premium: A payment to make up for the risk of not being repaid in full.

S

safety net: Nickname for the group of government programs that provide assistance to the poor and the near-poor.
savings account: A bank account that pays an interest rate, but withdrawing the money typically requires you to make a trip to the bank or an automatic teller machine.
savings deposits: Bank accounts where you can't withdraw money by writing a check, but can withdraw the money at a bank—or can transfer it easily to a checking account.
Say's Law: "Supply creates its own demand."
service contract: The buyer pays an extra amount and the seller agrees to fix anything that goes wrong for a set time period.
shareholders: Those who own at least some stock in a firm.
shares: The stock of a firm is divided into individual shares.
shift in demand: When a change in some economic factor related to demand causes a different quantity to be demanded at every price.
shift in supply: When a change in some economic factor related to supply causes a different quantity to be supplied at every price.
shortage: At the existing price, the quantity demanded exceeds the quantity supplied; also called "excess demand."
shutdown point: When the revenue a firm receives does not cover its average variable costs, the firm should shut down immediately; the point where the marginal cost curve crosses the average variable cost curve.
social costs: Costs that include both the private costs incurred by firms and also costs incurred by third parties outside the production process, like costs of pollution.
social surplus: The sum of consumer surplus and producer surplus.
soft peg: An exchange rate policy where the government usually allows the exchange rate to be set by the market, but in some cases, especially if the exchange rate seems to be moving rapidly in one direction, the central bank will intervene.
special-interest groups: Groups that are numerically small but well organized and thus exert a disproportionate effect on political outcomes.
specialization: When workers or firms focus on particular tasks in the overall production process for which they are well-suited.
spillover: When a market exchange affects a third party who is outside or "external" to the exchange; more formally called an externality.
splitting up the value chain: When many of the different stages of producing a good happen in different geographic locations.
stagflation: When an economy experiences stagnant growth and high inflation at the same time.
stock: A claim on partial ownership of a firm.
store of value: Something that serves as a way of preserving economic value that can be spent or consumed in the future.
substitutes: Goods that can replace each other to some extent, so that a rise in the price of one good leads to a greater quantity consumed of another good, and vice versa.
substitution bias: An inflation rate calculated using a fixed basket of goods over time tends to overstate the true rise in the cost of living because it doesn't take into account that the person can substitute away from goods whose prices rise by a lot.
substitution effect: When a price changes, consumers have an incentive to consume less of the good with a relatively higher price and more of the good with a relatively lower price; always happens simultaneously with an income effect.
sunk cost: Costs that were incurred in the past and cannot be recovered, and thus should not affect current decisions.
supply: A relationship between price and the quantity supplied of a certain good or service.
supply curve: A line that shows the relationship between price and quantity supplied on a graph, with quantity supplied on the horizontal axis and price on the vertical axis.
supply schedule: A table that shows a range of prices for a good or service and the quantity supplied at each price.
surplus: When at the existing price, quantity supplied exceeds the quantity demanded; also called "excess supply."

T

T-account: A balance sheet with a two-column format, with the T-shape formed by the vertical line down the middle and the horizontal line under the column headings for "Assets" and "Liabilities."
tariffs: Taxes imposed on imported products.
technology: All the ways in which a certain level of capital investment can produce a greater quantity or higher quality, as well as different and altogether new products.
tie-in sales: A situation where a customer is allowed to buy one product only if the customer also buys another product; also called "bundling."
time deposits: Accounts that the depositor has committed to leaving in the bank for a certain period of time, in exchange for a higher rate of interest; also called certificates of deposit.
time value of money: The cost of having to wait for repayment.
total cost: All the costs that a firm must incur in the process of production.
total revenue: The quantity of goods and services sold by the firm multiplied by the selling price of these goods and services.
trade balance: Gap between exports and imports.
trade deficit: When imports exceed exports.
trade secrets: Methods of production kept secret by the producing firm.
trade surplus: When exports exceed imports.
trademark: A word, name, symbol, or device that indicates the source of the goods and can only be used by the firm that registered that trademark.
Treasury bonds: Bonds issued by the federal government through the U.S. Department of the Treasury.
trough: During the business cycle, the lowest point of output in a recession, before a recovery begins.

U

unemployment rate: The percentage of adults who are in the labor force and thus seeking jobs, but who do not have jobs.
unit of account: The common way in which market values are measured in an economy.
usury laws: Laws that impose an upper limit on the interest rate that lenders can charge.
utility: The level of satisfaction or pleasure that people receive from their choices.

V

variable costs: Costs of production that increase with the quantity produced.
velocity: The speed with which money circulates through the economy, calculated as the nominal GDP divided by a measure of the size of the money supply.
venture capital: Financial investments in new companies that are still relatively small in size but that have potential to grow substantially.
voting cycle: When a majority prefers A over B, B over C, and C over A.

W

warranty: A promise to fix or replace the good, at least for a certain period of time.

Z

zero elasticity: The highly inelastic case in which a percentage change in price, no matter how large, results in zero change in the quantity demanded or supplied.

Index

Note: Page numbers in *italics* refer to exhibits.

A

B

C

D

F

G

H

I

J

K

L

M

N

O

P